1912—Stern (1871–1938)
Introduced the concept of mental quotient.

1916—Terman (1877–1956)
Published the *Stanford Revision and Extension of the Binet-Simon Intelligence Scale.*

1918—Otis (1886–1964)
Published the *Absolute Point Scale,* a group intelligence test.

1919—Monroe (1863–1939) and Buckingham (1899–   )
Published the *Illinois Examination,* a group achievement test.

1923—Kelly (1884–1961), Ruch (1903–   ), and Terman (1877–1956)
Published the *Stanford Achievement Test.*

1923—Kohs (1890–   )
Published the *Kohs Block Design Test* of nonverbal reasoning.

1924—Porteus (1883–1972)
Published the *Porteus Maze Test.*

1926—Goodenough (1886–1959)
Published the *Draw-A-Man Test.*

1928—Arthur (1883–1967)
Published the *Point Scale of Performance Tests.*

1931—Stutsman (1894–   )
Published the *Merrill-Palmer Scale of Mental Tests.*

1933—Thurstone (1887–1955)
Favored a multiple factor analytic approach to the study of human abilities.

1933—Tiegs (1891–1970) and Clark (1895–1964)
Published the *Progressive Achievement Tests,* which were later renamed the *California Achievement Tests.*

1936—Lindquist (1901–1978)
Published, with colleagues, the *Iowa Every-Pupil Tests of Basic Skills,* which were later renamed the *Iowa Tests of Basic Skills.*

1936—Piaget (1896–1980)
Published *Origins of Intelligence.*

1937—Merrill (1888–1978)
Published the 1937 revision of the *Stanford-Binet* with Terman.

1938—Bender (1897–   )
Published the *Bender Visual Motor Gestalt Test.*

1938—Gesell (1880–1961)
Published the *Gesell Maturity Scale.*

1939—Wechsler (1896–1981)
Published the *Wechsler-Bellevue Intelligence Scale.*

1940—P. Cattell (1893–   )
Published the *Cattell Infant Intelligence Scale.*

1959—Guilford (1897–   )
Proposed a Structure of Intellect model of intelligence based on factor analytic methods.

1961—Kirk (1904–   ) and J. J. McCarthy (1927–   )
Published the *Illinois Test of Psycholinguistic Ability.*

1963—R. B. Cattell (1905–   )
Proposed a theory of fluid and crystallized intelligence.

1969—Bayley (1899–   )
Published the *Bayley Scales of Infant Development.*

1972—D. McCarthy (1906–1974)
Published the *McCarthy Scales of Children's Abilities.*

Assessment of Children's Intelligence and Special Abilities

Assessment of Children's Intelligence and Special Abilities

2ND EDITION

Jerome M. Sattler
San Diego State University

Allyn and Bacon, Inc.
Boston   London   Sydney   Toronto

Portions of this book first appeared in
Assessment of Children's Intelligence by
Jerome M. Sattler, Copyright © 1974 by
Allyn and Bacon, Inc.

Series Editor: Bill Barke
Production Editor: Shirley Davis

Library of Congress Cataloging in Publication Data

Sattler, Jerome M.
    Assessment of children's intelligence and special
abilities.

    First ed. published in 1974 under title: Assessment
of children's intelligence.
    Bibliography: p.
    Includes indexes.
    1. Intelligence tests. 2. Ability—testing.
3. Psychological tests for children. I. Title.
BF431.S27   1981   155.4'13'0287   81-7882
ISBN 0-205-07362-X   AACR2

38,9 76

10 9 8   86 85 84
Printed in the United States of America.

To
BAXTER VENABLE
for his faith in the book, his friendship, and his fine editorial skills

to
WILLIAM A. HILLIX
for his friendship and willingness always to lend a helping hand

and to
the memory of my parents
NATHAN and PEARL

Contents

List of Tables

List of Figures

List of Exhibits

Preface

Writing a book is an adventure; to begin with it is a toy and an amusement, then it becomes a master, and then it becomes a tyrant; and the last phase is just as you are about to be reconciled to your servitude—you kill the monster and fling him . . . to the public.

SIR WINSTON CHURCHILL
Saturday Review (1963)

The second edition of *Assessment of Children's Intelligence* has an expanded title: *Assessment of Children's Intelligence and Special Abilities.* The change reflects coverage of a wider range of assessment procedures, including, in addition to intelligence tests, achievement tests, perceptual-motor tests, adaptive behavior scales, and behavioral assessment procedures. These tests and procedures were added because each one contributes to the assessment task, and it is important for the student to learn how they can be integrated into an assessment battery. The use of a battery approach is especially important now that Public Law 94-142 stipulates that no single procedure shall be the sole criterion for determining an appropriate educational program for a child. Clinical and psychoeducational assessments require the administration of a battery of tests in order (a) to arrive at a thorough description of the child's assets and limitations and (b) to formulate a treatment or remedial plan. Although personality tests are frequently included in clinical and psychoeducational assessment batteries, they are not covered in this edition because the text focuses on intelligence and special abilities.

The second edition is a thorough revision. There are over 1,800 references, with approximately 600 from between 1974 and 1981. Some chapters have been reorganized, and new chapters have been written to cover basic psychometric concepts useful for assessment, assessment of learning disabilities, and special ability testing. When one or two references document a point in the text, they are cited directly in the chapter. For ease of reading, when three or more references document a point, they are placed in the Notes at the end of the book. Technical information regarding various issues in the text is also included in the Notes. The Glossary, which is new to this edition, includes terms from the areas of assessment, child psychopathology, psychometrics, and special education.

The book is designed to teach clinical assessment skills to students in clinical, school, and counseling psychology and to enable students in special education to understand the assessment process. It also can serve as a reference book for practicing professionals in these areas. Other professionals, too, such as teachers, pediatricians, and speech therapists, will benefit from a study of the book. The text is recommended for courses in assessment of intelligence, assessment in clinical psychology, assessment in school psychology, psychoeducational assessment, assessment of learning disabilities, and assessment in special education. The book also may be used in specialized courses in tests and measurement.

The following measures are covered in the book:

AAMD Adaptive Behavior Scale (ABS)
AAMD Adaptive Behavior Scale–Public School Version (ABS-PSV)
Abbreviated Symptom Questionnaire
Adaptive Behavior Inventory for Children (ABIC)
AML Behavior Rating Scale
Auditory Discrimination Test (ADT)
Balthazar Scales of Adaptive Behavior
Bayley Scales of Infant Development
Behavior Problem Checklist
Bender Visual Motor Gestalt Test
Bilingual Syntax Measure and Bilingual Syntax Measure II
Boehm Test of Basic Concepts
Bruininks-Oseretsky Test of Motor Proficiency
Child Behavior Checklist
Child Behavior Scale
Classroom Adjustment Ratings Scale (CARS)
Classroom Reading Inventory
Columbia Mental Maturity Scale (CMMS)
Denver Developmental Screening Test (DDST)
Detroit Tests of Learning Aptitude
Developmental Test of Visual Motor Integration (VMI)
Developmental Test of Visual Perception (DTVP)
Devereux Adolescent Behavior Rating Scale
Devereux Child Behavior Rating Scale
Devereux Elementary School Behavior Rating Scale
Extended Merrill-Palmer Scale

Goldman-Fristoe-Woodcock Test of Auditory Discrimination
Goodenough-Harris Drawing Test (Draw-A-Man)
Halstead Neuropsychological Test Battery
Health Resources Inventory
Hyperkinesis Rating Scale
Illinois Test of Psycholinguistic Abilities, Revised Edition (ITPA)
Infant Psychological Developmental Scale
KeyMath Diagnostic Test
Kohn Problem Checklist
Kohn Social Competence Scales
Language Assessment Battery
Language Assessment Scales
Leiter International Performance Scale (LIPS)
Lindamood Auditory Conceptualization Test (LACT)
McCarthy Scales of Children's Abilities
Merrill-Palmer Scale of Mental Tests
Parent Symptom Questionnaire
Peabody Individual Achievement Test (PIAT)
Peabody Picture Vocabulary Test–Revised (PPVT-R)
Pictorial Test of Intelligence (PTI)
Preschool Attainment Record
Preschool Behavior Questionnaire
Progressive Matrices
Purdue Pegboard
Purdue Perceptual-Motor Survey
Quick Test
Reitan-Indiana Neuropsychological Test Battery for Children
Revised Visual Retention Test
San Diego Quick Assessment
Slosson Intelligence Test (SIT)
Southern California Sensory Integration Tests
Stanford-Binet Intelligence Scale (SB)
Sucher-Allred Reading Placement Inventory
System of Multicultural Pluralistic Assessment (SOMPA)
Teacher Behavioral Description Form
Teacher Questionnaire
T.M.R. School Competency Scales
Token Test for Children
Vineland Social Maturity Scale
Visual Aural Digit Span Test (VADS)

Wechsler Intelligence Scale for Children–Revised (WISC-R)

Wechsler Preschool and Primary Scale of Intelligence (WPPSI)

Wide Range Achievement Test (WRAT)

Woodcock-Johnson Psycho-Educational Battery

Woodcock Reading Mastery Tests

The book can be used in either a one- or a two-semester course in assessment. Various arrangements of chapters will meet the objectives of different courses. For example:

1. The entire text can be used in a comprehensive one-semester course designed for the assessment of intelligence and special abilities of children.
2. In a two-semester course, the material can be divided as follows. The first semester might cover theory, administration, and evaluation of intelligence tests, using Chapters 1 through 13 and Chapters 24 and 25; the second semester might cover test applications and special ability tests, using Chapters 14 through 23.

The second edition of *Assessment of Children's Intelligence and Special Abilities* is accompanied by two useful supplements. The *Instructor's Manual* contains information on how to organize an individual intelligence testing course; exercises covering clinical, technical, and professional skills; and essay, short answer, and multiple-choice questions. The *Student's Manual* contains an outline of each chapter; major terms and concepts for each chapter; review questions; sample multiple-choice questions; special exhibits to facilitate administering individual intelligence tests; supplementary tables to facilitate interpreting and using special tests; and appendixes with a discussion of the WAIS-R and tables to facilitate the interpretation of the WAIS-R. Because the WAIS-R is applicable for 16- to 18-year-olds, it is an important instrument in the assessment of children in late adolescence. While the WAIS-R could not be included in the text proper because it was published after the text was completed, it was included in the *Student's Manual.*

Acknowledg- ments

The present text evolved over a period of six years after the publication of the first edition of *Assessment of Children's Intelligence.* Throughout this period, my editor at W. B. Saunders, Baxter Venable, was a constant source of encouragement. In our numerous discussions, we planned a revision that would be even more useful, informative, and readable. His enthusiasm for the first edition, as well as for the new edition, matched mine. Shortly before the completion of the new edition, CBS transferred the college division of W. B. Saunders to another publishing subsidiary, which decided not to go along with our plans for the new edition. However, they graciously gave me a release and allowed me to select another publisher. Allyn and Bacon was my choice.

My colleague William A. Hillix has made a significant contribution to my growth and development as a psychologist and writer. During my sixteen years at San Diego State University, Al has given generously of his time to read and comment on my work. His breadth of knowledge and keen judgment gave me invaluable insights. I feel honored to know him. This book, in part, is dedicated to Al as a small token of my gratitude.

I have been extremely fortunate in obtaining guidance from some of our nation's outstanding authorities in the field of psychology and measurement. In addition, some of my students and former students also gave generously of their time to comment on the manuscript. The following individuals read every chapter of the manuscript and made many invaluable suggestions. Their help is much appreciated.

Dr. Kathryn C. Gerken
Dr. Terry B. Gutkin
Dr. William A. Hillix
Dr. Alan S. Kaufman
Ms. Chris Laitenieks
Mr. Christopher Maloy
Ms. Marilyn Moore
Dr. Louise S. Musser
Dr. Daniel J. Reschly
Dr. Cecil R. Reynolds
Dr. Joy Rogers
Dr. Jonathan Sandoval
Dr. Arthur B. Silverstein
Ms. Glenyth Turner
Dr. Fred H. Wallbrown

A number of individuals made useful comments and suggestions on one or more of the chapters. I wish to express my thanks for their help and advice. They are as follows:

Dr. Edward F. Alf, Jr.
Dr. Nicholas Aliotti
Ms. Linda Altes
Dr. Arthur Benton
Ms. Ann Bohanan
Dr. Rebecca B. Bryson
Ms. Donya Harvin
Ms. Sara Holland
Dr. Arthur Jensen
Dr. Catherine Johns
Dr. Robert L. Karen
Dr. Judith S. Kass
Ms. Barbara McNeil
Ms. Marjorie W. Matlock
Ms. Debra Murphy
Ms. Jackie Newcomb
Dr. Thomas Oakland
Ms. Jeanne Panell
Ms. Diane Rowland
Dr. Joseph J. Ryan
Dr. Melvin Schwartz
Mr. Leigh Scott
Dr. Alan L. Shanske
Dr. John R. Smith
Dr. John J. Spinetta
Mr. Gerald Sweeny
Ms. Shirley Wilson
Mr. Allen Workman

Many students at San Diego State University assisted me in locating references, reviewing test manuals, and performing many other tasks related to the preparation of the manuscript. I am grateful for their help. They are as follows:

Mr. Gerald S. Anderson
Mr. James Barter
Mr. Michael D. Basil
Ms. Debra J. Beach
Ms. Beverly J. Belliveau
Ms. Ann Bohanan
Mr. Gerald E. Bowman
Mr. David Charlton
Mr. Michael B. Cowen
Ms. Julie Engelhardt
Mr. Gary Feldman
Ms. Kathleen E. Gilbride
Mr. John Gwynn
Mr. William Huston
Ms. Barbara Kennedy
Ms. Carla H. McCann
Ms. Debra Murphy
Ms. Lucinda Nerhood
Ms. Lucille Patloff
Ms. Grace Rosa
Ms. Joyce Sprock
Ms. Linda Weiner
Ms. Sally R. Wenner
Ms. Lynn Zarbatany

Throughout the preparation of the manuscript, my able secretary and assistant, Jessica McDonald, was a constant source of strength. Her patience, friendliness, and willingness to type and retype the numerous drafts of the manuscript will always be appreciated. Thank you, Jessica, for being you. Our secretary at the Psychology Clinic at San Diego State University, Dorathe Frick, also was helpful in typing various sections of the manuscript. Thank you, Dorathe. I also wish to express my appreciation to Penny Goforth, Connie Liciow, Laura Zossani, Monica Noetling, and Amy McRoberts for their help in typing various parts of the manuscript. I have benefited from the excellent interlibrary loan service at the San Diego State University library. Thank you, Ann Wright, Karen Hogarth, and Valerie Edwards, for your invaluable help. All of you were always willing to lend a helping hand and to locate books and journals that were not available at our library.

I have also benefited from the generosity of many psychologists who willingly shared their cases with me. While it was not possible to use all of their cases in the text, their help enabled me to present some outstanding examples of psychological evaluations from a clinical or school psychology perspective. These individuals are as follows:

Dr. Wayne Adams
Dr. Nicholas Aliotti
Ms. Betty A. Biernat
Dr. Allan S. Bloom
Ms. Ann Bohanan
Mr. Rick Bruhn
Mr. Stephen Colombo
Ms. Carol J. Craig
Dr. Michael L. Dimitroff
Dr. Anne M. Eastman
Dr. Constance T. Fischer
Ms. Drina Fried-Roberts
Dr. Kathryn C. Gerken
Dr. Joan F. Goodman
Ms. Elaine Grover
Ms. Donya Harvin
Ms. Faye Hnath
Ms. Sara Holland
Mr. Michael P. Juskelis
Dr. Judith S. Kass
Mr. Gerald P. Koocher
Dr. Nadine Lambert
Dr. Margie Lewis
Ms. Nora C. McKay
Ms. Barbara McNeil
Dr. Judith Mazza
Ms. Marilyn Moore
Dr. Jack A. Naglierri
Dr. Patricia Nolen

Jerome M. Sattler. Photo by David N. Sattler.

Dr. Thomas
 Oakland
Dr. John C. Pappas
Dr. DeAnsin G.
 Parker
Sister Marie Rose
 Petrie
Dr. Lillie Pope
Dr. Larry M. Raskin

Dr. Dennis Saccuzzo
Dr. Alan L. Shanske
Ms. Janice Tonz
Dr. Hubert "Boony"
 Vance
Dr. Fred Wallbrown
Mr. Daniel B.
 Watkins
Ms. Shirley Wilson

I am especially indebted to Donya Harvin, not only for her willingness to share her evaluations, but for her efforts to locate, organize, and write reports that represented the assessment of various types of exceptional children. Thank you, Donya.

I have been fortunate in having the staff at Lifland et al., Bookmakers, design and copyedit the book. Thank you, Sally Lifland and Janice Ostock, for your careful attention to the manuscript. Both of you have made the text even more accurate and readable and have done an outstanding job of editing the manuscript.

I wish to thank the staff at Allyn and Bacon, including Bill Barke (Psychology Editor), Gary Folven (Senior Editor), Shirley Davis (Production Editor), and Wendy Ritger (Editorial Assistant), for their help in seeing this book through to its completion.

My family has been a constant source of support and encouragement during the writing of the text. I wish to express my thanks to my wife Bonnie Sattler; to my children Heidi, David, and Deborah; to my brother Paul Sattler; to my niece Suzan M. Sattler; and to my nephew Robert C. Sattler.

J.M.S.
San Diego State University
Psychology Department
San Diego, CA 921820350

June 1981

Assessment of Children's Intelligence and Special Abilities

CHAPTER 1

Introduction

It is in connection with intelligence and the tests which measure it that some of the most violent polemics in psychology and in all the behavioral sciences have raged. These polemics have concerned the nature of man's intellectual capacities, how they should be measured, how mutable they are, and what the implication of the decisions on these issues should be for educating and improving the race.

J. McVicker Hunt
Intelligence and Experience

EXHIBIT 1-1. Psychological Reports Do Count: The Case of *Daniel Hoffman v. the Board of Education of the City of New York*

The case of *Daniel Hoffman v. the New York City Board of Education* is instructive because it illustrates the important role that testing and psychological reports can play in people's lives. In this case, the report made a recommendation that was ignored by the school administrators. Years later when the case was tried, the failure to follow the recommendations became a key issue.

Daniel Hoffman, a 26-year-old man, brought suit against the New York City Board of Education to recover damages for injuries resulting from his placement in mentally retarded classes. The complaint alleged that (a) the defendant was negligent in its original testing procedures and placement of the plaintiff, causing or permitting him to be placed in an educational environment for mental defectives and mentally retarded children and consequently depriving him of adequate speech therapy which would have improved his only real handicap, a speech impediment; and (b) the defendant was negligent in failing or refusing to follow adequate procedures for the recommended retesting of the plaintiff's intelligence.

The Board of Education took the position that Daniel's IQ of 74, which he obtained on the Stanford-Binet when he was 5 years, 9 months old, indicated that his placement in a class for the mentally retarded was appropriate. They contended that the test was proper, that it was administered by a competent and experienced psychologist, and that it was the unanimous professional judgment of Daniel's teachers, based upon their evaluation and his performance on standardized achievement tests, that a retest was not warranted. The Board made clear that at the time Daniel was in school its policy was to retest only when retesting was recommended by teachers or requested by parents.

The psychological report became one of the key documents upon which the entire case rested. The key sentence in the report, written in 1957, was as follows: *"Also, his intelligence should be reevaluated within a two-year period so that a more accurate estimation of his abilities can be made"* (italics added). The psychologist recommended that Daniel be placed in a class for the mentally retarded on the basis of his IQ of 74. Daniel entered special education classes and remained in them during his entire school years.

The Board of Education argued that the psychologist did not literally mean "retesting" be-

EXHIBIT 1-1 (cont.)

cause he did not use this word in the report. A minority of the Appellate Justices concurred with this interpretation, being of the opinion that re-evaluation was carried out by the teachers in their routine administration of achievement tests. A majority of the court, however, disagreed and supported the plaintiff's position that reevaluation meant only one thing—administration of another intelligence test.

In a curious twist of fate, testing, which resulted in the assignment of Daniel to special education, also played an important role in removing him from a special workshop program during his late teenage years. Daniel had made poor progress during his school years, and there had been no significant change in his severe speech defect. At the age of 17 years, he entered a shop training school for retarded youths. After a few months in the program, he was given the Wechsler Adult Intelligence Scale and obtained a Verbal Scale IQ of 85, a Performance Scale IQ of 107, and a Full Scale IQ of 94. His overall functioning was in the normal range. On the basis of these findings, Daniel was not permitted to remain at the Occupational Training Center. On learning of this decision, he became very depressed, often staying in his room with the door closed. His mother testified at the trial that, when she entered the room, he would be sitting in the corner, brooding and crying, "What was he going to do, he wasn't a little child, he was a grown man."

Daniel then received assistance from the Division of Vocational Rehabilitation. At the age of 21 years, he was trained to be a messenger, but did not like this work. At 26 years of age, at the time of the trial, he had obtained no further training or education, had not made any advancement in his vocational life, and had not improved his social life.

During the trial it was shown that the psychologist who tested Daniel in kindergarten had not (a) interviewed Mrs. Hoffman, (b) obtained a social history, or (c) discussed the results of the evaluation with her. If a history had been obtained, he would have learned that Daniel had been tested ten months previously at the National Hospital for Speech Disorders and had obtained an IQ of 90 on the Merrill-Palmer Scale of Mental Tests.

The case was initially tried before a jury, which returned a verdict in favor of Daniel, awarding him damages of $750,000. This decision was appealed to the Appellate Division of

the New York State Supreme Court, which affirmed the jury verdict on November 6, 1978, but lowered damages to $500,000. The New York State Appeals Court overturned the Appellate Court's decision on December 17, 1979, finding that the court system is not the proper arena for testing the validity of educational decisions or for second guessing such decisions.

The Importance of the Case for the Practice of School and Clinical Psychology

Whatever the final outcome, the case of *Daniel Hoffman v. the Board of Education of the City of New York* is important for the practice of school and clinical psychology. It represents one of the first cases in which the courts carefully scrutinized psychological reports and the process of special education placements. The case touches on many important issues involved in the psycho-educational assessment process. Let us now consider some of these issues.

1. *Psychological reports do count.* Psychological reports are key documents which are used by mental health professionals, teachers, administrators, physicians, courts, and parents and children.
2. *Words can be misinterpreted.* A pivotal point in the case was the meaning of the words "re-evaluate" and "retest." Some participants in the case, as well as some justices, believed these words had different meanings. Therefore, careful attention must be given to the wording of reports. It is important to write clearly and to state as precisely as possible your findings and recommendations.
3. *IQs change.* Children's IQs do not remain static. While there is much stability after 6 years of age, IQs do change.
4. *Different tests may provide different IQs.* The three IQs obtained by Daniel at 5, 6, and 18 years of age may reflect differences in the content and standardization of the three tests rather than genuine changes in cognitive performance.
5. *Placement decisions must be based on more than one assessment approach.* A battery of psychological tests and procedures along with interviews with parents and reports from teachers should be used in the assessment process. All available information should be reviewed before placement recommendations are made.
6. *Use appropriate instruments.* A child who has a speech or language handicap may need to

EXHIBIT 1-1 (cont.)

be assessed with performance tests in addition to, or in place of, verbal tests.

7. *Review previous findings.* Before the formal assessment is carried out, it is necessary to determine whether the child has been previously tested, and if so, to review these findings.

Many other issues were involved in the case of Daniel Hoffman. However, the above points are particularly germane to the practice of school and clinical psychology. They illustrate that psychological evaluation requires a high level of competence. Finally, the case demonstrates the importance of recommendations made in psychological reports and the obligation on the part of administrators to carry out a report's recommendations. ■

Source: This case review was prepared by Jerome M. Sattler and Lucille Patlaf. The citations for this case are 410 N.Y.S.2d 99 and 400 N.E.2d 317–49 N.Y.2d 121.

Assessing the intelligence and special abilities of children is a complex, demanding, and yet rewarding activity. It requires a variety of skills and talents, including the ability to work with children (and adults), an understanding of the characteristics and makeup of various tests, the ability to interpret test findings, knowledge of child psychopathology and psychometric principles, consultation skills, and communication skills. But these skills, however well established and integrated, pale before the one quality that perhaps is the most important and that provides the foundation for all of the others, namely, a liking of children.

Many of these skills can be learned, and this book will provide much useful information to aid clinicians in their work with children. I use the term "clinician" to refer to any of a number of different individuals who have been trained in such professional areas as clinical psychology, school psychology, educational psychology, special education, and speech therapy. Physicians, social workers, and mental health workers, too, occasionally use some of the techniques employed in the assessment areas covered in the text.

The results of the assessment need to be closely interrelated, whenever possible, with treatment and remediation programs designed to meet the needs of the developing child. Our evaluations need to go beyond the mere presentation of test data. Data are important, but without interpretation they remain cold, sterile figures lying about like a corpse. The findings must be given a living body by including interpretations, diagnoses, and, where possible, suggestions for treatment and remediation.

The assessment process, especially when intelligence tests and other standardized tests form the basis of the evaluation, should never focus exclusively on just a score or a number. Children have a range of competencies that are evaluated by both quantitative and qualitative means. The clinician aims to assess competencies of the child; the focus should not be solely on handicaps or on areas of weakness. The following are important guidelines that should be followed in using intelligence and special ability tests. These guidelines form an important foundation for the clinical and psychoeducational use of tests:

1. Tests are samples of behavior.
2. Tests do not reveal traits or capacities directly.
3. Tests purporting to measure a particular ability or skill should have adequate reliability and validity.
4. Test results should be interpreted in light of the child's cultural background, primary language, and handicapping conditions.
5. Test scores and other test performances may be affected by temporary states of fatigue, anxiety, or stress; by basic disturbances in personality; or by brain damage.

6. Tests purporting to measure the same ability may provide different scores for that ability.
7. Test results should be interpreted in relationship to other behaviors and to case history information; test results should never be interpreted in isolation.
8. Test results are dependent on the child's cooperation and motivation.

Tests are tools which may be useful in accomplishing goals, and their effectiveness will depend on the skill and knowledge of the clinician. When used wisely and cautiously, they will assist us in helping children, parents, teachers, and other professionals obtain valuable insights. When used inappropriately, they may mislead and cause harm and grief. As we saw in the case of *Daniel Hoffman,* presented in Exhibit 1-1, test results do have an impact on many people, directly affecting the lives of children and their parents. As a result of psychological and psychoeducational evaluations, actions are taken and decisions made. We must be careful of the words that we choose (a) to write our reports and (b) to communicate with other professionals, the clients themselves, and their families. We are guardians of a tradition of clinical and psychological measurement, and are representatives of a professional community. We must never forget these obligations.

Our study of intelligence, which is the main focus of the text, should leave us with a feeling of humility. We still know little about how information is processed, stored, and retrieved; about how differing environments affect learning; and about how intellectual growth is best nourished. We must be mindful of the labels and classifications that we use to categorize our clients, for we believe in and respect their resiliency. When we affix a label of "mentally retarded" on children, we may be surprised at the countless ways in which children who have received this label differ from one another. We will be surprised at the intelligence and humanity manifested in many of their reactions. While labels are important in the assessment process, we must not allow the label to regiment and restrict our ways of observing and working with the individual child.

This text is designed to provide guidelines that will promote the usefulness and fairness of assessment procedures. I believe that assessment can and should provide one of the most effective ways of promoting the mental health and educational needs of children of all ethnic backgrounds. Each child represents a separate challenge for the examiner; this book aims to increase the examiner's ability to effectively rise to the challenge.

The clinician's greatest responsibilities to the client extend beyond the assessment room. When recommendations are made that require the child to be placed in a new "environment," a thorough knowledge of that environment is needed. For example, a child may be gifted, but not desire to leave the regular classroom. His or her needs must be considered. What happens to the child who is rejected from a gifted program? Can the regular classroom teacher learn to accommodate the child's special interests and abilities in the classroom? The assessment process calls for an understanding of the child's present environment and the new environments that may be created as a result of the placement decisions.

The philosophy of this book is that norm-referenced tests are extremely useful in the evaluation of intelligence and special abilities, such as reading, arithmetic, spelling, visual-motor skills, gross and fine motor skills, and adaptive behavior. Norm-referenced tests provide valuable information about a child's level of functioning in the areas studied by the tests. Tests are also relatively economical of time, permitting a sampling of behavior in a few hours. The appraisal allows for the application of a wealth of normative information unavailable to even the most skilled observer who does not use tests (Watson, 1951). However, the precautions of Robinson and Robinson (1976, p. 355) need to be heeded:

... test scores will be seriously misused if they are taken out of the context of a broad range of information about the child and his or her environment. Responsible test users are cautious and modest. They have no secret password to the child's mental development and they ask neither too much nor too little of the test score. They have data which can be exceedingly valuable if viewed in terms of the brief investment of time required of both tester and child, but which furnish only a single piece of the puzzle presented by any complex individual, whose history is unique and whose future is uncharted.

Norm-referenced tests also provide an index for evaluating change in many different aspects of the child's physical and social world, including developmental changes and the effects of remediation. However, these tests, at present, provide limited information about the ways children learn or about ways to ameliorate children's handicaps. Much has yet to be learned about tailoring remediation strategies to individual patterns of learning ability. Standardized tests need to be supplemented with new tests and techniques that are designed for such efforts.

However much we subscribe to the philosophy that well-normed standardized tests provide one of the most important means of assessment, we also must recognize that children come to us from many different ethnic and cultural backgrounds, and these differing backgrounds must be considered in selecting tests and in interpreting norms. We have, on the one hand, forces that continue to mold us into a more homogeneous society. On the other hand, subtle and not so subtle differences exist between various ethnic groups in our country, including differences in language styles and in patterns of family interaction. Such differences among blacks, whites, Hispanics, and American Indians, for example, may affect the kinds of knowledge acquired by children. These ethnic differences must be considered in interpreting test results and in working with children and their families.

The decade of the seventies has seen the profession of applied clinical and school psychology attacked from both within and without. Accusations arose from ethnic minority groups that those "standardized tests" used to allocate limited educational resources penalized children whose family, socioeconomic, and cultural experiences were different from those of white, middle-class normative groups. The very foundations of the profession have been questioned, including the tools that are used and the situations in which they are administered. Some members of minority groups maintain that intelligence tests and achievement tests are culturally biased and harmful to black children and other ethnic minority children. Others, such as Bersoff (1971), believe that many of the activities of school (and clinical child) psychologists are not in the best interests of the child. These include (a) labeling children, (b) testing children without their permission and without giving them full knowledge of the possible consequences of testing, and (c) removing children from regular classrooms and referring them to potentially damaging special classes. These criticisms have little merit, I believe, because they are not based on any foundation of research and merely skim the surface of clinical activities.

Many critics fail to consider that tests have many valid uses. Tests allow for accountability, for measurement of change, and for evaluating the effectiveness of programs. The diagnostic process helps children to obtain special programs that can contribute to their educational experiences. We must recognize that it is crucial for children of all ethnic groups to learn the basic cognitive and academic skills necessary for survival in our culture. Few of the critics have yet to propose reasonable alternatives to supplement present methods.

Clinical and school psychologists have reeled under the numerous attacks of the past decade. Courts have issued subpoenas limiting the freedom of psychologists to use and select tests for evaluation and placement decisions. These attacks have uncovered some real shortcomings. To label a Spanish-speaking child who does not speak English as mentally retarded, based on the administration of an English-language verbal intelligence test, is unconscionable and unforgivable. To keep poor records of the parental permission that acknowledged and authorized an evaluation is shoddy practice; to give tests to children without explanation and discussion is inconsiderate. These and other such practices must not continue.

We are accountable, as a profession, to the children we serve, to their parents, to the schools, and to the larger community. We must not ignore the many valid criticisms of tests and test practices simply because we do not like them. We must continue to develop procedures and instruments that will best serve our clients. Procedures now available to protect our clients must be adhered to scrupulously. While none of us like our shortcomings to be pointed out in private, much less in public, we must listen to our critics and make sure that we are following the best scientific and clinical practices. I believe that the discord of the seventies has had a cleansing and beneficial effect.

Behavioral Objectives of Text

This book emphasizes the technical as well as the clinical aspects of testing. The technical information on testing presented in this book provides the foundation for accurate and objective measurement. As mentioned earlier, tests are tools; so this book will also focus on the clinical skills that enhance the clinician's ability to use these tools meaningfully and effectively. Some important guidelines for evaluating tests are presented in Table 1-1.

All students training to become clinicians should have a background in tests and measurement, statistics, child development, and child psychopathology. The book is not meant to be a substitute for test manuals or for texts in child psychopathology. It supplements some of the material contained in test manuals, but goes further by considering many additional facets of tests and of the assessment process.

Mastery of the assessment process requires supervised experience. Supervision is needed especially in the beginning phase of a student's career. Supervision should cover all phases of the assessment process, including test administration, scoring, report writing, and consultation. Ideally, during the beginning phase of the student's course of study, the student should examine many different types of children—normal and emotionally disturbed, retarded and gifted, and physically handicapped children—in a variety of settings.

Selecting a Test Battery

A prerequisite for effective testing is the ability to plan assessment strategies and to choose tests to meet specific needs. This book is intended to provide clinicians with the knowledge that they will need in order to evaluate and to use a variety of individual intelligence and special ability tests. Information is included on test reliability, validity, and normative standardization.

In deciding whether or not to administer an individualized assessment battery, consider the appropriateness of the referral question and whether alternative assessment routes are available. How important is it for the battery to be administered? Will group tests be as effective as the individual battery in answering the referral question? Are there any motivational, personality, linguistic, or physically disabling factors that may impair the examinee's performance on group tests? Individual tests should be administered primarily when there is reason to question the validity of the results of group tests or when an extremely careful evaluation of the examinee's performance is needed. The examiner should also discuss the reasons for individual assessment with referral sources in order to familiarize them with the values and limitations of individual testing. Such discussions may lead to a reduction in the number of children unnecessarily referred for individual testing. In turn, children most in need of individual testing will be provided with prompt and intensive services.

Administering the Test Battery

Knowing what is in the test manuals and in the present text will aid examiners in learning how to administer the tests properly. This text contains information relevant to test administration, including sections on

TABLE 1-1. Guidelines for Evaluating a Test

General Identifying Information

1. What is the name of the test?
2. Who are its authors—by name and position if that information is available.
3. Who published the test, and when was it published?
4. Is there an alternative form available?
5. What does it cost?
6. How long does it take to administer?

Information About the Test

1. Is there a manual for the test (or other similar source) that is designed to provide the information that a potential user needs?
2. How recently has the test been revised? How recently has the test manual been revised?

Aids to Interpreting Test Results

1. Does the manual provide a clear statement of the purposes and applications for which the test is intended?
2. Does the manual provide a clear statement of the qualifications needed to administer the test and interpret it properly?

3. Do the test, manual, record forms, and accompanying materials guide users toward sound and correct interpretation of the test results?
4. Are the statements in the manual that express relationships presented in quantitative terms, so that the reader can tell how much precision or confidence to attach to them?

Validity

Does the manual report evidence on the validity of the test for each type of inference for which the test is recommended?

Reliability

Does the manual present adequate data in order to permit the reader to judge whether scores are sufficiently dependable for the recommended uses?

Administration and Scoring

1. Are the directions for administration sufficiently full and clear so that the administrator will be able to duplicate the conditions under which the norms were established and reliability and validity data were obtained?

2. Are the procedures for scoring set forth clearly and in detail, in such a way as to maximize scoring efficiency and minimize the likelihood of scoring error?

Scales and Norms

1. Are the scales used for reporting scores clearly and carefully described, so that the test interpreter will fully understand them and be able to communicate the interpretation to an examinee?
2. Are norms reported in the manual that are in an appropriate form, usually standard scores or percentile ranks in appropriate reference groups?
3. Are the populations to which the norms refer clearly defined and described, and are they populations with which you can appropriately compare your client?
4. If more than one form is available, including revised forms, are tables available showing equivalent scores on the different forms?
5. Does the manual discuss the possible value of local norms, and provide any help in preparing local norms?

Reprinted, in condensed form, and with modifications, by permission of the publisher and authors from R. L. Thorndike and E. Hagen, *Measurement and Evaluation in Psychology and Education* (4th ed.), pp. 108–110. Copyright 1977, John Wiley and Sons, Inc.

---

the completion of record booklets, general administrative procedures, specific test procedures, and examiner-examinee variables. Practical administrative suggestions, based on clinical experience and on research findings, are provided for many of the tests.

Scoring Tests

Concurrently with administering the test battery, examiners are required to score the child's responses. If they are going to score the tests accurately, they should be familiar with the research findings concerning scoring bias, halo effects, errors in test scoring, and use of scoring criteria.

Observing Behavior

Another activity that takes place concurrently with administering the test battery is the observation of the child's behavior. Such observation is an important part of the assessment process. Knowing how the child performs on the various tasks is extremely useful in individualizing the clinical evaluation and is a valuable supplement to the more objective evaluation. Behavioral observations focus on such areas as the child's interpersonal relations, attitude, language, motivation, and motor skills. Specific suggestions are made in the text for observing and evaluating the child's behavior during the evaluation.

Communicating Results

As mentioned earlier, clinicians using tests make a unique contribution to those dedicated to studying and encouraging child development. The value of their contribution will depend on their ability to communicate their findings clearly and meaningfully. Additionally, clinicians must direct their efforts on the basis of feedback they receive from others. At the time the referral is initiated, the clinician may confer with the referral source; read background information; interview teachers, parents, or other knowledgeable individuals; and study cumulative records in preparation for the formal testing. When the evaluation is completed, many different types of professionals—including teachers, psychiatrists, pediatricians, neurologists, social workers, and lawyers—may make use of the findings. In addition, the findings and recommendations need to be communicated to the child's parents and, where applicable, to the child as well.

After the testing has been completed, a psychological report usually is written. The report contains the psychologist's findings, interpretations, and recommendations. One of the best aids in learning how to write a report is the study of reports written by competent clinicians. In the text, several reports are included to demonstrate different styles and approaches to the evaluation task. They all have in common, I believe, clear writing, skillful analysis, and good clinical judgment. However, these reports should be used only as general guides, for each examiner needs to develop his or her own style and approach to report writing. The text also presents examples of communication problems that occur in reports.

Exhibit 1-2 illustrates how a test battery is used in the assessment of a child who is having difficulty in school.

After the report is written, examiners may want to meet with the child to discuss the results or they may discuss the results with the child's parents or with the referral source. In addition, examiners may be called upon to present their results at a staff conference. Such meetings require skill, because in some cases clients or parents may be defensive, and in hospitals and in other settings special problems may arise in working with other professionals. Examiners thoroughly familiar with the subject matter presented in this text will be in a firm position to present and defend their findings clearly and systematically.

The assessment should not stop with the writing of a report. Every attempt should be made to work continuously with the referral source. Interventions recommended in the report should be evaluated to determine their effectiveness.

Conducting Research

While not directly involved in the formal assessment process, research is an invaluable adjunct to our understanding of tests and the testing process. Progress in assessment cannot occur without research. Many factors bear investigation, such as determining test reliability and validity for various populations, evaluating clinical and educational theories, studying procedural changes in test administration, and evaluating different remediation strategies. Familiarity with research findings and the problems involved with such research will provide examiners with a base from which they can evaluate their own testing techniques and published research reports.

Finally, examiners may find themselves doing research on intelligence testing and on tests of special abilities. Much of the material in the text is relevant to this task. A knowledge of research and research problems may stimulate examiners to design and conduct their own investigations.

EXHIBIT 1-2. Psychological Evaluation: A Boy with Learning Problems

Name: Bill
Date of birth: April 10, 1971
Chronological age: 9-8
Date of examination: December 12, 1980
Date of report: December 15, 1980
Grade: Second

Tests Administered

Wechsler Intelligence Scale for Children–Revised:

VERBAL SCALE		PERFORMANCE SCALE	
Information	4	Picture Completion	13
Similarities	7	Picture Arrangement	9
Arithmetic	6	Block Design	12
Vocabulary	8	Object Assembly	14
Comprehension	7	Coding	6
(Digit Span)	(5)		

Verbal Scale IQ = 78
Performance Scale IQ = 105
Full Scale IQ = 89±6 at the 95% confidence level

Wide Range Achievement Test:

	STANDARD SCORE	PERCENTILE
Reading	67	1
Spelling	61	.9
Arithmetic	80	9

1. N (in)
2. gow (go)
3. cat (cat)
4. boe (boy)
5. dnb (and)
6. woll (will)
7. maek (make)
8. humo (him)
9. sae (say)
10. kut (cut)
11. kuk (cook)
12. loek (light)
13. mast (must)
14. dust (dress)
15. rech (reach)

Vineland Social Maturity Scale: SA = 6.9; DSQ = 76.

Draw-A-Man: Standard score = 99; Percentile = 47th.

Bender-Gestalt: 9-year-old level.

Reason for Referral

Bill was referred by his teacher because of learning problems at school.

EXHIBIT 1-2 (cont.)

Background

Bill, a 9-8-year-old boy, is enrolled in second grade, having repeated both first and second grades. A recent parental divorce, the death of a grandfather, and the return of Bill's two older brothers to the home has made for a tumultuous home setting. Bill's mother seems to be trying hard to deal with these numerous areas of frustration and tension.

Besides two older brothers, Bill has a 13-year-old sister with whom he is close. He is in good health and no serious childhood illnesses were reported. His mother recalled that some motor and speech milestones were delayed.

Behavioral Observations

Bill, who arrived with his mother, initially seemed shy and reticent with the examiner. Nevertheless, he willingly came with the examiner, and, except for intermittent anxious laughter, he seemed relatively at ease. Bill tended to be chatty with a somewhat disconnected conversational style. Numerous sound substitutions and omissions (such as "vorsed" for divorced, and "skies" for disguised) and syntax errors (often in tenses as well as subject-verb agreement) were noted in his spontaneous speech. He also displayed some word retrieval difficulties, such as labeling dresser knobs as "holes"; auditory discrimination difficulties, such as defining "contagious" as "cage"; and difficulty repeating short sentences (his rendering of the statement "How many things make a dozen?" was "How much make a bunch?").

Bill's work style tended to be slow and cautious, and he seemed to want to avoid all errors. Although generally cooperative, he sometimes gave up when tasks became difficult, but persisted with mild verbal encouragement. Overall, his level of activity was within normal limits and he reacted appropriately to success and failure.

Test Results

On the WISC-R, Bill, with a chronological age of 9-8, achieved a Verbal Scale IQ of 78 (8th percentile), a Performance Scale IQ of 105 (63rd percentile), and a Full Scale IQ of 89 ± 6. The chances that the range of scores from 83 to 95 includes his true IQ are about 95 out of 100. His overall score places him in the Below Normal range and at the 24th percentile. These, as well as other test results, appear to be reliable and valid. A 27-point disparity between his Verbal and Performance Scale IQs was noted, with borderline functioning overall in verbal areas and average functioning in performance areas. Bill has strengths in the areas of spatial reasoning and perceptual integration. His weaknesses are in short-term auditory memory, psychomotor speed, and general information.

Qualitatively, Bill's verbal responses on the WISC-R were marked by numerous confused and unusual responses. He seemed confused by temporal relationships, as he named days of the week when asked for seasons of the year. Further conceptual confusion was noted as he responded to the question "How many pounds make a ton?" with "Elephant." In general, his answers tended to be concrete and poorly organized, with a loose run-on sentence structure.

On the Draw-A-Man, he obtained a standard score of 99 (47th percentile). This result is somewhat higher than his score on the WISC-R.

On the WRAT, Bill functioned in the 1st percentile in reading and spelling skills. Although he knows numerous spelling rules, he has considerable difficulty in employing them at the right time and in the right place. For example, the word *boy* was spelled *b-o-e*. His reading does not reflect an effective use of phonetic skills (such as his reading the word "red" for "run" or "get" for "big"). He can identify letters reliably, and, in attempting to read words, he tended to fractionate each phonetic unit and was often unable to integrate them effectively. Arithmetical skills are at the 9th percentile. While he seems to have mastered simple addition and subtraction skills including borrowing and carrying skills, he has difficulty with age-appropriate arithmetic tasks.

It is not surprising that a young man who has difficulty in auditory discrimination and verbal sequencing (for example, saying "masic" for magic and "gammel" for gamble) would have difficulty spelling and reading phonetically. For example, he was unable to sequence all the sounds when asked the name of his school. Other common information which he seemed unable to give included his brother's age, his current address, and familial relationships, such as uncle.

On the Vineland Social Maturity Scale, with Bill's mother as informant, Bill received a Social Age of 6.9 years and a Deviation Social Quotient of 76. This suggests that some social immaturity may be present. Bill's scope of freedom and responsibility seems sharply limited at home, as his mother does not allow him to leave the yard. His chores at home are few and his mother still helps

EXHIBIT 1-2 (cont.)

him with many self-care activities, including combing his hair.

His performance on the Bender-Gestalt was close to the level of a 9-year-old child. Overall, visual-motor ability as measured on this test was well within normal limits.

Summary and Discussion

Bill showed unusually divergent strengths and weaknesses across intellectual areas, with verbal abilities being at a below average level and performance abilities being at an average level. Overall, he obtained a WISC-R Full Scale IQ of 89 ± 6, which is at the 24th percentile and in the Below Average range. He would fit the definition of a "learning disabled" child, and is no doubt experiencing considerable difficulty in a traditional school setting because of language processing difficulties. Correspondingly, little progress has been seen in spelling and reading (despite repeating first and second grades); however, some progress has been made in arithmetic. Socially, Bill also acts like a child younger than his age.

Recommendations

1. An individualized program of special education with particular emphasis on language and language-related skills is recommended. The program should be structured to emphasize the acquisition of reading and writing skills.
2. Speech and language therapy integrated with this special education curriculum would be desirable.
3. Bill's nonverbal spatial strengths should be used in the remediation program. For example, reading materials related to building models might be appropriate.
4. Bill's mother could use guidance to help sort out and resolve personal as well as family stress. Some possible areas of focus would be encouraging communication skills between family members, dealing with hostilities felt toward her husband and older children, learning how to cope with being a single parent, and helping her children deal with the issue of the divorce.

Examiner

Summary

1. The assessment of children's abilities is a complex activity that requires technical skills as well as interpersonal skills.
2. Tests are powerful tools and must be thoroughly understood before they are used as assessment instruments.
3. Labeling and classification, while important, must not cloud the examiner's ability to see the child as a unique individual.
4. Norm-referenced tests are important for the assessment of intelligence and special abilities.
5. Testing has become of public concern, particularly the assessment and placement of ethnic minority children. The attacks on testing during the 1970s should make us doubly vigilant about how we use tests in the future.
6. The assessment process, in part, consists of evaluating the referral question; selecting, administering, and scoring a test; observing behavior; designing interventions; writing reports; evaluating the success of interventions; and consulting.
7. Research, too, may be a by-product of assessment activities.

CHAPTER 2

Useful Statistics for the Assessment of Intelligence and Special Abilities

We conquer the facts of nature when we observe and experiment upon them. When we measure them we have made them our servants. A little statistical insight trains them for invaluable work.

EDWARD L. THORNDIKE
Educational Psychology

This chapter covers some useful statistics and measurement concepts that are needed for the assessment task. The concepts reviewed will enable you to evaluate more effectively the psychometric properties of intelligence and special ability tests and to approach test manuals and research reports with a keener and more discerning eye. Psychometric refers, in part, to the quantitative assessment of an individual's psychological traits or attributes. This chapter is presented as a review, and is not meant as a substitute for texts in statistics or tests and measurement.

Descriptive Statistics

Descriptive statistics provide means by which data obtained on a sample of individuals can be summarized. For an understanding of descriptive statistics we need to know about such things as the various scales that are used for measurement, types of distributions of scores, basic statistical notations, measures of central tendency, measures of dispersion, and correlations. The more commonly used symbols in statistics and psychometrics are shown in Table 2-1. These symbols are a shorthand way of describing important characteristics of a test formula or norm group.

Scales of Measurement

There are various methods by which data can be ordered. In most cases, measurement techniques fall into one of four types of scales: nominal, ordinal, interval, or ratio. A scale is a system for assigning numerical values to some measurable trait or characteristic. These values can then be subjected to various mathematical procedures in order to determine relationships between the traits or characteristics of interest and other measured behaviors.

Nominal scales. In a nominal scale a separate numeral or name, such as a number, letter of the alphabet, or Roman numeral, is assigned to each item being scaled. These labels ordinarily represent mutually exclusive categories and cannot be arranged in order. An example of nominal scaling would

"I THOUGHT THIS IS WHAT WE HAVE COMPUTERS FOR!"

Reprinted by permission of the Chicago Tribune–New York News Syndicate, Inc.

TABLE 2-1. Some Common Statistical and Psychometric Symbols and Abbreviations

Symbol	Definition	Symbol	Definition
a	Intercept constant in a regression equation.	r_{xy}	Validity coefficient (x represents test score and y the criterion score).
b	Slope constant in a regression equation.	SD or s	Standard deviation of the sample.
c	Any unspecified constant.	σ	Standard deviation of a population.
CA	Chronological age.	S^2	Variance.
f	Frequency.	s_m or s_{meas}	Standard error of measurement.
F	Test statistic in analysis of variance and covariance.	t	t test.
IQ	Intelligence quotient.	T	T score. Standard score with a mean of 50 and standard deviation of 10
M	Mean (see also $\bar{X}$).	X	Raw score.
Md or Mdn	Median.	x	Deviation score $= X - \bar{X}$. Indicates how far the individual falls above or below the mean of the group.
MA	Mental age.		
n	Number of cases in a subsample.	$\bar{X}$	Mean.
		Y	A second raw score.
N	Number of cases in a sample.	z	z score. Standard score with a mean of 0 and standard deviation of 1.
p	Probability.		
p	Proportion.	Σ	"The sum of." ΣX means add up all the Xs (scores).
P	Percentile.		
Q_1	The 25th percentile.	χ^2	Chi square.
Q_3	The 75th percentile.	$<$	Less than.
Q	Semi-interquartile range. Half the difference between Q_3 and Q_1.	$>$	Greater than.
		$\pm$	Plus or minus.
		$\sqrt{}$	Square root.
r	Correlation coefficient.	$\geq$	Greater than or equal to.
r_{xx}	Reliability coefficient.	$\leq$	Less than or equal to.

be the assignment of numbers to baseball players. These numbers have no meaning or use other than to identify the individual players. The scale is of limited usefulness because it allows only for classification.

Ordinal scales. In an ordinal scale the variable being measured is ranked or ordered, regardless of the difference in the magnitude between scores. An example of an ordinal scale would be the ranking of persons or scores for a particular measure, such as class standing, from first to last or highest to lowest. An ordinal scale would tell us, for example, who was first, second, or third; it would not tell us whether the distance between the first- and second-ranked scores was the same as the distance between the second- and third-ranked scores.

Interval scales. In an interval scale a specific unit of measurement is obtained. The unit of measurement is such that the distance or difference between any two adjacent numbers on the scale is the same as the difference between any other two adjacent numbers. The interval scale does not possess a true zero point, either because a true zero point exists but is unknown or because conceptual problems have not yet allowed its establishment. The measurement technique must specify a procedure for determining equal intervals, but it provides no operation allowing for the definition of "zero."

Ratio scales. In a ratio scale there are equal intervals and, in addition, a true or absolute zero point. A statement such as "X is twice as heavy as Y" is a legitimate statement when it refers to a measurement made on a ratio scale. Thus, an example of a measurement made on a ratio scale is the different weights of individuals. An individual who weighs 150 pounds is twice as heavy as one who weighs 75 pounds. This statement can be made because there is a meaningful zero point (no weight); thus a true ratio of the weights of the two individuals exists. Because most psychological characteristics do not permit the measurement of an absolute zero point (such as "zero intelligence"), ratio scales are found infrequently in psychology. We must be content with interval scales in many cases, and the weaker ordinal scales are also very common.

Measures of Central Tendency

The three most commonly used measures of central tendency are the mean, median, and mode. The mean is the arithmetic average of all of the scores or values in the distribution. It is found by dividing the sum of all the scores by the total number of scores in the distribution.

The median is defined as the middle point in a distribution when all of the scores have been arranged in order of magnitude. Fifty percent of the scores lie above and 50 percent of the scores lie below the median. The median may or may not be earned or ob-

MOMMA by Mell Lazarus. Courtesy of Mell Lazarus and Field Newspaper Syndicate.

tained. That is, if there is an even number of scores, the median is taken as the average of the two middlemost scores and therefore it is not actually earned by anyone. However, if there is an odd number of scores, the median is simply the middlemost score; as such, it is actually earned by someone.

The mode of a distribution of scores is that score occurring more often than any other score. In some distributions two scores occur more often than any other score and with the same frequency; in such cases the distribution is said to be bimodal. When more than two scores occur more than any other score and with the same frequency, the distribution is said to be multimodal.

Measures of Dispersion

The two most common measures of dispersion are variance and standard deviation. Variance (S^2) is a measure of the variability or dispersion of a group of scores. It is a statistical way of expressing the amount of spread in a group of scores; the greater the spread, the greater the variance, and the smaller the spread, the smaller the variance. For example, say we have two different sets of scores both normally distributed and with the same mean, but one with a large variance and the other with a small variance. The group of scores with the large variance will have a larger range or spread of scores than the group of scores with the small variance.

The standard deviation (SD), sometimes represented by the Greek letter σ, is another measure of the extent to which scores deviate from the mean. It is the square root of the variance, and is the most important and most commonly used measure of variability. It is also used in calculating the Deviation IQ, which is discussed later in this chapter.

Normal Curve

The normal (or bell-shaped) curve (see Figure 2-1) is the most common type of distribution. Many psychological traits are distributed roughly along a normal curve. Although a perfect normal curve is rarely achieved, small variations do not appreciably change the relevant statistical interpre-

tations. An important feature of the normal curve is that it tells us exactly how many cases fall between any two points on the curve.

We now have covered some of the basic concepts that can help us better understand the normal curve. Let us examine more carefully Figure 2-1. It can be seen that there is a precise relationship between the standard deviation and the proportion of cases in a normal curve. Notice, too, that Figure 2-1 shows the percentage of cases that fall within one, two, and three standard deviations above and below the mean. Approximately 34 percent of the cases fall within +1 SD (or −1 SD) of the mean. As we go further away from the mean, the number of cases diminishes. Thus, the areas covered from +1 SD to +2 SD and from −1 SD to −2 SD each represent approximately 14 percent of the cases. Between 2 and 3 SD from the mean are even fewer cases, approximately 2 percent of the distribution. We will return again to the normal curve when we consider standard scores.

Correlations

Correlations quantify the relationship between two (or more) variables. The relationship is presented in the form of a correlation coefficient, which is an index of both the strength and direction of the relationship between the two variables. The strength of the relationship is determined by the absolute magnitude of the coefficient; the maximum value is 1.00. The direction of the relationship is given by the sign preceding the number. A positive correlation indicates that a high score on one variable is associated with a high score on the second variable. Conversely, a negative correlation signifies an inverse relationship. That is, a high score on one variable is associated with a low score on the other variable. Thus, correlation coefficients range in value from −1.00 to +1.00.

A most important aspect of correlation is its close relationship to prediction. The higher the correlation between two variables, the more accurately one can predict the value of one variable when supplied only

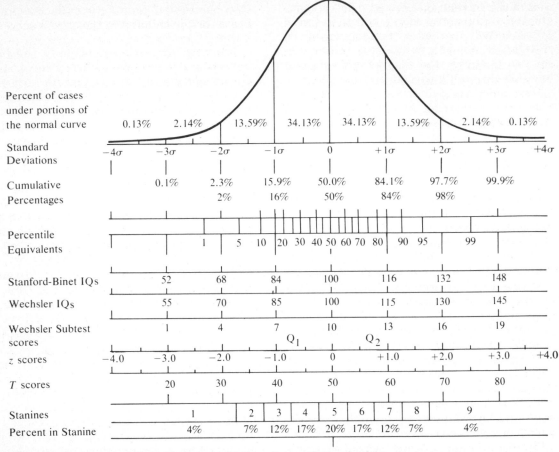

FIGURE 2-1. Relationship of Normal Curve to Various Types of Standard Scores.

with the value of the other variable. A correlation of −1.00 or +1.00 would enable one to predict perfectly a person's score on one variable if the score on the other variable were known. In contrast, a correlation of .00 indicates that there is no (linear) way of predicting one variable from knowledge of the other variable.

The Pearson product-moment correlation coefficient, symbolized by the letter r, is the most frequently used correlation coefficient. The assumptions underlying the Pearson r are that the two variables are continuous and normally distributed, that a linear relationship exists between these variables, and

that the predictions of scores on variable Y can be made about equally well, irrespective of scores on variable X.

Correlational data can be used to construct an equation that makes the best possible prediction about the unknown value of one variable when one has the value of the other variable. The equation used for prediction is called the regression equation, and has the general form $Y = a + bX$, where Y and X are the variables, a is the Y-axis intercept of the regression line, and b is the slope of the regression line. The values for the constants a and b are determined from the available scores. It should be realized that the accuracy of the estimate depends on the extent of the correlation between the two variables: a ± 1.00 correlation coefficient allows for a perfect prediction to be made; a .00 correlation makes it impossible to improve the prediction of the value of the unknown variable through knowledge of the value of the second variable.

Multiple Correlation

Multiple correlation is a statistical technique that allows us to determine the relationship between one variable and several others. The statistic used for this purpose is the coefficient of multiple correlation, R. Predictions based on a multiple correlation are likely to be more accurate than those based on a single variable because several different factors relevant to the prediction are considered. A principal drawback of using multiple correlations is that it takes very large samples, usually over one hundred, to arrive at a stable prediction equation when several variables are used. A good example of the proper use of multiple correlation is in prediction of performance in college. Measures of high school grades, intelligence test scores, and educational attainment of parents have been found to correlate positively with test performance. By using all of these measures in a multiple correlation analysis, it is possible to predict performance level in college more accurately than if only one of these measures were used.

Norm-Referenced Measurement

In norm-referenced testing an examinee's performance is compared with the performance of a specific group of subjects. A norm provides an indication of average or typical performance of the specified group. Norms are needed because the raw score in itself is not very meaningful. Knowing that a child scored 20 or answered correctly 70 percent of the items tells us very little unless we also know how other children performed on the same test; a relevant normative population is needed. We could compare the child's score with those of a representative population of children in the United States or the children in the child's school or a special population. The comparison is carried out by converting the child's raw score into some relative measure. These measures are termed derived scores, and they indicate the child's standing relative to the norm group. Derived scores also allow us to compare the child's performance on one test with his or her performance on other tests.

Before turning to a discussion of derived scores, let us consider some factors that are important in evaluating a normative group. These include (a) the representativeness of the group, (b) the number of cases in the group, and (c) the relevance of the group. Representativeness of the norm group refers to the extent to which the group is characteristic of a particular population. Ideally, the norm sample should match as closely as possible various demographic characteristics of the population as a whole. The most salient of these characteristics for psycho-educational assessment are age, grade level, sex, geographic region, ethnicity, and socio-economic status. The date the norms were established also is an important consideration in interpreting the norms.

The number of subjects in the norm group should be large enough (a) to ensure stability of the test scores and (b) to include various groups that are represented in the population. Usually, the larger the number of subjects used, the more stable the norms are. If the test is to span a number of age groups, then the size of the sample should contain at least one hundred subjects for each age level or grade level.

It is important to consider how relevant the norms are for the evaluation of the examinees. Proper test interpretation is vitally dependent on the selection of the correct norm group against which to evaluate the examinee's test results. For some purposes, national norms may be most appropriate, while for others, norms of a particular segment of the population may be most relevant. In all cases, the person interpreting a test must possess the skills and insight to select the proper norm group for each individual being evaluated. The report should clearly state the norm group that has been selected, especially when the norm group is different from the one that is customarily or routinely used by most testers.

Derived Scores

We now consider the major types of derived scores that are used in norm-referenced testing. Derived scores vary in their usefulness, as we will see below. The major types of derived scores are age and grade equivalents, ratio IQs, percentiles, standard scores, and stanines.

Age-Equivalent and Grade-Equivalent Norms

Age-equivalent and grade-equivalent norms are obtained by determining the average score obtained by children of various ages or grade placements. For example, if the average score of 10-year-old children on a test is 15 items correct out of 25 problems, then any child obtaining a score of 15 receives an age-equivalent score of 10. The age-equivalent norm is obtained by computing the mean raw score of a measure for a group of children with a specific age. Similarly, a grade-equivalent norm is obtained by finding the mean raw score obtained by children in each grade. If the mean score of seventh graders on an arithmetic test is 30, then a child obtaining a score of 30 would be said to have arithmetical knowledge at the seventh grade level. A grade-equivalent score is expressed in tenths of a grade (e.g., 5.5 refers to average performance at the middle of the fifth grade).

Other terms for age-equivalent scores are mental age (MA) and test age. For the 1972 norms on the Stanford-Binet, mental ages do not mean scores (or performances) that are associated with children of a certain age. MAs simply represent a certain number of points obtained by the child on the test. The interpretation of MAs is discussed more fully in Chapter 4. In the WISC-R and WPPSI manuals, test ages are presented for raw scores on each subtest.

Careful interpretation of age- and grade-equivalent scores is required. A number of problems are associated with these types of scores (Thorndike & Hagen, 1977). First, age- and grade-equivalent scores may not represent equal units. The difference between second and third grade-equivalent scores may not be the same as the difference between eleventh and twelfth grade-equivalent scores. Second, many grade-equivalents are obtained by means of interpolation and extrapolation. Consequently, the resulting scores do not reflect scores actually obtained by children. Third, when grade-equivalent scores of two or more kinds are compared, misleading conclusions may result because advancement does not occur uniformly in all subject areas. For example, it is not necessarily the case that a child who obtains a fifth grade equivalent on a mathematics test measuring addition and subtraction can also do fifth grade mathematics requiring knowledge of multiplication and division. Finally, age- and grade-equivalent scores tend to be based on ordinal scales, not interval scales, and therefore they are less amenable to the computation of important statistical measures, such as the standard error of measurement.

Ratio Intelligence Quotients

Before interpreting age-equivalent or grade-equivalent scores, we must know the child's chronological age (CA). Knowing the child's MA and CA allows us to make a judgment about the child's relative performance. For example, a child with a CA of 10-0 and an MA of 12-0 has performed at an above average level, while a child with the same CA and an MA of 8-0 has performed at a below average level.

When IQs were first introduced, they were defined as the ratio of mental age to chronological age, multiplied by 100 to eliminate the decimal: $IQ = MA/CA \times 100$. Substituting an MA of 12 and a CA of 10 in the formula yields a ratio IQ of 120 ($IQ = 12/10 \times 100 = 120$). This IQ was called a ratio IQ, because it was a ratio of the two ages. It was soon discovered that because the standard deviation of the IQ distribution did not remain constant with age, the IQs for different ages were not comparable: the same IQ at different ages had different meanings. The use of the Deviation IQ, however, which is a standard score (see section below on Standard Scores), effectively avoids this problem.

Percentiles

Percentile ranks or norms are derived scores that permit us to determine an individual's position relative to the standardization sample (or any other specified sample). A percentile is a score or point in a distribution at or below which a given percentage of individuals fall. If 63 percent of the cases fall below a given score, then that score is at the 63rd percentile. Quartiles are percentile ranks that divide a distribution into four equal parts, with each part containing 25 percent of the norm group. Deciles, a less common percentile rank, contain 10 bands, with each band containing 10 percent of the norm group.

Interpretation of percentile ranks is simple and straightforward. For example, a person who obtains a percentile rank of 35 on an intelligence test has scored as well as or better than 35 percent of the people in the norm sample. However, the psychometric properties of percentile ranks limit their usefulness in data analysis. The primary difficulty is that all parts along the percentile distribution do not represent equal units. Raw score differences between percentiles are smaller near the mean than at the extremes. Percentiles must be normalized by being converted to another scale before they are used in statistical tests.

Standard Scores

Standard scores are raw scores that have been transformed to have a given mean and standard deviation. They express how far an examinee's score lies from the mean of the distribution in terms of the standard deviation.

A z score is one type of standard score, with a mean of 0 and a standard deviation of 1. Frequently, z scores are transformed to other standard scores in order to eliminate the + and − signs. For example, a T score represents a standard score based on a distribution with a mean of 50 and a standard deviation of 10. The Deviation IQ is another example of a standard score. Instead of a mean of 50 and a standard deviation of 10, as in the T score distribution, the Deviation IQ has a mean of 100 and a standard deviation of 15 or 16, depending on the test used. All of the Wechsler scales (WISC-R, WPPSI, and WAIS-R) provide Deviation IQs with a mean of 100 and a standard deviation of 15. The Stanford-Binet, Form L-M, also provides Deviation IQs, with a mean of 100 and a standard deviation of 16.

Stanines

Stanines (a contraction of *standard nine*) provide a single-digit scoring system with a mean of 5 and a standard deviation of 2. The scores are expressed in whole numbers from 1 to 9. When scores are converted to stanines, the shape of the original distribution is changed into a normal curve. The percentages of scores at each stanine are 4, 7, 12, 17, 20, 17, 12, 7, and 4, respectively (see Figure 2-1).

Comment on Derived Scores

From our discussion of derived scores, it should be evident that the various types of derived scores are all based on raw scores. The different types represent different methods of expressing the child's performance. One type of derived score can be converted to another type. The most frequently used conversion in the area of intelligence testing is from standard scores (e.g., scaled scores or Deviation IQs) to percentiles. Standard scores are the preferred derived scores, but percentiles—and, on occasion, age equivalents—are also useful. The latter two scores may be helpful in describing the child's performance to parents or teachers.

The relationship among various types of derived scores is shown in Figure 2-1. If a test has a Deviation IQ of 100 and a standard deviation of 15 we can determine precisely the percentiles associated with each IQ. Let us see how we compute percentiles associated with IQs at various SD points.

First, let us begin with an IQ of 100. This represents the 50th percentile, because an IQ of 100 has been set as the mean of the distribution. An IQ of 115 represents the point that is +1 SD away from the mean in this example. The percentile associated with this IQ is the 84th percentile. It is obtained by adding 50 to 34 percent. The 50 percent represents the amount of population below the mean of 100, and the 34 percent represents the amount of population between the mean and +1 SD away from the mean. The key here is to recognize that an IQ of 115 is +1 SD above the mean because 15 is the SD of the distribution.

Using the same rationale, we can compute readily the percentile associated with an IQ of 130. An IQ of 130 is +2 SD away from the mean. We know (see Figure 2-1) that the area from the mean to +1 SD represents approximately 34 percent of the population, while the area from +1 SD to +2 SD represents approximately 14 percent of the population. To arrive at the percentile for an IQ of 130 we would add $50 + 34 + 14 = 98$th percentile. The 50, as we have just seen, represents the percent of the population below the mean; the 34 represents the percent of the population between the mean and +1 $SD;$ and the 14 represents the percent of the population between +1 SD and +2 SD. Now try to figure out the percentile associated with an IQ of 85. The answer you obtain should be the 16th percentile. This time we need to subtract 34 from 50, because 85 represents the score (or point) that is −1 SD below the mean. The percentile associated with an IQ of 70 is the 2nd percentile $(50 − 34 − 14 = 2)$.

The above examples hold only for tests that have a Deviation IQ with a $\bar{X}$ of 100 and a SD of 15 (e.g., WISC-R, WPPSI, and WAIS-R). For tests that have a $\bar{X}$ of 100 and a SD of 16, such as the Stanford-Binet, the percentiles associated with the various IQs are slightly different except at the mean. The IQ of 100 is still at the 50th percentile, but an IQ of 116 (not 115) is at the 84th percentile because the SD is 16.

Thus, the IQs on the two types of scales are not directly comparable. For example,

we have just seen that an IQ of 116 is at the 84th percentile on the Stanford-Binet, but at the 85th percentile on the WISC-R. While a one percentile difference may not appear to be a major difference, it may loom as an important factor when placement decisions are made. This is especially so when the one percentile difference places the child into a different classification. A glance at Table BC-1 on the inside back cover will show you the percentile ranks associated with the Deviation IQs found on the Stanford-Binet, Wechsler batteries, and other tests.

Statistical Significance

As part of a statistical analysis, the results are usually analyzed to determine the extent to which the findings differ from those to be expected on the basis of chance. Conventions establish the .05 level as the minimum significance level indicating that observed differences are real. This level means that such results would occur 5 percent of the time by chance. More stringent levels of significance can be reported, such as the .01 and .001 levels. Significance levels are used, for example, in evaluating differences between means, differences between a score and the mean of the scale, or whether correlations differ from zero. The expression $p < .05$ means that the results are at a probability level that is less than .05 (or 5 times in one hundred), whereas the expression $p > .05$ means that the results are at a probability level that is greater than .05.

It is important to evaluate not only whether the particular findings probably differ from chance, but also the absolute difference between the mean values or the absolute value of the correlation. For example, while the mean difference between two groups may be statistically significant, the difference may have no practical significance. Similarly, the correlation may be significant if the sample size is large enough, but the correlation may account for only a small percent of the variation in the criterion. Correlations used as validity coefficients must be squared in order to determine the amount of variance explained by the predictor (or test). Thus, a .60 correlation between IQs and school grades indicates that IQs account for 36 percent of the variance in school performance.

Reliability

"Reliability refers to consistency of scores obtained by the same persons when re-examined with the same test on different occasions, or with different sets of equivalent items, or under variable examining conditions" (Anastasi, 1976, p. 103). It is expressed by some form of reliability coefficient or by the standard error of measurement, which is derived from the reliability coefficient. A test whose reliability is too low simply cannot be trusted. High reliabilities are needed for tests used for individual assessment. For most tests of cognitive and special abilities, a reliability coefficient of .80 or higher is generally considered to be acceptable.

Reliability Coefficient

The reliability coefficient expresses the degree to which there is consistency in measurement of the test scores. The symbol used to denote a reliability coefficient is the letter r with two identical subscripts (e.g., r_{xx}). The reliability coefficient ranges from 1.00 (indicating perfect reliability) to .00 (indicating the absence of reliability). There are three types of reliability coefficients: test-retest, alternate forms, and internal consistency. The Pearson product-moment correlation procedure is used to determine test-retest and alternate-form reliability coefficients, while specialized formulas are used to compute internal consistency reliability.

Test-retest reliability. Test-retest reliability, the most common way of measuring reliability, is an index of stability. The usual procedure for obtaining a test-retest reliability coefficient is to test the same group on two different occasions with the same test, usually within a short period of time. The obtained correlation, sometimes referred to as a coefficient of stability, represents the extent to which the test is consistent over time. This correlation is affected, for example, by factors associated with the specific administrations of the test or with what the child has remembered or learned. Generally, the shorter the retest interval, the higher the reliability coefficient, since within a shorter span of time there are fewer reasons for an individual's score to change.

Alternate form reliability. Alternate form reliability, also called equivalent or parallel form reliability, is obtained when two equivalent tests are administered to the same group of examinees. If the two forms are equivalent, they should have the same means and variances and a high reliability coefficient. If there were no error in measurement, an individual would be expected to earn the same score on both forms of the test.

In obtaining alternate form reliability, a large sample is tested with two forms of the same test. Half of the sample is given form A, followed by form B, whereas the other half of the sample is given form B, followed by form A. Scores from the two forms are correlated in order to obtain the reliability coefficient. Alternate form reliability coefficients are subject to some of the same influences as test-retest reliability coefficients, such as lower reliability as the time interval between the tests is lengthened. However, because examinees are not tested twice with the same items, there is less chance of memory and specific item content affecting the scores than there is in the test-retest method.

Internal consistency reliability. Internal consistency, or split-half reliability, is a reliability coefficient based on the scores of one test. The internal consistency coefficient is obtained by administering the test to a group of individuals and then dividing the test into two equivalent halves. This division creates two alternate forms of the test. The most common way of dividing the test is to assign odd-numbered items to one form and even-numbered items to the other form.

In this procedure it is assumed that all of the items measure the same trait in question.

Generally, the size of the internal consistency coefficient is increased with greater test length. The internal consistency reliability coefficient is not used with timed tests, nor does it provide an estimate of stability over time.

Factors Affecting Reliability

There are several factors that affect the reliability of a test.

1. *Test length.* The more items and the more homogeneous a test, the greater the reliability is apt to be.
2. *Test-retest interval.* The greater the time interval between the two tests, the greater the chance of change and hence the lower the reliability is apt to be. Various changes may occur between testings that can affect the child's abilities or test-taking skills.
3. *Variability of scores.* The greater the variance of a test, the higher the reliability estimate may be. Small changes in performance have a greater impact on the reliability of a test when the range (or spread) of scores is narrow than when it is large. Therefore, samples with a small variance probably yield lower reliability estimates than similar samples with a large variance.
4. *Guessing.* The more guessing that occurs (i.e., responding to items randomly), the lower the reliability is apt to be. Even guessing that results in correct answers introduces error into the score.
5. *Variation within the test situation.* The more variations that occur in the test situation (such as misleading instructions, misunderstood directions, losing place on answer sheet, illness, and daydreaming), the lower the reliability is apt to be. Such factors introduce an indeterminate amount of error into the testing procedure.
6. *Other factors.* The greater the effects of memory and practice, the more reliability is affected.

Standard Error of Measurement

Because of the presence of measurement error associated with test unreliability, there is always some uncertainty about an individual's true score. The standard error of measurement provides information about the certainty or confidence with which the obtained test score can be interpreted, and also gives us the range in which an individual's true score is likely to lie. The larger the standard error of measurement, the larger the uncertainty associated with an individual's score. The standard error of measurement (s_m) is an estimate of the amount of error usually attached to an examinee's obtained score. The standard error of measurement, also called the standard error of a score, is the standard deviation of the distribution of error scores, and can be computed from the reliability coefficient of the test by use of the following formula:

$$s_m = SD\sqrt{1 - r_{xx}}$$

where the standard deviation (SD) of the test is multiplied by the square root of 1 minus the reliability coefficient (r_{xx}) of the test.

Confidence Intervals

In order to provide a statement about the probability that an examinee's score reflects his or her true score, we obtain a confidence interval or band—a range of scores around the examinee's obtained score. The standard error of measurement is the basis for forming the confidence interval. The interval may be large or small, depending on the degree of confidence desired. Usually points are selected that represent the 68 percent, 95 percent, or 99 percent levels of confidence, although the 85 percent and 90 percent levels are also used. If we construct a 95 percent confidence interval, then the chances are only 5 in 100 that a person's true score lies outside the confidence interval. Alternatively, we can think of the 95 percent confidence interval as the range in which a person's true score will be found 95 percent of the time. Confidence intervals represent a band or range of scores in which there is a high probability that the examinee's true score would lie. *No confidence interval can be constructed that can always predict with absolute certainty where a person's true score will lie.*

To construct a confidence interval, we first need to select the degree of confidence desired. Let us say that the 95 percent level is selected. The *z* score associated with this level is then obtained from a normal curve table. This table, which appears in most statistics books, shows a value of 1.96 for the 95 percent level. This value is then multiplied by the standard error of measurement to obtain one-half of the confidence interval. For example, if the standard error of measurement is 2.40, the confidence interval for the 95 percent level is ± 4.7, which is obtained by multiplying 1.96 by 2.40. The ± represents both halves of the interval—that is, its upper and lower limits. The value 4.7 is then added to and subtracted from the obtained score to obtain the specific band associated with the obtained score.

In clinical and psychoeducational assessment it is important to report the confidence interval associated with the child's scores, especially with the IQ. Special tables in this text provide the confidence intervals for the major individually administered intelligence tests, including the Stanford-Binet, WISC-R, WPPSI, and McCarthy Scales of Children's Abilities (see Appendix Tables C-1, C-5, C-16, and C-31).

Validity

The validity of a test refers to the extent to which a test measures what it is supposed to measure, and also the appropriateness with which inferences can be made on the basis of the test results. Test results are used for many different purposes, including placement in special training or educational programs, job qualification, and personality assessment, to name just a few. Unless the test is valid for the particular purposes for which it is being used, the results cannot be used with any degree of confidence. Because tests are used for many different purposes, there is no single type of validity appropriate for all testing purposes. It is important to recognize that no test is simply valid in general or in the abstract; tests are valid only for a specific purpose. Let us now consider the three principal varieties of validity: content, criterion-related, and construct.

Content Validity

Content validity involves the systematic evaluation and examination of the content of the test in order to determine whether or not the items are representative of the domain that is purported to be measured. In evaluating content validity, consider the appropriateness of the type of items, the completeness of the item sample, and the way in which the items assess the content of the domain involved. Questions relevant to these considerations include the following: (1) Are the questions appropriate test questions and does the test measure the domain of interest? (2) Does the test contain enough information to cover appropriately what it is supposed to measure? (3) What is the level of mastery at which the content is being assessed? If these three questions can be answered satisfactorily, the test is thought to have good content validity. Content validity can be built into a test by including only those items that measure the trait or behavior of interest. It is a major component in the validation process for any educational or psychological test.

Content validity, however, should not be confused with face validity. Face validity is not validity in the technical sense. It refers to what the test appears to measure, not what it actually does measure. Face validity is important to examinees, in that if the test does not appear to measure what it purports to measure, they may become skeptical, and the results may not accurately reflect their abilities. Although face validity is in itself a desirable feature of a test, it is not always necessary for good validity in the technical sense.

Criterion-Related Validity

Criterion-related validity refers to the relationship between test scores and some type of criterion or outcome, such as ratings, classifications, or other test scores. The criterion, like the test, must possess useful psychometric properties. It should be readily measurable, free from bias, and relevant to the purposes of the test. This complementary relationship between test and criterion is an obvious necessity, because without it, it becomes impossible to determine whether or not the test measures the trait or characteristic it was designed to measure. Let us now examine the two types of criterion-related validity: concurrent (or diagnostic) and predictive (or prognostic).

Concurrent validity. Concurrent validity refers to whether or not test scores are related to some currently available criterion measure. Let us say that we have a test that we would like to use to place children in a special math class. If we find that the test scores correlate with a teacher's assessment of the child's knowledge of math, the test is said to have concurrent validity. If a test is highly correlated with a currently used procedure, this is usually taken to mean that the test may be used to replace the longer, more laborious procedure formerly used for a selection process.

Predictive validity. Predictive validity refers to the correlation between test scores and performance on a relevant criterion, where there is a time interval between the test administration and performance on the criterion. It answers the following question: Is the score obtained on a test an accurate predictor of future performance on the criterion? The accuracy with which an aptitude or readiness test indicates future learning success in school depends on predictive validity. Thus, predictive validity is very important in many psychoeducational contexts.

Predictive validity is established by giving a test to a group that has yet to perform on the criterion of interest. The group's performance is subsequently measured on the criterion. The correspondence between the two scores provides a measure of the predictive validity of the test. If the test possesses high predictive validity, persons scoring high (or low) on the test should perform well (or poorly) on the criterion measure. If the test's predictive validity is low, there will be an erratic and unpredictable relationship between the test scores and subsequent performance on the criterion.

Construct Validity

Construct validity is associated with the extent to which a test measures a psychological construct or trait. It is evaluated by various procedures designed to determine how the items in the test relate to the theoretical constructs that the test purports to measure. The construct validity of an intelligence test can be evaluated by examining how the items relate to a theory of intelligence. Factor analysis also permits an examination of the construct validity of a test. On the Wechsler batteries, for example, factor analysis usually demonstrates that the batteries have verbal and performance components, thereby supporting the use of separate verbal and performance scores.

Factors Affecting Validity

Since validity coefficients are correlation coefficients, they too are affected by such factors as range of talent being measured and length of interval between the administration of the two measures. Predictive validity of the IQ (and other test scores) can be impaired in a number of ways (Deutsch, Fishman, Kogan, North, & Whiteman, 1964). First, there are test-related factors. These include test-taking skills, anxiety, motivation, speed, understanding of test instructions, degree of item or format novelty, examiner-examinee rapport, physical handicaps, bilingualism, deficiencies in educational opportunities, unfamiliarity with the test material, and deviation in other ways from the norm of the standardization group. Obviously, the test results are not valid with uncooperative or highly distractible examinees or with those who fail to understand the test instructions.

Second, there are factors related to the criterion. School grades, a commonly used criterion, are affected by motivation, classroom behavior, personal appearance, and study habits. If examinees are hampered in any of these areas, the predictive validity of intelligence tests may be lowered.

Third, intervening events and contingencies may affect predictive validity. This last general area is of special importance in testing handicapped children. Consideration should be given to the extent to which an emotionally disturbed examinee's condition is acute or chronic. Acute states of disturbance often disrupt intellectual efficiency, thereby leading to nonrepresentative test results. When therapeutic intervention—such as drugs, psychotherapy, foster-home placement, or environmental manipulation—is capable of improving the examinee's performance, the validity or representativeness of the initial test results should be questioned. However, chronic conditions, such as irreversible brain damage or chronic schizophrenia, may not necessarily invalidate the test results because in such conditions there may be little that can be done to improve the examinee's performance. If the examinee's performance is the best he or she is likely to achieve during the next few weeks, the examination can be considered to be representative (Roe & Shakow, 1942). Further,

if the time interval between the test administration and the criterial assessment is lengthy, a host of situational, motivational, and maturational changes may occur in the interim. An illness, an inspiring teacher, a shift in aspiration level or in direction of interest, remedial training, an economic misfortune, an emotional crisis, a growth spurt or retrogression in the abilities sampled by the test—any of these changes intervening between the testing and the point or points of criterion assessment may decrease the predictive power of the test. [Deutsch et al., 1964, pp. 136–137]

In some cases, it may be difficult to determine the validity of the test results on the basis of only one test session, especially when information about previous test results (e.g., from school records) is not avail-able. If there is sufficient reason to question the validity of the test results, such doubt should be clearly indicated in the report. Deviation from a premorbid level of functioning does not necessarily invalidate the results, because a level that is either lower than or higher than the premorbid level may be the accurate current level of functioning. The premorbid level may be obtained from prior test results or estimated from school grades or, in some cases, from parental reports.

Factor Analysis

Factor analysis is a mathematical procedure that is used to analyze a group of intercorrelations that are usually derived from a number of tests. Factor analysis reduces a larger number of variables to a smaller number that "explain" the variance of the respective variables in a more parsimonious way.

Briefly, when factor analysis is to be used, a group of subjects is given a large number of tasks. The tasks may be all the items in a particular test or, more commonly, all the items in a large number of separate tests. Correlations are computed between scores on all the possible combinations of the tasks. When this is done, the tasks are found to fall into clusters; each cluster includes tasks that are highly correlated with each other and not highly correlated with tasks forming other clusters. Tasks that are highly correlated (that is, tasks on which subjects show a high degree of consistency of performance) define a "factor"; in other words, each factor is defined as a cluster of intercorrelated tasks. The factors obtained vary with the tasks that are used, the subjects who are tested, and the computational technique that is employed. [Reese & Lipsitt, 1970, p. 516]

Information provided by factor analysis includes (a) an indication of the extent to which varying numbers of factors account for the correlations among tests, (b) communality, or the total amount of variability in test scores accounted for by common factors, and (c) factor loadings, the relative weight of each factor in determining the performance on each test. Thus, a major purpose of factor analysis is to simplify the description of behavior by reducing the number of factors or variables to the smallest number possible.

Factor analysis is also used to determine the homogeneity of a test and to develop better tests. In investigations of homogeneity, the input data are the scores of each individual on each item of the test. Intercorrelations of the items (not people) are computed and then subjected to the factor analytic procedure. Factor analysis can be used to determine whether one common factor underlies performance on all items. If one common factor is present, then the test is homogeneous; if it is not, the test is heterogeneous.

Factor analysis can also be applied to data other than test scores. For example, it can be applied to personality traits or behaviors of people, thus grouping individuals by their similarities. In addition, it is a useful procedure for studying the underlying constructs associated with a test or tests.

Summary

1. There are four types of scales for recording data: nominal, ordinal, interval, and ratio. Each scale is useful for answering different kinds of questions. Nominal scales simply identify individuals or things. Ordinal scales rank order the measured variable. Interval scales contain a unit of measurement and equal intervals. Ratio scales contain a unit of measurement as well as a true zero point.

2. The mean, median, and mode are the three principal measures of central tendency. The mean is the arithmetic average of the scores in a distribution. The median is the middle point, with 50 percent of the scores lying above the median and 50 percent below the median. The mode is the most frequently occurring score.

3. The standard deviation and variance are the two most common measures of dispersion.

4. The normal or bell-shaped curve reflects the distribution of many psychological traits.

5. Correlations provide an important means of describing the relationship between two (or more) variables or tests. Correlations range from +1.00 to −1.00. A positive correlation indicates that a high score on one variable is associated with a high score on the other variable, whereas a negative correlation indicates that a high score on one variable is associated with a low score on the other variable.

6. Multiple correlations assist in determining the relationship between one variable and several other variables.

7. Norm-referenced measurement is useful when we wish to compare an examinee's score with those of a known group of subjects. The characteristics of the normative group—such as its representativeness, size, and relevance—should be evaluated carefully.

8. Derived scores are the primary means by which the results of norm-referenced testing are conveyed. Age-equivalent and grade-equivalent norms have poor statistical properties and are potentially misleading. Ratio IQs, based on the ratio of mental age to chronological age multiplied by 100, also have poor statistical properties, particularly the uneven distribution of IQs at various ages. Percentiles are useful in expressing the examinee's position relative to a known sample. Standard scores are the preferred scores because they are designed to have a constant mean and standard deviation at all ages of the normative sample. Stanines are based on a nine-category system for grouping scores.

9. It is important to evaluate not only whether the findings of an investigation differ from chance, but also whether the results have any practical significance.

10. Reliability refers to consistency of measurement, a vital characteristic of a test. The three types of reliabilities are test-retest, alternate form, and internal consistency. Several factors affect reliability, including test length, test-retest interval,

variability of scores, guessing, and situational factors.

11. The standard error of measurement allows us to determine the amount of error associated with an examinee's score. Confidence intervals are developed on the basis of the standard error of measurement.

12. Validity refers to the extent to which a test measures what it is supposed to measure. Tests are valid for specific purposes. The principal types of validity are (a) content, (b) criterion-related, and (c) construct. They involve, respectively, (a) evaluation of test content, (b) correlations with specific criteria, and (c) evaluation of constructs underlying the development of the test. Predictive validity is affected by test-related factors, criterion-related factors, and intervening factors.

13. Factor analysis is a useful procedure for determining the underlying structure of a test or group of tests.

CHAPTER 3

Historical Survey and Theories of Intelligence

Only the history of science can clarify adequately the meaning of contemporary science. It alone can attach the fleeting present to man's long march toward the enrichment of mankind.

GEORGES GUSDORF
*Les Sciences Humaines
et la Pensée Occidentale*

EXHIBIT 3-1 (cont.)

tory continued to attract people, although not to the same extent, over the next eight years. ■

Source: From *Francis Galton: The Life and Work of a Victorian Genius,* by D. W. Forrest, p. 181. Reprinted by permission of Taplinger Publishing Co., Inc. and Paul Elek, Ltd. Copyright 1974.

The history of the study of intelligence reveals that there has been a general progression from a stage in which there was no accepted definition of intelligence or method of testing to a time of somewhat intuitional and trial-and-error approaches, superseded by the present stage of a gradually developing conception of intelligence based on more systematic, logical, and empirical approaches. A guiding principle in developing intelligence tests is to define intelligence, in part, by its correlations with various kinds of criteria. When items fail to correlate with these criteria, they are discarded and replaced with other items. A second guiding principle is to look at a task, a prototypical activity, and analyze the activities required for its proper execution. This analysis then leads to the development of specific kinds of items that collectively form a test.

As a result of empirical and theoretical work, factor analytic approaches to the study of intelligence evolved. Factor analysis, as we have seen in Chapter 2, is a statistical way of sorting out components that are related to overall task performance. Factor analytic approaches also went through trial-and-error phases. Factor analytic approaches have evolved from an analysis of "randomly" selected items to a situation in which logical analysis guides the selection of items and factor analytic techniques then test the logical analysis. Thus, at present, there tends to be a wedding of logical and statistical approaches.

Definitions of intelligence tend to follow from different theoretical views of intelligence. Some definitions emphasize correlations and some emphasize the functions which appear to be logically related to intelligence. Another approach is highly operational; it tells us that intelligence is what intelligence tests measure. This latter approach provides little in the way of a substantive contribution to our understanding of intelligence. The condensed history which follows shows us some of the people responsible for the trends that have taken place in the field of intelligence and summarizes some of the definitions of intelligence.

Nineteenth-Century Developments

Interest in intelligence and in intelligence testing was an inherent part of the movement, beginning in the latter part of the nineteenth century, that brought psychology into being as a separate discipline. Intelligence testing had its roots in the fields of general psychology and measurement. The psychophysical methods developed by E. H. Weber (1795–1878) and G. T. Fechner (1801–1887), the study of difference limens by G. E. Müller (1850–1934) and F. M. Urban, and the statistical studies of higher mental processes initiated by Sir Francis Galton (1822–1911) formed the background for much of the work that would take place in the twentieth century. (See the inside of the front cover for a listing of historical landmarks in cognitive and educational assessment.)

The need for a practical study of mental ability became apparent during the nineteenth century because there was confusion about the difference between "idiots" and "lunatics," with idiots being classed with lunatics and both being treated similarly to criminals (Shouksmith, 1970). Jean Esquirol, in 1838, was one of the first persons to make a clear distinction between mental incapacity and mental illness. He pointed out that idiots may have never developed their intellectual capacity, whereas mentally deranged persons have lost abilities that they once possessed. Furthermore, Esquirol tried to develop methods of differentiating defect from illness, focusing first on physical measurements and then turning to speech patterns as a way of distinguishing the two groups. His descriptions of verbal characteristics in various levels of idiocy may be regarded as the first crude, but effective, mental test.

Galton

Sir Francis Galton played an extremely influential role in the development of the testing movement. The psychometric field was able to flourish because he originated two very important statistical concepts: regression to the mean and correlation. These concepts allowed for the study of intelligence over time, and for the study of the relationship of intelligence test scores between parent and child (as well as other relationships).

Some regard Galton as the true father of the testing movement (Shouksmith, 1970). In 1869 he published an important psychological work *Hereditary Genius* in which he made a statistical analysis of inherited mental characteristics, estimating the number of geniuses expected to be found in a particular sample of people. In another publication in 1883, *Inquiries into Human Faculty*, he considered the problems involved in measuring mental characteristics, arguing that since our knowledge of the environment reaches us through the senses, those with the highest intelligence should also have the best sensory discrimination abilities. This belief led him to study mental capacity by developing tests of sensory discrimination and motor coordination.

His concern with individual differences led him to set up a psychometric laboratory at the International Health Exhibition in 1884, which later was reestablished at University College, London. (Exhibit 3-1, which introduces this chapter, presents an interesting description of the laboratory.) The laboratory was open to the public (see Figure 3-1), and for a small fee provided measures of physical and mental capacities. Galton assumed that the ability to make fine sensory discriminations was correlated with intelligence, and this assumption, which generally proved to be invalid, may have been instrumental in limiting the progress of his work (Akhurst, 1970).

Pearson

Karl Pearson (1857–1936), a close friend of Galton, was a professor of applied mathematics and mechanics at University College, London. On the basis of Galton's work, Pearson developed the product-moment for-

ANTHROPOMETRIC
LABORATORY

For the measurement in various ways of Human Form and Faculty.

Entered from the Science Collection of the S. Kensington Museum.

This laboratory is established by Mr. Francis Galton for the following purposes:—

1. For the use of those who desire to be accurately measured in many ways, either to obtain timely warning of remediable faults in development, or to learn their powers.

2. For keeping a methodical register of the principal measurements of each person, of which he may at any future time obtain a copy under reasonable restrictions. His initials and date of birth will be entered in the register, but not his name. The names are indexed in a separate book.

3. For supplying information on the methods, practice, and uses of human measurement.

4. For anthropometric experiment and research, and for obtaining data for statistical discussion.

Charges for making the principal measurements:
THREEPENCE each, to those who are already on the Register.
FOURPENCE each, to those who are not:— one page of the Register will thenceforward be assigned to them, and a few extra measurements will be made, chiefly for future identification.

The Superintendent is charged with the control of the laboratory and with determining in each case, which, if any, of the extra measurements may be made, and under what conditions.

FIGURE 3-1. An Announcement for Galton's Laboratory. Reproduced by permission of the Photo Science Museum, London, England.

mula for linear correlation. Pearson was active in the fields of eugenics, anthropology, and psychology, and in addition to the product-moment correlation (r), introduced the multiple-correlation (R), partial correlation, phi coefficient, and chi-square test for determining how well a set of empirical observations conforms to an expected distribution ("goodness of fit") (Du Bois, 1970).

James McKeen Cattell

James McKeen Cattell (1860–1944) studied with Wilhelm Wundt at Leipzig, where the first psychological laboratory was founded in 1879. Wundt believed that psychology should focus on a study of immediate experience, principally by means of self-observation (introspection). The aim of psychology was to analyze the content of consciousness. Cattell also was an assistant at Galton's anthropometric laboratory. Galton probably had a major influence on Cattell, who, instead of becoming a follower of Wundt's psychological approach to psychology, focused on the study of individual differences in behavior. On his return to the United States, Cattell established his own laboratory at the University of Pennsylvania. In an article published in 1890 in *Mind*, he used the term "mental test." Fifty different measures were described, most of them of a sensory and motor nature, and differing little from those designed by Galton.

Cattell stressed that psychology must rest on a foundation of measurement and experimentation. He foresaw the practical application of tests as tools for the selection of people for training and for diagnostic evaluations, and sought to develop a battery of tests that could be used to evaluate people. Some of the tests he considered included the following: Dynamometer Pressure; Rate of Movement (speed to move an arm a specified distance); Sensation-areas (two-point discrimination); Least Noticeable Difference in Weight; Reaction-time for Sound; Time for Naming Colors; Bi-section of a 50 cm line; Judgment of Ten Seconds Time; and Number of Letters Remembered on Once Hearing. In 1891 Cattell moved to Columbia University to continue his work on measurement. We now easily realize that these measures have little predictive validity for educational achievement or for other aspects of intellectual functioning, but at the time they made a valuable contribution by taking the assessment of mental ability out of the field of abstract philosophy and showing that mental ability could be studied experimentally and practically.

Other Developments in the United States

In the United States, psychological tests made their debut in public at the Chicago World's Fair in 1893, where Hugo Münsterberg and Joseph Jastrow collaborated on a demonstration laboratory with testing apparatus. For a small fee, visitors to the exhibit could take tests in "mental anthropometry" and learn about how their performance compared to that of others. In the early 1890s Franz Boas at Clark University and J. Gilbert at Yale University were also studying how children responded to various types of tests. Boas studied the validity of simple sensory-motor tests by using as a criterion teachers' estimates of children's "intellectual acuteness." Gilbert, also studying simple sensory-motor tests, found only two tests—rate of tapping and judgment of length of distances—to distinguish bright from dull children.

Clark Wissler (1901) was another investigator who sought to determine the validity of some of the tests that were thought to be related to cognitive processes. Most of the tests that he used were measures of simple sensory functions. Using the correlational methods of Galton and Pearson, he found that the relationships among the test scores and between the test scores and school grades were very low in a relatively homogeneous college-age population. Stella Sharp (1898) reported that tests similar to those used by Binet and Henri were measuring many different functions—a result which was contrary to the claim made for them —and were giving unreliable results. Sharp, however, studied only seven graduate students; it is not surprising that this small homogeneous sample yielded low correlations among the tests. These two studies, in spite of their methodological shortcomings, dealt early blows to the mental testing movement.

Developments in Germany

In Germany at the turn of the century, five individuals were making contributions to the field of assessment. In 1889, Emil Kraepelin (1855–1926), working in the field of psychopathology, was introducing complex tests (e.g., tests of perception, memory, motor functions, and attention) for measuring mental functions. Kraepelin was a psychiatrist, and had been one of Wundt's first pupils. Many of his tests were based on performance needed in everyday life. Kraepelin recognized the need to examine an individual a sufficient number of times in order to rule out chance variation.

H. Münsterberg (1891) was developing
various types of perceptual, memory, reading, and information tests for children. In
1897, H. Ebbinghaus (1850–1909) was working on tests of memory, computation, and
sentence completion. He anticipated the
development of group-administered intelligence tests by using a timed procedure to
administer his completion tasks. Passages
were presented with words left out, and the
examinee's task was to fill as many blanks
as possible within a five-minute period. His
tests were developed in response to a request from teachers in Breslau, Germany,
for help in evaluating the academic aptitude
of that city's school children.

Carl Wernicke (1848–1905), well known
for his investigations in Poland and in Germany of brain localization, developed a set
of questions in 1897 that were designed to
detect mental deficiency. The questions emphasized conceptual thinking (e.g., "What is
the difference between a ladder and a stair-
case?"). Ziehen (1862–1950) published in
Germany in 1908 a test battery that contained questions requiring generalizations,
such as "What have an eagle, a duck, a
goose, and a stork in common?"

Developments in France

At about the same time in France, Alfred
Binet (1857–1911), Victor Henri (1872–
1940), and Theodore Simon (1873–1961) were
developing methods for the study of a variety of mental functions. These investigators
found the key to the measurement of intelligence by focusing on higher mental processes instead of on simple sensory functions. Their work culminated in the 1905
Binet-Simon Scale. The scale was by no
means novel, since many of the items had
been developed earlier and were previously
reported in other papers. Its contribution
was as a new combination of the existing
tests, chosen and ranked in order of difficulty level, and published with careful instructions for administration. The 1905
scale might be considered the first modern
intelligence test. Unlike previous attempts,
the scale reflected some concern with normative data. It served the purpose of objectively diagnosing degrees of mental re-

tardation, and became the prototype of
subsequent scales for the assessment of
mental ability. (See Chapter 6 for a detailed
description of the development of the Stanford-Binet and for Binet's and Simon's contributions.)

Comment on Nineteenth-
Century Developments

Developments in the field of intelligence
testing proceeded in somewhat different
fashions in England, the United States, Germany, and France. English workers were
concerned with statistical analyses; the
Americans focused on implementation of
the Binet ideas for developing a scale and
statistical methods of treating test data; the
Germans emphasized the study of psychopathology and more complex mental functions; and the French focused on clinical
experimentation (McConnell, 1930).[1]

The early test constructors also had varied reasons for developing tests (Du Bois,
1972). Galton and Pearson developed tests
to aid them in their studies of heredity,
James McKeen Cattell was interested in the
study of individual differences in behavior,
and Binet was primarily interested in the
diagnosis of individuals.

The period from the 1880s to 1905 was the
"laboratory" period in mental measurement. Various devices enabled psychologists to formulate general psychological
principles and study individual differences.
The search for a means to measure intelligence focused on such psychological processes as sensation, attention, perception,
association, and memory (Du Bois, 1970).
The work of Binet, Ebbinghaus, and others
had a unifying thread—the application of
methods used in their experimental laboratory work to solve practical problems presented by educators from their communities. This interplay of forces created the
birth of applied psychology and ushered in a
new period in the field of psychometrics.

Twentieth-Century Developments

With the introduction of the Binet-Simon
Scales, the testing movement began to flourish in the United States. Lewis Terman

standardized the Binet-Simon Scales in 1916 and with Maud Merrill revised them in 1937 and 1960 (see Chapter 6). Robert Yerkes and his colleagues, however, found fault with the age-scale format of the Binet-Simon Scales and developed their own point scale (see section on Yerkes). In 1939, David Wechsler introduced the Wechsler-Bellevue Intelligence Scale (see section on Wechsler). Many other specialized tests were also developed to evaluate specific facets of cognitive ability. Testing in schools, clinics, industry, and the military became a common practice and influenced public affairs, business, and scientific psychology. Let us now look at the contributions of Yerkes and Wechsler.

Yerkes's Contribution

Soon after the Binet scales were introduced to the United States, discontent with the age-scale format appeared. The leading spokesman against the age-scale format was Robert M. Yerkes (1876–1956), who, with Bridges and Hardwick, published the Point Scale in 1915. Yerkes (1917) believed that the age-scale format was radically different from the point-scale format in three ways: the method of selecting the parts of the test; the method of standardizing the tests or combinations of tests; and the method of measuring the examinees' responses and of expressing their scores.

According to Yerkes, tests are selected for the age scale on the basis of proportions of successes and failures in selected age groups. This procedure assumes that important forms of behavior appear at various points in development. In contrast, tests are selected for the point scale on the basis of their ability to measure various functions; the tests in the scale are not considered in relationship to stages of development. The heterogeneity of tests within the Stanford-Binet suggests that measurements made on individuals who differ in age are not strictly comparable, whereas the ideal of a point scale is to measure the same aspects of behavior at every age.

The Stanford-Binet is internally standardized, i.e., tests are selected according to percentage of passes and are grouped according to year level. The Point Scale is externally standardized. Tests are selected that are independent of the development of specific norms. Therefore, the Point Scale is characterized as being more flexible than the Stanford-Binet.

The Stanford-Binet uses an all-or-none scoring procedure for each test, while the Point Scale uses a more-or-less scoring procedure. The point-scale format provides some credit for each correct answer, and thereby was thought to produce a more effective basis for statistical handling of data.

General comparisons between the Binet and point-scale formats are shown in Table 3-1. Many of the difficulties in the Stanford-Binet to which Yerkes alluded in Table 3-1 have been cleared up in subsequent revisions of the scale. Yerkes's overall criticism was that the constructors of the Binet not only avoided repeating tests, but also avoided including more difficult versions of the same tests. Tests appear to be distributed throughout the year levels in a haphazard manner. Yerkes believed their placement at particular year levels was not based on any scientific principle.

Wechsler's Search for Subtests

In designing the Wechsler-Bellevue Intelligence Scale, Form I (the forerunner to Form II of the Wechsler-Bellevue Intelligence Scale and the WISC-R, WPPSI, and WAIS-R), Wechsler studied the standardized tests that were available during the later 1930s and selected eleven different subtests to form the scale. Sources for the subtests included the Army Alpha (for Information and Comprehension), Stanford-Binet (for Comprehension, Arithmetic, Digit Span, Similarities, and Vocabulary), Healy Picture Completion Tests and other tests having picture completion items (for Picture Completion), Army Group Examinations (for Picture Arrangement), Kohs Block Design Test (for Block Design), and Army Beta (for Digit Symbol and Coding). Wechsler designed original material for all subtests, although in some cases items were only slightly modified from those appearing on other scales.

Wechsler's search for subtests was guided by his focus on the global nature of intelli-

TABLE 3-1. Comparisons Between Binet and Point Scales

Binet Characteristics	Point Scale Characteristics
Multiple-group, age or year scale	Single graded-test scale
Selection by relation of successes to age	Selection by function measured
Varied, unrelated, ungraded tests	Each test so graded as to be available for wide range of ages
Internally standardized and inflexible	Externally standardized and flexible
All-or-none judgments	More-or-less judgments
Qualitative	Quantitative
Measurements only slightly amenable to statistical treatment	Measurements wholly amenable to statistical treatment
Tests weighted equally	Tests weighted unequally
Implicit assumption, that of appearing functions	Implicit assumption, that of developing functions
Measurements for different ages relatively incomparable	Measurements for different ages relatively comparable

From R. M. Yerkes, "The Binet versus the Point Scale Method of Measuring Intelligence," *Journal of Applied Psychology, 1,* p. 117. Copyright 1917, American Psychological Association. Reprinted by permission

gence. Wechsler considered intelligence to be a part of the larger whole of personality itself. The Wechsler scales were designed to take into account factors contributing to the total effective intelligence of the individual. However, no attempt was made to design a series of subtests to measure "primary abilities" (the basic units that make up general ability or intelligence—see later section on Thurstone) or to order the subtests into a hierarchy of relative importance (Wechsler & Weider, 1953). The overall IQ obtained from the scale represented an index of general mental ability. A biographical profile of David Wechsler appears in Exhibit 3-2.

We now leave our historical overview and examine how intelligence has been defined by various theorists and how factor analysis and other approaches have contributed to our understanding of intelligence and to the development of tests. These materials, too, are related to the history of intelligence, for factor analysts have played a powerful role in shaping twentieth-century developments in the field of assessment.

Definitions of Intelligence

Three different meanings can be associated with the term "intelligence" (Vernon, 1969). One meaning is that intelligence refers to the innate capacity of individuals, their

genetic equipment. This meaning reflects the genotypic form of intelligence; it cannot be measured directly. A second meaning of intelligence refers to what individuals do, specifically to their behaviors involving learning, thinking, and problem solving. It results from an interaction of genes with the prenatal and postnatal environment, the phenotypic form. These two meanings, however, are not wholly separate or independent of each other, because the genotypic form enters into and is a necessary component of the phenotypic form (Hebb, 1966). A third meaning of intelligence refers to results obtained on intelligence tests that sample specialized abilities, such as verbal, nonverbal, or mechanical abilities. However, the Stanford-Binet or the Verbal Scale of the WISC-R, for example, do not fall under this third meaning. Rather, these omnibus tests, Vernon believes, sample the phenotypic form of intelligence of Western children because they contain material that deals with the grasping of relations and symbolic thinking.

Defining intelligence is not an easy matter. In a famous symposium conducted in 1921 (*Journal of Educational Psychology*), thirteen psychologists gave thirteen different views about the nature of intelligence, although there was much in common in their definitions. Terman (1921), one of the participating psychologists, defined intelligence

EXHIBIT 3-2.   Biographical Profile: David Wechsler

David Wechsler was born in 1896. He received his AB and MA at about the time that World War I was claiming center stage in the United States. The young scholar, as Private Wechsler, found himself involved in the large-scale intelligence testing program conducted by the Army. Thus began a fruitful interest in the measurement of intelligence, which has led to major contributions to theory and practice. After the war ended, Wechsler studied in London with Spearman and Pearson and in Paris with Henri Pieron and Louis Lapique. It was in Paris that he became interested in the psychogalvanic reflex. Later, he studied this reflex in depth in his doctoral dissertation "The Measurement of Emotional Reactions." He was awarded the PhD by Columbia University in 1925.

By 1932, Wechsler had become chief psychologist at Bellevue Psychiatric Hospital. He had already published papers in a variety of areas: studies in chronaxie, tests for taxicab drivers, the influence of education on intelligence, galvanic responses in preschool children, and others. An important article entitled "The Range of Human Capacities" was subsequently expanded and published as a book in 1935. This volume revealed that "the differences which separate the mass of mankind from one another, with respect to any one or all their abilities, are small . . . ." It also noted the decline of ability with age, a matter of special significance in Wechsler's later work with intelligence scales.

Starting in 1934 and continuing to the present day, he has devoted some of his enormous energy and talent to the development of the intelligence scales which are internationally known: the Wechsler-Bellevue I (1939), the Wechsler-Bellevue II or Army Wechsler (1942), the Wechsler Intelligence Scale for Children (1949), the Wechsler Adult Intelligence Scale (1955), the Wechsler Preschool and Primary Scale of Intelligence (1967), and the Revision of the Wechsler Intelligence Scale for Children (1974).

When Wechsler undertook to develop the first of his adult scales, the Wechsler-Bellevue I, he was responding to a need for an instrument that would measure adult intelligence in adult terms. He insisted that "adult intelligence cannot be evaluated in the same terms as those generally employed in defining juvenile intelligence," and

that the concept of mental age for adults was misleading. He wrote:

To calculate an I.Q. for a man of 60 by dividing his M.A. score by 15, is as incorrect as to obtain an I.Q. for a boy of 12 by dividing his M.A. score by 15 . . . . for a valid evaluation of an individual's brightness, one must compare his mental ability to that of the average individual of his own age.

He produced his IQ tables by taking the age of the subjects into consideration, and thus the deviation IQ was offered for the first time in a major individual test of intelligence for adults.

During this period in the 1930s, Wechsler was crystallizing his thoughts on the measurement of intelligence. Especially noteworthy was the apparently simple but very insightful definition of intelligence that emerged in 1939: "Intelligence is the aggregate or global capacity of the individual to act purposefully, to think rationally and to deal effectively with his environment." This has been the guiding principle in Wechsler's conception of intelligence. The definition conceives of intelligence as a global entity, multidetermined and multifaceted, rather than as an independent trait. Wechsler wished to avoid designating any single ability as crucial. In particular, he wished to avoid equating general intelligence with intellectual ability. He has consistently adhered to this view. In the Manual (1974) for his Revision of the Wechsler Intelligence Scale for Children, he wrote:

To the extent that tests are particular modes of communication, they may be regarded as different *languages*. These languages may be easier or harder for different subjects but it cannot be assumed that one language is necessarily more valid than another . . . . an intelligence scale, to be effective as well as fair, must utilize as many different languages (tests) as possible.

He pointed out the role of nonintellective factors at all levels of intelligence and inserted this note of caution: "Nonintellective factors are necessary ingredients of intelligent behavior; they are not, however, substitutes . . . for other basic abilities."

It should be noted that, over the years, Wechsler also found time to serve as Clinical Professor at the New York University College of Medicine, a Trustee of the American Board of

EXHIBIT 3-2 (cont.)

Examiners of Professional Psychology, President of Division 12 (APA), and President of the American Psychopathological Association. He has had more than 60 articles published in scientific journals and is the author of *The Measurement of Adult Intelligence.* This book was first published in 1939. It went through three editions and, in its fourth edition in 1958, it became *The Measurement and Appraisal of Adult Intelligence.* A fifth and enlarged edition of this book, by Joseph D. Matarazzo, was published in 1972.

Although he retired from his position as chief psychologist at Bellevue Hospital in 1967, it is obvious to all who know him that he has simply "changed jobs." With writing, lecturing, travel-ing, developing new test ideas, and researching new areas, he has been busier than before. Among topics that have been of interest to him are artificial intelligence, the problem of memory storage, and collective intelligence. His views on the last are in his paper, "The Concept of Collective Intelligence," published in the *American Psychologist,* October 1971.

David Wechsler has made major contributions to psychology for more than a half-century. Hopefully, he will continue to do so for many years to come." ∎

[Ed. Note: David Wechsler passed away in 1981.]

Source: *American Psychologist,* 1974, *29,* pp. 44–45. Copyright 1974 American Psychological Association. Reprinted by permission.

as the ability to carry on "abstract thinking." He was well aware of the danger of placing too much emphasis on the results of one particular test: "We must guard against defining intelligence solely in terms of ability to pass the tests of a given intelligence scale. It should go without saying that no existing scale is capable of adequately measuring the ability to deal with all possible kinds of material on all intelligence levels" (p. 131). His comments are still very appropriate today. A summary of some definitions of intelligence appears in Table 3-2.

Binet (Binet & Simon, 1905) regarded intelligence as a collection of faculties: judgment, practical sense, initiative, and the ability to adapt oneself to circumstances. However, his selection of tests was based on empirical criteria, namely, those tests which differentiated older from younger children. What he thought the tests were measuring was based only on his opinion; the tests were not originally selected on the basis of factor analysis.

Wechsler's (1958) definition (see Table 3-2) implies that intelligence is composed of qualitatively different elements or abilities. However, it is not the mere sum of abilities that defines intelligence, because intelligent behavior is also affected by the way in which the abilities are combined and by the individual's drive and incentive. Wechsler recognized that while it is possible to measure various aspects of intellectual ability, the obtained scores are not identical with what is meant by intelligence. Wechsler has taken a pragmatic view of intelligence, stating that intelligence is known by what it enables us to do. However, Wechsler failed to supply empirical referents for such terms as "aggregate," "global," "purposefully," and "rationally" (Guilford, 1967).

Part of the confusion concerning definitions of intelligence and ways of measuring intelligence results from the failure to understand (a) that intelligence is an attribute, not an entity, and (b) that intelligence is the summation of the learning experiences of the individual (Wesman, 1968). Tests with different names (e.g., intelligence, achievement, or aptitude) are for the most part measuring similar abilities; the name merely reflects different criteria that have been selected for investigation. All ability tests measure what the examinee has learned.

Factor Analytic Theories of Intelligence

Historically, the factor analytic theorists formed two camps: those who espoused a general theory of intelligence versus those favoring a faculty theory. Galton first proposed that individuals possess both a general intellectual ability, present in the whole range of their mental abilities, and some special aptitudes. In contrast, theorists such as Thorndike, Kelley, and Thurstone championed a faculty theory, asserting that the

TABLE 3-2. Some Definitions of Intelligence

Binet (in Terman, 1916)	"The tendency to take and maintain a definite direction; the capacity to make adaptations for the purpose of attaining a desired end; and the power of auto-criticism" (p. 45).
Binet & Simon (1916)	". . . judgment, otherwise called good sense, practical sense, initiative, the faculty of adapting one's self to circumstances. To judge well, to comprehend well, to reason well, these are the essential activities of intelligence" (pp. 42–43).
Spearman (1923)	". . . everything intellectual can be reduced to some special case . . . of educing either relations or correlates" (p. 300).
	Eduction of relations—"The mentally presenting of any two or more characters . . . tends to evoke immediately a knowing of relation between them" (p. 63).
	Eduction of correlates—"The presenting of any character together with any relation tends to evoke immediately a knowing of the correlative character" (p. 91).
Stoddard (1943)	" . . . the ability to undertake activities that are characterized by (1) difficulty, (2) complexity, (3) abstractness, (4) economy, (5) adaptiveness to a goal, (6) social value, and (7) the emergence of originals, and to maintain such activities under conditions that demand a concentration of energy and a resistance to emotional forces" (p. 4).
Freeman (1955)	". . . *adjustment or adaptation of the individual to his total environment,* or limited aspects thereof. . . . the capacity to reorganize one's behavior patterns so as to act more effectively and more appropriately in novel situations. . . . the *ability to learn.* . . . the extent to which [a person] is educable. . . . the *ability to carry on abstract thinking* . . . the effective use of concepts and symbols in dealing with . . . a problem to be solved" (pp. 60–61).
Wechsler (1958)	"The aggregate or global capacity of the individual to act purposefully, to think rationally and to deal effectively with his environment" (p. 7).
Das (1973a)	". . . the ability to plan and structure one's behavior with an end in view."
Humphreys (1979)	". . . the resultant of the process of acquiring, storing in memory, retrieving, combining, comparing, and using in new contexts information and conceptual skills; it is an abstraction" (p. 115).

Note. The first five definitions appeared in Snow (1978, p. 234).

intellect is composed of many independent faculties, such as mathematical, mechanical, and verbal faculties. Spearman introduced statistical techniques that allowed for the testing of these rival theories. Factorial methods used by the general theorists (e.g., Spearman and Vernon) allow for a large general factor to emerge as the first factor. In contrast, the methods used by the faculty theorists (e.g., Guilford and Thurstone) yield a number of independent or primary factors, but no large general factor. Both methods, however, may be reducible to each other (Bourchard, 1968).

While factor analysts differ as to how intelligence is organized—arguing whether intelligence is a general unitary function on the one hand or a composite of several or many more or less independent abilities on the other—many accept the theory of general intelligence (Urbach, 1974), with the belief that intelligent behavior is still multidimensional. Part of the difficulty with factor analytic approaches to the study of intelligence is that the outcomes of the factor analysis vary with the nature of the data, the type of correlation and statistical procedure, and the proclivities of the investigator in choosing names to designate the factors (Frank, 1976). Factor names should be viewed as descriptive categories and not as a reflection of underlying entities. Thus, while the factor analysts have made significant contributions to the field, there are pitfalls associated with their methods as well as with those of other theorists.

Spearman

Charles E. Spearman (1863–1945) was one of the early proponents of a factor analytic approach to intelligence. Spearman (1927) proposed a two-factor theory of intelligence to account for the patterns of correlations that he observed among group tests of intelligence. The theory stated that a general factor (*g*) plus one specific factor per test can account for performance on intelligence tests. Spearman thought of the *g* factor as a general mental energy, with complicated mental activities containing the highest amount of *g*. This factor is involved in operations of a deductive nature, linked with skill, speed, intensity, and extensity of a person's intellectual output. The cognitive activities associated with *g* are eduction of relations (determining the relationship between two or more ideas) and eduction of correlates (finding a second idea associated with a previously stated one). Any intellectual activity involves both a general factor, which it shares with all other intellectual activities, and a specific factor, which it shares with none.

Thorndike

Edward L. Thorndike (1874–1949) conceived of intelligence as a product of a large number of interconnected intellectual abilities, a view that is now known as a multifactor theory. Each of these intellectual elements represents a distinct ability. In addition, certain mental activities have elements in common and combine to form clusters. Three such intelligence clusters were identified: social (or dealing with people), concrete (or dealing with things), and abstract (or dealing with verbal and mathematical symbols) (Thorndike, 1927). However, factor analytic methods were not used to obtain these clusters.

Thurstone

Louis L. Thurstone's (1887–1955) view of human intelligence was the most divergent from Spearman's. Thurstone (1938) maintained that intelligence could not be regarded as a unitary thing. He assumed that human intelligence possesses a certain orderly organization, the structure of which could be inferred from a statistical analysis of the pattern of intercorrelations found in a group of tests. Using a method of factor analysis that was suitable for analyzing many factors at once (centroid method), he identified the following factors as being primary mental abilities: verbal, perceptual speed, inductive reasoning, number, rote memory, deductive reasoning, word fluency, and space or visualization. Intelligence, he believed, could be analyzable into these multiple factors, all of which have equal weight. He went on to develop the Primary Mental Abilities Tests to measure these group factors. While Thurstone's multidimensional theory at first eliminated *g* as a significant component of mental functioning, the primary factors were found to correlate moderately among themselves, leading Thurstone to postulate the existence of a second-order factor that may be related to *g*.

Guilford

The most prominent multifactor theorist in the United States is J. P. Guilford (1967). He developed a three-dimensional Structure of Intellect Model as a way of organizing intellectual factors into a system. One dimension represents operation categories, a second dimension represents content categories, and a third dimension represents product categories. Intelligence activities can be understood by the kind of *mental operation* performed, the type of *content* on which the mental operation is performed, and the resulting *product*. The model proposes five different kinds of operations (cognition, memory, divergent thinking, convergent thinking, and evaluation), four types of content (figural, symbolic, semantic, and behavioral), and six products (units, classes, relations, systems, transformations, and implications). Thus, 120 possible factors ($5 \times 4 \times 6$) are postulated in accordance with the model (see Figure 3-2). A cross between the three dimensions yields a factor, such as Cognition of Semantic Units. *Cognition* refers to the operations dimension, *semantic* to the content dimension, and *units* to the product dimension. This factor refers to knowing what a word means.

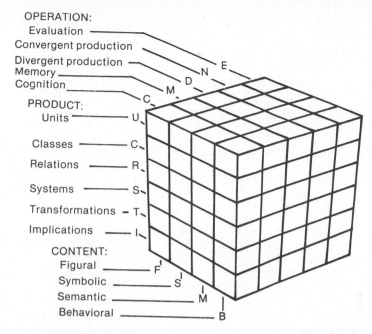

FIGURE 3-2. Guilford's Structure of Intellect Model.

Guilford's model has been criticized by Hans Eysenck (1967) for failing to reproduce the essentially hierarchical nature of intelligence test data. Eysenck, following Quinn McNemar (1964), noted that the one outstanding fact which recurs in studies of intelligence tests is the universality of positive correlations among all relevant tests, and the positive correlations between different factors. The failure to mention any central feature in the model thus reduces its value. Vernon (1965) also noted that a large number of Guilford's factors of intellect have failed to show any external validity that could not be accounted for by their general or group factors.

Vernon

In Philip E. Vernon's (1950) hierarchical theory of intelligence (see Figure 3-3), central importance is given to g, the highest level in the hierarchy. At the next level of generality, two major group factors represent skill in the Verbal-Educational and Spatial-Mechanical fields. At lower levels of generality are smaller subdivisions of these group

factors (or minor group factors), such as creative abilities, verbal fluency, and number factors under Verbal-Education, and spatial, psychomotor, and mechanical information factors under Spatial-Mechanical. Other more specialized skills (or specific factors) peculiar to certain tests emerge at the next level. Factors low in the hierarchy refer to narrow ranges of behavior, while those high in the hierarchy refer to a wide variety of behaviors. Vernon (1965) believes that a general group factor (g) must be considered in an attempt to understand intelligence. This is supported by findings which show that substantial positive intercorrelations are found when any cognitive tests are applied to a fairly representative population.

Cattell

Raymond B. Cattell and John Horn[2] have provided an innovative theory on the structure of intelligence. Their theory holds that there are two types of intelligence: fluid and crystallized. Fluid intelligence refers to essentially nonverbal, relatively culture-free

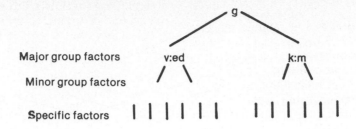

FIGURE 3-3. Vernon's Hierarchical Model of Intelligence (g = General; v:ed = Verbal-Educational; k:m = Spatial-Mechanical).

mental efficiency, while crystallized intelligence refers to acquired skills and knowledge that are strongly dependent for their development on exposure to culture.

Examples of tasks that measure fluid intelligence are figure classifications, figural analyses, number and letter series, matrices (e.g., Progressive Matrices), and paired associates. Crystallized intelligence is measured by such tests as vocabulary, general information, abstract word analogies, and mechanics of language. Tests that load equally on both factors include arithmetic reasoning, inductive verbal reasoning, and syllogistic reasoning. The Stanford-Binet, WISC-R, WPPSI, and WAIS-R contain measures of both fluid and crystallized intelligence. Tasks that measure fluid intelligence may require more concentration and problem solving than crystallized tasks, which tap retrieval and application of general knowledge abilities.

Fluid intelligence, in comparison with crystallized intelligence, is more dependent on the physiological structures that support intellectual behavior. It increases until sometime during adolescence and then declines thereafter, because of the gradual degeneration of physiological structures. Fluid intelligence is also more sensitive to the effects of brain injury. Crystallized intelligence reflects cultural assimilation, being highly influenced by formal and informal educational factors throughout the life span. It is only through the exercise of fluid intelligence that crystallized intelligence develops.

Other Approaches to Intelligence

Jensen

Arthur Jensen (1970a, 1980) has proposed that mental abilities fall into two major classes: associative (or level I) and cognitive (or level II). Associative ability involves rote learning and short-term memory, and is measured by tasks involving digit span memory, free recall, serial learning, and paired-associate learning. Cognitive ability involves reasoning and problem solving, and is measured by most tests of general intelligence, particularly those with tasks involving reasoning, problem solving, use of concepts, verbal and figural analogies, number series, and progressive matrices. Many tests of intelligence are likely to measure both levels, but different tests measure the abilities to different degrees.

The major difference between level I and level II is that in level I tasks there is little transformation of the input; a high degree of correspondence exists between the form of the stimulus input and the form of the response output. On the other hand, level II processes involve a transformation of the stimulus input; the input must be consciously manipulated in order to arrive at the correct output. The crucial distinction between levels I and II, according to Jensen (1980), involves a difference in the complexity of the transformation and mental manipulations that occur between the presentation of a given mental task and the response.

Das

An information processing model, based in part on Aleksandr Luria's (1966a, 1966b) work, has been proposed by Jagannath Das and his colleagues as a way of categorizing cognitive ability.[3] The model has two primary modes. In one mode, termed *simultaneous processing* (or *simultaneous synthesis*), stimuli are arranged in a simultaneous manner in order to make a decision. Processing is in an integrated, usually semi-spatial form. Examples of tasks measuring simultaneous processing are the Progressive Matrices, Figure Copying, and Memory for Designs. In the other mode, termed *successive processing* (or *successive synthesis*), stimuli are arranged in a sequence in order to make a decision. Processing is in a sequence-dependent, temporal-based series. Examples of successive processing tasks are auditory short-term memory, visual short-term memory, word reading, color naming, and Digit Span.

The two modes of processing are available to individuals for their use according to the demands of the task and their past experiences. No hierarchy is implied, so that equal status is given to simultaneous and successive modes. Complexity, too, is not tied to either mode. The model also assumes that a given task can be solved by more than one method (or mode). The occipitoparietal region of the cortex is probably involved in simultaneous processing, whereas the fronto-temporal region may be responsible for successive processing. It also may be that simultaneous processing of nonverbal information is carried out in the right hemisphere, whereas successive processing of both verbal and nonverbal information as well as verbal simultaneous information is carried out in the left hemisphere. (See Chapter 22 for further information regarding lateralization.) Intelligence is viewed as the ability to use information obtained through the simultaneous and successive transformation procedures in order to plan and structure behavior effectively for goal attainment.

Piaget

Jean Piaget conceives of intelligence as a form of biological adaptation between the individual and the environment. The individual is constantly interacting with the environment, trying to maintain a fit between his or her own needs and the demands that the environment makes. Cognition extends the scope of biological adaptation by allowing the individual to move from the immediate action level to a symbolic level through the process of internalization. Symbolic trial-and-error eventually can replace overt trial-and-error when necessary.

According to Piaget, cognitive processes emerge through a process of development that is neither a direct function of biological development nor a direct function of learning; rather, the emergence represents a reorganization of psychological structures resulting from organism-environmental interactions. Piaget regards social development, play, and art as all having large cognitive-structural components. These views have led Piaget to disregard the dichotomy between maturation and learning and between cognitive and social-emotional components of development.

Piaget (Ault, 1977) proposes that there are two inherent tendencies that govern one's interactions with the environment: organization and adaptation. Organization is the tendency to combine two or more separate schemes into one higher-order, integrated scheme. Schemes refer to individual structures that produce changes in cognitive development. They are a kind of mini-system forming a framework onto which incoming sensory data can fit.

Adaptation contains two complementary processes: assimilation and accommodation. Assimilation refers to "interpreting or construing external objects and events in terms of one's own presently available and favored ways of thinking about things" (Flavell, 1977, p. 7). Accommodation is a process of perceiving the structural attributes of environmental data by taking into account the real properties, and relationships among those properties, that external objects and events possess. Both assimilation and accommodation occur simultaneously whenever children adapt to environmental events, but the particular balance between the two is likely to vary from situation to situation.

TABLE 3-3. Outline of Piaget's Periods of Intellectual Development

Period	Approximate Ages	Characteristic Behaviors
I. Sensorimotor Period	Birth to 2 years	Child passes through six stages. Begins with the exercise of simple reflexes and ends period with the first signs of internal or symbolic representations of actions.
1. Exercising Reflexes	Birth to 1 month	Simple reflex activity; exercising ready-made sensorimotor schemes.
2. Primary Circular Reactions	1 to 4 months	Activities involve only the infant's own body and are endlessly repeated. First acquired adaptations, such as integration and coordination of activities (e.g., finger sucking or watching one's hands).
3. Secondary Circular Reactions	4 to 8 months	Procedures are developed to make interesting sights last; reactions also involve events or objects in the external world (e.g., shaking a rattle to hear the noise).
4. Coordination of Secondary Schemes	8 to 12 months	Two or more previously acquired schemes are combined to obtain a goal; acts become clearly intentional (e.g., reaches behind cushion for a ball).
5. Tertiary Circular Reactions	12 to 18 months	Trial-and-error behavior and goal-seeking activity are designed to produce novel results; movements are purposely varied and the results observed (e.g., pulls pillow nearer in order to get toy resting on it).
6. Invention of New Means through Mental Combinations	18 to 24 months	Mental combinations appear; the beginning of representational thought (e.g., use of stick to reach desired object).
II. Preoperational Period	2 to 7 years	Child acquires language and symbolic functions (e.g., able to search for hidden objects, perform delayed imitation, engage in symbolic play, and use language).
III. Concrete Operations Period	7 to 11 years	Child develops conservation skills; mental operations applied to real (concrete) objects or events.
IV. Formal Operations Period	11 years and upward	Child can think abstractly, formulate hypotheses, use deductive reasoning, and check solutions.

An example of assimilation is make-believe play with an object. Special features of the object are ignored and it is responded to as if it were something else. Accommodation is seen when a child learns a new scheme by imitating someone else's behavior. Assimilative processes permit intelligence to go beyond a passive coping with reality, while accommodative processes operate to prevent intelligence from constructing representations of reality which have no correspondence with the real world. Intelligence represents the rational processes, the processes that show the greatest independence of environmental and internal regulation.

TABLE 3-4.   Comparison of Piagetian and Psychometric Approaches to Intelligence

Similarities	Differences	
	Piagetian	*Psychometric*
1. Both accept genetic determinants of intelligence. 2. Both accept maturational determination of intelligence. 3. Both use nonexperimental methodology. 4. Both attempt to measure intellectual functions that the child is expected to have developed by a certain age. 5. Both conceive of intelligence as being essentially rational. 6. Both assume that maturation of intellectual processes is complete somewhere during late adolescence. 7. Both are capable of predicting intellectual behavior outside of the test situation.	1. Assumes that there are factors which give development a definite, nonrandom direction. Mental growth is qualitative and presupposes significant differences in the thinking of younger versus older children; concerned with intra-individual changes occurring in the course of development. 2. Views mental growth as the formation of new mental structures and the emergence of new mental abilities. 3. Genetic and environmental factors interact in a functional and dynamic manner with respect to their regulatory control over mental activity.	1. Tested intelligence is assumed to be randomly distributed in a given population, with the distribution following the normal curve; concerned with inter-individual differences. 2. Views the course of mental growth as a curve which measures the amount of intelligence at some criterion age that can be predicted from any preceding age. 3. Genetic and environmental contributions to intelligence can be measured.

Note. Similarity items 5, 6, and 7 obtained from Dudek, Lester, Goldberg, and Dyer (1969); the remainder of the table adapted from Elkind (1974).

EXHIBIT 3-3. Intelligence Tests in the Year 2000: What Form Will They Take and What Purposes Will They Serve?

John Horn

Realistic appraisal, based on historical analysis, suggests that in the year 2000 the tests used to measure intellectual abilities in applied settings will be very similar to the tests used today and 40 years ago. However, if the technology of measurement for applied purposes follows advancements in scientific understanding of human intelligence, then we can expect that intelligence tests of the future:

1. will be architectonically structured to provide for measurements of many separate abilities, ranging from very elementary processes to broad but distinct dimensions of intelligence;
2. will involve, perhaps be focused on, abilities to comprehend and assimilate information that comes to one via the continuous flow of TV-like presentations;
3. will contain subtests designed to indicate features of temporal integration of information, auditory organization, and elementary cognitive processing of information;
4. will derive more from the study of adulthood development than from the study of childhood development.

The mainstreams of cognitive psychology will be diverted more and more into the study of intelligence and thus will influence the shape of practical tests. Tests will be used less and less to measure global intelligence just for the sake of measuring it, or to make invidious distinctions, but more testing will be done to help identify particular ability strengths and weaknesses. Theory about intelligence will improve and more test construction will be based on sound theory.

Lauren B. Resnick

What is the likelihood that IQ tests as we currently know them will still be in use in the schools at the turn of the century? . . . What new kinds of tests of aptitude and intelligence can we reasonably look for? . . . IQ tests, or some very similar kind of assessment instrument, are likely to be functionally necessary in the schools as long as the present form of special education for the mentally handicapped remains with us—or

until we are prepared to spend substantially more public resources on education for all children than we are now doing. Further, I have suggested that there is a very real possibility of a *revival* of interest in IQ tests in the educational mainstream as a protective response by school people threatened with legal responsibility for ensuring that all children, even the very hard-to-teach, learn. I believe these two areas—special education and the school's legal responsibility—are the things to watch over the next twenty years for new developments in global IQ measurement . . . .

What kinds of tests can we expect? I have suggested the possibility of a serious shift in the science and therefore the technology of intelligence testing. Aptitude tests useful for monitoring instruction and adapting it to individual differences are essentially nonexistent today. Current work on the cognitive analysis of intelligence and aptitude tests may be able to provide the basis for much more systematic and refined matching of instructional treatments to aptitudes within two decades. We can particularly look forward to this development as work on the cognitive components of intelligence shifts attention from performance on the tests themselves to the *learning* processes that underlie both skillful test performance and skillful performance in school subject matters.

Ann L. Brown and Lucia A. French

By the year 2000 we would like to see an extension of the predictive power of intelligence tests so that we are able to (a) predict school failure prior to its occurrence and (b) predict potential adult competence by a consideration of performance on tests of everyday reasoning. To achieve these ends we will need to invest considerable energy in ethnographic surveys and experimental testing programs directed at improving our scanty knowledge in two main areas. First we need sensitive indices of early cognitive (in)competence that are related to subsequent academic intelligence. Secondly we need theories and measures of functional literacy, minimal competence, and mundane cognition, so that we can begin to predict life adaptation as well as academic success.

We would also like to see an increased emphasis on the diagnosis and remediation of cognitive deficits, of both the academic and everyday variety.

EXHIBIT 3-3 (cont.)

William W. Turnbull

My view . . . is that over the next twenty years or so we are likely to see evolutionary rather than quantum changes in intelligence tests, at least as they are used in academic settings. We are likely to see tests that provide separate scores on a variety of abilities. They are likely to be standard scores. The ratio defining the IQ may by then have been abandoned everywhere and the term IQ may have disappeared into psychological and educational history.   ■

Source: Horn (1979, p. 239); Resnick (1979, p. 252); Brown and French (1979, p. 270); Turnbull (1979, p. 281). Originally appeared in *Intelligence,* 1979, *3* (3), Norwood, New Jersey: Ablex Publishing Corporation.

There is at present no comprehensive battery of Piagetian tests of intelligence, although some success has been realized with the development of sensory-motor scales (Uzgiris & Hunt, 1975, see page 255). A variety of studies have shown that correlations between Piagetian and psychometric scales of intelligence in infant, preschool, and school-age populations are consistently positive and generally moderate in magnitude.[4] Intelligence, as measured by psychometric testing, is related to such Piagetian measures as ability to utilize formal operations, to understand the principle of conservation, and to use sensory-motor operations. There appears to be a general factor common to Piagetian tasks and to standard intelligence tests, although Piagetian tasks have their own uniqueness, and not all studies report a common underlying factor between Piagetian and psychometric measures of intelligence. Studies indicate that children who achieve high scores on psychometric tests of intelligence are not merely "good test-takers"; they have excellent levels of cognitive development in a variety of areas.

Comment on Modern Views of Intelligence

Emerging from these modern views of intelligence is a common trend stressing the importance of both innate and developmental influences (Shouksmith, 1970). A "fluid" kind of genetically determined mental ability is seen as always being modified by experience. Measures of intelligence sample only a limited spectrum of intellectual ability, and the test responses given by individuals are related to their unique learning history. Contemporary views suggest that intelligence is a more global concept than was earlier imagined. (For projections of what form intelligence tests will take in the year 2000, see Exhibit 3-3.) Whatever position you adopt toward definitions of intelligence, it is still important to recognize that the unique learning history of individuals determines the ways in which they use their intelligence.

Summary

1. The field of intelligence testing grew from the work of the early experimental psychologists, who were developing psychophysical methods (e.g., Weber, Fechner, Müller, and Urban), and from the pioneering efforts of Galton in England, Cattell in America, Kraepelin in Germany, and Binet and Simon in France. The focus on higher mental processes enabled Binet and Simon to develop a useful test of intelligence.

2. Other early pioneers were Pearson, who developed the product-moment correlation coefficient; Münsterberg and Jastrow, who developed various reaction-time tests; and Ebbinghaus and Wernicke, who worked on various types of cognitive tests.

3. Yerkes developed one of the first point-scales in the twentieth century, believing that a point-scale arrangement had better psychometric properties than an age-scale format.

4. Wechsler systematized and organized a series of subtests into a standardized scale, guided by a conception of intelligence that emphasized its global nature.

5. Various meanings are associated with the term intelligence, including (a) a measure of innate capacity, (b) a measure of observed

behavior, and (c) a measure of performance on specific tests of cognitive ability. Innate capacity, however, cannot be measured directly.

6. The definition of intelligence continues to be a problem. Terman focused on abstract thinking as the essential part of intelligence; Binet focused on a varied set of qualities including judgment, common sense, initiative, and adaptation; and Wechsler stressed the qualities of purposefulness, rationality, and ability to deal effectively with the environment.

7. Concurrently with the development of statistical methods for the evaluation of large amounts of data, factor analytic theories of intelligence arrived on the scene. Some theorists (e.g., Spearman and Vernon) proposed a general theory of intelligence, while others (e.g., Thorndike and Thurstone) viewed intelligence as being composed of many independent faculties. Many now accept the theory that general intelligence co-exists with separate independent abilities.

8. Spearman proposed a two-factor theory of intelligence, emphasizing a general factor (*g*) and one or more specific factors (*s*).

9. Thorndike described three kinds of intelligence—social, concrete, and abstract.

10. Thurstone described at least seven group factors, and in his later work postulated a second-order factor which may be similar to *g*.

11. Guilford's theory maintains that any account of intellectual abilities must consider three classes of variables: (a) the activities or operations performed (*operations*); the material or content on which the operations are performed (*content*); and the product which is the result of the operations (*products*).

12. Vernon's hierarchical approach to intelligence emphasizes the *g* factor, followed by Verbal-Educational and Spatial-Mechanical group factors, which are in turn further broken down into minor group factors.

13. Cattell postulated two types of intelligence: fluid (capacity independent of experience) and crystallized (learned knowledge).

14. Jensen's associative-ability and cognitive-ability theory is an attempt to demarcate two separate but partially dependent mental functions. Associative ability is represented by memory and serial learning tasks, while cognitive ability is represented by conceptual reasoning tasks.

15. Das proposes a simultaneous-successive information processing model as a way of categorizing cognitive ability. In simultaneous processing, processing occurs in an integrated, usually semi-spatial form; in successive processing, processing is sequence dependent and temporally based. No hierarchy is assumed in the model.

16. Piaget views intelligence as an extension of biological adaptation, consisting of assimilation (processes responsive to inner promptings) and accommodation (processes responsive to environmental intrusions). Assimilative processes permit intelligence to go beyond a passive coping with reality, while accomodative processes operate to prevent intelligence from constructing representations of reality which have no correspondence with the real world. Intelligence represents the rational processes which show the greatest independence of environmental and internal regulation.

17. Piaget views intellectual development as consisting of a series of stages that are marked by changes in adaptation. The stages reflect a series of progressively maturing cognitive structures marked by decreasing dependence on the immediately perceived environment and increasing ability to deal logically with abstract propositions.

18. Piagetian and psychometric approaches to intellectual assessment complement each other. They have similarities as well as differences. Both approaches accept genetic and maturational determinants and emphasize the rational nature of intelligence. The Piagetian approach emphasizes developmental changes and the emergence of new mental structures, while the psychometric approach emphasizes the normal distribution of intelligence and inter-individual differences.

CHAPTER 4

Issues Related to the Measurement and Change of Intelligence

For instinct dictates our duty and the intellect supplies us with pretexts for avoiding it.

PROUST

The assessment of intelligence requires not only the ability to administer and interpret tests, but also knowledge of some of the important variables associated with the measurement and change of intelligence. An understanding of the issues discussed in this chapter will enable you to interpret better the results of the psychological evaluation and will aid you in your consultation role. The chapter begins with a consideration of the measurement of intelligence, then turns to a discussion of heredity and how it may be related to intelligence, continues with a discussion of familial factors and intelligence, turns to other related matters, and ends with a discussion of the assets and limitations of intelligence testing.

Some of the primary abilities included in the concept of intelligence are conceptual learning ability, abstract or symbolic reasoning ability, and abstract or verbal problem-solving ability. However, these represent only a segment of the spectrum of intellectual abilities. They are emphasized on most standard intelligence tests because they are needed for school work and for many occupations. The similarity in the composition of different tests, observed through high intercorrelations among tests, indicates that there is a large general factor (g) which tests share in common.

The IQ is related to socially valued criteria. The prestige value of occupations, upward social mobility, and scholastic success, for example, are all substantially related to measured intelligence (see Table 4-1). However, the predictive validity of the IQ is much less for individuals than for groups. Unassessed traits or unpredictable unusual future circumstances may radically alter the course of an individual's intellectual development. Consequently, caution must be used in the assessment of individuals, especially in predicting future level of intellectual functioning.

Jensen (1970b) suggested that the concepts of intellectual breadth and altitude are useful in understanding the composition of intelligence tests. General information and vocabulary tests measure intellectual breadth (scope), while tests involving problem-solving measure altitude (mental pow-

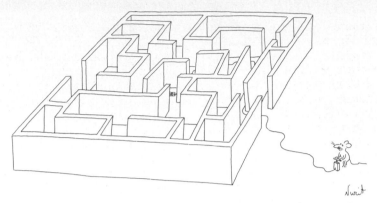

© 1979. Published by permission of *Saturday Review* and Nurit Karlin.

er). The breadth factor depends on amount and range of exposure to a stimulating environment as well as on the individual's interests and values. Breadth and altitude measures are highly correlated with *g*, but test content reflecting breadth, such as is found on the Peabody Picture Vocabulary Test, is extensively influenced by environment and training. The altitude factor seems to be more dependent on innate endowment than the breadth factor. Cattell's fluid intelligence is similar to the altitude component, while crystallized intelligence is similar to the breadth component.

The *g* factor is an index of general mental ability or intelligence (Jensen, 1979a). It represents the "inventive" as contrasted with the "reproductive" aspect of mental ability. Tests with high *g* loadings require conscious and complex mental effort, such as is found in reasoning, comprehension, or hypothesis-testing tasks. The stimuli for these tasks may be either perceptual or re-

trieved from memory. In contrast, tests with low *g* loadings are less complex, emphasizing such processes as recognition, recall, speed, visual-motor abilities, and motor abilities.

Intellectual Functioning: Hereditary and Environmental Influences

Heritability of Intelligence

An estimate of the heritability of a trait describes the proportion of the variation of a trait in a given population that is attributable to genetic differences in that population. The degree of heritability can range from 0 to 100 percent. If we say that the heritability of the IQ is .60 in a given population, we mean that 60 percent of the variation in IQs in that population is attributable to genetic differences among the members of the population and that 40 percent of the observed variation is attributable to other sources. A heritability estimate refers only

TABLE 4-1. Mean IQ of Different Professional and Occupational Groups

140	Higher Professional, Top Civil Servants, Professors and Research Scientists.
130	Lower Professionals, Physicians and Surgeons, Lawyers, Engineers (Civil and Mechanical).
120	School Teachers, Pharmacists, Accountants, Nurses, Stenographers, Managers.
110	Foremen, Clerks, Telephone Operators, Salesmen, Policemen, Electricians, Precision Fitters.
100+	Machine Operators, Shopkeepers, Butchers, Welders, Sheet Metal Workers.
100−	Warehousemen, Carpenters, Cooks and Bakers, Small Farmers, Truck and Van Drivers.
90	Laborers, Gardeners, Upholsterers, Farmhands, Miners, Factory Packers and Sorters.

Reprinted by permission of the author from H. J. Eysenck (Ed.), *The Measurement of Intelligence*, p. xi. Copyright 1973, H. J. Eysenck.

to population variance in a trait; it is not applicable to individuals.

A polygenic model is useful for understanding the heritability of intelligence. This model assumes that intelligence is the result of the combined action and influence of many genes. Techniques of biometrical genetics clearly indicate that intelligence is under polygenic control (Jinks & Fulker, 1970).

Heritability estimates for human intelligence are obtained using the correlations between groups of individuals of different degrees of kinship, such as between monozygotic and dizygotic twins. Heritability estimates must remain as *estimates* because experimental manipulations of human matings cannot be performed. Studies of European and North American Caucasian populations suggest that the heritability of intelligence varies from .40 to .80, although Jensen (1970b) believes that .80 is the best estimate. Table 4-2 shows that, as the genetic component between persons becomes more similar, their IQs also become more highly related.

A study of the Wechsler Preschool and Primary Scale of Intelligence (WPPSI) scores of 142 pairs of monozygotic and dizygotic white twins over a three-year period (4 to 6 years of age) indicated that genotype exerts a significant influence on cognitive patterning and development (Wilson, 1975). The correlations of WPPSI Verbal, Performance, and Full Scale IQs were higher for

monozygotic twins (.76 to .82) than for dizygotic twins (.49 to .68). The scores of the monozygotic twins also became more closely aligned in the direction and magnitude of difference between their Verbal and Performance IQs. The monozygotic correlations started out at a relatively high level and increased somewhat with age. Wilson suggested that shared genotype and experience apparently made an equal contribution to the intellectual functions measured by both scales.

The scores of the dizygotic twins displayed moderate correlations, but the pattern of correlations on the two scales differed. The Verbal IQ correlations had a high initial level followed by subsequent decline (.73 to .56), whereas the Performance IQ correlations had relatively consistent values around .50. The dizygotic twins also failed to show an increasing rate of concordance for the difference between Verbal and Performance IQs. Wilson concluded "that within a broad range of home environments, the genetic blueprint made a substantial contribution to cognitive patterning and development" (p. 126).

A high heritability index does not mean that the environment is not important or necessary for the expression of a trait. Furthermore, a heritability index does not provide answers "to such questions as the etiology of an individual's handicaps, the origin of ethnic differences in test performance, or the anticipated benefits of compensatory education or other programs of environmental intervention" (Anastasi, 1971, p. 1,037). Similar ideas are further elaborated in Exhibit 4-1, which focuses on infant tests as a way of understanding the relationship of genetics to intelligence.

The score on an intelligence test does not permit us to draw inferences about either genetic influences (or the biological substrate) or environmental influences (or the psychosocial substrate) (Humphreys, 1971). The independent contribution of these two components is extremely difficult to assess. Intelligence tests measure acquired behavior and yield an estimate of the child's current level of performance (or observed be-

TABLE 4-2. Median Correlation Coefficients Between IQs of Persons of Different Degrees of Relationship

Relationship	Number of Studies	Median Correlation
Twins, monozygotic,		
reared together	15	.88
reared apart	4	.75
Twins, dizygotic,		
reared together	21	.53
Siblings,		
reared together	39	.49
reared apart	3	.46
Unrelated children,		
reared together	7	.17

Adapted from Loehlin, Lindzey, and Spuhler (1975).

EXHIBIT 4-1. Implications of Infant Intelligence for an Understanding of Variations in Intelligence

First of all, the data on infant intelligence tests require that we look at the relation of genetics to intelligence in a dynamic rather than in a static manner. The discontinuity between infant and later intelligence suggests that mental ability changes qualitatively with age and that its genetic analogue is thus not a simply determined genetic trait such as eye, hair, or skin color. Rather, intelligence is much more likely to be controlled by an intricate system of gene complexes, such as those involved in the development of dentition and secondary sex characteristics. Put differently, human intelligence has to be thought of as closer to an evolving organ system than it is to a fixed physical trait.

The determining role of genetics in the evolution of such organ systems does not cease at the moment of conception, but continues to play a determining role in the gradual development of the system. It is because intelligence evolves with age that the question of *how much* heredity contributes to intelligence is unanswerable. That is to say, the contribution of heredity to the evolution and growth of intelligence is variable over time so that the hereditary contribution to infant intelligence might be more, less, or the same [as] the hereditary contribution to adolescent intelligence. Put differently, the relationship between genetics and intelligence is dynamic and not static so that [the] question of how much heredity contributes is analogous to the question of how much water flows over Niagara Falls[.] In both cases it is impossible to answer the question unless some time parameters are specified.

If intelligence is thought of as analogous to an evolving organ system, then the question as to the "fixity" of the IQ across the life cycle can also be answered in a dynamic way. If an individual is born with a good heart, the heart is likely to remain strong throughout life, barring an untoward incident. But if the individual becomes obese, smokes to excess, and fails to exercise, he can undo his good endowment. Contrariwise, a person with a heart murmur who watches his diet, and who exercises regularly, can have a long and productive life. Intelligence works in much the same way. Bright children are likely to stay bright unless, for whatever reason, they engage in activities destructive to mental prowess. Contrariwise, a youngster with average ability can, by dint of hard work, accomplish a good deal. He will never be a genius, no more than the person with a murmur is going to lose it, but he will make the most of what he has.

One last point has to be made when intelligence is thought of in dynamic biological terms rather than in static psychometric ones. Any measure of organ systems gives, for the most part, an index of current function, not innate capacity. The same holds true for intellectual ability. IQ tests assess current intellectual functioning and not innate intellectual capacity. Accordingly, IQ measures, like measures of heart rate or blood pressure, are useful for the experienced clinician who understands their value as well as their limitations. With all their failings, even infant tests may be of some value for purposes of gross discrimination. But they most certainly should not be used to assess the effects of early intervention programs, nor to predict later intelligence tests. As in the case of all clinical measures, it is not the infant intelligence test itself, but its misuse and misinterpretations that causes all the mischief. ∎

Source: Reprinted by permission of the publisher and author, from D. Elkind, "Infant Intelligence," *American Journal of Diseases of Children, 126*(2), p. 144, Copyright 1973, American Medical Association.

havior). It is dangerous to make inferences from this level of behavior to another level, termed "innate potential." We cannot observe potential—all we can observe is actual behavior. Furthermore, performance on a test reflects the complex and pervasive cumulative effects of education and upbringing. It has not been possible to arrive at an index or estimate of innate potential by abstracting it from the child's interactions with the environment and from something measurable in the child's behavior. In the assessment situation, the focus should be on what the child can or cannot do and not on the child's innate potential.

Environmental Influences

Perinatal influences. Interest in the effects of perinatal factors on behavior and learning problems in children has led to a considerable body of research. Perinatal factors include (a) prenatal variables (e.g., abnormal fetus, prenatal strain, or accident); (b) general birth process variables (e.g., abnormal delivery, instrument delivery, and delivery difficulties); and (c) neonatal variables (e.g., brain damage, hemorrhage, and other physical malfunctions to the neonate). Related, too, are factors originating from the mother, including illness, weight gain, blood pressure, smoking, anxiety, pelvic difficulties, and difficulties with previous pregnancies. Studies typically report low correlations between perinatal factors and various behavioral and learning problems (Rubin & Balow, 1977).

A study of the physical condition at birth of children of low socioeconomic status also reported that perinatal factors were not related to the Stanford-Binet IQs obtained at 3 years of age (Shipe, Vandenberg, & Williams, 1968). However, the group of children with a poorer physical condition at birth had a larger number of children with either high IQs or low IQs than the group of children with normal physical conditions. The finding of greater variability in the poor physical condition group is in accord with results of a study by Yacorzynski and Tucker (1960), who also reported a higher percentage of brighter, as well as duller, children in a group of children with complicated birth deliveries.

Perinatal anoxia refers to a reduction of oxygen level below the biophysiologic requirement of the infant during the perinatal period that begins at the onset of labor, continues with the expulsion of the neonate from the birth canal, and ends with the removal of the umbilical cord. While there is much controversy concerning the effects of perinatal anoxia on intellectual performance, some tentative conclusions may be advanced:

(a) intellectual impairment resulting from anoxia is most [sic] often found in infants and preschoolers than in older children and adolescents,
(b) anoxic subjects as a group are not mentally retarded,

(c) anoxia may increase the probability of being mentally retarded, and
(d) deficits in specific intellectual abilities in anoxic subjects are not known as yet.
[Gottfried, 1973, p. 231]

Rubin and Balow (1977) concluded from their research that perinatal anomalies do not provide a firm ground for making adequate predictions about school achievement or emotional status. Therefore, current efforts for the early screening of potentially handicapped children based on perinatal anomalies cannot be justified on the basis of the available evidence.

Birth weight. The weight of an infant at birth is an important developmental milestone, and provides a useful index of intrauterine growth. Difficulties occurring during intrauterine life may lead to a reduction in genetic potential for intellectual (and physical) development. Low birth weight (i.e., less than 2,500 grams or 5½ lbs), which may be associated with intrauterine difficulties, represents an increased risk factor. Factors associated with low birth weight include low socioeconomic status, extremes of maternal age, short stature, cigarette smoking, the presence of certain pathologic states, and low maternal weight gain during pregnancy (Hardy, 1973).

While low birth weight is associated with increased neonatal mortality as well as with relative mental and educational impairment in surviving infants (Wiener & Milton, 1970), there appears to be a demarcation between infants who weigh below 2,000 grams and those who weigh between 2,000 and 2,500 grams. Intellectual impairment is much more frequent in those below 2,000 grams (Caputo & Mandell, 1970). Improved care for premature infants appears to be leading to better levels of intellectual development (Francis-Williams & Davies, 1974).

Malnutrition. While research into the effects of malnutrition on intelligence is difficult to conduct because of ethical problems, there is sufficient evidence, from both human and animal studies, to lead to the conclusion that early malnutrition contributes to the incidence of mental retardation.[1] Vulnerability to malnutrition is greatest during the nine months of gestation and the first few years of life, the most critical periods in the growth of brain tissue. Nutritional stress can lead to learning difficulties by (a) affecting the central nervous system and (b) creating disturbances in social experiences. Malnutrition is thus linked to both organic changes (preventing the expression of the full genetic potential for mental development) and social learning factors (interfering with learning time, concentration, motivation, and social interaction). Nutritional inadequacy also increases the risk of infection and interferes with immune mechanisms. Much remains to be learned about the effects of malnutrition on learning, personality, and motor performance.

Childhood influences on intellectual development. Two long-term investigations have been conducted on the effects of a variety of familial influences on children's intellectual development—the Guidance Study and the Berkeley Growth Study.[2] Although the results showed that familial influences operate differentially as a function of sex and developmental stage, overall the findings indicated that higher IQs are associated with (a) higher socioeconomic status of parents; (b) superior play facilities; (c) parental concern that children get a good education; (d) parental harmony; and (e) mothers who appear worrisome, tense, highly active, and energetic.

A study by McCall, Appelbaum, and Hogarty (1973) reported that children who showed *decreases* in IQ in the preschool years tended to come from homes that had minimal stimulation and either a very severe or a very mild punishment regime. In contrast, children who showed *increases* in IQ, until approximately the age of 8 years, came from families that gave their children encouragement in a clear manner and provided structure and enforcement. Severity of penalties imposed by the parent when the child misbehaved was an important variable related to IQ change: children with the most

depressed IQ records had parents who were most severe in their penalties, while children whose parents were lax in their penalties showed some recovery in IQ during the middle school years; children who gained in IQ points had parents who seemed to adopt a middle-of-the-road policy on the severity of discipline.

A longitudinal study by Hanson (1975) across three time periods in childhood (0 to 3 years, 4 to 6 years, and 7 to 10 years), with a sample of 110 predominantly upper-middle-class male and female white children, showed that a number of home environmental variables were significantly related to Stanford-Binet IQs, highly consistent within a given time period, and extremely stable across the childhood years. Variables such as freedom to engage in verbal expression, language teaching, parental involvement, and provision of language development models were found to be related significantly to intelligence in each age period (see Table 4-3).

A study (Wolf, 1966) of home variables that may be related to intellectual development—such as quality of language models available to the child, opportunities for enlarging vocabulary, feedback about appropriate language usage, and opportunities for language practice—showed that the correlation between total ratings of the intellectual environment and general intelligence was extremely high ($r = .69$). Environmental ratings were also highly related ($r = .80$) to achievement test scores. The combination of tested general intelligence and environmental ratings produced a remarkably high correlation of .87. This study, like Hanson's (1975), showed that some of the best predictions of intelligence come from an analysis of environmental variables.

A study (Radin, 1972) of fathers' behaviors with their 4-year-old boys indicated that paternal nurturance ($r = .49$) and paternal restrictiveness ($r = -.36$) were significantly related to Stanford-Binet IQs. Paternal nurturance also was significantly correlated with IQs the boys obtained one year after the ratings were taken (Radin, 1973). These results indicate that paternal nurtur-

TABLE 4-3. Concurrent Relationships Between Environmental Variables and Stanford-Binet IQs ($N=110$)

Environmental Variable	Age		
	3 Years	5½ Years	9½ Years
Freedom to engage in verbal expression	.20*	.45**	.41**
Direct teaching of language behavior	.36**	.36**	.43**
Parental involvement with child	.31**	.36**	.38**
Emphasis on school achievement	.16	.38**	.31**
Emphasis on independent performance	.06	.05	.32**
Models of intellectual interests	.15	.43**	.45**
Models of language development	.25**	.34**	.43**
Emphasis on female sex role development	−.08	−.13	−.12
Freedom to explore the environment	−.10	.13	.12
Models of task orientation	−.02	.04	.04

*$p<.05$.
**$p<.01$.

Adapted from Hanson (1975).

ance probably fosters cognitive development, although the mechanisms by which this takes place are by no means clear. Perhaps nurturant paternal behavior suggests to the child that interaction with the environment is likely to be rewarding and thereby encourages the child to engage in exploratory behavior. Maternal behaviors reflective of warmth also have been found to be related to 4-year-old children's Stanford-Binet IQs ($r=.37$), PPVT receptive vocabulary scores ($r=.43$), motivation ($r=.56$), and general school behavior ($r=.35$) (Radin, 1971).

Another investigation (Marjoribanks, 1972) sought to determine the relationship between home environmental variables and various types of cognitive abilities in a sample of 185 11-year-old boys. The results (see Table 4-4) indicated that home environmental variables, such as press for achievement, press for activeness, press for intellectuality, and press for independence, were highly related to the verbal, number, and total ability scores of the SRA Primary Mental Abilities Test, moderately related to reasoning ability scores, and minimally related to spatial ability scores. The environmental variables also were a more powerful predictor of mental ability scores than either social status variables (occupation of father, educa-

tion of father, and education of mother) or family structure variables (size of family, ordinal position in the family, and crowding ratio in the home).

Zajonc (1976) has proposed a *confluence model* that relates intellectual development to a number of family configuration variables, including birth order, family size, and sibling birth intervals. The model provides important insights about how family configuration may affect intellectual development. It postulates that cognitive development is mediated by the intellectual environment to which the child is exposed. Specifically, it proposes that family size is negatively correlated with IQ and that later born children who are born into large families frequently obtain lower intelligence test scores than earlier born children. Family size affects intelligence because a large family is said to provide a less stimulating intellectual environment. While there is some evidence to support the model, further work is needed.

An additional familial configuration variable—father absence—also plays a role in cognitive development (Shinn, 1978). Children reared in father-absent homes (or in families in which fathers have little supportive interaction with their children) often do poorly on cognitive tasks. These findings,

TABLE 4-4. Correlations Between Mental Ability Test Scores and Environmental Variable Test Scores

| Environmental Variable | Ability | | | | |
	Verbal	Number	Spatial	Reasoning	Total
Press for achievement	.66**	.66**	.28**	.39**	.69**
Press for activeness	.52**	.41**	.22**	.26**	.47**
Press for intellectuality	.61**	.53**	.26**	.31**	.59**
Press for independence	.42**	.34**	.10	.23**	.38**
Press for English	.50**	.27**	.18**	.28**	.40**
Press for ethlanguage[a]	.35**	.24**	.09	.19**	.28**
Father dominance	.16*	.10	.09	.11	.15
Mother dominance	.21**	.16*	.04	.10	.16*

*$p < .05$.
**$p < .01$.

[a]Ethlanguage refers to any language spoken in the home other than English.

Reprinted, with a change in notation, from K. Marjoribanks, "Environment, Social Class, and Mental Abilities," *Journal of Educational Psychology, 63,* p. 106. Copyright 1972 by the American Psychological Association. Reprinted by permission.

while not easy to explain, may be associated with (a) reduced interaction affecting cognitive development, (b) anxiety, or (c) financial hardship.

Personality-emotional-social correlates of intelligence. Performance on cognitive tasks is likely to be in part a function of the child's social-emotional and cognitive functioning. Children most likely to use their cognitive processes in a productive way and to make gains in cognitive achievement are those who are active, curious, task involved, and well organized (Kohn & Rosman, 1974). Thus, a study of preschool children's social-emotional functioning and academic and intellectual achievement in the early elementary school grades revealed that children who showed interest, curiosity, and assertiveness as preschoolers obtained higher first and second grade achievement scores than those who showed withdrawal, lack of interest, and failure to elicit cooperation from peers (Kohn & Rosman, 1972). These findings suggest that curious, alert, and assertive children likely learn more from their environment than those who are passive, apathetic, and withdrawn. The findings also are consistent with those of Sontag, Baker, and Nelson (1958) and Kagan, Sontag, Baker, and Nelson (1958), who found

that emotional independence from peers and teachers, the ability to operate freely and constructively within a preschool setting, assertiveness, interest, and curiosity were predictive of subsequent gains in intellectual functioning.

Children with high test anxiety about school-related tasks are likely to have a history of school failure, while those with low test anxiety probably have had a general history of success in school (Hill, 1972; Hill & Sarason, 1966). There is evidence (Hill & Eaton, 1977) indicating that anxious children perform poorly on cognitive and ability tests because of motivational difficulties rather than because of learning or ability deficiencies. Highly test-anxious children have been found to perform rapidly and accurately on arithmetic problems when the threat of failure was removed and when they were allowed to pace themselves without time pressure. In general, situations experienced as highly evaluative are likely to result in lowered scores for highly anxious children. Therefore, ways are needed to optimize the testing procedure in order to arrive at less biased and more useful testing procedures for children with high test anxiety. A summary of research on the effects of anxiety on test performance is presented in Table 4-5.

TABLE 4-5.   Effects of Anxiety on Test Performance

1. A high level of anxiety generally causes impaired performance, but occasionally causes improved performance.
2. Subjects react differently to anxiety; some anxious subjects exhibit mental alertness, others, reduced functioning.
3. A critical factor is what the test situation means to a particular individual in terms of his learned patterns of response to anxiety. If the test is considered important to the individual and if he is anxious when taking tests, he is more likely to perform poorly on tests than one who is less anxious.
4. There is a negative relationship between level of ability and level of test anxiety. Poorer students tend to be most anxious when facing a test.
5. There is a positive correlation between level of anxiety and level of aspiration. Those who are least anxious when facing a test tend to be those who have the least need or desire to do well on it.
6. Extreme degrees of anxiety are likely to interfere with test performance; mild degrees of anxiety facilitate test performances.
7. The more familiar a student is with tests of a particular type, the less likely he is to suffer extreme anxiety.
8. Test anxiety can enhance learning if it is distributed at a relatively low level throughout a course of instruction rather than being concentrated at a relatively high level just prior to and during a test.
9. A high level of anxiety tends to be positively correlated with the following: [blacks], rural children, children with emotional problems, unpopularity with peers, low socioeconomic level.
10. There is generally no relationship between anxiety and sex at the elementary school level; however, junior high school girls score higher on anxiety measures than junior high school boys.
11. There is no consistent relationship between the anxiety scores of students and anxiety as rated by teachers and psychologists.
12. There are low to moderate negative relationships between measures of anxiety and performance on very complex tasks. This negative relationship tends to increase as the task becomes more test-like.
13. Test anxiety increases with grade level and appears to be long-range rather than transitory.
14. Relationships between anxiety and personality variables can generally be found: (a) both active and passive forms of dependency are positively related to anxiety; (b) aggression is negatively related; (c) a negative concept of self and general behavior constriction are positively related.

From Kirkland, M., "Effects of Tests on Students and Schools," *Review of Educational Research,* 1971, *41,* pp. 318–319. Copyright 1971, American Educational Research Association, Washington, D.C.

Developmental trends are evident in the personality patterns of children and adults who show increases or decreases in IQ. Gains in IQ are associated with independence and competitiveness during the preschool years; with independence, scholastic competitiveness, self-initiation, and problem-solving approaches during elementary school years; and with interpersonal distance, coldness, and introversion during adulthood. "These shifts may reflect the changing sources of educational experiences and motivation for intellectual achievement beginning with the family, then the competition with peers at school, and finally the self-education and intrinsic motivations that characterize maturity" (McCall, Appelbaum, & Hogarty, 1973, p. 71).

Sex correlates of intelligence. An extensive survey of sex differences in cognitive abilities was performed by Maccoby and Jacklin (1974). They concluded that there is good evidence that girls have somewhat greater verbal ability than boys and that boys excel in visual-spatial ability and mathematical ability during adolescence. However, there is no evidence that girls are better at rote learning or that boys are better at higher-level cognitive processing tasks or at analytic tasks. Furthermore, there is no evidence that girls are more affected by heredity or that boys are more affected by environment.

Socioeconomic correlates of intelligence. Members of high socioeconomic groups, on the average, have higher IQs than members of low socioeconomic groups (Havig-hurst & Janke, 1944; Janke & Havighurst, 1945). "The relationship of measured intelligence to socio-economic level is," according to Tyler (1965), "one of the best documented findings in mental-test history" (p. 336). Infant developmental status interacts with socioeconomic status (SES). Low scores on infant developmental scales are more likely to result in poorer intellectual performance at later ages (4 and 10 years) in the context of low socioeconomic status than in the context of high socioeconomic status (Werner, Honzik, & Smith, 1968; Willerman, Broman, & Fiedler, 1970). Urban children usually perform at a higher level than rural children, although in the WISC-R standardization group the difference between the two groups was slight.[3]

Comment on Hereditary and Environmental Influences

The evidence clearly indicates that intelligence is affected by both hereditary and environmental influences. Environmental influences come from (a) birth weight and nutrition, (b) numerous familial sources—including socioeconomic status, parental harmony, maternal personality characteristics, punishment regimes, modeling, paternal nurturance and restrictiveness, and father absence—and (c) the child's temperament and personality. Thus, hereditary and environmental factors continually interact to influence the child's level of cognitive development.

Stability and Change of Intelligence

The stability of IQs obtained during the course of development is a function of measurement factors, genetic factors, and environmental factors (Ausubel & Sullivan, 1970). Let us examine each of these as they might relate to the constancy of the IQ, that is, the extent to which the IQ fluctuates from one age to another.

Measurement factors. Errors of measurement associated with tests are major factors that can influence the obtained IQs. Included here are placement of test items, errors of test administration and scoring, situational factors (e.g., rapport, fatigue, physical well-being, attitude, motivation, attention span, frustration tolerance, self-confidence, level of aspiration, anxiety, and reaction to failure), variation in the standardization sample over the ranges covered by a test or tests, and test-taking experience (e.g., differential exposure to practice and coaching). In addition, when retests are carried out using different tests, changes may be related to the equivalency of scores provided by the different tests. The tendency of extreme scores to regress toward the mean can also affect stability.

Gains are likely to be larger on performance items than on verbal items. This occurs because examinees may develop a set of problem-solving strategies which they can apply to the same or similar problems. They therefore may solve the tasks more quickly by becoming familiar with the puzzles or other performance items. The susceptibility of performance tests to retest effects may also be accounted for by the fact that many are timed tests, and bonus points are awarded for correctly completing the test as quickly as possible.

Genetic factors. Changes in IQs may be related to genetically based developmental trends. Some children may have a continuous growth pattern, others may have spurts and pauses, and still others a discontinuous curve breaking at puberty and then showing a more gradual slope thereafter.

Environmental factors. Environmental factors can contribute to fluctuations in intelligence test scores in two ways. First, physical and emotional factors (e.g., physical illness, emotional trauma, or separation from parents), often transitory in nature, may affect the child's test performance. Second, changes in cognitive stimulation or motivation may alter the child's level of performance. The effects of extreme environments may change IQ scores by about 20 points (Bloom, 1964).

Prediction of IQs from Infant Tests

Infant tests cover a period of development in which there are important qualitative changes. The most important change is the transition from the assessment of sensorimotor functions during early infancy to the assessment of functions connoting intelligence around 18 months of age. One of the difficulties in the testing of infants, as we have just mentioned, is that some infants may be prone to developmental spurts and lags, resulting in a decrease in the reliability of test scores.

It is something of an overstatement to say that developmental tests in infancy have no relationship to intelligence test scores obtained in childhood (McCall, Hogarty, & Hurlburt, 1972). Although correlations are low for normal children and not adequate for clinical application, they do attain a level of statistical significance at certain ages, especially after 18 months of age (see Table 4-6).

A longitudinal study of infants (Wilson, 1978), who were tested at 3, 6, 9, 12, 18, and 24 months of age on the Bayley and at 3 years on the Stanford-Binet, showed an interesting pattern of correlations (see Table 4-7) The correlations were larger as the infants became older, with the highest correlation occurring between 24 and 36 months of age ($r = .73$). Wilson pointed out that "the pattern of correlations is coherent and orderly, and perhaps the most interesting feature is the substantial gain in predictive power at 18 months. It suggests an emerging dimension of cognitive functioning that becomes more fully operative with age, but that is only modestly related to earlier functions" (p. 138).

Infant Developmental Quotients that fall in the average or superior levels have more limited predictive power than those that are at mentally retarded levels (McCall et al., 1972). Willerman and Fiedler (1977), for example, found that infant developmental scores did not predict the unusual intellectual achievements of a group of gifted children tested at 4 years and at 7 years of age. The picture dramatically changes for developmentally disabled infants. Correlations are much higher between infant test scores and childhood IQs in developmentally disabled children.[4] For example, infants with serious developmental handicaps, such as Down's Syndrome or a major congenital malformation, who score in ranges below the average on infant tests during their first 20 months of life, are likely to obtain low IQs at later periods of development. Similarly, infants who score in mentally retarded ranges on developmental scales during their first year of life have a high probability of functioning in the mentally retarded range during the school years. These results are based on group findings. *However, it is imperative that a diagnosis of retardation never be made on the basis of a single test score in infancy.* Infants who are slow at an early age might gain rapidly at subsequent ages (Wilson & Harpring, 1972). Infant assessments

TABLE 4-6.   Median Correlations Across Studies Between Infant Test Scores and Childhood IQ

Age of Childhood Test (years)	Age of Infant Test (months)				
	1 to 6	7 to 12	13 to 18	19 to 30	
8 to 18	.06	.25	.32	.49	.28
5 to 7	.09	.20	.34	.39	.25
3 to 4	.21	.32	.50	.59	.40
	.12	.26	.39	.49	

Note. Decimal entries indicate median correlation. Marginal values indicate the average of the median *r*s presented in that row/column. Median *r*s based on 3 to 34 different *r*s and obtained from 3 to 12 studies.

Adapted from McCall (1979).

TABLE 4-7. Intercorrelations Between Mental Development Scores at Ages 3 Months to 36 Months

Months	Months						
	3	6	9	12	18	24	36
3		.57	.44	.44	.37	.22	.20
6			.58	.53	.42	.25	.26
9				.57	.43	.30	.34
12					.55	.43	.38
18						.61	.57
24							.73

Note. N between 177 and 335 for each correlation.

Reprinted, with a change in notation, from R. S. Wilson, "Sensorimotor and Cognitive Development," in F. D. Minifie and L. L. Lloyds (Eds.), *Communicative and Cognitive Abilities—Early Behavioral Assessment* (Baltimore, Md.: University Park Press, 1978), p. 138, Copyright 1978 by University Park Press.

in cases of handicapped (or developmentally disabled) children should always be followed by retesting when the child is older.

An extensive investigation of the relationship between early, preschool, and school-age mental development and social class indices in black and white children was carried out by the Collaborative Perinatal Project (Broman & Nichols, 1975). The project involved administering tests at three different age levels—the Bayley Mental Scale at 8 months, the Stanford-Binet at 4 years, and the WISC at 7 years—to 14,665 white children and 16,293 black children.

The major findings of this large-scale investigation were as follows: (1) Mental development, measured by correlations of mental test scores at ages 8 months, 4 years, and 7 years, was similar in black and in white children, although level of performance differed at 4 and 7 years of age. (2) Social class indices (SES and maternal education) were more highly related to IQs obtained at 4 and 7 years of age among white children than among black children. (3) Bayley Mental Development scores, although not highly related to IQs obtained at 4 and 7 years of age, were good predictors of severe mental retardation at 7 years of age. (4) A curvilinear relationship was found between social class indices and intellectual

level at 7 years of age. The curvilinear relationship probably occurred because profound retardation is usually a result of genetic factors or brain damage, thus being independent of SES, maternal education, and other demographic factors. However, mild mental retardation is not independent of these factors. (See Chapter 21 for further information on mental retardation.)

Childhood IQs as Predictors of Adult Educational and Occupational Success

IQs obtained on a sample of children between 3 and 18 years of age were found to predict significantly educational and occupational status when the sample was 26 years of age or older (McCall, 1977). The correlations between IQ and attained educational and occupational success rose until ages 7 to 8 years and thereafter remained fairly stable at about .50. IQs obtained by the age of 5 years were found to correlate highly with adult IQs (.50 and higher).

Comment on Stability and Change of Intelligence

The constancy of the IQ is greatly influenced by the age of the child at initial testing and by the length of the interval between the test and retest. The older the child when first tested and the shorter the interval between tests, the greater the constancy of the IQ. We have seen that infant scales have limited predictive power, except for handicapped children, because the items they contain are primarily of a perceptual-motor nature. Preschool intelligence tests have more content reflecting cognitive ability, and therefore have greater predictive value. However, even more stable correlations are found for IQs obtained after 5 years of age and those obtained in adulthood, as we have just read. Generally, while IQs obtained prior to the age of 5 or 6 years must be interpreted cautiously, those obtained during elementary school years tend to remain stable, although individual fluctuations may be great, with children with high IQs showing greater amounts of change than children with low IQs (McCall et al., 1973).

Although there are fluctuations in test scores, most children tend to retain their same relative position in their age group. *In spite of high correlations between tests, in assessing individuals it is necessary to have frequent and periodic testing, if test scores are to be used for guidance or placement decisions.* There is sufficient variability in individual growth patterns to warrant evaluation at the time decisions are to be made.

IQ constancy occurs partly because of genetic factors. Much of the constancy of the IQ is related to (a) the invariance of genetic factors; (b) the relative stability, within limits, of the environment for any particular individual; (c) developmental irreversibility (current developmental status exerts a strong influence on future development); and (d) the overlap of abilities measured by intelligence tests at different ages (Ausubel, Novak, & Hanesian, 1978).

Distinction Between Intelligence Tests and Achievement Tests

Intelligence tests and achievement tests have commonalities as well as differences. Both types of tests (a) sample aptitude, learning, and achievement to some degree and (b) sample responses in the child's repertoire at the time of testing. However, the two types of tests differ on a number of dimensions (Humphreys, 1971). Intelligence tests are broader in coverage than achievement tests and sample from a wider range of experiences. Because intelligence tests assess learnings that occur in a wide variety of life experiences, they are more valid measures of learning potential than are achievement tests. Achievement tests, such as reading and mathematical tests, are heavily dependent on formal learning experiences that are acquired in school or at home. They appear to be more culture bound and sample more specific skills than do intelligence tests. Intelligence tests stress the ability to apply information in new and different ways, while achievement tests stress mastery of factual information. Thus, intelligence tests measure less formal achievements than do achievement tests.

Criterion-Referenced vs. Norm-Referenced Testing

Norm-referenced testing, as we have seen in Chapter 2, is used to evaluate an individual's performance in relation to the performance of other individuals on the same measure. The individual's performance is compared with that of some normative group, hence the description norm-referenced testing. Another approach, criterion-referenced testing, is used to identify an individual's status with respect to an established standard of performance. Individuals are compared to some established criterion, rather than to other individuals, hence the designation criterion-referenced testing. This approach measures levels of mastery.

Criterion-referenced tests can provide information closely related to instructional decisions, such as (1) whether a child is ready to proceed to the next level of instruction; (2) whether there are certain subskills that require more attention than others; and (3) what curriculum materials might help the child master the necessary skills (Carver, 1972).

For instance, one could develop a series of tests with the following four levels of reading mastery:

Level I. Ability to read beginning-level basal readers and most of the curriculum materials found in grades one and two.

Level II. Ability to read all levels of basal readers and most of the curriculum materials found in elementary schools.

Level III. Ability to read most newspapers and most of the curriculum materials found in high school.

Level IV. Ability to read college-level material.

The following statements illustrate criterion-referenced interpretations:

"Jim can read 90 percent of the material at Level II of the reading mastery program."

"Bill can spell 80 percent of the words in the unit word list."

"Judith can subtract three-place numbers without error."

These statements refer to performance on a given criterion without reference to the level of performance of other members of the group. A level of performance is set for a group as part of the instructional objective. This level of criterion (e.g., mastery at the 90 percent level or 80 percent level) is used for describing the child's test performance.

Criterion-referenced measurements differ from norm-referenced measurements primarily in the scales used for measurement. In norm-referenced measurements the scale is usually anchored in the middle to an average level of performance for a particular norm group, with the units of the scale being a function of the distribution of scores above and below the average level. "In criterion-referenced measurement the scale is usually anchored at the extremities—a score at the top of the scale indicating complete or perfect mastery of some defined abilities; or at the bottom indicating complete absence of those abilities. The scale units consist of subdivisions of this total scale range" (Ebel, 1971, p. 282). Criterion-referenced and norm-referenced tests are compared further in Table 4-8.

Criterion-referenced testing has some dangers, especially when emphasis is placed on specifics rather than on structures of understanding. Rote learning may take the place of understanding. Other problems may occur with criterion-referenced testing (Ebel, 1975):

Criterion-referenced testing has the appeal of novelty and innovation. It may seem to offer more meaningful measures of achievement, as well as escape from some of the problems inherent in norm-referenced measurements. But it creates special problems. There is the problem of first selecting and later defending a unique set of ideas and abilities which each student will be expected to learn. There is the problem of rational definition of a particular level of test performance which will indicate attainment of each objective. There is the problem of repeated testing of those who do not reach the criterion at first, plus the problem of creating multiple parallel test forms for use in the repeated testing. There is the problem of reporting only two levels of an achievement that exists at many different levels, and of treating an achievement ever so slightly above the criterion as completely satisfactory, while an achievement ever so slightly below is treated as completely unsatisfactory. There is the problem of producing, distributing, and using detailed, bulky, and quite ephemeral re-

TABLE 4-8.   Comparison of Criterion-Referenced and Norm-Referenced Tests

Norm-Referenced Tests	Criterion-Referenced Tests
1. Interpret test scores in relation to established norms.	1. Report which, or how many, of a set of specific achievement goals the individual has reached.
2. Sample the domain of a particular achievement area broadly.	2. Sample a limited number of specifically defined goals.
3. Provide a concise summary of less clearly defined areas of achievement.	3. Report specific and detailed information on pupil achievement.
4. Encourage and reward individual excellence in achievement.	4. Emphasize mastery of specific subject matter by all pupils.
5. Treat learning as consisting of building a structure of numerous relations between concepts.	5. Treat learning as if it were acquired by adding separate, discrete units to the collection of things learned.

Adapted from Ebel (1975).

ports on which objectives a particular student achieved and which he did not. [p. 85]

Criterion-referenced tests may diminish, to some extent, the feeling of competition among children because the children are competing with themselves in striving to advance their own skills, regardless of where they stand in relation to other children. But criterion-referenced tests cannot eliminate all competition among children because those performing at lower levels are likely to feel inferior to those who are at more advanced levels. Substituting "levels of ability" for "percentiles" may be simply a cosmetic act. It is doubtful whether the replacement of norm-referenced tests with criterion-referenced tests can eliminate comparisons among children.

Both norm-referenced testing and criterion-referenced testing have relatively distinct roles to play, and both contribute to our understanding of the child's abilities. They should be viewed as complementary methods of evaluation. Criterion-referenced procedures aid when behavioral objectives and individual teaching programs are sought, whereas norm-referenced procedures are especially useful in measuring individual differences between children.

Mental Age

Mental age can be thought of as a developmental measure that indicates a level of cognitive functioning. It also can be conceived of as a level of achievement that may indicate a child's readiness to learn and level of cerebral development (Jensen, 1979b).

Mental age (MA) divided by chronological age (CA) and multiplied by 100 produces the ratio IQ which is still used on some tests and which was used on early editions of the Stanford-Binet. The MA provides an age-equivalent for the child's raw score, whereas the IQ indicates a child's performance relative to that of children who are at his or her own chronological age. Mental age can be defined as the degree of general mental ability possessed by the average child of a chronolog-

ical age corresponding to that expressed by the MA score.

Mental age scores, while easily calculated and easily understood, have limitations that are often overlooked (British Psychological Society, 1958; Greene, 1941).

1. Mental growth shows a decrement from year to year so that the difference between mental ages of 2 and 3 is much greater than the difference between mental ages of 10 and 11.
2. After the age of 13 years, the concept of mental age changes. The mean mental age does not increase as rapidly as chronological age. The highest mental age possible on the Stanford-Binet is 22-10, but this figure does not represent the achievement of an average American at an age of 22 years and 10 months; it is the mental age of a superior person. An average adult only achieves a mental age of 15-9. Thus, the original meaning of mental age, as representing the average of a particular age group, is lost for adults.
3. The abilities measured at different mental ages may not be the same.
4. The same mental ages at different chronological ages may have different meanings. For example,

   A ten-year-old with a mental age of six will differ from a normal six-year-old in physical development and skills; his interests and experience may be more like those of his age group although their range and his understanding of them will be poorer. He will perhaps be less curious, spontaneous and active; the quality of his learning and remembering will be poorer. [Tansley & Gulliford, 1960, p. 43]

5. Even the same mental age at the same chronological age may have different meanings. Thus, children with the same mental age may not be able to do the same grade of work or make the same rate of progress in school (Murdoch, 1918).

Hunt (1973) pointed out that Binet's and Simon's choice of MA as a measuring unit meant that any one success at an age level could be substituted for other successes at the same or other age levels. MA is simply the sum of all credits earned by a child (or adult) (see Chapter 7). If a child passes one test at year level VII and one test at year level VIII, a total of 4 months of MA credit is awarded. The 4 months could also be obtained if two tests were passed at year level VII only (each test receives 2 months of MA credit). Thus, MA is the sum of all the credits, regardless of where they occurred on the test. Similarly, it does not matter what two tests are passed to obtain 4 months of credits. The MA, therefore, may have served to distract investigators from studying the structural aspects of psychological development, namely, the stages of cognition that children pass through during their developmental period. Averaging tends to hide structural and hierarchical aspects of psychological development.

Cortical Evoked Potential and Intelligence

Since the beginning of electroencephalography, a relationship between brain-wave patterns and level of intelligence (or motor abilities) has been sought (Rhodes, Dustman, & Beck, 1969). The cortical evoked potential provides a measure of neural efficiency or spread of neural information processing. The two main sensory modalities that have been investigated are the visual and auditory, with most research concentrating on the visual modality. When the cortical evoked potential is derived from the visual modality, it is referred to as the visual evoked response or VER. VER latencies are obtained by placing electrodes over the occipital lobes of the cortex, presenting flashes of light, and then finding the latency of the response from the brain-wave recordings. The response is extracted from an electroencephalogram by means of computer summation techniques that enhance signals to a sensory stimulus. The VER is a useful measure of brain activity arising from sensory stimulation.

Overall, the research literature indicates that there is little evidence that the VER is related to intelligence test scores, although it is related to infant test scores.[5] However, because the technical problems associated with standardized recordings have not been ironed out completely, future research may alter present findings. Even in those instances in which a significant relationship between VER and IQ has been reported, the VER accounts for such a small proportion of the variance that it would be useless for the individual appraisal of intelligence. The VER, however, may be related to intelligence in neurologically impaired children, and there is some evidence that the VER is related to the developmental status of the central nervous system.

Reaction Time, Movement Time, and Intelligence

Early attempts by Galton and Cattell to use reaction time as a measure of intelligence were unsuccessful. However, recently there has been a revival of interest in reaction time as a measure of intelligence. Current interest focuses on reaction time and movement time in connection with theories of information processing. These variables depend on the complexity of the stimuli and the amount of information presented to the subject. Reaction time refers to the time elapsed between the presentation of a signal and the reaction, while movement time involves the time elapsed between the initial reaction and the final response. Both reaction time and movement time have been found to be correlated significantly with psychometric measures of intelligence in a variety of populations (Jensen, 1979b).

The Testing of Intelligence: Pro and Con

Intelligence testing has generated much controversy in recent years. Some writers maintain that the development of intelligence tests is one of the most significant contributions of the field of psychology, while others believe that intelligence tests have many serious shortcomings. Table 4-9 summarizes some of the major assets and limitations of intelligence tests, and Table 4-10 presents some important misconceptions about intelligence tests and testing.

It is important to recognize that intelligence tests, as presently constituted, cannot be divorced from the social order of our society which values academic excellence over other kinds of excellence. Our intelligence tests, which measure success in school quite effectively, are value-laden. They represent primarily such societal values as schooling, verbal abilities, and abstraction and concept formation skills. These are important skills in Western society, but they are not the only ones. Attempts are being made to find ways to measure and reward different kinds of skills (e.g., creativity) from those currently associated with intelligence tests (cf. Resnick, 1975). Such efforts are needed because our tests tap only part of the spectrum of human ability. Still, our current intelligence tests do their job well. They predict success

TABLE 4-9. Intelligence Testing: Pro and Con

Pro	Con
1. The IQ has a larger collection of correlates that are predictive of success in a wide variety of human endeavors than any other variable (Anderson & Messick, 1974; Kohlberg & Zigler, 1967).	1. Intelligence tests limit our understanding of intelligence (Dingman & Meyers, 1966; Nunnally, 1967).
2. Intelligence testing is the primary leveler preventing the classes from hardening into castes (Duncan, 1968).	2. IQs are used to sort children into stereotyped categories, thereby limiting their freedom to choose fields of study (Kagan, 1971).
3. Intelligence testing has revealed unsuspected talents in many individuals and has improved educational opportunity (Du Bois, 1972).	3. Knowledge of their IQs may inhibit children's level of aspiration and affect their self-concept (Holmen & Docter, 1972).
4. Intelligence tests provide standardized ways of comparing a child's performance with that of other children observed in the same situations represented by the test items (Anastasi, 1950).	4. Intelligence tests fail to measure the processes underlying the child's responses (Haeussermann, 1958; Sigel, 1963).
5. IQs may be regarded as a measure of the child's ability to compete in our society in ways that have economic and social consequences (Jensen, 1971).	5. Intelligence tests are culturally biased against ethnic minorities.
6. Intelligence tests provide a profile of strengths and weaknesses.	6. The single IQ does not do justice to the multidimensional nature of intelligence (Guilford, 1956; McFie, 1961; Sarason & Doris, 1969).
7. IQs are excellent predictors of scholastic achievement (Butcher, 1968).	7. IQs are limited in predicting occupational success (Hudson, 1971).
8. IQs measure the effects of changes associated with special programs, treatment, and training.	8. IQs are limited in predicting nontest or nonacademic intellectual activity (Masland, Sarason, & Gladwin, 1958).
9. Intelligence tests assess individual differences and provide useful reflections of cultural and biological differences among individuals (Hunt, Frost, & Lunneborg, 1973).	9. IQs are misused as measures of innate capacity (Earl, 1961; Gallagher & Moss, 1963; Sarason & Doris, 1969).
10. Intelligence tests are valuable tools in working with handicapped children.	10. Nonconventional, original, or novel responses are penalized on intelligence tests (Sigel, 1963).

TABLE 4-10.   Some Misconceptions About Intelligence Tests and Testing

Misconception	Comment
1. Intelligence tests measure innate intelligence.	1. IQs always are based on the individual's interactions with the environment; they never measure innate intelligence exclusively.
2. IQs are fixed and immutable and never change.	2. IQs change in the course of development, especially from birth through 6 years of age. Even after 6 years of age, significant changes can occur.
3. Intelligence tests provide perfectly reliable scores.	3. Test scores are only estimates. Every test score should be reported as a statement of probability (or odds): "There is a 90 percent chance that the child's IQ falls between ___ and ___."
4. Intelligence tests measure all we need to know about a person's intelligence.	4. Most intelligence tests do not measure the entire spectrum of abilities that are related to intellectual behavior. Some stress verbal and nonverbal intelligence, but do not adequately measure other areas, such as mechanical skills, creativity, and social intelligence.
5. IQs obtained from a variety of tests are interchangeable.	5. While there is some degree of overlap among intelligence tests, IQs are not always interchangeable, especially when the standard deviations of the tests are different.
6. A battery of tests can tell us everything that we need to know in making judgments about a person's competence.	6. No battery of tests can give us a complete picture of any person. A battery can only illuminate various areas of functioning.

in school, and they measure some of the important skills needed in our industrialized society.

The real importance of the IQ, as Jensen (1974d) points out, is the fact that it has something of a threshold character—below some very low point on the IQ distribution people do not function well in society nor can any of their other possible latent talents ever be manifested. "There seems to be no other human defect . . . as severely limiting as a very low intelligence. Deafness, blindness, physical deformity, paralysis—all are not incompatible with achievement, athletic enjoyment, and self-realization. Very low intelligence, on the other hand, seems a different order of misfortune . . ." (p. 434).

A central criticism, perhaps at the heart of many other criticisms, is that tests are used to allocate the limited resources of our society (Lewis, 1973). Intelligence-test results are used to provide rewards or privileges, such as special classes for the gifted, admission to college or advanced study, and jobs.

Those who do not qualify for these programs may readily direct their anger at the tests, because they see the tests as denying opportunity for success. Hudson (1972) points out that, for reasons that are still unclear, the IQ has come to be associated not only with an individual's ability to perform certain tasks, but with his or her essential worth as well: "To have a low IQ is seen as the equivalent of having low caste" (p. 15). This mystique surrounding the IQ must be squelched. It has no place in our society.

The IQ obtained from standardized intelligence tests can be extremely helpful in work with handicapped and severely handicapped children. Because the IQ is the best available long-range predictor of outcome and adjustment, it provides teachers and parents with a helpful timetable for planning the child's progress. Furthermore, because intelligence tests provide some measure of the child's developmental limitations or impairments, teachers and parents can develop individualized curriculums within the limits

— PITY THE TEST DOESN'T MEASURE ALL HER SKILLS..........

Cartoon by Tony Hall from *Of Children, An Introduction To Child Development,* Third Edition, by Guy R. LeFrancois. © 1980 by Wadsworth, Inc., Belmont, California 94002. Reprinted by permission of the publisher.

of the child's level of development and developmental expectations.

Du Bois (1972) concluded from his study of the testing movement that:

> Whether measurement leads to an increase in educational opportunity depends on administrators of education programs as well as on the psychometricians who devise the tests. In the past 60 years the applications of psychological and educational measurements have increased enormously through the joint efforts of both administrators and test technicians. By and large these applications have improved educational opportunity. [p. 55]

Summary

1. Intelligence is an important attribute of a person and is related to socially valued criteria.

2. Heritability of intelligence in European and North American Caucasian populations—the proportion of variation in the population that is attributable to genetic differences in the population—is estimated to vary from .40 to .80. There is a strong positive relationship between level of intelligence and degree of kinship.

3. A high heritability index does not mean that the environment is not an important determinant of intelligence. There is no way to separate the influence of genetic and environmental factors on the IQ (or on any test score).

4. Environmental influences on the development of intelligence indicate that while perinatal anomalies may not affect significantly the development of intelligence, low birth weight (below 2,000 grams) and malnutrition may have adverse effects. Higher IQs are associated with higher socioeconomic status of parents, superior play facilities, parental concern about their children's education, parental harmony, and mothers who are worrisome, tense, highly active, and energetic.

5. Children who show *decreases* in IQ during the preschool years tend to come from homes in which there is minimal stimulation and either very severe or very mild punishment regimes, while those who show *increases* tend to come from homes in which encouragement is given in a clear manner and with structure and enforcement.

6. Higher achievement scores in the first and second grades are associated with children who show interest, curiosity, and assertiveness as preschoolers.

7. Highly test-anxious children are likely to perform more poorly in test situations that are highly evaluative than in those that are less evaluative.

8. Substantial evidence indicates (a) that girls have somewhat greater verbal ability than boys and (b) that boys excel in visual-spatial ability and mathematical ability during adolescence. There is *no* evidence (a) that girls are better at rote learning, (b) that boys are better at higher-level cognitive processing tasks, (c) that girls are more affected by heredity, or (d) that boys are more affected by environment.

9. Members of high socioeconomic groups usually obtain higher IQs than members of low socioeconomic groups.

10. Hereditary and environmental factors continually interact to affect cognitive development.

11. Stability of the IQ is affected by errors of measurement, genetically based developmental trends, and environmental factors.

12. Correlations between infant test Developmental Quotients and IQs obtained later in childhood tend to be very low for those with average or superior intelligence. However, for developmentally disabled children, correlations tend to be substantial between IQs obtained in infancy and those obtained later in childhood.

13. Correlations between mental development scores in infancy and in early childhood tend to be similar for white children and for black children.

14. IQs obtained between 3 and 18 years have been found to be related significantly to educational and occupational status at 26 years of age and older. Correlations between IQ and attained educational and occupational success are about .50 from ages 7 and 8 years and thereafter.

15. While intelligence tests and achievement tests both sample learning, intelligence tests assess learnings that occur in a wider variety of settings and measure less formal experiences than do achievement tests.

16. Criterion-referenced testing is maximally sensitive to within-individual gain or growth, while norm-referenced testing is maximally sensitive to individual differences. Criterion-referenced testing complements norm-referenced testing.

17. Limitations associated with use of the mental-age concept include the following: (a) The concept of mental age (for test purposes defined as the degree of general mental ability possessed by the average child of a chronological age corresponding to that expressed by the MA score) breaks down for adults when it is used in the ratio IQ. (b) Different abilities may be measured at different mental ages. (c) The same mental age at different chronological ages may indicate different things. (d) Children with the same mental age at the same chronological age may have different abilities. However, in spite of these difficulties, mental age provides an index of the child's cognitive level and possesses a high degree of generality.

18. The measurement of visual evoked responses (VER) requires sophisticated computer technology. There is little evidence that VER is related to intelligence test scores.

19. Interest in reaction time as a measure of cognitive ability has been revived, and positive relationships have been found between reaction time and intelligence.

20. Intelligence testing has generated much controversy in recent years. Opponents argue that intelligence testing restricts children's opportunities, places minorities in an unfavorable position, and sorts children into stereotyped categories.

Proponents maintain that intelligence testing facilitates movement between classes, reveals unsuspected talents in many individuals, and assists in the diagnostic process.

21. It is important to recognize (a) that intelligence tests do not measure innate intelligence, (b) that IQs change, (c) that IQs are only estimates of ability, (d) that IQs reflect only a part of the spectrum of human abilities, (e) that IQs obtained from different tests might not be interchangeable, and (f) that a battery of tests cannot tell us everything we need to know about a child.

CHAPTER 5

The Examination Process

Everyone is a prisoner of his own experiences. No one can eliminate prejudices—just recognize them.

EDWARD R. MURROW

When administering a test, the examiner needs to first obtain the confidence and cooperation of the child, or the results may not accurately reflect the child's abilities. The setting should be one that allows the child to demonstrate the best of his or her capabilities. Even before the examination begins, some children will wonder about why they are being tested and how the results will affect their future. Children who feel apprehensive about the examination will need reassurance and support. Difficult questions may produce stress in the child. Examiners should help children through these and other difficult phases of the examination by use of various procedures, such as praise for their efforts, understanding comments, and explanations designed to help them understand the reasons for the evaluation. With young children, the test may be referred to as a game, and the examination carried out in a game-like spirit.

Administering tests to handicapped children requires much skill and patience. Emotionally disturbed children, psychotic children, brain-injured children, and physically handicapped children present particular problems; such children will test the resources of even the most competent and experienced examiner. The assessment instruments and administrative procedures must take into account the child's disabilities. While the general testing procedures used for nonhandicapped children are also used for handicapped children, additional procedures are needed. The material in this chapter describes some of these procedures, alerts examiners to problems that they may encounter in testing both normal and handicapped children, and provides ways to overcome testing problems.

Establishing Rapport

When you first meet a child, greet him or her by the first name and introduce yourself, giving your name to the child. A brief and frank account of the purpose of the examination may be helpful, especially with older children. Opening statements should not be standardized but flexible and adaptable to meet children's needs. Introductory talk can be kept to a minimum. Be confident and encouraging, making it clear that you want the children to make the best possible score. Convey to the children that you are sincerely interested in seeing them succeed, yet unconditionally accepting and supportive in the event of failure. While the children are working, observe them inconspicuously. You should not stare at them or do anything that might distract, embarrass, or irritate them. Try to be inconspicuous when recording observations and scoring responses.

The children should be helped to feel at ease. Encourage them to give a response to each question or to take a chance even when they are reluctant to respond. This type of encouragement may reduce some of the anxiety in the testing situation. Interest level should be maintained. If fatigue occurs, testing should be discontinued. If you sense that the child has experienced some frustration on a previous test item, you can say, "That was a bit difficult, but no one is expected to get them all right. Now let's try another one" (or something similar). Because directions cannot cover every situation, be prepared to use tact and common sense when difficulties arise. Stereotyped and routine manners of interacting with children should be avoided.

Rapport can be facilitated by starting immediately with the test material, giving brief, natural, and casual praise for the child's efforts. When administering the Stanford-Binet, you can help anxious children by beginning the examination with one or two tests below their probable basal level. A similar procedure can be used with the WISC-R, WPPSI, and WAIS-R on those subtests that have easier items that are not routinely administered.

Encourage children who are superficially cooperative to participate as fully as possible. Appropriate facial expressions and modulations of voice, in addition to supportive comments, may help. Early experiences of success in answering test questions should help children relax more quickly than almost any other procedure. The following incident illustrates an effective way of establishing rapport in cases in which it may not be appropriate to start with the test materials directly.

> The clinician approached the child sitting tensely by her mother in the waiting room. Quietly introducing himself (without maudlin gestures or syrupy promises of what fun this is going to be), he extended his hand expectantly to the child and they disappeared into an examining room. We watched through a one-way mirror as the clinician explored the room with the child. He talked softly, almost in a whisper, as he itemized the objects and structures visible in the room. Still talking softly, in short, simple sentences, he opened a small box containing several plastic farm animals. Arraying the creatures on the table top, the clinician named them, purposely confusing the pig and the goat. Sara smiled slightly and shifted her chair closer. The clinician then proposed an animal parade and pranced the horse and the cow closer and closer to Sara. In a short time, the child was playing eagerly with the animals and chatting freely with the therapist. [Emerick & Hatten, 1974, p. 49]

At times rapport may be affected in a number of ways, some of which are obvious and others not so obvious. For example, statements that are in conflict with the quality of the response may increase the incidence of blocking (impeding or preventing a response) and refusal to respond. When praise has been used excessively, it will be difficult to use it appropriately when the test questions become more difficult. Examiners then are faced with either abandoning their previous approach, with the obvious implication that praise is no longer deserved, or continuing to praise in situations where the children themselves are aware that their performance is inadequate (Cole, 1953).

Praising children *for their effort* rather than for the results of their effort, a subtle but important distinction, may help to reduce some of the problems associated with the use of praise. Blocking can be reduced by capturing children's frame of reference and by showing them that their situation is understood. This can be accomplished by

accepting their attitudes toward the examination, by recognizing that the questions are getting harder, and by acknowledging verbally their reactions. The characteristics of examiners that can lead to good rapport include empathy, genuineness, warmth, and respect for children. Helping children maintain a sense of self-esteem and self-acceptance is a key to ensuring a successful relationship.

Children, particularly older ones, are likely to have some idea about the purposes of tests, and do react to being tested. While we attempt to ensure the objectivity of tests by standardizing test procedures, we cannot be completely successful because children will react in different ways to the test items. Some may react slowly, others quickly. Some may need two trials before succeeding (i.e., on tests where two trials are allowed according to the standardized instructions), others only one trial. These and countless other variations preclude giving an exami-

"Mr. Merrill's real strength is his ability to empathize in one-to-one situations."

Cartoon first appeared in *New Era.* Used by permission.

nation that is strictly "objective." In addition, variations in the personalities, administrative skills, and scoring judgments of examiners can diminish the test results' objectivity. However, these examinee and examiner variables may not seriously or significantly diminish the reliability or validity of the results. They are sources of variability that contribute to the standard error of measurement of the test score and, in part, have been taken into account in standardizing the test.

Older children usually recognize that they are being judged, and that the test holds the possibility that they may be found wanting (Fiske, 1967). When such reactions occur, they may interfere with the children's performance or influence the kinds of responses they give. Positive reinforcement on such occasions is particularly desirable, along with brief explanations concerning the perceived apprehensions.

Children, being relatively unprotected by age, experience, skill, and insight, may attempt to control the test situation in indirect ways, while examiners try to accomplish their goals in more direct ways (Engel, 1960). For example, youngsters are seldom aware of their explicit role as examinees. Some may try to control the situation by requesting water frequently or by being silently negativistic. Examiners, on the other hand, may try to control the situation by never varying from the test procedures. These and other dynamics involved in the assessment relationship need to be recognized and understood by the examiner. To facilitate such understanding, be aware of nonverbal as well as verbal communications; where, when, and why the examination is occurring; and the child's age.

Many researchers have studied how different types of examiner-examinee relationships may affect children's performance on intelligence tests or tests of vocabulary.[1] The children in these studies represented a variety of normal and handicapped groups and ethnicities. The findings do not lend themselves to easy generalizations because no firm trends emerge. For example, in one study, contact with a warm examiner before the formal testing began led to higher scores, while in others the warmth or coldness of the contact did not affect scores. Overall, the examiner-examinee relationship may be influenced by such variables as the child's age, the type of test, and the type of rapport.

Testing Preschool Children

Preschool children are likely to be challenging to test. They have little interest in their performance, their social behavior is not advanced, they follow their own impulses, they are difficult to coerce, and they express their feelings easily. Some may be fearful or shy, especially those who are not accustomed to being alone with a stranger.

Approach the young child with an air of confidence. If you are tense or apprehensive, the child is likely to sense these feelings and may become resistant or negative, especially if you try too hard and too soon to get cooperation. At the opposite extreme, testing can be interfered with by prolonging the preliminary getting-acquainted time with overstimulating or entertaining play (McCarthy, 1972). In some cases, more than one session may be needed before adequate rapport is established. Every effort should be made to examine children without the mother or father present (McCarthy, 1972). If this is not possible, the parent should remain in the background out of the child's view. After the session is over, any questions raised by the parent about the child's performance should be answered.

Useful frameworks for testing and working with preschool children have been provided by Goodenough (1949) and by Read (1976). Their major points, as well as some additional ones, are summarized below. The reader is encouraged to consult both sources for detailed comments concerning preschool children.

1. Do not remove the child abruptly from an interesting activity in order to test.
2. Take an extra toy with you for the child to use, if necessary, to maintain rapport and protect testing materials.

3. Use an attractive testing room.
4. Arrange materials systematically.
5. Keep testing materials, toys, and other necessary equipment at hand but out of sight.
6. Do not urge the child to respond before he or she is ready.
7. Before beginning the examination, be sure that the child is physically comfortable.
8. Follow test instructions exactly.
9. Adjust the speed of administering the test to the child's temperament.
10. Keep voice low in pitch.
11. Prepare the child for each kind of test.
12. Do not ignore any remarks made by the child.
13. Give adequate praise.
14. Watch for early signs of boredom, fatigue, physical discomfort, or emotional distress, and take appropriate action before such conditions become acute.
15. Be playful and friendly, but always maintain control of the situation.
16. Try to have the child cooperate actively at all times.
17. Give the child a choice only when you intend to leave the situation up to him or her.
18. Use words and tone of voice that will help the child feel confident and reassured.
19. Never attempt to change behavior by acts that may make the child feel less respect for himself or herself.
20. Avoid motivating the child by making comparisons between him or her and another child or by encouraging competition.
21. Redirect activities in a way that is consistent with the child's motives or interests.
22. Handle problems by trying to foresee and forestall them.
23. Clearly define and consistently maintain limits on the child's allowable behavior. Be sure that the child clearly understands the limits that are set. However, although consistency is necessary, do not be inflexible. Accept the child's need to "test out" the limits and try to adapt the limits to the child's needs, giving him or her time to accept them while at the same time respecting his or her feelings.

Try to accept the children as they are, with their feelings and behavior, knowing that there are reasons for the ways they feel and act. Help them find acceptable outlets for their feelings and try to meet their needs. Skills you acquire in handling young children can aid you in helping them gain confidence in their abilities. Increased confidence may enhance their cooperativeness and willingness to respond to the tests. (Exhibit 5-1, which began this chapter, portrays the characteristics of a successful examiner.)

Preschool children may be referred for psychological evaluation because of delay in the onset of speech. Testing may be extremely difficult when a child is nonverbal. Obviously, a diagnostic label should not be given to such a child unless there is conclusive evidence that the obtained results are valid. It is better in such cases to have a period of observation before arriving at a diagnosis. Reasons for delayed speech include mental retardation, hearing defect, developmental aphasia, poor language model at home, emotional blocking, childhood schizophrenia, and autism (McCarthy, 1972).

McCarthy (1972) presented useful suggestions for working with children with speech defects and with young children with articulatory problems:

The testing of children with speech defects presents special challenges to examiners, as does the testing of very young children, many of whom are still developing articulatory skills. There is really no substitute for experience with young children and becoming attuned to baby talk, although some training in speech therapy can be extremely helpful. Noting a child's pattern of sound substitutions can often render poor speech comprehensible. Although quality of speech may be of special interest and should be noted in clinical reporting, a child should not be penalized for immature pronunciation if he has provided meaningful, correct responses. Children who stutter may require more time and perhaps more than one session. The examiner should be careful to maintain a relaxed atmosphere so as not to aggravate the presenting symptom. [pp. 27–28]

Finally, be aware of the feelings of the parents. Parents have limited experience with testing; they may lack knowledge about the meaning of test results, be anxious about their child's behavior, and defensive about their child's needing testing. Giving realistic reassurance and explanations whenever possible can help to alleviate some of their anxieties.

Testing Ethnic Minority Children

Establishing rapport may be difficult with some ethnic minority children and with some children from lower socioeconomic backgrounds, especially when the examiner is white and comes from the middle class. Adolescents from these groups may be negativistic or ingratiating in the test situation. Elkind (1973a) presented some excellent suggestions for dealing with these behaviors. (Additional information about testing ethnic minority children appears in Chapter 19.)

> Regardless of whether the young person is negativistic or ingratiating, one common characteristic that stands out in the testing situation is the language differences between the middle income examiner and the lower income examinee. Not only are there differences in articulation, vocabulary, and inflection, but there are also more subtle differences in phrasing and emphasis. The communication problem is a very real one that complicates testing and diagnosis.
> . . . a low income youngster may say something like "Humb" that turns out to be Humboldt Avenue, the street on which he lives. Sometimes the misunderstanding can be amusing, as in the case of the young person who makes a face when he hears "espionage" as "spinach." These language differences are very apparent to the examinee as well as to the examiner, and they pose an additional barrier to effective rapport and valid testing. In my own work I find that it is important to confront the issue directly, to restate words I feel have not been understood, and to have the adolescent repeat words I could not comprehend. If the young person realizes the ex-

aminer really wants to understand him and is not making aspersions about his speech, such little confrontations can be most helpful in aiding communication. Minor confrontations are equally effective with negativistic and ingratiating adolescents. [pp. 62–63]

Comments on Testing Handicapped Children

While every attempt should be made to administer a standardized test to handicapped children, there will be occasions when this is not possible. Children who are actively psychotic, severely cerebral palsied, or markedly deficient in attention and motivation may prove to be untestable. In such cases, observations of the child's behavior should be recorded and testing rescheduled.

Work with physically handicapped children (and other developmentally disabled children as well) requires an appreciation of the limitations associated with various disabilities. However, it is all too easy to generalize from the disability to all other behaviors. If the assumption is made that handicapped children are very limited in what they can do, we are likely to place unnecessary restrictions on what they are allowed or encouraged to do; such restrictions may harm the child's development. Wright's (1974) insightful discussion can help us understand how an exaggerated perception of limitation develops.

1. *The spread phenomenon.* A prime reason for biased perception of physically disabled children is the tendency to draw inferences about a child based on a single, prominent characteristic of that child. When the idea of disability is extended from one area to other areas of functioning—such as to hearing, to general health, and to emotional maturity, as in the case of a blind child—we have an illustration of the *spread phenomenon*, in which the abilities of physically handicapped children are underrated. The negative evaluation of disability spreads to the total child. Wright pointed out how universal the phenomenon of spread is in interpersonal relations:

It should be understood that the phenomenon of spread is not limited to physical disability. It is a general law of human perception that an observer will make wide-ranging judgments about a person on the basis of a single characteristic, especially when that characteristic is viewed as salient and the person himself is little known. Thus, it is common to make unwarranted inferential leaps about a person on the basis of the single fact of his sex, religion, nationality, and so on. [p. 109]

2. *Position of the observer.* A second reason for incomplete understanding of handicapped children stems from the position of the observer. The observer imagines what it must be like to be handicapped, and these imaginings are likely to be overly pessimistic. Problems and limitations dominate the imagination of the observer because of his or her inexperience and lack of knowledge. The observer fails to realize how fully life can be lived with the handicap, despite major limitations.

3. *Fitting perceptions to expectations.* A third factor that makes us believe that handicapped children are more dependent than they need be is related to the methods of resolving discrepancies in expectations. In instances in which handicapped children behave in a manner that is contrary to the observer's expectations, the observer may overlook or deny these behaviors. If forced to recognize the behaviors, the observer may believe that the particular behaviors are exceptions to the rule.

4. *Fitting environments to expectations.* Another factor involved in biased perception concerns the observer's control over the handicapped child's environment. Through the limiting of training and educational programs, for example, handicapped children are forced into a more dependent position by not being allowed to engage in activities commensurate with their abilities.

Clinicians must be aware of their attitudes toward, and social perceptions of, handicapped children, and attempt to change their negative attitudes about the competencies and independent-action potentials of children who are handicapped. Handicapped children's capabilities must be appreciated for what they are, and every attempt should be made to provide them with appropriate training and educational programs.

Wright (1974) described two possible orientations that people have toward handicapped individuals: a coping framework or a succumbing framework. The coping framework emphasizes an active engagement with life, while recognizing limitations, and stresses opportunities for constructive action; the succumbing framework focuses on the limitations and dire consequences associated with handicaps. Those working with handicapped children—including clinicians, teachers, parents, and the general public—would be well advised to incorporate the guidelines associated with the coping framework into their work with handicapped children.

Testing Emotionally Disturbed and Delinquent Children

While most emotionally disturbed children should not feel threatened by tests, they will demand extra patience and effort on the part of the examiner. When children are difficult to test, procedures should be explored that will help them be less resistant. Beginning the test with performance-type materials may be helpful in cases in which the child is reticent about speaking. Extremely shy children may need to meet with the examiner on more than one occasion before they are ready to respond to the test questions.

Delinquent children are likely to experience not only the situational stress induced by the authoritarian setting in which testing usually takes place (such as a juvenile detention center or jail), but also the real and immediate threat posed by the examination itself (Harari & Shwast, 1964). Delinquent children may feel that they have everything to lose and nothing to gain by revealing themselves to the examiner. Testing might cause the curtailment of their liberty, placement in an institution, or some other disposition they regard as punishment. As a consequence, they may consciously or unconsciously defend themselves against self-revelation. Every attempt must be made to understand and to work through these difficulties; if not, a valid picture of the delinquent's abilities may not be obtained.

Testing Psychotic Children

In administering tests to psychotic children, it is especially important to use tact, diplomacy, and ingenuity, and to have patience and understanding. Questions should be read slowly and clearly. In some cases two or more test sessions may be needed. Psychotic children may be difficult to test because they cannot concentrate well and because they may have preoccupations that impede their comprehension of the instructions.

Children who are suspected of being psychotic are easier to test when they have average or above-average intelligence, when they can speak, and when they are cooperative; the assessment situation is more complicated when intelligence is low or when there is mutism (Mehr, 1952). For those who are mute, the Merrill-Palmer Scale may prove to be more useful than the Stanford-Binet, WISC-R, or WPPSI (Rutter, 1966). Items from the Bayley Scales of Infant Development or Cattell Infant Intelligence Scale can be used to assess the general level of functioning of young psychotic children (see Chapter 14). In some cases when a psychotic child is "untestable," the child's parents may be able to provide information that will allow the examiner to make judgments concerning the child's developmental level in such areas as language, motor ability, social skills, self-sufficiency, mental development, and overall development. The Vineland Social Maturity Scale and other adaptive behavior scales can be used to assist in obtaining these judgments (see Chapter 17).

Testing Brain-Injured Children[2]

Because a brain-injured child may be more fearful than other children, the child's parents or teachers should inform him or her about the examination a day or two before it is scheduled. Similarly, the strangeness of the testing situation can be reduced by having the child visit the examining room shortly before the examination, meet the examiner, and handle the test materials. The test situation may pose a threat to the child's self-esteem, but the threat may be diminished by minimizing the "testing" features of the situation. A play atmosphere can be created with younger children, while with fear-ridden children or with frustrated children the examiner might begin playing with test-like materials (e.g., form boards or puzzles).

Some brain-injured children who know an answer to a problem may require an inordinately long time to organize an appropriate response. They may sit quietly for a long time before responding, or they may make tentative, hesitant responses. On such occasions, the children should be permitted to proceed at their own pace, without being urged to respond. However, when the delay is excessive (over a minute), the problem should be repeated, because they may have forgotten it.

Before beginning the examination, eliminate or minimize all potential sources of distraction in the testing room. A quiet room, with objects and toys removed, is preferred. If *perseveration* (a persistent continuation of a response despite its inappropriateness to a change in conditions) occurs, try to distract the child. This can be done, for example, by interjecting a comment about the weather, thereby giving the child time to reorganize before returning to the task.

When brain-injured children cannot cope with the test demands, they may become emotionally labile (unstable), which in extreme form is termed "catastrophic reaction." In catastrophic reactions, besides becoming extremely emotionally labile, brain-injured children may sit quietly and do nothing, blank out, or give an apparently aberrant response. These behaviors are attempts by the child to cope with a difficult situation. While ineffective as far as the goals of the examination are concerned, these strategies may help the child avoid further stress. The catastrophic reaction allows him or her to leave a difficult situation. These catastrophic reactions, and lesser forms of emotional lability, can be minimized by the following procedures:

1. Introduce the testing procedures slowly and casually and permit the child to play with toys very similar to the test materials.
2. Avoid any suggestions of inadequacy in the child's performance.
3. Avoid sudden movements or noises.
4. Introduce new materials gradually, reassuring the child that the new activities will be pleasant.
5. Stop testing if the emotional lability becomes too severe, and then sit quietly or go back to a test that the child has previously passed.

Testing Mentally Retarded Children

While mentally retarded children may behave during the examination (and on other occasions as well) in ways that are traditionally viewed as being negative, these same behaviors may have adaptive significance (as in the case of brain-injured children) by allowing the child to maintain self-esteem in the face of difficult intellectual or social demands (Hirsch, 1959). For example, aggressive, hyperactive behavior may represent a child's emergency reaction to finding himself or herself in a novel situation with very difficult tasks. Echolalia may serve as a way of establishing and maintaining a relationship, even though it is ineffective. Persistent questioning may be an effort to ensure stability. The child may also use perseveration to get through the situation. Finally, denial may be used to cover vulnerability.

A number of actions can be taken to cope with these behaviors. When mentally retarded children try to reverse roles, try to help them to become at ease and agree to alternate questions with them. By showing the children that they will be unconditionally accepted, you may diminish their need to keep control. Aggressive and hyperactive behavior may be reduced by beginning the examination with easy questions.

To prevent the children from being constantly confronted with inadequacy, difficult tasks can be alternated with easy ones. However, modifying test procedures may produce less reliable results.

Testing Physically Handicapped Children

The techniques used to test physically handicapped children encompass those used with normal children, but their application is more demanding. Normal children often need little encouragement. They are accustomed to answering test questions and are likely to find the tasks challenging. Physically handicapped children, in contrast, may feel at a disadvantage in the test situation. Their physical limitations may make them appear clumsy and awkward, resulting in feelings of self-consciousness. They must cope not only with the specific deficits associated with their disability (such as lack of sight or hearing), but also with the increased anxiety and uncertainty of their parents, anxiety associated with repeated medical examinations, peer difficulties, and other factors that may influence affective development and, indirectly, cognition and learning (cf. Wilson, Rapin, Wilson, & Van Denburg, 1975). Their reactions to the test situation may largely depend on how they perceive themselves outside of the test situation. They may be aware of their handicaps and reluctant to expose their disabilities in the examination. It will require patience and encouragement to elicit their optimum performance.

Testing physically handicapped children poses various kinds of problems (Russ & Soboloff, 1958). First, false impressions about the child's intellectual ability may be induced by any communication difficulties that exist, such as speech and hearing deficiencies. Second, because handicapped children may be unaccustomed to concentrated work for long periods of time, they may fatigue easily. Third, it may be difficult to decide whether attention difficulties, when present, are associated with physical deficiencies or with cognitive deficiencies.

SURVEY OF DEGREE OF PHYSICAL HANDICAP

Name _____ Date _____

Date of birth _____ Diagnosis _____

Age _____ Sex _____ Rater's name _____

	NON-HANDICAPPING		HANDICAPPING		Comments
	Minimal	Mild	Moderate	Severe	
VISION	☐ No trouble with vision; no glasses needed	☐ Some correction needed; may wear glasses; not handicapped in seeing	☐ Quite handicapped in seeing; vision not correctible by glasses	☐ Almost blind Totally blind	Left eye Rt. eye
HEARING	☐ No trouble with hearing	☐ Some difficulty in hearing; may wear hearing aid satisfactorily	☐ Quite handi-capped in hearing; has difficulty when wearing hearing aid	☐ Almost deaf Totally deaf	Left ear Rt. ear
SPEECH (verbal)	☐ Speech can be under-stood with-out difficulty by a stranger	☐ Some difficulty in being under-stood by a stranger; able to get ideas across in speech	☐ Speech hard for a stranger or imme-diate family to understand; hard to get ideas across in speech	☐ Almost totally unable to commu-nicate by speech; totally without speech	
SITTING BALANCE	☐ No difficulty in sitting in a chair or at a table	☐ Some difficulty in sitting in a chair or at a table, but not handicapped in doing so	☐ Quite handicapped in sitting in a chair or at a table; needs a relaxation chair and tray	☐ Unable to main-tain sitting balance unless fully supported	
ARM-HAND USE	☐ No difficulty in using arms and hands for self-help activity	☐ Some difficulty in using arms and hands for self-help, but not handicapped in doing so	☐ Quite handicapped in using arms and hands for many self-help activi-ties	☐ Unable to use arms and hands for any self-help activity	Left arm Rt. arm
WALKING	☐ No difficulty in walking	☐ Braces needed; unsteady gait; but able to get around	☐ Quite handicapped in walking; cannot walk independently	☐ Unable to walk	Left leg Rt. leg

Figure 5-1. Survey of Degree of Physical Handicap. Reprinted, with a change in notation, by permission of the publisher from E. Katz, "A Survey of Degree of Physical Handicap," *Cerebral Palsy Review, 15*(11), p. 10. Copyright 1954, Institute of Logopedics.

Fourth, it may be difficult to establish rapport with physically handicapped children who have heightened dependency.

Prior to testing a physically handicapped child, it is important to determine the degree to which the child is physically able to respond to the tests.[3] Informally evaluate the child's (a) vision, hearing, speech, sitting balance, and arm-hand use, (b) reading and writing skills, and (c) ability to indicate "yes" or "no" by either verbal or nonverbal means. Based on the results of these evaluations, an appropriate battery can be selected. A useful form for recording these observations is shown in Figure 5-1. Special procedures that can be used to administer the Stanford-Binet and WISC-R, WPPSI, and WAIS-R to handicapped children are discussed in the chapters of this book that cover these tests.

After you have become familiar with the child's problems and limitations associated with his or her disabilities, select tests that are appropriate and geared to the child's strengths and limitations. It may be necessary to omit certain test items. For example, items that require deftness in object manipulation or drawing may have to be eliminated when testing children with severe handicaps of the upper extremities. To counter the problem of fatigue and to obtain a more valid assessment, it may be advisable to schedule, if possible, several shorter test sessions spaced over several days. A scale for rating the adjustment of physically handicapped children is shown in Table 5-1.

TABLE 5-1. Rating Scale for Physically Handicapped Children

Directions: Place an "X" on the appropriate line.

1. Very poor mobility (needs constant aid in finding objects, locating places, etc.) ___:___:___:___:___:___ Superior mobility (needs no assistance in finding objects, locating places, etc.)

2. Very poor adjustment to handicap (denies the handicap, retreats, tries to outdo the nonhandicapped) ___:___:___:___:___:___ Superior adjustment to handicap (realistically accepts the disability without devaluing self, sets realistic goals)

3. Very poor social acceptance (disliked, rejected, or ignored by peers) ___:___:___:___:___:___ Superior social acceptance (preferred companion of almost all members of peer group)

4. Very dependent (expects others to do most things for him or her) ___:___:___:___:___:___ Very independent (self-reliant, does almost everything for himself or herself)

5. Very conforming (mild, obedient, a good follower) ___:___:___:___:___:___ Very nonconforming (prefers own decisions and ways of doing things)

6. Very rigid (self-opinionated, set, resistant to new ideas, new ways of doing things) ___:___:___:___:___:___ Very nonrigid (adaptable, flexible, accepts change, tries new ways of doing things)

7. Very little curiosity (very little desire to know about self and his or her environment, reluctant to seek and explore new elements in his or her environment) ___:___:___:___:___:___ Much curiosity (desires to know about self and his or her environment, seeks new experiences, examines and explores his or her environment)

8. Very poor academic achievement (has great difficulty or is failing in most school subjects) ___:___:___:___:___:___ Superior academic achievement (does outstanding work in most school subjects)

Reprinted, with a change in notation, from G. Halpin, G. Halpin, and M. H. Tillman, "Relationships between Creative Thinking, Intelligence, and Teacher-Rated Characteristics of Blind Children," *Education of the Visually Handicapped, 5*, p. 35. Copyright 1973. With permission of the Association for Education of the Visually Handicapped.

Visually Impaired Children

In testing visually impaired children it is important to try to determine the extent of the blindness, the quality of the vision present, and the extent of the field of vision. The term "blindness" encompasses a range from total lack of vision to the ability to see at 20 feet what persons of normal vision can see at 200 feet (20/200). In some school districts special programs for visually handicappd children may include those with 20/70 acuity. Individuals also may be classified as legally blind if their acuity is good, but their field of vision so narrow that it subtends an angle no greater than 20°.

Three broad groupings of blind children can be made (Bauman, 1974):

1. Vision is of no practical use in the test situation. This group includes the totally blind, those who can differentiate between light and dark only, and those who can distinguish shapes, but only when the shapes are held between the eyes and the source of light.
2. Vision can be used in handling large objects, locating test pieces, or following the examiner's hand movements during a demonstration, but cannot be used in reading even enlarged print effectively. These children may be able to use vision and touch in working with form boards, but are at a great disadvantage if they are required to read.
3. Vision can be used to read print efficiently, but only when the type is large, the page is held close to the eyes, or a magnifier or other special visual aid is used.

In testing partially sighted children examiners must take into account the amount of useful vision the child has and adjust the testing procedures accordingly. It is important that partially sighted children wear their glasses when they are tested and that the lighting conditions be adequate in the testing room. Some signs of the child's visual difficulty that may be apparent during the examination (as well as in the classroom and at home) are as follows:

BEHAVIOR
- Rubs eyes excessively
- Shuts or covers one eye, tilts head or thrusts head forward
- Has difficulty in reading or in other work requiring close use of the eyes
- Blinks more than usual or is irritable when doing close work
- Holds books close to eyes
- Is unable to see distant things clearly
- Squints eyelids together or frowns
- Loses place while reading
- Avoids close work
- Has poor sitting posture while reading
- Has difficulty judging distances

APPEARANCE
- Crossed eyes
- Red-rimmed, encrusted, or swollen eyelids
- Inflamed or watery eyes
- Recurring sties

COMPLAINTS
- Eyes itch, burn, or feel scratchy
- Cannot see well
- Dizziness, headaches, or nausea following close work
- Blurred or double vision

Other useful suggestions for testing partially sighted children include the following:

While it is certainly useful if the psychologist can have a copy of the ophthalmological report, even this provides only a general notion of how much vision the child will bring to the testing situation. Children with the same acuity rating may differ greatly in the effective use of their remaining vision because of real differences in field of vision, in sharpness of image, and in the strain involved in reading, because the age at which vision was lost might affect ability to interpret slight cues, and because some children do learn to use remaining vision far more efficiently than others do. With children of some maturity the wisest procedure may be to allow the child himself to decide whether he prefers to read or to have test material read to him. It is also sensible to have the child demonstrate his skill by reading aloud briefly, since some children overstate their ability to handle ink print. [Bauman, 1974, p. 161]

If the visual handicap is not too severe, intelligence tests such as the WISC-R, Stanford-Binet, WPPSI, and WAIS-R may be used. However, if the handicap is severe, only verbal items should be administered. It should be recognized that the ability to answer even verbal items may be reduced if information required by the items depends in part on visual experiences. The Hays-Binet and Perkins-Binet also are available for evaluating blind children.

Hearing Impaired Children

Hearing impairment is a general term that refers to hearing losses ranging from mild to profound. Children with hearing impairments are not a homogeneous group. This is so because hearing impairment is associated with various types of etiological factors, including maternal rubella, meningitis, Rh incompatability, and prematurity. On a broader level, deafness may be associated with brain damage, learning difficulties, aphasia, mental illness, and mental retardation. In many cases hearing impaired children are often multiply handicapped. Some signs of possible hearing difficulty are as follows:

GENERAL SIGNS

- Lack of normal response to sound
- Inattentiveness
- Inability to follow oral directions
- Failure to respond when spoken to
- Frequent requests to have speaker repeat what was said
- Intent observation of speaker's lips (lip-reading, speechreading)
- Habit of turning one ear toward the speaker
- Unusual voice quality (e.g., monotonous)
- Speech too loud or too soft
- Faulty pronunciation
- Poor articulation
- Frequent earaches or discharges from ears

EXAMPLES OF POSSIBLE HEARING DIFFICULTIES

- Difficulty discriminating consonant sounds; e.g., hears *mat* for *bat, tab* for *tap*
- Difficulty discriminating and learning short vowel sounds

- If given a word, has difficulty sounding it out, sound by sound, as *cat* is k-a-t
- Difficulty relating printed letters to their sounds, as "f," "pl," "ide"
- Cannot separate sounds that make up blends, as "fl" has sounds of f-f . . . l-l
- Spells and reads sight words better than phonetic words

Hearing represents a continuum from very acute perception, as in the case of a gifted musical conductor who can detect an out-of-tune instrument in an orchestra, to the total deafness of an individual who can only detect strong vibrations through tactile sensations. The following classification scheme, in order of severity, for hard-of-hearing individuals has been proposed by Vernon (1974):

1. The least hard-of-hearing are those children with a hearing loss of less than 15 db (decibels) in the speech range. These children can be given the same intelligence tests as those administered to non-hard-of-hearing children.
2. The middle group consists of children whose loss is between 20 and 70 db in the speech range. Some children in this group may require special procedures because of severe communication problems, while those with few communication problems can function in a normal environment. The procedures selected should be based on the child's degree of communication, because no set procedure is applicable to all children who are in this group. This group is the least clearly defined of the three groups.
3. The last group contains children with a severe hearing loss—75 db or more in the speech range. This group needs special evaluation procedures devised for deaf children or for those with profound hearing losses.

The greatest single handicap associated with hearing loss during the prelingual years is the barrier to learning language (Gerken, 1979). Hearing impairment impedes the normal acquisition of both receptive and expressive language skills. For example, it has been estimated that a normal 4-year-old child has a working vocabulary of between 2,000 and 3,000 words, while a prelingually deaf child of this age has fewer than 25 words (Meadow, 1968). This latter estimate may not be true for a deaf child of deaf parents who has been exposed to education programs as an infant. Hearing impaired children also have syntactical deficiencies in the use of language. Because normal sequences of language mastery are impeded, difficulties arise in acquiring communication skills, including reading, writing, and spelling skills.

In the assessment of hearing impaired children, it is important to consider the type of loss, degree of loss, age of onset, and etiologic components. It also is helpful to determine when the child was fitted with a hearing aid, if one was prescribed. Before beginning the assessment, try to learn about the child's functioning level. This includes the methods by which the child receives information and how he or she communicates (receptive and expressive skills). Interviewing parents and teacher can help one obtain this information.

Examiners who work with deaf children need special communication skills. As a first step, if you have not received special training, prepare for testing deaf children by observing classes for the deaf, noting how teachers communicate with their pupils (Levine, 1960). More importantly, a valuable procedure in testing deaf children is to use a total communication approach for those children familiar with it (Sullivan, 1978). This approach entails the simultaneous use of speech, sign language (a manual system of communication such as the American Sign Language or Signed English) (Bornstein, Hamilton, Saulnier, & Roy, 1975), and/or fingerspelling. Generally, to administer tests to deaf children a variety of techniques can be used including speech, gesture, pantomime, writing, signs, fingerspelling, and drawing.

Testing children with impaired hearing requires a high degree of skill and wide experience with deaf children (Reed, 1970). Because sight is the chief means by which deaf children receive stimuli, they are likely to seek visual clues, such as facial expressions or movements of hands, to gain understanding about their performance (Murphy, 1957). Examiners must realize that any slight movements they make may furnish cues to the deaf child. Facial expressions rather than tone of voice will convey the examiner's mood, and a frown or a grimace of impatience will be quickly noted and interpreted unfavorably (Falberg, 1967). Smiling, as though the child were being rewarded for a correct response, should be avoided when a wrong response has been given so that the child is not encouraged to make similar responses.

Not only are there difficulties associated with administering tests and with conducting the interview, but, in addition, it may be difficult to understand the answers of hearing impaired children with expressive difficulties. Hearing impaired children may give the impression of being able to understand directions and test questions, but on closer inspection their seeming comprehension may turn out to be an artifice. They may have learned how to play a role to avoid confronting a potentially embarrassing situation.

For children who lipread, it is important that the lighting in the room and the child's position in relation to the examiner be appropriate. Examiners must be able to make the instructions understood without giving away answers in the process. Pantomime is not always successful in conveying to the child what the examiner intends to communicate. While a simple demonstration will sometimes suffice, the demonstration itself may also indicate the answer. Responses given in pantomime by the child should be given credit only when there is no doubt about the accuracy of the answer (Bice & Cruickshank, 1966).

If you use speech, be sure that you are looking at the child while you are reading the test instructions and questions and that the child is watching your face (Sullivan & Vernon, 1979). Speech should be clear and distinct. Try to maintain a pleasant face. Be sure that there are no obstructions that block the child's view of your lips. Children who wear hearing aids should do so during the examination; the hearing aids should be in good working order. In some cases it may be necessary to use an interpreter skilled both in sign language and in English.

Vernon and Brown (1964) described the tragic case of a hearing impaired child who received an IQ of 29 on the Stanford-Binet, a score that led to her commitment to a hospital for the mentally retarded where she remained for five years. The case demonstrates what can occur when there has been a failure in the diagnostic process. No one realized that the child was deaf, so only the Stanford-Binet was administered for the initial intellectual assessment. It was only after she was administered a performance intelligence test and obtained an IQ of 113 that the staff discovered that she was not retarded. Upon dismissal from the institution, she entered a school for the deaf and made good progress.

The assessment of hearing impaired children poses special problems. Arriving at a valid measure of ability is difficult because many tests have large verbal components. Verbally based tests usually do not give an accurate picture of the hearing impaired child's level of ability. They are more likely to measure the extent of the hearing impaired child's language deficiency than the level of mental ability. Verbally oriented tests should be used with extreme caution, if at all.

The performance tests selected for hard-of-hearing children should not depend on verbal directions. Timed tests may be less valid for hard-of-hearing children because the added stress of time may interfere with their performance to a greater extent than it does with normally hearing children. Representative performance tests include the WISC-R, WPPSI, and WAIS-R Performance Scales, Ontario School Ability Examination, Leiter International Performance Scale, Hiskey-Nebraska Test of Learning Aptitude, the nonauditory/nonverbal subtests of the Illinois Test of Psycholinguistic Ability, and the Progressive Matrices.

While the audiologist is the major authority in determining the communication skills of hard-of-hearing children, the psychologist also makes observations, both formal and informal. Note should be made of where the observations occurred, e.g., a quiet one-to-one situation, classroom, job, or a social setting. The child's (a) ability to read and write, (b) speech intelligibility and pleasantness, and (c) skill in lipreading should be assessed. Note the extent to which the child is able to understand conversation during the examination. Do not assume that the communication difficulties of hard-of-hearing children indicate that they have limited intelligence. A congenital hearing loss can interfere with the development of many different kinds of skills that may not be related to cognitive ability. In examining hard-of-hearing children, select the most appropriate test, and use at least one performance measure of cognitive ability.

A primary goal in evaluating hard-of-hearing children is to determine the extent to which their performance resembles that of a normally hearing child or that of a deaf child. Vernon (1974) has stressed why this effort is needed.

By interrelating IQ, educational, and other facts about a deaf or hard of hearing child it is possible to derive a picture which reveals the role played by his hearing loss. If the youth's profile is similar to that of the normally hearing, his loss and the way it has been coped with is not particularly disabling. By contrast, if the profile is similar to that of a deaf child then the loss has had major effects on communication, language development, and education. Appropriate planning for the two kinds of children vary drastically. What would be constructive for one would in certain cases be devastating for the other. An evaluation which does not fully address itself to this issue has failed to serve one of its major functions. The issue cannot be handled without comprehensive information. Shortcuts will not suffice and hasty inadequately done evaluations are actually unethical and wasteful of human resources. [p. 209]

Cerebral Palsied Children

Cerebral palsied children present particular difficulties when being tested. Their motor, speech, visual, and auditory difficulties may limit the applicability of standardized tests and make caution mandatory in interpreting test results.[4] Because cerebral palsied children frequently perform motor tasks in a slow and laborious manner, they may be at a particular disadvantage when time limits are imposed. Furthermore, it is sometimes difficult to determine whether their test failures are due to physical disabilities or to cognitive deficits. Some writers are of the opinion that when standardized tests are given to severely handicapped cerebral palsied children, the scores may tend to underestimate the child's ability in proportion to the severity of his or her handicaps (Katz, 1955; McIntire, 1938). However, in spite of the difficulties in using standard tests, it is still important to compare the cerebral palsied child's performance with that of the normal child, because the latter sets the standards in the world at large.[5]

Because many cerebral palsied children talk adequately and have at least one good hand, modifications in administering the tests may not be necessary. However, when serious physical limitations exist, modifications are needed. Bice and Cruickshank (1966) suggested that tests requiring the least modification be used:

> If the subject has good hands and poor speech, performance tests are appropriate. If the opposite is true, verbal tests may have priority. In the majority of cases, the examiner will be able to give at least part of both these types of tests. At times it is necessary to omit tests. A child who can neither walk nor use a wheel chair cannot be asked to go to a chair to place a pencil, or go to a door and open it. Scores can be prorated as necessary. [p. 103]

While some writers have questioned whether the initial IQs obtained by cerebral palsied children are reliable and valid,[6] research studies and follow-up reports indicate that the initial test results have a satisfactory degree of reliability and validity.[7] However, caution is still needed in using the first scores as the sole criterion in long-range planning, not only for cerebral palsied children, but for all children examined by an intelligence test. Exhibit 5-2 presents a case of a child with mild cerebral palsy.

Examiner Halo Effects

Examiners must try to prevent their test administration from being influenced by their impression of the examinee—the "halo" effect. For example, examiners may overrate the responses of a child whom they perceive as "bright" and underrate the responses of a child who appears "dull." In the testing of handicapped children, the halo effect may occur in the following way:

> Motivated by a feeling of sympathy often reinforced by seeing the physical energy expended by so many palsied children in following instructions, the examiner easily believes his hope, i.e., that the child knows more than he can express, and hence overestimates the child's ability. [Burgemeister, 1962, p. 117]

Binet and Wechsler carefully sought to diminish halo effects by their standardization procedures. Yet Goodenough (1949) pointed out that most of us too rarely take precautions to avoid them.

There is some evidence from social-psychological literature that an experimenter's hypotheses (or expectancies) may exert some subtle influence over a subject's performance. An experimenter's hypothesis may affect how he or she behaves with a subject, and early data returns in an experiment may lead to the development of experimenter expectancies that can subtly affect the experimenter's behavior in later interactions with the subject (Rosenthal, 1966). Administering an individual intelligence test is somewhat analogous to conducting an experiment. Prior information about the examinee's ability level and classroom performance, and impressions resulting from

EXHIBIT 5-2.   Psychological Evaluation: Developmental Delay Coupled with Limited Cognitive Skills, Mild Cerebral Palsy

Name: Jim
Date of birth: January 10, 1974
Chronological age: 5-11
Date of examination: December 10, 1979
Date of report: December 11, 1979
Grade: Kindergarten

Tests Administered

Stanford-Binet (LM):
Chronological age: 5 years, 11 months
Mental age: 4 years, 5 months
IQ: 67 ± 5 at 95 percent confidence level
Classification: Mental Retardation.

Beery Test of Visual Motor Integration: In this test the child is asked to copy shapes of increasing complexity with a pencil. Age equivalent: 3 years, 2 months.

Selected nonverbal tests:
Seguin Form Board, age norm: 4 yrs (awkward performance)
Two-Hole Form Board: 4 yrs
Manikin: 3 yrs.

Draw-A-Man: Age equivalent: 4 to 4½ years (quality poor, begins to make repetitive marks and stray into story-telling).

Wide Range Achievement Test (readiness portions): Unable to coordinate counting and pointing; limited understanding of number concepts; markedly poor pencil control (e.g., was able to "draw" a few letters of his name laboriously). General grade level equivalent: Pre-kindergarten.

Developmental Test of Visual-Perception: Eye-motor Coordination Subtest, age equivalent: 3 years, 9 months.

Reason for Referral

Jim is an almost 6-year-old boy who has been having difficulties adjusting to kindergarten. He moves about constantly, has trouble following verbal instructions, and perseverates in his activities. Psychological-developmental assessment was requested as part of a more comprehensive evaluation of these problems.

Background

Jim had a normal birth, insofar as could be documented. Developmental milestones were delayed. He sat at 9 and a half months, walked at 19 months, and uttered his first words at 3 and a half years. When he began to walk, he ran in headlong fashion. Because he did not have enough control for speed, he fell frequently and needed restraints for his own safety.

   The neurological examination indicated that there were signs of diffuse neurodevelopmental disorder, including choreoform movements and many clumsy falls. The diagnostic impression was that the child probably would fall into the category of Mild Cerebral Palsy.

   Jim's school teacher reported the following observations:

1. Sucks on fingers or hand, emotionally immature.
2. Perseverative behavior. When told to put a mark on a picture, he marked them all. He hits other kids; once he begins, he cannot seem to stop. He sometimes seems to hurt on purpose.
3. Moves hands, feet, and arms constantly; makes strange noises and twists his mouth.
4. Unable to follow verbal commands.
5. "Wild fantasies"—draws and talks (unclearly) about monsters.
6. Unable to sustain attention long enough to complete screening assessment.

EXHIBIT 5-2 (cont.)

A summary of the speech pathologist's impressions are as follows:

It is my impression that Jim's most significant problems have had to do with poor impulse control and considerable difficulty relegating some stimuli to the background in order to attend selectively to a specific task. His attention frequently wandered, or he became over engrossed in coloring or marking as he wished, perseverating, and having difficulty shifting to a new task. Immediate memory problems and word finding difficulties were both noteworthy.

Given his language lags, his very considerable fine motor incoordination and attentional problems, he is likely to require special, highly structured educational management. Essential portions of management should include presenting one stimulus at a time and expanding his vocabulary and concepts. I understand that medical management will be explored with the family as well.

Behavioral Observations

In our one-to-one test setting (with either mother or father observing unobtrusively), Jim came across as a high-keyed, but reasonably cooperative little boy. His articulation, play-preferences, and the way he related to adults were more in keeping with an appealing, younger child. He tried hard to meet expectations, in terms of both test performance and social conduct. He beamed when his efforts were successful, and particularly when they were rewarded by approval. However, when he was pressed beyond his capabilities we began to see signs of the motor restlessness, perseverative responses, and mischievous limit-testing described in his kindergarten classroom. In the individual test setting these behaviors could be curtailed fairly readily by providing firm guidelines for acceptable activities, lowering the difficulty of the tasks, and pacing the procedures to allow for ample "recess time." Clearly, Jim is a youngster who works at maximum efficiency for just so long (roughly fifteen minutes at a stretch). After this, his mind begins to wander toward more active, playful, or imaginative pursuits.

Over and beyond these behavioral observations, I was struck by Jim's awkward gait and poor fine motor coordination. Even when working with large puzzles and form boards, which he enjoyed, he often had difficulty controlling manual movements sufficiently to receive time bonuses.

Conclusions

Present test findings and observations suggest moderate, generalized delays in cognitive development coupled with more significant deficits in both fine and gross motor functions. While it was indeed true that Jim could not stay put for long and sometimes needed close supervision to maintain attention (especially under stress of difficulty), I did not feel that "hyperkinesis" alone could explain the pervasive immaturity. Rather, these behaviors seemed to represent additional handicaps to adjustment and learning, especially in situations offering little chance for successful performance.

Judging from the information available, I suspect that a regular kindergarten curriculum is one of these situations. Jim is simply not capable at this time of understanding many of the teacher's verbal instructions, coping with the pencil work, or meeting the requirements for close attention. Many of the perseverative, aggressive, fantasy-oriented behaviors described may well represent his way of coping with expectations he cannot meet, and the sense of inadequacy which follows.

It is impossible to make specific recommendations at this point, without knowing what alternatives (if any) are available. Ideally, I would like to see Jim in a small, highly structured preschool setting where the program can be individually tailored to Jim's present capabilities—generally those of a 4-year-old—and build from there. As discussed with his physician, a trial of medication, designed to provide additional "outside" control of his attention and activity, might also be worthwhile.

After a period of optimal educational/medical intervention, it will be extremely important to evaluate Jim's progress, as well as to reassess his social-educational needs year by year. While it may be much too early to pinpoint primary handicaps, or assign diagnostic labels, it seems likely that this youngster will require special educational planning.

———————

Examiner

the information obtained from the responses to early test questions, may lead the examiner to formulate a hypothesis, albeit vague, regarding the examinee's level of intelligence. Consequently, it is imperative that examiners prevent the halo effect from affecting their test administration adversely.

Many studies have examined whether information given to examiners affects (a) their scoring of intelligence test responses provided on questionnaires or (b) the scores obtained by children in actual testing activities. Expectancy has been manipulated by providing various kinds of case history information, such as prior test scores, grades, academic achievement history, socioeconomic status, ethnicity, sex, and behavioral ratings. Most studies indicate that examiners are influenced by pretest information in the scores they give to responses, especially if the responses are ambiguous.[8] Examinees described as being bright are likely to receive more credit than examinees described as being dull for the exact same response.

Findings are not as clear-cut when examiners actually tested children. In some cases the positive expectancies led to children obtaining higher scores,[9] while in others they did not.[10] In the latter case, examiners probably resolved any discrepancies created by the referral information by relying on the child's actual test performance. An illustration of one such study is highlighted in Exhibit 5-3.

The studies reviewed indicate that pretest information plays a role in the overall evaluation of the examinee and, on occasion, in scoring responses and in administering the test. The existence of expectancies regarding an examinee's probable level of performance does not mean that scoring bias will necessarily occur. Rather, the research studies point out that examiners must guard against the occurrence of halo effects when administering intelligence tests. The processes by which pretest information affects the examiner's performance are still unclear.

Eliminating halo effects in administering, scoring, and evaluating intelligence tests is a difficult goal. It probably is impossible to eliminate completely your positive or negative evaluations of the child; however, it is possible and necessary to minimize the influence of these reactions on your test administration and rating of the child's test responses. You must become aware of your reactions to the child, and be especially alert to possible halo effects in your scoring of the child's ambiguous responses.

Suggestions for Administering Tests

You are likely to be anxious when you are first learning to administer tests. You must become a juggler, as you do such things as establish rapport, administer the appropriate items, keep the materials ready, respond appropriately to the child, record precisely the child's responses, observe the child's behavior, and score the responses. In time, many of these procedures become routine, but even the most experienced examiners will need to review their test procedures periodically. The test manuals usually present many useful and important suggestions for administering the tests; in each case they should be studied carefully. The following suggestions serve to supplement or to re-emphasize a number of selected points that are often presented in test manuals. If they are followed, along with the instructions in the various test manuals, it is likely that administrative errors, such as inaccurate scoring, incomplete recording of the child's responses, and failure to question ambiguous responses, will be reduced. (Detailed suggestions for administering various tests appear in other chapters of the book.)

Try to maintain control of the situation. Children should not be allowed to turn pages in the manual, to play with the test materials, or to have pencils, pens, or toys in their hands, except when they are needed for a test. Having an extra chair on which to place the test kit will facilitate the administration. If you are uncertain about what the child said, ask the child to repeat his or her response. To minimize this, pay close attention to the child's responses.

EXHIBIT 5-3.   Research Highlight: Expectancy Effects on IQs Obtained by Mentally Retarded Children

Dangel (1972) studied the possible biasing effects of pretest referral information on the intelligence test scores obtained by mentally retarded children. In a sample of fifty-four mentally retarded boys and girls between 8 and 12 years of age, (a) one third were assigned to a condition in which positive referral information was given to the examiner, (b) one third to a neutral referral information condition, and (c) one third to a negative referral information condition. In the positive expectancy condition, examiners were informed of fictitious IQs—that the children had obtained previous IQs in the 84 to 93 range and had positive behavior in the classroom. In the neutral expectancy condition, the children's actual previous

IQs were reported along with comments indicating that they had average behavior in the classroom. In the negative expectancy condition, fictitious previous IQs were again provided—IQs of 54 or 55 together with unfavorable classroom behavioral comments.

After the expectancies were created, examiners administered the WISC. The children obtained similar IQs in all three conditions—less than a two-point difference in Full Scale IQs, 72.96 to 74.92. These results indicate that the pretest referral information did not affect the scores obtained by the children. Sources of possible examiner errors—such as computational errors, frequency of questioning children, indications that a ceiling had not been properly established, and frequency of questionable scoring—and examinees' reactions to the examiners did not differ across the expectancy conditions.   ■

Ideally, the examination room should be one which minimizes external sources of distraction and maximizes the child's motivation. The many different conditions you will meet on the job will invariably fall short of the ideal. You therefore may have to settle for conditions that approximate the ideal, although you must *never* test when the conditions would adversely affect the child's performance.

General Suggestions

The instructions for the various tests should be read verbatim, in an even and relaxed manner; avoid a wooden or machine-like approach. Most beginning examiners have a tendency to read the test instructions and questions too quickly, although some read them too slowly. Pace your reading and conversation to the child's age, striving for clarity and a natural quality. Avoid unusual facial expressions or modulations in voice that may give cues to the children about their performance.

The suggestions that follow pertain to many individually administered tests. However, some tests have specific guidelines that may differ from those presented below. In such cases, the guidelines in the respective manuals should always be followed. The

instructions used for the first trial of a test or subtest can be repeated on succeeding trials or items. However, it is not permissible to explain any of the words that are used in the directions or in the questions on the various test items. Further, be sure not to add any additional words to the instructions, such as "Now here is . . . ." Memory items should not be repeated. The directions should be learned well; ideally, they should be memorized. In addition, you should become so familiar with the test materials that you can introduce and remove them without breaking the interaction between you and the child.

On tests that have time limits, unless the manual says otherwise, do not tell the children how much time is allotted to the task. If they ask, tell them to give their answer as soon as they know it, or something similar. Timing should begin as soon as the item is shown to the child. Seldom accept the first "I don't know" response given by the child. Ask the child to try to answer, unless the question appears to be too difficult for him or her. It is permissible to say something like "Try to give an answer" or "Try to answer it in some way, if you can."

Ask the child to explain his or her answer further when the response is incomplete or when it borders on a correct response but is not correct as it stands. However, obviously incorrect responses should not be probed. When a response contains one part that is correct and one that is wrong, ask the child for his or her preference and score the response accordingly. Avoid giving the child the impression that a test (or subtest) is being discontinued because of repeated failure. If the child asks to have part of a question repeated, it is preferable to repeat the entire question.

The child should not be told whether his or her responses are correct. If asked, you can say that it is against the rules to tell the answers, or say that he or she can ask about one or two of the answers at the end of the examination, if he or she is still interested in discussing them at that time.

Immediately record the child's answer in the appropriate space provided in the record booklet as accurately as possible. Exercise judgment in recording parts of the response that have limited relevance to the test question.

When administering items that appear in booklets, it is not necessary to hold the booklet, unless the manual so states. The booklet can be left flat on the table and pages (or cards) turned over for each succeeding item.

A general rule of thumb is to administer items from the child's left to right in the order given in the test manual. Even demonstration items should be so arranged. This rule simply brings some uniformity to the test administration. Cards should be placed one at a time, allowing the child to see the cards clearly. Some beginning examiners have been found to cover the cards inadvertently as they placed them on the table. The child should be able to see your complete movements when cards are being rearranged in demonstration items. Be sure to record the child's arrangements as soon as the item is completed.

It may be helpful to construct sample block designs by completing the first row from the child's left to right and then the second row, again from the child's left to right. Be sure that the child can reach the blocks or other necessary materials. Do not remove the blocks (or other materials) until the child says that he or she is finished.

The child's responses should be scored as soon as they are given. Try to shield the scores in the record booklet as unobtrusively as possible. The test protocol should be positioned in such a way that the child does not see answers to questions or get feedback as to the correctness of prior or current responses. Scoring can be facilitated by referring to the scoring section of the test manual when there is any doubt about scoring the child's response. On the Stanford-Binet, tests that may fall at the basal and ceiling levels *must* be scored during the examination proper. Failure to follow this procedure may result in an invalid test administration, because a basal level and a ceiling level need to be established if standard procedures are to be followed. Similarly, on the WISC-R, WPPSI, and WAIS-R, discontinuance procedures cannot be followed unless responses are immediately scored. However, on the Stanford-Binet, when responses that are difficult to score occur on tests falling between the basal and ceiling year levels, you may score or rescore them carefully after the examination is completed. A question mark can be placed to the left of such responses in order to allow you to identify them easily when they are checked. A similar procedure can be followed for the WISC-R, WPPSI, and WAIS-R. However, try to score as many responses as possible during the examination.

The examples shown in the various test manuals for scoring responses are guides. They are not meant to be the only correct answers, with the exception of those problems (a) that have only one correct answer or (b) for which the manual lists the only acceptable responses. The scoring criteria for each test or subtest should be studied so that you know what are correct, questionable, or incorrect answers. Try to discern the kind of correct response called for by the item. The scoring guides occasionally provide such guidelines. When they are not provided, the sample responses should be studied to ascertain the kinds of responses that should receive credit. On the basis of such study, appropriate decisions regarding the correctness or incorrectness of a response can be made.

When the examination is completed, children should be praised for their efforts. Because children may be diabetic and because some parents may have objections, it is recommended that candy not be given routinely to children at the completion of the examination. A balloon or other such toy may be given, if you desire. However, any materials used in the examination, such as the paper cuttings from the Stanford-Binet, should not be given because they may provide cues to other children. An excellent general outline of testing procedures appears in Table 5-2.

TABLE 5-2.   A General Outline of Testing Procedures

I. General testing precautions.
  A. Read, learn, and *reread* instructions.
  B. Always adhere to standardized procedures.
    1. Use exact wording.
    2. Maintain accurate timing.
    3. Present materials in the prescribed manner.
    4. Follow scoring instructions rigidly.
    5. Do not depend solely on reading the printed directions, but do have them available for ready reference.
  C. Be objective.
    1. Give no indication of the correctness or incorrectness of the child's responses.
    2. Give no clues about the answer you expect; watch your verbal intonation; remember you are testing, not teaching.
  D. Be natural.
    1. Be warm but impersonal.
    2. Learn to use standardized wording in a natural and informal manner.
    3. Achieve rapport and verbal give-and-take before the test begins; take a listening attitude.
  E. Prepare the environment.
    1. Avoid distractions.
      a. Visual: Have the child face away from doors and windows where movement and activity are going on. Have him or her face away from large open spaces that have distracting pictures, colors, toys, etc. Avoid clutter.
      b. Auditory: Avoid noisy areas, other voices, etc.; test in isolation.
      c. Emotional: Avoid testing when the child is hurried, troubled, or ill.
    2. Provide optimum conditions for good performance.
      a. See that the child is in a comfortable position and has a clear view of the materials.
      b. Provide a well-lit room with adequate ventilation and comfortable temperature.
      c. Avoid glaring lights, reflections from the pages, etc. Face the child away from the window if possible.
      d. Speak in a clear, audible voice at a moderate rate of speed.
      e. Maintain interest through enthusiasm, attention to the child, and smooth presentation of the material.
      f. Commend and encourage for general performance but never on specific items.
      g. Let the child know you want to see how well he or she can do.
II. Administering and scoring the intelligence test.
  A. Efficiency.
    1. Provide an efficient arrangement and method of manipulating materials for
      a. Recording.
      b. Viewing the manual *without its becoming a barrier between you and the child.*
      c. Putting away and bringing out materials.
      d. Avoiding delays and distractions for the child.
    2. Make smooth transition from test to test and from item to item. You must know at each point in the test what your next presentation will be.
    3. Know your materials and scoring well enough that you do not extend the test

(cont.)

TABLE 5-2 (cont.)

unnecessarily. Overtesting may create fatigue and/or disinterest.
   a. Know the scoring standards.
   b. Begin at the appropriate point.
4. Learn to handle extraneous behavior.
   a. Disregard or redirect irrelevant remarks.
   b. Minimize extraneous movements by developing interest, motivation, and task orientation. If extraneous movements do not interfere with the child's functioning, ignore them. If necessary, provide the child a positive outlet such as grasping the edges of the desk or folding his or her hands.
   c. Foresee fatigue and distraction.

B. Scoring.
1. It is essential that an examiner know the scoring standards well. This requirement applies particularly to the understanding of the *intent* of each test or subtest.
2. It must be remembered that the scoring standards are just what the label states: they are "standards" for scoring rather than all-inclusive right-or-wrong answers. It is often necessary to evaluate equivalent responses in the light of other responses listed in the scoring standards, since not all possible responses could be included.
3. A beginning examiner should check all answers with the manual in order to verify any doubtful responses.
4. Every step in the scoring process should be rechecked.
5. All figures and calculations should be double-checked. The chronological age, the number of correct items, additions, and arithmetic calculations—all should be double-checked.

C. Care of materials.
1. Whenever any of the materials presented to the child become marked or defaced in any way that might influence the child's response, they should be replaced.
2. If you, the examiner, must point to the pictures, be sure not to mark the page. Use the back end of your pen or pencil.
3. If any materials are lost or damaged, they should be replaced by objects *identical to the original*.

Reprinted, with a change in notation, by permission of the publisher and author from W. D. Kirk, *Aids and Precautions in Administering the Illinois Test of Psycholinguistic Abilities*, pp. 5–7, 13–14. Copyright 1974, University of Illinois Press.

Departures from Standard Procedures

There are major problems involved with departing from standard procedures during the actual test administration. For example, Cronbach (1960) pointed out that "any departure from standard administrative practice changes the meaning of scores" (p. 185). Other writers, too, have stated that test norms cannot be used when standardized tests have been altered (e.g., Braen & Masling, 1959; Strother, 1945). However, in requiring standard test procedures, test authors do not take into account variability among examinees or the possibility that a more accurate estimate of intellectual ability can be obtained, on some occasions, by "violation" of standard procedures. The examiner who deems it desirable to go beyond the standard test instructions in order to assess present or potential intellectual ability usually has read that such procedures may interfere with or affect the final test results.

Eisenson (1954) noted that there may be occasions when standard administrative procedures should not be followed. For example, tests administered to aphasic patients

should be used to aid in formulating clinical judgments rather than as a means of trying to get a quantitative index. . . . Modifications in administering the tests and of evaluating the responses are usually necessary, or at least desirable, in order to elicit the clearest picture of the patient's intellectual functioning. Time limits may be ignored and roundabout definitions accepted. [p. 4]

He recognized that such modifications preclude the use of test norms.

Newland (1963) illustrated other alternatives available to the examiner in making test adaptations:

... the examiner may read the standardized test items to blind subjects, may allow a child to use a typewriter in giving his responses if he has a major speech or handwriting problem, may observe the eye movements of the subject as he identifies parts of a test item (where other children might write or point with their fingers in responding), might start with motor items rather than with verbal items in the case of a child whose problem involves the communication area, or might even rearrange some Binet items into WISC form if research warranted taking such liberties with the material. [p. 69]

In order for the test norms to be used with confidence, the test items must be administered according to standard procedures. This means, for example, that you must use the exact words of the questions, the specific test materials, and the specified time limits. However, while test content and test materials are standardized, one does not really know about the effects of small deviations in test procedures. Each test has a standard error reflecting the nuances in the examiner-examinee relationship, the conditions of the examination, the time of day, and other similar factors. It is hoped that when small changes occur in rapport or in other aspects of the test situation, these changes will keep the resulting score within the range of the standard error, but this will never be precisely known.

Consider when standard norms can be used and when they cannot be used. What does it mean to use them and be wrong? Can intuitive or conventional wisdom serve as a partial guide in the absence of formal standardization procedures? The answer to the latter question is a qualified "yes," depending on the extent to which modifications or violations have occurred. We have seen that one cannot standardize every little test procedure. What is most crucial, however, is that standard procedures be followed in administration and in scoring.

Whether or not norms will be violated when modifications in test procedures are introduced will depend on the extent of the modifications. Most of the procedures suggested by Newland do not appear to hamper the use of the standardized norms. However, more serious modifications, such as altering the wording of questions, changing the scoring criteria, or using a multiple-choice procedure for items that call for definitions, are likely to jeopardize the use of test norms.

While standard administrative procedures are the rule, exceptions may occasionally be made in order to obtain some estimate of the child's ability without regard for norms. On those occasions when modifications must be used, such information should be clearly conveyed in the report and the resulting scores interpreted in light of the modifications. The scores may be less precise, and predictions about future levels of functioning are likely to be more gross than would otherwise be the case. Specific suggestions for modifying the Stanford-Binet and WISC-R appear in Chapters 7 and 9.

Incentives and their effects. The use of incentives and feedback does not seem to increase children's test scores. Incentives, such as praise, candy, or money—referred to as social or token reinforcement—were viewed as a possible means of increasing children's motivation in various studies. An analysis of twenty-two different studies indicates that in thirteen studies incentives or feedback did not affect the children's performance;[11] in five studies, the effects were mixed;[12] in four studies, significant effects were reported.[13] The populations included a variety of normal and handicapped children of various ethnic groups. This body of data suggests that social and token reinforcers operate in similar ways in various ethnic and social-class groups. It may be that the standard test situation is one that is viewed by most children as a rewarding one. They may enjoy the special attention of an adult examiner and the acceptance by the examiner. Thus, the standard condition in these various experiments was one in which most children apparently were motivated to perform at their maximum level. The additional social or token reinforcement or feedback did not usually result in improved performance.

Testing of limits. The standard administrative procedures should be followed, if possible, in all cases. The only exceptions are those discussed in the test manuals (e.g., changing order of tests if necessary, eliminating spoiled tests, etc.) or those necessary to test handicapped children. However, there are times at which examiners desire to go beyond the standard test procedures (testing of limits) in order to gain additional information about the child's abilities. These occasions may be infrequent, but when they occur, the information gained from testing-of-limits procedures can be helpful, especially in clinical settings. Any successes obtained during testing of limits, of course, cannot be credited to the child's scores. *All testing-of-limits techniques should be used only after the scale has been administered using standard procedures.* The reason why this principle should be followed is that the additional cues on one item may facilitate the child's performance on the remaining items of a test or subtest. Such findings have been reported for the Block Design and Picture Arrangement subtests of the WISC and Wechsler-Bellevue (Sattler, 1969). A number of different testing-of-limits procedures are now considered.

1. *Additional cues.* How much help is necessary for the child to answer a question correctly? To answer this question, you may provide a series of cues to the child. You can show the first step in solving the problem, after which you can provide a series of additional steps if needed. Or you might begin by asking the child how he or she went about trying to solve the problem. This question can be followed by asking the child to try to answer the problem again, or by providing the first step in reaching the correct solution, or by informing him or her where the method was wrong and then asking him

or her to try again. The more cues that are needed before success is achieved, the greater the degree of possible learning disability or cognitive deficit.

2. *Establishing methods used by the examinee.* There are many different ways of solving the test questions. To learn how the child went about solving the problem, you may simply ask what method was used. Some children will be able to verbalize their method, while others will not, even though they have answered correctly. On digit span tests, for example, the task can be solved by grouping the digits in pairs of two, three, or more digit sequences, by recalling them as a number (4–1–3 as four hundred and thirteen), or by recalling them as distinct digits in sequence. The method used may be related to learning efficiency or to personality features, or it may have no particular import. Asking how the child solved the problem may give you additional insight about how well the task was understood.

3. *Additional time limits.* When the child fails a test because of time limits, you can readminister the test without time limits (after the examination has been completed), in order to determine whether the child can solve the problem.

4. *Alternate scoring.* As a result of the help provided during the testing-of-limits phase, the child may pass tests. During the test proper, too, the child may solve a problem after the time limit has been reached. In such cases, an alternate IQ can be calculated, and both the standard and alternate scores reported. However, the alternate IQ must be interpreted cautiously because it has no normative basis. Little is known about the meaning of alternate scores, but it is possible that they are related to learning potential.

One of the problems associated with helping procedures introduced during the testing-of-limits phase is that these procedures may invalidate the results of retesting occurring at a later date. You must therefore carefully consider the benefits and costs of testing limits. If retesting may be needed in the near future with the same test, then the testing-of-limits procedure in all probability should not be used. However, if the goal is to evaluate the limits of the child's abilities on the test, and there is no reason to plan on a retest in the near future (say within the next twelve to twenty-four months), testing of limits may be quite useful.

General Comment
Concerning Testing Skills

We have seen that the administration of tests is much more than a routine automatic procedure. Not only must you be familiar with the test materials and procedures, but you also must be vigilant, making certain that examinees have the necessary physical abilities to proceed with the test, observing when examinees are or are not making their best effort, and deciding when to offer encouragement and praise. Encouragement and support should be given whenever necessary to maintain the child's interest in the tasks. Problem behaviors will be especially taxing to the examiner. For example, does a particular behavior reflect true helplessness or is it manipulative? And once a decision is reached, what is the most appropriate action to take? Appropriate timing of supportive comments and actions, and maintaining an appropriate flow of materials, are some keys to successful testing.

Examiners' competence is judged not only by their ability to establish rapport with the child, administer tests in a standardized manner, and write a useful report, but also by their ability to observe and record the child's behavior. Clinicians' skills lie in their ability to obtain cooperation from the most intractable child under conditions that depart as little as possible from standardized procedures (Shapiro, 1951). However, subjective factors—such as the examiner's style, the child's physical and mental condition, the physical environment, the interruptions during testing, the examiner's preparation, and the language facility of the child—invariably affect the testing situation and reduce its objectivity (Louttit, 1957).

Examiners should strive to understand their own personalities and attitudes toward handicapped, exceptional, or ethnic minority children. Not all examiners will be (or should be expected to be) equally effective in working with (a) all types of exceptional children, (b) every age group, and (c) all ethnic minority children. Whenever examiners recognize that they are not fully capable of establishing rapport with a child, they should disqualify themselves from the examiner role and ask a colleague to complete the evaluation. It is only through encounters with a variety of populations of children and through a willingness to be open to self-evaluation and feedback from others that you will learn the limits of your ability to work with various groups of children. You should continually seek such knowledge by evaluating your own behaviors and reactions and by requesting feedback from colleagues.

We know from a variety of reports that examiners often differ in the scores they give to the same responses,[14] but it is unlikely that the examiner's experience in giving tests plays a critical role in contributing to examiner variability.[15] In addition, examiners occasionally differ among themselves in the scores they obtain from children.[16] Female examiners at times have been found to obtain higher scores than male examiners, but no systematic trends are evident.[17] With ethnic minority children, the examiner's race plays a negligible role. (See Chapter 19 for further information about the examiner racial variable.) Little is known about the personality variables that are related to examiners' scoring or administration styles.[18]

The above research confirms the clinical observations that the examination setting has elements of subjectivity. Therefore, every attempt should be made to reduce any examiner sources that may affect the reliability of the test score. While "extraneous" sources that contribute to examinee variability are more difficult to control, there is no reason to accept extraneous sources that contribute to examiner variability. To assist in this effort, the following list of questions should be answered after every assessment completed during the early phases of your career. The list can also be used as a checklist by an observer. An understanding of child psychology and exceptionality, of test manuals, and of material in this book, coupled with a willingness to evaluate and reflect on your testing skills, will enable most of you to reach a high level of competence and skill.

EXAMINER-EXAMINEE RELATIONSHIP

1. Did the examiner prepare the child for the examination?
2. Was the examiner friendly?
3. Was the examiner free from distracting mannerisms?
4. Was the examiner sympathetic and interested?
5. Was the examiner's appearance appropriate?
6. Was the examiner's voice audible and pleasant?
7. Did the examiner accept the examinee's attitudes?
8. Was the examiner biased? If so, in what ways?
9. Did the examiner seem at ease?
10. Did the examinee seem at ease?

THE EXAMINATION

1. Was the atmosphere permissive?
2. Was the pace of the examination appropriate to the child's abilities?
3. Were the examiner's vocabulary and concepts suited to the child?
4. Were test procedures adequately explained to the child?
5. Was the examiner aware of signs of fatigue?
6. Was fatigue handled adequately?
7. Was the examiner aware of emotional upsets?
8. Was emotionality handled adequately?
9. Did explanations to the child include material that could help the child solve the problem?
10. Were additional questions used to have the child clarify vague responses?
11. Were inquiries made in a nonthreatening manner?
12. Was the child praised appropriately?
13. How did the examiner handle any disruptions that arose during the testing?
14. Were tests given hurriedly?
15. Were materials manipulated with ease and confidence?
16. Were standardized procedures followed carefully?
17. Were responses recorded in the record booklet and scored correctly?
18. How was the examination terminated?

Summary

1. Every effort should be made to establish rapport with the child. This can be done by using praise, understanding comments, and meaningful explanations. The assessment aims to elicit the child's best efforts.

2. Research studies on the examiner-examinee relationship do not provide firm generalizations regarding effects on test scores. Results, in part, depend on the child's age, the type of test, and the nature of rapport. On some occasions special procedures to facilitate rapport have been found to increase the child's scores.

3. Some of the keys to successful testing of preschool children include timing of communications, empathy and understanding, and maintaining limits.

4. In testing ethnic minority children, openness and frankness in acknowledging miscommunications may help to facilitate rapport.

5. Physically handicapped children's disabilities should not become the basis of generalizations to other aspects of their behavior.

6. The key to testing emotionally disturbed children is to understand their particular problems and try to adapt the testing techniques to their needs.

7. Because delinquent children are likely to be defensive, attempts must be made to maximize their cooperative efforts.

8. Psychotic children are likely to be the most difficult of all handicapped children to test. Flexibility will be needed to obtain an estimate of their abilities.

9. In testing brain-injured children it is important to try to reduce any anxiety that is generated by the test situation.

10. Mentally retarded children may try to avoid difficult questions by various means. By showing acceptance and reducing the threatening aspects of the test situation, you can enhance their performance.

11. The administration of standardized tests to handicapped children requires patience, understanding, and flexibility. The test items administered to physically handicapped children must be ones to which they can respond.

12. In testing visually impaired children be sure that you are able to identify the extent of their impairment and how it may interfere with their ability to take the tests.

13. While hearing impaired children differ as to their degree of hearing loss, it is likely that nonverbal tests provide the most valid means of assessing their intellectual potential.

14. Flexibility will be needed in the testing of cerebral palsied children. If tests are administered carefully, the results obtained with cerebral palsied children are likely to provide an accurate estimate of their level of cognitive functioning.

15. The halo effect is a problem that may arise in the course of conducting an examination. There is substantial evidence that halo effects may affect the scoring of test responses, with bright examinees receiving more credit than dull examinees for the same responses. When examiners are provided with information about the examinee's probable level of performance, they are on some occasions likely to obtain better scores from examinees purported to be bright than from examinees purported to be dull. Thus, pretest information may play a role in the overall evaluation of the examinee and, on occasion, in scoring responses and in administering tests. One of the ways to reduce halo effects is to recognize the possibility of their occurrence.

16. Skill in the administration of tests develops with experience. Practice is impor-tant, especially in learning how to read the directions, handle the test materials, and score the responses. The guidelines presented in the chapter serve to supplement those that appear in test manuals. Recognize that the scoring guidelines in test manuals are just guides and that the answers, in most cases, are not meant to be the only correct answers.

17. Departures from standard procedures may be needed when testing handicapped children. However, the resulting scores may yield less precise estimates of the child's level of ability, depending on the extent of the departure.

18. Incentives, such as special praise, candy, or money, often do not lead to higher test scores. There is little evidence to support the position that reinforcers act differentially in ethnic groups or in social classes.

19. On some occasions it is useful to test limits in order to determine whether the child can solve problems when given helping cues or special procedures. Testing of limits should be carried out only after the standard administration of the test. When retesting is planned soon after the initial testing, testing of limits may increase the chances of obtaining invalid scores.

20. A willingness to be open to self-evaluation and to receive feedback from others will help beginning examiners develop clinical skills.

21. Examiners have been found to differ among themselves in their scoring of test responses and in the scores that they obtain from examinees. However, the sources for these differences have not been established. The examiner's experience in giving tests does not appear to play a crucial role in the scoring of test responses. The examiner's sex is usually not a critical factor in affecting the child's performance. Examiners' personality variables have not been shown to be associated significantly with either scoring style or scoring accuracy.

CHAPTER 6

Development of the Stanford-Binet Intelligence Scale

All things are engaged in writing their history. The planet, the pebble, goes attended by its shadow. The rolling rock leaves its scratches on the mountain; the river, its channel in the soil; the animal, its bones in the stratum; the fern and leaf, their modest epitaph in the coal. The falling drop makes its sculpture in the sand or the stone. Every act of the man inscribes itself in memories, manners and face. Every object is covered with hints which speak to the intelligent.

EMERSON

EXHIBIT 6-1. Some of Binet's and Simon's Views About Intelligence

It seems to us that in intelligence there is a fundamental faculty, the alteration or the lack of which, is of the utmost importance for practical life. This faculty is judgment, otherwise called good sense, practical sense, initiative, the faculty of adapting one's self to circumstances. To judge well, to comprehend well, to reason well, these are the essential activities of intelligence. . . . Indeed the rest of the intellectual faculties seem of little importance in comparison with judgment. [1905] ■

Source: Reprinted in Jenkins & Paterson, 1961, p. 93.

Our study of the Stanford-Binet Intelligence Scale begins with the historical developments that shaped the scale. Alfred Binet, the man primarily responsible for the construction of the scale, was born in Nice, France, on July 8, 1857, to well-educated parents: a physician father and an artist mother. Throughout his career, Binet brought a varied set of skills and interests to the study of thinking and intelligence. Both science and art were open to him. He wrote in a lucid and entertaining style, was willing to inquire and question provocatively, and had a streak of both the journalist and the reformer (Reeves, 1965). Because of his many contributions to the field of intelligence, Binet has been referred to as the father of intelligence testing (Pintner, 1931).

Binet's interest lay first in law, later in biology, and finally in psychology. He was an indefatigable worker, publishing about 336 books and articles during his career. Unfortunately, however, Binet "scattered his activities in many fields and never succeeded in creating the final work in which he would have concentrated the result of his life's work" (Ellenberger, 1970, p. 356). Binet also met with failure in obtaining professorships, losing out to Pierre Janet at the College de France and to Georges Dumas at the Sorbonne.

Three phases in Binet's career in psychology can be distinguished (Varon, 1935). In the first part of his career (1880 to 1890),

FIGURE 6-1. Alfred Binet. Courtesy of Bettmann Archives.

he explored a variety of different interests. He entered his second phase (1890 to 1895) with an interest in mental development and organization but without a theoretical focus. In the third phase (1895 to 1911), he pursued the study of individual differences.

During the first part of Binet's career he was engaging in a variety of studies that would eventually aid him in the development of the Binet-Simon intelligence scales (Wolf, 1964). His work with Charcot and Féré at the Salpêtrière stimulated his interest in such areas as hallucinations and perception, hypnosis and suggestibility, abnormal psychology, and somnambulism. Early in this period he favored the approach of associationism, which emphasized contiguity and resemblance in memory. However, he soon found problems with this approach, and turned to the position that memory was influenced primarily by attention and will and not by contiguity.

In 1892, Binet became adjunct director of the Laboratory of Physiological Psychology at the Sorbonne; three years later, he be-

came director, a position that he held until his death on October 18, 1911 at the age of 54. In 1895 he founded the journal *L'Année Psychologique,* which became the primary source for his future publications. About 1890, Binet (1890a) began to observe carefully the development of his two young daughters. Experiments with his children enabled him to gain information about mental organization, mental development, mental measurement, and other phenomena, including instinctive behavior, individual differences, and personality. His first definition of intelligence was linked to perception: "What is called intelligence in the narrow sense of the word consists of two principal things: first, perceiving the external world, and then taking up these perceptions again in the memorial state, handling them again, and meditating on them" (Binet, 1890b, p. 582). Binet emphasized that in the process of perception the whole is genetically prior to its parts. He discovered that the 4-year-old child defines words primarily in terms of use; for example, "A fork is for eating." Thus, the foundation for the Vocabulary test was laid (Binet, 1890b).

During the early 1890s Binet not only studied mental organization, but also investigated consciousness, perception, movements in insects, individuals who possessed excellent powers of calculating, chess players, and speed in graphic movements. His work represented "a groping after a method of experimenting with normal subjects, and still more, a groping after the problems with which such experiments ought to deal" (Varon, 1935, p. 31). His work of this period culminated in the publication of *Introduction à la Psychologie Expérimentale* in 1894. Binet's approach to experimental psychology emphasized a study of complex functions, the use of reliable measures, observation, and comparative introspection.

From 1895 to 1911, Binet's primary interest was in the qualitative and quantitative study of individual differences. Psychology, for Binet, was empirical, a science of observation and experimentation, separated from metaphysics. In collaboration with Victor Henri (1872–1940), Binet set out to apply the scientific method to the study of individual differences. They wanted to devise tests that not only would differentiate among individuals but also would throw light on the particular makeup of each individual. Prior work had been ineffective in studying individual differences because it placed too exclusive an emphasis on sensory-motor factors, focusing on special, limited abilities of minor significance. Differences among individuals, Binet and Henri reasoned, are most marked in the complex and higher mental processes; individuals differ least in elementary processes. Memory, reasoning, and judgment best serve to differentiate individuals. Memory tests, for example, would provide information about powers of acquisition, concentration, attention, tastes and tendencies, general mental disposition (reflected, for example, in errors or omissions), and comprehension (Binet & Henri, 1895c).

Binet and Henri went further than mere theorizing. They proposed a series of specific tests to study individual differences, though these tests were not in all cases original. Furthermore, Binet and Henri were good test constructors; they held that tests should (a) be simple, clear, short, and reliable, (b) be given within a 60- to 90-minute testing period, (c) have clear scoring principles independent of the examiner, and (d) require no complicated apparatus.

They were also concerned with questions of validity, because they were interested in determining how the abilities measured by the tests improved with the age and school attainment of the child, and how the test scores were related to teachers' ratings. They recognized that test questions must be appropriate to the child's milieu (Wolf, 1969a). The tests they developed, which they believed were a key to the study of individual differences, focused on memory, mental images, imagination, attention, comprehension, suggestibility, aesthetic appreciation, moral sentiments, muscular force and force of will, and acuity of observation.

They defined higher mental processes primarily in functional terms. Memory was viewed as an intellectual process that was facilitated by understanding. Attention was seen as having the characteristics of a process; it was measured in terms of duration and scope. Comprehension referred to common sense and judgment, and included the talent of observation and the spirit of ingenuity. Suggestibility pertained to the influence that one person exerts over another. These seemingly simple views are remarkably current.

Mental tests, Binet and Henri concluded, ought to be sufficiently varied so as to measure a large number of higher complex functions. They recognized that their series of tests was tentative and in need of revision. Initially, results were not reported nor were suggestions made for standardization of the tests into a scale; but this work was a necessary beginning, serving as a basis for the development of the 1905 scale. The tests were remarkable for their breadth, and implied a much wider conception of human ability than was held by any other contemporary scientist (Shouksmith, 1970).

Binet and Henri gave continuous attention to the measurement of higher complex functions. The first extensive investigation of memory of words and of sentences appeared in two important papers published in 1895 by Binet and Henri (1895a, 1895b). Verbal memory received emphasis in their work, since it was seen as the chief foundation of school instruction and as a basic factor in all forms of language. The current resurgence of interest in memory span as an important component of intelligence indicates that their interest in it was not misplaced.[1]

Binet (1903) continued his study of attention by asking a principal and teacher to select children whom they considered to be either intelligent or not intelligent. Tests successful in differentiating the eleven children in the two groups involved copying digits, tactile sensibility, and cancellation of letters from a printed page; other tests, such as those of choice reaction time, quick perception of words, and speed of work, were not successful. On the basis of these studies, Binet defined attention as mental adaptation to a new situation. Speed of execution of routine acts, he concluded, was not related to intelligence.

Binet also sought to classify people into types (such as emotional, intellectual, and stable) through the study of such variables as memory, capillary circulation and pressure, suggestibility, graphology, and mental fatigue. Twenty tests measuring complex processes were described in his 1903 book on intelligence, *L'Etude Expérimentale de L'Intelligence.*

The 1905, 1908, and 1911 Scales

The impetus for the construction of the first scale, the 1905 scale, came from the Minister of Public Instruction in Paris in 1904, when he appointed a committee to find a method that could separate mentally retarded from normal children in the schools. Binet, a member of the committee, began work on the problem by assuming that the difference between the two groups was one of intelligence. In collaboration with Theodore Simon (1873–1961), Binet devised thirty objective tests that he hoped would differentiate mentally retarded from normal children (Binet & Simon, 1905).

The tests, which represented an evolution of those studied by Binet, Henri, Simon, and others, focused on the execution of simple commands, coordination, recognition, verbal knowledge, definitions, picture recognition, suggestibility, and completion of sentences. The tests, called the 1905 scale, were given to mentally retarded children at the Salpêtrière and to mentally retarded and normal children in the primary schools of Paris.

The object of the 1905 scale was to devise a measure of the intellectual capacities of school children. It was not to be used in the treatment of the mentally retarded, nor was it to be applied to the study of brain damage. Binet and Simon aimed, at first, simply to determine the level of intelligence of school children. The 1905 scale had many features that Binet and Simon believed to be important for an assessment of intelligence. The scale measured general mental development and judgment rather than an assort-

ment of specific functions. Administration time was short, tests were arranged in order of difficulty rather than by type, and they were scored with whole, half, or no credit. The scale, unlike previous attempts to measure intelligence, sought to measure a wide variety of complex mental processes, rather than simple sensory-motor functions.

Murphy (1968) observed that "It was a clinical purpose that Binet's work served, and it was a methodological sophistication, with fifteen years of prior work with testing, that made possible the 1905 scale" (p. 22). Exhibit 6-2 presents the thirty items used in the scale. Some of Binet's and Simon's views about intelligence and testing are found in Exhibit 6-1, which introduced the chapter.

In the 1908 scale (Binet & Simon, 1908), tests were grouped according to age levels, and the concept of mental age was introduced. The beginning of test standardization can be seen in the approach to item placement: each item was placed at an age level where 60 to 90 percent of normal children passed it. Placing the tests into age groups represented the most significant advance over the 1905 scale (Pintner, 1931). The 1908 scale, with its advances over the 1905 scale, is considered to be an important milestone in the chronology of intelligence testing (Peterson, 1925).

In the last revision, the 1911 scale (Binet, 1911), further refinements were made, particularly in selecting tests that would measure intelligence rather than academic knowledge. Tests too dependent on scholastic abilities such as reading and writing or on knowledge that had been incidentally acquired were eliminated. Other tests were shifted, and new ones were introduced.

Other Comments About Binet and Simon

Binet has been credited with popularizing the mental-age concept, although it did not originate with him.[2] One of the earliest references to the mental-age concept was made by Esquirol (1838), who noted that an idiot was not capable of acquiring knowledge common to other persons of his own

EXHIBIT 6-2.　Description of the 1905 Scale

The 1905 Scale

1. Visual coordination. Noting the degree of coordination of movement of the head and eyes as a lighted match is passed slowly before the subject's eyes.
2. Prehension provoked tactually. A small wooden cube is to be placed in contact with the palm or back of the subject's hand. He must grasp it and carry it to his mouth, and his coordinated grasping and other movements are to be noted.
3. Prehension provoked visually. Same as 2, except that the object is placed within the subject's reach, but not in contact with him. The experimenter, to catch the child's attention, encourages him orally and with appropriate gestures to take the object.
4. Cognizance of food. A small bit of chocolate and a piece of wood of similar dimensions are successively shown the subject, and signs of his recognition of the food and attempts to take it are noted carefully.
5. Seeking food when a slight difficulty is interposed. A small piece of the chocolate, as used in the previous test, is wrapped in a piece of paper and given to the subject. Observations are made on his manner of getting the food and separating it from the paper.
6. The execution of simple orders and the imitation of gestures. The orders are mostly such as might be understood from the accompanying gestures alone.
(This is the limit for idiots as experimentally determined.)
7. Verbal knowledge of objects. The child is to touch his head, nose, ear, etc., and also to hand the experimenter on command a particular one of three well-known objects: cup, key, string.
8. Knowledge of objects in a picture as shown by finding them and pointing them out when they are called by name.
9. Naming objects designated in a picture.
(This is the upper limit of 3-year-old normal children. The three preceding tests are not in order of increasing difficulty, for whoever passes 7 usually passes 8 and 9 also.)
10. Immediate comparison of two lines for discrimination as to length.
11. Reproduction of series of three digits immediately after oral presentation.
12. Weight discrimination. Comparison of two weights—of 3 and 12 grams, of 6 and 15 grams, and of 3 and 15 grams.
13. Suggestibility. (a) Modification of 7: an object not among the three present is asked for. (b) Modification of 8: "Where [in the picture] is the *patapoum?* the *nitchevo?*" (These words have no meaning.) (c) Modification of 10: the two lines to be compared are of equal length.
(Test 13 is admitted to be a test not of intelligence but of "force of judgment" and "resistance of character.")
14. Definitions of familiar objects—*house, horse, fork, mamma.*
(This is the limit of 5-year-old normal children, except that they fail on Test 13.)
15. Repetition of sentences of 15 words each, immediately after hearing them spoken by the examiner.
(This is the limit of imbeciles.)
16. Giving differences between various pairs of familiar objects recalled in memory: (a) *paper* and *cardboard,* (b) *a fly* and *a butterfly,* and (c) *wood* and *glass.*
(Test 16 alone effectively separated normal children of 5 and 7 years.)
17. Immediate memory of pictures of familiar objects. Thirteen pictures pasted on two pieces of cardboard are presented simultaneously. The subject looks at them for 30 seconds and then gives the names of those recalled.
18. Drawing from memory two different designs shown simultaneously for 10 seconds.
19. Repetition of series of digits after oral presentation. Three series of three digits each, three of four each, three of five, etc., are presented until not one of the three series in a group is repeated correctly. The number of digits in the highest series which the subject repeats is his score.
20. Giving from memory the resemblance among familiar objects: (a) *a wild poppy* (red) and *blood,* (b) *an ant, a fly, a butterfly,* and *a flea,* and (c) *a newspaper, a label,* and *a picture.*
21. Rapid discrimination of lines. A line of 30 cm is compared successively with 15 lines varying from 35 down to 31 cm. A more difficult set of comparisons is then made of a line of 100 mm with 12 lines varying from 103 to 101 mm.
22. Arranging in order five weights—15, 12, 9, 6, and 3 grams—of equal size.

EXHIBIT 6-2 (cont.)

23. Identification of the missing weight from the series in Test 22 from which one is removed. The remaining weights are not in the right order. This test is given only when Test 22 is passed.
    (This is given as the most probable limit of morons.)
24. Finding words to rhyme with a given word after the process has been illustrated.
25. Supplying missing words at the end of simple sentences, one for each sentence. This is the Ebbinghaus completion method simplified.
26. Construction of a sentence to embody three given words: *Paris, gutter, fortune.*
27. Making replies to 25 problem questions of graded difficulty, such as "What is the thing to do when you are sleepy?" "Why is it better to continue with perseverance what one has started than to abandon it and start something else?"
    (Test 27 alone reveals the moron.)
28. Giving the time that it would be if the large and the small hands of the clock were interchanged at four minutes to three and at twenty minutes after six. A much more difficult test is given those who succeed in the inversion; namely, to explain the impossibility of the precise transposition indicated.
29. Drawing what a quarto-folded paper with a piece cut out of the once-folded edge would look like if unfolded.
30. Giving distinctions between abstract terms as between *liking* and *respecting* a person, between being *sad* and being *bored*.   ■

age. Duncan and Millard (1866), as well as Down (1887), suggested that a useful method for understanding mental retardation was to compare a mentally retarded child with younger children, although tests were not used for this purpose. Another reference to mental age appeared in a report by Hall (1848), in which he cited the testimony of a psychiatrist who had stated that the defendant in a murder trial, an adult, had knowledge equal to that of a 3-year-old child. It remained for Binet, however, to refine the concept of mental age and to make it definite and concrete.

Binet and Simon recognized that mental abilities are independent and unequal within each subject. Although the tests in the 1905 scale were thought to measure various abilities, the scale yielded only one measure of general intelligence. The 1905 scale, like all later ones, did not provide scores for the mental processes measured by the separate tests. Only with the Vocabulary test was there an attempt to measure the same ability throughout the scale.

In developing their scale, Binet and Simon first approached the problem of defining intelligence by describing *judgment* (which included good sense, practical sense, initiative, and the ability to adapt oneself to events) as the *sine qua non* of normality or as the essential faculty of intelligence: "To judge well, to comprehend well, to reason well, these are the essential activities of intelligence" (Binet & Simon, 1905, p. 192). Intelligence was not considered to be the same as scholastic aptitude (Binet & Simon, 1908), but as a composite of such abilities as judgment, comprehension, invention, and direction.

Their study of the mentally retarded helped them to clarify further the concept of intelligence (Binet & Simon, 1909). Normal intellectual functioning is distinguished from retarded intellectual functioning by three distinct elements that work together and form part of a single process: *direction of thought* (its complexity and persistence), *adaptation* (ability to differentiate), and *self-criticism*. These three elements may be paraphrased as follows: (a) the ability to take and maintain a given mental set; (b) the capacity to make adaptations for the purpose of attaining a desired end; and (c) the power of auto-criticism (Terman, 1916). Although Binet and Simon did not have a well-formulated definition of intelligence, no earlier definition was as concise in emphasizing the active and organized properties of intelligence.

Binet's and Simon's interests extended beyond intellectual measurement. They wanted to classify individuals with reference to each other, not to measure purely in the physical sense. Even when working on the 1908 and 1911 revisions, Binet maintained his interests in many other areas. Research was conducted on teachers' preferences for academic subjects, language and thought, palmistry, mental deficiency, and insanity. Binet tried many different approaches (including head movements, graphology, and palmistry) before arriving at his final scales.

The scales represented a gradual evolution. They were successful because of their simplicity and practicality, exact directions, brief and varied tasks, age standards, provision of a general level of intelligence, and testing of complex instead of elementary processes (Mateer, 1924; Terman, 1916). It is ironic that while Binet was convinced that intelligence is embedded in the total personality, his tests have become instrumental in making "intelligence" seem to have a relatively independent existence (Wolf, 1969a).

The Binet-Simon scales, almost from their inception, were recognized as being extremely valuable for the diagnosis of mental retardation (Burt, 1914). The scales achieved great popularity in many countries, including France, Belgium, Switzerland, Italy, Russia, Sweden, England, and the United States. Butcher (1968) aptly summarized the work of Binet and Simon as follows:

> Binet and Simon were concerned to sample broadly the intellectual performances of which typical children at particular ages would be capable, including as little as possible that was distinctively scholastic, but taking equal pains to retain a broad conception of intellectual progress and, above all, to tie down the items to what children actually were found able to perform as distinct from any purely theoretical ideas of what they ought to be able to. [p. 220]

The Binet-Simon Scale in the United States

The Binet-Simon scales were accepted readily by many investigators in the United States, but revisions were needed.[3] Goddard

FIGURE 6-2. Lewis M. Terman. Courtesy of Stanford University.

(1908), the director of the Psychological Laboratory at the Vineland Training School, introduced the 1905 scale to the United States in 1908, and two years later, the 1908 scale (Goddard, 1910). He adapted the 1908 scale with as few revisions as possible, and standardized it on 2,000 American children. For many years this was the most commonly used version of the Binet-Simon scale. The early use of the scale was almost entirely restricted to the evaluation of the mentally retarded. Goddard also altered Binet's conception of intelligence, substituting for "Binet's *idea* of intelligence as a shifting complex of inter-related functions, the concept of a single, underlying function (faculty) of intelligence. Further, he believed that this unitary function was largely determined by heredity, a view much at variance with Binet's optimistic proposals for mental orthopedics" (Tuddenham, 1962, p. 490).

1916 Stanford-Binet Scale

Terman (1911) observed that the 1908 scale had great practical and theoretical value, and suggested a number of additional tests that could be used to supplement the Binet-Simon scale. He became interested in the intelligence testing of school children, and after studying Goddard's work, collabo-

EXHIBIT 6-3. Biographical Profile: Lewis M. Terman (1877–1956)

Several features of Lewis Madison Terman's origins seem hardly to have pointed toward his developing into an eminent scientist. He was born on January 15, 1877, to a farm family, eleventh of fourteen children and eighth of ten surviving infancy. The world of his youth, Johnson County, Indiana, was at the time a cultural backwater. Yet Terman had the advantages of a precocious intellect, an older brother and sister who sponsored his rapid development, and a sympathetic father who possessed both a relatively large library and, ultimately, the wherewithal to loan his son the means for securing an excellent education. Terman earned three degrees at the Central Normal School of Danville, Indiana, spent three years as a high school principal, and took an AB and an AM at Indiana University by 1903. In 1905 he took a Ph.D. in educational psychology at Clark University, having studied under Hall, Sanford, and Burnham.

Terman's teaching career started out rather modestly. Suffering from tuberculosis and requiring a dry climate, Terman assumed the principalship of a San Bernardino, California, high school in 1905. A year later he accepted the position of Professor of Child Study and Pedagogy at the Los Angeles Normal School, a position he held for five years. In 1910, however, things took a vital turn with his acceptance of an assistant professorship in the School of Education at Stanford University. Interestingly, a former Clark classmate, E. B. Huey, deserves credit both for recommending Terman for the position and for suggesting, in the same year, that he undertake the work on the 1908 Binet-Simon Intelligence Scale which culminated in the Stanford Revision of 1916, and in the securing of Terman's fortunes. Terman was promoted to Associate Professor of Education in 1912, and in 1916 to Full Professor.

In 1917 he initiated contacts with the leading psychologists of the country, and, like many of them, left academic life to participate in the war effort. As a civilian member of the general psychological staff of the Surgeon General's Office, Terman contributed in several significant ways. He had already worked as a member of the volunteer committee of seven that developed the historic Army Alpha and Army Beta tests. After the war he wrote a full fifth of the enormous official report on the testing experience, published in 1921. Terman was commissioned a major in October of 1918.

The recognition accorded Terman after the war was equaled by his administrative, professional, and polemical productivity. In 1923 he was elected president of the American Psychological Association. The year before, without consultation, President Wilbur of Stanford moved Terman from the School of Education to head up the school's Department of Psychology, a post he maintained for twenty years. Terman turned out to be a propitious choice. Whereas in the thirty years of his predecessor's chairmanship only one Ph.D. had been awarded in Psychology, during the Terman regime fifty-five doctorates were granted and Stanford developed one of the top programs in the country. Moreover, Terman was consummately helpful to his graduate students, inviting their collaboration on his numerous research projects, arranging positions for them across the country, and publishing their work in the eleven journals he edited and in the Measurement and Adjustment Series he directed from 1921 to 1946 for the World Book Company.

All these administrative efforts seem hardly to have interfered with Terman's output. In addition to the ten tests he devised (with others) beyond the Stanford-Binet, and the revision he and Maud Merrill produced for that scale in 1937, Terman launched a longitudinal (and lifelong) study of 1,528 gifted California children in 1921. Near the end of his career he conducted massive investigations of psychological sex differences and of marital compatibility. Terman's most important publications included the two books published in connection with the introduction of the Stanford-Binet, the *Measurement of Intelligence* (1916) and *The Stanford Revision and Extension of the Binet-Simon Scale for Measuring Intelligence* (1917); the five volumes concerned with his study of gifted children, *Genetic Studies in Genius,* Volumes 1 through 5 (1925–1959); *Sex and Personality* (1936); and *Psychological Factors in Marital Happiness* (1938).

In addition, Terman attracted public notice throughout his career as a consistent and rather combative defender of the hereditarian interpretation of intelligence test results, doing battle with challengers ranging from Walter Lippmann, William Bagley, and Charles Judd in the 1920s to George Stoddard and the Iowa School in the early 1940s and Allison Davis in the late 1940s. Moreover, in 1928 Terman chaired the editorial committee of the National Society for the Study of Education, overseeing the assembly of the Society's twenty-seventh yearbook as a collection of investigations of the nature-nurture issue,

EXHIBIT 6-3 (cont.)

and either wrote, or directed the writing of, one third of that volume's contents.

Three years after Terman's death on December 21, 1956, the American Psychological Association selected the ten outstanding psychologists in American history. Terman ranked third on the list. Certainly this eminence must have reflected various things, such as the breadth of Terman's interests and investigation and the clarity of his writing style and investigative design. For the most part, however, this high station must have resulted from the vital nature of the scale Terman provided his profession in 1916. Intelligence testing at that time greatly needed one scale to stand above the rest, to function as a measuring stick for the testing and validation of all others. That Terman's scale was able to serve this function for over fifty years, that it could be become, in E. G. Boring's words, "the operational definition of intelligence" throughout the United States, more than assured his enduring fame.   ■

Source: This profile was written especially for this text by Gerald Sweeney.

---

rated with Childs in publishing a tentative revision of the Binet-Simon scale in 1912 (Terman & Childs, 1912). (See Exhibit 6-3 for a biographical profile of Terman.) This revision was modified, extended, and standardized during the next four years. The 1916 Stanford-Binet used the ideas of Binet and Simon, but Terman deserves credit for his thorough and accurate working-out of the method suggested by Binet and his co-workers. A major contribution of the 1916 scale was its standardization.

Terman adopted Stern's mental quotient, which is arrived at by dividing mental age by chronological age. Stern had originally introduced the mental quotient in a paper delivered at the German Congress of Psychology in Berlin in April 1912 and described it in his book *The Psychological Methods of Testing Intelligence* (Stern, 1914). Stern's rationale for the development of the mental quotient was, in part, as follows:

It is perfectly clear how valuable the measurement of mental retardation is, particularly in the investigation of abnormal children. It has, however, been shown recently that the simple computation of the absolute difference between the two ages is not entirely adequate for this purpose, because this difference does not mean the same thing at different ages . . . . Only when children of approximately equal age-levels are under investigation can this value suffice: for all other cases the introduction of the *mental quotient* will be recommended . . . . This value expresses not the difference, but the ratio of mental to chronological age and is thus partially independent of the absolute magnitude of chronological age. The formula is, then: mental quotient = mental age ÷ chronological age. [pp. 41–42]

Terman and his associates renamed this ratio the intelligence quotient (IQ) when they produced the 1916 version of the Binet-Simon scale. This version was called the Stanford Revision and Extension of the Binet-Simon Intelligence Scale. Although the IQ has become an extremely useful means for classifying persons, Wolf (1969b) noted that it is questionable whether Binet "would have accepted even Terman's elaborate standardizations as a valid basis for calculating IQ's" (p. 236).

1937 Revision

After twenty-one years, the 1916 scale was revised (Terman & Merrill, 1937). (See Exhibit 6-4 for a biographical profile of Merrill.) The revision was recognized as a milestone in the progress of the individual testing of intelligence (Flanagan, 1938). Additional items were introduced, the scale was better standardized, two forms were made available, and there were more performance tests at the earlier levels. New types of tests were more prevalent at the preschool and adult levels, and more use was made of differential scoring of the same test. Improvement was made in memory tests, in the wording of questions, in year-level assignments, and in

FIGURE 6-3. Maud Merrill James. Courtesy of Stanford University.

the scoring of the Vocabulary test. The scale was extended downward to year level II, with tests appearing at half-year levels between years II and V, and upward to the Superior Adult III level. Tests were also provided for year levels XI and XII.

The scales had excellent reliability (ranging from .98 for those with IQs below 70 to .90 for those with IQs above 129) and acceptable validity (*r*s of .40 to .50 with school success) (Terman & Merrill, 1953). Factor analytic studies indicated that most of the tests loaded heavily on a common factor (McNemar, 1942), although group factors (e.g., verbal, memory, visualization, spatial, and reasoning) were also reported.[4]

The 1937 scales represented a significant improvement over the 1916 scale and were greeted favorably by many reviewers.[5] The scales were improved statistically and had many clinical applications. They were seen as efficient instruments for diagnosing mental retardation and for providing insights about the child's temperament. Reviewers characterized the Stanford-Binet as combining the facets of the clinical interview with those of an objective assessment. How-

ever, the scales did not escape all criticism. Some said that the scales placed too much emphasis on verbal material (Krugman, 1939; McCandless, 1953), while others believed that there was an overweighting of practical tests (Burt, 1939). There also was dissatisfaction with the age-scale format, ceiling procedure, item placements, emphasis on rote memory, administration procedures, incomplete statistical data, use of one score only, inadequate measurement of *g*, use with adults, and use in clinical situations.[6] Despite these criticisms, the 1937 scales were extremely popular, yielding acceptable validity coefficients and serving as the standard for the development of other tests. The scales, although by no means perfect instruments, served as important tools in clinical and educational settings.

1960 Revision, Form L-M

In 1960 a new revision appeared (Terman & Merrill, 1960). In many ways the 1960 edition was not a genuine revision. The revision was carried out by selecting the best items from Form L and Form M and combining them into a new form. A new standardization group was not obtained; instead, a sample of 4,498 subjects who had taken the scale between 1950 and 1954 was used to check on changes in item difficulty. New material was not introduced, nor were the essential features of the scale changed. With the 1960 revision, only one form was available. Validity data were not presented with the revision; its validity rested on the fact that the same types of tests were used as in the 1937 scales (Balinsky, 1960).

One of the most important developments in Form L-M was the replacement of the 1937 scale's IQ tables, which represent the conventional ratio IQ, by tables devised by Pinneau, which present Deviation IQs for ages 2 through 18 years. The Deviation IQ is basically a normalized standard score with a mean of 100 and a standard deviation of 16. It expresses the deviation of the ratio IQ from the mean ratio IQ at each age level. The Deviation IQ controls for the variability in IQ distributions that was found to exist in various levels of the former revisions. A

EXHIBIT 6-4.   Biographical Profile: Maud Merrill James (1888–1978)

Maud Merrill James died at her home on the Stanford University campus on January 15, 1978. She was 90, having been born at Owatonna, Minnesota, April 30, 1888. As a child she lived in an orphanage of which her father was director, and her life's work as a professional psychologist was with children.

After receiving a BA at Oberlin College in 1911, the then Miss Merrill worked for the Minnesota Bureau of Research until 1919. She came to Stanford for graduate work in that year, earning her MA in 1920 and her PhD in psychology in 1923. She continued her association with Stanford as a faculty member until her retirement in 1954.

In the early 1920s, Dr. Merrill established a small psychological clinic for children and then soon became a regular consultant to the Juvenile Court in San Jose. Both services provided an opportunity for Stanford graduate students to gain firsthand experience with disturbed or delinquent children. In the Psychology Department itself, Dr. Merrill took the responsibility for training both undergraduate and graduate students in the administration of the newly constructed Stanford-Binet Intelligence Scale. For the next two decades she was an acknowledged authority on the proper use of the test.

Dr. Merrill's clinical work in the Juvenile Court led her to write a book on delinquency. It also brought her into a working relationship with Judge William F. James, who was strongly supportive of the psychological study of children. In 1933 Judge James and Dr. Merrill were married, and they were campus residents thereafter. Judge James died in 1966.

In 1926, Dr. Merrill and Dr. Lewis M. Terman had begun collaboration on a major revision of the Stanford-Binet, a formidable task that took 11 years to complete. During the first 4 years they constructed and pilot tested hundreds of new items. Then the most promising were tested on a national sample of 3,000 children, aged 2 through 18. The testing was done by six highly trained examiners who kept verbatim records of all responses. With these reports as data, the two collaborators then spent a year selecting the final test items. Finally, after two more years of statistical analysis—there were no electronic computers then—two parallel forms of the test emerged. These constituted the 1937 revision, and the two forms were initialed L and M, after the first names of the two collaborators. Twenty years later, after her retirement, Dr. Merrill herself constructed a second but less major revision. In 1940 she and Professor Quinn McNemar edited a volume of research papers in honor of Professor Terman's retirement.   ■

Source: R. R. Sears, "Obituary: Maud Merrill James (1888–1978)," *American Psychologist,* 1979, *34,* p. 176. Copyright 1979 by the American Psychological Association. Reprinted by permission.

---

specific IQ at different ages in Form L-M indicates close to the same relative ability or standing regardless of the age of the examinee.

However, Berger (1970) was unhappy with the manner in which the Deviation IQs were constructed. He pointed out that Deviation IQs are different from deviation scores, which are linear transformations of raw score "distances" from the mean. He noted that the Deviation IQ tables in the Stanford-Binet manual should not be accepted as being valid until it has been demonstrated that (a) L-M ratio IQs have the same distribution statistics as those observed on the 1937 scales and (b) the 1960 revision employed representative samples.

The revision procedures used with Form L-M prevented either of these conditions from being fulfilled. Consequently, Berger concluded that "there would appear to be no justification in interpreting L-M 'IQs' according to standard practice" (p. 24). Berger's analysis serves to remind us of the shortcomings of the Deviation IQ as it is used on the Stanford-Binet (L-M), and of the necessity to employ careful standardization procedures in constructing new tests or in revising old ones.

Berger also found fault with the procedures that were used to substitute for restandardization. For example, he believed that item difficulty could not be properly determined because an inappropriate mental age criterion was used to select the sample for the revision. Second, because the demographic characteristics of the sample were not sufficiently detailed, the extent of bias in the sample could not be determined. Berger concluded that Form L-M provides MAs and IQs that are of limited accuracy, a limitation that exists in addition to those usually associated with intelligence test scores.

The 1960 scale also has weaknesses common to all former revisions. It has been criticized for being too heavily weighted with verbal materials, making it useless for some purposes. Like other tests of intelligence, it does not measure creative abilities. It is inadequate for superior students, although the latest revision is more effective than former ones for use with superior adolescents (Kennedy, Moon, Nelson, Lindner, & Turner, 1961). Also, it has abstract material at too low a level, and rote memory tests at too high a level.

However, the 1960 revision, despite some of the difficulties associated with its standardization, still produces acceptable validity coefficients (cf. Himelstein, 1966) and remains as one of the standard instruments for the assessment of children's intelligence.

Table 6-1 summarizes some of the major characteristics of the three Binet-Simon scales and of the three Terman and Terman-Merrill scales.

1972 Norms

During the 1971–1972 period the norms for the Stanford-Binet Intelligence Scale, Form L-M, were revised, and one year later they were published (Thorndike, 1973). Except for two minor changes in the test procedures (a more attractive female doll card was used and the word "charcoal" was substituted for "coal"), the tests in the scale and the directions for scoring and administration are the same. The standardization group for the revision consisted of a representative sample of 2,100 children, with approximately 100 subjects at each Stanford-Binet year level. A special procedure, based on test scores from the group-administered Cognitive Abilities Tests, was used for stratifying each age sample to ensure proportionate representation of all ability levels. Unlike the 1960 norms, which did not include nonwhites in the standardization group, the 1972 norms contained nonwhites (including black and Spanish-surnamed individuals)

TABLE 6-1. Some Characteristics of the Binet-Simon and Stanford-Binet Scales

Scale Year	Authors	Number of Tests	Year Levels Covered	Modifications Made in Revisions	Difficulties
1905	Binet and Simon	30	Very low grade idiots to upper elementary grades		Poorly standardized ($N=50$) Inadequate range Tests did not always discriminate No objective method for arriving at a total score
1908	Binet and Simon	59	III to XIII	New tests added Some tests eliminated, especially those at the idiot level Tests grouped according to age commonly passed Mental-age concept introduced	Inadequate standardization ($N=203$) No credits given for fractions of a year Lower year level tests too easy, higher year level tests too difficult Scoring and administrative procedures inadequate Unequal number of tests at different year levels
1911	Binet and Simon	54	III to Adult	New tests added, some eliminated Credit given for fraction of a year	Almost same difficulties as those noted for 1908 scale; there were no fundamental changes

(cont.)

TABLE 6-1   (cont.)

Scale Year	Authors	Number of Tests	Year Levels Covered	Modifications Made in Revisions	Difficulties
1911 (cont.)				Tests shifted More detailed scoring instructions Adult year level included	
1916	Terman	90	III to Superior Adult I	New tests added Some tests revised Location changed for some tests Scoring and administrative procedures changed and better organized Introduced alternate tests Introduced IQ concept Representative sampling attempted	Poor standardization at extremes Only single form Inadequate standardization ($N=1000$ native-born Californian children and 400 adults) Inadequate measure of adult mental capacity Too heavily weighted with verbal and abstract materials Inadequate scoring and administrative procedures at some points Some tests dated in the 1930s Some tests misplaced Too much credit for rote memory
1937	Terman and Merrill	129	II to Superior Adult III	Better standardization ($N=3184$) Two forms (L and M) More performance tests at earlier year levels	Equal variability at all ages not present Sample somewhat higher in socioeconomic level than general population, and more urban than rural subjects included Some tests difficult to score Low ceiling with above-average adolescents
1960	Terman and Merrill	142	II to Superior Adult III	One form (L-M) which incorporates best tests from Forms L and M New group of children used to check changes in test difficulty ($N=4498$) Some tests relocated, dropped, or rescored Substitution of Deviation IQ for ratio IQ— standard score with $M=100$ and $SD=16$ Use of age 18 years as ceiling level rather than 16 years Clarification of scoring principles	Too heavily weighted with verbal materials Originality and creative abilities not measured Inadequate for very superior students Abstract verbal tests appear at too low a level and rote memory tests appear at too high a level Restandardization procedures not appropriate
1973	Thorndike	—	—	Restandardized in 1972 ($N=2100$)	—

and whites. However, subjects were excluded from the normative sample if English was not the primary language spoken in the home.

A study of the 1937 and 1972 standardization samples indicated that most items decreased in difficulty from the 1930s to the 1970s, especially at the younger age levels

TABLE 6-2.   Comparison of IQs Yielded by the 1960 and 1972 Stanford-Binet (L-M) Norms for Selected Chronological Ages

CA	MA	SD	1960 Norm IQs	1972 Norm IQs	Change	Mean Change[a]
2-0	2-0	—	98	87	−11	
	2-4	+1	114	104	−10	−10.4
	2-8	+2	131	121	−10	
	3-0	+3	147	137	−10	
	2-10	−3	52	45	−7	
	3-6	−2	67	59	−8	
	4-3	−1	83	74	−9	
5-0	5-0	—	100	91	−9	−9.7
	5-9	+1	116	106	−10	
	6-6	+2	132	122	−10	
	7-2	+3	147	136	−11	
	5-2	−3	52	52	0	
	6-11	−2	68	68	0	
	8-7	−1	84	83	−1	
10-0	10-3	—	100	98	−2	−1.9
	12-0	+1	116	113	−3	
	13-8	+2	132	127	−5	
	15-4	+3	148	142	−6	
	7-0	−3	52	51	−1	
	9-6	−2	68	66	−2	
	12-0	−1	84	81	−3	
15-0	14-6	—	100	96	−4	−3.9
	17-0	+1	116	111	−5	
	19-6	+2	132	126	−6	
	22-0	+3	148	141	−7	
	8-6	−3	52	52	0	
	10-11	−2	68	66	−2	
	13-4	−1	84	80	−4	
18-0	15-9	—	100	94	−6	−6.9
	18-1	+1	116	108	−8	
	20-6	+2	132	122	−10	
	22-10	+3	147	136	−11	

Note. The standard deviation units were selected for the 1960 norm IQs. In some cases, there are no IQs in the 1960 norm tables that perfectly match the standard deviation units. Consequently, the IQ closest to the standard deviation unit was selected in these cases.

[a]Mean change obtained from Table 11 of *Stanford-Binet Intelligence Scale, 1972 Norms Tables.* Change obtained by subtracting 100 from the smoothed estimates of means and placing a minus sign by the remainder.

(Garfinkel & Thorndike, 1976). Of the 122 items, 89 were easier, 1 showed no change, and 32 were more difficult.

Like the 1960 norms, the 1972 norms yield a mean Deviation IQ of 100 and a standard deviation of 16. Therefore, direct comparisons can be made between the two sets of norms. A comparison of both norms reveals some interesting trends in changes in intelligence. Changes are related to chronological age and to ability level. The largest mean changes from the 1960 to the 1972 norms are at the youngest levels of the scale (mean changes of −9.7 to −10.8 IQ points in the age range from 2 to 5 years). These changes mean that a 2-year-old child, for example, who obtains a mental age of 2-0 receives an IQ of 98 on the 1960 norms but only an IQ of 87 on the 1972 norms. The changes in IQs become progressively smaller until the age of 10 years (mean changes of −7.1 to −1.9 IQ points in the age range from 6 to 10 years) and then rise again for the remaining ages (mean changes of −2.2 to −6.9 IQ points from 11 to 18 years). The changes are not as marked for the older ages as they are for the younger ones. (See Table 6-2, which shows changes for five selected age levels.)

The IQ changes from the 1960 to the 1972 norms for ages 2 to 5 years are about the same throughout the range of ability. However, after the age of 5 years, the changes are greater for children with average and above-average ability than for children with below-average ability. Thus, for example, at age 10-0 years there is no change for a child with an MA of 6-11 (IQ of 68 on both norms), whereas for a child with an MA of 13-8 there is a change of −5 IQ points (IQ of 132 on the 1960 norms and 127 on the 1972 norms). At the chronological age of 18 years, the change is −2 IQ points for a child with an MA of 10-11 (IQ of 68 on the 1960 norms and 66 on the 1972 norms) and −8 IQ points for a child with an MA of 18-1 (IQ of 116 on the 1960 norms and 108 on the 1972 norms).

We have seen that (a) the 1972 norms provide IQs that are usually *lower* than those provided by the 1960 norms for the same MA levels for a specific CA, particularly for younger children at all ability levels and for those of average or above-average ability who are more than 5 years of age; and (b) the traditional relationship between CA and MA (which, prior to the 1972 norms, resulted in an IQ of close to 100 when both were the same) does not hold for the 1972 norms. To account for the downward shift in IQs, Thorndike (1973) suggested that the cultural background of children had changed from the 1930s to the 1970s. The increased exposure to television in particular may be one of the major factors causing large shifts at the preschool level. Thus, the downward adjustment in IQs may suggest that children in the most recent normative sample are brighter than those in prior normative samples.

Concluding Comment on the Binet-Simon Scale

The Binet-Simon scale helped to stimulate the development of clinical psychology in the United States and in other countries as well.   Jenkins and Paterson (1961) have noted that "probably no psychological innovation has had more impact on the societies of the Western world than the development of the Binet-Simon scales" (p. 81). Tuddenham (1962) expressed a similar opinion:

> The success of the Stanford-Binet was a triumph of pragmatism, but its importance must not be underestimated, for it demonstrated the feasibility of mental measurement and led to the development of other tests for many special purposes. Equally important, it led to a public acceptance of testing which had important consequences for education and industry, for the military, and for society generally. [p. 494]

With the introduction of the Binet-Simon scale, intelligence testing became a popular technique in many types of institutions throughout the country. The 1960 revision, together with the 1972 renorming, represents the latest and most modern development of Binet's original idea.

The intelligence testing movement, which developed without the backing of any particular school or system, grew because of practical demands (Heidbreder, 1933). The IQ concept, too, generated interest in the testing movement. Success came to Binet and Simon when they attempted to measure intelligence in general terms, abandoning the attempt to analyze intelligence into component parts. While there were many workers in the field of test construction during the Binet-Simon period (see Chapter 3), it was Binet's and Simon's work during the years from 1905 to 1911 that led to their scale's receiving universal recognition as a practical means for the measurement of mental ability.

Summary

1. Alfred Binet, considered the father of intelligence testing, developed a valuable tool for the assessment of intelligence. His range of interests was wide, including developmental, clinical, and experimental concerns. His collaborations with Victor Henri and Theodore Simon were guided by a concern for tests that could shed light on higher mental processes. These were alert and flexible investigators, willing to discard tests that proved to be unreliable and willing to modify others when necessary.

2. The first Binet-Simon scale—the so-called 1905 scale—developed from a practical need of the public school system in Paris. The Minister of Public Instruction desired a means of separating mentally retarded from non–mentally retarded children, and it was to this problem that Binet and Simon addressed their work. The first scale represented the culmination of years of previous experimentation.

3. The 1905 scale consisted of thirty tests arranged in order of difficulty. The year-level format of tests was introduced in the 1908 scale, which contained fifty-nine tests. The 1911 scale represented a further refinement of the scales and increased the range to include an adult year level while simultaneously decreasing the number of tests to fifty-four.

4. Binet and Simon considered judgment, comprehension, and reasoning as the essential parts of intelligence. The process of thinking was conceived of as having three interrelated parts: the ability to adopt and maintain a given set, the ability to make adaptations, and the ability to criticize oneself. While this conception of intelligence was not a precise one, it did emphasize the active and organized properties of intelligence. Through the use of the mental-age concept, Binet and Simon found a means of ranking individuals.

5. The Binet-Simon scales were warmly received in many countries. Goddard, in the United States, was one of the leading proponents of the scales, and contributed by translating, adapting, and standardizing them.

6. Terman and Childs produced a revision of the Binet-Simon scale in 1912, and during the next four years completed a thorough standardization of the revised scale which, when published in 1916, was termed the "Stanford Revision and Extension of the Binet-Simon Intelligence Scale." With the 1916 scale, Terman introduced the IQ concept, borrowed from Stern, who had referred to it as "mental quotient." Terman can be credited for his thorough and accurate working-out of the procedures originally formulated by Binet and his co-workers.

7. The first thoroughly American version of the scale, the 1916 Stanford-Binet, consisted of ninety tests, thirty-six of which were new. It ranged from year level III to Superior Adult I level.

8. The 1937 Stanford-Binet extended the range from year level II to Superior Adult III level, increased the number of tests to 129, and had two forms, L and M.

9. The 1960 Stanford-Binet (Form L-M) combined tests from the two 1937 forms, and, in place of a restandardization, used a sample of subjects who had previously taken the scale to evaluate difficulty levels of the tests. Form L-M replaced the ratio IQ with the Deviation IQ.

10. In 1972, the norms for the Stanford-Binet Intelligence Scale (Form L-M) were revised. White and nonwhite children were included in the standardization group. The Deviation IQ was maintained, with a mean

of 100 and a standard deviation of 16. The 1972 norms usually yield, for comparable MAs, *lower* IQs than the 1960 norms. The shifts are a function of both the child's age and ability level, with the largest changes occurring with younger children (2 to 5 years of age) at all ability levels and with older children (above 5 years of age) with average or above-average ability.

11. The 1937 and 1960 forms of the Stanford-Binet have proved to be extremely reliable and valid instruments. However, the Stanford-Binet, like any measuring instrument, is far from perfect. The scales have been criticized for (a) placing too heavy emphasis on verbal and rote memory tests, (b) providing too few tests of *g*, (c) providing only one score (the IQ) to represent the complex nature of cognitive functions, (d) failing to measure creative abilities, and (e) being unsuitable for testing adults. Technical criticisms of all forms include the cumbersomeness of the age-scale format, scoring and administration difficulties, and the low ceiling for gifted adolescents. In the 1960 form, revision procedures were found to be inadequate, especially with respect to the construction of the Deviation IQs and the determination of difficulty levels for the tests.

12. The Binet-Simon scale was influential in stimulating the development of clinical psychology in the United States and in many other countries. The scales demonstrated that mental measurement was possible and, by so doing, led to the development of many other types of tests and to an acceptance by the public of testing. The Binet-Simon scales and their successors have had an important impact on Western society, especially for education, industry, and the military.

CHAPTER 7

Administering the Stanford-Binet Intelligence Scale

There are thresholds which thought alone can never permit us to cross. An experience is needed.

GABRIEL MARCEL

EXHIBIT 7-1. Some of Binet's and Simon's Suggestions for Administering an Intelligence Test

The examination should take place in a quiet room, quite isolated, and the child should be called in alone without other children. It is important that when a child sees the experimenter for the first time, he should be reassured by the presence of someone he knows, a relative, an attendant, or a school superintendent. The witness should be instructed to remain passive and mute, and not to intervene in the examination either by word or gesture.

The experimenter should receive each child with a friendly familiarity to dispel the timidity of early years. Greet him the moment he enters, shake hands with him and seat him comfortably. If he is intelligent enough to understand certain words, awaken his curiosity, his pride. If he refuses to reply to a test, pass to the next one . . . ; if his silence continues, send him away until another time. These are little incidents that frequently occur in an examination of the mental state, because in its last analysis, an examination of this kind is based upon the good will of the subject. [1905] ∎

Source: Reprinted in Jenkins & Paterson, 1961, p. 94.

On the part of the experimenter, some conditions are necessary. He must not allow himself to be influenced by information regarding the child obtained from other sources. He must say to himself that nothing he already knows about the child counts at all. He must consider the child as an X to be solved by this means alone. He must be entirely convinced that by using this method, he will be able by it alone to obtain a thorough knowledge of the child without depending on any outside help. But this self-confidence is liable to many fluctuations. In the beginning everything seems easy; it is the period of illusions. After a few trials, if one has at all the critical spirit, errors are seen everywhere, and this leads to discouragement. But if one keeps at it faithfully, patiently, confidence will return little by little; it is no longer the optimism of the beginner, but a confidence grounded upon deliberate reason and proof; one has a consciousness of his own power as well as of his limitations. [1908] ∎

Source: Reprinted in Jenkins & Paterson, 1961, p. 98.

The procedures used to administer the Stanford-Binet have been carefully developed over the years and have proven to be workable and efficient. (See Exhibit 7-1 for some of Binet's and Simon's suggestions for administering their test.) However, they cannot cover all contingencies. Some children fail to obtain a basal level (the highest year level at which all tests have been passed when no tests have been failed below that level) or a ceiling level (the highest year level at which all tests have been failed when no tests have been passed above that level), while others have physical handicaps that may interfere with their ability to respond to the test items. This chapter discusses ways in which these and other administrative problems can be met. Topics include the appropriate year level at which to begin testing, modifications in test procedures, use of short forms, and the mechanics of completing the record booklet.

Where to Begin Testing

The test should be started at the earliest year level that contains questions challenging for the child but having a high probability of being answered correctly. Starting with very easy tests may induce boredom and loss of interest, while starting with very difficult tests may produce anxiety and discouragement. Testing time, too, can be reduced when a single basal level is found. The following points should prove to be helpful when you are faced with deciding where to begin the examination.

First, consider the child's chronological age. Most children with average intelligence usually will pass all of the tests at a year level close to their chronological age. Testing may be begun at their chronological year level or at a level one year below their chronological age.

Second, consider starting with the Vocabulary test for children six years old or above. This test provides a vocabulary age, which can be found on the lower right-hand corner on the next to the last page of the record booklet. The examination can then be continued at the year level corresponding to or close to the vocabulary age level. For chil-

dren younger than six years, the Picture Vocabulary test serves a similar purpose.

Third, consider the child's background and the reason for referral. Because children being tested for possible placement in educable mentally retarded classes may have a mental age that is considerably below their chronological age, it may be best to begin at a year level lower than their chronological age. If placement in a gifted class is the purpose of the examination, the child's mental age may be considerably above the chronological age.

These three factors—the child's chronological age, initial Vocabulary test performance, and background information—will aid in selecting an appropriate year level. When one of the Vocabulary tests is administered first, testing can be continued at the year level indicated by the vocabulary age, especially if this year level is close to the child's chronological age. For children whose vocabulary age is considerably above their chronological age, the examination can be begun at a year level midway between the vocabulary age year level and the chronological age year level. A possible entry point for a 10-year-old who obtains a vocabulary age of 14 is at year level XII, a level that is halfway between year level X (representing the child's chronological age) and year level XIV (representing the child's vocabulary age). If there is reason to believe that the child has superior intellectual ability, testing could be continued at the vocabulary age year level, which, in the present example, is XIV. When children obtain a vocabulary age considerably below their chronological age, testing can be continued at a year level midway between the two ages. If testing has begun at a year level that is either too high or too low, you can always change to another year level and continue testing at that level.

Effects of Not Having a Basal Level or a Ceiling Level

The Stanford-Binet requires that one basal level and one ceiling level be obtained to administer the scale. However, occasionally neither a basal level nor a ceiling level can be obtained. The former can occur in testing

FIGURE 7-1. Stanford-Binet Intelligence Scale, Form L-M. Courtesy of Houghton Mifflin Company.

young mentally retarded children (and occasionally young normal children as well), while the latter can occur in testing gifted adolescents. In such cases, you have the choice of either disregarding the results and turning to another test that may be more valid or using the test results, recognizing that they may not be valid. Although there is no definitive answer concerning the procedure to follow when a basal or ceiling level is not obtained, there are some helpful guidelines.

The most difficult decision is what to do in those cases in which a basal level cannot be established. In such cases, if the child passes at least one test at year level II, a basal age of 1-6 can be assumed and one month credit added for each test passed at year level II. Research suggests that this procedure yields valid results (Sternlicht, 1965). A less serious problem arises when a ceiling level is not obtained. In such cases the IQ can be reported, followed by a statement such as "minimal estimate." In a study (Kennedy et al., 1961) of adolescents with superior intelligence who had passed

one or more tests at the last year level of the scale, the results indicated that the IQs they obtained were highly correlated with their IQs obtained on other tests. This finding led the investigators to conclude that Form L-M of the Stanford-Binet is an effective though not ideal research instrument for the study of superior adolescents.

Generally, the larger the number of tests passed at year level II or failed at the Superior Adult III year level, the greater the probability that the results are valid. When many (say four out of six) tests are passed at year level II, the child is showing that he or she has most of the expected abilities at this level. However, when only one or two tests are passed, there is less evidence that the child has the expected abilities and, therefore, less confidence can be placed in the estimated IQ. At the Superior Adult III year level, failing most of the tests probably indicates that the child's limit has been reached on the scale and that the score adequately reflects his or her abilities. However, if all or most of the tests are passed, the resulting score may underestimate the child's IQ by a considerable amount because the child might have succeeded on more difficult items, if they had been available.

General Administrative Suggestions

In presenting the test materials to children, a good procedure to follow is to arrange them from the child's left to right, unless other instructions are given in the manual. This arrangement serves to standardize this aspect of the test procedure. On tests requiring children to mark their response in the record booklet, expose the one page that is needed by folding the record booklet at the centerfold. When a screen is needed, the white side of the cardboard doll may be used. All materials should be returned to the the test kit immediately after they are used. Although a stopwatch is not mandatory in administering the test, it can be helpful.

Of the 142 tests in the scale (including alternates), only 15 tests are timed. Instructions should be repeated for each new trial or part of a test, unless it is evident that the child understands the test requirements. Suggestions for administering specific tests, supplementing those that appear in the test manual, are found in Table 7-1.

The test procedures in the manual must be followed carefully and the record booklet filled out accurately. Unfortunately, some examiners make errors. Examples of common errors include the following (Pierce, 1948):

TABLE 7-1. Suggestions for Administering Specific Stanford-Binet Tests

Year Level	Test Name	Suggestion
II,2	Delayed Response	Use the three boxes that are closed on the top side and on four sides.
II,3	Identifying Parts of the Body	Place the doll face up and flat on the surface of the table.
III-6,1	Comparison of Balls	For each trial, alternate the horizontal position of the balls by using a 180-degree rotation.
III-6,3	Discrimination of Animal Pictures	Do not touch the card after it is placed on the table. However, ask children to point to the animal if their response is not clear.
VI,6	Maze Tracing	In pointing to the sidewalk, examiners can run the top of their pencil back and forth horizontally over a small area of the top of the maze, or they can run their pencil up and down vertically in approximately the same area.
VIII,2	Memory for Stories: The Wet Fall	Give the child a copy of the story *after* reading the instructions and the title of the story.
VIII,4	Similarities and Differences	Do not probe on items *c* and *d*. If the child fails to give *both* a similarity and a difference for each item, the item is failed.
IX,1	Paper Cutting	Remove scraps from the table after the test has been completed.
IX,3; XI,1	Memory for Designs I	Show the child the designs *after* reading the instructions. Give the child a blank portion of the record booklet for his or her drawings.
XIV,2	Induction	Leave the cut sheets of paper unfolded, one on top of another. Do not ask for the rule unless the last response is correct.
VI–SAIII	Vocabulary	Older children may find it disconcerting to have the card pulled away from them after six consecutive failures. The children can be asked to look at the list to see if they know any other words. Credit should be given for any successes.

1. Records are not readable. (Readable records are important because (a) they provide a record of the child's performance that is helpful for study and evaluation and for comparison with future performance, (b) they permit the checking of scoring and calculations, and (c) they can be used for research purposes.)
2. Minus signs and plus signs are not filled in.
3. Some examiners credit a child who refuses to respond if they believe that the child could adequately respond, while other examiners judge refusals as failures. (Refusals should not be counted in the scoring. However, try to identify the reasons for the refusals.)
4. The halo effect is evident when examiners overestimate intelligence on tests that have inconclusive results.
5. Examiners undertest; they do not expend the time and effort necessary to obtain maximum scores.
6. Testing is stopped prematurely when the child fails five of the six tests at a given year level.
7. Troublesome tests or time-consuming tests are omitted.

Scoring the child's responses, for the most part, is a relatively easy procedure. The manual provides helpful guidelines for each test. However, because no manual can cover all conceivable responses, you must use judgment in scoring responses that deviate from those in the manual. When such deviations occur, you can easily become perplexed, especially in attempting to decide on a score for borderline responses, that is, those that are vague or ambiguous or just not quite right. We do know that psychologists do not always agree in assigning scores to ambiguous responses (Sattler & Ryan, 1973a). When ambiguous responses occur, you are encouraged to study carefully the sample responses in the manual, to discuss them with colleagues, and to consult supplementary scoring guides, such as those by Pintner, Dragositz, and Kushner (1944) and by Wrightstone (1941).

Modifying Test Procedures

Because the Stanford-Binet requires adequate vision, hearing, speech, and arm-hand use, some items may be inappropriate for physically handicapped children. Whenever children's physical handicaps impede their ability to respond to the test questions, the test should not be administered unless appropriate modifications are possible. In some cases, it may be preferable to administer another test that is more suitable for physically handicapped children in place of the Stanford-Binet (see Chapter 14).

Various types of test modifications have been proposed that make it possible to administer the Stanford-Binet to handicapped children.[1] Some test items can be presented in pantomime or in a multiple-choice or enlarged format. Children who cannot speak can be encouraged to write their answers, while those who cannot hear can be shown the test questions, if they are able to read. Children who have limited arm-hand use may be able to substitute a pointing response or another type of nonverbal response. If you evaluate the physical skills needed for each test item, appropriate modifications will become evident. Many of the tests in the early year levels, for example, require vision and arm-hand use. Suggested modifications for tests at these levels are shown in Table 7-2.

Modifications are valuable because they enable one to evaluate a child who otherwise could not be administered the Stanford-Binet. IQs obtained by using modified procedures, however, such as selecting only certain tests or changing methods of administering the tests, should be viewed cautiously. For example, a multiple-choice administration may result in an easier test because of the elimination of some of the recognition and recall elements required by the standard presentation (Burgemeister, 1962). The results obtained by use of modified procedures should be considered only as an approximate estimate of the child's level of intellectual functioning, since there is no way of determining to what extent standard norms apply.[2]

TABLE 7-2.   Examples of Modifications for Stanford-Binet Tests at Year Levels II Through V

Three-Hole Form Board (Year Level II,1 and Year Level II-6, Alternate)	Vision is necessary but the examiner helps by actually placing the blocks in the form board recesses for the child. The blocks are removed in the child's presence and each one is placed above its appropriate recess. Orally or by pantomime the examiner indicates that each block is to be reinserted into its recess. Examiner points to the first block, the square, and then to the first recess, the square, and asks if it belongs there. Regardless of the "yes" or "no" signal, the examiner goes on to the triangle and the circle recesses in turn, inquiring if the square block belongs in either of these recesses. If the child selects the correct recess the block is appropriately placed. The same is done for the triangle and the circle blocks in that order.
Identifying Objects by Use (Year Level II-6,1)	The instructions for the test are given: "Show me the one we drink out of." Then pointing to the shoe the examiner asks, "Is it this one?" and waits for the prearranged response signal for "yes" or "no." Whether the choice is correct or not, the examiner continues in a clockwise rotation, stopping at the cup, penny, iron, knife, and the auto, inquiring, "Is it this one?" The same procedure is followed for each of the six objects on the card.
Picture Memories (Year Level III,4)	After the instructions are given for Card (A), the examiner starts at the corner of the card and points to the dog, inquiring, "Is it this one?" This is continued until the child has seen and responded to all the pictures on Card (A). The correctness of the choice is recorded. The same procedure is repeated with cards (b) and (B) until one correct answer is given.
Comparison of Sticks (Year Level III-6, Alternate)	The examiner arranges two sticks in proper order and asks which of the two is longer. Pointing to the top one he or she says, "Is it this one?" After the visible response signal of "yes" or "no," the examiner indicates the stick below it and repeats the question. The reply is noted and the entire procedure is continued until the criterion of three correct responses in three trials or five in six is met. In each instance the examiner should point to the top and bottom sticks so as to avoid cuing the child to the correct choice.
Picture Identification (Year Level IV,4)	The pictures are placed before the child. The examiner directs, "Show me the one that we cook on." Starting at the top, he or she points to each picture asking, "Is it this one?" and moves across the four rows pointing to each of the 12 pictures.

From Allen and Jefferson (1962, pp. 42–44) with changes in notation.

One modification that appears to have little effect on test scores is the enlargement of visual items (Livingstone, 1957). Another modification, which can be used with cerebral palsied children, is to administer only tests that can be answered by pointing and then to compute a mental age by prorating (Katz, 1956). A nonverbal pointing or "yes-no" format modification of tests located at year levels II through V also appears to hold some promise for use with cerebral palsied preschool children (Sattler & Anderson, 1973).

Testing of Limits

Testing of limits, as we have seen in Chapter 5, may prove helpful in obtaining additional insights about the child's cognitive capacities. Items passed as a result of such procedures are not counted in computing the child's mental age. The most thorough and systematic procedures for testing of limits on the Stanford-Binet (and on other tests as well) have been presented by Taylor (1961). Because her detailed suggestions are too numerous to summarize, you are encouraged to consult her work whenever there is a need for testing of limits. Following, however, are her suggestions for the Picture Vocabulary test. As we see below, the flexible testing-of-limits procedure recommended by Taylor generates excellent guidelines for assisting in a more thorough assessment of handicapped children (and perhaps other children as well).

. . . GESTURES. The same picture material may be used to study more specifically children's ability to express themselves without words. Show a knife (or airplane, ball, spoon) and ask, "Show me what it does" or "Show me what we do with it." For children who do not seem to understand language, show by a sample what is wanted of them.

Note: Does the child use varied appropriate gestures, or does he or she tend to use the same gestures with all pictures? Are the child's means of expression mostly manual, facial, or both? Is there any sign that the child indicates objects of the same category in similar ways? Does he or she, for instance, describe animals by their sounds and movements, tools by their use, or point to a chair in the room to indicate a stool or chair? Observations of a child's use of gestures can be of considerable diagnostic significance with respect to development of communication.

. . . ALTERNATE NAMING. If the child has designated an object either in words or through gestures, examiner may ask, "What else could it be?" The child may or may not find a second response, produce a synonym, a better word, or a better gesture.

. . . POINTING. This picture material may also be used to investigate comprehension of language. Use all cards of a series at one time, or use them in groups of four to six. Present the material by asking, "Where is the spoon?" etc. . . . . The child can indicate by pointing or nodding at the pictures, or in any other way he or she chooses. For a severely handicapped child who is unable to point accurately or to turn his or her head freely, the pictures may be spread far enough apart to avoid equivocal responses, yet near enough so that they all remain in the line of vision.

Note whether the child scans the field for the proper picture or responds haphazardly, pointing first to one, then to another. Does the child point to the correct picture only? Does the child know at least the general area in which it belongs? (Does he or she point to a fork when asked for a knife, for instance?) Does the child seem to see all the pictures correctly, or does he or she make unexpected errors? Are such errors possibly attributable to sensory difficulties? Check whether a wrong picture is pointed to because of poor perception, eyesight, or hearing. Does the child not *understand* or does he or she not *see* (or *hear*) the difference in the looks of a gun and knife, or the words house and horse? . . . Experience shows that, in general, normal children are able to point out all pictures adequately before, or at least at the same age as, they can find names for them. Often one may find children who can point correctly to something long before they are able to name it. It may be important for the clinician to discover whether a child understands more language than he or she is able to express. The procedure is therefore of considerable value in all cases of speech retardation, as well as in those where sensory difficulties are suspected. [Taylor, 1961, pp. 309–310, with changes in notation]

Short Forms of the Stanford-Binet

Short forms of the Stanford-Binet have been considered as potential timesavers. However, if we view the test questions themselves as important stimuli useful for obtaining information about the child's cognitive makeup and temperament, then shortening the examination will limit the amount of potential information. Short-form reliabilities and validities must be considered too. While acceptable correlations between abbreviated scales and the full scale are usually reported, few investigators actually have used the short form. In most cases, the full scale is administered and the MAs and IQs are obtained for the short form from the full scale. This procedure presents problems in interpreting the correlation coefficient because of overlapping tests in both forms. In addition, there is no way of assessing the effects of the altered order of test administration on the resulting score.

In studying abbreviated and full scales, it is important to distinguish between correlations obtained for a group, mean scores obtained on the scales, and differences in the IQs obtained by any one individual child. A correlation coefficient of .99 between two scales still could result in a significant difference between the means obtained on the scales. Even when the correlation is high and mean difference between the two scales is small, any one child may have large differences between the scores he or she obtains on the two scales.

The short form proposed by Terman and Merrill (1960), in which the four starred tests designated for each year level and half-year level of the scale are administered, is the most conventional. It saves approximately 33 percent of the time usually needed to administer the test. Highly significant correlations, ranging from .92 to .99, have been reported between this abbreviated scale and the full scale for a variety of children's groups.[3] Another proposed modification consists of administering all six tests at the basal and ceiling level and the four starred tests at other year levels (Wright, 1942). This procedure only saves about 20 percent of the time usually needed but is somewhat more reliable than the Terman-Merrill abbreviated procedure.[4]

A short-form screening procedure—the Cattell-Binet Short Form—combines the Cattell Infant Intelligence Scale (Cattell, 1950) and the Stanford-Binet (Alpern & Kimberlin, 1970). At year levels II through X, two specific tests are administered, while after year level X, any two tests may be given. The short form is administered by obtaining a triple basal level and a triple ceiling level, and the IQs are obtained from the Stanford-Binet manual. The Cattell-Binet Short Form has satisfactory reliability (.97) and validity (.73 to .83) and is efficient and economical, since it takes about 75 percent less time than the standard form and uses 37 percent of the tests of the full scale. However, the IQs obtained by this short form differed from the standard form IQs by 6 or more points in 34 percent of a group of developmentally disabled children, with discrepancies in IQ classifications in over 40 percent of the cases (Bloom, Klee, & Raskin,

1977). In addition, in a group of normal children, MAs come within three months of the full scale MAs in only 48 percent of the cases (Gordon & Forehand, 1972). Thus, this short form, if selected, should be used only as a rough screening instrument; it should not be used to classify children.

While the abbreviated scales will usually provide a valid estimate of intelligence, it is advisable to administer the entire scale except when continuing the examination will cause a hardship to the examinee. This recommendation applies particularly to those situations in which the IQ and test performance will be used in conjunction with other material to make important decisions about the child, and when the scale is used as an assessment device to observe, record, and evaluate the child's ability. In screening situations, short forms may be acceptable as a means of arriving at a crude estimate of intelligence. However, it is important to recognize that, while administration and scoring time is relatively short for a short form, the time involved in preparation, arranging for a meeting, and the like is similar for both long and short forms. The amount of time saved when using short forms, therefore, is overestimated when everything involved is considered.

Completing the Record Booklet

The record booklet is the key record of the child's performance. It is both a working tool and a record for the future. It contains space for recording the child's responses; for assigning appropriate credits; for calculating the CA, MA, and IQ; and for noting relevant personal information and behavioral observations. The importance of completing the record booklet thoroughly and accurately cannot be overemphasized. Since the record booklet is the clinician's working document, it may be referred to many times, not only in the writing of the report, but in future consultations and in research.

Completing the record booklet requires attending to many minor details, including recording and scoring responses, tallying the number of correct items, and summing months' credit. In the beginning stages of your career, it is important to pay close attention to these many details. They will soon become routine and you will be able to execute them quickly.

We now turn to the steps necessary to complete the record booklet properly. The basic principles that apply to completing the Stanford-Binet record booklet are also applicable to other tests. Accordingly, the procedures that follow illustrate the care that should be taken in completing the record booklets of all tests.

Cover Page

On the cover page of the record booklet (see Figure 7-2) complete the identifying information section. Be sure to write in the child's name, sex, address, date of test, birthdate, age, and your name. These are usually necessary as a minimum. Below the identifying information, there is a section labeled "Factors Affecting Test Performance." The completion of these ratings is optional because similar material should be discussed in the report, and because the record booklet is often not available to the reader of the report. However, the factors listed do provide useful guidelines for evaluating the child's performance.

On the upper right-hand side of the cover page there is a small rectangle with the terms CA, MA, and IQ. This section of the cover page is completed after administration of the examination. For a child who is 4 years and 6 months of age and who has achieved a mental age of 5 years and 2 months, the CA and MA are expressed as follows: CA 4-6; MA 5-2. The first numeral indicates years; the second, months. It is not necessary to write "four years and six months" or some other expression, since it is assumed that those having access to the record booklet will understand the meaning of the two numerals. Figure 7-2 also shows how the IQ is written. Confidence intervals for the Stanford-Binet IQs are shown in Table C-1 in the Appendix.

The rectangle on the right-hand side of the cover page labeled "Testing Summary" should also be completed after the test has been administered. Figure 7-2 illustrates, for a child of CA 4-6, the proper completion of this section of the booklet. The Arabic numerals in the "Yrs." column represent the basal age, which is the *highest* level of the examination at which *all* tests were passed. No other numerals are written in the "Yrs." column. Since the basal age was at the IV-6 year level, the number 4 appears in the "Yrs." column and the number 6 in the "Mos." column. In the column labeled "Mos." credit is also allotted for those tests passed *above* the basal year level. As illustrated in Figure 7-2, 4 months' credit was given at year level V because four tests were passed and each test passed is equivalent to *one* month's credit at this level. Opposite year level VI, a 4 appears, since two tests were passed and each test at this year level is allotted *two* months' credit. A zero (0) appears opposite year level VII, indicating that all tests were failed here. Opposite the term "Total," separate scores appear in the years and months columns. The 4 indicates the years' credit, and the 14 reflects the total months' credit. The MA then becomes the sum of these two credits, 5-2. The 5-2, indicating five years and two months, is obtained by adding the number of months' credit from the basal year to the number of months' credit obtained from the remaining year levels ($6 + 8 = 14$ months), and then adding this figure to the year's credit of the basal year (adding 1 year and 2 months to 4 years results in a total of 5 years and 2 months). Of course, there are other ways to compute the MA. For example, the basal credit can be converted to months (in Figure 7-1, 4-6 is equal to 54 months); then the additional months earned (eight months) are added, giving the total months' credit (54 months + 8 months = 62 months). The total months' credit is then converted to years and months (62 months = five years and two months, 5-2). A record of the amount of time required for testing completes the "Test Summary" section.

Inside the Record Booklet

In order to assist you in mastering the numerous details that are involved in complet-

RECORD BOOKLET — Form L-M

Stanford-Binet Intelligence Scale

9-74149

Name .... Sex .... Date of test .... Year .... Month .... Day

Address .... Birthdate ....

School .... Grade .... Examiner .... Age ....

Parent .... [From .... Agency ....]

Birthplace .... of father .... of mother ....

Occupation of father .... of mother ....

TEST SUMMARY		
	Yrs.	Mos.
II		
III		
III-6		
IV		
IV-6	7	6
V		4
VI		4
VII		0
VIII		
IX		
X		
XI		
XII		
XIII		
XIV		
AA		
SA I		
SA II		
SA III		
Total	4	14
MA Score	5	2
Testing time	55 minutes	

CA 4-6
MA 5-2
IQ 115

FACTORS AFFECTING TEST PERFORMANCE

OVERALL RATING OF CONDITIONS

	Optimal	Good	Average	Detrimental	Seriously detrimental

Attention
a) Absorbed by task .... Easily distracted

Reactions During Test Performance
a) Normal activity level .... Hyperactive or depressed
b) Initiates activity .... Waits to be told
c) Quick to respond .... Urging needed

Emotional Independence
a) Socially confident .... Shy, reserved, reticent
b) Realistically self-confident .... Distrusts own ability or overconfident
c) Comfortable in adult company .... Ill-at-ease
d) Assured .... Anxious about success

Problem Solving Behavior
a) Persistent .... Gives up easily or can't give up
b) Reacts to failure realistically .... Withdrawing, hostile, or denying
c) Eager to continue .... Seeks to terminate
d) Challenged by hard tasks .... Prefers only easy tasks

Independence of Examiner Support
a) Needs minimum of commendation .... Needs constant praise and encouragement

Was it hard to establish a positive relationship with this person? ....

FIGURE 7-2. **Cover Page of Stanford-Binet Record Booklet.** Reprinted, with a change in notation, by permission of the publisher. Copyright 1960, Houghton Mifflin Company. All rights reserved.

ing the inside of the record booklet, let us focus on year levels II and II-6. The procedures needed to fill out the record booklet for these two half-year levels are similar to those that are encountered at the other year levels of the test. Therefore, there should be little difficulty in generalizing from these two year levels to the remainder of the record booklet.

Allotment of credit. On the first page and on all the remaining pages of the record booklet, space is provided for recording and scoring the child's responses. Figure 7-3 shows how to complete properly year levels II and II-6. The number of months' credit allotted for the passing of a test at year level II is shown in the parentheses after "Year II." Similar information is provided at every year level. The differential credit within any year level is a function of the number of tests administered. Usually, either all tests are administered (omitting the alternate) or only those tests that make up the short form. When all tests are administered, the first piece of information in the parentheses is applicable; when the short form of the examination is administered, the second piece of information applies. At year level II, one month's credit is allotted for each test passed when six tests are administered; one and one-half months' credit is allotted when four tests are administered. Six months' credit is the maximum allotted for this year level. If, in exceptional cases, only three tests are administered, credit for each test is prorated (two months are credited for each test passed, in order to obtain the total of six months' credit).

The allotment of months' credit is partly a function of the specific year level of the examination. The overall distribution of months' credit can be seen by studying Table 7-3, which presents the year levels, the number of months' credit allotted for each test, and the total number of months' credit allotted for the standard tests. As can be seen in Table 7-3, tests at the half-year levels (II through V) are each allotted one month's credit. The total number of months' credit allotted for any full year level from II

through V is the same as the allotment for each of the next nine year levels (VI through XIV). Because year levels between II and V are divided into two parts (e.g., II and II-6), a total of 12 months can be earned in any one full year. After year level XIV, the total months' credit allotted to each year level changes. Beginning with SA I, while the number of tests remains constant, more weight is given to each test. Thus, the allotment is 24 months' credit at SA I, 30 months at SA II, and 36 months at SA III. There are six tests at every half-year level and at every year level except at the AA year level, where eight tests are present.

When all tests are passed at year level II, 24 months of credit is given. Mental-age credits of 18 months are assumed, and 6 months are added for the six tests successfully completed at year level II. The Stanford-Binet is so constructed that whenever a basal year level is established, mental age credits are assumed for all year levels of the scale below the basal year level. This procedure automatically includes the initial 18 months of mental age credit. At year levels IV-6 and V, a total of 12 months' credit is given for the 12 tests. If all tests of the scale are passed through year level V and none at higher year levels, five years and zero months (5-0) of mental-age credits are given. Since year level VI provides 12 months of mental age credit, it bridges the apparent gap between year level V and year level VI (i.e., not having a half-year level between year level V and year level VI). A basal year level established at V and one success at

TABLE 7-3.   Credit Allotted for Stanford-Binet (L-M) Year Levels

Year Levels	Number of Tests	Individual Test Months' Credit	Total Months' Credit
II-V	6	1	6
VI-XIV	6	2	12
AA	8	2	16
SA I	6	4	24
SA II	6	5	30
SA III	6	6	36

YEAR II (6 tests, 1 month each; or 4 tests, 1½ months each)

| 1 | 1. *Three-hole form board (1+) [1] a)....✓.. b)....⌃

| 1 | 2. Delayed response (2+) [3] a) Middle...✓.. b) Right...✓.. c) Left...✓.

| 1 | 3. *Identifying parts of the body (same as II-6, 2) (4+) [5]

a) Hair...✓.. b) Mouth...✓.. c) Feet...✓.. d) Ear...⌃e) Nose...✓.. f) Hands...✓.. g) Eyes...✓..

| 1 | 4. Block building: Tower (±) [+]

| 1 | 5. *Picture vocabulary (same as II-6, 4; III, 2; IV, 1) (3+) [4]

1. airplane...✓..   4. ball...✓..   7. horse...✓..   10. ship...⌃..   13. flag...⌃..   16. pocket knife...✓..

2. telephone...✓..   5. tree...✓..   8. knife...✓..   11. umbrella...✓..   14. cane...⌃..   17. pitcher...✓..

3. hat...⌃..   6. key...⌃..   9. coat...✓..   12. foot...⌃..   15. arm...✓..   18. leaf...⌃..

| 1 | 6. *Word combinations (±) [+] Example .... *I go home.* ....

.. .. Alternate. Identifying objects by name (5+) [ ]

a) Dog......... b) Ball......... c) Engine......... d) Bed......... e) Doll......... f) Scissors.........

_6_ **Mos. credit at Year II**

YEAR II-6 (6 tests, 1 month each; or 4 tests, 1½ months each)

| 1 | 1. *Identifying objects by use (3+) [3]

a) Cup...✓.. b) Shoe...⌃.. c) Penny...✓.. d) Knife...✓.. e) Automobile...⌃.. f) Iron...⌃..

| 0 | 2. Identifying parts of the body (same as II, 3) (6+) [5]

| 0 | 3. *Naming objects (5+) [3]

a) Chair...⌃.. b) Automobile...✓.. c) Box...⌃.. d) Key...✓.. e) Fork...✓.. f) Flag...✓..

| 0 | 4. *Picture vocabulary (same as II, 5; III, 2; IV, 1) (8+) [4]

| 1 | 5. *Repeating 2 digits (1+) [1]

a) 4-7 _3-7_ b) 6-3 _7-8_ c) 5-8 _5-8_

| 0 | 6. Obeying simple commands (2+) [1] a)....✓.. b)....✓.. c)...⌃..

..... Alternate. Three-hole form board: Rotated (II, 1 must precede) (2+) [ ] a)......... b)......... c).........

_2_ **Mos. Credit at Year II-6**

FIGURE 7-3. Year Levels II and II-6 of Stanford-Binet (L-M) Record Booklet. Reprinted, with a change in notation, by permission of the publisher. Copyright 1960, Houghton Mifflin Company. All rights reserved.

year level VI results in mental-age credits of 5-2 (five years and two months).

Returning again to Figure 7-3, notice that four of the six tests (Tests 1, 3, 5, and 6) have an asterisk preceding the name of the test, denoting that these tests are to be administered in·the short form. In the rec-

tangle preceding the name of the first test, Three-Hole Form Board, a 1 is written to indicate that the child received one month's credit for his or her performance on this test. The 1s appearing in all of the rectangles of year level II mean that the examinee was successful on all tests at this year level.

After the name of the first test, Three-Hole Form Board, a 1+ is printed, which indicates the minimum number of parts of the test that must be passed before credit is given. Thus, before credit is earned, one of the two parts of the first test must be passed; for the second test, Delayed Response, two of the three parts must be successfully completed. Additional credit is not assigned when more than the minimum number of parts of a test are passed. For example, one month's credit is assigned for success either on both trials of the Three-Hole Form Board or on one trial only. When all six tests are administered at year levels II through V, no more than one month's credit can be assigned to a single test.

The number 1 is written in the bracket after the (1+) to indicate that performance was satisfactory on one of the two trials of the test. A 2 is written when both trials a and b are successfully completed. The examinee's success on trial a and failure on trial b is shown by a "correct mark" (√) on the line after the a and an "incorrect mark" (√) on the line after the b.

The notations printed in the booklet for Test 2, Delayed Response, are very similar to those appearing for Test 1. Note, however, that two of the three trials must be correct before credit is given. Note also that Test 2 is not administered in the short form, as shown by the absence of an asterisk before the name of the test.

Tests at more than one year level. Test 3, Identifying Parts of the Body, contains a statement after the name of the test. The statement "same as II-6,2" means that Test 3 is also administered as the second test (the 2 after the comma means second test) at year level II-6. Similar information appears after the test names for all other tests occurring at more than one year level. When the same test appears at more than one year level, additional parts of the test must be correctly answered in order for the examinee to receive credit at the higher year level. However, test content, administration, and scoring criteria do not change. The 4+ appearing after "same as II-6,2" for Test 3

at year level II indicates that four parts must be passed in order to give credit; whereas at year level II-6, the 6+ in the parentheses after "same as II,3" specifies that at least six parts must be passed to give credit. The number of parts needed for credit on each test is always indicated in the record booklet and in the test manual.

A useful procedure to follow when reaching a test that appears at more than one year level is to record the score at the level at which the test first appears and then at each of the other year levels at which it also appears. Space for recording responses to a test appearing at more than one year level is always provided only at the year level at which the test first appears. Thus, for example, if the examination is begun at year level II-6, responses to the Identifying Parts of the Body test are recorded at year level II,3. However, no tests at year level II are actually administered when the basal year level is established at year level II-6. Although the space in the record booklet at year level II is used to record the responses to the Identifying Parts of the Body test, the scoring criteria used to establish success or failure are, in this example, those indicated for year level II-6. There are eleven tests (excluding alternates) appearing at more than one year level of the examination. The Vocabulary test, for example, occurs at all even-year levels from VI through XIV, and then at every year level from SA I to SA III.

Notice in Figure 7-3 that at year level II-6, a 5 appears in the booklet after Test 2. The 5 represents the number of correct responses given by the child when the test was first administered at year level II. The 5 is recorded twice, once at year level II and once at year level II-6. However, no credit is given at year level II-6 for this performance because six correct answers are needed at this year level and the child had only five correct answers. In the parentheses after Identifying Parts of the Body at year level II-6, information is given that shows where the test initially appeared (at year level II,3). The same procedure is followed for Picture Vocabulary at year level II-6 because this test also appears at year level II.

Plus or minus scoring. Test 4, Block building: Tower, differs from the preceding three tests in that it does not have trials or parts. This is indicated by the ± in the parentheses after the name of the test (see Figure 7-3). The + recorded in the bracket after the (±) indicates that the child passed the test.

Further comments on tests at more than one year level and establishing a ceiling. The year levels of the examination at which Test 5, Picture Vocabulary, is administered are shown immediately after the name of the test. Test 5 occurs at four different year levels; namely II, II-6, III, and IV. The examiner must be alert to the fact that a score on the Picture Vocabulary test may indicate that credit for passing the test is assigned to *more than one year level.* As suggested earlier, it is important to note the score needed for credit at each of the year levels at which the Picture Vocabulary test appears so that credit can be recorded and a valid test ceiling can be reached. For example, if 14 parts of the Picture Vocabulary test are passed, the examination usually should be continued to at least year level IV-6 in order to establish a ceiling, even though all tests may have been failed at year level III-6. Although all tests at the lower year level were failed, since a test at year level IV was passed (14 correct answers to the Picture Vocabulary test), the ceiling level should be established at a year level *above* IV. To recapitulate: continue testing in order to obtain a ceiling year level whenever a test is passed at a year level above the level at which all tests have been *first* failed.

Further comments on tests at more than one year level and establishing a basal. In establishing a basal, be alert to the possibility that even though all tests are passed at a particular year level, there still may be a failure below that level. This situation arises because some tests, as we have seen, occur at more than one year level. For example, if a child passes all of the tests at year level X and then fails the Memory for Designs test at year level XI (with zero credit), go back to year level VIII in order to establish a

basal. This is recommended because the Memory for Designs test also appears at year level IX. Since zero credit was obtained, a failure was also recorded at year level IX. Consequently, year level VIII tests should be administered to establish a basal. In addition, all tests at year level IX should be administered.

Test 6 and mos. credit. Test 6, Word Combinations, contains space for recording the specific word combination(s) produced by the examinee. In the example in Figure 7-3, the alternate test Identifying Objects by Name was not administered, and thus this part of the booklet remains incomplete. The number 6 preceding "Mos. credit at Year II" indicates the sum of months credited for the child's performance at year level II.

Major Points to Remember in Filling Out the Record Booklet

As an overall guide to filling out the record booklet, the following points should be considered:

1. Record the child's responses to the test questions verbatim as soon as they are made. If additional paper is used, always indicate the test name or test number and year level at which the response occurred. Always use discretion in recording remarks that are not directly pertinent to the test questions. Such remarks may occasionally be noted if they provide useful information about the examinee's personality or test performance.
2. Indicate scores clearly by a check mark or a plus sign ($\checkmark$, +) or by a modified check mark or a minus sign ($\checkmark\!\!\!\!$, −) in the booklet.
3. Fill in the brackets with the appropriate number. This number depends on the number of *trials* or *parts* that have been successfully completed. It will vary from 0 to a maximum of 40, depending on the specific test administered.
4. In the rectangle preceding each test, write the number of months credited. This number ranges from 0 to 6, except when the short form is administered or

when credit is prorated. Writing a number rather than a plus (+) or minus (−) reduces the possibility of miscalculating months' credit.

5. Write the letter Q after those responses of the child that were probed.

6. When there is uncertainty about the scoring of a response, place a question mark in the margin and review the scoring after the examination has been completed.

7. Double-check all scoring and calculations (months' credit, CA, MA, and IQ) after completing the examination. This always should be done to avoid serious errors in scoring.

8. Double-check the entries in the summary section of the cover page of the record booklet with the entries at all year levels inside the booklet in order to guard against errors in transcribing credits from the year levels to the cover page.

These steps will help to ensure that the record booklet will serve as an accurate record of the child's performance. Obviously, the proper completion of the record booklet will not ensure that the test was administered properly and competently or that the results were reliable and valid. However, a competent administration of the test can be tarnished by mistakes in addition and subtraction and by other clerical errors. Developing the correct administrative procedures early in your career will pay many dividends in the future.

Summary

1. A first step to consider in administering the Stanford-Binet is to determine whether the child has the necessary sensory and motor abilities required by the various tests. If physical handicaps impede the child's ability to perform, the scale should not be administered unless appropriate modifications are possible. Modification of some test procedures may produce scores that do not differ significantly from those obtained with standard test procedures, but each modification must be evaluated separately.

2. In starting to administer the test, find a year level that is of moderate difficulty. The child's chronological age and vocabulary age serve as useful guideposts.

3. The effects of not having a basal or ceiling year level are difficult to evaluate. In such cases, the IQ can still be reported, with a statement indicating that the results may not be completely valid. The larger the number of tests that are passed at year level II or failed at year level Superior Adult III, the greater the probability that the results are valid.

4. Administering and scoring the Stanford-Binet requires considerable skill and judgment and requires careful study of the test manual.

5. Testing-of-limits procedures, which are to be used only after the entire examination has been administered, may be useful on some occasions.

6. Short forms of the Stanford-Binet generally appear to provide reliable and valid IQs. However, the resulting loss of information may not be compensated for by the gain in time.

7. A record booklet that is properly completed provides a useful test record, aids in the writing of a report, and facilitates a review of the scoring. A usable record booklet is an important contribution to the assessment process.

CHAPTER 8

Interpreting the Stanford-Binet Intelligence Scale

To confront a blank wall may be the first step toward seeing around it.

J. S. BIXLER

EXHIBIT 8-1 (cont.)

and talkative throughout the testing session. As preparation was being made to begin testing, she displayed great curiosity regarding the contents of the examiner's kit, inquiring whether or not she would be allowed to play with some of the "toys." She appeared to be quite excited over the prospect of taking the test.

Karla's enthusiasm diminished somewhat when she discovered that the test involved more than just playing with toys. She became quite restless after a short time and it was necessary to interrupt the testing session in order to allow her to walk around and get a drink of water. She frequently shifted about in her chair and, at times, asked to have a question repeated, saying that she had not heard it the first time.

Karla handled failure well. Only on one occasion was there any indication that failure disturbed her. When she was copying a square, she assumed a pouting expression and said, "That's not the same but it's as good as I can do it." She usually responded quickly to the questions, and only rarely did she say that she didn't know an answer. When asked to complete the statement "The snail is slow, the rabbit is _____," Karla replied quickly, "Elephant." Even when providing such a purely fanciful answer, however, she did not appear to be disturbed by the thought of failure.

Test Results

With a chronological age of 3-11 and a mental age of 4-7, Karla achieved an Intelligence Quotient of 104 ± 10 on the Stanford-Binet Intelligence Scale, Form L-M. This places her in the Normal classification and indicates that in this respect she exceeds 60 percent of the children of her age in the standardization group, which was roughly representative of the population of the United States. The chances that the range of scores from 94 to 114 includes her true IQ are about 95 out of 100. The present measure of her level of intellectual functioning appears to be valid, in spite of the fact that there was some restlessness and possible impulsivity during the examination.

Karla passed all of the tests at year level IV, three of the six tests at year level IV-6, and four of the six tests at year level V. She failed all of the tests at year level VI. She generally performed at the average level for her age in the various areas of the test.

Karla demonstrated adequate language usage, general reasoning, and visual-motor coordi-

nation. In language usage she was able to define such words as ball, hat, and stove: ball—"you throw with it"; hat—"to wear it"; and stove—"to cook supper on." Although failing the Vocabulary test at year level V, she was able to define four words from the vocabulary list: orange ("you eat it"), envelope ("to put what you write in"), straw ("you drink with"), and eyelash (pointed to her own eyelash).

Her average general reasoning ability was shown by her correctly joining two pieces of paper to form a rectangle. However, some evidence of perseveration or lack of adequate comprehension was noted on a general reasoning test at year level IV-6. When asked to identify the dissimilar object in a series of pictures in which three objects were identical and the fourth different, Karla correctly pointed to the left-hand object on the first picture and then continued to point, but incorrectly, to the same location on each of the following pictures. These responses were given very quickly and carelessly; the perseveration was in all likelihood only a reflection of restlessness and immaturity.

Her normal visual-motor coordination was shown when she correctly made two folds in a square piece of a paper to form a triangle, a feat of which she seemed quite proud. However, other tasks requiring visual-motor ability were failed at year level V—copying a square and completing a drawing of a man. She approached these tasks in a quick and careless manner. Noting that the man had only one leg, she quickly drew another and said, "There now, he's all done because he has two legs."

Karla showed adequate memory (being able to carry out three simple commands in order) and social intelligence (being able to state that we have eyes "to look with them"). Conceptual thinking ability also is average. She completed such statements as "In daytime it is light; at night it is _____," and "The sun shines during the day; the moon at _____." Karla responded correctly by saying "dark" and "night," respectively.

Summary

In summary, with a CA of 3-11 and an MA of 4-7, Karla achieved an IQ of 104 ± 10 on the Stanford-Binet Intelligence Scale, Form L-M. This places her in the Normal classification and indicates that in this respect she exceeds 60 percent of the children of her age in the standardization group, which was roughly representative of the population of the United States. The chances that the range of scores from 94 to 114 includes her true IQ are about 95 out of 100. The test results

A number of different strategies are available for interpreting the child's performance on the Stanford-Binet. One procedure for interpretation consists of qualitative observations focusing on the child's verbal and nonverbal responses, visual-motor productions, interactions with the examiner, and other behaviors that occur during the evaluation. An introduction to qualitative interpretations on the Stanford-Binet is presented in this chapter, while additional information on general assessment and assessment of handicapped children is presented in Chapters 18–23.

A second procedure is to examine the results of factor analytic investigations in order to obtain guidelines for evaluating tests. However, while factor analytic approaches are adequate for a number of purposes (such as a study of the composition of test items), they usually are not adequate for the practical purposes envisioned by examiners who are using the Stanford-Binet. It is important to recognize that naming factors is a subjective process and may lead to interpretations that are just as "subjective" as those resulting from content analyses of the cognitive skills brought into play by various test items.

A third interpretive procedure is to classify the items by content analysis and to profile the child's successes and failures. In order to assist in profile analysis, I have developed the Binetgram, which presents a graphic picture of the child's performance.

A fourth procedure that can guide interpretations is to determine areas of strengths and weaknesses. This can be accomplished by the use of the standard deviation method. This method stresses the notion that there is a band of normal variability around every score, and only tests falling outside of this band should be considered to indicate strengths and weaknesses reliably.

Finally, a fifth type of interpretation simply consists of attaching a descriptive label to the IQ, such as "Normal" or "Mentally Retarded" or "Gifted" and a percentile equivalent. Table C-37 in the Appendix and Table BC-1 on the inside back cover sheets of this text provide the necessary information for converting IQs to these types of classifications.

None of the existing intelligence tests permit us to determine the types of cognitive processes used by the child in arriving at an answer. All we have is the final output, the test response, which can result from different ways children process information. Even the same type of test at different ages may require different strategies for successful performance. For example, repeating digits at early ages may primarily involve following directions, while at later ages immediate memory may be more important (McNemar, 1942).

Let us take another example. Stringing beads (at year levels III and XIII) is a complex and multifaceted task involving much more than visual-motor dexterity, as the following analysis indicates:

The child's response will indicate first whether he has understood an instruction to observe a demonstration of what he himself will be asked to attempt afterwards; secondly, whether he has grasped the principle of "threading," which will involve comprehension of the fact that a sufficient length of the tag must be pushed through the hole before it is possible to change from "pushing" to "pulling"; thirdly, if he can begin on the task, his response will demonstrate his ability to remember instructions and maintain his initial purpose for a period appropriate to the age level at which the test is placed. Even at this early stage therefore, the problem is one of comprehension and direction of attention as much as of purely mechanical skill. . . . The test has now become [at the higher level] a test of form perception and discrimination and of spatial relations and visual memory, rather than merely manipulation. [Dunsdon, 1952, p. 36]

Still another example illustrates why it is so difficult, with present measuring devices, to account for a child's cognitive acts or behaviors by one "pure" factor name or label.

A 6-year-old who assembles three alphabet blocks to spell out "cat" has employed, at a minimum, verbal and spatial skills; if he is aware that there are three blocks or letters, he has engaged in numerical perception as well. The ability to perform the task has required cognition, memory, convergent thinking, and evaluation. The product is figural, symbolic, and semantic. All this, and we have not yet taken into account such considerations as the motor-manipulative activity, the perception of color, the earlier learning experiences which enabled him to perform the task successfully, or the imagery which the concept "cat" induces in him. We, as analysts, may choose to attend to only a single aspect of the behavior—but the behavior itself remains multifaceted and complex. To assume that we can abstract from a host of such activities a pure and simple entity is to ignore the psychological meaning of intelligent behavior. [Wesman, 1968, p. 273]

Qualitative Observations

Important information about children is acquired from a careful study of the responses given to specific test items, the behaviors accompanying the responses, and the overall test performance. While in theory there is little ambiguity in the test questions, they are open to children's interpretation (Lejeune, 1955). Because of inherent ambiguity in any test question, responses may reveal personality dynamics. In addition, "Even

seemingly neutral stimuli, such as the incomplete man or the mutilated pictures on the Binet, may evoke threatening associations to some children" (Palmer, 1970, p. 105).

The examiner has numerous opportunities to observe children's behavior in the course of administering the Stanford-Binet. Because there are varied test materials, children have the opportunity to react in many different ways, and in the process may reveal some facets of their personality.[1] Tests found at the lower year levels of the Stanford-Binet, primarily below year level IX, can be classified into four general categories that serve to demarcate the kinds of materials with which the child deals (Brown, 1941).

First, there are tests with *materials* (e.g., Sorting Buttons and Stringing Beads), which have a game-like quality and which possess a minimum of authoritative elements. The examiner's attention seems to center on the materials rather than on the child. Some children may resist these materials by simulating active sabotage; buttons or beads may be swept off the table onto the floor. Other children may go beyond the requirements of the tests by making something of their own with the materials. Competition with the examiner, such as seeing who can get the most beads strung, may be triggered. Having the child return the materials at the end of a test may reveal such behaviors as tidiness, aggressiveness upon being asked to do a job, or carelessness.

Second, there are *pictorial* tests (e.g., Picture Vocabulary, Discrimination of Animal Pictures, Pictorial Similarities and Differences, Mutilated Pictures, and Picture Absurdities) that direct the child's attention to the pictures. In the process of responding to picture items, the child may free associate or may produce "projective material," which can be helpful in gaining some insight into his or her personality.

Third, there are *performance* tests (e.g., Picture Completion: Man, and Patience: Rectangle) that require the child to respond actively. These tests, more than other types of tests found in the Stanford-Binet, may reveal children's attitudes toward themselves (e.g., degree of self-confidence and self-criticism, aspiration level, or pride in achievement). The drawing tests may bring out confidence in a child who in verbal situations is shy and hesitant.

Fourth, there are tests with questions of *comprehension, memory, definition,* and so forth (e.g., Comprehension I, Repeating 2 Digits, and Definitions). These questions clearly bring out the testing nature of the situation. Reactions to these tests may differ from those to the performance tests.

An analysis of a child's performance on the Picture Vocabulary test (year levels II through IV) can be facilitated by the following guidelines. The guidelines can also be applied to other Stanford-Binet tests or other individual scales of intelligence.

> . . . Note all responses obtained. Does the child find some responses for every picture, or is he apt to say, "I do not know"? Does he try to find a new word for each picture, or does he use the same word several times, successively or at intervals? Does he seem to grope for the correct word, or does he seem to say the first word that comes to his lips? Do his errors show associations easily recognizable as such (spoon for fork) or meaningful to those around him? ("Daddy go" for airplane)? Does his naming show that he tends to perceive pictures in a primitive, diffuse, global way, paying attention to "qualities of the whole" rather than fine details (stick for knife)?
>
> Are his errors the result of a carryover from a previous picture or from other familiar verbal patterns? Carefully observe the child's enunciation; note which of the consonants may be missing or defective. Watch for dropped consonants (coa- for coat, fla- for flag). For children with very poor articulation, note and check with the mother on nuances in sound productions which may mean different words to the child even if only barely perceptible to outsiders. Observe gestures and whether they accompany or replace verbal responses. Are they relevant and meaningful or only incidental? If they are the child's only form of response, do they indicate that he is, or is not, familiar with the picture? [Taylor, 1961, pp. 308–309]

Some tests are more likely than others to reveal the child's attitudes. (See Chapter 18 for examples of interpretations.)

1. Responses to the Identifying Objects by Use test at year level II-6 may be especially informative about social factors in the child's environment (Ross, 1959).
2. Attitudes toward the home may be reflected in many responses and, in particular, in those given to the Comprehension test at year levels III–6 and IV (Ross, 1959).
3. Current interests, family conditions, school relationships, and alertness may be revealed on the Word Naming test at year level X (Freeman, 1962).
4. Tests requiring the interpretation of pictures may bring out attitudes such as hostility, moralistic preoccupations, and submissiveness (Freeman, 1962).
5. On the Verbal Absurdities test, which appears at year level IX, examinees' responses may reflect their attitudes toward death and toward bodily injury. Some examinees may fail to appreciate the illogicality contained in the statements because of their need to moralize, while other examinees may refuse to accept the statements as even being hypothetical (Kessler, 1966).
6. Replies to the Comprehension IV test questions, appearing at year level VII, may reflect the child's inordinate dependency on his or her mother, a moral or a religious outlook, or an inability to arrive at any solution (Kessler, 1966).
7. Analysis of responses to Proverbs (year levels AA, SA I, and SA III) may prove useful for the following reasons (Dearborn, 1926). First, failure may be associated with lowered attention and concentration. Second, bizarre or irrelevant interpretations may indicate disturbances in conceptual associations. Third, responses may suggest suspicion, evasion, lack of cooperation, negativism, or incoherence. Fourth, responses may reveal the examinee's rational process of inference. Thus, the test involves many pro-

cesses, including attention, awareness of a whole situation, appreciation of fine shades of meaning, memory, judgment (both practical and ethical forms), interest, vocabulary, and imagination.

A number of scoring and interpretation systems have been developed for tests that are in some ways similar to those found in the Stanford-Binet. These systems, if applied with caution, can be helpful in interpreting a child's performance on the Stanford-Binet. The administration and standardization procedures used with other tests differ from those used in the Stanford-Binet. Therefore, information gained by applying such systems to performance on the Stanford-Binet must be viewed in a very tentative light; primarily, the material should be used to generate hypotheses about the examinee's performance.

The examinee's drawings that appear on tests such as Copying a Circle at year level III, Copying a Square at year level V, and Copying a Diamond at year level VIII can be analyzed by applying methods of interpretation associated with the Bender-Gestalt (see Chapter 16). The drawings should be examined for perseveration, closure difficulties, tremor, and other signs of visual-motor impairment.

Guidelines developed for the Children's Apperception Test (see Haworth, 1966) and for other children's tests containing thematic material can be used for interpreting the responses given to picture tests (e.g., Responses to Pictures at year level III and Picture Absurdities at year level VII). The child's performance on the Picture Completion: Man test at year level V can be evaluated for signs of body-image disturbances or confusion of spatial relations (see Machover, 1949, for information about interpreting figure drawings).

The report (Exhibit 8-1) which began this chapter presents many verbatim responses given by the child to specific test questions. The recommendations are developed by considering her level of test performance, her test behavior, and her developmental age.

The report illustrates how test-oriented statements can be incorporated with subject-oriented material.

Factor Analysis

Factor analyses of the Stanford-Binet, Form L-M, have yielded various findings, depending on the age levels studied. At the upper age levels (e.g., 15 years of age), the scale primarily taps verbal fluency and verbal reasoning and neglects spatial ability (Stormer, 1966). At the younger age levels (e.g., 3 to 7 years of age), it taps a variety of factors including verbal, visual-motor, figural, visualization, control of impulsivity, and cognition (Hallahan, Ball, & Payne, 1973; Ramsey & Vane, 1970). Thus, the scale appears to be factorially more complex at the lower year levels than at the upper year levels. Overall, a general factor appears to carry most of the variance in the Stanford-Binet, although there are also many group factors whose makeup depends on the age level studied.

Classification Systems and Profile Analysis

The items in the Stanford-Binet can be grouped into various descriptive categories on the basis of a particular theoretical system or content analysis. A classification scheme is a convenient way of describing clusters of items in categories that have some face validity. Classification schemes aid in evaluating the child's performance, especially the pattern of successes and failures, and enable the examiner to make recommendations based on these patterns.

Classification schemes should not be used to report special abilities. They are simply rough guides for describing various cognitive functions, such as verbal fluency, conceptualization, reasoning, memory, and visual-motor perception. Careful attention is given to the child's pattern of performance in order to establish a basis for making detailed recommendations. The IQ by itself cannot satisfy the demands of differential assessment of learning failures, since it can be the result of various patterns of successes and failures. Let us now examine two different ways of classifying Stanford-Binet items.

Structure of Intellect Classification

Meeker (1969) developed an approach to test classification based on Guilford's Structure of Intellect model to classify tests in the Stanford-Binet and Wechsler batteries. Each item is classified according to operations, contents, and products (see Appendix C-4). Templates for the entire scale are available to provide a quick and convenient way of classifying a child's test performance. Meeker also discussed how the Structure of Intellect classifications can be useful in analyzing an examinee's strengths and weaknesses and in planning educational programs.

However, in a study (Dyer, Neigler, & Milholland, 1975) of the Structure of Intellect operations categories, psychologists' modal assignments agreed with Meeker's assignments on only 57 percent of the 142 Stanford-Binet items. This level of agreement may not be high enough to justify using the Structure-of-Intellect operations categories. Other reports, too, have questioned the categories proposed by Meeker (Stormer, 1966; Wikoff, 1971), and there is little information with which to evaluate the system's usefulness. In addition, the criticisms associated with Guilford's model, which are discussed in Chapter 3, may also affect the usefulness of the proposed classifications for the Stanford-Binet and Wechsler tests.

The Binetgram

The Binetgram, which profiles the child's performance, is based on grouping items into one of seven categories: language, memory, conceptual thinking, reasoning, numerical reasoning, visual-motor, and social intelligence (Sattler, 1965). It is both a means of ordering data from the Stanford-Binet and a convenient way of describing what the child has done in categories that have some face validity. The scheme is based on somewhat arbitrary groupings of tests according to test content. Some tests could be placed in categories other than those shown and

other categories could be developed, if desired. A factor analysis was not performed, nor were judges used for a reliability check on the categorizations. Cronbach (1970) observed that some of the distinctions are subtle, and other interpreters of the scale would no doubt modify the categories used. However, the classifications are in the tradition of those presented for previous Stanford-Binet editions. Silverstein (1965) noted that Sattler's scheme is similar to the one presented by Valett (1964), so that there appears to be a satisfactory degree of reliability for Sattler's categorizations. Significant correlations have also been reported (Wiebe & Harrison, 1977) between Sattler's categories and the subtests of the McCarthy Scales of Children's Abilities.

The Binetgram is shown in Figure 8-1. The first two lines in the upper left-hand corner of the Binetgram are available for recording "identifying data." To facilitate evaluation of strengths and weaknesses, the standard deviation (SD) bands can be entered in the spaces provided in the upper right-hand corner. (See the next part of this chapter, entitled "Determining Strengths and Weaknesses," for a discussion of the standard deviation method.)

The rows of the Binetgram present the seven areas, while the columns present the year levels. At year level II, for example, tests 3, 5, 6, and A appear in the language category; test 2, in the reasoning category; and tests 1 and 4, in the visual-motor category. No tests have been classified in the remaining four categories at this year level.

After the examination is finished and all scoring and calculations have been checked, complete the Binetgram. The mechanics of completing the Binetgram are relatively simple. First record identifying data, then circle the Roman numerals for the basal year level and for the ceiling year level (e.g., ⑦ when this is the basal year level and ⑪ when this is the ceiling year level). Then circle all of the tests passed by the child.

The purpose of the Binetgram is to assist in making interpretations. For example, children who consistently fail visual-motor tests while passing other types of tests may

BINETGRAM

Instructions: First circle basal year level and ceiling year level and then circle all tests passed by examinee.

Name _____ Date of testing _____

Date of birth _____ Grade _____ IQ _____ CA _____ MA _____

Bands for SD Method*

CA Reference: _____

MA Reference: _____

*See Table C-2 in Appendix in Assessment of Children's Intelligence and Special Abilities (2nd ed.).

YEAR LEVEL

CATEGORIES	II	II-6	III	III-6	IV	IV-6	V	VI	VII	VIII	IX	X	XI	XII	XIII	XIV	AA	SA I	SA II	SA III
Language	3 5 6 A	1 2 3 4	2		1 4	A	3	1		1	4 A	1 3 5	3	1 5 6	2 5	1	1 3 8	1 3 5	1	1
Memory	5	5	4 A		2 A	5			6 A	2	3 6	6	1 4	4 A	3 6		5 7	4	6	6
Conceptual Thinking					3	2		2 5	2 5	4			6			6		6 A	3 5	2 3 A
Reasoning	2			1 2 3 5 A	5	3	5 6	3		3	2	A	2	2	1 4	3 5	6		2 A	4 5
Numerical Reasoning							1 2 4 A	4			5	2				2 4 A	2 4	2	4	
Visual-Motor	1 4	A	1 3 5 6					6	3		1			A	A	A	A			
Social Intelligence	6	6		4 6	6	1 4 6		A	1 4	5 6 A		4	5 A	3						

FIGURE 8-1. The Binetgram. Developed by Jerome M. Sattler.

need further testing to evaluate their visual-motor skills. The classifications are to be used to generate hypotheses about the child's performance in order to make more meaningful recommendations; they are not to be used to make diagnoses about special abilities.

All of the difficulties associated with classification systems, of course, apply to the Binetgram. The Binetgram must be used with caution. It shows that there are many year levels at which categories are not tapped. For example, tests in the conceptual thinking category do not begin until year level IV. Numerical reasoning tests, which begin at year level VI, do not appear again until year level IX. Language is the most systematically represented category; it appears at every year level, with the exception of year levels III-6 and VII.

The classification scheme used in the Binetgram also appears in Table C-4 in the Appendix. The first description of functions and processes in the second column of Table C-4 refers to the category from Sattler's classification scheme. Other relevant descriptions that pertain to test functions and processes are also described.

The seven areas covered in the Binetgram are as follows:

Language. This category includes tests related to maturity of vocabulary (in relation to the prekindergarten level), extent of vocabulary (referring to the number of words the child can define), quality of vocabulary (measured by such tests as abstract words, rhymes, word naming, and definitions), and comprehension of verbal relations.

Memory. This category contains meaningful, nonmeaningful, and visual memory tests. The tests are considered to reflect rote auditory memory, ideational memory, and attention span.

Conceptual thinking. This category, while closely associated with language ability, is primarily concerned with abstract thinking. Such functions as generalization, assuming an "as if" attitude, conceptual thinking, and using a categorical attitude are subsumed.

Reasoning. This category contains verbal and nonverbal reasoning tests. The verbal absurdity tests are the prototype for verbal reasoning tests. The pictorial and orientation problems represent a model for the nonverbal reasoning tests. Reasoning includes the perception of logical relations, discrimination ability, and analysis and synthesis. Spatial reasoning may also be measured by the orientation tests.

Numerical reasoning. This category includes tests involving arithmetic reasoning problems. The content is closely related to school learning. Numerical reasoning involves concentration and the ability to generalize from numerical data.

Visual-motor. This category contains tests concerned with manual dexterity, eye-hand coordination, and perception of spatial relations. Constructive visual imagery may be involved in the paper folding test. Nonverbal reasoning ability may be involved in some of the visual-motor tests.

Social intelligence. This category strongly overlaps with the reasoning category, so that consideration should be given to the tests classified in the latter as also reflecting social comprehension. Social intelligence includes social maturity and social judgment. The comprehension and reasons-finding tests are seen to reflect social judgment, whereas obeying simple commands, response to pictures, and comparison tests likely reflect social maturity.

Table 8-1 shows the rank order of categories by percentage for each category for the total number of tests ($N = 142$), total number of tests without alternates ($N = 122$), alternates ($N = 20$), and starred tests ($N = 80$) that are used in the short form. The 142 tests are not separate and distinct tests, because many of them have the same item content, but receive differential scoring based on the number of correct responses. Table 8-1 shows that language tests are more frequent than other kinds of tests (rank 1 for the total number of tests, with and without alternates, and rank 1 for starred tests). Numerical reasoning tests, on the other hand, are the least frequently represented tests (rank 7 for the total number of tests, with

TABLE 8-1. Rank Order of Categories in Stanford-Binet (L-M)

Rank	Total No. of Tests			Total No. of Tests Without Alternates			Alternates			Starred Tests		
	Category	N	%	Category	N	%	Category	N	%	Category	N	%
1	L	35	25	L	32	26	M	4	20	L	31	39
2	R	25	18	R	22	18	VM	4	20	R	11	14
3	M	21	15	M	17	14	L	3	15	M	11	14
4	CT	18	13	CT	16	13	R	3	15	CT	10	12
5	SI	17	12	SI	14	11	SI	3	15	VM	6	8
6	VM	16	11	VM	12	10	CT	2	10	NR	6	8
7	NR	10	7	NR	9	7	NR	1	5	SI	5	6
	Total	142	101		122	99		20	100		80	101

Note. Abbreviations are as follows: CT = Conceptual Thinking, L = Language, M = Memory, NR = Numerical Reasoning, R = Reasoning, SI = Social Intelligence, VM = Visual-Motor.

Reprinted, with a change in notation, by permission of the publisher and author from J. M. Sattler, "Analysis of Functions of the 1960 Stanford-Binet Intelligence Scale, Form L-M," *Journal of Clinical Psychology, 21,* p. 175. Copyright 1965, Clinical Psychology Publishing Co., Inc.

and without alternates, and rank 7 for alternate tests).

Determining Strengths and Weaknesses

Obtaining a profile of the child's strengths and weaknesses on the Stanford-Binet is a difficult task because the age-level format of the scale does not permit a simple way of calculating significant differences between those tests that are passed and those that are failed. However, some guideposts can be obtained by use of the standard deviation technique (SD) in connection with the examinee's CA and MA.

The SD technique is needed because differences between successive year levels do not mean the same thing throughout the scale. For example, the difference between year level II and year level III represents approximately a 50 percent increase in mental development, whereas the difference between year level X and year level XI represents approximately a 10 percent increase in mental development. Thus, a 2-year-old child who obtains an MA of 3-0 receives an IQ of 147, whereas a 10-year-old child who obtains an MA of 11-0 receives an IQ of 107. The statement "Tests were passed on a year level one above the examinee's chronological age," while literally accurate, does not describe the level of mental functioning represented by the successes. For a 2-year-old, passing tests "one year above" may indicate superior functioning, while for a 10-year-old, passing tests "one year above" may indicate normal functioning. Therefore, such a statement needs elaboration.

The use of the SD technique guards against overinterpretation of minor fluctuations or unwarranted interpretations of chance deviations in a child's performance. The SD technique is based on the premise that tests passed within 1 SD of the child's chronological age or mental age represent normal (i.e., expected) fluctuations in ability. Tests passed or failed within these boundaries, therefore, should not be considered as indicative of strengths or weaknesses.

Two different reference points can be used for the SD technique. The CA reference point is used for comparing the child's performance with that of children of similar chronological age. This is an *intergroup comparison* or normative group comparison. The MA reference point is an *intraindividual comparison* and is used for interpreting strengths and weaknesses in relation to the child's own level of performance. In the psychological report it is important to indicate clearly which reference point is being discussed; however, both reference points are potentially useful.

Table C-2 in the Appendix provides a quick and convenient way for determining the band of year levels surrounding the child's chronological age (CA) and mental age (MA) that reflects normal variability or typical functioning. Only tests passed or failed outside of these bands should be considered to reflect significant strengths or weaknesses. The table has three columns. When CA is used as the reference point, the left-most column is entered with the child's chronological age and then read horizontally across to the center of the table to determine the band of normal variability. When MA is used as the reference point, the right-most column is entered with the child's mental age and the band is again determined from the center of the table.

The steps needed to use Table C-2 are as follows:

1. Enter the table with the child's MA or CA or both.
2. Find the year levels indicating normal variability from the center of the table appropriate for the child's MA or CA or both.
3. On the front page of the Stanford-Binet record booklet, draw a box (or boxes) around the year levels indicating normal variability. Label the box (or boxes) MA or CA to indicate which reference point was used.

In interpreting the child's performance, strengths and weaknesses should always be evaluated in reference to the child's overall level of functioning, namely, the IQ. Therefore, the SD technique cannot be used in a mechanical fashion. When the CA reference point is used, the interpretation tends to be more direct. Tests passed above the boxed levels reflect well-developed abilities or strengths, while those failed below the boxed levels reflect poorly developed abilities or weaknesses. Tests passed or failed within the boxed levels suggest chance fluctuations in performance and should not be interpreted as strengths or weaknesses.

When MA is the reference point, tests passed above the boxed levels reflect *rela-*

tively well-developed abilities or strengths for the child, but the actual level of success may still be below average, especially when the child is mentally retarded. These abilities, in the case of mentally retarded children who fail to obtain any successes near their chronological age, can be described as being better developed than their other abilities, but still at a level that is below average for children of the same chronological age. They are strengths only in relation to the child's general level of functioning.

When MA is used as the reference point, tests passed below the boxed levels reflect *relatively* poorly developed abilities or weaknesses because the actual level of failure may still be average or above, as in the case of a gifted child. These failures should be described as reflecting abilities that are less well developed than others. They are weaknesses only in relation to the child's overall level of functioning.

The Binet profile in Table 8-2 portrays a girl with a CA of 10-0, an MA of 13-8, and an IQ of 127. To make an intergroup comparison, the CA column is entered in Table C-2 in the Appendix (row 9-10—10-05), and the respective normal variability band is located (years IX through XIII). A band is then drawn around these year levels, as shown. Using the CA reference point (for the intergroup comparison), the girl's successes above the top of the band are on tests in years XIV, AA, SA I, and SA II. These successes demonstrate well-developed abilities when compared to the average child of the same CA. Since there were no failures below year IX, weaknesses are not present in this profile using the CA reference point.

To make an intraindividual comparison, the MA column is entered in Table C-2 in the Appendix (row 13-05—14-07), and the respective normal variability band located (years XII through SA I). A band is then drawn around these year levels, as shown in Table 8-2. Using the MA reference point, items failed by the girl at year X and year XI indicate a weakness in relation to her overall level of functioning. Items passed at year SA II demonstrate a strength in relation to her other abilities.

TABLE 8-2.   Sample Calculation of Variability in Stanford-Binet Scores

Year Level	Total Credits Years	Total Credits Months
IX (Basal)	9	0
X		10
XI		8
XII		8
XIII		10
XIV		10
AA		6
SAI		2
SAII		2
SAIII (Ceiling)		0
		9-56
		MA = 13-8

CA is bracketed next to IX (Basal), X, XI. MA is bracketed next to XIV, AA, SAI.

The SD method is simply a convenient way of evaluating a child's performance on the Stanford-Binet. It focuses on tests or groups of tests to determine strengths and weaknesses.

Another method of evaluating a child's performance is to examine the variability of successes and failures, disregarding the content of tests or groups of tests. For the most part, this type of "scatter analysis" has not been shown to be useful as a valid interpretive device on the Stanford-Binet.[2] In some cases, however, scatter has been found to be greater (a) in emotionally disturbed than in nonemotionally disturbed children, (b) in organic mentally retardated than in familial mentally retarded or normal children, and (c) in exogenous brain-injured than in endogenous brain-injured children.[3] These findings have been based on limited samples of children and, for the most part, have not been replicated.

Interpreting Mental Age on the 1972 Stanford-Binet Norms

With the restandardization of the Stanford-Binet norms in 1972, mental age lost its meaning as a score that reflects children's ability to do things that children of their age normally do. This is because the average mental age for a particular chronological age no longer numerically corresponds to that chronological age. For example, a 5-year-old child needs a mental age score of 5-6, not 5-0, in order to obtain an IQ of 100. Thus, "average" 5-year-old children have a mental age that is six months higher than their chronological age.

The changes in the relationship between chronological age and mental age for the 1972 norms indicate that the mental age is an MA in name only. The MA on the test is simply a raw score (Goodman, 1978). However, a conversion table can be used to obtain a true mental age (shown as *corrected* MA in the table), which reflects the performance of an average child (see Table C-3 in the Appendix). By entering the child's obtained mental age score in the first outside column and row of the table, the true mental age score is obtained. The true (or corrected) mental age score reveals more accurately the age-level performance of the child and seems more interpretable, both practically and theoretically, than the mental age used to compute the child's IQ.

Sex Differences

Sex differences in IQ on the 1937 forms tend to be small (McNemar, 1942). This finding supports the intent of the standardization procedure, which was to eliminate sex differences from the scales. Girls are somewhat higher at preschool ages (three points), while boys are somewhat higher at later ages (about two points). In the final two forms of the scales, six tests showed girls significantly surpassing boys, and eighteen tests showed boys significantly surpassing girls. The fact that a greater number of tests favored boys rather than girls is accounted for by repetition of the same or similar tests at various year levels and in both forms. Many of the significant findings (and lack of consistent significant findings) could not be explained easily.

Stanford-Binet and Other Intelligence Tests

The Stanford-Binet is often used as a criterion measure to evaluate the concurrent validity of a variety of other intelligence tests. These studies are described in the various chapters of the book that discuss other tests. The findings often indicate that IQs provided by other tests are not directly interchangeable with Stanford-Binet IQs.

The relationship between the Stanford-Binet and WAIS holds some interest, especially for longitudinal studies of intelligence and for work in the field of mental retardation.[4] The correlations between the Stanford-Binet and WAIS in samples of mentally retarded individuals are uniformly high, ranging from .74 to .90 (median correlation of .75). However, differences between mean IQs may be large—as much as 23 points in favor of the WAIS. Binet IQs are lower than WAIS IQs in mentally retarded groups. In contrast, with normal college freshmen and normal adults, the Stanford-Binet has been found to yield higher IQs than the WAIS, with correlations ranging from .40 to .83 (median correlation of .77). The Stanford-Binet correlates more highly with the Verbal Scale than with the Performance Scale. These studies were based on pre-1972 norms. It is likely that the extent of IQ differences between the Stanford-Binet and WAIS has changed with the 1972 norms.

Bradway and Thompson (1962) studied a group of 111 subjects who as children had been administered the Stanford-Binet and twenty-five years later the WAIS. Some tests were found to predict significantly the Verbal Scale IQ; other tests, the Performance Scale IQ; and still other tests, both the Verbal and Performance Scale IQ. Only one test, Counting Four Objects, was found to be a negative predictor of the Performance Scale IQ, while none of the tests were a negative predictor of the Verbal Scale IQ. The best predictors of adult abilities were verbal tests and memory tests, while number concept tests were unreliable in predicting adult abilities.

Test Your Skills

Now that you have finished reading the three chapters on the Stanford-Binet and the previous five chapters of the book, you should be able to describe and interpret a child's performance on the Stanford-Binet. To sharpen your interpretation and communication skills, look at the excerpts from reports in Exhibit 8-2. In each case there is some inadequacy of description or interpretation. Find the mistakes in the sentences. After you have completed your analysis, check your evaluations with those shown in the Answers section on p. 541.

Summary

1. Strategies for interpreting the Stanford-Binet include obtaining information from qualitative observations, factor analytic findings, content and profile analysis, and the pattern of strengths and weaknesses; attaching a descriptive label to the IQ also provides a means of interpretation.

2. A child's response to a question may result from many different ways of processing information. Tests require complex be-

---

EXHIBIT 8-2. Exercises for the Stanford-Binet

1. "At the Superior Adult 1 level she failed a test requiring filling in the missing word."
2. "The results from the Vocabulary section indicated that the examiner start Cheryl at the Average Adult level."
3. "At the Superior Adult I level Bill started showing signs of scatter."
4. "On the Stanford-Binet, Allen's basal age was established at age 4 and his ceiling was at age 6. This places him considerably below his chronological age."
5. "There was some scatter in the judgment and reasoning area, as seen by the successes at IX-4 and X-1."
6. "With a chronological age of 8-0, the test results indicated a mental age of 7-8. This would place her about half a year behind in the classroom, which she is according to her teacher."
7. "Observation of the student in the classroom and from her tests correlates the fact that her weak areas are judgment and reasoning."
8. "Julie is immature, and this is substantiated by the Stanford-Binet score in judgment and reasoning."
9. "Testing began on the Stanford-Binet with the Vocabulary test. Alice was able to give the correct meaning for 8 words. This is the minimum number to pass the test at year level VIII. Testing continued at year level VIII."
10. "One could not predict her abilities in the general comprehension area because only two tests were administered at year level VIII."
11. The following statements were written for a child with a Stanford-Binet IQ of 115, CA = 4-5 and MA = 5-8.

    "Jill appeared to have difficulty with tasks involving memory. She received credit for repeating 5 digits at year VII, but was only able to repeat the last series of digits. She answered three questions involving memory at year VIII, but this was not enough to receive credit."
12. "She received no credits at the Superior Adult II level in vocabulary (23) and ingenuity (2)."
13. "The administration of the Stanford-Binet supported the findings revealed by the Draw-A-Man and the Bender as that of visual-motor development."
14. "Her ability of verbal fluency and a general comprehension did assist with Lilly's overall IQ of 112."
15. "With a CA of 5-3, Bill earned an MA of 5-6 (IQ = 97) on the Stanford-Binet. This indicates that his potential probably falls within the average range."
16. "Bill did quite well on the vocabulary portion of the Stanford-Binet Intelligence Scale, scoring 18."
17. "Her scores on the Vocabulary and Abstract Words tests were significant." ∎

---

haviors, and a simple name to describe a test's function is usually not satisfactory.

3. The varied materials on the Stanford-Binet provide opportunities for the child to react in different ways and for the examiner to obtain a sampling of behaviors.

4. A general factor appears to account for most of the variance on the Stanford-Binet. At the upper levels, the Stanford-Binet primarily measures verbal abilities, while at the lower levels, the test is factorially more complex.

5. Classification systems can serve as provisional, tentative guides for grouping tests in the scale in order to formulate hypotheses about the child's pattern of abilities. If classification systems are used, they should be thought of as crude guidelines. Cognitive acts require complex and multifaceted behaviors—reducing the act to a simple category name or factor name does not do justice to the psychological processes involved in the task.

6. One interesting classification system, based on Guilford's Structure-of-Intellect model, has been developed by Meeker. Another system, by Sattler, classifies Stanford-Binet tests into seven categories. The Binetgram provides a visual picture of the child's pattern of scores.

7. The standard deviation method is a useful procedure for evaluating children's strengths and weaknesses on the Stanford-Binet. The children's chronological age and mental age can serve as guidelines for evaluating their pattern of performance.

8. Scatter analysis, as applied to the Stanford-Binet, was once thought of as a useful tool that could aid in the diagnostic process. While many different measures of scatter have been proposed, numerical measures of scatter generally have not proved to be valid clinical tools.

9. The MA on the 1972 Stanford-Binet norms is a raw score; it does not reflect a child's true MA. A conversion table (C-3) in the Appendix facilitates the rapid conversion of the obtained MA to a true MA.

10. Sex differences are minimal on the Stanford-Binet.

11. While correlations between the Stanford-Binet and the WAIS are generally satisfactory, large differences between mean IQs, with WAIS IQs higher, have been reported in some studies with mentally retarded children.

12. Verbal and memory tests on the Stanford-Binet are good predictors of WAIS IQs, while number concept tests are less reliable predictors.

CHAPTER 9

Wechsler Intelligence Scale for Children– Revised (WISC-R): Description

Mind is the great lever of all things; human thought is the process by which human ends are ultimately answered.

DANIEL WEBSTER

EXHIBIT 9-1.   Illustrations and Descriptions of Items Like Those on the WISC-R

Information (30 questions)

How many legs do you have?
What must you do to make water freeze?
Who discovered the North Pole?
What is the capital of France?

Similarities (17 questions)

In what way are pencil and crayon alike?
In what way are tea and coffee alike?
In what way are inch and mile alike?
In what way are binoculars and microscope alike?

Arithmetic (18 questions)

If I have one piece of candy and get another one, how many pieces will I have?
At 12 cents each, how much will 4 bars of soap cost?
If a suit sells for ½ of the ticket price, what is the cost of a $120 suit?

Vocabulary (32 words)

ball	poem
summer	obstreperous

Comprehension (17 questions)

Why do we wear shoes?
What is the thing to do if you see someone dropping their packages?
In what two ways is a lamp better than a candle?
Why are we tried by a jury of our peers?

Digit Span

Digits Forward contains seven series of digits, 3 to 9 digits in length (Example: 1-8-9).
Digits Backward contains seven series of digits, 2 to 8 digits in length (Example: 5-8-1-9).

Picture Completion (26 items)

The task is to identify the essential missing part of the picture.
A picture of a car without a wheel.
A picture of a dog without a leg.
A picture of a telephone without numbers on the dial.
An example of a Picture Completion task is shown on the next page.

EXHIBIT 9-1   (cont.)

Courtesy of The Psychological Corporation.

Picture Arrangement (12 items)

The task is to arrange a series of pictures into a meaningful sequence. An example of a Picture Arrangement item is shown in the photograph of the WISC-R (Figure 9-1).

Block Design (11 items)

The task is to reproduce stimulus designs using four or nine blocks. An example of a Block Design item is shown below.

Object Assembly (4 items)

The task is to arrange pieces into a meaningful object. An example of an Object Assembly item is shown above in column 2.

Courtesy of The Psychological Corporation.

Coding

The task is to copy symbols from a key. An example of the Coding task is shown below.

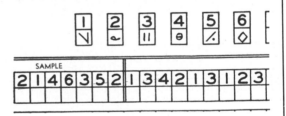

Courtesy of The Psychological Corporation.

Mazes

The task is to complete a series of mazes. An example of a maze is shown in the photograph of the WISC-R (Figure 9-1).

Note. The questions resemble those that appear on the WISC-R, but are not actually from the test. Chapter 10 describes each subtest in more detail.

The Wechsler Intelligence Scale for Children–Revised (WISC-R) (Wechsler, 1974) was published in 1974, twenty-five years after the original publication of the WISC. Its predecessor, the WISC (Wechsler, 1949), was developed as a downward extension of the adult intelligence test, the Wechsler-Bellevue Intelligence Scale. To make the adult scale more suitable for children, easier items were added to the low end of the subtests. The WISC-R covers an age range from 6-0 to 16-11 years and contains twelve subtests (as shown in Exhibit 9-1). Six of the tests form the Verbal Scale (Information,

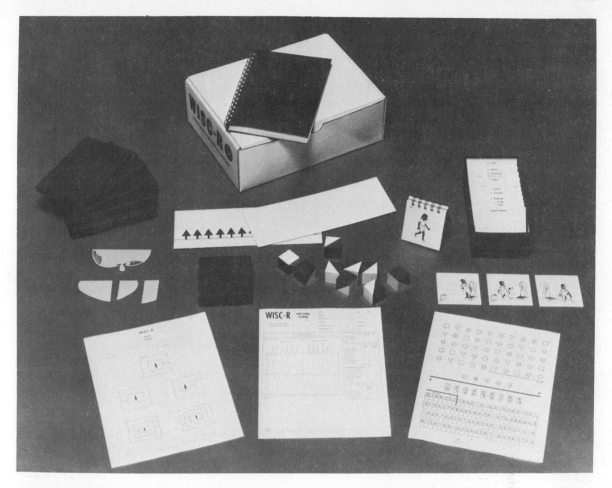

FIGURE 9-1. Wechsler Intelligence Scale for Children–Revised. Courtesy of The Psychological Corporation.

Similarities, Arithmetic, Vocabulary, Comprehension, and Digit Span) and the other six form the Performance Scale (Picture Completion, Picture Arrangement, Block Design, Object Assembly, Coding, and Mazes). A total of 72 percent of the WISC items are retained in the W1SC-R, either intact (64 percent) or with a substantial modification (8 percent), and the items in the Coding subtest remain the same as in the original.

Standardization

The WISC-R was standardized on 2,200 white and nonwhite American children selected to be representative of the population to be covered by the scale on the basis of 1970 U.S. census data. In the standardization sample, there were eleven different age groups, ranging from 6 and one-half to 16 and one-half years, with 200 children in each group. Unlike the WISC, which did not include nonwhites in the standardization group, the WISC-R included nonwhites (e.g., blacks, American Indians, Orientals, and some Puerto Ricans and Mexican-Americans) in approximately the same proportions as in the U.S. population, as shown by the 1970 census data. The proportions in the WISC-R sample do approximate those in the census data more closely for the white sample than for the nonwhite (the discrepancy between the standardization sample and the census data is no greater than 1 percent for the white sample, but is as high as 4.5 percent for the nonwhite sample). However, there is no way of assessing the extent to which the discrepancies affect the test scores. At worst, the effects should not be large.

Deviation IQs, Scaled Scores, and Test-Age Equivalents

The WISC-R (and the other Wechsler scales as well) provides three separate IQs: a Verbal Scale IQ, a Performance Scale IQ, and a Full Scale IQ. All three IQs are Deviation IQs, which are obtained by comparing the examinees' scores with the scores earned by a representative sample of their own age group. Because Deviation IQs are standard scores, the mean IQs and standard deviations at each age level are equal. Each of the three IQs has a mean of 100 and standard deviation of 15.

When the WISC-R is administered, raw scores are first obtained on each subtest. The raw scores are then converted to normalized standard scores (or scaled scores) within the examinee's own age group by use of a table in the WISC-R manual that is based on four-month age intervals between 6-0-0 (years, months, days) and 16-11-30. The scaled scores for each subtest have a mean of 10 and standard deviation of 3.

The IQ tables in the WISC-R manual are based on ten of the twelve subtests. The two supplementary subtests, Digit Span and Mazes, are excluded. Even when Digit Span and Mazes are administered, the manual recommends that they not be included in the tabulation of the IQ. When fewer than 10 subtests are administered, prorating is necessary, or else a specialized short-form procedure, described later in this chapter, can be used to compute the IQ. The WISC-R manual provides a table for prorating the scores when four of the subtests are administered in each scale. However, I recommend that when fewer than four subtests are administered, IQs be computed using the short-form procedure described in this chapter.

FIGURE 9-2. David Wechsler. Courtesy of The Psychological Corporation.

Wechsler developed the WISC-R and the other Wechsler scales without using mental age to calculate IQs because he believed that the concept was potentially misleading. (See Chapter 4 for criticisms associated with the mental-age concept.) He rejected the notion that mental age represents an absolute level of mental capacity or that the same mental age in different children represents identical intelligence levels. However, soon after the initial publication of the WISC, he recognized that mental-age or test-age equivalents (average age associated with a score) would be useful for some purposes. Therefore, in subsequent publications of the WISC manual and in the WISC-R manual, a table of test-age equivalents was provided. Wechsler considered the test-age equivalents only as guides to facilitate interpreting the child's performance.

Reliability

The WISC-R has outstanding reliability. Each of the three IQ scales has a reliability coefficient of .89 or above in the standardization group over the entire age range covered by the scale. Average reliability coefficients, based on the eleven age groups, are .96 for the Full Scale IQ, .94 for the Verbal

Scale IQ, and .90 for the Performance Scale IQ.

Subtest reliabilities, while adequate, are less satisfactory than scale reliabilities, as can be seen in Table 9-1, which summarizes average reliabilities and standard errors of measurement for the twelve subtests and three scales. The average subtest reliability coefficients range from a low of .70 for Object Assembly to a high of .86 for Vocabulary. The highest reliabilities are generally found among the Verbal Scale subtests, although one Performance Scale subtest, Block Design, has one of the highest reliability coefficients in the scale (.85). The average reliability coefficients range from .77 to .86 (median of .80) for the Verbal Scale subtests and from .70 to .85 (median of .72) for the Performance Scale subtests. When the relia-

bility coefficients are considered for each of the eleven age groups separately, they range from a low of .57 for Mazes at the 16½ age level to a high of .92 for Vocabulary at the 16½ age level. The reliability coefficients are similar, for the most part, across the eleven age groups.

Standard errors of measurement. The standard errors of measurement (S_m) in IQ points, based on the average of the eleven age groups, are 3.19 for the Full Scale, 3.60 for the Verbal Scale, and 4.66 for the Performance Scale. Thus, more confidence can be placed in the IQ based on the Full Scale than in the IQ based on either the Verbal or Performance Scale. The Verbal Scale subtests (S_m ranges from 1.15 to 1.44) usually have smaller standard errors of measurement than the Performance Scale subtests (S_m ranges from 1.17 to 1.70). Within the Verbal Scale, Vocabulary and Information have the smallest S_m (1.15 and 1.19, respectively), while, within the Performance Scale, Block Design and Picture Completion have the smallest S_m (1.17 and 1.45, respectively). (The S_m for each subtest is expressed in scaled score points and is based on the average of the eleven age groups.)

Stability. The stability of the WISC-R was assessed by retesting a group of 303 children from six age groups in the standardization sample after a one-month interval (Wechsler, 1974). For the retest sample, the stability coefficients were .95 for the Full Scale IQ, .93 for the Verbal Scale IQ, and .90 for the Performance Scale IQ, while those for the twelve subtests ranged from .65 (Mazes) to .88 (Information), with a median coefficient of .78. The mean test-retest IQs and standard deviations for the Verbal, Performance, and Full Scales for the three groups are shown in Table 9-2. The average increase in IQ from the first to the second testing was about 7 IQ points for the Full Scale, about 4 IQ points for the Verbal Scale, and about 10 IQ points for the Performance Scale. These differences, which can be considered practice effects, are much greater for the Performance Scale than for the Verbal Scale. The stability coefficients

TABLE 9-1. Average Reliability Coefficients and Standard Errors of Measurement for WISC-R Subtests and Scales

Subtest and Scale	Average Reliability Coefficient	Average Standard Error of Measurement
Information	.85	1.19
Similarities	.81	1.34
Arithmetic	.77	1.38
Vocabulary	.86	1.15
Comprehension	.77	1.39
Digit Span	.78	1.44
Picture Completion	.77	1.45
Picture Arrangement	.73	1.57
Block Design	.85	1.17
Object Assembly	.70	1.70
Coding	.72	1.63
Mazes	.72	1.70
Verbal Scale IQ	.94	3.60
Performance Scale IQ	.90	4.66
Full Scale IQ	.96	3.19

Note. Reliability coefficients for ten of the twelve subtests (except Digit Span and Coding) are split-half correlations. For Digit Span and Coding the reliability coefficients are test-retest coefficients obtained on a sample of about fifty children in six different age groups who were retested after a one-month interval. Verbal, Performance, and Full Scale reliability coefficients are based on a formula for computing the reliability of a composite group of tests.

Adapted from Wechsler (1974).

TABLE 9-2.   Test-Retest WISC-R IQs for Three Groups of Children

Age	Scale	First Testing		Second Testing		Change
		Mean IQ	SD	Mean IQ	SD	
6½–7½	Verbal	98.3	12.3	102.2	12.7	+ 3.9
(N = 97)	Performance	97.9	14.5	106.5	15.0	+ 8.6
	Full	97.9	13.2	104.5	14.0	+ 6.6
10½–11½	Verbal	99.0	13.4	102.4	13.8	+ 3.4
(N = 102)	Performance	98.5	13.9	109.3	16.3	+10.8
	Full	98.6	13.7	106.2	15.1	+ 7.6
14½–15½	Verbal	96.8	16.1	100.0	17.1	+ 3.2
(N = 104)	Performance	96.2	14.4	105.4	18.2	+ 9.2
	Full	96.1	15.4	103.0	18.0	+ 6.9

suggest that the WISC-R provides stable IQs for each of the three scales.

Precision range. Table C-5 in the Appendix shows the confidence intervals for the 68, 85, 90, 95, and 99 percent levels for each scale. The confidence intervals are provided for separate age levels as well as for the average of the age levels. *The child's specific age group, and not the average of the eleven age groups, should be used to obtain the most accurate confidence interval.* The precision ranges of the WISC-R IQs are similar throughout the age levels covered by the scale. (For further discussion of precision range, see Chapter 24.)

Validity

The criterion validity of the WISC-R has been investigated in a variety of studies by correlating it with the WPPSI, WAIS, Stanford-Binet L-M, other intelligence tests, and measures of achievement and school grades. These studies are now reviewed.[1]

WISC-R and WPPSI. Because the WISC-R overlaps with the WPPSI in the age range of 6-0-0 to 6-7-15, either of the two tests can be used to evaluate children in this age range. The WISC-R manual cites a study in which a

representative sample of fifty children (males and females who were 6 years, 0 months of age) were given the two tests in counterbalanced order. The correlations between each of the three scales on the two tests were .80 for the Verbal Scale, .80 for the Performance Scale, and .82 for the Full Scale. While the mean IQs on the Verbal, Performance, and Full Scales were higher on the WPPSI than on the WISC-R (1.5, 2.8, and 2.5 IQ points, respectively), the differences were small.

In a study (Rasbury, McCoy, & Perry, 1977) of 5- to 6-year-old middle-class children, the WISC-R yielded IQs that were 5 points lower on the average than those of the WPPSI over a one-year test-retest interval. Correlations between the two tests were .81 for the Verbal Scales, .80 for the Performance Scales, and .94 for the Full Scales. An analysis of individual subtests indicated that the difference between the two forms was approximately one scaled-score point across the subtests (with the WISC-R lower than the WPPSI). In ten percent of the cases, differences between the two tests were larger than 10 IQ points. In retest situations, consequently, when the WISC-R follows the WPPSI, it is important to recognize that differences in the two IQs may reflect errors of measurement and not any changes in the child's ability.

WISC-R and WAIS. Because the WISC-R overlaps with the WAIS in the age range 16-0-0 to 16-11-30, either of the two tests can be used to test children in this age range. The WISC-R manual cites a study in which a representative sample of forty children (boys and girls who were 16 years, 11 months of age) were given the two tests in counterbalanced order. The correlations between each of the three scales on the two tests were .96 for the Verbal Scale, .83 for the Performance Scale, and .95 for the Full Scale. Differences between the mean IQs obtained on the two tests for the Verbal, Performance, and Full Scales were 5.3, 5.2, and 6.2 IQ points, respectively, with higher IQs on the WAIS than on the WISC-R.

In retest situations, it is likely that children older than 16 years of age who have previously been given the WISC-R will be given the WAIS. When this occurs, there is evidence that the WAIS will yield IQs that are considerably higher than those obtained on the WISC-R. For example, Nagle and Lazarus (1979) reported that in a sample of thirty 16-year-old mentally retarded children, the WAIS yielded Verbal, Performance, and Full Scale IQs that were 14, 9, and 13 IQ points higher than those on the WISC-R. In this study the tests were administered in counterbalanced order. In another study (Craft & Kronenberger, 1979) with a sample of fifty 16-year-old educably mentally handicapped children, the WAIS was again found to yield considerably higher IQs than the WISC-R for the Verbal, Performance, and Full Scales (77 vs. 64, 78 vs. 69, and 75 vs. 64). The two tests were administered twenty-nine to forty-seven days apart. These differences indicate that children are likely to receive different classifications depending on whether the WAIS or WISC-R is administered. In addition, children previously tested by the WISC-R may fall into a different classification on the WAIS. In cases of mental retardation, such differences may have great import for eligibility in special programs. The nonequivalent scores provided by the WAIS and WISC-R give great urgency to the principle that decisions concerning children's programming needs must be based on all the available facts, and not on the IQ exclusively.

Other concurrent validity studies. Table 9-3 summarizes the results of studies that have compared the WISC-R with a variety of ability and achievement tests and grades. The studies indicate that when intelligence tests, receptive vocabulary tests, achievement tests, and school grades are used as criteria, the WISC-R has satisfactory concurrent validity. Median correlations range from the upper .30s to low .80s.

An evaluation of the IQs provided by the WISC-R and other tests indicates that for group purposes, IQs on the Stanford-Binet and WISC-R are generally similar. The Slosson Intelligence Test, on the average, yields IQs that are about 5 points higher than those of WISC-R. The McCarthy Scales of Children's Abilities, on the average, yields GCIs (General Cognitive Indexes) that are lower by about 6 points. There are no trends evident with respect to whether or not group tests yield higher or lower IQs than the WISC-R does. Although many studies report small mean differences between the WISC-R and other intelligence tests, IQs should not be considered interchangeable for a particular child.

The Peabody Picture Vocabulary Test generally yields higher scores than the WISC-R by about 3 points. The Quick Test has been found to be about 9 points lower than the WISC-R with a low-ability group and 5 points higher with a normal-ability group. These two tests are measures of receptive vocabulary; their scores should not be viewed as IQs. (See Chapter 15 for an evaluation of the PPVT-R and Quick Test.)

Intercorrelations Between Subtests and Scales

Intercorrelations between subtests and scales permit us to observe the degree of relationship between the various parts of the WISC-R. Intercorrelations between the twelve subtests range from a low of .19 to a high of .69, with a median of .40. The six

TABLE 9-3. Concurrent Validity Studies for the WISC-R

Criterion	Median Correlations		
	Verbal Scale	Performance Scale	Full Scale
Stanford-Binet	.75	.68	.82
Slosson Intelligence Test	.81	.50	.61
McCarthy Scales of Children's Abilities	—	—	.68
Group Intelligence Tests[a]	.61	.59	.66
Peabody Picture Vocabulary Test	.66	.32	.58
Quick Test	.73	.74	.76
Wide Range Achievement Test			
Reading	.61	.35	.60
Spelling	.60	.26	.56
Arithmetic	.64	.48	.58
Peabody Individual Achievement Test	—	—	.60
Other Achievement Tests[b]			
Reading	.66	.47	.65
Arithmetic	.56	.48	.58
School grades	—	—	.39

[a]Group intelligence tests include Lorge-Thorndike, Otis-Lennon, Pintner Cunningham, Revised Beta, and Culture Fair Intelligence Test.
[b]Other achievement tests include California Achievement Test and Metropolitan Achievement Tests.

highest subtest intercorrelations are between Vocabulary and Information (.69), Vocabulary and Similarities (.67), Vocabulary and Comprehension (.66), Information and Similarities (.62), Block Design and Object Assembly (.60), and Similarities and Comprehension (.59), while the six *lowest* subtest intercorrelations are between Picture Completion and Coding (.19), Picture Completion and Digit Span (.21), Object Assembly and Digit Span (.21), Coding and Mazes (.21), Picture Arrangement and Digit Span (.22), and Mazes and Digit Span (.22). These coefficients indicate that the Verbal Scale subtests are more highly intercorrelated than are the Performance Scale subtests.

Average correlations between the Verbal Scale subtests and the Verbal Scale range from .45 to .78 (median of .70), while those between the Performance Scale subtests and the Performance Scale range from .33 to .68 (median of .53). Intercorrelations between the individual subtests and the Full Scale show similar trends. Vocabulary has the highest correlation of any of the subtests with the Full Scale (.74), followed by Information (.70) and Block Design (.68), while

Digit Span (.43) and Coding (.38) have the lowest correlations with the Full Scale. Within their respective scales, Vocabulary (.78) and Block Design (.68) have the highest correlations with the Verbal and Performance IQs.

Comparability of WISC-R and WISC IQs and Coding Scores

Using the standardization samples for the WISC-R and WISC, Doppelt and Kaufman (1977) reported that, on the average, WISC-R IQs are 4 points lower than WISC IQs. The largest differences (7 to 8 points) are for children between ages 6½ and 10½ in the Low Average through Mentally Retarded ranges. The smallest differences (2 to 3 points) are for children 11½ to 15½ years of age, regardless of ability level. In addition, WISC-R Performance Scale IQs are considerably lower than WISC Performance Scale IQs (5 to 9 points throughout the 6½ to 15½ age range studied), while WISC-R Verbal Scale IQs are lower than WISC Verbal Scale IQs only in the 6½- to 10½-year age range. These data indicate that the WISC-R sample would have obtained higher scores on the WISC than those obtained by the original standardization group. These results are for group differences; in the case of a given child, the estimated differences may be in error by considerable amounts. Therefore, these findings should be used only as guidelines for understanding differences between the WISC and WISC-R when such comparisons are needed.

Since the publication of the WISC-R, numerous studies have been published that have compared the WISC-R and WISC within a variety of populations.[2] Correlations in these studies between the two Verbal Scales ranged from .21 to .96 (median = .84); Performance Scales, from .41 to .96 (median = .80); and Full Scales, from .42 to .95 (median = .89). These studies almost uniformly indicate that the WISC-R provides lower scores than the WISC by about 5 IQ points for the Full Scale, 4 IQ points for the Verbal Scale, and 6 IQ points for the Performance Scale. Thus, in retest situations, changes within these limits on the WISC-R should be viewed as a reflection of changes in the test norms and not as a decrement in the child's level of intellectual functioning. We would anticipate that the updated WISC-R norms would lead to lower IQs than the WISC norms, because over the twenty-five-year period between the two sets of norms there have been expanded educational opportunities and widespread exposure to television and other media.

Normative changes over a twenty-five-year period can be directly measured on the Coding subtest because it is the only subtest in both the WISC and the WISC-R that has exactly the same stimuli, scoring procedure, and time limits. An analysis of the original and revised tests reveals that scaled-score equivalents are almost always either the same or *lower* on the WISC-R than on the WISC for the same raw score. The extent of change is a function of both ability level and age, as shown in Table 9-4, which illustrates the normative changes for three age groups. Overall, the greatest changes occur for scaled scores higher than 1 and for ages 8-0

TABLE 9-4. Illustrations of Normative Changes on the WISC-R Coding Subtest

| Age | Raw Score | Scaled Score | | Change |
		WISC-R	WISC	
6-0	0	1	2	−1
	4	3	4	−1
	13	7	7	0
	25	10	10	0
	36	12	13	−1
	46	16	16	0
	49	19	19	0
8-0	0	1	1	0
	9	2	4	−2
	19	5	7	−2
	25	7	10	−3
	33	11	13	−2
	40	14	16	−2
	48	17	19	−2
15-0	19	1	1	0
	29	1	4	−3
	42	5	7	−2
	53	8	10	−2
	66	11	13	−2
	76	13	16	−3
	83	15	19	−4

through 15-0 years (i.e., Coding B rather than Coding A). For those with very low scores between 6-0 and 8-0 years, there is little change in the norms. However, for those older children who are especially talented at the Coding task, the norms have been changed so that they must obtain more raw-score points in order to receive the same scaled score. In general, children tested with the WISC-R Coding subtest have to be more proficient than they were on the WISC Coding subtest in order to maintain the same relative position.

WISC-R IQs and Stratification Variables

The relationship of WISC-R IQs to various stratification variables used in the standardization sample is shown in Table 9-5 (Kaufman & Doppelt, 1976). Differences between the boys' and girls' mean IQs on the three scales were less than 3 points. Consequently, sex differences are not large enough to assume any practical significance on the scale. White children obtained mean IQs that were about one standard deviation higher than those of black children (*M* IQs of 102 vs. 86).

Mean IQs show a clear relation to parental occupation group, with a difference of 21 Full Scale IQ points (*M* IQ of 108.2 vs. *M* IQ of 87.3) between the highest (children of professional and technical workers) and lowest (children of unskilled workers) groups. Urban-rural differences on the three scales were small—less than 3 points. Differences associated with geographic region indicate that children from the south obtained mean IQs that were about 6 points lower than

TABLE 9-5. Relationship of WISC-R IQs to Sex, Race, Occupation of Head of Household, Urban-Rural Residence, and Geographic Residence

Demographic Variables		N	Verbal IQ		Performance IQ		Full Scale IQ	
			M	*SD*	*M*	*SD*	*M*	*SD*
Sex	Boys	1,100	101.2	15.4	100.4	15.1	100.9	15.4
	Girls	1,100	98.8	14.3	99.8	14.9	99.1	14.6
Race	White boys	945	103.3	14.7	102.2	14.3	103.1	14.5
	Black boys	143	87.6	12.4	87.9	13.7	86.7	12.5
	White girls	925	100.7	13.5	102.1	13.9	101.4	13.5
	Black girls	162	88.0	13.7	86.5	13.0	86.2	12.9
Parental occupation group	*Whites*							
	1. Professional and technical	308	109.7	12.8	107.1	13.7	109.4	12.9
	2. Managerial, clerical, sales	538	104.2	14.0	104.0	14.6	104.4	14.1
	3. Skilled	446	100.5	13.2	101.3	13.1	100.9	12.9
	4. Semi-skilled	499	97.9	13.5	99.2	13.4	98.3	13.2
	5. Unskilled	79	92.3	13.3	93.4	13.8	92.1	13.3
	Blacks							
	1. Professional and technical	20	92.0	12.7	90.8	10.4	90.7	11.4
	2. Managerial, clerical, sales	51	91.7	11.5	90.9	12.5	90.5	11.1
	3. Skilled	47	89.6	10.6	87.4	11.1	87.5	10.2
	4. Semi-skilled	129	87.4	13.6	87.0	14.2	86.0	13.6
	5. Unskilled	58	82.6	13.5	82.8	13.3	81.5	12.5
	Total Group							
	1. Professional and technical	329	108.6	13.5	106.1	14.1	108.2	13.6
	2. Managerial, clerical, sales	594	103.1	14.2	102.9	14.8	103.2	14.4
	3. Skilled	495	99.5	13.3	100.1	13.6	99.6	13.3
	4. Semi-skilled	639	95.7	14.3	96.9	14.6	95.9	14.4
	5. Unskilled	143	87.8	14.3	88.8	14.6	87.3	14.1
Urban-rural residence	Urban	1,557	100.6	14.7	100.5	15.1	100.6	14.9
	Rural	643	98.5	15.4	99.0	14.8	98.6	15.2
Geographic residence	Northeast	478	102.8	14.6	101.3	14.4	102.3	14.6
	Northcentral	641	100.0	14.0	101.0	14.6	100.5	14.2
	South	696	96.9	15.7	96.7	15.9	96.6	15.9
	West	385	101.8	14.3	103.1	13.6	102.6	13.8

Adapted from Kaufman and Doppelt (1976).

TABLE 9-6. Factor Loadings of WISC-R Subtests for Eleven Age Groups (Varimax Rotation)

Subtest	6½[a]	7½	8½	9½	10½	11½	12½	13½	14½	15½	16½	Mdn.
					Factor A—Verbal Comprehension							
Information	35	49	65	57	63	63	65	77	60	72	57	63
Similarities	44	60	63	64	69	65	67	74	62	65	62	64
Arithmetic	32	38	31	29	41	37	33	53	37	40	32	37
Vocabulary	58	69	74	67	73	72	64	82	75	78	71	72
Comprehension	49	55	67	62	63	64	67	70	69	63	66	64
Digit Span	18	23	04	23	13	17	16	27	27	20	16	18
Picture Completion	39	29	22	27	40	34	35	36	31	35	39	35
Picture Arrangement	38	31	44	44	27	26	34	42	33	25	25	33
Block Design	28	30	27	30	26	22	33	39	23	20	22	27
Object Assembly	19	24	20	34	33	21	22	20	20	14	22	21
Coding	06	12	23	10	14	16	17	23	13	15	31	15
Mazes	21	08	18	06	08	20	15	−06	08	13	12	12

Subtest	6½[a]	7½	8½	9½	10½	11½	12½	13½	14½	15½	16½	Mdn.
					Factor B—Perceptual Organization							
Information	18	33	20	25	22	38	35	19	34	22	32	25
Similarities	23	30	24	38	33	44	35	26	38	34	34	34
Arithmetic	21	20	19	24	19	38	27	23	19	19	16	20
Vocabulary	17	22	24	26	33	31	36	19	24	18	29	24
Comprehension	28	28	30	37	26	33	27	21	31	35	32	30
Digit Span	18	20	14	12	11	07	14	04	07	12	13	12
Picture Completion	27	52	48	63	55	60	62	57	60	57	54	57
Picture Arrangement	38	49	51	49	41	41	61	41	29	49	41	41
Block Design	44	66	58	63	66	73	54	70	70	72	76	66
Object Assembly	57	66	69	65	58	70	61	68	64	64	70	65
Coding	12	23	24	20	17	13	₁6	22	12	24	20	20
Mazes	60	60	47	49	47	42	47	47	32	48	48	47

Subtest	6½[a]	7½	8½	9½	10½	11½	12½	13½	14½	15½	16½	Mdn.
					Factor C—Freedom from Distractibility							
Information	55	51	31	48	32	41	28	24	47	23	46	41
Similarities	37	27	28	38	32	23	26	23	30	28	31	28
Arithmetic	59	59	51	63	48	44	61	45	58	48	64	58
Vocabulary	36	31	16	53	25	33	44	29	33	39	45	33
Comprehension	33	28	08	28	12	30	28	22	19	15	24	24
Digit Span	54	50	56	52	57	54	59	59	39	56	62	56
Picture Completion	13	06	33	18	01	02	20	05	11	08	12	11
Picture Arrangement	27	28	09	12	19	25	12	07	16	10	09	12
Block Design	25	27	32	36	35	28	50	27	18	33	27	28
Object Assembly	18	25	19	16	12	12	22	05	12	11	09	12
Coding	20	25	46	42	45	53	42	45	15	40	31	42
Mazes	21	23	15	24	22	12	26	30	04	24	18	22

[a]This row indicates age level.

From A. S. Kaufman, "Factor Analysis of the WISC-R at 11 Age Levels between 6½ and 16½ Years," *Journal of Consulting and Clinical Psychology*, 1975, *43*, pp. 138–140. Copyright 1975 by the American Psychological Association. Reprinted by permission.

those of children from the west (96.6 vs. 102.6).

Factor Analysis

A factor analysis of the total standardization group revealed that three factors—Verbal Comprehension, Perceptual Organization, and Freedom from Distractibility—could efficiently describe the WISC-R (see Table 9-6) (Kaufman, 1975a).[3] The term "Verbal Comprehension" describes the hypothesized ability underlying the factor for both item content (verbal) and mental process (comprehension). This factor appears to measure a variable common to the Verbal Scale subtests. Vocabulary, Information, Comprehension, and Similarities have high loadings on the Verbal Comprehension factor, followed by Arithmetic, which has a moderate loading. Two Performance Scale subtests—Picture Completion and Picture Arrangement—also have moderate loadings on the Verbal Comprehension factor, thus suggesting that these two subtests may require verbal mediation to a greater degree than the other Performance Scale subtests.

The term "Perceptual Organization" describes the hypothesized ability underlying the factor for both item content (perceptual) and mental process (organization). This factor appears to measure a variable common to the Performance Scale subtests. Block Design, Object Assembly, and Picture Completion have high loadings on the Perceptual Organization factor, followed by Picture Arrangement and Mazes, which have moderate loadings.

While there is some difficulty in interpreting the meaning of the third factor, the name "Freedom from Distractibility" appears to be most appropriate. The Arithmetic and Digit Span subtests have high loadings on the Freedom from Distractibility factor, followed by Information and Coding B, which have moderate loadings. (Coding A has only a minimal loading on this factor.)

The factor analytic results give strong empirical support to interpretation of the Verbal and Performance IQs as separately functioning entities in the WISC-R. The factor structure of the scale closely agrees with the actual organization of the tests in the battery.[4]

Using a procedure that allows for the measurement of a general factor (g), Kaufman (1975a) found that the WISC-R subtests cluster into three groups, as shown in Table 9-7.[5] The subtests having the highest g load-

TABLE 9-7. WISC-R Subtests as Measures of g

Good Measure of g[a]			Fair Measure of g			Poor Measure of g		
Subtest	Median Loading of g	Proportion of Variance Attributed to g	Subtest	Median Loading of g	Proportion of Variance Attributed to g	Subtest	Median Loading of g	Proportion of Variance Attributed to g
Vocabulary	.80	64%	Arithmetic	.65	42%	Digit Span	.49	24%
Information	.76	58%	Object Assembly	.62	38%	Mazes	.45	20%
Similarities	.76	58%	Picture Completion	.61	37%	Coding	.41	17%
Block Design	.73	53%	Picture Arrangement	.60	36%			
Comprehension	.72	52%						

Note. The square of the median coefficients provides the proportion of each subtest's variance that may be attributed to g.

[a]For children ages 6 to 7 years, there are only three good verbal measures of g (Information, Arithmetic, and Vocabulary) and two good nonverbal measures of g (Block Design and Picture Arrangement).

Adapted from Kaufman (1975a).

ings are Vocabulary, Information, Similarities, Comprehension, and Block Design, while the subtests with the lowest g loadings are Digit Span, Mazes, and Coding.

Other factor analytic studies. Other factor analytic studies of the WISC-R with males and females, black children, Mexican-American children, lower-middle-class children, mentally retarded children, adolescent psychiatric patients, children referred for academic difficulties, learning disabled, and emotionally disturbed children indicate that the factors found in these subgroups are similar to those found in the standardization group.[6]

Subtest specificity. Subtest specificity refers to the proportion of a subtest's variance that is both reliable (i.e., not due to errors of measurement) and distinctive to the subtest. Although the subtests overlap in their measurement properties (i.e., the majority of the reliable variance for most subtests is common factor variance), many of the subtests also have a relatively high degree of subtest specificity which allows for interpretations of specific subtest functions, as shown in Table 9-8 (Kaufman, 1979c). Although a firm ground for profile analysis of scaled scores is also afforded by the relatively high degree of subtest specificity, constraints still must be placed on interpreting subtest functions. These include determin-

ing which subtest scaled scores are significantly different from one another (see Chapter 11 for a discussion of profile analysis) and analyzing all relevant subtests before drawing any conclusions about unusual ability or weakness. For example, a low score on Digit Span together with low scores on Arithmetic and Coding (and average or high scores on other subtests) may indicate that the child is highly distractible (Kaufman, 1975a). However, a low score on Digit Span, but not on Arithmetic and Coding, suggests a pattern reflecting difficulty with auditory memory or one indicating anxiety.[7]

Factor scores. Factor scores can also be obtained from the WISC-R, permitting the identification of meaningful psychological dimensions (Kaufman, 1975a). The Verbal Comprehension factor score measures verbal knowledge and comprehension, knowledge obtained in part by formal education and reflecting the application of verbal skills to situations that are new to the child. The Perceptual Organization factor score is a nonverbal factor involving perceptual and organizational dimensions and reflects the ability to interpret and organize visually perceived material while working against a time limit. The Freedom from Distractibility factor score measures the ability to remain undistracted (to attend or concentrate), but also may involve numerical ability. Short-term memory may be an im-

TABLE 9-8.   Amount of Specificity for WISC-R Subtests

Ample Specificity		Adequate Specificity		Inadequate Specificity	
Subtest	Ages	Subtest	Ages	Subtest	Ages
Information	all ages	Vocabulary	all ages	Similarities	9½ to 16½
Similarities	6½ to 8½	Comprehension	all ages	Object Assembly	all ages
Arithmetic	all ages	Picture Completion	9½ to 16½		
Digit Span	all ages				
Picture Completion	6½ to 8½				
Picture Arrangement	all ages				
Block Design	all ages				
Coding	all ages				
Mazes	all ages				

Adapted from Kaufman (1979c).

portant component of the Freedom from Distractibility factor, but it is not certain to what extent this is so.

The three factor scores can be obtained as follows:

Verbal Comprehension = Verbal Scale IQ

Perceptual Organization = Performance Scale IQ

Freedom from Distractibility = Sum of scaled scores on Arithmetic, Digit Span, and Coding.[8]

Since the Verbal and Performance IQs are already in the form of Deviation IQs, all that need be done to make the Freedom from Distractibility factor score directly comparable to these two factor scores is to use a conversion procedure. Table C-8 in the Appendix permits the rapid conversion of the sum of scaled scores on Arithmetic, Digit Span, and Coding directly into a Freedom from Distractibility Deviation IQ.

Gutkin (1978) suggests that somewhat purer factor scores can be obtained by using only Information, Similarities, Vocabulary, and Comprehension for the Verbal Comprehension factor score and Picture Completion, Picture Arrangement, Block Design, and Object Assembly for the Perceptual Organization factor. He based his proposal on the factor analytic findings that show that Arithmetic and Coding have low loadings on the Verbal Comprehension and Perceptual Organization factors, respectively. Deviation IQs for these two factor scores are shown in Table C-8 in the Appendix.

Administering the WISC-R

The general procedures discussed in Chapter 5 for administering psychological tests and the procedures discussed in Chapter 7 for the Stanford-Binet should be helpful to you in administering the WISC-R. However, there are problems associated with the administration and scoring of the WISC-R that are not encountered with the Stanford-Binet; for each different test, the special pro-

cedures must be mastered. Some confusion may arise in administering the WISC-R because there are some subtests on the WAIS and WPPSI that are similar to those on the WISC-R but have different instructions and time limits. Extreme care is needed to make sure one is using procedures that are appropriate for the particular tests. Specific and detailed suggestions supplementing those in the WISC-R manual are presented in Chapter 10 for each WISC-R subtest. This section discusses some general issues.

Considerable practice is necessary in order to gain familiarity with the test materials before the scale is actually administered to a child. The Verbal Scale subtests are generally easier to administer than the Performance Scale subtests, but they are more difficult to score. A stopwatch is very useful in administering the timed WISC-R subtests.

The details associated with test administration, test scoring, and completing the record booklet, which were pointed out in Chapter 7, also pertain to the WISC-R and other similar individually administered tests. The record booklet should be clearly and accurately completed and responses recorded verbatim. Checking all calculations is an absolute necessity, as is the checking of the conversion of raw scores to scaled scores and of scaled scores to IQs. The correct calculation of the child's chronological age is also, of course, important. Examiners should try to develop proper administrative procedures early in their testing career. A copy of the cover page of the record booklet is shown in Figure 9-3.

General problems in administering the WISC-R. Beginning examiners as well as professionals have been observed to have some of the following problems in administering the WISC-R:

1. Reading questions too quickly or too slowly.
2. Enunciation difficulties.
3. Failure to clear table of unessential materials.

WISC-R

RECORD FORM

**Wechsler Intelligence Scale
for Children—Revised**

NAME_____ AGE_____ SEX_____

ADDRESS_____

PARENT'S NAME_____

SCHOOL _____ GRADE_____

PLACE OF TESTING_____ TESTED BY_____

REFERRED BY_____

WISC-R PROFILE

Clinicians who wish to draw a profile should first transfer the child's *scaled scores* to the row of boxes below. Then mark an X on the dot corresponding to the scaled score for each test, and draw a line connecting the X's.*

VERBAL TESTS   PERFORMANCE TESTS

	Information	Similarities	Arithmetic	Vocabulary	Comprehension	Digit Span		Picture Completion	Picture Arrangement	Block Design	Object Assembly	Coding	Mazes	
Scaled Score	☐	☐	☐	☐	☐	☐	Scaled Score	☐	☐	☐	☐	☐	☐	Scaled Score
19	•	•	•	•	•	•	19	•	•	•	•	•	•	19
18	•	•	•	•	•	•	18	•	•	•	•	•	•	18
17	•	•	•	•	•	•	17	•	•	•	•	•	•	17
16	•	•	•	•	•	•	16	•	•	•	•	•	•	16
15	•	•	•	•	•	•	15	•	•	•	•	•	•	15
14	•	•	•	•	•	•	14	•	•	•	•	•	•	14
13	•	•	•	•	•	•	13	•	•	•	•	•	•	13
12	•	•	•	•	•	•	12	•	•	•	•	•	•	12
11	•	•	•	•	•	•	11	•	•	•	•	•	•	11
10	•	•	•	•	•	•	10	•	•	•	•	•	•	10
9	•	•	•	•	•	•	9	•	•	•	•	•	•	9
8	•	•	•	•	•	•	8	•	•	•	•	•	•	8
7	•	•	•	•	•	•	7	•	•	•	•	•	•	7
6	•	•	•	•	•	•	6	•	•	•	•	•	•	6
5	•	•	•	•	•	•	5	•	•	•	•	•	•	5
4	•	•	•	•	•	•	4	•	•	•	•	•	•	4
3	•	•	•	•	•	•	3	•	•	•	•	•	•	3
2	•	•	•	•	•	•	2	•	•	•	•	•	•	2
1	•	•	•	•	•	•	1	•	•	•	•	•	•	1

*See Chapter 4 in the manual for a discussion of the significance of differences between scores on the tests.

NOTES

	Year	Month	Day
Date Tested	___	___	___
Date of Birth	___	___	___
Age	___	___	___

	Raw Score	Scaled Score
VERBAL TESTS		
Information	___	___
Similarities	___	___
Arithmetic	___	___
Vocabulary	___	___
Comprehension	___	___
(Digit Span)	(___)	(___)
Verbal Score		___
PERFORMANCE TESTS		
Picture Completion	___	___
Picture Arrangement	___	___
Block Design	___	___
Object Assembly	___	___
Coding	___	___
(Mazes)	(___)	(___)
Performance Score		___

	Scaled Score	IQ
Verbal Score	___	* ___
Performance Score	___	* ___
Full Scale Score	___	___

*Prorated from 4 tests, if necessary.

FIGURE 9-3. Cover Page of WISC-R Record Booklet. Copyright © 1971, 1974 by The Psychological Corporation, New York, N.Y. All Rights Reserved.

4. Failure to record all responses.
5. Failure to calculate chronological age correctly.
6. Providing too much help to the child.
7. Failure to adhere to directions.
8. Errors in timing.
9. Failure to question ambiguous or vague responses.
10. Failure to credit all responses.
11. Errors in converting raw scores to scaled scores.
12. Errors in prorating.
13. Use of incorrect time-bonus credits.
14. Use of wrong norms.
15. Crediting an incorrect response.
16. Errors in adding raw scores.
17. Errors in adding scaled scores.
18. Failure to check all Coding subtest responses.
19. Failure to credit nonadministered passed items.
20. Failure to score a subtest.
21. Errors in converting scaled scores to IQ.

It is important that examiners study their testing practices carefully in order to ensure that these and other administrative problems do not occur.

Subtest sequence. The WISC-R manual indicates that, while it should be convenient to administer the subtests in the order indicated in the manual, it is permissible to change the order when the needs of a particular child must be met, or when the examiner has a personal preference. *I strongly urge that the subtests be administered in the order specified in the manual unless there is some compelling reason to use another order.* The order in the manual was the order used in obtaining the standardization data. A rearranged order constitutes a departure from standard procedures, and there is evidence that such departures do affect the child's scores.[9]

Starting rules. A specific rule must be followed in scoring items that are failed below the entry-point items (Wechsler, 1974, page 59). (The entry-point items are those that the child must pass in order for the examiner

to administer more difficult items.) The rule applies in situations in which the examiner has some doubts about whether or not the items at the entry point have been passed, and subsequently decides to administer earlier items in the series. The rule, which applies only to normal children aged 8 years and above (because these are the children who have entry points that are above the first item on certain subtests), is as follows: "*If subsequent scoring of the test reveals that some of the earlier items were administered unnecessarily, the child should be given full credit for these items—even if he earned partial or no credit* (p. 59) (italics added). This rule means that when an item (or items) below the entry point is failed (or when partial credit is received), *full credit* is given to the item (or items) when further checking has indicated that, in fact, the child correctly answered the items at the entry point.

Here is an example. After administering words 4 and 5 on the Vocabulary subtest to a normal 8-year-old child, the examiner is not certain of the scoring of the responses that were given to these two entry items. The examiner therefore decides to administer words 3 and 2 and then word 1 because word 3 was definitely failed. The child passes words 1 and 2, and the subtest is continued with word 6. After the examination, checking of the responses indicates that the child should receive full credit for words 4 and 5. The application of the rule means that the child is given full credit for defining word 3 (as well as words 1 and 2), even though the definition of word 3 was incorrect, because word 3 is a word that occurs *below* the entry words which were defined correctly. This rule favors the child, since it was the examiner's decision to administer the earlier word which the child subsequently failed. The rule is an attempt to maintain standardized scoring procedures.

Discontinuance rules. Another scoring rule applies to situations in which the examiner has some doubts as to whether or not the items at the discontinuance point have been failed, and then subsequently decides to administer additional items in the series (Wechsler, 1974, page 59). (The discontinuance-point items are those that the child fails in a series [e.g., five consecutive items], indicating, according to the manual, that the subtest should be discontinued.) The rule is as follows: *If subsequent scoring of the items indicates that the additional items were administered unnecessarily, the child should not be given credit for items passed after the discontinuance point.*

A concrete example shows the application of the rule. The examiner administered the first 15 words of the Vocabulary subtest, but is not certain of the scoring of some of the responses that the child gave to words 11 through 15. The examiner therefore decides to administer additional words, and the child definitely passes words 16 and 17 but fails words 18 through 22. The subtest is, therefore, discontinued after word 22. After the examination, checking of the responses indicates that the child should not receive credit for definitions of words 11 through 15. The application of the rule means that the child is not given credit for definitions of words 16 and 17, even though these definitions were correct, because they are words that occur *after* the discontinuance criterion has become applicable. In contrast to the scoring rule described in the previous section on "Starting Rules," this rule does not favor the child. The rule indicates that the child should not be given additional points because of the examiner's uncertainty in scoring items during the regular administration of the subtests. This rule also is an attempt to maintain standardized scoring procedures.

Repetition of items. The WISC-R manual encourages examiners to use judgment in deciding whether an "I don't know" response reflects a child's lack of knowledge or lack of desire to respond. If examiners decide that it is the latter, especially if the "I don't know" response is given to an easy question, they are encouraged to ask the question again at some later point. Credit is given if the child correctly answers the ques-

tion. This suggestion does not pertain to timed subtests or to the Digit Span subtest.

Use of probing questions and queries. The WISC-R manual encourages flexibility in administering test items. The examiner is instructed to acknowledge negativistic or mistrustful responses, for example, and to continue to probe in order to determine whether the child knows an answer. For example, if the child responds to the Comprehension question "Why are criminals locked up?" with "Society labels people criminals who shouldn't be so labeled," the examiner can say, "Well, try to give some answers that other people think are reasonable." The examiner will have to be alert in order to recognize responses that indicate a need for these kinds of probes. Probes are also required on verbal responses that are incomplete or indefinite or vague.

Spoiled responses. An explicit scoring rule on the WISC-R is that spoiled responses are scored 0. A spoiled response is one that initially was partially right, but was spoiled (i.e., an incorrect reply was given) after the child elaborated on his or her initial response. For example, the response "Goes ticktock" (for the Vocabulary word "clock") was elaborated as "It's the engine on a motorcycle." The elaboration spoiled the response, revealing the child's misconception about clocks.

Modifying standard procedures. Deviations in administering the subtests are likely to result in scores that differ from those obtained under standard administrative procedures.[10] For example, children have been found to obtain higher scores on some of the subtests when they were encouraged (a) to talk about the procedure they were using while solving the problems or (b) to think about their answers before responding or (c) to explain their picture arrangements. Children given a series of cues after failing Picture Arrangement or Block Design items were found to benefit from the extra help (Sattler, 1969). Thus such modifications, if used, should only be attempted *after* the standard administration. The results of such procedures may be helpful for clinical purposes in assessing the child's potential for learning.

Scoring WISC-R responses. Arriving at a score for some WISC-R subtests is by no means a simple matter. Judgment is important especially for handling ambiguous responses that occur on the Vocabulary, Comprehension, and Similarities subtests.[11] A careful study of the scoring criteria, scoring guidelines, and scoring examples is needed. The supplementary WISC-R scoring manual can assist one in scoring these three subtests (Massey, Sattler, & Andres, 1978).

Even authorities who have published scoring manuals do not always agree on the score to a response. In a study by Sattler, Squire, and Andres (1977), eleven scoring discrepancies were noted between the WISC-R manual and two other scoring guides for Vocabulary and Similarities words (see Table 9-9). Fortunately, however, such differences appear to be relatively few in number.

In scoring responses, some examiners are more lenient than others, and, at times, examiners may not even adhere consistently to their own relative standards (Scottish Council for Research in Education, 1967). For example, examiners who are strict on some occasions may be lenient on others. Dramatic differences in the scoring standards of examiners have been illustrated in a number of reports. In one study, ninety-nine school psychologists gave IQs ranging from 63 to 117 to the same WISC protocol (Massey, 1964). Both graduate-student examiners (Miller, Chansky, & Gredler, 1970) and members of the American Psychological Association (Miller & Chansky, 1972) have been found to vary in the scores given to WISC responses. The graduate students gave IQs ranging from 76 to 93 to the same protocol, whereas the professional raters gave IQs ranging from 78 to 95.

Extrapolated IQs. When children obtain a sum of scaled scores that is either too low or too high to allow the examiner to determine their IQ from the tables in the WISC-R manual, Table C-9 in the Appendix can be used. This table extends the IQ table down to the minimum possible sum of scaled scores and up to the maximum possible sum of scaled scores. In using Table C-9, remember that Wechsler recommends that a child's Full Scale IQ not be determined unless he or she obtains raw scores greater than 0 on at least

TABLE 9-9. Eleven Scoring Discrepancies Between WISC-R Manual and Two Scoring Guides

Subtest	Item and Response	WISC-R Score	Jastak and Jastak Score	Scottish Council Score
Vocabulary	8. donkey—"a mule"	1	2	—
	12. diamond—"can cut glass" (or "a rock or an object that can cut glass")	1	2	2
	12. diamond—"mineral"	1 (Q)	2	—
	13. gamble—"a game"	0 (Q)	1	—
	21. stanza—"a phrase"	0	1	—
	22. seclude—"opposite of include"	0	1	—
	25. belfry—"a tower"	1	2	—
Similarities	7. cat—mouse—"both pets"	1	—	2
	13. mountain—lake—"both in country"	0	—	1
	15. first—last—"places"	0 (Q)	—	1
	17. salt—water—"chemicals"	0	—	1

Reprinted with permission of the publisher and authors from J. M. Sattler, L. Squire, and J. Andres, "Scoring Discrepancies between the WISC-R Manual and Two Scoring Guides," *Journal of Clinical Psychology, 33,* p. 1059. Copyright 1977, Clinical Psychology Publishing Co., Inc.

three Verbal and three Performance Scale subtests.

The values presented in Table C-9 are for the purpose of assisting those who must use a specific intelligence quotient in their work. Clearly, the values in this table are outside the range of the children who were tested in the standardization sample. Therefore, it was necessary to extrapolate to these values using linear regression methods. *The reader should be warned that the possibility of error in extrapolations such as these may be disconcertingly large.* Nevertheless, these values may be of some use to those examining children who fall in the very low or very high IQ ranges. The examiner should also consider using another test (such as the Stanford-Binet) to evaluate children whose IQs do not fall in the range covered by the WISC-R.

Short Forms of the WISC-R

Since the publication of the WISC-R (and WISC), there has been much interest in developing short forms or abbreviated versions of the scale. The usual procedure for evaluating a short form has been to rescore complete tests; seldom have the proposed combinations been administered separately. Several methodological problems exist with short forms, including adequacy of sampling, validity, reliability, equivalence of means and agreement in intellectual classifications between short and standard forms, and methods for conversion of scores into IQs. Even short forms with high validities may misclassify individuals. Goh (1978), for example, found that a short form of the WISC-R misclassified 45 percent of a group of 142 children. In addition, short forms limit profile analysis and reduce the opportunity to observe the child's problem-solving methods.

Selecting the short form. The ten best short-form combinations of two, three, four, and five WISC-R subtests, arrived at by using the standardization data and a formula that takes into account subtest unreliability, are

shown in Table C-12 of the Appendix. Because the validities of the various short forms are high, clinical considerations can guide you in the choice of the short form. For example, when using a tetrad, you may select a combination consisting of two Verbal and two Performance Scale subtests in order to obtain some representation of both verbal and performance skills in the short form.

Converting the composite scores into Deviation Quotients. After the specific combination of subtests has been selected, it is necessary to convert the child's scores on the short form to an estimate of the Full Scale IQ. Simple prorating and regression procedures are not applicable because they do not deal adequately with the problem of subtest reliability (Tellegen & Briggs, 1967). The more acceptable procedure is to transform the short-form scores into the familiar Wechsler-type Deviation Quotient, which has a mean of 100 and a standard deviation of 15. The procedure to follow in converting the short-form scores to a Deviation Quotient is shown in Exhibit 9-2. While this approach does not eliminate the many problems associated with short forms, it does appear to provide fairly reliable IQs.

Yudin abbreviated procedure. The Yudin (1966) short form of the WISC-R consists of administering every other item on most subtests. The specific procedures, which have been modified by Silverstein (1968a), are shown in Table C-13 of the Appendix. After the test has been administered, the scaled scores and IQs are obtained from the manual in the usual way. The Yudin procedure differs from other short-form procedures in that all of the subtests are used. The advantages are that a representative sample of items is administered, scatter analysis can be applied to the examinee's scores, and the procedure uses approximately 56 percent of the items that are used in the Full Scale.

While satisfactory reliability coefficients have been reported for the Yudin procedure,[12] shortcomings also have been noted,

EXHIBIT 9-2.   Obtaining Deviation Quotients for Short Forms

The following formula is used to compute the Deviation Quotient for a short form:

Deviation Quotient = $(15/S_c)(X_c - M_c) + 100$,

where
$S_c = S_s\sqrt{n + 2\Sigma r_{jk}}$
X_c = composite score
M_c = normative mean, which is equal to $10n$
S_c = standard deviation of composite score
S_s = subtest standard deviation, which is equal to 3
n = number of component subtests
Σr_{jk} = sum of the correlations between component subtests.

This equation considers the number of subtests that were given, the correlations among the subtests, and the total scaled score points that were earned by the examinee. Table C-26 in the Appendix can assist you in calculating the Deviation Quotient. Two constants are used, with constant $a = 15/S_c$ and constant $b = 100 - n(150)/S_c$. Substituting these constants into the formula leads to the following:

Deviation Quotient = (composite score $\times a$) + b.

In using Table C-26, first select the appropriate heading corresponding to the number of subtests that are used in the short form. The first column under each heading is Σr_{jk}. This term represents the sum of the correlations between the subtests making up the composite score. To obtain Σr_{jk}, the WISC-R correlation table of the group closest in age to the examinee is used (Table 14 on pages 36 through 46 of the WISC-R manual). With two subtests in the short form, only one correlation is needed. With three subtests in the short form, three correlations are summed (1 with 2, 1 with 3, and 2 with 3). With four subtests in the short form, six correlations are summed (1 with 2,

1 with 3, 1 with 4, 2 with 3, 2 with 4, and 3 with 4). With five subtests in the short form, 10 correlations are summed (1 with 2, 1 with 3, 1 with 4, 1 with 5, 2 with 3, 2 with 4, 2 with 5, 3 with 4, 3 with 5, and 4 with 5). After Σr_{jk} is calculated, the values for the two constants are obtained under the appropriate heading.

The following steps then are needed to obtain the Deviation Quotient.

1. The scaled scores of the subtests in the short form are summed. This constitutes the composite score.
2. The correlations between the subtests are summed to obtain Σr_{jk}.
3. After Σr_{jk} is obtained, Table C-26 in the Appendix is consulted to find the appropriate a and b constants.
4. The Deviation Quotient is computed using the composite score and the a and b constants.

An example: The examiner selected a three-subtest short form composed of the Arithmetic, Vocabulary, and Block Design subtests. The examinee was 6 years old, and had obtained scaled scores of 7, 12, and 13, respectively, on the three subtests. The steps described in the previous paragraph are illustrated.

1. Summing the three scaled scores yields a composite score of 32.
2. From Table 14 (page 36) of the WISC-R manual, the correlations between the three subtests are obtained (Arithmetic and Vocabulary, .52; Arithmetic and Block Design, .47; Vocabulary and Block Design, .43). These are summed to yield 1.42 (Σr_{jk}).
3. The appropriate row in Table C-26 in the Appendix is the fourth one under the heading "3 Subtests." There we find the values for the constants a and b (2.1 and 37, respectively).
4. Using the formula Deviation Quotient = (composite score $\times a$) + b, we obtain a Deviation Quotient of (32 $\times$ 2.1) + 37 = 104. ■

such as a moderate degree of loss of validity and reliability, less reliable profile data, and IQs that differ from those obtained on the Full Scale.[13] Examiners need to consider carefully the assets and liabilities of the Yudin abbreviated procedure in deciding whether or not it should be used.

Vocabulary plus Block Design short form. A popular two-subtest combination for use as a short form for screening purposes is the Vocabulary plus Block Design subtests. These two subtests have high correlations with the Full Scale over a wide range, have consistently high reliabilities, and are good measures of *g*. If this combination is chosen, Table C-27 in the Appendix can be used to convert the sum of scaled scores on the two subtests directly to an estimate of the Full Scale IQ. This is a good screening combination (Kilian & Hughes, 1978), but should not be used for classification purposes (King & Smith, 1972).

Arithmetic, Vocabulary, Picture Arrangement, and Block Design short form. A potentially useful short form for screening purposes is composed of two Verbal Scale subtests (Arithmetic and Vocabulary) and two Performance Scale subtests (Picture Arrangement and Block Design) (Kaufman, 1976b). This short form takes longer to administer than Vocabulary plus Block Design, but provides somewhat more clinical and diagnostic information.

Comment on short forms of the WISC-R. Now that we have considered some of the factors involved in the use of short forms, a concluding comment is in order. Short forms are practical, save time, and can serve as screening devices. However, coupled with these advantages are many disadvantages. For example, the IQs obtained with short forms may be less stable than those obtained with the standard form (Baumeister, 1964). When short forms are used, information about cognitive patterning is lost. For example, the use of the Verbal Scale alone, as a quick estimate of intelligence, does not allow for the assessment of both verbal and performance abilities (Witkin, Faterson, Goodenough, & Birnbaum, 1966). When there is intersubtest scatter, the savings in time may be hazardous and expensive in terms of lost information (Burstein, 1965). Reliability of the estimated IQ is reduced when subtests are eliminated (Piotrowski, 1976).

Those interested in using short forms must consider time saved vs. the extent to which validity is lost (Levy, 1968). In addition, it is important to identify the nature of the decision that is to be made on the basis of the test scores. The most efficient testing strategy for a particular situation will depend, in part, on the goal of the evaluation—that is, whether it is for (a) a general evaluation of intelligence, (b) classification, or (c) selection.

Although it will be up to each examiner to decide on the applicability of short forms to the task at hand, it is important to understand that even when all of the subtests are administered, the IQ obtained on the WISC-R (and all other intelligence tests) is but an estimate of the different kinds of abilities possessed by a child. With small numbers of subtests, the estimate may be far less adequate than that provided by the Full Scale. *Educational and clinical situations call for more, rather than less, extensive cognitive evaluation. Therefore, examiners are encouraged to administer the Full Scale, unless there is some compelling reason to administer a short form. I do not recommend short forms for any decision-making purposes.*

Choosing Between the WISC-R and the WPPSI and Between the WISC-R and the WAIS

The WISC-R overlaps with the WPPSI for the age period 6-0-0 to 6-7-15 and overlaps with the WAIS for the age period 16-0-0 to 16-11-30. The overlap in ages between the WISC-R and the WPPSI and between the WISC-R and the WAIS will be helpful especially in retesting situations. A child first administered the WISC-R at age 6-0-0 can be retested with the WPPSI at any time during the next seven-month period. Similarly, a child tested with the WAIS at age 16-0-0 can be retested with the WISC-R up until about his or her seventeenth birthday. For these overlapping age periods, the WISC-R manual indicates that "the examiner should choose the Scale that is most appropriate for his purposes" (p. 53). However, it is difficult to see how this statement can guide the examiner's choice. In order to select a scale, we need to have some information about the advantages and disadvantages of the various scales. To this end, it would be helpful to have more studies that compare the WISC-R with the WPPSI and the WISC-R with the WAIS in their overlapping age ranges, using samples of both normal and exceptional children.

The choice of a test depends on the validity of the inferences that can be made from scores on it. In addition, the personal preferences of the examiner will likely determine which test will be used. However, the choice ought to depend on which test yields the smallest standard errors of measurement for scores at the levels obtained. Because standard errors of measurement are provided in the Wechsler manuals for age and not for ability level, the needed information is not completely available. In the case of the WISC-R vs. the WPPSI, the standard errors of measurement for the Verbal, Performance, and Full Scale IQs are smaller for the WPPSI than for the WISC-R at age 6½ years. In the case of the WISC-R vs. the WAIS, there are no standard errors of measurement provided in the WAIS manual for the 16½ age level. However, using the 18 to 19 age level for the WAIS and the 16½ age level for the WISC-R, we find that the standard errors of measurement for the Verbal, Performance, and Full Scale IQs are smaller for the WAIS than for the WISC-R.

The child's estimated level of intelligence also should be considered in selecting a test. A 6½-year-old child who obtains an IQ that is below the normal level will be administered a greater number of WPPSI items than WISC-R items (e.g., nine correct WPPSI Information items but only three correct WISC-R Information items are needed to obtain a scaled score of 5). Similarly, a 16-8-year-old child needs many more successes on the WISC-R than on the WAIS to obtain the same scaled score (e.g., thirteen correct WISC-R Information items but only five correct WAIS Information items are needed to obtain a scaled score of 5). Consequently, a more thorough sampling of ability can be obtained from the WPPSI than from the WISC-R and from the WISC-R than from the WAIS in their overlapping age ranges for children with below-normal ability. For normal and gifted children, all three tests appear to provide an adequate sampling of ability.

Administering the WISC-R (and WPPSI and WAIS-R) to Handicapped Children

Various physical abilities are necessary in order for the child to respond to each WISC-R subtest. Vision or hearing (or both) is necessary for most of the Verbal Scale subtests, while vision and arm-hand use are necessary for the Performance Scale subtests. In administering the WISC-R (and WPPSI and WAIS-R) to children with physical disabilities, attempts must be made to find ways to give the test without, in the process, providing cues to the child. However, when modifications are needed that go beyond simply permitting the child to respond in a different manner, it is likely that the results must be reinterpreted in the light of the modifications used. The point-scale format of the WISC-R (and WPPSI and WAIS-R) reduces the need to shift constantly from one test to another, thus making the WISC-R (and WPPSI and WAIS-R) more convenient than the Stanford-Binet for adaptive administration.

All of the Verbal Scale subtests can be administered orally if the children can hear. However, if they cannot hear but can read, the Information, Comprehension, Similarities, and Vocabulary questions can be typed on cards and presented one at a time. Visually presenting the Arithmetic and Digit Span items presents more difficulties because of the time limits involved in these subtests and because visual presentation of the items seems drastically different from oral presentation, especially with Digit Span items. Therefore, these two subtests may have to be omitted from the battery in testing deaf children who have reading skills. Detailed instructions for administering the Performance Scale subtests to deaf children are shown in Appendix B. If the child cannot respond orally, written replies to any of the Verbal Scale subtests can be accepted.

WISC-R (and WPPSI and WAIS-R) Performance Scale subtests require the child to have adequate vision. Adaptations, where possible, center on the child's methods of responding. The Picture Completion subtest can be given only to a child who is able to see and who can describe the missing part orally or in writing, or point to it. Block Design, Object Assembly, Coding, Mazes, Animal House, and Geometric Design are not easily adaptable when the child has severe impairment of arm-hand use. Adaptation of the Picture Arrangement subtest is possible when there is only impairment of arm-hand use. The examiner can arrange the cards in the order indicated by the child.

The distribution of the subtests into the Verbal and Performance Scales is helpful in testing handicapped children. For example, the Verbal Scale can be administered to blind children and to children with severe motor handicaps. The Performance Scale can be administered to hard-of-hearing children and to children who have little or no speech. In the case of hard-of-hearing children, if the Verbal Scale can also be administered, a comparison between the two scales may reveal the extent of the child's verbal deficit.

Without empirical findings there is no way of knowing how the suggested modifications affect the reliability and validity of the subtest scores. Yet, when standard procedures cannot be used because sensory handicaps prevent the child from comprehending the instructions, modifications in instructions should be considered. *When modifications are used, the resulting score should be considered only as a rough estimate of the child's intelligence.*

Speed of correct response on the WISC-R Picture Arrangement, Block Design, and Object Assembly subtests is related significantly to chronological age and to problem-solving ability (Kaufman, 1979b). Older children solve the tasks more quickly than younger children, and those who solve the problems quickly also tend to solve more problems than those who solve the problems slowly. Speed plays only a limited role in enabling children below 10 years of age to earn bonus points. Therefore, Kaufman suggested that it is reasonable to administer these subtests to orthopedically handicapped children who are able to manipulate

the materials and who are between 6 and 10 years of age, because they would not be unduly penalized for failure to earn bonus points.

Assets of the WISC-R

The WISC-R is an extremely well-standardized test, with excellent reliability and adequate validity. It continues in the tradition of the WISC and other Wechsler scales (e.g., WAIS and WPPSI) by dividing the twelve subtests into two sections and providing three IQs—Verbal, Performance, and Full Scale. This procedure is especially helpful in clinical work and aids in the assessment of brain-behavior relationships. A valuable feature of the scale is that all children take a comparable battery of subtests.

1. *Good validity.* The WISC-R, as we have seen, has adequate validity using a variety of ability and achievement measures.
2. *High reliabilities.* The reliabilities of the WISC-R Full Scale IQs are extremely high (average r_{11} of .96), with standard errors of measurement of the IQs on the three scales being less than 5 points. The WISC-R manual, by providing reliability data, standard errors of measurement, and intercorrelations of subtest scores by one-year age intervals as well as for the average of the eleven age groups, permits evaluation of the scale's properties throughout its entire age range. This procedure allows confidence intervals to be established for IQs for each of the eleven separate age groups, thereby providing estimates that are specifically applicable to each child's chronological age level.
3. *Excellent standardization.* The standardization procedures were excellent, sampling four geographic regions, both sexes, white and nonwhite populations, urban and rural residents, and the entire range of socioeconomic classes.
4. *Good administration procedures.* The prescribed procedures for administering the WISC-R are excellent. Examiners actively probe the child's responses in order

to evaluate the breadth of the child's knowledge and determine whether the child really knows the answer. On items that require two reasons for maximum credit, the child is asked for another reason when only one reason is given. These procedures do not penalize children for not understanding the demands of the questions. The emphasis on probing questions and queries is extremely desirable.

5. *Good manual.* The WISC-R manual is easy to use; it provides clear directions and tables. Reading of the directions is facilitated by the fact that the examiner's instructions are in a different color from the other information in the manual. Helpful abbreviations are provided for recording the child's responses, such as "Q" for Question, "DK" for Don't Know, "Inc." for Incomplete, and "NR" for No Response. The test materials are interesting to children.

6. *Helpful scoring criteria.* The criteria for scoring replies have been carefully prepared. The Similarities and Vocabulary scoring guidelines, for example, detail the rationale for use of 2, 1, and 0 scores and are accompanied by a number of examples that demonstrate the application of the principles. Many typical responses are scored, and those deemed to need further inquiry are indicated by a "Q." A study of the scoring sections will aid examiners not only in scoring responses but also in administering the scale.

Limitations of the WISC-R

The WISC-R, as we have seen, is an excellent instrument, yet there are a number of difficulties with the test and with the manual that should be recognized.

1. *Limited applicability of norms for children younger than 6 years, 4 months of age and for children older than 16 years, 8 months of age.* One of the major questions about the WISC-R concerns the applicability of the norms for children 6-0 to 6-3 years of age and for those between 16-8 and 16-11 years of age. In standardizing

the WISC-R, the only children tested were those whose birthdates were at midyear, plus or minus 1.5 months. Consequently, at the 6-year-old age level, no children were included who were between 6 years, 0 months of age and 6 years, 3 months of age. (A footnote on page 48 of the WISC-R manual indicates that there was a small norms group [$N = 50$] at age 6 years, 0 months, and this group was used as a guide in extrapolating norms for the 6-0 to 6-3 age group.) The same type of gap occurs for children between 16 years, 8 months of age and 16 years, 11 months of age. Nevertheless, the WISC-R manual presents norms for these two three-month age periods. Therefore, the standardized normative scores, arrived at by extrapolation, may not yield correct results for these two age groups.

2. *Limited floor and ceiling.* Another difficulty with the WISC-R is that the range of Full Scale IQs (40 to 160) is insufficient both for severely retarded children and for extremely gifted children. The test is designed so that a 6-year-old child receives up to three scaled-score points for having given *no* correct answers for some subtests. Throughout the entire age range of the test, children receive at least one scaled-score point on every subtest, even though they have a raw score of zero. Wechsler recognized that this can be a problem in computing IQs and therefore recommended that IQs for each scale be computed only when the child obtains a raw score greater than zero on at least three of the subtests on each of the scales. Similarly, a Full Scale IQ should not be computed unless raw scores greater than zero are obtained on three Verbal and three Performance subtests. However, these are only recommendations and must be considered as such until validity data show that other procedures for computing IQs are not valid.

Following Wechsler's recommended procedure, let us determine what the lowest possible IQ would be for a 6-year-old child. Let us say that the child obtained raw scores of 1 on the Information, Vocabulary, Comprehension, Picture Completion, Object Assembly, and Coding subtests and a raw score of zero on each of the remaining four subtests. The resulting IQs would be as follows: Verbal Scale IQ = 57 (15 scaled-score points), Performance Scale IQ = 48 (11 scaled-score points), and Full Scale IQ = 48 (26 scaled-score points). Six 1-point successes thus yielded an IQ of 48. Therefore the WISC-R may not provide precise IQs for young children who are functioning at two or more standard deviations below the mean of the scale. Even for IQs between 70 and 80 only a very small sample of a child's ability is tested because so few items are administered. The test provides a sparse sample of the abilities of children of limited intelligence in the lower age ranges of the scale.

The highest IQ that can be obtained by children aged 16 years, 8 months and older is 158, a ceiling score that probably is too low to make the test appropriate for use with extremely gifted children.

3. *Nonuniformity of scaled scores.* The range of scaled scores on all subtests is not uniform throughout the age range covered by the scale. It is only in the 6-through 10-year age range that children can receive up to 19 scaled-score points on all subtests. After 10 years of age it is not possible for a child to receive 19 scaled-score points on some subtests. For example, at age 11 years, the highest raw score on the Arithmetic subtest (18 points) receives a scaled score of 18. At age 16 years, 8 months, this same raw score receives a scaled score of 16. On only five of the twelve subtests can children aged 16 years, 8 months and older receive the highest scaled score. The lack of uniformity of available scaled scores throughout the entire age range makes scatter analytic techniques more difficult to apply to the profiles of older gifted children.

Scatter analytic techniques can be applied appropriately throughout the entire range of scaled scores for five subtests only (Similarities, Vocabulary, Digit Span, Picture Arrangement, and Coding); for older gifted children they can be ap-plied only when all scaled scores are 16 or below. *It would be dangerous and misleading to apply scatter analytic techniques uniformly to all subtests for individual cases because the same number of scaled-score points cannot be obtained on all subtests.*

4. *Difficulty in scoring responses.* When responses on the Similarities, Comprehension, and Vocabulary subtests differ from those that appear in the WISC-R manual, they are difficult to score. Such difficulties may lead to halo effects in scoring and contribute to examiner bias (cf. Sattler & Ryan, 1973b).

5. *Difficulty in interpreting norms when a supplementary subtest is substituted for a regular subtest.* With the norms based on the ten regular subtests only, there is no way of knowing precisely what the scores mean when one of the supplementary subtests (Digit Span or Mazes) is substituted for a regular subtest. A substitution of this kind, therefore, should be made only in unusual circumstances and the results labeled "tentative" when the scores are reported.

6. *No normative data for raw scores.* The WISC-R manual fails to give means, standard deviations, and frequency distributions for the raw scores.

7. *Failure to describe procedure for establishing cutoff criteria.* The WISC-R manual fails to provide information concerning how the cutoff criteria were determined (i.e., empirically or intuitively).

Concluding Comment on the WISC-R

The WISC-R has been well received by those who use tests to evaluate children's intellectual ability. It has excellent standardization, reliability, and validity, and much care has been taken to provide useful administrative and scoring guidelines. While some minor problems exist in the WISC-R manual, it is, on the whole, excellent. A valuable addition to the manual would have been data about the standard errors of measurement of IQ scores on the Verbal, Performance, and Full Scales at IQ levels of 70,

100, and 130 (if not others). The WISC-R will serve as a valuable instrument in the assessment of children's intelligence for many years to come.

Summary

1. Twenty-five years after its original publication, the WISC was revised. The new scale, the WISC-R, is similar to its predecessor, with 72 percent of the items retained, plus the same Coding subtest stimuli. The WISC-R is applicable to children from 6-0-0 to 16-11-30 years of age. Standardization of the scale was excellent, and included both white and nonwhite children.

2. Although Wechsler objected to the use of mental ages in the calculation of IQs, he included a table of test-age equivalents for the scaled scores in the WISC-R manual.

3. The WISC-R provides Deviation IQs for the Verbal, Performance, and Full Scales, with a mean of 100 and standard deviation of 15. The norms for the twelve subtests also are standard scores, with a mean of 10 and standard deviation of 3.

4. The reliabilities of the Verbal, Performance, and Full Scales are excellent (average of .94, .90, and .96, respectively), with a standard error of measurement for the Full Scale of about 3 IQ points. Subtest reliabilities range from .70 to .86.

5. Practice effects (after a one-month test-retest interval) are about 10 IQ points on the Performance Scale, 4 IQ points on the Verbal Scale, and 7 IQ points on the Full Scale.

6. The WISC-R has acceptable concurrent validity. Median correlations with selected cognitive measures are as follows: .88 with the WPPSI, .95 with the WAIS, .82 with the Stanford-Binet, .61 with the Slosson Intelligence Test, .58 with the PPVT, .68 with the McCarthy Scales of Children's Abilities, .76 with the Quick Test, and .66 with group-administered tests.

7. The WISC-R tends to provide lower IQs than the WPPSI and the WAIS. The various Wechsler scales do not appear to provide interchangeable IQs.

8. The WISC-R has acceptable validity using as criteria (a) achievement tests, with median correlations between .56 and .60, and (b) school grades, with a median correlation of .39.

9. Normative changes on the WISC-R Coding subtest indicate that for the equivalent performance children usually obtain lower scaled scores than on the WISC Coding.

10. A study of WISC-R IQs in relation to various stratification variables showed the following: (a) mean differences between girls and boys were less than 3 points; (b) white children obtained higher IQs than black children by about 1 standard deviation (102 vs. 86); (c) children in the highest parental occupation group had a mean IQ that was on the average 21 points higher than that of those in the lowest parental occupation group (108 vs. 87); (d) urban-rural differences were small; and (e) geographic region differences were largest between the west and the south (103 vs. 96).

11. A factor analysis of the WISC-R standardization data indicated that three factors account for the scale's structure: Verbal Comprehension, Perceptual Organization, and Freedom from Distractibility. The Verbal Scale subtests load primarily on Verbal Comprehension; Performance Scale subtests load primarily on Perceptual Organization; and Arithmetic, Digit Span, and Coding load primarily on Freedom from Distractibility. The best subtests of g are four Verbal Scale subtests—Vocabulary, Information, Similarities, and Comprehension—and one Performance Scale subtest—Block Design.

12. Because most WISC-R subtests have an adequate degree of subtest specificity, interpretation of profiles of subtest scores generally is on firm ground.

13. The Deviation IQs associated with the Verbal and Performance Scale IQs can be used as factor scores. Somewhat purer factor scores can be obtained by using Information, Similarities, Vocabulary, and Comprehension for the Verbal Comprehension factor and Picture Completion, Picture Arrangement, Block Design, and Object Assembly for the Perceptual Organization factor. The three subtests that comprise Freedom from Distractibility also provide a factor score.

14. Examiners should try to develop proper administrative procedures early in their career.

15. Beginning examiners tend to make a variety of errors, including improper completion of the record booklet, failure to adhere to directions, failure to probe ambiguous responses, and giving items beyond the discontinuance points.

16. It is recommended that, except in unusual cases, the standard order of administering the subtests be followed.

17. The WISC-R manual describes a number of administrative procedures that must be followed carefully in order to ensure standardized scoring. These procedures, in part, concern items that are failed below the entry point and items that are passed above the discontinuance point. If the entry-point items are passed, credit is given to items failed below the entry-point items. Contrariwise, no credit is given to items passed above the discontinuance-point items.

18. The WISC-R requires the use of many probing questions and queries. Spoiled responses are scored 0.

19. Modifications in test procedures have been found to increase children's scores. Any modifications, if used, should be administered after the standard administration.

20. Scoring WISC-R Vocabulary, Comprehension, and Similarities subtests requires considerable skill. A careful study of the scoring criteria is needed to reduce errors in scoring.

21. Extrapolated IQs present serious problems because of the possibility of error in determining the IQ. However, if IQs are needed for a sum of scaled scores that is not shown in the WISC-R manual, Table C-9 in the Appendix can be consulted.

22. Short forms of the WISC-R, while practical, have serious disadvantages associated with them. IQs may be less stable, scatter analysis is difficult, and many misclassifications may result. If short forms are needed for screening purposes, the procedures advocated by Tellegen and Briggs should be followed to overcome some of the statistical problems associated with short forms. Table C-12 in the Appendix shows the best combinations of two, three, four, and five WISC-R subtests. Other tables in the Appendix also provide information about short forms.

23. The WISC-R and WPPSI can be viewed as alternate forms for children aged 6-0 to 6-7 years, and the WISC-R and WAIS for children aged 16-0 to 16-11 years. Although the choice of a test in the overlapping age groups will likely depend on the examiner's personal preference, the WPPSI is preferred to the WISC-R while the WISC-R is preferred to the WAIS for below-normal-ability children. In the overlapping age levels, the standard errors of measurement are smaller for WPPSI IQs than for WISC-R IQs and smaller (perhaps) for WAIS IQs than for WISC-R IQs.

24. Hearing is necessary for most of the WISC-R Verbal Scale subtests, although vision may be used as a substitute modality for some subtests. Arm-hand use is a prerequisite for almost all of the Performance Scale subtests, although some adaptations are possible. The Verbal and Performance Scale arrangement of the subtests facilitates the selection of scales for testing handicapped children. Special procedures, which are described in the chapter, are usually needed in administering the Performance Scale to deaf children.

25. The assets of the WISC-R include its excellent reliability, validity, and standardization; good administrative procedures; good manual; and helpful scoring criteria.

26. The limitations of the WISC-R include the limited applicability of norms for ages 6-0 to 6-3 years and for ages 16-8 to 16-11 years, limited range of IQs (40 to 160), nonuniformity of scaled scores, difficulty in scoring some subtests, difficulty in interpreting norms when a supplementary subtest is substituted, lack of normative data for raw scores, and failure to describe procedures for establishing cutoff criteria.

27. Overall, the WISC-R represents a major contribution to the field of intelligence testing of children. It serves as one of the most important instruments for the evaluation of children's intelligence.

10

WISC-R Subtests

The true art of memory is the art of attention.

SAMUEL JOHNSON

This chapter focuses on each of the twelve WISC-R subtests. A brief description is given of each subtest, followed by its interpretative rationale, factor analytic findings, reliability and intercorrelational highlights, and administrative considerations. (All factor analytic findings are from Kaufmann, 1975a and 1979c). The abilities measured by each subtest, background factors influencing performance, implications of high and low scores, and suggested training activities to improve scores on each subtest are summarized in Table C-15 in the Appendix. Table C-15 is a useful guide for report writing and deserves careful study and evaluation. Readers interested in the Structure-of-Intellect classifications can refer to Table C-14 in the Appendix. The supplementary scoring guide by Massey, Sattler, and Andres (1978) also presents many additional responses to help in scoring the Similarities, Vocabulary, and Comprehension subtests.

Many of the subtests have an adequate degree of subtest specificity (see Chapter 9) and therefore are likely to provide reliable estimates of some specific abilities. The most reliable estimates of specific abilities employ combinations of individual subtests. For example, the Verbal Scale IQ, which is derived from a combination of five subtests, yields more accurate data about a child's verbal skills than does a single subtest score, such as the Vocabulary scaled score.

As part of the administrative considerations, a number of questions are posed for some subtests to aid you in observing the child's performance. The answers to these questions, as well as to similar ones that appear in other chapters of this text, will serve as a data base for the testing of clinical hypotheses once the test is completed. You may not have many specific questions in mind at the beginning of the testing, but you will (or should) at the end. Therefore, you will have to make as complete a record as possible in order to be able to answer any questions that may arise.

Information

The Information subtest contains thirty questions which sample a broad range of general knowledge. The subtest is started at

different points, depending on the child's age. Children aged 6 to 7 years are started with item 1; 8 to 10 years, item 5; 11 to 13 years, item 7; and 14 to 16 years, item 11. All items are scored 1 or 0 (pass-fail), and the subtest is discontinued after five consecutive failures.

The questions usually can be answered with a simply stated fact. Correct answers may be brief. Children simply must demonstrate whether or not they have these facts at their command; they need not find relationships between facts.

Rationale. The amount of knowledge children possess may depend on their natural endowment, the extent of their education (both formal and informal), and their cultural opportunities and predilections (cf. Rapaport et al., 1968). In general, the Information subtest samples the kind of knowledge that average children with average opportunity should be able to acquire for themselves (cf. Matarazzo, 1972). The child's responses provide clues about the child's general range of information, alertness to the environment, and even social or cultural background. High scores should not be interpreted as indications of mental effi-

ciency and competence, since individuals may acquire isolated facts without being able to use them appropriately or effectively (Taylor, 1961). However, intellectual drive may account for high scores. The type of memory required for successful performance on the Information subtest involves memory primarily based on habitual, overlearned responses, especially in the case of older children.

Factor analytic findings. The Information subtest ties with Similarities as the second-best measure of *g* (58 percent of its variance may be attributed to *g*). The subtest has an ample amount of subtest specificity to permit specific interpretation of its functions. The Information subtest contributes substantially to the Verbal Comprehension factor (median loading of .63).

Reliability and correlational highlights. Information is a reliable subtest ($r_{11} = .85$) and correlates more highly with Vocabulary ($r = .69$) than with any other subtest. It has a moderate correlation with the Full Scale ($r = .70$) and with the Verbal Scale ($r = .74$), but a somewhat low correlation with the Performance Scale ($r = .56$).

Administrative considerations. The Information subtest is easy to administer. The questions are simple and direct, and timing is not required. Credit should be given to the examinee if questions are answered correctly at any time during the course of administering the scale (Rapaport et al., 1968). Scoring usually, but not always, proves to be straightforward. A correct response receives 1 point; an incorrect response, 0. The examinee should always be asked to decide on the best answer whenever two or more answers, one of which is ambiguous or incorrect, are given to the question. Answers should be recorded verbatim.

If children are hesitant to respond, they should be encouraged to guess or take a chance. Note the quality of their answers. Are they precise or wordy, well thought out or simply a guess? Responses that are overly long and filled with information beyond that required by the demands of the question are suggestive of an obsessive-compulsive orientation—children may feel compelled to show the examiner how much they know. Or an ostentatious display of knowledge may simply reflect the examinee's desire to impress the examiner by showing his or her breadth of knowledge. Which interpretation is appropriate should be decided on by considering the child's entire test protocol and other relevant information. Inhibition, too, may be noted. For example, a child may not be able to recall an answer because the question may be associated with conflict-laden material.

Similarities

The Similarities subtest contains seventeen pairs of words; the child must explain the similarity within each pair. All children begin with the first item. The first four items are scored 1 or 0 (pass-fail), while items 5 through 17 are scored 2, 1, or 0, depending on the conceptual level of the response. The subtest is discontinued after three consecutive failures.

Rationale. At one level, the questions on the Similarities subtest require children to perceive the common elements of the terms they are asked to compare. At another level, they must be able to bring these common elements together in a concept. The latter ability, termed "concept formation," is an ability to place objects and events together in a meaningful group or groups; thus, the Similarities subtest may measure the ability for verbal concept formation (or abstract thinking ability). While concept formation can be a voluntary, effortful process, it can also reflect well-automatized verbal conventions (Rapaport et al., 1968). Performance on the Similarities subtest also may be related to cultural opportunities and to interest patterns. In addition, memory may be involved.

Factor analytic findings. The Similarities subtest ties with Information as the second-best measure of g (58 percent of its variance may be attributed to g). The subtest has ample subtest specificity for ages $6\frac{1}{2}$, $7\frac{1}{2}$, and $8\frac{1}{2}$ years, but not for ages above $8\frac{1}{2}$ years. Thus, specific interpretation of the subtest's functions is appropriate only for the three earliest ages. The Similarities subtest contributes substantially to the Verbal Comprehension factor (median loading of .64), making it interpretable as a measure of verbal comprehension.

Reliability and correlational highlights. Similarities is a reliable subtest ($r_{11} = .81$) and correlates more highly with Vocabulary ($r = .67$) and with Information ($r = .62$) than with any other subtests. It has a moderate correlation with the Full Scale ($r = .71$) and with the Verbal Scale ($r = .72$), but a somewhat low correlation with the Performance Scale ($r = .58$).

Administrative considerations. Responses to the first four questions are generally easy to score, while those for items 5–17 are more difficult. For items 5–17, a higher conceptual response (e.g., general classification) receives a 2, a more concrete response (e.g., specific property of the item) receives a 1, and an incorrect response receives a 0. That the items on the Similarities subtest are difficult to score is shown by a study of 187 ambiguous WISC-R Similarities (and Vocabulary and Comprehension) responses (Sattler, Andres, Squire, Wisely, & Maloy, 1978). At least 80 percent of the experienced psychologists and graduate students participating agreed on the scoring of only 51 percent of the responses. Scoring difficulties, in part, arise from the limited number of examples in the manual and from the difficulty in establishing precise criteria that can be applied to a vast variety of responses, some of which may be highly idiosyncratic. However, a careful study of the scoring guide will help you become more proficient in scoring.

Be sure to note whether the child understands the task. Children who state that they do not know the answer to a question should be encouraged to think about the question, but as in any subtest, the child should not be pressed unreasonably. When many responses are given to one question, examinees should be asked to select the response that they think best represents the essential similarity (e.g., "Tell me the one best way in which they are alike"). The score should be based on this answer.

When the child gives a 1-point answer to items 5 or 6 (or both), tell the child the 2-point answer, in order to encourage the child to give 2-point responses on later items. Give the child the correct answers to items 1 and 2 when the child fails either or both of these items.

Two parts of Appendix A in the WISC-R manual ("Scoring Criteria" for the Similarities subtest) need careful study. First, the general scoring principles, which elucidate the rationale for 2, 1, and 0 scores, should be thoroughly mastered. Second, the "Sample Responses" section, which lists many responses that should be queried, as shown by a "(Q)," should be studied carefully so that this type of response can be recognized readily.

Responses to the Similarities subtest may provide insight into the logical character of the child's thinking processes. The scoring takes into account whether or not the responses are essential likenesses (2 points) or superficial likenesses (1 point). Observe the child's typical level of conceptualization throughout the subtest. Are the answers on a concrete, functional, or abstract level? Concrete answers refer to qualities of the objects (or stimuli) that can typically be seen or touched (apple-banana: "Both have a skin"). Functional answers typically concern a function or use of the objects (apple-banana: "Give you energy"). Finally, abstract answers typically refer to a more universal property or to a common classification of the objects (apple-banana: "Both fruits").

A 2-point response, while on an abstract level, may not necessarily reflect the examinee's ability to perform at an abstract level of thinking. A 2-point response may simply be a conventional, perhaps overlearned response. There is a difference between the 2-point response "Both fruits" for apple-banana and the 2-point response "Social qualities" for liberty-justice. The former may be a conventional response, whereas the latter is likely to reflect a more abstract level of conceptualizing ability.

Also observe how the examinee handles frustration that may be induced by the subtest questions. Is the examinee negativistic and uncooperative, or is there a genuine inability to see the similarity involved? Responses such as "They are not alike" may be an indication of (a) negativism, (b) an attempt to avoid the task demands, (c) suspiciousness, (d) a coping mechanism, or (e) a failure to know the answer. Try to determine the reasons for the response. Compare the style of responding on the Similarities subtest with that on other subtests.

Arithmetic

The Arithmetic subtest contains eighteen orally presented problems, many of which are similar to ones often faced by children. Children are required to give their answers without using paper and pencil. The child's age determines where the subtest is started. Children aged 6 to 7 years (and older children suspected of mental retardation) are started with item 1; 8 to 10 years, item 5; 11 to 13 years, item 8; and 14 to 16 years, item 10. All of the problems are timed, with the first thirteen items having a thirty-second time limit; items 14 and 15, a forty-five-second time limit; and items 16 to 18, a seventy-five-second time limit. All items are scored 1 or 0, with the exception of items 2 and 3, which also can be given ½ point. The subtest is discontinued after three consecutive failures.

The problems on the Arithmetic subtest reflect various kinds of skills. Problems 1, 2, and 3 require direct counting of concrete quantities. Problems 4, 6, 7, 8, 9, 11, and 12 require simple addition or subtraction. Problems 5, 13, and 15 involve simple division. Problem 10 involves multiplication. Problems 14, 16, 17, and 18 require automatized number facts and subtle operations, such as immediately seeing relevant relationships at a glance. In problems 13 and 15, the answers may come intuitively to children experienced with facts, while for children who have not yet automatized simple arithmetic facts, the problems may require reflection and mental operation (cf. Taylor, 1961).

Rationale. The problems on the Arithmetic subtest require the child to follow verbal directions, to concentrate on selected parts of the questions, and to use numerical operations. In order to solve the problems, children must have knowledge of the basic arithmetical operations of addition, subtraction, multiplication, and division. The emphasis of the problems is not on mathematical knowledge per se, but on mental computation and concentration. Concentration is especially necessary for complex problems.

The Arithmetic subtest measures the ability to solve arithmetical problems (numerical reasoning ability). The subtest requires the use of noncognitive functions (concentration and attention) in conjunction with cognitive functions (knowledge of numerical operations). Success on the subtest is influenced by education, interests, fluctuations of attention, and transient emotional reactions. Like Vocabulary and Information, Arithmetic depends on memory and prior learning; however, it requires concentration to a greater extent than Vocabulary and Information and the active application of select skills to cope with new and unique situations (Blatt & Allison, 1968).

Factor analytic findings. The Arithmetic subtest is a fair measure of g (42 percent of its variance may be attributed to g). The subtest has an ample amount of subtest specificity to permit specific interpretation of its functions. Arithmetic has a high loading on the Freedom from Distractibility factor (median loading of .58) and a moderate loading on the Verbal Comprehension factor (median loading of .37).

Reliability and correlational highlights. Arithmetic is a somewhat reliable subtest ($r_{11} = .77$) and correlates more highly with Information ($r = .54$) and Vocabulary ($r = .52$) than with the other subtests. It has a somewhat low correlation with the Full Scale ($r = .58$) and Verbal Scale ($r = .58$), and a low correlation with the Performance Scale ($r = .48$).

Administrative considerations. The last three Arithmetic items appear in the Picture Completion/Block Design booklet. If examinees need additional time to complete the problems, let them have it. The time elapsed from the expiration of the time limit until the solution of the problem should be recorded. While a correct response after the time limit has expired does not receive credit, such information is important in attempting to differentiate between failures due to "temporary inefficiency" and those due to limited knowledge. Successful performance after the time limit has expired may indicate temporary inefficiency or a slow, painstaking approach to problems. Inquiry about the failures after the test is completed may also help to determine the reasons for failure (e.g., poor knowledge of arithmetical operations, inadequate conceptualization of the problem, temporary inefficiency or anxiety, poor concentration, or carelessness). Another testing-of-limits procedure—allowing the child to use paper and pencil—may shed further light upon the child's arithmetical knowledge.

Vocabulary

In the Vocabulary subtest, which consists of thirty-two words arranged in order of increasing difficulty, the child is asked to explain orally the meaning of each word (e.g.,"What is a _____?" or "What does _____ mean?"). The subtest is started at different points, depending on the child's age. Children aged 6 to 7 years (and older children suspected of mental retardation) are started with item 1; 8 to 10 years, item 4; 11 to 14 years, item 6; and 14 to 16 years, item 8. All words are scored 2, 1, or 0. The subtest is discontinued after five consecutive failures.

Rationale. The Vocabulary subtest, a test of word knowledge, may involve a variety of cognitive functions or features—including learning ability, fund of information, richness of ideas, memory, concept formation, and language development—that may be closely related to the child's experiences and educational environment. The number of words known by children likely reflects their ability to learn and to accumulate information. The subtest provides an excellent estimate of intellectual capacity. Performance on the subtest is stable over time and relatively resistant to neurological deficit and psychological disturbance (Blatt & Allison, 1968). Vocabulary is valuable in deriving an index of the examinee's general mental ability.

Factor analytic findings. The Vocabulary subtest is the best measure of *g* in the scale (64 percent of its variance may be attributed to *g*). The subtest has an adequate amount of subtest specificity across the entire age range to permit specific interpretation of its functions. The Vocabulary subtest contributes substantially to the Verbal Comprehension factor (median loading of .72).

Reliability and correlational highlights. Vocabulary is the most reliable subtest ($r_{11} = .86$) in the scale. It correlates more highly with Information ($r = .69$), Similarities ($r = .67$), and Comprehension ($r = .66$) than with the other subtests. It has a moderate correlation with the Full Scale ($r = .74$) and with the Vebal Scale ($r = .68$), and a somewhat low correlation with the Performance Scale ($r = .58$).

Administrative considerations. Care should be taken to pronounce each word clearly and correctly. While this suggestion holds for all subtests, it is especially important on the Vocabulary subtest because the stimuli (or questions) consist of one key word only and the word cannot be spelled for the child. It is important to record carefully the examinee's responses to the words.

A careful qualitative analysis of the children's responses to the Vocabulary subtest may tell us something about their background, cultural milieu, social development, life experiences, responses to frustration, and thought processes. Inquiry is especially important whenever peculiar responses, mispronunciations, and peculiar inflections are given. The basis for the examinee's incorrect responses should be determined, since it is important to distinguish among the many possible types of responses, including, for example, guesses, clang associations, idiosyncratic associations, or bizarre associations. In children with late-onset psychosis or early infantile autism, language disturbances occasionally can be seen in word definitions (see Chapter 23 for a discussion of childhood psychosis).

The nature of the response should determine whether or not the inquiry occurs during or after the standard administration. For example, if the answer is clearly in response to a homonym, repeat the question by saying "What does _____ also mean?" However, if the response is possibly indicative of disordered thinking, further probing of the response should be delayed until the standardized portion of the testing has been completed. During the testing-of-limits phase you might say, "To the word _____ you said _____. I wonder if you could tell me about your answer."

The following guides, presented by Taylor (1961), are useful for observing and evaluating responses to the Vocabulary subtest.

Note all responses, whether correct or not. Note whether the child is familiar with the word or whether he knows only about in which area it might belong. If he explains a word, does he try to find one description or definition only, does he try to be precise and brief or does he embark on lengthy explanations? Does he keep it objective or does he get involved in relating personal experiences? Note whether he thinks he knows the word but confuses it with another that sounds like it to him. If he does not know the word, does he try to guess its meaning? Is he ready to say, "I do not know" and try to shake off further demands, or is he puzzled? Note whether or not showing him the word printed helps him to recognize it.

Watch for possible hearing difficulties; listen carefully how he repeats the word, if he does. Has he heard it correctly or with some distortion? Note how he expresses himself. Does he find it easy or difficult to say what he means? Does he have mechanical difficulties getting words said properly or does he seem uncertain about how best to express what he thinks? Does he use gestures to help him illustrate his statements or does he even depend on them exclusively?

Note the content of his definitions. Does he choose a synonym for the stimulus word ["Thief"—"a burglar"], or does he describe an action ["Thief"—"takes stuff"]? Does he describe some special feature ("Donkey"—"it has four legs"), or does he try to fit it into some category ("Donkey"—"a living creature that is kept in some kind of enclosure or in a special building called a barn")?

Note any emotional overtones, personal experiences or feelings ["Alphabet"—"I hate to write"]. [p. 485]

The scoring system (2, 1, or 0 for all words) takes into account the quality of the response. While, in general, any recognized meaning of the word is acceptable, disregarding elegance of expression, poverty of content (e.g., a response indicating vague knowledge of what the word means) results in a lowered score. Two points are awarded to answers that are a good synonym, a major use, or a general classification, while one point is given for a vague response, a less pertinent synonym, or a minor use.

Vocabulary is one of the more difficult subtests to score. Often it is not easy to implement Wechsler's criteria for scoring the responses. In the study by Sattler et al. (1978), 80 percent of the raters gave the same score to only 38 percent of the 352 ambiguous Vocabulary responses that were

used in the task. You are encouraged to probe borderline responses and to study carefully the scoring guide in the WISC-R manual. These sources will help you to resolve some of the scoring problems that arise in the course of administering the subtest, but not all problems. You must try to do the best job possible with the available guides.

In administering the first word of the Vocabulary subtest give the 2-point answer when young children or older children suspected of mental retardation give a 0- or 1-point response. This procedure, designed to encourage 2-point responses, is not followed on subsequent items. Responses suggestive of regionalism or slang should be probed further (e.g., "Give me another meaning for _____"). The "Sample Responses" section of Appendix B of the WISC-R manual, which lists many responses that should be queried, as shown by a "(Q)," should be studied carefully so that this kind of response can be recognized readily.

The Vocabulary subtest, together with Block Design, can be used to estimate intelligence in research studies and in clinical screening batteries. (See Chapter 9 for further discussion of the Vocabulary plus Block Design short form and see Table C-27 in the Appendix for the estimated Full Scale Deviation IQs for this short form.)

Comprehension

The Comprehension subtest consists of seventeen questions that deal with a variety of problem situations, involving subjects such as one's body, interpersonal relations, and social mores. All children begin the subtest with the first item, and all items are scored 2, 1, or 0. The subtest is discontinued after four consecutive failures.

Rationale. The Comprehension subtest involves comprehending given situations and providing answers to specific problems. Success depends, in part, on possession of a certain amount of practical information plus an ability to draw on past experiences in reaching solutions to a variety of situations. Responses, in part, reflect the child's knowledge of conventional standards of behavior, extensiveness of cultural opportunities, and development of conscience or moral sense. Success suggests that the child has social judgment or common sense and a grasp of social conventionality. These skills imply an ability to use facts in a pertinent, meaningful, and emotionally appropriate manner.

Factor analytic findings. The Comprehension subtest is a good measure of *g* (52 percent of its variance may be attributed to *g*). The subtest has an adequate amount of subtest specificity across the entire age range to permit specific interpretation of its functions. The Comprehension subtest has a high loading on the Verbal Comprehension factor (median loading of .64).

Reliability and correlational highlights. Comprehension is a somewhat reliable subtest ($r_{11} = .77$) and correlates more highly with Vocabulary ($r = .66$) and Similarities ($r = .59$) than with the other subtests. It has a moderate correlation with the Full Scale ($r = .66$) and with the Verbal Scale ($r = .68$), and a somewhat low correlation with the Performance Scale ($r = .53$).

Administrative considerations. The Comprehension subtest is difficult to score because children give a variety of responses that differ from those found in the manual. The difficulty in scoring Comprehension responses has been shown in the Sattler et al. (1978) study where 80 percent of the raters gave the same score to only 49 percent of the 187 ambiguous Comprehension responses that were used in the study.

The most complete or best response receives a 2; a less adequate response, a 1; and an incorrect response, a 0. If inquiry into a response receiving credit alters the meaning of that response, the initial response, not the reply to the inquiry, determines the amount of credit given (Rapaport et al., 1968).

In administering the Comprehension subtest, for the first item only, when children do not give a 2-point response, tell them the 2-point answer. This procedure is designed to encourage children to give 2-point responses. On the nine items (3, 4, 7, 8, 9, 12, 14, 16, and 17) that require two ideas for full credit (2 points), you are required to ask for a second idea when children give only one idea. Consequently, children are not routinely penalized when they do not give two reasons. However, on other items where an adequate 1-idea answer will gain 2 points, obvious 1-point responses should not be probed in an attempt to make them 2-point responses.

Study carefully the "Sample Responses" section of Appendix C of the WISC-R manual so that you will know what responses need further inquiry "(Q)". The examples indicate that many 0- and 1-point responses should be queried. (When the 2-point responses include a "(Q)," it indicates that the entire response [including the elaboration] is worth 2 points.) The additional queries offer you an opportunity to evaluate more thoroughly the extensiveness of the child's knowledge.

Responses to the Comprehension questions may be especially valuable in providing information about the child's personality style and social and cultural background. Unlike the Information questions, which usually elicit precise answers, the Comprehension questions may elicit more complex and idiosyncratic replies. Because the questions, in part, require or involve judgment of social situations, answers may reflect the child's attitudes. Some responses reveal understanding *and* acceptance of social mores, whereas others reveal understanding *but not* acceptance of social mores. Knowledge of social mores does not automatically mean that such knowledge will be carried out into action. A child may know the right answers but may not necessarily put them into practice. Some children may maintain that they do not have to abide by social conventions, believing that such matters do not pertain to them personally.

Children may reveal dependent tendencies by indicating that they would seek help from their mothers or others when confronted with the various problem situations.

Initiative, self-reliance, independence, self-confidence, helplessness, and other traits also may be revealed in their replies. For example, replies to questions 6 and 9, which ask the examinee what should be done when a younger child starts a fight with him or her and why criminals are locked up, may reveal independence, manipulatory tendencies, naïve perceptions of problems, cooperative solutions, hostility, or aggression (Robb, Bernardoni, & Johnson, 1972).

The following questions are useful for observing the children's manner of responding to the questions (Taylor, 1961). Are questions failed because the meaning of a word or the implication of a particular phrase is misunderstood? Is a complete answer given or just part of a phrase repeated? Does the child respond to the entire question or only to a part of it? Does the child seem to be objective, see various possibilities, and then choose the best way? Is the child indecisive, being unable to come to firm answers? Are responses given too quickly, indicating failure to consider the questions in their entirety? Does the child recognize when answers are sufficient?

Unusual responses may be probed by asking children to explain their responses further. Inquiry provides material that may give insight into the examinee's thought processes, but it should not be a routine procedure or be conducted on every response. Extensive inquiry can be conducted as part of the testing of limits after the examination has been completed. It is especially important that the examinee's responses be recorded verbatim during the initial presentation of the items and during the inquiry phase in order to facilitate restudy and qualitative evaluation.

Digit Span

On the Digit Span, a supplementary subtest, the child listens to a series of digits given orally by the examiner and then is required to repeat the digits. There are two parts to the subtest. The Digits Forward part contains series ranging in length from three to nine digits, while the Digits Backward part contains series ranging in length from two to eight digits. There are two series of digits for each sequence length. Digits Forward is administered first, followed by Digits Backward.

The subtest is not counted in obtaining the IQ when the five standard Verbal Scale subtests are administered. All items are scored 2, 1, or 0. The subtest is discontinued after failure on both trials of any item for both parts of the subtest. Scaled scores are not provided separately for Digits Forward and Digits Backward.

Rationale. The Digit Span subtest is a measure of short-term memory and attention (Rapaport et al., 1968). An effortless and relaxed performance may enable a child to achieve a high score on the subtest, whereas excessive anxiety may result in a low score. The task assesses the child's ability to retain in mind several elements that have no logical relationship to one another (Kubota, 1965). Because auditory information must be recalled and repeated orally in proper sequence, the task has been described as involving "auditory vocal sequencing memory" (Bannatyne, 1974).

Digits Forward involves primarily rote learning and memory, whereas Digits Backward requires considerably greater transformation of the stimulus input prior to recall. Not only is memory involved in Digits Backward, but also remanipulation and reorganization of encoded information. The mental image of the numerical sequence not only must be held longer (usually) than in the Digits Forward sequence, but must be manipulated before it is restated. Digits Backward may indicate flexibility, good tolerance for stress, and excellent concentration. Thus, Digits Backward involves more complex cognitive processing than Digits Forward. Digits Backward has also been shown to have higher loadings on *g* than Digits Forward (Jensen & Osborne, 1979).

Factor analytic findings. The Digit Span subtest is a poor measure of *g* (24 percent of its variance may be attributed to *g*). The subtest has ample subtest specificity across the entire age range to permit specific interpretation of its functions. Digit Span has a high loading on the Freedom from Distractibility factor (median loading of .56).

Reliability and correlational highlights. Digit Span is a somewhat reliable subtest ($r_{11} = .78$) and correlates more highly with Arithmetic ($r = .45$) than with any other subtest. It has a low correlation with the Full Scale ($r = .43$), with the Verbal Scale ($r = .45$), and with the Performance Scale ($r = .34$).

Administrative considerations. Be sure that the examinee cannot see the digits in the manual or on the record blank. The digits should be read clearly at the rate of one per second, with the inflection dropped on the last digit in the series. It is a good idea to practice reading speed with a stopwatch. It is never permissible to repeat any of the digits on either trial of a series. After the subtest has been completed, it is worthwhile to ask examinees about their method of recalling the digits. "How did you go about recalling the numbers?" is one way of phrasing the question. Record whether, for example, examinees visualized the digits, said the digits to themselves and reproduced them by use of verbal or motor or auditory techniques, or grouped the digits. Some types of grouping may introduce meaning into the task, in that instead of separate entities, the digits become numbers or are grouped into hundreds, tens, or other units. If grouping occurs, the function underlying the task may be changed from one of attention to one of concentration (Rapaport et al., 1968).

In the record booklet, the actual number of digits in each series correctly recalled should be recorded either by placing a correct mark above or on each digit correctly recalled or by placing an incorrect mark on each digit missed. This procedure provides another source of qualitative material. For example, an examinee who consistently misses the last digit in a series and then successfully completes the second series in the sequence may differ from one who fails to recall any of the digits in the first series, but successfully completes the second series. The quantitative scores do not distinguish between these two patterns. This is true particularly for the number of digits failed. For example, for scoring purposes, an examinee who misses one digit in the eight-digit sequence receives the same score as one who misses all eight digits. A qualitative analysis of the two patterns suggests that there is more inefficiency in the performance of the second examinee than in the first examinee's performance. The second examinee thereby reveals lapses in attention that may be due to anxiety or to other factors.

Observe also whether failures were due to leaving out one or more digits, transposing digits, interjecting incorrect digits, or producing more digits than the number originally given. Does the child perform in an effortless manner or with a great deal of concentration? Note whether the child views the task as interesting, boring, or difficult (Taylor, 1961). When errors are made, does the child notice them, or does the child think that the answers are correct? When the Digits Backward series is presented, does the child understand the difference between this task and the previous one? Are the same types of errors made or do they change? As the series proceeds, does the child become stimulated and encouraged, or more tense and anxious?

Both trials of each series are routinely administered on the subtest. The child receives credit for each trial that is passed. On Digits Backward, if the child passes the sample three-digit series (either on the first or second trial), proceed to the two-digit series. If the child fails the sample series, read specific directions that explain how the series should be repeated correctly. Whenever there is any doubt about the child's auditory acuity skills, an audiometric examination should be requested.

Picture Completion

The Picture Completion subtest consists of twenty-six drawings of objects from everyday life. The pictures, which are lacking a single important element, are shown one at a time. The child's task is to discover and name (or point to) the essential missing portion of the incompletely drawn picture within the twenty-second time limit.

The subtest is started at different points, depending on the child's age. Children aged 6 to 7 years (and older children suspected of mental retardation) are started with item 1, while those aged 8 to 16 years are started with item 5. All items are scored 1 or 0 (pass-fail), and the subtest is discontinued after four consecutive failures.

Rationale. The Picture Completion subtest involves recognizing the object depicted, appreciating its incompleteness, and determining the missing part. The child must know what the picture represents and must be able to appreciate that the missing part is in some way essential to the form of the object on the picture. It is a test of the ability to differentiate essential from nonessential details, and requires concentration, reasoning (or visual alertness), and visual organization and visual memory. The subtest may measure the child's perceptual and conceptual abilities in so far as they are involved in the visual recognition and identification of familiar objects. Perception, cognition, judgment, and delay of impulse all may enter into the child's performance (Taylor, 1961). The concentration required is directed toward an externalized form, a visual stimulus, whereas the concentration required on the Arithmetic subtest is a more internalized process. The time limit on the subtest is important, since it places additional demands on the examinee. The richness of the child's experiences, such as extensiveness of contact with the environment, may affect performance on the subtest.

Factor analytic findings. The Picture Completion subtest is a fair measure of g (37 percent of its variance may be attributed to g). The subtest has an ample or adequate amount of subtest specificity at all ages to permit specific interpretation of its func-

tions. Picture Completion contributes substantially to the Perceptual Organization factor (median loading of .57).

Reliability and correlational highlights. Picture Completion is a somewhat reliable subtest ($r_{11} = .77$) and correlates more highly with Block Design ($r = .52$) than with any other subtest. It has a somewhat low correlation with the Full Scale ($r = .57$), with the Performance Scale ($r = .54$), and with the Verbal Scale ($r = .50$).

Administrative considerations. Some of the points to consider in administering the Picture Completion subtest are as follows: Do children understand the task? Do they say anything that comes to mind or do they search for the right answer? When they fail, do they find fault with themselves or with the picture (Taylor, 1961)? Whenever there is any doubt about a child's visual skills, a visual examination should be requested. In presenting the pictures, a useful procedure is to leave the booklet flat on the table and simply turn the card over for each succeeding item.

Examinees should be aware that they are being timed, because it is important for them to realize that speed is expected. Allowing them to see the stopwatch is all that is necessary. After the subtest is completed, inquire into the examinee's perception of the task. "How did you go about solving the task and deciding when to give the answer?" is one way of inquiring. Children's behavior during this subtest may provide insight about how they react to time pressure. Inquiry also should be made concerning any peculiar answers. If a testing-of-limits phase is conducted, children can be asked to look again at those pictures that they missed. You can say, "Look at this picture again. Before, you said that _____ was missing. That's not the part that's missing. Look for something else."

If examinees have speech difficulties, such as those that occur in aphasia, the subtest can be administered by having them point to the place where the part is missing. Observe whether or not perseveration occurs. For example, perseveration is present when the response "mouth" is given to each picture portraying a person (pictures 2, 12, 15, 17, and 19). "Mouth" is the correct answer for picture 2, but it is not the correct answer for the subsequent pictures showing people.

In all cases, incorrect responses as well as the time taken to make the responses should be recorded. Examinees who characteristically respond correctly in less than five seconds may be brighter than examinees who take more than five seconds. Similarly, examinees who uniformly respond correctly in between twenty-one and thirty seconds do not receive credit, yet they may be brighter than those who respond incorrectly. Because the all-or-none scoring (scoring is either 1 or 0) makes no provision for such individual variations, qualitative factors (e.g., receiving no credit but answering the item correctly) should be carefully evaluated in each case and discussed in the report.

You are instructed to give, if necessary, and on one occasion only, each of three guiding statements to help the child understand the requirements of the subtest. You can ask (1) for the most important part that is missing when the child mentions an unessential missing part; (2) for what is missing when the child names the object pictured; and (3) for what is missing when the child names a part that is off the card.

On five items (6, 14, 22, 23, and 24), the WISC-R manual indicates that the child should be asked to point to the missing part on the card when certain kinds of ambiguous responses are given. In other cases, whenever there is any doubt about the child's verbal or pointing response on any item, ask for clarification.

Picture Arrangement

The Picture Arrangement subtest requires the child to place a series of pictures in a logical sequence. The twelve series (or items) are similar to short comic strips. The examiner places the individual pictures (or cards) in a specified disarranged order, and the child is asked to rearrange the pictures in the "right" order to tell a story that makes sense. One set of cards is presented at a time. The motor action required to solve the problems is simply to change the position of the pictures so that they make a meaningful story.

All children are started with the sample item, after which children aged 6 to 7 (and older children suspected of mental retardation) are given item 1, while children aged 8 to 16 are given item 3. Items 1 to 4 are scored 2, 1, or 0, while items 5 to 12 receive 3 points for the correct arrangement, with up to 2 additional time-bonus points. The subtest is discontinued after three consecutive failures.

Rationale. The subtest measures the child's ability to comprehend and size up a total situation. In order to accomplish the task, the child must grasp the general idea of a story. While trial-and-error experimentation is sometimes involved, the overall task requires an appraisal of the total situation depicted in the cards.

The Picture Arrangement subtest is a nonverbal reasoning test, which may be viewed as a measure of planning ability involving anticipation and visual organization. The anticipation required is an ability to anticipate the consequences of initial acts or situations and to interpret social situations. The capacity to anticipate, judge, and understand the possible antecedents and consequences of events is important in providing meaningful continuity in everyday experiences (Blatt & Allison, 1968).

Factor analytic findings. The Picture Arrangement subtest is a fair measure of *g* (36 percent of its variance may be attributed to *g*). The subtest has ample subtest specificity across the entire age range to permit specific interpretation of its functions. Picture Arrangement has a moderate loading on the Perceptual Organization factor (median loading of .41).

Reliability and correlational highlights. Picture Arrangement is a somewhat reliable subtest ($r_{11} = .73$) and correlates more highly with Block Design ($r = .46$) than with any other subtest. It has a somewhat low correlation with the Full Scale ($r = .55$), with the Performance Scale ($r = .52$), and with the Verbal Scale ($r = .49$).

Administrative considerations. All Picture Arrangement items are arranged from the examinee's left to right in the order given in the manual. In the demonstration items, be sure not to cover the pictures. The examinee should be able to see all of the pictures and follow your movements when you are rearranging the pictures. Record the examinee's Picture Arrangement sequence as soon as the cards are picked up.

If children do not say when they are finished, ask if they have finished. When children are extremely compulsive, tell them that the cards do not have to be perfectly straight (or aligned) so that they will not be penalized (i.e., lose time-bonus points) for their compulsive tendencies.

The subtest is useful in observing how children approach a performance task involving planning ability. How do the children proceed with the task? Do they look the cards over, come to some decision, and reassess it while they arrange the cards (Taylor, 1961)? Or do they proceed quickly without stopping to reconsider their decision? Are their failures to understand the task revealed by their leaving the pictures in the order in which they were placed by the examiner?

The child's persistence, trial-and-error patterns, degree of discouragement, impulsiveness, or rigidity should be noted. It may be valuable to compare the child's approach to the Picture Arrangement items with that used on the Block Design and Object Assembly items. Does the child consistently employ the same patterns in searching for the solutions? If they are not consistent, what may account for the changes? Consider the extent to which the content of the task, fatigability, and mood changes are involved in the child's approach to the various items.

Inquiry into the child's arrangements may elicit useful material, particularly on those items that have been failed. In order to keep the test administration as standard-

ized as possible, inquiry should be conducted after the entire scale has been administered. Select items from those that have been failed or passed, if there is reason to believe that they may reveal insight into the examinee's thought pattern. The last two items attempted can routinely be subjected to inquiry. Even in the case of items that have been correctly arranged, incorrect anticipations or lack of understanding may be present (Rapaport et al., 1968). Set up the Picture Arrangement cards for each item separately in the order given by the child. Ask the child to "tell what is happening in the pictures," or to "make up a story," or to "tell the story," or to "tell what the pictures show."

The following questions should be considered in evaluating the stories (Taylor, 1961): Are they logical, fanciful, or bizarre? Is there originality in them or are they conventional? Are emotional attitudes revealed, such as self-oriented or socially-oriented themes? Are incorrect arrangements due to incorrect perceptions of details in the pictures or failure to consider some details? Were all relationships in the pictures considered?

Useful testing-of-limits procedures include (a) giving the child additional time to complete the arrangement and (b) arranging one or more pictures on items that have been failed. Children who solve the problems with the aid of one or more cues may have greater ability than those who fail in spite of the additional guidance. It is important that graded help be introduced only after the standard examination has been completed, because it has been demonstrated that such help significantly raises Picture Arrangement scores (Sattler, 1969).

The child can earn bonus points for speed on items 5 through 12. In order to help children understand the importance of speed, encourage them to work quickly and tell you when they are finished.

Block Design

In the Block Design subtest, the child is shown two-dimensional, red-and-white pictures of abstract designs. The task requires using blocks to assemble a design that is identical to the design on each picture. There are eleven items on the subtest, which is started at different points depending on the child's age. Children aged 6 to 7 years (and older children suspected of mental retardation) are started with item 1, while children aged 8 to 16 years are started with item 3. The child is required to reproduce the designs from a model constructed by the examiner for the first two items. For the remaining nine items, the patterns are shown on cards. Two-color (red and white) plastic blocks are used. The patterns are arranged in order of increasing difficulty. Four blocks are used for the first eight designs, and nine blocks are used for the last three designs.

All of the items are timed. The first four items are given a maximum of 45 seconds; the next four items, 75 seconds; and the last three items, 120 seconds. Items 1 to 3 are scored 2, 1, or 0, while items 4 to 11 receive 4 points for a correct completion and up to 3 additional time-bonus points for quick execution. The subtest is discontinued after two consecutive failures.

Rationale. Block Design involves the ability to perceive and analyze forms by breaking down a whole (the design) into its component parts and then assembling the component parts into the identical design, a process referred to as analysis and synthesis. The subtest combines visual organization with the reproductive aspects of visual-motor coordination. Success involves the application of logic and reasoning to spatial relationship problems. Consequently, Block Design can be conceived of as a nonverbal concept formation task requiring abilities for perceptual organization, spatial visualization, and abstract conceptualization.

Performance may be affected by rate of motor activity and vision. Inadequate performance should not be interpreted as direct evidence of inadequate visual form and pattern perception, because the ability to discriminate block designs (i.e., to perceive the designs accurately at a recognition level) may be intact even though the ability to reproduce the designs is impaired (Bortner & Birch, 1962).

Factor analytic findings. The Block Design subtest is the best measure of g among the Performance Scale subtests and is the fourth-best measure of g among all twelve subtests (53 percent of its variance may be attributed to g). The subtest has ample subtest specificity across the entire age range to permit specific interpretation of its functions. The Block Design subtest contributes substantially to the Perceptual Organization factor (median loading of .66).

Reliability and correlational highlights. Block Design is a reliable subtest ($r_{11} = .85$) and correlates more highly with Object Assembly ($r = .60$) and with Picture Completion ($r = .52$) than with the other subtests. It has a moderate correlation with the Full Scale ($r = .68$) and with the Performance Scale ($r = .68$) and a somewhat low correlation with the Verbal Scale ($r = .58$).

Administrative considerations. In arranging the blocks for the demonstration, be sure that the area being used is clear of other blocks and materials. A useful procedure in constructing the design is to complete, from the examinee's left to right, first the first row and then the second row. The blocks should be scrambled before each new design is administered. Only the number of blocks needed for the item should be placed before the examinee.

It is important to have the children indicate when they have completed each item. On the first three designs it may be necessary, therefore, to ask them to indicate when they have finished ("Tell me when you have finished"). The instructions also ask the children to state when they have finished on designs 4 to 11.

Block Design is an excellent subtest for observing the children's methods of working. Are the children hasty and impulsive or deliberate and careful? Do the children give up easily or become disgusted when faced with possible failure, or do they persist and keep on working even after the time limit has been reached? Do the children use one kind of approach or do they alter it as the need arises (Taylor, 1961)? Do they study the designs first? Do they have a plan? Do they construct units of blocks and arrange them in proper relationship, or do they work in piecemeal fashion?

Excessive fumbling or failure to check the pattern is suggestive of anxiety. Visual-perceptual difficulties may be indicated if the children rotate their bodies to get a better perspective on the design or if space is left between the blocks in the assembled design (Robb et al., 1972). Try to differentiate between excessive cautiousness as a personality style and excessive slowness as a possible indication of depression.

If testing of limits is indicated or desired, the specific item or items should be presented *after* the entire examination has been completed. Research has shown that a series of cues administered to children during the standard administration of the Block Design subtest significantly raises subtest scores (Sattler, 1969). However, when only one cue was administered, significant changes were not observed. A useful procedure to follow is to place one block in its correct position (or one row) for those designs that were failed. Say, depending on the cue, "Let's try some of these again. I'm going to put together some of the blocks. I will make the top row. Now you go ahead and finish it. Now make one like this. Tell me when you have finished." If the examinee still fails, additional blocks can be arranged. The amount of help needed to complete the designs accurately should be recorded.

Object Assembly

The Object Assembly subtest involves the presentation of four jigsaw problems. The task consists of assembling the pieces correctly to form common objects: a girl (seven pieces), a car (seven pieces), a horse (six pieces), and a face (eight pieces). The items are given one at a time, with the pieces presented in a specified disarranged pattern. There also is one sample item, an apple, which consists of four pieces. All children receive all items, beginning with the sample and continuing with items 1 through 4.

All items are timed. The first item is given a maximum of 120 seconds; the next two items, 150 seconds; and the fourth item, 180 seconds. Two items (girl and face) receive 6 points for perfect performance, and the other two items (horse and car) receive 5 points for perfect performance. In addition, children can earn time bonuses of up to 3 points for quick performance. The girl, horse, and car items each have a maximum score of 8, and the face item, 9. Points are also awarded for performances that are only partially correct.

Rationale. The assembling of pieces into a whole is mainly a test of synthesis—putting things together to form familiar objects. Object Assembly requires visual-motor coordination, with the motor activity being guided by visual perception and sensory-motor feedback. Object Assembly is a test of perceptual organization ability. The visual organization seems to play a "productive" role, in that something must be produced out of parts that may not be immediately recognizable. In solving the jigsaw puzzles, examinees are required to grasp a whole pattern by anticipating the relationships among the individual parts. The tasks, therefore, require some constructive ability as well as perceptual skill. Performance also may be related to rate and precision of motor activity.

Factor analytic findings. The Object Assembly subtest is a fair measure of *g* (38 percent of its variance may be attributed to *g*). The subtest has an inadequate amount of subtest specificity across the entire age range, thereby preventing interpretation of the specific underlying ability measured by the subtest. The Object Assembly subtest has a high loading on the Perceptual Organization factor (median loading of .65), making it interpretable as a measure of perceptual organization.

Reliability and correlational highlights. Object Assembly is a somewhat reliable subtest ($r_{11} = .70$) and correlates more highly with Block Design ($r = .60$) than with any other subtest. It has a somewhat low correlation with the Full Scale ($r = .56$), a moderate correlation with the Performance Scale ($r = .60$), and a low correlation with the Verbal Scale ($r = .46$).

Administrative considerations. It is important that the child not see the WISC-R manual, which contains pictures of the assembled objects. The screen used to set up the individual puzzle parts can be used to cover the manual, if desired. Be sure to place the pieces close to the child so that the child does not lose time in attempting to reach the pieces. As in other subtests, it is sometimes necessary to ask examinees to indicate when they are finished. In requesting this information, be careful not to give any cues to the examinee that indicate approval or disapproval.

Object Assembly is an especially good subtest in which to observe the child's thinking and work habits. Some children have the idea of the complete object almost from the start and either recognize the relations of the individual parts to the whole or have an imperfect understanding of the relations between the parts and the whole. Other children merely try to fit the pieces together by trial-and-error methods. Still others may have initial failure, followed by trial-and-error and then sudden insight and recognition of the object.

Observe how the child responds to errors and how the child handles frustration that may result from the errors. Are low scores a result of temporary inefficiency, such as reversal of two parts, with the resulting loss of time-bonus credits, or are they due to other reasons? Anxiety or rigidity may be revealed when a child continues to work with one piece, trying to position it in an incorrect location. Inquiry should be made concerning constructions that appear to be peculiar or unusual.

Testing of limits can also be used after the entire examination has been completed. Procedures similar to those described for the Picture Arrangement and Block Design subtests can be used. A series of graduated cues or steps can be introduced, such as placing one or more pieces in the correct location and noting how much help is needed before the task is completed successfully.

Coding

The Coding subtest requires the copying of symbols that are paired with other symbols. The speed and accuracy with which the task is performed are a measure of the child's intellectual ability. Estes (1974, p. 745) describes the task as follows: "At each step in the task the subject must inspect the next digit, go to the proper location in the table, code the information distinguishing the symbol found, and carry this information in short-term memory long enough to reproduce the symbol in the proper answer box." This analysis suggests that Coding can be, in part, conceptualized as an information processing task involving the discrimination and memory of visual pattern symbols (Royer, 1977).

The Coding subtest consists of two separate and distinct parts. Coding A is administered to children under the age of 8 years, and Coding B to those who are 8 years of age and over. Each part uses a sample (or key). In Coding A, the sample consists of five shapes (star, circle, triangle, cross, and square). Within each shape, a special mark appears (vertical line, two horizontal lines, horizontal line, circle, and two vertical lines, respectively). The child is required to place within each shape the mark that appears in the sample. Five practice shapes are presented, followed by forty-three shapes in the subtest.

In Coding B, the sample consists of boxes containing the numbers 1 through 9, and a symbol below each number. The child is required to write the symbols shown in the sample in boxes that contain a number in the upper part and an empty space in the lower part. There are seven practice boxes, followed by ninety-three boxes in the subtest proper. The time limit for each Coding task is 120 seconds.

The Coding subtest appears in a separate booklet (the last page of the Mazes booklet). Both you and child use a pencil with red lead, without an eraser, and the subtest should be administered on a smooth drawing surface. One point is allotted for each correct item, with up to 5 additional time-bonus points given to children with a perfect score on Coding A. There are no time-bonus points for Coding B.

Rationale. Coding requires the ability to learn an unfamiliar task, and involves speed and accuracy of eye-hand coordination, attentional skills, short-term memory, and, possibly, motivation. The subtest, therefore, involves visual-motor coordination, speed of mental operation (psychomotor speed), and, to some extent, visual acuity. Success, too, depends not only on the child's comprehending the task, but also on the child's skill with pencil and paper.

Coding involves a verbal-encoding process as a major component (Estes, 1974). The encoding process refers to the fact that many of the symbols have distinctive labels readily available. For example, a + symbol may be labeled as a "plus sign" or "cross" and the V symbol as the letter "V." Performance may be enhanced when the symbols are recoded in terms of verbal labels. Consequently, Coding also can be described as measuring the ability to learn combinations of symbols and shapes and the ability to make associations quickly and accurately.

Factor analytic findings. The Coding subtest is the poorest measure of *g* in the scale (17 percent of its variance may be attributed to *g*). It has ample subtest specificity across the entire age range to permit specific interpretation of its functions. Coding has a moderate loading on the Freedom from Distractibility factor (median loading of .42).

Reliability and correlational highlights. Coding is a somewhat reliable subtest ($r_{11} = .72$) and correlates more highly with Block Design ($r = .33$) than with any other subtest. It has a low correlation with the Full Scale ($r = .38$), with the Performance Scale ($r = .33$), and with the Verbal Scale ($r = .36$).

Administrative considerations.   Children with visual defects or with specific motor disabilities may be penalized on this subtest. In such cases the subtest should not be given, or if it is given, it should not be counted in the final score.

The examinee's method of proceeding with the task should be observed. A child who stops working after the first line should be told to complete the task by continuing on the next line ("Continue on the next line"). These instructions should be counted as part of the two-minute time limit. If examinees skip around, filling like shapes or like numbers first, tell them to proceed in order.

Left-handed children may be penalized on the Coding subtest. They may bend their wrists when writing, cover the sample immediately above the line of writing, and lift their hands repeatedly during the task. Either of two procedures can be used to counteract these difficulties. One method consists of showing the child the sample from another record booklet. A more satisfactory procedure is to cut the sample from another record booklet, mount it on a strip of cardboard, and then position it in a convenient place for viewing (McCarthy, 1961).

Observe whether the child is impulsive or meticulous, or whether tremor is evident. Note the pace of the child's performance. Are there increases or decreases in speed? An increase in speed, coupled with correct copying of symbols, suggests good ability to adjust to the task. A decrease in speed, coupled with correct copying of symbols, suggests that fatigue may be present (Rapaport et al., 1968).

Other useful questions are as follows (Taylor, 1961): Are the child's marks well done, just recognizable, or wrong? Is the child penalized for lack of speed, for inaccuracy, or for both? Does the child understand the task? Does the child fail because of inadequate form perception or poor attention? Does the child check each figure with the samples, or are the samples remembered? Does the child pick out one figure only and skip others? Does the child work smoothly, or is there confusion as the child goes along? Does the child understand and proceed correctly after explanations have been made? Thus, opportunity is provided to study the child's attention, especially when attention difficulties are suspected in a child who has had a recent head injury and who previously had no attention difficulties.

The actual symbols written by the child should be examined for types and frequency of distortions. Do they appear with one figure only, occasionally, or each time the figure appears? Do distortions appear randomly among the correct markings? Distortions of forms may suggest difficulties in perceptual functioning (Taylor, 1961). Inquiry should be made into any symbol that is peculiarly written, and a determination made of whether the peculiarity is associated with inadequate visual-motor coordination or whether it has some symbolic meaning to the child.

Mazes

On the Mazes subtest children are required to draw a line showing how to find their way out of a series of mazes without becoming blocked (i.e., not going through a line that demarcates a wall). Each maze is presented separately.

Mazes is a supplementary test that consists of nine test mazes and one sample maze. The subtest is not counted in obtaining the IQ when the five standard Performance Scale subtests are administered.

The subtest is started at different points, depending on the child's age. Children aged 6 to 7 years (and older children suspected of mental retardation) are started with the sample maze, followed by maze 1, while children aged 8 to 16 years are started with maze 4. The examiner uses a pencil with black lead to demonstrate the sample item, while the child uses a pencil with red lead, without an eraser. The subtest should be administered on a smooth drawing surface.

All items are timed. The first four mazes are given a maximum of 30 seconds; the fifth maze, 45 seconds; the sixth maze, 60 sec-

onds; the seventh and eighth mazes, 120 seconds; and the last maze, 150 seconds. The number of errors made determines the child's score. The range of scores is from 0 to 5 points, with mazes 1 to 3 having a maximum score of 2; mazes 4 and 5, a maximum score of 3; mazes 6 and 7, a maximum score of 4; and mazes 8 and 9, a maximum score of 5. The subtest is discontinued after two consecutive failures.

Rationale. On the Mazes subtest the child must (a) attend to the directions, which include the requirements of locating a route from cross to exit arrow, avoiding blind alleys, crossing no lines, and holding pencil on paper; and (b) execute the task, which involves remembering and following the directions, executing adequate visual-motor coordination, and resisting the disruptive effect of an implied need for speed (Madden, 1974). Thus, the Mazes subtest appears to measure planning ability and perceptual organization (following a visual pattern). Visual-motor control and speed combined with accuracy are, in part, needed for success.

Factor analytic findings. The Mazes subtest is a poor measure of g (20 percent of its variance may be attributed to g). The subtest has ample subtest specificity across the entire age range to permit specific interpretation of its functions. Mazes has a moderate loading on the Perceptual Organization factor (median loading of .47).

Reliability and correlational highlights. Mazes is a somewhat reliable subtest ($r_{11} = .72$) and correlates more highly with Block Design ($r = .44$) than with any other subtest. It has a low correlation with the Full Scale ($r = .44$), with the Performance Scale ($r = .47$), and with the Verbal Scale ($r = .34$).

Administrative considerations. The child's performance should be observed carefully. Is there tremor, difficulty with control of the pencil, or a problem with nonuniformly drawn lines? Does the child correctly solve the mazes, but not receive credit because the time limit has expired? Is the crossing of lines related to poor visual-motor coordination or to impulsivity?

When certain errors occur for the first time, inform the child that an error has been made. The cues that you need to give the child when he or she makes certain errors are conveniently listed in the manual. Although they require careful study, they should be helpful, especially for the child who does not fully understand the task requirements. A table in the manual shows clearly the number of points allotted for the child's performance. The sample responses, which illustrate the various rules regarding the scoring of errors, should help you score the child's performance.

Summary

Chapter 10 discusses the interpretative rationale, factor analytic findings, reliability and subtest correlations, and administrative considerations for each of the twelve WISC-R subtests. The proposed interpretative rationales and possible implications of high and low scores are summarized in Table C-15 in the Appendix.

The following is a short summary of some of the important features of each subtest:

1. *Information.* Information measures the wealth of available information acquired as a result of native ability and early cultural experience. Memory is an important aspect of performance on the subtest. The subtest ties with Similarities as the second-best measure of *g*, and contributes to the Verbal Comprehension factor. Subtest specificity is ample at all ages. Information is a reliable subtest ($r_{1I} = .85$). It is relatively easy to administer.

2. *Similarities.* Similarities measures verbal concept formation and ties with Information as the second-best measure of *g*. Subtest specificity is adequate only between ages 6½ and 8½ years. Similarities is a reliable subtest ($r_{1I} = .81$). Scoring requires con-

siderable judgment on some items; therefore, the child's responses should be evaluated carefully.

3. *Arithmetic.* Arithmetic measures numerical reasoning ability. It is a moderately good measure of *g*, and contributes to the Freedom from Distractibility and Verbal Comprehension factors. Subtest specificity is adequate at all ages. Arithmetic is a somewhat reliable subtest ($r_{1I} = .77$). The subtest is relatively easy to administer.

4. *Vocabulary.* Vocabulary measures a variety of functions, including language development, learning ability, and fund of information. The subtest is an excellent measure of *g*, and contributes to the Verbal Comprehension factor. Subtest specificity is adequate at all ages. Vocabulary is a reliable subtest ($r_{1I} = .86$). The subtest requires skill to administer and score. The child's responses should be evaluated carefully.

5. *Comprehension.* Comprehension measures social judgment: the ability to use facts in a pertinent, meaningful, and emotionally appropriate manner. The subtest is a moderately good measure of *g*, and contributes to the Verbal Comprehension factor. Subtest specificity is adequate at all ages. Comprehension is a somewhat reliable subtest ($r_{1I} = .77$). Scoring requires considerable judgment; therefore, the child's responses should be analyzed carefully.

6. *Digit Span.* Digit Span measures short-term memory and attention and forms part of the Freedom from Distractibility factor. It is a poor measure of *g*. Subtest specificity is ample at all ages. Digit Span is a somewhat reliable subtest ($r_{1I} = .78$) and is relatively easy to administer.

7. *Picture Completion.* Picture Completion measures the ability to differentiate essential from nonessential details. It requires concentration, visual organization, and visual memory. The subtest is a fair measure of *g*, and contributes to the Perceptual Organization factor. Subtest specificity is ample or adequate at all ages. Picture Completion is a somewhat reliable subtest ($r_{1I} = .77$) and is relatively easy to administer.

8. *Picture Arrangement.* Picture Arrangement measures nonverbal reasoning

ability. It also may be viewed as a measure of planning ability, i.e., the ability to comprehend and size up a total situation. The subtest is a fair measure of g, and contributes to the Perceptual Organization factor. Subtest specificity is ample at all ages. Picture Arrangement is a somewhat reliable subtest ($r_{1I} = .73$). The subtest is easy to administer, and it is amenable to testing-of-limits procedures.

9. *Block Design*. Block Design measures visual-motor coordination and perceptual organization. The subtest is the best single measure of g among the Performance Scale subtests, and contributes to the Perceptual Organization factor. Subtest specificity is ample at all ages. Block Design is a reliable subtest ($r_{1I} = .85$). It requires skill to administer.

10. *Object Assembly*. Object Assembly measures perceptual organization ability. The subtest is a fair measure of g, and contributes to the Perceptual Organization fac-

tor. Because it has an inadequate amount of subtest specificity, its specific underlying ability should not be interpreted. However, it can be interpreted more generally as a measure of perceptual organization. Object Assembly is a somewhat reliable subtest ($r_{1I} = .70$). It requires skill to administer.

11. *Coding*. Coding measures visual-motor coordination, speed of mental operation, and short-term memory. The subtest is the poorest measure of g in the scale, but it contributes to the Freedom from Distractibility factor. Subtest specificity is ample at all ages. Coding is a somewhat reliable subtest ($r_{1I} = .72$) and is easy to administer.

12. *Mazes*. Mazes measures planning ability and perceptual organization. The subtest is a poor measure of g, but it contributes to the Perceptual Organization factor. Subtest specificity is ample at all ages. Mazes is a somewhat reliable subtest ($r_{1I} = .72$) and is easy to administer.

CHAPTER 11

Interpreting the WISC-R

The first of our senses which we should take care never to let rust through disuse is that sixth sense, the imagination. . . . I mean the wide-open eye which leads us always to see truth more vividly, to apprehend more broadly, to concern ourselves more deeply, to be, all our life long, sensitive and awake to the powers and responsibilities given to us as human beings.

CHRISTOPHER FRY
Vogue, January 1956

Exhibit 11-1. Psychological Evaluation: An Emotionally Disturbed Seven-Year-Old Examined with the WISC-R

Name: Jim
Date of birth: July 17, 1972
Chronological age: 7-4
Date of examination: November 20, 1979
Date of report: November 21, 1979
Grade: Second

Test Administered

Wechsler Intelligence Scale for Children–Revised (WISC-R):

VERBAL SCALE		PERFORMANCE SCALE	
Information	14	Picture Completion	12
Similarities	12	Picture Arrangement	13
Arithmetic	15	Block Design	14
Vocabulary	13	Object Assembly	8
Comprehension	12	Coding	6

Verbal Scale IQ=119
Performance Scale IQ=104
Full Scale IQ=113± 7 at the 95% confidence level

Reason for Referral

Jim is a 7-year-old boy who was referred to the clinic for evaluation because of involuntary defecation, fecal smearing, enuresis, and stealing.

Background

Jim, an illegitimate child who never knew his natural father, was separated from his mother at six months of age, when she developed leukemia from which she died a year later. Since that time Jim has lived with a paternal aunt and her three children, who range in age from 8 to 18 years. At this time, the aunt has been divorced twice. Jim does call his aunt "mother" and thought of her first husband as his father. This man, who had been in the family as long as Jim had, left when he divorced the aunt; Jim was then two and a half years old. During this period of turmoil, incomplete and ineffectual attempts at toilet training were made. Last year Jim's aunt remarried. During the six months that the marriage lasted, Jim formed no attachment to his second step-uncle.

Jim is routinely reported to have bowel movements in the bathtub; he smears feces on the walls or leaves them in trash cans around the house. He also soils himself frequently. He wanders around the house at night and some-

EXHIBIT 11-1 (cont.)

times vanishes for a number of hours from the park or on his way home from school. He has been known to steal food, money, and a stopwatch from the principal's office. He steals routinely and seems to make an effort to be discovered.

Jim is an excellent student, although he is very difficult to handle because of his opposition and defiance. His behavior in the past three months has been changing. There has been a decrease in encopresis and fecal smearing, and an increase in stealing and aggressive behavior.

General Observations

Jim is a small, thinly built child who appears to be energetic. He was cooperative and friendly during the testing session. His test behavior was characterized by competitiveness, tenacity, and anxiety. He seemed to want to answer all of the questions correctly and was reluctant to give up on any question. For example, on the Information subtest, he responded to "What are the four seasons of the year?" with "Spring" and "Fall," but he could not remember winter and summer. He had to be encouraged to go on to the next question, and three items later he spontaneously returned to the question, adding "Winter" and "Summer." Jim seemed constantly to need assurance from the examiner that he was answering the items correctly. He often asked, "Have I gotten them all right?"

Test Results

With a chronological age of 7-4, Jim achieved a Verbal Scale IQ of 119, a Performance Scale IQ of 104, and a Full Scale IQ of 113±7 on the WISC-R. This places him in the Bright Normal classification and indicates that in this respect he exceeds 81% of the children in the standardization group, which was roughly representative of the population of the United States. The chances that the range of scores from 106 to 120 includes his true IQ are about 95 out of 100. The present measure of his level of intellectual functioning appears to be valid.

While there was a 15-point difference between the Verbal and Performance Scales, this difference was primarily associated with his low scores on two Performance Scale subtests. Therefore, while verbal skills are uniformly well developed, performance skills show more variability, with some abilities that are well developed and others that are less well developed. Overall, with the exception of two of the Performance subtest scores, Jim consistently obtained above-average scores on the test.

Within the verbal area, his numerical reasoning ability, range of knowledge, and language usage are excellent, while social comprehension and concept formation ability are very adequate. Within the performance area, his analytic and synthetic ability, planning and anticipation ability, and ability to differentiate essential from nonessential details are all well developed. His less adequate skills are associated with visual-motor coordination and with psychomotor speed. It is difficult to account for his lowered scores in these two areas in light of his overall above-average ability. Perhaps the scores reflect temporary inefficiency, such as inefficiency due to fatigue, or perhaps they simply indicate that his abilities in these areas are less adequate than are his other abilities.

A number of responses were particularly interesting. To the question, "Why are criminals locked up?" he said, "Because they steal things that are expensive." In reference to another question concerning charity and a beggar, he said, "Because the beggars might be a burglar." His mention of "stealing" and the specification of "expensive" and "burglar" are notable responses in view of his behavior pattern, which includes stealing. Preoccupation with stealing seems to be intruding into his outlook toward life. One response differed from his general pattern of rather clear-cut, detailed, well-oriented, and direct responses. He said that apple and banana are alike because they "feel the same." The above responses were the only ones that were noteworthy of idiosyncratic tendencies. Overall, he approaches problems by giving detailed answers that are descriptive and include meaningful phrases.

The test results suggest that Jim's behavioral problems, for the most part, have not interfered with his intellectual functioning. While psychomotor speed and visual-motor coordination are less adequately developed than are his other abilities, his overall functioning is very satisfactory. There were some suggestions of preoccupations with stealing, but it is difficult to determine the extensiveness of such preoccupations or the degree to which they may interfere with other forms of cognitive thinking that were not measured by the present test.

Recommendations

On the basis of the present limited evaluation, it is recommended that a personality evaluation be conducted. Further, the seriousness of his behavioral disturbance suggests that therapy should be initiated. Every attempt should be made to obtain further information about his home environment

EXHIBIT 11-1   (cont.)

and to determine what factors in the home may be reinforcing his deviant behavior pattern. His aunt should be actively engaged in the development of a treatment program.

Summary

In summary, with a chronological age of 7-4, Jim achieved an IQ of 113±7 on the WISC-R. This places him in the Bright Normal classification and indicates that in this respect he exceeds 81% of the children in the standardization group, which was roughly representative of the population of

the United States. The chances that the range of scores from 106 to 120 includes his true IQ are about 95 out of 100. The test results appear to give a valid indication of his present level of functioning. Verbal skills were uniformly well developed, while there was some variability in his performance skills. There was no evidence that his behavioral problems are significantly interfering with his cognitive skills. An evaluation of personality was recommended, as well as the development of a treatment program that would involve Jim and his aunt.

Examiner

Interpreting a child's performance on the WISC-R is like interpreting any other psychological test. It requires a synthesis of all available data observed during the evaluation, and an analysis of the data in light of the child's background. The material presented in the previous chapter on the twelve WISC-R subtests should help with the process of test interpretation. Many of the administrative suggestions were made to assist the examiner in obtaining a better picture of the child's performance and abilities. The insights thus gained are a starting point for interpreting the child's performance.

The information gained in the course of administering the test must be supplemented by knowledge of the structure of the WISC-R in order for the examiner to understand the underlying properties of the subtests and scales and how the subtests cluster. The factor analytic studies covered in Chapter 9 help us in test interpretation. Other important approaches to test interpretation involve the study of (a) Verbal-Performance discrepancies and (b) the pattern of subtest scores, technically called profile analysis or "test scatter." Because the WISC-R (and other Wechsler scales) have Deviation IQs with a mean of 100 and standard deviation of 15 and subtests with the same mean ($M = 10$) and standard deviation ($SD = 3$), statistical approaches to evaluating profiles can be readily applied.

After the Verbal-Performance discrepancy and profiles are statistically evaluated,

it is necessary to interpret the findings, particularly when significant differences are established. The information presented in the two previous chapters about the scales and subtests forms the basis for these interpretations. This chapter explains how interpretative rationales can be developed for Verbal-Performance comparisons and for subtest comparisons.

The psychological evaluation in Exhibit 11-1, which began the chapter, illustrates how the WISC-R can contribute to the assessment of an emotionally disturbed youngster. The report focuses on only the WISC-R for illustrative purposes. A thorough assessment would be based on a battery of tests.

Many guidelines needed for interpreting the WISC-R are included in Chapters 9, 10, and 11. However, a more complete interpretation of the WISC-R requires knowledge of clinical and psychoeducational approaches to test interpretation; these approaches are discussed in detail in later chapters of the book, which focus on general assessment and child psychopathology.

A Successive Level Approach to Test Interpretation

Many different kinds of information are obtained from a child's performance on the WISC-R and other Wechsler scales. In order to place the information in perspective it is useful to follow a successive level approach to test interpretation. This approach is valuable, especially for the development of hypotheses that are useful for clinical and psychoeducational purposes. The approach, formulated by Rabin and McKinney (1972), is presented in a modified fashion below.

The five levels of analysis are as follows:

Level I. The Full Scale IQ. The Full Scale IQ forms the basis for the entire evaluation. In most cases, it is the most reliable and valid estimate of intellectual ability provided by the scale. The Full Scale IQ is the primary or major numerical and quantitative index. It gives us information about the child's relative standing in the general population, as represented by the standardization group. The Full Scale IQ is a global estimate of the child's level of cognitive ability. The ranges and percentiles associated with Full Scale IQs are shown in Table C-37 in the Appendix and Table BC-1 on the inside back cover sheets of this text.

Level II. Verbal and Performance IQs. The second level focuses on the Verbal and Performance IQs and the extent to which there are significant differences between the two scales. As we have seen, the Verbal Scale provides information about verbal comprehension skills, while the Performance Scale covers perceptual organization skills. Tables BC-1 and C-37 can also be used to obtain the percentiles and ranges associated with the Verbal and Performance Scale IQs.

Level III. Intersubtest scatter. The third level focuses on deviations of the various subtests from the mean of the Verbal Scale or Performance Scale *and* comparisons between subtests. Hypotheses about strengths and weaknesses can be developed from these analyses.

Level IV. Intrasubtest scatter. The fourth level focuses on the pattern of performance within each individual subtest. Since the items are arranged in order of difficulty, deviations of successes and failures from the prearranged order of difficulty need to be evaluated carefully. For example, a child who passes the first item, fails the next four, passes the next one, fails the next four, and

overall passes a total of four items is showing a different pattern from one who passes the first four items and fails the remainder. In these two cases, each child receives 4 raw-score points, even though the 4 points were obtained in different ways. The child with the markedly uneven pattern may have cognitive or attentional inefficiencies that should be explored further.

Level V. Qualitative analysis. The last level focuses on the content of the responses, or qualitative analysis. (Chapter 18 discusses this aspect of test interpretation in more detail.) Careful attention to unique or highly personal responses may be especially informative. Both verbal and nonverbal responses should be evaluated.

Profile (or Scatter) Analysis

The evaluation of irregular performance on intelligence tests has been of interest to psychologists almost from the beginning of the testing movement. We have seen in Chapter 8 that profile analysis applied to the Stanford-Binet has proven to be, for the most part, of limited value. However, profile analysis is used frequently with the Wechsler scales, although with caution. The cardinal rule for use of profile analysis is that *profile analysis is dependent upon the presence of statistically significant differences between Verbal and Performance Scale IQs and between subtest scaled scores.* Thus, before any statements are made about whether the examinee obtained higher (or lower) IQs (or scaled scores) on one scale (or subtest) than on another scale (or subtest), significant differences between IQs (or scaled scores) should be present.

The WISC-R has an advantage over the Stanford-Binet for the purposes of profile analysis. The items on the WISC-R are already grouped into subtests that might be revealing of specific mental operations. The subtest scaled scores permit ready comparisons and preparation of profiles. Scatter, the pattern or configuration formed by the child's subtest scaled scores, is not fortuitous. Several possible factors may account for the performance. Ideally it would be necessary to consider to what extent age, sex, racial or ethnic group membership, socioeconomic status, occupation, education, special training, social and physical environment, family background, and nationality have affected the examinee's performance on the scale. Only after the above factors have been considered should diagnostic interpretative hypotheses be sought to account for the examinee's performance (Ogdon, 1967).

The intent of profile analysis is to determine whether a child is more adept in one area or skill than in another. Such information is used by psychologists and educators to evaluate a child's strengths and weaknesses and to plan programs of instruction most suitable for the child's needs. If a child's profile on an intelligence or special ability test is flat and significantly above average, it likely indicates that the child is gifted and would profit from instruction that capitalizes on these exceptional skills. Conversely, a profile that is flat and significantly below average may be indicative of limited intellectual ability. Special instructional programs might best meet the needs of children with this type of profile. Profiles with peaks and valleys may be indicative of special strengths and weaknesses, and may provide cues about the child's cognitive style and possible remediation efforts.

It is important to reiterate that, before any statements are made about cognitive strengths and weaknesses, the following be determined:

1. that the IQs on the Verbal and Performance Scales are significantly different from each other;
2. that subtest scaled scores are significantly different from the mean of their respective scales;
3. that subtest scaled scores (of interest) are significantly different from one another;
4. that cultural factors are taken into account; and
5. that other important factors (e.g., sex, age, special training, and socioeconomic status) are considered in evaluating the test scores.

The possibility must be considered that scatter simply is a reflection of the unreliability of the individual subtest scores, examiner variability, or situational variability, rather than a reflection of cognitive strengths and weaknesses.

In the early days of the Wechsler and Wechsler-type scales, it was hoped that profile analysis would contribute to the diagnostic process by allowing the clinician to classify examinees into diagnostic categories or to pinpoint their cognitive deficiencies. Soon after the Point Scale (Yerkes et al., 1915) was published, Pressey and Cole (1918) pointed out that irregularity on the scale might have a number of implications, including poor cooperation, deterioration, negativism, retardation, temporary psychotic disturbance, physical disease or disability, malingering, and illiteracy. Which, if any, of these implications is appropriate must be determined on an individual case basis. Unfortunately, research studies have failed to provide any firm basis for making diagnostic classification decisions from profile analysis. The use of profile analysis for the WISC-R and WPPSI (and other Wechsler scales) presents problems because the subtests are not as reliable as the three IQs obtained on the test.

While profile analysis has difficulties, it still is useful to evaluate routinely the pattern of scores obtained by the examinee. The goal of profile analysis is not to classify or categorize children; rather, it is to seek clues about their abilities. Ideas generated from profile analysis must be viewed simply as hypotheses to be checked against other information about the examinee. Profile analysis may assist the examiner in arriving at recommendations for clinical treatment, educational programs, or vocational placement. The functional nature of the child's learning problems can be better understood by use of profile analysis.

Many different patterns are, of course, possible. Some configurations have all subtest scaled scores within three or four points of each other, while other configurations have greater variability, with subtest scaled scores differing from each other by many points. Marked intersubtest variability, as we have seen, may be due to temporary inefficiencies, permanent incapacity, or disturbed school experiences (Blatt & Allison, 1968). Psychologists believe that profiles showing much scatter may reflect more potential than profiles showing limited scatter (Sattler & Kuncik, 1976). However, research is needed to support this belief. You will, in each case, have to seek out the best explanation of the child's profile by using all of the test data and the case history material.

When a child's profile of subtest scores is within normal limits, it should not be considered diagnostic of any exceptionality. However, even when scatter is outside of "normal limits," it does not necessarily indicate the presence of pathology. It may simply be a reflection of the child's cognitive style. There is no evidence to support the assumption that pathology and scatter are necessarily linked.

Primary Methods of Profile Analysis

The primary methods of profile analysis are the following:

1. comparing the Verbal and Performance IQs,
2. comparing each Verbal subtest scaled score to the mean Verbal scaled score,
3. comparing each Performance subtest scaled score to the mean Performance scaled score,
4. comparing each subtest scaled score to the mean subtest scaled score, and
5. comparing sets of individual subtest scores.

Notice that the first method compares IQs, whereas the other four methods compare scaled scores. Now let us examine each of these methods in more detail.

Comparing Verbal and Performance IQs. Table C-6 in the Appendix should be consulted to obtain the differences between the Verbal and Performance IQs that are needed to satisfy the .05 and .01 significance levels. Because differences between the two IQs generally are similar throughout the WISC-R age levels to reach the .05 or .01

significance levels, the values based on the average of the eleven age groups are used. The critical values are as follows:

.05	.01
12	15

Thus, if a child has a difference of 12 points between his or her Verbal and Performance IQs, it can be assumed that it is a statistically significant difference at the .05 level of significance. Similarly, a 15-point difference is needed between the two scales at the .01 level of significance. Exhibit 11-2 describes the procedure used to obtain the critical values shown in Table C-6. This procedure can be used to determine the needed critical values for any comparison involving two scales, subtests, or tests.

Comparing each Verbal subtest scaled score to the mean Verbal scaled score. Table C-7 in the Appendix allows you to compare each Verbal subtest scaled score with the mean Verbal scaled score. It shows the deviations from the mean that are needed at the .05 and .01 significance levels for comparisons involving five or six Verbal subtests. The critical values range from 2.74 to 3.15 for the 5 percent level and from 3.29 to 3.78 for the 1 percent level for the five Verbal subtests.

In order to use Table C-7 the following steps are necessary:

1. When the five standard Verbal subtests have been given, compute the mean of the five scaled scores by summing the scaled scores and dividing by 5, the number of subtests.
2. Compute the deviation from the mean for each subtest.
3. Check column 1 of Table C-7, the column for the five standard subtests, to determine whether the deviations from the mean are significant.
4. Use column 2 when six Verbal subtests have been given.

EXHIBIT 11-2.   Procedure Used to Determine Whether Two Scores in a Profile Are Significantly Different

In order to establish whether differences between scores in a profile are reliable, it is necessary to apply some statistical procedures to the profile. As always, we cannot be 100 percent certain that the differences between any two subtest scores are reliable. A confidence level must therefore be selected, such as a 95 percent level of certainty that the differences are significant. In order to determine whether the difference between two scales or subtests or tests is reliable, the following formula can be used:

$$\text{Difference Score} = z\sqrt{s_{mA}{}^2 + s_{mB}{}^2}$$

The Difference Score refers to the magnitude of the difference between scales or subtests A and B. The z refers to the the normal curve value associated with the desired confidence level. If we select the 95 percent level, the associated z value is 1.96. The terms under the square root sign refer to the standard error of measurement associated with each scale or subtest (or test).

Many test manuals provide these standard errors of measurement.

The following example illustrates how to determine whether there is a significant difference between two scaled scores. Let us say that we are interested in determining the value needed to represent a significant difference between the WISC-R Verbal and Performance Scales for children in the standardization group. The average standard errors of measurement associated with these two scales are 3.60 and 4.66, respectively, as indicated in the WISC-R manual. We know that at the 95 percent confidence level the z value is 1.96. Substituting these values into the formula yields the following:

$$\underset{\text{Score}}{\text{Difference}} = 1.96 \; \sqrt{3.60^2 + 4.66^2} = 12.$$

Differences between these two scales that are at or above this value are significant at the 95 percent level of confidence. A larger difference (15) is needed for the 99 percent confidence level. This value, as well as the value of 12, appears in the small rectangle of Table C-6 in the Appendix. All values in Tables C-6 and C-17 in the Appendix were obtained by following the above procedure. For the 99 percent confidence level, the z value of 2.58 is used in the equation. ■

Table 11-1 is an example of how to determine whether each Verbal subtest scaled score differs from the mean of the Verbal scaled scores. In Table 11-1, we see that the deviations for Information and Vocabulary are the only ones that exceed the critical values (shown in Table C-7 at the .01 level of significance). Information is significantly higher than the average, while Vocabulary is significantly lower. To determine whether a scaled score is significantly different from the mean, the plus or minus sign is disregarded. We are now in a firm position to infer that the differences between Information, Vocabulary, and the child's mean Verbal scaled score are attributable to something other than chance.

The critical values used in the preparation of Table C-7 are based on the assumption that the scores on all subtests in a scale are to be compared with the average score for that scale. Therefore, only one significance level (either .05 or .01) should be used to determine the critical values; mixing levels of significance is not recommended.[1]

Comparing each Performance scaled score to the mean Performance scaled score. The procedure for this comparison is the same as that described for the Verbal scaled scores. In Table C-7 in the Appendix either column 3 or column 4 is used, depending on whether five or six subtests are included in the average.

Comparing each subtest scaled score to the mean scaled score. This procedure is the same as that described for the Verbal scaled scores. However, in Table C-7 in the Appendix column 6, 7, 8, or 9 is used, depending on whether ten, eleven, or twelve subtests are included in the average.

TABLE 11-1.   Sample Procedure for Comparing Subtest Scaled Scores to Mean

Verbal Subtest	Scaled Score	Deviation from Average
Information	14	+5*
Similarities	11	+2
Arithmetic	6	−3
Vocabulary	4	−5*
Comprehension	10	+1
	45	

Mean Verbal scaled score: $\dfrac{45}{5} = 9$

*Significant at the .01 level.

Comparing sets of individual subtest scores. Table C-6 in the Appendix shows differences between sets of scaled scores on the twelve WISC-R subtests that are required for the .05 and .01 significance levels for the average of the eleven age groups. The table indicates that the statement "The child obtained a higher score on the Information than on the Similarities subtest" should not be made unless there is a 4-point scaled-score difference between the Information and Similarities subtests. The values in Table C-6 are overly liberal when subtests are involved in multiple comparisons. However, they are more accurate when a priori planned comparisons are made involving pairs of subtests, such as Information vs. Comprehension or Digit Span vs. Arithmetic. The procedure described in Exhibit 11-2 also is used to obtain the needed critical values between subtests.

Silverstein advises that if multiple subtest comparisons are made, the examiner first determine the difference between the highest and lowest subtest scores.[2] A difference of 7 scaled-score points indicates a significant difference at the .05 level. Those differences that are 7 scaled-score points or greater can then be interpreted. If the difference between the highest and lowest subtest scaled scores is less than 7 scaled-score points, then multiple comparisons between individual subtest scores should not be made.

Other Approaches to Profile Analysis

A number of supplementary approaches to profile analysis have been developed. These approaches, for the most part, examine the kinds of scatter found in the normative group. They allow you to compare an individual child's performance with that of the normative group. The approaches described below provide base rates for examining various kinds of scatter.

Subtest scaled-score ranges. An analysis of the scaled-score ranges—that is, the size of the difference between the highest and lowest WISC-R subtest scores—in the standardization group indicates that the median scaled-score range was 7 points for the Full Scale, 4 points for the Verbal Scale, and 5 points for the Performance Scale (Kaufman, 1976c). The median Full Scale range was similar across age groups, sexes, whites, blacks, parental occupations, and intelligence levels.

The range scatter index, however, is not too helpful because it is difficult to interpret. Many factors may influence the range between the highest and lowest subtest scores. Further, the range index deals with only two scores and fails to take into account the variability among all ten (or eleven or twelve) subtest scores. Yet, the range information is useful because it provides base rate information about what did occur in the standardization sample.

Number of subtests deviating from child's own average. An analysis of the number of subtest scores in the standardization sample that deviated from the child's own mean by 3 or more points indicated that the average child had about zero subtests deviating from his or her own Verbal Scale mean by at least 3 points, about one subtest deviating from the Performance Scale mean, and about two subtests deviating from the Full Scale mean (Kaufman, 1976c). For the ten standard subtests, 63 percent of the children in the standardization sample had no deviations of 3 or more scaled-score points on the Verbal Scale and 46 percent had no deviations on the Performance Scale.

Verbal-Performance Scale base rate differences. In our discussion of primary approaches to profile analysis we considered the minimum differences between the Verbal and Performance Scales that are statistically significant for the various age levels covered by the WISC-R. By extending the method previously used, we can determine the probability from .001 to .50 associated with various Verbal-Performance Scale differences. These probabilities are shown in Table C-10 of the Appendix. They reflect the reliability of the difference score, that is, the extent to which the difference is likely to be due to error of measurement. If the probability is at or below the .05 level, you can entertain the hypothesis that the difference is a "real one."

In addition to using the above approach for evaluating Verbal-Performance differences, we can also determine the extent to which a given discrepancy occurs in the standardization population (probability-of-occurrence approach). This approach also provides us with an expectancy table, as is shown in Table C-11 of the Appendix.

It is also of interest to consider the extent to which Verbal-Performance discrepancies occurred in the standardization sample in relation to IQ level and various demographic variables. The median discrepancy was 8 IQ points for the total group (Kaufman, 1976d). Brighter children had somewhat higher discrepancies (median discrepancy of 9 IQ points) than duller children (median discrepancy of 6 to 7 points).

Verbal-Performance IQ differences were not related significantly to either sex or race, but were related significantly to parental occupation and to intelligence level. Children of professional parents tended to have higher Verbal than Performance IQs, while children of semiskilled and unskilled workers tended to have higher Performance than Verbal IQs. More Verbal-Performance differences were observed in the brighter

groups than in the duller groups. At all levels of intelligence, it was about as likely that Verbal IQ would be higher than Performance IQ as that it would be lower.

We have just reviewed two different approaches to evaluating Verbal-Performance differences. One focuses on the reliability of the discrepancy, the other on the probability of occurrence in the standardization group. Both approaches can be used, and it is up to you to determine which approach is best suited to your needs. Research in this area would be most welcome. The reliability-of-difference approach tells us the probability that a difference between two scores is statistically significant. Whether or not such a difference has practical significance is still open to question. The probability-of-occurrence approach provides us with the frequency of occurrence. While a difference between the Verbal and Performance IQs may be statistically significant, if it occurs in a large proportion of the standardization sample it may take on less diagnostic significance.

In summary, Verbal-Performance differences may be significant and yet occur with some frequency in the population. Thus, the discrepancy may be a reliable one but not a unique one. The probability-of-occurrence approach is dependent on the correlation between the two scales, while the reliability-of-difference approach is based on the standard error of measurement of each scale. I recommend that when reliable (significant) differences occur between the child's Verbal and Performance Scales, hypotheses about the child's cognitive strengths and weaknesses be formulated. This recommendation is made because discrepancies may provide a meaningful profile (or pattern) of abilities, even though they may occur in a large segment of the population.

Comment on Profile Analysis

A statistically significant difference between subtests or scales tells us that the difference is large enough so that it cannot be attributed to measurement error. When the difference is significant, it means that the difference is one that can be reliably measured through the abilities tapped by the respective subtests or scales. I recommend, in contrast to the WISC-R manual, that, as a minimum, the .05 level of significance be used to determine whether or not there are significant differences between scaled scores and between Verbal and Performance Scale IQs. This recommendation is made in order to reduce the chances of making a Type I error (accepting differences between scores as true differences when they are not in fact true differences).

The WISC-R manual states that a Verbal-Performance difference of 15 points or more calls for "further investigation." However, no further information is given. Does Wechsler mean, for example, that the child be administered additional special tests, receive a neurological examination, or be observed in the classroom? While a Verbal-Performance Scale difference that is significant at the .05 or .01 level should be considered somewhat unusual, it should not necessarily mean that there is a need for further investigation. The child's entire performance should always be evaluated carefully, especially the scatter on the individual subtests, together with case history material and background factors (e.g., interests, cultural factors, physical disabilities, home environment, minority group status, or bilingualism) whenever WISC-R scores are interpreted.

Profile analysis is a useful tool for comparing intraindividual differences in various ability and achievement areas. It must be kept in mind that profile differences represent only uneven skill development. Taken alone, they do not permit one to make decisions about pathological conditions or possible causes and cures of the uneven development. Rather, they serve as an adjunct to other assessment strategies used by clinicians and educators in performing a diagnostic evaluation and in developing remediation programs.

Comparisons Between WISC-R Scales That Can Guide Interpretations

The evaluation of the WISC-R Verbal and Performance Scales is dependent primarily on the assumptions made for the individual subtests that comprise the respective scales. However, some general observations can be made concerning the two scales. The Verbal Scale is dependent on the child's accumulated experience, and usually requires an automatic response with what is already known. The scale involves auditory verbal input and vocal verbal output. The Performance Scale is more dependent on the child's immediate problem-solving ability and requires the child to meet new situations and apply past experience and previously acquired skills to a new set of demands. The scale involves visual nonverbal input, some verbal input, and motor nonverbal output. It might be considered to be an index of nonverbal ability or of fluid intelligence. A summary of the interpretative rationales, possible implications of high and low scores, and instructional implications for the Verbal, Performance, and Full Scales and for the Freedom from Distractibility factor score is presented in Table C-29 in the Appendix.

Discrepancies between the Verbal and Performance Scales lend themselves to the development of various hypotheses. However, before any hypotheses are formulated, the discrepancies should be at a significance level of .05 or below, as was previously mentioned. Significant Verbal-Performance discrepancies may indicate any one of a number of possibilities, including the following:

1. an expression of interests,
2. an expression of cognitive style,
3. an expression of psychopathology (such as emotional disturbance or brain damage),
4. deficiencies (or strengths) in processing information,
5. deficiencies (or strengths) in certain modes of expression,
6. deficiencies (or strengths) in working under conditions of pressure (such as time constraints on the Performance Scale), or
7. sensory deficiencies.

Which possibilities are appropriate must be decided on the basis of background information and the child's entire performance.

Some hypotheses to consider relative to Verbal-Performance discrepancies are found in Table 11-2. These hypotheses must be formulated in relationship to the absolute IQs obtained by the child. We would not say, for example, that a child with a Verbal IQ of 150 and a Performance IQ of 125 had a performance deficit. In this case both abilities are well developed, with verbal skills even better developed than performance skills.

In addition to the hypotheses presented in Table 11-2, hypotheses about Verbal-Performance discrepancies have been developed in relation to various forms of psychopathology. Juvenile delinquents, for example, tend to have higher Performance Scale IQs than Verbal Scale IQs. In some cases of brain damage, there is a significant decrement in the Performance Scale. These and other clinical applications of the Verbal-Performance discrepancy are discussed in the chapters of this book that cover the field of psychopathology and learning disabilities.

Comparisons Between WISC-R Factor Scores That Can Guide Interpretations

In Chapter 9 we discussed how factor scores can be developed for the WISC-R. These factor scores are somewhat purer measures of verbal comprehension and perceptual organization than the Verbal and Performance IQs. The Freedom from Distractibility factor score also can assist one in evaluating the child's ability to attend and concentrate. As with the Verbal and Performance Scale IQs, it is necessary to determine whether the factor scores are significantly different from one another before interpretations are made about the child's strengths and weaknesses. Table C-6 in the Appendix presents the differences between sets of Deviation IQs on the Verbal Comprehension, Perceptual Organization, and Freedom from Distractibility factor scores that are needed to satisfy the .05 and .01 significance levels.

The Verbal Comprehension and Perceptual Organization factors can be interpreted in a manner similar to that used for the interpretation of the Verbal and Performance Scales, respectively. These interpretations were considered in the preceding section. The Freedom from Distractibility factor score is somewhat more difficult to interpret. It may involve attention, concentration, numerical ability, and short-term memory. If the child's three subtest scores (Arithmetic, Digit Span, and Coding) are not consistent (e.g., high Digit Span and low Arithmetic and Coding), the factor score may be especially difficult to interpret. If the child performed consistently, the examiner may have more confidence in his or her interpretation of the Freedom from Distractibility score. Table C-29 in the Appendix presents guidelines for interpreting this factor score.

It is not necessary or desirable to report factor scores in the psychological evaluation. As Kaufman (1979a) points out, the three standard IQs are sufficient. The factor scores simply are a way of generating hypotheses to interpret the child's pattern of performance.

Kaufman also suggested that the mean on the Freedom from Distractibility factor can

TABLE 11-2.   Illustrations of Hypotheses Developed from Verbal-Performance Discrepancies

Verbal > Performance	*Performance > Verbal*
1. Verbal skills better developed than performance skills.	1. Performance skills better developed than verbal skills.
2. Auditory processing mode better developed than visual nonverbal mode.	2. Visual nonverbal mode better developed than auditory processing mode.
3. Possible difficulty with practical tasks.	3. Possible difficulty with reading.
4. Possible performance deficit.	4. Possible language deficit.
5. Possible limitations in motor nonverbal output skills.	5. Possible limitations in auditory conceptual skills.

be compared with the means on the other two factors to determine whether or not there is a meaningful discrepancy. As a rule of thumb, he advised that the means should differ by 3 or more scaled-score points. Let us look at an example of how this can be done. A child obtains scaled scores of 8, 10, 11, 11 on the Information, Comprehension, Similarities, and Vocabulary subtests ($M = 10$); scaled scores of 4, 5, 6, and 9 on Picture Completion, Picture Arrangement, Block Design, and Object Assembly ($M = 6$); and scaled scores of 6, 7, and 8 on Arithmetic, Digit Span, and Coding ($M = 7$). Using Kaufman's suggested rule of thumb, we find that there is a meaningful discrepancy between Freedom from Distractibility and Verbal Comprehension ($10 - 7 = 3$) but not between Freedom from Distractibility and Perceptual Organization ($7 - 6 = 1$).

Kaufman (1979a) also advises that if the Freedom from Distractibility factor score is used to formulate interpretations, it should be compared to the Verbal Comprehension and Perceptual Organization factor scores instead of to the Verbal Scale and Performance Scale IQs. This recommendation is made because the Verbal and Performance Scale IQs contain subtests that are also in the Freedom from Distractibility factor. Consequently, comparing the three factor scores does not involve overlapping subtests. Finally, the mean scaled score on any of the three factors can be reported as a percentile in the report (by use of Table C-28 in the Appendix), if so desired.

Comparisons Between WISC-R Subtests That Can Guide Interpretations

In the section on profile analysis, detailed procedures were described for making comparisons between sets of subtest scaled scores. Interpreting the meaning of differences between subtest scores is not an easy matter. Once significance has been established, one needs to translate the statistical findings into meaningful descriptions. Careful study of the material that has been presented for each subtest in Chapter 10, and of the material presented in this chapter, will facilitate making such interpretations. The interpretations that follow should be viewed as hypotheses that may prove to be useful in the evaluation of a child's performance, but that need further investigation through study of the child's entire test performance and through research. The hypotheses should be treated as tentative, *formulated in relation to the child's absolute scaled scores*, and *not* referred to as "verified insights."

The following examples illustrate how subtests can be compared. However, neither are they an exhaustive list of comparisons, nor do they reflect all possible interpretations. You should be able to develop and formulate other interpretations, building from these examples and from the material covered in Chapter 10.

1. *Information and Comprehension.* This is a comparison of the amount of information retained (Information) and the ability to use information (Comprehension). Information requires factual knowledge, while Comprehension requires both factual knowledge and judgment.

   I > C: High Information and low Comprehension may suggest that children have general knowledge but are not able to synthesize and use information to solve problems involving the social world.

   I < C: Low Information and high Comprehension may suggest that children have been limited in their exposure to factual material, but use their limited knowledge to make appropriate judgments.

2. *Comprehension and Arithmetic.* Both the Comprehension and Arithmetic subtests require reasoning ability or, more specifically, the ability to analyze a given set of material and then to recognize the elements that are needed for the solution of the specified problem.

   C > A: High Comprehension and low Arithmetic may suggest that reasoning ability is adequate in social situations but not in situations involving numbers.

3. *Arithmetic and Digit Span.* Both the Arithmetic and Digit Span subtests

require facility with numbers and ability in immediate recall. Comparing the two subtests may provide an index of the relative balance between attention (Digit Span) and concentration (Arithmetic).

DS>A: High Digit Span and low Arithmetic may suggest that attention is better developed than concentration.

4. *Similarities and Comprehension.* S>C: High Similarities and low Comprehension may suggest that children have the ability to do abstract thinking but cannot apply their conceptualizing ability to solve problems in the social world.

5. *Vocabulary and Similarities.* Both Vocabulary and Similarities measure level of abstract thinking and ability to form concepts, but Similarities is a better measure of these abilities.

S>V: High Similarities and low Vocabulary may suggest that children have the mental ability to do abstract thinking but have had restricted opportunities to learn new words.

6. *Vocabulary, Information, and Comprehension.* V, I>C: High Vocabulary and Information coupled with low Comprehension may suggest that the individuals are not able to use fully their verbal facility and general knowledge in life situations; they therefore may have impaired judgment (Rapaport et al., 1968).

7. *Digit Span—Forward versus Backward.* DF>DB: High Digits Forward and low Digits Backward may indicate that the child did not put forth the extra effort needed to master the more difficult task of recalling digits backward in sequence.

DB>DF: High Digits Backward and low Digits Forward may occur when children see Digits Backward as a challenge rather than as a task which consists of a mere repetition of numbers.

8. *Similarities and Digit Span.* S>DS: High Similarities and low Digit Span may reflect good conceptualizing ability coupled with poor rote auditory memory for digits. Children with this pattern may do poorly in acquiring reading

decoding skills that are highly dependent on memorization of sound-symbol relationships. However, their listening comprehension may be strong (Malter, 1977).

9. *Comprehension and Picture Arrangement.* Both the Comprehension and Picture Arrangement subtests contain stimuli that are concerned with social interaction. Scores on the two subtests permit comparison of knowledge of social conventions (Comprehension) with the capacity to anticipate and plan in a social context (Picture Arrangement).

PA>C: High Picture Arrangement coupled with low Comprehension may indicate that the individuals are sensitive to interpersonal nuances, but disregard social conventions (Blatt & Allison, 1968).

C>PA: An adequate Comprehension score coupled with a poor Picture Arrangement score suggests that the children can understand social situations in the abstract, but once they are involved in them they may be unable to decide what they may mean or how to act (Palmer, 1970).

10. *Picture Completion and Picture Arrangement.* This comparison provides an estimate of attention to detail versus organization of detail. Both tasks involve perception of details, with Picture Arrangement requiring logical ordering of details or sequencing.

PC>PA: High Picture Completion and low Picture Arrangement may suggest that perception of details in nonsequencing tasks is better developed than that in tasks requiring sequencing and organization.

11. *Picture Completion and Block Design.* This comparison involves an estimate of visual perception versus visual-motor-spatial coordination.

PC>BD: High Picture Completion and low Block Design may suggest that children have adequate nonspatial visual perceptual ability but have difficulty in spatial visualization.

12. *Object Assembly and Picture Arrangement.* This comparison provides an esti-

mate of inductive reasoning versus sequencing. Both tasks require synthesis into wholes without a model to follow, with Picture Arrangement involving sequencing in addition.

OA > PA: High Object Assembly and low Picture Arrangement may suggest that visual inductive reasoning skills are better developed than visual sequencing skills.

13. *Object Assembly and Block Design.* This comparison provides an estimate of inductive reasoning (Object Assembly—working from parts to a whole) versus deductive reasoning (Block Design—working from a whole to parts). Both tasks involve perceptual organization and spatial visualization ability.

OA > BD: If Object Assembly is higher than Block Design, it may suggest that nonverbal inductive reasoning skills are better developed than nonverbal deductive reasoning skills.

14. *Block Design, Object Assembly, and Coding.* The Block Design, Object Assembly, and Coding subtests require visual-motor coordination; that is, they involve motor activity guided by visual organization. A visual direction is involved in the execution of the tasks. The role of visual organization differs in the three subtests (Rapaport et al., 1968). In the Block Design subtest, visual organization is involved in a process consisting of analysis (breaking down the pattern) and synthesis (building the pattern up again out of the blocks). In the Object Assembly subtest, the motor action consists of arranging parts into a meaningful pattern. In the Coding subtest, visual organization is of the same kind that is found in such activities as writing or drawing. Thus, the name "visual organization" does not refer to the same function in every case.

BD > CO: High Block Design and low Coding may suggest that visual organization skills involving analysis and synthesis are better than those involving visual-motor coordination.

Studies Evaluating Correlates of WISC-R Subtests

Research into some of the correlates associated with WISC and WISC-R subtests, although limited and with small samples, has produced some interesting findings. Comprehension has been found to be related to Vineland Social Maturity Scale scores (Krippner, 1964) and to teacher ratings of interpersonal maturity (Brannigan, 1975), but not to need-for-approval (Brannigan, 1976). Although Picture Arrangement was not found to be related to either interpersonal maturity or need-for-approval (Brannigan, 1975, 1976), it was found to be related to analytical ability (Kagan, Rosman, Day, Albert, & Phillips, 1964). Digit Span was not found to be related to degree of classroom distractibility (Nalven, 1969; Nalven & Puleo, 1968). Object Assembly does not appear to be related to concerns about body intactness and integrity (Marsden & Kalter, 1969; Rockwell, 1967).

Performance on the Coding subtest is facilitated by the learning of appropriate number-symbol pairs, memory, and speed of writing, but not by ability to discriminate between shapes, ability to label figures, response to incentives, time taken to refer to the code, or tendency to scan completed work.[3] Coding, too, has been found to be related to achievement orientation (Oakland, 1969). High scores on Block Design, Picture Completion, and Object Assembly appear to be related to field-independence—the ability to overcome embedding contexts by readily separating an item from its context (Goodenough & Karp, 1961). Reflective children have been found to obtain higher scores on Information, Comprehension, Digit Span, Picture Completion, Picture Arrangement, Block Design, and Object Assembly than impulsive children (Brannigan & Ash, 1977).

Estimated Percentile Ranks and Test-Age Equivalents for Raw Scores

In working with the subtest scaled scores, it is sometimes helpful to obtain their respective percentile ranks. Table C-28 in the

EXHIBIT 11-3. Exercises for the WISC-R

1. "The 15-point discrepancy between Mary's Verbal and Performance Scale IQs indicates that she has a learning disability."
2. "The 40-point difference between Greg's Verbal and Performance IQs can probably be accounted for by the fact that at age 6, Greg's visual-motor skills are not yet adequately developed to enable him to do his best on the nonverbal part of the WISC-R."
3. "Her high Verbal subtest scores indicate that she is able to express herself with little difficulty."
4. "His average scaled score was 9.8 on the WISC-R."
5. "His score on the WISC-R was equivalent to an IQ of approximately 98."
6. "Bill achieved a Verbal Scale score of 65, a Performance Scale score of 60, and a Full Scale IQ of 118."
7. "Mark did not score zero on any Comprehension items. He had twelve 2-point responses and five 1-point responses."
8. "On the WISC-R, the majority of her scores hovered around 12."
9. "It was not until the last two most difficult Comprehension items that Bill received scores of zero."
10. "The Digit Span is an optional subtest and was not used in computing the IQ."
11. A child obtained the following scores on the WISC-R: Information—1; Similarities—4; Arithmetic—7; Vocabulary—1; Comprehension—5; (Digit Span)—(3); Picture Completion—4; Picture Arrangement—3; Block Design—1; Object Assembly—7; Coding—5; (Mazes)—(1). The mean of the six Verbal Scale subtests was 3.8, and the mean of the six Performance Scale subtests was 3.5. The examiner reported the following: "Jim fell below his mean in the areas of Information, Vocabulary, and Digit Span."
12. "Bill scored high on Object Assembly because he was persistent in his attempt to assemble the objects."
13. "Her Verbal IQ is indicated to be 66."
14. "Henry scored in the average intellectual range on the WISC-R with a mental age of 7-2 and a chronological age of 7-6."
15. "Frank appears to be weak in the areas dealing with Freedom from Distractibility."
16. "A lower score on Information (scaled score 9) shows poor range of knowledge."
17. "Lack of social judgment and immature responses were noted on the Comprehension subtest (scaled score 8)."
18. "She showed a retarded score on the ability to see spatial relationships."
19. "John has average verbal concept formation as reflected by his ability to find the similarities between two seemingly opposite words."
20. "Discrepancies between this WISC-R administration and the one given three years ago may be due to Henry's variable attention and memory span or possible examiner differences."
21. "On the Coding subtest the child is asked to attach a meaningless symbol to a number."
22. "A high Picture Completion subtest score and a low Coding subtest score may predict difficulty in reading."
23. "Bill's Full Scale IQ was achieved with a 10-point difference between his Verbal and Performance Scale scores, in favor of the latter. This difference suggests an action-oriented person."
24. "A high score on Coding reflects a high and sustained energy level."
25. "His low Information score reflects potential repressive mechanisms at work."
26. "A total scaled score of 52 yielded a Performance IQ score of 102."
27. "She scored 12 in both Arithmetic and Similarities."
28. "Five of the twelve WISC-R subtests were two standard deviations from the mean, indicating that her performance was in the very superior range."
29. "A mean scaled score of 9 was obtained on the ten subtests."

Appendix shows the estimated percentile ranks for each WISC-R (and WPPSI and WAIS-R) scaled score. Scaled scores also can receive a qualitative description, and these descriptions, too, are shown in Table C-28. It is recommended that IQs never be estimated on the basis of only one subtest score.

Raw scores can be translated into approximate developmental levels or test-age equivalents, as was noted in Chapter 9. Thus, a raw score of 6 on the Information subtest may be roughly equivalent to a developmental age level of 6-6 years (see Table 21 in the WISC-R manual). In some settings and for some purposes, test-age scores may facilitate communication. However, they have many drawbacks, as was shown in Chapter 2. Their routine use is not recommended.

Test Your Skills

Exhibit 11-3 presents a series of exercises designed to sharpen your skills in writing reports and in interpreting the WISC-R. These exercises are similar to those that were presented at the end of Chapter 8 for the Stanford-Binet. Read each excerpt shown in Exhibit 11-3. In each case there is some inadequacy of description or interpretation. Find the mistakes in the sentences. After you have completed your analysis, check your evaluations with those that are shown in the Answers section on p. 542.

Summary

1. A successive level approach to test interpretation is helpful in the development of hypotheses. The five levels of the approach are as follows: (1) the Full Scale IQ, (2) Verbal and Performance IQs, (3) intersubtest scatter, (4) intrasubtest scatter, and (5) qualitative analysis.

2. Profile analysis should be based on a statistical approach, designed so as to evaluate differences between Verbal and Performance Scale IQs and between sets of subtest scaled scores. However, even after such differences are established as significant, it is necessary to consider a variety of factors that may account for a specific profile. Profile analysis is a method of generating hypotheses about the organization of intellective functions. Profile analysis is one form of test interpretation, and it must be looked at in relation to the entire test performance and background data.

3. The primary approaches to profile analysis include (a) comparing Verbal and Performance Scale IQs, (b) comparing Verbal and Performance subtest scaled scores with the average scores on the respective scales, and (c) comparing sets of individual subtest scores.

4. Secondary approaches to profile analysis include an evaluation of subtest scaled-score ranges, number of subtests deviating from child's own average, and Verbal-Performance Scale differences based upon frequency of occurrence in the population.

5. Interpreting the findings of profile analysis requires considerable judgment and skill.

6. Scale differences and subtest differences should be intrepreted only when the differences are statistically significant.

7. Verbal-Performance Scale differences may reflect the child's interest or cognitive style or be an indication of some type of deficit.

8. Studies evaluating the correlates of WISC and WISC-R subtests suggest that various subtests are related to behavioral ratings, associative learning, and cognitive style.

9. It is helpful to translate scaled scores to percentile ranks and occasionally to test-age equivalents.

CHAPTER *12*

Wechsler Preschool and Primary Scale of Intelligence (WPPSI): Description

From the child of five to myself is but a step. But from the new-born baby to the child of five is an appalling distance.

TOLSTOY

EXHIBIT 12-1. Illustrations and Descriptions of Items Like Those on the WPPSI

Information (23 questions)

Show me your eyes. Touch them.
How many legs does a cat have?
In what kind of store do we buy meat?
What is the color of an emerald?

Vocabulary (22 words)

boot
book
nice
annoy

Arithmetic (20 problems)

Card with squares of different sizes. Card is placed in front of child. Examiner says, "Here are some squares. Which one is the biggest? Point to it."
Bill had one penny and his mother gave him one more. How many pennies does he now have?
Judy had 4 books. She lost 1. How many books does she have left?
Jimmy had 7 bananas and he bought 8 more. How many bananas does he have altogether?

Similarities (16 questions)

You can read a book and you can also read a ___.
Apple pie and ice cream are both good to ___.
In what way are a quarter and a dollar alike?
In what way are a cow and a pig alike?

Comprehension (15 questions)

Why do you need to take a bath?
Why do we have farms?
What makes a sailboat move?

Sentences (10 sentences)

The task is to repeat sentences given orally by the examiner.

Mother loves me.
Ted likes to eat apples.
Martha likes to visit the museum. She will go there today.

Animal House

The task is to place appropriate colored cylinders in the corresponding holes on a board. The colored cylinders are matched with four different animals. The Animal House task is shown in the photograph of the WPPSI (Figure 12-1).

EXHIBIT 12-1   (cont.)

Picture Completion (23 items)

The task is to identify the essential missing part of the picture (see Figure 12-1).

A picture of a tricycle without handlebars.
A picture of a doll without a leg.
A picture of a swing without a seat.

Mazes (10 mazes)

The task is to complete a series of mazes. An example of a maze is shown in the photograph of the WPPSI (Figure 12-1).

Geometric Design (10 designs)

The task is to copy geometric desgins which are shown on printed cards. The designs include a circle, square, triangle, and diamond.

Block Design (10 designs)

The task is to reproduce the stimulus designs using three or four blocks. The blocks are shown in the photograph of the WPPSI (Figure 12-1). ■

Note. The questions resemble those that appear on the WPPSI but are not actually from the test. Chapter 13 describes each subtest in more detail.

In 1967 the Wechsler Preschool and Primary Scale of Intelligence (WPPSI) was published for use with children between the ages of 4 and 6½ years (Wechsler, 1967). It is a separate and distinct scale, although similar to the WISC-R in form and content. The WPPSI contains eleven subtests (as shown in Exhibit 12-1), eight of which (Information, Vocabulary, Arithmetic, Similarities, Comprehension, Picture Completion, Mazes, and Block Design) also appear on the WISC-R and three of which (Sentences, Animal House, and Geometric Design) are unique to the WPPSI. Excluded from the WPPSI are the Digit Span, Picture Arrangement, Object Assembly, and Coding subtests that are found on the WISC-R. The methods of computing the IQ and evalu-

FIGURE 12-1. Wechsler Preschool and Primary Scale of Intelligence. Courtesy of The Psychological Corporation.

ating scores are similar to those employed on the WISC-R. The WPPSI can be considered a downward extension of the WISC-R.

Standardization

The WPPSI was standardized on 1,200 children, 100 boys and 100 girls in each of six age groups, ranging by half-years from 4 to 6½ years. The 1960 U.S. census data were used to select representative children for the normative sample. Whites and nonwhites were included in the sample, based on the ratios found in the census for four geographic regions in the United States.

Reliability

The WPPSI has excellent reliability. Reliabilities for each of the three IQs range from .91 to .96 over the range covered by the scale. Average reliability coefficients, based on the average of the six age groups, are as follows: .96 for the Full Scale IQ, .94 for the Verbal Scale IQ, and .93 for the Performance Scale IQ.

The reliabilities for the subtests are not as satisfactory as those for the three scales (see Table 12-1). The average subtest reliabilities range from a low of .77 for Animal House to a high of .87 for Mazes. Reliabilities are similar for Verbal and Performance Scale subtests. When the reliability coefficients are considered separately for each of the six age groups in the standardization sample, they range from a low of .62 for Animal House at 4 years of age to a high of .91 for Mazes at 5½ years of age. The reliability coefficients are similar across the six age groups.

Satisfactory split-half Full Scale reliabilities have been reported for a variety of populations, including Mexican-American children ($r = .95$) (Henderson & Rankin, 1973), gifted children ($r = .93$) (Ruschival & Way, 1971), mentally retarded children ($r = .88$) (Richards, 1970), and English children ($r = .97$) (Brittain, 1969). A test-retest study over a one-year time period revealed satisfactory reliability ($r = .89$) for the WPPSI Full Scale IQ for a group of twenty-five

TABLE 12-1.   Average Reliability Coefficients and Standard Errors of Measurement for WPPSI Subtests and Scales

Subtest and Scale	Average Reliability Coefficient	Average Standard Error of Measurement
Information	.81	1.34
Vocabulary	.84	1.21
Arithmetic	.82	1.23
Similarities	.83	1.24
Comprehension	.81	1.32
Sentences	.85	1.18
Animal House	.77	1.46
Picture Completion	.83	1.20
Mazes	.87	1.08
Geometric Design	.82	1.29
Block Design	.82	1.26
Verbal IQ	.94	3.57
Performance IQ	.93	3.85
Full Scale IQ	.96	2.88

Note. Reliability coefficients for all subtests except Animal House are odd-even correlations corrected by the Spearman-Brown formula. For Animal House the reliability coefficients are test-retest coefficients.

Adapted from Wechsler (1967).

black, lower socioeconomic class children (Croake, Keller, & Catlin, 1973).

Increases on the average of 3, 6.6, and 3.6 IQ points for the Verbal, Performance, and Full Scales, respectively, were found for fifty children in the standardization group when the test was readministered after a period of approximately eleven weeks (see Table 12-2). Respective test-retest correlations were .86, .89, and .91 for the Verbal, Performance, and Full Scales. The changes in subtest scaled scores, which probably were for the most part due to practice effects, ranged from −.2 (Sentences) to +1.3 (Mazes), and were significant on the Information (+.7), Similarities (+.7), Animal House (+.4), Picture Completion (+.7), Mazes (+1.3), and Block Design (+1.0) subtests, but not on the others (Wasik & Wasik, 1970). Generally, the Performance Scale subtests showed greater practice effects than the Verbal Scale subtests.

TABLE 12-2.   Test-Retest WPPSI IQs for Fifty Children Between 5¼ and 5¾ Years of Age

Scale	First Testing		Second Testing		Change
	Mean IQ	SD	Mean IQ	SD	
Verbal	104.5	14.7	107.5	13.9	+3.0
Performance	103.8	14.1	110.4	13.7	+6.6
Full	105.6	14.8	109.2	13.3	+3.6

Adapted from Wechsler (1967).

Validity

The WPPSI manual presents minimal information about the validity of the scale. However, since the publication of the WPPSI, there have been a number of concurrent and predictive validity studies.

WPPSI and Stanford-Binet. Most of the studies correlating the WPPSI and the Stanford-Binet used the 1960 Stanford-Binet norms instead of the 1972 norms, because the studies were published prior to 1973 when the new norms became available. Those studies using the 1960 Stanford-Binet norms indicated that the WPPSI had satisfactory concurrent validity, with a median correlation of .82 between the two scales.[1] The WPPSI Verbal Scale correlates more highly with the Stanford-Binet than does the Performance Scale (median *r* of .81 vs. .67).

Before the Stanford-Binet was renormed, in many cases it yielded substantially higher IQs than the WPPSI. Therefore, IQs provided by the 1960 Stanford-Binet norms were not interchangeable with those of the WPPSI. With the 1972 norms, the Stanford-Binet yields IQs that are on the average about 7 to 10 IQ points lower than they were in the 1960 norms for children in the 4- to 6-year-old age range. Therefore, it is likely that the two scales now yield more similar IQs. However, this statement must be tempered with the fact that there are few published research studies on the 1972 Stanford-Binet norms and the WPPSI. In one study with thirty-five black children, the WPPSI yielded somewhat higher IQs than the Stanford-Binet (*M* of 96 vs. 91), and a correlation of .71 (Sewell, 1977).

WPPSI and WISC. Because the WPPSI and the WISC overlap between the ages of 5 and 6½ years, it is of interest to review the studies that have compared the two scales. Correlations between the two scales run from .57 to .91 for the Verbal Scale, from .41 to .82 for the Performance Scale, and from .54 to .90 for the Full Scale (median correlation of .81).[2] These results suggest that the two scales are related to a significant degree. However, this conclusion is somewhat tentative because of the limited number of studies and the restricted populations (primarily Head Start children) that have been used. Full Scale IQs appear to be very similar, differing by 6 points or less in most studies.

WPPSI and WISC-R. As we have seen in Chapter 9, the WPPSI and the WISC-R overlap for a six-month period, from 6-0 to 6-6 years. The two studies cited in that chapter indicated that the WPPSI tends to provide somewhat higher IQs than the WISC-R. Thus, WPPSI and WISC-R IQs may not be directly interchangeable. Further research is needed to explore the comparability of these two tests.

WPPSI and achievement tests. The relationship between the WPPSI and a number of achievement tests has been studied in a variety of populations. Predictive validity coefficients appear to be satisfactory for white middle-class populations. A coefficient of .58 was reported between the WPPSI Full Scale and the Gray Oral Reading Test, administered one to three years after the WPPSI, for a group of twenty-eight white middle-class children (White & Jacobs, 1979). Kaufman (1973b) reported correlations of .30 and .37 between the WPPSI and the Metropolitan Achievement Tests Mathematics and Reading parts, respectively, which were administered approximately four months after the WPPSI, for a group of thirty-one white middle-class 6-year-olds. Pasewark, Scherr, and Sawyer (1974) reported a significant correlation between the WPPSI and the Metropolitan Achievement Tests total score ($r = .58$) for a sample of thirty normal 6-year-olds.

Krebs (1969) investigated the effectiveness of the WPPSI in predicting reading scores. At kindergarten age, seventy children (thirty-four boys and thirty-six girls), equally divided into lower and upper socioeconomic status groups, were administered the WPPSI. One year later in first grade, the Stanford Achievement Test, which contains sections on reading, and the Gilmore Oral Reading Paragraphs Test were administered. As Table 12-3 shows, all of the subtests and scales were found to be related significantly to reading scores on both tests. When breakdowns were made for socioeconomic class, the WPPSI scores were found to have higher correlations with reading scores in the lower socioeconomic status group than in the upper socioeconomic status group. For example, in the lower socioeconomic status group, the correlations with the total reading score on the Stanford Achievement Test for the Verbal, Performance, and Full Scales were .59, .61, and .66, respectively, whereas in the upper socioeconomic status group, they were .32, .35, and .40, respectively. In the total sample, the two best subtests for predicting the total reading achievement score on the Stanford Achievement Test were Arithmetic and Geometric Design ($R = .63$).

With ethnic minority children or with children of lower socioeconomic status the predictive validity of the WPPSI is somewhat more variable than it is for white middle-class children. In one study (Crockett, Rardin, & Pasewark, 1976), a sample of Head Start children were administered the Metropolitan Achievement Tests three to four years after the WPPSI. The only significant correlations were between Mathematics and the Full Scale IQ ($r = .43$) and between Mathematics and the Performance Scale IQ ($r = .52$). The investigators indicated that the WPPSI Verbal Scale must be viewed with caution in the evaluation of Head Start children because many of these children are of lower socioeconomic status, bilingual, and may evidence atypical development of language skills during primary school years. In another study of the validity of the WPPSI with a group of fifty black, thirty-two white, four Hispanic, and one Oriental child, all of whom were of lower socioeconomic status and had been referred to a special setting because of personal and social difficulties, the WPPSI Full Scale IQ was found to be significantly associated with gross assessments of speech development ($r = .61$), motor development ($r = .41$), and perceived improvement in a specialized program ($r = .73$) (Dlugokinski, Weiss, & Johnston, 1976).

Henderson and Rankin (1973), from their work with Mexican-American 5½-year-old

TABLE 12-3. Correlations Between WPPSI and Two Reading Tests

WPPSI Subtest	Gilmore Oral Reading Paragraphs Test	Stanford Achievement Test: Reading
Information	.49	.52
Vocabulary	.52	.53
Arithmetic	.54	.58
Similarities	.48	.53
Comprehension	.36	.38
Sentences	.54	.55
Animal House	.41	.46
Picture Completion	.43	.47
Mazes	.42	.47
Geometric Design	.52	.54
Block Design	.44	.49
Verbal Scale IQ	.57	.61
Performance Scale IQ	.58	.63
Full Scale IQ	.62	.68

Reprinted by permission of the author from E. G. Krebs, "The Wechsler Preschool and Primary Scale of Intelligence and Prediction of Reading Achievement in First Grade" (Doctoral dissertation, Rutgers State University). Ann Arbor, Mich.: University Microfilms, 1969, pp. 73a-73b, No. 70-3361. Copyright 1970, E. G. Krebs.

children from economically depressed areas, suggested that it is ill-advised to use the WPPSI as a routine tool for the identification of children to be placed in special classes. They found that there was an 18-point difference between the children's Verbal and Performance Scale IQs (74 vs. 92), and that the predictive validity of the WPPSI, using third grade Metropolitan Reading Tests scores as the criterion, was poor ($r = .27$). The WPPSI, therefore, appears to have dubious utility as a predictor of later school performance for this group of children. Unfortunately, since separate correlations for the Verbal and Performance scales were not reported, there is no way of knowing which of the scales is the more valid predictor of future academic performance.

The few studies available on the predictive validity of the WPPSI indicate that much attention must be given to the type of children studied; the WPPSI scale studied (Verbal, Performance, or Full Scale); and the length of time between the administration of the WPPSI and the criterion measure. Overall, the WPPSI appears to have some predictive validity for both white children and ethnic minority children, although more work is needed to arrive at any firm conclusions

about the predictive validity of the WPPSI for Mexican-American children.

WPPSI and other tests. The relationship between the WPPSI and tests other than the Stanford-Binet, WISC, WISC-R, and achievement tests also has been studied. Correlations between the WPPSI and a variety of other tests have ranged from a low of .30 (Progressive Matrices) to a high of .82 (Primary Mental Abilities Test), with a median correlation of .64.[3] In eight of the nine investigations, lower-class or ethnic minority group or Head Start children were studied; therefore, it is difficult to know whether the findings are generalizable to other groups of children. WPPSI scores also have been found to be related significantly both to perceptual development and to creativity (Lichtman, 1969; Yule et al., 1969).

Factor Analysis

A factor analysis of the WPPSI, using the standardization sample, yielded two principal factors: Verbal and Performance (Carlson & Reynolds, 1980). The factor loadings associated with the two factors are shown in Table 12-4. The Verbal factor is best repre-

TABLE 12-4. Factor Loadings of WPPSI Subtests for Six Age Groups (Varimax Rotation)

Subtest	Factor A—Verbal							Factor B—Performance						
	4[a]	4½	5	5½	6	6½	Mdn	4[a]	4½	5	5½	6	6½	Mdn
Information	71	74	66	74	69	74	72	32	29	37	40	34	31	33
Vocabulary	63	70	63	68	70	62	65	31	18	31	31	32	35	31
Arithmetic	50	56	54	61	54	55	54	45	42	51	51	46	54	48
Similarities	75	69	57	66	61	72	67	17	26	13	17	31	23	21
Comprehension	71	77	73	71	75	71	72	29	17	28	31	25	22	27
Sentences	66	66	53	61	55	65	63	27	28	29	30	39	21	28
Animal House	46	40	25	32	25	25	28	29	43	60	56	63	42	49
Picture Completion	43	49	37	37	42	31	40	51	42	50	53	54	49	50
Mazes	15	07	29	30	42	10	22	77	65	57	61	58	65	63
Geometric Design	27	27	24	17	25	20	24	62	57	73	80	75	62	67
Block Design	32	29	22	35	45	34	33	50	56	72	68	55	61	58

Note. Decimals omitted.

[a]This row indicates age level.

From Carlson and Reynolds (1980).

sented by the six Verbal Scale subtests (Information, Vocabulary, Comprehension, Arithmetic, Similarities, and Sentences), while the Performance factor is best represented by the five Performance Scale subtests (Block Design, Mazes, Geometric Design, Picture Completion, and Animal House). While the factor loadings vary somewhat across age levels, the general trends noted can be applied to the various age levels covered by the scale. The results support the division of the WPPSI into Verbal and Performance Scales, provide construct validity for the test, and suggest that for children between the ages of 4 and 6 the WPPSI may be a more sensitive instrument for the purpose of assessing the structure of intelligence than is the Stanford-Binet.

WPPSI subtests as measures of g. A hierarchical factor analysis, using the WPPSI standardization sample, indicated that all of the eleven WPPSI subtests have strong loadings on a general intelligence factor (*g*), as is shown in Table 12-5 (Wallbrown, Blaha, & Wherry, 1973). The loadings are relatively similar across the age levels of the test, suggesting that differentiation of abilities is not

apparent during the ages covered by the scale. Although the Verbal subtests tend to have the highest *g* loadings, the range of median loadings for the eleven subtests is relatively narrow (.55 to .72). The *g* factor accounts for the largest percentage of subtest variance (39 percent).

WPPSI subtest specificity. WPPSI subtests, with the exception of Information and Comprehension, have enough specificity to warrant specific clinical interpretation across the age range covered by the scale (Carlson & Reynolds, 1980). Thus, most subtests allow for individual interpretation of a child's strengths and weaknesses.

Factor analysis of WPPSI compared to WISC-R. The primary difference between WPPSI and WISC-R factor analytic findings is that a Freedom from Distractibility factor emerges on the WISC-R but not on the WPPSI. Conceivably, sustained directed attention, partly measured by the Freedom from Distractibility factor, is a part of every subtest at younger age levels and only emerges as a separate factor for older ages. It appears that the factor structure of the WPPSI is generally similar to that of the WISC-R, particularly in regard to the Verbal Comprehension and Perceptual Organization factors.

Factor structure for black children and white children. In a factor analysis of the WPPSI scores of black children and white children in the standardization sample, the same two factors, Verbal and Performance, were found in each group (Kaufman & Hollenbeck, 1974). Various statistical procedures used to test the similarity of factor loadings also indicated that the WPPSI has virtually the same structure for black children as it does for white children. These results suggest that WPPSI is a fair instrument, in the sense that it is measuring the same dimensions of intellect in both ethnic groups.

Factor structure for two cultural groups. A study (Heil, Barclay, & Endres, 1978) of the WPPSI factor structure of two groups of

TABLE 12-5.   WPPSI Subtests as Measures of *g*

Subtest	Median Loading	Percent Proportion of Variance Attributed to g
Information	.72	52
Vocabulary	.64	41
Arithmetic	.68	46
Similarities	.63	40
Comprehension	.68	46
Sentences	.64	41
Animal House	.55	30
Picture Completion	.60	36
Mazes	.57	32
Geometric Design	.64	41
Block Design	.62	38

Note. The square of the median coefficient provides the percent proportion of each subtest's variance that may be attributed to *g*.

Adapted from Wallbrown, Blaha, and Wherry (1973).

white preschool children, one of which was "educationally deprived" (educationally handicapped due to poverty, neglect, delinquency, or cultural or linguistic isolation from the community at large) and the other normal, found essentially the same three factors in both groups: a Verbal factor, a Performance factor, and a factor limited to the Picture Completion subtest. These results, which support those found for samples of black and white children, indicate that cultural differences do not produce differences in intellectual structure on the WPPSI.

Demographic Correlates

Sex differences have been found on some WPPSI subtests. In the standardization sample, boys obtained significantly higher scores than girls on the Mazes subtest, while girls obtained higher scores than boys on the Animal House, Geometric Design, Block Design, and Sentences subtests (Herman, 1968). Thus, Performance IQs may be achieved in different ways by boys and girls. In a sample of 5½-year-old English children, boys obtained higher WPPSI IQs than girls (M IQs of 104 vs. 98), thus indicating that

the test may be biased in favor of boys when used in England (Brittain, 1969). However, significant sex differences in IQ were not found by Ruschival and Way (1971) in an American sample. Generally, for purposes of individual assessment, sex differences do not appear to play an important role.

A study of the relationship of WPPSI IQs to socioeconomic status (SES) (as determined by father's occupation), urban vs. rural residence, and geographic region of children in the standardization group revealed some important trends (Kaufman, 1973c). With respect to SES, the largest difference, about 18 points, was found between children of unskilled laborers and those of professional men, while differences between SES levels 2, 3, and 4 were not significant (see Table 12-6). Urban-rural residence was not a significant factor, but geographic region was. Children from the west had significantly higher IQs than children in the other regions, while those in the other three regions did not differ significantly from one another. There is no readily available explanation to account for the one regional difference. SES differences corroborate those found on the WISC-R (Kaufman & Doppelt,

TABLE 12-6. Means and Standard Deviations of WPPSI IQs for SES, Residence, and Region

Demographic Variable	N	Verbal IQ		Performance IQ		Full Scale IQ	
		M	SD	M	SD	M	SD
SES (Father's occupation)							
1. Professional & Technical	78	110	13	108	12	110	12
2. Manager, Clerical, & Sales	78	102	13	102	13	102	12
3. Skilled	78	100	15	100	14	100	15
4. Semiskilled	78	98	14	99	15	99	14
5. Unskilled	78	93	14	93	16	92	15
Residence							
Urban	325	99	14	98	15	98	15
Rural	325	99	14	99	14	99	14
Region							
Northeast	178	101	14	102	14	102	14
North Central	178	101	15	100	15	102	16
South	178	98	15	98	16	98	15
West	178	105	13	104	13	105	13

Reprinted, with a change in notation, by permission of the publisher and author from A. S. Kaufman, "The Relationship of WPPSI IQs to SES and Other Background Variables," *Journal of Clinical Psychology, 29,* p. 356. Copyright 1973, Clinical Psychology Publishing Co., Inc.

1976), WISC (Seashore, Wesman, & Doppelt, 1950), and Stanford-Binet (McNemar, 1942).

Kaufman (1973a) compared the performances of 132 matched pairs of black children and white children in the WPPSI standardization group. The children were matched on age, sex, geographic region, father's occupation, and urban-rural residence. The white children obtained significantly higher Verbal (99 vs. 88), Performance (97 vs. 88), and Full Scale (98 vs. 87) IQs at all of the age levels studied, on the average by about 11 IQ points.

On the Performance Scale only, differences between the two ethnic groups were significant at the 4-year-old level, but not at the 5- and 6-year-old levels. Differences in the Performance IQ decreased with increasing age almost in a linear fashion: 16 points at 4 years, 11 points at 4½ years, 8 points at 5 years, 7 points at 5½ years and 6 years, and 5 points at 6½ years. This trend suggests that a cumulative deficit was not shown by this sample of preschool and primary children. It is not easy to explain why the older black children performed at a level so much above that of their younger peers.

Assets of the WPPSI

The WPPSI has many assets, as well as some limitations. Reviewers and investigators have commented favorably on these aspects of the WPPSI (Eichorn, 1972; Oldridge & Allison, 1968).

1. *Excellent psychometric properties.* The WPPSI has excellent reliability and validity and has been carefully standardized. The features that are common to other Wechsler tests—such as separate Verbal and Performance Scales, Deviation IQs, and a convenient manual—also are part of the WPPSI.
2. *Provides useful diagnostic information.* The WPPSI provides useful diagnostic information for the assessment of cognitive abilities of preschool children. It is an excellent instrument that can be used in clinical and school settings, and it pro-

vides useful information for the assessment of preschool mentally retarded children (Richards, 1968). The test is useful in planning special school programs, perhaps tapping more developmental or maturational factors important for school success in the lower grades than the Stanford-Binet does (Corey, 1970).
3. *High interest.* Children have been reported to enjoy taking the test. The mixture of verbal and performance items maintains their interest (Yule et al., 1969).

Limitations of the WPPSI

We now turn to the limitations of the WPPSI, some of which are the same as those previously discussed for the WISC-R. As we consider the limitations of the WPPSI, we also should bear in mind the many assets that the scale possesses.

1. *Long administration time.* Administration time may be too long for some children, although fatigue is not often a problem.[4] With younger children or with handicapped children, two test sessions may be needed. When this procedure is followed, there is no way of determining whether the break between testing sessions affects a child's scores, since the procedure differs from that used in standardizing the scale. Empirical data would be helpful in clarifying the effect of two test sessions on test scores. In the standardization sample, approximately 10 percent of the children needed one and one-half hours or more in which to complete the test. Other reports have indicated a mean administration time of sixty-two minutes (McNamara, Porterfield, & Miller, 1969) or of more than one hour (Fagan et al., 1969).
2. *Limited floor and ceiling.* The WPPSI, like the WISC-R, is limited by having an inadequate floor, i.e., it does not clearly differentiate abilities at the lower end of the scale. The IQ equivalents of the scaled scores shown in the manual range from 45 to 155. However, this range is

not applicable until the 5½-year-old level. For example, at the 4-year-old level the lowest Full Scale IQ shown in the manual is 51, the lowest Verbal Scale IQ is 55, and the lowest Performance Scale IQ is 55. A child receives up to 4 scaled-score points for having given *no* correct answers. Wechsler (1967) recognized this problem and therefore recommended that IQs for each scale be computed only when the child obtained a raw score greater than zero on at least two of the subtests on each of the scales. Similarly, a Full Scale IQ should not be computed unless raw scores greater than zero are obtained on two Verbal and two Performance subtests.

What is the lowest possible IQ that a 4-year-old child can receive on the WPPSI? Following Wechsler's recommended procedure, let us calculate IQs for each of the three scales for a 4-year-old child who obtained raw scores of 1 on the Information, Vocabulary, Animal House, and Picture Completion subtests and a raw score of 0 on each of the remaining six subtests. The resulting IQs would be as follows: Verbal Scale IQ = 59 (17 scaled-score points), Performance Scale IQ = 60 (21 scaled-score points), and Full Scale IQ = 55 (38 scaled-score points). Four 1-point successes thus yielded an IQ of 55. This example demonstrates that the WPPSI may not provide precise IQs for children who are functioning two or more standard deviations below the mean of the scale. Further research is needed to determine the validity of the WPPSI for moderately mentally retarded children.

The WPPSI not only has a limited floor but also a limited ceiling. Between 11 and 19 percent of a sample of gifted children have been found to obtain the maximum possible scores on the Arithmetic, Mazes, and Block Design subtests (Rellas, 1969). Consequently, the WPPSI may be limited in the assessment of gifted children.

3. *Difficulty in scoring responses.* As in the WISC-R, the scoring of responses on some subtests is difficult.[5] This is especially true for the Geometric Design sub-test, which appears to rely on examiners' subjective scoring decisions (Sattler, 1976), and for the Vocabulary, Similarities, and Comprehension subtests. Consultation with colleagues is recommended when responses are difficult to score.

4. *Difficulties with disadvantaged children.* Disadvantages of the WPPSI, at least with lower-class children, include the ambiguity and possible emotional loadings of several Comprehension subtest questions and the need to ask for additional reasons on several questions, making some of the children uncomfortable (Fagan et al., 1969).

5. *Failure to provide information about cut-off criteria.* Finally, the WPPSI manual fails to provide information about whether the cutoff criteria were determined empirically or intuitively (Oldridge & Allison, 1968).

Summary

1. The WPPSI, designed to be used with children between 4 and 6½ years of age, follows the basic format of the WISC-R, providing Verbal, Performance, and Full Scale IQs.

2. Three new subtests developed for the WPPSI—Sentences, Animal House, and Geometric Design—do not appear on other Wechsler tests.

3. The standardization sample was good, with average reliabilities ranging from .77 to .87 for the individual subtests, and from .93 to .96 for the three scales.

4. Comparative validity studies between the WPPSI and Stanford-Binet indicate that the two scales correlate highly (median $r = .81$). However, more information is needed about the comparability of IQs yielded by the two scales.

5. The WPPSI appears to correlate highly with the WISC-R.

6. The WPPSI has adequate predictive validity for both white children and black children, using achievement scores as the criterion. However, for Mexican-American children more work is needed to establish its predictive validity.

7. Factor analytic studies support the division of the scale into Verbal and Performance sections. All eleven WPPSI subtests have strong *g* loadings. The factor structure for black and white children is similar.

8. Sex differences are minimal on the subtests; when they occur, they are more pronounced on Performance than on Verbal subtests.

9. The relationship between WPPSI IQs and demographic characteristics indicates that there is an 18-point difference between the highest and lowest socioeconomic status groups (110 vs. 92). Urban-rural differences are not significant. Children from the west obtained significantly higher IQs than those from other regions of the country.

10. In the standardization group white children obtained higher IQs than black children by about 11 points on the average (98 vs. 87).

11. While the WPPSI has some limitations—such as long administration time, limited floor and ceiling (IQ range of 45 to 155), difficulty in scoring some subtests, and minor administration problems—it is, overall, a well-standardized, carefully developed instrument that is a valuable tool for the assessment of children's intelligence.

13

WPPSI: Subtests and Applications

Dogma is for those who need to be governed; thought is for men who can rule themselves and others.

GIORDANO BRUNO

EXHIBIT 13-1.   Psychological Evaluation: A Child with Developmental Immaturity Evaluated by the WPPSI

Name: Debbie
Date of birth: November 25, 1966
Chronological age: 5-6
Date of examination: June 12, 1972
Date of report: June 15, 1972
Grade: Kindergarten

Test Administered
Wechsler Preschool and Primary Scale of Intelligence (WPPSI):

VERBAL SCALE		PERFORMANCE SCALE	
Information	8	Animal House	5
Vocabulary	13	Picture Completion	6
Arithmetic	10	Mazes	8
Similarities	7	Geometric Design	7
Comprehension	9	Block Design	9

Verbal Scale IQ = 96
Performance Scale IQ = 80
Full Scale IQ = 87 ± 6 at the 85 percent confidence level

Reason for Referral

The evaluation was requested by Debbie's parents, who were concerned about her rate of development. Her parents described her as being a slow learner, and as having a short attention span. In addition, she has motor difficulty, with an unsteady gait and awkwardness of balance. Developmental landmarks were all reached slightly later than the average. The results of a neurological examination were essentially negative. She is described as being a fairly well adjusted child who is happy with other children. There is one other sibling in the family, a boy, who is said to be gifted.

Debbie's kindergarten teacher described her as a willing worker when supervised by an adult. However, on her own, her attention often wanders aimlessly. In class, her retention appears to be limited, and she is distracted by anything that crosses her vision. She tends to perceive situations as parts, not wholes, and because she fixes her attention upon small details she fails to understand many situations. Speech problems also are evident. In class she speaks slowly and uses phrases that are more characteristic of a 3-year-old than a 5-year-old.

The background information suggests that the major concerns focus on patterns which reflect developmental immaturity. Learning difficulties also may be present. Clear-cut patterns of brain injury have not been reported.

EXHIBIT 13-1   (cont.)

General Observations

Debbie is an attractive youngster, of average height and weight for her age. Although a speech impediment was evident, her speech was understandable. She exhibited some awkwardness in motor coordination. Her walking gait was uneven, and she had some difficulty in turning the pages of a test booklet. At times she was restless during the testing. However, she was cooperative and attempted to answer the questions and do the tasks asked of her.

Test Results

The WPPSI results were as follows: Verbal Scale IQ of 96, Performance Scale IQ of 80, and Full Scale IQ of 87±6. Her IQ is in the Dull Normal classification and falls at the 20th percentile rank of children of her age in the normative group, which was roughly representative of the United States population. The chances that the range of scores from 81 to 93 includes her true IQ are about 85 out of 100. The good rapport which existed between Debbie and the examiner and the child's ability to follow directions and to attempt to respond to the items suggest that the present results are valid.

Debbie's performance skills are not as well developed as are her verbal skills. The 16-point difference between her scores on the verbal and performance parts of the scale suggest that visual-motor ability, perceptual ability, ability to attend to perceptual details, and persistence are at a level of development that is below normal. In contrast, not only do her verbal skills show more variability than her performance skills, but also the overall level of verbal development is within the normal range. Her outstanding strength was her word knowledge. She was able to define words at a level that was higher than normal and above the average of her verbal scaled scores. Thus, for example, she gave satisfactory definitions to such words as "fur," "join," and "diamond." Arithmetic skills appear to be at an average level.

Debbie's answers were usually short, precise, and direct. Her failures were manifested both by incorrect answers and by her saying "No" when she did not know an answer. She seemed to experience more difficulty on the Similarities subtest questions than on most other verbal subtests. Instead of giving analogies, she would repeat part of the question in her answer or give associations. For example, to the question "You ride in a train and you also ride in a ——," she said, "Choo-choo." This one verbal subtest, more than any of the other verbal subtests, reflected her difficulty in grasping concepts and suggested some immaturity in reasoning. She also at first refused to complete the Animal House subtest, but with encouragement and support finally proceeded with the task.

Recommendations

The results suggest that Debbie's principal cognitive handicap is a gap between visual-motor skills and verbal skills, in favor of the latter. In school situations she will not likely be perceived as being extremely slow because of her average verbal skills. However, she will need encouragement and attention, because she may tend to remove herself from difficult situations by inattention or by simply refusing to try. Her parents should be helped to accept her present level of development and not place unrealistic demands on her. Special programs to improve her muscle coordination and speech are recommended.

Summary

In summary, on the WPPSI, Debbie, with a chronological age of 5-6, obtained an IQ of 87±6, which is in the Dull Normal classification and at the 20th percentile rank. The chances that the range of scores from 81 to 93 includes her true IQ are about 85 out of 100. The results appear to give a valid estimate of her present level of intellectual functioning. Case history material suggested a pattern of developmental immaturity. The examination revealed that she has better verbal skills than performance skills. Visual-motor coordination and other perceptual skills are less well developed than her vocabulary ability. Immaturity was suggested by some of her responses and behavior patterns. She will need support and encouragement, and her parents should be helped to accept her at her present level of functioning. Special programs were recommended to improve her muscle coordination and speech.

Examiner

The WPPSI contains an excellent collection of tasks that allow for the assessment of a variety of cognitive processes. After some introductory comments, this chapter discusses general administrative procedures, and then turns to a thorough examination of each WPPSI subtest with respect to its interpretative rationale, factor structure, reliability, correlations with other subtests, and administrative procedures. Factor analytic findings were obtained from Carlson and Reynolds (1980) and from Wallbrown et al. (1973). The last part of the chapter presents correlates of WPPSI scales and subtests, profile analysis, and clinical and educational uses.

Table C-25 in the Appendix is an important table that will facilitate the interpretation of the WPPSI subtests and aid in the writing of reports. This table summarizes the abilities measured by each subtest, background factors that may influence subtest performance, and implications of high and low scores; it deserves careful study. In order to obtain the percentiles and classifications associated with WPPSI IQs, see Table C-37 in the Appendix and BC-1 on the inside of the back cover. Percentiles associated with the scaled scores are shown in Table C-28 in the Appendix. The WPPSI Structure-of-Intellect classifications can be obtained from Table C-24 in the Appendix.

The individual subtests should not be viewed as a means of determining specific cognitive skills with precision. Rather, subtest scores are to be used as a means of generating hypotheses about the child's abilities. The most reliable estimates of specific abilities are derived from the Verbal Scale IQ (verbal comprehension) and the Performance Scale IQ (perceptual organization) and not from individual subtest scores.

Because there is a great deal of overlap between the WPPSI and the WISC-R, especially for the eight common subtests, you are encouraged to become familiar, if you have not done so, with Chapter 10, which discusses the WISC-R subtests, before further reading of this chapter. This is recommended because much of the WISC-R presentation is pertinent to the WPPSI.

The evaluation in Exhibit 13-1 illustrates the application of the WPPSI to a problem involving developmental immaturity. The report summarizes information obtained from the parents and from a kindergarten teacher and cites both qualitative and quantitative information obtained during the evaluation. Profile analysis is used to develop some assessment information. The recommendations are based on the test results and background information.

General Administrative Considerations

The general administrative suggestions that have been described for the WISC-R in Chapter 10 are also appropriate for the WPPSI. Both scales have common problems in administration and scoring. Because both scales also have subtest names that are the same, it is important that you do not substitute WISC-R directions for WPPSI directions or vice versa. Figure 13-1 presents the cover of the record booklet.

Physical abilities necessary for the WPPSI. The physical abilities that are necessary for children to be administered the WPPSI are, for the most part, the same as those required for the WISC-R. Adequate visual-motor skills are needed to handle the Performance Scale materials. Alternative ways of administering the WPPSI items are restricted because young children have limited writing and reading skills. Children who cannot speak usually will not be able to write their answers, while those who cannot hear usually will not be able to read the test questions. Still, the specific suggestions for administering the WISC-R to handicapped children are also useful for the WPPSI; this material should be reviewed carefully before the WPPSI is administered to physically handicapped children (see Chapter 9).

Testing the limits on the WPPSI. The general testing-of-limits suggestions presented in Chapter 5 also are useful with the WPPSI.

WPPSI

RECORD FORM

Wechsler Preschool and Primary
Scale of Intelligence

NAME_____ AGE_____ SEX_____

ADDRESS_____

PARENT'S NAME_____

SCHOOL_____ GRADE_____

PLACE OF TESTING_____ TESTED BY_____

REFERRED BY_____

NOTES

	Year	Month	Day
Date Tested	____	____	____
Date of Birth	____	____	____
Age	____	____	____

	Raw Score	Scaled Score
VERBAL TESTS		
Information	____	____
Vocabulary	____	____
Arithmetic	____	____
Similarities	____	____
Comprehension	____	____
(Sentences)	____	____
Verbal Score		____
PERFORMANCE TESTS		
Animal House	____	____
Picture Completion	____	____
Mazes	____	____
Geometric Design	____	____
Block Design	____	____
(Animal House Retest)	____	____
Performance Score		____

	Scaled Score	IQ
Verbal Score	____*	____
Performance Score	____*	____
Full Scale Score	____	____

*Prorated if necessary

FIGURE 13-1. Cover Page of WPPSI Record Booklet. Copyright 1949, renewed 1976; © 1963, 1967 by The Psychological Corporation, New York, N.Y. All Rights Reserved.

Extrapolated IQs. Extrapolated IQs are provided in Table C-19 in the Appendix for scaled scores that are either below or above those shown in the WPPSI manual. However, as noted in the discussion of extrapolated IQs for the WISC-R in Chapter 9, extrapolated IQs must be used cautiously.

WPPSI short forms. Short forms of the WPPSI have the same disadvantages as those of the WISC-R (see Chapter 9). Short forms should never be used for classification or selection purposes. However, there may be occasions when a short form is useful for screening purposes. In order to assist in the selection of a short form, Table C-22 in the Appendix has been prepared. This table is based on the standardization data, and shows the best WPPSI short forms for two, three, four, and five subtests. The short forms of a given length, for all practical purposes, are mutually interchangeable. Consequently, clinical considerations, on some occasions, can be used in selection of the short form.

After the short form is selected, the procedures outlined in Chapter 9, dealing with conversion of WISC-R composite scores to Deviation Quotients, should be followed. Table C-26 in the Appendix can be used to obtain the appropriate a and b constants. The same procedure presented for the WISC-R should be followed for the WPPSI, with the exception that the WPPSI correlation table of the group that is closest in age to the examinee should be used to obtain Σr_{jk} (i.e., one of the tables on pages 26 through 31 of the WPPSI manual).

Kaufman (1972a) proposed a four-subtest short form that consists of the Arithmetic, Comprehension, Picture Completion, and Block Design subtests. This short form takes longer to administer than does the Vocabulary plus Block Design short form (soon to be described), but it does provide somewhat more clinical and diagnostic information.

Other investigators (Dokecki et al., 1969) have found that for middle-class children the four subtests that made the best short form were Information, Comprehension, Arithmetic, and Geometric Design ($r = .94$ with the Full Scale). The best two-subtest short form for predicting reading achievement in a group of lower-class children was Information and Geometric Design (Plant & Southern, 1968).

Yudin's (1966) short-form method for the WISC-R, which reduces the number of items within the subtests, has been applied to the WPPSI by Silverstein (1968a). Table C-23 in the Appendix shows the specific procedures. Raw scores are multiplied by a constant and, as Silverstein suggested for the WISC-R, a correction factor is not needed. Silverstein suggested that Sentences be excluded from the short form, because the subtest was omitted in establishing the IQ tables. The following reliabilities were reported for the short form: .91 for the Verbal Scale, .91 for the Performance Scale, and .94 for the Full Scale.

The Vocabulary plus Block Design combination is useful as a two-subtest screening short form. When this combination is used, Table C-27 in the Appendix can be used to convert the sum of scaled scores on the two subtests directly to an estimate of the Full Scale IQ. Silverstein (1970b) reported a .82 correlation between the Vocabulary plus Block Design short form and the Full Scale. King and Smith (1972), however, reported that the Vocabulary plus Block Design short form only agreed with the IQ classifications obtained from the Full Scale in about 33 percent of their cases. These results reinforce my recommendation that short forms should never be used for classification or selection purposes. We now turn to an examination of the eleven WPPSI subtests.

Information

The WPPSI Information subtest contains twenty-three questions, twelve of which, with minor changes in wording, come from the WISC. Most questions require the child to give a simply stated fact or facts. All items are scored 1 or 0 (pass-fail), and the subtest is discontinued after five consecutive failures.

Rationale. The rationale presented for the WISC-R Information subtest appears to apply to the WPPSI Information subtest (see Chapter 10). However, the WPPSI questions appear to assess that part of the child's knowledge of the environment that is gained from experiences rather than from education, especially formal education.

Factor analytic findings. The Information subtest is the best measure of *g* (52 percent of its variance may be attributed to *g*) in the scale. The subtest contributes substantially to the Verbal factor (median loading of .72).

Reliability and correlational highlights. Information is a reliable subtest ($r_{II} = .81$) and correlates more highly with Vocabulary and Comprehension ($rs = .60$) than with any of the other subtests. It has a moderate correlation with the Full Scale ($r = .70$) and the Verbal Scale ($r = .73$), but a rather low correlation with the Performance Scale ($r = .56$).

Administrative considerations. The administrative considerations presented for the WISC-R Information subtest also are relevant for the WPPSI Information subtest. In addition, some WPPSI items require special scoring considerations. For example, in question 4 ("What comes in a bottle?"), things that come in plastic bottles are not mentioned as acceptable answers. However, because the term "etc." appears in the manual after the acceptable answers, it seems logical to assume that "shampoo," "liquid soap," and other things that come in plastic bottles should receive credit. Acceptable answers to question 9 ("What shines in the sky at night?") do not include "planet"; yet a planet shines in the sky at night. It is recommended that "planet," "comet," and other astronomical terms be given credit.[1]

Vocabulary

The WPPSI Vocabulary subtest contains twenty-two words, fourteen of which are from the WISC. The child is asked to explain orally the meaning of each word. All words receive a score of 2, 1, or 0, and the subtest is discontinued after five consecutive failures.

Rationale. The rationale presented for the WISC-R Vocabulary subtest generally applies to the WPPSI Vocabulary subtest (see Chapter 10). However, for many preschool children, formal education is less likely to be an influence in enabling them to develop a vocabulary than it is for older children. Their experiences are likely to be the major contributing factor in the development of their vocabulary.

Factor analytic findings. The Vocabulary subtest is a moderately good measure of *g* (41 percent of its variance may be attributed to *g*). The subtest contributes substantially to the Verbal factor (median loading of .65).

Reliability and correlational highlights. Vocabulary is a reliable subtest ($r_{II} = .84$), and correlates more highly with Information ($r = .60$) than with any other subtest. It has a moderate correlation with the Full Scale ($r = .65$) and with the Verbal Scale ($r = .66$), but a somewhat low correlation with the Performance Scale ($r = .51$).

Administrative considerations. The subtest is started with the first word for all examinees. This procedure differs from the one used in the WISC-R, where the subtest is started with different words, depending on the child's age.

The general administrative considerations presented for the WISC-R Vocabulary subtest should be followed for the WPPSI Vocabulary subtest. Scoring requires considerable judgment, and the WPPSI manual provides too few sample responses. Because many of the Vocabulary words have near homonyms (words 1, 13, 14, 15, 16, 17, and 22), diction should be watched carefully when one is pronouncing these words (Yule et al., 1969).

Arithmetic

The WPPSI Arithmetic subtest consists of twenty problems, six of which are from the WISC. For the first four items the child points to the correct answer on a card, for the next four items blocks are used, and for the last twelve items oral answers are required.

The subtest is started at different points, depending on the child's age and possible level of intellectual functioning. Children under 6 years of age (and older children where mental retardation is suspected) are started with item 1, while children 6 years of age and older begin with item 7. The first eight problems have no time limit, while the last twelve problems have a thirty-second time limit. All items are scored 1 or 0, and the subtest is discontinued after four consecutive failures.

The problems on the Arithmetic subtest reflect various kinds of skills. Problems 1 through 4 entail perceptual judgments involving the concepts of "biggest," "longest," "most," and "same." Problems 5 through 8 require direct counting of concrete quantities. Problems 9 through 20 involve simple addition or subtraction, although simple division and multiplication also can be used to solve these problems.

Rationale. The rationale described for the WISC-R Arithmetic subtest appears to apply generally to the WPPSI Arithmetic subtest (see Chapter 10). However, the skills required for the WPPSI Arithmetic subtest are likely to be less dependent on formal education than those required for the WISC-R Arithmetic subtest. The first four WPPSI questions, which require the child to make comparisons and perceptual discriminations, appear to measure nonverbal reasoning ability; these four problems measure quantitative concepts without involving the explicit use of numbers.

Factor analytic findings. The Arithmetic subtest is a moderately good measure of g (46 percent of its variance may be attributed to g). The subtest has a high loading on the Verbal factor (median loading of .54) and a moderate loading on the Performance factor (median loading of .48). Its loading on the Performance factor may be accounted for by the fact that some items employ pictures of sets of objects that must be visually analyzed before verbal comparisons are made.

Reliability and correlational highlights. Arithmetic is a reliable subtest ($r_{11} = .82$), and correlates more highly with Information ($r = .58$) than with any other subtest. It has moderate correlations with the Full Scale ($r = .68$), Verbal Scale ($r = .62$), and Performance Scale ($r = .60$).

Administrative considerations. The administrative considerations discussed for the WISC-R Arithmetic subtest generally apply to the WPPSI Arithmetic subtest. Scoring, as in the WISC-R, is for the most part direct, 1 or 0 points. The time taken by the child to solve all of the problems should be recorded. Correct answers to the problems after the time limit has expired on problems 9 through 20 also should be noted.

Similarities

The WPPSI Similarities subtest consists of sixteen questions, seven of which are found in the WISC. The first ten questions require simple analogies, whereas the remaining questions are similar to those found in the WISC-R Similarities subtest. Items 1 through 10 are scored 1 or 0 (pass-fail), while items 11 through 16 are scored 2, 1, or 0, depending on the conceptual level of the response. The subtest is discontinued after four consecutive failures.

Rationale. The rationale described for the WISC-R Similarities subtest generally applies to the WPPSI Similarities subtest (see Chapter 10). However, because over half of the WPPSI questions (1 to 10) require analogies, the subtest may be measuring logical thinking rather than verbal concept formation, especially for the earlier levels of the test (i.e., below 5 years of age).

Factor analytic findings. The Similarities subtest is a moderately good measure of g (40 percent of its variance may be attributed to g). The subtest contributes substantially to the Verbal factor (median loading of .67).

Reliability and correlational highlights.
Similarities is a reliable subtest ($r_{11} = .83$),
and correlates more highly with Comprehension ($r = .55$) than with any other subtest. It
has a somewhat low correlation with the
Full Scale ($r = .58$), a moderate correlation
with the Verbal Scale ($r = .62$), and a low correlation with the Performance Scale ($r = .44$).

Administrative considerations. The administrative considerations discussed for the
WISC-R Similarities subtest apply
generally to the WPPSI Similarities subtest. Scoring procedures, however, differ.
Because responses to the first ten questions
are scored 1 or 0, few scoring problems
should be encountered for these questions.
However, as in the WISC-R, questions 11
through 16, which deal with similarities, are
difficult to score. It is recommended that
the scoring guidelines be studied carefully.

Comprehension

The WPPSI Comprehension subtest contains fifteen questions, six of which, with
minor changes in wording, are from the
WISC. A wide variety of situations are
covered, including health and hygiene,
knowledge of environment, and knowledge
of activities in society. Items are scored 2, 1,
or 0. The subtest is discontinued after four
consecutive failures.

Rationale. The rationale presented for the
WISC-R Comprehension subtest appears to
apply generally to the WPPSI Comprehension subtest (see Chapter 10). However, linguistic skill and logical reasoning may play
a more important role on the WPPSI Comprehension subtest than on the WISC-R
Comprehension subtest.

Factor analytic findings. The Comprehension subtest is a moderately good measure
of *g* (46 percent of its variance may be attributed to *g*). The subtest contributes substantially to the Verbal factor (median loading of
.72).

Reliability and correlational highlights.
Comprehension is a reliable subtest
($r_{11} = .81$), and correlates more highly with
Sentences ($r = .53$) than with any other subtest. It has moderate correlations with the
Full Scale ($r = .65$) and Verbal Scale
($r = .69$), and a low correlation with the Performance Scale ($r = .44$).

Administrative considerations. The administrative considerations discussed for the
WISC-R Comprehension subtest generally
apply to the WPPSI Comprehension subtest. Because Comprehension responses will
occasionally be difficult to score, judgment
is especially needed in arriving at appropriate scores. The content of the response,
not the quality of the verbalization, should
be considered in evaluating the child's response (Wechsler, 1967); this is true, of
course, for all scoring decisions made for
WPPSI and WISC-R responses.

Sentences

On the WPPSI Sentences, a supplementary
subtest, the child listens to sentences given
orally by the examiner and then is required
to repeat each sentence verbatim. There are
thirteen sentences of increasing length,
ranging from two to eighteen words. The
subtest is discontinued after three consecutive failures.

The subtest is not counted in obtaining
the IQ when it is administered as a sixth
Verbal Scale subtest. Items receive 1, 2, 3,
or 4 points, depending on the length of the
sentence and the number of errors made.
Errors in reproducing the sentences include
omissions, transpositions, additions, and
substitutions of words.

Rationale. The Sentences subtest is a memory test, measuring immediate recall and
attention. Because success may depend upon verbal facility (Wechsler, 1967), failure
may not necessarily reflect poor memory
ability. It has been hypothesized that scores
are related primarily (a) to memory ability
for children 5 years of age and older, and (b)
to verbal knowledge and comprehension,

rather than to immediate recall ability per se, for children younger than 5 years (Lutey, 1967).

Factor analytic findings. The Sentences subtest is a moderately good measure of *g* (41 percent of its variance may be attributed to *g*). The subtest contributes substantially to the Verbal factor (median loading of .63).

Reliability and correlational highlights. Sentences is a reliable subtest ($r_{1I} = .85$), and correlates more highly with Comprehension ($r = .53$) than with any other subtest. It has moderate correlations with the Full Scale ($r = .61$) and Verbal Scale ($r = .64$), but a low correlation with the Performance Scale ($r = .47$).

Administrative considerations. Scoring the child's responses on the Sentences subtest is an exacting procedure because of the variety of errors that can occur. Responses must be analyzed carefully in order to determine the type of error that has been made. In addition to recording the number of errors that have been made, the examiner must evaluate the child's responses qualitatively. For example, were any idiosyncratic or peculiar words added? Did errors occur toward the beginning, middle, or end of the sentences? Were sentences completely missed or were only a few errors made in each sentence? The child who misses a few words may be revealing minor temporary inefficiencies, while the one who cannot recall any words in the sentences may have more serious memory problems.

Animal House and Animal House Retest

The WPPSI Animal House subtest, a replacement for the WISC Coding subtest, requires the child to place a cylinder of the appropriate color (the "house") in a hole on a board. The subtest's name is derived from the fact that four animals are depicted in various colored houses (e.g., dog with black house and chicken with white house). It is a timed subtest (maximum time of five minutes) in which a premium is placed on speed. A perfect performance in nine seconds or less is credited with 70 raw-score points, while one obtained in five minutes is credited with 12 raw-score points.

Animal House Retest is exactly the same test as Animal House. The word "retest" indicates that when the subtest is administered a second time, separate normative scaled scores are available for the retest performance. While any subtest can be administered a second time, Animal House is the only one in the scale that has separate normative scaled scores for the retest.

Rationale. The Animal House task requires the child to associate sign with symbol. Memory, attention span, goal awareness, concentration, and finger and manual dexterity may all be involved in the child's performance (Herman, 1968; Wechsler, 1967). The subtest may also be a measure of learning ability (Wechsler, 1967).

Animal House has been found to correlate significantly with a measure of learning ($r = .71$) and a measure of motor skill ($r = -.69$) in a sample of thirty-six 5- to 6-year-old children (Sherman, Chinsky, & Maffeo, 1974). The combination of learning and motor scores leads to a better prediction of Animal House scores than the learning scores by themselves. The results suggest that motor abilities, in addition to learning abilities, may be involved in the performance on the Animal House subtest.

Perry et al. (1976) offered an interesting hypothesis, in need of verification, about how children's cognitive style may affect performance on the Animal House subtest. They observed that:

> . . . Animal House requires only a relatively primitive cognitive association; so that highly impulsive children who would deal with the task with considerable speed (even though making some errors) would be at an advantage compared with children who, performing in a more reflective or cautious manner, would perform much more slowly due to a tendency to check their response for possible errors before proceeding. [p. 328]

Yule et al. (1969) cautioned against accepting Wechsler's statement that performance on the Animal House Retest may differentiate between slow and fast learners. They believe that this statement is potentially misleading, because it is difficult to assess and predict rate of learning and because there are no validation studies to support Wechsler's position. Yule and his co-workers pointed out that an assessment of learning ability on the Animal House Retest needs to take into account the child's age and initial score. For example, children who are 4½ years old and who achieve a raw score of 3 on initial testing maintain their initial status on retest by improving their performance by 2 raw score points, whereas children of the same age with a raw score of 18 on the initial subtest need an increase of about 10 raw score points to maintain their position. At age 6¼ years, still other relationships are found. In addition to the child's age and initial score, motivational factors, magnitude of retest change, and overall level of ability must be considered as possible factors that can affect learning ability. Yule and his co-workers concluded that empirical work is needed before meaningful interpretations can be made of scores on the Animal House Retest.

Factor analytic findings. The Animal House subtest is a moderately good measure of g (30 percent of its variance may be attributed to g). The subtest has a moderate loading on the Performance factor (median loading of .49).

Reliability and correlational highlights. Animal House is a somewhat reliable subtest ($r_{11} = .77$), and correlates more highly with Geometric Design ($r = .43$) than with any other subtest. It has somewhat low correlations with the Full Scale ($r = .53$) and Performance Scale ($r = .50$), and a low correlation with the Verbal Scale ($r = .46$).

Administrative considerations. It is important to determine whether the child is right- or left-handed before administering the subtest. Children should be encouraged to use their preferred hand. As on all timed subtests, it is not permissible to stop timing once the subtest has begun. However, if for any reason the subtest is spoiled, do not include it in the final calculations. (This is true, of course, for all subtests in the scale.)

The WPPSI manual does not provide adequate guidance about what to do when a child stubbornly reinserts a wrong color peg or refuses to take the examiner's hints during the demonstration items. In such situations, it is advisable, when a child puts a yellow peg under the same dog for the second time, to simply say, "No, it should be a black one," insert the peg yourself, and go on to the next sample item.[2]

The Animal House Retest does not enter into the calculation of the IQ. When the Animal House subtest is administered a second time, the examiner can compare the child's two performances, and possibly obtain some indication of the child's learning ability or ability to benefit from practice. In the WPPSI manual, Table 20 is used to obtain raw scores for the Animal House and Animal House Retest, but a separate part (last column) of Table 21, "Scaled Score Equivalents of Raw Scores," is used to obtain the Animal House Retest scaled scores.

An inspection of the scaled scores for Animal House and Animal House Retest indicates that the child needs a higher raw score on the Animal House Retest in order to obtain a scaled score that is equivalent to the one earned on the initial Animal House administration. For example, a raw score of 16 on Animal House is equivalent to a scaled score of 10, but the same raw score on Animal House Retest is equivalent only to a scaled score of 9, meaning a loss of 1 scaled-score point.

Picture Completion

The WPPSI Picture Completion subtest consists of twenty-three drawings of common objects (e.g., doll, roses, and door), each of which lacks a single important element. Twelve of the drawings appear on the WISC. It is the child's task to discover and name (or point to) the essential missing portion of the incompletely drawn picture. While there is no exact time limit for each picture, the examiner is instructed to proceed to the next picture if there is no response after fifteen seconds.

Rationale. The rationale described for the WISC-R Picture Completion subtest appears to hold for the WPPSI Picture Completion subtest (see Chapter 10).

Factor analytic findings. The Picture Completion subtest is a moderately good measure of g (36 percent of its variance may be attributed to g). The subtest has a moderate loading on the Performance factor (median loading of .50) and on the Verbal factor (median loading of .40).

Reliability and correlational highlights. Picture Completion is a reliable subtest ($r_{11} = .83$), and correlates more highly with Information ($r = .47$) than with any other subtest. It has a moderate correlation with the Full Scale ($r = .60$) and somewhat low correlations with the Verbal Scale ($r = .54$) and Performance Scale ($r = .55$).

Administrative considerations. The administrative considerations discussed for the WISC-R Picture Completion subtest generally apply to the WPPSI Picture Completion subtest, with the exception of the material related to the time limits. Unlike the WISC-R Picture Completion subtest, which has a maximum of twenty seconds per card, there is no absolute time limit on the WPPSI Picture Completion subtest. Even though the WPPSI Picture Completion subtest is not timed, it may prove to be valuable for qualitative analysis to record the amount of time taken by children to make their response.

In administering the second card, it is advisable to repeat the directions given for the first card: "Look at this picture. Some important part is missing. Tell me what is missing." Children are given credit if they correctly point to the missing part. However, if a pointing response is accompanied by a verbal response, the verbal response is given precedence over the pointing response. Therefore, an incorrect verbal response (for example, "hair" to number 1) accompanied by a correct pointing response (pointing to the missing tooth) receives a score of 0.

Mazes

The WPPSI Mazes subtest consists of ten mazes, seven of which are from the WISC. Three new horizontal mazes intended for younger children have been introduced at the beginning of the subtest. The WPPSI Mazes subtest is a standard subtest, while in the WISC-R it is a supplementary one. The subtest is discontinued after two consecutive failures.

Rationale. The rationale described for the WISC-R Mazes subtest appears to apply to the WPPSI Mazes subtest (see Chapter 10).

Factor analytic findings. The Mazes subtest is a moderately good measure of g (32 percent of its variance may be attributed to g). The subtest contributes substantially to the Performance factor (median loading of .63).

Reliability and correlational highlights. Mazes is a reliable subtest ($r_{11} = .87$), and correlates more highly with Geometric Design ($r = .48$) than with any other subtest. It has somewhat low correlations with the Full Scale ($r = .54$) and Performance Scale ($r = .57$), and a low correlation with the Verbal Scale ($r = .44$).

Administrative considerations. While the administrative considerations described for the WISC-R Mazes subtest apply to the WPPSI Mazes subtest, the administrative *procedures* used in the WPPSI Mazes subtest are not the same as those used in the WISC-R Mazes subtest. Changes have been made in timing, scoring, and other details. For example, Mazes 1A, 1B, 2, 4, 5, and 6 each are given a maximum of 45 seconds; mazes 3 and 8, 60 seconds; and maze 10, 135 seconds. Therefore, the examiner must make sure to use the procedures appropriate to the scale being administered.

The child should be allowed to finish each maze, regardless of the errors made (Yule et al., 1969). Interruptions may generate some anxiety and confusion and leave the child with a sense of failure.

Scoring the WPPSI Mazes subtest requires considerable judgment. The examiner must become familiar with special terms, such as "blind alley," "false exit," "alley wall," and "false start," which designate specific features of the mazes or of the child's performance. The types of errors made by the child may be a valuable source of qualitative material. The child's failures should be studied carefully. The examiner should note whether there is a pattern to the child's failure, or whether there are signs of tremor or other visual-motor difficulties. After the entire examination has been administered, the examiner may desire to return to the Mazes subtest to inquire into the child's performance. "Why did you go that way?" is a question that may be asked. Inquiry may be made about the child's performance on any of the mazes that have been failed or about any of the mazes that may be of interest to the examiner.

Geometric Design

On the WPPSI Geometric Design subtest the child is asked to copy ten designs, such as a circle, a square, or a diamond. There is no time limit. Scores for items 1 to 5 range from 0 to 2, for items 6 and 7 from 0 to 3, and for items 8 to 10 from 0 to 4.

Rationale. The Geometric Design subtest is considered to measure perceptual and visual-motor organization abilities (Wechsler, 1967). Low scores may indicate lags in the developmental process. High scores may be difficult even for bright young children to obtain, because the motor ability needed for successful performance is associated in part with maturational processes that may be

independent of the development of cognitive processes.

Factor analytic findings. The Geometric Design subtest is a moderately good measure of g (41 percent of its variance may be attributed to g). The subtest contributes substantially to the Performance factor (median loading of .67).

Reliability and correlational highlights. Geometric Design is a reliable subtest ($r_{11} = .82$), and correlates more highly with Mazes ($r = .48$) and Block Design ($r = .48$) than with any other subtests. It has a somewhat low correlation with the Full Scale ($r = .58$), a moderate correlation with the Performance Scale ($r = .60$), and a low correlation with the Verbal Scale ($r = .48$).

Administrative considerations. The Geometric Design subtest is difficult to score. At least eight different general criteria must be used to score the designs; each design requires special scoring criteria. Sattler (1976) demonstrated that there is seldom unanimous agreement among examiners in the scores given to the drawings of normal children. He reported that unanimous agreement among a sample of eighteen school psychologists occurred on only seven out of fifty drawings. Lowering the agreement criterion to 78 percent of the group (fourteen out of eighteen) still resulted in agreement on only twenty-three of the fifty drawings. Similar results were found for a group of fourteen inexperienced graduate students. These results indicate that examiners will need to study the Geometric Design scoring criteria carefully in order to become proficient in scoring the designs.

The special copyrighted blank paper obtained from the test publisher for the administration of the Geometric Design subtest is not necessary (Yule et al., 1969). All that is needed is to fold a sheet of paper in half and on each drawing write the appropriate number of the design and "top" and "bottom" relative to the child.

Block Design

On the WPPSI Block Design subtest the child is required to reproduce designs using flat blocks—from a model constructed by the examiner for the first seven items and from cards for the last three items. Children who are under 6 years of age (and older children suspected of mental retardation) are started with item 1, while children 6 years of age and older are started with item 3.

All of the items are timed. The first four items are given a maximum of thirty seconds; the next two, forty-five seconds; the next two, sixty seconds; and the last two, seventy-five seconds. Unlike the WISC-R, there are no time-bonus credits. A score of 2 is given for a successful performance on the first trial, a score of 1 on the second trial, and a score of 0 when both trials are failed.

Rationale. The rationale described for the WISC-R Block Design subtest appears to apply to the WPPSI Block Design subtest (see Chapter 10).

Factor analytic findings. The Block Design subtest is a moderately good measure of g (38 percent of its variance may be attributed to g). The subtest contributes substantially to the Performance factor (median loading of .58).

Reliability and correlational highlights. Block Design is a reliable subtest ($r_{11} = .82$), and correlates more highly with Arithmetic ($r = .50$) than with any other subtest. It has a moderate correlation with the Full Scale ($r = .61$) and somewhat low correlations with the Performance Scale ($r = .59$) and Verbal Scale ($r = .52$).

Administrative considerations. The administrative considerations described for the WISC-R Block Design subtest generally apply to the WPPSI Block Design subtest.

Correlates of WPPSI Scales and Subtests

Studies have examined the relationship between the WPPSI and various psychological constructs and processes. In one investigation (Brown, Matheny, & Wilson, 1973), 5-year-old children with more mature moral judgment had significantly higher WPPSI Performance IQs, but not Verbal IQs, than those with less mature moral judgment (IQs of 101 vs. 92, respectively). The results suggest that appraisal of the interpersonal elements of social situations in young children is related to accurate perceptual activities in the impersonal world as well. The Performance IQ also is a better predictor of color-form association learning than the Verbal IQ (r of .65 and .33, respectively) (Van Duyne, 1974). The Block Design and Geometric Design subtests load on a Perceptual-Analytic factor (a measure of field independence) in young children (Coates, 1975). Finally, Geometric Design subtest scores (a visual-motor reproduction task) are related ($r = .55$) to scores on a visual-recognition task (Cutler, Hirshoren, & Cicirelli, 1973).

Profile Analysis

Because profile analysis applied to the WPPSI is similar to that on the WISC-R, the material in Chapter 11 that discusses WISC-R profile analysis should be reviewed. Much less is known about the clinical use of scatter on the WPPSI than on other Wechsler scales. However, profile analysis is still useful in generating hypotheses about a child's strengths and weaknesses.

The five approaches to profile analysis on the WPPSI described below are the same as those for the WISC-R. The only change is that different tables in the Appendix must be used. An explanation of each of the approaches appears in Chapter 11. The approaches are as follows:

1. comparing the Verbal and Performance IQs (see Table C-17 in the Appendix—the critical values are 11 at the .05 level and 14 at the .01 level);

2. comparing each Verbal subtest scaled score to the mean Verbal scaled score (see Table C-18 in the Appendix);

3. comparing each Performance subtest scaled score to the mean Performance scaled score (see Table C-18 in the Appendix);

4. comparing each subtest scaled score to the mean subtest scaled score (see Table C-18 in the Appendix); and

5. comparing sets of individual subtest scores (see Table C-17 in the Appendix).

Silverstein advises that if multiple subtest comparisons are made, the examiner first determine the difference between the highest and lowest subtest scores.[3] A difference of 6 scaled-score points indicates a significant difference at the .05 level. Those differences that are 6 scaled-score points or greater can then be interpreted. If the difference between the highest and lowest subtest scaled scores is less than 6 scaled-score points, then multiple comparisons between individual subtest scores should not be made.

In the Appendix, Table C-20 presents the probabilities from .001 to .50 that are associated with a given Verbal-Performance Scale discrepancy, and Table C-21 presents the percentage of individuals obtaining a given discrepancy between the Verbal and Performance Scales. The interpretation of these tables is similar to that of the WISC-R tables (see Chapter 11).

Clinical and Educational Uses of the WPPSI

The administration of the WPPSI, like the administration of any other psychological or educational test, requires careful observation of the child's performance. Behaviors suggestive of, for example, emotional disturbance, language difficulties, perceptual problems, or visual-motor difficulties should be noted carefully and reported. (See Chapter 18 for further assessment considerations.) There is little published research about the clinically meaningful use of scat-

ter on the WPPSI, and research in this area is needed. The statement by Wechsler (1967) that very poor performance on the Animal House subtest will at times be associated with organic deficit should not be accepted until research studies are available; it should be regarded as an unconfirmed hypothesis (Yule et al., 1969).

Learning Disabilities and the WPPSI

An interesting contribution by Hagin, Silver, and Corwin (1971) illustrated how the WPPSI can be used in the assessment of cognitive functioning of children with learning disabilities. These investigators reported a representative WPPSI profile, where possible, for three different subgroups of learning-disabled children: specific language disability, brain damaged, and developmental immaturity. These three subgroups are now considered.

Specific language disability. Children in the specific language disability subgroup have problems in developing body-image concepts, in establishing cerebral dominance for language, and in orienting figures in space and sounds in time. Richard (see Table 13–1) is representative of this subgroup. While the neurological examination was negative, there were some minor soft signs (equivocal signs of brain damage) such as gross errors in right-left orientation and mild difficulties in movement. Visual-motor skills were good, but some difficulties were evident in auditory discrimination and sequencing. On the WPPSI, he earned an average IQ (98), but showed a 23-point spread between his Verbal and Performance IQs (87 and 110, respectively). Within the Verbal Scale, his major difficulties were in areas requiring quantitative reasoning, logical thinking, and social judgment. Range of knowledge and linguistic skill were adequate, although ideas were sometimes awkwardly expressed. His above-average Performance Scale IQ suggests that he has good potential for learning. It was recommended that educational intervention stress the auditory modality.

TABLE 13-1. Illustrations of WPPSI Deviations from Mean Scaled Scores for Children with Learning Disabilities in First Grade

Subtest	Richard: Specific Language Disability		Karl: Brain Injured		Rosemary: Developmental Immaturity	
	Score	Deviation[a]	Score	Deviation	Score	Deviation
Information	10	+ 2	11	− .8	7	+ .3
Vocabulary	11	+ 3*	14	+ 2.2	6	− .7
Arithmetic	6	− 2	11	− .8	7	+ .3
Similarities	6	− 2	15	+ 3.2*	7	+ .3
Comprehension	7	− 1	11	− .8	7	+ .3
Sentences	8	0	9	− 2.8	6	− .7
Animal House	10	− 1.2	9	− 1.8	11	+ 3.6*
Picture Completion	13	+ 1.8	11	+ .2	7	− .4
Mazes	12	+ .8	15	+ 4.2*	6	− 1.4
Geometric Design	11	− .2	13	+ 2.2	7	− .4
Block Design	10	− 1.2	11	+ .2	6	− 1.4
M Verbal scaled score	8		11.8		6.7	
M Performance scaled score	11.2		10.8		7.4	
Verbal Scale IQ	87		106		80	
Performance Scale IQ	110		112		82	
Full Scale IQ	98		110		79	

[a]The deviations are from the mean of the respective scales.
*These are significant deviations (see Table C-15 in the Appendix).

Adapted from Hagin, Silver, and Corwin (1971).

Brain damaged. A second subgroup is the brain damaged. These children demonstrate many of the behaviors of the specific language disability group, but in addition show abnormality on the standard neurological examination. Some children are hyperkinetic, while others are hypokinetic. Generally, the findings do not point to focal brain damage, and specific etiological factors are rarely found in the child's history. The children in this subgroup present special educational problems because of poor impulse control, limited attention span, inadequate motor coordination, and anxiety.

Karl (see Table 13-1) is an example of a child in the brain-damaged subgroup. Because there is no typical "brain-damaged child," he was selected simply to illustrate how one brain-damaged child performed on the WPPSI. The neurological examination disclosed poor fine and gross motor coordination and severe praxic difficulties. There was confusion in right-left discrimination, restless motion, tremors, and hyperactivity. His verbal communications were, at times, incoherent and circumstantial. On the WPPSI, he obtained a Full Scale IQ of 110. Conceptual thinking, memory, and attention and concentration were areas that were below his average level of performance. His motor problems were especially evident in his difficulty in grasping the pegs in the Animal House subtest and in his four-finger, non-oppositional grip on the pencil in the Geometric Design subtest. His best performances were on the Mazes and Vocabulary subtests, subtests that reflect planning ability and word knowledge, respectively. His performance improved when he became familiar with the task requirements. It was

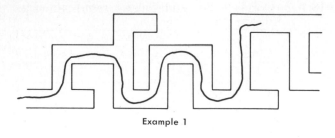

Example 1

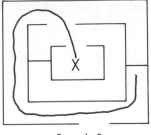

Example 2

FIGURE 13-2. Two Examples of Failures on the Mazes Subtest. WPPSI Mazes reprinted by permission of the publisher. Copyright 1949; © 1963, 1967, The Psychological Corporation, New York, N.Y. All Rights Reserved.

recommended that educational effort emphasize visual-motor and organizational skills.

Developmental immaturity. A third subgroup focuses on children with developmental immaturity. In this subgroup, there is no clinical or historical evidence of central nervous system damage, but there is slowness in reaching developmental landmarks. In physical appearance, in gross and fine motor development, in language, and in social awareness, these children seem to be younger than their chronological ages. Low birth weight appears frequently in their histories.

Rosemary (see Table 13-1) can be considered to be representative of this subgroup. Neurological difficulties were absent. On the WPPSI, she performed in the Borderline range. Her profile of deviations of subtest scaled scores from the mean of her scaled scores is essentially flat; the only significant variation occurred on the Animal House subtest. Recommendations centered on general enrichment, with particular emphasis on language stimulation.

Reading Disability and the WPPSI

Attempts have been made to determine whether there are differences in patterns of intellectual abilities, as measured by the WPPSI, in preschool and school-aged children who differ in their reading skills. The results suggest that the WPPSI profiles for adequate and inadequate readers are essen-

tially similar (Barron, 1971; Kavajecz, 1969). This statement holds for both Anglo-American and Mexican-American children.

Qualitative Analysis of Performance on the WPPSI Mazes Subtest

A careful evaluation of the failures that occur on the Mazes subtest may prove to be useful. Two examples are shown in Figure 13-2. In example 1, a girl failed to complete the maze, but made no errors as far as her performance goes. In example 2, another girl entered a blind alley and therefore made an error. The first performance makes one wonder why the girl stopped short before reaching the goal. Perhaps her perseverance is limited, or perhaps she takes things for granted and hopes that others will understand her, or perhaps she was distracted. In contrast, the second performance may be that of an impulsive girl who works well until she is about to complete the task, and then is unable to do so correctly. These analyses are, of course, only tentative, subject to modification by a study of the child's performance on the entire subtest and other subtests on the scale, and of other sources of data.

Summary

1. The administrative considerations that apply to the WISC-R generally apply to the WPPSI. Because of the younger age group for which the WPPSI is appropriate, there

are some problems in adapting the subtests to alternative sensory modalities.

2. Table C-22 in the Appendix shows the best combination of two, three, four, and five WPPSI subtests, and Table C-27 in the Appendix shows IQs for the sum of the scaled scores for the Vocabulary plus Block Design short form.

3. The interpretative rationale, factor analytic findings, reliability and subtest correlations, and administrative considerations for each of the eleven WPPSI subtests are presented in the chapter. The proposed interpretative rationales and possible implications of high and low scores are summarized in Table C-25 in the Appendix.

4. *Information subtest*. The rationale for the WISC-R Information subtest probably applies to the WPPSI Information subtest, but WPPSI questions may be related more to the child's experiences than to formal education. The subtest is the best measure of g in the scale and contributes to the Verbal factor. It is a reliable subtest $(r_{1I} = .81)$. Judgment is required in scoring responses.

5. *Vocabulary subtest*. The rationale for the WISC-R Vocabulary subtest probably applies to the WPPSI Vocabulary subtest. Formal education probably has less of an influence on the WPPSI than on the WISC-R. The subtest is a moderately good measure of g and contributes to the Verbal factor. It is a reliable subtest $(r_{1I} = .84)$. Scoring requires considerable judgment.

6. *Arithmetic subtest*. The rationale for the WISC-R Arithmetic subtest probably applies to the WPPSI Arithmetic subtest. Formal education probably has less of an influence on the WPPSI. The subtest is a moderately good measure of g and contributes to the Verbal and Performance factors. It is a reliable subtest $(r_{1I} = .82)$. Scoring is direct.

7. *Similarities subtest*. The WPPSI Similarities subtest appears to measure logical thinking to a greater extent than the WISC-R Similarities subtest. The subtest is a moderately good measure of g and contributes to the Verbal factor. It is a reliable sub-test $(r_{1I} = .83)$. Judgment is required in scoring the last six items.

8. *Comprehension subtest*. The rationale for the WISC-R Comprehension subtest probably applies to the WPPSI Comprehension subtest, although linguistic skill and logical reasoning may play a more significant role on the WPPSI. The subtest is a moderately good measure of g and contributes to the Verbal factor. It is a reliable subtest $(r_{1I} = .81)$. Scoring requires considerable judgment.

9. *Sentences subtest*. Sentences is the only supplementary subtest in the WPPSI. It is a memory test, measuring immediate recall and attention. The subtest is a moderately good measure of g and contributes to the Verbal factor. It is a reliable subtest $(r_{1I} = .85)$. Scoring requires considerable skill.

10. *Animal House subtest*. Animal House is considered to measure memory, attention span, goal awareness, concentration, and finger and manual dexterity. It is a moderately good measure of g and contributes to the Performance factor. It is a somewhat reliable subtest $(r_{1I} = .77)$. Administration is relatively easy. The abilities measured by the Animal House Retest are not known at this time.

11. *Picture Completion subtest*. The rationale for the WISC-R Picture Completion subtest probably applies to the WPPSI Picture Completion subtest. The subtest is a moderately good measure of g and contributes to the Performance factor. It is a reliable subtest $(r_{1I} = .83)$. Administration is relatively easy.

12. *Mazes subtest*. The rationale for the WISC-R Mazes subtest probably applies to the WPPSI Mazes subtest. The subtest is a moderately good measure of g and contributes to the Performance factor. It is a reliable subtest $(r_{1I} = .87)$. Scoring requires considerable judgment. Administrative procedures differ from those used on the WISC-R.

13. *Geometric Design subtest*. Geometric Design is considered to measure perceptual and visual-motor organization abilities. It is

a moderately good measure of g and contributes to the Performance factor. It is a reliable subtest ($r_{11} = .82$). This subtest may be the most difficult of all WPPSI subtests to score.

14. *Block Design subtest.* The rationale for the WISC-R Block Design subtest probably applies to the WPPSI Block Design subtest. The subtest is a moderately good measure of g and contributes to the Performance factor. It is a reliable subtest ($r_{11} = .82$). The subtest requires skill to administer.

15. The WPPSI Performance IQ is a better predictor than the Verbal IQ of children's moral judgment and ability to form color-form associations. Block Design and Geometric Design are related to field independence. In addition, Geometric Design is related to visual-recognition ability.

16. The same considerations that apply to profile analysis on the WISC-R apply to profile analysis on the WPPSI. However, even more care should be taken with the WPPSI than with the WISC-R in using profile analysis because limited research findings are available.

17. Illustrations of the clinical use of the WPPSI were presented.

18. For the most part, WPPSI profiles of adequate and inadequate readers are similar.

Assessment of Intelligence and Infant Development with Specialized Measures

An "intelligence quotient" may be of provisional value as a first crude approximation when the mental level of an individual is sought; but whoever imagines that in determining this quantity he has summed up "the" intelligence of an individual once and for all . . . leaves off where psychology should begin.

WILLIAM STERN

EXHIBIT 14-1. Psychological Evaluation: Fetal Alcohol Syndrome (Initial Evaluation)

Name: Tim
Date of birth: January 19, 1976
Chronological age: 1-5
Date of examination: June 10, 1977
Date of report: June 12, 1977

Tests Administered

Bayley Scales of Infant Development
Vineland Social Maturity Scale

Background

Tim, a black youngster, was referred by the Catholic Home Bureau because of developmental difficulties. Little is known about Tim's prenatal history, although it is believed that his mother was an alcoholic and involved in a methadone treatment program. However, no information is available about the amount of alcohol consumed during the pregnancy. Tim was born prematurely, at 32 + weeks gestation, with birth weight at 2 lbs., 3½ oz. At the time of his discharge from the Intensive Care Unit three months later, he weighed 5 pounds and was given a diagnosis of fetal alcohol syndrome, with accompanying physical manifestations including cleft palate and congenital heart murmur. A recent physical examination also indicates that he has numerous physical stigmata consistent with the fetal alcohol syndrome, such as microcephaly, distinctive epicanthal folds, and a depressed nasal bridge. Tim has been living with foster parents since he was 3 months old.

Observations

Tim is a tiny 17-month-old baby who seems more like a 5- or 6-month-old. He has a markedly small head and a misshapen right ear. During the examination he tilted his head backward to see, using only the lower portion of his eyes. He tracked objects in vertical, horizontal, and circular patterns adequately but in a somewhat lazy fashion, often dropping his head to the right. Tim generally used his right hand to grasp objects.

Tim responded well to social approaches by quieting down and seeming to listen intently, occasionally smiling in response. He was accepting of the examiner and affectionate with his foster mother. He was interested in the test stimuli and played with sustained attention on each item presented. Tim generally played in a rather immature fashion, exploring the toys by mouthing, fingering, or banging them. His emotional

EXHIBIT 14-1   (cont.)

tone was generally happy, as he cooed and gurgled happily and only occasionally expressed displeasure. Tim made persistent attempts at goals and his responses were satisfactory to auditory, visual, and tactile stimulation.

Test Results

On the Vineland Social Maturity Scale, which was administered to his foster mother, Tim achieved a Social Age of 7 months (Deviation Social Quotient = 68), which represents a 10-month delay in independent self-help skills. While he has mastered such skills as the ability to pull his socks off, pull himself upright, and sit unsupported, he cannot imitate sounds, drink from a cup assisted, or grasp with his finger and thumb opposed as would be expected of a 17-month-old child.

On the Bayley Scales of Infant Development, Tim achieved a mental-age level of 5 months and a motor-age level of 7 months. These results indicate that his psychomotor development is extremely delayed, by as much as 12 months. Positive trends observed in the testing session were Tim's delight in play and persistent reaching toward objects, his frequent seeking of the source of sounds, and his manipulation and exploration of toys. Tim, in addition, is able to crawl and stand up holding onto furniture.

Summary

Tim is quite delayed in psychomotor development, but is interested in exploring his environment. The positive mother-child interaction is an important factor in furthering Tim's development.

Recommendations

1. Tim's foster parents should be counseled about the results of the testing; the counselor should stress the developmental delays but indicate the need for yearly reassessment before any long-term prognostic statements are made.
2. The Infant Training Program should be offered to Tim's foster parents; it would help them to work more positively with Tim's specific handicaps and assets.
3. Reassessment to evaluate Tim's progress and adjust therapeutic goals is advised after one year.

_____
Examiner

(See Exhibit 17-1 [p. 307] for a reevaluation of Tim.)

Many of the individually administered tests of intelligence surveyed in this chapter make valuable additions to the examiner's basket of techniques, especially when it is not feasible or practical to administer the Stanford-Binet, WISC-R, or WPPSI. Some tests, such as the McCarthy Scales of Children's Abilities or Extended Merrill-Palmer Scale of Mental Tests, deserve consideration in their own right. The infant tests, while placed in this chapter, are for the most part best seen as measures of development rather than of intelligence. However, as we have seen in Chapter 4, developmental scores have prognostic value for evaluating the cognitive abilities of some handicapped infants.

The intelligence tests, achievement tests, and special ability tests covered in this book serve a number of different purposes, including screening, classification/placement, and program planning/remediation. Tests vary in the extent to which they are useful in meeting one or more of these purposes. In your reading about the tests covered in this and other chapters of the text, keep in mind the different purposes that tests may serve, and try to determine the purposes for which the test is best suited.

The tests covered in this chapter can be used for screening devices, for follow-up evaluations, and for assessing handicapped as well as normal children. Some of the tests require a simple pointing response, and if this response is not possible for the child, there are other means of obtaining a response from the child. Eye movements may be used in some cases. In others, the examiner may point to each alternative choice and ask the child to indicate "yes" or "no" by a prearranged signal. Instructions for some tests can be pantomimed.

Although some of the tests covered in the chapter provide limited material for qualitative analysis, it is still important for the examiner to try to understand the reason for the child's failures (as well as successes). For example, failures may represent limited cognitive ability or inability to understand the directions. These and other possibilities should be evaluated carefully.

It is important to recognize that critical decisions should not be based on any of the tests described in the present chapter, with the possible exception of the McCarthy Scales. Some of the tests have limited validities and reliabilities, others have limited normative groups, and still others measure only a limited aspect of intelligence. In addition, large discrepancies for individual children have been reported between IQs obtained on some of these tests and those obtained on the Stanford-Binet or WISC-R, even though mean IQs may not be significantly different. It is recommended that when a child has the necessary physical capacities and when time is not at a premium, the examiner select the Stanford-Binet, WISC-R, or WPPSI for the assessment of intelligence. This is particularly important when the IQ is to be used to make decisions about the child. However, when verbal responses cannot be elicited from the child, when motor handicaps limit the child's performance, or when time is at a premium and only a screening procedure is needed, brief intelligence tests can be useful instruments. (Appendix D presents the highlights of the tests covered in this and other chapters of the book.)

Assessment of Intelligence with Tests Containing Verbal and Nonverbal Items

McCarthy Scales of Children's Abilities

The McCarthy Scales of Children's Abilities (McCarthy, 1972) is a well-standardized and psychometrically sound measure of the cognitive ability of young children. It should find a useful place in the clinician's battery. It is individually administered, covers the age range from 2½ to 8½ years, and takes approximately forty-five to fifty minutes for

children below the age of 5 years; it requires about one hour for older children. The scales have some unique features that may prove to be valuable, especially in the evaluation of young children with learning problems and with other types of exceptionality (Sattler, 1978).

The McCarthy Scales provide a general level of intellectual functioning, the General Cognitive Index (GCI), and a profile of abilities. The profile includes measures of verbal ability, nonverbal reasoning ability, number aptitude, short-term memory, and coordination. Several items also assess hand dominance. No important sex differences have been found on the scales for any age groups in the standardization sample (Kaufman & Kaufman, 1973).

The McCarthy Scales contain eighteen tests grouped into one or more of six scales (see Table 14-1). The five verbal tests, seven perceptual-performance tests, and three quantitative tests are also included in the General Cognitive Scale. All four memory tests also appear in other scales. Among the five motor tests, two are found in other scales and three are exclusive to the scale. These latter three tests measure gross coordination and are not included in the General Cognitive Scale. The abilities thought to be measured by the scales and subtests are also shown in Table 14-1.

An Index, which is a standard score, is computed for each scale. The GCI has a mean of 100 and a standard deviation of 16, while the five remaining scale Indexes have means of 50 and standard deviations of 10. McCarthy interprets the GCI as representing the child's ability to integrate his or her accumulated knowledge and adapt it to the tasks of the scales. This functional definition is strikingly similar to definitions associated with the Intelligence Quotient, a term McCarthy deliberately avoids. Further evidence suggesting that the two terms are comparable comes from the fact that (a) the descriptive classifications associated with the GCI are almost the same as those used for IQs on Wechsler's tests, and (b) mental ages (ranging from 1-4 to 12-6 years), which are available for the GCI, can serve,

TABLE 14-1.   Abilities Thought to Be Measured by McCarthy Scales and Subtests

Verbal Scale (Ability to understand and process verbal stimuli and to express thoughts)				
Pictorial Memory	*Word Knowledge*	*Verbal Memory*	*Verbal Fluency*	*Opposite Analogies*
Short-term memory (auditory and visual) Early language development Attention	Verbal concept formation Early language development Verbal expression (Part II)	Short-term memory (auditory) Verbal comprehension Attention Concentration (Part II) Verbal expression (Part II)	Verbal concept formation Logical classification Creativity (divergent thinking) Verbal expression	Verbal concept formation Early language development Verbal reasoning

Perceptual-Performance Scale (Visual-motor coordination and nonverbal reasoning through manipulation of concrete materials)						
Block Building	*Puzzle Solving*	*Tapping Sequence*	*Right-Left Orientation*[a]	*Draw-A-Design*	*Draw-A-Child*	*Conceptual Grouping*
Visual-motor coordination Spatial relations	Visual perception Nonverbal reasoning Visual-motor coordination Spatial relations	Short-term memory (primarily visual) Visual-motor coordination Attention	Spatial relations Verbal concept formation Nonverbal reasoning Directionality	Visual perception Visual-motor coordination Spatial relations	Nonverbal concept formation Visual-motor coordination Body image	Logical classification Nonverbal reasoning Verbal concept formation
						(cont.)

McCarthy suggests, as indications of mental competence and can be used for other legal decisions. For all practical purposes, the GCI and the IQ are barely distinguishable.

Standardization. The standardization of the McCarthy Scales was excellent, with the sample closely matching the 1970 census data. Stratification variables included age, sex, color, geographic region, father's occupation, and urban-rural residence. A total of 1,032 children between the ages of 2½ and 8½ years were tested; 100 to 106 children, equally divided by sex, were tested for each of the ten age levels included in the sample.

Reliability. Coefficients of reliability, standard errors of measurement, and intercorre-

lations between the scales are reported for ten different age levels in the standardization sample for each of the six scales. The average split-half reliability of the GCI is excellent ($r = .93$), while average split-half reliabilities for the other five scales, which range from .79 to .88, are satisfactory. The GCI has an average standard error of measurement of 4 points. The lowest intercorrelations occur between the Motor Scale and the other five scales. Stability of the McCarthy Scales, measured over a retest interval of approximately thirty days in a sample of 125 children, is adequate, with coefficients of .90 for the GCI and of .69 to .89 for the other scale Indexes. The GCI also has been found to have adequate stability ($r = .85$) over a one-year period (Davis & Slettedahl, 1976).

TABLE 14-1   (cont.)

Quantitative Scale (Facility in dealing with numbers and understanding of quantitative concepts)		
Number Questions	*Numerical Memory*	*Counting and Sorting*
Numerical reasoning	Short-term memory (auditory)	Rote counting
Computational skills	Attention	Number concepts
Number facts and concepts	Reversibility (Part II)	Numerical reasoning
Concentration		
Verbal comprehension		

Memory Scale (Short-term memory across a wide range of visual and auditory stimuli)			
Pictorial Memory	*Tapping Sequence*	*Verbal Memory*	*Numerical Memory*
Short-term memory (auditory and visual)	Short-term memory (primarily visual)	Short-term memory (auditory)	Short-term memory (auditory)
Early language development	Visual-motor coordination	Verbal comprehension	Attention
Attention	Attention	Attention	Reversibility (Part II)
		Concentration (Part II)	
		Verbal expression (Part II)	

Motor Scale (Gross and fine motor coordination)				
Leg Coordination	*Arm Coordination*	*Imitative Action*	*Draw-A-Design*	*Draw-A-Child*
Gross motor coordination	Gross motor coordination	Gross motor coordination	Fine motor coordination	Fine motor coordination
Balance	Precision of movement	Fine motor coordination		

General Cognitive Scale[b] (Reasoning, concept formation, and memory when solving verbal and numerical problems and when manipulating concrete materials)

[a]For ages 5 and above.
[b]The fifteen separate tests included in the General Cognitive Scale are described in the Verbal, Perceptual-Performance, and Quantitative Scales.

Adapted from Kaufman and Kaufman (1977).

Validity. Concurrent validity is acceptable, using the Stanford-Binet, WISC, WISC-R, and WPPSI as criteria, with correlations ranging from .45 to .91 (median of .75).[1] Predictive validity also is satisfactory, using the Metropolitan Achievement Tests (*r* from .34 to .54) (McCarthy, 1972).

Construct validity appears to be good, at least as established by factor analytic techniques. Factor analytic findings indicate that the tests possess a certain amount of uniqueness, with the following five factors, for the most part, appearing throughout the age levels covered by the tests: Verbal, Motor, General Cognitive, Memory, and Perceptual-Performance. Additional factors also are found at selected age levels (Kaufman, 1975b). The McCarthy appears to be tapping the same theoretical abilities for both black and white children (Kaufman & DiCuio, 1975). However, studies are needed concerning the extent to which the test is fair for various cultures and whether or not the test will be *used fairly*.

While concurrent validity coefficients are satisfactory, large differences have been reported between McCarthy GCIs and Stanford-Binet or WISC-R IQs in samples of gifted children (Gerken, Hancock, & Wade, 1978), mentally retarded (Levenson & Zino, 1979), and learning disabled (Goh & Youngquist, 1979). With the gifted children, means differed by 10 points (*M* GCI = 105, *M* IQ = 115), but individual discrepancies were as much as 20 to 30 points (lower McCarthy GCIs than Stanford-Binet IQs). With the mentally retarded children, the mean Stanford-Binet IQ was 64, whereas the mean McCarthy GCI was 44, a difference of 20 points. With learning-disabled children, GCIs were lower than WISC-R IQs by 8 to 15 points, on the average. These results suggest that GCIs are not interchangeable with Stanford-Binet and WISC-R IQs.

Some useful administrative and interpretative guidelines. Confidence intervals for the five scales and GCI by age level are shown in Table C-31 in the Appendix. Table BC-1 on the inside back cover can be used to obtain the percentile ranks for GCIs, while Table C-37 in the Appendix shows the classifications associated with the GCIs.

Kaufman (1977) proposed a short form of the McCarthy consisting of the following subtests: Puzzle Solving, Word Knowledge, Numerical Memory, Verbal Fluency, Counting and Sorting, and Conceptual Grouping. Equations to convert the short form to an estimated GCI are available in his article. Taylor, Slocumb, and O'Neill (1979) offered a short form containing the following six subtests: Counting and Sorting, Pictorial Memory, Number Questions, Verbal Fluency, Numerical Memory, and Tapping Sequence. Both of these short forms, if needed, should be used only for screening purposes.

Extrapolated GCIs above 150 and below 50 are found in a study by Harrison and Naglieri (1978).

Differences required for significance when comparing a child's Index on one scale with his or her mean Index can be obtained in Table C-32 in the Appendix. In comparing a single Index with the child's overall average Index on the five scales, a difference of 8 points can be considered significant for the Verbal Index, 9 for the Perceptual-Performance Index, and 10 for the Quantitative, Memory, and Motor Indexes.

Significant scatter in 62 percent of the profiles of the standardization sample has been reported. That is, one or more of the five scale Indexes differed significantly from the mean score (Kaufman, 1976a). This finding suggests that caution must be used in interpreting scatter on the McCarthy, especially when testing exceptional children. The clinical applications of scatter on the McCarthy Scales await further research.

Without resort to statistical methods, McCarthy has suggested that about a 15-point difference is needed between the Verbal and Memory, Perceptual-Performance and Motor, and Quantitative and Memory Scales to be considered "noteworthy." However, differences as low as 10 points between the scale Indexes have been found to be significant (Ysseldyke & Samuel, 1973). Since significant differences between scale Indexes vary by as much as four scaled-score points at various ages, it is preferable to use the table presented by Ysseldyke and Samuel (1973), which shows the significant differences between scales by age level rather than just average difference values.

Limitations of the McCarthy Scales. While the McCarthy Scales have many strengths, they also have a number of limitations (Kaufman & Kaufman, 1977). First, much clerical work is involved in transforming scores on the eighteen separate tests into Indexes on the six scales. Second, the test does not include social comprehension and judgment tasks, and few tasks assess abstract problem-solving skills. Third, the test may not be suitable for school-age children because some of the procedures are too cumbersome. Fourth, there is a lack of a sufficient ceiling on many of the tests for children aged 7 years and older. Consequently, the test is not effective in assessing the abilities of older gifted children. Fifth, the unavailability of a McCarthy-like battery for older children and adolescents makes the McCarthy of limited use for follow-up evaluations; there is less than adequate continuity with other available instruments. Sixth, the internal consistency reliabilities of some of the Indexes are lower than might be desired (below .80). Seventh, some of the scales overlap in content. Eighth, the GCI floor of 50 limits its usefulness for severely mentally retarded children. Ninth, the test is not adequate for evaluating below-average 2½-year-olds because it has a limited floor. Consequently, it is not possible to obtain an adequate ability profile. Finally, the McCarthy makes no provision for tests that are spoiled or not administered. When this happens, the computation of Indexes is not possible for all scales that include the spoiled or omitted test. Fortunately, however, Kaufman and Kaufman (1977) describe proration procedures that permit the estimation of scores when there are spoiled or omitted tests.

Comment on the McCarthy Scales of Children's Abilities. Because there is some evidence that the McCarthy Scales do not provide scores that are equivalent to those on the Stanford-Binet and WISC-R, it is recommended that caution be exercised in using GCIs for placement decisions, especially in the assessment of mental retardation and giftedness. An important question is whether the GCI on the McCarthy Scales is more valid than the IQs provided by the Stanford-Binet and WISC-R. More research is needed to answer this question. McCarthy states that the individual tests are not sufficiently reliable by themselves to permit meaningful evaluation. However, it is impossible to judge the reliabilities of the individual tests because they are not presented. The lack of standard scores for each test by age level limits the diagnostic usefulness of the McCarthy Scales. In addition, the extent to which the scaled scores will assist in educational or clinical treatment decisions is unknown. The manual provides no guidelines for such decisions, nor does it provide help in interpreting profiles of scaled scores.

However, in spite of its limitations, the McCarthy Scales of Children's Abilities has great potential because it provides a profile of abilities that may be particularly useful in evaluating children with learning disabilities. In addition, the manual is convenient to use, the general guidelines for testing are thorough, the materials are well constructed, and the tasks are likely to appeal to children. It is a very promising tool for assessing the cognitive and, to a lesser extent, the motor abilities of young children, and therefore deserves serious consideration. (See Kaufman & Kaufman (1977) for a detailed approach to the interpretation of the McCarthy Scales of Children's Abilities.)

Extended Merrill-Palmer Scale

The Extended Merrill-Palmer Scale (Ball, Merrifield, & Stott, 1978) is an individually administered test of cognitive ability for preschool children between the ages of 3-0 and 5-11 years. It attempts to evaluate both the content of thinking (i.e., the material that is actually processed by the child) and the process of thinking (i.e., the way in which this material is used to form new concepts) in young children. It was based on the Merrill-Palmer Scale, but only nine of the original thirty-eight tests are included in the new version. The tests retained are the three copying tests, the two pyramid building tasks, the pink tower, questions, matching colors (directions), and action-agent (word meaning). All timed tests in the original version were excluded, as were tests that failed to meet adequate statistical standards or other criteria. The scale takes approximately one hour to administer.

The scale, based on Guilford's Structure of Intellect model, assesses two types of thought content (semantic and figural) and two types of thought processes (productive thinking and evaluative). The two content categories and the two process categories are combined to define four dimensions: Semantic Production, Figural Production, Semantic Evaluation, and Figural Evaluation (see Figure 14-1). Semantic Production involves the use of language or other means of communication. Tests in this area tap the availability and flow of ideas. Semantic Evaluation requires judging whether a given action, statement, or configuration

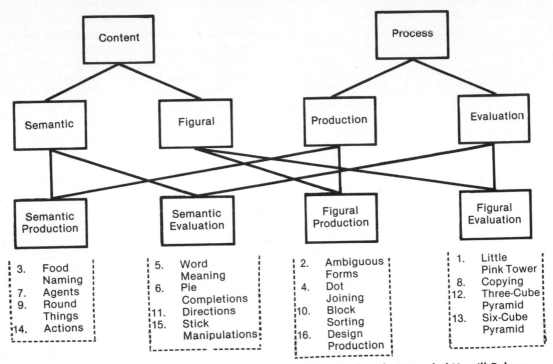

FIGURE 14-1. Cognitive Components of the Four Dimensions Measured on the Extended Merrill-Palmer Scale.

fits a given criterion. Figural Production involves producing a variety of responses by using a crayon or pencil or sticks or by describing ink blots. Figural Evaluation requires matching a configuration by using a crayon or pencil or by moving objects.

Each of the sixteen tasks presented in the Extended Scale measures one of the four dimensions. There are four tasks within each dimension. A brief description of the tasks follows:

1. *Little Pink Tower.* Building a five-block tower from memory.
2. *Ambiguous Forms.* Naming things seen in ink blots.
3. *Food Naming.* Naming things that people eat.
4. *Dot Joining.* Joining dots.
5. *Word Meaning.* Giving the use or meaning of words.
6. *Pie Completion.* Cutting a pie into parts from the center outward.

7. *Agents.* Naming several agents for each of ten different actions (e.g., "What runs?").
8. *Copying.* Copying a circle, cross, star, and diamond.
9. *Round Things.* Selecting round objects from a visual display.
10. *Block Sorting.* Sorting sixteen blocks by color, shape, and size.
11. *Directions.* Following directions, using knowledge of colors, and understanding concepts (e.g., "Put the red and green cars inside the blue box").
12. *Three-Cube Pyramid.* Building a pyramid from three blocks.
13. *Six-Cube Pyramid.* Building a pyramid from six blocks.
14. *Actions.* Giving several actions for each of seven different objects.
15. *Stick Manipulation.* Reproducing figures constructed by the examiner.
16. *Design Production.* Making designs with a set of sticks.

The record form provided in the Extended Scale is designed to facilitate administration of the test. Each task has its own record form, complete with instructions for the task and space for recording the child's responses. The forms are convenient, making it unnecessary to refer to the manual while administering the test. The manual presents forty-two cases describing various profiles.

Raw scores are transformed into weighted composite scores for each dimension. Each weighted score is then converted into a percentile range, which is presented on a bar graph. Children are evaluated separately on each dimension on the basis of how they compare to their same-age peer group. Percentile bands are provided by six-month intervals between ages 36 months and 71 months. However, the scale does not give specific percentiles or an overall score.

Standardization. The Extended Merrill-Palmer Scale was standardized on a group of 1,124 white preschool children from Ohio and New York. Children were selected whose mothers represented three different educational levels—one-quarter college graduates, one-half high school graduates, and one-quarter with not more than a ninth grade education.

Reliability. Reliabilities are presented as part-whole coefficients for the four separate scores by six-month age levels. The median part-whole reliability is .74 (range of .54 to .81). However, these coefficients are not acceptable as reliability estimates, because the tasks are not parallel forms of the same test.

Validity. No validity indices are reported for the scale.

Comment on the Extended Merrill-Palmer Scale. The Extended Merrill-Palmer Scale has potential for the assessment of the cognitive ability of preschool children. However, the scale is deficient on a number of grounds.

First, the standardization sample is not representative of the country. Minorities were entirely excluded from the norm group,

and only a crude method was used to classify the socioeconomic status of the sample.

Second, the psychometric properties of the scale are questionable. No information is given about test-retest reliabilities. The part-whole reliabilities are less than .80, in one case as low as .54, and are not appropriate estimates. In addition, standard errors of measurement are not provided.

Third, no validity data are presented.

Fourth, the percentile bands do not allow for a precise evaluation of a child's performance. In some instances, the range may be as great as 20 percentage points, making it impossible to tell exactly where the child's abilities fall. A child who exceeds 32 percent of the children in the normative group on Figural Production is obviously not as well developed in this skill as one whose score falls at the fifty-second percentile. Yet, this differentiation cannot be made by referring to the bar graphs. As a result, it is difficult in some cases to determine whether a child's performance is below average or average.

Finally, an extensive scoring guide is not provided. As a result, scoring difficulties are likely to arise.

Despite the above difficulties, the scale deserves consideration in the assessment battery. The breakdown of the tests into four cognitive components is useful. The nonverbal scores can be used in the assessment of language-handicapped children, and the verbal scores can be used for the assessment of motorically handicapped youngsters. However, the authors' attempt to replace a general estimate of ability with component scores does not appear to do justice to a large body of evidence which indicates the importance of the construct of *g* as an underlying component of intellectual ability.

Merrill-Palmer Scale of Mental Tests

The Merrill-Palmer Scale of Mental Tests (Stutsman, 1931) is primarily a nonverbal test designed to evaluate children between 18 months and 71 months of age. However, Stutsman recommends that it be used only for children between 24 and 63 months because of norming problems below and above this age range. The test contains items related to fine motor coordination, spatial discrimination, manipulation of materials, and memory for words or for groups of words.

The test can easily be adapted for use with deaf children by using pantomime, and can be used with handicapped or difficult-to-manage children because of the flexible scoring procedures.

The Merrill-Palmer contains thirty-eight tests, with sixteen graded on a pass-fail basis and twenty-two on a partial-credit basis. The tests are arranged in six-month intervals, starting at 18 months, and ranked according to difficulty. Time limits are used for some tests. The scale takes approximately thirty to forty minutes to administer.

Standardization. The Merrill-Palmer was standardized on 631 children (331 males and 300 females) from 18 to 77 months of age. The children were selected from twenty different sources including private nursery schools, public schools, child care agencies, and health agencies. No information is provided about the ethnicity or socioeconomic status of the sample.

Instructions are given verbally, and the order of administration may be varied so as to allow the examiner to use a flexible administrative approach when necessary. Scores are reported as a mental age or a percentile rank. IQs are not recommended, but they can be computed using the ratio method (MA/CA × 100 = IQ).

Reliability. The manual fails to report any reliability data. Later studies, however, reported test-retest reliability coefficients that ranged from .39 to .92 (median $r = .60$).[2]

Validity. Correlations between the Merrill-Palmer and the Stanford-Binet range from .22 to .79 (median $r = .51$). Correlations are high between the Merrill-Palmer and other preschool tests.[3] Several group factors have been found in a sample of 3- to 4-year-old

nursery school children: Willingness to Cooperate, Finding Relations, Fine Motor Coordination, Persistence, Perceptual Speed, and Space (Hurst, 1960).

Comment on the Merrill-Palmer Scale of Mental Tests. The Merrill-Palmer, despite its limited standardization and seriously outdated norms, is still a useful instrument that provides a crude measure of the nonverbal skills of young children, especially those who are extremely handicapped (e.g., autistic). It has a flexible administration, which is especially useful with nonspeaking children or those who are minimally cooperative (Mittler, 1966). It is a test that is interesting to children, requires a minimum of spoken instructions, and has a wide range of items that require no speech from the child (Berger & Yule, 1972). However, the scale may not be appropriate for physically handicapped or slow children, because many tests are timed (Honzik, 1967). The test appears most useful for ages 18 to 42 months, after which its use is limited, except with mentally retarded children (Goodenough, 1940).

Slosson Intelligence Test

The Slosson Intelligence Test (Slosson, 1963) is an age-scale test that provides mental ages from .5 month to 27 years. The two major sources for the items were the Stanford-Binet and the Gessell Institute of Child Development Behavior Inventory. For children over 4 years of age, all questions are presented verbally and require spoken responses. There are no time limits. The test takes between ten and thirty minutes to administer and scoring is fairly objective. The test can be given by relatively untrained examiners.

The test places heavy emphasis on language skills for children between 2 and 3 years of age, and consequently may not be valid for those children in this age group who have delayed language development. A major problem with the test is in the age period of .5 to 24 months. There are few items at each month's level, and placement of the items does not agree with the placement of similar items on the Bayley Scales of Infant Development.

The Slosson Intelligence Test still maintains the ratio IQ. This type of IQ, as we have seen, has many disadvantages. While the mean is set at 100, the standard deviations vary considerably throughout the age range covered by the scale. Thus, IQs are not equally distributed throughout the scale.

Standardization. The standardization group is poorly described, and no systematic attempt was made to get a representative norm group.

Reliability. Test-retest and split-half reliabilities are in the .90s.[4]

Validity. Correlations with the Stanford-Binet are in the .60s to .90s.[5] However, these correlations are spuriously high because the Slosson contains items that are essentially adaptations from the Stanford-Binet. With other tests of intelligence, correlations are in the .40s to .90s.[6] Acceptable concurrent and predictive validity coefficients (.30s to .60s) have been found using a variety of achievement tests.[7]

Comment on the Slosson Intelligence Test. The Slosson Intelligence Test has merit as a quick screening device. Advantages include the short administration time and relative ease of use by personnel with minimal training in the administration of individual intelligence tests. However, the poor standardization and use of the ratio IQ are major difficulties. The test should not be used as a substitute for the Stanford-Binet, WISC-R, or WPPSI or for decision-making purposes, such as for making the classification of mental retardation.

Detroit Tests of Learning Aptitude

The Detroit Tests of Learning Aptitude (Baker & Leland, 1967) is an omnibus test containing nineteen subtests that measure various abilities, including reasoning and comprehension, practical judgment, verbal ability, time and space relationships, number ability, auditory and visual processing skills, and motor ability (see Table 14-2). The battery was first published in 1935, and a revised manual was published in 1967. However, the norms are still based on the 1935 sample.

The battery covers an age range from 3 years through adult, although not all tests are administered at every age. Separate mental ages are available for each subtest. For the entire battery, an intelligence quotient can be obtained by the ratio method. The manual recommends that a minimum of nine and maximum of thirteen subtests be administered to any one examinee. The test is individually administered, and requires about sixty to ninety-five minutes.

Standardization.   The Detroit Tests of Learning Aptitude was standardized on 150 Detroit public school students at each age level from 3 to 19 years. The subjects in the

TABLE 14-2.   Detroit Tests of Learning Aptitude

Subtests
1. Pictorial Absurdities
2. Verbal Absurdities
3. Pictorial Opposites
4. Verbal Opposites
5. Motor Speed
6. Auditory Attention Span for Unrelated Words
7. Oral Commissions
8. Social Adjustment A
9. Visual Attention Span for Objects
10. Orientation
11. Free Association
12. Designs
13. Auditory Attention Span for Related Syllables
14. Number Ability
15. Social Adjustment B
16. Visual Attention Span for Letters
17. Disarranged Pictures
18. Oral Directions
19. Likenesses and Differences

standardization sample were selected on the basis of their having obtained IQs in the average range on standardized group intelligence tests. However, sex, race, and socioeconomic level of the sample were not reported.

Reliability. Test-retest reliability for IQs reported in the manual is .96 for 48 students (age not reported) retested at an interval of five months and .68 for 792 students, aged 7 to 12 years, retested at an interval of two to three years. The number of subtests used to compute these reliability coefficients was not reported. Separate reliabilities for each subtest are not reported in the manual, nor are standard errors of measurement.

Validity. Intercorrelations reported in the manual among sixteen of the subtests appropriate for 8- to 12-year-olds ($N = 100$) range between .20 and .40, which indicates relative independence of the subtests. Chiappone (1968), with a small sample of mentally retarded subjects, found satisfactory correlations between the Detroit and the Stanford-Binet ($r = .70$), and between the Detroit and the WISC Full Scale ($r = .68$) and Verbal Scale ($r = .78$). The correlation between the Detroit and the WISC Performance Scale, however, was only .38.

Comment on the Detroit Tests of Learning Aptitude. The Detroit has some assets but many limitations. On the positive side, it provides mental-age equivalents for each subtest, covers a wide age range, and provides a profile of relative strengths and weaknesses. However, on the negative side, the norms are out of date, the standardization group is inadequate, administration time is long, standard scores are not available for each subtest, and reliability and validity data are not extensive. In spite of these difficulties, the Detroit does have some merit in some cases as a supplementary diagnostic instrument (Chiappone, 1968).

Assessment of Intelligence with Tests Containing Nonverbal Items Only

Progressive Matrices

The Progressive Matrices test is a nonverbal, individually or group administered test of reasoning ability based on figural materials. The test measures the ability to form comparisons, to reason by analogy, and to organize spatial perceptions into systematically related wholes. The Progressive Matrices comes in three different series: Standard Progressive Matrices (Raven, 1938), Coloured Matrices (Raven, 1947b), and Progressive Matrices Sets I and II (Raven, 1947a). In each form, the child is presented with a matrix-like arrangement of figural symbols, and must complete the matrix by selecting the appropriate missing symbol from a group of symbols. The test takes between fifteen and thirty minutes to administer. Raw scores are converted to percentiles.

The Standard Progressive Matrices is used for both children (6 years and older) and adults. It contains sixty items that are presented in five sets, with twelve items per set. In each item there is a matrix (or design) in black and white, with one part missing. In the first set, the design is shown with a piece appearing to have been cut out. In the other sets, there are individual pieces arranged in either a 2×2 or a 3×3 matrix. In each matrix one piece (or design) is left out, and the examinee must select, from a group of from six to eight choices, the one piece that best completes the matrix.

The rule or principle that will solve each item can either be formulated in verbal terms or be derived from a visual perceptual discovery of the internal structure of the stimulus. In the former case, an analytic approach is used in which logical operations are applied to features contained within the elements of the problem matrix (Hunt, 1974). In the latter case, a Gestalt approach is used to problems involving visual perception.

Testing-of-limits procedures can be applied to the Progressive Matrices (Carlson &

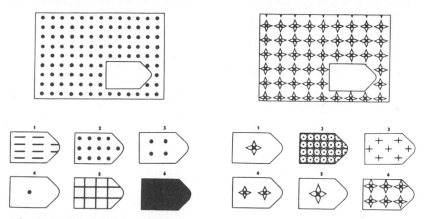

FIGURE 14-2. Sample Progressive Matrices Items. Reprinted by permission of J. C. Raven, Ltd.

Wiedl, 1979). Examples are as follows: (a) ask children to verbalize while they are solving the problem; (b) ask children to describe the principles or reasons for their solutions after the answer is given; (c) give children feedback for correct performance, incorrect performance, or both; and (d) show children the correct solution if they fail.

Standardization. The Standard Progressive Matrices was standardized on a representative sample of British people from 6 to 65 years of age (Raven, 1960). For the individual administration, the Standard Progressive Matrices was standardized on 735 British children between 6 and 13½ years of age. For self-administration or for group administration, the Standard Progressive Matrices was standardized on 1,407 children, 3,665 militiamen, and 2,192 civilians. The Coloured Matrices was standardized on 627 British children from 5 to 10½ years of age, and 271 people from 60 to 89 years of age (Raven, 1960). The Progressive Matrices Sets I and II were standardized on 471 British 10½-year-olds, 596 12½-year-olds, and 304 20-year-olds.

Reliability. Test-retest reliabilities are adequate for each form. They range from .71 to .92. The lowest reliabilities are for young children.[8]

Validity. Numerous studies indicate that the three forms have adequate concurrent validity using various intelligence tests as criteria with a variety of populations (white, black, Mexican-American, Indian, deaf, and mentally retarded).[9] Correlations with the Stanford-Binet and Wechsler tests range from .55 to .86 in these studies.

Factor analytic studies report conflicting results.[10] Some studies report that the Progressive Matrices contains primarily a *g* (Inductive or Reasoning) factor, while others indicate that it contains more than one factor, such as (1) Concrete and Abstract Meaning, (2) Continuous and Discrete Pattern Completion, and (3) Patterning Through Closure.

Comment on the Progressive Matrices. While the Progressive Matrices is a useful measure of nonverbal reasoning ability, it is unfortunate that its norms are dated. The test needs to be standardized on a representative sample of United States children (and adults). However, the ease of administration (instructions can be pantomimed) and limited sensory demands make it a useful supplementary screening test for children (and adults) with severe language, auditory, or physical disabilities. In addition, it is useful in testing children who do not speak English or who have limited command of English, as it represents a culturally reduced test. But even in these situations, the norms may not provide a valid estimate of ability.

The Progressive Matrices should not be used as a substitute for the Stanford-Binet or the Wechsler tests because it is less reliable and less valid. Its main limitation is that it attempts to measure general intelligence through one modality. Children can be incorrectly assessed if they are not capable of doing a figural-reasoning task. Supplementing the Progressive Matrices with a vocabulary test may prove to be helpful in the assessment of children who can speak English.

Goodenough-Harris Drawing Test

The Goodenough-Harris Drawing Test (Harris, 1963), also referred to as the Draw-A-Man Test, is a brief, nonverbal test of intelligence that can be administered either individually or in a group. Individual administration is recommended for preschool children and for children tested in clinical settings. The test covers ages 3-0 through 15-11 years, but the preferred ages are 3 to 10 years. The test has less ability to discriminate for children who are older than 10 years of age.

The purpose of the test is to measure intellectual maturity, which Harris defines as the ability to form concepts of an abstract character. The abilities involved in forming these concepts are (a) perception (discrimination of likenesses and differences), (b) abstraction (classification of objects), and (c) generalization (assigning newly experienced objects to the correct class). Evaluation of the child's drawing of the human figure serves as a way of measuring the complexity of his or her concept formation ability. The human figure is used because it is the most familiar and meaningful figure for the child.

The Draw-A-Man Test is based upon Goodenough's (1926) assumption that the intelligence of early school-age children can be estimated from their drawings of the figure of a man. The Harris revision includes (a) a more extensive and objective scoring system, (b) the introduction of the Draw-A-Woman Test as an alternative form, (c) the

Drawing of the Self as a possible third alternative form and a possible vehicle for exploring self-concept, and (d) the attempt to extend the usefulness of the test through 15-11 years of age.

Harris suggested that the following instructions be used to begin the test: "I want you to make a picture of a man. Make the very best picture you can; take your time and work very carefully. Try very hard and see what a good picture you can make. Be sure to make the whole man, not just his head and shoulders." Almost identical instructions are given for the drawing of the woman and the drawing of the self. For the drawing of the self, children are also told: "So take care and make this last one the very best of the three." In individual examinations, the examiner clarifies any ambiguous aspects of the drawing by asking the child to identify the body parts and describe the picture. The three drawings take between five and fifteen minutes to complete.

Two IQs can be derived from the child's drawing of a man and woman. One IQ is based on the Point Scale, an expanded version of the scale originally proposed by Goodenough (1926). Harris added twenty-two items to Goodenough's original fifty-one items. Each of the seventy-three items is rated on a pass-fail basis (0 or 1 point) for the presence or absence of a body part or for the presence of specific detail (e.g., hair styling). The Draw-A-Woman Test contains seventy-one items. Each drawing can be scored in three to four minutes. A thorough scoring guide is provided in the manual. Table 14-3 summarizes the major scoring guidelines for the Draw-A-Man test.

A second IQ is available from the Quality Scale, which is based on a 12-point scale, with 1 indicating the lowest category and 12 the highest. It is a rapid scoring procedure that is carried out by comparing the child's drawing with twelve model drawings that represent a continuum from least excellence to greatest excellence. For more precision, it is also possible to use a finely graded twenty-three-step Quality Scale, which ranges from .5 to 11.5, in .5 intervals. The Quality Scale was standardized by having

TABLE 14-3.   Short Scoring Guide for Draw-A-Man Test

1. Head present	25. Correct number of fingers shown	50. Proportion: face
2. Neck present		51. Proportion: arms I
3. Neck, two dimensions	26. Detail of fingers correct	52. Proportion: arms II
4. Eyes present	27. Opposition of thumb shown	53. Proportion: legs
5. Eye detail: brow or lashes	28. Hands present	54. Proportion: limbs in two dimensions
6. Eye detail: pupil	29. Wrist or ankle shown	55. Clothing I
7. Eye detail: proportion	30. Arms present	56. Clothing II
8. Eye detail: glance	31. Shoulders I	57. Clothing III
9. Nose present	32. Shoulders II	58. Clothing IV
10. Nose, two dimensions	33. Arms at side or engaged in activity	59. Clothing V
11. Mouth present		60. Profile I
12. Lips, two dimensions	34. Elbow joint shown	61. Profile II
13. Both nose and lips in two dimensions	35. Legs present	62. Full face
	36. Hip I (crotch)	63. Motor coordination: lines
14. Both chin and forehead shown	37. Hip II	64. Motor coordination: junctures
	38. Knee joint shown	
15. Projection of chin shown; chin clearly differentiated from lower lip	39. Feet I: any indication	65. Superior motor coordination
	40. Feet II: proportion	66. Directed lines and form: head outline
	41. Feet III: heel	
16. Line of jaw indicated	42. Feet IV: perspective	67. Directed lines and form: trunk outline
17. Bridge of nose	43. Feet V: detail	
18. Hair I	44. Attachment of arms and legs I	68. Directed lines and form: arms and legs
19. Hair II		
20. Hair III	45. Attachment of arms and legs II	69. Directed lines and form: facial features
21. Hair IV		
22. Ears present	46. Trunk present	70. "Sketching" technique
23. Ears present: proportion and position	47. Trunk in proportion, two dimensions	71. "Modeling" technique
		72. Arm movement
24. Fingers present	48. Proportion: head I	73. Leg movement
	49. Proportion: head II	

From *Children's Drawings as Measures of Intellectual Maturity*, by Dale B. Harris. Copyright 1963 by Harcourt Brace Jovanovich, Inc. Reprinted by permission of the publisher.

judges rate the level of maturity of 240 drawings from children ages 5 through 15 years.

Norms for the Point Scale are provided separately for boys and girls from age 3 through age 15 in whole-year intervals. Raw scores are converted into standard scores, with a mean of 100 and a standard deviation of 15. There are no norms for the Drawing of the Self Test. Norms also are available for the Quality Scale for ages 5 through 15 years. These norms, too, are standard scores, with a mean of 100 and a standard deviation of 15.

Standardization. The standardization sample for the Point Scale consisted of 2,975 boys and girls in the United States, selected so as to be representative of the 1960 census. Four geographical areas of the country were sampled. At each age level, from 5 through 15 years, 75 children were included.

Reliability. Test-retest reliabilities are in the .50s to .70s, while alternate-form (man, woman) reliabilities range from .72 to .90.[11] Interrater reliabilities on the Point Scale are satisfactory (in the .80s to .90s), while those for the Quality Scale are somewhat lower (in the .70s to .90s).[12]

Validity. Correlations between the Draw-A-Man Test and various intelligence tests in normal and handicapped populations range from .24 to .88 (with a median correlation of

.49) in Anglo groups[13] and from .22 to .85 (median of .57) in ethnic minority groups.[14] Correlations are somewhat higher with the Wechsler Verbal IQ than with the Performance IQ (median of .62 vs. .50).[15]

Correlations between the Draw-A-Man Test and various perceptual-motor tests range from .39 to .83, with a median correlation of .46.[16] Correlations between the Draw-A-Man Test and academic performance and teacher ratings range from .03 to .57, with a median correlation of .36.[17]

Comment on the Goodenough-Harris Drawing Test. The Draw-A-Man Test appears to be an acceptable screening instrument for use as a nonverbal measure of cognitive ability, particularly with children under 10 or 11 years of age. Its popularity is due to its nonverbal nature, its adaptability to group administration, and the ease of its integration into a battery of tests. Although the reported reliabilities are good, the validities are less acceptable. Therefore, the Draw-A-Man Test should not be used as the only measure of intelligence. The Draw-A-Man Test tends to provide lower IQs than the Stanford-Binet and Wechsler tests in a variety of white populations.

The Draw-A-Man Test seems to be an acceptable instrument for use with minorities, since it may not be as culturally loaded as are other tests. This is especially true for American Indian children (Cundick, 1970). However, cultural backgrounds may influence test scores, since different cultures place varying emphasis on body parts and clothing.

While the standardization sample was excellent, the norms need to be refined into half-year and quarter-year intervals for young children. Another necessary revision is a modernization of the scoring guidelines for the Draw-A-Woman Test. Many of the criteria for appropriate dress and hairstyling date back to the 1950s.

Leiter International Performance Scale

The Leiter International Performance Scale (Leiter, 1948) is a nonverbal test of intelligence that can be used to evaluate children who have sensory or motor defects or who have difficulty in speaking or reading. The scale also has been purported to be a culture-free measure of intelligence, although it appears to be no more culture-free than the Stanford-Binet (Tate, 1952). The scale contains fifty-four tests arranged in an age-scale format from year II to year XVIII. The MA obtained on the scale is used to obtain an IQ by the ratio method.

The tasks on the Leiter consist of having the child select the blocks bearing the appropriate symbols or pictures and insert them into the appropriate recess of a frame that is used in administering the scale. There is no time limit, and instructions are given in pantomime. The scale, which takes approximately thirty to forty-five minutes to administer, appears to require perceptual organization and discrimination ability. The tests at the lowest levels of the scale are considered to be tests of the ability to learn, rather than tests of learned material (Arthur, 1949). In principle, the Leiter is a nonverbal Binet scale.

The 1948 revision is the latest in a series of revisions. The initial version of the scale was reported in 1929 in Leiter's master's thesis. The 1948 revision was adapted by Arthur (1949), who supplemented the revision with tests from the Revised Form II of the Point Scale of Performance Tests. The Arthur Adaptation covers the age range between 3 and 8 years, and the tests cover year levels II through XII. The adaptation was needed because Arthur found the norms too high for children between the ages of 3 and 8 years. However, the test materials for the 1948 revision of the Leiter and the Arthur Adaptation are exactly the same through year level XII, where the Arthur Adaptation ends.

A Leiter profile is available to assist in qualitative analysis (Levine, Allen, Alker, & Fitzgibbons, 1974). However, care must be taken when using the profile because the areas covered by the Leiter are not uniform throughout the age range of the scale.

Standardization. The manual fails to describe the standardization sample adequately.

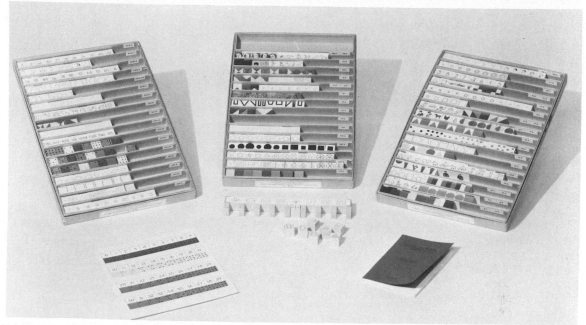

FIGURE 14-3. Leiter International Performance Scale. Courtesy of C. H. Stoelting Company.

Reliability. The manual fails to present reliability data or standard deviations for the various age levels. However, satisfactory test-retest reliabilities (in the .80s and .90s) have been reported for populations of handicapped children.[18]

Validity. Correlations with the Stanford-Binet and WISC range from .56 to .92, with a median correlation of .83.[19] The Leiter correlates more highly with the WISC Performance Scale than with the Verbal Scale. While correlations may be high, large differences in IQs between tests are occasionally observed. For example, in a study (Bonham, 1974) of deaf children, the Leiter yielded a mean IQ that was 17 points *lower* than the WISC Performance IQ (79 vs. 96).

Comment on the Leiter International Performance Scale. The scale has a number of limitations, including uneven item difficulty levels, outdated pictures, a small number of tests at each year level, and use of the ratio IQ. The most serious difficulties are the out-dated norms, inadequate standardization, and lack of information about the reliability of the scale for various age levels. Because the norms underestimate the child's intelligence, Leiter (1959) recommended that five points be added to the IQ obtained on the scale.

While the Leiter has a number of limitations, it does merit consideration as an aid in clinical diagnosis (rather than as a measure of general intelligence), especially in testing language handicapped children who cannot be evaluated by the Stanford-Binet, WISC-R, or WPPSI. However, although the test may be less culturally loaded than some other intelligence tests, there is no evidence that it is a culture-fair measure of intelligence.

Pictorial Test of Intelligence

The Pictorial Test of Intelligence (French, 1964) assesses intelligence of normal and handicapped children between the ages of 3 and 8 years. There are six subtests in the scale: Picture Vocabulary, Form Discrimination, Information and Comprehension,

Similarities, Size and Number, and Immediate Recall. The subtests are not timed, and the test takes approximately forty-five minutes to administer.

The items are presented in multiple-choice fashion, thereby making scoring a simple procedure. The arrangement of the alternatives on the response cards facilitates the use of eye movements for recording responses for those children who are not capable of pointing to their choices. Raw scores are converted to MA units and then to Deviation IQs ($M = 100$, $SD = 16$).

Standardization. The standardization sample consisted of 1,830 children stratified by regional area, community size, and father's occupational level to conform with the 1960 census. Although race was not used as a stratification variable, children from various races were included in the sample.

Reliability. The manual reports test-retest and internal consistency reliabilities in the high .80s and low .90s. However, other studies (Howard & Plant, 1967; Sawyer, 1968) found reliabilities in the .70s and .80s. Test-retest reliabilities may not be as adequate as split-half reliabilities, with the test being least reliable at age 8 years (Himelstein, 1972).

Validity. Correlations with other tests of intelligence range from .42 to .75 (median of .65), while with tests of achievement they range from .23 to .79 (median of .56).[20]

Comment on the Pictorial Test of Intelligence. The Pictorial Test of Intelligence sustains children's interest (Pasewark et al., 1967), although some of the instructions are confusing. Generally, the items appear to be arranged in ascending order, although some easy items appear in the later portions of the subtests (Sawyer, 1968). The need to start each subtest with the first item may add to testing time, and the norms may not be sufficiently specific. The test appears to be useful in evaluating children with motor and speech handicaps (Himelstein, 1972) and in evaluating the learning aptitude of children from 3 to 6 years of age (Newland, 1972).

Columbia Mental Maturity Scale

The Columbia Mental Maturity Scale (CMMS), Third Edition (Burgemeister, Blum, & Lorge, 1972), is useful in evaluating children who have sensory or motor defects or who have difficulty in speaking and, to some extent, in reading. The test does not depend on reading skills. It provides age deviation scores (standard scores) for chronological ages between 3 years, 6 months and 9 years, 11 months. The age deviation scores range from 50 to 150, with a mean of 100 and standard deviation of 16. The standard error of measurement is 5 points for ages 3½ through 5½ years, and 6 points for ages 6 through 9½ years. A second score, the Maturity Index, which indicates the standardization age group most similar to that of the child in terms of test performance, also is provided.

The test contains ninety-two cards (6 by 19 inches), fifty of which are completely new to the Third Edition. The task is simple—namely, to have the child select the one drawing on each card that is different from the others. However, young or deaf children may have difficulty in understanding the concept of pointing to the "one that does not belong." If deaf children do understand the directions, the test is useful as a screening device.

The test, which is untimed, usually takes between fifteen and twenty minutes to administer, and is simple to score. The child is required to make perceptual discriminations involving color, shape, size, use, number, missing parts, and symbolic material. Tasks include simple perceptual classifications and abstract manipulation of symbolic concepts. The CMMS appears to measure general reasoning ability, although there is some evidence that it may be more of a test of the ability to form and use concepts than a test of general intelligence (Reuter & Mintz, 1970).

Standardization. The standardization sample for the Third Edition consisted of 2,600 children residing in twenty-five states. The norming procedures were designed to ensure a representative national sample on the variables of geographic region, race, parental occupation, age, and sex of the 1960 census.

Reliability. Test-retest and split-half reliabilities are in the high .80s.

Validity. Correlations with other tests of intelligence range from the .30s to .60s, with many in the .50s. Concurrent validity is satisfactory ($r = .74$) using the Stanford-Binet as the criterion with below-average children (Ritter, Duffey, & Fischman, 1974). There is also some evidence that the scale provides similar scores for black and white 4- to 5-year-old children (Ratusnik & Koenig-sknecht, 1976). However, with Mexican-American children, the scale resulted in scores that were 6 points lower than those obtained by Anglo children (83 vs. 89) (Melear & Boyle, 1974).

Comment on the Columbia Mental Maturity Scale. The Third Edition of the CMMS is an improved version of the scale. The scale provides a means for evaluating intelligence through the use of nonverbal stimuli. It can be useful as an aid in evaluating handicapped children, and may be less culturally loaded than some other intelligence tests. However, the scores obtained on the CMMS are not interchangeable with those on the Stanford-Binet, WISC-R, or WPPSI.

Assessment of Infant Development

Bayley Scales of Infant Development

The Bayley Scales of Infant Development (Bayley, 1969) is a carefully developed measure of infant development for the age period from 2 months to 2½ years. Two standard scores are provided: a Mental Developmental Index, obtained from the Mental Scale, and a Psychomotor Developmental Index, from the Motor Scale. An Infant Behavior Record rating scale also is available.

The Mental Scale contains 163 items that are arranged by tenths of months. The scale evaluates a variety of activities and processes including shape discrimination, sustained attention, purposeful manipulation of objects, imitation and comprehension, vocalization, memory, problem solving, and naming objects. The 81 items in the Motor Scale cover gross and fine motor abilities, such as sitting, standing, walking, and grasping. The two scales take approximately forty-five minutes to administer, although approximately 10 percent of the children require seventy-five minutes or more. Table 14-4 shows some representative items on the two principal scales.

The Infant Behavior Record is a systematic way of assessing and recording observations of the child's behavior during the examination. Ratings are made for the following eleven areas: social orientation, cooperativeness, fearfulness, tension, general emotional tone, object orientation, goal directedness, attention span, endurance, activity, and reactivity. Behaviors that are oriented toward cognitive tasks (e.g., goal directedness, attention span, object orientation, and reactivity) have been found to be related to mental scores, while those related to social extroversion (e.g., social orientation to the examiner, cooperation, and emotional tone) had little predictive power (Matheny, Dolan, & Wilson, 1974).

Standardization. The Bayley was standardized on a representative national sample of 1,262 normal infants and children in fourteen age groups, from 2 months to 30 months of age. The stratification variables included geographic area, urban-rural residence, sex, race, and education of head of household. The Mental Developmental Index and the Psychomotor Developmental Index are normalized standard scores (with a mean of 100 and a standard deviation of 16) that have the same characteristics as a Deviation IQ.

TABLE 14-4.   Illustrative Items on the Bayley Scales of Infant Development

Age (in months)	Mental Scale	Motor Scale
2	Visually recognizes mother	Elevates self by arms: prone
4	Turns head to sound of rattle	Head balanced
6	Looks for fallen spoon	Sits alone 30 seconds or more
8	Uncovers toy	Pulls to standing position
10	Looks at pictures in book	Walks with help
12	Turns pages of book	Walks alone
14	Spontaneous scribble	Walks sideways
16	Builds tower of 3 cubes	Stands on left foot with help
18	Initiates crayon stroke	Tries to walk on walking board
20	Differentiates scribble from stroke	Walks with one foot on walking board
22	Names 3 pictures	Stands on left foot alone
24	Names 3 objects	Jumps from bottom step
26	Train of cubes	Walks down stairs alone: both feet on each step
28	Understands 2 prepositions	Jumps from second step
30	Builds tower of 8 cubes	Walks on tiptoe, 10 feet

Reliability. Split-half reliability coefficients for the fourteen age groups range from .81 to .93 (median of .88) on the Mental Scale and from .68 to .92 (median of .84) on the Motor Scale. Reliabilities on the Mental Scale are fairly consistent throughout the age periods covered by the test. However, on the Motor Scale, reliabilities tend to be lower for the first four months (ages 2 through 5 months). Split-half reliability also is satisfactory for black infants on both the Mental and Motor Scales (King & Seegmiller, 1973).

Correlations between the Mental and Motor Scales vary widely for the fourteen age groups, ranging from .18 to .75 (median of .46). Because the correlations tend to decrease with age, there may be a clearer differentiation between mental and motor skills as the child develops.

Validity. A correlation of .57 was obtained with the Stanford-Binet for a sample of 120 children, ages 24 to 30 months, in the standardization group. The manual, however, fails to report any validity coefficients for the younger age groups.

Comment on the Bayley Scales of Infant Development. Administration of the Bayley Scales requires considerable practice and experience. The Bayley Scales is an ex-

cellent addition to the area of infant assessment (Holden, 1972). It is, at present, by far the best measure of infant development (Collard, 1972), and provides valuable information about patterns of early mental development.

Other Infant Assessment Measures

Various procedures are available for assessing infants soon after birth and throughout the entire stage of infancy. At birth, a procedure for evaluating the neonatal status of the newborn child, known as the Apgar score, can be obtained. The score is derived by an evaluation of five indices: heart rate, color, respiration, muscle tone, and reflexes. The examination is conducted at one minute and again at five minutes after delivery. Each factor is rated on a 3-point scale (0, 1, and 2—weak to strong). An extremely low score indicates that there may be a potential problem in the newborn child (Chinn, Drew, & Logan, 1975).

A more detailed scale, the Rochester Research Obstetrical Scale (ROS) (Sameroff, 1979), contains three scales—a prenatal scale, a delivery scale, and an infant scale—with twenty-seven items, one of which is the Apgar rating. The scale holds promise in evaluating factors surrounding the birth process that may be related to the child's developmental status. Another useful procedure for evaluating infants during the early months of development is the Neonatal Behavioral Assessment Scale (Brazelton, 1973), which contains items that range from the evaluation of neurological reflexes to the evaluation of alertness. A monograph edited by Sameroff (1978) reviews this scale.

In addition to the Bayley Scales of Infant Development, there are other infant scales such as the Gesell Developmental Schedule (Ilg & Ames, 1965) and the Cattell Infant Intelligence Test (Cattell, 1940). The primary value of infant scales is that they provide a basis for establishing the child's current status and any deviations from normal expectancy. Exhibits 14-1 (p. 235) and 17-1 (p. 307) illustrate how psychological evaluations contribute to infant assessment. Note how the successive evaluations provide a basis for observing change and progress.

An infant assessment scale developed on the basis of Piagetian theory is the Infant Psychological Development Scale (Uzgiris & Hunt, 1975). It is designed to measure intellectual growth between the ages of 2 weeks and 2 years. There are eight subscales, each consisting of a number of separate ordinal steps. Each step delineates a stage in the development of the ability measured by the subscale:

1. object permanence (fifteen steps);
2. use of objects as means (nine steps);
3. learning and foresight (five steps);
4. development of schemata (eleven steps);
5. development of an understanding of causality (ten steps);
6. conception of objects in space (eleven steps);
7. vocal imitation (eight steps);
8. gestural imitation (five steps).

The scale attempts to measure underlying intellectual processes that are associated with natural stages of development.

A study (Wachs, 1975) of the relationship between the Infant Psychological Development Scale administered at 12, 15, 18, 21, and 24 months of age and the Stanford-Binet administered at 31 months of age indicated that most subscales of the Infant Psy-

chological Development Scale were not significantly related to the Stanford-Binet until the 18-month level. However, one subscale, Object Permanence, was significantly related to later Binet performance at each age level studied. This subscale also showed the most consistently significant pattern of relationships across all five age levels. These results indicate that the development of object permanence may play an important role in cognitive development.

Assessment of infants and young children also can be facilitated by an understanding of normal developmental sequences in adaptive, motor, language, and personal-social behavior. Table C-34 in the Appendix presents some important milestones in each of these areas.

Summary

1. Some of the tests reviewed in this chapter are useful in the assessment of handicapped children or children with limited knowledge of English. They also can serve as screening instruments, and supplement tests such as the Stanford-Binet, WISC-R, and WPPSI.

2. The McCarthy Scales of Children's Abilities, applicable for children between 2½ and 8½ years of age, contains eighteen tests grouped into six scales. It is well standardized and has excellent reliability. However, until more information is available about its validity, placement decisions should be based on the Stanford-Binet, WISC-R, or WPPSI.

3. The Extended Merrill-Palmer Scale covers the age period from 3 to 6 years. It provides opportunities to evaluate the content and the process of thinking, following Guilford's Structure of Intellect model. Unfortunately, little is known about the validity of the scale. The manual also fails to provide standard scores for any of the measures. Although the scale has some limitations, it does provide assessment information that is not easily obtainable from other instruments.

4. The Merrill-Palmer Scale of Mental Tests has not been restandardized since 1931. The Extended Scale may, in part, be

considered as its replacement. However, some of the tests in the Merrill-Palmer can still be useful in evaluating extremely handicapped children.

5. The Slosson Intelligence Test can be used as a screening instrument for the assessment of intelligence. It should not be used as a substitute for the Stanford-Binet, WISC-R, or WPPSI. Poor standardization and use of the ratio IQ are major limitations.

6. The Detroit Tests of Learning Aptitude contains nineteen subtests. Although its standardization is inadequate and norms dated, it does provide some supplementary diagnostic information.

7. The Progressive Matrices, Leiter International Performance Scale, Pictorial Test of Intelligence, and Columbia Mental Maturity Scale all require a pointing response. These tests tap various reasoning processes.

8. The Progressive Matrices is a nonverbal test of reasoning ability that comes in three editions. Unfortunately, there are no norms for United States children (or adults). However, the English norms serve as useful guidelines. The test may provide misleading results for children who are not able to do figural-reasoning tasks.

9. The Goodenough-Harris Drawing Test (Draw-A-Man) provides a quick estimate of children's ability, particularly between the ages of 3 and 10 years. It may have some use in the evaluation of ethnic minority children.

10. The Leiter International Performance Scale is a nonverbal intelligence test that taps perceptual organization and discrimination skills. Its outdated norms and inadequate standardization are major shortcomings. There is no evidence that the test is culture-fair. However, it does merit consideration for testing children with language deficiencies.

11. The Pictorial Test of Intelligence serves to evaluate the learning aptitude of children, primarily from 3 to 6 years of age. It is useful in evaluating children with motor or speech handicaps.

12. The Columbia Mental Maturity Scale is a nonverbal test of intelligence designed for children between 3 and 10 years of age. It requires perceptual discriminations and probably measures the ability to form and use concepts.

13. The Bayley Scales of Infant Development is excellent for assessing infants. It covers the age period from 2 months to 2½ years of age. A Mental Scale and a Psychomotor Developmental Index are provided. It is a well-standardized test.

14. Other infant assessment devices include the Gesell Development Schedule, the Cattell Infant Intelligence Test, and the Infant Psychological Development Scale.

CHAPTER 15

Assessment of Academic Achievement and Other Special Abilities

Have you ever considered what the mere ability to read means? That it is the key which admits us to the whole world of thought and fancy and imagination? To the company of saint and sage, of the wisest and wittiest at their wisest and wittiest moment? That it enables us to see with the keenest eyes, hear with the finest ears, and listen to the sweetest voices of all time?

JAMES RUSSELL LOWELL

EXHIBIT 15-1. Psychological Evaluation: Auditory and Visual Processing Deficits

Name: Ricky
Date of birth: March 5, 1968
Chronological age: 10-11
Date of examination: February 5, 1979
Date of report: February 6, 1979
Grade: 5th

Tests Administered

WISC-R:

VERBAL SCALE		PERFORMANCE SCALE	
Information	11	Picture Completion	13
Similarities	10	Picture Arrangement	10
Arithmetic	8	Block Design	8
Vocabulary	11	Object Assembly	7
Comprehension	11	Coding	7
Digit Span	9		

Verbal Scale IQ = 100
Performance Scale IQ = 92
Full Scale IQ = 96±6 at the 95 percent confidence level

Wide Range Achievement Test:

	STANDARD SCORE	PERCENTILE
Reading	65	1
Spelling	70	2
Arithmetic	86	18

1. *go* (go)   16. _____ (order)
2. *cat* (cat)   17. _____ (watch)
3. *in* (in)   18. _____ (enter)
4. *boy* (boy)   19. *Gow* (grown)
5. *an* (and)   20. _____ (museum)
6. *will* (will)   21. _____ (precious)
7. *make* (make)   22. _____
8. *Hm* (him)   23. _____
9. *Say* (say)   24. _____
10. *sat* (cut)   25. _____
11. *cook* (cook)   26. _____
12. *lite* (light)   27. _____
13. _____ (must)   28. _____
14. *driss* (dress)   29. _____
15. _____ (reach)   30. _____

Motor-Free Visual Perception Test: 25/36 correct; Perceptual Age = 6 years, 11 months.

Visual-Aural Digit Span Test:
Auditory-Oral span = 5 digits
Auditory-Written span = 6 digits
Visual-Oral span = 6 digits
Visual-Written span = 0.

Lindamood Auditory Conceptualization Test: 2nd half of 1st grade level.

EXHIBIT 15-1   (cont.)

Bender-Gestalt: Standard score = 48; percentile = 1st.

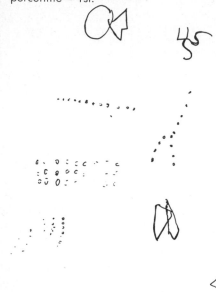

Reason for Referral

Ricky has had a history of learning problems since entering school. All of his teachers have considered him to be an intelligent and well-behaved boy who is cooperative and motivated to learn. His parents state that he has never had any behavior problems.

Background Information

In 3rd grade, when he was 8-4, a psychological evaluation was performed. He obtained a WISC-R Verbal IQ of 114, Performance IQ of 95, and Full Scale IQ of 105. His Wide Range Achievement Test scores were as follows: Reading—6th percentile, Spelling —4th percentile, and Arithmetic—9th percentile. On the Bender-Gestalt his performance was at a 5½-year-old level. After being in a special class for learning handicapped children for the past two and one-half years, he is still unable to read, write, or spell commensurate with his intellectual level. His parents requested the present reevaluation.

Test Results

Ricky was pleasant and cooperative. He seemed to want to succeed, and worked in a careful and methodical manner. His intellectual skills are within the average classification. Verbal comprehension and perceptual organization abilities are about equally developed. The pattern of his scores suggests no outstanding strengths or weaknesses. His present level of functioning is somewhat lower than his previous level (96 vs. 105), but this difference may simply be due to chance fluctuations in his performance.

Ricky's visual-motor abilities still show some maturational delay, being at a level that is similar to 6½-year-olds. In his drawings, angulation and integration difficulties were present, and circles were drawn for dots.

On the Wide Range Achievement Reading Test he displayed few word attack skills; he either knew a word or did not know it. He mainly relied on initial letter clues to guess at a word. Of his three miscalled words, two had incorrect vowel sounds. On the spelling test, he displayed a similar pattern; he either knows how to spell a word or he doesn't, except for dress (driss) and grown (gow).

Ricky was unable to remember words visually. He was also unable to listen to a syllable and analyze how many sounds he heard or to determine whether any sounds were repeated within the syllable.

Recommendation

Since Ricky has both visual and auditory processing difficulties, a multisensory approach to reading is recommended, using visual, auditory, kinesthetic, and tactile senses.

_____

Examiner

The assessment of academic achievement plays an important part in a psychoeducational evaluation. Reading, arithmetic, and spelling, of course, form the three major skill areas. The tests covered in this chapter are designed for individual administration. Many group-administered tests are also available for measuring academic achievement and reading skills (such as the California Achievement Test, Iowa Tests of Basic Skills, Metropolitan Achievement Tests, Stanford Achievement Test, Gates-MacGinitie Reading Tests, and Nelson Reading Skills Test), but they are not reviewed because the focus of this book is on individual assessment. Nevertheless, these and other group-administered achievement tests should be considered in the psychoeducational battery. They often provide a more thorough sampling of achievement than individual screening achievement tests. Other types of instruments also are covered in the chapter. Included are tests of language processing and receptive vocabulary, visual-oral processing, and SOMPA, a system that attempts to integrate data obtained from a variety of sources. (Appendix D presents the highlights of the tests covered in this and other chapters of the book.)

Assessment of General Achievement

Wide Range Achievement Test

The Wide Range Achievement Test (WRAT) (Jastak & Jastak, 1978) is a brief, individually administered achievement test that measures reading, spelling, and arithmetic skills. The reading skills measured are recognizing and naming letters and pronouncing words; the spelling skills include copying marks resembling letters, writing one's name, and writing single words from dictation; and the arithmetic skills cover counting, reading number symbols, solving oral problems, and performing written computations. The WRAT is concerned primarily with mastery of the mechanics of these three subject areas.

The WRAT was originally published in 1936. Revisions appeared in 1946, 1965, 1976, and 1978. However, the items in the last three revisions are exactly the same. The 1978 edition differs from the 1976 edition in that new scaling techniques were used to develop the WRAT norms and grade ratings. In the latest revisions, the test is divided into two age spans: Level I for ages 5-0 to 11-11 and Level II for ages 12-0 to 64-11. The items in each area of the test are arranged in ascending order of difficulty. The test is timed and takes approximately twenty to thirty minutes to administer.

Three types of scores are provided: grade ratings, percentiles, and standard scores. The grade ratings refer to the approximate grade levels associated with the raw scores. Grade ratings should be used only as a rough guide to performance on the test (see Chapter 2). Percentiles, too, are used to guide interpretations. The standard scores are the preferred scores to use. They are based on a mean of 100 and a standard deviation of 15, and range from 55 to 145.

Standardization. The most recent normative sampling was reported in the 1976 revision. This group also was used for the renorming published in 1978. The normative sample contained children and adults from five eastern and two western states. Although efforts were made to ensure that all ethnic groups were proportionally represented, no representative national sampling was conducted. An attempt was made to select subjects on the basis of their IQs, in order to have below-average, average, and superior levels of ability represented in the sample.

The standardization for Level I involved 7,800 children between the ages of 5-0 and 11-11 years, divided into six-month age groups. The normative group for Level II involved 7,400 children and adults between the ages of 12-0 and 64-11, divided into thirteen age groups. In both levels, the size of each age group ranged from 400 to 600 individuals, and groups were equally divided between the sexes.

A comparison (Silverstein, 1978b) of the 1976 WRAT Reading and Arithmetic norms with those of a representative national sample indicated that, except for raw scores above the mean on the Level I Reading subtest, the WRAT norms tend to underestimate achievement levels. The largest discrepancies (by as much as 8 points) were found on Level II of the Arithmetic subtest. Thus, while the current norms are likely to be adequate for many purposes, they may not accurately reflect a child's level of achievement relative to the general population.

Reliability. Split-half reliabilities reported in the manual are excellent, ranging from .94 to .98 for the three subtests at both levels. Standard errors of measurement range from 1.05 to 1.70 for the Reading subtest, .86 to

1.34 for the Spelling subtest, and .88 to 1.42 for the Arithmetic subtest. Generally, the standard errors of measurement are lower at Level I than at Level II.

Test-retest reliabilities (two- to twenty-two-week intervals) for samples of emotionally disturbed and slow learning children range from .96 to .98 for the Reading subtest, .92 to .95 for the Spelling subtest, and .87 to .88 for the Arithmetic subtest (Woodward, Santa-Barbara, & Roberts, 1975).

Levels I and II were found to be highly correlated (median r of .91, .90, and .86 for the Reading, Spelling, and Arithmetic subtests, respectively) in a group of 9- to 14-year-old children (Jastak & Jastak, 1978).

Validity. Numerous studies have compared the WRAT with other achievement, intelligence, and ability tests.[1] The results of these studies suggest that the WRAT has adequate concurrent validity. Examples of other achievement tests that have been used as criterion measures include the Stanford Achievement Test, Metropolitan Achievement Test, and Peabody Individual Achievement Test. Correlations between the WRAT and these tests are in the vicinity of .60 with various groups of children, including normal, learning disabled, economically deprived, and mentally retarded.

The intelligence tests used as criterion measures included the WISC, WISC-R, WAIS, and Stanford-Binet. Median correlations between the WRAT and the WISC and WISC-R Verbal and Full Scales are about .60, but only about .40 with the Performance Scale. Thus the Performance Scale is less adequate in predicting academic achievement than is the Verbal Scale. Children in these studies came from various ethnic groups, including white and black, and normal and mentally retarded groups. The WISC predicts WRAT scores of white children and black children equally well (Hartlage & Lucas, 1976; Ryan, 1973). Median correlations between the WRAT and Stanford-Binet are about .55.

In addition to these intelligence tests, other measures that have been used as criterion measures for the WRAT include the Slosson Intelligence Test, Leiter International Performance Scale, Peabody Picture Vocabulary Test, and Illinois Test of Psycholinguistic Abilities. Correlations with these measures, too, are satisfactory, in the vicinity of .40.

A comparison of the 1965 and 1978 norms indicates that the 1978 norms generally provide lower standard scores on the Reading and Spelling subtests but higher scores on the Arithmetic subtest (Sattler & Feldman, 1981). The 1978 norms also yield grade ratings that are as much as seven full grades lower than the 1965 norms for high raw scores. Studies are needed to evaluate the validity of the revised grade ratings.

Comment on the Wide Range Achievement Test. The WRAT provides limited information about reading, arithmetic, and spelling skills. The only form of reading measured consists of recognizing individual letters or words. There are no specific breakdowns provided to enable one to determine specific types of reading, arithmetical, or spelling difficulties. In addition, the test does not provide specific instructional objectives. Its normative sample, too, is less representative of the population than is desirable, and the norms may tend to underestimate children's achievement levels. However, the WRAT is popular because it is quick and easy to administer, provides standard scores, and measures three different ability areas. It appears to be a useful screening device when a quick estimate of reading, arithmetic, and spelling skills is needed.

Peabody Individual Achievement Test

The Peabody Individual Achievement Test (PIAT) (Dunn & Markwardt, 1970) is an individually administered screening measure of achievement. It covers mathematics, reading recognition, reading comprehension, spelling, and general information for grades kindergarten through high school. It takes about thirty to forty minutes to administer. The Mathematics, Reading Comprehension, and Spelling subtests use a multiple-choice format. The Reading Recognition subtest employs a combination of multiple-choice items and letters or names to be read aloud to the examiner, while the General Information subtest requires oral answers only. Overall, half of the items use a multiple-choice pointing format.

The PIAT provides grade equivalents, age equivalents, percentile ranks, and standard scores ($M = 100$, $SD = 15$) for the total test and for each of the five subtests. The general format of the test, the manual, and the record booklet is superior (Lyman, 1971). While the administration of the test generally requires minimal training, the Spelling and Reading Comprehension subtests, in particular, do require some skill to administer.

A brief description of each subtest follows. The *Mathematics* subtest ranges from testing early skills of matching, discriminating, and recognizing numerals to measuring concepts in geometry and trigonometry. The *Reading Recognition* subtest requires matching letters of the alphabet with identical stimuli, naming individual letters, and reading aloud individual words. The *Reading Comprehension* subtest contains sentences that the children read silently, after which they select the best meaning of the sentence. The *Spelling* subtest requires the identification of printed letters and the correct spelling of words. The *General Information* subtest measures general knowledge of science, social studies, fine arts, and sports. The PIAT manual justifies the double weighting of reading by stating that reading is a key tool of academic learning.

Standardization. The standardization sample was a national sample of 2,889 male and female school children attending regular classrooms in public schools and living in nine geographic divisions. The sample generally conformed to the 1967 U.S. Bureau of Census data. There were approximately 200 children for each of the thirteen grade levels, from kindergarten through grade 12.

Reliability. Median test-retest reliabilities, with retest intervals of one month, are .89 for Total Test, .74 for Mathematics, .88 for Reading Recognition, .64 for Reading Comprehension, .65 for Spelling, and .76 for General Information. The median standard error of measurement for the Total Test is 12; for the five subtests, the median standard errors of measurement range from 3.06 to 6.51. Satisfactory test-retest and split-half reliabilities for the scale also have been reported in other studies with samples of Anglo, Mexican-American, and handicapped children.[2] Table C-33 in the Appendix shows the differences required for significance when each PIAT subtest is compared to the mean score for any individual child.

Validity. The concurrent validity of the PIAT, using a variety of achievement and ability tests in a variety of populations, is excellent.[3] Thus, the evidence indicates that the PIAT measures general achievement areas. However, the scores cannot always be used interchangeably with those provided by the Wide Range Achievement Test.

Studies of the WISC-R and the PIAT indicate that there is much overlap between the two tests (Bretzing, 1977; Dean, 1977b). They share a general factor of verbal-educational development. The WISC-R is the preferred test, and can be supplemented with the two PIAT reading subtests for an estimate of the child's reading skills.

Factor analyses of the PIAT suggest that it contains two factors (Reynolds, 1979; Wikoff, 1978). One factor, termed "Verbal Comprehension and Reasoning Skills" or "Word Recognition," is covered by the two reading subtests and the Spelling subtest. The second factor is termed "Acquired Practical Knowledge" or "School-related Knowledge," and is covered by the Mathematics and General Information subtests.

Comment on the Peabody Individual Achievement Test. Although the item content for each of the five subtests seems appropriate and although there are advantages to having an individual achievement test, the PIAT suffers in comparison to its group competitors (Lyman, 1971) because reliability coefficients are somewhat low and because it has no subtests for science, social studies, or study skills. The PIAT serves to locate the child's general level of achievement, after which a longer, more comprehensive achievement test is needed (French, 1972). More confidence can be placed in the total score than in the subtest scores.

The multiple-choice pointing format on three of the five subtests makes it possible to obtain an achievement measure for children who otherwise would be impossible to examine. The high concentration of items suitable for lower grade levels adds to the discriminating power of the PIAT in more accurately determining academic achievement of educable mentally retarded children (Burns, Peterson, & Bauer, 1974). An extension of the norms downward would greatly increase the potential of the PIAT for use with educable mentally retarded children.

Woodcock-Johnson
Psycho-Educational Battery

The Woodcock-Johnson Psycho-Educational Battery (Woodcock, 1977) is a comprehensive, individually administered set of twenty-seven tests that assesses three areas of functioning: cognitive ability, achievement, and interest. The Tests of Cognitive Ability in Part I are composed of twelve subtests that cover a variety of domains, such as vocabulary, spatial relations, memory, quantitative concepts, and concept formation. The Tests of Achievement in Part II cover ten achievement areas, including reading, spelling, capitalization, punctuation, and knowledge of science, humanities, and social studies. The Tests of Interest Level in Part III cover five areas: preference for participation in reading, mathematics, language, physical activities, and social activities.

While the battery covers ages 3 years through adult, not all tests are administered at every age. At the preschool level, only six of the twelve cognitive ability tests and only five of the ten achievement tests are applicable. None of the five interest tests were designed for children below grade three. The entire battery can be administered in approximately two hours, with Part I taking about one hour; Part II, thirty to forty minutes; and Part III, about fifteen minutes.

The Cognitive Ability subtests are arranged in various combinations to form clusters. A cluster represents two or more subtests that are grouped together. The Full Scale cluster contains twelve subtests, while the Perceptual Speech cluster contains only two subtests. The groupings of subtests appear to have been made on the basis of subtest content rather than on the basis of factor analysis. In addition, the clusters are not independent of one another because the same subtests appear in more than one cluster.

Each cluster score can be converted into a percentile rank, which, in turn, can be converted into a standard score with a mean of 100 and standard deviation of 15, or with a mean of 50 and standard deviation of 10. However, there are no tables that convert the raw scores directly into standard scores for each subtest or for each cluster. In addition to percentile ranks, grade-level scores are also provided for subtests and cluster scores. Finally, a Relative Performance Index is provided for the Full Scale, Preschool Scale, and Brief Scale clusters. The Relative Performance Index indicates the percent of mastery predicted for an examinee when the reference group performs at a 90 percent level of success. For example, a 50/90 Relative Performance Index indicates that when the reference group shows 90 percent mastery, the examinee would demonstrate only 50 percent mastery.

The ten Tests of Achievement subtests are grouped into five clusters, while the five Tests of Interest Level subtests are grouped into two clusters. The cluster scores can be converted into percentile ranks and standard scores. Relative Performance Indexes are provided for all of the achievement cluster scores, but not for the interest clusters.

The Woodcock-Johnson also provides an Achievement Aptitude Profile, which is based on a comparison between the Tests of Cognitive Ability (aptitude) and the Tests of Achievement. The Profile provides Relative Performance Indexes for Reading, Mathematics, Written Language, and Knowledge. These indexes are interpreted in the same manner as the Relative Performance Index for the Tests of Cognitive Ability.

Standardization. The battery was standardized on 4,732 subjects from 3 years through 80 years of age living in forty-nine communities across the United States. The sample was carefully chosen to be representative of the population of the United States, and matched on such variables as sex, race, occupational status, geographical region, and community (urban, non-urban) with the census data.

Reliability. Reliabilities(split-half or test-retest) range from .57 to .96 for the Cognitive Ability subtests. The Cognitive Ability cluster scores, the Tests of Achievement, and the Tests of Interest Level have reliabilities in the .80s and .90s. Unfortunately, the technical manual fails to provide standard errors of measurement for any of the scores.

Validity. Several concurrent and predictive validity coefficients are reported in the manual, using various intelligence, ability, and achievement tests as the criteria. Coefficients are satisfactory, and range from the .40s to the .80s. However, the test has been found to yield a mean Full Scale score that was almost 12 points lower than the WISC-R score for a sample of children with learning disabilities (86.65 vs. 98.61) (Reeve, Hall, & Zakreski, 1979). Thus, Woodcock-Johnson scores may not be comparable to those obtained on the WISC-R.

Comment on the Woodcock-Johnson Psycho-Educational Battery. The Psycho-Educational Battery appears to be a well-standardized, reliable, and valid measure of cognitive ability, scholastic achievement, and interest. The manual is written in a clear and understandable manner. Nevertheless, the battery is still too new for us to know how it may contribute to the psycho-educational evaluation. Its primary failure is a lack of standard errors of measurement for the subtests and scales, which impedes profile analysis. Furthermore, cognitive ability scores on the battery may not be interchangeable with those provided by the WISC-R for children with learning disabilities.

Assessment of Specific Achievement

Woodcock Reading Mastery Tests

The Woodcock Reading Mastery Tests (Woodcock, 1973) battery includes five individually administered reading tests: Letter Identification, Word Identification, Word Attack, Word Comprehension, and Passage Comprehension. Letter Identification measures the child's ability to name letters of the alphabet shown in common and uncommon styles of type. Word Identification requires the child to name words with a range in difficulty from kindergarten to advanced twelfth grade reading level. Word Attack measures the child's ability to identify nonsense words through application of phonetic and structural analysis skills. Word Comprehension measures the child's knowledge of word meanings using an analogy completion format. Passage Comprehension requires the child to read silently a passage that has a word missing, and then provide the appropriate missing word. A Total Reading Index of overall skill also can be obtained, based on all 400 items.

Test items are open-ended, rather than multiple-choice, to minimize the possibility of guessing. Two alternate forms are provided. The test can be administered in twenty to thirty minutes and is used in kindergarten through grade twelve. Raw scores can be converted to grade scores, age scores, percentile ranks, and standard scores ($M = 50$, $SD = 10$).

A Mastery Scale provides useful information about children's success potential on a reading task at any given level of difficulty. It predicts their expected level of success in each of the five test areas and for the total test by comparing the difference between their ability level and the difficulty of the task.

Standardization. Norms are provided for the total group as well as separately by sex. Special norms also are provided for such community socioeconomic characteristics as occupation, education, family income, and race. Examiners must obtain these demographic characteristics for their community in order to use these norms.

A stratified random sample of communities throughout the United States was used, with 50 school districts and 141 schools with a total of 5,252 children in grades kindergarten through twelve. The children were administered the complete set of five tests, except for kindergarten children who were administered only the two easiest tests, Letter Identification and Word Identification. The standardization group was weighted for six variables—size and type of community, racial distribution, number of persons per household, years of school completed, occupation, and family income—to conform with the 1970 U.S. census data.

Reliability. Split-half and test-retest reliabilities range from .02 to .99 for the five subtests. Letter Identification has the poorest reliability at the level of seventh grade. Standard errors of measurement are much larger for very low and very high scores than for scores in the midrange.

Validity. No information on concurrent validity was provided in the manual.

Comment on the Woodcock Reading Mastery Tests. The Woodcock Reading Mastery Tests has excellent standardization. Reliabilities are satisfactory for most subtests and for the total score. However, little is known about the test's validity. Overall, the test appears to be useful in evaluating children's reading skills.

Sucher-Allred Reading Placement Inventory

The Sucher-Allred Reading Placement Inventory (Sucher & Allred, 1973), developed in 1968 and revised in 1973, is an individually administered reading test that contains selections ranging from primer level to ninth grade level. It contains a Word-Recognition Test and an Oral Reading Test. Administration time is approximately twenty minutes.

The Word-Recognition Test consists of twelve lists of words. The test is used to find a starting level for the Oral Reading Test and to determine achievement of word recognition. Two of the lists contain fifteen words each and are used for the primer and first reader levels. The remaining ten lists contain twenty words each and are used for the second through ninth grade levels.

The test is begun by selecting a level at which the child is unlikely to make errors. The child is encouraged to read quickly each word. Mispronunciations or hesitations longer than two seconds are recorded as errors. The child's instructional level is designated as the level at which five or more errors occur.

The Oral Reading Test contains twelve reading selections that range from primer through ninth grade levels. This test is designed to identify three reading levels: the independent level, the instructional level, and the frustration level.

At the independent level the child is able to read without aid and is also able to answer questions that test comprehension. The performance criteria are as follows: 97 percent or better word recognition; 80 percent or better comprehension; few or no head movements; and good phrasing and expression in oral reading. This level is used as a guide to provide the child with appropriate independent reading materials.

At the instructional level the child is developing new reading skills and vocabulary. This level must be challenging but not too difficult. The performance criteria are as follows: 92 to 96 percent word recognition; 60 to 79 percent comprehension; few or no head movements; and good phrasing and expression in oral reading. This level is used as a guide to provide the child with appropriate instructional materials.

At the frustration level the child has difficulty in recognizing words or in comprehending much of what is read. The performance criteria are as follows: less than 92 percent word recognition; less than 60 percent comprehension; excessive head movements; finger pointing; labored, slow oral reading; tension; and frequent self-correction. This level is used as a guide to avoid giving the student reading material that is too difficult.

The Oral Reading Test is begun at one level below the level of the Word-Recognition Test at which the student made five or more errors and is completed when the frustration level is reached. Six types of word-recognition errors are scored: mispronunciations; nonpronunciations; omission of a word; insertion of a word; substitution of a word; and repetition of three or more words. Two other types of errors (self-corrections and poor phrasing) are recorded, but not scored.

After each selection is read, five comprehension questions are administered. These questions cover the main idea (title), facts, sequence, inference, and critical thinking. Full, partial, or no errors are recorded for each question. For instance, a full error would be recorded if the student did not respond to the question, or gave an answer unrelated to the question. A key is provided that indicates the number of errors associated with each reading level. The test is stopped when the frustration level is reached.

Standardization, reliability, and validity. Unfortunately no data regarding standardization, reliability, or validity are provided. Word frequencies in graded readers were used to select the words in the Word-Recognition Test. For the Oral Reading Test special formulas were used to determine the readability of each selection.

Comment on the Sucher-Allred Reading Placement Inventory. The manual is easy to comprehend and the tests are easy to administer; however, there are a number of problems with the Sucher-Allred Reading Placement Inventory. First, because no specific data about standardization, reliability, or validity are provided, the psychometric properties of the test cannot be evaluated. Second, the test does not provide an indepth assessment of reading difficulties. Third, the starting level of the Oral Reading Test may be too high, and no instructions are provided as to what the examiner should do if a child is at the frustration level on the first selection (Johnson, 1978). Fourth, there are not enough reading selections at any one level to provide a reliable pattern of comprehension errors (Stafford, 1978). Fifth, scoring criteria are vague (Wardrop, 1978). Finally, silent reading selections are not included. While oral reading requirements are

acceptable for the primary grades, silent reading becomes more important at the upper grade levels (Johns, 1978).

Overall, the Sucher-Allred may be applicable as a gross measure of a child's reading ability (Johnson, 1978). However, standardization, reliability, and validity data, more complete administrative procedures, and more complete scoring instructions are needed.

Classroom Reading Inventory

The Classroom Reading Inventory (Silvaroli, 1976) is an individually administered, diagnostic reading inventory designed for screening children in grades two through ten. The inventory assists in placing children at their appropriate reading level, in pinpointing particular reading problem areas, and in developing appropriate remedial instruction. There are three parts to the inventory: the Graded Word Lists, the Graded Oral Paragraphs, and the Graded Spelling Survey. Three forms also are available.

The Graded Word Lists consist of a series of twenty words, from preprimer through grade six level, that the child reads aloud. This aids the examiner in identifying specific word recognition errors and in estimating a starting level for the Graded Oral Paragraphs.

The Graded Oral Paragraphs are short reading selections that the child also reads aloud. Upon completion of the reading, three types of comprehension questions are asked: (a) factual (e.g., "What was the name of the horse in the story?"), (b) vocabulary (e.g., "What does the word 'grind' mean?"), and (c) inferential (e.g., "Why is sky diving like being in a dream?"). Reading selections are available for grades preprimer through eight.

The Graded Spelling Survey consists of ten words for each level from grades one through six. This section of the inventory can be individually or group administered. The entire inventory takes about fifteen minutes to administer.

The two major ratings provided for the Graded Oral Paragraphs are word recognition and comprehension. For each rating the child is classified in one of three areas of proficiency: independent reading level, instructional reading level, and frustration reading level. The independent reading level is the grade level at which the child reads comfortably. The instructional level is the one at which the child can read a textbook with a teacher's guidance at a 95 percent accuracy level in word recognition and at a 75 percent or better accuracy level in comprehension. Frustration level is the level beyond the previous one, where comprehension of concepts and questions is poor.

A third type of rating also can be obtained for the Graded Oral Paragraphs—the hearing capacity (listening comprehension) score. This score refers to how many grade levels above the instructional level the child can comprehend 75 percent of the reading material read to him or her. However, Silvaroli does not recommend this rating for routine use.

The Graded Oral Paragraphs require considerable judgment to score because the list provided in the manual does not cover all possible responses (Johnson, 1978). The Graded Word Lists are scored by calculating the percentage of words correctly read.

In addition to the above scores, qualitative observations of the child's performance can be noted. For example, possible errors that can be observed include omissions, insertions, repetitions, substitutions, transpositions, and weaknesses in consonants, vowels, and syllables.

Standardization, reliability, and validity. Unfortunately, the manual fails to provide any data concerning the standardization sample, reliability, or validity. Various techniques were used by Silvaroli to obtain readability levels. One study (Johns, 1975), however, does report satisfactory validity for the Classroom Reading Inventory using the Gates-MacGinities Reading Test as the criterion (correlations between .70 and .80 for a sample of fourth grade children).

Comment on the Classroom Reading Inventory. The major limitations of the Classroom Reading Inventory are its failure to provide any reliability, validity, and normative information. Minor difficulties (John-

son, 1978) are (a) that some of the child's deficiencies may pass unnoticed because there are only five comprehension questions for each selection, and (b) that the test does not tap higher-level thinking abilities. Overall, Johnson believes that the Classroom Reading Inventory is adequate in providing teachers with information about children's reading levels, word recognition, and reading comprehension abilities. Its assets are that it can be quickly administered, classifies children as to their degree of reading readiness, and measures various reading skills.

San Diego Quick Assessment

The San Diego Quick Assessment (La Pray & Ross, 1969) is a graded reading word list from preprimer to eleventh grade. The ten words at each grade level were obtained from basal reader glossaries and from the Thorndike list. The test can be used as a screening device (a) to obtain a rough reading level and (b) to detect errors in word analysis. Unfortunately, standardization, reliability, and validity data were not presented in the report.

KeyMath Diagnostic Arithmetic Test

The KeyMath Diagnostic Arithmetic Test is an untimed, individually administered diagnostic test that assesses mathematical skills (Connolly, Nachtman, & Pritchett, 1971). It contains fourteen subtests that are classified into the following three major areas: content, operations, and applications. The test is used primarily in grades one through six, but there is no upper limit for clinical or remedial use. The content area measures basic mathematical concepts (such as numeration, fractions, and geometry and symbols) that are necessary to perform mathematical operations and to make meaningful mathematical applications. The operations area covers computational processes (addition, subtraction, multiplication, and division), mental computation, and numerical reasoning. The applications area contains problems involving the use of mathematical processes in everyday life. Administration time is approximately thirty minutes.

Scores are provided for four diagnostic levels—total test performance, area performance, subtest performance, and item performance. Total test performance provides a grade-equivalent score. Area performance refers to the child's strengths and weaknesses in content, operations, and applications. Subtest performance indicates relative performance on the fourteen subtests. Unfortunately, the manual does not provide any information that allows the user to determine whether there are significant discrepancies between subtest scores. Item performance provides information about the child's performance on each item. Criterion-referenced information also is available from an appendix in the manual that gives the behavioral objective of each item in the test.

Standardization. The 1,222 children in the standardization sample were in grades kindergarten through seven, and lived in twenty-one school districts in eight states. They came from a wide range of urban, suburban, and rural settings and from varied ethnic backgrounds. The sample was weighted to conform to U.S. proportions of race and community size.

Reliability. The reliability of the KeyMath total score is satisfactory, as noted by a median split-half reliability coefficient of .96 for a sample of 934 children in kindergarten through seventh grade. Subtest reliabilities are substantially lower, with median reliabilities ranging from .64 to .84. The median standard error of measurement is 3.3 for the total score and .6 to 1.3 for the subtest scores.

Validity.   Validity information available about the KeyMath is limited. A correlation of .63 has been reported between the KeyMath and the Metropolitan Achievement Test for a sample of children with learning disabilities (Kratochwill & Demuth, 1976). A factor analysis (Greenstein & Strain, 1977) of the KeyMath with a sample of adolescents with learning disabilities established two factors: Operations and Applications. The content items were assimilated into these two areas.

The KeyMath has been found to be a satisfactory preliminary screening instrument for assessing strengths and weaknesses in general mathematics of educable mentally retarded children (Goodstein, Kahn, & Cawley, 1976). However, because there are too few items at the middle range of difficulty, the test may not provide sufficient diagnostic information to affect programming decisions for children whose difficulties lie in this range. The KeyMath also has been found to discriminate between the performance of learning-disabled and normal children (Greenstein & Strain, 1977).

Comment on the KeyMath Diagnostic Arithmetic Test. The KeyMath test provides useful information that can guide teachers in their selection of appropriate procedures for remediation of arithmetic deficiencies. The broad range and diversity of item content and the lack of reading and writing requirements make the KeyMath attractive for use with exceptional children (Kratochwill & Demuth, 1976). The test appears to be a useful addition to the clinician's assessment battery for working with children in the elementary school grades.

Boehm Test of Basic Concepts

The Boehm Test of Basic Concepts (Boehm, 1971) is a pictorial multiple-choice test designed to measure knowledge of various concepts—such as direction, amount, and time—thought to be necessary for achievement in the first few years of school. It is a screening and teaching instrument, and is not intended as a measure of mental ability. The test can be individually or group administered. There are two forms (A and B), each containing fifty picture items arranged in increasing order of difficulty. For each item, the child selects the one picture from a set that is most appropriate to a statement read by the examiner. For example, one item is "Look at the trees; select the largest tree." Items cover various concepts of relative relationships, such as space (next to, farthest), quantity (few, most, equal), or time (always, after).

The test is intended for use in kindergarten through second grade, and takes approximately thirty minutes to administer. Percentile ranks are available for the raw scores.

Standardization. Form A of the Boehm was standardized on 9,737 children in kindergarten through second grade from sixteen cities across the United States. While norms are provided for children in high, middle, and low socioeconomic classes, the manual fails to describe the criteria used for placing children in these classes. Norms also are available for the start and the middle of the academic year, and include the percentage of children passing each item by grade level. While the norms are not representative of the country as a whole (Proger, 1970), they appear to be reasonably representative of school systems (McCandless, 1972).

Form B was constructed to parallel Form A, and like-numbered items on the two forms are considered to measure the same concepts. It was standardized on 1,192 students. Means and standard deviations are similar on the two forms.

Reliability. Split-half reliability coefficients for Form A range from .68 to .90, with a median of .82. The higher coefficients are generally for the kindergarten children. For Form B, split-half reliability coefficients range from .12 to .94, with a median of .78. Alternate-form reliability coefficients, with intervals between one and seven days, range from .55 to .92, with a median of .76.

Validity. The manual fails to present any validity studies. It simply suggests that the validity of the test rests on its relevance to the school curriculum. However, face validity of the test is good, as the items appear to tap concepts children need to know for school (McCandless, 1972) and studies report that the Boehm has acceptable concurrent validity (.84 with the PPVT) and predictive validity (.54 and .72 with Spelling and Language of the Stanford Achievement Test; .27 to .72 with the Reading, Listening, Work Analysis, and Mathematics tests of the Cooperative Primary Tests).[4]

Comment on the Boehm Test of Basic Concepts. The Boehm is useful in providing information not readily obtainable from other tests about children's knowledge of certain basic concepts (Proger, 1970). However, the test appears too easy for first graders from the middle or higher socioeconomic level and for most second graders (McCandless, 1972). The manual fails to provide information on how necessary the concepts are to school achievement in the early grades (Noll, 1970). Finally, the Boehm appears to have acceptable validity but only minimally adequate reliability; it should be used with caution (Proger, 1970).

Assessment of Psycholinguistic Ability and Receptive Vocabulary

Illinois Test of Psycholinguistic Abilities

The Illinois Test of Psycholinguistic Abilities (ITPA) (Kirk, McCarthy, & Kirk, 1968) is designed to assess verbal and nonverbal psycholinguistic ability. It is an individually administered test used with children between 2-4 years and 10-3 years. There are twelve subtests, ten standard and two supplementary (see Table 15-1), divided into two levels of organization, the representational level and the automatic level. The test was constructed following Osgood's (1957) psycholinguistic model.

The representational level focuses on language symbols, and includes subtests that measure auditory and visual reception, auditory and visual association, and verbal and manual expression. The automatic level focuses on highly organized and integrated habitual patterns of retention and retrieval of language. Subtests included in this level are auditory, grammatical, and visual closure; sound blending; and auditory and visual sequential memory. The battery takes about one hour to administer.

The ITPA provides three types of scores: (a) scaled scores for each subtest, with a mean of 36 and a standard deviation of 6, (b) psycholinguistic ages, and (c) a psycholinguistic quotient. The psycholinguistic quotient is derived by dividing the psycholinguistic age by the chronological age and multiplying by 100. Unfortunately, the psycholinguistic quotient and psycholinguistic ages do not have consistent variances at each age level of the scale.

TABLE 15-1.   Description of ITPA Subtests

Subtest	Description
Auditory Reception	Ability to understand spoken words. Example: "Do chairs eat?"
Visual Reception	Ability to gain meaning from familiar pictures. Example: Match picture stimulus with picture from same category.
Auditory Association	Ability to relate concepts presented orally. Example: Verbal-analogies test (e.g., "Grass is green, sugar is __."
Visual Association	Ability to relate concepts presented visually. Example: Relate a pictorial stimulus with its conceptual counterpart (e.g., bone goes with dog).
Verbal Expression	Ability to express concepts verbally. Example: Describe common objects verbally.
Manual Expression	Ability to demonstrate knowledge of the use of objects pictured. Example: Express an idea with gestures (e.g., "Show me what to do with a hammer").
Grammatic Closure	Ability to use proper grammatical forms to complete statement. Example: "Here is a dog. Here are two __."
Visual Closure	Ability to identify common objects from an incomplete visual presentation. Example: Locating specific objects in scene filled with distracting stimuli.
Auditory Sequential Memory	Ability to reproduce orally a sequence of digits from memory. Example: Repeating digits.
Visual Sequential Memory	Ability to reproduce sequences of geometrical forms from memory. Example: Placing geometric shapes in proper sequence from memory.
Auditory Closure	Ability to complete a word when only fragments of it are orally presented. Example: Complete the word DA__Y.
Sound Blending	Ability to synthesize into words syllables spoken at half-second intervals. Example: "What word is D—OG?"

Standardization. The ITPA was standardized on 962 boys and girls with normal intelligence, ages 2-7 years to 10-1 years, living in five predominantly middle-class midwestern communities. Fathers' occupations closely matched those in the 1960 U.S. census data.

Reliability.   Paraskevopoulos and Kirk (1969) report internal consistency reliabilities that range from .67 to .95 for the ten principal subtests. Test-retest reliabilities, at five- to six-month intervals, range between .28 and .90 for the ten principal subtests for samples of 4- to 6-year-old children. Other test-retest reliabilities have been reported that range from .70 to above .90 for normal children at an interval of three months (Wisland & Many, 1967), and .95 for retardates at an interval of one year (Hubschman, Polizzotto, & Kaliski, 1970). Differences between subtest scores that are significant at the .05 and .01 levels of confidence can be obtained by use of a table published by Ysseldyke and Sabatino (1972).

Validity. Newcomer and Hammill (1975) surveyed twenty-eight studies that investigated the concurrent validity of the ITPA, using a variety of achievement tests as criteria. Median subtest correlations ranged from nonsignificant (below .21) to .42, while median total score correlations ranged from .30 to .51. Highly significant correlations have been found between the ITPA and various measures of intelligence.[5]

Factor analytic studies report varied findings.[6] In general, three major factors have been found: Verbal Comprehension, Vocal-Motor Expression, and Meaningful Figural Comprehension. There is little, if any, evidence that the ITPA measures ten independent areas.

Comment on the ITPA. The ITPA has frequently been criticized.[7] Criticisms include the inadequate normative sample, use of incorrect reliability procedures, middle-class emphasis of speech patterns, and limited educational usefulness of the test. Silverstein (1978a) wonders whether the test is anything more than another individual test of general intelligence. However, the breakdown of different aspects of linguistic functioning into comprehension (decoding) and production (encoding), and the distinction between input and output channels involved in the communication process, appear to be potentially valuable (Mittler & Ward, 1970). Overall, the ITPA appears to have limited use in the assessment battery.

Peabody Picture Vocabulary Test–Revised

The Peabody Picture Vocabulary Test–Revised (PPVT-R), developed by Dunn in 1959, was revised in 1981 (Dunn & Dunn, 1981). It is a nonverbal, multiple-choice test designed to evaluate the receptive vocabulary ability of children and adults. It covers an age range from 2½ years through adult. The examinee must have adequate hearing and be able to indicate "yes" or "no" in some manner. The test was designed to provide an estimate of an individual's hearing vocabulary or receptive knowledge of vocabulary.

In revising the test, excellent item analysis procedures were used to select new items. Words were selected to include a relatively good balance of nouns, gerunds, and modifiers in nineteen content categories. Items favoring one sex were eliminated entirely or counterbalanced by including an item favoring the opposite sex. Words from the prior edition that were found to be culturally, regionally, sexually, or racially biased were eliminated. The manual, however, fails to indicate the basis of these "findings."

Of the 300 items in the 1959 edition, 111 (37 percent) were included in the 1981 edition. The PPVT-R has two forms, L and M, with 175 plates in each form. Each plate contains four pictures, arranged in increasing levels of difficulty. The two forms differ only in that they use different words.

The pictures are clearly drawn, free of fine detail, and pose no figure-ground problems. (A figure-ground problem occurs when the background interferes with the key stimulus or figure of the picture.) The test is untimed; it requires no reading ability, and neither pointing nor oral response is essential. Test-ing time is between ten and fifteen minutes. If the child cannot point, the examiner can administer the test by pointing to each picture and asking the child to designate whether it is correct or incorrect by means of some prearranged signal. These qualities make the test suitable for testing a variety of exceptional children.

Raw scores are converted to standard scores, with a mean of 100 and standard deviation of 15. The standard scores range from 40 to 160.

Standardization. The normative group was based on a representative national sample of 4,200 children, ages 2½ through 18 years, and 828 adults, ages 19 through 40 years, based on the 1970 U.S. census data. Two hundred children, equally divided by sex, were included within twenty-one age groups. These groups were at half-year intervals from ages 2-6 to 6-11 and at one-year intervals for ages 7 through 18. The sample was stratified on sex, geographic region (northeast, south, northcentral, and west), occupation of major wage earner, race, and community size.

In the adult sample, four age groups were used: 19 through 24, 25 through 29, 30 through 34, and 35 through 40. The sample was stratified by age, sex, and occupation. However, while four geographic regions were sampled, a proportionate allocation was not used. Adults were tested in a group setting (with the exception of eleven adults who were tested individually) via slide presentation.

Reliability. Split-half reliability coefficients for ages 2-6 through 18-0 years range on Form L from .67 (at the 2-6 year level) to .88 (at the 18 year level) (median $r = .80$). On Form M they may range from .61 (at the 7-0 year level) to .86 (at the 12 year level) (median $r = .81$). For the adult sample, Form L has a median split-half reliability coefficient of .82, while no split-half reliability coefficient was reported for Form M. The median standard error of measurement for the standard scores is 7 points for Forms L and M, for both children and adults.

Alternate-form reliabilities for a sample of 642 children given both forms in counterbalanced order ranged from .74 to .89 (median of .81) for the standard scores. In a sample of 962 children given Forms L and M within nine to thirty-one days, alternate-form reliabilities ranged from .50 to .89 (median of .76) for the standard scores.

PPVT-R internal reliability estimates and alternate-form reliabilities are somewhat lower than preferred, with half of the estimates being less than .80 (or .81). Studies with the 1959 edition of the PPVT reported test-retest and alternate-form reliabilities in the .70s, although in some groups they ranged from the .20s to the .90s.[8] For the PPVT, the lowest alternate-form reliabilities were with preschool and Head Start children, whereas the highest were with cerebral palsied and mentally retarded children. Stability of the PPVT was especially high for mentally retarded children. Future research will be helpful in determining whether similar trends occur on the PPVT-R.

Studies with Forms A and B of the PPVT indicated that the two forms may not provide equivalent scores. For example, children have been found to differ on Forms A and B by as much as 37 points (McWilliams, 1974; Nicolosi & Kresheck, 1972). These results indicate that Forms A and B, in some cases, are not parallel and should not be used in test-retest situations. We need to learn about the extent to which Forms L and M of the PPVT-R provide equivalent IQs.

Validity. Since the PPVT-R is new, no validity studies are yet available. However, because the test is similar in many ways to the PPVT, it is of interest to review validity studies of the PPVT.

Many studies have compared the PPVT with tests of intelligence, ability, and achievement. With tests of intelligence, median correlations are in the .60s, with a range from the .20s to the .90s.[9] While concurrent validity is generally satisfactory, using intelligence tests as criteria, differences between PPVT and Stanford-Binet or Wechsler IQs are considerable in some cases. This is particularly true for ethnic minority children, for whom the PPVT consistently has been found to yield *lower* IQs than the Stanford-Binet, and for samples of gifted children. In some cases, differences as large as 30 to 40 points are observed. With achievement tests, correlations range between .00 to .90, with the median in the .40s.[10]

Zigler, Abelson, and Seitz (1973) attempted to account for the finding of lower PPVT scores in "disadvantaged" ethnic minority children by noting that the Stanford-Binet requires the examiner to interact personally with the child throughout the test. The PPVT, in contrast, entails a simple repetitive response format wherein the child only points to one of the four pictures. On the PPVT, a child's wariness or desire to terminate the task can lead to stereotypic or other maladaptive forms of responding that can result in a low score. These investigators concluded that *the dangers of using the PPVT "IQ" as a valid indicator of disadvantaged children's cognitive abilities appear to be considerable.*

The studies involving intelligence tests indicate that *PPVT "IQs" are not interchangeable with IQs obtained on the Stanford-Binet, WISC-R, or WPPSI for any groups of children.*

This conclusion raises an intriguing question: What does the PPVT (and other picture vocabulary tests) measure? The answer is not a simple one. The test has been described as measuring language ability, semantic comprehension, vocabulary ability, receptive language, recognition vocabulary, verbal intelligence, vocabulary comprehension, vocabulary usage, comprehension of single words, single word hearing vocabulary, single word receptive vocabulary, and intelligence. One common thread in these descriptions is that vocabulary, and language to some extent, is involved. The response, in part, involves recognition ability and visual comprehension because pictures are provided. In addition, perceptual scanning is also involved. The vocabulary tests on the Stanford-Binet and Wechsler batteries involve retrieval of information to a greater extent than does the

PPVT. Obviously, receptive (or recognition) vocabulary ability is related to general intelligence, but it is by no means the same. Thus, the practice of using the PPVT as an estimate of general intelligence does not appear to be justified. The test is much too limited in its scope, measuring only one facet of a child's ability repertoire.

Equivalence of original and revised editions. Equivalence of Form A of the PPVT (1959 edition) and Form L of the PPVT-R (1981 edition) was studied in a sample of 1,709 children, ages 3 through 16 years. Correlations, using standard scores, ranged from .50 to .85 across the age ranges. Standard scores tend to be lower on Form L than on Form A for equivalent raw scores.

Comment on the Peabody Picture Vocabulary Test–Revised. The PPVT-R is a vastly improved instrument, especially with regard to standardization. The manual is excellent, providing users with much valuable information. Reliability coefficients (split-half and alternate forms) and standard errors of measurement are provided for raw scores and standard scores by age group. A table is available that permits conversion of raw scores and Deviation IQs from Form A (1959 edition) to Form L (1981 edition). A summary of the vast literature on reliability and validity of the PPVT also is included in the manual.

The PPVT-R is useful in measuring extensiveness of receptive vocabulary and may serve as a screening device for children with a limited expressive vocabulary or for children who are verbally inhibited in a testing situation. However, PPVT-R scores should not be considered in isolation from measures of intelligence or other measures of language ability. They are not substitutes for IQs obtained on the Stanford-Binet or Wechsler batteries. When examiners evaluate language-impaired children, differences between scores on the PPVT-R and Leiter International Performance Scale or Columbia Mental Maturity Scale or Progressive Matrices might be valuable aids in obtaining

an estimate of language deficit. Special care must be given in examining ethnic minority group children, because they have been found to obtain lower scores on the PPVT than on intelligence tests. Their lower PPVT scores may in part be a reflection of their verbal and experiential deficiencies.

The PPVT-R now uses the designation "standard score" in place of "Deviation IQ" for the derived score. This change is important because receptive vocabulary ability measured by a multiple-choice pointing procedure represents only a limited part of the cognitive ability domain. Those familiar with the PPVT should note this change.

Quick Test

The Quick Test (Ammons & Ammons, 1962) is a brief, nonverbal, multiple-choice measure of receptive vocabulary. There are three forms of the test described in the manual, each containing fifty words. In addition, three other forms are available (C. H. Ammons, personal communication, February 1973). Three plates of four drawings each are used, with two forms of the test used for each plate. The words on each of the three forms described in the manual do not overlap with one another, nor with the Stanford-Binet or Full-Range Picture Vocabulary Test. Norms are provided from age 2 years to adult level. The Quick Test is similar to the Full-Range Picture Vocabulary Test (Ammons & Ammons, 1948), but it was independently standardized. There are also several group formats of the test.

A single form of the test can be given in three minutes or less. However, the manual recommends that either two or three forms be used if the test is the only measure of "intelligence" being used, whereas one form is sufficient if only general information about cognitive ability is desired. The Quick Test is a recognition test for word meaning using pictures of objects and activities.

The test can be administered by persons not specifically trained to administer individual ability tests. Suggestions for handling guessing are included in the manual. Since only a pointing response is required, children (and adults) with a variety of handicaps (e.g., speech or motor difficulties) can be evaluated.

Mental age norms are available for the total sample, but IQs are only available for adults. The manual suggests, however, that IQs can be calculated by the ratio method. Providing Deviation IQs would have been a more satisfactory procedure. MAs below 2.5 years are to be interpreted with extreme caution.

Standardization. The standardization sample consisted of 458 white children and adults living in parts of Montana and Kentucky. An attempt was made to control for age, grade, occupation of parents, and sex.

Reliability. Test-retest and alternate-form reliabilities usually are in the .70s to .80s, and range from the .60s to .90s.[11] Unfortunately, standard errors of measurement are not presented for IQs but only for raw scores.

Validity. Correlations with the Stanford-Binet and WISC range from the .10s to the .80s. The median correlations are in the .40s; with other ability tests, the median correlations are in the .30s.[12] With other picture vocabulary tests, correlations run much higher: from the .30s to .90s, with a median coefficient of .81.[13] With achievement tests, correlations range from .13 to .93, with a median correlation of .48 (Ammons & Ammons, 1962). Large discrepancies have been observed between Quick Test scores and individual intelligence test scores.

Comment on the Quick Test. There are a number of difficulties associated with the Quick Test, including its dated norms, less-than-adequate standardization group, and use of the ratio IQ. In addition, a drawback of the test is its complex and poor-quality drawings. On the positive side, the test is a good rapport builder, and can be administered in a short period of time by individuals not specifically trained to administer individual intelligence tests. The Quick Test appears to be useful as a screening device, particularly when precise estimates of ability are not of crucial importance. *The test should not be used as a substitute for the Stanford-Binet, WISC-R, WPPSI, or WAIS-R.* The Quick Test also appears to be useful in large-scale research studies where a simple and quick assessment of ability is needed.

Other Assessment Procedures

Visual Aural Digit Span Test

The Visual Aural Digit Span Test (VADS) (Koppitz, 1977) attempts to measure, in a standardized manner, aural and visual short-term memory for children between the ages of 5-6 years and 12-11 years and to provide some information about intersensory and intrasensory integration. The test presupposes that the child is able to read and write numbers. Administration time is approximately ten minutes.

The VADS consists of four subtests that measure short-term memory:

1. The Aural-Oral subtest requires oral repetition of an orally presented series of digits. It is similar to the Digit Span subtest on the Stanford-Binet and the WISC-R. The digits are presented at the rate of one per second.
2. The Visual-Oral subtest requires that the child be able to read printed digits and repeat them from memory. A card showing all of the digits is presented for ten seconds.
3. The Aural-Written subtest requires the child to write digits that are presented orally, again at the rate of one per second.
4. The Visual-Written subtest requires the child to read the digits and write them from memory. As in the Visual-Oral subtest, the digits appear on a card and ten seconds are allotted for each card.

Scoring is a relatively simple procedure. The score given for each subtest equals the longest digit sequence successfully completed without error. The highest score a child can receive on any of the four subtests is 7, since the longest series presented contains seven digits.

The VADS yields eleven different scores. Four scores are obtained from the four subtests. An additional four scores are obtained by summing (a) the two aural subtest scores, (b) the two visual subtest scores, (c) the two oral subtest scores, and (d) the two written subtest scores. Two additional scores are obtained by summing (a) the two like-modality scores—Aural-Oral and Visual-Written—to form an Intrasensory Integration score and (b) the two different-modality scores—Visual-Oral and Aural-Written—to form an Intersensory Integration score. Finally, the eleventh score, the Total score, is based on the sum of the four subtest scores.

The VADS manual provides means and standard deviations for the eleven scores for children ages 5-6 to 12-11 years and for kindergarten through sixth grade levels. The raw scores are converted to percentiles for age and for grade levels. However, the manual fails to provide standard scores or standard errors of measurement.

Because the range of scores for each subtest is extremely small, 0 to 7, the resulting conversion to percentiles is highly inadequate. For example, at the 5-5-year-old level, a raw score of 4 on the Aural-Oral subtest represents percentiles of 25, 50, *and* 75. Thus, the same raw score is shown in the conversion table as representing three different percentiles, covering a range from the 25th to the 75th percentile. The same problems occur at every age level for one or more of the subtests or combination scores. In addition, a raw score of 4 on the Aural-Oral subtest is at the 25th percentile for ages 5 through 8 years. Thus, from 5 through 8 years there is no age differentiation for this raw score. Similar problems occur on the other subtests.

The larger raw-score range for the VADS Total score (0 to 28) reduces the problems associated with converting the raw scores to percentiles. However, problems still are present in these conversions, especially at the older ages. In many cases, a change of one raw-score point results in a change of 25 percentiles. For example, at the age of 10 years, a raw score of 25 is at the 50th percentile, while a raw score of 26 is at the 75th percentile. Another problem with the Total score is that its distribution is highly skewed at ages 9 years and above. The median raw scores at ages 9, 10, 11, and 12 years are 23, 25, 25, and 26, respectively, with the maximum score being 28.

The grade-norm percentiles suffer from the same problems observed for the age-norm percentiles.

Standardization. The VADS was standardized on 810 normal public school children 5-6 years to 12-11 years of age, living in five states (New York, Ohio, California, Virginia, and Texas). The sample consisted of approximately equal numbers of boys and girls at each age level. The children came from upper middle, middle, and lower middle classes, and from economically deprived home environments. Of the total sample, 81 percent were white, 13 percent black, 6 percent Hispanic, and less than 1 percent Oriental. No children with serious physical or mental handicaps were included in the sample.

Reliability. Test-retest reliabilities are reported for two groups of children with learning and behavior problems ($N = 35$, 6- to 10-year-olds; $N = 27$, 11- and 12-year-olds). The interval between tests ranged from one day to fifteen weeks ($\bar{X} = 6.5$ weeks). Correlations for the eleven separate scores for the 6- to 10-year-old children ranged from .74 to .92 ($Md = .84$) and from .72 to .90 ($Md = .85$) for the 11- and 12-year-old children. The Total score had the highest reliability in each group. Correlations between the four subtest scores and the Total score range between .65 and .79.

Validity. Correlations between the VADS Total score and the WRAT Reading, Spelling, and Arithmetic scores in four samples of children with learning disabilities (two samples at 8 years of age and two at 10 years of age) indicated validity coefficients ranging from .29 to .65 (Koppitz, 1977). Median coefficients were .60 for Reading, .62 for Spelling, and .56 for Arithmetic. VADS subtest scores and combination scores were, for the most part, significantly related to WRAT scores. However, the VADS was not found to be related significantly to WRAT Reading and Spelling scores in a sample of upper-middle-class second grade pupils (Baldwin, 1976).

Correlations between the VADS Total score and WISC IQs in a sample of fifty children with learning disabilities were significant with the Verbal IQ ($r = .45$) and Full Scale IQ ($r = .39$) but not with the Performance IQ ($r = .26$) (Koppitz, 1977). Individual VADS subtest and combination scores also were significantly related to the Verbal and Full Scale IQs, with the exception of the Aural-Oral subtest. As might be expected, the VADS Total score was more highly related to Digit Span ($r = .68$) than to any other WISC subtest.

Koppitz (1977) reported that the VADS discriminated children with learning disabilities from normal children in the second, third, and fourth grades, with the children with learning disabilities obtaining lower scores. However, she also reported that the VADS was not able to differentiate among a sample of normal first to fifth grade children with average and above-average ability.

Comment on the Visual Aural Digit Span Test. The VADS is an interesting attempt to measure in a standardized way various components of short-term memory. It provides two methods of presentation of digits (aural and visual) and two methods of response (oral and written). However, the limited range of raw scores on each subtest seriously reduces the diagnostic usefulness of these scores. Koppitz recognized this and therefore suggested that the subtest scores be used only for differentiating between high, low, and average test performance.

The visual presentation also has some potential difficulties. The digits are presented simultaneously rather than sequentially. This form of visual presentation allows for grouping of digits. The visual presentation of 2 4 1 9 may be viewed as two thousand four hundred and nineteen. This subtest, then, may be tapping a different kind of memory than that measured by the visual presentation of digits spaced at one-second intervals.

While there is some information to suggest adequate reliability for the Total score, more studies are needed. This recommendation also holds for studies on validity. The VADS does not appear to be useful for children with normal intelligence, because of its limited ability to discriminate among normal children. Similarly, the test is not applicable for physically handicapped children who have serious visual, hearing, or motor impairments.

Overall, the VADS is still too new for us to evaluate its role in the assessment of children. Its psychometric properties are less than adequate. It may be useful in providing some additional information in the assessment of children with learning disabilities. However, using the Digit Span subtest from the WISC-R or Stanford-Binet in combination with other memory tests may provide similar types of information to that obtained on the VADS. Rosenthal (1979), too, concluded that the VADS adds little to the information obtainable by the use of larger test batteries.

Denver Developmental Screening Test

The Denver Developmental Screening Test (DDST) (Frankenburg, Dodds, Fandal, Kazuk, & Cohrs, 1975) was designed as an aid in identifying delays in the development and behavior of children from birth to 6 years of age. The test is a screening instrument and should not be used as a substitute for a diagnostic evaluation.

The DDST provides information about four areas of development: personal-social (twenty-three items), fine motor (thirty items), language (twenty-one items), and gross motor (thirty-one items). Personal-social items deal with the child's ability to get along with others, to play, and to initiate self-care; fine motor items are concerned with the ability to pick up objects and to draw objects; language items assess the ability to hear, understand, and use language; and gross motor items measure body control, balance, and coordination. The test requires approximately twenty minutes to administer and score.

Items are administered that are appropriate for the child's age. The basic scores are pass or delay. A delay score is given to items failed by the child that have been successfully completed by 90 percent of the children in the normative group younger than the child. Scores are interpreted as "abnormal," "questionable," or "normal," based on the number of delays on each area of the test.

The 1975 edition differs from the 1967 edition (Frankenburg & Dodds, 1967) in its interpretation of scores. Some scores interpreted as abnormal or questionable in the 1967 edition are classified as questionable or normal in the revised edition. In all other respects, the two editions are the same.

Standardization. The Denver Developmental Screening Test was standardized on 1,036 children (543 male, 493 female) between the ages of 2 weeks and 6.4 years living in Denver, Colorado. The sample was closely representative of the racial-ethnic and occupational-group characteristics of the Denver population according to 1960 census data, although stratified random sampling techniques were not used (Frankenburg & Dodds, 1967).

Reliability. Test-retest reliability coefficients, for thirteen age groups over a one-week interval, are reported to range from .66 to .93 for 186 Colorado children between 1.5 and 49 months of age (Frankenburg, Camp, Van Natta, Demersseman, & Voorhees, 1971). These reliabilities are somewhat low. Rate of agreement for four examiners who participated in the standardization ranged from 80 to 95 percent agreement.

Validity. The manual claims a high degree of agreement between the DDST ratings and Stanford-Binet IQs and Bayley Scales of Infant Development DIs. Normal and questionable DDST scores of 236 children led to the finding that 7 percent would be overreferred and 3 percent would be under-

referred if the group were formed on the basis of scores above 70 on the Stanford-Binet or Bayley Scales. A correlation of .97 was reported between the DDST and the Yale Developmental Examination for 18 children aged 4 to 68 months (Frankenburg & Dodds, 1967). Correlations ranging from .84 to .95 have been reported between the DDST and Stanford-Binet, Revised Yale Developmental Schedule, and Bayley Scales for 236 normal and retarded children (Frankenburg, Camp, & Van Natta, 1971). Woodcock (1977) reported correlations of .82, .65, and .52 between the DDST and Developmental Indicators for the Assessment of Learning, the Stanford-Binet, and the PPVT, respectively.

A study of 250 preschool and primary students with the Quick Neurological Screening Test, the DDST, and a neurological examination found that the DDST was not an appropriate instrument for kindergarten-primary neurodevelopmental screening (Sterling & Sterling, 1977). The DDST was able to identify clearly only three of eighteen children with significant neurological-neurodevelopmental disorders, diagnosed on the basis of the neurological examination, and flagged only five additional children.

Comment on the Denver Developmental Screening Test. Moriarty (1972) suggested that the DDST is a useful and acceptable screening device, especially for children between the ages of 3 months and 4 years. It is inexpensive, quick, easy to administer, and requires relatively little training or experience in testing. However, Werner (1972) pointed out that the DDST has several weaknesses. The standardization sample contains more white and upper-middle-class children than the census distribution warranted. Further, the correlation reported between the DDST and the Yale Developmental Schedule is inflated because the sample was not representative. Another problem with the DDST is that the authors maintain that the DDST is not an intelligence test; yet they use an intelligence test to validate their instrument. Caution is therefore needed in using the DDST as a screening instrument.

System of Multicultural Pluralistic Assessment

The System of Multicultural Pluralistic Assessment (SOMPA) (Mercer, 1979; Mercer & Lewis, 1978) is a battery of measures that attempts to incorporate medical, social, and pluralistic information in the assessment of the cognitive, perceptual-motor, and adaptive behavior of black, white, and Hispanic children between ages 5-0 and 11-11 years. SOMPA attempts to provide a comprehensive and balanced assessment that will allow educational and placement decisions to be made that are not racially or culturally discriminatory. However, as we shall see, this effort has not been entirely successful because no attempt was made to alter test content or to deal with bilingualism on the intelligence test. Furthermore, there are questions concerning the appropriateness of the standardization group for use nationwide, and about the validity of the Estimated Learning Potential score.

Assessment Models

SOMPA utilizes a multidimensional approach in which ten measures are used within three assessment models: the medical model, the social system model, and the pluralistic model.

Medical model. Six SOMPA measures are used within the medical model paradigm: the Physical Dexterity Tasks, the Bender Visual Motor Gestalt Test, Weight by Height, Visual Acuity, Auditory Acuity, and the Health History Inventories. This model attempts to answer the question "Is the child a biologically normal individual?" where "normal" is defined as the absence of pathological organic symptoms. Thus, two assumptions of this model are apparent: pathological signs are caused by a biological condition in the child, and the sociocultural characteristics of the child are not essential for accurate diagnosis of biological normalcy. A third assumption is that the six measures that make up the medical model battery assess behaviors or traits that are affected by biological dysfunction.

The Physical Dexterity Tasks consist of twenty-nine tasks that measure the integrity and capabilities of the child's sensorimotor pathways. These tasks are grouped into six scales—Ambulation, Equilibrium, Placement, Fine Motor Sequencing, Finger-Tongue Dexterity, and Involuntary Movement. Representative tasks include walking on heels, hopping on one foot, placing index fingers to nose with eyes open and then closed, touching heel to shin, opening and closing hands alternately, moving tongue from one side of the mouth to the other, and standing on one foot with eyes open. The six raw scores obtained are converted into scaled scores, which are based on a mean of 50 and standard deviation of 15. The standard errors of measurement for the six scales range from 3.93 (Placement) to 7.70 (Finger-Tongue Dexterity).

Split-half reliability coefficients for the Physical Dexterity Tasks scaled scores range from .61 to .94 for the seven age levels and from .71 to .90 for the total sample. Because the correlations between the scaled scores on the Physical Dexterity Tasks and raw scores on the Sociocultural Scales are low, the Physical Dexterity Tasks, Mercer indicates, can be interpreted without reference to the child's sociocultural background.

The Bender Visual Motor Gestalt Test provides a measure of the child's perceptual maturity and is scored according to the Koppitz (1964) procedure (see Chapter 16). The total error raw scores are converted into scaled scores, which are based on a mean of 50 and standard deviation of 15. The standard errors of measurement range from a low of 6.02 for white 10-year-old children to a high of 11.99 for black 5-year-olds. The median standard error of measurement is 8.55 for the total sample.

Split-half reliability coefficients for the Bender-Gestalt raw scores have been computed for the total sample and for each ethnic group by age. Reliabilities, which range between .65 and .74 for the total sample at each age level and between .54 and .77 within each ethnic group, are low. No consistent pattern in the size of the coefficients exists across age or ethnic groups.

The Bender-Gestalt has significant positive correlations with all of the Physical Dexterity Tasks. However, the amount of variance accounted for ranges from 0 to 1 percent. This indicates that the Bender-Gestalt is tapping a set of behaviors that appear to be independent, for the most part, from those measured by the Physical Dexterity Tasks.

Auditory Acuity is measured by a trained audiometrist. Scoring consists of recording the uncorrected hearing levels, in decibels, at frequencies of 250, 500, 1000, 2000, and 4000 Hertz for each ear. If the child wears a hearing aid, the test is administered in both aided and unaided conditions. The child's hearing is considered to be subnormal if there is a hearing threshold level in one ear of 35 decibels or greater for any one frequency or 25 to 34 decibels for any two frequencies.

The results of the standard Snelen Test, obtained from the records of school nurses, comprise the Visual Acuity score. The Snelen scores are recorded directly on the SOMPA profile, with 20/40 or poorer vision being considered subnormal. If the child wears corrective lenses, he or she should be tested both with and without them.

The Weight by Height ratio is considered to be a good indicator of the overall health of the child. The child's height is recorded to the nearest inch and weight to the nearest pound. The corresponding scaled scores are provided separately for boys and girls and again are based on a mean of 50 and standard deviation of 15.

The Health History Inventories consist of a set of forty-five structured, precoded questions asked of the principal guardian during a home interview. This measure provides systematic scorable information on the health history of children that will aid in identifying high-risk cases. Although placed within the medical model, it should not be taken as a medical index, since it is based entirely on the responses of the child's guardian. Questions deal with events surrounding pregnancy, the number and types of severe illnesses and injuries the child has suffered, and any chronic health problems that may

exist. Examples of these items include: "How much did the child weigh when he/she was born?" "Were you sick or did you have any complications while you were pregnant with the child?" "Has the child ever had a temperature of 104 degrees or higher for more than a few hours?"

Social system model. The purpose of the social system model is to evaluate the child's role performance relative to various social groups. It is based on a social deviance model. As such, the emphasis is on determining whether or not a child's behavior is normal for a given situation. Normal behavior is defined as behavior that conforms to the expectations of other members of the group, whereas abnormal behavior is that which violates these expectations (Mercer, 1979). The first of the two assumptions of the social system model extends the concept of normalcy by stating that there are multiple definitions of "normal" because of the existence of different social systems and their social roles. The consequence of this assumption is that a child can be judged normal in one social setting and subnormal in another. It should be noted that normalcy is not a trait of the child, but a definition of a performance within a certain social system with respect to a specific social role.

The SOMPA measures that are placed in the social system model are the WISC-R and the Adaptive Behavior Inventory for Children (ABIC). The WISC-R is administered in the usual fashion. The Verbal, Performance, and Full Scale IQs are viewed as being accurate predictors of the child's academic performance in public schools and are termed the School Functioning Level (SFL) in the SOMPA. For children to be considered "at risk," their IQs must fall in the lowest three percent of the WISC-R standardization group. The ABIC is reviewed in Chapter 17.

Pluralistic model. The pluralistic model uses multiple norms to estimate a child's learning potential. In this approach, the fact that children have different social and cultural backgrounds is taken into consideration by evaluating them in the context of their own social and cultural group rather than by the standards of the prevailing culture. It has two complementary assumptions: (a) all tests are culture-specific and measure learning, and (b) children must be compared with other children from a similar cultural background before any conclusions concerning intelligence can be reached.

The WISC-R is the sole measure in the pluralistic model; it will be recalled that it is also used in the social system model. In the latter model, however, the WISC-R is interpreted in terms of its standard norms. In the pluralistic model, interpretation is aided by the use of the Sociocultural Scales, which contain eleven questions on four areas —Family Size, Family Structure, Socioeconomic Status, and Urban Acculturation. These four scales measure the social and cultural characteristics of the child's family. The weighted raw scores for the scales are converted to scaled scores appropriate to the child's ethnic background. A multiple regression equation, using scores from these four areas, adjusts the standard WISC-R IQs so that an Estimated Learning Potential (ELP) can be derived.

This adjustment in WISC-R scores is intended to allow for differences in children's sociocultural background. To help you better understand the basis for ELP scores, a description of each of the four scales and its role in arriving at an ELP will now be given.

The single Family Size question is presented in two parts: (a) "How many full brothers and sisters does __ have?" (b) "How many persons live in the household, including __ and yourself?" The two numbers so obtained are added together and constitute the raw score for this scale. The ELP converted scale equivalent of the raw score is obtained from the manual.

The Family Structure Scale consists of two clusters of questions. The first cluster defines the parent-child relationship by asking "What relation are you to __?" The second cluster establishes the marital status determination with two questions: (a) "What relation are you to the head of the

household?" and (b) "What is the child's relation to the head of the household?" It should be noted that family structure makes no contribution to Hispanic children's ELPs, as it is not used in estimating their WISC-R scores. This is the sole instance in which there is no contribution from the sociocultural scales to a child's ELP.

The Socioeconomic Status Scale has three questions: (1) "Does the head of the household help support the family by working?" (2) "What is the chief source of income for the family?" and (3) "Does the family have any other sources of income?" It is especially important to obtain an explicit description of the type of work done by the head of the household so that a proper classification can be made relative to the nature of the work and the amount of skill involved, since this description will be used to classify the occupational level on a 0- to 9-point scale, after which the converted scale equivalents are obtained.

The Urban Acculturation Scale consists of four items. The first consists of three questions which yield a "sense of efficacy factor." This factor attempts to characterize the respondent's attitude toward the future. The second item is in four parts and determines the respondent's participation in various types of community groups. The third item concerns the extent of formal education and the nature of the community in which the respondent and the head of the household spent their childhoods. The last item rates the population size of the towns in the previous question, the larger community getting the higher score. The items are multiplied by various factor weights and summed to obtain the total raw score. This score is used to determine the converted score equivalents. The converted score equivalents for the raw scores of the four sociocultural scales are assigned differential weights within each ethnic group.

Let us compute an ELP in the hypothetical case of a black youngster who obtained IQs of 70, 70, and 69 on the three WISC-R scales, respectively. If this youngster came from a very large family and had an inadequate family structure, low socioeconomic status, and limited urban acculturation (obtaining zero raw scores on each of the latter three scales), the ELP given this child would be an IQ of 108 for the Verbal Scale, an IQ of 102 for the Performance Scale, and an IQ of 108 for the Full Scale. The ELP Full Scale IQ is 39 points higher than the child's actual obtained IQ. The ELP changes the child's Full Scale IQ from the 2nd percentile to the 70th percentile.

Standardization

The standardization sample for the SOMPA consisted of 2,085 California public school children aged 5-0 to 11-11 years. Three racial ethnic groups were represented in approximately equal numbers: 696 black children, 690 Hispanic children, and 699 white children. The children were randomly sampled from pre-selected school districts.

Administration

The administration of the SOMPA battery is divided into two parts: an interview with the child's principal guardian in the home and the direct testing of the child at school. The home interview consists of three measures: the Adaptive Behavior Inventory for Children, the Sociocultural Scales, and the Health History Inventories. The child is tested with the WISC-R, the Bender Visual Motor Gestalt Test, and Physical Dexterity Tasks. Visual Acuity (Snellen Test), Auditory Acuity, and a Weight by Height ratio are also obtained. Thus, the administration of the complete SOMPA is an involved and time-consuming task (usually taking about five hours total time).

Comment on the System of Multicultural Pluralistic Assessment

Considerable controversy has arisen about certain crucial aspects of SOMPA. The most salient of these concern the effectiveness of its tripartite model scheme, the lack of adequate national norms and the representativeness of the California sample, and the lack of evidence for the validity of its measures as evidenced by the lack of empirical support for SOMPA's performance in prac-

tical assessment situations. Of particular interest in this last regard are the Estimated Learning Potential (ELP) scores. These scores, which are derived by transforming WISC-R scores according to SOMPA-devised sociocultural norms, may be the most misused and controversial aspect of SOMPA. The effect of sociocultural factors on Bender-Gestalt performance also needs to be considered more fully.

It is important to recognize that nowhere in the SOMPA system is any provision made to observe the child in school, to interview the teacher, to observe the teacher, to use school grades, or to evaluate the curriculum (Oakland, 1979b). It is regrettable that a system designed to facilitate the assessment of school children entirely neglects school performance and school agents for the assessment task.

Effectiveness of tripartite model. Brown (1979) pointed out that empirical evidence is needed about the relationship between SOMPA medical model measures and school variables. He questioned whether the medical model measures should be used at all in making educational decisions until supporting empirical evidence is presented. Similarly, little is known about the effectiveness of the adaptive behavior measure and school achievement. Much more information is needed before we can evaluate the usefulness of the tripartite model for educational planning.

Pitfalls of ELP-based prediction. The validity of ELPs as predictors of achievement is suspect. Oakland (1979b) reported that ELPs correlate in the high .40s with reading and mathematics, while IQs correlate in the high .60s with these two achievement areas. Thus, IQs predict achievement better than ELPs. Additionally, Mercer's own data show that the sociocultural scales account for less than 15 percent of the variance in WISC-R scores among blacks and Hispanics. Thus, the evidence suggests that use of the ELP violates the provision of Public Law 94-142 that requires tests to be valid for the purposes for which they are used (Clarizio, 1979a).

Goodman (1979b) pointed out that "SOMPA would have us believe that to discover learning potential all we need to know are a few facts about size and structure of a family along with its socioeconomic status and urban acculturation" (p. 51). On the basis of the available evidence, ELPs do not appear to measure potential.

Clarizio (1979b, p. 87) faults Mercer with trying to exclude mentally retarded children from the special educational programming that they need.

Once these retarded children are declared ineligible, they will lose the advocacy of exceptional parent groups, government funding, and, most regrettably, special programs and services. From the standpoint of providing special help to EMR children, Mercer's scale, the SOMPA, will prove far more discriminatory than the use of traditional IQ tests. Given the objective of reducing bias, it seems strange to attach greater significance to less reliable and less valid and potentially more discriminatory sources of information. Ironically, the assumption made by test critics is that use of more subjective measures will benefit minority groups.

Goodman (1979a, p. 220) addresses still another side of the question of use of the ELP, emphasizing its danger to children whose scores are not raised by the various transformations:

The notion that we are now provided with a means of tapping a person's innate or biological potential is, in my view, both unwarranted and dangerous: unwarranted because there is no way to verify the claim and because Mercer offers no evidence that her calculation of a child's potential correlates with any observable behaviors; dangerous because labeling a group of children "defective"—biologically impaired with poor potential—both stigmatizes them and discourages remedial efforts that might have a chance of success.

Furthermore, the regression equations used to obtain the ELPs are based entirely on data from California (see Chapter 2 for more information on regression equations). Utmost caution is needed in applying these equations in other parts of the country. Oakland (1979b) reported that with a Texas sample, Mercer's regression equations produced ELPs that were 7 to 8 points different from those obtained with regression equations based on Texas sample data.

In summary, while the ELP IQ may be of some interest, its use in placement and clinical situations is not supported by current studies. The use of the ELP and other unvalidated procedures violates the widely accepted test standards of the American Psychological Association. The predicted IQs may create misleading expectations for the child, parents, and teacher. Children who are led to believe that they can achieve in the society at large, on the basis of predicted scores based on norms that do not represent the culture at large, may be placed in situations with which they cannot cope. They may experience disappointment and frustration and come to resent school systems and psychologists who have led them to such expectations. The publication and use of SOMPA is premature, given its inadequate validity.

Is renorming necessary? A second major criticism of SOMPA concerns the adequacy of the California-based norms and the appropriateness of applying these norms to other areas of the country. No information is presented in the manual regarding the socioeconomic distribution of the sample. Because of this lack, there is no way to evaluate the representativeness of the sample. Furthermore, use of any norms based on the total sample obviously gives a distorted picture of the school-based population of California children. The three major racial-ethnic groups are almost equally represented in the total sample, and equal representation does not exist in the state population.

Considerable doubts about the validity of SOMPA for other areas of the country have been raised. Therefore, a key question is whether it is psychometrically justifiable to generalize from the California sample to samples of children in other parts of the country. This question threatens the very foundations of SOMPA. It has not yet received an affirmative response; indeed, some evidence has accrued that suggests that SOMPA norms may be inappropriate in other parts of the country (Oakland, 1979b). Critics (e.g., Brown, 1979; Clarizio, 1979a) have stated that renorming is essential for SOMPA to have nationwide validity.

Problems with the ABIC. As you will read in Chapter 17, the ABIC's principal strength is that it is a well-standardized instrument for measuring adaptive behavior. However, it has certain drawbacks, such as (a) items that may discriminate against children of lower socioeconomic class and (b) norms that may not be applicable nationwide, because its sample also is limited to California.

Medical model problems. A criticism of the medical model, as a predictor of school achievement, concerns the lack of empirical evidence of the relationship between scores on medical measures and school variables. Such evidence must be presented or the use of these measures to make educational decisions about children cannot be justified.

Additionally, an unnecessary complication exists with respect to the scoring of these tests. The Physical Dexterity and Bender-Gestalt scores are first converted into scaled scores and then profiled as percentiles. This involves fitting highly skewed data into a model that assumes a normal distribution. For example, at ages 11-0 to 11-3 Ambulation raw scores from 9 to 120 are assigned a scaled score of 10, while raw scores from 0 to 8 are assigned scaled scores from 16 to 61. In addition, the profile for the Physical Dexterity Tasks and the Bender-Gestalt only ranges from the 1st to the 50th percentile. All scaled scores over 50 are lumped together as being at "over 50th percentile." Brown (1979) wonders why it is necessary to derive scaled scores if the scaled scores are not profiled in their entirety. Three of the other medical model measures—Visual Acuity, Auditory Acuity, and Health History Inventory—are only profiled for two categories: "Not at Risk" and "At Risk." For the "At Risk" category, the lowest 16 percent of the distribution has been chosen to receive this designation. Brown (1979) proposed that scores on all medical model scales be reported in terms of a critical "At Risk" level. The use of several broad categories, such as borderline, normal, and above normal, could further enhance this effort.

Bender-Gestalt norms. The Bender Visual Motor Gestalt Test is included in SOMPA without any provision of separate ethnic norms. Yet a study (Sattler & Gwynne, 1982) of the data presented in Table 16 in the SOMPA manual clearly shows that black children at every age made significantly more errors on the Bender-Gestalt than did white children, while Hispanic children made significantly more errors than did white children at two of the ages (8 and 10 years). The black children also made significantly more errors than did the Hispanic children at six of the seven age levels. Thus it appears that the use of one set of norms for all ethnic groups does not fit in with SOMPA's attempt at pluralistic assessment.

Concluding Comment on the System of Multicultural Pluralistic Assessment

As Oakland (1979a) observed, there is no evidence that the use of SOMPA will lead to educational decisions that are not racially or culturally discriminatory. In fact, no guidelines are presented in SOMPA that show how it can be used in making educational decisions. While SOMPA is an interesting attempt to standardize a number of procedures used in an assessment battery, we must not be misled by claims that have not been empirically supported.

Comment on Tests of Achievement and Special Abilities

Screening achievement tests, such as the WRAT and the PIAT, measure only a limited aspect of reading ability. For example, a child with exceptional individual word recognition skills may obtain high scores, although his or her ability to read with meaning may be limited. Reading in context is a different skill from reading or recognizing individual words. Typical classroom reading allows for the use of contextual cues. Reading assessment instruments, such as the Sucher-Allred Reading Placement Inventory, Classroom Reading Inventory, and San Diego Quick Assessment, are poor instruments for classification or placement, but are useful in pinpointing specific areas of deficit that can be the focus of remediation.

In deciding on the relative merits of the Wide Range Achievement Test versus the Peabody Individual Achievement Test, consider the two different formats that they use for measuring ability. The WRAT requires expressive skills, while the PIAT requires receptive or recognition skills. In the PIAT Reading Comprehension subtest, children who are good visually and who are shrewd at guessing may perform beyond their true reading level. As you become more familiar with each instrument, many of its assets and limitations will become more apparent to you.

In research studies, as well as in school and clinical practice, it is a poor practice to use a test of specific ability, such as the Peabody Picture Vocabulary Test or Quick Test, to estimate the child's mental ability. Wheldall and Jeffree (1974) pointed out that in research studies an insidious process takes place. A child's raw score is transformed into a Vocabulary Age, which then is confused with Verbal Age, and then may become an MA—a measure of general ability. This procedure is particularly unfortunate with mentally retarded children, because receptive vocabulary is unlikely to reflect their general level of ability. Receptive vocabulary may be acquired in a relatively automatic, very mechanical way, much as the mechanics of reading can be learned without comprehension.

Williams, Marks, and Bailer (1977) also strongly recommended that the PPVT not be used as a measure of intelligence in any research study that involves a relationship between intelligence and visual comprehension. This recommendation was made because the PPVT itself is in part a measure of visual comprehension. Therefore, using two supposedly different measures could result in criterion contamination.

In administering multiple-choice picture vocabulary tests (or other multiple-choice tests), an "eyeblink" response procedure can be used with children who have severe motor handicaps. First, explain the nature of the items, illustrate their administration, and acknowledge the child's response method (Allen & Jefferson, 1962). Second, place the plates in front of the child so that he or she can see them easily. Then say the first word, followed by "I want you to let me know which picture shows __? I'll point to each picture, and you blink your eyes once for 'no' and twice for 'yes.' Is it this one?" Point to the picture in the upper-left corner (as the child views it) and wait for the child's response. Then point to the upper-right corner, asking "Is it this one?" After the child's response, proceed to the lower-left and then the lower-right corner drawings. Record the answer on the answer sheet. The next word is sounded, and the same technique followed until the test is discontinued. In order to standardize the procedure, be sure to point to all four pictures on a card for each word until the test is finished.

For a deaf or hard-of-hearing child, the stimulus words can be shown individually on 3 × 5 cards. This requires reading ability, because the stimulus words should not be pantomimed. The directions, however, can be pantomimed. Point to the word on the 3 × 5 card and then point to each of the pictures on the plate, shaking your head while pointing to the incorrect picture and nodding while pointing to the correct picture. The child should easily grasp the idea of pointing.

Summary

1. The tests covered in this chapter are useful for the assessment of academic achievement, psycholinguistic and receptive

vocabulary skills, and processing skills, and for developmental screening. A system of integrating various assessment tools is also considered.

2. The Wide Range Achievement Test provides measures of reading, spelling, and arithmetic. There is some evidence that the WRAT norms tend to underestimate achievement levels. The WRAT does not provide for an in-depth study of academic skills. It should only be considered as a screening instrument.

3. The Peabody Individual Achievement Test is a screening test measuring mathematics, reading and spelling ability and general information. Over half of the items use a multiple-choice format. It is useful as a screening test, but its content overlaps with that of the WISC-R.

4. The Woodcock-Johnson Psycho-Educational Battery is an omnibus test that covers cognitive ability, achievement, and interest. Its reliability and validity appear to be satisfactory. However, cognitive scores may not be comparable to those on the WISC-R. Furthermore, the battery fails to provide standard errors of measurement for the subtests and scales. More information is needed to evaluate its effectiveness.

5. The Woodcock Reading Mastery Tests, Sucher-Allred Reading Placement Inventory, Classroom Reading Inventory, and San Diego Quick Assessment can be useful as screening instruments to determine a child's reading level.

6. The KeyMath Diagnostic Arithmetic Test is a useful instrument that provides diagnostic information about children's arithmetic skills.

7. The Boehm Test of Basic Concepts measures concepts related to space, quantity, and time for children in kindergarten through second grade.

8. The Illinois Test of Psycholinguistic Abilities provides information about various areas of linguistic functioning. The test is controversial, because it may be a test of intelligence rather than a test of linguistic functioning. The test has limited usefulness in the assessment battery.

9. The Peabody Picture Vocabulary Test–Revised and the Quick Test provide measures of receptive vocabulary ability. They should not be used as measures of intelligence. Both tests require only a pointing response and use a multiple-choice format.

10. The Visual Aural Digit Span Test, while attempting to measure intersensory and intrasensory integration, fails to provide a sufficient range of scores. It is difficult to evaluate its place in the assessment battery.

11. The Denver Developmental Screening Test attempts to measure developmental delays in children between birth and 6 years of age. However, its validity is questionable.

12. The System of Multicultural Pluralistic Assessment combines medical, social, ethnic, cognitive, perceptual-motor, and adaptive behavior information. The unique aspect of SOMPA is its attempt to estimate learning potential (ELP) by applying family size, family structure, socioeconomic status, and urban acculturation variables to WISC-R scores. There is no evidence that the ELP measures "potential" or that SOMPA makes any additional contribution to the assessment process. Furthermore, there is no evidence that SOMPA is culturally nondiscriminatory.

Assessment of Visual-Motor Perception, Auditory Perception, and Motor Proficiency

What should be remembered is that many less than perfect measures have proven to be useful in psychology . . . .

EDWARD F. ZIGLER

EXHIBIT 16-1. Psychological Evaluation: Auditory Processing Deficit

Name: Henry
Date of birth: May 31, 1964
Chronological age: 15-3
Date of evaluation: September 14, 1979
Date of report: September 15, 1979
Grade: 9th

Tests Administered

WISC-R:

VERBAL SCALE		PERFORMANCE SCALE	
Information	7	Picture Completion	16
Similarities	11	Picture Arrangement	12
Arithmetic	7	Block Design	18
Vocabulary	7	Object Assembly	15
Comprehension	12	Coding	11
Digit Span	7		

Verbal Scale IQ = 92
Performance Scale IQ = 131
Full Scale IQ = 111 ± 6 at the 95 percent confidence level.

Wide Range Achievement Test:

	STANDARD SCORE	PERCENTILE
Reading	83	13
Spelling	72	4
Arithmetic	85	16

1. _Cat_ (cat)
2. _run_ (run)
3. _arm_ (arm)
4. _train_ (train)
5. _Shout_ (shout)
6. _Crear_ (correct)
7. _cil_ (circle)
8. _heaven_ (heaven)
9. _educate_ (educate)
10. _____ (material)
11. _rulih_ (ruin)
12. _fastioh_ (fashion)
13. _belive_ (believe)
14. _Sugjustion_ (suggestion)
15. _equitment_ (equipment)
16. _majorite_ (majority)
17. _____
18. _____
19. _____
20. _____
21. _____
22. _____
23. _____
24. _____
25. _____
26. _____
27. _____
28. _____
29. _____
30. _____

Gray Oral Reading Test: (Form A) 3.0 grade equivalent.

Lindamood Auditory Conceptualization Test: Mid-3rd grade level.

Visual Motor Integration Test: (21) 12 years, 8 months level.

Reason for Referral

Henry was referred for a psychoeducational evaluation by a psychiatrist who was consulted

EXHIBIT 16-1   (cont.)

by the parents. His parents were concerned because Henry's behavior was deteriorating at home as well as at school. He has never done well academically, despite being motivated to learn and generally liking school. He had previously been enrolled in a learning center program to increase his low reading ability, but was believed still to be reading at about a 3rd or 4th grade level. He would not complete assignments or participate in class, was excessively tardy, and showed a lack of interest in subjects over the past year. Grades were all poor, except for physical education.

Observations

Henry is a very tall, good-looking youth. He had good eye contact and was relaxed and comfortable about being tested. He seemed to care about whether his performance was correct, and frequently asked if he was "right." Self-concept appeared to be very well developed, and motivation was strong throughout testing.

Discussion

Although Henry's Full Scale IQ was in the High Average range, this fact obscured the highly unusual 39-point difference between his Performance IQ of 131 (98th percentile) and his Verbal IQ of 92 (30th percentile). Except for abstract verbal reasoning ability and practical judgment, Henry's verbal abilities were all below average. On the other hand, his nonverbal cognitive skills were highly developed, particularly visual-spatial ability and alertness to details.

Reading of separate words on the Wide Range Achievement Test revealed errors of substitution (whole words or vowels), omissions of parts of words, and insertions of additional syllables. Oral reading of paragraphs allowed him to use contextual clues, but he substituted words so often that the meaning was changed. Paragraph reading was at the beginning 3rd grade level, with comprehension at about the 5th grade level.

Spelling was also below average, with seven words spelled correctly. Spelling showed a pattern of auditory discrimination errors. For example, correct was spelled "crear," circle was "cil," ruin was "rulin," and equipment was "equitment." Omissions and insertions were the most

frequent errors. As is typical in cases of a severe auditory processing deficit, it would have been difficult to guess in some cases which word he had spelled, because the sound-letter relationships were so poor.

Arithmetic was at the 16th percentile. Henry could perform the four basic operations on numbers, but he was weak in fractions, decimals, and percentages. There appeared to be no severe disability in this area.

Ability to analyze how many sounds he had heard and where he had heard same and different sounds within a syllable was very poor (mid-3rd grade level). He could correctly represent the sounds about 75 percent of the time. Integration of auditory and visual-motor modalities was poor. Visual processing skills appear to be superior to auditory processing skills.

Summary and Recommendations

Henry is an intelligent and likable young man with good motivation for school-related tasks, despite a long history of unsuccessful efforts. He was willing to try harder at a task upon receiving encouragement. Henry's auditory processing is exceptionally weak when compared with his visual-spatial processing. The difference between his Verbal IQ and Performance IQ of 39 points indicates language impairment of a slight to moderate degree. For purposes of educational remediation, Henry needs to increase the following auditory abilities: auditory discrimination, sequencing, auditory analysis of sounds within a syllable, auditory closure, auditory-motor integration, auditory-visual integration, and auditory memory.

Reading and spelling remediation should be approached in a multisensory way; that is, combining his strong and weak modalities—visual, tactile, kinesthetic, and auditory senses. Auditory discrimination training that incorporates oral-motor feedback is often quite effective in cases such as this. Without strengthening Henry's weak auditory system, it is likely that reading and spelling will be difficult to improve, since his word attack skills are quite poor. He has only been able to learn words as wholes.

Prognosis is guarded, dependent upon improvement of auditory processing ability.

Examiner

The tests reviewed in this chapter focus on visual-motor perception and integration, visual perception, auditory perception, and motor proficiency. The measurement of these expressive and receptive functions helps us to understand, in part, how the child processes information. Some of the tests covered are particularly useful in evaluating children with possible learning disabilities or neurological difficulties. The most popular and important test covered in the chapter is the Bender Visual Motor Gestalt Test.

Let us consider what factors may be involved in copying simple geometric designs. They probably include appropriate motor development, perceptual discrimination ability, and ability to integrate perceptual and motor processes. Poor performance may be due to (a) misperception (faulty interpretation of input information), (b) execution difficulties (faulty motor response output), or (c) integrative or central processing difficulties (faulty memory storage or retrieval systems). Inadequate visual-motor performance may be associated with maturational delay, limited intellectual stimulation, unfamiliarity with testing situations, or neurological impairment.

Sometimes it is possible to discern whether the difficulty lies in the output (motor) or the input (perceptual) process. Generally, if children struggle to reproduce the designs, the difficulty is likely to be expressive or motor, while if they draw them quickly and easily, but with errors that are not recognized, the difficulty may be receptive or perceptual and not entirely motor (Palmer, 1970). If children cannot see their errors, the trouble may lie in the input mechanisms, whereas children who can acknowledge their errors, but cannot correct them, may have difficulty with the output mechanisms (Stellern, Vasa, & Little, 1976).

Tests of visual-motor, auditory, or motor ability should help us to determine which modalities are intact and which one or ones are not. This information may provide leads useful in developing remediation programs. Let us now turn to the tests themselves, and evaluate their possible contribution to the assessment task. (See Appendix D for the highlights of tests covered in this and other chapters of the book.)

Assessment of Visual-Motor Ability and Visual Perception

Bender Visual Motor Gestalt Test

The Bender Visual Motor Gestalt Test (Bender, 1938) is one of the most widely used psychological tests and certainly the most popular of the visual-motor tests (e.g., Lubin, Wallis, & Paine, 1971). It was developed in 1938 by Loretta Bender for use as a visual-motor test with adult clinical populations and as a developmental test for children. The test was derived from Gestalt configurations devised by Wertheimer in 1923 to demonstrate principles of Gestalt psychology in relation to perception.

The Bender-Gestalt, an individually administered, paper-and-pencil test, contains nine geometric figures drawn in black (see Figure 16-1) on 4 × 6 inch white cards. The designs are presented one at a time, and the child is required to copy the designs on a blank sheet of paper. The test serves as a good "ice breaker" with which to begin the testing session—the task is innocuous, nonthreatening, interesting, and appealing to children. Our discussion of the Bender-Gestalt focuses primarily on its use as a test of visual-motor perception in children, although some attention also is given to how the test may provide indices of emotional difficulties.

Administration. To take the test, the child needs a number 2 pencil with an eraser and a blank, unlined sheet of 8½ × 11 paper, which is placed vertically before the child. A number of extra sheets of paper, usually equal to the number of cards, also should be available on the table, along with an extra pencil in case of breakage. Examinees are told that they will be shown nine cards, one at a time, each with a design, and that they are to copy them as well as they can on the paper.

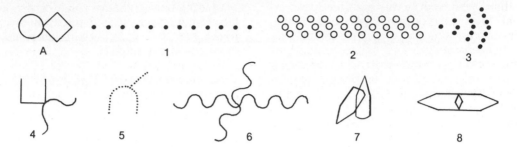

FIGURE 16-1. Designs on the Bender Visual Motor Gestalt Test.

Recommended instructions include the following:

1. "I have nine cards here with designs on them for you to copy. Here is the first one. Now go ahead and make one just like it" (Koppitz, 1964, p. 15).
2. "Now I would like you to draw some designs for me. [Place pencil, paper, and cards in front of child.] There are nine cards here and each card has a drawing on it. I want you to copy the drawings. Make them the best you can" (Clawson, 1962b, p. 7).

Questions raised by the child should be given a noncommittal reply, such as "Make it look as much like the picture on the card as you can" or "Try to do it the way you think is best" or "Do the best you can."

The examiner then presents each card individually. They are shown in a specific order, beginning with card A, and followed by cards 1 to 8. The cards are numbered sequentially in terms of approximate difficulty. The examinee is permitted to erase, but the drawings must be done freehand, without the use of any mechanical aids, such as rulers.

The nine designs take approximately five minutes to complete. Any large deviation in the time required to complete the designs should be noted. For example, children who require fifteen minutes to copy the designs might have a slow, methodical approach to situations, compulsive tendencies, or depressive features, while those who finish in less than two or three minutes might have

an impulsive style. Place a caret (∧) next to any design that appears to be rotated. The caret indicates the direction of the top of the page, and allows you to distinguish between those designs that were correctly reproduced and those that were rotated. Finally, the child's approach to the task (e.g., degree of impulsiveness or compulsiveness or ability to cope with frustration) should be noted.

Variations in administration. Several variations are possible in administering the Bender-Gestalt. Two of the most widely used are (a) the tachistoscopic procedure and (b) the memory phase procedure. In the tachistoscopic procedure, each card is shown for five seconds. It is then removed, and the child is asked to draw the design from memory. In the memory procedure, children first complete the standard procedures. After all the designs have been copied, the children are asked to draw as many of the figures as they can remember.

The Bender-Gestalt also can be administered as a group test. Four methods of administration have been used: (a) presentation of enlarged Bender-Gestalt cards at the front of the room; (b) presentation of special Bender-Gestalt test booklets in which the designs are drawn and the children copy the designs in blank spaces; (c) presentation of the designs by an opaque, overhead, or slide projector; and (d) presentation of individual decks of Bender-Gestalt cards. The most successful method with large numbers of children is the first method, the presentation of enlarged Bender-Gestalt cards. The projector methods, too, are popular, but they have the disadvantages of requiring special equipment and requiring that the children draw their designs in semi-darkness. Individual decks have been most successful with hyperactive or immature children who require extra attention, although only two or three children should be tested at one time. Overall, research has demonstrated that group administration of the Bender-Gestalt yields reliable protocols that are comparable to those obtained under individual administration (Koppitz, 1975).

Koppitz Developmental Bender Scoring System. The Koppitz Developmental Bender Scoring System (Koppitz, 1964) for evaluating the Bender-Gestalt drawings of young children is probably the most popular objective scoring system for the test. It is composed of two parts: (a) developmental scoring and (b) scoring of emotional indicators. The first part has most relevance for the evaluation of visual-motor perception. There are thirty developmental scoring items, with each item receiving 1 or 0 points,

depending on whether or not an error occurs. The items are classified into four types of errors: (1) distortion of shape, (2) rotation, (3) integration difficulties, and (4) perseveration. A scoring sheet can be used to record 1 point for each distortion made by the child. The points are summed to obtain a total score, which is then compared to norms for the child's age. Percentile norms are available for children aged 5-0 through 11-11 years (Koppitz, 1975). A table of standard-score equivalents (see Table C-35 in the Appendix), based on a mean of 100 and standard deviation of 15, is most useful for ages 5-0 through 8-0. In addition, standard scores are available for the SOMPA standardization sample (Mercer & Lewis, 1978), with a mean of 50 and standard deviation of 15.

A comparison (Sattler & Bowman, 1981) of the Koppitz and SOMPA standard-score equivalents indicates that the two sets of norms do not provide equivalent standard scores for the same raw scores. In some cases, the same raw score results in standard scores that are as much as one stan-

YOU SEE —
— AT THIS AGE THEY CAN'T COPY A DIAMOND PROPERLY!

Cartoon by Tony Hall from *Of Children, An Introduction To Child Development,* Third Edition by Guy R. Lefrancois. © 1980 by Wadsworth, Inc., Belmont, California 94002. Reprinted by permission of the publisher.

dard deviation apart. For example, a raw score of 9 (for an 8-year-old child) is about 1 *SD* below the mean on the SOMPA norms, and about 2 *SD* below the mean on the Koppitz norms. Until further validity evidence is available, I urge caution in making any placement decisions based on either set of norms.

Let us consider the four classifications of errors used by the Koppitz scoring system.

1. *Distortion of shape* involves destruction of the gestalt, such as misshapen figures, disproportion between the sizes of the component parts of the figure; substitution of circles or dashes for dots; substitution of distinct angles for curves or total lack of curves where they should exist; extra angles; and missing angles. Distortion of shape may be scored for Figures A, 1, 3, 5, 6, 7, and 8, for a possible total of 10 points.

2. *Rotation* is scored when the figure or any part of it is rotated by 45 degrees or more, or when the Bender-Gestalt card is rotated even if it is copied correctly as shown on the rotated card. This error may be scored for Figures A, 1, 2, 3, 4, 5, and 8, for a possible total of 8 points.

3. *Integration* involves (a) failure to connect properly the two parts of a figure, either by leaving more than ⅛ inch distance between them or causing them to overlap; (b) two lines crossing not at all or in an incorrect place; and (c) omission or addition of rows of dots or loss of the overall shape in the case of figures composed of dots or circles. Integration difficulties may be

scored with Figures A, 2, 3, 4, 5, 6, and 7, for a possible total of 9 points.

4. *Perseveration* involves increase, continuation, or prolongation of the number of units in the design. It is scored for three of the designs: (a) when there are more than fifteen dots in a row in Figure 1; (b) when there are more than fourteen columns of circles in a row in Figure 2; and (c) when there are six or more complete curves in either direction in Figure 6. A total of 3 points is possible. This type of perseveration is known as "within-card perseveration." There is a second type of perseveration, much rarer, called "card to card perseveration," which occurs when a preceding design or parts of it influence succeeding designs. However, this type of perseveration is not scored in the Koppitz system.

The twelve emotional indicators provide ways of evaluating the child's performance qualitatively, but should not be used to make specific diagnoses. A brief description of the emotional indicators follows:

1. *Confused order* is scored when the designs are arbitrarily placed on the paper; any sort of logical sequence is not counted as a confused order.

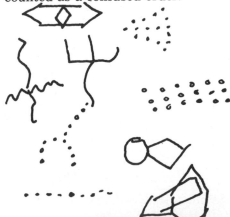

2. *Wavy line* is scored for only Figures 1 and 2. It involves abrupt changes in the direction of dots or circles; a gradual curve or rotation is not counted as a wavy line.

3. *Dashes for circles* involves substituting dashes for circles on Figure 2.

4. *Increasing size* (Figures 1, 2, and 3) is scored when the last dots or circles are at least three times as large as the first dots or circles.

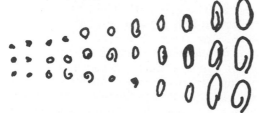

5. *Large size* is scored when the figure is drawn at least ⅓ larger in each direction than the one on the card.

6. *Small size* occurs when the drawings are half as large as on the card.

7. *Fine line* is seen when drawings are done with a very faint, thin pencil line.

8. *Overwork* or *reinforced lines* is scored when the entire figure, or part of a figure, is redrawn or when it is reinforced with heavy lines.

9. *Second attempt* refers to leaving a partially completed or finished drawing and starting a new drawing of the same figure. This indicator is not scored when the figure is erased and redrawn in the same spot.

10. *Expansion* refers to the use of two or more sheets of paper, regardless of the size of the drawings.

11. *Box around design* refers to drawing a box around one or more of the designs after it is copied.

12. *Spontaneous elaboration* or *addition to design* occurs when the child spontaneously makes changes on one or more figures, turning it into an object or bizarre design.

Koppitz (1964) suggested that personality and temperament characteristics are associated with the various emotional indicators, such as low frustration tolerance, acting-out behavior, aggressiveness and impulsivity, timidity, and anxiety or shyness. However, these emotional indicators should only be used to formulate hypotheses about the child; they should not be used to make definitive statements about the child's personality.

Standardization. The 1975 Koppitz norms are based on a sample of 975 elementary school children, aged 5-0 to 11-11 years, living in rural areas, small towns, suburbs, and large metropolitan centers in the west, south, and northeast. The composition of the sample was 86 percent white, 8.5 percent black, 4.5 percent Mexican-American and Puerto Rican, and 1 percent Oriental. The sample is not representative of the country, as its geographic distribution was highly skewed to the northeast. Further, the socioeconomic characteristics of the sample were not reported.

Reliability. Test-retest reliabilities for the Developmental Scoring System, with intervals ranging from the same day to eight months, and with samples of 19 to 193 children in kindergarten through sixth grade, have ranged from $r = .50$ to $r = .90$, with a median r of .77 (Koppitz, 1975). The median correlation suggests that while the total score has adequate reliability, its level of reliability is not high enough to permit basing diagnostic decisions on the test alone, or on only one administration of the test.

Interscorer reliabilities are highly acceptable, ranging from .79 to .99, with a median coefficient of $r = .91$ (Koppitz, 1975). These reliabilities were based on samples of normal and mentally retarded children.

The reliabilities of the four separate error scores (perseveration, distortion, rotation, and integration) are much lower than those of the total score (Engin & Wallbrown, 1976; Wallbrown, Wallbrown, & Engin, 1976). Therefore, the focus in interpreting the Bender-Gestalt should be on the total score and not on the individual sources of error.

Validity. The validity of the Developmental Scoring System depends on how the test is used. When used as a test of perceptual-motor development in children, the Bender-Gestalt appears to have acceptable validity. Copying errors decrease steadily between ages 5 and 9 years because of maturational changes. However, for children over 8 years of age, the Developmental Scoring System only distinguishes those with below-average perceptual-motor development from those with normal development, since near-perfect performance falls within the normal range (Koppitz, 1964).

Concurrent validity for the Developmental Scoring System has been established by correlating it with various tests of visual-motor perception (Koppitz, 1975). Correlations with the Frostig Developmental Test of Visual Perception range from .39 to .56, with a median correlation of .47; a correlation of .82 was found with the Beery Developmental Test of Visual-Motor Integration. Correlations with a variety of intelligence tests range from $-.19$ to $-.66$, with a median coefficient of $-.48$. (The negative correlations occur because the Developmental Scoring System gives error scores.)

In recent years there has been an increased interest in evaluating the ability of the Bender-Gestalt to predict educational readiness (Koppitz, 1975). Studies report that correlations between kindergarten Bender-Gestalt scores and later achievement scores range from −.19 to −.57, with a median of −.29. Bender-Gestalt scores obtained in grades one through three correlate with later achievement in the range of −.17 to −.58, with a median of −.35. Concurrent validity coefficients between the Bender-Gestalt Developmental Scores and school achievement for grades kindergarten, one, two, three, and six range from −.13 to −.58, with a median of −.34. These results suggest that while the Developmental Scoring System has both concurrent and predictive validity using achievement scores, the correlations are too low to warrant its use for predicting school achievement for any one individual child.

The predictive validity of the Bender-Gestalt appears to be somewhat better for predicting arithmetic achievement than reading achievement. Correlations between the Bender-Gestalt and arithmetic scores range from −.25 to −.51, with a median of −.43, while those with reading scores range from −.17 to −.57, with a median of −.29 (Koppitz, 1975).

Studies investigating concurrent validity of the Bender-Gestalt report that correlations with measures of arithmetic proficiency range from −.13 to −.49, with a median of −.36; while with measures of reading, they range from −.14 to −.58, with a median of −.32 (Koppitz, 1975). These results, too, indicate that the Bender-Gestalt should not be used as a screening instrument for either reading proficiency or arithmetic proficiency. It is important to recognize that school success depends upon many factors, including cognitive ability, level of maturity, experience, school atmosphere, pedagogy, perceptual-motor development, motivational variables, and familial factors. Perceptual-motor skills, therefore, are only one part of the total picture.

The Bender-Gestalt as a diagnostic tool. The Bender-Gestalt is considered to be primarily a perceptual-motor test. The child's performance is regarded as a function of visual perception, motor coordination, and visual-motor integration. However, frequently Bender-Gestalt protocols have also been interpreted diagnostically, especially to assess the possibility of brain damage. Diagnostic indicators have been proposed that are considered to be indicative of organicity (brain damage) or psychosis. However, any specific indicator may be associated with one or more kinds of difficulties. Thus, while these indicators are helpful in formulating hypotheses, they should never be used alone to make a diagnosis.

When using the Bender-Gestalt diagnostically, it is important to remember that it should be used as part of an assessment battery. Further cautions will be emphasized in the following sections as they apply to the use of the Bender-Gestalt in evaluating brain damage, mental retardation, psychosis, and various other handicapping conditions.

Brain damage: Many of the signs that have been suggested as possible diagnostic indicators of brain damage are incorporated within the Developmental Scoring System. Some of the signs that may be associated with brain injury are as follows.[1] (For signs 1, 3, 4, and 6, see examples earlier in this chapter.)

1. Rotation.
2. Difficulties with angles, such as adding extra angles or "dog-ears."

3. Destruction of the gestalt or loss of shape.
4. Perseveration.
5. Disproportion between the parts of a figure.

6. Difficulties in integrating parts of a figure.

7. Substituting circles for dots.

8. Addition or exclusion of one or more rows of circles.

9. Gross oversimplification or primitization, such as substituting a line for a row of separate dots.

10. Fragmentation, such as treating the parts of the design as separate entities.

11. Crowding or overlapping the figures (i.e., collision).

In addition to the above indices, other aspects of the child's performance should be considered, including the time taken to copy the designs, the space used, the child's be-

havior, and the child's recognition of error (Koppitz, 1964). Each of these is now considered.

1. *Time.* Observe how quickly the child completes the designs. Some brain-injured children work impulsively, completing the test in less than three minutes. Others may require a large amount of time and effort, drawing slowly and compulsively in an attempt to compensate for their deficiencies.
2. *Space.* The use of more than one sheet of paper, *expansiveness,* also appears in the performance of some brain-injured children.
3. *Behavioral observations.* Certain behavioral tendencies may also appear: (a) tracing the design with a finger before drawing it, (b) "anchoring" the design with a finger, (c) briefly glancing at the card and then drawing from memory, (d) rotating the card and paper, (e) excessive counting, and (f) checking and correcting drawings. In addition, some brain-injured children may try to divert attention from the task through disruptive behavior.
4. *Recognition of error.* Through inquiry it can be determined whether children can recognize or correct their errors.

The difficulty with this list of signs is that normal children also make some of these errors. For example, as many as 24 percent of a group of normal children with no medical evidence of brain injury had some of these signs in their drawings (Koppitz, 1975). Therefore, the signs must be viewed with caution and studied along with other aspects of the child's performance.

The Bender-Gestalt has questionable validity in the diagnosis of brain damage. First, although there are many different types of brain damage, the Bender-Gestalt only evaluates damage that may interfere with visual discrimination and visual-motor coordination. Second, the supposed "neurological indices" frequently appear in the performance of children who may be neurologically immature but who do not have demonstrable damage. In addition, these indices may be associated with pathology other than brain damage. Finally, the presence of visual-motor difficulties is not sufficient to diagnose brain injury.

Thus it seems obvious that a diagnosis of brain damage should never be made on the basis of the Bender-Gestalt alone. However, if several of these signs exist accompanied by some significant behavioral indices (see Chapter 22), the hypothesis of possible visual-motor impairment can be entertained. Assessment information obtained from medical, developmental, educational, and psychological evaluations would then be needed to determine whether neurological impairment may be present.

Mental retardation: There are no special signs or diagnostic indicators associated with mental retardation. However, Bender-Gestalt developmental scores of retarded children tend to be poorer than those of non-retarded children (Koppitz, 1964). In severe cases, signs similar to those for brain damage may appear, such as expansion, perseveration, primitivization, and oversimplification (Halpern, 1951; Koppitz, 1975). However, the presence of one or more of these signs does not imply intellectual retardation.

Psychosis: There has been no widescale attempt to use the Bender-Gestalt as a test for diagnosing psychosis, as has been done with brain damage. Still, a number of diagnostic indicators may be associated with psychosis. These involve serious errors or distortions of the figures, reflecting impaired reality testing (the inability to test or explore the nature of one's social and physical environment). Many of the errors found in the Bender-Gestalt reproductions of psychotic children are similar to those that occur with brain-damaged children. These include fragmentation, primitivization or oversimplification, and crowding or overlapping (Halpern, 1951; Stellern et al., 1976). Errors that are more specific to the reproductions of psychotic children include collision, elaboration or bizarre doodling, and scribbling (Halpern, 1951; Stellern et al., 1976).

The examiner should never rely on these signs alone to make a diagnosis of psychosis. First, they overlap with indices of brain damage. Second, they may be by-products of temporary states of inefficiency. Finally, a diagnosis of psychosis must be based on many sources of data, and not on the Bender-Gestalt exclusively.

Variables affecting Bender-Gestalt performance: We have seen that brain damage, psychosis, and mental retardation may interfere with perceptual-motor functioning and affect Bender-Gestalt test performance. Some of the factors associated with these conditions (as well as other factors that may lead to poor perceptual-motor functioning) include physiological limitations, sensory deprivation, muscular weakness, and other physical handicapping conditions; physiological "disruptions," such as illness, injury, or fatigue; immediate, temporary environmental stress; poor motivation; affective disruptions; intellectual retardation; social or cultural deprivations; and experiences that differ from those of the normative group (Koppitz, 1975; Palmer, 1970). Social and cultural factors are considered in more detail below.

Physical handicaps may affect Bender-Gestalt performance. Some children with poor Bender-Gestalt drawings have undetected visual problems, while others, who demonstrate difficulties in motor control, may be suffering from the first signs of disorders such as muscular dystrophy or multiple sclerosis. Hyperactive children, who have difficulty sitting still, may make serious errors on the Bender-Gestalt. Certain medical conditions, such as low birth weight, cerebral palsy, and sickle cell anemia, can interfere with performance. Obviously, children with severe visual impairments are not able to take the Bender-Gestalt unless they wear glasses. Bender-Gestalt scores of deaf children have been found to be lower than those of children with normal hearing (Gilbert & Levee, 1967; Keogh, Vernon, & Smith, 1970). Deafness has many etiologies, including brain damage which could affect visual-motor ability.

Social and cultural influences: Ethnic minority children, especially black children, tend to score lower on the Bender-Gestalt than white children (Koppitz, 1975). A number of reasons have been proposed to account for their poorer performance, including slower perceptual-motor development, delayed maturation, difficulty in understanding the task requirements, insufficient motivation, limited perceptual-motor experiences, cognitive deficits, and insufficient experience in the use of verbal mediation in solving nonverbal tasks (Greenberg & Alshan, 1974; Vega & Powell, 1970).

There is some evidence to suggest that when IQ is held constant across ethnic groups, no significant differences emerge between black children and white children (Zuelzer, Stedman, & Adams, 1976). Consequently, perceptual-motor differences between ethnic groups may be related to differences in level of measured intelligence or to some other variable or variables that may be mediated by level of measured intelligence, such as motivation or task orientation.

There are few differences between the perceptual-motor skills of Mexican-American children and those of Anglo-American children (Zuelzer et al., 1976). However, American Indian children between 5 and 10 years of age have less well-developed visual-motor skills than Anglo-American children (Price, 1976; Taylor & Thweatt, 1972). By the age of 11 to 12 years, the two groups perform at a similar level. Perceptual immaturity and differences in school experiences might account for the group differences at the younger ages. Overall, the Bender-Gestalt appears to be less culturally loaded than are most tests of cognitive ability.

Sex differences: Minor sex differences appear on the Bender-Gestalt (Koppitz, 1975). Girls in kindergarten may score slightly higher than boys, but the differences disappear by first grade. Although girls mature earlier in their visual-motor development, these differences disappear over time.

Comment on the Bender-Gestalt. The Bender-Gestalt is a useful part of an assessment battery. However, it should not be used to make definitive diagnoses. Rather, it can guide us in developing hypotheses about the child's perceptual-motor ability. It provides useful indices about the perceptual-motor development of children, particularly those between 5 and 8 years of age, and perceptual-motor deficits.

Developmental Test of Visual Motor Integration

The Developmental Test of Visual Motor Integration (Beery, 1967) is a perceptual-motor ability test for children from ages 2 through 15 years. It contains twenty-four geometric forms, arranged in order of increasing levels of difficulty, which are copied by the child. The test can be either individually or group administered in about 15 minutes. Each design is scored on a pass-fail basis. The total raw score is converted into developmental-age equivalents, with separate tables for boys and girls.

Standardization. The standardization group consisted of 1,039 normal children, 3 to 14 years of age, from suburban, urban, and rural areas in Illinois (Beery, 1967). No other information was given about the standardization sample.

Reliability. Test-retest reliabilities, with intervals of two to eight weeks, range in the low .80s, while internal consistency reliabilities range from the .70s to the low .90s. Interrater reliabilities are in the .90s.

Validity. The concurrent validity of the test is satisfactory, using such criteria as chronological age ($r = .89$), reading achievement ($r = .50$), mental age (r from .38 to .59), perceptual skill ($r = .80$), and psycholinguistic skills (r from .20 to .81).

Comment on the Developmental Test of Visual Motor Integration. The Visual Motor Integration test is a useful test for measuring visual-motor ability. In spite of the high interrater reliability, a large number of subjective scoring judgments are required. The test would benefit if scaled scores and a more representative standardization sample were made available. Many of the interpretative rationales described for the Bender-Gestalt also apply to the Developmental Test of Visual Motor Integration.

Purdue Perceptual-Motor Survey

The Purdue Perceptual-Motor Survey (Roach & Kephart, 1966) provides a qualitative assessment of perceptual-motor abilities of second, third, and fourth grade children. The survey is based on the premise that the development of adequate perceptual-motor skills is necessary for acquiring academic skills. It consists of twenty-two items (eleven subtests) divided into five behavioral areas: balance and posture, body image and differentiation, perceptual-motor match, ocular control, and form perception. The survey takes approximately ten to fifteen minutes to administer.

Balance and posture items identify rhythm, coordination, and balance in bilateral activities. Body image and differentiation items assess the child's knowledge of body parts, ability to imitate and move the body as directed, and physical strength. Perceptual-motor match items require the accurate reproduction of patterns. Ocular control requires maintaining visual contact with a moving penlight. Form perception requires copying seven simple geometric forms. Scores are assigned on the basis of qualitative judgments. The resulting scale is primarily ordinal.

Standardization. The survey was standardized on 200 normal children, randomly selected from the first, second, third, and fourth grades in one school serving a wide range of socioeconomic levels. No information was given about the racial composition of the normative group.

Reliability. A test-retest reliability coefficient of .95 was reported for a small sample of thirty children over an interval of one week.

Validity. The manual fails to provide adequate validity data for the survey. A factor analysis (Dunsing, 1969) generally supported the divisions of the survey, but found six factors instead of five. Another factor analysis also supports the construct validity of the survey (Neeman, 1972). Correlation coefficients of .75 and higher have been found between the survey and reading and arithmetic grades at two- and three-year follow-ups (Dunsing, 1969). Advantaged kindergarten children perform better than disadvantaged kindergarten children on the survey (Lietz, 1972).

Comment on the Purdue Perceptual-Motor Survey. The theoretical basis of the test may be invalid. Salvia and Ysseldyke (1978) find no support for the claim that the development of adequate perceptual-motor skills is a necessary prerequisite to the acquisition of academic skills. Further, Jamison (1972) stresses that the skills assessed by the survey may not be necessary for academic learning; also, it is not known what specific levels (if any) of perceptual-motor development are attained by various age groups. However, some research demonstrates construct validity for the survey (Dunsing, 1969; Lietz, 1972).

Landis (1972) suggests that another problem with the survey is that it is unusable by all except experienced clinicians; the manual includes minimal interpretative data. The test apparently is useful only for those knowledgeable about perceptual functioning. In summary, although the Purdue Perceptual-Motor Survey is easy to administer and has high reliability, it is difficult to interpret and validity is still not sufficiently well established. The survey assists in identifying specific perceptual and motor behaviors, but it cannot be used to recommend perceptual-motor training as a way of enhancing academic success.

Developmental Test of Visual Perception

The Frostig Developmental Test of Visual Perception (DTVP) (Frostig, Maslow, Lefever, & Whittlesey, 1964) is a nonverbal test designed to evaluate visual perception in children aged 3-0 years to 9-0 years. The test is intended to serve as a measure of visual-motor maturity and as a basis for developing remedial programs.

The DTVP consists of five subtests designed to measure various areas of visual perception and visual-motor integration. Eye-hand Coordination involves drawing lines between boundaries of varied widths. Figure-ground Perception requires discriminating between intersecting shapes and finding hidden figures. Form Constancy involves the identification of circles and squares in a variety of visual contexts. Position in Space requires differentiation between figures in an identical position and those in a reversed or rotated position. Perception of Spatial Relationships involves copying patterns by connecting dots.

The DTVP may be individually or group administered, takes approximately forty minutes, and is objectively scored. Because the test requires minimum use of language, it can be used with deaf, hard-of-hearing, and non-English-speaking children.

The test yields three types of scores: scaled scores, perceptual-age equivalents, and a perceptual quotient. Perceptual-age equivalents are available for each subtest, while the perceptual quotient is based on the overall performance. Unfortunately, the scores are not uniformly scaled throughout the age levels of the test. For example, while the mean scaled score for each subtest is approximately 10, the standard deviations range from .99 to 2.71. These statistics are only for ages 5-0 to 8-0 years; no means or standard deviations are given for ages below 5-0 years or above 8-0 years. For each age group the perceptual quotient has a median of about 100 and a standard deviation of about 16. However, the median varies from 96 to 104 for the various age levels covered by the scale. Standard errors of measurement are not presented either for the scaled scores or for the perceptual quotient. The psychometric properties of the Frostig are poor and do not meet acceptable levels needed for a diagnostic instrument.

Standardization. The DTVP was standardized on a population of 2,116 nursery school and public elementary school children, primarily middle class and living in Southern California, between the ages of 3-0 years and 9-0 years. Unfortunately, the standardization was not even representative of Southern California, let alone the United States. There were no black children in the

norm group, and other minority groups were poorly represented. The poor standardization group again limits the usefulness of the DTVP.

Although the standardization sample ranged from ages 3-0 years to 9-0 years, it appears that the DTVP is most applicable for children 4-0 years to 7-0 years, since it is within this age range that maximum perceptual development occurs. Also, the reliability of the test for children below 4-0 years and above 7-0 years is not reported in the manual.

Reliability. Test-retest reliabilities of the perceptual quotient and total scale scores obtained from the manual and from other studies range from .69 to .80 for groups of children in kindergarten, first, and second grade.[2] These reliabilities are somewhat low. Subtest reliabilities are even less satisfactory, ranging from .22 (Position in Space) to .80 (Form Constancy). Thus, the test-retest reliability of the total test, and especially of the individual subtests, is somewhat questionable.

Split-half reliability was not determined for ages under five years. For ages 5 through 9, split-half reliability of the DTVP ranged from .78 to .89 based on the total raw scores. Individual subtest split-half correlations ranged from .35 (Position in Space) to .96 (Figure-ground Perception). Boyd and Randle (1970) and Silverstein, Ulfeldt, and Price (1970) found split-half reliability coefficients similar to those reported in the manual for the five subtests, using samples of first grade and mentally retarded children. In addition, the latter researchers found the reliability of the test as a whole to be .95, which is considerably higher than that reported in the manual.

Validity. Validity studies are reported in the manual, using teacher ratings of classroom adjustment, motor coordination, and intellectual functioning for a sample of 374 kindergarten children. The validity coefficients were .44, .50, and .50, respectively. Correlations between the DTVP and the Goodenough Draw-A-Man Test ranged from

.32 to .46 for 715 kindergarten, first, and second grade children. Sprague (1963) reported a correlation of .24 between the DTVP and the Goodenough for 111 kindergarten children and a correlation of .27 for the same children a year later. These correlations indicate that the two tests measure relatively distinct factors, although some overlap is evident.

The authors claim, without presenting confirming evidence, that the five subtests measure different visual perceptual processes. A variety of factor analytic studies of the DTVP fail to verify the authors' claim. In most cases only one general visual perceptual factor is found,[3] although in a minority of instances two or three specific factors also appear.[4] Silverstein (1972a), however, has reanalyzed various factor analytic studies and reported that, on the average, 40 percent of the total variance of the DTVP subtests is common variance. Silverstein's results suggest that there is some support for interpretation of visual perceptual abilities based on individual subtest scores. However, the overall perceptual quotient appears to be the best measure of perceptual development derived from the DTVP.[5]

Several studies have investigated the ability of the DTVP to predict reading readiness and achievement in samples of children in kindergarten, first, and second grades.[6] While some of these investigations report significant but low correlations (.23 to .67) between the DTVP and reading achievement, the majority indicate that the DTVP subtests and perceptual quotient are not significantly related to reading achievement. Consequently, the DTVP should not be used as a predictor of reading readiness or later reading skill.

The DTVP has been found to correlate significantly with IQs from the Stanford-Binet and Wechsler Intelligence Scale for Children (.41), with the American School Intelligence Test (.64), and with the Slosson Intelligence Test (.33 and .49).[7] Among mentally retarded children, those with average perceptual abilities achieve better WISC IQs on all three scales than do those with poor perceptual abilities (Allen, Haupt, & Jones, 1965).

The Frostig training program was developed to teach children with visual perceptual difficulties certain basic learning skills which are presumed to determine later learning and academic achievement. The DTVP manual, however, provides few guidelines for determining when a child is in need of such remediation. There appears to be no justification for offering remedial programs based on the results of the DTVP alone.

While several investigations have found the Frostig training program to be effective in increasing scores on the DTVP, none have found the program to be influential in improving reading achievement skills,[8] and few have found support for using the Frostig program to improve visual perceptual abilities (Anderson & Stern, 1972; Beck & Talkington, 1970).

Comment on the Developmental Test of Visual Perception. The DTVP seems best interpreted as a general measure of visual perception, with the perceptual quotient being the most stable measure available from the test. The test may be useful as a screening instrument for perceptual development in preschool children, but should not be used as a measure of reading readiness or to predict reading skill. Further, specific types of remediation should not be recommended on the basis of particular subtest scores, as individual subtests are not sufficiently reliable. There is little if any justification for use of training programs based on the DTVP with children with learning disabilities (Mann, 1972).

Assessment of Auditory Perception

Auditory Discrimination Test

The Auditory Discrimination Test (Wepman, 1973) measures children's ability to hear accurately differences in phonemes. The test consists of forty word-pairs matched for familiarity, length, and phonetic category. Ten of the word-pairs do not differ, while thirty word-pairs differ in a single phoneme (initial consonants, final consonants, or medial vowels). The examiner reads each pair, and the child must indicate whether the words are the same or different.

The score is determined by the total number of correctly identified unidentical pairs. There are controls for guessing and ability to follow instructions. If the score is less than ten, or if the child identifies seven of the identical pairs as unidentical, the test is considered to be invalid. A 5-point scale is used to classify the scores. The test comes in two forms. Administration time is approximately five to ten minutes.

Standardization. No information is presented in the manual about the norm group.

Reliability. Test-retest and parallel-form reliabilities are in the .90s.

Validity. Various attempts have been made to validate the test. First, the Auditory Discrimination Test scores increase with age level (median score at age 5 years is 24 and at age 8 years it is 27). This range, however, is very limited. Second, scores obtained from children in first grade have slight predictive validities (*r* in the .20s and .30s) with Metropolitan Achievement Tests scores obtained from children in the fourth through sixth grades. Third, low scores tend to be obtained by children who have poor reading scores and below-average intelligence. Finally, first grade children with known articulatory problems obtained lower scores than those without articulatory problems.

Comment on the Auditory Discrimination Test. The Auditory Discrimination Test, Locke (1979) observed, has a number of major faults. First, its failure to describe the normative group is a major limitation. Second, there is no evidence that performance on the test is related to reading or to articulation or to language. Third, the test fails to sample many important contrasts of English. Fourth, children may fail some items and yet be able to say syllables correctly when they are asked to imitate them. Locke concluded that the test is not valid. He also observed that "all of the popular discrimina-

tion tests suffer—more or less equally—from the problem of phonemic irrelevance and insufficient trials" (p. 126).

Lindamood Auditory Conceptualization Test

The Lindamood Auditory Conceptualization Test (Lindamood & Lindamood, 1971) is an individually administered test designed to evaluate the child's ability (a) to discriminate speech sounds and (b) to perceive the number and order of sounds within a spoken pattern. The test, which is designed for use with children from kindergarten through grade twelve, assists in the identification of auditory perceptual deficiencies. Two alternate forms of the test are available.

The test has two parts. The first part requires discrimination of individual sounds, such as /g/ /b/ /v/, while the second part requires discrimination of longer sound patterns, such as /op/ from /vop/. The second part entails the identification of omissions, substitutions, shifts, repetitions, and differentiations.

A unique method is used to administer the test. Eighteen blocks, with six different colors, are used by the child to indicate sounds. The child selects a color to represent a sound. For example, if the examiner says "Show me /g/ /g/," the child is required to pick out any two blocks of the same color to represent this sound. An audio-tape is available to train examiners to administer the test.

Before the test proper is begun, a pretest is administered which is designed to determine whether or not the child knows the following concepts needed for the test: (a) left and right, (b) first and last, (c) same and different, and (d) counting to four. If the child does not know these concepts, the test cannot be administered. The test takes approximately twenty to thirty minutes to administer, pretest included.

Each item is scored either pass or fail (1 or 0). The raw scores for each part are multiplied by a constant to obtain a converted score. The total raw scores, by deciles, can be converted to percentiles for kindergarten through grade six; however, there are no conversion tables for grades seven through twelve. In addition, there are no tables for converting raw scores on the separate parts to percentiles. Recommended minimum scores are also provided for kindergarten through grade twelve, but the test reaches a ceiling after grade six. There are no standard scores available.

Standardization. The standardization sample consisted of 660 boys and girls in kindergarten through grade twelve from a large heterogeneous school district in Monterey, California. The sample included a range of socioeconomic classes, ethnic backgrounds, and linguistic backgrounds. There were 420 children from kindergarten through grade six, and 240 children from grades seven through twelve. The children were selected from groups rated by their teachers as performing well or poorly in school.

Reliability. Alternate-form reliability with a sample of fifty-two children was high, $r = .96$. No information is available about within-grade reliabilities.

Validity. Correlations between the combined reading and spelling subtests of the Wide Range Achievement Test and the Lindamood Auditory Conceptualization Test for the standardization sample ranged from .66 to .81, with a median of .75. In another sample of fifty-two children, the correlations ranged from .72 to .78.

Comment on the Lindamood Auditory Conceptualization Test. A possible shortcoming of the test is that examiners must have excellent diction skills. Since differences among examiners in their diction skills is a possible source of test unreliability, it is important that the test be administered only by competent speakers.

The major problem with the Lindamood Auditory Conceptualization Test is its failure to provide normative data. The lack of means, standard deviations, and scaled scores prevents an evaluation of the test's psychometric properties. Reliability and validity data, too, are insufficient. Furthermore, the test cannot be used unless the child has knowledge of certain concepts, thus limiting its use with preschool children. Finally, adequate vision is required.

In spite of the shortcomings of the Lindamood Auditory Conceptualization Test, it does provide a unique method of assessing auditory skills in such areas as sound discrimination, short-term memory, and sequencing (Butler, 1978). The test should be viewed as a screening device, rather than as an instrument that provides a precise estimate of auditory ability. Further work is needed to evaluate its psychometric properties.

Goldman-Fristoe-Woodcock Test of Auditory Discrimination

The Goldman-Fristoe-Woodcock Test of Auditory Discrimination (Goldman, Fristoe, & Woodcock, 1970) provides standardized measures of speech-sound discrimination ability for children (as young as 4 years of age) and adults. Measures of auditory discrimination are obtained (a) under ideal conditions (Quiet Subtest) and (b) in the presence of a controlled background noise (Noise Subtest). The test consists of the presentation of individual words by means of a cassette tape. The examinee is required to point to one of four pictures on a plate that best corresponds to the word.

The test has three parts:

1. *Training procedure.* During the training procedure the examinee is familiarized with the pictures and names that are used on the two subtests.
2. *Quiet Subtest.* Individual words are presented in the absence of any noise. This subtest provides a measure of auditory discrimination under ideal conditions.
3. *Noise Subtest.* The words are presented in the presence of a distracting "cafeteria" background noise on the tape. This subtest provides a measure of auditory discrimination under conditions similar to those encountered in everyday life.

The Goldman-Fristoe-Woodcock is relatively easy to administer, requiring a minimum of preparation and training. A tape recorder and a set of earphones are needed to monitor what the examinee is hearing. A quiet and adequately lighted testing room is recommended. The test takes approximately ten to fifteen minutes to administer.

The primary method of scoring consists of determining the number of errors made by the examinee. This number is then converted to a standard score (by age level), with a mean of 50 and standard deviation of 10 for each subtest. A supplementary clinical method for evaluating errors is also presented. This method differentiates errors made on particular types of words, such as voiced sound words (those involving use of vocal cords) or unvoiced sound words.

Standardization.   The Goldman-Fristoe-Woodcock was standardized on 745 individuals, 3 years to 84 years of age, with varying numbers of individuals (from 6 to 83) at each age level. They resided in three states—Minnesota, New Jersey, and Tennessee. Individuals with moderate or severe hearing losses were excluded from the sample. No information is given about the socioeconomic status or ethnicity of the sample.

Reliability. The internal consistency (split-half reliability) coefficient in the standardization sample is .79 for the Quiet Subtest and .68 for the Noise Subtest. The authors believe that these low reliabilities are due to the shortness of the test. In a clinical sample of 242 children, ages 4 to 12 years, the split-half reliability coefficients were .87 for the Quiet Subtest and .68 for the Noise Subtest. Test-retest reliability coefficients (interval of two weeks) for a sample of seventeen preschool speech-handicapped children yielded coefficients of .87 for the Quiet Subtest and .81 for the Noise Subtest.

Validity. The manual reports a variety of validity indices. Point-biserial correlations of .68 for the Quiet Subtest and .72 for the Noise Subtest were found between the Goldman-Fristoe-Woodcock and auditory-discrimination ability (i.e., individuals clas-

sified as having good or poor auditory discrimination ability). The two subtests had correlations of .39 in the standardization group and .53 in clinical samples. Correlations with the Stanford-Binet in a sample of forty preschool culturally disadvantaged children yielded coefficients of .60 for the Quiet Subtest and .52 for the Noise Subtest. In a sample of educable mentally retarded children, correlations were extremely low with the Peabody Picture Vocabulary Test: .15 for the Quiet Subtest and .00 with the Noise Subtest. In a sample of 122 kindergarten children, correlations with the Primary Mental Abilities Test were .48 for the Quiet Subtest and .24 for the Noise Subtest. Finally, correlations with the Auditory Attention Span for Related Syllables subtest from the Detroit Tests of Learning Aptitude were .34 for the Quiet Subtest and .20 for the Noise Subtest.

Comment on the Goldman-Fristoe-Woodcock Test of Auditory Discrimination. The psychometric properties of the Goldman-Fristoe-Woodcock are less than adequate. The reliability coefficients are not up to acceptable standards and the standard errors of measurement are quite large. Discrimination among age groups is extremely poor for various scores. For example, an error of 3 results in the exact same standard score for children ages 11 through 18. Furthermore, the test has limited validity (Bannatyne, 1975). While the test may be helpful as a crude measure of auditory discrimination, it fails to differentiate adequately among some age groups. It may be, however, that auditory discrimination skills reach a peak at some time during the preadolescent period so that only those who severely deviate from the norm can be reliably diagnosed.

Assessment of Motor Proficiency

Bruininks-Oseretsky Test of Motor Proficiency

The Bruininks-Oseretsky Test of Motor Proficiency (Bruininks, 1978) is an individually administered test that assesses gross and fine motor functioning of children from 4½ to 14½ years of age. The test contains forty-six items that are grouped into eight subtests (see Table 16-1), four of which measure gross motor skills (subtests 1, 2, 3, and 4); three, fine motor skills (subtests 6, 7, and 8); and one, both gross and fine motor skills (subtest 5). In addition to scores for each subtest, composite scores are obtained for the gross motor subtests, fine motor subtests, and total battery. A short form of fourteen items is also available that can be used as a brief survey of motor proficiency. The complete test takes between forty-five and sixty minutes to administer.

The Bruininks-Oseretsky is based on the United States adaptation of the Oseretsky Tests of Motor Proficiency (Doll, 1946). About 60 percent of the items are new, and the remainder are from the Oseretsky Tests of Motor Proficiency. The Bruininks-Oseretsky reflects advances in content, structure, and technical qualities over former versions of the tests.

Standardization. The Bruininks-Oseretsky was standardized on a population of 765 boys and girls selected from various schools, day-care centers, nursery schools, and kindergartens in the United States and Canada. A stratified sampling procedure, based on the 1970 U.S. census, was used to select the children. Stratification variables included age, sex, race, community size, and geographic region.

The test provides subtest scores, a Gross Motor Composite score, a Fine Motor Composite score, and a Battery Composite score. For each of these areas, standard scores, percentile ranks, and stanines are available. In addition, age equivalents are available for the subtest scores. Each subtest has a mean of 15 and standard deviation of 5. The composite scores have a mean of 50 and standard deviation of 10.

Reliability. Test-retest reliabilities range from .86 to .89 for the Battery Composite, and from .68 to .88 for the Fine and Gross Motor Composites. The Gross Motor Composite yields somewhat higher reliabilities than the Fine Motor Composite. Average test-retest reliabilities range from .56 to .86. Reliabilities associated with the individual subtests suggest that extreme caution is needed in using individual subtest scores as a basis for clinical interpretation. Average standard errors of measurement are 4.0 for the Battery Composite, 4.6 for the Gross Motor Composite, and 4.7 for the Fine Motor Composite.

Validity. Construct validity of the Bruininks-Oseretsky was evaluated by the follow-

TABLE 16-1.   Description of Tests on the Bruininks-Oseretsky Test of Motor Proficiency

Test	Description
1. Running Speed and Agility (one item)	Running speed
2. Balance (eight items)	Static balance and maintaining balance while executing various walking movements
3. Bilateral Coordination (eight items)	Sequential and simultaneous coordination of upper with lower limbs, and upper limbs only
4. Strength (three items)	Arm and shoulder strength, abdominal strength, and leg strength
5. Upper Limb Coordination (nine items)	Visual tracking with movements of arms and hands and precise movements of arms, hands, or fingers
6. Response Speed (one item)	Ability to respond quickly to a moving visual stimulus
7. Visual-Motor Control (eight items)	Ability to coordinate precise hand and visual movements
8. Upper Limb Speed and Dexterity (eight items)	Hand and finger dexterity, hand speed, and arm speed

ing methods: (a) relationship between test scores and chronological age, (b) internal consistency of the subtests, and (c) factor structure of the items in each subtest. Product-moment correlations between subtest scores and chronological age for the standardization sample range from .57 to .86, with a median of .78. These correlations indicate that there is a close relationship between subtest scores and chronological age. Subtest scores show the expected increase from one age group to the next. Internal consistency measures indicate that the correlations between items and their respective subtest scores are closer than between items and the total test scores.

A factor analysis, performed on the standardization sample, provides limited support for grouping the items into the various subtests. Five factors were found, with one factor (general motor ability) accounting for approximately 70 percent of the total common factor item variance. The remaining factors represented specific factors associated with the various subtests. Most of the items measuring fine motor ability (fourteen out of seventeen) loaded on the general motor ability factor. The fine motor subtests did not cluster together on clearly identifiable factors as did the gross motor subtests.

Comment on the Bruininks-Oseretsky Test of Motor Proficiency. The Bruininks-Oseretsky Test should prove to be useful in assessing gross and fine motor skills, developing and evaluating motor training programs, and screening for special purposes. It is a refinement of the previous scale which has proved to be useful for the clinical evaluation of motor skills. The manual and materials are attractive and well designed. The variety of scores available facilitates the use and interpretation of the scale.

Southern California Sensory Integration Tests

The Southern California Sensory Integration Tests (Ayres, 1972) battery is designed to assist in the diagnosis of dysfunctions of four areas of perceptual and perceptual-

motor functioning: (a) form and space perception, (b) postural and bilateral integration, (c) tactile perception, and (d) motor skills. The battery covers an age range from 4 through 10 years.

The battery contains seventeen tests: Space Visualization, Figure-Ground Perception, Position in Space, Design Copying, Motor Accuracy, Kinesthesia, Manual Form Perception, Finger Identification, Graphesthesia, Localization of Tactile Stimuli, Double Tactile Stimuli Perception, Imitation of Postures, Crossing Mid-line of Body, Bilateral Motor Coordination, Right-Left Discrimination, Standing Balance: Eyes Open, and Standing Balance: Eyes Closed. Included in the battery are the former Ayres Space Test, Southern California Motor Accuracy Test, Southern California Figure-Ground Visual Perception Test, Southern California Kinesthesia and Tactile Perception Tests, and the Southern California Perceptual-Motor Test.

All of the tests are reasonably brief, most of them are timed, and the entire battery can be administered in seventy-five to ninety minutes, although two sessions of approximately forty-five minutes each are recommended. The battery should be administered only by persons thoroughly familiar with the nature of sensory integrative dysfunctions.

Raw scores are converted to standard scores ($\bar{X} = 0$, $SD = 1$) for each test. However, some scaled scores were obtained by extrapolation, thereby reducing the reliability and validity of the norms. Consequently, the norms should be used with extreme caution.

Standardization. The battery was standardized using several different groups of tests, each administered at different times to different but similar samples of children throughout the area in and around Los Angeles, California. The norm groups were selected from public and private schools, organizations, and children's centers. Each group varied in size, with thirty to fifty children for each age from 4 through 8 years.

Unfortunately, the demographic characteristics of the normative samples are not given.

Reliability. Test-retest reliabilities (time interval unknown) are reported for sixteen of the seventeen tests, the exception being the Motor Accuracy Test. Reliabilities ranged from a low of .01 to a high of .89 (median = .49). For the Motor Accuracy Test, internal consistency reliability coefficients ranged from .67 to .94 (median = .86). Standard errors of measurement reported for the battery ranged from .80 to 58.5. The extreme range of reliabilities indicates that many scores are too unreliable to be of value. It is therefore imperative that before any test is interpreted its reliability and standard error of measurement be obtained from the test manual. There is no simple way to interpret profiles, because the standard errors of measurement are not consistent among the tests.

Validity. No validity data are reported in the manual.

Comment on the Southern California Sensory Integration Tests. The Southern California Sensory Integration Tests battery measures perceptual and perceptual-motor skill areas (e.g., kinesthesia and tactile perception) that are not usually measured by other tests. However, the battery's psychometric properties are extremely poor. The absence of any validity data, the large spread of reliability coefficients, and the wide range of the standard errors of measurement associated with the tests indicate that the battery cannot be used with any degree of confidence.

In order to use the battery, the examiner should become familiar with the various behaviors assessed by the tests; this limits the number of persons who can use it properly without special training. Because of the weak normative and reliability data, heavy reliance must be placed on personal intuition (Westman, 1978). Still another disadvantage is that the demographic characteristics of

the normative samples are lacking. The battery should be viewed only as a rough screening guide for purposes of measuring various sensory abilities. Overall, the battery fails to meet acceptable psychometric standards.

Comment on Tests of Visual-Motor Perception, Auditory Perception, and Motor Proficiency

Many of the tests covered in this chapter do not meet acceptable psychometric standards. Their standardization samples are limited, reliabilities are below acceptable standards, and little is known about their validity. In addition, there is some evidence that tests of auditory discrimination may not correlate highly with one another (Koenke, 1978). However, each one contributes in some way to the assessment process. Further refinements are needed, particularly in the area of assessment of auditory perception. Thus, the results obtained from many of these instruments should be viewed as tentative, subject to verification through a more detailed study of the child's abilities.

Summary

1. This chapter covered nine tests that were designed to measure visual-motor integration, visual perception, auditory perception, or motor proficiency.

2. The Bender Visual Motor Gestalt Test is the most popular of all the visual-motor tests, and has received much study. The Koppitz Developmental Scoring System is helpful in evaluating the maturational skills of children, primarily from 5 through 8 years of age. The major errors studied in the system are (a) distortion of shape, (b) rotation, (c) integration, and (d) perseveration. Indicators of possible emotional difficulties also can be obtained. The reliability of the Developmental Scoring System is not adequate for the purpose of individual diagnosis. The system has acceptable validity when used to assess perceptual-motor development, but concurrent and predictive validities are too

low for predicting school achievement or achievement in reading or arithmetic.

3. Possible diagnostic indicators of brain damage on the Bender-Gestalt are as follows: rotation, difficulties with angles, destruction of the gestalt, perseveration, disproportions, integration difficulties, additions or exclusions, gross oversimplification, fragmentation, and crowding. These signs, however, also appear in the records of normal children. A diagnosis of brain damage should never be made on the basis of the Bender-Gestalt alone. It has not been possible to differentiate accurately Bender-Gestalt indications of immaturity from those of pathology. Black children tend to obtain lower scores on the Bender-Gestalt than white children, whereas there are relatively few differences between the scores of Mexican-American and Anglo-American children. Sex differences are minor on the Bender-Gestalt.

4. The Developmental Test of Visual Motor Integration is a useful test for measuring visual-motor ability.

5. The Purdue Perceptual-Motor Survey has unsatisfactory psychometric properties, but provides some qualitative indices of perceptual-motor abilities.

6. The Developmental Test of Visual Perception may have some usefulness as a test of visual perception. However, recommendation of training programs based on the test does not appear to be warranted.

7. The Auditory Discrimination Test has serious shortcomings, but it may provide a rough estimate of auditory discrimination in children between 5 and 8 years of age.

8. The Lindamood Auditory Conceptualization Test has some shortcomings and limitations, but still can serve as a screening device for assessing auditory skills.

9. The Goldman-Fristoe-Woodcock Test of Auditory Discrimination has poor psychometric properties, but may serve as a crude measure of auditory discrimination.

10. The Bruininks-Oseretsky Test of Motor Proficiency is a useful test for assessing gross and fine motor skills of children ages 4½ to 14½ years.

11. The Southern California Sensory Integration Tests battery has poor psychometric properties. However, the battery can be useful as a rough screening device for examiners who are specifically trained in the area of perceptual and perceptual-motor functions.

CHAPTER

17

Assessment of Adaptive Behavior and Behavior Problems

One may say broadly that all animals that have been carefully observed have behaved so as to confirm the philosophy in which the observer believed before his observation began. Nay, more, they have all displayed the national characteristics of the observer. Animals studied by Americans rush about frantically with an incredible display of bustle and pep, and at last achieve the desired result by chance. Animals observed by Germans sit still and think, and at last evolve solutions out of their own inner consciousness.

BERTRAND RUSSELL

EXHIBIT 17-1. Psychological Evaluation: Fetal Alcohol Syndrome (Second Reevaluation)

Name: Tim
Date of birth: January 19, 1976
Chronological age: 3-7
Date of examination: September 5, 1979
Date of report: September 5, 1979

Tests Administered

Vineland Social Maturity Scale:

	6/77	8/78	9/79
Chronological Age	1-5	2-7	3-7
Social Age	7 mo.	1-2	1-4
Deviation Social Quotient	68	68	62

Bayley Scales of Infant Development:

	6/77	8/78	9/79
Mental Age	5 mo.	10 mo.	12 mo.
Motor Age	7 mo.	1-1	1-6

History and Referral

This is our second reevaluation of Tim. Previous evaluations indicated that Tim was suffering from a fetal alcohol syndrome. Initial evaluation (6/77) indicated rather severe developmental delay. The first follow-up reevaluation in August 1978 found some improvement, but Tim was still at least 50 percent delayed in development.

Observations and Interview

Tim came with his foster mother for the interview. He was described by his foster mother as being highly mischievous. He likes to throw things around and occasionally scratches other children. Tim also plays with his excrement, and punishment has not been effective in getting him to stop this behavior. As a result of a recent operation to correct his cleft palate, his speech has improved so that he now is able to say "Ma ma" and "Da da."

Tim is still a very small child for his age, and still has some physical stigmata. During the interview he walked around the room freely and investigated various objects without hesitancy. When his mother was asked to leave, Tim was momentarily upset, but he soon became engaged in various activities. Tim was silent throughout the testing session. His attention span was adequate for most of the tasks, with the exception of the more difficult ones. He responded to these difficult tasks by knocking the test materials on the floor.

Current test results reveal that Tim's mental and motor progress in the last year appears to be minimal. Although he is now able to stand on

EXHIBIT 17-1   (cont.)

one foot with slight support, tries standing on a walking board, and stands up from the supine position without first turning to his stomach, he cannot, as would be expected from a child his age, stand on either foot without support or walk up or down stairs even with support. He is able to remove a pellet from a bottle, put six of eight beads in a box, and turn the pages of a book. However, he is unable to put cubes in a cup on command, build a tower of blocks, or complete a peg board.

Tim's social progress likewise has been limited. As mentioned by his mother, he frequently throws things, behaves aggressively toward other children, and smears feces. While the cleft palate operation seems to have helped his constant drooling to some degree, it is still not completely under control. Tim still cannot use a spoon for eating or drink from a cup unassisted. He can now, however, mark with a pencil or crayon and walk around a room unattended.

Summary

Tim, a 3-7-year-old child, has been diagnosed as having a fetal alcohol syndrome. His psycho-motor and social development are extremely slow. Test results over a two-year period show a marked decline in mental growth rate. He is cur-

rently functioning at the 12 month level mentally, the 18 month level motorically, and the 16 month level socially. The prognosis does not appear favorable, given these levels of functioning and the extremely small amount of improvement over the past two years.

Recommendations

1. Parental counseling is advisable in order to inform Tim's foster parents of his declining mental growth rate and to assist them in finding an appropriate educational placement. Parental counseling, in addition, should include a program to teach Tim's parents appropriate behavior modification techniques that are designed to help them control his fecal smearing and hostile behavior toward others.
2. Tim should be evaluated by a physical therapist. He appears to need a program of physical therapy that can capitalize on his existing motor skills and build on his improved mouth and tongue control.
3. Tim should be reevaluated next year to reassess his progress and adjust therapeutic and educational goals accordingly.

_____

Examiner

(See Exhibit 14-1 [p. 235] for the initial evaluation.)

Assessment of Adaptive Behavior

Adaptive behavior has been defined by the American Association on Mental Deficiency (Grossman, 1973) as behavior that is effective in meeting the natural and social demands of one's environment. The assessment of adaptive behavior focuses on two major functions: (a) the degree to which individuals are able to function and maintain themselves independently, and (b) the degree to which they meet satisfactorily the culturally imposed demands of personal and social responsibility. Thus, adaptive behavior reflects a person's competence in meeting independence needs and the social demands of his or her environment. These definitions, while important, are broad and somewhat vague because there is no way of knowing the kinds of environments in which

individuals will be required to function. Furthermore, there is no one instrument that can measure all of the relevant domains of adaptive behavior.

Adaptive behavior may be reflected primarily in terms of maturation during the preschool years, academic performance during the school years, and social and economic independence in adulthood. Adaptive behavior covers a wide range of behaviors including perceptual abilities, motor skills, physical fitness, speech proficiency, vocational competence, and academic achievement. Adaptive behavior scales have been developed to provide information about individuals, primarily those who are mentally retarded, that is helpful for classification, training, and treatment decisions. An instrument used to measure adaptive behavior, however, should never be the sole criterion for evaluating a child's adaptive abilities. The child's culture, socioeconomic status, motivation, and parental expectations, to give just a few examples, must be considered. While adaptive behavior scales provide one approach to the assessment of social adjustment, they do not measure all aspects of social adjustment. Adaptive behavior scores are complex products of a myriad of personal, social, cognitive, and situational variables (Brooks & Baumeister, 1977).

Children who have delayed or deficient development likely will have more difficulty in adapting to the environment than normally developing children, and will be less able to meet societal demands. It is important to recognize that adaptive rating scales and other behavioral rating scales cannot be entirely objective, because behaviors may be viewed differently by parents and by teachers, and the same behavior may be judged adaptive in one setting and maladaptive in another (Leland, 1978). Leland is of the opinion that adaptive behavior scales cannot depend upon norm-referenced standardization, because the behaviors themselves are not "standard."

The assessment of adaptive behavior usually is performed by interviewing a parent or teacher or caretaker who knows the individual. Informants are required to make judgments about the child's (or adult's) functioning. These judgments, however, are subject to bias and distortion. Therefore, it is important that the informants' credibility be evaluated. If there is doubt about their credibility, the obtained estimates of adaptive behavior should not be used. Informants also reveal during the interview their own attitudes toward the child (or adult) and toward the various areas of adaptive behavior and social competence incorporated in the scale.

Well-normed adaptive behavior scales have a variety of applications, including (a) identifying areas of behavioral (and sometimes affective) strength and deficiency of an individual (or group); (b) providing an objective basis for comparisons of an individual's ratings over time in order to plot progress or to evaluate a training program; (c) comparing ratings on the same individual under different situations (e.g., home, school, ward); (d) comparing the ratings of different raters; (e) providing a standardized way of reporting information between and within organizations; and (f) stimulating the development of new training programs and research. Some scales also provide schedules of normal development. Although there are many instruments used to assess adaptive behavior, only some of the more popular ones are discussed in this chapter.

AAMD *Adaptive Behavior Scale*

The American Association on Mental Deficiency Adaptive Behavior Scale (ABS) (Nihira, Foster, Shellhaas, & Leland, 1974) is a behavior rating scale for use with mentally retarded, emotionally maladjusted, and developmentally disabled individuals who are institutionalized. It covers an age range from 3 to 69 years. Two types of competencies are assessed: behavioral and affective. The scale provides information that is useful in evaluating the personal and social resources of institutionalized individuals. The 1974 version is a revision of the first scale, published in 1969.

Part I of the ABS covers ten behavioral domains and measures basic survival skills and habits considered to be important to the maintenance of personal independence in daily living (see Table 17-1). In Part II, the fourteen domains focus primarily on maladaptive behavior related to personality and behavioral disorders. Part I is organized along developmental lines, while Part II focuses on maladaptive behavior.

The ABS, which takes approximately fifteen to thirty minutes to administer, can be administered by persons with minimal training. Information about the individual (subject) is obtained by using one of three methods. In first-person assessment, the informant must be familiar with the individual and have had enough professional training to make appropriate ratings. In the interview method, which is most useful with parents, the interviewer completes the scale based on the information provided by the parents. In third-party assessment, more than one informant may be used to obtain the desired information, including ward attendants, parents, and nurses.

Standardization. Standardization of the ABS was based on approximately 4,000 persons residing in sixty-eight facilities for the mentally retarded throughout the United States. The manual presents percentile norms for eleven age groups from 3 to 69 years. These norms, however, do not take into account differing cognitive ability levels (Sundberg, Snowden, & Reynolds, 1978).

Reliability. Unfortunately, the manual fails to provide test-retest reliability or estimates of internal consistency reliability for the scale. This is a serious limitation of the ABS.

Interrater reliabilities, however, are reported. Interrater reliability is acceptable for Part I, with r ranging from .71 to .93 ($\bar{X} = .86$), but it is questionable for Part II, since r ranges from a low of .37 to a high of .77 ($\bar{X} = .57$). No other reliabilities were reported. The manual states that these reliabilities can be regarded as conservative estimates of the true reliability coefficients, as they may have been influenced by the restricted range of the sample population.

Correlations between the domain scores indicate that only a few of the domains tend

TABLE 17-1.   AAMD Adaptive Behavior Scale Domains

Part I *(10 behavior domains)*	
I. Independent functioning	VIII. Self-direction
A. Eating	A. Initiative
B. Toilet use	B. Perseverance
C. Cleanliness	C. Leisure time
D. Appearance	IX. Responsibility
E. Care of clothing	X. Socialization
F. Dressing and undressing	
G. Travel	
H. General independent functioning	
II. Physical development	
A. Sensory development	*Part II*
B. Motor development	*(14 domains related to personality and behavior disorders)*
III. Economic activity	
A. Money handling and budgeting	I. Violent and destructive behavior
B. Shopping skills	II. Antisocial behavior
IV. Language development	III. Rebellious behavior
A. Expression	IV. Untrustworthy behavior
B. Comprehension	V. Withdrawal
C. Social language development	VI. Stereotyped behavior and odd mannerisms
V. Numbers and time	VII. Inappropriate interpersonal manners
VI. Domestic activity	VIII. Unacceptable vocal habits
A. Cleaning	IX. Unacceptable or eccentric habits
B. Kitchen duties	X. Self-abusive behavior
C. Other domestic activities	XI. Hyperactive tendencies
VII. Vocational activity	XII. Sexually aberrant behavior
	XIII. Psychological disturbances
	XIV. Use of medications

Reprinted by permission of the publisher and author from C. J. Fogelman (Ed.), *AAMD Adaptive Behavior Scale Manual, 1974 Revision*, pp. 6–7. Copyright 1974, American Association on Mental Deficiency.

to overlap. In a study (Leva, 1976) of 338 mentally retarded institutionalized children, the scales that were significantly related were Self-destruction and Socialization (*r* = .73), Self-destruction and Responsibility (*r* = .50), and Responsibility and Socialization (*r* = .68). These findings suggest that most of the scales are generally measuring different facets of adaptive behavior.

Validity. The ABS has been found to discriminate between individuals (a) who are classified at different adaptive behavior levels by clinical judgment and (b) who differ as to type of placement within the institution (Nihira et al., 1974). The scale is sensitive to changes related to a rehabilitation program. Performance on the ABS also is related to intelligence. In a study (Christian & Malone, 1973) of 129 institutionalized, mentally retarded individuals, the ABS (1969 version) and IQ were highly correlated (*r* = .75).

Factor analyses on the domain scores for the ABS (1969 version) delineated three major dimensions: Personal Independence, Social Maladaptation, and Personal Maladaptation (Nihira, 1969a, 1969b). The obtained factor structure was found to be relatively stable across a wide span of age ranges. These findings provide some construct validity for the ABS.

While the ABS possesses some validity, a report by Millham, Chilcutt, and Atkinson (1976) indicates that serious discrepancies exist between ratings made on the ABS and those obtained by behavioral ratings. In 400 ratings of adaptive behavior levels across ten behavior domains in a sample of mentally retarded persons, more than half (56 percent) of the ratings were found to differ from those obtained by direct observation of the individuals' performance. Millham et al. recommended that neither placement decisions nor behavioral statements be made on the basis of ABS scores alone.

Comment on the AAMD Adaptive Behavior Scale. The ABS is a clinically useful scale that provides information about important areas of competence for mentally retarded persons. Practitioners and researchers have

found the scale to be useful, especially in describing individuals' daily living performance and adequacy of complex social and interpersonal behavior.

Despite the useful applications of the ABS, it has some drawbacks. Its standardization group is limited, as it contained only mentally retarded individuals residing in institutions. Reliability data are limited, and validity, too, is not sufficiently established. Much work is needed to determine how useful the scale will be as a measure of adaptive behavior.

AAMD Adaptive Behavior Scale–Public School Version

The AAMD Adaptive Behavior Scale–Public School Version (ABS-PSV) (Lambert, Windmiller, Cole, & Figueroa, 1975) is a re-standardization of the Adaptive Behavior Scale (ABS) originally constructed for and normed on an institutionalized, mentally retarded population. The ABS-PSV is used with children ages 7-3 years to 13-2 years in the second through sixth grades. The scale aids school personnel in obtaining a measure of the child's adaptive behavior level and in determining areas of functioning where remediation may be applied. The ABS-PSV is similar to the ABS, except that some of the domains, not applicable to behaviors in the school setting, have been eliminated (Domestic Activity for Part I, Self-Abusive Behavior and Sexually Aberrant Behavior for Part II). The remainder of the domains in Part I and Part II of the scale are the same as those in the ABS.

The ABS-PSV is administered in the same manner as is the standard version, taking approximately fifteen to thirty minutes. Parents, as well as teachers, are encouraged to fill out the ABS-PSV in order to make the record as complete as possible (Lambert, 1978b).

Standardization. The ABS-PSV was standardized on a sample of 2,600 children, ages 7 years to 13 years (second through sixth grades) in fourteen school districts in California. The sample was chosen so as to be representative of the school population in

California. Percentile norms are available for sex, age, ethnic status, and level of school-classroom placement (regular class, educable mentally retarded class, and trainable mentally retarded class).

Reliability. The manual does not present reliability data for the ABS-PSV. However, a later report by Lambert (1978a) indicates that internal consistency reliabilities for Part I range from .70 to .92 ($\bar{X} = .88$) and from .80 to .92 ($\bar{X} = .87$) for Part II.

A study (Lambert, 1978b) of the agreement between parents and teachers who rated educable mentally retarded children of white or Hispanic background indicated that there were no significant differences in their ABS-PSV ratings. This led Lambert to conclude that these educable mentally retarded children could not simply be considered to be "six-hour retardates." (This term has been coined to characterize children who function in the retarded range at school but apparently not in their homes. The validity of this concept remains to be proved.)

Validity. Validity of the domain scores is reported by significance levels rather than by correlations. Therefore, there is no way to evaluate the extent to which the domain scores correlate with class placement (mentally retarded or regular classes). The manual does report, however, that most correlations were significant between the domain scores and class placement, with the exception of some correlations at the 12-year-old level. Furthermore, the manual notes that the domain scores are valid indicators of whether or not a child is likely to be classified as a regular or educable mentally retarded pupil.

The magnitude of the relationships between adaptive behavior measured in the nine domains in Part I and intelligence range from about .10 (Vocational Activity, Self-Direction, and Responsibility) to about .60 (Number and Time Concepts, Economic Activity, and Language Development) (Lambert, 1978b). Correlations between intelligence and Part II range from −.01 to

−.21. These results indicate that there are low to moderate relationships between adaptive behaviors, as measured by Part I of the ABS-PSV, and measured intelligence. Ratings of personality and behavior disorders covered in Part II do not appear to be related to intelligence.

Factor analysis of the ABS-PSV yielded four dimensions of adaptive behavior: Functional Autonomy, Interpersonal Adjustment, Social Responsibility, and Intrapersonal Adjustment (Lambert & Nicoll, 1976). These dimensions appear to be associated with adaptations to the school environment, to interpersonal behavior, and to intrapersonal stress. They provide some construct validity for the scale.

A study (Bailey & Richmond, 1979) of black and white rural South Carolina elementary school children, who were referred for possible placement in special education classes, indicated that the ABS-PSV failed to distinguish between those who were slow learners (IQs of 70 to 89) and those who were mentally retarded (IQs of 47 to 69). These results led the investigators to question the validity of the scale. They suggested that more refined instruments are needed for measuring adaptive behavior, and advised that intelligence tests and other data be used to distinguish slow learners from educable mentally retarded children.

Comment on the AAMD Adaptive Behavior Scale–Public School Version. The ABS-PSV appears to have satisfactory reliability but questionable validity for the specific populations that it is intended to serve. While the behavioral domains in Part I are more highly related to intelligence than are the domains in Part II, the entire ABS-PSV complements the assessment of intelligence. Part I of the scale may be inappropriate for children (a) who have physical handicaps, such as deafness, blindness, or orthopedic difficulties, (b) who show evidence of emotional disturbance, or (c) who have not had the opportunity to learn the adaptive behaviors being assessed (Mastenbrook, 1977). Overall, the scale provides a profile of adaptive behavior strengths and weaknesses that may be useful to the examiner in evaluating children and in developing possible educational plans.

Adaptive Behavior Inventory for Children

The Adaptive Behavior Inventory for Children (ABIC) (Mercer & Lewis, 1978) is an adaptive behavior scale that measures six areas of adaptive behavior: Family, Peers, Community, School, Earner/Consumer, and Self-Maintenance. The items in the ABIC deal with the child's family life, peer relations in school, ability to function in a variety of settings and roles, types of activities engaged in during leisure time, and extent to which the child performs routine household chores. Representative ABIC items are as follows: "How does the child get along with the children in the neighborhood?" "How often does the child become afraid at night because of bad dreams, fear of the dark, or things like that?" "Does the child use a can or bottle opener?" "How often does the child pool his/her money with other children to buy candy, soda, or other things?" The ABIC is available in both English and Spanish.

Standardization. The ABIC was standardized on a sample of 2,085 California public school children 5-0 years to 11-11 years of age. The children were randomly chosen from preselected school districts. Three ethnic groups were represented in approximately equal numbers (696 blacks, 690 Hispanics, and 696 whites).

Administration and scoring. Administration of the ABIC consists of an interview with the principal guardian of the child, usually the mother. The interview uses 242 questions, divided into two sections. Those in the first section (1 to 35) are asked of all respondents; those in the second section (36 to 242) are graded by age, and only those questions appropriate for the age of the child are administered.

Each item is scored with one of five types of responses: 0 (never), 1 (sometimes), 2 (often), N (no opportunity or not allowed), and DK (don't know). Administration is discontinued after eight consecutive 0 or N responses in any combination.

Six raw scores, one for each area, are obtained by following a seven-step procedure set out in the manual. These raw scores are then converted to scaled scores, using tables appropriate to the age of the child. The scaled-score equivalents for the six subscales and for the total score are based on a mean of 50 and standard deviation of 15. Standard errors of measurement range from 1.95 to 2.59 for the total score and from 3.83 (Community at age 6 years) to 6.88 (Self-Maintenance at age 8 years) for the six subscales.

Reliability. Split-half (odd-even) reliabilities for the scaled scores were calculated for each age level from 5 to 11 years for the entire standardization sample and separately for each ethnic group. Reliabilities for the Total Score for the complete sample and for each ethnic group were .95 or above. For the separate scales, reliabilities range from .78 (Earner/Consumer at age 5 years) to .92 (Community at ages 10 and 11 years), with a median r of .86. The manual reports intercorrelations among the subscales ranging from .66 to .87 (median $r = .77$).

Validity. Correlations between the ABIC and the WISC-R for white and black children in the standardization sample yielded coefficients of .16 with the Verbal Scale, .14 with the Performance Scale, and .17 with the Full Scale IQ. In a study of thirty-six (eighteen white and eighteen black) Alabama children 8 to 11 years of age, with IQs of 90 or less, the ABIC also was found to have a low correlation with the WISC-R ($r = .19$) and with the California Achievement Test ($r = .18$ with reading and $r = .12$ with Mathematics) (Sapp, Horton, McElroy, & Ray, 1979).

Another study (Tebeleff & Oakland, 1977) correlated the ABIC with the California Achievement Test and the WISC-R with a sample of children from Austin, Texas. Coefficients of .25 for Reading and .21 for Mathematics were reported between the ABIC and the California Achievement Test. For the WISC-R, the correlations were .28 for the Full Scale IQ for the total sample; for each ethnic group they were .31 for whites, .21 for blacks, and .27 for Mexican-Americans.

The manual reports few significant correlations between the ABIC and the four sociocultural scales (Family Size, Family Structure, Socioeconomic Status, and Urban Acculturation). The only significant correlations were between the ABIC and the Urban Acculturation scale: .03 to .19 for the total sample, .06 to .15 for blacks, .08 to .22 for Hispanics, and .06 to .18 for whites.

Correlations between the ABIC and the Bender-Gestalt were .08 for the Total Score and .04 to .14 for the subscale scores. Correlations between the ABIC and Visual Acuity were .06 for the Total Score and −.06 to −.09 for the subscale scores.

The ABIC makes no provision for consideration of the child's opportunities to learn adaptive behaviors. In fact, low-income Mexican-American children have been found to score lower than other groups on the ABIC (Gridley & Mastenbrook, 1977). Their lower scores might be associated with their having fewer opportunities and lower parental expectations for acquiring adaptive behavior skills than other groups of children (Mastenbrook, Scott, & Marriott, 1978). One of the scores on the ABIC (no opportunity or not allowed) results in a lowering of the adaptive behavior score, not in an explanation of why there is no opportunity.

The ABIC not only fails to identify lack of opportunity due to socioeconomic or cultural background, but (a) fails to single out factors in the child's home environment, apart from socioeconomic status or culture, that may inhibit the acquisition of adaptive behavior and (b) fails to consider motivational factors that contribute to failure to learn some adaptive behaviors (Mastenbrook et al., 1978). The answers to some questions on the ABIC may depend on the opportunities existing in the child's environment, and not on the child's ability or lack of it. For example, whether or not a child joins clubs or collects for charities may be contingent upon the family's attitude toward such things, and whether the child has had such an opportunity.

Comment on the Adaptive Behavior Inventory for Children. The principal strength of the ABIC is that it is a standardized instrument that measures factors such as role behavior in the home, the neighborhood, and the community. It appears to measure children's performances in six areas of adaptive behavior fairly accurately, and it constitutes a potentially strong assessment for adaptive behavior (Oakland, 1979a). It also provides opportunities for pattern analysis among the six separate areas. Scott (1979) believes that the ABIC is a better scale than either the Adaptive Behavior Scale–Public School Version or the Vineland Social Maturity Scale for determining the eligibility of children for placement in classes for the mentally retarded.

The ABIC, like other measures of adaptive behavior, still has some drawbacks. First, it relies exclusively on a guardian's report, which is not always accurate. Second, it contains some middle-class items that may discriminate against lower socioeconomic class children and ethnic minority children. Third, the norms may not be applicable nationwide, as Buckley and Oakland (1977) found that children in two Texas school districts obtained significantly lower scores on the ABIC than did the California sample.

The validity of the ABIC is said to be "judged by its ability to reflect accurately the extent to which the child is meeting the expectations of the members of the social systems covered in the scales . . . " (Mercer, 1979, p. 109), implying that the evaluation of a child's adaptation within each social system rests upon our knowledge of the expectations that surround the child within that social system. To evaluate a child's adaptation in the community, we should know the expectations that the community has for the child. Unfortunately, the ABIC does not provide a way of acquiring information about these different expectations; therefore, the ABIC is unable to evaluate the child's adaptive behavior against these expectations for each social system (Oakland, 1979b).

Vineland Social Maturity Scale

The Vineland Social Maturity Scale (Doll, 1953) is a standardized developmental schedule that measures level of social competence. It covers an age range from birth through maturity. The scale is arranged as a combination point and age scale containing 117 items that are in order of increasing difficulty. The items are divided into eight categories: Self-help General, Self-help Eating, Self-help dressing, Self-direction, Occupation, Communication, Locomotion, and Socialization. During infancy and early childhood, the scale reflects self-help skills; in adolescence, self-direction activities; in adulthood, assumption of responsibility for others. The ordering of the items reflects an increasing capacity to lead an independent life as an adult. Examples of the items are shown in Table 17-2.

A guided interview is used to obtain the information needed to complete the scale. In the case of children, the child's parent or guardian usually serves as the informant.

With older individuals, the individual himself or herself can serve as the informant. The examiner, on the basis of the information obtained in the interview, rates the items in the scale. The ratings are done by making certain inferences about the presence or absence of the behavior relevant to the items in question.

A qualified examiner is needed to administer the scale, which takes approximately twenty to thirty minutes to administer. The recommended method is to go through the items in each category until two consecutive failures are reached. The basal score is determined by two consecutive successes within each category. Scoring takes into account successes, failures, temporary failures, and no opportunity to perform activity. The examiner must determine the extent to which the child is capable of performing the various activities in order to score the items accurately. It is therefore helpful if the examiner has some opportunity to observe the child. Children with physical handicaps should not be penalized if their disability prevents them from performing the activity. The final score is computed from the total number of items successfully completed by the child, with consideration given for lack of opportunity to perform an

---

TABLE 17-2.   Sample Items from the Vineland Social Maturity Scale

Category	Sample Items[a]
Self-help General	Balances head (0–1), asks to go to toilet (2–3).
Self-help Eating	Drinks from cup or glass assisted (0–1), cares for self at table (9–10).
Self-help Dressing	Pulls off socks (1–2), bathes self assisted (5–7).
Locomotion	Moves about on floor (0–1), walks upstairs unassisted (1–2), goes to distant points alone (18–20).
Occupation	Occupies self unattended (0–1), uses tools or utensils (8–9), creates own opportunities. (25 +).
Communication	"Crows" and laughs (0–1), talks in short sentences (1–2), makes telephone calls (10–11), follows current events (15–18).
Self-direction	Is trusted with money (5–6), goes out unsupervised in daytime (15–18), assumes personal responsibility (18–20), purchases for others (25 +).
Socialization	Reaches for familiar persons (0–1), disavows literal Santa Claus (7–8), assumes responsibility beyond own needs (20–25), advances general welfare (25 +).

[a]Expected age range (in years) for item appears in the parentheses.

activity and for performances that are in a transitional stage.

Standardization. The standardization sample was limited and not based on representative sampling procedures. There were 620 persons in the standardization group, 10 males and 10 females at each year from birth to 30 years of age, white, living in New Jersey. Two types of scores are provided by the Vineland: a Social Age (SA) and a Social Quotient (SQ). A table in the manual is used to convert the total number of points earned by the examinee to an SA. The SA and Chronological Age (CA) are then used to obtain an SQ by use of the following formula: $SQ = SA/CA \times 100$. For adults 25 years of age and older, a CA of 25 is used in the formula.

Because SQ is a ratio, it has the same problems that are associated with a ratio IQ. The major difficulty is that the standard deviations of the SQ are not constant with age; therefore, they are not directly comparable at the different ages of the scale. However, using the table developed by Silverstein (1971), the SQs can be converted to Deviation SQs (DSQs), thereby standardizing the variability at each age. The DSQ has a mean of 100 and standard deviation of 9.

Reliability. Test-retest reliabilities, after an interval of approximately two years, for 250 individuals from the normative sample are satisfactory for the SA ($r = .98$), but less satisfactory for the SQ ($r = .57$). When 196 members of this sample were tested again after another year, the test-retest coefficients ranged from .94 to .99 for SAs. Mothers and teachers, however, have been found to differ in their reports of preschool children's social competence, with mothers reporting higher levels of competence than teachers, $\bar{X}$ SQs of 138 and 115, respectively (Kaplan & Alatishe, 1976).

Validity. Median correlations between the Vineland and intelligence tests are in the .40s to .50s.[1] With cerebral palsied children, high correlations have been found between the Vineland and the Preschool Attainment Record ($r = .88$) and the Gesell Developmental Schedule ($r = .97$) (Krasner & Silverstein, 1976). Social competence is moderately related to intelligence.

Comment on the Vineland Social Maturity Scale. The major difficulties with the Vineland are (a) its inadequate standardization and (b) its limited psychometric properties. The ratio SQ must be converted to a Deviation SQ in order to have comparable scores throughout the age ranges covered by the scale. Even with this conversion, standard errors of measurement of the DSQs at each age level are unknown.

Overall, the Vineland is a useful instrument for providing information about social competence, a very important facet of behavior. While the scale does not measure all aspects of social competence and may not be as applicable to children with physical handicaps, it is an important adjunct to the clinical evaluation (Watson, 1951). It is especially useful for interview and counseling purposes. However, its usefulness is primarily based on the reliability of the informant. Despite its limitations, when used wisely, the Vineland adds to our clinical insight (Teagarden, 1953).

Preschool Attainment Record

The Preschool Attainment Record (Doll, 1966) is a 112-item survey that evaluates physical, social, and intellectual functions of children from birth to 7 years, 6 months. It represents an extension of the Vineland Social Maturity Scale. The record contains eight scales which fall into three developmental areas: (1) Physical (Ambulation and Manipulation), (2) Social (Rapport, Communication, and Responsibility), and (3) Intellectual (Information, Ideation, and Creativity). Each scale contains one item at each age level.

An informant provides information to the examiner about how well a child can perform each task. Representative items include the following: "stands in place on each foot alternately," "reproduces or echoes words or sounds," "tells names of primary colors," and "tries new or unusual ways of doing things." All items are administered, regardless of the child's age. On the basis of a 3-point scoring system—(a) credit (child can perform task), (b) half-credit (doubtful if child can perform task), and (c) no credit (child cannot perform task)—an Attainment Age and an Attainment Quotient are calculated. The ratio method is used to obtain the Attainment Quotient.

Standardization, reliability, and validity. Standardization, reliability, and validity data are not provided in the manual. Items were placed in the Record by using a developmental frame of reference. However, there are some reports about the Record's reliability and validity. Owens and Bowling (1970) report reliability coefficients of .52 to .84 for the individual scales and .96 for the total score for a sample of institutionalized mentally retarded individuals. Concurrent validity coefficients are acceptable, using as criteria the Denver Developmental Screening Test ($r = .89$), the Vineland Social Maturity Scale ($r = .88$), and the Gesell Developmental Schedules ($r = .86$) (Krasner & Silverstein, 1976; Ritter, 1977). One factor analytic study (Owens & Bowling, 1970) reported that the Record contains two factors (Physical-Developmental and Social-Intellectual), while another study (Hug, Barclay, Collins, & Lamp, 1978) reported that a single factor accounts for most of the variance.

Comment on the Preschool Attainment Record. The Preschool Attainment Record does not meet acceptable psychometric standards because of (a) its failure to describe a normative group and (b) its use of the ratio method to compute the Attainment Quotient. However, it does serve as a research or experimental scale for evaluating the adaptive behavior of young children. Some items appear to be placed at arbitrary points, and there are too few items for each scale at each age level.[2] The Preschool Attainment Record needs better standardization, and more complete information about its reliability and validity before it can be used in individual assessment situations.

T.M.R. School Competency Scales

The T.M.R. School Competency Scales (Levine, Elzey, Thormahlen, & Cain, 1976) are designed to measure the following social and personal skills of trainable mentally retarded children in a school setting: Perceptual-Motor, Initiative-Responsibility, Cognition, Personal-Social, and Language. There are two separate forms: one for 5 to 10 years, and one for 11 years and over. Both forms consist of a total of 128 items, with 66 items in common.

The scales are completed by the child's teacher. Each item has four levels of competence. Percentiles are obtained for each subscale and for the total score.

Standardization. The scales were standardized on 302 randomly selected trainable mentally retarded students attending public schools in suburban and urban communities in California.

Reliability. Split-half reliabilities for all age groups were in the high .80s to .90s for the subscales, and in the high .90s for the total score. Subscale and total score intercorrelations for each age group ranged from the high .60s to the low .90s.

Validity. No validity data are presented in the manual.

Comment on the T.M.R. School Competency Scales. The T.M.R. Scales are similar to the Cain-Levine Social Competency Scale (Cain, Levine, & Elzey, 1963). Both contain many of the same items. The T.M.R. Scales contain an additional Cognition subscale and an extended age range. The scales have limited psychometric properties. However, they may be useful in evaluating the progress of trainable mentally retarded children.

Balthazar Scales of Adaptive Behavior

The Balthazar Scales of Adaptive Behavior (Balthazar, 1976) are designed for the assessment of severely and profoundly mentally retarded institutionalized individuals. They can be used to measure a range of functional abilities, and to evaluate the effectiveness of treatment and training programs. The scales are divided into two sections. Section I, the Scales of Functional Independence, assesses how well an individual can perform basic self-care activities. It contains three scales: Eating, Dressing, and Toileting (see Table 17-3). In completing the scales, the rater observes the individual directly over several days, if necessary.

The Eating Scales are designed to assess the individual's representative eating skill behavior. They measure how well individuals can feed themselves, eat finger foods, handle a spoon and fork, and drink from a glass or cup. There is also a supplementary checklist for evaluating other aspects of eating behavior. The Dressing Scales focus on various types of abilities required for dressing. The Toileting Scales are used to obtain information about the individual's behavior when using the toilet. The information

about these activities can be obtained from the individual or from an informant.

Section II, the Scales of Social Adaptation, provides an objective measure of interpersonal behaviors. The eight scales in the section (see Table 17-3) evaluate the individual's interpersonal adjustment and social interactions. They take approximately sixty minutes to administer, with at least six sessions of ten minutes each.

Standardization. The norms were based on ambulant institutionalized residents at a state training school in Wisconsin. Their ages ranged from 5 years to 57 years (median of 17 years), and all had IQs below 35. There were 122 subjects tested for the Eating Scales, 200 for the Dressing Scales, 129 for the Toileting Scales, and 288 for the Scales of Social Adaptation. The manual strongly encourages users of the scales to develop their own norms. This precaution is

---

TABLE 17-3. Illustrations of Items on the Balthazar Scales of Adaptive Behavior

Scales of Functional Independence	*Scales of Social Adaptation*

Eating Scales
  I. Dependent Feeding: opens mouth voluntarily; removes food from spoon with lips
  II. Finger Foods: eats finger foods (e.g., bread, fruit, etc.); reaches for finger foods (initiates reaching for food)
  III. Spoon Usage: eats tray foods with spoon; manipulates spoon with precision; does not stuff mouth
  IV. Fork Usage: same as spoon usage but with fork
  V. Drinking: takes liquids from cup; lifts cup off table with one hand to drink
Dressing Scales
  Consists of a list of clothing (e.g., shoes, socks, shirt, and pants). Subjects are graded on how well they put on and take off clothing.
Toileting Scales
  Questionnaire used for interview. Example: "Adjusts clothing appropriately before toileting":—"For an average ten times that the subject eliminates, how often does he (she) pull his (her) pants down by himself (herself)?"
	1. Unadaptive Self-directed Behaviors: failure to respond to staff or peers; disorderly or nonsocial behavior
	2. Unadaptive Interpersonal Behaviors: aggression; withdrawal
	3. Adaptive Self-directed Behaviors: generalized, exploratory, recreational activity
	4. Adaptive Interpersonal Behaviors: fundamental social behaviors; noncommunication
	5. Verbal Communication: verbalization
	6. Play Activities: playful contact
	7. Response to Instructions: cooperative contact; response to firmly given instructions
	8. Checklist: clothing adjustment; drinking; napping on ward

Adapted from Balthazar (1976).

given because Balthazar recognizes that the scales are not well standardized.

Reliability. There are no standard reliability coefficients reported for any of the scales. Interrater agreements in scoring the Scales of Functional Independence were high (.94 or higher). Less agreement was found for two raters scoring the Scales of Social Adaptation (42 to 100 percent, with a median of 81 percent agreement).

Validity. The manual fails to present any validity data. Validity for the scales is assumed to be inherent in and limited to the behaviors observed by each rater.

Comment on the Balthazar Scales of Adaptive Behavior. The Balthazar must be completed by a treatment-trainer person or someone closely involved with the individual. While one of its strongest and most appealing features is the direct observation of behavior, there is limited information given to raters about how to use the rating categories. Another limitation is that a satisfactory level of rater agreement may be difficult to achieve on the Scales of Social Adaptation.

The Balthazar Scales of Adaptive Behavior attempt to provide a standardized way to monitor the training and treatment of severely and profoundly mentally retarded individuals living in an institution. The scales provide finely grained measures; they are potentially one of the best tools for their purpose (Meyers, 1978). They also appear to be one of the better designed instruments of their type (Proger, 1973). Silverstein (1972b), however, suggested that further research is needed before the Balthazar Scales of Adaptive Behavior can be accepted as being any better than other adaptive behavior assessment techniques. These scales are still in an experimental stage, and revisions and improvements are needed.

Assessment of Behavior Problems

Behavioral checklists are useful in identifying problem behaviors in children. They provide a basis for evaluating behavior in a structured format, and are useful for measuring change and improvement. Some checklists are designed for parents, others for teachers, and others for both parents and teachers. Because parents and teachers are likely to see different aspects of the child, both sources are needed to obtain a comprehensive clinical picture.

There are several rating instruments useful in obtaining behavioral ratings of children. They can be distinguished by the age group covered by the checklist, the setting that the questions are directed to (school or family), and the type of classifications they provide (e.g., broad-band syndromes or more differentiated syndromes). The checklists referred to in this chapter are representative of the many that are available. The failure to include other checklists is no reflection on their merits; it simply was a matter of time or space or availability of information.

Behavioral checklists have some of the following uses: (a) they permit a study of how each parent views the child's problems and how parents' views compare with teachers' views; (b) they may be sensitive to changes in behavior that occur as a result of therapeutic or remedial interventions; (c) they are helpful in describing clinically relevant dimensions of behavior; and (d) they are useful as screening instruments.

Behavioral checklists should be evaluated on the same dimensions as other measuring devices. Unfortunately, the same care that has gone into standardizing individually administered intelligence tests has not gone into the standardization of behavioral checklists. None of the checklists referred to in this chapter have been based on a nationwide representative sample. Yet, many do provide valuable information that can be used in a variety of settings. Information gained from behavioral checklists can supplement that obtained from standardized tests and adaptive behavior scales.

Parents and teachers completing a behavioral checklist should be given some guidelines for recording their observations (Spivack & Swift, 1973). What kind of sampling of behavior should be used for the observations? How frequently does the behavior occur? Over what period of time has the rater observed the child? In what settings have the observations occurred? These are just a few of the many rater variables that must be considered. The reliability and validity of the checklist are affected, in part, by the specificity of the rating task. For example, do items require observations of specific behavior (e.g., "Has the child fought with another child on at least three occasions during the last month?") or do they require a judgment (e.g., "The child is depressed.")? Some teachers may be inaccurate judges of students' behavior; they may disregard actual behavior and be influenced by the child's race, socioeconomic status, or appearance. In such cases, teachers' observation skills must be sharpened before checklists can be used in the assessment process.

Behavior problems also can be evaluated by direct observation methods.[3] (See references in note 3 for reports on direct observation methods.) Direct observation methods, or what has been termed "behavioral assessment" techniques, must be evaluated not only with respect to such issues as content, criterion-related, and construct validity, but also with respect to observer training; bias and drift; observer accuracy; and behavior, subject, situation, and time sampling variables (Haynes & Kerns, 1979). Unfortunately, the teacher rating scales and direct observation methods may not provide congruent scores (Vincent, Williams, & Elrod, 1977). Discrepancies occur, in part, because the samples of behavior are usually not the same for the two methods. Teacher rating scales sample a broad range of behaviors, with the incidence of certain behaviors tending to be exaggerated relative to the actual rates of occurrence. Direct observations focus on a more limited segment of behavior. Teacher ratings also are based on contact with the child over a long period of time, while direct observations are made over a much shorter period of time. Because it is difficult to determine which method is more valid, and because each method gives a different perspective on problem behaviors, it is recommended that both methods be used when there is a need to assess behavior traits.

Behavioral Checklists Summarized in Appendix D

Appendix D summarizes the principal features associated with the following behavioral checklists: AML Behavior Rating Scale, Behavior Problem Checklist, Child Behavior Checklist, Child Behavior Scale, Classroom Adjustment Ratings Scale, Devereux Adolescent Behavior Rating Scale, Devereux Child Behavior Rating Scale, Devereux Elementary School Behavior Rating Scale, Health Resources Inventory, Hyperkinesis Rating Scale, Kohn Problem Checklist, Kohn Social Competence Scales, Parent Symptom Questionnaire, Preschool Behavior Questionnaire, Teacher Behavioral Description Form, and Teacher Questionnaire. Appendix D also provides information about where each checklist can be obtained.

Examples of Behavioral Checklists

Examples of four different behavioral checklists are shown in Tables 17-4 through 17-7. The Classroom Adjustment Ratings Scale is an example of a scale rating behavior problems. It measures three factors: Learning Problems, Acting-Out, and Shy-Anxious. The Preschool Behavior Questionnaire also measures behavior problems, but is designed for young children. It, too, measures three factors: Hostile-Aggressive, Anxious-Fearful, and Hyperactive-Distractible. The Health Resources Inventory has five health or competence factors: Good Student, Gutsy, Peer Sociability, Rules, and Frustration Tolerance. It was designed to temper the emphasis on pathology that is present in many behavioral checklists. The Hyperkinesis Rating Scale focuses on the evaluation of hyperkinesis exclusively. The following additional checklists are presented in other chapters of the book: (a) a checklist for evaluating various degrees of handicap (Figure 5-1) in Chapter 5, (b) a rating scale for evaluating handicapped children (Table 5-1) in Chapter 5, (c) a behavior rating scale for evaluating psychotic children (Table 23-2) in Chapter 23, and (d) a behavior and attitude checklist for evaluating the child's behavior during the examination (Table 24-1) in Chapter 24.

TABLE 17-4. Classroom Adjustment Ratings Scale

Child's name: _____   Rater's name: _____   Date: _____

Section I: Please rate *every* item on the following scale: 1 = not a problem   2 = very mild problem
3 = moderate problem   4 = serious problem   5 = very serious problem

Child's classroom behavior:
1. ___ disruptive in class
2. ___ fidgety, hyperactive, can't stay in seat
3. ___ talks out of turn, disturbs others while they are working
4. ___ constantly seeks attention, "clowns around"
5. ___ overly aggressive to peers (fights, is overbearing, belligerent)
6. ___ defiant, obstinate, stubborn
7. ___ impulsive, is unable to delay
8. ___ withdrawn
9. ___ shy, timid
10. ___ does not make friends
11. ___ overconforms to rules
12. ___ daydreams, is preoccupied, "off in another world"
13. ___ unable to express feelings
14. ___ anxious
15. ___ worried, frightened, tense
16. ___ depressed
17. ___ cries easily, pouts, sulks
18. ___ does not trust others
19. ___ shows other signs of "nervousness," specify: _____
20. ___ specific fears, specify: _____

Other behaviors:
21. ___ lacks self-confidence
22. ___ overly sensitive to criticism
23. ___ reacts poorly to disappointment
24. ___ depends too much on others
25. ___ pretends to be ill
26. ___ other, specify: _____
27. ___ poor grooming or personal hygiene

Child's academic performance:
28. ___ underachieving (not working up to potential)
29. ___ poorly motivated to achieve
30. ___ poor work habits
31. ___ difficulty following directions
32. ___ poor concentration, limited attention span
33. ___ motor coordination problem
34. ___ other, specify: _____

Child has specific academic problems in:
35. ___ reading   36. ___ math   37. ___ numbers
38. ___ writing   39. ___ colors   40. ___ concepts
41. ___ language skills problems, specify: _____

Section II: From your experiences with this child, please check (√) any of the following which you believe relate to the problems you have reported:
42. ___ separation or divorce of parents
43. ___ illness or death of a family member
44. ___ lack of educational stimulation in the home
45. ___ economic difficulties
46. ___ under family pressure to succeed
47. ___ family difficulties

Section III: From your experiences with this child, please check (√) where he or she would lie on the following dimensions taking into account the direction of each item:

Know child well   Barely know child
48. 1   2   3   4   5   6   7

Child seems easy to like   Child seems difficult to like
49. 1   2   3   4   5   6   7

Child has significant   Child has no school
school adjustment problems   adjustment problems
50. 1   2   3   4   5   6   7

Note. Item numbers for the three factor scores are as follows: Learning Problems (24, 28, 29, 30, 31, 32, 33, 35, 36, 37, 38, 39, 40, 41), Acting-Out (1, 2, 3, 4, 5, 6, 7, 9 [scoring reversed], 18, 30), and Shy-Anxious (8, 9, 10, 13, 14, 15, 16, 17, 18, 21, 22, 23).

TABLE 17-5.   The Preschool Behavior Questionnaire by Lenore Behar, Ph.D., and Samuel Stringfield

Child's Name _____   School Attending _____

Parents' Name _____   Sex (circle)   M   F

Address _____   Present Date _____
                (Street)   Month   Day   Year

_____   Child's Birthday   ____   ____   ____
        (City, State, Zip Code)

Rated by _____   Age of Child   ____   ____   ____

Title of Rater _____

Length of Time Rater Has Worked with Child (months
or weeks) _____

Following is a series of descriptions of behavior often shown by preschoolers. After each statement are three columns, "Doesn't Apply," "Applies Sometimes," and "Certainly Applies." If the child shows the behavior described by the statement frequently or to a great degree, place an "X" in the space under "Certainly Applies." If the child shows behavior described by the statement to a lesser degree or less often, place an "X" in the space under "Applies Sometimes." If, as far as you are aware, the child does not show the behavior, place an "X" in the space under "Doesn't Apply."

Please put ONE "X" for EACH statement.

	Doesn't Apply	Applies Sometimes	Certainly Applies	For Scorer's Use Only			
1. Restless. Runs about or jumps up and down. Doesn't keep still	__	__	__	__..	....	....	__
2. Squirmy, fidgety child	__	__	__	__..	....	....	__
3. Destroys own or others' belongings	__	__	__	__..	....	....	
4. Fights with other children	__	__	__	__..	__		
5. Not much liked by other children	__	__	__	__..	__		
6. Is worried. Worries about many things	__	__	__	__..	....	__	
7. Tends to do things on his own, rather solitary	__	__	__	__..	__		
8. Irritable, quick to "fly off the handle"	__	__	__	__..	__		
9. Appears miserable, unhappy, tearful, or distressed	__	__	__	__..	....	__	
10. Has twitches, mannerisms, or tics of the face and body	__	__	__	__..	....	__	
11. Bites nails or fingers	__	__	__	__			
12. Is disobedient	__	__	__	__..	__		
13. Has poor concentration or short attention span	__	__	__	__..	....	....	__
14. Tends to be fearful or afraid of new things or new situations	__	__	__	__..	....	__	
15. Fussy or over-particular child	__	__	__	__..	....	__	
16. Tells lies	__	__	__	__..	__		
17. Has wet or soiled self this year	__	__	__	__			
18. Has stutter or stammer	__	__	__	__			
19. Has other speech difficulty	__	__	__	__..	....		__

(cont.)

Reprinted with permission of the authors, from L. Behar and S. Stringfield, "A Behavior Rating Scale for the Preschool Child," *Developmental Psychology, 10,* pp. 601–610. Copyright 1974 by L. Behar. Copies of the scale, scoring sheet, and instruction manual can be obtained from Lenore Behar, Ph.D., 1821 Woodburn Road, Durham, North Carolina 27705.

TABLE 17-5   (cont.)

	Doesn't Apply	Applies Sometimes	Certainly Applies	For Scorer's Use Only			
20. Bullies other children	—	—	—	—..	—		—
21. Inattentive	—	—	—	—..	—	....	....
22. Doesn't share toys	—	—	—	—..	—	....	
23. Cries easily	—	—	—	—..	—	....	
24. Blames others	—	—	—	—..	—		
25. Gives up easily	—	—	—	—..	—	....	
26. Inconsiderate of others	—	—	—	—..	—	....	—
27. Unusual sexual behaviors	—	—	—	—..	—		
28. Kicks, bites, or hits other children	—	—	—	—			
29. Stares into space	—	—	—	—..	—	....	
30. Do you consider this child to have behavior problems?	—	—	—	—			
TOTALS				Total	1	2	3

Scoresheet

Date: _____   Child's Name: _____

Rater's Name: _____

The scoring system for the PBQ is as follows:

All items marked "Doesn't Apply" are scored "0."
All items marked "Applies Sometimes" are scored "1."
All items marked "Certainly Applies" are scored "2."

For each behavior, fill in the appropriate score in the column. If this blank has to its right a series of dots followed by a second blank, then also fill in that second blank with the child's score on that item. Add all of thenumbers in each of the four columns and transfer those totals to the following table. If the exact score appears on the table, circle it. If not, enter the exact score in the appropriate place and circle it.

Percentile Rank		TOTAL Behavior Disturbed		Scale 1 Hostile-Aggressive		Scale 2 Anxious		Scale 3 Hyperactive-Distractible		Percentile Rank
99	—	29	—	14	—	9	—	8	—	99
		26		11		8 7		7		
95	—	23	—	10 9	—	6	—	6	—	95
		20		8		5		5		
90	—	17	—	7	—		—		—	90
		15		6 5		4		4		
80	—	13	—	4	—	3				80
		11		3						
65	—	9	—	2	—	1	—	3	—	65
50	—	7 6	—	1	—	0	—	2 1	—	50
		4		0						
25	—	2	—						—	25
		1								
0		0								0

TABLE 17-6. Health Resources Inventory I

Child's Name _____   Date _____

School _____   Teacher's Name _____

Please rate each of the listed behaviors according to how well it describes the child:

1 = not at all   2 = a little   3 = moderately well   4 = well   5 = very well

1 ___ functions well even with distractions
2 ___ feels good about himself or herself
3 ___ applies learning to new situations
4 ___ has a good sense of humor
5 ___ is interested in schoolwork
6 ___ shares things with others
7 ___ is well behaved in school
8 ___ is mature
9 ___ approaches new experiences confidently
10 ___ is a happy child
11 ___ does original work
12 ___ can accept things not going his or her way
13 ___ is pleased with accomplishments
14 ___ defends his or her views under group pressure
15 ___ mood is balanced and stable
16 ___ resolves peer problems on his or her own
17 ___ copes well with failure
18 ___ follows class rules
19 ___ participates in class discussions
20 ___ is able to question rules that seem unfair or unclear to him or her
21 ___ uses teacher appropriately as resource
22 ___ is affectionate toward others
23 ___ is generally relaxed
24 ___ is a self-starter
25 ___ plays enthusiastically
26 ___ completes his or her homework

27 ___ has a lively interest in his or her environment
28 ___ anger, when displayed, is justified
29 ___ is trustworthy
30 ___ works well without adult support
31 ___ expresses ideas willingly
32 ___ carries out requests and directions responsibly
33 ___ uses his or her imagination well
34 ___ well liked by classmates
35 ___ is good in arithmetic
36 ___ tries to help others
37 ___ is well organized
38 ___ faces the pressures of competition well
39 ___ has many friends
40 ___ works up to potential
41 ___ thinks before acting
42 ___ accepts legitimate imposed limits
43 ___ knows his or her strengths and weaknesses
44 ___ adjusts well to changes in the classroom routine
45 ___ expresses needs and feelings appropriately
46 ___ accepts criticism well
47 ___ is a good reader
48 ___ is comfortable as a leader and follower
49 ___ functions well in unstructured situations
50 ___ is spontaneous
51 ___ works well toward long-term goals
52 ___ works for own satisfaction, not just rewards
53 ___ rarely requires restrictions or sanctions
54 ___ is polite and courteous

Please specify any other strengths or competencies which your mental health team should be aware of:_____

_____

_____

Note. Item numbers for the five factor scores are as follows: Good Student (1, 3, 5, 11, 24, 26, 30, 35, 40, 47), Gutsy (14, 19, 20, 31, 45, 48, 50), Peer Sociability (4, 6, 10, 22, 25, 27, 34, 36, 39, 43), Rules (7, 18, 29, 32, 42, 53, 54), and Frustration Tolerance (2, 9, 12, 15, 16, 17, 23, 26, 27, 38, 44, 46).

Reprinted by permission of the author, from E. L. Gesten, "A Health Resources Inventory: The Development of a Measure of the Personal and Social Competence of Primary-Grade Children," *Journal of Consulting and Clinical Psychology,* 1976, *44,* 775–786.

TABLE 17-7.   Hyperkinesis Rating Scale

Child's Name _____   Birth Date _____

Rater's Name _____   Date of Rating _____

Please rate the child on each of the characteristics (or behavior) listed on the following scales. Place a check mark at the point on the scale indicative of your estimate of the degree to which the child possesses the particular characteristic.

As you make each rating, judge the child in comparison with other children of the same sex and age. That is, the ratings should indicate your estimate of the child's behavior in comparison with the behavior displayed by other "normal children."

For each of the characteristics, which are defined below, place a check mark at one of the six points on the scales running from "much less than most children" to "much more than most children." Do not mark the midpoint on any of the scales. Even though it may sometimes be difficult to make a judgment, please make a rating on one or the other side of the scale.

1. *Hyperactivity*—Involuntary and constant overactivity; advanced motor development (throwing things, walking, running, etc.); always on the move; rather run than walk; rarely sits still.

Much Less Than Most Children	Less	Slightly Less	Slightly More	More	Much More Than Most Children

2. *Short Attention Span and Poor Powers of Concentration*—Concentration on a single activity is usually short, with frequent shifting from one activity to another; rarely sticks to a single task very long.

Much Less Than Most Children	Less	Slightly Less	Slightly More	More	Much More Than Most Children

3. *Variability*—Behavior is unpredictable, with wide fluctuations in performance; "sometimes he (or she) is good and sometimes bad."

Much Less Than Most Children	Less	Slightly Less	Slightly More	More	Much More Than Most Children

4. *Impulsiveness and Inability to Delay Gratification*—Does things on the spur of the moment without thinking; seems unable to tolerate any delay in gratification of his (her) needs and demands; when wants anything, he (she) wants it immediately; does not look ahead or work toward future goals; thinks only of immediate present situation.

Much Less Than Most Children	Less	Slightly Less	Slightly More	More	Much More Than Most Children

5. *Irritability*—Frustration tolerance is low; frequently in an ugly mood, often unprovoked; easily upset if everything does not work out just the way he (she) desires.

Much Less Than Most Children	Less	Slightly Less	Slightly More	More	Much More Than Most Children

(cont.)

TABLE 17-7   (cont.)

6. *Explosiveness*—Fits of anger are easily provoked; reactions are often almost volcanic in their intensity; shows explosive, temper-tantrum type of emotional outbursts.

Much Less Than Most Children	Less	Slightly Less	Slightly More	More	Much More Than Most Children

7. *Poor School Work*—Has difficulty participating successfully in school work; cannot concentrate on school work; has some specific learning difficulties or blocks (e.g., poor in arithmetic, poor in reading, etc.); poor visual-motor coordination (e.g., awkward gestures, irregular handwriting, poor in drawing, etc.).

Much Less Than Most Children	Less	Slightly Less	Slightly More	More	Much More Than Most Children

Comment on Adaptive Behavior Scales and Behavioral Checklists

The reviews of the various adaptive behavior scales indicate that we are only at a beginning stage in the assessment of adaptive behavior and social competence. At present, there are no nationally standardized and well-normed scales of adaptive behavior that cover birth through adulthood. All of the available scales have been found to have one or more major difficulty. Many adaptive behavior scales are normed only on a retarded population. In such cases, norms are limited in that the examinee is being compared with norms that in themselves embody deviance instead of normalcy (cf. Silverstein, 1972b). In spite of their limitations, each of the adaptive behavior scales reviewed in this chapter has a place in the assessment of adaptive behavior.

While there are many adaptive behavior scales, it is important to recognize that each scale covers only certain types of behaviors, and that no one scale covers all areas. When the assessment of adaptive behavior is necessary, the examiner must select the most appropriate scale for the assessment task. Caution also should be used in making sure that the standardization group for the scale being used is appropriate for the examinee. Much further work is needed in the development of adaptive behavior scales.

Content analysis of the various checklists referred to in Appendix D suggests that the same factor label includes different behaviors, and that similar behaviors are given different labels. For example, some scales isolate hyperactive behavior as a separate scale, while others include hyperactive behavior under a conduct-problem factor. Also, some checklists present a small number of broad-band factors (e.g., Conduct Problem, Personality Problem, Immaturity), while others present a large number of narrow-band factors (e.g., Hyperactivity, Withdrawal, Aggressive). In general, broad-band factors appear to be more reliable than narrow-band factors. Narrow-band factors, however, provide information about specific problems that may be of interest to teachers and clinicians. Another complicating factor in evaluating behavioral checklists is that raters, too, may use different frames of reference, depending on whether the children are clinic patients or school children. Thus, care must be taken in evaluating the results of studies when different scales are used.

In selecting among the many available behavioral checklists, consider the applicability of the checklist for the assessment or screening task. Many factors should be considered, including availability of raters, time involved in completing the checklist, the psychometric properties of the checklist, and how the information will be used in the assessment task. While much more information is needed about behavioral checklists, they do serve as an important adjunct to the assessment process.

Summary

1. The AAMD Adaptive Behavior Scale (ABS) assesses two major areas—basic survival skills and maladaptive behaviors—for mentally retarded, emotionally maladjusted, and developmentally disabled individuals residing in an institution. It covers an age range from 3 to 69 years.

2. The AAMD Adaptive Behavior Scale–Public School Version (ABS-PSV) is a modified version of the ABS for use with children in school between the ages of 7 and 13 years (second to sixth grade). It assesses most of the same behavior domains as the ABS, with the exception of those areas that are not applicable to the school setting. The scale can assist in the evaluation of different kinds of handicapped children.

3. The Adaptive Behavior Inventory for Children is used to assess the behavior of noninstitutionalized school-age children between 5 and 11 years of age in kindergarten through fifth grade. It provides scores for six areas of adaptive behavior (Family, Peers, Community, School, Earner/Consumer, and Self-Maintenance). It is useful in evaluating children.

4. The Vineland Social Maturity Scale is designed to measure an individual's ability to look after his or her own practical needs, covering areas such as self-help, self-direction, occupation, communication, locomotion, and socialization. It covers an age range from birth to 25 years and can be used for nonhandicapped, handicapped, or mentally retarded individuals. The scale provides an overall social age and a social quotient. It and the Preschool Attainment Record are particularly useful for children under 5 years of age because most other scales do not cover this age period.

5. The T.M.R. School Competency Scales measure various personal and social skills of trainable mentally retarded school children, including perceptual-motor, initiative-responsibility, cognition, personal-social, and language. The scales may have some usefulness, but more information is needed about their validity.

6. The Balthazar Scales of Adaptive Behavior contain two separate scales, each dealing with different areas of behavior. They are similar to the AAMD-ABS in that Part I assesses basic self-help skills and Part II assesses maladaptive and adaptive coping behaviors. The Balthazar is used for the assessment of ambulant severely and profoundly mentally retarded children and adults, less retarded young children, and emotionally disturbed children. Coverage begins at 5 years of age. One difference between the Balthazar and the ABS is that the Balthazar was standardized on institutionalized individuals with IQs below 35 residing in one institution, while the ABS was standardized on individuals in sixty-eight institutions across the United States.

7. The behavioral checklists referred to in this chapter and described in Appendix D can be completed by the child's parent, teacher, guardian, or attendant. They are designed for school-age children or for preschool children. While most of the checklists focus on deviant behavior, some also evaluate the child's competencies. Many of the checklists were designed on the basis of factor analysis.

CHAPTER *18*

The Assessment Process

It is probably unwise to spend much time in attempts to separate off sharply certain qualities of man, as his intelligence, from such emotional and vocational qualities as his interest in mental activity, carefulness, determination to respond effectively, persistence in his efforts to do so; or from his amount of knowledge; or from his moral or esthetic tastes.

E. L. THORNDIKE

General Assessment Considerations

The assessment of a child is often based on information obtained from a variety of sources. These include records and reports; interviews with parents, teachers, and child; observations of the child; standardized tests; and other special procedures. Standardized tests provide a means of observing and assessing abilities in a systematic way. On the basis of what is observed on tests, results are reported and inferences are made. Since the test stimuli and scoring procedures are standardized, norms can be established.

The usual steps in the assessment process are as follows (Gerken, 1979):

1. Review referral information. Any material that is not clear should be checked with the referral source (e.g., physician, teacher, parent, or court).
2. Interview parent. Obtain information relevant to developmental, health, familial, and environmental factors that may be pertinent to the child's problem.
3. Obtain information from other agencies, including previous psychological evaluations.
4. Obtain current medical assessment.
5. Observe child in various settings, if at all possible.
6. Perform psychological evaluation.
7. Conduct interdisciplinary staff conference after all materials have been obtained.

These steps will result in the following kinds of information: (a) *developmental* (including information about cognitive and perceptual achievement, social abilities and skills, adaptive behavior, and emotional and personality characteristics); (b) *behavioral* (including observations from the test situation, school, and family); (c) *medical* (including neurological work-up); and (d) *environmental* (including information about school and family). The information will be used to describe the problem, to estimate its severity, to identify factors related to the problem, to suggest areas for improvement, and to help develop treatment or remediation suggestions.

Working with Relevant Adults

A comprehensive assessment of a child's behavior requires the assessment of relevant adults' behavior as well. Significant adults usually play an important role in the development of the child's behavior. Ideally, one should observe how the behavior of parents and teachers affects the child.

The interview with the parents or teacher should elicit information about (a) how they view the problem, (b) what they have done to alleviate the problem, and (c) their role in maintaining the problem. When the test findings do not agree with the parents' account of what the child can do, investigate further the reasons for the disagreement.

Observing the Child's Behavior

It is important to observe the child's behavior not only in the testing room but also in the waiting room and, if possible, in a play room. The following are some questions that can guide your observations (Eaton & Menolascino, 1970):

- How does the child relate to his or her parents?
- How does the child react to the examiner?
- How does the child approach the new situation?
- How does the child react to the play materials?
- Does the child show normal curiosity for his or her age?
- Does the child use toys in an age-appropriate way?
- Does the child need support or reassurance to continue playing?
- Are themes developed in the child's play and, if so, what themes?
- How long does the child persist at various tasks?
- Is fantasy used?

During testing, observe the child's ability to participate actively, to take the initiative, and to assume responsibility for responses. On those occasions when a child is asked for further information, observe how he or she complies with the request, such as whether the child can rephrase or elaborate on the original response. Such information provides insight about children's flexibility and willingness to extend themselves by trying to make their communications clear to others. Observations should also be made of how the child approaches the test materials, how the tasks are attempted, and what factors lead to success and failure.

Complexities of the Assessment Task

The assessment task is a complex activity. It requires the integration of data obtained from such sources as the child, parents, teachers, and physicians. Many of the techniques available for the assessment task have an adequate degree of reliability and validity. However, we still are faced with the task of (a) integrating, organizing, and interpreting the data and (b) making treatment or remedial suggestions. Some of the difficulties that are faced in the assessment of children include the following:

1. Classification systems are not uniform, and overlapping symptoms are present in various diagnostic categories.
2. The behavior displayed by a child that is of concern to the adult may not be of concern to the child.
3. The child's behavior is highly dependent on significant adults, so that these adults must also be interviewed and informally evaluated.
4. Because of rapid developmental changes in children, problems at one age may not be evident at another. Problems may be associated simply with developmental lags rather than with psychopathology.
5. Assessment is time consuming, and may not be readily accepted by some parents or schools.

Interpreting test results. A useful model that provides some understanding of the factors that influence the test score is shown in Figure 18-1. In this model the test score is viewed as the end product (the output), which is influenced by innate factors and background and environmental factors (input); and personality, situational test demands, and random variation factors (intervening variables). Not all variables are equally important, and on some occasions and for some examinees some variables will play a more important role than others. An accurate assessment of intelligence and other abilities requires consideration of the variables illustrated in the model plus other factors that are unique to the examinee.

The model begins with a consideration of innate factors—general and special inherited abilities—and their contribution to test performance. The contribution of inherited ability to the intelligence test score has been of concern since the inception of the testing movement, and while there is still no definitive answer about the exact contribution of heredity, there is strong evidence that it does make a significant contribution (see Chapter 4). We also do not know the extent to which genetic limitations can be penetrated by environmental programs.

The process of interpreting the test results can be conceptualized as a chain with three major links (Appelbaum, 1975): (1) the test responses proper, (2) a theory with which to integrate and conceptualize the responses, and (3) knowledge of what to do on the basis of this information (e.g., remediation or treatment). In working with children, it is especially important to know the age-appropriate behavior and to determine to what extent the child's behavior deviates from the norm.

Developing treatment and remediation plans. A diagnostic assessment provides hypotheses upon which treatment should be based. Assessment and treatment are inextricably intertwined. Assessment involves the formulation of a diagnostic label, a careful delineation of the child's strengths and weaknesses, a description of temperament and personality, and appropriate recommendations. In the course of treatment or

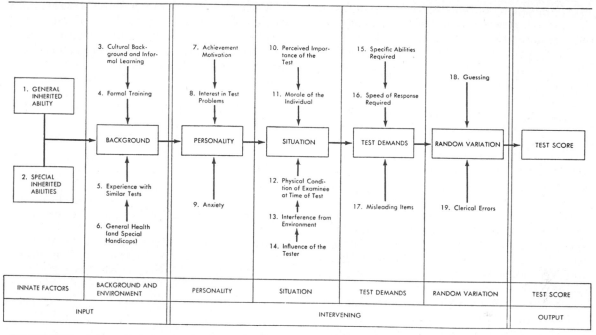

FIGURE 18-1 . A Paradigm for the Analysis of Influencing Variables. Reprinted by permission of the publisher from D. A. Goslin, *The Search for Ability: Standardized Testing in Social Perspective,* p. 130. Copyright 1963, Russell Sage Foundation.

remediation, the hypotheses proposed in the assessment can be tested out. As a result of such feedback, the original appraisal is modified and further issues that may require additional assessment are delineated. Short-term follow-up (say two to six weeks) is strongly recommended, since treatment recommendations may be ineffective just two weeks after implementation because the situation has changed or because the recommendations were inadequate from the beginning. Effective delivery of services requires close monitoring of recommendations.

Assessment is not a once-and-for-all matter. Children change as a result of development, life experiences, and treatment. An evaluation conducted when the child is 2 years of age may have little meaning four years later, except as a basis for comparison with the findings obtained at that time. Both short- and long-term follow-up are im-

portant parts of the psychological assessment process.

The psychological evaluation aims to assess the child's performance and capabilities and to guide in establishing appropriate educational and remediation programs. For example, with brain-injured children or with children handicapped by other physical disabilities, the medical evaluation and diagnosis may provide information about the etiology of the child's exceptionality, areas of deficit or diminished skill, and need for special environmental considerations or prosthetic aids. While medical treatment is necessary for various types of handicapping conditions, focus must also be given to helping the child function in an optimal manner in everyday life situations; it is in this area that psychological assessment can serve a valuable function. The plasticity of the child's central nervous system may enable the child to compensate for the loss of certain functions, either through the natural course of development or by means of special educational programs and training.

Comment on General Assessment Considerations

Interviews, tests, checklists, and observations are behavior sampling tools. They aid in providing a profile of strengths and weaknesses, a profile which is derived in relationship to a normal population. There is little if any value in establishing norms based on a selected group of handicapped children. However, such norms may be useful as adjuncts to norms based on the population as a whole, or sometimes for children already known to be below normal in intelligence (e.g., for measurement of adaptive behavior skills).

We have seen that the psychological evaluation aims to provide an understanding of the child's abilities and to provide suggestions that may assist in the child's development. The evaluation is based on information obtained from objective testing; interview material; observations in a controlled setting; observations in the classroom or at home; classroom performance; information obtained from parents, teachers, and other individuals who know the child well; and a medical evaluation. The results of the evaluation become part of the child's file and, as such, become a data base for evaluating present, as well as future, performance.

To be effective assessors, clinicians need the following skills (Goldman, 1961):

1. They must know their tests and a great deal about people.
2. They must develop hypotheses and be willing to modify or reject a hypothesis in the light of new data, recognizing that creative skill, scientific rigor, and cautiousness are involved in such procedures.
3. They must know the situations about which they make inferences.
4. They must study themselves as interpreters of test performance and of human behavior.

Murphy's (1975) insightful suggestions are a fitting way to close this general introduction to the assessment process. They alert us to the need to discover each child's unique coping strategies:

... we need to focus on and better understand the nature of ongoing current coping struggles; how to support them, how to help the child to extract the strength and insight that successive experiences may make available to him. We need to understand the positive strategic values of withdrawal in certain situations, and be very cautious about talking about a "withdrawn child." Similarly we need to respect and value children's protests, resistances, attempts to change or control situations, and all the other active coping efforts that can give us cues to what the child finds intolerable, unsuitable, boring, distasteful or threatening to his integrity. . . . I am pleading . . . that each clinician, each teacher, use all of the available resources along with his

From *Mainstreaming Series: Individualized Educational Programming* (IEP), © 1977 by Judy A. Schrag, Thomas N. Fairchild, and Bart L. Miller, published by Teaching Resources Corporation, Hingham, Massachusetts. Reproduced by permission. All rights reserved.

own fresh look at the child in his situation in order to discover the meaning of the child's behavior from the child's own point of view. [p. 42]

Assessment Process in Schools

Everything we have discussed previously about the assessment process also pertains to the assessment of children with learning or behavior problems in school. We can reformulate the objectives of the assessment process for these children in the following way:

1. to determine the nature of the learning or behavior problem,
2. to determine the child's strengths and weaknesses in abilities related to learning,
3. to evaluate the type of behavior problem,
4. to develop an educational plan which takes the child's abilities and personality resources into account,
5. to assess the child's response to educational and remedial efforts, and
6. to recommend modifications in programs and class placements.

The kinds of diagnostic problems faced by school psychologists and educators are illustrated for three children in Exhibit 18-1, which is presented at the beginning of the chapter. Diagnosing educational handicaps in these and other types of children is a complex and difficult task. It will call for many skills and will involve collaboration with other professionals. Whatever the etiology of these children's difficulties, special educational procedures will still be needed.

The assessment should not be merely a catalogue of deficits or areas of failure, but should specify abilities that might be used to master tasks (Keogh, 1971). Through identification of compensatory abilities a basis can be established for remedial and teaching strategies. Emphasis should be on what the child can do, rather than on what was failed. It is unlikely, however, that the test results will provide the precise causes of the child's school failure (that is, the etiol-

ogy of the specific learning deficits). The following outline presents the types of questions that should be covered in a history of a child's school problem (Kinsbourne & Caplan, 1979, pp. 83–84, with changes in notation).

I. Summary of problem presented, with ramifications concerning:
  A. Learning of school subjects
  B. Classroom behavior
  C. Emotional problems of child, such as ones resulting from fear of repeated failure
  D. Relationship with peers
  E. Relationship with parents and siblings
II. Learning problems and hyperactivity in parents, grandparents, and siblings
III. Prenatal history
IV. Developmental milestones before school entry
  A. Motor development
    1. Gross
    2. Fine
  B. Language development
  C. Other cognitive development
V. Sleeping and eating patterns since birth
VI. Interpersonal style since birth
  A. As baby—cuddly or rigid? overactive or underactive? tantrums? rocking? headbanging?
  B. As child—relationships with peers and siblings?
VII. School history—Basic school subjects (the three R's)
  A. Has any teacher recommended special help for the child?
  B. Has the child ever received special help?
    1. In or out of school?
    2. From whom?
    3. How long was each session, and how many did the child have?
    4. What was the child's emotional response to it?
    5. Did the child make any progress because of it?

VIII. Family relations
  A. Number and ages of parents and siblings
  B. Who lives in the home?
  C. Who is close to whom?
  D. Does child have own room?
  E. Amount of time each parent spends with child
  F. Nature of each parent's relationship with child
  G. Each parent's goals for child
  H. Each parent's disappointments with child
  IX. Child's strengths
  A. Skills
  B. Personality
  X. School circumstances
  A. What kind of classroom is the child in?
    1. Structured
    2. Open
  B. What is available?
    1. Is any other kind of classroom available in that school?
    2. Is any special help (small-group or individual teaching) available in that school?
  XI. How many professionals have been seen before and why? What were their verdicts? (This should be explored right away, if necessary, to expose parents' feelings of guilt, of ignoring the child's needs, and of assuming the interviewer to be omnipotent)
  XII. Who instigated the visit (school, parents, child, or physician)? Why (what was the immediately precipitating factor)?
  XIII. What decisions need to be made?
  A. Official-educational and medical decisions
  B. Family-related decisions involving reality testing, expectations, existing pressures, help with homework, etc.

In school settings, the formal assessment should be supplemented with visits to the child's classroom. The characteristics of the particular classroom environment should be observed and intervention strategies tailored to this environment. Classroom visits provide an added benefit—consultation with the teacher. In implementing such visits, consider the following precautions (Bardon, Bennett, Bruchez, & Sanderson, 1976):

1. Excellent rapport is needed between the psychologist and the teacher.
2. Visits should not interfere with regular classroom procedures.
3. The teacher must be assured that the focus of study is the child, not the teacher's performance.
4. The child under study should not be stigmatized.

The problem of assuring teachers that their performance is not the focus of study is a subtle consultation issue. On the one hand, we do not want to threaten teachers when the classroom is visited. On the other hand, teachers must come to understand that their behavior may be part of the problem and that changes in their behavior may be part of the solution. The child's and teacher's behavior (and the child's and parents' behavior) are usually so intertwined that it is almost impossible to examine one without the other.[1]

The two primary goals of a psychological evaluation in school are similar to those in other settings: (1) an accurate description of the child's level of functioning, and (2) treatment and remediation suggestions. The first goal is easier to accomplish than the second. Information gained during the evaluation allows us to describe the positive qualities of the child's functioning, the difficulties he or she faces in mastering problems, and the quality and style of his or her intellectual and social functioning. However, we are much more handicapped in knowing (a) the classroom procedures that will ameliorate the child's problems, (b) the conditions needed to create appropriate conditions for learning, (c) the conditions that can contribute to the child's social adjustment and successful participation in the community, (d) the kinds of assignments and materials that can foster the child's psychological development, (e) the teaching procedures that will be effective in bringing positive changes in the child's learning, personality, and social adjustment, and (f) what it takes, over and above standard classroom procedures, to help the child acquire additional skills and knowledge.

The field of clinical and school psychology is shifting from relying on traditional approaches to evaluation, with remediation when possible, to a more dynamic approach, emphasizing relevancy. There is a greater concern with goals. While this is an important shift, I believe that we must not be hasty in attempting to go beyond the limits of our present knowledge. The results of the assessment do not furnish us with well-validated remediation techniques. Remediation procedures are as much an art as they are a science.

In spite of the limitations associated with developing remediation suggestions, psychologists should work with teachers to establish a plan of instructional objectives. These objectives can include determining the tasks that are to be taught, arranging a hierarchy of instructional objectives, eliminating behaviors incompatible with effective instruction, and teaching the tasks most needed by the child.

The assessment and the recommended activities, or prescriptive programs, are not meant to be the final solution to the child's difficulties. They are starting points for the clinician and teacher. Assessment should be a continuous activity, with modifications made in the initial prescriptive teaching plans when the child's needs change or when the plans are not working effectively. All too often, tests are given, recommendations are made, and the psychologist vanishes until the reevaluation three years later. Effective consultation requires short-term follow-up contacts.

Classification and Labeling

Every description, in some sense, implies a label. When we say "normal range of functioning," we are labeling the child. But this label should be thought of only as a point of reference, not as a means of denying the child an opportunity to learn or to enter into a program. Standardized tests do not tell us how much the child can learn. While they provide a valuable yardstick, which shows a relative level of accomplishment in certain kinds of cognitive activities, they do not sample the complete range of cognitive abilities. We do not know the limits of our examinees' abilities.

Some clinicians object to the term "diagnosis," maintaining that it should be avoided because of its medical, disease-oriented connotations (Ross, 1974). Ross advocates that the task of psychologists and educators is to train, teach, and rehabilitate children who have a limited behavioral repertoire and who cannot cope successfully with their environment. Furthermore, diagnostic labels provide no explanation of the child's difficulties and tell us nothing about the steps necessary for remediation. Ross concludes that clinicians should cease their preoccupation with finding the "right" label and focus on the child, attempting to find ways to alleviate problems and develop more adequate behavior. Assessment is the starting point for training and teaching, not for speculations about etiology and labels.

Classifications, such as trainable mentally retarded (e.g., IQ of 30 to 49) or educable mentally retarded (e.g., IQ of 50 to 69), are simply arbitrary cut-offs on a continuum of intelligence test scores. It is important to recognize that a child with an IQ of 48 is very similar to one who has an IQ of 50, even though they may receive different classifications, whereas a child with an IQ of 68 is more similar to a child with an IQ of 70 than to a child with an IQ of 50. We should be guided by the child's performance, not by a classification system that has arbitrary cut-offs.

While these objections to classification have merit, it is also important to consider that classification is an integral part of the psychological evaluation. Classification aims to provide some organization to the complex and heterogeneous area of exceptionality. Classification aids us in the study of etiology, in the development of programs,

---

EXHIBIT 18-2.   Research Highlight: Effects on Teachers' Expectancies of Labeling a Child "Educable Mentally Retarded"

In a study of the effects of labeling on teachers' expectancies (Yoshida & Meyers, 1975), eighty teachers—forty teachers of regular class elementary children and forty teachers of educable mentally retarded (EMR) children—viewed a videotape of a black child answering concept formation questions ("How are ___, ___, and ___ the same?"). One-half of the teachers were told that the child was in a regular sixth grade class and the other half that he was in an EMR class. At four intervals during the presentation, the teachers were asked to predict how the child would perform on the concept formation questions that were to be administered later in the series. Predictions of future performance were not found to be influenced by the child's label (i.e., whether the child was designated as being in a regular class or as being in an EMR class). In addition, both groups of teachers made similar predictions. The results suggest that it was the teachers' personal evaluations of the student's performance, and not the educational-diagnostic label, that contributed to their expectations of how the student would perform on the tasks.   ∎

---

in evaluations of the outcomes of intervention programs, in communication with professionals, and in problem solving (cf. Hobbs, 1975). The diagnostic label is a quick and convenient device for communicating a set of concepts. It is helpful for record keeping and for statistical reporting.

It has been alleged that placing a label on a person, such as "mentally retarded," initiates a self-fulfilling prophecy. That is, the label supposedly induces individuals who come in contact with the labeled person to treat the person in accord with the label, thereby producing a change in the person's status which may or may not be reversible. We all know that negative stereotypes are often associated with behavioral deviancy labels and with labels indicating low levels of intellectual functioning. However, studies indicate that children's classroom performance is a much more potent force in influencing teachers' expectancies than labels that are given to them.[2]

Let us consider why these results appear to be reasonable. Observation of the child's classroom behavior over weeks and months probably plays the crucial role in the formation of expectancies. When a teacher is told that a child is mentally retarded, certain initial expectations are likely to be generated by this label. However, these expectations will be modified if the child obtains successes in his or her school work—such as reading at grade level or solving 80 percent of the arithmetic and geography problems

correctly. The initial impression will be tempered by the child's *actual* classroom performance. Thus, while labels often initiate expectations, they hold little power once the observer has had a chance to obtain information about the child's abilities, as illustrated in the Research Highlight in Exhibit 18-2.

However, the previous discussion should not make us complacent about the effects of labeling. Labels do set up expectancies, and such expectancies may influence the observer's behavior, especially when there is limited contact with the child. In some situations, it is conceivable that the expectations generated by labels may be so powerful that they may lead to severe restrictions of the child's opportunities. We still know little about the frequency of such occurrences, but even the thought of such a possibility should make us alert to some of the dire consequences of inappropriate labeling.

Psychosituational Assessment

Bersoff calls for replacing traditional forms of psychometric testing with psychosituational assessment (Bersoff, 1973; Ellett & Bersoff, 1976). In a psychosituational assessment, the child's behavior is analyzed, together with "the immediate antecedent and consequent conditions that evoke, reinforce, and perpetuate that behavior" (Bersoff, 1973, p. 896). The assessment focuses on children as they interact and are affected by the environment. Direct measurement of performance takes place continuously in the situations where behavior naturally occurs. When they are getting continuous feedback about the child's level of performance, teachers are in a position to restructure their instructional strategy more quickly.

Bersoff (1973) finds fault with traditional testing:

> In educational settings, testing removes both the child and the psychologist from the natural situation of the classroom, restricting the psychologist's contact with the child's teacher, a primary agent of behavior change. Thus, the teacher is isolated from the information-gathering process, and the psychologist is prevented from gathering data concerning those events that may be evoking academic failure (antecedent conditions) and those that are consequating it (reinforcing events). [pp. 896–897]

The criticisms of standardized testing voiced by Bersoff do have some merit. However, many psychologists are aware of these difficulties and are attempting to deal with them. Other criticisms made by Bersoff may not have much substance. First, he calls the classroom "a natural setting." Would children and parents (and educators and psychologists) agree to this description? The classroom, in many instances, is a highly unnatural setting. Children are expected to be there, and frequently have to follow inflexible procedures. Second, psychologists do have direct contacts with teachers in many settings. Often the child's teacher must be present during the staff conference. There is communication via the referral form and psychological report. Continuous contact is always possible. Third, who is the primary agent of behavior change—the teacher, the parent, the child's siblings, or the child's peers? Fourth, how are teachers isolated from the information-gathering process? They know about the tests, often see the reports, interact with the psychologist, and may have had courses in psychological testing. Where is the isolation?

I do agree that behavior in a standard testing situation may differ from that which occurs in the classroom, and classroom be-

havior is useful in understanding the child. I believe that psychosituational assessment can be a valuable adjunct to the standardized assessment process, but it should not be used, with our present state of knowledge, as the sole means by which to evaluate intelligence, perceptual-motor skills, memory, and a host of other cognitive and academic skills.

Behavioral Assessment

In behavioral assessment, samples are obtained of the child's behavior in specific situations. Many varied assessment procedures are used, including interviews, problem checklists and rating scales, direct observation procedures, psychophysiological data, and intelligence and achievement testing. Some of the goals of behavioral assessment are (a) describing antecedent, situational, and consequent events associated with problem behaviors in order to determine the specific environmental correlates of the problem behavior; (b) designing interventions based on the assessment behavior; and (c) using the assessment data to evaluate the effectiveness of the intervention or to revise the intervention (Bergan, 1977). In a behavioral assessment approach, the focus is on phenomena that can be observed by the clinician, rather than on inferring "mental" entities. The emphasis is placed on children's *present* response capabilities, the stimuli in their environment that are currently effective, and the reinforcers, both positive and negative, that are currently capable of maintaining their behavior (Ross, 1974).

Some of the features of behavioral assessment include the following (Ciminero & Drabman, 1977):

1. Behaviors should be measured in a variety of settings, especially in those settings in which they normally occur, because behavior does change from setting to setting.
2. Ideally, multiple response measures should be obtained from the child. These may include verbal, perceptual, motor, and psychophysiological responses.

3. The assessment data collected should be related directly to treatment decisions.

Standardized tests, from a behavioral analysis perspective, assess various abilities, such as the child's labeling repertoire, discrimination skills, imitation abilities, ability to attend and to follow instructions, and indirectly the child's motivation (e.g., ability to produce sustained effort on a task when the reinforcers are social reinforcement from the examiner and intrinsic reinforcement from being correct) (Nelson, 1975). The frequency, intensity, persistence, and location of the behavior are important to evaluate, as well as the events that precipitated the problem behavior and the events that follow from the behavior. The following are examples of questions that should be considered in a behavioral assessment (Gardner, 1974, p. 256, with a change in notation).

1. What behavior (or behaviors) is (are) creating difficulty?
2. In what setting does the behavior occur (place, time, conditions)?
3. What is the strength of the behavior (frequency, rate, duration, magnitude)?
4. What consequences does the behavior produce which may be maintaining the behavior? (Remember that reinforcement may occur only infrequently and still maintain the behavior—getting attention, avoiding unpleasant duties or situations, etc.)
5. Is the presumed reinforcement positive or negative?
6. Can the presumed reinforcing consequences be eliminated?
7. Can the presumed reinforcing events be used to strengthen acceptable competing behaviors?
8. Does the child have acceptable alternative behaviors in his or her repertoire which would be suitable in the situation?
9. Does the environment provide sufficient opportunity to obtain positive consequences for acceptable behavior?
10. What behaviors should be taught which will replace the excessive behaviors?

A Behavioral Analysis Perspective on Intelligence Testing

From a behavioral analysis perspective, intelligence tests sample general behavioral skills that have been acquired through learning. Intelligence tests can help identify certain treatable behavioral deficits (Ciminero & Drabman, 1977). Items on intelligence tests can be considered to reflect samples of behavior; they are not considered to be indices of internal qualities. The skills measured by intelligence tests enable children to be successful in school (Staats, 1975). Intelligence can be conceived of as learned basic behavioral repertoires. Vocabulary, for example, is an illustration of the labeling repertoire, which in turn is part of the language repertoire. Behaviors, such as placing a block in the appropriate recess on the request of the examiner, are under the explicit control of verbal instructions, and form part of the verbal-motor repertoire. If children are to succeed in the block task (and other tasks as well), a number of abilities are required, including (a) attentional behaviors (listening and following the examiner), (b) understanding the terms used by the examiner, and (c) integrating the instructions with motor movements. Success, therefore, requires that complex verbal-motor units be present in the child's basic behavioral repertoire.

Behavioral Uses of Tests

Standardized ability and achievement tests have a number of advantages for behavioral assessment (Nelson, 1974, 1975). First, they provide built-in comparison norms for children on whom the test was standardized and thereby provide a ready-made control group. Second, they elicit samples of children's academic behaviors in response to standardized stimuli. Third, they assess children's behavioral assets and deficits in comparison with the behavior of other children of their same chronological age. Fourth, they provide baseline measures useful in planning treatment. Fifth, they can be used for screening purposes. Finally, they can be used for prescriptive teaching purposes.

EXHIBIT 18-3.   Psychological Evaluation: A Borderline Child Evaluated with a Behavioral Assessment Focus

Name: Bob   Date of birth: March 3, 1972
Chronological age: 6-4
Date of examination: July 5, 1978
Date of report: July 10, 1978   Grade: 1st

Test Administered

WISC-R (scaled scores):

VERBAL SCALE		PERFORMANCE SCALE	
Information	7	Picture Completion	7
Comprehension	4	Picture Arrangement	5
Arithmetic	6	Block Design	9
Similarities	4	Object Assembly	8
Vocabulary	4	Coding	4
Digit Span	8		

Verbal Scale IQ = 69
Performance Scale IQ = 77
Full Scale IQ = 71 ±5 at the 90 percent confidence level.

Other assessment strategies:
    Behavioral interviews
    Conner's parent and teacher questionnaires
    Behavioral observations at home and at school

Referral

Bob is a 6-year, 4-month-old Caucasian male referred for intellectual and psychological evaluation by his teacher. He was brought to the testing center by his mother.

Behavior

At the time of testing, Bob was neatly dressed and well-groomed. He is the appropriate weight and height for his age and appears to be healthy. His mother expressed concern that his behavior would interfere with attempts to test Bob and remarked that previous testing generally proved inconclusive because of his behavior problem.

The testing took place at a university clinic. Initially, Bob eagerly accompanied the examiner to the small testing room. The first test administered was the Wechsler Intelligence Scale for Children–Revised (WISC-R). During the first thirty minutes of the WISC-R administration, Bob was alert, cooperative, and friendly. He maintained good eye contact and tried to answer the questions presented, although he seemed to have trouble understanding what was required on some of the verbal tasks. However, after approximately thirty-five minutes of testing, his behavior began to change dramatically (about midway through the Vocabulary subtest). He became easily distracted by the metal shelves in the

room, he constantly traced his finger along the walls, and he was frequently out of his seat, wandering about the room. Eye contact and on-task behavior began to disappear, and the examiner had to command him to sit down and pay attention. After Bob answered a question, he would ask, "Is that all?" and stand up, ready to leave. During the last four performance subtests, Bob's behavior was such that the examiner had to coax him continuously to do the items.

Test Results

Bob's WISC-R Full Scale IQ of 71 ± 5 falls within the Borderline range of intellectual functioning and is at the 2nd percentile. There is no significant difference between the verbal and performance portions of this test. In addition, his scaled scores were similar regardless of whether or not he was inattentive.

Behavioral Assessment Results

Bob was observed for approximately two hours in the home/family environment. It was noted that Bob frequently argued with his siblings and would not comply with their requests to leave their toys and other belongings alone. On occasion, he played cooperatively but only as long as he seemed to be getting his own way. Also, interactions between Bob and his mother revealed his tendency to defy her commands. Bob's mother reports that her reprimands were consistently followed by episodes when he "stares at her" defiantly. The father interacted little with his son; however, on one occasion, Bob obeyed his father's command to stop misbehaving, and he did not "stare" at his father as he did at his mother.

Bob was observed at school in his morning classroom for approximately two and a half hours. During this time, his behavior significantly disrupted classroom functioning. He made loud noises during the pledge of allegiance and refused to stand or to repeat it. His frequent silliness was apparently reinforced by the laughter of others in his class. He generally did not comply with his teacher's commands and threw tantrums whenever he was physically forced to participate in a task or denied freedom to do as he pleased. His teacher constantly pleaded with him to behave and frequently threatened him with spankings and not being able to earn tokens. She reported that "nothing seemed to work." She said that she had tried spanking, time out, tokens for appropriate behavior, and even, on occasion, sending him home, but none of these procedures seemed effective.

EXHIBIT 18-3 (cont.)

During classroom activities, Bob constantly demanded his teacher's undivided attention. When he failed to win this he responded by wandering about the room or throwing tantrums.

Thus, Bob does what he wants, when he wants, in the classroom situation. Because of his extremely disruptive behavior in the classroom, it seems that the amount of material Bob is learning is limited. Bob has learned how to avoid putting effort into something he does not like, and this may have also caused deficits in many pre-academic areas as a result of these avoidance tactics.

Most of the items checked as problems on the Conner's Behavior Checklist revolve around issues of noncompliance and disruptive behavior (e.g., picks on other children, throws or breaks things, will not obey school rules).

Recommendations

At this time, it is difficult to assess Bob's intellectual functioning because of his problem behaviors. The WISC-R seems to be an accurate indicator of his current intellectual functioning. However, it was difficult to distinguish what he could not do from what he did not want to do. At this time, it does not appear that placement away from home is necessary, provided that Bob's parents and teacher can carry out the necessary behavioral programs needed to improve his behavior.

The following recommendations need to be carried out under the supervision of a behavior therapist. It is recommended that the mother initiate a "time out" procedure in the home. This would entail sending Bob to an unstimulating portion of the house for a preset period of time contingent upon noncompliance with her requests. The details of this procedure can be worked out in conjunction with the behavior therapist. In addition to instruction in this system for dealing with disruptive or inappropriate behavior, the mother should receive instruction on how to immediately and generously reinforce Bob when he is "good" and "on-task." Reinforcements may consist of praise or simple treats.

Efforts should be made to enlist Bob's father in the program. Also, Bob's siblings should be alerted to the procedure and prevented from interfering in the use of time outs.

Any behavioral system in the classroom should be consistent. Whatever the target behavior, the punishment for transgression should be quick and consistent (every time it occurs). The teacher should not allow Bob to cajole her into letting him off, nor should she allow his attempts at "good" behavior after transgression to keep her from paddling him. Initially, she can expect his tantrum behavior to increase significantly, but if she is consistent, Bob will learn the consequences for his disruptive behaviors, and the rate should decline.

An immediate token/reward system should also be initiated for Bob in the classroom. Shaping appropriate behaviors in Bob will require immediate verbal praise and material reinforcement, rather than the once a week system now used in his classroom. In addition, he should be given tokens that can be exchanged for small trinkets or prizes from a grab bag at the end of each hour.

The behaviors desired and the reinforcement system should be explained to Bob. Each time he is reinforced for appropriate behavior, the behavior should be mentioned as the reinforcers are distributed. This procedure will allow him to become quickly acquainted with what is required of him and the consequences of performing the desired behaviors.

It is recommended that after his disruptive behavior has been brought under control, he be retested in about a year to provide a more accurate estimate of his intellectual functioning and abilities.

Summary

In conclusion, the results of the assessment reveal that Bob is currently functioning in the Borderline range of intellectual functioning. Disruptive behaviors, including fidgeting, poor eye contact, and defiance, were noted during the test session as well as during home and classroom observations. Recommendations focused on the need to bring Bob's disruptive and inappropriate behaviors within tolerable limits. Specific behavior modification programs were suggested for both the home and school environment.

Examiner

Adapted with permission of the publisher and authors from A. R. Ciminero and R. S. Drabman, "Current Developments in Behavioral Assessment of Children," in B. B. Lahey & A. E. Kazdin (Eds.), *Advances in Clinical Child Psychology* (Vol. 1), Copyright 1977, Plenum, pp. 70–75.

Nelson (1974) wisely suggested that "Behaviorists could replace their motto of 'teach, don't test,' with 'test in order to teach'" (p. 283). Exhibit 18-3 presents a psychological evaluation with a behavioral assessment focus.

Applying Behavioral Analysis to the Development of Remediation Strategies

In working with teachers (and other professionals and parents as well), the procedures developed in the area of applied behavior analysis can be very useful. The psychologist, on the basis of data obtained from the psychological evaluation, group-administered tests, and classroom observations is in an excellent position to develop remediation strategies. As remediation proceeds, new information is constantly being elicited, which in turn leads to the continuous updating of diagnostic impressions throughout the remediation period.

It is a good principle to start the remediation procedure at or slightly below the level of the child's strengths. By starting at this level, you give the child an opportunity to make progress at the outset and to be reinforced by his or her efforts. In a behavioral program assessments are also made of the remediation program, including teaching materials, response contingencies, response requirements, and contextual factors, in order to permit change in procedures where necessary. At the end of training, assessments of the child's competencies are again carried out.

Observation of Language and Speech Development

The assessment of language and speech development requires careful attention to the child's speech. In addition, the child's parents can provide valuable information about their child's language and speech development. Some of the major deviations in language and speech that may occur during the preschool and early school years are as follows (cf. Lillywhite, 1958):

1. During the preschool years (3 to 5 years of age), deviations include lack of speech, unintelligible speech, and failure to speak in sentences.
2. At about 5 to 6 years of age, deviations include substitutions of easy sounds for difficult ones, consistent dropping of word endings, faulty sentence structure, noticeable nonfluency, and abnormal rhythm, rate, and inflection of speech.
3. By the age of 7 years, deviations include distortions, omissions, or substitutions of any sounds.

Other signs of difficulties that are not specifically age related include individual speech sounds more than a year late in appearance; use of vowel sounds to the exclusion of almost all other sounds; embarrassment or disturbance by speech; consistently monotonous, inaudible, or poor-quality voice; consistent use of pitch inappropriate for child's age; noticeable hypernasality or lack of nasal resonance; and unusual confusions, reversals, or telegraphic speech (type of speech in which connectives, prepositions, modifiers, and refinements of language are omitted). When some of the above deviations are observed, the child should be referred for speech evaluation.

The tempo of the child's verbal responses and the quality and content of the responses also are important guideposts in the assessment process. Language usage is a guide to personality style and to thought processes. Answers to the following questions will provide cues about the child's general language style and communication skills.

• Are imitation and symbolization used in play?
• Are vocalizations normal?
• Does the child understand what is being said?
• Is gesture understood?
• Are gestures or mime used to communicate?
• Does the child attend to faces or watch lips when people speak?

- Is there any speech?
- What is the child's competence in the use of words and grammar?
- Does the child echo what is said or use words inappropriately?
- Is articulation normal?
- Are words used for social communication?
- Are the responses direct and to the point, vague, roundabout, or free associative?
- What is the usual tempo of the responses? Are they quick or slow?
- Is time taken to consider the responses?
- Is thinking done aloud or is only the final answer given?
- Are the responses self-critical?

Also consider the presence of any language distortions evidenced in the content of the responses. When severe language distortions occur, it may be in the context of severely neurotic or psychotic conditions or brain damage. Examples of major kinds of language distortions are the following:

1. *Automatic phrases* are repetitive statements that do not serve communication purposes. They may reflect defensiveness or inability to rely on one's own resources.
2. *Bizarreness* is revealed when responses show signs of inconsistency, illogical reasoning, or idiosyncratic associations, or when there is a juxtaposition of disconnected ideas.
3. In *blocking,* an attempt is made to recall the answer but it is not successful. Blocking also may be seen when one word is substituted for another when children cannot remember the one for which they are searching.
4. *Circumlocution* is shown when there are roundabout answers.
5. *Circumstantiality* is noted in responses that are indirect. The child proceeds indirectly to the answer with many tedious details and parenthetical and irrelevant additions.
6. *Clang associations* are words linked with one another only on the basis of sound.

7. *Confabulation* is noted in responses that indicate some farfetched association elaborated on the basis of some superficial similarity to the stimulus.
8. *Ellipsis* occurs when there is "omission of one or more words (sometimes only syllables) necessary to complete the meaning in a phrase or sentence" (Wechsler, 1958, p. 181).
9. In *fragmentation,* incomplete thoughts are presented for complete ones, and the examiner is left to fill in the missing ideas.
10. *Irrelevant speech* is similar to rambling, except that the degree of disorganization is more intense. Inappropriate topics may be introduced or statements of self-reference may appear.
11. *Over-elaboration* is "the tendency to give alternate meanings and irrelevant details, or to be overly and unnecessarily descriptive" (Wechsler, 1958, p. 181).
12. *Perplexity* is signaled by confusion, by an inability to understand the questions, or by an inability to understand what is called for.
13. *Rambling* is seen when a topic is introduced after another to which it has little logical relationship; words are not used precisely.
14. A *self-reference* occurs when personalized elements or details reflecting self-involvement are incorporated into a definition (Wechsler, 1958).
15. *Speech difficulty* may be shown by stammering, stuttering, or by other types of speech problems, which may indicate aphasic or dysarthric conditions.
16. *Verbal perseveration* is demonstrated by similar definitions to different words.

Assessment of Visual-Motor Ability

As we have seen in Chapter 16, visual-motor ability is assessed by means of special tests, such as the Bender-Gestalt or the Visual Motor Integration Test. However, some items on intelligence tests and other special ability tests also require visual-motor skills.

Particular attention should be given to children's reaction time and to their trial-and-error methods. Signs of visual-motor difficulty include much trial and error, fumbling, tremor, repetition of copying errors, perseveration, rotation, and variable line quality. Visual-motor difficulties may be associated with defects in visual, auditory, or muscular functions, with poor physical condition, with anxiety, or with other conditions.

Innovative Assessment Procedures

A number of procedures have been developed that permit us to go beyond the standard assessment techniques in evaluating special children. Because these techniques are not well standardized, they must be used cautiously. They are recommended as supplementary techniques that can provide additional information useful in evaluating handicapped children and children referred because of poor school performance, and in developing remediation strategies. Some of the techniques (e.g., learning-potential assessment) are similar to the testing-of-limits procedures described in Chapter 5.

Learning-Potential Assessment

In the learning-potential assessment strategy the child is first tested, then given specialized training, then tested again. Budoff and his associates have used this approach with primarily nonverbal techniques, such as the Wechsler Block Design subtest and the Progressive Matrices.[3] Feuerstein (1979) has developed a similar approach termed the Learning Potential Assessment Device. It is designed to assist in the assessment of low-functioning children. The examiner evaluates the extent to which the child is able to benefit from teaching procedures. The examiner becomes a teacher-observer and the child a learner-performer. Research has shown that some children are able to improve their performance as a result of such training. However, we still need more information about how the ability to profit from this form of specialized training generalizes

to other tasks, especially those that are related to classroom activities.

Paired-Associate Learning

A paired-associate learning task provides a direct measure of learning ability. In this type of task children may be required to learn noun pairs or pairs of visually presented objects. Attempts are also made to discover ways in which such learning can be improved. However, paired-associate learning tasks are limited because they are not highly related to either school achievement or the wider range of conceptual skills needed in school (Kratochwill, 1977).

Diagnostic Teaching

The diagnostic teaching procedure is similar to the paired-associate learning procedure. It goes beyond the latter by attempting to teach children various skills, such as sight reading. Retention is measured, and strategies to facilitate learning are evaluated. Kratochwill (1977) observed that little is known about the usefulness of diagnostic teaching methods as formal assessment devices. In addition, the tasks have been limited and need to be extended to broader areas of ability.

Child Development Observation

The child development observation procedure focuses on gauging the potential of different strategies to facilitate learning; it does not assess learning potential per se. Various strategies are used to enable the child to experience success. The child is encouraged to inform the clinician about what improves his or her learning. Unfortunately, there is little information about the reliability or validity of the assessment sequence (Kratochwill, 1977).

Contingency Reinforcement Procedures

The incident in Case 18-1 demonstrates how a contingency reinforcement procedure (i.e., a procedure that involves the use of reinforcers when certain responses are given) can be effective in enhancing the performance of some problem children in the testing situation. It illustrates the importance of occasionally using flexible procedures that are designed to encourage an exceptional child to participate in the testing situation, and the importance of comparing the test results with the child's behavior outside of the testing situation.

CASE 18-1. The Effectiveness of Contingency Reinforcement

An 11-year-old girl achieved an IQ in the normal range (IQ = 101) when first tested with the WISC, and IQs in the mentally retarded range (IQs = 62, 51, and 65) when tested on three other occasions over a period of two years (Miller, 1969). However, outside of the testing situation, she seemed to function in the normal range. On the Verbal Scale subtests, she failed many items by saying that she did not know the answer or by making inaccurate replies. On the Performance Scale subtests, she haphazardly manipulated many of the materials and generally made little effort to complete the items. Neurological evidence was negative. When she was tested for a fifth time, a monetary reward incentive procedure was used. Chips, which were to be exchanged for money, were given for correct responses and for bonus credits. This procedure resulted in the child's achieving an IQ of 106. Interestingly, performance on the Digit Span subtest at first did not improve. However, she performed at a normal level when the contingency was changed from one chip per correct series to one chip for each digit in the series when the entire series was repeated without error. ∎

Experimental Assessment Techniques

It may be of value to supplement standardized cognitive measures with experimental tests that measure abilities not directly measured by standardized cognitive and achievement tests. One such measure that has received attention is the Unusual Uses Test. In this test children are asked to identify different ways to use specific common objects. Instructions that have been used for the test are as follows (Price-Williams & Ramirez, 1977, p. 7): "Let's see how clever you can be about using things.

For instance, if I ask you how many ways an old tire could be used, you might say: fix up an old car, for a swing, to roll around and run with, to cut up for shoe soles, and so on. Now if I asked you: 'How many ways can you use a pebble?' What would you say?" After these instructions are given, the child is asked to give uses for a *newspaper*, a *table knife*, a *coffee cup*, a *clock*, and *money*.

Two scores are obtained: an ideational fluency score (the number of uses mentioned for all five objects is summed) and an ideational flexibility score (the number of different categories of usage for each object is summed). The scoring is illustrated in the following example. A response to newspaper, "To read, to make a mat, and to use as an umbrella," receives a fluency score of 3 and a flexibility score of 3. A response to table knife, such as "cut your meat and cut other things" receives a fluency score of 2 and a flexibility score of 1. The two scores also form an efficiency index (ratio of flexibility score to fluency score).

General Diagnostic Examples

In testing children, one should be aware that there are many possible reasons for a child's failure. Take the case, for example, of a child who fails to stack blocks when asked to do so by the examiner. Failure may mean that the child has limited hearing, vision, comprehension, or motor capacities, or that the child's language development was too low to translate the commands, or that the child was behaving negatively, or that the child has some degree of neurological damage (Curtis & Donlon, 1973). To arrive at a possible explanation of the child's failure, a careful analysis of the child's entire performance is required. Reporting that there was failure to stack blocks, without providing any explanation, is not sufficient for the assessment task.

The child's performance in a standardized test situation, while providing valuable information, may not reflect how the child might perform if he or she were more comfortable, stimulated or inspired, healthier, or less bogged down by family anxieties. Tests give us information about how children are performing at a specific moment and under specific conditions. The overall score may not reveal some of the underlying dynamic trends that are developing in the child, as Murphy (1975, p. 41) illustrated:

> . . . we need to recognize that the *specifics* of the test may be much more illuminating than the IQ, which is the average of all the functions. One little girl who barely passed the seventh-year-level tests on routine items passed twelfth-year-level tests involving insight and comprehension. Although she was retarded in reading at that time, she has become an expressive and original writer and a remarkably intuitive and creative mother. She was considered a "slow learner" in the second grade, while all the time she was storing away observations and reflections in her independent sensitive way.

The examples presented in this section and in the remaining sections of the chapter are meant to illustrate how *tentative hypotheses* are developed from the child's responses and performance. Hypotheses developed from performance on a few items or from a few test responses usually must be verified via other data sources before being accepted and/or reported. While we must be careful not to overinterpret every miniscule aspect of the child's test responses or performance, there are occasions, as some of the examples in this section indicate, when hypotheses developed from particular patterns may prove to be valuable.

The following examples are illustrations of how hypotheses about temperament, personality, and level of ability can be developed from a careful analysis of the child's responses and behavior. The examples indicate that both physical and psychological factors should be considered in attempting to understand the child's performance. These general examples are followed by diagnostic examples that specifically pertain to the Stanford-Binet and the WISC-R.

EXAMPLES BASED ON BEHAVIORAL CUES

1. *Inability to respond at the moment,* rather than lack of knowledge, may be indicated when a child stares blankly ahead and does not respond to one or more questions.
2. *Distress,* rather than joy, may be shown by laughter in some emotionally labile children (Mecham et al., 1960).
3. *Aggressiveness* may be indicated when a child smashes blocks.
4. *Failure to understand directions* or *feelings of dependency* may be seen when the child builds a design directly on the examiner's model.
5. *Loss of motivation and interest* or a *passive-aggressive expression of defiance* may be indicated when increasing amounts of time are needed in order for the child to complete the trials on some subtests (such as on pegboards). The expectation is that performance should improve with practice, not get worse.
6. *Difficulty in finding a solution, depression, perfectionism, difficulty in making a decision,* or the child's habitual coping style may be revealed by excessive slowness.
7. *Impulsiveness* (particularly when the solution is not correct) or the child's habitual coping style may be indicated by excessive speed. (Impulsiveness may reflect difficulty in postponing action until the solution is thought out.)
8. *Hypomanic qualities* are noted by an expansive, outpouring, and excited response style.
9. *Limited intelligence, shyness or timidity, or deliberate intention to be sure, though slow,* may be revealed by failure to answer a question within an allotted period of time (Burt, 1914).

EXAMPLES BASED ON QUALITY OF VERBALIZATION

10. *Artistic talent* may be shown by responses to vocabulary words that are given in highly sensory terms (Murphy, 1948).
11. *Obsessive tendencies* may be indicated by (a) four or five explanations of courses of action in reply to questions; (b) three, four, or more likenesses given to the similarities questions; (c) elaborate and quibbling definitions of vo-

cabulary words; and (d) overdetailed and doubt-laden responses (Freeman, 1962).

12. *Depressive* features may be indicated by slow, hesitant, and blocked responses, interspersed with self-deprecatory remarks.

13. *Paranoid* qualities are suggested by querulous, distrustful, and legalistic responses.

14. *Dependency* may be revealed by answers such as "Ask my mommy" or "Ask my daddy."

15. *Hypochondriachal preoccupations* may be suggested by constant reference to the body or by responses such as "I should rest."

16. *Fearfulness* may be expressed by responses such as "They all hurt you." In such cases, the child may be expressing his or her fear that the world is a dangerous place.

17. *Exhibitionism* may be revealed by responses referring to dress, parties, and ornaments.

18. *Aggressiveness* may be expressed by responses referring to weapons or battles.

EXAMPLES BASED ON TYPE OF VERBALIZATION

19. *Hearing difficulty* may be disclosed on memory items if words or numbers are distorted, consonants dropped, or prepositions and other connecting words omitted (Taylor, 1961).

20. *Misleading results* occur when a child with severe speech defects substitutes one word for another simply because the second word is easier to say. For example, the child says *knife* instead of *scissors* to a picture vocabulary card simply because it is easier to say *knife* at the moment (Berko, 1953).

EXAMPLES BASED ON ITEM CONTENT

21. *Boredom* may be present when a child passes difficult items but fails easier ones. This type of child may be bored by easy material and stimulated by hard material (Murphy, 1948).

22. *Dependency or submissiveness* may be indicated by ready and assured responses to routine materials, but anx-

ious, hesitant, and tentative responses to questions that require judgment and evaluation (Freeman, 1962).

23. *Compulsive tendencies* may be revealed when a child passes tests requiring meticulousness but then fails others because the child is either more meticulous than the test requires or too inflexible in his or her thinking (Fromm, Hartman, & Marschak, 1957).

24. *A pedantic urge to accuracy* may enhance performance on memory tasks (Cronbach, 1949).

25. *Inhibition and a fear of being incorrect* may be shown when a child fails tasks requiring insight and imagination but not other tasks (Cronbach, 1949).

26. *Difficulty with handling aggression* may be indicated when a child becomes disorganized when reading a passage that has aggressive content (Brooks, 1979).

The demarcation between style of responding and content of the responses often is not clear, but this should not be too much of a problem. Both content and style intermesh to provide some insights about the child's personality and temperament. However, judgment must be used in deciding whether a response reflects the child's habitual style or whether it is a temporary and transient expression.

Diagnostic Illustrations for the Stanford-Binet

We now turn to some examples that illustrate how interpretations of the Stanford-Binet are developed. Illustrations for specific handicapped groups and for mentally retarded children are presented in Chapters 20 to 23. Chapter 8 also presents useful interpretative guidelines for the Stanford-Binet.

Illustration Number 1—Discrepancy Between Mental Age and Vocabulary Age

A quiet, rather retiring 10-year-old girl, who had no significant behavioral problems other than enuresis and whose school performance was average, had considerable variability on the Stanford-Binet. The variability was evident in her obtaining a mental age of 12-5 years (IQ = 120) and a Vocabulary age of 6 years (only seven vocabulary words were defined correctly). Shapiro (1951) proposed the following four hypotheses and methods for evaluating the hypotheses to account for the discrepancy between her mental age and Vocabulary age.

1. The child's poor social and economic environment has caused her poverty of vocabulary. This first hypothesis can be tested by having a social worker visit the home and evaluate the family environment.
2. An extreme degree of emotional inhibition has produced a breakdown on the Vocabulary items, but not on other items. A group vocabulary test can be administered, and if the obtained score is higher than the Binet Vocabulary score, the second hypothesis would receive some confirmation.
3. The variability is due to a temporary disturbance, and therefore has no diagnostic significance. This hypothesis can be evaluated by administering the Vocabulary test again at the end of the examination.
4. An aphasic disturbance exists. Additional language tests or tests for aphasia may be given to investigate this hypothesis.

Further investigation revealed that the girl's vocabulary ability was commensurate with her IQ, but that a combination of personality factors and peculiarities of the test situation depressed her Vocabulary score. The second and third hypotheses were therefore partly supported. Shapiro's example is a good illustration of how clinical hypotheses are formed and how they may be tested.

Illustration Number 2—Interpretation of Successes and Failures

A study of successes and failures can provide helpful cues about differential cognitive functioning (Palmer, 1970).

Thus, the seven-year-old child who on the Binet can repeat digits, copy a diamond, answer questions about a story, but has less than a six year old's vocabulary, cannot make the simplest verbal similarities and is not able to fathom "what's foolish about this picture?" may be doing well or even above average work on tasks involving routine learning of one-to-one concrete associations, but the development of his independent judgment and analysis of a situation may be quite retarded. [p. 104]

Palmer hypothesized that the child who displays the above pattern may be too dependent emotionally on others to begin to make independent intellectual judgments, or that severe emotional or physiological handicaps deter more complex thought processes. These hypotheses can be tested by examining the quality of the child's responses and types of failures, and by administering other tests designed to measure social and emotional adjustment.

Illustration Number 3—Interrelationships Among Several Variables

The examiner should integrate the child's entire performance to arrive at an appraisal of personality.

The child who overcautiously stays within limits on the drawing tests, . . . shows poor insight, defines "obedience" but not aggressive words, may be giving important clues to a personality structure; he may be anxious about authority to the extent of inhibition of normal childish spontaneity, and this would affect work as well as social relations in a modern school. [Murphy, 1948, p. 17]

Illustration Number 4—Analysis of Performance on Paper Cutting

The interplay of various dynamics involved in the child's attempt to arrive at a solution on the Paper Cutting test at year level IX is illustrated in the following example (Fromm, 1960).

On the Paper Cutting test an eight year old struggled for a while with the solution. She drew one cut incorrectly, looked at it critically and said, "No, I don't think I have it right."

She erased it. She thus showed that, among other variables, she employed *judgment* and *self criticism* in striving for the correct solution. Had she stopped after the first trial with the remarks "Oh, well, I never can do things right," her self criticism would have been an unhealthy one and would have been involved in her failing the item. Instead, she asked the examiner: "Do you know how to do it?" The examiner said she did. The little girl replied in an eager voice, "If you can do it, I want to be able to learn to do it by myself too." Thus she also used the mechanism of *identification* in spurring herself on towards success. She sat there thinking for a few more moments, and suddenly, with a flash of *insight* . . . , exclaimed, "Oh, I know how it goes!" Then she drew the correct pattern. In addition to the variables already discussed, others were involved in her success: *language understanding*—she understood the instructions; *reality-centered concept formation*—she asked herself what is the thing, what does the paper look like when it is opened; and *flexibility of thinking,* which is necessary in order to proceed from the actual stimulus, the folded paper, to the imagined visualization of the opened paper. [p. 233]

Illustration Number 5—Physical Disability vs. Emotional Disturbance

Escalona (1945) showed how a qualitative analysis of test responses and a comparison of the child's performance on several tests were useful in determining whether failures were a function of physical disability or of emotional disturbance. The examinee, a 6½-year-old girl whose mother had died shortly before she was seen for testing, was in good health, with the exception of severe myopia.

While she obtained an IQ of 97 ± 4 on the Stanford-Binet, Form L (CA = 6-6, MA = 6-4), emotional disturbance was reflected by irrelevant and absurd fantasy material appearing in a variety of responses. To the "Man with umbrella" item on the Picture Absurdities I test (year level VII) she replied, "Nothing is funny about it . . . his hand . . . he has got it cut off . . . sure, when the finger is cut off it hurts." When she was asked to repeat the sentence "Fred asked his father to take him to see the clowns in the circus" (Memory for Sentences III, year level VIII), she said, "Fred lost his father." She performed poorly on the Copying-a-Square test (year level V) and failed the Copying-a-Diamond test (year level VII). The failures on the visual-motor tests might be attributed to her visual handicap, if it were not for the fact that other tests requiring visual acuity were passed (e.g., Maze Tracing, year level VI; Mutilated Pictures, year level VI). She adorned the incomplete drawing of a man (Picture Completion: Man, year level V) with a gun and showed the "smoke from shooting" by violent scribbles across the entire page.

Escalona noted that the Stanford-Binet alone did not reveal the degree to which the child differed from normal children in her capacity to deal with everyday situations. It was the Stanford-Binet in conjunction with other tests that provided a comprehensive picture of the child's psychological functioning. Escalona concluded that the child was emotionally disturbed.

Illustration Number 6—Analysis of Vocabulary Definitions

This illustration demonstrates how an analysis of vocabulary definitions is useful for forming hypotheses about the examinee (Moriarty, 1961). Compare the two following definitions for the word *orange:* (a) "Well, it's something that has juice in it and you squeeze it in the squeezing room and then you get the whole juice." (b) "That you eat." Both responses are equally correct. However, the first response suggests that the child is aware of uses and values of things, and that he or she has some original phrases. The second response is short. It "might reflect efficiency, inhibition in verbalizing or a functional orientation in the pattern of thinking" (p. 8).

Illustration Number 7—Analysis of Verbal Absurdities Responses

Fromm (1960) provided interesting illustrations of how responses to the Verbal Absurdities II test (year level IX) may reveal personality dynamics. It must be emphasized that any interpretations about personality that are made from one or two responses must be tentative, subject to revision or abandonment after a thorough and systematic analysis is made of all available material.

A 10-year-old boy revealed his impulsiveness in his response to the fireman item ("The fireman hurried to the burning house, got his fire hose ready, and after smoking a cigar, put out the fire." "Why is that foolish?"): "Boy-oh-boy, he'll start a second fire with his cigar! And pretty soon the houses next door will burn down, and then the whole city will burn up like Chicago did when Mrs. O'Leary's cow kicked over the kerosene lamp." To the melting icebergs item ("One day we saw several icebergs that had been entirely melted by the warmth of the Gulf Stream." Why is that foolish?"), he said: "They couldn't have told you that, because when the icebergs melted the water rushed all over the boat and everybody drowned." This latter answer suggested the presence of hostile-aggressive impulses, as well as wild, destructive fantasy; the question does not include any reference to a boat or to drowning people.

The following response to the iceberg item by an adolescent girl revealed her anxiety and a religious defense against the anxiety: "God would not allow icebergs to melt when I am so near that I could see them, because God does not want me to get drowned."

Illustration Number 8—Perseveration

The following two examples show how perseveration can occur on Similarities and Comprehension items (Wells & Kelley, 1920). One example is that of an examinee who gave the answer "Burning" to the question "In what way are wood and coal alike?" (Similarities: Two Things, year level VII). Then to the next question, "In what way are apple and peach alike?" he said, "They'll burn all the time." A second example is that of a child who replied to the question "What's the thing for you to do when you have broken something that belongs to someone else?" (Comprehension IV, year level VII) with "Return it and have it fixed." Then to the next question, "What's the

thing for you to do when you are on your way to school and see that you are in danger of being late?" he answered, "Hurry up and fix it as quick as I could."

Illustration Number 9—Plan-of-Search Test

The Plan-of-Search test at year level XIII is valuable for observing how children perform on a relatively minimally structured task. The test requires that the child develop a plan for a practical situation that is, however, fictitious and imagined (Bühler, 1938). Failures may be due to defective ability to visualize or to difficulty in working systematically.

The Plan-of-Search test can be solved in various ways (Bühler, 1938; Lejeune, 1955). Some solutions reflect normal coping attempts, while others may reflect emotional problems or personality styles. For example, neurotic children (a) may have difficulty in organizing their solutions, (b) may become stuck in the middle of the field, (c) may give up, (d) may make random and futile attempts, or (e) may be obsessive and unadaptable.

Illustrations 1 and 2 in Figure 18-2 are examples of a "helplessly confused" solution and an "ornamentally involved" solution that may be the products of neurotic children. Illustration 3 represents a "giving up helplessly" solution that may appear in the performance of mentally retarded children. Illustration 4 is an advanced and thoughtful solution. Examples of solutions that may reflect personality dynamics are seen in Illustrations 5 and 6. Illustration 5, "going out of the field," may be the performance of a timid child whose parents have encouraged his or her fears and flight reactions, while Illustration 6, "success followed by flight from field," may represent the effort of an overconscientious child or one who has conversion symptoms or school difficulty.

The personality descriptions for the solution types are interesting and potentially useful, but must be viewed as speculations. Utmost caution is urged in interpreting personality dynamics from a child's performance on the Plan-of-Search test (or from performance on any single test item). The

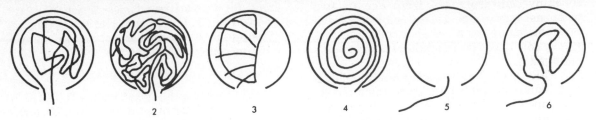

FIGURE 18-2. Illustrations of Types of Solutions on the Plan-of-Search Test.

approaches of Bühler and Lejeune, neverthe-less, are valuable, for they enable us to formulate tentative hypotheses that are amenable to further investigation.

Illustration Number 10—A Variety of Interpretative Hypotheses for the Stanford-Binet

a. On the Obeying Simple Commands test (year level II-6), *negativism* may be elicited to a greater extent than on other tests.
b. The presence of repetition compulsion, perseveration, or stimulus boundness in children with a *compulsive neurosis* may cause them to fail the Paper Cutting test (year level IX) and other similar tests. These defenses may lead to blocking, overwhelming anxiety, unrealistic wild flights of fantasy, or compulsive meticu-lousness—reactions that can impede per-formance (Fromm, 1960).
c. *Overmeticulous, neurotic children* may be absorbed in and anxious about details on reasoning tests (e.g., Reasoning I at year level XIV, Ingenuity I at year level XIV). They may become concerned about the burglary itself or about the danger of spilling water, but still may be able to get to the nucleus of the problem and proceed correctly (Taylor, 1961).
d. Children with *body-image problems* may fail or exhibit anxiety on the Mutilated Pictures test at year level VI or on the Picture Completion: Man test at year level V (Fromm et al., 1957).
e. *Aggressive, practical children* with a "know-how" for solving problems may have an advantage over *passive, contem-*

plative children on the Ingenuity tests found at year levels XIV and above (Taylor, 1961).
f. Children who are *dependent on authority and precise tangible accomplishments* may have success on digits and on other precisely defined tasks, but fail tests that require insight, while the opposite pat-tern suggests that "anxiety may have stimulated a concentrated effort to understand and deal with social relations at the expense of routine learning" (Murphy, 1948, p. 17).
g. The following pattern of failures and suc-cesses on tests at year levels IV through VI may suggest *sexual inhibition:* failing tests that deal directly or indirectly with sex differences (Opposite Analogies at year level IV; Pictorial Similarities and Differences at year level IV-6; Picture Completion: Man at year level V; Muti-lated Pictures at year level VI), while passing other tests of equal difficulty. The sexual inhibition is reflected by the child's denying that there are differences or missing parts (Kessler, 1966).

Diagnostic Illustrations for the WISC-R

The diagnostic illustrations presented for the Stanford-Binet are also valuable in working with the WISC-R (and WPPSI and WAIS-R). In addition to those in the follow-ing examples, other assessment considera-tions are presented in the chapters on psy-chopathology and mental retardation and Chapters 11 (for the WISC-R) and 13 (for the WPPSI). The principles of interpretation illustrated in this section can be generalized to many different types of responses and patterns that occur on the WISC-R. The illustrations, like those for the Stanford-Binet, cover only a few selected points.

Cognitive variables involved in the WISC-R (and WPPSI and WAIS-R) subtests, such as planning, anticipation, attention, and concentration, are a good source for understanding personality organization. The pattern of scores may reflect general modes of adaptation. The general procedure is to look for consistency among the various aspects of test performance (profile of scores, content of responses, and style of responses).

Illustration Number 1—A Variety of Interpretative Hypotheses for the WISC-R

a. Some children may show a pattern of missing easy items and succeeding on more difficult items. This pattern may occur in the case of a bright child who is bored by the easy items and thus gives careless or even nonsense replies, only to become challenged by more difficult items where he or she can demonstrate his or her skills (Palmer, 1970).

b. Various questions and words may arouse associations of violence or hostility (Palmer, 1970). Two such words are knife and affliction, which appear on the Vocabulary subtest.

c. The response to the Comprehension question "What is the thing to do if a boy (girl) much smaller than yourself starts to fight with you?" may reveal the child's ability for social impulse control (Palmer, 1970).

d. A child struggling with issues of aggression and retribution gave the following reply to the Comprehension question "What would you do if you cut your finger?"—"Fingers can fall off or be cut off and maybe they could be sewed on" (Brooks, 1979).

e. A child struggling with separation issues may be unable to answer any Picture Completion items because of incapacitating anxiety. The child might ask the examiner why something has to be missing (Brooks, 1979).

f. Children who constantly recheck their work with the Block Design model, a possible indication of doubt and uncertainty, may be revealing obsessive tendencies.

g. The painstaking Coding task may be more difficult for the alert, creative, and intuitive normal child than for the more pedantic, passive, and slow-moving one (Taylor, 1961).

Illustration Number 2—Example of a Paranoid Structure

Blatt and Allison (1968) demonstrated how content of responses, style of responses, and pattern of scores are interrelated in a paranoid individual. The content of the responses may reflect suspiciousness regarding the recording of the responses or feelings of being tricked. The style may be cautious, rigid, and legalistic. The pattern of scores may show high scores in areas related to hyperalertness to details (Picture Completion or Picture Arrangement) and to bringing together and relating disparate things (Similarities).

Illustration Number 3—Interpreting Comprehension Subtest Responses

The following are possible interpretations of Comprehension subtest responses (Taylor, 1961). The interpretations should be viewed as tentative, subject to modification after an analysis of the child's performance on the entire test.

a. A moralistic response: "What is the thing to do if a boy (girl) much smaller than yourself starts to fight with you?" Answer, "He should not hit you."

b. A moralistic response: "What is the thing to do when you cut your finger?" Answer, "You should be more careful and not cut your finger."

c. A defensive response: "What is the thing to do if a boy (girl) much smaller than yourself starts to fight with you?" Answer, "I should not fight."

d. A need-for-help response: "What is the thing to do if a boy (girl) much smaller than yourself starts to fight with you?" Answer, "I would tell my mother."

Illustration Number 4—Diagnostic Aspects of the Picture Arrangement Subtest

Correct as well as faulty solutions on the Picture Arrangement subtest allow for an evaluation of the child's developmental level of reasoning (Taylor, 1961). Most failures are due to difficulties in logical reasoning. However, faulty solutions also may be due to inattention (e.g., on the SLEEPER item, failure to see the time on the clock), minimal experience with common events (e.g., on the BURGLAR item, prison picture is placed before court session), or emotional attitudes and preoccupations (e.g., on the BURGLAR item, "He is in prison, he got out again, holds up a guy, then tells judge that he did not do it"). The last arrangement, however, may not be an indication of emotional preoccupations because it actually depicts what occurs in many real situations. Children who "miss" the item by using this arrangement may be very close to the experience.

Reasoning difficulties are suggested when distorted infantile arrangements occur with regularity in a child who is older than 8 years. This can occur with mentally retarded children, with brain-injured children, and perhaps with psychotic children. Emotionally disturbed children usually produce stories that are logical. However, their anxieties and preoccupations may be revealed by unusual arrangements, such as neglecting details for the sake of a particular theme.

Illustration Number 5—Picture Arrangement Subtest as a Thematic Technique

Craig (1969) described a method that can be used to obtain thematic material from the WISC-R Picture Arrangement subtest. (Although Craig's procedure was illustrated for the WISC, it also applies to the WISC-R.) The method may serve as a useful screening device; it is not intended to replace other thematic techniques, such as the Thematic Apperception Test (TAT) or Chil-

dren's Apperception Test. It is used *after* the entire WISC-R has been administered. The procedure involves randomly placing the FIGHT sequence of cards before the child and then asking him or her to make up a story about *one of the cards* in standard TAT fashion. After the story is completed, the cards are removed and the PICNIC sequence of cards is placed randomly before the child. The child is asked to tell a story about one of the cards. This procedure is followed for each of the Picture Arrangement sequences. The procedure differs from the one suggested by Rapaport et al. (1968) and Wechsler (1958), which involves having the examinee make up a story that is based on the arrangement of cards in each sequence. The stories are interpreted by following usual methods applied to thematic material.[4]

Summary

1. The assessment process brings together all available relevant information gathered from past records, interviews, observations, and test results.

2. The assessment considers developmental, behavioral, medical, and environmental data.

3. The aims of the assessment process include a description of the problem, an estimate of its severity, identification of relevant factors, prognosis, and treatment suggestions.

4. It is important to observe the child in a variety of settings, not just in the test situation.

5. It is important to obtain information from relevant adults, particularly parents and teachers, about their knowledge of the child's problems.

6. The assessment of children presents some difficulties because (a) classification systems are not uniform, (b) behavioral disorders are not always clear, (c) the child's behavior is highly dependent on adults, (d) assessment is time consuming, and (e) there are rapid developmental changes in children.

7. Assessment and treatment are intertwined, with treatment results providing feedback for the assessment hypotheses. Re-evaluation and follow-up are important parts of the assessment process.

8. The assessment process in schools incorporates the general principles of assessment, but focuses more directly on learning and educational remediation. The evaluation should focus on the child's strengths and compensatory abilities as well as on areas of deficiency.

9. While visits to the classroom may provide valuable information, it is necessary that the teacher approve and support such visits.

10. There are better tools for evaluating children's ability than there are for pre-scribing remediation programs.

11. Although classification and labeling have potential negative consequences, they serve many useful functions, such as aiding in the study of exceptionality and facilitating communication and record keeping.

12. Psychosituational assessment—that is, the observation of children in their environment—serves as a valuable addition to psychometric testing; it should not serve as a replacement for psychometric testing.

13. In behavioral assessment, a variety of techniques are used in order to (a) evaluate the child's present level of functioning, (b) design appropriate interventions, and (c) evaluate the effectiveness of the interventions.

14. Standardized tests, from a behavioral assessment perspective, (a) provide built-in comparison norms, (b) elicit samples of academic behavior in response to standardized stimuli, (c) assess behavioral assets and deficits, (d) provide baseline measures, (e) serve as screening devices, and (f) serve prescriptive teaching purposes.

15. Language and speech assessment must rely heavily on developmental norms. Deviations during preschool years include failure to develop speech, unintelligible speech, and failure to speak in sentences. During school years speech deviations include distortions, omissions, or substitutions of sounds.

16. A variety of innovative assessment procedures have been proposed, including (a) learning-potential assessment, (b) paired-associate learning, (c) diagnostic teaching, (d) child development observation, (e) contingency reinforcement procedures, and (f) experimental assessment techniques.

17. The diagnostic examples presented in the chapter illustrate how hypotheses can be developed from an analysis of the child's responses, performance, and behavior.

CHAPTER *19*

Assessment of Ethnic Minority Group Children

IQ and achievement tests are nothing but updated versions of the old signs down South that read "For Whites Only."

ROBERT L. WILLIAMS (1974)
Psychology Today

Moreover, it is precisely the black students who need IQ tests most of all, for it is precisely with black students that alternative methods of spotting intellectual ability have failed.

THOMAS SOWELL (1973)

EXHIBIT 19-1   (cont.)

he went on to tell her how he had changed his opinion of her on the day of the birthday party because of the close relationship he had seen between her and the Black psychologist.

This little story illustrates a number of things. First, it shows that the test is a social situation. The testing situation, whether it be a psychological test or any other kind of test for that matter, reflects a relationship between people, a relationship that is often remarkably subtle. And when anything hampers this relationship, the result is likely to show in the test score itself. This can occur on an individual test as well as a group test, an IQ test as well as a personality test, a subject-matter examination as well as a psychological measure.

The story also shows how the behavior evidenced in the clinical situation tends to be seen by the psychologist as indicative of the basic personality of the child. This is frequently done with little awareness of how much this behavior is a product of the particular relationship between the psychologist and the child, and of the testing situation as such. Children from different cultural backgrounds respond very differently to clinical situations and to the idea of being tested or evaluated.

The anecdote also points up the fact that a well-meaning, clinically trained, unprejudiced psychologist can have poor rapport with an inner-city child, not because of deficient psychological technique, but because of limited knowledge about certain cultural attitudes. In this case, the attitude in question is the feeling held by many Black people that the informality intended by nicknames signifies a lack of respect when it takes place across cultural lines. This does not suggest that the child himself was aware of this reasoning, but rather that he was simply reflecting his mother's wish that he be called by his full name. ■

Reprinted, with a change in notation, by permission of the publisher and author from F. Riessman, *The Inner-City Child*, pp. 53–55. Copyright 1976, Harper & Row.

The label "ethnic minority group children" is used to designate children who belong to a recognized ethnic group and whose values, customs, patterns of thought, or language are significantly different from those of the majority of the society in which they live. The groups from which ethnic minority children come include blacks, Mexican-Americans, American Indians, Puerto Ricans, and Asian Americans. The use of such labels as "culturally handicapped," "culturally disadvantaged," or "culturally deprived" to designate ethnic minority group children has been unfortunate, because these terms have value implications. No one has the right to degrade a subculture that does not conform to the patterns of the majority group. Certain unstandard behaviors in minority groups may be both healthy and justified, because life conditions of these groups differ markedly from those of the dominant culture (Barnes, 1971). The extent to which a group is handicapped may lie in the eyes of the beholder. This chapter therefore uses the term "minority group" instead of alternatives which may have pejorative connotations.

In working with ethnic minorities it is important to gain an appreciation for each ethnic minority's culture—including values, styles, language, mores, motivations, and attitudes—because cultural factors may affect the assessment situation. These variables, as we have seen in the incident described in Exhibit 19-1, are powerful forces that shape the child's attitudes toward the test situation, including the test materials, the examiner, and the reasons for the assessment. Ethnic minorities have developed coping patterns that, in part, are a response to an environment that has been less than hospitable. It is important to understand how these coping patterns facilitate or hinder children's adjustments to their own subculture, as well as to the culture at large.

We shall see that the issues concerning intelligence testing (and special ability testing) of ethnic minority group children are complex, for they are woven into the very fabric of society. Test results have an impact on children's self-esteem and influence their life chances (Brim, 1965). If tests are detrimental to ethnic minority children, then they must be changed or eliminated. However, if tests are beneficial to ethnic minority children, then their elimination may be a disservice to countless children. Whenever tests are used, examiners must ensure that the results are used for the good of the child. Let us now look at the arguments and the evidence.

Arguments Against the Use of Intelligence Tests in Assessing Ethnic Minority Children

Many allegations have been made about the inappropriateness of tests, and in particular of intelligence tests, for use with ethnic minority children.[1] The major ones are listed below and then are considered in more detail.

1. Standard intelligence tests have a strong white, Anglo-Saxon, middle-class bias— tests are culturally biased.
2. National norms are inappropriate for use with ethnic minority group children.
3. Ethnic minority children are handicapped in taking tests because of (a) deficiencies in motivation, test practice, and reading; (b) failure to appreciate the achievement aspects of the test situation; and (c) limited exposure to the culture.
4. Rapport and communication problems exist between white examiners and ethnic minority children.
5. Test results are the main reason why ethnic minority children are segregated into special classes that provide them with inadequate and inferior education; test results induce negative expectancies in teachers.

Cultural Bias Argument

There are many definitions of test bias, each of which has some value in helping us to understand the properties of tests and how they are used. In examining the issue of test bias, we must first consider the meaning of a test score. Is the test score an indication of past achievement or is it an indication of aptitude for future achievement? This distinction is extremely important because many arguments concerning the bias of tests rest on which of these interpretations is considered correct. It is, in part, a distinction between achievement tests and aptitude tests.

We should view intelligence tests and other special ability tests as measures of achievement. The tests covered in this book are not viewed as pure measures of aptitude or as measures of the capacity for accomplishment. Scores reflect past learnings, representing the interplay of biological factors (genes) and environmental factors (experiences). Low scores obtained by ethnic minority children should be a call for improved educational systems and not for the abandonment of those "lying tests" (see Flaugher, 1978). Let us now examine some of the definitions of test bias, reviewed by Flaugher and supplemented with additional studies, as they relate to ethnic minorities.

Test bias as mean differences. Test bias is seen by some when a group makes scores that are lower, on the average, than scores made by other groups. However, this definition is not acceptable as a definition of bias. Mean differences are not a legitimate standard for identifying bias. Because of the disparities, socioeconomic and otherwise, among various groups in our society, it would be surprising if intelligence and achievement tests did not show mean differences in favor of some groups.

We know that when disparities between black and white groups are reduced, IQs become more similar. For example, 7-year-old black children obtained IQs that were less than 5 points below those of white 7-year-olds when both groups came from the same socioeconomic level, lived in the same city, and had mothers who had gone to the same hospital for prenatal care (Nichols & Anderson, 1973). The 5-point difference contrasts with a 15-point difference that is often reported between black and white children (in favor of white children).

Test bias as overinterpretation. This type of bias is seen when test users generalize from a limited domain of measurement to a broad range of ability, a tendency to overinterpretation. For example, it is a great leap to say that a child "lacks practical judgment" simply because he or she was unable to answer correctly a few problems on a test. The issue of test bias is legitimately raised in such cases.

Test bias as single-group or differential validity. This issue of test bias focuses on whether a test can predict equally well for two ethnic groups within the United States. Two related ways of comparing validity coefficients are used to examine this form of test bias. "Single-group validity" occurs when a validity coefficient is significantly different from zero for one ethnic group but not for another, while "differential validity refers to the finding of a significant difference *between* two validity coefficients" (Flaugher, 1978, p. 674). The majority of research with ethnic minorities in our country indicates that this form of test bias does not exist. That is, neither single-group validity nor differential validity is generally found. Although there are instances when single-group or differential validity is found, "the fact that they are so elusive, difficult to detect, and debatable is good evidence that they are not very potent phenomena relative to all other possible sources of problems in the interaction of minorities and testing" (Flaugher, 1978, p. 674).

Recent studies with the WISC-R, Stanford-Binet, PPVT, and Progressive Matrices all indicate that the regression lines for black children and white children (and in the Reschly and Sabers' study of Mexican-American children as well) were similar using Wide Range Achievement Test scores and other achievement indices as criteria.[2] In addition, recent studies have shown that the WISC-R, Stanford-Binet, and Slosson Intelligence Test have excellent concurrent validity for black, white, and, in some studies, Mexican-American and/or American Indian children, using such criteria as the California Achievement Test, Wide Range Achievement Test, Metropolitan Achievement Tests, teacher ratings, Stanford Achievement Test, and California Test

of Mental Maturity.[3] Validity coefficients usually are in the .50s or higher in these studies. Recent studies support the conclusion that intelligence tests generally predict equally well for black and white children.

Test bias as content. This form of test bias focuses on the content of the test items, whether they are in some sense unfair to some groups of the population. Inspection of items in standardized intelligence tests reveals few, if any, that appear to be systematically biased in favor of one group over another. Agreement among the members of a panel of experts as to what items are biased tends to be very low. A useful empirical approach in investigating content bias is to examine item performance statistics group by group. In this method the difficulty level of each item is examined. "If a particular item is extraordinarily difficult for minority-group members relative to the difficulty of other items in the same test, then that item is a good candidate for suspicion of this kind of bias" (Flaugher, 1978, p. 675). Studies cited by Flaugher suggest that the elimination of such items from standardized tests makes little if any difference in test scores.

Several different types of internal criteria are available for studying test bias (Jensen, 1974c). These include (a) similarity in the rank order of the percent passing each item in each of the groups; (b) similarity between groups in the differences between the percent passing values of adjacent items in the test; (c) differences between groups in the number of persons passing each item when both groups are equated for total score; and (d) systematic differences in the types of item content that discriminate most and least between the two groups. Applications of these methods to the intelligence test and ability test performance of black and white children (and adults) indicate that there is no evidence that differences between blacks and whites are due to cultural bias as reflected by these internal criteria.[4] Tests in these investigations included the Stanford-Binet, WISC-R, PPVT, and Progressive Matrices.

Miele (1979) reported that the WISC Comprehension item 4 "What should you do if a child smaller than you begins to fight with you?" singled out by Robert Williams as a blatant manifestation of cultural bias, proved to be the 42nd easiest item for black children and the 47th easiest item for white children. Thus, this item was found to be easier for black children than for white children. Sandoval and Miille (1980) reported that black, Mexican-American, and Anglo judges were not able to determine accurately which WISC-R items were more difficult for minority students. The ethnic background of the judges also made no difference in accuracy of item selection. These results suggest that subjective judgments cannot be used to determine bias.

Test bias as the selection model. This form of test bias, or more accurately *selection bias*, refers to the extent to which a test is used to allow examinees to enter certain programs (e.g., special classes, college, vocational training, or jobs). Various statistical models have been offered to reduce selection bias (see, for example, Petersen & Novick, 1976). However, these models do not function in a vacuum; they are tied to ethical and social value systems. Flaugher believes that the prospects are dim for universal acceptance of a set of values concerning fair selection.

Test bias as the wrong criterion. This form of test bias focuses on the criterion used to investigate the validity of a test. The criterion itself is open to many problems. How important is the criterion? What is the reliability of the criterion measure? To what extent have innovative and nontraditional criterion measures been used? While the criterion problem is a difficult one, attempts should be made to examine thoroughly the criterion used to validate tests.

Test bias as atmosphere. This form of test bias examines the extent to which the examinees feel out of place or unwelcome when taking a test. If examinees' real capacities are inhibited when they are confronted by a test, then the test scores are biased. However, this type of bias appears to play a limited role, if any, because much care is taken to obtain the child's best performance in the testing situation. A very important atmosphere-type factor currently in use is "the application of nationally normed examinations to certain areas of the American education system, e.g., large inner-city school systems that are in fact not in the same population, academically speaking, as the rest of the system" (p. 677). Such norms bring bad news to teachers and students and cause much concern, anxiety, discouragement, and despair. The very process of testing creates these feelings. Flaugher believes that criterion-referenced testing promises to provide an effective solution to this type of bias.

Other aspects of the culture-bias argument. Another way to evaluate the possible test bias of intelligence tests is to study the extent to which tests measure similar abilities in various ethnic groups. A number of studies have examined the factor structure of the WISC, WISC-R, WPPSI, and McCarthy Scales of Children's Abilities for samples of black, Mexican-American, and white children.[5] In almost every case the results indicated that the groups have comparable factor structures. This led investigators to conclude (a) that the intelligence tests under study measure the same abilities in white, black, and Mexican-American children, and (b) that the Verbal-Performance distinction is appropriate for the three ethnic groups.

One of the main thrusts of the culture-bias argument has been that intelligence tests are not relevant to the experiences of ethnic minority children. Black children, for example, are said to develop unique verbal skills that are neither measured by conventional tests nor accepted by the middle-class-oriented classroom (Williams, 1970b). There has been little, if any, research to support this contention. Further, Ebel (1975) pointed out that items on intelligence tests represent important aspects of competence in the *common* culture; the items are not reflective of simply middle-class values. For a democratic society to exist, these common cultural forms and practices need to be maintained and extended to the culture as a whole. Ebel wisely observed that *"cultural apartheid ought not to be encouraged in this society"* (p. 86, italics added). He believes that

> The bias which accounts for poor test performance by some minority persons is not in the tests so much as it is in the culture, and thus is another problem altogether. So long as the tests under scrutiny truly measure the skills necessary to success in the prevailing culture, minority interests are not well served by blaming "test bias" for poor performance.
>
> The tests we use in education ought to be as free of bias as we can make them. But the extent and seriousness of bias in our current educational tests can be, and probably has been, exaggerated. The "well-known" bias of tests against minority group members seems to be more fanciful than factual. [p. 87]

Attempts to develop tests that are relevant for black children have not been successful. Williams (1972), for example, developed a 100-item multiple-choice test termed the Black Intelligence Test of Cultural Homogeneity (BITCH), based on items drawn from the black culture. It is a culture-specific test measuring special information about the world of the inner city. Many of the items deal with black slang, which is itself not uniform throughout the country. The following are two items from the test:

> Boot refers to a (a) cotton farmer, (b) black, (c) Indian, (d) Vietnamese citizen.
> Yawk (a) gun, (b) fishing hook, (c) high boot, (d) heavy coat.

Williams (1972) reported low correlations between the BITCH and the California Achievement Test (Reading, $r = .39$, Language, $r = .33$, and Mathematics, $r = .18$) in a sample of twenty-eight blacks, aged 16 to 18 years. However, two other studies failed to provide evidence that the test is useful for assessing the abilities of black children. One study (Long & Anthony, 1974) of a group of thirty black 16-year-old high school students enrolled in educable mentally retarded classes in Florida showed that their scores were below the 3rd percentile on the WISC and at the 1st percentile on the BITCH. Thus, these black children did no better on the BITCH. In another study (Andre, 1976) of 150 black and white seventh graders in a southeastern urban school system, the black middle-class adolescents obtained higher scores than the white middle-class adolescents on the BITCH, while lower-class whites and blacks obtained the same score. These results do not provide differential validity for the BITCH.

Milgram (1974) pointed out that the BITCH may be useful for building black pride, but is useless as a predictor of success in the majority culture. The test measures only knowledge of black slang, not problem-solving or reasoning abilities. At present, the BITCH does not appear to be useful in the assessment of black children.

The argument that intelligence tests are not valid because ethnic minorities have not had the same experiences as Anglo middle-class children becomes difficult to accept when we consider the fact that the mean scores of children in Japan on many of the Performance Scale subtests of the various Wechsler scales are higher than those of the American standardization samples (Lynn, 1977). These results clearly show that a population quite far removed from white middle-class America actually does better on nonverbal tests than do American children themselves. Lynn believes that these findings indicate that tests such as the Performance Scale of the Wechsler scales may be much fairer culturally than many critics have been willing to allow.

Humphreys (1973) believes that

> there is every reason to accept a single biological species for blacks and whites and a high degree of cultural similarity as well. While there are obvious environmental differences, these differences are not as profound as to require different principles in the explanation of black and white behavior. The two groups use a highly similar (if not identical) language, attend similar schools, are exposed to similar curricula, listen to the same radio

programs, look at the same commodities, etc. Cultural differences are a question of degree, not of kind. [p. 3]

Thus, we see that there are opposing views about the extent to which intelligence tests are appropriate for ethnic minority children. The evidence, gathered from many studies and with a variety of intelligence tests and ethnic minority groups, points to one conclusion: *Intelligence tests are not culturally biased. They have the same properties for ethnic minority children as they do for white children.* While there are some limited exceptions to this conclusion, it appears to be warranted from an impartial assessment of the data.

Inappropriateness of National Norms Argument

The argument that national norms are inappropriate for ethnic minority children has led some writers (e.g., Mercer, 1976) to advocate establishing pluralistic norms. Pluralistic norms may be important if one believes that it is useful to know how a child's performance compares to that of others in his or her own ethnic group. However, pluralistic norms are potentially dangerous because (a) they provide a basis for invidious comparisons among different ethnic groups, (b) they may lower the expectations of ethnic minority children and reduce their level of aspiration to succeed, (c) they may have little relevance outside of the child's specific geographic area, and (d) they furnish no information about the complex reasons why ethnic minority group children tend to score lower than Anglos on intelligence tests (DeAvila & Havassy, 1974b). Bernal (1972) believes that renorming tests is a dishonest undertaking because the renorming does not involve test modifications nor does it take into account whether or not the test should even be used with ethnic minority children. What norms should be used for a child who has a Mexican father and a Hungarian mother?

The charge that norms for the major individual intelligence tests are based *entirely* on the performance of middle-class whites simply is not true. All current versions of the Stanford-Binet, WISC-R, WPPSI, WAIS-R, and McCarthy have used excellent sampling procedures to obtain their standardization populations. Ethnic minority children are represented in each of the norm groups in proportion to their representation in the general population.

If ethnic minority children are to succeed in the majority culture, they will need to acquire the skills that would enable them to do so. National norms reflect the performance of the population as a whole. They are important because they describe the typical performance of our nation's children. They are an important frame of reference and provide a guidepost for decision-making. This is not to say that other norms should not be used. Test results may be interpreted from several frames of reference. But it is important that test users and consumers of test information clearly recognize which norms are being used.

Handicapped in Test-Taking Skills Argument

Ethnic minority group children may be deficient in employing test-taking skills, choosing proper problem-solving strategies, and balancing speed and power. They may also have test anxiety. Western culture emphasizes achievement and problem solving, and by the time children begin school, it is usually necessary for them to accept intellectual challenge. However, some ethnic minority children may fail to comprehend or to accept the achievement aspects of the test situation (Palmer, 1970). They may view it as an enjoyable child-adult encounter, rather than as a time to achieve; or, if the problem-solving aspects of the situation are recognized, they may be ignored. North American Indian children, in particular, may not work quickly because of a desire not to compete with others.

Zigler and Butterfield (1968) suggested that while ethnic minority children may have an adequate storage and retrieval system to answer questions correctly, they may fail in practice because they have not been exposed to the material. For example, to the question "What is a gown?" they may respond incorrectly because they have never heard the word "gown." Motivational factors may affect the performance of some ethnic minority group children; they know what a gown is, but respond with "I don't know" in order to terminate as quickly as possible the unpleasantness of interacting with a strange and demanding adult. Thus, low IQs may be associated with limited exposure to test content or with motivational factors, neither of which has much to do with a child's thinking abilities.

Studies have suggested that ethnic minority group children, in comparison with Anglo middle-class children, are more wary of adults, more motivated toward securing adults' attention and praise, less motivated to be correct for the sake of correctness alone, and willing to settle for lower levels of achievement success (cf. Zigler & Butterfield, 1968). The results of Zigler's and Butterfield's own investigation suggested that ethnic minority group children suffer from emotional and motivational deficits which decrease their usual intellectual performance.

Johnson (1974) tested the assumption that some ethnic minority group children express themselves best in spontaneous, unstructured settings, whereas in testing settings they are likely to be more inhibited, that is, to talk less and to be less verbally responsive (e.g., see Riessman, 1962; Zigler, Abelson, & Seitz, 1973). He compared language samples obtained during the administration of the WPPSI and Illinois Test of Psycholinguistic Abilities with those obtained in natural settings. The sample of children consisted of forty 4-year-olds who differed in race (black or white), social class (middle class or lower class), and sex. The samples were matched for age and WPPSI Performance IQ. Spontaneous speech samples were gathered in nursery school settings and on playgrounds, and were analyzed by various language-complexity measures. The results indicated that there were few differences between the groups either on the spontaneous speech measures or on the test language measures. The study provided no support for the assumption that black lower-class children express themselves better in natural settings than in test settings.

There is sufficient evidence that some ethnic minority children have limited test-taking skills. But this limitation is also true of some non–ethnic minority children as well. We do not know how pervasive this limitation is among ethnic minority children, or to what degree it lowers their performance on tests. (The Research Highlight in Exhibit 19-2 illustrates many methodological flaws in a study that attempted to demonstrate that the WISC is not valid for assessing black children because it allegedly does not take into account their cultural and test-taking background.)

Racial Examiner Effect Argument (with Black Children)

The anxiety, insecurity, latent prejudice, and other reactions to contemporary black-white relations that are experienced by white clinicians in their work with black children may be transmitted to the children in any of a number of different ways. For example, some examiners may show one or more of the following reactions: (a) paternalism, (b) overidentification, (c) overconcern or excessive sympathy or indulgence; (d) reactive fear, or (e) inhibition. Black children, in turn, may show fear and suspicion, verbal constriction, strained and unnatural reactions, and a façade of stupidity to avoid appearing "uppity." Some may even deliberately score low to avoid personal threat, and others may view the test as a means for white persons, not blacks, to get ahead in society. While many of these behaviors, patterns, and perceptions are likely to exist and are important phenomena in their own right, there is still no way of knowing to what extent they affect black children's scores (Sattler, 1970, 1973a).

Another possible source of difficulty that white examiners may have in working with

EXHIBIT 19-2.   Research Highlight: Pitfalls in the Measurement of Intelligence of Urban Children—An Example of Inadequate Methodology

A. Introduction

Hardy, Welcher, Mellits, and Kagan (1976) claimed that the WISC fails to provide a valid measure of the intelligence of inner-city black children. They arrived at this conclusion by testing a sample of 200 7-year-old children, 88 percent of whom were black. The children were initially administered the complete WISC, after which parts of five subtests were once again administered by using special procedures. For the Information, Comprehension, and Vocabulary subtests (a) selected questions were readministered and scored in the standard manner, (b) probing questions were then asked to ascertain the reason for the child's response, and (c) the response was scored after the probing questions. For Digits Backward, the child's name was reversed to familiarize him or her with the task, and for Picture Arrangement, the children were asked to tell what they were doing while arranging the pieces.

Incorrect responses were classified by the following scheme: (a) lack of knowledge, (b) failure to comprehend the total question, (c) failure of speech perception (enunciation)—i.e., the child failed to "hear" the question correctly or misheard a key word so that more than the standard correction permitted by the protocol was needed, (d) an incorrect frame of reference—i.e., the child's experience was other than that upon which the question was based, and (e) inability to verbalize (possibly due to vocabulary limitations—the child seemed to know what was required but could not find appropriate words for a precise definition).

B. Methodological Weaknesses

Sattler (1979) critically evaluated their study and found it to be deficient in a number of areas.

1. The major methodological weakness was the failure of the investigators to present any evidence that the higher scores resulting from their testing-of-limits procedures were actually more valid than those obtained during the standard administration.
2. The investigators failed to include other types of children in their study or to recognize that almost any group of children would obtain higher scores under the altered procedures and more liberal scoring standards than under standard administrative conditions.
3. The children did not serve as their own controls, nor was there a separate control group for the Digits Backward and Picture Arrangement subtests. A repeated administration of these two subtests was not given in a standard manner, so that any changes on retest could simply have been a result of practice.
4. The report failed to give information about the raters or how reliable they were in using the classification scheme for rescoring the items.
5. Children who failed an item as a result of "failure of speech perception" may have been penalized because examiners failed to administer the test appropriately during the initial administration.
6. The investigators claimed that errors which fell into the "an incorrect frame of reference" category reflected the children's limited experience and not their limited cognitive capacities. But this interpretation is open to question, because their study does not permit one to determine whether the children's failures were due to limited experience or to their inability to learn.
7. The investigators reported that their altered procedures resulted in significantly higher subtest scores. However, on two of the five subtests, Information and Digits Backward, the mean increases were .20 and .18, respectively. While these increases are significant in a statistical sense, they may have no practical significance in the calculation of an individual child's IQ.

C. Conclusion

The above analysis points to only one conclusion: the investigators have failed to support their assertion that the WISC underestimates the level of intellectual capability of inner-city children. Their report does a disservice to countless inner-city children who need the benefits of techniques that can assess their level of cognitive functioning, guide them in their choice of careers, and facilitate the diagnostic and remediation process within the school and larger community. Creating misleading doubts about existing intelligence tests, as their study has done, can be of no service to inner-city children.   ■

black children involves the communication process (Sattler, 1973c, 1977). Communication may be interfered with when there are misunderstandings of verbal and nonverbal cues. A misreading of verbal and nonverbal cues in interethnic communication may result in mistrust, sustain stereotypic judgments, and contribute to conflict. Therefore, every attempt should be made by clinicians to communicate as clearly and effectively as possible with black children (and children from other ethnic groups as well).

A view held by some psychologists is that white examiners impair the intelligence test performance of black children.[6] However, a careful study of the research literature refutes the myth of racial examiner effects. In twenty-five of the twenty-nine published studies dealing with racial examiner effects on individual intelligence tests or other cognitive measures, no significant relationship was found between the race of the examiner and the examinee's scores.[7] Thus, it is apparent that in the overwhelming majority of cases white examiners have not been found to impair the intelligence test performance of black children.

The result is all the more impressive when one considers the wide range of tests, grade levels, geographic areas, and dates of administration encompassed by these studies. The tests covered included the WISC, WAIS, WPPSI, Stanford-Binet, PPVT, Draw-A-Man, Iowa Test of Preschool Development, and several other tests of cognitive ability. The grade level of the children in these studies ranged from preschool through grade twelve. The geographic locations, though largely urban, included eastern, midwestern, southern, and western cities. The years of publication ranged from 1964 to 1977. Thus, the scope of these studies is comprehensive, rendering their results all the more forceful.

Differences in dialect are another source of potential difficulty between white examiners and black examinees. The argument goes that black children do not clearly understand white examiners, and this causes their scores to be lower than those they obtain when tested by black examiners.

Studies, however, have failed to provide any support for this position. Quay (1972, 1974), for example, reported that black children failed to obtain higher scores when, instead of being administered in standard English, the Stanford-Binet was administered by a black examiner in black dialect. There is increasing evidence that black children are bidialectical, in that they have the ability to comprehend equally well black dialect and standard English.[8]

Even though white examiners have not usually been found to affect black children's performance on intelligence tests, examiners cannot be indifferent to the examinee's race. They must be alert to any nuances in the test situation that suggest that an invalid performance is in the making. Testing children from cultures different from that of the examiner is a demanding task. At times it may be difficult to understand children's responses, and every effort must be used to enlist their best efforts.

Inadequate and Inferior Education Argument

Test results, it is claimed, are used to place black children in special education classes (or tracks), which are considered to be inadequate and inferior. This argument is based on a number of premises. One premise is that black children who are placed in special classes would achieve at a higher level if they were not removed from the regular class. Tests are held accountable since they are one of the means by which schools place children in special classes. A second premise is that test results produce negative expectancies in teachers—when teachers learn that black children have low scores, they then begin to treat children as if they will perform at a below-average level.

The position of the Association of Black Psychologists (Williams, 1970a) with regard to standardized tests is as follows:

The Association of Black Psychologists fully supports those parents who have chosen to defend their rights by refusing to allow their children and themselves to be subjected to achievement, intelligence, aptitude and performance tests which have been and are being used to—A. Label Black people as uneducable. B. Place Black children in "special" classes and schools. C. Perpetuate inferior education in Blacks. D. Assign Black children to educational tracks. E. Deny Black students higher educational opportunities. F. Destroy positive growth and development of Black people. [p. 5]

We all would agree that test results may be one link in the educational chain that leads teachers and school administrators to assign children to special classes or programs. However, what Williams (and others) fails to acknowledge is that children are usually referred for individual assessment only *after* they have performed poorly in school. Most black children (or any other group of children) are never seen for a comprehensive individual assessment.

The premise that test results contribute to the development of expectancy effects also has some merit. However, we again must consider the strength of such expectancy effects. The claim that the initial negative expectancies produce a self-fulfilling prophecy has little merit. The self-fulfilling prophecy received great impetus from the work of Rosenthal and Jacobson (1968), which supposedly demonstrated that children who were characterized as "late bloomers" performed better than other children on ability tests. However, this study has so many pitfalls that its results cannot be accepted (see, for example, Snow, 1969; Thorndike, 1968). As Cronbach (1975) observed:

> In my view, *Pygmalion in the Classroom* merits no consideration as research. The "experimental manipulation" of teacher belief was unbelievably casual—one sheet of paper added to the teacher's in-basket, which apparently moved within seconds to the wastebasket. The technical reviews indicate that the advertised gains of the "magic" children were an artifact of crude experimental design and improper statistical analysis. (No doubt there are expectancy effects in the classroom. The question ought to be whether tests add to bias or instead bring expectations closer to the

truth. On that there is no direct evidence.) [pp. 6–7]

Further, additional studies have failed to document this type of self-fulfilling prophecy (or expectancy) effect.[9] Thus, research studies indicate that, for the most part, children's intellectual growth is not influenced when teachers know children's intelligence test scores.

We must also carefully examine the premise that special education classes for the mentally retarded do not provide the kinds of intervention programs needed for ethnic minority children who are functioning in the mentally retarded range. These children may need programs emphasizing enrichment and verbal stimulation rather than the usual type of program designed for the mentally retarded. Children who are not learning adequately in school and who may not be mentally retarded need such opportunities as resource rooms, tutoring, nongraded classes, or learning centers. "Such programs tend to deemphasize labels and focus on remediating deficiencies or teaching needed skills in order that the child can be integrated into regular school classes at or near his age level" (Garrison & Hammill, 1971, p. 20). This is appealing advice, but we need to know a great deal more about the differential effectiveness of these special programs when compared with traditional programs designed for the mentally retarded.

Arguments for the Use of Intelligence Tests in Assessing Ethnic Minority Children

We have just surveyed the principal arguments against the use of intelligence tests in the assessment of ethnic minority children. While some of the arguments have value, the crucial ones surrounding culture bias were found to have little, if any, merit. Now let us explore some of the arguments that have been offered for the continued use of intelligence tests (and other ability tests) for assessing ethnic minority children:

1. Test scores of ethnic minority children are useful indices of immediate or present

functioning. Tests provide valuable information about their strengths and weaknesses. Doing away with tests would deprive clinicians and educators of vital information needed to assist children. A report sponsored by the American Psychological Association's Board of Scientific Affairs (Cleary, Humphreys, Kendrick, & Wesman, 1975) stressed the importance of evaluation in education: *"Diagnosis, prognosis, prescription, and measurement of outcomes are as important in education as in medicine"* (p. 18, italics added).

2. Standardized intelligence tests serve a useful purpose by providing good indices of future levels of academic success and performance as defined by the majority culture.

3. Tests can be useful in obtaining special enrichment programs and services for ethnic minority children (and other children as well). Abandoning formal assessment procedures may deprive handicapped ethnic minority children of the opportunity to obtain appropriate attention and services to which they are legally entitled (Tolor, 1978). The problem of poor achievement of black inner city children is real. It has not been caused by tests. Tests have been helpful in documenting the severity of the educational deficits. "The tests are not bigoted villains but color-blind measuring instruments that have demonstrated a social problem to be solved" (Green, 1978, p. 669).

4. Tests serve to evaluate the outcomes of school or special programs. For example, tests might be used to determine whether children have learned to read or to perform arithmetical operations. For this purpose, tests serve as a means of providing objective evidence that the school is accountable. *"As such, far from being a part of the problem, tests are an absolutely essential part of the solution"* (Flaugher, 1974, p. 14, italics added). Those calling for the elimination of testing altogether would in fact be allowing the educational system to be released from any accountability at all.

5. Tests serve as a corrective device by providing information that cannot be obtained easily by other means. Tests have helped to prevent misplacements of many ethnic minority children. This is so because teachers cannot reliably judge children's level of intelligence.

6. Because tests may reveal the inequalities of opportunity available to various groups, they may also provide the stimulus for social intervention to facilitate the maximum development of each child's potentialities. Thus, knowing that differences exist may lead to the gradual disappearance of some kinds of bias.

7. Ethnic minority groups should be favorably inclined toward use of ability tests, because tests constitute a universal, objective rather than prejudicial, standard of competence and potential (Brim, 1965). Other selection methods may decrease the opportunities of ethnic minority children. Jensen (1975) observed that "objective means of revealing talents stand to benefit talented members of disadvantaged groups the most, since in their cultural circumstances certain talents are more apt to go unrecognized and underdeveloped" (p. 67).

8. Concern about the social consequences of not using educational tests has been expressed (Ebel, 1964; Messick & Anderson, 1970). If educational tests are abandoned, it will become more difficult to encourage and reward individual efforts to learn. Programs will be difficult to evaluate, and educational opportunities might be based more on ancestry and influence, and less on aptitude and merit. Decisions on curriculum would be based less on evidence, and more on prejudice and caprice.

In summary, we have seen that intelligence tests (and other ability tests) measure the abilities that they were designed to measure with reasonable accuracy for ethnic minority children and for children from the dominant culture as well. Tests have the potential to do much good in our society. Tests assess a child's current intellectual functioning irrespective of race or social status. Thus, the consequences of not testing might be to increase bias and discrimination.

Black American Children

Black Americans are bicultural and bidialectical, and, far from being either deficient or merely different in culture, often possess a richer repertoire of life styles than middle-class whites (Valentine, 1971). Valentine suggested that neither the deficit model (cf. Zigler & Butterfield, 1968) nor the difference formulation (cf. Baratz & Baratz, 1970) is adequate in accounting for Afro-American behavior. Instead, he argued for a biculturation model. Biculturation is the

> key concept for making sense out of ethnicity and related matters: the collective behavior and social life of the Black community is bicultural in the sense that each Afro-American ethnic segment draws upon both a distinctive repertoire of standardized Afro-American group behavior and, simultaneously, patterns derived from the mainstream cultural system of Euro-American derivation. [p. 143]

The cultural diversity existing within the black community makes any generalizations about black children suspect. However, the pattern of race relations in our country is likely to have had similar effects on black children, regardless of their particular individual cultural style.

The withering effect of racism has been cited as the major and overriding psychiatric problem of black individuals (Pierce, 1974). The family patterns developed in the inner city, which may be adaptive for occupational and economic survival, may be unsuitable to the task of socializing children to achieve in the middle-class culture (Rodman, 1968). The Black Power movement has developed as one attempt to eradicate racism (Pinderhughes, 1969), and a remarkable effect of the movement is that it has helped to affirm psychologically the fact of being black. The movement has helped rectify some of the negative imagery attached to blackness in the years since slavery (Pierce, 1968; White, 1970).

A cumulative deficit hypothesis has been proposed to account for the performance of black children. It postulates that, relative to the standardized norms, there is an increasing decrement in intelligence test scores with age. Studies examining this hypothesis in large samples of white and black school children in California (Jensen, 1974a) and in rural Georgia (Jensen, 1977) have found that there was little decrement in intelligence in either ethnic group in the California sample, whereas in the Georgia sample the black children, but not the white children, showed significant and substantial decrements in both verbal and nonverbal intelligence. To account for these differential findings, Jensen suggested that the progressive IQ decrement of the rural Georgia children was likely associated with the cumulative effects of a poor environment.

Layzer (1972) offered a slightly different explanation to account for the cumulative deficit hypothesis. If intelligence represents an adaptation to one's environment, a suburban child will have stronger incentives to develop certain cognitive skills (as measured by intelligence tests) than a ghetto child, because the skills assessed by intelligence tests are less relevant to the environmental challenges faced by ghetto-dwellers. These considerations would explain the findings that the IQs of children living in urban ghettos and depressed rural areas tend to decrease as children grow older. Kamin (1978) offered still another explanation of these findings. He suggested that the measured intelligence of recently born black children has been facilitated by changed social conditions. Therefore, younger black children have higher IQs than older ones. Additional research, such as longitudinal investigation, is needed in order to determine which explanation accounts for the performance of black children.

Hispanic-American Children

Hispanics, a term referring to persons of Spanish-speaking origin, are the second largest ethnic group after blacks in the United States. There are approximately 14.6

million people of Spanish origin living in the United States, roughly 6 percent of the total population. The major Hispanic groups are the Mexican-Americans (Chicanos), Puerto Ricans, Cubans, and people from Central and South America.

Mexican-Americans are the largest Hispanic group, with approximately 9 million concentrated in five southwestern states—California, Texas, Arizona, Colorado, and New Mexico. The largest percentage of Mexican-Americans, 35 to 40 percent, live in California. One important feature of the Mexican-American population is that its median age is 18 years, compared with the median age of 27 years in the United States population as a whole. This demographic factor suggests that the Mexican-American population can be expected to increase substantially in the next several decades.

Puerto Ricans are the second largest group of Spanish-speaking persons in the United States. New York City accounts for about 60 percent of the total Puerto Rican population in the United States. There are approximately 2.0 million Puerto Ricans on the mainland, compared with 3.0 million inhabiting the island of Puerto Rico. On the mainland, they reside mostly in the northeast (e.g., New York, New Jersey, Connecticut, Pennsylvania, and Massachusetts); some also live in Illinois. They are an economically deprived group, being at a great disadvantage with respect to income, employment, and education. The island of Puerto Rico was ceded to the United States in 1898, was a territory until 1948, and then became a commonwealth. Puerto Ricans became citizens of the United States in 1917 with the passage of the Jones Act.

Approximately 1 million Cubans live primarily in Florida and in other states on the East Coast. There are approximately 2.5 million other Latin Americans who live in the United States, with the largest numbers coming from the Dominican Republic, Colombia, and Chile.

Hispanic groups share a similar language and Spanish heritage, but maintain their autonomy and are clearly distinguishable from one another. While it is important to recognize that there are differences among Hispanics, especially between those born in the United States and those born in other countries, and between lower and middle classes, some generalizations about the Hispanic culture, as dangerous as they may be, appear relevant to the assessment situation.

First, in evaluating Hispanic children it is important to consider such factors as cultural practices, bilingualism, speech, rapport, and translation of test items. Each of these factors may affect the validity of the test results in some manner, and their impact is likely to vary, depending on the child's degree of cultural assimilation. We will shortly examine these factors more closely.

Second, attitudes toward mental health also will affect how Hispanics perceive psychological services, including the psychological evaluation and recommendations. Because they are more tolerant of deviant behavior than Anglo-Americans and fear hospitalization and possible removal of the child from the family, Hispanics tend to underuse mental health services and to institutionalize their mentally retarded children at rates somewhat lower than those found in Anglo-American families (Dohrenwend & Chin-Shong, 1967; Eyman, Boroskin, & Hostetter, 1977). Furthermore, the strong group and family orientations of Hispanics may work against them in educational and psychotherapeutic settings, which are predicated upon strong individualistic orientations. Traditional Hispanics prefer to solve emotional problems within a family context (Edgerton & Karno, 1971). The possibility, too, must be considered that mental health services are not meeting the needs of Hispanic families.

Third, Hispanics share economic and social difficulties, such as poverty, inadequate employment, poor educational opportunities, segregation in housing, inequality before the law, and various kinds of social discrimination. Hispanic children tend to come from homes with less education and less income than the average Anglo-American home. In school they have a lower level of achievement, a higher percentage of drop-outs, and poorer reading skills. Factors that may contribute to their difficulties in school include lower socioeconomic status, inadequate mastery of English, and cultural traits and customs that conflict with the Anglo culture. In addition, boys are sometimes forced to find work in order to help support their families, and girls may drop out of school to help care for younger brothers and sisters. Assimilation is more difficult for Hispanics than for some other ethnic groups because they are physically distinguishable, use a foreign language, and have cultural practices that are not always compatible with those of the majority culture.

The following list of suggestions for working with Hispanic children emphasizes that psychologists and educators must examine their own values and become familiar with Hispanic culture if they are to be successful in their work with Hispanic children (cf. Christensen, 1975).

1. *Learn about the culture.* Study and learn about the various Hispanic groups that you are working with. Stereotypes are likely to interfere with your ability to work with Hispanic clients.
2. *Call children by their right names.* Hispanics are given two last names, the first representing the father's side of the family and the second the mother's side. It is important that you recognize that the child's second name is the beginning of the last name; therefore, it represents part of the family name.
3. *Work with the family.* The family plays an important role in Hispanic culture. It is especially important to work with the family during the evaluation and remediation process.
4. *Refrain from using the child as an interpreter during a family conference.* If the child is used as an interpreter, undue strain may be placed on the family and the obtained information may be distorted.
5. *Understand that to the Hispanic, the Anglo-American clinician is the stranger (or foreigner).* Anglo-American clinicians may have difficulty in establishing rapport with Hispanic clients. A number of interviews may be needed before the formal examination is begun. In some cases, clinicians may need to visit the child's home and share information about their personal background with the child and the other family members in order to permit the family to get to know the clinician as a person. Skill is required in order to establish rapport with children of different cultures. In some cases, Hispanics have many obstacles to overcome in adjusting to the Anglo-American culture. To be effective, clinicians must demonstrate their credibility, honesty, and reliability. Some Hispanic children and families may expect that the clinician will be prejudiced, arrogant, and lacking in knowledge about Hispanics. Clinicians who are patient, understanding, competent, and tolerant will be able to diminish these feelings and help the family see that the child's welfare is the concern of all involved.
6. *Understand the concept of "hijo de crianza"* ("a child who is raised by someone else"). Occasionally someone other than the child's parents may raise the child. Clinicians should be tolerant of these and other living situations.

Bilingualism

In one sense, bilingualism can be understood as second-language learning, although other meanings are also associated with the term, such as the learning of two languages simultaneously. Research on second-language learning in children indicates that there is no evidence that bilingualism affects general intelligence, although in some cases verbal scores may be lowered and classroom performance may be impeded because of ignorance of words, ideas, and grammatical structures (McLaughlin, 1977).

The effects of bilingualism depend in part on whether children are adding a second language to a well-developed first language or whether a second language is gradually replacing their first language. Hispanic children usually have to learn English as a second language, and then are required to use this second language in their school work (Manuel, 1965). Spanish, however, is the language they use outside of school. It is spoken at home and in the community, but is seldom used in reading. Because of this form of bilingualism, many children fail to develop a sufficient mastery of either language, and learning is more difficult under such conditions. Linguistically, Mexican-American children are a very heterogeneous group, with wide variations in the combinations in which the two languages are known.

Speech Difficulties

Because Hispanic children often speak Spanish as their primary language, the Anglo-American examiner may have difficulty communicating with the Hispanic examinee. The patterns of speech inculcated by use of the primary language, Spanish, can interfere with the correct speaking of English.[10] Speech patterns of bilingual Hispanic children often are a complex mixture of English and Spanish, and the children may never become proficient in speaking either language (Holland, 1960). Language barriers arise from (a) the different sound that the same letters have in Spanish and English (e.g., *i* in "hit" or "miss" may be pronounced *ee* as in "meet"), and (b) the variations in concepts that exist between the two cultures (e.g., "nose" in some Spanish localities is plural, so that a child may say "I hit *them* against the door") (Chavez, 1956).

Spanish-speaking children can encounter three types of difficulties when they speak their own language (Perales, 1965). First, because their Spanish vocabulary is limited, they may borrow from a limited English vocabulary to complete expressions begun in Spanish. Students may use such expressions as *"yo le dije que* I wouldn't do it" (I said to him that I wouldn't do it) and *"El fue,* but I stayed in *la casa"* (He went, but I stayed in the house). Second, they may give English words Spanish pronunciations and meanings (called *pochismos*). For example, a Spanish speaker may use the word *huachar*

(from the English verb "to watch") instead of the correct Spanish verb *mirar,* or the word *chuzar* (from the English verb "to choose") instead of the correct Spanish word *escoger.* Third, they may have difficulties in pronunciation and enunciation. They may say, for example, *"Nos juimos con eos"* for *"Nos fuimos con ellos"* (We went with them). The problem of language mixing, illustrated in the first example, should not be construed to mean that bilingualism is necessarily detrimental to the mastery of either language; little is known about the reasons for such linguistic interactions (Padilla, 1977).

Classifying children's degree of language proficiency is a difficult task. While there are a large number of instruments available for evaluating Spanish-speaking children's language proficiency, none meet acceptable psychometric standards. (Appendix D reviews the Bilingual Syntax Measure Bilingual Syntax Measure II, Language Assessment Battery, and Language Assessment Scales.) After the child has been evaluated, some attempt should be made to classify the child's degree of language proficiency. The following 5-point scale is an example of a classification scheme (DeAvila & Duncan, 1976):

1. Monolingual speaker of a language other than English (speaks the other language exclusively).
2. Predominantly speaks a language other than English (speaks mostly the other language, but also speaks some English).
3. Bilingual (speaks both the other language and English with equal ease).
4. Predominantly speaks English (speaks mostly English, but also speaks some other language).
5. Monolingual speaker of English (speaks English exclusively).

Although bilingualism per se does not affect intelligence, there is some evidence that Mexican-American children may have linguistic difficulties. Preschool Mexican-American children have been found to vary widely in their understanding of English and Spanish, with many children having diffculty in both languages (Carrow, 1971; Zimmerman, Steiner, & Pond, 1974). Six-year-old Mexican-American children perform better on vocabulary tests, but not on an achievement test, if their parents speak both English and Spanish in the home rather than Spanish only (Spence, Mishra, & Ghozeil, 1971). Bilingual Mexican-American high school juniors and seniors have greater difficulty in learning lists of words in Spanish than in English (Lopez & Young, 1974), a result that may be related to the learning history of the children. Because they are expected to learn in English in school, Mexican-American children are more likely to develop the coding strategies that are necessary for rapid acquisition of verbal material in English than in Spanish.

Examiner Effects

Stereotypes held by the Anglo examiner toward the Mexican-American examinee, or by the Mexican-American examinee toward the Anglo examiner, may interfere with rapport. The two ethnic groups are keenly aware of the differences that divide them, and feelings of resentment—stemming from a mutual lack of understanding—are prominent (Madsen, 1964). Anglos generally do not know much about Mexican-American customs and values (Clark, 1959), nor are they knowledgeable about the conditions that exist in the *barrio* (section of a town in which Mexican-Americans live) (Burma, 1954). The examinee's language may serve as a reduced cue for group identification and, like skin color, it may influence the examiner-examinee relationship (Anastasi & Cordova, 1953). Every attempt must be made by examiners to overcome any of their stereotypes.

The assertion that Anglo-American examiners are not as effective as Mexican-American examiners in testing Mexican-American children has not received support in studies by Gerken (1978) and by Morales and George (1976). Gerken reported that neither the examiners' ethnicity (Mexican-American or Anglo-American) nor their language facil-

ity (bilingual or monolingual) was a significant factor in the IQs obtained by Mexican-American kindergarten children on the WPPSI and on the Leiter International Performance Scale. Morales and George found that bilingual Mexican-American first, second, and third graders obtained higher WISC-R Performance IQs when tested by monolingual non-Hispanic examiners than when tested by bilingual Hispanic examiners who gave the test directions in both English and Spanish. The children tested by non-Hispanic examiners also obtained significantly higher scores on the ITPA Grammatical Closure subtest, but not on the Screening Test of Spanish Grammar. These two studies, while limited, do point out that Anglo-American examiners may not necessarily impair the test performance of Mexican-American elementary school children.

While the studies above provide no support for the assertion that Anglo-American examiners are less effective than Hispanic examiners, examiners of both ethnic groups must still be aware of stereotyped attitudes toward Mexican-American children that may interfere with their clinical judgments. For example, a study of teachers' attitudes toward Mexican-American third and fourth graders who spoke with minimally accented, moderately accented, or highly accented English speech showed that most favorable ratings were given to the minimally accented speakers and least favorable ratings to the highly accented speakers (Carter, 1977). Although Mexican-American teachers had more favorable attitudes than Anglo-American teachers, both groups had more unfavorable attitudes to the highly accented speakers. This study points out that clinicians must be aware of possible stereotypes that they hold toward children with accented speech. Such stereotypes, if they exist, must not be allowed to color test interpretations and recommendations or to impair the examiner-examinee relationship.

Translations

In an attempt to make intelligence tests more appropriate for Spanish-speaking children, tests or test directions have been translated into Spanish. However, translations have some inherent difficulties.[11]

1. Many concepts either have no equivalent in another language or are difficult to render without engendering ambiguity. Thus, the meaning of important phrases may be lost in translations.
2. Translations are usually made into standard Spanish, with no provision for dialectical or regional variations. The word "kite," for example, may be translated as *cometa, huila, volantin, papalote,* or *chiringa,* depending on the country of origin.
3. The language familiar to Spanish-speaking children may be a combination of two languages ("Pocho," "pidgin," or "Tex-Mex"), so that a monolingual translation may be inappropriate.
4. Some words may have different meanings for Mexican-Americans, Puerto Ricans, Cubans, and other Hispanics. For example, *tostón* refers to a half dollar for a Chicano child, but to a squashed section of a fried banana for a Puerto Rican child.
5. The difficulty level of words may change as a result of translation. For example, the word *pet,* a common English word, becomes in its Spanish equivalent *animál doméstico,* an uncommon word.
6. Translation can alter the meanings of words. For example, seemingly harmless English words may translate into Spanish profanity. *Egg* translated as *huevón* may be literally correct, but the Spanish term has more earthy connotations.

The major problem in translations is to ensure that each translated phrase is equivalent to the phrase in the original language. An important rule in translating is that the translator have good acquaintance with the language as used by the prospective test respondents. It is important to recognize that no matter how carefully the translation is done from the standpoint of the language involved, the translation is likely to be ineffective if both cultures do not share similar ex-

periences and concepts (Sechrest, Fay, & Zaidi, 1972).

While recognizing the many problems involved in translating tests, researchers still have attempted to discover how translations affect children's scores. When intelligence tests or vocabulary tests have been translated into Spanish, no consistent trend emerges. The Spanish version may result in higher, similar, or lower scores than the English version.[12] Thus, translations are no panacea for obtaining more valid results. In fact, Hispanic school children often have been found to have poorly developed language skills in both English and Spanish. This is especially true during the preschool and kindergarten period. Both English and Spanish language skills of Hispanic children improve during the elementary school years.

Heavily weighted language-based tests do not appear to provide the most effective way of evaluating Hispanic children's cognitive skills. Furthermore, the results of many studies suggest that Hispanic children reared in a bilingual environment do not have a "native" language. While Hispanic children often learn Spanish in their early years of life, English becomes, in many cases, the predominant mode of communication in their school years. For these children, what is their native language?

Mexican-Americans

While it is difficult to generalize about cultural groups, there is some evidence that Anglo-Americans tend to value efficiency, task-centeredness, and individual accomplishment, whereas Mexican-Americans stress human relations, person-centeredness, and open acceptance of affective temperament (Garza & Lipton, 1978). Many Mexican-American families possess a number of characteristics in common with many Mexican families, including father dominance, a belief in masculine superiority, strict disciplining of children, separation of sex roles, and emphasis on submission and obedience to authority figures (Ramirez, 1967). One of the most pronounced clashes between Anglo and Hispanic cultures centers on the family. The concept of *machismo* runs counter to the Anglo concept of a democratic family, in which, at least theoretically, the female is equal to the male. The traditional Hispanic male, for example, would not share household duties with his wife—*En mi casa, yo mando* (In my house, I command). However, the dominance-submission patterns are much less universal than previously assumed (Hawkes & Taylor, 1975).

The traditional traits are undergoing change as a result of increased urbanization and higher levels of assimilation. Younger Mexican-Americans, those with more education, and those who have attained relatively high occupational positions possess value orientations that are closer to those held by Anglo-Americans (Chandler, 1974). They believe that people can actively control their fate, that planning for the future brings rewards, that trust can be placed in people other than the family or friends, and that family ties should not hamper a person's individual career. Younger Hispanic men are sharing child-care responsibilities and important decisions with their wives, and birth control methods are increasingly being used, despite church doctrine. The traditional traits, however, still exert a powerful force, and must be considered in working with Mexican-American children and their families.

Although assimilation is on the increase, Mexican-Americans have difficulty in becoming assimilated into American culture because the customs, language, and values of the Mexican culture are continually reinforced by newly arrived aliens who settle in the same area of the country (Adkins & Young, 1976). In addition, because of the close proximity to Mexico, Mexican-Americans have comparatively easy access to the land of their ethnic origins. The relative isolation of some of the communities in which Mexican-Americans live also contributes to the continued use of Spanish.

Mexican-Americans may be caught between two cultures and experience severe value conflicts. When such conflicts occur, various reactions, which may create adjustment difficulties, are possible, such as (a) rebellion (e.g., the desire to be seen as an American and disassociate oneself from the folk culture) or (b) in-group identification (e.g., affiliation with the folk culture and hostility toward American values and symbols) (cf. Ramirez, 1969).

The pride of the Mexican-American family, manifested, for example, by a family's not wanting to lose face by admitting that a child is handicapped, may make it extremely difficult even to arrange for an evaluation (Adkins & Young, 1976). Other cultural factors, too, may interfere with the family's acceptance of emotional or even physical disability. When the family recognizes handicaps, the handicapped child may receive special treatment, such as excessive sympathy and overindulgence, resulting in few demands being placed on the child. Special classes may be mistrusted because they are for "sick" or "crazy" children. "How long will it take to make the child well?" is often the most immediate concern. Much care and attention may be needed to help Mexican-American families accept the need for evaluation and treatment. Program objectives should be explained so that the family understands them fully. It is the welfare of the child that is of primary consideration, and this must repeatedly be stressed. The family needs much support. Conflicts that involve clashes of values should be resolved, if at all possible, to the satisfaction of the family. The family must learn to accept the child's handicap, and to be realistic about the disability. Useful approaches in achieving these goals include (a) making initial contacts for the intervention program in the home setting, (b) having Spanish-speaking parents who have children in special programs assist in orienting new Mexican-American families, and (c) establishing discussion groups for Spanish-speaking parents.

Mexican-American children have a higher dropout rate from school and have less formal schooling than blacks (Grebler, Moore, & Guzman, 1970), with as many as 50 percent of Spanish-speaking students leaving school permanently by the time they reach eighth grade (Ortego, 1971). Many explanations have been offered to account for their poor school performance, including lower socioeconomic status, bilingualism, negative attitudes toward school, negative self-image, lower aspirations, feelings of external control, cultural values, overt prejudice, culturally biased testing, lower teacher and community expectations for Mexican-American students, lower quality of schools attended, lack of appreciation in schools for Mexican cultural heritage, and differences in cognitive style (Kagan & Zahn, 1975). Which, if any, of these explanations are valid is still a matter for future research, but some are likely to play a more important role than others. Further, some of these factors may in part be associated with the culture of poverty and not with ethnic cultural patterns per se.

There is evidence to suggest that the longer Mexican-Americans are acculturated by the Anglo-American culture, the more likely they are to prepare the Mexican-American child for life in a highly competitive setting (Knight & Kagan, 1977). However, Mexican-American children are still more cooperative and altruistic than Anglo-American children (Kagan, 1977). These values clash with those dominant in American primary schools, which use competitive motives to promote and reward academic achievement (McClintock, 1974). The strong individualistic orientation of our nation's schools, which runs counter to the group and family orientations of Mexican-Americans, may in part contribute to the poor school performance of Mexican-American children.

Another possibility that holds some promise for our understanding of the Mexican-Americans' school performance is further study of their way of processing information—their cognitive style. The field independent versus field dependent cognitive style dimension is particularly relevant. The *field independent individual* experiences parts of the field as discrete from the organized background. Such an individual is able to differentiate objects from embedding contexts, and his or her analytic functioning is combined with an impersonal orientation. The *field dependent individual*'s perception is strongly dominated by the overall organization of the field; parts of the field are experienced as fused. Events are experienced globally in an undifferentiated fashion, and a social orientation predominates. Thus, the field independent—field dependent cognitive style dimension defines a continuum from an analytic, articulate, or differentiated style to a more global way of experiencing. This dimension can also be referred to as the analytic cognitive style versus global cognitive style dimension.

Mexican-American children appear to use a more global cognitive style, while Anglo-Americans use a more analytic cognitive style. Schools favor the analytic mode in teaching, an approach that may interfere with the learning ability of Mexican-American children. Mexican-American children are significantly more field dependent than Anglo-American children. The greater field dependence of Mexican-American children is probably associated with (a) the more traditional childrearing practices of the Mexican culture, which emphasize adherence to convention, respect for authority, and a continued identity with the family, and (b) an authoritarian childrearing orientation, including arbitrary and coercive parental demands that may discourage children's independence, assertiveness, or aggressive behavior (Witkin, Price-Williams, Bertini, Bjorn, Oltman, Ramirez, & Van Meel, 1973). Anglo-American culture, in contrast, typically emphasizes greater assertiveness, autonomy, and a more individualistic sense of self-identity (Ramirez & Castañeda, 1974).

While there are differences in the cognitive styles and value orientations of Mexican-Americans and Anglo-Americans, neither pattern should be the preferred mode of functioning. Value orientations of children in each culture are adaptive or nonadaptive depending primarily on the specific situation (Kagan, 1975). Limited competitive strivings may result in fewer possessions, but too much competition may also result in loss of possessions. A global cognitive style limits the ability to see abstractions, but it allows for greater contact with important perceptual qualities, a contact that may be lost by those with an analytic cognitive style. High need for achievement has important benefits, such as greater productivity, but associated with it is a tendency to make more errors on certain tasks and to be anxious and compulsive. Schools and other public institutions will need to develop more responsive programs that take into consideration the social motives and cognitive style of Mexican-Americans (Kagan, 1977).

Ramirez and Castañeda (1974) hypothesize that educational institutions have failed to meet the needs of Mexican-American children because they are not cognizant of the cognitive styles of the children. They suggested that teachers use a field-sensitive approach to teach Mexican-American children. This approach emphasizes the expression of warmth, sensitivity to personal feelings and interests, use of social rewards, humanization and personalization of curriculum materials, and use of structured guidance and a deductive curriculum approach. The field-sensitive approach contrasts with a field-independent approach, which emphasizes formality and aloofness, the use of formulas and graphs, independent work, and the use of an inductive curriculum approach. Although much research is needed in order to evaluate the effectiveness of the field-sensitive approach, incorporation of at least some of these features may prove to be useful in teaching Mexican-American children.

Reliability and Validity of Intelligence Tests and Tests of Special Abilities with Hispanic Children

Most research on the intelligence test performance of Hispanic children has focused on the WISC-R (or WISC). The WISC-R Verbal, Performance, and Full Scale IQs have been found to be reliable for the assessment of Mexican-American children (Dean, 1977e, 1979b). The three IQs on the WISC-R also have been found to have predictive validity for Mexican-American children using such criteria as the Peabody Individual Assessment Test, Wide Range Achievement Test, and Iowa Test of Basic Skills.[13] In addition, factor analysis of the WISC-R supports its construct validity for Mexican-American school children who have been referred for psychological testing (Gutkin & Reynolds, 1980).

The Block Design subtest may have the most cross-cultural validity of any of the WISC-R subtests for Mexican-American children. This subtest has been found to correlate significantly with classroom performance (Morales & George, 1976) and with mathematical ability (Buriel, 1978). Studies almost universally report that Mexican-American children obtain higher Performance than Verbal IQs.[14] This latter finding is probably associated with the language difficulties experienced by Mexican-American children.

I recommend that the PPVT never be used to obtain an estimate of young Hispanic children's intelligence. As we have seen in Chapter 15, this test is a measure of receptive vocabulary, not general intelligence. There is no evidence with which I am familiar that indicates that the test provides a valid measure of young (that is, preschool and kindergarten age) Hispanic children's intelligence.

Any results obtained on verbal intelligence and special ability tests administered in English to Spanish-speaking children without taking into account their degree of proficiency in English should be highly suspect. Because some Hispanic children may be reluctant to reveal their deficiencies in English, they may pretend to understand the instructions. If there is any hint that such may be the case, an interpreter should be employed. Similarly, because some Hispanic children have never learned to read in Spanish, it is inappropriate to give all Spanish-speaking children written tests in Spanish. For those who have a poor command of English, a Spanish language test and a nonverbal test, such as the Progressive Matrices, Wechsler Performance Scales, Leiter International Performance Scale, or Draw-A-Man, can be administered to obtain an estimate of cognitive ability. A verbal test in English is useful for an estimate of proficiency in English.

North American Indian Children

According to the 1980 U.S. census, there are about 1.4 million American Indians, constituting about .60 percent of the U.S. population. Because of undercounting, two million may be a more accurate estimate of the American Indian population, including Alaskan natives. The term "American Indian" is a broad, almost arbitrary category covering over 500 tribes or Indian groups in the United States (Valencia-Weber, 1977). The primary identification that Indians make is with their particular group, such as Navajo, San Juan Pueblo, or Eastern Band Cherokee. It is important to recognize that there is great cultural diversity among various Indian groups; they should not be treated as a homogeneous group. Those working with Indians will need to learn about the histories and traditions of particular Indian communities if they are to achieve success with Indians and respect from them.

Indians are an impoverished group in our society. Their infant mortality rate is twice as high as it is for other American infants (32.2 deaths per 1,000 live births), and after the first twenty-seven days of life, the death rate for Indian infants is four times that of white infants (Farris & Farris, 1976). The outlook for Indian children in our schools is poor, and work opportunities are limited. Indian school dropout rates are double the national average. The median educational level for American Indians is 9.8 years as contrasted with 12.1 years for the white population. Median educational levels for various Indian groups vary from 3 years among some non-urban groups to 11 years or more among some urban and other non-urban groups. Their poor scholastic achievement may be related to cultural conflict, motivational differences, and emotional maladjustment, including alienation from self and the community. Indian children face a limited future (as shown below), and unless radical changes are made in our society's treatment of the Indian, few, if any, significant changes will occur.

The Indian child can look forward to little more than a fifth-grade education; he and 95 percent of his classmates will probably drop out before high school. His self-image reflects this if, indeed, it is not the cause of his failure. More than any other group, Indian children believe themselves to be of below-average intelligence. Boarding schools and long separations from family are commonplace. It is not unheard of for an Indian child in Alaska to be sent to a school run by the Bureau of Indian Affairs in Oklahoma. In 1973 there were over 33,000 children living away from their homes and families. And these schools, where his teachers are usually non-Indian, will further erode his self-esteem.

Because of the poor quality of his education and the likelihood that he will drop out of school early, the Indian has few marketable vocational and professional skills. The unemployment rate for this group may be as high as 90 percent. The average family income for the American Indian is frequently under $2,000 a year. Ninety percent of the housing available to him is substandard. Furthermore, he can anticipate that he and his family will have major problems with crime, drugs, and alcohol. The suicide rate for the American Indian is twice the national average; among teenagers, however, it is more than five times as high.

The transition from an uncomplicated tribal life-style to a pressure-oriented, complex, industrial society has taken a tragic toll on the American Indian. [Farris & Farris, 1976, p. 386]

Part of the cultural conflict involves differences in values between Indians and the majority culture. The values of the Indian child may include (a) a desire for harmony with nature instead of a mastery over nature, (b) a present time orientation rather than a future time orientation, (c) an explanation of natural phenomena by mythology and sorcery rather than by science, together with fear of the supernatural, (d) an aspiration to follow in the ways of old people, and to cooperate and maintain the status quo rather than to compete and climb the ladder of success, (e) a choice of anonymity and submissiveness over individuality and aggression, and (f) a desire to satisfy present needs and to share, rather than to work to "get ahead" and save for the future (Zintz, 1962).

Testing Indian children may pose some difficulties. Their command of English may be limited, so that they may have difficulty in understanding test questions. English-speaking examiners, in turn, may experience communication difficulties in those instances in which Indian children speak a native language and have limited knowledge of English. Some Indian children may be hesitant to speak, or they may speak softly, and their responses may be short and lack important details. They may work slowly, attempting to be sure that they make few errors. Some Indian children may be more fearful than white children of making a mistake.

Studies of the intellectual ability of Indian children uniformly indicate that they obtain higher scores on performance tests than on verbal tests.[15] This pattern of achievement may be a reflection of a visual style of learning and limited familiarity with English (Krywaniuk & Das, 1976). The degree of discrepancy between verbal and performance abilities also may be an indication of the degree of acculturation that has taken place. Schubert and Cropley (1972) suggest that the Indians' pattern of exhibiting better performance than verbal skills is adequate for their traditional ways, but inadequate for the requirements of a highly technological society.

In some cases, Indian children obtain IQs that are as much as 25 to 30 points higher on the WISC Performance Scale than on the Verbal Scale.[16] Thus, it is important to examine carefully IQs generated by different scales and tests. In addition to the Stanford-Binet and Wechsler tests, it is valuable to administer the Draw-A-Man

From Arkava, M. L., and Snow, M., *Psychological Tests and Social Work Practice*, 1978, p. 39. Courtesy of Charles C. Thomas, Publisher, Springfield, Illinois.

EXHIBIT 19-3.   Psychological Evaluation (Brief Report): A Navajo Adolescent

Name: Mark
Date of birth: Oct. 15, 1966
Chronological age: 13-0
Date of evaluation: Oct. 15, 1979
Date of report: Oct. 18, 1979
Grade: 8th

Tests Administered

Bender-Gestalt:

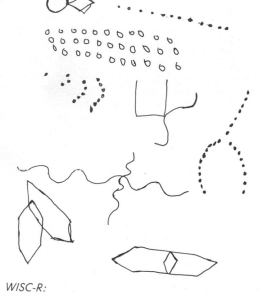

WISC-R:

VERBAL SCALE		PERFORMANCE SCALE	
Information	3	Picture Completion	8
Similarities	4	Picture Arrangement	10
Arithmetic	7	Block Design	.7
Vocabulary	1	Object Assembly	8
Comprehension	3	Coding	7
Digit Span	9	Mazes	14

Verbal Scale IQ—not valid
Performance Scale IQ = 95 ± 10
Full Scale IQ—not valid

Wide Range Achievement Test:

	STANDARD SCORE	PERCENTILE
Reading	81	10
Spelling	77	6
Arithmetic	69	2

1. *cat* (cat)
2. *run* (run)
3. *arm* (arm)
4. *train* (train)
5. *shout* (shout)
6. *correct* (correct)
7. *circle* (circle)
8. *heaven* (heaven)
9. *educate* (educate)
10. *material* (material)
11. *ruin* (ruin)
12. *fashion* (fashion)
13. *believe* (believe)
14. *suggestion* (suggestion)
15. *equipment* (equipment)
16. *majority* (majority)
17. *institute* (institute)
18. *literature* (literature)
19. _____
20. _____
21. _____
22. _____
23. _____
24. _____
25. _____
26. _____
27. _____
28. _____
29. _____
30. _____

Mark is a 13-0-year-old Navajo Indian whose primary language is Navajo, although he also speaks English. His teachers referred him for possible placement in an educable mentally retarded class. During the evaluation, he seldom spoke, and when he did, it was mostly in short statements. His nonverbal skills are within the average range (37th percentile), whereas his verbal skills are only at the 1st percentile. Because of his limited English language proficiency, the best estimate of his ability is the Performance Scale IQ. The Verbal and Full Scale IQs are not valid estimates of his cognitive functioning. Academically, his skills are poor, being at or below the 10th percentile in reading, spelling, and arithmetic. Visual-motor development is adequate. Mark needs intensive remedial work, if he is to increase his English language and academic skills. Placement in an educable mentally retarded class is not considered appropriate.

Examiner

Test and, on some occasions, other nonverbal tests, such as the Progressive Matrices, to evaluate the cognitive skills of Indian children. Because their visual-spatial abilities are much better developed than their verbal skills, misleading results can occur when reliance is placed primarily on the scores provided by verbal tests. Thus, for example, Indian children obtain scores on the PPVT that are much below those they obtain on performance tests (Cundick, 1970; Thurber, 1976). A brief report of a Navajo adolescent is shown in Exhibit 19-3.

Indian children begin school with less developed verbal concept ability (as measured by the Boehm Test of Basic Concepts) (Mickelson & Galloway, 1973). If they are to function adequately in school, special programs aimed at developing verbal concepts may have to be implemented, together with special training in English. Training in English should be aimed at supplementing their native language, not replacing it (Bowd, 1972). Because of their better developed spatial and perceptual skills, more visual-oriented techniques of teaching should be adopted for Indian children. Finally, the introduction of topics on Native American history and culture into the school curriculum may be one method of developing a sense of cultural pride (Van der Keilen, 1977).

The Culture of Poverty and Its Effects on the Test Performance of Ethnic Minority Children

Ethnic minorities in our country suffer from many forms of economic deprivation. The resulting poverty affects rates of learning, which in turn influence intelligence and academic success. Poverty, for example, affects maternal health, infant mortality, and the child's health and social functioning, all of which may be related to school failure. Figure 19-1 shows the relationship among various environmental variables and poverty and educational failure. The assaults that may affect inner-city children's central nervous systems include prematurity, perinatal disease, malnutrition, infection, anemia, and ingestion of lead (Needleman, 1973). Research, too, has shown that blacks have a considerably higher rate of prematurity and a higher incidence of abnormalities of pregnancy than whites.[17]

Birch and Gussow (1970) stressed that "the links which bind the poor into this repeating cycle of failure can be broken at any one of a number of points" (p. 267). Vocational training, adequate family allowances, and health care programs are some examples of ways to break the link between unemployment and poverty or between physical risk factors and school failure. Whatever procedures are instituted, dramatic changes cannot be expected:

> . . . environmental equalization must be viewed as a longer term process, stretching across two or three generations at least, and we must not expect to overcome within a single lifetime the entire consequence of 15 generations of suboptimal conditions for life. Our neglect will not be so cheaply or so hastily repaired. [Birch & Gussow, 1970, pp. 268–269]

Bruner's (1975, p. 47) penetrating analysis of the culture of poverty emphasizes that the poor must be provided with opportunities to gain a sense of power and pride:

> Persistent poverty over generations creates a culture of survival. Goals are short range and restricted. The outsider and the outside are suspect. One stays inside and gets what one can. Beating the system takes the place of using the system.
>
> Such a culture of poverty gets to the young early—how they learn to set goals, mobilize means, delay or fail to delay gratification. Very early too they learn in-group talk and thinking and just as their language use reflects less long-range goal analysis, it also tends toward a parochialism that makes it increasingly difficult to move or work outside the poverty neighborhood and the group. Make no mistake about it: it is a rich culture, intensely personalized and full of immediate rather than remote concerns. The issue is certainly not cultural deprivation, to be handled, like avitaminosis, with a massive dose of compensatory enrichment.
>
> Rather the issue is to make it possible for the poor to gain a sense of their own power—through jobs, through community activation, through creating a sense of project in the future. Jobs, community action under community control, a decent revision of preschool and early school opportunities—all of these are crucial. But just as crucial is a sense of the changes in the times—the insistence of the powerless that their plight is *not* a visitation of fate, but a remediable condition. If we cannot produce that kind of change, then our system that has worked fairly well (if exploitatively) since the industrial revolution will doubtless collapse, probably to be replaced by something premised far more on coercion for all rather than just for some. That is why the

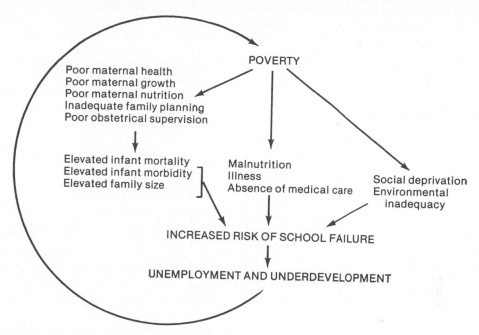

FIGURE 19-1. Environmental Relationships Between Poverty and Educational Failure. Reprinted by permission of the publisher and authors from H. G. Birch and J. D. Gussow, *Disadvantaged Children: Health, Nutrition, and School Failure,* p. 268. Copyright 1970, Grune & Stratton.

generation to be raised is so crucial a resource. It may be our last chance.

Montagu (1972) emphasizes that poverty, as such, is neither a necessary nor a sufficient condition to produce intellectual deficits, especially if nutrition and the home cultural environment are adequate. It is only when these factors are inadequate that there are likely to be learning deficits. Take, for example, the following conditions—poor nutrition and health care, substandard housing, low family income, prevalent family disorganization, anarchic discipline, diminished personal worth, low expectations, frustrated aspiration, as well as other environmental handicaps—and imagine what the consequences may be for the development of adequate intellectual skills.

Elkind's Premature Structuring and Alternate Elaboration Hypothesis

Elkind (1973a) offered two intriguing concepts to account for the poor test scores of low income and ethnic minority youth. These concepts are termed *premature structuring* and *alternate elaboration*. Premature structuring occurs when children "are forced to apply their abilities to practical matters before these abilities are fully realized or elaborated. The effect is to stunt or limit growth" (p. 79). Low income youth may have to direct their intellectual abilities to practical issues, such as assuming responsibility for their siblings at an early age, and such early application to real life matters may inhibit the future growth of cognitive skills. Premature structuring is most likely to occur when children have little or no opportunity to develop their mental abilities.

Alternate elaboration occurs when children develop mental abilities in ways that are different from those of most other children. Children who function in the underworld subculture acquire a kind of cognitive language that may make it difficult for them to elaborate their abilities "or to learn academic material in a traditional school setting" (p. 81). Case 19-1 illustrates how a low income youth may appear to have limited ability, as assessed by standard tests, but function quite well in his community.

CASE 19-1.   A Low Income Youth's "Alternate Elaboration" Development

One young man . . . came to the court clinic because he was not going to school and was suspected of pushing dope and of having a couple of girl friends doing "tricks" for him. He was well dressed and smooth talking with a vocabulary rich in the argot of the street and the underworld. He was alternatively amused and annoyed at the test questions, and he did best in arithmetic and worst on the test of general information and vocabulary.

His poor performance on information and vocabulary, however, does not reflect deficiency but rather alternate elaboration. This young man was far from lacking in general information. Indeed, his fund of information in many areas was much greater than mine. The same was true for his vocabulary, which was rich in words not found on intelligence tests. To call this young man deficient in ability would be a gross error. On the contrary, his at least average intellectual abilities were elaborated in a subcultural domain that is virtually unknown to the middle-class test maker and user. ■

Source: Elkind (1973a), p. 80.

Elkind proposed the premature structuring and alternate elaboration models as possible replacements for the various deficit models that have been proposed to account for the poor test performance of low income youth. He suggested that "from a developmental standpoint the mental growth of some low income youth may simply be different in direction and elaboration than that of the offspring of more affluent parents" (p. 81).

Poverty and Testing

Leland (1971) believes that formal testing procedures appear to identify those individuals who cannot compete in our technologically oriented culture. Tests can become major instruments for casting out the phys-

ically sick, the uneducated, and those with special personal problems. The poor, as a group, are the most vulnerable, and it is *poverty* that is the main characteristic of minority groups. The adaptive strategies of the poor are not always conducive to good test performance. They may cope poorly with external pressures and experience failure—even in areas where they have some cognitive strengths—because they feel that things often happen to them in spite of themselves and without their participation. Testing situations may arouse tension and feelings of suspicion in poor children. They may react with aggression or with passivity, but simultaneously may feel that it is important to establish a friendly relationship with the examiner. A heightened preoccupation with their relationship with the examiner may, in turn, reduce the saliency of the test questions. Such strategies leave the poor child ill-equipped to cope with tests. Leland made the telling observation that when children who perform adequately in their own environment are given a label as a result of testing, the label makes otherwise unlabeled children visible and begins to create social problems where previously none had existed.

Racial Differences in Intelligence

In 1969 Arthur Jensen published an article in the *Harvard Educational Review,* "How Much Can We Boost IQ and Scholastic Achievement," which raised a storm of controversy that has yet to be quieted. This article, McGuire and Hirsch (1977) maintain, was responsible for the resurgence of racist thinking in the United States. Others maintain that Jensen's views must not be dismissed lightly.[18] In the ensuing decade, Jensen has published numerous books and articles defending and elaborating on his position, culminating in his text *Bias in Mental Testing,* published in 1980.

The major thrusts of Jensen's 1969 article were as follows:

1. Intelligence tests measure a highly relevant dimension of general ability.

2. This dimension has a high degree of heritability (about 80 percent).

3. Educational programs have not been effective in bringing about significant changes in this ability.

4. Genetic factors are strongly indicated in the average black-white intelligence difference (about 15 points in favor of whites), although environmental factors still may play a role in accounting for this difference.

5. Teaching methods should be tailored to the child's particular learning skills.

In a careful analysis of the problem of racial differences in intelligence, Loehlin, Lindzey, and Spuhler (1975) pointed out that the heritability estimate of .80 for intelligence is based on studies of white persons; consequently it is difficult to know how accurate this estimate is for other racial groups. Heritability estimates, based on studies within one specific group, may have little relevance to an understanding of how genetic variation can account for differences in a trait between two or more groups. Consequently, the heritability of IQ differences *between* racial or ethnic groups cannot be estimated at present. Further, as Tyler (1978) observed: "Even if heritability coefficients for both blacks and whites were as high as the highest estimate made heretofore, namely .80, they would still tell us nothing about the extent to which the difference between the racial groups arises from genetic sources" (p. 89).

Valid inferences cannot be drawn about genetic differences among races as long as there are relevant systematic differences in cultural patterns and in the psychological environment (Layzer, 1974). These differences influence the development of cognitive skills in complex ways, and no one has succeeded in either estimating or eliminating their effects. Centuries of discrimination have made direct comparisons of mental ability traits between blacks and whites not biologically meaningful (Lerner, 1968). Hebb (1971) elaborates on this view:

The data from which heritability is established come, in general, from studies of white children attending school or in families in which the value of schooling for a child's future is taken for granted. In general, that environment lacks at least one fundamental feature of the black child's: prejudice, with effects cumulative over generations. The black child is not only exposed to it himself; he is brought up also by parents who are already defeated by it. We have simply no way of estimating the extent of its effect on cognitive development. The direct effect of poverty is the lack of toys and books, and parents with time to talk to the child. The effect must be multiplied in an environment in which hope has been lost. There is no justification for generalizing to this environment from that of the ordinary white child. [p. 736]

Even when social class and economic variables are equated between ethnic groups, there are still important differences in life style and experience (Gallo & Dorfman, 1970).

Loehlin et al. (1975) concluded that during the first year or two of life there are few differences in intellectual functions related to race or social class. However, by the age of 3 or 4 years, one can observe race and social class differences which remain fairly stable during the school years. These findings suggest that "the schools can mostly be exonerated from the charges of creating the black-white difference in average IQ-test performance or of increasing it during the period of school attendance" (pp. 156–157). The lower scores of black children may be associated with the increased *g* loading of intelligence test items between 2 and 5 years of age or with certain environmental differences in the black home or community (Jensen, 1975).

The debate about the relative importance of genetic and environmental influences on differences between black and white groups in our country should not obscure the facts that (a) within both the black and white populations there are wide individual variations in genetic potential and (b) there are wide variations in educational opportunity. Further, we must not be complacent and allow a heritability hypothesis to be a convenient rationalization for poor schooling or for our failure to cope with the following:

... the emergence of a growing and self-per-petuating lower class, disproportionately Afro- and Latin-American in its ethnic compo-sition, excluded from the mainstream of American life and alienated from its values, isolated in rural areas and urban ghettos, and dependent for the means of bare survival on an increasingly hostile and resentful majority. [Layzer, 1972, p. 267]

Ethnicity and Patterns of Mental Abilities

A number of studies have investigated the organization of mental abilities in various ethnic groups. One of the first studies, by Lesser, Fifer, and Clark (1965), found that patterns of intellectual ability differed in Chinese, Jewish, black, and Puerto Rican children. Chinese children were found to have excellent spatial ability, but were con-siderably weaker, relative to the other groups, in verbal ability. Jewish children's verbal skills were superior to the verbal ability of the other three groups. Black chil-dren were weak in spatial skills and average in verbal ability. The Puerto Rican children had weaker verbal skills compared to their other abilities.

Other studies, however, have failed to replicate the above findings. Sitkei and Meyers (1969), using a battery of twenty-two tests, reported that the pattern of abili-ties of black and white children from the lower and middle socioeconomic classes was essentially similar. Flaugher and Rock (1972) found that a battery of nine cognitive tests given to junior high school students —who were of black, white, Mexican-Amer-ican, and Oriental backgrounds—yielded similar patterns of abilities, regardless of the children's ethnic background. Finally, Hennessy and Merrifield (1976), in an exten-sive study of 2,985 Afro-American, His-panic, Jewish, and Caucasian-gentile high school seniors with a battery of ten mental ability and achievement tests, reported that there are highly similar structures of mental abilities in the four groups. These findings suggest that intelligence and achievement tests measure the same abilities in a variety of ethnic groups.

The Development and Use of Culture-Fair Tests for Assessing Ethnic Minority Children

Attempts have been made to develop cul-ture-fair tests, such as the Davis-Eells Test of General Intelligence on Problem Solving Ability and the Culture Fair Intelligence Test. Other tests, too, have been charac-terized as being culture fair, such as the Leiter International Performance Scale and Progressive Matrices. These tests tend to emphasize pictorial, spatial, or figural con-tent, because it is believed that problems in-volving this content may be answered from experiences that have been more nearly equal in different ethnic and racial groups. Verbal content is minimized in the belief that verbal content is more biased against ethnic minorities than nonverbal content. However, these attempts to create culture-fair tests have not been successful. An ex-amination of the available research findings indicates that ethnic minorities do not per-form any better on supposedly culture-fair tests than on the more conventional tests of intelligence (see Arvey, 1972, for a review). In fact, nonverbal tests (or subtests) and cul-ture-fair tests have been found, on occasion, to be as difficult as or more difficult than verbal tests for black children.

Ethnic minorities may have even less chance of entering educational institutions or of being considered for a job or a training program when culture-fair tests rather than more traditional tests of cognitive abilities are used as the selection instruments. The available evidence suggests that culture-fair tests do not show greater validity for ethnic minorities than do more verbally loaded tests, such as the Stanford-Binet and the WISC-R. Culture-fair tests are not the panacea that some believed they would be for the assessment of ethnic minorities.

Wesman (1968) observed that culture-fair tests have not been successful because of the failure to recognize that intelligence, in part, is based on the learning experiences of the individual. As far as we know, no test can be created that will entirely eliminate the influence of learning and cultural experiences. The test material, the language in which the questions are phrased, the manner of asking the child to respond, the categories of classifying the responses, the scoring criteria, and the validity criteria are all culture bound. In fact, all human experience is affected by the culture from birth on and even prenatally. As Scarr (1978) observed: "Intelligence tests are not tests of intelligence in some abstract, culture-free way. They are measures of the ability to function intellectually by virtue of knowledge and skills in the culture of which they sample" (p. 339).

Every test is *culturally loaded* to some extent, and it is important to distinguish between a test that is *culturally loaded* and one that is *culturally biased* (Jensen, 1974c). We have seen in this chapter that *cultural bias* is a complex concept that has various meanings. Generally, there is little evidence that individual intelligence tests are culturally biased, according to most definitions of bias. However, tests may vary in their degree of cultural loading. On the one hand, picture vocabulary tests, such as the PPVT, are highly culturally loaded because they use as stimuli pictures that call for specific information associated with a given culture, such as familiarity with the language of the culture and objects representative of the linguistic terms. On the other hand, the matrices tests (such as the Progressive Matrices), digit span memory tests, and maze tests are *culturally reduced* tests, because they are less dependent on exposure to specific language symbols. However, even these types of tests have some degree of cultural loading—they are not culture fair or culture free.

Recommendations for Assessing Ethnic Minority Children

Many different kinds of recommendations have been made for assessing ethnic minority children.[19] Some recommendations advocate a moratorium on testing, while others advocate ways in which testing can become a more useful tool in the educational process. Let us now examine various recommendations.

1. The most radical recommendation is for a complete moratorium on intelligence and ability testing, or for the banning and elimination of intelligence tests in schools. This recommendation is elaborated on by Williams and Mitchell (1977):

> [a] Administrators should discontinue all standardized testing of minorities until formal investigations into the validity of each test can be conducted. (This includes public and private schools, colleges, universities and employment offices.)
>
> Obviously, calls for a moratorium on testing are not enough. Parents must be continually warned of the danger inherent in the testing process and must bring heavy pressure on school districts to halt the use of achievement testing of their children. We suggest that they use a form letter which implements this recommendation. For example:
>
> Dear Principal or Superintendent:
> We are requesting that you do not administer any standardized tests to our children. We feel that because of the problems in the tests, they may unnecessarily penalize our child; we do not wish to take such a chance. If you insist, we may be forced to file a lawsuit charging you with the violation of our child's rights under the 14th Amendment.
>
> [b] A federal investigation of the testing industry should be conducted. Far too many of the corporate executives in the testing industry may also be on educational boards which determine which tests are to be used. A federal regulatory law must be enacted through legislation and vigorously enforced. In sum, an attempt must be made to reorganize and regulate the corporate structure of the testing industry.
>
> Tests are tools. When a tool does not fit or work for you, it should be returned to the tool box. Current ability, achievement and aptitude tests neither fit the Black experience, nor do they work for us. *Res Ipsa Loquitur* ("The situation speaks for itself"). [pp. 39–40]

Williams (1970b) earlier had issued the following warning:

> In conclusion, I make one simple proposal to my critics: It is either time now to halt the dehumanization and genocide of Black minds using psychological instruments as tools, or Black psychologists have no alternative but to develop our own strategies. One possibility is the publication in the Black community of answers to all ability and achievement tests. [p. 7]

2. Assessment should focus on discovering ways to help children. The aim should be on gaining knowledge about children, on improving instruction, and on helping children best develop their potentialities. Eliminating the focus on screening, classification, and selection and replacing it with these aims may reduce some of the objections to intelligence and achievement tests.

3. Every effort must be made to enlist children's motivation and interest by helping them feel as comfortable and at ease as possible. Examiners should take as much time as needed to ensure the child's cooperation. If at all possible, the examiner should be someone who is familiar to the child.

4. It is important that a wide range of mental tasks be used when testing ethnic minority children. Neither a single score nor any small number of scores can provide an adequate picture of the intellectual abilities of a child. The sampling of cognitive abilities is especially important in order to discover the strengths and weaknesses of children from educationally disadvantaged backgrounds, since there may be more variability in their pattern of abilities than in the patterns of children who are not disadvantaged.

5. In assessing ethnic minority (and nonminority) children we need to seek a better balance between formal and less formal assessment techniques. Standardized tests should be supplemented, for example, with information obtained through observing and interviewing children and through narrative self-reports, autobiographic reports, actual work samples, and anecdotal information.

6. The use of more extensive testing-of-limits procedures may be helpful. We need to know to what extent children can profit from help and from extra testing procedures.

7. Criterion-referenced testing should supplement normative testing. One focus is on individualized instruction involving self-paced learning. The curriculum consists of units of instruction or modules that are linked together. Testing consists of evaluating the extent to which the child has met the training objectives (e.g., the learning of modules), rather than normative testing for measuring individual differences.

8. Separate norms for various ethnic groups (and sociocultural groups) have been advocated. Test scores can be used for a within-group analysis. That is, they can be used to compare ethnic minority children with one another or to compare children's current test performance with their previous test performance. For these comparisons, the standardization norms would not be used.

9. In testing Hispanic children who have learned only Spanish in the home, a Spanish language test and a nonlanguage performance scale should be administered; a nonlanguage performance test should not be exclusively relied on. For a bilingual child, it is preferable to administer intelligence tests in both languages on the assumption that the ability repertoires in the separate languages will rarely overlap completely. Unfortunately, there are few objective psychometric techniques to accomplish this goal.

10. Children who have limited command of English should not be recommended for special education classes for the mentally retarded unless there is no doubt about their level of cognitive functioning. Psychologists should be extremely wary of identifying children whose na-

tive language is not English as "mentally retarded" when the tests require understanding of English (either in the test items or in the test directions). If nonverbal tests are used, the examiner must be certain that the child understands the test directions, and that the test items do not require familiarity with the English language.

11. Only after careful consideration has been given to the test results, adaptive behavior information, classroom performance, medical and family history, and cultural patterns should special class placement be considered. This recommendation holds for all children, but especially for those children who are from ethnic minority groups.

12. Clinicians must acquire knowledge and understanding of ethnic minority children's culture and community. Those who are able to help children feel pride in their native language and culture will be making important strides in facilitating the educational process. The ability to speak Spanish, in testing Hispanic children with minimal proficiency in English, may also contribute to the assessment process.

13. Clinicians who work with ethnic minority children will have to (a) evaluate carefully their feelings about the child's ethnic group, (b) understand the ethnic group's viewpoint, and (c) accept the goal that each child should have an equal opportunity to achieve to the limits of his or her capacity.

14. We need to develop tests that will help to evaluate the psychological processes by which children learn. Present tests sample primarily what children have learned. New tests or procedures are needed that will lead to prescriptions for each individual child.

15. Tests developed in the future should be properly constructed and empirically validated on ethnic minority children. These children should also be represented in the standardization sample. Ideally, tests are needed that can evaluate the thought processes, modes

of perceiving, and modes of expression of different cultures, and that also accord some recognition to the differing contents in different cultures.

16. The development of culture-specific tests for the distinctive cultural groups in America may assist in the assessment process. However, at present, there is no evidence that such tests have a sufficient degree of reliability and validity or that they can assist in furthering our understanding of the abilities of ethnic minority children.

17. Assessments may improve when educational systems become more responsive to the attitudes, perceptions, and behaviors of ethnic minority children. In addition, parents should be encouraged to become more involved in the educational process and should be helped to learn more effective ways of reinforcing their child's achievements.

18. Teachers must come to understand that the educational difficulties displayed by ethnic minority children represent a difference rather than a special kind of intellectual deficit. Teachers should concentrate on how to get children to transfer skills they already possess to the tasks at hand, rather than attempt to create new intellectual structures.

19. Gains in scholastic aptitude should be encouraged through educational strategies such as (a) instruction in the use of concepts and in the development of verbal problem-solving strategies and other intellectual strategies, (b) training in study habits, and (c) development of achievement motivation, field independence, reflectivity, and delay of gratification. We must remember that ethnic minority children who perform poorly on intelligence and ability tests are still growing intellectually; they need the best educational programming available to increase their academic skills.

20. We need to strive to eliminate social inequalities and prejudice from our society. Rather than attack intelligence and other ability tests, we should focus on the environmental problems that have

created the intellectual and academic disparities. Improving the quality of education and changing attitudes toward learning in the home may go a long way toward improving test scores and changing attitudes toward testing. As Wesman (1972) observed: "If tests reveal that the disadvantaged have been deprived of opportunities to learn fundamental concepts, the remedy is to provide those opportunities—not do away with the source of the information" (p. 401). "The remedy for the ills of society is not to dispense with diagnosis; it is to treat the ills" (p. 402).

21. Test scores should never be viewed as an index of the child's personal worth; this is the most pernicious use of tests.

Comment on Assessment of Ethnic Minority Group Children

It is important to reiterate that intelligence tests only deal with a certain part of the broad spectrum of abilities labeled "intelligence." They focus primarily on problem-solving and abstract abilities. Furthermore, the results of intelligence testing should not be regarded as all-important. This is especially true for ethnic minority children. These children must be given the full benefits of a battery approach to assessment, and all available information must be considered. As Eysenck (1971) pointed out, IQ tests, imperfect as they undoubtedly are, are a first step toward better understanding and a proper measurement of important aspects of human nature.

Changes in intelligence may come about by (a) new environmental conditions that do not presently exist; (b) advances in our understanding of the physiology and biochemistry of neural functions that will lead to beneficial forms of environmental intervention, such as what has already occurred with phenylketonuria and diabetes; or (c) new ways of transmitting information (e.g., new techniques in teaching) that do not require the preexistence of high intelligence (Vernon, 1979). The most efficacious way of reducing scholastic differentials may be to develop teaching procedures that are geared to the individual strengths of each child. We need a diversity of learning situations geared to the individual, and tests can aid in determining the kinds of learning approaches best suited to each child. Humphreys (1975) pointed out that "We need to know . . . the extent to which deficits . . . can be overcome for a given function, in a given person, at a given period of development. Related to these needs are the choice of techniques to use, how long the remediation will take, and the amount the remediation will cost" (p. 126).

If there is a need to evaluate ethnic minority children, which test or tests can be used? Many minority group members do not appear to accept any of the available standard intelligence tests. Although educators and psychologists must be responsive to the needs of minority group children and acknowledge the pleas of individuals such as R. L. Williams, they will likely continue to need to use tests in their educational programs. The shortcomings and hazards of using standardized intelligence tests with ethnic minority children have been discussed in this chapter. In addition, excellent recommendations have been presented that may pave the way for more appropriate uses of tests. I believe that standardized intelligence and special ability tests should be used, but only with recognition of their shortcomings and difficulties when applied to the evaluation of children coming from ethnic minority groups. Tests should never be used if they do not contribute to the development of the child or to the body of knowledge of a field of study. Obviously, no tests should be used in ways or under conditions that would physically or emotionally harm any child. However, it is difficult to spell out convincingly how tests *do* contribute, especially if the audience represents ethnic minority group members.

All we can do is hope that we do not lose sight of the importance of our nation's children and of ways to help them reach their potentials. I do not believe that the elimination of intelligence and special ability tests from the schools of our nation will contribute to this goal. If decisions must be made about the use of tests, they should be based on methodologically sound investigations. The evidence from many divergent studies indicates that individual intelligence tests are not culturally biased, and provide a profile of abilities that is valid for black, Hispanic, and white children.

Summary

1. "Ethnic minority group children" designates children who come from ethnic groups having sociocultural patterns that differ from those of the predominant society. These groups include blacks, Hispanic Americans, American Indians, and Asian Americans.

2. Arguments against the use of intelligence tests in assessing ethnic minority children include the following: (a) Tests have a white, Anglo-Saxon, middle-class bias. (b) National norms are inappropriate. (c) Ethnic minority children are deficient in motivation, test practice, reading, and exposure to the culture and therefore are handicapped in taking tests. (d) Examiner-examinee rapport problems exist. (e) Test results lead to the placement of ethnic minority children in inferior special education classes and create negative expectancies in teachers.

3. Research suggests the following: (a) There is little, if any, evidence to support the position that intelligence tests are culturally biased, using either external or internal procedures to evaluate bias. (b) Although pluralistic norms may have a limited use, national norms are important because they reflect the performance of the population as a whole. (c) While there is some evidence that ethnic minority children may have motivational deficits that interfere with their test performance, it is not known to what extent these deficits lower their test scores. (d) There is no evidence that white examiners impair the intelligence test performance of black children. (e) There is no evidence that special education classes are necessarily

harmful or that test results create self-fulfilling prophecies.

4. Arguments for the use of intelligence tests in assessing ethnic minority children include the following: (a) Test scores are useful indices of present functioning. (b) Tests provide good indices of future levels of academic success. (c) Tests are useful in obtaining special services. (d) Tests serve to evaluate the outcomes of programs. (e) Tests help to prevent misplacement of children. (f) Tests serve as a stimulus for change. (g) Tests provide a universal standard of competence. (h) Tests help to reward individual efforts to learn.

5. Black Americans are bicultural and bidialectical, and share with one another the effects of racism. The cumulative deficit hypothesis, which proposes that black children have an increasing decrement of test scores with age, receives some support for black children in Georgia, but not in California.

6. Factors that may affect the test performance of Hispanic children include cultural practices, bilingualism, speech, rapport, and test translations. For example: (a) Hispanics may be reluctant to permit their child to be evaluated. (b) Bilingualism, per se, does not affect general intelligence, although many Hispanic children fail to gain mastery of either language. (c) The child's speech difficulties may interfere with the examination. (d) Anglo examiners have been found to be effective with Mexican-American children. (e) Translating tests or test directions is fraught with difficulties. Spanish test versions have been found to produce higher, similar, or lower scores than English test versions.

7. The WISC-R, but not the PPVT, has been found to be a reliable and valid measure of the intelligence of Mexican-American children. Mexican-American children usually obtain higher Performance IQs than Verbal IQs, a result which, in part, may be related to their limited proficiency in English.

8. The sociocultural values of North American Indian children—such as a deemphasis on competitive individualism and achievement motivation and an emphasis on

harmony with nature and the present time—are likely to interfere with their performance on many standardized intelligence tests. Indian children often score higher on performance tests than on verbal tests.

9. The culture of poverty may interfere with the development of intelligence. Low income youth may develop intellectual skills in ways that deviate from those of the majority culture, such as through premature structuring (attending to practical matters instead of developing intellectual skills) and alternate elaboration (developing mental abilities in ways that differ from those of most other children).

10. The heritability estimate of .80 for intelligence is based on studies of white persons. This estimate may have little relevance for accounting for IQ differences between groups. As long as there are systematic differences between blacks and whites in cultural patterns and in the psychological environment, valid inferences cannot be drawn about genetic differences between the two groups.

11. Research suggests that many ethnic groups have similar ability patterns.

12. Culture-fair tests do not provide more valid measures of the cognitive abilities of ethnic minority children than standard tests. All tests are culturally loaded to some extent.

13. The following kinds of recommendations have been made for the use of tests with ethnic minority children:

    a. Place an immediate moratorium on all testing.

    b. Focus on ways to improve instruction, rather than on classification, and increase children's motivation.

    c. Administer a wide range of tests using informal as well as formal assessment techniques, use extensive testing-of-limits procedures, and supplement normative testing with criterion-referenced testing.

    d. Establish separate norms for various sociocultural groups.

    e. Administer Spanish language tests and nonverbal tests to Hispanic children who have a poor command of English, and tests in Spanish and in English to bilingual children.

    f. Recommend special education only after all relevant data have been evaluated.

    g. Know as intimately as possible ethnic minority children's culture, and strive to help children feel proud of their culture.

    h. Develop tests that will better measure the psychological processes by which children learn.

    i. Develop and construct tests that have been validated on ethnic minorities and that include items reflective of their culture.

    j. Improve the educational system so that it becomes more responsive to the needs of ethnic minorities.

    k. Strive to eliminate social inequalities and prejudice from our society.

    l. Make certain that test scores are never viewed as an index of the child's personal worth.

14. A responsible use of tests in the assessment of ethnic minority children, and all other children too, mandates that their assets as well as their limitations be recognized.

CHAPTER 20

Assessment of Learning Disabilities, Hyperactivity, Behavior Disorders, and Sensory Impairments

The mind of man is keener than it is rational and embraces more than man is able to clearly explain.

VAUVENARGUES
Reflection 2

EXHIBIT 20-1. Psychological Evaluation: Visual-Spatial Dyslexia (Visual-Spatial Processing Deficit)

Name: Norman
Date of birth: July 24, 1970
Chronological age: 8-10
Dates of examination: May 24 & 26, 1979
Date of report: June 28, 1979
Grade: 4th

Reason for Referral

Norman has had behavior problems ever since kindergarten. He has not adjusted well to school or to his peers. There have been many incidents of fighting, lying, and stealing. His therapist referred him for a psychoeducational evaluation because of continued poor performance.

Tests Administered

Wechsler Intelligence Scale for Children–Revised (WISC-R):

VERBAL SCALE		PERFORMANCE SCALE	
Information	9	Picture Completion	9
Similarities	11	Picture Arrangement	8
Arithmetic	9	Block Design	3
Vocabulary	11	Object Assembly	5
Comprehension	16	Coding	5
Digit Span	7		

Verbal Scale IQ = 107
Performance Scale IQ = 73
Full Scale IQ = 89 ±5 at the 90 percent confidence level.

Wide Range Achievement Test (WRAT):

	STANDARD SCORE	PERCENTILE
Reading	75	5
Spelling	83	13
Arithmetic	102	55

1. *go* (go)	16. *order* (order)
2. *cat* (cat)	17. *woch* (watch)
3. *in* (in)	18. *etter* (enter)
4. *boy* (boy)	19. *gone* (gone)
5. *and* (and)	20. *eacher* (nature)
6. *will* (will)	21.
7. *make* (make)	22.
8. *him* (him)	23.
9. *sac* (say)	24.
10. *cut* (cut)	25.
11. *cwck* (cook)	26.
12. *liht* (light)	27.
13. *must* (must)	28.
14. *dres* (dress)	29.
15. *rcch* (reach)	30.

EXHIBIT 20-1   (cont.)

Lindamood Test of Auditory Conceptualization: Mid-kindergarten level.

Developmental Test of Visual Motor Integration: 7 years, 4 months level.

Sucher-Allred Reading Placement Inventory: Instructional Reading Level = Primer.

Behavioral Observations

Norman is a small, friendly youngster who showed an unusual ability to relate to a strange adult. His conversation was interesting, and he displayed a fine sense of humor. Cooperation and effort were strong throughout both testing sessions.

Discussion

The unusually wide difference of 34 points between his Verbal IQ (68th percentile) and his Performance IQ (4th percentile) suggests that language-based abilities are generally average (except for rote auditory memory), whereas visual-spatial abilities are poorly developed. Norman was exceptionally poor at determining part-whole relationships, whether they were meaningful or abstract. Perceptual processing and concept formation, based upon visual-spatial relationships, and speed of eye-hand coordination were also poor.

Auditory discrimination (ability to tell whether sounds/words are same or different) was adequate. Ability to blend separate sounds into words was poor (partly due to very short auditory recall of only 3 to 4 items). Norman also had extreme difficulty representing sounds and their order of occurrence.

Reading of separate words on a list was extremely poor, with only 80 percent of Primer words and 66 percent of First Reader words recognized. He was able to use initial and final consonant clues if a word was not known, but generally could not sound out words he did not know. Oral paragraph reading was limited to the mid-1st grade selection only. His errors were mispronunciations, omissions, and substitutions. He also made characteristic *b/d* reversals and transposed the letter order of words. Comprehension was much better than decoding, a pattern probably associated with his adequate language abilities.

Spelling was also poor. Auditory analysis was relatively easier than visual analysis of words, but neither skill was very well developed.

Arithmetic was better than either spelling or reading, although numbers were poorly written. He could add and subtract with regrouping, and was able to do some multiplication problems. Division was not performed correctly, however.

Recommendations

Norman's verbal abstract reasoning ability and vocabulary knowledge are average, indicating that he has underlying strengths for academic learning and for reading comprehension. Since auditory abilities are stronger than visual ones, a structured, phonics-based multisensory approach is suggested to help develop his reading skills.

Remediation is also needed to help Norman develop better visual processing and decoding of visual symbols representing words. Since his recent optometric examination proved him normal, it is suggested that he be trained in visual-spatial analysis coupled with verbalization. He needs guided practice in matching, manipulating, drawing, feeling shapes and space with eyes shut (visualizing), and visual memory. The visual-spatial items should be both meaningful, nonmeaningful, and letter/word forms. Continuation in therapy is also recommended.

_____

Examiner

Children who have difficulty learning present complex diagnostic and assessment problems. One primary reason for the diagnostic difficulty is that we are not sure in many cases whether the learning difficulty is primarily an educational or a medical problem. Children who have learning problems in school are likely to be labeled as "minimally brain damaged" if seen by physicians and as "learning disabled" if seen by educators. In this chapter we first review the area of learning disability and then turn to an evaluation of children with an "attention deficit disorder with hyperactivity," the current classification of children who manifest symptoms that formerly might have received a classification of "minimal brain damage" or "hyperkinetic syndrome of childhood." The last sections of the chapter focus on children with behavior disorders and children with sensory impairments.

Learning Disabilities—An Introduction

One of the first descriptive studies of learning disabilities, by Morgan, a physician, appeared in the *British Medical Journal* in 1896. He described the case of an intelligent 14-year-old boy who had unusual reading and writing difficulties and termed the difficulty "word blindness." The boy's difficulties included confusion of the sequential order of the letters in his name, spelling errors, and difficulty in learning the letters of the alphabet as a young child. Another early report was furnished by Hinshelwood (1917), who provided a more extensive description of "word blindness."

The term "learning disability" can be used in both a broad and a narrow sense. In the broad sense it refers to learning difficulties that can be associated with any type of factor, including mental retardation, brain injury, sensory difficulties, or emotional disturbance. In the narrow sense, which is the meaning adhered to in this chapter, it refers to the failure to learn a scholastic skill by a child who has adequate intelligence, maturational level, and cultural background. The narrower meaning is termed "specific learning disability." It is defined as follows in Public Law 94-142 (*Federal Register*, December 29, 1977):

"Specific learning disability" means a disorder in one or more of the basic psychological processes involved in understanding or in using language, spoken or written, which may manifest itself in an imperfect ability to listen, think, speak, read, write, spell, or to do mathematical calculations. The term includes such conditions as perceptual handicaps, brain injury, minimal brain dysfunction, dyslexia, and developmental aphasia. The term does not include children who have learning problems which are primarily the result of visual, hearing, or motor handicaps, of mental retardation, of emotional disturbance, or of environmental, cultural, or economic disadvantage.

The most prominent learning disability is reading disability. Other learning disabilities are associated with writing, spelling, and arithmetic skills. According to learning-disability specialists, the five disabilities that best differentiate learning-disabled from non-learning-disabled children are disabilities in reading comprehension, attention, auditory-visual coordination, writing, and auditory speed of perception (Wissink, Kass, & Ferrell, 1975).

In studying specific learning disabilities, it is important to distinguish the behavioral and psychological level from the etiological level. The former category includes such terms as "reading disability" and "dyslexia," while the latter includes terms related to the brain and its dysfunctions, such as "brain damage," "minimal brain dysfunction," and "genetic dyslexia."

A second important distinction focuses on learning difficulties that are associated with limited general intelligence versus those that are related to specific types of processing or organizing difficulties within the child. This distinction does not rule out the possibility that children who are functioning in below-average intellectual ranges also have processing difficulties that impede their learning ability.

Cruickshank (1977), in particular, objects to the inclusion of "adequate intelligence" as a necessary condition for a child to be classified as learning disabled. He conceives of learning disability as a *perceptual processing deficit* which results in a specific learning problem of some sort and involves one or more sensory modalities. Children who have learning difficulties due to poor teaching, mother-child separation, and other similar types of problems should be separated from those whose learning disability is due to a perceptual processing deficit, which Cruickshank believes is likely to have a neurological origin. He further states that learning disability can occur at every intellectual level because perceptual processing deficits are not bound by intellectual levels of functioning. Consequently, it is illogical to establish an arbitrary cut-off level of, say, an IQ of 80 or higher for defining learning disability. Learning disability is a psychoeducational problem and deserves special study.

The etiology of specific learning disability is by no means clear. Some favor a neurologically based hypothesis, others a maturational hypothesis, and still others a motivational hypothesis. Whatever the etiology might be, the disability appears to be related to a disturbed interaction between various cognitive and perceptual functions within the cerebral hemispheres. Often associated with specific learning disability are various kinds of secondary problems, including hyperactivity, impulsiveness, phobias, and lack of self-confidence. Delinquency, too, may be a concomitant of specific learning disability during the adolescent years. It is not known to what extent behavioral disorders associated with specific learning disability may be (a) a cause of the learning disability, (b) a consequence of the learning disability, (c) from the same origin as the learning disability (e.g., minimal brain dysfunction or inadequate maturation of the central nervous system), or (d) simply behaviors that occur concurrently with the learning disability (Matějček, 1977).

Theories to account for learning disability include (a) *neurological difficulties* (e.g., mixed cerebral dominance, maldevelopment or disease of the brain, or vestibular difficulties), (b) *integrative problems* that may have a neurological basis (e.g., sequencing difficulties, difficulty in processing visual or auditory input, memory difficulty, and slow maturation or developmental lag), (c) *emotional and behavioral problems* (e.g., anhedonia, depression, anxiety, and hypermobility), and (d) *failure of schooling* (e.g., failure of schools to teach children adequately, or erratic educational history). It is important to recognize that learning disability is not a unitary diagnostic category or a homogeneous one. There are subgroups within the population of learning-disabled children, even though all share a common problem with school learning.

Learning-disabled children may show deficits in auditory and visual memory, temporal sequencing, auditory and visual figure-ground relationships, reauditorization, revisualization, symbolization, abstraction, conceptualization, linguistic processing, conceptual synthesis, logical processing, control of morphology and syntax, and retrieval of verbal labels and verbal associations. Deficits in language processing may be shown in (a) reductions in short-term memory and immediate recall, (b) reductions in the acquisition of linguistic rules and in linguistic processing, and (c) reductions in cognitive-semantic and logical processing. Language production may reveal problems in word retrieval and sentence formulation.

Perhaps a key to the difficulties of some learning-disabled children is their failure to develop increased attentional efficiency to visual stimuli with age. The failure is especially noteworthy because the school makes increasing demands on children to pay attention to visual stimuli as a variety of reading, mathematical, and other learning tasks are introduced (Quay & Weld, 1980). In addition to having attentional deficits, learning-disabled children may employ inefficient memorization strategies (Torgesen, 1979). They may fail to use mnemonic strategies, such as verbal rehearsal or categorization of stimuli, when dealing with memory tasks. Short-term memory deficits have been found to exist, especially when material is presented at a fast pace (Cohen & Netley, 1978). Consequently, learning-disabled children might benefit from special help in developing selective attention to visual stimuli and in using more efficient memory strategies.

Dyslexia

Reading is a complex cognitive-linguistic skill. It is influenced by a variety of factors, such as intelligence level, language ability, neurological and sensory development, family background, personality, and quality of school instruction. According to Gibson (1968), the child goes through three sequential phases in the process of learning to read: (1) learning to differentiate graphic symbols

---

EXHIBIT 20-2.   Our Incredible Language

When the English tongue we speak
Why is "break" not rhymed with "freak?"
Will you tell me why it's true
We say "sew" but likewise "few?"
And the maker of a verse
Cannot cap his "horse" with "worse."
"Beard" sounds not the same as "heard."
"Cord" is different from "word."
Cow is "cow," but low is "low."
"Shoe" is never rhymed with "roe."
Think of "hose" and "dose" and "lose."
And think of "goose" and yet of "choose."
Think of "comb" and "tomb" and "bomb."
"Doll" and "roll" and "home" and "come."
And since "pay" is rhymed with "say,"
Why not "paid" with "said," I pray?
We have "blood" and "food" and "good,"
"Mould" is not pronounced like "could."
Wherefore "done" but "gone" and "lone."
Is there any reason known?
And, in short, it seems to me
Sounds and letters disagree.   ■

Author Unknown

---

the process by responding to the printed word patterns with the appropriate sound sequences. Thus, the acquisition of reading skills may be dependent on a complex constellation of many different abilities, including auditory sequencing, visual sequencing, visual-motor-spatial integration, visual discrimination, short-term memory, and auditory and visual integration. Exhibit 20-2 illustrates some of the complexities involved in learning how to read English.

Dyslexia defined. Dyslexia may be defined as "a severe retardation in reading and writing in children who otherwise have at least average intelligence, educational opportunity and freedom from gross neurological sensory or cultural handicap" (Satz, Friel, & Rudegeair, 1974a, p. 176). Another definition of reading retardation is that it is a "syndrome of learning disability in children who are bright enough to learn, and who have had the usual learning opportunities" (Lyle & Goyen, 1969, p. 106). Both definitions, then, suggest that an exploration of reading retardation per se is of minimal concern when children are dull, have sensory handicaps, or have missed schooling. Lyle and Goyen also pointed out that

the term "reading retardation" may in fact have four meanings: (a) slow reading speed, (b) limited vocabulary, (c) failure to master basic processes such as letter recognition and sound blending, and (d) lack of comprehension despite adequate fluency in the mechanics of reading. [p. 106]

In studies of children with reading retardation, it is rare to find any who fall into the fourth type. The first and second types can occur through lack of reading practice at older age levels. Therefore, Lyle and Goyen believe that it is the third meaning which should form the basis for the selection criteria in studies of reading retardation.

The following types of deficits have been thought to be associated with reading disability: directional confusion (or right-left confusion), deficient visual information processing, auditory-perceptual difficulties, de-

(e.g., ability to discriminate the distinctive features of letters), (2) learning to decode letters to sounds (e.g., ability to analyze the conventional phonetic value of letters), and (3) learning to use higher-order units of linguistic structure (e.g., ability to group letters into words).

Reading requires the transformation of visual symbols into verbal language, be it audible or covert. Both the ability to analyze visual constructs—printed words—and the ability to analyze acoustical constructs —spoken words—into their component parts appear to be critical skills. These abilities are derived from basic perceptual processing skills and are essential in learning to read (Rosner, 1973). At the decoding level, children must learn to relate auditory patterns in speech to the spatially ordered visual patterns in print and must also reverse

ficient intersensory transfer of information, attentional difficulties, impairment in verbal intelligence, calculation difficulty, problems with finger-differentiation, spontaneous writing and spelling impairment, form perception impairment, inefficient memorization strategies (such as verbal rehearsal), difficulties in gross and fine motor coordination, delayed lateral awareness or crossed dominance, speech difficulties, social-emotional disturbance, and neurological difficulties.[1] It is important to recognize that no one particular child is likely to have all of these deficiencies and that no one deficiency invariably has been observed in all reading-disabled children.

In addition to the deficits mentioned, the following instructional and sociocultural factors may be associated with reading disability (Sartain, 1976):

1. *Instructional factors* (failure of schools) include (a) failure to adjust rate of instruction to the progress of individuals because of large class size or lack of teaching skill, (b) failure to relate reading to pupils' personal needs and interests, (c) inadequate introduction and maintenance of necessary component skills, (d) lack of reinforcement of learning through psychological and material rewards (inadequate motivation and behavior modification), (e) inadequate rapport between instructor and pupils, (f) inadequate amount of time scheduled for reading instruction, and (g) lack of instructional materials that can be used in making program adaptations for different individuals.

2. *Sociocultural factors* include (a) home factors—family distrust of schools, lack of family models of good education, low family expectations, vocational expectations not requiring education, problems related to family disintegration; (b) community factors—anti-intellectual peer pressures, limited vocational opportunities; and (c) cultural background factors—lack of familiarity with language styles and social customs used in school, and lack of instructional materials depicting the pupil's real life.

Research findings with dyslexic children. Benton (1975) carefully reviewed studies dealing with various perceptual, motor, linguistic, cognitive, and neurological factors that may be associated with dyslexia. His conclusions, which are summarized in Table 20-1, suggest that dyslexic children, in comparison to normal readers, are more likely to have (a) impaired directional sense, (b) impaired intersensory integration, (c) impaired linguistic facility, and (d) impaired sequential perception. However, not all dyslexics will show these difficulties and with age some of these difficulties may diminish. In contrast to these significant trends, Benton observed that research does not support the view that dyslexics have significantly impaired (a) visuoperceptual ability, (b) finger recognition, (c) laterality, (d) electrophysiological functioning, or (e) neurological functioning.

Benton (1975) hypothesized that the overall findings suggest that a neurological or at least a constitutional explanation of developmental dyslexia is tenable, even though specific findings are weak. As for support for his conclusion, he pointed out that there is a striking sex difference, with males being four to five times more frequently represented than females. In addition, there are indications of a significant hereditary factor operating. The behavioral correlates associated with dyslexia (such as right-left confusion and defects in intersensory integration) also support his hypothesis.

Vellutino (1978) concluded that there is increasing evidence that dyslexia is primarily associated with verbal mediation or verbal processing deficiencies, possibly associated with basic language problems, and that the apparent perceptual problems are only a secondary manifestation. Consequently, he holds little justification for a perceptual-deficit explanation of reading disability. This view does not take into account the child's age, and, as Satz and his colleagues (see next section) have observed, age is an

TABLE 20-1.   Reported Correlates of Developmental Dyslexia

Correlate	Comment
Impairment in directional sense (particularly lateral or right-left discrimination)	Studies suggest that faulty right-left discrimination may be associated with reading failure in first to third grade children but not in older dyslexic children. Directional orientation difficulties may be of a general nature and not restricted to the right-left dimension.
Defects in intersensory integration (particularly in the equivalence matching of visual and auditory stimuli)	Studies indicate that crossmodal matching is deficient in some dyslexics. Whether the difficulty indicates a specific deficiency in audiovisual matching ability or poor memory or some other factor has not been determined. The mechanisms involved in crossmodal matching are not well understood.
Generalized language disability	Studies indicate that many dyslexics have a relatively poor general linguistic development, including poor development of oral language skills.
Deficiency in sequential perception (faulty perception and retention of organized stimulus patterns)	Studies indicate that dyslexics have more difficulty than normal readers in identifying the temporal sequence of presented digits or figures.
Visuoperceptual defects (reflected in poor form discrimination, poor visuomotor performance, and poor visual memory)	Studies do not provide conclusive evidence that dyslexics are inferior to normal readers in visuoperceptive and visuomotor functions. Even when findings are significant, only a relatively small proportion of dyslexics are found to be deficient in these areas.
Disturbances in finger recognition	Studies are inconsistent as to whether or not defective finger recognition is a significant correlate of dyslexia.
Less clearly defined laterality (reflected, for example, in mixed hand and eye preference)	Studies do not allow for any simple generalizations concerning laterality characteristics and reading skill. While many nonsignificant findings have been reported, there is a weak trend in the direction of a higher frequency of deviant lateral organization in poor readers.
Abnormalities in the electroencephalogram	Studies are inconclusive about the relationship between EEG abnormality and dyslexia.
Neurological abnormalities	Studies do not provide any conclusive evidence that neurological abnormalities are greater in dyslexic children than in other groups of children.

Adapted from Benton (1975).

important variable in evaluating deficiencies associated with dyslexia.

A developmental theory of dyslexia. Satz and his colleagues have hypothesized that specific reading disability is not a unitary syndrome.[2] Rather, they propose that the disability reflects a lag in the maturation of the left hemisphere of the brain. Maturational lag refers to a slow or delayed development of those brain areas which facilitate the acquisition of age-linked developmental skills. It is postulated that the disabled reader has a lag or delay in acquisition, rather than an impairment or loss of function. However, the underlying mechanism associated with the delay remains obscure.

From a developmental perspective, the skills affected are those that are in a period of most rapid change. At the early school years (e.g., first and second grades) these skills center on visual spatial abilities (e.g., visual-perceptual, visual-motor, and directional-spatial or cross-modal integration), whereas in the later elementary school years (e.g., sixth to eighth grades) they center on verbal cognitive abilities (e.g., language and formal operations). The theory, which postulates that dyslexic children have a central processing disorder that varies with the age and developmental stage of the child, is compatible with those developmental positions which hypothesize that the child goes through consecutive stages of thought development, each of which incorporates the processes of the preceding stage into a more complex and hierarchically integrated form of adaptation.[3]

Research provides some support for Satz's theory. Younger dyslexic children appear to have poor visual-perceptual or perceptual-motor skills, which are important to the early phases of reading, whereas older dyslexic children do not evidence any significant delay in these earlier developing skills, but rather lag on a number of language skills that are important to the later phases of reading.

Syndromes in dyslexic children. Efforts to delineate subtypes within the broad classification of dyslexia are only beginning. However, some promising proposals have appeared that may enable us to classify reading difficulties more precisely. Four such attempts are shown in Table 20-2. These proposals are not mutually exclusive. They emphasize that the primary difficulty for some dyslexic children appears to be in language-related areas, whereas for others it appears in visual-spatial areas. The syndromes illustrated in Table 20-2 are by no means pure. Symptoms overlap, and not all children in any one group display all of the

symptoms. In addition, not all dyslexics fall into one of the syndromes shown in the table. Yet, these classification systems have potential because they may lead to the development of remediation efforts that are tailored to the specific deficiencies of the dyslexic child.

Three psychological evaluations in the text illustrate some of these syndromes. Exhibit 16-1 (Chapter 16) concerns an adolescent who may have an auditory processing deficit (dysphonetic dyslexia). Exhibit 15-1 (Chapter 15) describes a child with auditory and visual processing deficits. The evaluation that began this chapter portrays a boy with a visual-spatial processing deficit (Exhibit 20-1).

Improving research on dyslexia. The following suggestions will aid those who perform research with dyslexic children (Benton, 1975). They involve delineating children's disabilities more carefully and establishing more homogeneous groups.

1. First, it is necessary to differentiate between specific reading disability and reading retardation associated with more general factors, such as mental retardation or lack of educational opportunity.
2. Second, the types of errors shown by children, or their particular difficulties, should be specified. Differences in laterality or right-left confusion, to take just two examples, have been found to be associated with certain types of reading errors, such as reversal errors or errors on sequential reading tasks, but not with other types (Belmont & Birch, 1965; Shankweiler, 1964). Benton believes that such performance characteristics may be more closely related to cognitive, perceptual, and neurological factors than to overall reading level, which is influenced by a variety of social factors, such as cultural background, family size, and special tutoring.
3. Third, "pure" dyslexics, i.e., those who have no other types of learning problems, should be distinguished from those who have a concomitant deficiency in other

TABLE 20-2. Syndromes in Dyslexic Children

I. Mattis, French, and Rapin (1975) Classification	
Language Disorder	1. Defects in both understanding and expression of oral language—anomia is the major critical factor. 2. Intact visual and constructional skills and adequate graphomotor coordination. 3. Blending of speech generally intact. 4. Verbal IQ poorer than Performance IQ.
Articulatory and Graphomotor Dyscoordination Syndrome	1. Deficiencies in speech articulation. 2. Poor copying of designs. 3. Normal receptive language. 4. Verbal IQ approximates Performance IQ.
Visuo-spatial Perceptual Disorder	1. Poor visuo-spatial perception. 2. Intact language, graphomotor coordination, and speech blending skill. 3. Performance IQ poorer than Verbal IQ. 4. Poor Progressive Matrices and Visual Retention Test scores.
II. Boder (1973) Classification	
Dysphonetic Dyslexia	1. Difficulty in integrating symbols with their sounds (or difficulty in learning what letters sound like). 2. Words are read globally rather than analytically. 3. Difficulty in sounding out and blending the component letters and syllables of a word.
Dyseidetic Dyslexia	1. Difficulty in perceiving letters and whole words as configurations or gestalts (or difficulty in learning what the letters of the alphabet look like) because of poor memory for visual gestalts. 2. Reading occurs through a process of phonetic analysis and synthesis. 3. There is a sounding out of combinations of letters instead of recognition of whole-word visual gestalts.
Mixed Dysphonetic-Dyseidetic Dyslexia	1. Combinations of the first and second types. 2. These children have extreme difficulty in reading either by sight or "by ear."
III. Ingram, Mason, and Blackburn (1970) Classification	
Audio-phonic Difficulties	1. Inability to synthesize letters correctly sounded individually into the appropriate words (*b u n* sounded but the word uttered as *but*). 2. Confusion of vowel sounds in recognition of words (*bed* read as *bad*). 3. Poor phonic knowledge (lack of acquaintance with the sound of diphthongs). 4. General inability to analyze words into their natural auditory units.
Visuo-spatial Difficulties	1. Confusion of letters of the same shape but different orientation (b, d, p). 2. Slow recognition of even simple words. 3. Poor visual discrimination of words closely similar in shape (*road* and *read*). 4. Directional errors (*saw* read as *was*), although this type of error may also occur as a result of an audio-phonic difficulty.
IV. Kinsbourne and Warrington (1963) Classification	
Language Retardation	1. Verbal IQ lower than Performance IQ. 2. Impaired language, reading, and writing skills. 3. Delay in the acquisition of speech.
Developmental Gerstmann Syndrome	1. Verbal IQ higher than Performance IQ. 2. Deficits in finger differentiation and order, in arithmetic, in right-left orientation, and in mechanical and constructional tasks (e.g., copying drawings and match-stick patterns). 3. Difficulty in performing written additions and subtractions.

skills. Studies have shown that the latter group has more neurological abnormalities than "pure" dyslexics.

Remediation and Prognosis of Learning Disabilities

While a discussion of remediation techniques is beyond the scope of this book, some comments are in order about remediation, prognosis, and assessment. Remediation is likely to be most effective when the instructional techniques are geared to the child's strengths and weaknesses and formulated in relation to the child's developmental level, individual learning style, and task requirements. This philosophy is illustrated by Vellutino, Steger, Moyer, Harding, and Niles (1977, p. 383):

> We strongly advocate that the behavioral concept of maximum transfer be substituted for process dysfunction theories which currently dominate our approach to evaluating and correcting learning disabilities. For optimal effect, diagnostic and treatment procedures should (1) focus upon performance and task variables in units that most closely approximate the skill to be learned, (2) emphasize direct instruction rather than discovery methods of learning, (3) ascertain and capitalize upon competencies already possessed by the learner, (4) incorporate no assumptions about the learner's ability to acquire a specific

skill—as a result of tenuous or ill-founded etiological theories, or prior to attempts at teaching him that skill, and (5) facilitate development of individualized programs.

Also implied in this discussion is a call for using well-established principles of learning such as cueing to effect discrimination and correct association, teaching unifying concepts to facilitate synthesis and transfer, providing adequate opportunity for practice and review, and structuring for high motivation and success. These ideas are neither new nor profound but, to the detriment of the children they are to serve, seem to have suffered from disuse.

In addition to the above factors, the teacher's style may have to be considered in developing remediation programs. The age of the child, too, is a critical factor in any work with children, because with age there is increased maturation of the brain and a corresponding differentiation and growth of cognitive functions. Early identification programs, particularly in the first two grades, coupled with appropriate remediation programs have a much better rate of success than programs in later grades (Satz, Friel, & Rudegeair, 1974b). Psychologists working in schools will have to become familiar with resource rooms, learning centers, teacher consultants, itinerant programs, and special education programs in order to recommend the best program for a child.

"Your feelings of insecurity seem to have started when Mary Lou Gurnblatt said, 'Maybe I don't have a learning disability—maybe you have a teaching disability.'"

Courtesy of Tony Saltzman.

Although the performance of dyslexic children may improve with time, the children may remain slow readers and poor spellers. Improvement has been associated with socioeconomic status and with verbal intelligence—children from the higher socioeconomic classes and those with higher verbal intelligence make better progress than those from lower classes and those with lower verbal intelligence (Benton, 1975; Safer & Allen, 1973).

Studies indicate that attempts to improve cognitive development and subsequent academic success of learning-disabled children by use of perceptual-motor training programs—such as those developed by Frostig and Horne (1964), Kephart (1971), and Getman, Kane, Halgren, and McKee (1968) —have questionable success (Hammill, Goodman, & Weiderholt, 1974). Studies also indicate that psycholinguistic training, using the ITPA scores as a criterion of improvement, does not generally improve reading performance (Hammill & Larsen, 1974). The reasons for the limited success of this approach are still unknown. It may be that (a) the skills required by the ITPA subtests are difficult to teach, (b) the training programs were inadequate, or (c) the ITPA is not an appropriate tool to measure psycholinguistic constructs. Only future research will clarify these issues. Hammill and Larsen advise that until further research is available, programs designed to improve psycholinguistic functioning be viewed cautiously and monitored with care.

Assessment of Learning Disabilities

The assessment of learning-disabled children has three major aims. One aim is to obtain an estimate of general intelligence in order to determine whether the child has the ability for higher achievement despite past or present performance. A second aim is to determine areas of impaired functioning that may lend themselves to remediation. A third aim is to find areas of strength that may prove helpful in remediation efforts. In working with learning-disabled children, it is especially important to enlist their cooper-

ation and motivation. If these are not obtained, the test results may not be valid, as Case 20-1 demonstrates.

CASE 20-1. Effects of Motivation on Test Scores

Michael, a ninth-grade boy with a Peabody Picture Vocabulary IQ of 100, was about to be labeled as having a "learning disability" on the basis of his scores on a standard test battery. According to the test results, Michael was functioning several years below his grade level, and plans were being made to refer him to a special learning disability program. At about the same time, Michael had also been referred to the school counselor because of disruptive behavior in the classroom, and, as a result, the counselor observed him in the classroom on several occasions and kept a written record of his disruptive behavior. These observations confirmed that Michael was indeed frequently disruptive, but he was also observed to attend to movies for long periods of time and to draw elaborately detailed pictures of sport cars. Such observations tended to contradict the "hyperactive-distractible" label tentatively ascribed. Consequently, it was decided to readminister the learning disability test battery, this time offering incentives for good performance. Specifically, Michael was offered two cents for each correct response. The results of the second administration indicated Michael to be near grade level or above on all three subtests. His average gain on the three subtests was four years! Had it not been for these circumstances, Michael would have been referred to a learning-disability classroom. A disturbing question is how many children like Michael have been misplaced.

This illustration indicates the value of distinguishing between a learning disability and a "motivational disability." A child for whom academic tasks have low intrinsic interest would not need the same kind of training program as a child who lacks ability to process or assimilate sensory input. Ideally, an aptitude or ability test might yield both an ability or aptitude score *and* a motivation score. Then the diagnostician would have a means of distinguishing between two often imperceptibly different kinds of problems, with a resultant improvement in the definitiveness or appropriateness of the therapeutic prescription. ■

Source: Adapted from Kubany and Sloggett (1971, pp. 427–428).

Approaches to Classification of Learning Disabilities

Establishing whether or not a child has a learning disability is not a simple task. All relevant factors must be considered. The U.S. Office of Education provided the following guidelines, as part of Public Law 94-142, for determining the existence of a specific learning disability (*Federal Register,* December 29, 1977, p. 65083, 121a.541):

(a) A team may determine that a child has a specific learning disability if:
   (1) The child does not achieve commensurate with his or her age and ability levels in one or more of the areas listed in paragraph (a)(2) of this section, when provided with learning experiences appropriate for the child's age and ability levels; and
   (2) The team finds that a child has a severe discrepancy between achievement and intellectual ability in one or more of the following areas:
      (i) Oral expression;
      (ii) Listening comprehension;
      (iii) Written expression;
      (iv) Basic reading skills;
      (v) Reading comprehension;
      (vi) Mathematics calculation; or
      (vii) Mathematics reasoning.
(b) The team may not identify a child as having a specific learning disability if the severe discrepancy between ability and achievement is primarily the result of:
   (1) A visual, hearing, or motor handicap;
   (2) Mental retardation;
   (3) Emotional disturbance; or
   (4) Environmental, cultural or economic disadvantage.

The guidelines, however, *do not indicate how a severe discrepancy between achievement and intellectual ability should be determined.* While various proposals, described below, have been offered to help determine whether the child's performance is significantly below expectation for his or her age level and intelligence, these proposals should be viewed simply as helpful guideposts. *In the final analysis, clinical and psychoeducational considerations must come together in a diagnosis of learning disability.*

Let us examine some of the proposals for establishing the presence of a learning disability and, in particular, reading retardation.

1. The most acceptable procedure entails establishing a regression equation (Thorndike, 1963; Yule, Rutter, Berger, & Thompson, 1974). Reading ability does not exactly parallel intellectual ability (e.g., the correlation is not perfect: $r \neq 1.00$). When the correlation between two measures (such as mental age and reading age) is less than perfect, a "regression effect" appears. This means that children who are above average on one measure will be less superior on the other, while those who are below average on the first measure will be less inferior on the second. A regression equation permits one to take into account the regression effect when evaluating achievement level.

2. A second method involves a ratio of reading age to chronological, mental, or oral language age (Benton, 1975). Ratios less than .80 may be considered as suggestive of reading retardation. The ratio method takes into account the fact that a retardation of, for example, 2 years is more severe for a fourth grade child than for a tenth grade child.

3. Reynolds (1981) proposed a method that takes into account the reliabilities of the intelligence and reading tests. The child's scores are entered into a formula that determines whether or not a significant discrepancy exists between the scores. In order to use the formula, scores must be expressed as standard scores.

4. The least preferred method is simply to determine the extent to which the child's reading level is below his or her chronological age or mental age or grade level. This method fails to take into account the relative differences between reading level and chronological age or mental age or grade level.

All of the above methods are dependent on reliable and valid measuring instruments. Further, different instruments are likely to yield different estimates of intelligence and achievement skills. These factors, therefore, should be taken into account in arriving at a classification and in comparing different groups of learning-disabled children.

Guidelines for the Assessment of Learning Disabilities

While there is no one standard battery for the assessment of learning disability, many of the tests reviewed in Chapters 14 through 17 have proved useful. As always, the selection of tests should be based on the referral question. Evaluating auditory skills as well as visual-perceptual processing skills, in addition to intelligence and achievement skills, may often be important. Ideally, ongoing diagnostic procedures should become part of the regular classroom activity rather than be conducted outside of the classroom. This is particularly necessary after psychoeducational and related studies have been completed.

On a battery of tests there is no one characteristic pattern of test performance associated with learning-disabled children in general or with reading-disabled children in particular. Children may have (a) a deficiency in reading primarily, (b) a deficiency in arithmetic primarily, (c) a deficiency in reading and spelling, but not arithmetic, or (d) a deficiency in each of these skill areas.

The assessment of reading-disabled children should focus on the child's skills in reading—such as repertoire of words identified on sight; knowledge of speech sounds, such as vowels, consonants, and blends; comprehension skills; silent reading skills; and oral reading skills—and should incorporate trial remediation procedures in the assessment process (Vellutino et al., 1977). The most important tools in the assessment of learning-disabled children are (a) a reliable and valid intelligence test and (b) reliable and valid achievement tests that assess major content areas such as reading, mathematics, and spelling.

In the assessment of reading skills, it is important to determine (a) the extent of the reading deficit, (b) the type of reading deficit, and (c) the possible reasons for the reading deficit. In the earlier part of the chapter we saw that numerous deficiencies may be associated with reading disability. Generally, these deficiencies may reflect limited intelligence; below-average skills in decoding words; below-average knowledge of the meanings of words heard or of the names of things seen pictured; below-average skills in remembering ideas heard and understood; and below-average capability for weaving together ideas heard and understood (Davis, 1972). More specific symptoms are shown in Table 20-3. Because teachers often do not know precisely the child's deficiency (or

---

TABLE 20-3.   A Composite Behavioral Symptomatology of Reading Disorders

A. Oral Reading Behavior
  1. Confusion in letter, syllable and word recognition
  2. Reversal of letters and syllables
  3. Loses place easily
  4. Confusion of similar verbal and/or visual configuration
  5. Many errors in omissions, additions, substitutions, and transpositions
  6. Poor use of word-attack skills
  7. Perseveration of beginning sounds
  8. Lacks fluency
  9. Points to words
  10. Moves head
  11. Poor concentration
  12. Lacks interest, poor motivation
  13. Words and phrases lack meaning
  14. Tense, can't sit still, overactive
B. Silent Reading Behavior
  1. Loses place easily
  2. Points to words
  3. Moves head
  4. Erratic eye movements, fixations, and tracking
  5. Lip movement
  6. Subvocalization (whispering)
  7. Poor concentration
  8. Can't sit still, overactive

From Bloom and Jones (1970, p. 608).

deficiencies), appropriate remediation programs are difficult to develop. The assessment aims at determining which deficiency (or deficiencies) is present.

Learning disabilities and the Stanford-Binet. On the Stanford-Binet, learning-disabled children may demonstrate difficulty with verbal materials, perceptual difficulty, poor recall of visual patterns, poor copying and reproduction of forms, and short memory span. Studying the child's pattern of successes and failures (see the Binetgram in Chapter 8) may provide clues to various kinds of cognitive difficulties.

Learning disabilities and the WISC-R. Attempts have been made to determine whether or not various WISC-R (or WISC) patterns—such as Verbal-Performance discrepancy, pattern of subtest scores, and range of scatter—can distinguish learning-disabled children from normal children, behavior problem children, and mentally retarded children. The evidence indicates that these attempts have not been successful.[4] There is no one particular WISC-R (or WISC) pattern that is reliably diagnostic of learning disability. The WISC-R should be used to assess the child's intelligence and patterns of cognitive efficiency; it should not be used in the absence of other tests and information to make a differential diagnosis.

There are trends emerging, however, from studies that have evaluated the rank order of WISC and WISC-R subtest scores in heterogeneous groups of reading-disabled children.[5] An inspection of thirty studies indicates that the average subtest ranks of inadequate readers, from highest to lowest, are the following:

1. Picture Completion
2. Picture Arrangement
3. Block Design
4. Object Assembly
5. Similarities
6. Comprehension
7. Vocabulary
8. Coding
9. Digit Span

10. Arithmetic
11. Information.

The four most difficult subtests form the acronym ACID (Arithmetic, Coding, Information, and Digit Span). In nearly every study that reported Verbal Scale and Performance Scale IQs, Verbal Scale IQs were lower than Performance Scale IQs. This discrepancy could be expected from the rank order data, which showed that the four easiest subtests were Performance Scale subtests. The low Coding score may reflect the failure to use an effective labeling strategy as a memory aid, thereby increasing the time needed to complete the task (Lyle & Goyen, 1969).

Bannatyne (1974) proposed that the WISC subtests be recategorized as an aid in evaluating learning-disabled children. Subtests are recombined into Spatial, Conceptual, Sequential, and Acquired Knowledge categories as follows:

Spatial: Picture Completion, Block Design, and Object Assembly
Conceptual: Comprehension, Similarities, and Vocabulary
Sequential: Arithmetic, Digit Span, and Coding
Acquired Knowledge: Information, Arithmetic, and Vocabulary.

The Spatial category involves the ability to manipulate objects in multidimensional space, either directly or symbolically. The Conceptual category represents abilities related to language development. The Sequential category reflects the ability to retain and use sequences of auditory and memory stimuli in short-term memory storage. Acquired Knowledge represents abilities that are usually learned in the school or home. The Sequential category is the same as the Freedom from Distractibility factor found in factor analytic studies of the WISC and the WISC-R.

Bannatyne's recategorization was based on an inspection of the subtests, not on factor analytic findings. It is simply a heuristic model that may aid in test interpretation. While children with reading difficulties frequently have a Wechsler pattern of Spatial > Conceptual > Sequential (Rugel, 1974), this pattern is by no means evident in a majority of reading-disabled children.[6] In addition, the recategorizations have not been successful in differentiating children with visual-perceptual learning disorders from those with auditory-perceptual learning disabilities (Miller, 1977). There is no reason to expect *all* reading-disabled children to show any one pattern on the WISC-R (or other tests), because reading disability is symptomatic of many different kinds of underlying difficulties.

The findings of these studies suggest that the Bannatyne recategorized scores may be of little value in the assessment of learning disability in children. The existence of the pattern does not establish a learning disability. Contrariwise, the absence of a Spatial > Conceptual > Sequential   pattern should not be taken as an indication that a learning disability is not present.

The ability structure of learning-disabled children has been compared with that of normal children by means of factor analyzing the WISC-R (or WISC). Lombard and Riedel (1978) and Lowrance (1977) have found the WISC-R factor structure of learning-disabled children to be similar to that of normal children. However, Wallbrown, Blaha, Counts, and Wallbrown (1974) reported that reading-disabled children have a WISC factor structure characterized by a weaker general factor and by more primary factors. These results were interpreted to mean that learning-disabled children have less effective ability integration than normal children and a more complex arrangement of abilities.

Investigators have been interested in determining the correlates of Verbal-Performance discrepancies in learning-disabled children. First, three groups usually are established, namely, (a) those whose Performance Scale is greater than their Verbal Scale by a specific number of points (e.g., 9 or more points) (P > V), (b) those whose Verbal and Performance Scales are similar (e.g., within ± 5 points) (V = P), and (c) those

whose Verbal Scale is greater than their Performance Scale (e.g., 9 or more points) (V > P). The three groups usually are matched on Full Scale IQ.

The findings of a number of different studies are by no means clear-cut, although some trends appear to exist.[7]

1. Learning-disabled children with P > V tend to do better on visual-perceptual tasks, complex motor and psychomotor tasks, and tactual performance tasks than those with V > P. However, they perform more poorly on reading tasks and tasks requiring language expression.
2. Learning-disabled children with V > P tend to do better on verbal and auditory-perceptual tasks than those with P > V. However, they tend to be more impaired neurologically and have impaired finger differentiation, constructional ability, and left-right orientation.

The above trends must be tempered by a number of other findings. First, they are more likely to hold for older learning-disabled children (e.g., 9 to 14 years) than for younger ones (e.g., 5 to 8 years). Second, not all investigators have been able to replicate these trends. For example, in two studies of learning-disabled children most of the neuropsychological measures failed to discriminate between the P > V and V > P groups (Larsen, Tillman, Ross, Satz, Cassin, & Wolking, 1973; Wener & Templer, 1976).

Attention Deficit Disorder with Hyperactivity

The term proposed by the American Psychiatric Association (1980) in their third edition of the *Diagnostic and Statistical Manual of Mental Disorders* (DSM III) for conditions previously referred to as hyperkinesis or minimal brain dysfunction is "attention deficit disorder with hyperactivity." The proposed criteria for this condition are as follows:

The essential features are signs of developmentally inappropriate inattention, impul-

EXHIBIT 20-3.   Psychological Evaluation: Attention Deficit Disorder with Hyperactivity

Name: Craig
Date of birth: March 5, 1969
Chronological age: 10-3
Date of examination: June 6, 1979
Date of report: June 7, 1979
Grade: 4th

Tests Administered

Draw-A-Man:

Wechsler Intelligence Scale for Children–Revised (scaled scores):

VERBAL SCALE		PERFORMANCE SCALE	
Information	10	Picture Completion	13
Similarities	11	Picture Arrangement	10
Arithmetic	7	Block Design	12
Comprehension	13	Object Assembly	10
Vocabulary	11	Coding	7
(Digit Span)	(9)		

Verbal Scale IQ = 102
Performance Scale IQ = 102
Full Scale IQ = 102±5 (90 percent confidence level).

Wide Range Achievement Test:

	STANDARD SCORE	PERCENTILE
Reading	111	77th
Spelling	96	39th
Arithmetic	93	32nd

Bender-Gestalt: Designs were over-drawn, small circles substituted for "dots," and two errors noted in integrating tangential figures; problems primarily apparent in fine-motor precision. Age norm (Koppitz standards)—8½ years.

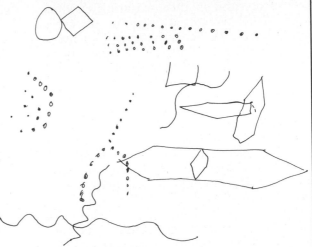

Reason for Referral

Craig has a long, complicated history of social behavioral problems which have manifested themselves both at home and at school. From a very early age he was considered "hyperactive," not only physically but verbally as well. As his mother put it: "He walked, ran, and talked early, and has never stopped."

In short, Craig continues to be a challenging management problem—what with his impulsivity, high activity level, and inclination to test, if not defy, limits when disciplinary measures are imposed. Incidents of petty stealing, followed by vigorous denials (even when found with "hard evidence"), have cropped up again recently. It may be significant that medication (Ritalin) prescribed by his pediatrician two years ago has recently been discontinued on a trial basis. The mother and school personnel feel that re-instituting the medication should be considered in formulating recommendations from this study.

Background Information

Craig's parents were divorced when he was six weeks old. For the first six years of his life he was cared for by his mother, a single parent, and his maternal grandmother, who lived in the home. He has two older siblings, who present no behavior or school difficulties.

Craig has been an extremely active child. Because scolding did not work, corporal punishment was often needed to keep him in line. In

EXHIBIT 20-3 (cont.)

the early school years he was sent home at least once a week for disrupting class. His mother began to resent this, and tensions built up because she needed to work to support the family.

In the 2nd and 3rd grades, Craig's behavior did not improve. In addition, he fell farther and farther behind in school work because he would not complete assignments (usually written), and his anger and frustration made matters worse. The situation became so unbearable at one point that he was placed in a foster home.

Upon Craig's return to the family a year later, his mother sought the help of his pediatrician. The pediatrician found him to be in generally good health, but an extended neurological examination revealed many "soft" signs, consistent with a mild neurodevelopmental disorder. Craig's history suggested "Hyperkinetic Syndrome," and a regimen of Ritalin was instituted. The medication seemed to result in moderate improvement, at least to the extent that his behavior was more manageable.

Observations from his teachers and the school psychologist indicate that Craig can be worked with easily on a one-to-one basis. He sponges up information and responds in a rewarding, delightful way. However, he does not like to be angered or asked to do something that does not suit him ("I'm not gonna read that out loud and you can't make me.") When reprimanded for throwing a workbook into the ash can, he "fell apart in anger" and threatened to throw his chair at the teacher (he would have, if it had not been too heavy).

Children are afraid of Craig. They will give him candy, lunches, and money—anything to keep from being attacked, especially when he is angry. They have learned to recognize a "certain look in his eye." He has displayed many outbursts of behavior, including kicking a custodian in the hall (unprovoked) and then tearing up a field trip notice into little pieces.

Test Results

The test results indicate that Craig is a competent reader, even though he stated vehemently that he "hates reading." This was one of the few test areas where he complained openly and worked grudgingly. His writing is awkward and enlarged, and his spelling appears to be almost strictly phonetic. For example, "brief" is printed as "breaf" and "light" as "lite," suggesting poorly developed visual memory processes.

His mathematical skills appear to be shaky, although further testing may be warranted in this area. When faced with two-digit number combinations, he had to stop and think as to whether each problem required borrowing or a carrying process. He performed at a below-average level on the oral arithmetic items of the WISC-R, which may in part have resulted from hastily given responses. His Wide Range Achievement Test arithmetic score was also somewhat below average.

So far as his intellectual functioning is concerned, Craig again evidenced irregularities in his ability pattern, but performed, overall, well within the normal range. It is interesting that on the WISC-R he obtained a high score on Comprehension, a verbal task involving practical-social reasoning and judgment. He gave quick, sensible explanations to questions such as: "Why are criminals locked up?" and "Why should a promise be kept?" The only items which gave him significant trouble were arithmetic items and those which relied upon rapid visual-motor dexterity with a pencil.

Throughout both of our test sessions, Craig came across as congenial, articulate, if not a rather "verbally glib" young man. While not hyperactive, in the sense of being motorically mobile, he impressed me as somewhat edgy and almost "super-alert." Almost all of his test responses were characterized by unreflective haste or undercurrents of impatience. In fact, his intellectual efficiency as a whole may well have been depressed by the headlong quality of his reactions.

Recommendations

In an attempt to put together my own observations with those reported by the school staff through the years, the following tentative impressions and recommendations are offered.

1. Craig appears to be an intellectually capable boy who, at the same time, may manifest subtle weaknesses in his neurodevelopmental makeup, which render him more vulnerable to environmental stress and cause him to over-respond to external stimulation. I suspect that these problems were far more conspicuous when he was a young child, but even now may be reflected to some degree in his impulsive reactions and the undercurrents of restlessness observed in his behavior. The question of re-institution of medication is apparently a crucial one, and the mother is awaiting medical opinion.

EXHIBIT 20-3   (cont.)

2. Situational conditions of his early family life may not have been conducive to the formation of stable emotional ties or behavioral expectations, which for the "vulnerable" child, especially, are a dire necessity. It should be said, however, that in recent years, the mother has tried many different alternatives in an effort to meet his emotional and behavioral needs, but, as mentioned earlier, feels that her own resources have been exhausted. I think that all of us who are acquainted with Craig, and the severity of his behavioral problems, agree that psychotherapeutic counseling should be an integral part of a comprehensive medical-emotional treatment plan. My own bias is toward family therapy, with Craig being seen individually as necessary. This suggestion would have to be presented carefully, stressing the need for "mutual learning" among family members. Whatever combination of treatment is de-cided upon, there should be close coordination with the school to ensure consistency of management strategies.

3. Although Craig may well have experienced "primary" learning disabilities at one time, I suspect that behavioral-emotional components have taken over, and now constitute the most serious handicap to his adjustment in an educational setting. Judging from the information at hand, placement in a regular class situation next fall would eventually lead to more failure, both academically and socially. Clearly, he is a youngster who needs a highly structured situation, with explicit goals for achievement and agreed-upon limits for conduct. It is hoped that the school will be able to provide such a program for Craig, as well as continued counseling designed to help him realize these goals for improved behavior and achievement.

Examiner

---

sivity, and hyperactivity. In the classroom, attentional difficulties and impulsivity are evidenced by the child's not staying with tasks and having difficulty organizing and completing work. The children often give the impression that they are not listening or that they have not heard what they have been told. Their work is sloppy and is performed in an impulsive fashion. On individually administered tests, careless, impulsive errors are often present. Performance may be characterized by oversights, such as omissions or insertions, or misinterpretations of easy items even when the child is well motivated, not just in situations that hold little intrinsic interest. Group situations are particularly difficult for the child, and attentional difficulties are exaggerated when the child is in the classroom, where sustained attention is expected.

At home, attentional problems are shown by a failure to follow through on parental requests and instructions and by the inability to stick to activities, including play, for periods of time appropriate for the child's age.

Hyperactivity in young children is manifested by gross motor activity, such as excessive running or climbing. The child is often described as being on the go, "running like a motor," and having difficulty sitting still. Older children and adolescents may be extremely restless and fidgety. Often it is the quality of the motor behavior that distinguishes this disorder from ordinary overactivity in that hyperactivity tends to be haphazard, poorly organized, and not goal-directed.

In situations in which high levels of motor activity are expected and appropriate, such as on the playground, the hyperactivity seen in children with this disorder may not be obvious.

Typically, the symptoms of this disorder in any given child vary with situation and time. A child's behavior may be well-organized and appropriate on a one-to-one basis but become dysregulated in a group situation or in the classroom; or home adjustment may be satisfactory and difficulties may emerge only in school. It is the rare child who displays signs of the disorder in all settings or even in the same setting at all times.

Associated features. Associated features vary as a function of age and include obstinacy, stubbornness, negativism, bossiness, bullying, increased mood lability, low frustration tolerance, temper outbursts, low self-esteem, and lack of response to discipline. . . .

Nonlocalized "soft" neurological signs, motor-perceptual dysfunctions (e.g., poor eye-hand coordination), and EEG abnormalities may be present. However, in only about 5% of the cases is Attention Deficit Disorder associated with a diagnosable neurological disorder. . . . [pp. 41–42]

Thus, we see that the attention deficit disorder with hyperactivity is a behavioral syndrome marked by hyperactivity, impulsivity, distractibility, excitability, and short attention span. Other symptoms, which occasionally occur in some children, are aggression, conceptual deficits, perceptual deficits, learning disorders, speech difficulties, poor self-concept, and depression. The syndrome becomes most evident when children reach school age and have difficulty meeting the demands of the classroom. Overactivity is a major part of the syndrome in early childhood. The syndrome is more common in boys than in girls, with some estimates as high as a 9:1 ratio of boys to girls (Campbell, 1976). The psychological evaluation in Exhibit 20-3 (p. 404) illustrates a child with an attention deficit disorder with hyperactivity.

It is difficult to decide which children are hyperactive (Campbell, 1976). Restlessness and overactive behavior are common in normal children, especially in boys between 6 and 12 years of age. Some "problem" children are never referred for hyperactive behavior because they have (a) parents who are tolerant of their behavior, (b) teachers who do not perceive their behavior as a problem, or (c) optimal environments that provide structure for their behavior. Conversely, there are essentially normal but active children who are referred for evaluation because of less tolerant environments. Estimates of hyperactivity in clinical populations of children range from 23 percent to 50 percent, depending on the criteria used to define hyperactivity. Hyperactivity appears to account for a large proportion of the problems treated at child mental health clinics. In the school-age population as a whole, estimates of hyperactivity range from 3 percent to 20 percent (Cantwell, 1975).

Adolescence continues to be a difficult period for hyperactive children, although the manifestations of the disorder appear to change with age (Campbell, 1976). While restlessness, distractibility, and poor concentration may diminish, they do remain problems for some adolescents. The major shift appears to be in the emergence of difficulties associated with social behavior and interpersonal relationships. Particularly evident are rebelliousness, antisocial behavior, and low self-esteem. Problems with academic achievement and problem solving remain. Hyperactive children in adolescence repeat more school grades, perform more poorly in academic subjects, and obtain lower intelligence test scores on group-administered tests than do normal children. Studies of the cognitive style of adolescent hyperactive children indicate that, in comparison to normal adolescents, (a) they are more impulsive and field-dependent, (b) they tend to respond without thinking, and (c) they are easily distracted by incorrect but compelling cues. In the classroom, hyperactive adolescents continue to show problems in attention and concentration, but these problems are less disruptive than in earlier years.

Hyperactive children tend to do more poorly than non-hyperactive children on tests of perceptual-motor functioning, measures of sustained attention (especially in situations in which the stimulus is unpredictable), and measures requiring delay of impulse, such as the Matching Familiar Figures Test, which is a visual matching test (Campbell, 1976). In these and other situations hyperactive children tend to respond more quickly and make more errors than control group children do. Possibly, their poorer performance reflects problems of attention and impulse control rather than problems of perceptual-motor control. Hyperactive children can be helped in these and other areas by use of stimulant medication and predictable positive reinforcement (e.g., praise) and by training in the use of self-directed verbal commands to remind themselves to slow down and pay attention.

Etiology of Attention Deficit Disorder with Hyperactivity

The etiology of hyperactivity is unknown. Various theories attribute hyperactivity to a dysfunction of the brain or central nervous system (such as an underarousal of the central nervous system), delayed maturation of the central nervous system, genetic variation, metabolic disturbance, emotional disturbance, or an allergic reaction to certain foods such as those that contain artificial coloring and food additives (Baxley & Leblanc, 1976). These factors may occur either alone or in combination. While brain impairment or dysfunction is a possible etiologic factor, studies indicate that there is no clear correspondence between traditional signs of brain damage and the attention deficit disorder with hyperactivity (Campbell, 1976). Though hyperactive children usually present a similar clinical picture, they may differ greatly with regard to physical and neurological factors, psychological factors, neurophysiological functioning, familial patterns of psychiatric illness, and developmental history.

EEG and Hyperactivity

There is little evidence that hyperactive children with abnormal EEGs have poorer intellectual functioning, greater impairment in learning, more severe problems in the classroom or at home, or a poorer prognosis (as measured by response to stimulant medication) than those with normal EEGs.[8] Consequently, it should not be assumed that signs of organicity (such as an abnormal EEG) in hyperactive children necessarily indicate a more pathological condition and a poorer prognosis. Since there appears to be no relationship between the presence of an EEG abnormality and psychological test performance, little emphasis should be placed on an abnormal EEG—in the absence of some known brain damage or retardation—for diagnostic or placement purposes with children manifesting the attention deficit disorder with hyperactivity.

Treatment of Attention Deficit Disorder with Hyperactivity

The most popular treatment for hyperactivity is a psychostimulant medication (most often amphetamines), such as methylphenidate (Ritalin) or dextroamphetamine (Dexedrine). Methylphenidate is more frequently administered (Krager & Safer, 1974). Hyperactive children taking stimulant medication often show dramatic behavioral changes, with noticeable improvement in attention and impulse control. Stimulant drugs have a much more complex effect than a simple reduction of activity level (Conners, 1973b). They may alter children's activity, goal-directedness, mood, personality, concentration, perception, and motor coordination, and changes in these areas, in turn, can affect the children's relationship to their family, school, and peers. However, it is unlikely that their performance will improve in language development, reading, arithmetic, or other related school subjects. Unfortunately, once the medication is withdrawn, the gains associated with behavioral control often disappear.

When hyperactive children are not responsive to chemotherapy, alternative

From Washington Star Syndicate, May 9, 1974. Copyright 1974, Universal Press Syndicate. All rights reserved.

forms of therapy should be sought and the medication discontinued. The use of chemotherapy does not mean that special school services are not needed. Remediation is required for all children who have serious academic deficiencies.

The extent to which drugs affect the intelligence test performance of hyperactive (and learning-disabled) children appears to be quite variable. Some studies report improvements in Verbal IQ or Performance IQ, while others reveal few or no changes (see Whalen & Henker, 1976, for a review). The major effect of stimulants given to hyperkinetic children appears to be an improvement in classroom manageability rather than in academic performance (Barkley & Cunningham, 1979). Consequently, additional educational assistance must be provided for these children.

The picture changes markedly on laboratory tasks of attention, memory, and learning: the use of psychostimulants markedly improves the performance of hyperactive children. These tasks require sustained attention and are regulated by an examiner. The findings indicate that broad-gauged cognitive abilities—such as reasoning and problem-solving skills—do not appear to be affected directly by stimulants, whereas more refined skills—such as attentional skills—are enhanced by drugs. Drugs appear to help hyperactive children plan and control their responding.

Approximately 70 percent of hyperactive children respond positively to stimulant medication (Satterfield, Cantwell, & Satterfield, 1974). Methylphenidate does not appear to be particularly useful in the treatment of hyperactivity in preschoolers, although more research is needed about the effects of stimulants on preschool children (Campbell, 1976). Other treatment approaches include psychoactive drugs (e.g., chlorpromazine and imipramine), lithium carbonate, behavior modification, low sugar diets, megavitamins, avoidance of artificial food additives, exercises, and optometric treatment. Hyperactive children who respond best to stimulant medication appear to be those who have low central nervous system arousal levels as measured by EEGs, low evoked cortical response, or low skin conductance levels (Satterfield et al., 1974). Stimulant medications may restore both central nervous system arousal levels and inhibitory levels to normal, thereby providing the child with better controls and permitting a wider range of behaviors. Appropriate educational management and counseling of parents appear to be useful in conjunction with drug management.

The principal aim in treating hyperactive children and other children with similar problems is to help them to focus and sustain their attention and to keep impulsive responding under control. A useful method is to teach children to verbalize to themselves effective problem-solving strategies, such as planning ahead, stopping to think, and being careful (Meichenbaum & Goodman, 1971). Self-verbalizations of these kinds help hyperactive children bring their behavior under their own verbal control, and also make it possible for them to reinforce themselves for employing appropriate strategies. A structured and predictable environment with clear, consistent expectations and immediate feedback can also help in the treatment of hyperactivity (Campbell, 1976).

Improving Research on Attentional Deficits with Hyperactivity

One of the difficulties in studying hyperkinesis is that research designs are often inadequate. To assist clinicians in evaluating and performing research in this area, useful guidelines are shown below (Dubey, 1976). The guidelines indicate that research on hyperactivity requires a study of the interrelationship of organic and behavioral deviations, coupled with attention to proper control groups and experimental procedures.

1. Use both normal control groups and deviant (i.e., disturbed) control groups.
2. Use a generalizable population (i.e., do not generalize from findings using an institutionalized group to hyperkinetic children in general).
3. Use a "blind" examination (examiners should be unaware of child's diagnostic status).
4. Investigate interjudge reliability.

5. Investigate the reliability of the measures used (e.g., repeat blood tests and compare the results of the two tests).
6. Investigate the relationship between severity of organic signs and behavioral deviations.
7. Investigate whether the biological indicators of organicity may be a result, rather than a cause, of the behavioral difficulties.

Assessment of Hyperactivity

Many of the considerations involved in the assessment of learning-disabled children hold for those with an attention deficit disorder. In addition, there is evidence that hyperactive children perform better in an individual test situation than in a group test situation (Minde, Weiss, & Mendelson, 1972). In the individual test situation, examiners can be responsive to lapses in attention—making sure that they have the child's attention before administering the test questions. These findings suggest that group intelligence tests may underestimate the ability level of hyperactive children; consequently, IQs obtained by hyperactive children on group-administered tests must be cautiously interpreted.

The major difficulties of hyperactive children, as we have seen, lie in their inability to focus, sustain, and organize attention, and to inhibit impulsive responding. These difficulties are likely to be reflected in their performance on some but not all psychological tests. On individual intelligence tests their scores may be more variable than those of normal children. Lower scores may be obtained on the Bender-Gestalt, Bruininks-Oseretsky, Developmental Test of Visual Perception, and Draw-A-Man. However, patterns of test scores (e.g., Verbal-Performance discrepancies or lowered abstract reasoning scores) that might be associated with hyperactivity have not been found on the WISC-R or on other intelligence tests. In addition, performance on a variety of other special ability tests may not be impaired (Douglas, 1974). An important cue in evaluating hyperkinesis is to examine the child's performance on cognitive tasks that require concentrated effort over a period of time. Because attentional factors probably permeate these tasks, children with hyperkinesis may do more poorly on them. Useful rating scales that can be completed by teachers and by parents for the assessment of hyperactivity in children are described or referred to in Chapter 17.

Behavior Disorders

Behavior disorders in childhood are relatively undifferentiated and have little continuity with adult neuroses (Rutter, Shaffer, & Shepherd, 1975). The major emotional disturbances specific to childhood and adolescence include anxiety and fearfulness, misery and unhappiness, sensitivity, shyness and social withdrawal, and relationship problems. The following symptoms may be suggestive of emotional disturbance in children, especially if they are present to a marked extent and occur over a prolonged period of time (Silverman, 1970):

1. difficulty in learning, not readily explainable by intellectual or physical factors;
2. unsatisfactory interpersonal relationships with peers, teachers, or parents;
3. inappropriate behavior;
4. depression or unhappiness that is relatively pervasive, and
5. the development of physical symptoms, pain, or fears that likely stem from psychological factors.

In a comprehensive review of research on sex differences in childhood behavior disorders, males were found to outnumber females in every major category, including adjustment reactions, antisocial disorders, gender identity disorders, learning disorders, neurotic disorders, and psychotic disorders (Eme, 1979). Culturally determined role expectations and biological differences are two possible explanations for these findings. Consequently, the male child appears to be more at risk for maladjustment than the female child. Beginning with adolescence and continuing into adulthood, a different pattern emerges: females out-number males in neurotic disorders and affective psychotic disorders, males continue to outnumber females in personality and gender identity disorders, and no sex differences emerge in schizophrenic disorders.

Using a statistical approach to the classification of behavior disorders in children, Quay (1969, 1972, 1979) arrived at a classification scheme in which the vast majority of deviant behaviors of children and adults can be covered by four headings: (a) conduct disorder, (b) anxiety-withdrawal, (c) immaturity, and (d) socialized-aggressive disorder. Table 20-4 presents a description of

each type, characteristics that are frequently found in each type, and guides to educational programming. The patterns within each type are homogeneous, independent, persistent over time, and reliably judged. Basic psychological processes and social behavior differ among the types. Most children with behavior disorders differ from their normal peers in the number, not the kind, of deviant behaviors.

Kohn (1977), taking a slightly different approach to classifications of childhood behavior disorders, concluded that a vast amount of research suggests that two major syndromes characterize emotionally disturbed children: (1) the *apathy-withdrawal*

TABLE 20-4.   Characteristics Associated with Four Major Patterns of Deviant Behaviors in Children, and Suggested Educational Programming[a]

Type	Description	Frequently Found Characteristics	Guide to Educational Programming
Conduct disorder	Pattern involving aggressive behavior, both verbal and physical, associated with poor interpersonal relationships	Fighting, hitting, assaultive; temper tantrums; disobedient, defiant; destructive of own or others' property; impertinent, "smart," impudent; uncooperative, resistive, inconsiderate; disruptive, interrupts, disturbs; negative, refuses direction; restless; boisterous, noisy; irritable, "blows-up" easily; attention-seeking, "show-off"; dominates others, bullies, threatens; hyperactive; untrustworthy, dishonest, lies; uses profanity, abusive language; jealous; quarrelsome, argues; irresponsible, undependable; inattentive; steals; distractible; teases; denies mistakes, blames others; pouts and sulks; selfish.	Contain behavior in a highly structured setting, work toward the extinction of the disordered behavior by non-reinforcement, and replace undesirable behaviors with more prosocial and academically efficient forms of behavior. Use concrete reinforcers (e.g., candy, trinkets, and toys) paired directly with social reinforcers (e.g., praise and approving gestures) and use of novelty and frequent activity changes.

(cont.)

Note. Characteristics are listed in rank order from most to least frequently found.
[a]Excluding psychosis.

Adapted from Quay (1969, 1972, 1979).

TABLE 20-4 (cont.)

Type	Description	Frequently Found Characteristics	Guide to Educational Programming
Anxiety-withdrawal	Pattern involving withdrawal, with general and specific fears	Anxious, fearful, tense; shy, timid, bashful; withdrawn, seclusive, friendless; depressed, sad, disturbed; hypersensitive, easily hurt; self-conscious, easily embarrassed; feels inferior, worthless; lacks self-confidence; easily flustered; aloof; cries frequently; reticent, secretive.	Encourage child to emit behavior that can be reinforced. Expose child to an increasing variety of situations, attempting to ensure that his or her responses are those of participation and mastery rather than anxiety and withdrawal. Use social rewards frequently and use criticism and disapproval sparingly, if at all.
Immaturity	Pattern of behaviors inappropriate to the chronological age of the child and society's expectations of him or her	Short attention span, poor concentration; daydreams; clumsy, poor coordination; preoccupied, stares into space, absentminded; passive, lacks initiative, easily led; sluggish; inattentive; drowsy; lacks interest, bored; lacks perseverance, fails to finish things; messy, sloppy.	Create classroom situation in which immature behavior does not result in positive consequences, while more mature forms of behavior predictably do. Use primary reinforcers at first (e.g., candy) coupled with verbal and social reinforcers and then switch to verbal and social reinforcers exclusively.
Socialized-aggressive disorder	Pattern of behavior in response to environmental circumstances—reinforcement by peers and modeling of behavior of adults and peers	Has "bad companions"; steals in company with others; loyal to delinquent friends; belongs to a gang; stays out late at night; truant from school; truant from home.	Substitute other reinforcers for approval of peers. Work with the entire group so that they will reinforce the more appropriate behavior of their associates.

syndrome (similar to Quay's anxiety-withdrawal classification), characterized by shy, withdrawn, and inhibited behavior, and (2) the *anger-defiance syndrome* (similar to Quay's conduct disorder classification), characterized by antisocial, aggressive, and dominating behavior. Both of these syndromes represent ineffective ways of coping with the environment. The coping strategy of the apathy-withdrawal syndrome is *flight*, while for the anger-defiance syndrome, it is *fight*.

Kohn (1977) followed up for a period of five years (until the oldest children had com-

pleted the fourth grade) a group of 1,232 preschool children who had demonstrated emotional difficulties during their preschool years. The children were found to have considerable academic difficulties. The preschool children characterized by the apathy-withdrawal syndrome had the most difficulty in school, especially in verbal achievement, arithmetic achievement, and general academic achievement. Those characterized by the anger-defiance syndrome also did poorly in school, but their performance was not as uniformly low. Their poorest performance was in arithmetic achievement, followed by verbal achievement. Achievement in other academic areas, however, was satisfactory. To account for these findings, Kohn hypothesized that shy and inhibited children reduce their opportunities for learning by isolating themselves from contact with people, events, and objects. Since learning, in part, is a function of exposure to the environment and ability to process information and formulate assumptions about the world, apathetic-withdrawn children are likely to become listless and sluggish in their mode of thinking. An important addition to this study would be a determination of the extent to which these findings hold true during junior high and high school.

It is also important to recognize that elementary school children (and other school-aged children as well) with maladaptive school reactions may be reacting to crisis events within their families. Among children with behavioral or educational problems, those who have experienced *parental death* are more likely to have heightened shyness, timidity, and withdrawal, while children with histories of *parental separation* or *divorce* are more likely to show aggression and acting-out problems (Felner, Stolberg, & Cowen, 1975). Each behavioral pattern can be viewed as a different resolution to early crisis experiences; the type of crisis also may be related to the type of school maladaptation. Appropriate preventive and interventive steps are needed to help children who experience these and other crises.

Delinquency and Level of Intelligence

IQs among delinquents, on the average, are about 8 points lower than among nondelinquents (Gath & Tennent, 1972). Among delinquents, there are more dull normals and fewer of superior intelligence. While the reasons for these findings are not clear, it may be that (a) bright delinquents are more apt to escape detection, (b) high intelligence may influence the police in deciding whether or

"His Freudian therapist says he has Oedipal conflicts, his Rogerian therapist says he has trouble with self-actualization, his Eriksonian therapist says he has identity-diffusion, and I say he is a brat!"

Courtesy of Ford Button.

not to prosecute, or (c) individuals of superior intelligence are less likely to commit delinquent acts. The school performance of highly intelligent delinquents is less satisfactory than that of nondelinquents. Among delinquents, rate of recidivism does not appear to be related to intelligence level (Tennent & Gath, 1975).

Brighter delinquent boys are more leniently treated by the courts (e.g., not as frequently institutionalized) than duller delinquents (Gath & Tennent, 1972). Evidence is inconclusive about how intelligence level of delinquents is related to responsiveness to treatment. Overall, studies indicate that bright delinquents share the same criminological, educational, and social characteristics as the great majority of other delinquents. However, they are less frequently encountered, they are treated differently by the courts, and they are more often presented to the courts as emotionally disturbed. Their comparative rarity may be a result of differential immunity given to them because of higher social class and higher intelligence.

A study by Berman and Siegal (1976) suggested that some delinquents have less adequate neuropsychological abilities than nondelinquents. The 15- to 18-year-old delinquents performed more poorly than the matched controls on the WAIS and on the Halstead-Reitan Neuropsychological Battery. An intriguing hypothesis is that some individuals may become delinquent as a consequence of consistent failures caused by deficits in adaptive abilities which are needed for success in our society.

Assessment of Behavior Disorders

Attitudes displayed during the examination that are suggestive of emotional disturbance include irritability and suspiciousness, restlessness, lack of spontaneity, variable mood, apathy, regarding the test as "kid stuff," euphoria, and dysphoria. Language difficulties suggestive of emotional disturbance (or of a behavior disorder) include speech difficulty, rambling, blocking, circumstantiality, clang associations, circumlocution, confabulation, overelabora-

tion, and self-reference. Behaviors suggestive of anxiety include restlessness; apprehensiveness; impaired attention and concentration; bodily expressions suggesting discomfort (e.g., tics, nailbiting, fidgeting, and coughing); difficulty in finding words; impulsively blurting out unfinished, unchecked, or inappropriate replies; and fumbling about for adequate formulations.

Using the Stanford-Binet in the Assessment of Behavior Disorders

The Stanford-Binet, as we have seen, is an excellent clinical instrument for observing the child's performance in a standardized situation. Chapter 18 presented many examples useful in interpreting children's Stanford-Binet performance, especially for children with behavior disorders. However, no systematic patterns have been found on the Stanford-Binet that are indicative of either emotional disturbance or juvenile delinquency.

Using the WISC-R in the Assessment of Behavior Disorders

The WISC-R (and the WISC) appears to be a reliable and stable instrument for evaluating children with behavior disorders.[9] However, there are no WISC-R (or WISC) patterns that have been found that can reliably distinguish between various groups of emotionally disturbed children, although there may be greater variability of scores in some emotionally disturbed children.[10] There appears to be no qualitative difference in the structure of intellectual abilities of normal children and those with behavior disorders, as indicated by factor analytic studies of the WISC-R (DeHorn & Klinge, 1978; Petersen & Hart, 1979).

However, there is conclusive evidence that delinquents, on the average, obtain higher Wechsler Performance IQs than Verbal IQs.[11] Thus, on the average, the perceptual organization abilities of delinquents are better developed than their verbal comprehension abilities. But the fact that a Verbal-Performance discrepancy is likely to appear in samples of delinquent children does not mean that this pattern can be used as a diagnostic sign of delinquency. Many

CASE 20-2.   Billy, a Child with Learning and Adjustment Problems

Billy, a 9-year-old boy with a long history of learning and adjustment problems, was found during a psychoeducational assessment (involving cognitive, educational, intellectual, neuro-maturational, and projective tests) to be a very needy, emotionally starved child with low self-esteem who could not tolerate failure. He appeared to be of average intelligence. His lack of interest in learning was understood as a retreat from an ongoing failure situation—a retreat that was becoming increasingly dominant. His lack of trust, which was so striking during the evaluation, made it difficult for him to invest in a cooperative learning task with another person. He argued that the tests were being used to trick him but would not elaborate on this contention.

In planning his program, the teacher was informed of the Herculean task of forming an alliance with this youngster. She was prepared for the weeks of testing limits that Billy would demonstrate and of performing the delicate task of removing him from the classroom when he became too disruptive without intensifying his feelings of rejection. Because she was alert to his sense of vulnerability and failure, which he frequently attempted to manage through control, she structured his program in ways that afforded him some sense of control (e.g., he was given the choice of what order to do three assignments—but he was requested to do all of them). Since the evaluation also indicated that Billy was slightly less anxious and less resistant when a task had only one or two problems on a page, the teacher cut up workbook pages and repasted them to ease Billy's turmoil.

The teacher's preparation and the way in which she managed the situation helped Billy settle down to some extent, but he basically remained unmotivated and too frightened to learn. Since hunger was such a prominent feature of Billy's psychological makeup, a decision was made to develop curricula around this hunger and to provide him with tasks that would allow him to feed others, thereby offering an active solution to his more passive longings. Given Billy's propensity for expressing feelings in the action modality, he was engaged in planning and building a birdhouse. He became involved in reading about birds and how to construct a birdhouse, measuring the dimensions, buying wood, accepting help while doing the building, waiting a day for the paint to dry, making a peanut butter ball with seeds, and then putting everything up on a tree outside.

These different components of Billy's project served multiple purposes, and they illustrate the comprehensive positive impact of a psychoeducational approach. For a child accustomed to failure, it invited him to demonstrate mastery and competence and then to feel comfortable in displaying his finished product for all to see (and admire). For a child hesitant to read or engage in learning, it provided the motivation to discover the benefits and excitement of taking in and then using new information—another example of the significant role that emotions and motivation play in learning. The motivation in this case came from offering a task that resonated with Billy's own needs for nourishment. Also, almost every phase of the work required Billy to learn to plan and to delay action, not an easy undertaking for such an impulsive, nonreflective child. Finally, for a child who was always poised for attack, experiencing others as ready to spot his mistakes and ridicule him, the project helped him relate in a trusting and cooperative interaction with other people.

While the overall task was far from easy, it helped to dislodge some of Billy's barriers to learning and trusting. Subsequent learning tasks aroused less resistance and less hostility. The information about this child's cognitive and affective functioning that was gained from the psychoeducational assessment was instrumental in planning this particular program. The evaluation findings served as guideposts to assist the specialist in understanding and planning activities that addressed both Billy's educational and cognitive lags and emotional needs.   ∎

Source: Reprinted, with permission of the publisher and author, from R. Brooks, "Psychoeducational Assessment: A Broader Perspective," *Professional Psychology, 10,* pp. 717–718. Copyright 1979, American Psychological Association, Inc.

different types of normal and exceptional children may show this same type of discrepancy. The discrepancy may have no diagnostic significance, especially when it is not statistically significant, or it may be a reflection of poor education, reading disability, bilingualism, cognitive style, or some other factor. Perhaps the Performance> Verbal pattern is a reflection of the learning handicaps that are a relatively frequent concomitant of delinquency, rather than of delinquency itself.

The WISC-R provides an opportunity to obtain many insights about the child from the pattern of subtest scores and from the content of the responses. The material presented in Chapter 18 provides many examples of how interpretations can be developed from a careful analysis of the child's performance, particularly for a child with a behavior disorder. Case 20-2 illustrates how a psychoeducational remediation plan, in part based on the results of a psychological evaluation, helped to diminish a child's learning and adjustment problems.

Differential Diagnosis

It is important to distinguish learning-disabled children from those who are hyperactive, particularly because different approaches to treatment may be required (Campbell, 1976). Hyperactive children show no specific pattern of cognitive deficits independent of their difficulties with attention or impulse control. While learning-disabled children may also be impulsive or have attentional difficulties, there is no one-to-one relationship between learning disabilities and specific behavior patterns. Children with hyperactivity, however, often show a constellation of problems, including restlessness, poor impulse control, and disobedience. If these groups are not properly diagnosed, improper treatment may result. Campbell emphasizes that

> it is important to keep in mind the distinction between academic under-achievement and a specific learning disability. Children who do not attend may do poorly in school, but in the absence of clear patterns of deficits in particu-

lar areas of cognitive functioning it would be misleading to assume that the poor school achievement was the result of a learning disability. [p. 226]

Learning-disabled children may be given stimulant medication because they are thought to be overactive and distractible. While this type of medication produces short-term decreases in impulsivity and inattentiveness, it does not improve overall cognitive functioning. Remedial work appears to be the most appropriate therapeutic approach for learning-disabled children, whereas drug therapy for short-term treatment and behavioral approaches are preferred for hyperactive children.

Arriving at a diagnosis of hyperactivity is fraught with difficulties. There are disagreements as to what constitute the necessary criteria for diagnosis. Different procedures may be used to arrive at a diagnosis, including neurological methods, psychological tests, and behavioral criteria. Consistent diagnoses are not likely to be obtained when different criteria are used. Another complicating factor is that children with learning disabilities and those with the attention deficit disorder with hyperactivity both often have difficulty with attention and impulsivity. However, in spite of these diagnostic difficulties, tests do contribute to the assessment process by providing a baseline for the measurement of change following therapy and for the evaluation of current performance.

Children with behavior disorders also have symptoms that are similar to those that appear in learning-disabled children and in hyperactive children. However, the symptoms may be more diffuse and cover a wider range of emotions. Children with behavior disorders have symptoms that are less severe than children with autistic and schizophrenic disorders.

Assessment of Sensory Impairments

The two major sensory impairments are blindness and deafness. Children with these handicaps not only are restricted in their activities, but also are limited in their opportunities for social, cultural, and intellectual stimulation. These limitations may affect the development of intelligence and other abilities.

Visual Impairment

Blind children usually obtain a mean IQ in the normal range, but their distribution of scores tends to be bimodal: there are more superior as well as inferior children in the blind group than in the normal group (Crowell, 1957). Partially sighted children tend to obtain IQs that are slightly below those of normally seeing children (Myers, 1930; Pintner, 1942).

On the WISC Verbal Scale, blind children perform best on the Digit Span subtest, poorest on the Similarities, and slightly better on the Comprehension subtest.[12] These results suggest that blind children have well-developed rote memory capacities but are less adequate in conceptual thinking and in social comprehension. Because of the variability in subtest scores, it is important to examine both the Verbal Scale IQ and the individual subtest scores. It is possible that the Verbal Scale IQ may not provide as adequate a measure as some of the individual subtests (Tillman & Bashaw, 1968).

A factor analysis of the WISC Verbal Scale indicated that blind children had fewer factor loadings and weaker communalities on all subtests, with the exception of Arithmetic, than sighted children (Tillman, 1967b). Perhaps blind children have a greater specificity in the organization of abilities sampled by the subtests than sighted children.

Studies of the WISC Verbal Scale with blind children report satisfactory reliability (Tillman, 1973). However, much less is known about the validity of the WISC (and the WISC-R) for blind children.

The WISC Verbal Scale and the Hayes-Binet (a special form of the Stanford-Binet that is used with blind children) have been compared in various samples of blind children. In one sample of children who were between 9 and 15 years, the two scales were highly correlated ($r = .86$), but WISC IQs ($M = 110$) were about 8 points lower than

Hayes-Binet IQs ($M = 118$) (Hopkins & McGuire, 1966). These results were essentially confirmed in another study (Hopkins & McGuire, 1967). The two scales also have been found to yield similar IQs (M of 78 and 75 for the Verbal Scale and Hayes-Binet, respectively) in a study of children between the ages of 6 and 14 years (Gilbert & Rubin, 1965) and in a study of young children ($r = .94$; M of 98 and 99 for the Verbal Scale and Hayes-Binet, respectively) (Lewis, 1957). The Hayes-Binet has been found to be somewhat more valid than the WISC when teachers' ratings were used as the criterion (r of .51 and .37, respectively) (Denton, 1954).

However, these studies also indicate that the WISC and Hayes-Binet cannot be considered to be interchangeable for above-average-ability blind children. For blind children with average or below-average ability, the scales do appear to yield more comparable IQs. Additional studies are needed about the prediction of academic achievement in blind children (Goldman, 1970).

An investigation of the first two years of gross motor development of infants blind from birth revealed that while adequate neuromuscular maturation was demonstrated, there was a considerable delay in self-initiated mobility (Adelson & Fraiberg, 1974). Perhaps the prolonged period of immobility during the first year of life of blind infants lessens their ability to explore independently and to discover by themselves the objective rules that govern things and events in the external world. An intervention program carried out by Adelson and Fraiberg, which focused on human relationships, adaptive hand behavior, and coordination of tactile and auditory schemas, was partially successful in increasing the mobility of the youngsters.

Suppes (1974) pointed out:

Educating blind children is a difficult task because the normal mode of taking in information is heavily dependent on the printed word. The cognitive deficits present in blind children may simply be due to the relatively simple fact of not having an alternative input channel that can match the rate of visual processing, and thus they are "information poor," deprived in the quantitative sense of the amount of information transmitted to them. [p. 149]

Hearing Impairment

Developing competence in a standard natural language is of critical importance for hearing-impaired children. Their ability to develop a language generally varies directly with the magnitude of their hearing loss. Although deaf children develop a normal pattern of vocalizations (e.g., babbling, crying, and cooing) until about 6 to 9 months of age, their ability to communicate orally decreases after this time (Suppes, 1974).

There is some evidence that those deaf children who have an early, severe hearing loss do not have the same lateral specialization for language that has been established for the hearing population (Kelly & Tomlinson-Keasey, 1977). It appears that without the auditory processing of speech, the left hemisphere does not develop a specialization for language. Instead, deaf children are likely to process cognitive information with right hemisphere structures (i.e., with visual codes rather than with language-oriented auditory codes). While this type of research is only in its rudimentary stages, it holds much promise for a better understanding of the cognitive processing of deaf children.

Deaf children usually obtain scores within the normal range on nonverbal intelligence tests, although their mean scores are somewhat lower than those of hearing children (Meadow, 1975). For example, a national sample of 1,228 deaf children obtained a mean IQ of 95.70 on the WISC-R Performance Scale (Sisco & Anderson, 1978). The subtests, from easiest to most difficult, were Object Assembly ($M = 10.32$), Mazes ($M = 10.03$), Picture Completion ($M = 9.51$), Block Design ($M = 9.48$), Picture Arrangement ($M = 8.71$), and Coding ($M = 8.03$). In contrast, the general level of academic achievement of deaf children was much below that which could be expected from their performance on intelligence tests. Reading achievement was especially below the expected level. The limited access to language stimulation is perhaps the key to why

deaf children perform poorly on reading tests and on verbal intelligence tests.

There is also a disproportionately higher prevalence of low IQs among hard-of-hearing children than among normal children. One explanation for this finding is that the etiologies of profound hearing loss also are associated with other neurological impairments that frequently interfere with cognitive processes. Thus, for example, maternal rubella, purulent meningitis of early onset, premature birth, and tuberculous meningitis may lead to deafness and to mental retardation.

The Performance Scale of the WISC-R (and the WISC) has been found to be a reliable and valid instrument in the assessment of deaf children.[13] *The Verbal Scale and other verbal tests appear to be inappropriate for measuring the intelligence of deaf children* (Vernon, 1968). However, a comparison of the Verbal IQ with the Performance IQ in deaf children provides an estimate of the degree to which the child has mastered verbal concepts.

A study of the sensorimotor development of sixteen deaf children 23 to 38 months of age using the Infant Psychological Development Scale showed that the children were progressing normally except in the area of vocal imitation, where the deaf children performed below age expectation (Best & Roberts, 1976). The six scales showing normal development were Object Permanence, Objects as Means, Schemas, Causality, Objects in Space, and Motor Imitation. The scale is easily adapted for use with deaf children, because it requires little or no language for administration (see p. 255).

Social maturity of deaf children also is generally behind that of their hearing peers (Meadow, 1975). Within the deaf population, social maturity appears to be dependent on at least two factors. First, deaf children with adequate communication skills are likely to be more socially mature than those with poor communication skills. Second, deaf children of deaf parents are relatively more mature than deaf children of hearing parents. The delayed language acquisition experienced by most deaf children probably leads to more limited opportunities for social interaction. This, in turn, may cause frustration for both children and parents. Generally, deaf children appear to have more adjustment problems than hearing children.

To improve the performance of hearing-impaired children, it may be useful to employ multisensory experiences, such as emphasizing the auditory dimension in conjunction with a good oral technique or focusing on transformations within a single mode. For example, "Sesame Street" (Children's Television Workshop) often uses multiple visuals of an object, transformed into the word for that object (Kelly & Tomlinson-Keasey, 1976). In addition, as much diversity as possible should be provided for visual and auditory processing (Kelly, 1978). Deaf children with good communication skills are likely to be those who have been exposed to both oral and manual training at an early age (Meadow, 1968). Early intervention programs with deaf children will need to focus more strongly on the area of vocal imitation, "improving communication abilities and developing curriculum materials which better teach those concepts which are usually transmitted through social interaction with the environment" (Best & Roberts, 1976, p. 564).

Summary

1. Specific learning disability is a term used to refer to children who have difficulty in mastering one or more basic scholastic skills, but who have adequate intelligence, maturational level, and cultural background.

2. The etiology of specific learning disability is not known. Various hypotheses have been proposed, including neurological dysfunction, delayed maturation, or inadequate motivation.

3. Attention deficits may be a key to understanding the difficulties displayed by some learning-disabled children.

4. Research on learning-disabled children indicates that heterogeneity of symptoms is common in this group.

5. Dyslexia, or reading disability, is best defined as a syndrome of learning disability in children with adequate intelligence who have failed to master basic processes, such as letter recognition and sound blending.

6. While a variety of deficits may be associated with reading disability, the primary deficits, supported by research, include impairments in directional sense, intersensory integration, linguistic facility, and sequential perception.

7. Satz proposed that dyslexia is associated with delayed maturation of the left hemisphere of the brain.

8. The delineation of specific syndromes in dyslexic children is still at a rudimentary stage.

9. Remediation should take into account the child's developmental level, strengths and weaknesses, learning style, and task requirements.

10. A diagnosis of learning disability is arrived at through a study of clinical and psychoeducational data obtained during the assessment process.

11. While there is no one preferred battery of tests for the assessment of learning disability, an intelligence test, an achievement test, and a visual-motor test usually should be included in the battery.

12. There is no WISC-R pattern that can reliably diagnose learning disability or reading disability. However, on the average, the four most difficult WISC-R subtests for reading-disabled children are Arithmetic, Coding, Information, and Digit Span (ACID).

13. The key behavioral features of the attention deficit disorder with hyperactivity syndrome are excessive motor activity, attentional difficulties, and impulsivity. Most children in this classification do not have diagnosable brain damage.

14. Many different theories have been proposed to account for hyperactivity, including brain damage, delayed maturation, genetic variation, metabolic disturbance, emotional disturbance, and allergic reaction to certain foods.

15. Ritalin is frequently used in the treatment of hyperactive children. Educational

management focuses on helping hyperactive children to sustain their attention and keep impulsive responding under control.

16. Behavior disorders in children are relatively undifferentiated. The major symptoms are difficulty in learning, unsatisfactory interpersonal relations, inappropriate behavior, depression, and the development of physical symptoms. Males outnumber females in every major category of childhood behavior disorders.

17. A useful classification scheme for behavior disorders in children postulates four major types: (a) conduct disorders, (b) anxiety-withdrawal, (c) immaturity, and (d) socialized-aggressive disorder. Another classification scheme proposes two major syndromes of childhood behavior disorders: (a) apathy-withdrawal syndrome and (b) anger-defiance syndrome.

18. Maladaptive reactions in school may reflect crises within the child's family. For example, parental death may lead to withdrawal reactions, whereas parental divorce may lead to aggressive reactions.

19. Delinquent children, on the average, obtain IQs that are about 8 points lower than those of nondelinquents. The comparative rarity of delinquents with superior intelligence may be a result of differential immunity given to them by the courts.

20. During the assessment, indicators of emotional disturbance can be observed in children's attitudes (e.g., irritability and suspiciousness), language (e.g., speech difficulty and rambling), and bodily expressions (e.g., tics and nail biting).

21. No systematic patterns have been found on the Stanford-Binet that are suggestive of emotional disturbance or juvenile delinquency.

22. The WISC-R, too, cannot reliably distinguish between various groups of emotionally disturbed children. However, delinquents, on the average, obtain higher Performance than Verbal IQs. The discrepancy may be more a reflection of learning difficulties than of delinquency per se.

23. It is important to attempt to differentiate learning-disabled children from those who are hyperactive, because different treatment approaches may be called for in each condition. Children with behavior disorders share similar symptoms with learning-disabled and hyperactive children, but the symptoms may be more diffuse.

24. While the WISC-R Verbal Scale and Hayes-Binet are not interchangeable, they appear to be reliable instruments for the assessment of the intelligence of blind children.

25. Children who are deaf from an early age may have a right hemisphere lateralization for cognitive information rather than a left hemisphere lateralization.

26. The Performance Scale of the WISC-R is a reliable and valid instrument for assessing the intelligence of deaf children.

CHAPTER

21

Assessment of Mental Retardation and Giftedness

The gifts of nature are infinite in their variety, and mind differs from mind almost as much as body from body.

QUINTILIAN

EXHIBIT 21-1. Psychological Evaluation: A Slower Learner

Name: Roger
Date of birth: April 16, 1971
Chronological age: 8-2
Date of examination: June 15, 1979
Date of report: June 17, 1979
Grade: 1st

Assessment Procedures

Wechsler Intelligence Scale for Children–Revised (scaled scores):

VERBAL SCALE		PERFORMANCE SCALE	
Information	6	Picture Completion	7
Similarities	1	Picture Arrangement	3
Arithmetic	3	Block Design	2
Vocabulary	5	Object Assembly	6
Comprehension	4	Coding	6
Digit Span	(5)	Mazes	(4)

Verbal Scale IQ = 60
Performance Scale IQ = 67
Full Scale IQ = 60±6 at 95 percent confidence level

Peabody Picture Vocabulary Test (PPVT) (Form A):
CA: 8–2
MA: 5–5
IQ: 76

Draw-A-Person (G-H Scoring): Time: 3′ 14″; standard score: 71.

Wepman Auditory Discrimination Test (Form I):
X-errors: 7; Y-errors: 3.

EXHIBIT 21-1 (cont.)

Bender-Gestalt: Time: 8′ 31″; Koppitz score: standard score = 77, percentile = 6th.

Wide Range Achievement Test (WRAT):

	STANDARD SCORE	PERCENTILE
Reading	77	6th
Arithmetic	70	2nd

Peabody Individual Achievement Test (PIAT):

	STANDARD SCORE	PERCENTILE
Mathematics	82	12th
Reading Recognition	74	4th
Reading Comprehension	—	—
Spelling	84	14th
General Information	72	3rd

(Parent interview, teacher interview by phone, informal information, play activities, and trial teaching were also used in the assessment.)

Referral Problem

Roger was referred by his pediatrician, who wished to obtain an estimate of the child's level of mental development.

Family Background

Roger is the third child from an intact family of four children. Roger's older brother (age 14) and sister (age 12) as well as his younger brother (age 6) are described by the mother as good students. There were no birth complications that the mother was aware of. Both parents agreed that Roger had always been a healthy, happy child who was easy to care for and manage, although he seemed to lag consistently a year or more behind his brothers and sister in language acquisition, toilet training, self-help, and play activities.

The parents appeared to be open and honest with each other and strongly committed to family-type activities, such as church, sports, camping, and fishing. Both parents have completed high school and specialized vocational training. Roger's mother is an office manager, a position she has held for sixteen years. The father is employed as a machinist in a local aircraft plant where he has a history of steady, stable employment since the beginning of the marriage.

Educational History

The parents reported that they had waited until Roger was six to enroll him in a public school kindergarten on the advice of their pediatrician, who had expressed concern over Roger's slowness to develop, his lack of readiness, and his general immaturity. The pediatrician was concerned that Roger not be subjected to academic pressure before he was mature enough to cope with the school curriculum.

Kindergarten was a pleasant, stimulating experience for Roger. School records indicated not only that he was cooperative, friendly, and willing to share, but also that he had shown significant improvement in fine and gross motor skills, listening skills, cooperative play, oral language, and ability to follow simple directions. It was noted, however, that because Roger had scored low on a reading readiness test, difficulty with first grade work was predicted. In the first grade he fell farther and farther behind the other children until mid-year, when he was the only student still working on readiness skills. Despite daily two-hour tutoring sessions for the remainder of first grade, Roger did not show much progress. A major concern of his teacher was Roger's emerging pattern of withdrawal, isolation, and daydreaming, which the teacher attributed to self-disgust because others were already reading.

Diagnostic Summary

The results of the assessment suggest that Roger is currently functioning within the mild range of retardation in measured intelligence. This finding is suggested by a broad configuration of behavioral data, as well as a consistent pattern of scores from standardized tests of intelligence, perceptual development (auditory and visual), and academic achievement.

First, the IQ scores from the WISC-R and Draw-A-Person are relatively consistent in that they all fall within the mild-borderline range of retarda-

EXHIBIT 21-1   (cont.)

tion. The PPVT receptive vocabulary score also is in this range. In addition, the scaled scores for all twelve of the WISC-R subtests are well below average (7 or less). The fact that Roger consistently scored below average on a wide range of different ability-type tasks provides strong support for inferring mild mental retardation in measured intelligence.

Second, the background data provided by the parents and school officials are consistent with the ability estimates reported. Specifically, both parents agreed that Roger was much slower than their other three children in many areas.

Third, the observations of the kindergarten and first grade teachers indicated that Roger's response to classroom instruction is much slower than that of his age mates, despite a positive attitude and a sincere effort to learn. His first grade teacher observed that, "Roger seems to have reached a plateau. He can't go from letters to words and he can't go any farther with his counting."

Fourth, testing of limits procedures (being shown, being told, or being given similar examples) did not cause a substantial increase in Roger's performance on any of the WISC-R subtests.

Finally, Roger comes from a stable, child-centered home which has provided adequate stimulation for intellectual development.

The pattern of evidence summarized above indicates a mild degree of retardation in academic aptitude or general intelligence (the ability to master the academic aspects of the school curriculum). In terms of age level, it appears that Roger's overall level of perceptual-cognitive development falls around 6-0 years. Instructionally speaking, a realistic expectancy for academic work would be for Roger to respond somewhat like an average 5½- to 6-year-old child. As compared to others his age, Roger's performance on the Bender-Gestalt indicates immaturity in visual-motor perception and is congruent with the mental age suggested above. Similarly, scores for the Wepman suggest difficulties in discriminating between common speech sounds and a short attention span for auditory material, which is congruent with the overall developmental level of the average 5-6- to 6-year-old child.

Analysis of performance on the WRAT and PIAT along with the observations of the first grade teacher and examining psychologist suggest that Roger's level of academic (readiness)

skills is comparable to that of the average student beginning first grade (6-0 to 6-6). During the assessment Roger demonstrated the following skills: (1) repeated letters of the alphabet in correct sequence and named all letters of the alphabet in isolation; (2) wrote capital letters (manuscript) in correct sequence; (3) counted meaningfully through 29; (4) wrote the numerals in correct sequence through 39; (5) recognized and named the colors red, white, orange, yellow, black, green, brown, blue, pink, and gray; (6) sequenced objects by height and size; and (7) described what was happening in pictures. This information, as well as most of the achievement test scores, suggests that Roger's overall level of academic (readiness) skills is somewhat higher than the overall level of perceptual-cognitive development.

Substantial information available from Roger's parents and teachers precluded the need for a formal behavioral assessment. The information that they provided is in general agreement with the observations of the examining psychologist. That is, Roger seems to be functioning at an adaptive level commensurate with most of his age mates. The only exceptions are found when Roger is involved in tasks requiring academic-type skills, such as making purchases, counting change, reading signs, and looking up telephone numbers. Thus, Roger is quite capable of carrying on an intelligent conversation as long as it does not involve academic material. Roger discussed the family vacation, fishing trips, campsites, gardening, church activities, and automobiles during the assessment sessions in a manner that could not be distinguished from the conversation of a normal 8-year-old boy. As noted earlier, Roger gets along well with his classmates and is generally well-liked. Stated alternatively, Roger is retarded to the extent that he has severe difficulty mastering the academic aspects of the school curriculum.

Recommendations

1. The parents should seriously consider enrolling Roger in the class for the educably mentally handicapped children in the neighborhood public school. However, there are several regular class activities that he should be able to benefit from, such as physical education, music, and art. Consistent participation in regular classroom activities is of critical importance for Roger if he is to continue developing and enhancing his already adequate social skills.

EXHIBIT 21-1   (cont.)

2. Roger's tendency to withdraw and daydream may be counteracted by having him respond actively in the classroom (e.g., answer a question, collect papers, and draw a picture). Verbal praise and nonverbal reinforcement (e.g., smile, happy face, or pat on shoulder) should be used to reinforce Roger for raising his hand and volunteering to participate in class at appropriate times.

3. Special attention should also be given to helping Roger learn to pay closer attention to verbal directions, such as having him repeat directions. Further, the teacher should take care to establish eye contact, physical contact, and physical proximity to help Roger to focus and sustain his attention on verbal directions.

4. Activities designed to help Roger improve his oral comprehension should incorporate the activities suggested above as well as other activities, such as listening to high interest simple stories, songs, and rhymes. These activities should be followed by asking Roger elementary questions about the stories.

5. A pictorial approach can be used effectively to help expand Roger's vocabulary and expressive skills.

6. Overlearning (initial thorough learning, relearning, and consistent review and practice) before new tasks are introduced may enable Roger to retain newly learned skills.

7. Improvement in arithmetic skills is probable if the work assignments center around money

values and making change and are broken down into small segments ensuring frequent successes.

8. An inductive approach should be used to help Roger learn abstract verbal concepts such as same, different, and opposite. Probably the best way to teach these concepts is to use pictures to provide Roger with an increasing number of examples.

9. It would probably be unwise to discontinue efforts to teach Roger words even though his overall level of perceptual-cognitive development is substantially below the level we ordinarily think of as being necessary for the initiation of formal reading instruction. Roger is highly motivated to read, and his teacher believes that he is becoming discouraged and starting to develop a negative self-concept because of his inability to learn words. If reading instruction is terminated, Roger may feel that he is being rejected and removed from the parochial school because he has not been successful in learning to read. In view of Roger's high motivation, some reading instruction with Roger in the special class or allowing him to join a first grade class working at the appropriate level is desirable to forestall further feelings of failure and rejection. In addition, a continuance of his tutoring sessions at his original school seems advisable.

———————

Examiner

Assessment of Mental Retardation

Definition of Mental Retardation

The term "mental retardation" describes a heterogeneous group of conditions characterized by low or very low intelligence and deficits in adaptive behavior. The most widely used definition of mental retardation is the one proposed by the American Association on Mental Deficiency (AAMD) (Grossman, 1973):

Mental Retardation refers to significantly subaverage general intellectual functioning existing concurrently with deficits in adaptive behavior, and manifested during the developmental period. [p. 11]

This definition refers to a level of behavioral performance without reference to etiology. The key terms in the definition bear closer inspection.

- *Significantly subaverage* refers to performance that is two or more standard deviations below the population mean on a standardized intelligence test.
- *General intellectual functioning* refers to performance on a standardized intelligence test that measures, as far as is possible, general cognitive ability rather than one limited facet of ability, such as receptive vocabulary only or spatial-analytic skills only.
- *Adaptive behavior* refers to the effectiveness with which individuals meet the stan-

dards of personal independence and social responsibility expected of individuals of their age and cultural group. Deficits in adaptive behavior are evaluated according to developmental age. During *infancy and early childhood,* adaptive behavior deficits are evaluated in relationship to sensory-motor skills, communication skills, self-help skills, and socialization skills. During *childhood and early adolescence,* the focus is on the application of (a) basic academic skills in daily life activities, (b) appropriate reasoning and judgment in interacting with the environment, and (c) social skills. During *late adolescence and adult life,* adaptive behavior centers on vocational and social responsibilities and performances.

• *The developmental period* is regarded as the period between birth and about 18 years of age.

The AAMD definition indicates that two criteria—level of intelligence and level of adaptive behavior—must be evaluated in making classifications. The classification of mental retardation is appropriate only when an individual falls into the retarded category in both intellectual functioning *and* adaptive behavior functioning. Intelligence is assessed through objective measurement, whereas adaptive behavior can be assessed clinically or by means of an objective scale.

The AAMD definition has several implications. First, the assessment must focus on a description of *present behavior;* prediction of later intelligence is a separate process and fraught with many difficulties. Second, the contribution of individually administered intelligence tests is specifically recognized. Third, diagnosis is tied to a developmental process, with behavioral descriptions anchored to the individual's own age level. Fourth, it is recognized that mental retardation can exist together with other forms of childhood disorders; the definition "*avoids specific differentiations of mental retardation from other childhood disorders* such as childhood schizophrenia or brain damage" (Robinson & Robinson, 1976, p. 31). Fifth, the definition avoids the implication that mental retardation is irreversible. Finally, a diagnosis of mental retardation is not given when individuals are adequately meeting the demands of their environment.

Classification of Mental Retardation

The AAMD classification of mental retardation contains four categories—mild, moderate, severe, and profound—based on levels of intelligence used in conjunction with the classification of adaptive behavior (see Table 21-1). In using the AAMD classification system, it is important to recognize that level of retardation arrived at by an intelligence test is dependent upon the standard deviation (*SD*) of the test. For example, if the −2 *SD* criterion is used, then the IQ just below the −2 *SD* point is 69 for the WISC-R (or WPPSI or WAIS-R), but 67 for the Stanford-Binet. These different IQs meet the criterion because the WISC-R (and the other Wechsler tests) has an *SD* of 15,

TABLE 21-1. Classification of Mental Retardation

Level of Mental Retardation	Educational Equivalent Description	Range in Standard Deviation Value	Range in IQ for Stanford-Binet, Form L-M	Range in IQ for WISC-R, WPPSI, and WAIS-R[a]	Approximate Mental Age at Adulthood	Approximate Percent in the Population
Mild	Educable	−2.01 to −3.00	67–52	69–55	8-3 to 10-9	2.7
Moderate	Trainable	−3.01 to −4.00	51–36	54–40	5-7 to 8-2	0.2
Severe	Trainable (Dependent)	−4.01 to −5.00	35–20	39–25	3-2 to 5-6	0.1
Profound	Custodial (Life Support)	< −5.00	<20	<25	<3-2	0.05

[a]The IQs shown for the severe and profound levels for the Wechsler tests are extrapolated.

whereas the Stanford-Binet has an *SD* of 16. Still other cut-off points may be appropriate depending on the *SD* of the test. While the WISC-R (and other Wechsler tests) and the Stanford-Binet have been standardized so that the *SD*s are the same throughout the ages covered by the scales, such may not be the case for other instruments. It is therefore important that the examiner study test manuals carefully in order to become knowledgeable about the psychometric properties of each test.

A tentative classification system of adaptive behavior that parallels the classification of measured intelligence has been developed by Sloan and Birch (1955); it is shown in Table 21-2. The system is presented in reference to developmental ages and degree of debility. The emphasis is on sensory-motor skills, language and communication, learning, degree of self-sufficiency, and vocational potential. The assessment of adaptive behavior may result in a classification that differs from the one arrived at from an assessment of intelligence. For instance, an individual may receive a *mildly* retarded adaptive behavior classification, but a *moderately* retarded intelligence classification.

TABLE 21-2.   Levels of Adaptive Behavior for the Mentally Retarded

Level	Preschool Age: Birth to 5 Years	School Age: 6 to 21 Years	Adult: over 21 Years
Mild retardation	Can develop social and communication skills; minimal retardation in sensorimotor areas; rarely distinguished from normal until later age.	Can learn academic skills to approximately 6th grade level by late teens. Cannot learn general high school subjects. Needs special education, particularly at secondary school age levels.	Capable of social and vocational adequacy with proper education and training. Frequently needs guidance when under serious social or economic stress.
Moderate retardation	Can talk or learn to communicate; poor social awareness; fair motor development; may profit from self-help; can be managed with moderate supervision.	Can learn functional academic skills to approximately 4th grade level by late teens if given special education.	Capable of self-maintenance in unskilled or semi-skilled occupations; needs supervision and guidance when under mild social or economic stress.
Severe retardation	Poor motor development; speech is minimal; generally unable to profit from training in self-help; little or no communication skills.	Can talk or learn to communicate; can be trained in elemental health habits; cannot learn functional academic skills; profits from systematic habit training.	Can contribute partially to self-support under complete supervision; can develop self-protection skills to a minimal useful level in controlled environment.
Profound retardation	Gross retardation; minimal capacity for functioning in sensorimotor areas; needs nursing care.	Some motor development present; cannot profit from training in self-help; needs total care.	Some motor and speech development; totally incapable of self-maintenance; needs complete care and supervision.

Reprinted, with a change in notation, by permission of the publisher and authors from W. Sloan and J. W. Birch, "A Rationale for Degrees of Retardation," *American Journal of Mental Deficiency, 60,* p. 262. Copyright 1955, American Association of Mental Deficiency.

The assessment of intelligence is a much more precise procedure than is the assessment of adaptive behavior. The Stanford-Binet and Wechsler scales are well-normed instruments, with excellent reliability and validity. Their respective normative groups are relatively up-to-date. In contrast, there are no nationally standardized instruments available for the assessment of adaptive behavior during the developmental period that meet acceptable psychometric standards. Instruments such as the AAMD Adaptive Behavior Scale and the Vineland Social Maturity Scale can assist in the assessment of adaptive behavior, but they can serve only as guidelines. Precise estimates of adaptive behavior are not provided by these scales. (These and other adaptive behavior scales are reviewed in Chapter 17.) Therefore, in assessing adaptive behavior the clinician must weigh all relevant data.

The assessment of adaptive behavior is highly dependent on the reliability of the informant. The informant's ability to observe and to report reliably the child's skills, behavior, and temperament will determine the accuracy of the adaptive behavior ratings in many cases. In contrast, the child himself or herself actually performs on the intelligence test; no intermediary is necessary. In the final analysis, the determination of the presence or absence of mental retardation rests on clinical judgment. Therefore, a careful assessment of all relevant factors is necessary.

Etiology of Mental Retardation

Mentally retarded individuals should not be viewed as a homogeneous group. They fall into two broad classes.

1. The *familial type* of mental retardation represents the milder forms of mental retardation, in the IQ range of 50 to 69. Familial retarded persons are primarily individuals in the lower portion of the normal distribution of intelligence. As such, their performance reflects normal intellectual variability. The variability is likely to be the result of normal polygenic variation, that is, the combined action of many genes. Performance in this range can also be associated with pathological factors or with the combined effect of below-average heredity in interaction with a markedly below-average environment. A psychological evaluation of a familial retarded child is shown in Exhibit 21-2.

The familial retarded frequently do not come to the attention of the professional community as adults. Although we are not certain why this occurs, various explanations have been offered (Clarke & Clarke, 1974). One possibility is that intellectual limitation is more obvious in school settings than in employment settings, where there is less of a need for certain types of cognitive skills. A second possibility is that mildly retarded persons gradually acquire many skills needed for adaptation to the community. Finally, some of these individuals may improve their intellectual ability in adolescence and in early adult years.

2. The *organic type* of mental retardation represents primarily the more severe forms of mental retardation, in the IQ range below 50, although it is seen in some milder forms as well. The etiology of the organic type may be associated with (a) a genetic component linked to single gene effects, (b) chromosomal abnormalities, or (c) brain damage. These children usually have severe and often diffuse brain damage or malformations commonly originating during the prenatal period. They show a severe lag in behavioral development, sometimes accompanied by an abnormal appearance. Identification of the more severe forms of retardation is relatively easy because the children fail to reach normal motor and language developmental milestones.

Most mentally retarded children (85 percent) are mildly retarded, with etiologies associated with social, cultural, psychological, or perhaps genetic factors. The remaining 15 percent of retarded children have moderate to severe deficits, such as microcephaly, Down's syndrome (mongolism), phenylketonuria, and cerebral agenesis;

EXHIBIT 21-2.   Psychological Evaluation: Mental Retardation of Unknown Etiology

Name: Jolene
Date of birth: May 1, 1971
Chronological age: 8-5
Date of examination: October 10, 1979
Date of report: October 12, 1979
Grade: 2nd

Test Results

Stanford-Binet (L M):

Chronological Age: 8 years, 5 months
Mental Age: 5 years, 7 months
IQ: 64 ± 5 at the 95 percent confidence level
Classification: Mental retardation

Boehm Test of Basic Concepts: (The test measures a child's understanding of "key" words and prepositional phrases commonly used in instructional language, such as "equal to," "a pair of," and "in order".) Results: 30th percentile for children *entering first grade.*

Bender Visual Motor Gestalt Test:
Standard score = 53; Percentile = 1st.

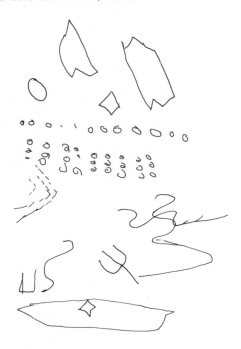

Human Figure Drawing: Age equivalent: Roughly 6 years.

Wide Range Achievement Test:

	STANDARD SCORE	PERCENTILE
Reading	80	9th
Spelling	79	8th
Arithmetic	79	8th

Vineland Social Maturity Scale: Deviation Social Quotient = 68.

Reason for Referral

Jolene's mother is concerned about an appropriate school placement for the coming year. From what Jolene's mother says, there are only two choices available: either a program for the mentally retarded or a second-third grade combination in an "open classroom" situation. She hopes that the evaluation can provide more information about her daughter's learning problems and educational needs because she believes that neither of these alternatives would be particularly appropriate.

Background Information

Jolene is the only child of middle-aged parents who are of Southern European extraction. The father is part owner of a restaurant, while the mother is a housewife. The mother appears to be fully in charge of child rearing and discipline. She recognizes Jolene's learning/educational difficulties, and appears to accept them remarkably well. There is a question, however, of whether she is fully aware of the long-term implications of her child's difficulties.

The mother finds Jolene a likable companion for shopping excursions and household projects, especially cooking. The father spends much time away from home working, in the company of friends, and at ball games.

There are no pertinent prenatal findings, with the exception that a Caesarean section was done because of slow dilation and mother's age. She

EXHIBIT 21-2   (cont.)

was 40 years old when Jolene was born, and it was her first pregnancy. Jolene was a "good baby." She walked and sat up at age-appropriate times, but talked "baby talk" until she was 3½ years old.

The first indication that anything was wrong came in kindergarten. The teacher's impression was that Jolene was a "spoiled only child." Assessment by learning specialists in the first grade revealed gaps in language understanding and poor visual-motor skills; testing was believed to be inadequate because of poor attention. Jolene repeated the first grade and participated in a perceptual-motor training program.

Observations

Jolene is a big, sturdy, handsome child who comes across as pleasant, if not a "super-friendly" little girl. She was intrigued by the possibilities of game-like activities, eager to talk about her own experiences, and full of questions for me (e.g., Where did I live? and Where did I get the picture books in the testing kit?). Although she seemed genuinely interested in this lively social give-and-take, I believe that she also used conversational tactics to avoid the inevitable: having to deal with questions and school-related tasks that would prove embarrassing and frustrating.

Needless to say, during formal testing it was often difficult to hold her interest and attention. Faced with even minimal challenge, she began changing the subject, wiggling in her chair, and, in some instances, simply putting her head down on the desk and bowing out altogether. Given constant individual encouragement, as well as some "bribes" (i.e., "Just one more thing and you can take a recess"), she managed to struggle through three half-hour work sessions. It was interesting, however, and perhaps significant, that her span of attention and energy level increased immediately when the tasks were sufficiently simple and structured to offer an opportunity for success, namely, those designed for a child of 5 or 5½ years of age.

Discussion and Impressions

Jolene impressed me as an outgoing buoyant little girl, displaying a knack for verbal expression in the form of lively, spontaneous conversation. She demonstrated relative strengths in both auditory and visual memory—recalling the facts of a short paragraph read to her (year level VIII), and scoring a near success on the "Memory for De-

signs" item at year IX on the Binet. It may well be that these selective skills account in part for relatively faster progress in sight reading than in subjects requiring conceptual learning.

On the other hand, she demonstrates substantial limitations for her age in functions calling for cognitive language reasoning, such as the ability to store information and generalize from what she has learned to new situations. She performs far better on tasks involving isolated visual and motor skills than on those demanding more complex integration or coordination of visual-motor processes. In addition, there appear to be sizeable gaps in her understanding of language concepts, especially those related to ideas of quantity, such as "equal to" or "less than." Certainly, Jolene's short attention span and limited staying power, noted particularly under stress of difficulty, are also additional liabilities in a classroom situation.

Her social and self-help skills are commensurate with that of her cognitive level of functioning. She functions at a level that is approximately two years younger than expected for her age.

Summary and Recommendations

Jolene impressed me as a personable child whose intellectual level of functioning in a conventional learning setting is currently in the mentally retarded range. We would probably all agree that Jolene is one of those youngsters who "fall between the cracks" when it comes to meeting diagnostic criteria for special education programs. I am sure that she would continue to struggle with little reward if she were to remain in a regular classroom even if the time allotted for specialized help were increased. She is simply too far behind, and her needs go beyond remedial assistance. On the other hand, it is hard to envision a satisfactory adjustment socially or academically in a program designed for more seriously handicapped youngsters.

Ideally, I would like to see Jolene in a small, highly structured, ungraded classroom; one geared to the developmental readiness level of a "rather special" 5- to 6-year-old. If a suitable program can be made available to her—namely, one that can provide successful learning experiences—her progress should be evaluated in another year or so. We will then be in a better position to take a harder look at "intellectual potential" and talk about long-term adaptive/education goals.

_____
Examiner

these are primarily associated with organic etiologies (Philips, 1967).

This discussion points out that it is important to recognize that there is a great heterogeneity of performance in individuals labeled "mentally retarded." A child who obtains an IQ of 67 and who is a slow learner is obviously far different from one who exhibits no language or self-help skills, yet both may be described as mentally retarded (Baumeister & Muma, 1975). Much more is understood about the etiology of organic retardation than about that of familial retardation.

Prevalence Rates of Mental Retardation as a Function of the Relationship Between Measured Intelligence and Adaptive Behavior

We have seen that the AAMD's definition of mental retardation requires that a child be below the population average by at least two standard deviations on (a) a measure of intelligence and (b) a measure of adaptive behavior. Because intelligence and adaptive behavior are not perfectly correlated, children who fall below $-2\,SD$ on an intelligence test may have adaptive behavior skills that do not fall into this range. Silverstein (1973)

and Mastenbrook (1978) have reported how the application of both criteria affects the number of children classified as mentally retarded. Silverstein estimated various hypothetical prevalence rates as a function of the correlation between measures of intelligence and adaptive behavior. As can be seen in Table 21-3, rates increase markedly as one moves from a correlation of .00 to a correlation of 1.00. Nationwide prevalence rates, using $-2\,SD$ as the cutting score on each measure, range from 104,000 to over 4,500,000, depending on the correlation between the two measures.

Mastenbrook (1978) administered both the WISC-R and an adaptive behavior scale to a large number of children. Of those 300 children who obtained an IQ between 50 and 70, less than 35 percent had adaptive behavior scores that also were lower than two standard deviations below the mean. Consequently, the joint use of the two criteria—IQ and adaptive behavior—for the classification of mental retardation eliminated 65 percent of those who would be so classified by the exclusive use of the IQ criterion.

Educational Programming and Consultation

Educational programs must be geared to the age of the children and to their level of functioning. Preschool and school-aged children functioning in the mild range of retardation can benefit from programs offered in regular schools, either in special education programs or, when appropriate, in regular classes. Much, too, can be done to help those families that are not able to take advantage of opportunities to help their children develop properly. Intervention strategies for those families include better incomes, better housing, preschool education for their children, further education for the parents, and effective family planning. In order to facilitate development of appropriate educational programs for a mentally retarded child, a battery of tests should be used for the assessment task. The battery should include an intelligence test, an achievement test, and one or more special ability tests.

TABLE 21-3.   Hypothetical Prevalence Rates of Mental Retardation per 1,000 Population and Hypothetical Nationwide Prevalence Using −2 Standard Deviation Cutting Score for Estimates of the Population Correlation Between Measured Intelligence and Adaptive Behavior

Correlation	Hypothetical Prevalence Rate per 1,000	Hypothetical Nationwide Prevalence
.00	.5	104,000
.20	1.4	274,000
.40	2.9	584,000
.60	5.5	1,100,000
.80	9.8	1,965,000
1.00	22.8	4,550,000

Note. These data are based on an assumed population of 200,000,000.

Adapted from Silverstein (1973).

Rehabilitation programs are more difficult to implement for those who are severely retarded. Yet, there are opportunities even for children functioning at the severely retarded levels. Effective methods are available to teach retarded children who are functioning in the 25 to 50 IQ range.

Popovich (1977) developed an excellent set of guidelines for working with severely and profoundly retarded individuals in such areas as motor development, eye-hand coordination, and language development. A criterion-referenced battery, designed to aid in the assessment of profoundly handicapped children, also is available. It covers twelve different areas of functioning, including self-help skills, communication, perceptual problem solving, and play (Kiernan & Jones, 1977).

It has been alleged that psychologists are primarily responsible for assigning children to classes for the mentally retarded. Yet Ashurst and Meyers (1973) reported that in large metropolitan school districts, psychologists in 43 percent of the cases *failed* to confirm teachers' judgments of children who were referred for possible placement in mentally retarded classes. Furthermore, when children were actually placed in special classes, the children's ethnicity or sex was not related to the frequency of placements. Placement decisions appeared to be made on the basis of the child's needs, rather than on the basis of test results per se. This study showed that referral to school psychologists may have prevented the incorrect placement of many children in classes for the mentally retarded.

Ingalls (1978) presented ten themes that characterize the present field of mental retardation. The themes, which follow, suggest that current efforts are focusing on integrating mentally retarded persons into our society, recognizing their rights for individualization, and providing opportunities for growth and development.

1. An emphasis on the similarities between retarded and nonretarded people rather than on their differences.

2. A recognition that retarded people can improve their level of functioning if they are given a proper opportunity.
3. A questioning of the concept of mental retardation.
4. A deemphasis on labeling.
5. Increased individualization.
6. Expansion of legal rights for the mentally retarded.
7. An increased tolerance of deviance.
8. The recognition that some mental retardation arises out of conditions in society.
9. An emphasis on prevention.
10. Planning and coordination of services.

Some General Considerations in Understanding Mental Retardation

Mentally retarded children are more vulnerable to the development of maladaptive behavior than normal children in all periods of their life (Garfield, 1963; Philips, 1967). They also may exhibit psychotic symptoms and have emotional disorders that are similar to those occurring in children of normal intelligence. As with normal children, there is considerable variability in the personality and behavior of individuals considered to be retarded.

Mental retardation is not a disease (Payne, 1968); rather, it is a symptom of a wide variety of conditions which interfere with the normal development of the brain, and intellectual impairment is a functional expression of the interference. It also is important to recognize that a low IQ is not synonymous with being passive, acquiescent, and helpless. In an impressive series of experiments, Braginsky and Braginsky (1971) demonstrated that mentally retarded children have the interpersonal awareness and manipulative skills necessary to control, to some extent, their own fate. In one of the experiments, for example, the children were able to appear either "dumb" or "bright" on the Quick Test according to whichever strategy was appropriate to satisfy their personal goals. Mental retardation represents a complex field of study. Simple generalizations about cognitive processes and personality are as difficult to make in the field of mental retardation as they are in any other field of psychology.

Mental Retardation and Intelligence Testing

As early as the first decade of the twentieth century, the National Education Association was concerned with the proper use of intelligence tests in the study of mentally retarded children. A committee of the association formulated a policy concerning the use of tests that is as appropriate today as it was when it was first issued:

> Tests of mental deficiency are chiefly useful in the hands of the skilled experimenter. No sets of tests have been devised which will give a categorical answer as to the mental status of any individual. In nearly every instance in which they are used, they need to be interpreted. [Bruner, Barnes, & Dearborn, 1909, p. 905]

The committee noted that the tests proposed by DeSanctis, and by Binet and Simon, were of considerable value as tests of general capacity. Today, the testing of intelligence is still one of the important functions in schools and in institutions for the mentally retarded.

In individuals who are institutionalized for mental retardation there is often a direct relationship between level of intelligence and numerous types of behaviors. In a study (Ross, 1972) of over 11,000 individuals residing in institutions for the mentally retarded, higher levels of intelligence were found to be associated with fewer physical handicaps, greater self-help skills, and fewer behavior problems. These results indicate that level of measured intelligence needs to be taken into consideration in developing programs for institutionalized mentally retarded individuals.

Although the IQ is an important factor in arriving at recommendations for mentally retarded children, Wallin (1940) emphasized the importance of attempting educational programs, regardless of the specific IQ that is found.

An IQ should never serve as an excuse for complacency or justification for inaction. Ample opportunities should be afforded young retardates and deficients in the literary subjects, using the best remedial techniques, concrete procedures, and interest-provoking activity programs, before such instruction is abandoned and the emphasis diverted to motor training. [p. 220]

If retarded children are to be helped to reach their potentials, test scores should not be used as a basis for prohibiting a child from participating in programs which can be stimulating. Studies have shown that many children whose test scores fall into the mentally retarded range develop into self-sufficient and desirable citizens as adults.[1] Further, as Masland, Sarason, and Gladwin (1958) noted, "The criteria customarily used to define mental retardation are not adequate to predict social and occupational success or failure except at the extremes" (p. 303).

The results of a psychological evaluation usually are accepted without extensive questioning. We assume that the examiner was competent, and that pertinent factors were considered in arriving at decisions concerning the examinee. However, the results of a study by Garfield and Affleck (1960) suggest that such assumptions are not always accurate. Many problems were found with the psychological reports of twenty-four individuals who were released from an institution for the mentally retarded because reexamination showed that they were not mentally retarded. The original examinations were inadequate, personality factors were neglected, and the IQ, by itself, was too exclusively relied on when decisions were made about the examinee. Their study, however, was not complete, for they failed to note whether psychological reports of children not released from the hospital had similar inadequacies, although similar problems might have been expected. Their study, too, should not be misconstrued to mean that psychological evaluations are more adequate for children who are not in an institution. The current focus on adaptive behavior reduces, but does not eliminate, the possibility that similar errors will occur with present examination techniques.

The Stanford-Binet, WISC-R, WPPSI, and WAIS-R are the most popular instruments for the evaluation of mental retardation. The Stanford-Binet is the preferred instrument in cases of severe mental retardation because it allows for a more accurate estimate of the child's ability. The Wechsler tests do not have as low a floor as the Stanford-Binet and were not designed for the assessment of severely retarded children.

Stability of the IQ. The question of the stability of the IQ in mentally retarded individuals has been of considerable interest. Studies agree generally that mentally retarded persons tend to obtain lower scores and to show less change in IQ when retested than persons who are not mentally retarded.[2] This generalization, however, is in part dependent on the time interval between tests and on the types of tests used for each evaluation. IQs are likely to be more similar when the interval between testings is short and when the same test is administered each time.

Goal in evaluating mentally retarded children. The principles of test interpretation illustrated throughout this text also apply to mentally retarded children. It is important to evaluate children's relative strengths, even though the children are mentally retarded. One of the goals in evaluating mentally retarded children is to contribute to an understanding of why they do not function socially, if that is their problem, and to determine their assets and limitations, so that remedial action can be taken (Gunzburg, 1970). The intelligence test plays a crucial role in the evaluation of a mentally retarded child. Consequently, the utmost care and attention must be exercised in the testing of children suspected of functioning in the mentally retarded range. In such cases, there must be no doubt about the reliability and validity of the obtained IQ.

Mentally retarded and normal children of similar mental age. Children who achieve the same mental age on a test but have different chronological ages can be considered to have reached similar levels of intellectual development. The labels "bright" and "dull," for these children, however, imply some differences in intellectual functioning in that the bright children have reached the same level of functioning as the dull children at an earlier age. Some differences, therefore, between bright and dull children may be due to their different rates of intellectual development (Sullivan & Skanes, 1971).

Many investigators have reported differences between mentally retarded and normal children of equal mental ages, but no strong trends have been noted.[3] In a study of Form L-M of the Stanford-Binet (Achenbach, 1970), few of the test results (seven out of thirty-three) were found to differ significantly in fifty-four matched pairs (on the basis of mental age) of 5-year-old nonretarded (M IQ = 126) and retarded children (M IQ = 52). The significant differences suggested that the retarded children excelled on concrete and practical tests, while the nonretarded children excelled on abstract tests and on tests involving general intelligence. Other comparisons indicated that the amount of scatter was not significantly different between the two groups and that the performance of black and white retarded children was not significantly different. Achenbach concluded that overall the results suggested that "individuals differing in IQ and CA but matched for MA differ little in their performance on the Stanford-Binet, Form L-M" (p. 493). In addition, "Binet performance by individuals obtaining the same MA scores may be generally similar even if they are of different races" (p. 494). However, in situations requiring new strategies, transfer of learning, generalization, and abstraction, retarded individuals are not always as efficient as their MA-matched nonretarded peers (Das, 1973b).

Using the Stanford-Binet for the assessment of mental retardation. One of the Stanford-

Binet's principal missions since its inception has been to be of aid to examiners in determining whether children should be placed in mentally retarded classes in the school. Over the years this purpose has been served remarkably well. The latest revision of the Stanford-Binet (Form L-M), like its predecessors, has been found to have substantial relationships with scholastic achievement, social maturity measures, and developmental schedules for mentally retarded children, thus indicating that Form L-M is a good predictor of learning and other facets of intelligence (Himelstein, 1968). Also, the internal consistency of Form L-M with retarded individuals appears to be satisfactory (Silverstein, 1969).

Stanford-Binet patterns that can reliably differentiate brain-injured from non-brain-injured mentally retarded children generally have not been found.[4] Similarities between the two groups are much greater than their differences. Overall, there is no single test pattern that clearly differentiates non-brain-injured mentally retarded children from other groups (cf. Sarason, 1953). Although the Stanford-Binet is not sensitive to factors that differentiate brain-injured from non-brain-injured mentally retarded children (cf. Himelstein, 1968), qualitative observations of the child's test performance and behavior may provide clues useful in making a differential diagnosis.

Using the WISC-R for the assessment of mental retardation. The WISC-R is a reliable and valid instrument for use in the assessment of mental retardation. Factor analytic studies indicate that the factor structure of the WISC-R for mentally retarded children is similar to that for normal children, although some minor differences emerge.[5] It appears that the Freedom from Distractibility factor (Arithmetic, Digit Span, and Coding) is less stable for retarded children than for normal children. However, in general, the factor analytic studies suggest that there may be no qualitative differences in the structure of intelligence for normal and mentally retarded children.

The relative difficulty of WISC-R subtests for mentally retarded children, from easiest to hardest, is as follows: (1) Object Assembly, (2) Picture Completion, (3) Block Design, (4) Coding, (5) Similarities, (6) Comprehension, (7) Picture Arrangement, (8) Information, (9) Arithmetic, and (10) Vocabulary.[6] These ranks indicate that both Verbal and Performance Scale subtests are about equally placed in the distribution. The psychological evaluation (Exhibit 21-1) that began this chapter illustrates how the WISC-R can be used in the assessment of mental retardation.

There is no evidence that the WISC-R can reliably differentiate brain-injured from non-brain-injured mentally retarded children. What is still needed, however, is a careful description of the child's performance. The results of the evaluation, in conjunction with other test results and qualitative data and case history information, are likely to be very useful in assessing the child's abilities.

Alternative Modes for the Assessment of Profoundly Retarded Children

Standardized tests, with well-developed norms, may not always be useful in the assessment of severely retarded children. This situation arises when children do not speak, or when they can not succeed on even the simplest performance tasks that appear on tests. In such cases, alternative modes of evaluation should be considered. Operant methods are potentially useful for the assessment of the learning potential of mentally retarded children (or psychotic children) who cannot be tested by traditional psychometric methods because of their severe language deficit or social withdrawal. In an operant procedure, the child receives reinforcement for making a correct response, such as pulling a lever when a light of a specific color is shown. The examiner measures response rate as well as quality of response (e.g., number of pauses). Better response rates and smoother, steadier rates of responding have been found to correlate with mental age in retarded children (Carter

EXHIBIT 21-3.   Effects of Behavioral Training on the Functioning of a Profoundly Retarded Microcephalic Teenager

History

John is a 17-year-old adolescent who has been institutionalized since he was 6 years old. He had spent 9 years in a private institution in the northeast and then was transferred, at his parents' request, to a large state institution for the mentally retarded in southern Florida.

The medical, psychiatric, neurological, and psychological records indicated minor disagreements concerning the specific primary diagnosis. Typical diagnostic impressions were "profoundly retarded with chronic brain syndrome associated with congenital cranial anomalies" and "microcephaly with cerebral palsy, mental deficiency severe with behavioral reaction." However, all of the evaluations over the years were in complete agreement that John possessed little possibility for behavioral, intellectual, and social development. There was agreement also that he would require lifelong custodial care within an institution. The psychologists' views concerning the possibilities of training the boy were usually the most pessimistic of all of the evaluations. For example, when John was 15 years of age, one psychologist wrote that further intellectual development was "quite unlikely."

Initial Level of Functioning

John was observed and interviewed at considerable length prior to the study. The observation period indicated that he did not possess intelligible speech, nor was he able to respond to verbal directions, unless these directions were accompanied by physical demonstrations of the actions desired. It was apparent that John was imitating modeled behavior; he was not able to respond to verbal directions alone. Therefore, it was concluded that he did not possess language and that he was not able to follow verbal directions. In addition, he lacked simple behavioral skills, such as an ability to sustain attention or to point his finger at an object.

Procedure

John was required to learn thirty-four problems in a program that employed a two-choice discrimination learning procedure. The stimuli pre-

sented in the two-choice problems varied on attributes of five dimensions: shape, size, quantity, color, and position. The program consisted of fourteen one-dimensional (e.g., red), ten two-dimensional (e.g., blue square), and ten three-dimensional (e.g., small, yellow triangle) conceptual problems.

For each concept problem, there were twenty instances, divided into two trial blocks, each with ten trials. The correct concept (e.g., red) was presented on each of the twenty learning trials. The alternative stimulus consisted of other possible concepts and was varied randomly (e.g., blue, triangle, two). Criterion performance for each problem was defined as 90 percent correct responding in a single trial block. John proceeded through the program, beginning with the first of the one-dimensional problems and continuing consecutively with the more complex two- and three-dimensional problems.

Prior to the learning of each concept, ten correct responses were modeled for John. Similar modeling occurred after every two trial blocks completed without concept attainment. Both frosted cereal and social praise were employed as reinforcers for correct responding. Two examiners worked with John. One examiner presented the stimuli and the other served as the model.

Results and Discussion

Effects of Program Participation

During the early hours of the program, pointing on cue and attending to the stimuli presented were modeled for John. By the end of the fifth hour both examiners judged that these skills had been learned.

The mean number of trial blocks to concept attainment for each problem is presented in Figure 21-1. It is apparent that rapid learning occurred during the first nine problems. In addition, the more complex two-dimensional problems (problems 15–24) and three-dimensional ones (problems 25–34) learned later in the program were solved more rapidly than the less complex one-dimensional problems learned earlier in the program (problems 1–14). Thus, John demonstrated the acquisition of a learning set.

Generalization to Linguistic and Intellectual Functioning

As John progressed through the program, the examiners noted that he had begun to speak in-

EXHIBIT 21-3   (cont.)

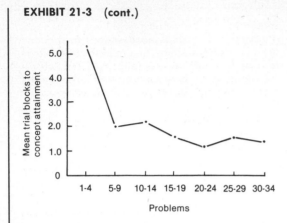

Figure 21-1. Mean Number of Trial Blocks to Concept Attainment over Problems.

telligible words. In order to provide a measure of the extent to which language was acquired, the two examiners conducted an interview with John following program completion. The interview consisted of a twenty-minute question-and-answer period. John was asked to respond to a series of questions concerning the names of objects present in the room, the parts of his body, and the clothing he wore. For example, an examiner would point to John's hand and ask: "What is this called?"

A response was scored as correct if it was a word whose meaning was intelligible to both examiners. Using this criterion, John verbalized forty-five one- and two-syllable words. Among the words given were "ball, car, beard, sky, tree, watch, hello, daddy, dollar, window, and mommy." Thus, some linguistic skill was acquired by John although it was not trained directly.

Prior to the study, it would not have been possible to evaluate the child with a standard intelligence test. However, given his progress in acquiring behavioral, conceptual, and language skills, the Stanford-Binet Intelligence Scale was administered to John in order to further evaluate his progress. He attained a basal level of 2-0, a ceiling of 4-6, and a mental age of 3-2. As expected, he performed most effectively on the nonverbal subtests. ■

Source: Reprinted, with a change in notation, with permission of the publisher and authors from *Behavior Research and Therapy, 11*, pp. 143–145, by L. I. Jacobson, G. Bernal, and G. N. Lopez, "Effects of Behavioral Training on the Functioning of a Profoundly Retarded Microcephalic Teenager with Cerebral Palsy and Without Language or Verbal Comprehension." Copyright 1973, Pergamon Press, Ltd.

& Clark, 1973; Ellis, Barnett, & Pryer, 1960) and in autistic children (Clark, 1971). The development of normative data for specific task and reinforcement procedures would greatly facilitate the use of operant procedures.

A behavioral training procedure that was found to be successful in assessing the intellectual ability of John, a profoundly retarded microcephalic teenager, is described in Exhibit 21-3. Prior to the behavioral training program, John demonstrated neither language nor an ability to comprehend and follow verbal directions. After the program was completed, he was able to say some words and obtain some successes on selected items of the Stanford-Binet.

Differential Diagnosis of Mental Retardation

As we will see in Chapters 22 and 23, severely disturbed children may display forms of behavior similar to those of mentally retarded children. Psychotic children and brain-damaged children, too, may function at mentally retarded levels. Mental retardation, then, should be seen as a description of performance and not as a replacement for some other designation.

Assessment of Gifted Children

The term "gifted" can be defined in a number of different ways, including (a) those who already have achieved outstanding prominence in an area, (b) those who have an extremely high IQ (e.g., above 130), (c) those who excel in art or music, or (d) those who score high on tests of creativity. The definition of gifted and talented children offered by the U.S. Office of Education is as follows (Marland, 1972, p. 10):

Gifted and talented children are those identified by professionally qualified persons who by virtue of outstanding abilities are capable of high performance. These are children who require differentiated educational programs and services beyond those normally provided by the regular program in order to realize their contribution to self and society.

Children capable of high performance include those with demonstrated achievement and/or potential ability in any of the following areas.

1. General intellectual ability
2. Specific academic aptitude
3. Creative or productive thinking
4. Leadership ability
5. Visual and performing arts
6. Psychomotor ability

Essentially, the term "giftedness" can refer to those children with exceptionally high IQs, to those who have creative talents, or to those who achieve highly on both dimensions. It is estimated that this definition would result in identification of approximately 3 to 5 percent of the population as being gifted and talented.

Identifying gifted children is a challenging activity. Various methods are available, including (from most to least preferred) (1) individual intelligence tests, (2) teacher observation and nomination, (3) previous accomplishments, (4–5) group achievement test scores, (4–5) creativity test scores, and (6) group intelligence tests (Martinson, 1973). While teacher nomination of gifted children is used more extensively than any other approach, it is successful only about 45 percent of the time in identifying gifted children (Gear, 1976). Group intelligence tests are about as successful as teacher nomination in identifying gifted children;

they tend to provide lower IQs than individually administered intelligence tests. Similarly, group achievement tests tend to underestimate the attainment of many bright students. The single best method available for the identification of children with superior cognitive abilities appears to be a standardized individually administered test of intelligence, such as the Stanford-Binet or those in the Wechsler series (French, 1974; Martinson, 1973). An evaluation of a gifted child appears in Exhibit 21-4.

In addition to selecting gifted children on the basis of an overall IQ, it is important to determine their abilities in various academic areas. Because not all gifted children are equally talented in every academic area, special ability tests should be used to supplement intelligence tests (Stanley, 1979). Some gifted children may have exceptional talent in mathematics or the language arts, while others have specific learning disabilities which interfere with their ability to realize their potentials (see Case 21-1 below). Once gifted children are identified, it is important that they receive accelerated educational opportunities.

CASE 21-1.   Spelling Disability in a Gifted Child

Paul, aged 13 years, 2 months, was referred because of a severe spelling disability (1st percentile on the Stanford Achievement Test). His teachers indicated that his specific deficits in spelling and writing were interfering with his academic performance. Other achievement scores indicated average to above-average reading skills (44th to 88th percentiles) and average to above-average arithmetical skills (54th to 94th percentiles). Reading comprehension scores were better than word recognition scores. On the WISC-R he obtained a Verbal IQ of 135, a Performance IQ of 127, and a Full Scale IQ of 134. The results suggested that Paul is a gifted youngster with a specific learning disability. ■

EXHIBIT 21-4. Psychological Evaluation: A Gifted Child

Name: Fred
Date of birth: May 30, 1970
Chronological age: 9-2
Date of examination: July 31, 1979
Date of report: August 2, 1979
Grade: 3rd

Test Administered

Stanford-Binet Intelligence Scale, Form L-M

Reason for Referral

Fred's parents requested the evaluation in order to gain a better understanding of his intellectual strengths and weaknesses.

Background Information

Fred is an active and healthy 9-year-old boy. He is the only son of parents who are both lawyers. In reference to being an only child Fred commented, "When I want privacy it's nice, but sometimes it's a little lonely."

Fred enjoys scholastic activities, especially reading, and his main complaint is "I've read all the kids' books they have." He also enjoys singing and spending time with his best friend. Although Fred is quite content with his abilities in most areas, sports is one area in which he would like to be more proficient. Some slight motor difficulties were previously noticed by his parents, and an evaluation is being made of his motor skills.

Behavioral Observations

Fred appeared self-confident and friendly. He went readily to the testing room with the examiner and talked freely, making excellent use of his extensive vocabulary, expressing himself clearly in a very adult fashion. He showed unusual sophistication in his use of humor by relating inflation to the value of his allowance, and also seemed to enjoy especially the verbal absurdities portion of the test.

When confronted with reasoning problems involving orientation and directionality, Fred balked and simply stated, "I'm not good at directions." Although Fred complied dutifully with all instructions, on tasks that he perceived to be difficult he was quick to accept his limitations and did not persevere in order to figure out the more challenging questions. With encouragement, he would eventually answer, often after

first trying to ascertain more information as an aid from the examiner.

In addition, Fred was rather physically active during the testing session. His attention frequently wandered as we changed to a different task, and he asked the examiner several times about the length of the test. He would, however, easily return to the task at hand with a little encouragement. The rapport maintained between Fred and the examiner was excellent, as were the testing conditions.

Test Results

On Form L-M of the Stanford-Binet Intelligence Scale, Fred, with a chronological age of 9-2, achieved a mental age of 13-2. This score yields an IQ of 136 ± 10. The chances that the range of scores from 126 to 146 includes his true IQ are about 95 out of 100. His Very Superior level of intelligence exceeds that of 99 percent of the children his age in the standardization group, which was roughly representative of the United States population.

Fred's greatest strength lies in conceptual thinking, an ability he demonstrated by defining essential differences at the Average Adult level. Also very well developed are his word knowledge and numerical reasoning skills, which equal those of the average 14-year-old. Fred's general reasoning ability, as revealed by problems of fact requiring deduction and the ability to analyze the logical requirements of a problem, is also well developed at the XIII year level. It is noteworthy that at the XI, XII, and XIII year levels, Fred passed all subtests except for nonverbal memory items, such as memory for designs, reproducing a sequence of shapes with beads, and repeating five digits in reverse order. He was able to complete all other tasks at these levels. This suggests that Fred's abilities are all equally well developed at a very superior level, with the sole exception of his memory for nonverbal material, which is, nonetheless, above average.

Impressions

This evaluation shows Fred to be functioning at a very superior intellectual level. Although Fred's interest in the test waned occasionally, simple encouragement was sufficient to focus him on the tasks. For this reason, and since excellent rapport was maintained during the exam, this measure of Fred's present level of intellectual functioning is thought to be valid.

EXHIBIT 21-4   (cont.)

Fred's level of functioning is very high in all areas except memory for nonverbal material which, although his weakest ability, is still above average. Test performance does suggest that Fred is rather aware of his abilities and may almost too nonchalantly accept his weaknesses with little effort toward strengthening them.

In conclusion, Fred is clearly a very bright child with an engaging sense of humor and unique charm. He is inclined to work hardest in areas where he already enjoys some success and tends to dismiss or avoid difficult tasks. He can probably be expected to function best in verbal activities and show a great deal of independence and responsibility. Successful completion of nonver-

bal tasks will probably require more structure and more encouragement.

Recommendations

Fred would probably benefit from a program designed for gifted children, which could offer projects and materials on a level in keeping with his intellectual abilities. Encouragement and additional structure might be useful in helping Fred to overcome his reluctance to attempt difficult tasks and to develop more perseverance. Participation in physical activities with an emphasis on self-improvement rather than on competition might also prove beneficial.

Examiner

Terman's Study of the Gifted

One of the most extensive longitudinal investigations of children (Terman, 1925; Terman & Oden, 1959) studied a sample of 1,528 (857 males and 671 females) gifted children (Stanford-Binet IQs ranging from 135 to 200 and group test IQs of 135 and above) who were approximately 11 years of age at the initiation of the project. The children were rated by physicians as physically superior to a group of unselected children. On tests of achievement, they were superior to other children in such areas as reading, arithmetical reasoning, and information, but not as superior in computation and spelling. The gifted children also were more interested in abstract subjects (e.g., literature, debating, dramatics, and history) and somewhat less interested in practical subjects (e.g., penmanship, manual training, drawing, and painting).

Teachers rated the gifted children as above the mean of the control group on intellectual traits, volitional traits, emotional traits, aesthetic traits, moral traits, physical traits, and social traits. Only in one area, mechanical ingenuity, were the gifted children rated slightly below the control group.

On follow-up in middle age (Terman & Oden, 1959), the gifted group, in comparison to a random sample of the population, were

found to have more education, higher incomes, more desirable and prestigious occupations, more entries in *Who's Who,* better physical and mental health, a lower suicide rate, a lower mortality rate, a lower divorce rate, and brighter spouses and children. The follow-up demonstrates that IQs do relate to accomplishments outside of school. As Brody and Brody (1976) observed: "It is doubtful that the attempt to select children scoring in the top 1% of any other single characteristic would be as predictive of future accomplishment" (p. 109).

A similar, but less extensive, study was carried out in England with a sample of fifty-five English boys and girls, ages 8 to 12 years, with WISC Verbal IQs above 140 (Lovell & Shields, 1967). Teachers rated the children *outstandingly high* in general intelligence and desire to know; *very high* in originality, desire to excel, truthfulness, common sense, will power and perseverance, and conscientiousness; *rather high* in prudence and forethought, self-confidence, and sense of humor; and *close to the average* in traits such as freedom from vanity and egotism. Sex differences were few. The mean ratings given by the British teachers were very close to those given by American teachers to the children in Terman's sample over forty years prior to Lovell and Shield's study. A correlation of .90 was found between the rank orders of traits in the two studies. Thus, despite changes over time and between countries in education and in life generally, teachers in the United States in the 1920s and in England in the 1960s saw the gifted child in very similar ways. The results also indicated that tests of creativity did not measure intellectual functions that were independent of those measured by the WISC or by tests of logical thought.

Creativity and Intelligence

The term "creativity," like intelligence, is a loosely defined, broad, and multifaceted concept; neither corresponds to a precisely defined or distinct entity (Anastasi & Schaefer, 1971). The relationship between creativity and intelligence is also complex, complicated with problems of measurement and definition. Measures of creativity that emphasize divergent thinking (e.g., Guilford-type tests that measure unusual uses, consequences, and problem situations) correlate only very modestly with tests of intelligence (between .25 and .30). However, tests of creativity correlate just as little with each other as they do with measures of intelligence. What little common variance they have may be accounted for by *g*, the general intelligence factor (Thorndike, 1963). Some tests of creativity likely measure cognitive abilities that are not reliably distinguished from intelligence, while others measure attributes that are different from those measured on intelligence tests (Madaus, 1967).

Another way to look at creativity is to study those individuals who have made creative contributions to society. The evidence suggests that individuals who have made creative contributions in art, literature, and science are more intelligent than those who have not made such contributions (Ausubel & Sullivan, 1970). It is likely that a critical level of intelligence is necessary for creative potentials to be actualized, but beyond this level the relationship between intelligence and creativity is approximately zero.

The major attributes associated with creativity can be grouped into three areas (Ross-

man & Horn, 1972): *abilities* (intelligence, originality, flexibility, fluency, memory, sensitivity to problems, and perceptual receptivity), *motives* (need for achievement, striving for novelty, striving to test self [risk taking], and preference for complexity), and *temperament traits* (independence of judgment, tendency to dominate, attitudinal openness, lack of anxiety, affective or aesthetic sensitivity, and playfulness). Different theorists emphasize one or more of the three areas. For example, Guilford (1967) stresses the ability area, maintaining that divergent thinking is the *sine qua non* of creative potential. Roe (1953) suggests that creativity is primarily the outcome of motivation, while Cattell and Drevdahl (1955) emphasize temperament or style in accounting for creative behaviors. It is useful to think of creativity and intelligence as the outgrowths of distinct (although overlapping) sets of influences (Rossman & Horn, 1972).

Summary

1. The most widely used definition of mental retardation is as follows: "Mental retardation refers to significantly subaverage general intellectual functioning existing concurrently with deficits in adaptive behavior and manifested during the developmental period." This definition implies that the diagnosis is only a description of present behavior, acknowledges the contribution of intelligence tests, ties diagnosis to the developmental process, and minimizes problems of differential diagnosis.

2. The definition of mental retardation also specifies that two criteria—level of intelligence and level of adaptive behavior—must be used in arriving at a diagnosis of mental retardation. Adaptive behavior is more difficult to assess than intelligence.

3. Four levels of mental retardation are identified—mild, moderate, severe, and profound. These levels fall two or more standard deviations below the mean of the intelligence test used in the evaluation.

4. There are two broad classes of mental retardation: the familial type and the organic type. The familial type represents the milder forms of mental retardation, reflecting primarily normal polygenic variation. The organic type represents the more severe forms of mental retardation as well as some milder forms, and is associated with genetic or chromosomal defects or with brain damage.

5. It is important to recognize that there are large and meaningful differences among individuals labeled "mentally retarded."

6. The correlation between adaptive behavior and intelligence affects the estimated prevalence rates of mental retardation. Depending on the correlation, estimated prevalence rates, using a $-2\ SD$ cut-off point, range from 104,000 to 4,500,000. The higher the correlation between adaptive behavior and intelligence, the larger the estimated prevalence rate.

7. Every attempt should be made to provide the best educational programming available for mentally retarded children. A battery of tests should be used for the assessment task. Even children at the moderate, severe, and profound levels of retardation can benefit from educational training.

8. Psychologists often do not confirm teachers' judgments that children referred for testing are in need of special education.

9. Current efforts are focusing on ways to integrate mentally retarded individuals into society.

10. Mentally retarded children are more vulnerable than normal children to the development of maladaptive behavior.

11. In institutionalized mentally retarded individuals, those with higher levels of intelligence are likely to have fewer physical handicaps, greater self-help skills, and fewer behavior problems than those with lower levels of intelligence.

12. Mentally retarded individuals tend to have more stable IQs over time than individuals who are not mentally retarded.

13. Intelligence tests probably play a more important role in the assessment process in the area of mental retardation than in other areas of exceptionality. Therefore, every attempt must be made to ensure the reliability and validity of the test results.

14. Mentally retarded and normal children of the same mental age show similar performances on the Stanford-Binet. However, when compared with normal children of the same mental age, mentally retarded children are likely to be less efficient in situations requiring new strategies, transfer of learning, generalization, and abstraction.

15. The Stanford-Binet is a useful and valid instrument for the assessment of mental retardation. However, there are no Stanford-Binet patterns that can reliably differentiate brain-injured from non-brain-injured mentally retarded children.

16. The WISC-R is another popular, useful, and valid instrument for the assessment of mental retardation. The WISC-R factor structure is similar for normal and mentally retarded children, although some minor differences have been found. Object Assembly and Picture Completion appear to be somewhat less difficult for mentally retarded children than Arithmetic and Vocabulary. The WISC-R, like the Stanford-Binet, cannot reliably differentiate brain-injured from non-brain-injured mentally retarded.

17. Behavioral training procedures are useful adjuncts for the assessment of profoundly retarded children.

18. The term mental retardation, when used as a designation to indicate level of cognitive performance, can also be included in other diagnoses.

19. Children who fall into the gifted classification may have exceptionally high IQs (over 130 or 140), creative talents, or both.

20. Individual intelligence tests are the preferred method of identifying children with superior cognitive abilities.

21. Intelligence tests should be supplemented with achievement tests in the assessment of gifted children.

22. Gifted children should be provided with accelerated educational opportunities.

23. Gifted children are not only brighter than the general population of children, but also tend (a) to perform better in school, (b) to be better adjusted, and (c) to have better

physical health. In later life, they tend to make many contributions to society.

24. "Creativity" is a difficult concept to define. One difficulty with tests of creativity is that they correlate only moderately with both tests of intelligence (between .25 and .30) and other tests of creativity.

25. The primary determinants of creativity include abilities (e.g., intelligence and originality), motives (e.g., need for achievement and striving for novelty), and temperament traits (e.g., independence of judgment and tendency to dominate).

CHAPTER 22

Assessment of Brain Damage

If the brain were so simple that we could understand it, we would be so simple that we couldn't.

EMERSON M. PUGH

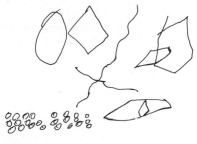

EXHIBIT 22-1 (cont.)

When he was well enough, John received intensive physical, occupational, and speech therapy at a rehabilitation center. Four months after the accident, a psychological evaluation was attempted. However, the evaluation was difficult to perform. John tired quickly, and his attention was inconsistent. It appeared at that time that his verbal abilities were well below average, with some performance skills closer to the average. He had an abnormal gait and his right hand was practically nonfunctional. On a second evaluation two years later, there was virtually no change in his performance. John currently is attending public school. His school records indicated that he was functioning at a high normal level prior to the accident.

Behavioral Observations

John did not remember me initially, but as rapport built he began to recognize and remember that I was connected somehow with the rehabilitation center. He looked very much the same as when I saw him two years ago, although somewhat taller. John seemed more alert, attentive, and coordinated than in the past. The test results appear to be valid, as John was quite cooperative and patient.

John did not talk much, tending to give one word responses to questions. Pencil-and-paper activities were executed with his right hand. Most visual-motor tasks were done slowly. When assembling multi-colored blocks into designs, several rotations of designs were observed. Yet, he never became frustrated and kept at the tasks. Many times John would surprise me with the sudden capability of solving complex problems. This was especially evident when arranging cut-up cartoon pictures into meaningful stories.

Test Results

John, whose chronological age is 13-2, earned a Verbal Scale IQ of 55, a Performance Scale IQ of 64, and a Full Scale IQ of 55 ± 5 on the Wechsler Intelligence Scale for Children–Revised. The latter score places him in the 1st percentile rank and is descriptively classified as Mentally Deficient. The chances that the range of scores from 50 to 60 includes his true IQ are about 90 out of 100.

The majority of John's subtest scores on the WISC-R are extremely below average. Only in one area, ability to arrange pictures into a meaningful arrangement, was his performance at an average level. Psychomotor speed was especially poor, as was his ability to define words.

He also performed poorly on the Coloured Progressive Matrices, Peabody Picture Vocabulary Test, and Bender Visual Motor Gestalt Test. John's performance on the Coloured Progressive Matrices was similar to that of an average 8-year-old and slightly better than his WISC-R performance. This test measures nonverbal or nonlanguage abilities and is closely related to some of the WISC-R Performance subtests, but it requires only pointing and eliminates almost completely the demand for a motor output.

His Peabody Picture Vocabulary performance was somewhat better, with a mental age level of 9-4 and a receptive vocabulary score of 78 (5th percentile). The PPVT does not require expressive language; only a pointing response is needed. The test measures receptive language ability and is sensitive to cultural factors and school learning experiences. Slightly better performance on this test magnified the expressive language deficit displayed by John.

His Bender-Gestalt performance revealed poor visual-motor skills. His performance was similar to that of 6-year-olds. The designs were drawn slowly and he had difficulty with curvature, angulation, and closure.

Impressions

John is a 13-year-old boy who is functioning at a mentally retarded level. He displays an expressive language disorder and visual-motor deficits. It appears that his deficits are a result of the damage sustained in the automobile accident. Improvement has been minimal since the initial evaluation four years ago.

The prognosis in my opinion is guarded to poor as to whether John can be a self-sufficient adult. Probably extensive rehabilitative procedures and care will be needed in the future. Certainly, special education will be necessary. Re-evaluations are recommended every two years to determine his degree of progress.

Examiner

Brain damage refers to any structural (anatomical) or physiological change of a pathological nature in the nerve tissue of the brain. Included under the heading of brain damage are at least nine kinds of brain disorders: physical trauma, metabolic dysfunction, toxicity, degenerative brain disease, cerebral infections and demyelinating disease, congenital malformations and heredito-familial disease, cerebral vascular disease, convulsive disorders, and tumors (Haywood, 1968). Some types of brain damage may produce focal lesions (e.g., intrinsic tumor, cerebral vascular accident, and focal head injury), while others may include generalized or diffuse cerebral involvement (e.g., closed head injuries, generalized degenerative disease, and metabolic disorders). Brain damage may produce different types of effects in individuals, including (a) a general deterioration in all aspects of functioning; (b) differential effects, depending on such variables as location, extent, type of injury, and age of individual; or (c) highly specific effects in certain locations.

The assessment of brain damage, especially in children, should be a joint venture between the neurologist and the psychologist. The accurate assessment of brain damage is a complex and exacting task and therefore requires a high degree of professional knowledge and cooperation. The neurological examination usually begins with a case history. It also includes a study of cranial nerves, reflexes, posture, sensory and sensorimotor functions, body balance, coordination of trunk and extremities, fine manipulative ability, gross motor functions, quality of motility, and a brief mental status examination. A variety of laboratory procedures may augment the examination, including CAT scans (computerized axial tomography), electroencephalograms (EEGs), skull x-rays, spinal taps, and cerebral angiograms.

The neuropsychological evaluation, a complement to the neurological examination, is usually based on a battery of tests of selected sensory, motor, language, and other cognitive and mental functions (Smith, 1975). The tests provide objective base line measures for evaluating the course of various neuropathological processes, as well as the effects of different therapeutic programs on cerebral functions. A variety of tests should be used to obtain an adequate assessment of brain-behavior relationships, as no single test can adequately assess the behavioral consequences of widely variable cerebral lesions. There is a higher probability of understanding the psychological correlates of brain functions when a more complete sample of brain-related behavior is elicited. The neuropsychological evaluation aims in part to draw inferences about the organic integrity of the cerebral hemispheres and the adaptive strengths and weaknesses of the child. While the goal of both the neurological and neuropsychological examinations is to assess brain damage accurately, one of the major differences between the two is that the former focuses primarily on the intactness of lower level functions (e.g., motor system and reflexes), whereas the latter deals more extensively with higher level cognitive processes (e.g., language and memory). Consequently, the neuropsychological examination probably is more sensitive to higher level cognitive dysfunction than the neurological examination (Selz & Reitan, 1979).

Standard neurological histories and examinations, coupled with an EEG, brain scan, and other ancillary diagnostic studies, usually are effective in establishing the presence and locus of intracranial disease or damage, although they are by no means perfect diagnostic tools. The neuropsychological evaluation is not sufficiently precise to permit definitive diagnosis, but it can aid in cases of equivocal findings, and can even be of assistance when there is clear evidence of brain damage, by defining the nature and the severity of specific defects in higher (cognitive) and lower (motor and perceptual) cerebral functions (Smith, 1975). In cases of equivocal findings, or when there is brain disease or trauma early in life, the effects of the underlying acute or chronic cerebral damage may not be readily apparent. However, they may manifest themselves through slight defects in different psychological tests or through marked impairment in selected performances on certain tests.

Clinical neuropsychology also makes other contributions to the diagnostic process (Davison, 1974). Where there is suspicion of brain damage, but insufficient evidence to warrant medical procedures that have potential risk to the patient (e.g., angiography), behavioral measures may contribute information relevant to an understanding of possible brain damage. Not infrequently, behavioral measures may reflect brain damage even though the neurological examination fails to demonstrate such damage. A neuropsychological examination, in cases of civil liability suits involving head injuries, may provide objective measures of adaptive deficits. Neuropsychological assessment procedures increase our understanding of the psychological effects of brain damage and, more generally, of brain-behavior relations. A battery of neuropsychological tests provides a comprehensive, objective, and quantified series of measures useful in assessing initial and later effects of various neuropathological conditions, neurosurgical procedures, and the course of drug therapy.

The signs obtained from the neurological examination that are suggestive of brain damage are sometimes referred to as "hard" or "soft." The hard signs are those that are fairly definitive indicators of cerebral dysfunction (e.g., abnormalities in reflexes, cranial nerves, and motor organization; pathological reflexes; asymmetrical failures in sensory and motor responses; and EEG abnormalities), and are usually highly correlated with other independent evidence of brain damage, such as that from CAT scans. The soft or equivocal signs are associated with more complex behaviors, including mental activities, coordination, and sensation. Representative soft signs include awkwardness, impaired auditory integration, atypical sleep patterns, and visual-motor difficulties. The term soft signs was originally applied because brain injury was suggested when such soft signs were present, but the signs were considered to be uncertain indicators of brain injury when verification could not be established by other diagnostic methods. Even though these signs may not have any systematic relationship to demonstrated neuropathology, some investigators believe that they are suggestive of neurological impairment (White, 1974), while others believe that they may reflect immaturity of development (Weithorn, 1973) or relate to a continuum of dysfunction (Schwartz & Dennerll, 1970). Thus, age norms for these soft signs are of crucial significance for their interpretation.

Young children are especially susceptible to head injuries, with boys more vulnerable than girls. Head injuries may result from falls from heights, play injuries, parental beatings, and automobile accidents. The clinical signs most frequently associated with head injuries include loss of consciousness and amnesia. A follow-up study of thirty-four children under the age of 16 years, four to ten years after they incurred brain damage as a result of automobile accidents, revealed that half the children were doing poorly in school, with eight unable to attend school since the injury and nine others functioning below their pre-traumatic levels (Heiskanen & Kaste, 1974). The children had been unconscious for more than twenty-four hours. These findings suggest that brain injury associated with automobile accidents may have serious consequences in children, as we have seen in the case of John (Exhibit 22-1) at the beginning of this chapter.

The following factors have an important bearing upon the assessment of behavioral effects associated with brain damage:

1. laterality of lesion—right or left hemisphere;
2. site of lesion within hemisphere;
3. causal agent(s) creating lesion(s);
4. course, size, and severity of lesion(s);
5. age of child when lesion was incurred;
6. time interval between damage and testing;
7. condition of child at the time of testing, apart from brain damage (e.g., associated physical [orthopedic] and health problems);

8. premorbid condition of the child; and
9. the home and school environments in which the child functions.

These factors interact to produce highly complex behavioral effects. Because of the complexity of the interactions, similar forms of brain damage do not always produce the same behavioral effects, nor do behavioral differences among brain-damaged children always relate directly to severity of damage or to premorbid personality characteristics. To complicate matters further, some individuals with brain damage are often able to compensate for deficits, and may not show impaired performance on psychological tests. Conversely, impaired performance on psychological tests does not necessarily mean that brain damage is present. Each case must be thoroughly studied in order to identify the factors that are responsible for the behavioral effects.

Lateralization of Cognitive, Perceptual, and Motor Activities

Lateralization refers to the specialization of the hemispheres of the cerebral cortex for various cognitive, perceptual, and motor or sensory activities. The sensorimotor activities are mediated by the side of the brain contralateral to the peripheral location examined. Consequently, a lesion in the right cerebral hemisphere may result in weakness or insensitivity on the left side of the body, while a left cerebral hemisphere lesion may produce similar deficits on the right side of the body. Examination procedures for lateralized differences include motor functioning tests (e.g., finger tapping rate, strength of grip, and motor dexterity), bilateral simultaneous stimulation (touching both sides of the body simultaneously), dichotic listening, and standard neurological techniques for assessing tactile, visual, and auditory senses.

The two hemispheres also appear to have specialized functions with respect to a variety of cognitive and perceptual processes. The *left hemisphere* (for nearly all right-handed and about two-thirds of left-handed individuals) is primarily responsible for verbal functions and verbal abstracting ability, including verbal sounds and language comprehension, spelling, and certain kinds of arithmetic. The *right hemisphere* is specialized for nonverbal, perceptual, and spatial functions, including spatial visualization, visual memory, and complex visual-motor organization. In addition, left hemisphere processing is analytic, sequential, serial, and differential, while right hemisphere processing is holistic, gestalt-like, parallel, and integrative (Wada & Davis, 1977). With simple tasks, nonverbal stimuli can be processed holistically by either hemisphere. Within the cerebral hemispheres, the temporal lobe is associated with auditory perception, the parietal lobe with somatosensory functions and visual-spatial ability, the occipital lobe with visual perception, and the frontal lobe with planning and expressive verbal behavior. Figure 22-1 presents a view of the cerebral hemisphere.

Hemispheric differences in the reactions of the brain to different stimuli may be present as early as the first year of life.[1] For example, 3-month-old infants have been reported to have a pattern of auditory perceptual asymmetries much like those found in older children and adults (Glanville, Best, & Levenson, 1977), which is consistent with the theory that the left hemisphere is superior at processing speech and the right hemisphere superior with nonspeech sounds. However, it is still unclear how specialization of brain functions occurs, whether specialization changes during development, and, if so, at what stage of development it changes. While there is some evidence that lateralization for expressive speech is completed by the age of 5 years (Krashen, 1973) and that some speech lateralization is present as early as 3 years of age (Hiscock & Kinsbourne, 1978), other studies suggest that the comprehension of speech (auditory lateralization) continues to increase until the age of 11 years.[2] Lateralization for visual stimuli also may not be complete until adolescence (Tomlinson-Keasey et al., 1978), although lateralization of spatial operations

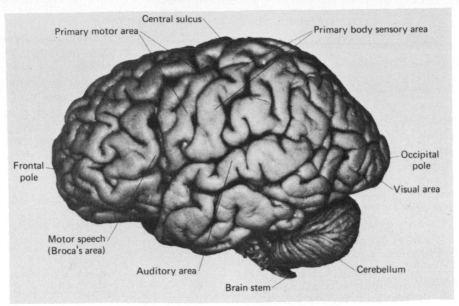

FIGURE 22-1. Lateral View of the Cerebrum, Cerebellum, and Part of the Brain Stem. From *Neuropsychological Assessment* by Muriel Deutsch Lezak. © 1976 by Oxford University Press, Inc. Reprinted by permission.

in the right hemisphere appears to be complete by 5 years of age (Carter & Kinsbourne, 1979).

Aphasia in Children

Childhood aphasia may be defined as a central nervous system dysfunction manifested by disorders in the perception and production of language. Three subgroups may be delineated: *congenital aphasia*, marked by an almost complete failure to acquire language; *developmental aphasia*, having a later onset and associated with less pervasive cognitive and developmental impairment; and *acquired aphasia*, resulting from some specific neurological damage, such as trauma, cerebrovascular accident, tumor, or infection (Cohen, Caparulo, & Shaywitz, 1976). These three subgroups appear to reflect the same basic language dysfunction, but differ from one another mainly in severity and age of onset.

The major forms of aphasia in children (as well as in adults) include *expressive aphasia*, defined as impaired ability to use spoken or written language, and *receptive aphasia*, defined as impaired ability to understand spoken or written language. *Auditory aphasia* refers to an incapacity to comprehend the meaning of spoken words. *Alexia* refers to a loss of ability to read written or printed language despite adequate vision and intelligence. *Agraphia* refers to impairment in the ability to write. Brain injury may also manifest itself in *agnosia*, defined as disturbance in the perception of the significance of or recognition of sensory stimuli or defects of imagination, and in *apraxia*, defined as disturbances in the ability to understand commands or in the production of movements in the absence of paralysis.

Children with aphasia have an impaired ability to acquire language symbols (Eisenson, 1972). One theory is that their major difficulty is in decoding, that is, in processing speech (or auditory information), especially when rates of presentation are rapid (Tallal & Piercy, 1973). They may even have difficulty in perceiving auditory information at a normal rate. Similar difficulties, however, may not be evident in their ability to process visual stimuli. Thus, we see that impaired speed of auditory processing may be one factor associated with aphasic children's language impairment, which, in turn, leads to communication difficulties.

Prognosis and Treatment of Brain-Damaged Children

The prognosis for children who have experienced brain injury depends on a number of factors, including the severity of the injury, the age at which the child incurs the injury, the localization of the brain damage, and the occurrence of post-traumatic complications, such as seizures. Certain types of difficulties resulting from brain injury, such as hemiplegias or visual field defects, may show little or no improvement after many years. On the other hand, mental processes, which are of a more complex order than sensory or motor processes and which are not as circumscribed or anatomically restricted as those underlying motor and sensory functions, may gradually recover even years after the initial insult. With respect to the development of intelligence, some evidence suggests that *lower IQs are associated with (a) more severe trauma, (b) early damage, (c) damage to the fronto-temporal area, and (d) the development of post-traumatic epilepsy* (Kleinpeter, 1976).

The effects of brain damage in young children are different from those in adults because the young child's brain is physically immature and still in a process of development (Ingram, 1969). When an adult sustains brain injury, there may be a loss or dissolution of previously acquired functions, such as impairment of language, memory, social relations, or general intelligence. When a child sustains brain injury, rather than a striking loss of function, there may be an interference with development. If the interference is global, mental retardation may be the result; if region-specific, difficulties with speech or in learning to recognize shapes, for example, may be the result.

Developmental disorders tend to be less specific in children, partly because damage to the immature brain is likely to affect the development of the whole brain rather than to produce localized abnormalities (functional specialization of given cortical regions has not yet been completed), and partly because there may be a greater possibility for the transfer of function from one part of the immature brain to another. Young children who receive unilateral injury to either hemisphere may have most of the functions of the injured hemisphere taken over by the noninjured hemisphere, or may rely on subcortical (lower) regions of the same hemisphere. Furthermore, brain damage in children may have more than a simple depressing effect on their ability structures; it may alter the basic pattern of ability development (Boll & Reitan, 1972), with large unilateral injuries in infants tending to produce a more widespread deficit in intellectual functions than similar injuries in adults.

The relationship between the age at which the child sustains damage and the seriousness of the consequences is a complex issue which depends on the kind and extent of lesion and on other similar factors. In cases in which early injury limits the course of further development, brain damage may result in more dysfunction than similar damage sustained at a later age. The notion that the young child always has great plasticity to permit adaptation to the damage is now being questioned. It may be, for example, that a greater mass of cortex is required for original learning than for retention of learned material (Hutt, 1976). If this is so, massive brain injuries during infancy may impose a limitation on the acquisition of abilities during the developmental years of childhood. Overall, there is some evidence, although it is by no means conclusive, that the consequences are more serious in children who sustain damage at an early age than in those who sustain damage after a long period of normal growth and development.[3] This tentative conclusion is based on studies with heterogeneous samples of brain-damaged children.

Older children with brain damage show a more mixed pattern of deficits, with deficits being similar to those found in adult patients. This is particularly so for older children (above the age of 11 or 12) and to some extent for children above 5 years of age as well, especially once speech has developed (Fedio & Mirsky, 1969; McFie, 1969). Thus, for example, classical patterns may be present, such as lesions in the left hemisphere associated with verbal disorders, and lesions in the right hemisphere with nonverbal or visuospatial disorders.

Brain-damaged children may differ from normal children not only in their capacity to learn but also in their approach to learning. For teaching brain-damaged children, the following procedures are recommended (Haskell, Barrett, & Taylor, 1977):

1. Do not "overload" the child with information.
2. Present information in a controlled and manageable fashion.
3. Determine the optimum level for reception of information for each child individually.
4. Use repetition and practice to consolidate previously learned material.
5. Avoid unnecessary alternative choices in learning tasks.

Behavioral deficits may be related to widely differing causative agents and, therefore, may require different remediation strategies. For example, a reading disability may be the result of (a) faulty learning (or education) in a child who is otherwise normal or (b) a structural or biochemical anomaly of the brain. For treatment purposes, it is important to detect the cause of the observed behavioral deficit. However, it must be acknowledged that even with such differential diagnostic knowledge, appropriate treatment programs are difficult to design. There are gaps in our knowledge of the relationship between the condition of the nervous system and appropriate treatment techniques, and even between patterns of adaptive functioning and treatment alternatives (Davison, 1974). In designing educational programs, it is important to determine the child's strengths and to use these strengths in planning the programs.

Neuropsychological Assessment

A wide spectrum of psychological deficits, varying in nature and degree, accompany brain injury in children. While a neuropsychological assessment may not be able to establish the specific nature, site, and extent of the various underlying brain lesions, it can determine with considerable accuracy the types of sensory, motor, and mental deficits that may be present. Such determinations are of critical importance in designing specific educational programs based on intact or impaired areas of functioning. An aggregate score, such as the total IQ, will not aid us greatly in evaluating the effect of brain lesions on various mental processes. To complement the IQ, we need information obtained from specific tests or sections of tests that provide separate scores for verbal and nonverbal performance, memory, perception, motor skills, and other cognitive and perceptual-motor areas. Age-appropriate normative standards are extremely important to use in the assessment of brain damage in children. Repeated psychological testing, where needed and indicated, is an excellent means of monitoring the evolving clinical picture for possible mental changes in the course of the disease process. The assessment also attempts to specify the probable course of development, when warranted, and to indicate possible remediation procedures and how the child may progress in school.

Several inferential methods are used to analyze the data obtained from a battery of tests. These include level of performance, pattern of performance, pathognomonic signs of brain impairment, and comparison of performance on the two sides of the body (Reitan, 1974). The findings resulting from each method need to be compared in arriving at a diagnostic impression. No one method should be used exclusively. Let us examine each of these methods in more detail.

1. Level of performance refers to using scores obtained on a test or group of tests. The child's score is compared to the normative sample. The strategy is to establish cut-off points that will distinguish brain-damaged from non-brain-damaged children.
2. The pattern of performance approach considers the relationships among a group of tests or subtests in an effort to discover specific combinations of strengths and deficits that may relate to specification of lesion or to outcome criteria.
3. The pathognomonic signs of brain damage approach focuses on signs of pathology (a) in the child's performance (e.g., attentional deficits, perseveration, rotation of a drawing, failure to draw the left half of a figure) or (b) on neurological tests (e.g., electroencephalographic abnormalities).
4. Comparison of performance on the two sides of the body provides valuable information that can be used in determining lateralization of deficits, i.e., relative efficiency of right versus left side of the body. Lateralization of brain damage is better diagnosed by sensory or motor deficits, if present, than by cognitive deficits.

Disturbances associated with brain damage revealed in the neuropsychological evaluation may occur in various spheres of functioning, including motor, sensory, affective, cognitive, social, and personality. Intellectual deficits may be seen in a global reduction of IQ or in reduced efficiency in certain performance or verbal areas. During the early stages of brain damage, subtle forms of behavioral change may occur that may even mimic psychiatric disorders. Children with brain damage involving a lesion in the higher cortical (or subcortical) centers (i.e., above the brain stem) have a rate of psychiatric disorder that is several times greater than that for children in the general population, and greater than that for children with chronic physical handicaps that do not involve brain pathology (Rutter,

1976). Brain damage itself, therefore, appears to play a major role in predisposing children to psychopathology. Brain lesions, too, may result directly in changes in personality.

In evaluating children for brain injury, particularly acute brain injury, observe carefully whether there have been any recent changes in their life style, level of functioning, or emotional stability. For example, instability, irritability, or lethargy may precede other symptoms of a brain tumor, while a progressive decline in academic functioning may be an early sign of degenerative brain disease. Sudden and inadequately explained changes in behavior are likely to be associated with acute, as opposed to chronic, brain disorders.

There is no simple one-to-one relationship between the presence of a demonstrable brain lesion and discernible sensory, motor, mental, or emotional symptoms (Smith, 1975). In some cases in which cerebral dysfunction is manifested through or restricted to either specific deep reflexes or superficial reflexes, no apparent deficits may be revealed on psychological tests. In other cases, psychological tests may reveal marked impairment in some areas of functioning, even though the neurological examination indicates intact functioning. Diagnostic difficulties arise, in part, because in evolving cerebral lesions there may be an interval when pathological processes in various parts of the brain develop without affecting the specific functions tapped by neurological or neuropsychological examinations. Also, early in the pathological development, compensation for deficits may mask clinical manifestations of progressive dysfunction. In addition, it is often difficult to distinguish brain-damaged individuals with vague complaints—such as loss of memory, dizziness, and irritability—from those with symptoms for which no ultimate cerebral lesion can be demonstrated.

The psychological evaluation may reveal a variety of overt and subtle symptoms that may be associated with brain damage (see Table 22-1). Clinicians are well advised to develop an awareness of these behavior pat-

TABLE 22-1. Possible Signs and Symptoms of Brain Damage Observed on the Neuropsychological Examination

Area	Sign or Symptom
Motor	Hyperkinesis (constant movement, inability to sit still; fingering, touching, and mouthing objects; voluble and uninhibited speech); awkwardness in locomotion (clumsiness, atypical arm swing, incoordination, tremors, involuntary movements, asymmetry of facial musculature and expressive gestures while talking); awkwardness in skilled movement (poor printing, writing, and drawing); impaired copying of geometric designs; postural rigidity; speech difficulties (e.g., dysarthria, slow speech); mixed dominance; repetitive movements; and perseveration
Sensory	Short attention span; poor concentration; distractibility; perceptual difficulty (e.g., closure difficulty, visual-motor disturbances, use of fingers to guide movements, turning materials around); and unusual episodic sensory experiences (e.g., occurrence of odd odors or vision of lights)
Affective	Reduced frustration threshold; emotional lability (impulsivity, irritability, aggressiveness, easily moved to tears, loss of control of emotions); anxiety (occasional panic reactions); and depression
Cognitive	Some intellectual deficit; impaired judgment; conceptual difficulties (e.g., in abstracting, planning, organizing, anticipating, analyzing and synthesizing, and integrating); specific learning deficit (in reading, spelling, or arithmetic); language difficulties (e.g., malapropisms, imprecise synonyms, truncated sentences, mispronunciations, circumstantiality); attraction to minute details; impaired right-left orientation; perseveration; concrete, rigid, and inflexible thinking; difficulty in shifting; and memory difficulty (recent, remote, or both; visual, auditory, or both)
Social	Interpersonal difficulties; immaturity (e.g., may regress to more childlike forms of behavior); negativism; and antisocial behavior (lying, stealing, truancy, sexual offenses)
Personality	Disturbed self-concept; disturbed body concept or body image; changes in personality (e.g., a previously fastidious child becomes unkempt and careless); hypochondriacal preoccupations; compulsive tendencies; denial (e.g., children may deny that they have any problems); and indications of insecurity (e.g., expressions of weakness, uncertainty, and inadequacy in dealing with test materials)

terns suggestive of brain damage, if only to rule them out; the earlier brain injury is detected, the better are the possibilities for treatment and rehabilitation. Especially consider the extent to which (a) special techniques have been used to secure the child's attention, (b) instructions have to be repeated before the child does what is asked, and (c) extraneous activity has to be prevented. Be especially alert for behaviors indicative of motor restlessness. However, hyperactivity (or any other behavioral sign) should *never* be taken by itself as indicative of cerebral damage or dysfunction (Werry, 1979).

The child's history also should be studied carefully for signs that may be suggestive of brain damage. Events surrounding the birth processes (prenatal, at birth, and postnatal) should be considered. Prematurity, Rh incompatibility, difficult labor, and a low Apgar score are relevant factors to evaluate. Developmental events that may have etiological importance include prolonged high fevers, injuries to the head, use of anesthetics during surgery, and poisoning associated with foods, chemicals, or medications (Small, 1973). With respect to history taking, the following guidelines should be considered:

In addition to the usual milestones history, the clinician will need to have very specific information regarding the following points: (a) any injury to the head, including the precise location, whether the child lost consciousness and for how long, and whether medical attention was available; (b) the child's behavior both immediately and for several days following the injury, and whether or not there was a noticeable personality change; (c) any occasions of ingestion of toxic substances, and the sequelae; (d) occasions of prolonged nausea and vomiting, which could not be related to eating habits or severe emotional upset; (e) periods of very high body temperature, including if possible the precise temperatures reached and the duration of these, as well as whether there were febrile convulsions; and (f) any sudden changes in levels of energy expenditure. [Haywood, 1968, p. 14]

Let us consider the behavior of aphasic children as illustrative of what may occur during the evaluation of brain-damaged children. When confronted with difficult material during testing, they have a tendency to perseverate, to display inappropriate anger and hostility toward the materials or test administrator, and to be hyperactive (Eisenson, 1972). Some may withdraw from further involvement with the testing situation, while others may fail to carry over a principle from one item to another. For example, on the Columbia Mental Maturity Scale, a developmentally aphasic child forgot the task requirements. On each card, he needed to be reminded to "point to one that is not alike." Without this repetition of the instructions, he could not have coped with the task.

Neuropsychological Test Batteries for Children

Two batteries for evaluating children suspected of brain damage are the Halstead Neuropsychological Test Battery for Children, designed for children aged 9 to 14 years, and the Reitan-Indiana Neuropsychological Test Battery for Children, designed for children between 5 and 8 years of age.[4] Both batteries, which are described in Table 22-2, contain a variety of cognitive and perceptual-motor tests, some of which also appear in the adult battery and some of which were especially designed for young children. The complete Halstead battery also includes the administration of an intelligence test.

Information about the reliability and validity of the two batteries is scarce. In addition, norms are extremely limited. Therefore, their use depends on the clinical sophistication of the examiner. In one study (Selz & Reitan, 1979), the Halstead Neuropsychological Test Battery, together with some additional tests, was successful in classifying children, ages 9 to 14 years, into one of three groups (normal, learning-disabled, and brain-damaged) with 73 percent accuracy. Selz and Reitan also present a useful table for scoring the child's performance on the battery and on other tests. Exhibit 22-2 (p. 455) presents a case illustrating the use of the Halstead battery, the WISC-R, and other assessment tools.

Individual Intelligence Tests and Brain Damage in Children

We now focus briefly on how the Stanford-Binet and WISC-R can aid in the assessment of brain damage. These representative tests, as well as others, provide a standardized series of tasks that can be used to evaluate the cognitive and visual-motor skills of brain-injured children. Brain-injured children may show extreme variability in their subtest scores (Rudel, Teuber, & Twitchell, 1974). In some cases there may be as much as a 30-point difference between the Verbal and Performance Scale IQs, while in others there is little difference. Subtest scores may range from considerably above average to below average or even retarded levels. Consequently, there is no single pattern of scores that is revealing of brain damage. Even though brain-damaged children may perform in the average range, they may have difficulties in sustaining attention and in filtering salient stimuli from their background (Hutt, 1976).

Intelligence tests permit the study not only of patterns of test performance but also of numerous qualitative indices that reveal difficulties with cognitive efficiency and control, such as perseveration, confusion, conceptual and reasoning difficulties, attention difficulties, memory difficulties, and visual-motor difficulties. Some of these difficulties may reflect compensatory adjustments associated with brain damage, while others are a more direct expression of the

TABLE 22-2. Description of the Halstead Neuropsychological Test Battery for Children and the Reitan-Indiana Neuropsychological Test Battery

Test	Description
Category Test[a]	Measures concept formation and requires child to find a reason (or rule) for comparing or sorting objects.
Tactual Performance Test[a]	Measures somatosensory and sensorimotor ability; requires child to place blocks with dominant hand alone, nondominant hand alone, and with both hands in appropriate recess while blindfolded.
Finger Tapping Test[a]	Measures fine motor speed and requires child to press and release a lever like a telegraph key as fast as possible.
Matching Pictures Test[b]	Measures perceptual recognition and requires child to match figures at the top of a page with figures at the bottom of the page.
Individual Performance Test[b] Matching Figures	Measures perception and requires child to match different complex figures.
Star	Measures visual-motor ability and requires child to copy a star.
Matching Vs	Measures perception and requires child to match "Vs."
Concentric Squares	Measures visual-motor ability and requires child to copy a series of concentric squares.
Marching Test[b]	Measures gross motor control and requires child (a) to connect a series of circles with a crayon in a given order with right hand alone and with left hand alone and (b) to reproduce examiner's finger and arm movements.
Progressive Figures Test[b]	Measures flexibility and abstraction and requires child to connect several figures, each consisting of a small shape contained within a large shape.
Color Form Test[b]	Measures flexibility and abstraction and requires child to connect color shapes, first by color and then by shape.
Target Test[b]	Measures memory for figures and requires child to reproduce a visually presented pattern after a three-second delay.
Rhythm Test[c]	Measures alertness, sustained attention, and auditory perception and requires child to indicate whether two rhythms are the same or different.
Speech Sounds Perception Test[c]	Measures auditory perception and auditory-visual integration and requires child to indicate, after listening to a word on tape, which of four alternative spellings represents the word.
Aphasia Screening Test[a]	Measures expressive and receptive language functions and laterality and requires child to name common objects, spell, identify numbers and letters, read, write, calculate, understand spoken language, identify body parts, and differentiate between right and left.
Trail Making Test (Parts A and B)[c]	Measures appreciation of symbolic significance of numbers and letters, scanning ability, flexibility, and speed and requires child to connect circles that are numbered.
Sensory Imperception[c]	Measures sensory-perceptual ability and requires child to perceive bilateral simultaneous sensory stimulation for tactile, auditory, and visual modalities in separate tests.
Tactile Finger Recognition[c]	Measures sensory-perceptual ability and requires child, while blindfolded, to recognize which finger is touched.
Fingertip Number Writing[c]	Measures sensory-perceptual ability and requires child, while blindfolded, to recognize numbers written on fingertips.
Tactile Form Recognition[c]	Measures sensory-perceptual ability and requires child to identify through touch alone various coins in each hand separately.
Strength of Grip[c]	Measures motor strength of upper extremities and requires child to use Smedley Hand Dynamometer with preferred hand and nonpreferred hand.

Note. The WISC-R (or WAIS-R) is often administered as part of the complete battery.

[a]This test appears both on the Halstead Neuropsychological Test Battery for Children and on the Reitan-Indiana Neuropsychological Test Battery.
[b]This test appears only on the Reitan-Indiana Neuropsychological Test Battery.
[c]This test appears only on the Halstead Neuropsychological Test Battery for Children.

EXHIBIT 22-2.   Psychological Evaluation: Brain Damage as a Result of a Brain Tumor

Name: Steve
Birth date: January 2, 1965
Age: 15 years, 4 months
Dates of examination: May 3–5, 1980
Date of report: May 5, 1980
Grade: 10th

Tests Administered

Trail-Making Test:
Part A—74 seconds 0 errors
Part B—253 seconds 3 errors

Strength of Grip:
Dominant hand—12 kilograms
Nondominant hand—11 kilograms

Reitan-Kløve Tactile Form Recognition Test:
Dominant hand—0 errors, 27 seconds
Nondominant hand—2 errors, 26 seconds

Category Test: score—108.

Seashore Rhythm Test: raw score—23.

Finger Oscillation Test:
Dominant hand—29
Nondominant hand—16

Tactual Performance Test:
Dominant hand—greater than 15 minutes
Nondominant hand—discontinued

Wechsler Intelligence Scale for Children–Revised:

VERBAL SCALE		PERFORMANCE SCALE	
Information	7	Picture Completion	1
Similarities	7	Picture Arrangement	1
Arithmetic	11	Block Design	1
Vocabulary	7	Object Assembly	1
Comprehension	8	Coding	1
Digit Span	12		

Verbal Scale IQ = 89
Performance Scale IQ = 39
Full Scale IQ = 63 ± 5 at the 90 percent confidence level

Wechsler Memory Scale: Informally administered
McCarthy Scales of Children's Abilities—Verbal Memory subtest
Raven's Progressive Matrices: Rank = 5th percentile
Detroit Test of Learning Aptitude—Visual Attention Span for Objects subtest
Aphasic Screening Test

Bender Visual Motor Gestalt Test:

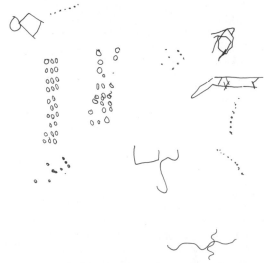

Reason for Referral

Steve was referred for a neuropsychological evaluation in order to assist in establishing treatment and educational planning efforts. The evaluation will provide base line levels of current performance that can be used to measure the extent of change as a result of remediation efforts.

Background Information

Approximately one year ago Steve underwent brain surgery when a tumor (pineal body tumor) was removed. Additional intervention included twenty-seven cobalt treatments. Two months after the operation, Steve went into a semicomatose state that lasted for almost five months. Before the surgery, he was performing adequately in school.

Behavioral Observations

Steve is a 15-year-4-month-old male who was seen on several occasions during the first week of May, 1979. When seen initially, he was wheelchair-bound due to difficulties with balance, but on later visits ambulation was independent with only minimal guidance necessary. Balance was still awkward, and weakness on the left side remains a prominent feature.

Steve's speech was generally flat, with little variation in stress or spacing of words. Specific features included a tendency to "trail off," slur words, and search for words. In general, his speech was intelligible, although concrete and with an impaired understanding of verbal metaphor, analogy, and humor.

EXHIBIT 22-2   (cont.)

Considerable fluctuations in attention and concentration were noted, ranging from an alert state to drowsy dozing off. Work periods were generally limited to thirty or forty-five minutes by Steve's fatigability. Periodic repetitive motor acts, such as brushing a paper on the desk or snatching at the air, as well as oscillating eye movements prior to dozing off suggest the presence of some seizure activity. When Steve was alert, he was cooperative and highly motivated, as evidenced by his concern over his performance and level of achievement. He frequently made self-derogatory comments, particularly when he was unable to remember answers that he thought he should know.

Steve demonstrated marked impairment in both visual and verbal memory functions. He was unable to remember the location of his bed or recall information about just finished conversations. Steve is relating at an appropriate social level, given his status. However, his range of overt affective response appears quite limited.

Test Results

On the WISC-R, Steve showed a marked discrepancy between his Verbal Scale IQ of 89 (24th percentile) and his Performance Scale IQ of 39 (less than 1st percentile). His Full Scale IQ of 63 ± 5 falls into the Mentally Retarded range of functioning. In light of the fact that his functioning prior to the surgery was at a normal level, the present results indicate that there has been a significant loss of functioning, particularly in performance skills. The Verbal IQ would appear to be a better estimate of his learning potential than either the Full Scale IQ or Performance IQ.

His performance on verbal tasks that rely on previously learned information was at a below-average level. He displayed a marked tendency for concreteness on the Aphasic Screening Test and whenever understanding of metaphor was required. For example, when he entered my office as I was finishing a project, I stated that I would meet with him as soon as I "put the last bit of icing on this cake." Steve then replied, "Make mine strawberry."

Tasks that require flexible thinking and rapid adjustment of set were performed with significant difficulty. For example, it took him five times longer to complete the Trail Making Test than most children of his chronological age. In addition, hypothesis testing and concept formation, as measured by the Category Test of the Halstead-Reitan Battery, are considerably hampered.

Visual field testing indicated that Steve is unable to see material presented within his left visual field. Thus, his visual constructive skills, such as construction of puzzles or comic strips, were severely impaired. Successful performance on the Raven's Progressive Matrices Test was limited to those items requiring numerical reasoning or a simple match-to-sample. More complex problems requiring visual-spatial orientation or abstract visual problem-solving skills were failed.

Further evidence of visual-spatial difficulties was shown on the Bender Visual Motor Gestalt Test. A slow response style, momentary absences, and errors of rotation and integration attest to his extremely inadequate visual-constructive abilities, which were at the level of an average 6-year-old child.

Steve's ability for immediate visual memory was at a 7-year-3-month-old level as measured by the Visual Attention Span for Objects subtest of the Detroit Tests of Learning Aptitude. More severe impairment was noted when there was a short lapse between the presentation of stimuli and the request for recall. Informal corroboration of the severity of his visual memory deficit was illustrated by an inability to remember how to return to his ward when standing in the corridor next to the ward. His marked anxiety over "getting lost" is seen to be a reflection of his current visual-spatial memory deficit.

In one area of short-term memory ability (measured by the Digit Span subtest on the WISC-R), his performance was average. This suggests that he at least can mobilize his attention adequately for a short-term immediate memory task. However, as noted above, other forms of memory are impaired. The decay in memory abilities over time demonstrated for visual memory tasks was also shown on verbal memory tasks. When required to recall details from a story immediately, he was able to respond with six of a possible eleven (a 6 year level); however, when a fifteen to thirty second delay was introduced, he could recall none of the story details. His memory impairment appears to be in areas requiring the ability to consolidate or organize incoming stimuli for relatively long-term retention.

The above findings, along with his performance on the sensory-perceptual tests of the Halstead-Reitan Battery, suggest that right hemisphere cerebral dysfunction is present to an even greater extent than left hemisphere dysfunction. Stimulation of the left side of his body was frequently not perceived. Likewise, inability to identify shapes and numbers tactually, as well as

EXHIBIT 22-2   (cont.)

only 50 percent accuracy in finger recognition, bears witness to hampered right cerebral functioning.

Summary and General Impressions

In summary, Steve is a 15-year-2-month-old male who was seen for a neuropsychological evaluation in order to determine areas of strengths and weaknesses following excision and cobalt treatment of a brain tumor. Steve manifests evidence of diffuse cerebral dysfunction, with the most specific impairment found on tasks requiring right cerebral hemispheric integrity.

Vebal cognitive skills on the Wechsler Intelligence Scale for Children–Revised were in the Low Average range, while nonverbal cognitive skills were extremely deficient. A left visual field impairment was found (homonymous hemianopsia). Neuropsychological tests of the Halstead-Reitan Battery examining lateralized functioning consistently indicated difficulty in perceiving tactual stimuli to the left side of the body, compared to the right side.

Recent memory skills in both visual and verbal modalities currently are significantly impaired, with the exception of adequate short-term memory for digits. Illustrative of his memory difficulties are Steve's inability to remember the location of his bed in his room, to draw geometric designs from memory, to recall aspects of previous conversations, or to recall tasks worked on when questioned following the evaluation session.

Alertness varies, and Steve frequently "falls asleep" during work periods. Repetitive behavior that may have represented seizure activity was observed. Essentially, Steve related well given the above-mentioned deficits. However, on several occasions, episodes of anxiety were observed, seemingly as a result of his current memory impairment.

Recommendations

1. Various approaches to assist Steve in coping with his current memory impairment should be attempted. For example, writing out a schedule of daily activities and noting who is responsible for those activities would be quite helpful (e.g., "school meets at 10:00 a.m.," "the teacher's name is . . . "). Using words, simple pictures, stick figures, or other ways of presenting a schedule to Steve should be explored. Identifying possessions by a simple color code may help Steve identify his bed or other possessions. Using Polaroid snapshots as a visual memory aid should also be explored. These techniques would allow him to review his schedule and to keep track of significant people in his environment, his possessions, and day-to-day activities. Hospital personnel and family might be helpful in reviewing his activities with him. Having Steve carry a pad or jot down concerns, questions, or issues that he would like clarified might help in reducing episodic anxiety.

2. Training Steve to compensate for his left visual defect by scanning his environment should be undertaken. It might prove helpful to place objects in front of him, both to his right and left side, and ask him to place them where they are comfortable for him.

3. Memory training could consist of having him first describe objects in the room from left to right and then close his eyes and repeat the description.

4. Obviously, special consideration will be required to locate an appropriate school curriculum for Steve for the next semester. He will require a full complement of therapeutic interventions, including occupational therapy, physical therapy, speech and language therapy, and perhaps psychological counseling. A diagnostic-prescriptive approach with accurate base line data will prove invaluable for those therapists and teachers who are charged with the responsibility of educating and rehabilitating this youngster and planning for his future placements.

   A multidisciplinary approach will be required to maximize generalization of training from one aspect of his daily curriculum to another. In addition, a highly coordinated effort will be required so that one discipline can reinforce what another discipline is working on. Such an approach should be explored prior to inpatient discharge. Additional educational recommendations should be sought during interdisciplinary planning meetings.

5. The results of the psychological evaluation should be discussed with Steve's parents. They should have a clear understanding of his strengths and weaknesses. The need for counseling should also be explored, although I suspect that, minimally, several follow-up visits would be in order.

6. Steve should be seen for a re-evaluation prior to leaving the hospital and again in a year's time in order to determine his status at that time.

_____

Examiner

injury. Illustrations of how some of these indices appear on the Stanford-Binet are shown in Table 22-3, while those for the WISC-R are shown in Table 22-4. It is important to reiterate that on these and other tests the child's entire performance must be evaluated, along with other available life history data.

The psychological evaluation (Benton, 1955) in Exhibit 22-3 (p. 461) shows how the Stanford-Binet can be helpful in the evaluation of brain damage. The evaluation describes a child whose disturbances in behavior were the first symptoms of an expanding brain tumor. As can be seen in the report, the nature of John's behavior disorder was so congruent with his life situation that a psychogenic etiology was repeatedly suggested. A close study of the results of psychological testing disclosed an intellectual impairment of an organic type in the earliest stages, when physical and neurological signs of a decisive or convincing nature were not observable. Benton pointed out that the disturbance in visual perception was elicited by a memory task and not by a visual copying task. Further, the boy did not have a general disturbance in memory but one primarily involving visual memory.

The case illustrates the principles that (a) complex behavioral processes are sensitive to the effects of a cerebral lesion and (b) psychogenic and organic factors can interact to cause behavioral deviations. The presence of a cerebral disease was established soon after the psychological evaluation. In succession, the child had a grand-mal seizure and displayed perseveration in speech and behavior. A progressive behavioral deterioration ensued, and, after some months, an exploratory craniotomy was performed. It revealed the presence of a large tumor occupying the greater portion of the left parietal lobe and parts of the left temporal lobe. Thus, the test findings accurately predicted the presence of serious cerebral disease.

While recognizing the valuable role intelligence tests play in the neuropsychological battery, it is still important to recognize that most tests and subtests do not allow us to specify the exact function that is required to perform the test. For example, the written responses to the Coding subtest are the end product of the integration of visual, perceptual, oculomotor, fine manual motor, and mental functions. Disturbances in any or all of these functions may result in poor performance. Consequently, there is no simple way of establishing which one or combination of the multiple possible factors accounts for the deficit. Attempts must be made to rule out separately defects in each of the possible component areas that are related to performance on the subtest (or test) (Smith, 1975).

Intelligence tests (and also other ability tests) can be varied in order to evaluate the adequacy of performance using different sensory modalities (Smith, 1975). For example, on the Digit Span subtest of the WISC-R or Stanford-Binet, the child's spoken responses can be compared with those that are written in order to examine the adequacy of different response modalities to the same stimulus (or test of mental function—short-term auditory memory). A child might also be asked to copy a circle from a stimulus figure or to draw a circle from an oral request only.

Other Procedures Useful in the Assessment of Brain Damage in Children

In addition to the Halstead and Reitan-Indiana batteries, other assessment procedures are useful in the assessment of brain damage in children. Chapter 16, which discusses the Bender-Gestalt, also presents guidelines for the assessment of brain damage. The Bender-Gestalt also can be administered first as a memory test and then as a copying test. This is an example of testing different mental functions—short-term visual memory and visual perception—that involve the same modalities in perception and task execution.

The Revised Visual Retention Test (Benton, 1963) assesses visual memory, visual perception, and visuoconstructive abilities. It has three forms, with ten designs in each form. The child is required to copy the designs directly and to draw them from memory. The test is scored by counting the number of correct responses or the number

TABLE 22-3.   Possible Indications of Brain Damage on the Stanford-Binet

Sign	Description
Perseveration	Perseveration may be shown on the Mutilated Pictures test when the child correctly answers the teapot item by stating that the handle is missing, and then says that the handle is missing from the glove item. The mental set to answer by looking for missing details, a set which is correct for the Mutilated Pictures test, may also carry over to other tests. For example, the first test at year level VII, Picture Absurdities I, requires that children state what is funny about the picture. If they are perseverating, they might look for missing details on the Picture Absurdities items instead of looking for funny or foolish details (Mecham et al., 1966).
Signs of Confusion	Brain-injured children may demonstrate more confusion on the Similarities, Pictorial Likenesses and Differences, Repeating Digits, Memory for Sentences, Memory for Stories, and drawing tests than on other Stanford-Binet tests (Burgemeister, 1962).
Conceptual and Reasoning Difficulties	Reasoning difficulties may be shown by brain-injured children on the Similarities, Opposite Analogies, Verbal Absurdities, Orientation, Problem Situation, and Picture Absurdities tests. Failures arise because the children may not be able to coordinate multiple relationships. They may cling to practical details and only attend to one or several parts of a problem without seeing the correct interrelationships among the parts (Taylor, 1961).
Attention to Small Details	Brain-injured children may solve problems involving a small missing detail more easily than problems involving a large missing detail. For example, on the Multilated Pictures test, pictures may be solved with greater ease if they show the missing handle on the teapot or the missing shoelace than if they contain more obvious incongruities (Taylor, 1961).
Memory Difficulty	Brain-injured children may obtain considerably higher scores on Repeating Digits Forward than on Repeating Digits Backward (Taylor, 1961). Auditory memory facilitates recall on Digits Forward, but the difficulty brain-injured children have in organizing and in remanipulating mentally what they have memorized may lead to failures on Digits Backward. Digits Backward is also a more demanding task than Digits Forward, and the trauma or illness associated with the brain injury may impede the child's ability to sustain the effort needed for successful completion of the task. While a significant and consistent discrepancy between Digits Forward and Digits Backward, in favor of Digits Forward, may suggest organic involvement, it is important to recognize that failure on Digits Backward also may be a function of attention difficulties which stem from causes other than brain injury.
Visual-Motor and Visual-Perceptual Difficulties	Children with visual-motor difficulties may establish a basal year level which is several years below their chronological age, because many early year levels include a test requiring well-integrated visual-perceptual-motor skills and organization (Coleman & Dawson, 1969). Example of tests requiring visual-motor skills are Picture Completion: Man (year level V), Paper Folding: Triangle (year level V), Maze Tracing (year level VI), Copying a Diamond (year level VII), and Paper Cutting (year level IX). Visual-motor handicaps also may be revealed by failures on the Three-Hole Form Board: Rotated (year level II-6) and on the Block Building: Bridge (year level III) tests in the context of successful performance on other tests at the same year levels (Reynell, 1970). Children with visual-motor handicaps who are between 2 and 3 years old may refuse to do the spatial tasks on the Stanford-Binet, but not other tasks (Gibbs, 1959). On the Picture Vocabulary test, young children with visual-perceptual difficulties may not be able to name the objects, although they may know the objects; instead, one part of the picture may be named.

TABLE 22-4. Possible Indications of Brain Damage on WISC-R Subtests and Scales

Subtest or Scale	Possible Indications of Brain Damage
Similarities	Integration difficulties—difficulty in abstracting essential from nonessential attributes for the two stimulus words and then relating them and verbalizing their relationship (Ross, 1959)
Digit Span	Obtaining considerably higher scores on Digits Forward than on Digits Backward
Picture Completion	(a) This subtest may be relatively resistant to brain impairment; therefore it may be used as a basis by which to infer the child's premorbid intellectual level. (b) Some children may have more successes with items involving small missing details than with other items, while other children may respond to irrelevant details.
Block Design	(a) Distractibility—difficulty in ignoring irrelevant stimuli; (b) perseveration—continuation of behavior after it is no longer appropriate; (c) integration difficulties—responding to stimuli in terms of parts or segments, with difficulty in bringing the parts together to form a whole; fumbling; angulation difficulties; grossly inaccurate reproductions; spacing isolated blocks far apart, lined in a row, or joined at their angles; (d) figure-ground disturbance—difficulties in differentiating foreground from background; (e) shifting difficulties—may not know when they have finished with the design, may have difficulty attending simultaneously to color and pattern, may get stuck at certain parts of the design; (f) may be able to discriminate the Block Design patterns, but not reproduce the designs because of an inability to translate a correct perceptual recognition into an appropriate action pattern (Bortner & Birch, 1962)
Object Assembly	(a) Integration difficulties—difficulty in integrating the memory of the percept, the discrete pieces, and the motor performance necessary to assemble the pieces correctly (Ross, 1959); (b) may be able to say what the object is supposed to be, but may not be able to assemble the pieces or to complete the entire picture (Ross, 1959)
Coding	(a) Perseveration—copying the same symbol for different numbers (may suggest failure to understand directions); (b) integration difficulties—difficulty in integrating visual perception and motor performance; (c) rotation of figures; (d) extreme caution and slowness
Verbal-Performance Discrepancy	(a) Brain damage is not necessarily associated with lower scores on the Performance Scale than on the Verbal Scale (McFie, 1969). However, a Verbal IQ that is 25 or more points above the Performance IQ may be suggestive of brain injury in children suspected of brain injury (Holroyd & Wright, 1965). (b) While the Verbal-Performance discrepancy cannot be used by itself as a reliable method for detecting the lateralization of cerebral lesions (Smith, 1975), there is some evidence that in brain-damaged children, those with Verbal IQs higher than Performance IQs by 10 or more points are more likely to have right hemisphere symptoms, whereas those with Performance IQs higher than Verbal IQs by 10 or more points have symptoms that appear equally in the left and right hemispheres (Rudel, Teuber, & Twitchell, 1974).

of errors. The Revised Visual Retention Test is similar to the Bender-Gestalt, but contains more complex stimuli. Detailed norms have been developed by Rice (1972). The Bruininks-Oseretsky Test of Motor Proficiency (see Chapter 16) may also contribute to the assessment of neurological dysfunction.

McFie (1975) suggested that the child's Bender-Gestalt performance be compared to his or her performance on the Revised Visual Retention Test. The Bender-Gestalt, according to McFie, may involve a greater degree of constructional ability (left parietal lobe) than the Revised Visual Retention Test, which may tap spatial perception (right

EXHIBIT 22-3.   Psychological Evaluation: Psychogenic Symptoms Mask Cerebral Disease in a Nine-Year-Old Boy

Name: John
Date of birth: July 10, 1942
Chronological age: 9-3
Date of examination: October 15, 1951
Date of report: October 18, 1951
Grade: 3rd

Tests Administered

Stanford-Binet, Form L
Visual Retention Test
Draw-A-Man

Reason for Referral

John, a 9-year-old boy, was referred for evaluation by his family physician to a child guidance clinic because of a longstanding emotional instability, tremulousness that had been noted during the past two months, and a decline in the quality of his school work, especially in arithmetic, over the past year.

Background Information

Early physical development followed normal milestones, with no serious illnesses. John talked quite early and was toilet trained easily. Progress through school was normal.

John's mother is a socially and financially ambitious woman who appears to be the dominant family member, often speaking not only for her children but also for her husband. She believes in firm, authoritarian discipline, which takes the form of corporal punishment and restriction. She tolerates little deviation from the "right way." John's rude conduct in front of her friends often precipitates conflict between mother and son. John's conduct problem at home is not seen at school, where his teacher reported that he had never presented a conduct problem. John's father gave the impression of a pleasant, well-meaning, but anxious man.

John has a younger 2-year-old brother and shows no overt hostility toward him. However, John's behavior disorder started shortly after his brother's birth. His tremulousness was first observed when he tried to feed his baby brother and his hand shook so much that he was not able to bring the spoon directly to the baby's mouth.

John had been seen by a psychologist and two pediatric neurologists. Their impression was that his behavioral symptoms were attributable to psychogenic factors, especially the intense conflict between John and his mother.

Behavioral Observations

During the examination John was posturally tense and showed a variety of anxious movements. Speech was often explosive, as if delivered under great tension. His manner of answering questions betrayed considerable insecurity and lack of confidence. Occasionally there were inexplicable delays in responding to a question or a request. Nevertheless, good rapport appeared to be present and John showed no anxiety in relation to the examiner. Physical contacts, such as pats on the shoulder or holding his hand in tests of stereognosis and of the finger schema, seemed to relax him. He showed no appreciable reaction to verbal praise. He worked steadily and without signs of fatigue throughout a long examination session. In working on problems and drawings John showed a certain "stickiness"—a tendency never to finish with them—which suggested to the examiner some rigidity and perseveration.

Test Results and Clinical Impressions

On the Stanford-Binet, Form L, John, with a chronological age of 9 years, 3 months, attained a mental age of 7 years, 1 month. The resulting IQ of 77 ± 7 places him at the 8th percentile and in the Borderline range. The chances are about 95 out of 100 that his true IQ lies in the 70 to 84 range. In view of John's history of essentially normal intellectual functioning, this finding suggests a significant decline in intellectual functioning.

The details of his performance on the Binet revealed some striking incapacities. He passed all tests on Year V. On Year VI he failed the Maze Tracing subtest, showing complete inability to grasp the implications of the problem. In the Pictorial Likenesses and Differences subtest of Year VI, he "inexplicably" equated a table and a chair, this gross error suggesting a serious oscillation in level of visual perception. Absurdities, of both pictorial and verbal type, and questions of practical judgment were consistently failed. Even vocabulary level was strikingly poor, being no higher than the obtained mental age. In contrast, tests of auditory memory were done fairly well. He was able to repeat five digits and to reverse four digits. Repetition of Sentences was successful through the level of Year VIII, and he succeeded on the ideational memory test (Memory for Stories) at Year VIII. That his inefficiency was not caused by undue emotional tension was suggested by his good performances on repetition of digits, reversal of digits, and repetition of

EXHIBIT 22-3   (cont.)

sentences, tasks which are believed to be particularly susceptible to the influence of emotional disturbance.

Arithmetic calculation was extremely poor. He was able to do simple single-digit addition but had difficulty with single-digit subtraction, even when the calculations were given in written form. It was evident that a significant impairment in this area was present.

The disturbance in visual perception that was suggested by the failure to discriminate between a table and a chair in the test of Pictorial Likenesses and Differences was strikingly confirmed by the boy's performance on the Visual Retention Test, a memory-for-design task primarily devised to disclose impairment in perceptual-motor functions resulting from cerebral lesions. On Form D of the test, John not only failed to reproduce a single design correctly, but also showed a number of difficulties that suggested an organic defect. These difficulties included omissions of major elements of designs, inversions, misplacements of parts of the design within a figure, fragmentation, disproportionate size, and omission of a figure without leaving space for it.

John's performance on the Visual Retention Test was so poor that the examiner wondered if perhaps he might be suffering from a basic visual handicap or graphomotor disability. To check this possibility, he was asked to copy some of the designs. He copied the designs quite accurately, the only deviant feature of performance being a certain degree of tremulousness. On the Draw-A-Man test his performance was appropriate for his age.

He read fluently and with understanding. Stereognostic capacity was unimpaired. He was able to point to all parts of his body and showed no disturbances in the identification of his fingers or in right-left identification, functions that may be impaired in children with brain injury.

Recommendations

1. In view of the pattern of John's performance on the psychological test battery, further neurological evaluation and follow-up seems warranted.
2. Special school placement is recommended to accommodate John's specific learning disabilities. The educational program should include an emphasis on auditory learning and remediation efforts directed at arithmetical calculations and vocabulary, with small increments assigned to ensure success and mastery.
3. Family counseling including not only John and his mother but also his father is strongly recommended. Positive parenting methods should be presented in order to increase parental options in child-raising techniques.

Summary

John is a 9-year-old boy who was referred for psychological evaluation following a period of declining school performance and behavior disorders. He achieved a mental age of 7-1 on the Stanford-Binet, Form L and an IQ of 77 ± 7, which places him at the 8th percentile and in the Borderline range. Although disturbed family relations, negative neurological findings, and the constellation of his behavioral symptoms initially suggested a psychogenic etiology, extensive psychological testing revealed a distinct visual impairment involving memory, which suggested the presence of an organic defect. Specifically, John confused a table and chair, copied designs but was unable to reproduce designs from memory, showed a certain degree of perseveration, and failed simple subtraction problems. Recommendations included further neurological testing, special school placement, and family counseling.

Examiner

Source: Adapted from Benton (1955).

parietal lobe). He cautions that neither of these two tests permits us to differentiate among (a) visual perception, (b) retention of the material perceived, and (c) the motor response.

The Purdue Pegboard test provides measures of sensorimotor functions, particularly fine motor coordination, that are essentially independent of educational achievement. In the first three parts of the test, the child places pegs in a pegboard with the preferred hand, with the nonpreferred hand, and with both hands for thirty-second periods. In the fourth part of the test, the child forms "assemblies" consisting of a peg, a washer, a collar, and another washer.

The test is a quick, simple instrument that has value for predicting the presence and laterality of cerebral lesions (Smith, 1975). Norms for children aged 5 through 16 years are presented by Gardner (1979). Tests such as the Purdue Pegboard may reveal deficits indicating the presence of neurological disease in children (or adults) who have high intellectual capacities and who are only slightly impaired. These tests also permit comparison of lower level functions with measures of higher level cognitive functions, and provide information about lateralized or bilateral deficits.

A useful procedure for obtaining information about the child's understanding of right and left is shown in Table 22-5. The results must be interpreted in relation to the child's age. Another procedure that may be used is the Finger Localization Test which is shown in Table 22-6. The results of this test, too, must be considered in relation to the child's age.

Another test that may prove to be useful in the assessment of brain damage is the Progressive Matrices (see Chapter 14 for a description of the test). Individuals who perform more poorly on the Progressive Matrices than on verbal intelligence tests, and who are suspected of having brain damage, may be suffering from spatial difficulties. Such spatial difficulties may be suggestive of lesions in the occipitoparietal area of the cortex (Luria, 1966a) or occasionally in the frontal lobes. Brain-injured individuals who perform poorly on the test may only be able to concentrate on one aspect of the stimulus array, and thus be unable to integrate the necessary spatial relationships to arrive at a correct response. In such cases, the score on the Progressive Matrices should not be used as an indication of intelligence.

The Token Test for Children (DiSimoni, 1978) also is useful as a screening test of receptive language (auditory comprehension) for children between the ages of 3-0 and 12-5 years. The test requires children to manipulate tokens in response to commands given by the examiner, such as "Touch the red circle." The tokens vary along the dimensions of color, shape, and size. It is a sensitive measure for identifying mild receptive disturbances in aphasic children who have passed other auditory tests. While the test is only a screening device because its psychometric properties are not well established, it appears to be a useful instrument for the assessment of aphasia.

Comment on Neuropsychological Assessment

All sources of information should be considered in the neuropsychological evaluation, including case history material, neurological evaluation, current test results, previous test results (where available), and behavioral observations. After a careful consideration

---

TABLE 22-5.   Right-Left Discrimination Test

1. Raise your right hand.
2. Touch your left ear.
3. Point to your right eye.
4. Raise your left hand.
5. Show me your right leg.
6. Show me your left leg.
7. Point to your left ear with your right hand.
8. Point to the wall on your right.
9. Examiner touches the child's left hand: "Which hand is this?"
10. Examiner touches his or her own right eye: "Which eye is this?"
11. Examiner touches his or her own right hand: "Which hand is this?"
12. Examiner touches his or her own left ear: "Which ear is this?"
13. With the child's eyes closed, the examiner touches the child's left ear: "Which ear is this?"
14. Examiner touches his or her own left hand: "Which hand is this?"
15. Examiner touches his or her own left eye: "Which eye is this?"
16. Examiner touches child's right hand: "Which hand is this?"

Scoring: One point for each correct response.

Adapted from Belmont and Birch (1965) and from Croxen and Lytton (1971).

TABLE 22-6. Finger Localization Test

In administering the three subtests in the Finger Localization Test, two numbered diagrams of a right and left hand are shown to the child. The child "localizes" by indicating the finger touched by pointing to it on the diagram, or by indicating its number, or by naming it.

I.	Visual Subtest	With the child's hand visible to him or her, the child is asked to localize single fingers that have been tactually stimulated. Ten stimulations are given to each hand. Each finger is touched twice in a randomized order. Maximum Score = 20.
II.	Tactual Subtest	With the child's hand hidden from his or her view, the child is asked to localize single fingers that have been tactually stimulated. Ten stimulations are given to each hand. Each finger is touched twice in a randomized order. Maximum Score = 20.
III.	Tactual Pairs Subtest	This subtest is like the Tactual Subtest, but the child localizes two fingers that have been simultaneously tactually stimulated. Ten stimulations are given to each hand. Every possible combination is touched on each hand. Maximum Score = 20.

Scoring: One point for each correct response. For the Tactual Pairs Subtest, a misidentification of either one or both of the fingers is counted as a single error. Maximum Score = 60.

Adapted from Benton (1959) and from Croxen and Lytton (1971).

of all relevant sources, judgments should be made about many different cognitive and perceptual-motor functions, including the following (Rie, Rie, Stewart, & Ambuel, 1976):

1. *integrative-synthesizing skills* (ability to organize, combine, and restructure data so as to be able to arrive at a correct solution or conclusion);
2. *degree of perseveration* (continued use of a response when it has ceased to be relevant);
3. *ability to make conceptual shifts* (ability to change focus from one concept or idea to another, to alter boundaries or limits of an idea, and to avoid continued preoccupation with a thought that is no longer relevant);
4. *degree of concrete thinking* (extent to which there is undue focus or dependency on immediately present stimuli, failure to think abstractly or to generalize relative to age expectations, and excessively literal interpretations);
5. *word recall ability* (ability to select and use words with reasonable fluency, ability to recall words immediately in a brief interchange, ability to use words to convey adequately the desired meanings);
6. *degree of word misuse* (degree to which words are selected and used that are incorrect but have some irrelevant or tangential relation to the word intended, such as a word having a similar sound or slightly different meaning or one referring to the same general class of objects but to an incorrect subgroup—e.g., "doggie" for animals of different species).

The more problems that are revealed in these and other areas, the greater the possibility of cognitive dysfunction suggestive of brain damage. This statement, however, must be tempered by a consideration of the extent to which the environment may have contributed to the development of any cognitive, perceptual-motor, or behavioral deficits (Rie et al., 1976). Environmental considerations are important, especially when working with children coming from adverse environments. In such cases, the environment may have contributed to their poor performance, and some judgment must be made concerning the extent to which this is so. If the environment looms large as a possible contributing factor to the child's poor performance, then a diagnosis of brain damage may be less appropriate, unless there are conclusive signs of brain damage forthcoming from the neurological examination and other medical procedures.

Some major assessment findings with brain-damaged children are as follows:

1. The effects of brain damage on test performance may be general (i.e., a global reduction in intelligence) or specific (i.e., impairment of selective areas of cognitive functioning).
2. Brain-damaged children often show lower IQs than normal children (Benton, 1974; Rutter, 1976). Perhaps the best single index of the presence of brain damage is lower than expected total scores (for age, education, socioeconomic status, and related factors) derived from a test or battery of tests.
3. There are a variety of possible impairments in brain-damaged children, including impairments in visual and auditory memory, constructional performance, motor skills and motor control, right-left discrimination, and finger recognition (Benton, 1974).
4. Similar test and behavioral patterns or scores may be related either to psychogenic or to organic factors. Therefore, it is essential to investigate thoroughly the child's entire performance and history before inferring from certain indices that brain damage may be present. For example, low test scores may be related to such factors as motivational difficulties, anxiety, educational deficits, physical handicaps (such as impaired hearing or vision), cultural factors, developmental delays, or cerebral impairment. Therefore, the level of performance, per se, should not be stressed as a key diagnostic method to evaluate brain damage, unless other factors are ruled out.
5. There are no patterns on the WISC-R—such as Verbal-Performance discrepancies, subtest patterning, or individual subtest scores—that reliably differentiate brain-damaged children from emotionally disturbed children, normal children, or both.[5]
6. WISC-R patterns do not have much relation to the extent of EEG deviations from normality.[6]

Differential Diagnosis of Brain Damage

While some of the symptoms of brain-injured children also are associated with non-brain-injured children who have psychiatric problems, closer examination sometimes reveals subtle differences between the two. For example, the compulsive behavior of children with organic dysfunction is qualitatively different from that of obsessive-compulsive children (Kernberg, 1969). Strict routines, constancy, and perseveration of sameness are ways brain-injured children cope with the enviroment; for neurotic children they may reflect personality styles. For example, anxiety in neurotic children may be aroused by the symbolic meaning of order and disorder and not by the physical disarrangement of objects.

Some of the symptoms that handicapped children display, such as hearing deficits, mental retardation, autism, emotional instability, and delayed speech, are similar to those displayed by aphasic children, thus making a differential diagnosis difficult (McGinnis, 1963). For example, the emotionally disturbed behavior of the aphasic child, which may be a consequence of frustration caused by the inability to communicate and to understand language, is difficult to differentiate from the emotionally disturbed behavior of the child who does not have brain damage. Children with aphasia share with autistic children abnormal responses to sounds, delay in language acquisition, and articulation difficulties. However, they usually do not manifest the perceptual or motor disturbances characteristic of autistic children. Further, aphasic children can relate to others by nonverbal gestures and expressions; they are sensitive to gestures and expressions of others; they can learn to point toward desired objects; and they show communicative intent and emotion when they acquire speech (Ornitz & Ritvo, 1976).

Other conditions can be distinguished from aphasia more easily. Children with psychosis display aberrant social behavior that sets them apart from aphasic children. Psychotic children who do not speak by 4 or 5 years of age may acquire speech and language rapidly once training has begun. Aphasic children, in contrast, will need much help. A trial teaching or evaluation period should be used whenever there is doubt about diagnosis or prognosis. A possible means of differentiating cerebral palsied children with normal intelligence from mentally retarded children with delayed motor development is an analysis of overall developmental patterns: cerebral palsied children may have normal social, personal, and language development coupled with motor difficulties, whereas mentally retarded children may show a generalized delay of developmental abilities. However, in practice this differentiation may prove to be difficult because the motor deficits in cerebral palsy often produce delays in social and personal development. In addition, cerebral palsied children may have expressive disorders as part of their motor difficulties.

Summary

1. Brain damage refers to a structural or physiological change of a pathological nature in the nerve tissue of the brain. Brain injury may result from varied causes, including congenital problems, traumas, disease, and tumors. There is no one-to-one relationship between type of damage and associated deficits.

2. Both the neurologist and the psychologist contribute to the assessment of brain damage. The neurological examination is primarily concerned with the intactness of lower level functions (such as reflexes), while the neuropsychological evaluation focuses on higher level cognitive processes. Several tests are needed to evaluate brain-behavior relationships.

3. The hard signs (such as pathological reflexes) observed on a neurological examination are fairly definitive indicators of brain damage, while the soft signs (such as perceptual-motor difficulties) are not clearly associated with brain damage.

4. Many factors must be considered in evaluating the behavioral effects associated with brain damage, including (a) laterality of lesion; (b) site of lesion; (c) causal agent creating lesion; (d) course, size, and severity of lesion; (e) age when lesion occurred; (f) time between damage and testing; (g) general condition of child; (h) premorbid condition of child; and (i) child's environment.

5. Many cognitive, perceptual, and motor activities are specialized within the left and right hemispheres. The hemisphere controlling a function is contralateral to the side involved in the activity. The *left hemisphere* is seen as mediating verbal functions and uses analytic, sequential, serial, and differential processing. The *right hemisphere* is seen as mediating nonverbal functions and uses holistic, gestalt-like, parallel, and integrative processing. Some specialization of function can be detected as early as the first year of life.

6. Childhood aphasia refers to disorders in the perception and production of language that may accompany brain damage. There are two general forms of aphasia—expressive and receptive—and a number of specific forms that involve cognitive, perceptual, or motor functions. In all varieties of aphasia, the deficit usually involves the use (or interpretation) of language (or language-related) symbols.

7. The prognosis for brain-damaged children is dependent on a number of factors, including the severity of the damage, the child's age, localization of brain damage, and the occurrence of post-damage complications.

8. Brain damage in children differs from brain damage in adults in several important respects. With adults, there may be a loss of or interference with previously acquired functions; with children, there may be interference with development. Major localized

lesions, too, are less common in children than in adults. There is some evidence that children who sustain brain damage at an early age have more deficits than those who sustain damage at a later age. The older the child, the more likely it is for the deficits to be similar to those observed in adults.

9. Teaching and remediation strategies should be individually tailored to each brain-damaged child.

10. Several inferential methods are used to interpret the results of a neuropsychological evaluation, including (a) level of performance, (b) pattern of performance, (c) pathognomonic signs, and (d) comparison of performance on the two sides of the body.

11. Brain damage and its sequelae may be significant factors in increasing children's vulnerability to emotional problems.

12. There is no one-to-one relationship between brain damage and symptom formation. Moreover, because some symptoms of brain injury mimic psychiatric symptoms, the assessment process is further complicated. However, there are many symptoms in the motor, sensory, affective, cognitive, social, and personality spheres that may be suggestive of brain damage. Representative symptoms include hyperkinesis, short attention span, lability of mood, intellectual deficits, interpersonal difficulties, and disturbed self-concept.

13. The Halstead Neuropsychological Test Battery and the Reitan-Indiana Neuropsychological Test Battery for Children are excellent batteries for use in the assessment of brain damage in children.

14. Intelligence tests serve as useful tools for the assessment of brain damage. The IQ, pattern of test performance, and qualitative indices should be evaluated. Suggestive indicators of brain damage on intelligence tests include perseveration, signs of confu-

sion, conceptual and reasoning difficulties, attention to small details, memory difficulty, visual-motor difficulty, integration difficulty, distractibility, figure-ground disturbance, and shifting difficulty. Generally, there is no one pattern of scores that is indicative of brain damage.

15. Other tests useful in the assessment of brain damage include the Bender-Gestalt, Purdue Pegboard, Progressive Matrices, Revised Visual Retention Test, Bruininks-Oseretsky Test of Motor Proficiency, Token Test for Children, a right-left discrimination test, and a finger localization test.

16. On the basis of the neuropsychological evaluation, it should be possible to assess the child's abilities in each of the following areas: integrative-synthesizing skills, degree of perseveration, ability for conceptual shifts, degree of concrete thinking, word recall ability, and degree of word misuse. Difficulties in these areas are suggestive of cognitive dysfunctions that are often associated with brain damage.

17. Some of the major assessment findings with brain-damaged children indicate that in some, but not all, cases there may be a lowering of intelligence and possible impairments in perceptual, motor, and perceptual-motor areas. There are no intelligence test patterns that reliably differentiate brain-damaged children from emotionally disturbed or normal children.

18. It is not always easy to differentiate brain-injured from non-brain-injured children. The symptoms of brain-injured children may reflect their attempts to cope with the environment, while those of neurotic children may reflect their personality. Aphasic children share language disturbances with autistic children. However, aphasic children are better at relating to others than are autistic children.

CHAPTER 23

Assessment of Childhood Psychosis

Nature reveals some of her deeper secrets through the abnormal.

EDUARD C. LINDEMAN
The Democratic Way of Life—Book II

EXHIBIT 23-1. Psychological Evaluation: A Profoundly Disturbed Youngster, Possibly Classified as Childhood Schizophrenic

Name: Mark
Date of birth: January 11, 1972
Chronological age: 7-1
Date of examination: February 9, 1979
Date of report: February 13, 1979
Grade: 2nd

Reason for Referral

Mark was referred for psychological reevaluation by the Center for the Developmentally Disabled, where he has been followed since his initial evaluation when he was four years, eight months old.

Tests Administered

Wechsler Intelligence Scale for Children-Revised:

VERBAL SCALE		PERFORMANCE SCALE	
Information	6	Picture Completion	8
Similarities	9	Picture Arrangement	1
Arithmetic	6	Block Design	1
Vocabulary	2	Object Assembly	11
Comprehension	4	Coding	6

Verbal Scale IQ = 72
Performance Scale IQ = 70
Full Scale IQ = 69±3 at the 68 percent confidence level

Vineland Social Maturity Scale

Bender Visual Motor Gestalt Test:

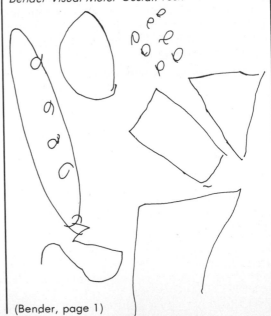

(Bender, page 1)

EXHIBIT 23-1   (cont.)

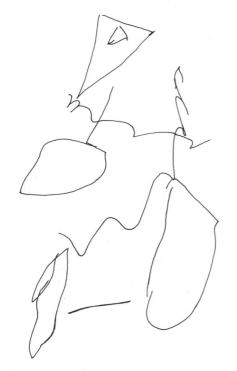

(Bender, page 2)

History

Mark was initially evaluated in 1976 because the day care center he was attending reported that his fine motor coordination appeared to be delayed. The results of the initial evaluation not only confirmed the center's suspicion, but also revealed a Borderline range of intelligence (IQ of 79 on the Stanford-Binet), accompanied by some depression and inappropriate affect. Expressive and receptive speech and language were delayed, with short incomplete sentences often marked by neologisms and jargon. There was no suggestion of a hearing loss, nor were there any positive neurological signs.

In both the first and second grades Mark has experienced problems with comprehension, especially in arithmetic. His parents are concerned, because their son is unable to answer many of his teacher's questions. However, his language has somewhat improved since the first evaluation. Mark has been having nightmares several times weekly, and frequently wets his bed. In addition, he often refuses to obey his parents and teachers and has frequent aggressive temper tantrums. He has only one friend, whom he sees only on a limited basis.

Test Observations

Mark is a tall, attractive boy. He appeared sullen and negative at first, resisting entrance to the testing room, and failing to answer questions. When he did respond, there were long hesitations between questions and responses as he appeared to ponder one single aspect or word in the question. Thus, his responses were unrelated to the questions, and his thought processes appeared to be fragmented and illogical. Periodic neologisms, frequent associative responses, and often bizarre responses were observed. For example, when asked to define a "hat," Mark said, "A hat makes brains." When asked what to do if he cut his finger, he replied "If you cut your finger you should break your hand; iron it on."

Sometimes Mark acted silly and laughed hysterically when he played with a series of words or neologisms that he had created. Echoing the examiner's words or rhyming them endlessly caused peals of humorless laughter. Often he could not focus on the essential elements of a task. He would become absorbed in irrelevant details, such as the difference in color of the fronts and backs of puzzle pieces, exclaiming, "I feel much better on the pink side."

His behavior also shifted rapidly and unpredictably from aggression to affection. For example, Mark pummeled, strangled, and swore at a stuffed bear in the room and shortly thereafter began to stroke the bear affectionately and hug it while whispering into its ear. Similarly, frequent verbal aggressive outbursts ("You stupid big mouth") were followed by friendly exchanges.

When Mark was presented with verbal items that he initially failed to understand, he became anxious and angry, and yelled at the examiner, "You stupid big mouth." When asked about this frequent remark, Mark said a big mouth is a monster. He then trailed off into illogical associative thoughts, forgetting his initial statement. Mark often seemed preoccupied during testing. Several times it seemed as though he was trying to shut out auditory stimulation by closing his eyes, or covering his face with his hands, showing a confusion in modalities. Throughout the test session, Mark seemed most comfortable when provided with gentle but firm structure. He became most anxious and disturbed when he was presented with an unstructured task.

Test Results

Mark, with a chronological age of 7-1, achieved a Verbal IQ of 72, a Performance IQ of 70, and a Full Scale IQ of 69 ± 3 on the WISC-R. This places him in the Mentally Retarded range. The chances that the range of scores from 66 to 72 includes his

EXHIBIT 23-1 (cont.)

true IQ are about 68 out of 100. His level of functioning exceeds 2 percent of the children in the standardization group, a group which is roughly representative of the United States population.

Much variability was evident in his WISC-R performance. He ranged from extremely inadequate performance in areas requiring word knowledge, interpretation of social situations, and spatial visualization (all within the 1st percentile) to average performance in verbal concept formation (37th percentile) and perceptual organization (63rd percentile). Within subtests, he often missed easy items and passed more difficult ones later. The often bizarre content and the extreme variability of scores suggests that there is impairment in his cognitive functioning.

On the Vineland Social Maturity Scale, Mark achieved a Social Age of 6-2, which is a year behind his chronological age level, and a Deviation Social Quotient of 90. He is able to bathe with assistance, go to school unattended, and print simple words. However, he cannot tell time or comb his hair. His visual-motor coordination, as measured by the Bender-Gestalt, was at the 4th percentile (Koppitz norms), indicating a serious delay in the development of these skills. His errors included collision, rotation, fragmentation, distortion of shape, and expansion.

In a free play situation, Mark continued to evidence loose thinking. While playing with a puppet, he excitedly described how a live pig went inside the skin of another pig. Although he was vague about himself and his relationships, unable to answer such questions as what grade he was in and where he lived, he talked lucidly and in detail about the book "The Wizard of Oz."

Clinical Impressions

Mark, who is functioning in the Mentally Retarded range, shows numerous social adjustment difficulties. Unevenness in development is apparent, with gross immaturities characterized by atypical and bizarre behavior. He is experiencing significant learning difficulties in a regular second-grade class. Throughout the test session there were indications of a marked behavior disorder and expressions of an aggressive and disorganized nature. Mark relates poorly to others, and is extremely sensitive to minimal pressure, either becoming verbally aggressive or attempting to screen out sounds by covering his eyes. The possibility of a childhood psychosis exists. Mark's intellectual deficits, coupled with marked behavioral and thought disturbances, suggest a diagnosis of childhood schizophrenia, which should be confirmed by psychiatric evaluation.

Recommendations

In view of the present test results and observations, it is recommended that Mark be referred for a psychiatric evaluation. EEG and neurological exams should be conducted to rule out organicity. Based on the results of this and previous evaluations, a more appropriate school setting needs to be explored for Mark (placement in an emotionally disturbed classroom). Psychotherapy for Mark and counseling for his parents is also suggested.

_____
Examiner

Childhood psychosis represents the severest form of psychopathology in childhood. Reported prevalence rates of childhood psychosis in the United States and England range from 2 to 5 per 10,000.[1] Although it is difficult to differentiate precisely among various types of childhood psychoses, four types have been described. *Infantile autism* and *childhood schizophrenia* are the two most frequent forms, while *disintegrative psychosis* and *other psychoses of childhood* are seen less frequently. (See Table 23-1 for a description of the clinical symptoms in each type of childhood psychosis.) The latter classification is used for cases that do not fit easily into the first three categories. Controversy still exists over whether or not infantile autism and childhood schizophrenia are two distinct conditions or part of the same syndrome, since they appear to have some similar as well as some distinct features. While the above classification scheme is but one of several, it is a useful working model. (Exhibit 23-1, which begins this chapter, presents a case of a 7-year-old boy who probably would be classified as having childhood schizophrenia.)

Psychotic children carrying any one of the four designations show marked deviations (a) in relationships to people and to the environment, (b) in emotional maturation, and (c) in the acquisition and integration of per-

TABLE 23-1.   Clinical Symptoms of Four Types of Childhood Psychoses

Type	Clinical Symptoms
Infantile Autism (birth to about 30 months)	Abnormal responses to auditory and visual stimuli; severe problems in the understanding of spoken language; delayed speech; echolalia, reversal of pronouns, immature grammatical structure, inability to use abstract terms; impaired social use of verbal and gestural language; impaired social relationships (impaired eye-to-eye gaze, social attachments, and cooperative play); ritualistic behavior (abnormal routines, resistance to change, attachment to odd objects, and stereotyped patterns of play); diminished capacity for abstract thought and imaginative play; intelligence variable (from mentally retarded to above normal); better rote memory and visuospatial skills than symbolic or linguistic skills
Disintegrative Psychosis (approximately 3 to 7 years of age)	Impoverishment or loss of speech and language; deterioration of language comprehension; decline of intelligence; loss of social skills; impairment of interpersonal relations; loss of interest in objects; development of stereotyped mannerisms
Schizophrenia (approximately 7 to 15 years of age)	Distortion of thinking; a sense of being controlled by alien forces; bizarre delusions; disturbed perception; abnormal affect; hallucinations; perplexity; vague, elliptical, and obscure thinking; attribution of special, usually sinister, meaning to everyday objects and situations
Other Psychoses of Childhood (after 30 months of age)	Loss of reality sense, but not as profound as in disintegrative psychosis; nonspecific disorders of psychotic intensity in mentally retarded or brain-damaged children; some features of infantile autism

Adapted from Rutter (1972).

ceptual, motor, and cognitive skills. Signs of severe behavioral disturbance change with developmental age. During the first few months of life the major source of behavioral disturbance is in deviations in the mother-child relationship. During preschool years, signs of disturbance may appear in areas related to the child's newly acquired physical and cognitive capacities. These new signs may occur in children who have already shown earlier disturbance or in those who have seemed to be developing normally. During the later ages of childhood, the symptoms approximate those found in adolescents and adults, such as hallucinations and delusions.

Types of Childhood Psychoses

We now turn to a discussion of the four types of childhood psychoses. More coverage is given to infantile autism than to the other three types because this condition has received considerable attention in the literature. A study of Table 23-1 will facilitate understanding of the four types of childhood psychoses.

Infantile Autism

Infantile autism is a severe behavioral disorder of children that appears before 2½ years of age. Autistic children may show poor response to sensory stimuli, such as sound or light, may not recognize their parents, and may lack interest in the environment. Some children appear distressed for long periods of time and cry continuously, while others appear apathetic. Feeding and sleeping may be erratic and unpredictable. In time, the child may show obsessional features, aloofness and lack of interest in people, language disturbances, and retarded intellectual functioning (Hermelin & Frith, 1971). The following three symptoms are most characteristic of children with infantile autism (Rutter, 1978):

EXHIBIT 23-2. Psychological Evaluation: An Autistic Child

Name: Sara
Date of birth: January 1, 1976
Chronological age: 3-9
Date of examination: September 10, 1979
Date of report: September 15, 1979

Tests Administered

Vineland Social Maturity Scale
Bayley Scales of Infant Development (selected items)
Cattell Scale of Infant Intelligence (selected items)
Informal observations of play

Background Referral Information

Sara was referred by her pediatrician, who was concerned about her development. He believes that she may be retarded and have possible emotional problems.

The parents have been concerned for some time about Sara's slow language development. Although she achieved motor milestones at the usual times, the family began to worry about her lack of speech and limited personal-social competency at the age of 3 years, when she failed to respond to toilet training and continued to prefer isolated play. At about the same time, she began to display "nervousness," tensing up and screaming at the slightest frustration. It was then that they consulted their pediatrician, insisting something was wrong, although a "wait-and-see" policy was suggested.

Medical-Social History

No significant prenatal or subsequent medical problems were reported. However, in their search for possible causes, both parents recall the early "play pen" stage with some guilt. Because of the demands of an elder (3-year-old) sister, they would leave Sara for long periods, hoping she could amuse herself. Mother and father are both professional people (dentist and junior college teacher), and have done considerable soul-searching, as well as much reading about developmental problems. Nonetheless, they have been inclined to hide their fears from one another to avoid worrying one another. The mother had miscarried a previous pregnancy, and had been "relieved" at the time. She may still be harboring some guilt about the miscarriage.

Observations and Impressions

Sara is a beautiful, physically well-developed little girl of almost 4 years of age. In a "formal" test setting her attention to people or the usual array of material was virtually nil. To the onlooker, Sara appears to wander aimlessly about, touching first one object and then another in a rather ritualistic way. Efforts to direct her activities seem to be regarded as an intrusion to which she responds with irritation.

Most observations and data were obtained by simply watching her behavior in the playroom (a kind of free play setting with other children), and from a parental report of her everyday functioning at home (rating on the Vineland Social Maturity Scale).

Sara's locomotor skills are not significantly out of line for a child of her age. She walks adeptly, climbs stairs, and on occasion has pedaled a tricycle (3 years of age). The very few attempts she made to manipulate simple puzzles or peg boards suggested some knowledge of size-shape discrimination (i.e., roughly at the 2½ year level), but the slightest obstacle would bring about marked frustration.

No vocal attempts were heard during the time I spent with her, nor did she respond to words or any verbal overtures. The parents report, however, that she has recently begun to associate words and action at home ("put that away") as well as use a few single, but highly selective, words and combinations—"strawberry" and "sex appeal" (mimicking a toothpaste ad). She also hums nursery rhymes in perfect intonation and pitch. Sara will feed herself, using both fingers and utensils, put on some of her own clothes, and, on occasion, tend to her toilet needs. (Until the last month or so she would hide her "BMs.")

On the Vineland, she obtained a social age of about 2 years. This score suggests that she is significantly below average in her personal-social level of functioning.

Summary

In summary, Sara comes across as one of those youngsters who is tuned into her environment in deviant and fragmented ways. While she *functions* as a retarded child, her developmental idiosyncrasies could not be explained on the basis of "simple mental retardation" alone. Rather, it seems, we are dealing with a pervasive communication problem which entails not only expressive speech and language comprehension, but many facets of her relationship with the outside world.

EXHIBIT 23-2   (cont.)

The mother did raise the question of infantile autism. We discussed the likelihood that Sara's behavior was consistent with that of many children described under this rubric. I pointed out the hazards of premature labeling, that experts held divergent opinions as to causality, but that most would agree that many complex factors play a role. Even though this was an initial diagnostic evaluation, it seemed important to allow the mother an opportunity to air her feelings of worry about the future, guilt, and confusion as to etiology. I could sincerely empathize with her plight, since it is so difficult to relate to these children, so few parental rewards are forthcoming, and we know so little about the basis of these formidable problems.

Recommendations

1. Further evaluation of neurological functions by a qualified pediatric neurologist.
2. Further evaluation of psycho-environmental aspects, including counseling with parents as to appropriate management and alleviation of guilt.
3. Explore preschool programs which could offer ongoing evaluation and appropriate training and special emphasis on social communication and early language development.

———————
Examiner

---

1. failure to develop social relationships,
2. deviant and delayed language development, and
3. various ritualistic and compulsive activities.

Other symptoms include

4. stereotyped repetitive movements,
5. short attention span,
6. self-injurious behavior, and
7. delayed bowel control.

Autism can be thought of as a behaviorally defined, specific syndrome that is manifested at birth or shortly thereafter. The various symptoms associated with autism appear to be expressive of an underlying neuropathophysiological process that affects developmental rate, perception, language, cognition, intelligence, and ability to relate (Ornitz & Ritvo, 1976). Prognosis is guarded, as almost all children manifest severe symptomatology throughout their lives. The psychological evaluation in Exhibit 23-2 shows how some of these characteristics are revealed during an evaluation.

Etiology of infantile autism. One of the most prominent views about the etiology of autism is that autism is a disorder of the central nervous system which manifests itself in a cognitive deficit (Damasio & Maurer, 1978; Rutter, 1974). The primary objectively observable deficit is impaired comprehension and use of language. The cause of the cognitive deficit, however, remains unknown. Brain damage may be present in some cases, while in others dysfunction due to developmental or genetic factors may be implicated. Another view is that autism involves a dysfunction of the complex circuitry providing the central connections of the vestibular system to the cerebellum and the brain stem (Ornitz, 1976). This last proposal attempts to account for the strange sensorimotor behavior observed in autistic children (e.g., spontaneous spinning and flicking of objects, flapping and oscillating of their extremities, and whirling and rocking of their bodies). There is some evidence that autistic children are more proficient at right hemisphere processing than at left hemisphere processing (Blackstock, 1978) and that they have a longer response latency of the auditory nerve than do normal children (Student & Sohmer, 1978).

Case illustrations of infantile autism. The following two cases show how autism manifests itself in various children. In Bill's case (Case 23-1) we are reminded to look beyond the immediate behavior and physical appearance. In James's case (Case 23-2), which traces the course of language, cognitive, and

CASE 23-1.   Bill, an Autistic Child

Bill is a blond-haired, blue-eyed boy of 4 years. He runs with fast, graceful movements. He is bright, good-looking and shows . . . an intense interest in mechanical toys. However, upon closer inspection unusual patterns of behavior become evident. Bill often sits for hours staring into space, motionless as if in deep thought. His interest in inanimate objects appears to be an obsession. Bill doesn't respond when you speak to him and tends to withdraw whenever he is approached. Speech is almost completely absent except for some unintelligible phrases. Bill becomes extemely upset by any environmental changes, e.g., changes in routine, rearrangement of furniture or the order in which everyday acts are carried out. He displays many of the typical behaviors one observes in "autistic children." ■

Source: Mulcahy, 1972–3, p. 73, with change in name.

CASE 23-2.   James, an Autistic Child

James was the third of four children, born following an uncomplicated pregnancy and labor. His health during the first 3 months of life was good, but shortly thereafter his mother expressed concern because of his sensitivities to light and sound, his failure to make an anticipatory response to being picked up, his fluctuating moods between inconsolable crying and extreme passiveness, and his failure to look at her when she fed him. She reported that he preferred lying in his crib, staring at the mobile, to being held or played with. Because his motor milestones appeared at the appropriate times, James's pediatrician reassured his mother that his development was fine. By age 16 months, James had not begun to babble or say single words, and spent most of his time in a corner repetitively moving toy cars back and forth. At 20 months, other symptoms emerged: he developed unusual hand movements and body postures; his obliviousness to people increased; he reacted to even the most subtle interruption in his routine or other changes in the world with extreme disorganization and panic; he developed a fascination with light switches and with studying tiny bits of paper and twigs.

At 4 years, James had not yet begun to speak socially to others, but could identify by name many numbers and all of the letters of the alphabet. He was able to execute the most graceful maneuvers, spinning in circles about a room without touching a piece of furniture, but often, at other times, appeared clumsy and uncoordinated. He persisted in lining up objects in the most complex patterns, but could never use objects appropriately. His parents complained about how difficult it was to buy birthday and Christmas gifts that could replace the tiny bits of paper and pieces of string he preferred playing with. At about the age of 4½ years, he began to echo long and complicated sentences, some of which his mother reported he may have heard days or even weeks before. He was able to complete puzzles designed for 8- and 9-year-olds quickly, but was unable to reproduce a line or circle.

At about age 5, James made his first spontaneous statement. His mother reported that he had been looking at the sky and said, "It looks like a flower." He did not speak again for 8 months, but then began talking in full sentences. Most often, the content was concerned with numbers—he read encyclopedias and reported, for example, to whoever would listen that a certain river was 1,000 miles long and had 200 tributaries. When he met strangers, he mechanically introduced himself without ever establishing eye contact, and then rushed on to ask what the person's birthday, anniversary, and social security number were, often appearing not to pause long enough to get the answers. Years later, upon remeeting the person, he was able to recite back these facts.

James was remarkably talented musically, and could sing the lyrics to popular tunes and TV commercials. While he could read well, he was unable to abstract from written information, to draw inferences or make conclusions. At age 9, he remained socially distant, although he had learned many of the rules for social situations. He received superior scores on the WISC Object Assembly, Picture Completion, and Block Design subtests, but fell many years below age level on the Comprehension, Similarities, and Information subtests. ■

Source: Caparulo and Cohen, 1977, pp. 623–624, with a change in notation.

social development, we find the simultaneous presence of remarkable talents and profound deficits.

Intelligence and infantile autism. In the past, IQs obtained from autistic children were often considered to be invalid. The hope was that with the right treatment, intellectual ability could develop to a normal level. Unfortunately, however, therapy with autistic children has not resulted in significantly improved levels of intellectual performance.

Research on autistic children's intellectual functioning points to several important findings.

1. As many as three-fourths of autistic children obtain IQs that are in the mentally retarded range of functioning.[2]
2. IQs obtained by autistic children have the same properties as do those obtained by other children.[3] Thus, for example, (a) IQs show moderate stability throughout childhood and adolescence (correlations between IQs obtained over periods of two to fifteen years have been found to range from .63 to .90), especially if the children are tested after 5 years of age, and (b) IQs provide a reasonable predictor of later educational attainments.
3. IQs fail to change markedly even after autistic children's social responsiveness greatly improves. Poor motivation, consequently, does not appear to be an explanation for autistic children's below-average performance on intelligence tests.
4. Initially untestable autistic children later have been found to perform in a manner similar to that of severely retarded children.[4] In addition, those who appear to be untestable may be testable when given items representing sufficiently low mental age levels.
5. IQs obtained by autistic children are higher when they have adequate conversational speech or adequate social relationships (DeMyer, Barton, Alpern, Kimberlin, Allen, Yang, & Steele, 1974).
6. The cognitive skills shown by autistic children suggest a specific cognitive defect involving the use of language—namely, they have relatively good visual-spatial and memory abilities coupled with poor sequencing and language abilities.

On the basis of the above findings, it is important to recognize that autistic children with low IQs are as retarded as any other children having low IQs. The intellectual level obtained by autistic children, therefore, should not be dismissed simply as a result of some temporary impairment that is easily reversible.

The effectiveness of treatment, as determined by increases in IQs, also is related to the autistic child's IQ at the beginning of treatment (DeMyer et al., 1974). Treated children with IQs equal to or over 50 had a better chance of improving their IQs than untreated children in the same IQ range. However, treatment did not improve the intelligence level of children who had IQs at or below 40. The brighter autistic children who received treatment improved their (a) Performance IQ by about 13 points (70 to 83), (b) Verbal IQ by about 23 points (42 to 65), and (c) general IQ by about 17 points (57 to 74). No such changes were evident in the children with IQs below 40. If the research design had not separated the children according to IQ level (over 50 and below 40), treatment would have been found to have no effect at follow-up for the total group.

Comparison of autistic children who were functioning in the mentally retarded range with those functioning at higher levels showed that both groups had (a) serious impairment in the development of social relationships; (b) delayed speech and marked impairment in imaginative or pretended play in early childhood; (c) some form of stereotyped, ritualistic, or compulsive behavior; and (d) disruptive or socially embarrassing behavior in public situations or in the company of other people (Bartak & Rutter, 1976). However, differences between the two groups also emerged. The autistic children who functioned in the mentally retarded range, when compared with the other autistic children, were more likely to show impaired physical responsiveness in infancy, delayed motor development, neurological dysfunctions (including epileptic seizures during adolescence), retarded language development, poor educational progress (including poor reading ability), difficulties in sequencing, impaired social behavior with adults, inappropriate behavior when in shops and when in buses and trains, resistance to environmental change, minimal concern with rituals, self-injurious behavior (such as head banging or wrist biting), hand and finger gestural stereotypes, and poor adjustment and limited gainful employment in adult life.

Thus, mentally retarded autistic children showed greater language difficulties, more severely disturbed interpersonal relationships, and more disruptive behavior than autistic children of higher intelligence, who showed more sensitivity to noise and exhibited more rituals. Overall, the findings suggest (a) that different etiological factors may be present in autism, depending on the presence or absence of mental retardation, and (b) that level of intelligence is associated with autistic children's scholastic progress, social competence, work opportunities, neurological intactness, and symptom formation.

Disintegrative Psychosis

Children diagnosed as having disintegrative psychosis (see Table 23-1) usually have a period of normal development for the first three or four years, after which profound regression and behavioral disintegration occur (Rutter, 1977). The children become restive, irritable, anxious, and overactive. Speech and language deteriorate, intelligence declines, and social skills diminish. The psychosis occasionally develops after measles, encephalitis, or some other organic illness that damages the brain; however, in many cases there are no clinical signs of brain damage. The prognosis is poor; the children remain severely mentally handicapped.

Childhood Schizophrenia

Childhood schizophrenia most often begins during the preadolescent or adolescent period, but can begin as early as 7 years of age (see Table 23-1). The symptomatology is generally similar to that seen in adults (see Exhibit 23-3 for a composite description of symptoms found in childhood schizophrenia), with such symptoms as thought association disorder, blocking, delusions, hallucinations, mood disorder, perplexity, blunting of affect, and grimacing (Rutter, 1977). Many of the children obtain IQs in the normal range, but most are likely to be in the low average range.

In Karl's case (see Exhibit 23-4) we observe many symptoms that suggest that he is involved in an intense struggle to maintain some hold on reality. It is possible that if he does not master this struggle, a full-blown psychotic episode may ensue. At present, he appears to be in a preschizophrenic state, displaying many behaviors characteristic of a schizoid personality.

Other Psychoses of Childhood

Children placed in the category *other psychoses of childhood* (see Table 23-1) have less well defined symptoms than those who fall into one of the three other more clearly defined types of childhood psychoses (Rutter, 1977). These children may show symptoms similar to those that are observed in infantile autism, although the symptoms develop after 30 months of age instead of before 30 months of age. Some children in this category may show a loss of reality when tested at 3 or 4 years of age, but they do not display the profound regression that is characteristic of children with disintegrative psychosis. Other children are placed in this category if they have nonspecific psychotic disorders that do not fit the criteria for infantile autism, childhood schizophrenia, or disintegrative psychosis.

Etiology of Childhood Psychosis

Theories related to the etiology of childhood psychosis fall into one of three categories: nonorganic, organic-experiential interaction, and organic (Hingtgen & Bryson, 1972). The *nonorganic theories* assume that the child is normal at birth. However, these theories postulate that personality deficits and defects in parental behaviors—especially in the mother-child relationship—may induce the psychotic behavior. Within this theoretical framework, maternal behaviors that may

EXHIBIT 23-3.   A Composite Description of Childhood Schizophrenic Children

The following composite description of childhood schizophrenic symptoms is based on a study of fifty-seven children, twenty-five boys and thirty-two girls. Eleven of these children developed the condition between 7 and 10 years of age, the remainder between 10 and 13 years of age.

Symptoms in Children Before Age 10

These children grew up quite unobstrusively until the onset of their psychosis, and then unexpectedly showed strange personality changes. These included increasing loss of contact with reality, reduced activity, diminishing of interests or narrowing of interests to those no longer appropriate to the child's age, indifference to the usual games and pursuits, disturbed motility (stereotypy, hyperkinesia, peculiar mannerisms, bizarre postures), negativism, disturbed contacts, retreat into their own autistic world, speech disturbances (echolalia, . . . neologism) leading to disintegration of speech, and often a modification of the personality toward dementia. Emotional changes manifested themselves as moodiness, often accompanied by anxiety, excessive distrust, and affective bluntness. Emotional changes also included coldness and even brutality. Some children who had loved animals tortured their own pets without reason. Previously affectionate children suddenly turned unkind, cold, and stubborn, and showed no more affection toward beloved persons in their surroundings.

Some children were compulsively disinhibited. They destroyed objects aimlessly, defecated openly, masturbated without embarrassment in front of strangers, ate unreasonable quantities of food, injured themselves with sharp and pointed objects, often to the point of endangering their lives with unmotivated suicide attempts.

The symptomatology showed special features determined by the stage of development: The earliest age at which our patients experienced delusions and hallucinations was 7 years, but these typical schizophrenic symptoms were rare in children of this age. One form of delusion characteristic of childhood schizophrenia was loss of identity. The young patients identified themselves with other persons, animals, or inanimate objects in their surroundings, or even pretended to have been transformed into such objects.

Coenesthetic [sensations arising from bodily organs through which one perceives his or her body] symptoms were also observed. For example, a little boy expressed fears such as "my navel is bursting," "my heart stops beating," "my penis bursts," and "lightning shoots through my body."

The delusional symptoms in children who became ill before the 10th year of life often appeared in the form of irrational, diffuse fears, or even cosmic threats: e.g., "the sun is falling from the sky," "the rain will never stop and everybody will drown." In several of the eleven children under 10 years of age there was evidence that the child had developed transitory paranoid ideas and in one case delusions of being poisoned. Obsessional hallucinations were also, though very seldom, observed in children under the age of 10.

Symptoms in Prepubertal Cases

In prepubertal cases (i.e., between 10 and 14 years), delusions became more persistent. Paranoid and hypochondriac ideas prevailed. At this age, religious and depressive themes sometimes appeared for the first time. On the whole, ideas of reference were most frequent among the delusions and the most frequent type of hallucinations were auditory. However, visual hallucinations were also found in half the children examined. These may be due to the affinity of children for eidetic phenomena.

Another change determined by development concerned the structure of delusional symptoms. With the increasing capacity for rational and critical reflection during the prepubertal phase, delusional themes became more abstract and were formulated more precisely. In 10 children, during this phase a more or less far-reaching *systemization* of delusional ideas was already observed; all of these children were above average in intelligence and sensitivity. They had pursued philosophical questions unusual for children of their age long before the psychotic breakdown. For example, a 5-year-old boy said, 6 years before the onset of psychosis at 11, "I regard my life only as a transition stage." Similarly, 3 years before becoming psychotic, a 10-year-old girl announced, "We must always be aware of the autumn of life."

With increasing age, childhood and prepubertal psychoses began to resemble those of the adult.   ∎

Source: Reprinted, with a change in notation, by permission of the publisher from C. Eggers, "Course and Prognosis of Childhood Schizophrenia," *Journal of Autism and Childhood Schizophrenia, 8,* pp. 24–25. Copyright 1978, Plenum.

EXHIBIT 23-4. Psychological Evaluation: Schizoid Personality or Possible Pre-Schizophrenic Reaction

Name: Karl
Date of birth: April 15, 1964
Chronological age: 14-2
Date of examination: June 6, 1978
Date of report: June 7, 1978
Grade: 10th

Tests Administered

Wechsler Intelligence Scale for Children-Revised:

VERBAL SCALE		PERFORMANCE SCALE	
Information	15	Picture Completion	11
Similarities	13	Picture Arrangement	9
Arithmetic	14	Block Design	10
Vocabulary	11	Object Assembly	15
Comprehension	9	Coding	7

Verbal Scale IQ = 114
Performance Scale IQ = 102
Full Scale IQ = 109±5 at the 90 percent confidence level

Bender Visual Motor Gestalt Test:

His performance was neat, accurate, and well organized. He also appeared to be relatively at ease in tackling this perceptual-motor task.

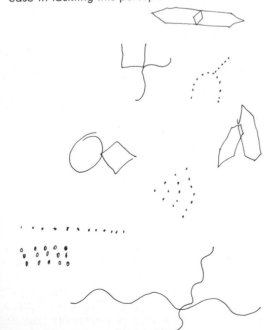

Wide Range Achievement Test:

	STANDARD SCORE	PERCENTILE
Reading (isolated word recognition)	133	99th
Spelling	118	88th
Arithmetic	84	14th

1. cat
2. run
3. arm
4. train
5. shout
6. correct
7. circle
8. heaven
9. educate
10. material
11. ruin
12. fashion
13. believe
14. suggestion
15. equipment
16. majority
17. institute
18. literature
19. reverence
20. museum
21. precious
22. illogical
23. decision
24. quantity
25. executive
26. necessity
27. opportunity
28. conscience
29. physician
30. courteous
31. possession
32. lucidity
33. exaggerate
34. pedolege
35. loquacious
36. medieval
37. resiliant
38. sovereignty
39. effeminate
40. aciduous
41. irresistible
42. aqueos
43. anxiety
44. charlatan
45. pusillonimous
46. irredescence

Rorschach

Background Data

Karl is a Caucasion 14-year-old boy who has a sister aged 18 and a brother aged 12. Both of his parents work at clerical jobs. Karl's parents noticed differences between him and his siblings since early infancy. He seemed to repulse human contacts, with the exception of occasional cuddlings by his father. By the age of 6 months, he was extremely active and prone to uncontrollable fits of screaming and temper tantrums, which became increasingly difficult to manage, especially after he began to walk at 9 months of age. He often bumped into things and appeared to be accident prone, seeming to be heedless of objects in his path. He spoke his first words at 18 months, but no sentences until the age of 4 years.

Karl was seen by a psychiatrist at 2½ years of age and was given a tentative diagnosis of "possible autism." During school years his learning and behavior fluctuated. He mastered sight reading early, but comprehension and mathematics were difficult for him. He alternately played the class clown and the recluse. In junior high school he shunned group activities, describing his classmates as uncivilized.

Karl spends hours poring over astronomy books and playing games involving military strategy, working out tactics well into the night. He still has occasional rage reactions for no apparent reason. They may be precipitated when he stands in crowded lines or when he rides a bus.

EXHIBIT 23-4   (cont.)

The present evaluation was initiated by Karl's parents. While they recognize that he has always had behavioral difficulties and was an under-achiever, they are becoming increasingly concerned about his scholastic performance and social/emotional well-being.

Behavioral Observations

Karl is a tall, rather pale and ascetic looking boy. While agreeable and cooperative, he remained tense, if not super-controlled, throughout the lengthy test session. At times he seemed almost immobilized by the fear of saying "the wrong thing" or "using the wrong word." He seemed a little more comfortable when faced with questions calling for factual answers, as opposed to those where several alternatives were available.

Impressions

Karl's overall intellectual functioning is well within the average range. However, there are some suggestions that his social judgment, planning and anticipation skills, and ability to persist at a visual-motor task requiring new learning are not as well developed as are his other skills. His somewhat lower social comprehension skills may be a reflection of some of the emotional turmoil that he is experiencing. His lowered visual-motor performance appeared to be a result of his perfectionism and super-control.

There were several qualitative features of his "cognitive style" which deserve mention. First, Karl has obviously absorbed a large vocabulary and fund of factual information, possibly as a result of his reading and solitary pursuits. Long pauses often preceded his answers to questions; it was as if he needed time to find substantial "grown-up words" and to organize his thoughts. Second, I often had the feeling that he placed a premium on being right and on how his answers sounded, perhaps sacrificing logical thinking

operations to some extent as a result. He was virtually never able to say, "I don't know," but would rather circumvent the question by a string of slightly tangential, pedantic phrases. What with all these efforts to appear intellectual, mature, and self-possessed (the latter took some doing), he often missed the point of a problem, or at least over-complicated it unnecessarily.

On an abbreviated Rorschach, there were long pauses between the presentation of each card and Karl's response. He seemed to be exerting a great deal of effort in maintaining composure, organizing his perceptions and weighing his words before replying. The results were a protocol of initially conventional, reasonable, controlled responses. Toward the end, however, as color stimuli became more prevalent, his controls weakened. As was not surprising, his responses then gave us glimpses of what might be interpreted as significant emotional turmoil.

Finally, judging from the history, together with the current medical/developmental findings, it seems likely that a combination of etiological factors contribute to the escalating problems. I suspect, for example, that Karl began life, as well as his school career, with subtle deviations in his neurological makeup, which in turn left him more vulnerable to learning problems and social/psychological insult.

In summary, for perhaps a combination of reasons, Karl gives the impression of a boy who has worked pathetically hard, for a very long time, not only to keep feelings and impulses under tight rein, but also to preserve the image of scholastic and intellectual excellence. I strongly agree with the other consultants that without some kind of shift in academic curriculum and/or expectations, as well as therapeutic intervention, his controls may one day break down under accumulating pressures. We all share the parents' concerns about the possible consequences.

_____

Examiner

---

contribute to the child's pathological behavior include overprotection, rejection, emotional deprivation, inappropriate somasthetic stimulation, and inappropriate reinforcement.

The *organic-experiential theories* focus on the interaction of child (deviations in the child or some unspecified vulnerability) and mother (failure of mother to compensate for child's deviations or pathological mother-child relationship). The following formula might characterize these theories: Severity of psychotic behavior = f (degree of organic damage $\times$ degree of environmental stress).

However, little is known about the degree to which each factor contributes to the child's psychopathology.

The *organic theories* range from those that postulate diffuse organic damage to those that postulate specific sites of impairment in the central nervous system. Defects in the arousal and integrative mechanisms in particular, such as problems with the reticular activating system or homeostatic regulation within the central nervous system, have been proposed to account for psychotic behavior. These theories hold that the psychotic child's inappropriate behavior is a way of adapting to an environment that is incomprehensible to the child.

The three theoretical positions regarding etiological factors in childhood psychosis are all limited to one degree or another. The nonorganic theories have not been supported, since there is limited evidence, at best, of parental psychopathology in the families of psychotic children. This is especially true in the case of infantile autism. Stresses in infancy (such as maternal depression in the child's early years or parental coldness, obsessionality, and social withdrawal) are not usually found. The organic-experiential theories are vague in defining the nature of the underlying vulnerability, the nature of the environmental stress, and the interaction between the two. Finally, the organic theories are inconclusive, because the evidence does not tend to support one organic theory over another. Thus we are left with the good possibility that childhood psychoses are associated with not one etiology, but a number of different etiologies.

Treatment and Prognosis in Childhood Psychosis

Treatment programs and goals in childhood psychosis must take into account etiology, intellectual level, biological factors, psychosocial factors, and the type of disorder displayed by the child (Rutter, 1972). In infantile autism, the goal is to develop better social and language skills in children who have cognitive handicaps. In childhood schizophrenia, where there has been a period of normal development, the focus is on restoring equilibrium. In disintegrative psychosis, the goal is to restore function and aid development in children who have severely regressed, often following the onset of brain damage. (See Exhibit 23-5 for an illustration of how assessment and treatment are interwoven in the case of a 7½-year-old autistic boy.)

The treatment of childhood psychosis should be individualized as much as possible, using the child's strengths and preferred modalities.

While the therapeutic outlook has brightened considerably, the general prognosis for most childhood psychotics is still poor in terms of developing levels of normal functioning. Significant expansion of their behavioral repertoires can be achieved, but spontaneity may remain absent, especially in the area of speech. At an even lower level many of these children do not seem able to make various types of simple cross-modal associations. Whether these major therapeutic roadblocks can be eliminated will be answered by further intensive study. What is clear at this point is that abilities vary widely from child to child, no matter what the diagnosis. Until each child's specific limitations of learning are objectively determined, all methods of proven effectiveness must be used to enable him to reach his highest level of performance. At best, these therapeutic approaches could allow the child to function well in home and school settings; at the very least, they could provide for the construction of prosthetic environments, designed for the individual child according to his maximum abilities. [Hingtgen & Bryson, 1972, p. 33]

In school, autistic children can be helped if these guidelines are kept in mind (Gallagher & Wiegerink, 1976, p. 329):

1. Autistic children are educable.
2. Their unique learning characteristics are due to basic cognitive deficits in information processing.
3. Such deficits can be compensated for, in part, by carefully structured educational programs with specified developmental learning sequences and enhanced reinforcing stimuli.

EXHIBIT 23-5.   The Interweaving of Assessment and Treatment in a Seven-and-a-Half-Year-Old Autistic Boy

This close interweaving between diagnosis and treatment is well illustrated by the clinical transaction with a seven-and-a-half-year-old boy who had been seen over several years by many specialists. He had only spoken, on rare occasion, three or four words, and at various times had been diagnosed as hard of hearing, mentally retarded, brain damaged, and autistic. Psychological testing was requested to aid in clarifying the problem and to assist in the development of a treatment plan. The boy was healthy and physically robust, but he was deeply engrossed in the repetitive and highly personalized rhythmic chant of nonsense syllables. Seen for the first time, he was seated at the child's table in the waiting room, loudly singing a repetitive, primitive chant. He was banging the tune on the table, tapping it out with his feet, and it seemed as if his entire body were involved in this rhythmic activity. His singing seemed to serve as a very primitive form of speech by which he communicated his apprehension. When he felt most threatened, the chanting would increase in intensity and in tempo. He did not speak at all and any attempts to communicate with him were ignored or met by increased singing. He was an intensely frightened, apprehensive child who had or wanted little, if any, contact with his environment. His entire organization seemed focused around the reduction of his fears and apprehension, and his primitive and rhythmic singing seemed to soothe and pacify him. If he were to interact at all, it would be on his terms and at a pace he could tolerate.

In the first two testing sessions the diagnostician sat quietly and unobtrusively on the side of the room playing with some material from the Merrill-Palmer Scale. Slowly the child began to move out from his incessant chanting and his scrawling with a crayon. He walked around the room, touched objects, came over to the diagnostician, and while looking directly into his face, touched and pinched his arm and then quickly returned to his drawings and humming of nonsense syllables. Any attempts to approach him directly were met by an increase in chanting.

In the third testing session the child came over and watched the diagnostician place objects in the form board and at one point directed the diagnostician's hand to the proper slot on the form board, indicating where blocks should be placed. Later, he cautiously accepted pieces and placed them himself. All this proceeded with a minimum of verbal contact, and communication was primarily through gestures or by the increase or decrease of his chanting.

On those subtests he participated in, he was able to function at the highest level of the Merrill-Palmer Scale. Although any IQ estimate of this performance would be highly unreliable, one could say with assurance that this child was not mentally retarded. Also, his manual dexterity was good, his perceptual motor skills were intact, as was his memory, and there were no indications of central nervous system damage. Rather, he seemed to be a seriously disturbed autistic child who had never made the decision that contact with people and with the world was worthwhile and desirable. He found more safety, security, and satisfaction in his rhythmic singing and banging.

During the six diagnostic testing sessions the child began to relate more readily to the examiner. When taken to the candy closet after each hour he would carefully select a piece of candy for himself and then select one for the diagnostician. In the last testing session he hummed "Happy Birthday" and the diagnostician sang the words along with him. Shortly thereafter, this supposedly inarticulate child sang the first two lines of the song, words and all. Aside from its rich symbolic meaning, the song communicated the very important message that, in fact, this child could speak. As he began to experience feelings of trust and security, the child emerged from his autistic chanting and rocking to explore and experience a very limited segment of his environment.

In the process of understanding how and why this child behaves the way he does, the diagnostician and the patient shared poignant moments and one might say, that in the sharing of these poignant moments, psychotherapy had begun. The initial contacts in the diagnostic relationship devoted to an appraisal of the problem have blended into therapy and the diagnostician could either continue with the child, or gradually make the transition to another person who would function as the therapist. The gains made early in the diagnostic relationship, however, would serve as a major impetus for the psychotherapeutic process, if the transition were skillfully handled.

In reviewing the diagnostic evaluation process with this child, it seems that diagnostic testing could facilitate treatment not only by presenting the therapist with the analysis of test responses, but also by having a direct and highly significant effect of facilitating communication with the

4. Structured education programs should begin early in life, with the parent or parent surrogate as the primary teacher.
5. Educational programs for these children are feasible, and, in the long run, less costly than institutional care.
6. The provision of appropriate educational programs for these children is not a manifestation of public generosity but rather a reflection that these children, too, have a clear right to an appropriate education.

Current evidence indicates that children receiving a diagnosis of childhood psychosis have a poor prognosis.

Contrary to the theory of normal "potential," the large majority of psychotic children demonstrate severe deficits in intellectual, perceptual, and language development. Followup studies indicate that, even when bizarre behaviors diminish and social relatedness increases, gross deficits in other areas of functioning remain. Many recent reports also indicate that, regardless of the treatment program followed, these children show more improvement in affective contact than in intellectual, perceptual, and language skills. Thus, it now appears that their deficits in social behavior are less a cause than a reflection of deviations in other areas of development. [Hingtgen & Bryson, 1972, p. 38]

Autistic children face extreme interpersonal, behavioral, intellectual, and neurological difficulties when they reach adolescence and early adulthood.[5] In adolescence and adulthood a majority of autistic individuals (about 60 percent) remain severely handicapped and are unable to lead an independent life; about 15 percent make a good social adjustment, holding a job and getting along in society; and about 25 percent have an intermediate outcome, with some degree of independence and only minor problems in behavior (Rutter, 1977). Even those with a good social adjustment have interpersonal difficulties and display oddities of behavior. A substantial minority of autistic children develop epilepsy during adolescence, especially those who are severely retarded.

The evidence is substantial that the IQ of autistic children in early childhood is an excellent predictor of their later educational attainments and social adjustment. Autistic children with IQs below 50 have a very poor prognosis, while approximately half of those with IQs above 70 show a good adjustment in adolescence and adult life (Rutter, 1977). A second important prognostic factor is level of language development. A good outcome is more likely if language comprehension is not severely impaired in the preschool years, or if the child has useful speech by the age of 5 years. Other prognostic factors include the severity of the behavioral disturbance in early childhood, the variety of play patterns, the type of schooling, and family interactions. Prognosis is better with less severe behavioral disturbance, with some constructive play, with good schooling, with a harmonious family, and with normal EEGs. The Research Highlight in Exhibit 23-6 shows how some of these factors are related to prognosis.

Assessment Considerations in Childhood Psychosis

A thorough assessment of childhood psychosis requires an evaluation of language,

EXHIBIT 23-6.   Research Highlight: Follow-up Studies of Autistic Children and Schizophrenic Children

A study by Lotter (1974) of thirty-two autistic children, identified at 8 to 10 years of age and followed up eight years later, illustrates how substantial the relationships are between outcome and speech, IQ, social maturity, and years of schooling. The best predictors of outcome (defined in terms of social adjustment, employment, and placement) were the ability to use speech communicatively ($r = .86$), IQ ($r = .78$), Vineland Social Quotient ($r = .78$), and years of school ($r = .86$). Speech and IQ together correlated more highly with outcome than did any other combination of variables ($R = .89$). Speech and IQ were also highly related ($r = .73$). Strong evidence of neurological abnormality was present in about 33 percent of the sample, while no evidence was present in 53 percent of the children. Most children with neurological abnormalities also had IQs in the mentally retarded range.

In a follow-up study by Eggers (1978) of fifty-seven children with a diagnosis of childhood schizophrenia, 20 percent were found to have recovered completely, 30 percent reached a relatively good social adjustment, and 50 percent had moderate or poor remission. In this study, stringent criteria were used to select the children, such as age at which symptoms developed (7 years of age or later), type of symptoms (similar to those of adult schizophrenia), and absence of mental retardation or obvious brain damage. Average length of follow-up was fifteen years. A more favorable prognosis was associated with (a) later onset (e.g., after the age of 10 years), (b) better premorbid personality development (e.g., warmhearted, capable of making contact with others, and developing interests), and (c) average or above-average intelligence. Prognosis was not related to family incidence of schizophrenic psychoses, to disturbed family atmosphere, or to frequency of psychotic episodes.   ∎

behavior, intelligence, neurological status, and familial factors, as well as of how these separate factors interrelate. During the evaluation, attention should be given to the child's language, affect, interpersonal relations, and perceptual-motor performance. Any extreme deviations should raise questions about the possible presence of impaired ability. Let us now consider some speech and language characteristics of children with childhood psychosis.

Speech and Language of Psychotic Children

There are several kinds of language disorders in psychotic children. Autistic children, in particular, usually show delayed acquisition of speech, and many are suspected of having a hearing deficit because they do not respond to sounds. In psychotic children the incidence of mutism has been reported to range from 28 to 61 percent, while adequate or normal speech development was reported in 5 to 53 percent of the cases (Hingtgen & Bryson, 1972). The most common characteristic of psychotic children who do speak is echolalia, either immediate or delayed. Those autistic children who are echolalic have a better chance to improve

their language skills than those children who have not developed speech. A comparison of the speech of psychotic children with that of other types of disturbed children indicates that

the speech of psychotic children is generally characterized by low developmental level, lack of questions and informative statements, few personal pronouns, greater use of imperatives, limitations in verbal output, and more frequent idiosyncratic uses of words. There is little comprehension of the speech of others, little gestural reinforcement of speech, and there are many deviations in articulation, pitch, stress, rhythm, and inflection, as well as poor coordination of speaking and breathing. [Hingtgen & Bryson, 1972, p. 19]

A study of the child's level of speech development is important, since speech is the primary form of communication between individuals. In psychotic children the level of speech development has been found to be closely related to (a) development of intelligence, (b) response to treatment, and (c) ability to develop relationships with people (Hingtgen & Bryson, 1972). The lower the development of speech, the less able the children are in each of these areas. As infants, psychotic children are more apt to show limited verbalization, reduced alertness and responsiveness to sounds, some autistic behaviors, self-mutilative behaviors, and evidence of other perceptual deficits. Therefore, it is likely that when psychotic children have difficulties in language, they will also have difficulties in affective and interpersonal areas and in other cognitive areas.

During the assessment a variety of language distortions may be revealed. These include echoing, circumlocution, rambling, fragmentation, irrelevant speech, bizarreness, neologisms, blocking, automatic phrases, confabulation, circumstantiality, clang association, over-elaboration, ellipsis, self-reference, confusion or omission of pronouns and connecting words, and mixtures of concrete and abstract words. Many of these terms have been described in Chapter 18 on p. 342.

Observations of the Behavior of Psychotic Children

Observing the toy play of psychotic children also can provide useful information. The toy play of psychotic children differs from that of normal children and other groups of disturbed children. Psychotic children's toy play shows fewer combinational, appropriate, constructive, and functional uses; more restricted repertoires of toy play; longer latencies in approaching toys; and more repetitive manipulations of toys and their own bodies (Hingtgen & Bryson, 1972). Examiners should be alert to these (and other) aspects of the toy play of children.

A useful rating scale for evaluating fourteen different behavioral dimensions of psychotic children is shown in Table 23-2. A scale such as this can be completed after the diagnostic evaluation, and the results can be incorporated into the pyschological report. It also can be used to rate children in a variety of other situations.

Intelligence Test Performance of Psychotic Children

Intelligence, as we have seen, plays an important role in the prognosis of psychotic children. It is a measure of the psychotic child's current overall level of organization and integration and is the best single measure of integrative functioning (Goldfarb, 1970). Frequently, psychotic children do not perform well on intelligence tests. Between one-third and one-half obtain IQs lower than 70, and less than one-quarter obtain IQs above 90 (Pollack, 1967). The critical variable determining the level of intelligence of psychotic children seems to be their age when they first come to the attention of mental health professionals: *the younger they are when first seen, the lower their obtained IQ*. Thus, preschool children diagnosed as psychotic usually have lower IQs than those so diagnosed in preadolescent years. No doubt the more severe cases are seen earlier.

Level of intelligence is related to childhood psychosis in a number of different ways. First, there is some evidence that in a family predisposed to schizophrenia, the child with the lowest IQ is most vulnerable (Offord & Cross, 1971). Second, level of intelligence may be related to etiology: those psychotic children with nonorganic etiologies tend to obtain higher IQs than those with organic etiologies (Gittleman & Birch, 1967; Goldfarb, 1961). Third, level of intelligence may be related to symptom content, with the more intelligent psychotic children demonstrating more complex and involved rituals and compulsions than those with less intelligence (Rutter & Lockyer, 1967). Finally, the higher the intelligence, the better the prognosis.[6]

On intelligence tests there is no one pattern of test performance that is diagnostic of childhood psychosis. Some children differ little in performance from normal children, while others show considerable unevenness in functioning. In some cases performance tests may be the only way to obtain an estimate of the psychotic child's intelligence level. The Merrill-Palmer, the Block Design and Object Assembly subtests of the WISC-R, or some of the WPPSI performance subtests are likely choices. Some illustrations of psychotic children's performance on the Stanford-Binet follow (Des Lauriers & Halpern, 1947):

1. A run of successes and then an unexpected and unpredictable failure followed

TABLE 23-2.   Behavior Rating Scale for Psychotic Children

No.	Variable — Item	Age appropriate	2 Mild deviation	3 Moderate deviation	4 Severe deviation
1	Relationship to people	Appropriate responsiveness to examiner; eye contact, communicates	Partial avoidance	Relating tenuous, must be initiated by examiner	Pervasive detachment or avoidance
2	Imitation: verbal and motor	Readily imitates adult on verbal or motoric tasks	Partial or delayed imitation	Very little imitation	No verbal or motor imitation
3	Affect	Appropriate pleasure, displeasure, interest, etc.	Some signs of deviant affect: inhibition, lack of responsiveness, some silliness	Excessive or minimal indications of pleasure, displeasure, or interest	Evidence of pleasure, displeasure absent or grossly inappropriate
4	Body awareness	Appropriate use of body and movements	Minimal peculiarities such as stereotyped movements, lack of coordination	Moderate peculiarities: posturing, rocking, self-directed aggression	Extreme or pervasive peculiarities: stereotypy, lack of coordination, posturing, rocking, self-directed aggression
5	Relation to non-human objects	Appropriate use of and interest in objects	Some preoccupation with objects, also like a younger child	Peculiar and obvious preoccupation with objects or significant lack of interest in objects	Extreme preoccupation or repetitive use of objects or pervasive absence of interest in objects
6	Adaptation to environmental change	Appropriate response to change in activities	Some resistance to changes in activity, persistence in the same response pattern	Active resistance to change, signs of irritability, frustration, avoidance, difficult to distract	Severe avoidance, negative reactions to change, extreme resistance
7	Visual responsiveness	Appropriate use of and interest in visual cues (not ability to see)	Some lack of attention to visual stimuli, does not make use of visual cues	Moderate visual inattention, generally avoids eye contact	Pervasive visual avoidance of people and objects

(cont.)

Reprinted, with a change in notation, by permission of the publisher and authors from R. Reichler and E. Schopler, "Observations on the Nature of Human Relatedness," *Journal of Autism and Childhood Schizophrenia, 1,* p. 285. Copyright 1971, Scripta Publishing Corporation (Plenum).

TABLE 23-2 (cont.)

No.	Item	1 Age appropriate	2 Mild deviation	3 Moderate deviation	4 Severe deviation
	Variable		*Ratings*		
8	Auditory responsiveness	Appropriate responsiveness to auditory cues	Some lack of responsiveness to sounds and speech, may also be delayed responsiveness	Moderate unresponsiveness to auditory cues or moderate hypersensitivity	Pervasive auditory avoidance or extreme hypersensitivity
9	Near receptor responsiveness	Appropriate response to pain, normal tactual exploration	Mild preoccupation with tactual exploration, some lack of appropriate response to pain or touch	Moderate preoccupation with tactual exploration or smelling, moderate unresponsiveness to pain or touch	Excessive preoccupation with tactual exploration, smelling, severe deficit in or lack of response to pain
10	Anxiety reaction	No excessive crying, screaming, giggling, or withdrawal	Some anxiety in specific situations	Prolonged anxiety in many situations	Prolonged anxiety pervasively present
11	Verbal communication	Appropriate speech	Speech retarded, some echolalia, slight peculiarity	Speech absent or somewhat peculiar, much echolalia, perseveration of ideas	Speech very peculiar and bizarre, jargon, complete absence of intelligible words
12	Non-verbal communication	Appropriate communication (gestures, facial expressions)	Communication mildly retarded	Communication absent, inappropriate, nonmeaningful	Communication severely peculiar and bizarre
13	Activity level	Motility of child is average	Mildly hypoactive or hyperactive	Moderately hypoactive or hyperactive	Severely hypoactive or hyperactive
14	Intellectual functioning	No evidence of retardation	Retardation with hints of potential	Retardation with obvious discrepancies	Retardation across the board

by later successes. The failures are not related to the difficulty of the task and may occur in an unpredictable manner. The poor responses may be the result of a sudden preoccupation with some small irrelevant detail with neglect of the main issue. The responses may also be manifestations of inner, uncontrollable pressures, with atypical associations and formulations. The answers, therefore, may be not only incorrect, but often illogical.

Questioning may show how the response was arrived at. This can be seen in the following example. To the statement,

"A man called one day at the post office and asked if there was a letter waiting for him. 'What is your name?' asked the postmaster. 'Why,' said the man, 'you will find my name on the envelope' [Verbal Absurdities II, year level IX]," the child responded with, "He shouldn't have called. There was a strike. The people have to work hard." Further questioning revealed that the child had responded to the word "called," had associated this word with telephoning, and from that had gone on to the threatened telephone strike.

2. Correct responses, too, may be arrived at by unusual lines of reasoning. For example, to the question, "What should you do if you found on the streets of a city a three-year-old baby that was lost from its parents? [Comprehension IV, year level VIII]," a schizophrenic child replied, "Take it to the cops." When asked why he would do this he said, "Blue, they all wear blue." When further questioned, he said that his father was a sailor and that he felt lost. It appeared that he had associated the blue uniforms of the police with the blue sailor uniforms. Thus, answers which on the surface may appear to be satisfactory may be found to be deviant once the reasoning behind the answer is elicited.

3. Disturbances in thinking may appear in response to any test item and are not confined to certain specific ones. The responses seem to indicate that the child is reacting to what catches his awareness at the moment and to what kind of associations the particular stimulus arouses.

4. On the Picture Completion: Man test (year level V) the child may reveal the confusion that he manifests concerning himself as a person and the confused distinction between himself and his environment. Disturbed spatial relations, elongated parts, omission of parts, and over-emphasis on parts may be noted.

On the Wechsler tests (WISC-R, WPPSI, and WAIS-R), and on other assessment instruments, the types of illogical reasoning illustrated for the Stanford-Binet also may appear. Scatter on the WISC has not been shown to be a useful index in differentiating childhood psychosis from other conditions (e.g., Kissel, 1966). The following short case of a schizophrenic child's WISC performance (Case 23-3) illustrates the importance of evaluating carefully children's behavior in the test situation, and how they respond to the test questions.

CASE 23-3.   A Schizophrenic Child's Performance on the WISC

The first hint of Phillip's fulminating schizophrenia came during his responses to the WISC. He was a highly verbal youngster (age ten) who was considered to be potentially very brilliant by his teachers but was labeled as "underachiever" because of his unsatisfactory school performance. He talked incessantly about his interest in science, and it was difficult to get him to respond to anything else. He went into great length to explain why there were four seasons in the year, but he was not clear in his explanation, forgot the question, and actually forgot to name one of the four seasons. "What the stomach does?" and "Why oil floats on water?" similarly set him off on a frantic flight of ideas. On other items of this and other subtests, he tended to give only perfunctory responses. All of his subtest scores were in the low average range. Qualitatively, his failures seemed to result either from a disinterest in the topic or a highly cathe[c]ted but very confused concern with how things work and why.   ■

Source: Palmer, 1970, p. 221.

Differential Diagnosis of Childhood Psychosis

Generally, efforts to differentiate childhood psychosis from other conditions such as mental retardation, epilepsy, aphasia, brain damage, psychoneurosis, and responses to early deprivation have not been very productive (Goldfarb, 1970). The difficulty, in part, occurs because the diagnosis of childhood psychosis is a symptomatic diagnosis;

other childhood behavior disorders also are diagnosed by symptoms that may overlap with those of childhood psychosis. In addition, childhood behavior disorders themselves are not precisely defined classes of deviation. Children who are mentally retarded and manifest symptoms of psychosis may be placed in either of the categories. However, the *Diagnostic and Statistical Manual of Mental Disorders* (DSM-III) recommends that when mental retardation *and* a mental disorder coexist, both conditions be given a code in the classification. Autistic children who lack speech may sometimes be diagnosed as mentally retarded. Severely retarded children may also resemble autistic children in being inaccessible. However, the severely retarded child can respond successfully if the appropriate level of testing can be found.

Infantile Autism vs. Childhood Schizophrenia

A consideration of the clinical features of infantile autism and of childhood schizophrenia indicates that there are marked differences between the two disorders.[7]

1. In infantile autism there is a failure of development, whereas in childhood schizophrenia there is loss of reality after development is better established. The schizophrenic child may retreat from reality into fantasy, whereas the autistic child, rather than retreating, may fail to develop social relationships. Further, the young autistic child has a *deficiency* of fantasy rather than an excess of fantasy.
2. Symptoms differ in the two conditions. In childhood schizophrenia hallucinations and delusions frequently occur, whereas in infantile autism these symptoms usually are not present. Children with infantile autism more frequently have such symptoms as gaze avoidance, stereotyped movements, resistance to change, and serious delays in speech and communication.
3. The male-female ratio is about 3:1 or 4:1 in infantile autism, but about 1:1 in childhood schizophrenia.

4. In infantile autism the disorder shows a relatively steady course, whereas in childhood schizophrenia the disorder is marked by remissions and relapses.
5. Mental retardation is more common in infantile autism than in childhood schizophrenia.
6. In infantile autism there is a higher frequency of perinatal risk factors, evidence of cerebral dysfunction, and occurrence of epilepsy than in childhood schizophrenia.
7. Parents of children with infantile autism have higher socioeconomic status than parents of children with childhood schizoprenia, whose social background is the same as that of the general population.
8. Parents of children with childhood schizophrenia have a higher rate of schizophrenia than parents of children with infantile autism.
9. Oddities of parental personality appear more frequently in parents of children with childhood schizophrenia than in parents of children with infantile autism.

Infantile Autism vs. Aphasia

In both childhood aphasia and infantile autism there are severe language disturbances, including abnormal responses to sounds, delay in language acquisition, and articulation difficulties. Both syndromes have a severe impact on development and affect language skills and social relations. However, there are some important differences between the two syndromes.[8] In comparison with children with infantile autism, aphasic children are more likely (a) to attempt to establish meaningful relationships with others; (b) to engage in imaginative play; and (c) to have less impaired language skills (e.g., use fewer pronomial reversals and have less echolalia). Overall, children with infantile autism and aphasia both share a central language disorder, with the autistic children having a more severe handicap.

Infantile Autism vs. Developmental Language Disorder

Children with infantile autism, although differing in behavioral and social characteristics from children with developmental language disorders, have some language problems in common, particularly in regard to delayed speech. However, the language difficulties of the autistic child are more severe, extensive, and deviant, involving both the understanding and the use of spoken language, gesture, written language, sequencing, and abstraction (Rutter, 1978).

Childhood Schizophrenia vs. Other Adolescent Disorders

The schizophrenic syndrome in adolescence is difficult to distinguish from adolescent depressive disorders and transient adolescent crises (Kolvin, 1972). Adolescent crises are marked by irritability, moodiness, depression, affective expression difficulties, philosophical ruminations, and rebellion and conflict with parents and authorities. These symptoms are possible signs of turmoil. However, they usually prove to be transient and can be differentiated from the schizophrenic syndrome by the absence of hallucinations and delusions. It is important to remember that active psychotic episodes in adolescence may be induced by drugs, such as amphetamines or hallucinogenic drugs.

Childhood Schizophrenia vs. Mental Retardation

Childhood schizophrenia may be differentiated from mental retardation in that the child who develops schizophrenia may at first have a normal period of development and then deteriorate, whereas the mentally retarded child may remain at the same level throughout the developmental period (Mehr, 1952).

Childhood Schizophrenia vs. Brain Damage

Children with brain damage may differ from those with childhood schizophrenia by having a history of difficult birth, postnatal anoxia, whooping cough, encephalitis, or other conditions that may lead to brain damage (Mehr, 1952).

Summary

1. Children receiving a diagnosis of childhood psychosis usually display marked deviations in their relationships to people and to the environment, in their emotional maturation, and in their development of perceptual, motor, and cognitive skills. Childhood psychosis is the severest form of child psychopathology.

2. Symptoms of childhood psychosis are developmentally based. Symptoms occurring at the younger ages are associated with areas involving the child's newly acquired skills, while those occurring at older levels reflect areas of more mature development.

3. There are four types of childhood psychosis: infantile autism, childhood schizophrenia, disintegrative psychosis, and other psychoses of childhood.

4. *Infantile autism* appears between birth and 2½ years of age. The primary symptoms include failure to develop social relationships, deviant language, and ritualistic and compulsive activities. The most prominent view of the etiology of infantile autism is that it is associated with a neuropathophysiological process. Almost 75 percent of autistic children obtain IQs that are in the mentally retarded range of functioning. IQs obtained by autistic children are as valid as those obtained by normal children.

5. Children with *disintegrative psychosis* usually develop normally for their first three or four years of life and then display profound regression and behavioral disintegration. The prognosis is poor.

6. *Childhood schizophrenia* is a diagnosis primarily given to preadolescent or adolescent children. Symptoms are similar to those that occur in adults, including delusions and hallucinations.

7. Children who receive a diagnosis of *other psychoses of childhood* are more difficult to classify because their symptoms are less clearly defined.

8. Theories associated with the etiology of childhood psychosis include nonorganic theories, organic-experiential theories, and organic theories. Each theory has some difficulties in accounting for some of the findings associated with childhood psychosis. It is likely that a number of different etiologies may account for childhood psychosis.

9. Treatment goals are dependent in part on the psychotic child's symptoms and intellectual level and on the etiology of the condition. Attempts are made to restore impaired areas of functioning.

10. The prognosis for children with childhood psychoses is guarded. A majority remain severely handicapped in adolescence and in adulthood.

11. The most favorable prognostic indicators in autistic children are (a) IQs over 70, (b) useful speech by 5 years of age, (c) less frequent and less severe pathology, (d) ability to attend school, (e) appropriate use of play material, and (f) normal EEGs.

12. The assessment of children with childhood psychosis is similar to that of other children, with particular focus on the child's language, thought, affect, interpersonal relations, and perceptual-motor performance.

13. Language disorders are a primary area of dysfunction in childhood psychosis, with echolalia being a prominent symptom.

14. Observations of psychotic children's toy play indicates that it is less functional, more restricted, and more repetitive than that of normal children.

15. The IQ is the best single measure of integrative functioning in psychotic children.

16. Psychotic children perform poorly on intelligence tests. The younger psychotic children are when first seen by mental health professionals, the lower is their obtained IQ.

17. Some of the signs suggestive of childhood psychosis on intelligence tests include (a) a series of successes and then unpredictable failures, followed by later successes; (b) correct responses that have unusual lines of reasoning behind them; (c) other types of disturbances in thinking; and (d) body-image disturbances. Scatter has not proved to be a useful diagnostic procedure in differentiating psychotic children from other types of children.

18. While it is difficult to differentiate children with childhood psychoses from those with other types of psychopathology, some differences emerge. Within the area of childhood psychosis, there appear to be differences between children with infantile autism and those with childhood schizophrenia. In infantile autism there is failure of development, speech difficulties, a steady course of symptomatology, and a preponderance of males to females; in childhood schizophrenia there is a loss of reality after development is better established, hallucinations and delusions, an unsteady course of symptomatology, and an equal distribution of males and females. Aphasic children are more social than autistic children. Brain-injured children, in comparison to psychotic children, may have a more clear-cut history of illness.

24

Report Writing

Writing is, for most, laborious and slow. The mind travels faster than the pen; consequently, writing becomes a question of learning to make occasional wing shots, bringing down the bird of thought as it flashes by. A writer is a gunner, sometimes roaming the countryside hoping to scare something up. Like other gunners, he must cultivate patience; he may have to work many covers to bring down one partridge.

WILLIAM STRUNK, JR., and E. B. WHITE
The Elements of Style

Report writing is a challenging activity. It is a difficult and demanding skill to acquire, particularly in the early phases of a student's career. The writing of a report involves analyzing, synthesizing, and integrating numerous sources of data, including the child's test scores, previous test scores, teachers' reports, behavioral observations, interview material, social and family history, and medical findings. The report is one of the principal vehicles of communication, serving as a medium through which findings are described and impressions conveyed as clearly and as concisely as possible. Even before the report is begun, an attempt is made to make some kind of coherent whole of all of the available information. The report should clearly present findings, interpretations, and recommendations and should meet acceptable writing standards.

The report should be written soon after the evaluation is completed. Even though there may be some situations in which only an oral report is needed, it is recommended that a written report also be completed, because at some future date there may be a need for it. Details observed during the examination are likely to be forgotten unless they have been recorded at, or shortly after, the time of the evaluation. The results of the evaluation may be presented at staff conferences, to the child's parents, and to the child himself or herself. At these times, too, a written report is valuable.

Examiners assume many roles in writing the psychological report (Appelbaum, 1970). They may play the role of politician, diplomat, group dynamicist, salesperson, artist, and finally, psychologist. Which one or ones of these roles will be displayed is in part dependent on the particular setting in which the report is written. The key elements or features involved in report writing, according to Appelbaum, include the ability (a) to balance between data and abstraction, (b) to use modulation, (c) to be assertive or modest when necessary, (d) to keep the interest of the reader, (e) to use illustrations wisely, (f) to discuss systematically the individual parts of the report, and (g) to facilitate the decision-making process. Appelbaum views reports as being political, diplomatic, and strategic persuasions that function in a com-

EXHIBIT 24-1.   Some Prescriptions for Good Report Writing

Prescription	Symptom	Cure
1. *Use definite, specific, concrete language. Prefer the specific to the general, the definite to the vague, the concrete to the abstract.* The discipline of this rule forces the clinician to report particulars instead of generalizations.	"The child appeared to be mentally retarded."	"Tom's performance on the Stanford-Binet Intelligence Scale falls into the Mentally Retarded range. He obtained an IQ of 62 ± 5."
2. *Do not take shortcuts at the cost of clarity.* Avoid the use of initials unless they will be easily and accurately translated by all readers. Even sophisticated readers appreciate having test names written out in full until they get their bearings.	"The PPVT, VSMS, WISC-R, and SBIS-LM were administered."	"The following tests were administered: Peabody Picture Vocabulary Test, Vineland Social Maturity Scale, Wechsler Intelligence Scale for Children–Revised, and Stanford-Binet Intelligence Scale, Form L-M."
3. *A participial phrase at the beginning of a sentence must refer to the grammatical subject.* The sentence to the right is puzzling. Who administered the Vineland Scale? Who was enuretic?	"Administering the Vineland Social Maturity Scale, the mother admitted that enuresis was still a problem."	"Replying to questions on the Vineland Social Maturity Scale, the mother said that the child was enuretic."
4. *Avoid fancy words.* The line between the fancy and the plain is sometimes alarmingly fine. It is a question of "ear." During the ear-training process, the wise report writer will avoid an elaborate word when a simple one will suffice. The clinic report must not become a two-page exhibition of the writer's professional vocabulary. The best report writers use vocabulary true to their own experience. How does the ear respond to the example presented to the right?	"The patient exhibited apparent partial paralysis of motor units of the superior sinistral fibres of the genioglossus resulting in insufficient lingual approximation of the palatoalveolar regions. A condition of insufficient frenulum development was noted, producing not only sigmatic distortion but also obvious ankyloglossia."	"The patient was tongue-tied."
5. *Omit needless words. Make every word tell.* Overweight in clinic reports is as undesirable as overweight in people.	"the question as to whether" "he is a man who" "call your attention to the fact that" "his brother, who is a member of the same firm" "due to the fact that" "Although it can not be definitely established, it is quite probable that the patient, in all likelihood, is suffering some degree of aphasia."	"whether" "he" "remind you (notify you)" "his brother, a member of the same firm" "because" "The patient is probably aphasic."

EXHIBIT 24-1   (cont.)

Prescription	Symptom	Cure
6. *Express coordinate ideas in similar form.* The content, not the style, should protect the clinic report from monotony.	"The patient sat alone at six months. At eight months crawling began. Walking was noted at twelve months."	"The patient sat alone at 6 months, crawled at 8 months, and walked at 12 months."
7. *Do not affect a breezy manner.* Be professional, avoid pet ideas and phrases, and cultivate a natural rather than a flippant style of writing.	"Would you believe, Ma and Pa had a fuss right in the middle of the interview over when the child began to walk."	"The patient's parents disagreed on the date of walking."
8. *Do not overstate.* When you overstate, the reader will be instantly on guard, and everything that preceded your overstatement, as well as everything that follows it, will be suspect in his or her mind because he or she has lost confidence in your judgment or your poise.	"There is no tension in the home." "The patient is absolutely brilliant."	"The father reported no tension in the home." "The patient scored 141 on the Stanford-Binet Intelligence Scale, presented an all 'A' report card, and was voted 'most intelligent' by the high school faculty."
9. *Avoid the use of qualifiers.* Rather, very, little, pretty—these are the leeches that infest the pond of prose, sucking the blood of words.	"The patient was very attentive." "She was a pretty good student." "a pretty important rule"	"The patient was attentive." "She was a good student" *or* "She was a mediocre student" *or* "She had a grade point average of 3.4." "an important rule"
10. *Put statements in positive form. Make definite assertions. Avoid tame, colorless, hesitating, noncommittal language.* Consciously or unconsciously, the reader is dissatisfied with being told only what is not; he or she wishes to be told what is. Let's go over the last sentence again: Tell what is as well as what is not. If the clinician can delineate the threshold between what a patient can and can not do, and if he or she can accurately report this threshold to another person, the danger of a confused or confusing report is negligible.	"The child did not know his colors." "The patient did not have good motor control."	"The child did not name the colors of the red and blue blocks. However, he did separate the blocks by color and matched them to other red and blue objects in the room." "The patient stacked two blocks. He was not able to stack three blocks."

Adapted from Moore (1969). The prescriptions were originally obtained from Strunk and White (1959). Permission to reprint the material in this exhibit was obtained from the publisher and author from M. V. Moore, "Pathological Writing," *Asha, 11,* pp. 535–537. Copyright 1969, American Speech-Language-Hearing Association.

plex sociopsychological context, rather than as being solely technical and scientific documents.

Paralleling the approach of Appelbaum, yet slightly different, is the interesting and valuable approach to report writing proposed by Fischer (1973, 1979). The approach, while not radically different from those offered by other writers or from that offered in this chapter, emphasizes a contextual approach as an alternative to the psychodynamic approach. The social/descriptive/contextual approach highlights the relationship between the examinee and the examiner, the circumstances under which the testing took place, the limited range of opportunities for observation and interaction, and the behavioral bases for the statements made in the report. Concrete recommendations, which have been discussed with the examinee, are emphasized. The report is descriptive and requires extensive samples; it eliminates constructs, causal interpretations, and jargon. The necessity to select specific examples and make recommendations confronts examiners with the issue of values. They must try to balance the needs of the examinee, of society, and of themselves.

By the time you have reached this chapter, you have been exposed to many different types of reports. At the beginning of the book, there is a list of psychological evaluations under the *List of Exhibits*. It may be helpful at this time to read these reports again and to study the various styles used in the reports. Let us now examine a typical report outline and then consider each part in more detail.

Suggested Report Outline

Psychological Evaluation

Name:
Date of birth:
Chronological age:
Date of examination:
Date of report:
Grade:
Test(s) administered:

1. *Reason for referral.* Note the problem indicated by the referral source, such as suspected retardation, speech difficulty, behavior problem, or perceptual-motor handicap. Also note relevant background information.
2. *General observations.* Include a brief description of the examinee. Note any physical characteristics that might affect test performance and describe atypical behaviors, attitudes, and feelings.
3. *Test results.* Present CA, IQ, precision range, classification, percentile rank, and representativeness of the results. In addition, for the Stanford-Binet, present the MA and, if desired, basal and ceiling levels; for the WISC-R, WPPSI, and WAIS-R present, if desired, Verbal and Performance IQs. [Subtest scores and drawings shown in exhibits are for illustrative purposes only.] Comment on the variability of tests passed and failed if noteworthy or if desired. Note any factors that may have distorted the results. Consider how educational, emotional, and cultural factors may have affected the examinee's test performance. Discuss the examinee's strengths and weaknesses, personality characteristics, diagnostic implications of findings, and other related material.
4. *Recommendations.* Be as specific as possible. Always try to answer the referral questions. Indicate your level of confidence in the predictions and in the recommendations.
5. *Summary.* If included, make the summary a short, one-paragraph integrated statement of test findings and recommendations.

Examiner's Name

Reason for Referral

The reason for referral places a perspective on the report. Information obtained from the referral source—including teachers, physicians, or parents—can be included in this section.

General Observations

The behavioral observations usually focus on a number of different areas (Watson, 1951). The child's appearance; adjustment to the test situation; degree of cooperation, effort, and attention; and attitude toward the tests and his or her own abilities are observed. Other areas include observation of the child's speech, including pitch of voice; vocabulary level and ability to express himself or herself; spontaneity and initiative during testing; general mood and sociability; evidence of anxiety; and ability to shift from one activity to another. Overall, the clinician evaluates the nature of the rapport during the evaluation and arrives at a general impression of the child.

Skilled observation of behavior requires training. Good observational skills do not follow automatically from simply being placed in a situation where one is required to observe. The clinician must develop various kinds of skills. One, for example, involves the accurate reporting of behavior, and this requires that the clinician be alert and attentive to the child's behavior. A second involves the making of relevant inferences from these observations. It is important to recognize that conclusions based on the samples of behavior obtained in the test situation may not generalize to behavior outside of the test situation. The test situation is a relatively narrow and, to some degree, artificial situation. It is imperative that the clinician evaluate the behaviors obtained in the test situation in light of the entire case study (Watson, 1951). The following behavioral cues are important to consider. The many cues may bewilder the novice; however, with increased experience the beginning examiner will notice a greater number of them.

LIST OF BEHAVIORAL CUES

Attitudinal Features

Attitude toward examiner:

1. How does the examinee relate to the examiner and the examiner to the examinee?
2. Is the examinee shy, frightened, aggressive, or friendly?
3. Is the examinee negativistic, normally compliant, or over-eager to please?
4. Is there a change from the initial meeting between the examinee and the examiner to the later part of the test situation?
5. Does the examinee try to induce the examiner to give answers to questions?
6. Does the examinee watch the examiner closely to discover whether his or her responses are correct?

Attitude toward test situation:

1. Is the examinee relaxed and at ease, tense and inhibited, or restless?
2. Is the examinee interested or uninvolved?
3. Does the examinee seem confident of his or her ability?
4. Is the examinee an eager or perfunctory participant?
5. Are the tasks enjoyable to the examinee as games, challenging as chances to excel, or threatening as possible sources of failure?
6. How well does the examinee attend to the test?
7. Is it necessary to repeat instructions?
8. Is it easy or difficult to regain the examinee's attention once it is lost?
9. Does the examinee appear to be exerting his or her best effort?
10. Does the examinee try only when urged on by the examiner?
11. Does the examinee give up easily or does he or she insist on continuing to work on difficult items?
12. Does the examinee's interest vary during the examination?

Attitude toward self:

1. Does the examinee have poise and confidence?
2. Does the examinee make frequent self-derogatory or boastful remarks or is he or she fairly objective toward his or her achievement?

Work habits:

1. Has the examinee a characteristic fast or slow work tempo?
2. Does the examinee appear to think about and organize his or her answers or does he or she give them impulsively or carelessly?
3. Does the examinee revise any of his or her answers?
4. Does the examinee think aloud or will he or she give only his or her final answer?

Reaction to test items:

1. What type of test item produces such reactions as anxiety, stammering, or blushing?
2. Are there any areas of the test in which the examinee feels more comfortable or less comfortable?
3. Is the examinee more interested in some types of items than in others?

Reaction to failure:

1. How does the examinee react to failure?
2. Does he or she apologize, rationalize, or accept failure calmly?
3. When faced with difficult items, how does the examinee react? Does the examinee retreat, become aggressive, work harder, try to cheat, become evasive, or openly admit failure?
4. If the examinee becomes aggressive, toward whom or what does the examinee direct the aggression?
5. If questioned further about an item, does the examinee reconsider the answer, defend the first answer, or become silent?

Reaction to praise:

1. How does the examinee react to praise?
2. Does the examinee accept it gracefully or awkwardly?
3. Does it motivate the examinee to work harder?

Language

1. How clearly and accurately does the examinee express himself or herself?
2. Is the examinee's speech fluent, halting, articulate, inexact, or precise?
3. Are the examinee's responses direct and to the point, or vague, roundabout, or free associative?
4. Does the examinee make any free, spontaneous conversation or does the examinee limit himself or herself to responding only to questions?
5. Does the examinee's conversation appear to derive from friendliness or from a desire to evade the test situation?

Visual-Motor

1. Note the movements the examinee makes with his or her hands, feet, and face, and how the examinee handles the testing material.
2. Note the examinee's handedness.
3. Is the examinee's reaction time fast or slow?
4. Does the examinee proceed in a trial-and-error manner?
5. Is the examinee skillful or awkward?
6. Are bilateral movements skillfully executed?

A convenient way of recording the examinee's reactions in the testing situation is to use the Behavior and Attitude Checklist, which is shown in Table 24-1. The Checklist, which was developed in part from the material described in this section of the chapter, has eleven divisions with twenty-eight 7-point scales. The Checklist, completed by placing an "X" in the appropriate space, can be filed with the record booklet for each examinee. The psychological report should include a discussion of the highlights of the Checklist data.

The Behavior and Attitude Checklist, as well as other material discussed in this text, is not meant to cover and cannot cover all contingencies that can arise during the course of the examination. On some occasions the examinee may be described easily by the categories found on the Checklist; however, the examiner should be prepared to encounter examinees who display behaviors that are not covered by the categories described on the Checklist. *The goal in all cases is to capture the examinee's uniqueness.* Statements that describe the examinee's behavior should be distinguished clearly from statements that interpret this behavior; however, observations and inferences are both valuable.

Test Results

The test results should be presented clearly and succinctly. Any doubts about the reliability and validity of the results should be clearly stated. In reporting the results of intelligence tests, it is advisable to note the

TABLE 24-1.   Behavior and Attitude Checklist

Name: Examiner:
Age: Date of report:
Test(s) administered: Date of examination:
IQ: Grade:

Instructions: Place an "X" on the appropriate line for each scale.

I. Attitude toward examiner and test situation:
   1. cooperative   __: __: __: __: __: __: __   uncooperative
   2. passive   __: __: __: __: __: __: __   aggressive
   3. tense   __: __: __: __: __: __: __   relaxed
   4. gives up easily   __: __: __: __: __: __: __   does not give up easily
II. Attitude toward self:
   5. confident   __: __: __: __: __: __: __   not confident
   6. critical of own work __: __: __: __: __: __: __   accepting of own work
III. Work habits:
   7. fast   __: __: __: __: __: __: __   slow
   8. deliberate   __: __: __: __: __: __: __   impulsive
   9. thinks aloud   __: __: __: __: __: __: __   thinks silently
   10. careless   __: __: __: __: __: __: __   neat
IV. Behavior:
   11. calm   __: __: __: __: __: __: __   hyperactive
V. Reaction to failure:
   12. aware of failure   __: __: __: __: __: __: __   unaware of failure
   13. works harder after
      failure   __: __: __: __: __: __: __   gives up easily after failure
   14. calm after failure __: __: __: __: __: __: __   agitated after failure
   15. apologetic after failure __: __: __: __: __: __: __   not apologetic after failure
VI. Reaction to praise:
   16. accepts praise gracefully __: __: __: __: __: __: __   accepts praise awkwardly
   17. works harder after
      praise   __: __: __: __: __: __: __   retreats after praise
VII. Speech and language:
   18. speech poor   __: __: __: __: __: __: __   speech good
   19. articulate language __: __: __: __: __: __: __   inarticulate language
   20. responses direct   __: __: __: __: __: __: __   responses vague
   21. converses
      spontaneously   __: __: __: __: __: __: __   only speaks when spoken to
   22. bizarre language   __: __: __: __: __: __: __   reality oriented language
VIII. Visual-motor:
   23. reaction time slow __: __: __: __: __: __: __   reaction time fast
   24. trial-and-error   __: __: __: __: __: __: __   careful and planned
   25. skillful movements __: __: __: __: __: __: __   awkward movements
IX. Motor:
   26. defective motor
      coordination   __: __: __: __: __: __: __   good motor coordination
X. Overall test results:
   27. reliable   __: __: __: __: __: __: __   unreliable
   28. valid   __: __: __: __: __: __: __   invalid
XI. Other:

Developed by Jerome M. Sattler; revised 1981.

precision range associated with the obtained IQ. The precision range is based on the standard error of measurement and the confidence level selected. The appropriate bands for the precision range are located in Table C-1 for the Stanford-Binet and Tables C-5 and C-16 for the WISC-R and WPPSI, respectively, in the Appendix. Table C-1 is entered with both the examinee's chronological age and his or her IQ, whereas in Tables C-5 and C-16 only the child's age is needed.

Suppose that Joe, a 4-year-old examinee, obtained an IQ of 100 on the Stanford-Binet, and the examiner wishes to use the 68 percent level of precision. Table C-1 shows that for the 68 percent confidence level the appropriate confidence interval for this age and IQ level is 5. (The actual standard error is 5.3, but all numbers have been rounded off for ease of expression in the report.) The recommended way of reporting this precision range is as follows:

"*Joe obtained an IQ of 100 ± 5. The chances that the range of scores from 95 to 105 includes his true IQ are about 68 out of 100.*"

If the 85, 90, 95, or 99 percent level is selected, the range and probability statement will change. The recommended ways of expressing these levels for Joe are as follows:

- "Joe obtained an IQ of 100 ± 8. The chances that the range of scores from 92 to 108 includes his true IQ are about 85 out of 100."
- "Joe obtained an IQ of 100 ± 9. The chances that the range of scores from 91 to 109 includes his true IQ are about 90 out of 100."
- "Joe obtained an IQ of 100 ± 10. The chances that the range of scores from 90 to 110 includes his true IQ are about 95 out of 100."
- "Joe obtained an IQ of 100 ± 14. The chances that the range of scores from 86 to 114 includes his true IQ are about 99 out of 100."

Notice that as the confidence level becomes more stringent, the precision range becomes wider.

In addition to reporting the test results, it is necessary to interpret the findings and to arrive at some synthesis of the overall pattern of scores and test performance. A greater degree of confidence can be placed in the interpretations when there is consistency in behavioral observations, qualitative analysis, pattern of performance on the tests, and case history material. However, when there is much inconsistency among the various sources of data, caution is needed in arriving at a diagnostic formulation. *Diagnostic statements should never be made on the basis of insufficient data.*

Recommendations

The recommendation section of the report is an important part of the psychological evaluation. The recommendations are based on the child's pattern of strengths and weaknesses and on the implications that this pattern has for remediation, treatment, and rehabilitation. The aim is not so much to look for a "cure" or "label," but to offer a flexible approach for remediation.

An important aim of the recommendations (and of the assessment as a whole) is to try to find ways to help children help themselves and to involve teachers and parents directly in the educational and therapeutic efforts (Fischer, 1976). The emphasis is on the child, on the child's situation, and on identifying avenues for growth and enrichment. Suggestions for change should be practical, concrete, and individualized. The child's active involvement in influencing his or her own life should be encouraged by the psychologist.

Recommendations can focus on many different factors, such as (a) covering specific suggestions for stimulating and enhancing the child's psychological growth and development, (b) providing information about possible patterns of developmental disturbances, (c) indicating a need for retesting or for further evaluation, (d) suggesting specific forms of treatment or remedial education, (e) pointing out vocational aptitudes and areas of strength, and (f) making predictions about future behavior. Recommendations should enable the reader to plan a program suitable to the child's needs and level of functioning.

Making predictions about future levels of attainment is difficult and risky. Further, predictions are potentially damaging to the child because the reader of the report may be lulled into thinking that a course of development is fixed or unchangeable. Tyler (1965) rightly cautioned: "Those responsible for the guidance of children need to realize that a single intelligence test can never be used as a basis for a definite judgment about what a child will be able to do several years later. Each new decision, at successive stages of development, calls for a recheck" (p. 71). Therefore, while it is important to indicate the examinees' present level of functioning and to make suggestions about what can be expected of them, statements dealing with performance in the far distant future must be made cautiously, if at all.

The recommendation section of the report should be written so that the reader recognizes clearly the examiner's degree of confidence in the predictions. Occasionally, it is helpful to cite test data or behavioral data to enable the reader to understand the recommendations better. Recommendations serve to highlight the findings and their implications and to individualize the report.

Summary

A summary is optional. While a summary reviews and integrates the test findings, it also may be repetitious, may unnecessarily lengthen the report, and may detract from the report by allowing the reader to forgo reading the main body of the report. Ideally, the report itself should be a summary: precise, compact, and to the point. If a summary is written, include all pertinent material. Limit the summary to a short, organized, and integrated paragraph. Do not include any new material in the summary.

Comment on Report Outline

The suggested report outline is meant to serve as a guideline, not as a fixed, unalterable way of organizing a report; other formats also are acceptable. The report's organization depends on the preference of the examiner, which, in turn, may be partly governed by the users of the report. The organization of the report should be logical and convey as clearly as possible the test findings, interpretations, and recommendations. In some cases, examiners place the recommendation section after the summary. This may occur when they desire to highlight or emphasize the recommendations. A summary in such instances, if written, would focus on the test results and on related information and not on the recommendations.

Considerations in Report Writing

We have just read about the structure of the psychological report. Now let us consider some of the more subtle points that are involved in the process of developing a report.

Focus of Report

Reports may have a *test* orientation or a *subject* orientation. Test-oriented reports rely primarily on the presentation of factual material, such as test questions, year levels, and other technical aspects of the examinee's performance. The subject-oriented report makes use of the same data, but instead of referring to the data directly, it uses them to describe the examinee. For example, "John passed the Vocabulary test at year level VIII of the examination" is a test-oriented statement, while "John's vocabulary knowledge is at the level of an average 8-year-old" is a more subject-oriented statement. Regardless of where the focus is placed, the report should aim to describe the examinee as carefully as possible. For example, how does the examinee with an IQ of 100 differ from other examinees with the same IQ? Answering such a question fulfills one of the primary objectives of the report: to present a description of the examinee that portrays his or her unique pattern and style of performance. While this objective may not always be achieved, it is worth striving for.

The subject-oriented report is probably more satisfactory for a psychological evaluation. However, the test-oriented report is not directly opposed to the subject-oriented report; the difference is a matter of emphasis. Even if an agency requires test-oriented reports or, for that matter, if the examiner prefers to write test-oriented reports, examinee characteristics should be included. Subject-oriented reports should, in turn, include test data. Subject-oriented reports may require more effort to write than test-oriented ones.

The goal of the report is to answer the referral questions and to present an integrated and meaningful picture of the examinee's abilities. Therefore, to answer such referral questions as "How can I best deal with John's behavior?" or "What factors are associated with John's low level of academic performance?" the report should discuss material related to the examinee's aptitudes, personality, and other pertinent factors, in addition to the quantitative data obtained from the examinee's performance on the test. In arriving at appropriate recommendations, all relevant factors, such as background information that includes school and medical records and family history, must be considered—not just the test results.

Deciding What Material to Include in the Report

At times it will be difficult to determine whether or not to include certain material in the report. At these times, judgment and discretion are required. Helpful guideposts include the nature of the referral problem, the object of testing, and the background of the persons for whom the report is written (Sargent, 1951).

When is it worthwhile, for example, to describe the child's grooming, handedness, or body structure? Each case must be considered individually. In some cases, the child's handedness may provide information helpful in determining whether mixed dominance exists. In other cases, a discussion of the child's grooming may contribute to an understanding of the child's self-concept,

attitudes, or family environment. In still other cases, neither handedness nor grooming will be of importance. Emphasize material that pertains to the referral question, that conveys the child's individuality, and that reflects unusual behaviors and attitudes. Avoid giving interpretations without supporting evidence. The formulation of every report is a process of incorporating those details, over and above the standard data, that highlight the examinee's unique level of psychological functioning. An important question that can guide the examiner about choice of material is "Does it serve to *individualize* the child?" (Lodge, 1953).

The steps used in arriving at inferences, conclusions, recommendations, and diagnostic formulations should not be presented in the report. "In scanning the test items successfully completed by the client, it was apparent that . . . " is superfluous. The statement should start with the information which follows after "that." Similarly, it is generally unnecessary to refer to the raw data upon which the inferences were based. Occasionally, however, carefully selected examples from the examinee's responses can enhance the meaningfulness of the report by serving to illustrate the diagnostic formulations. If, for instance, an examinee is described as giving over-elaborated responses, including an example would be helpful. Sometimes it may be necessary to cite the test question together with the examinee's response in order to facilitate the reader's understanding. It may not be enough to refer to specific tests or subtests by name, because test or subtest names may have limited meaning to the reader; instead, *describe* what they measure or require.

Deciding on the Degree of Certainty of the Statements

Phrases and words such as "probably," "it appears," "perhaps," and "it seems" are often used in reports when we are not completely confident of our predictions, conclusions, or inferences. However, when definitive data are available, present them confidently. One could write: "The child's IQ is in the Superior classification. The chances that the range of scores from 130 to 140 includes her true IQ are about 68 in 100." As Foster (1951) observed: "Be positive when sure, qualify when in doubt" (p. 195).

The degree of certainty we have about our conclusions will depend on the available data. Examinees' test behavior and responses are the observed data, whereas inferred behavior or predicted behavior has not yet been demonstrated. Recognizing the difference between what examinees actually *did*, that is, their test performance, and what they *may* be able to do may help in reducing the amount of ambiguity contained in the report and may also help in reducing errors of interpretation. For example, the examiner usually is certain that the child has brown eyes or that the child obtained an IQ of 110. The examiner is only reasonably sure that the range from 100 to 120 includes the child's true IQ. Finally, the examiner is less sure that the child will improve his or her performance if transferred to another teacher.

Noting Examination Conditions That May Help Explain Performance

Once the specific focus of the report has been decided on, material should be selected that describes and elucidates the main theme or themes. The aim is to give a consistent and integrated account of the examinee's abilities. However, data that diverge from the main theme should be included, especially if they have important implications. Discrepancy in performance—or, more likely, variability in performance—is especially useful in guiding predictions, inferences, and recommendations. Suppose, for example, that there is a general pattern of memory difficulty, but not a consistent one. In such a case, the variable efficiency should be noted. Diagnostic formulations should take into account the degree of consistency in the test performance. Degree of consistency alerts us to factors present during the examination, such as fatigue, anxiety, or lack of interest, that may partially explain the examinee's successes and failures.

Inferences are based on many different forms of information, including the quality of the interaction between the examinee and examiner, the examinee's responses, and the examinee's case history, which may include previous test results. *Everything observed from the initial encounter to the termination of the contact with the examinee constitutes data for analysis. The examination is to be viewed not merely as a question-and-answer session, but as an opportunity for interaction between two individuals. This interaction is as much a part of the examination as are the test questions and the examinee's responses.* Examiners must consider how they affect examinees and how, in turn, the examinees affect them. The nature of the interaction may play an important role in influencing interpretations. It may very well be that on some occasions the examinee's behavior is primarily a reaction to the examiner's behavior rather than a reaction to the test demands. Administration, scoring, and interpretation of intelligence and special ability tests are by no means so standardized that we can neglect individual differences among examiners and examinees.

Anchoring the Report to the Intelligence Level

When the goal of the evaluation is to estimate the child's intelligence, the obtained IQ serves as the anchor point for the development of the report. Primary emphasis should be given to the child's general level of intellectual functioning. A child with an IQ of 130 should appear superior in the report, while one with an IQ of 70 should appear dull. *The examinee's pattern of performance usually should be analyzed with reference to his or her general range of intellectual ability.* In presenting the examinee's strengths and weaknesses, it is helpful to use such terms as "relatively less developed," "relatively more developed," "in relation to his level of functioning," "in relation to the average child of her age," and "above average in her . . . [a specific area such as language, visual-motor, or memory may be cited] functioning." When the child's abilities are superior or retarded, terms such as strength or weakness can be used.

Some Helpful Questions for Report Writing

As an overall guide to report writing, the following questions can help you think about the various elements of the report.

1. How representative are the test results?
2. Have all relevant materials been considered in arriving at your recommendations and impressions, including the present test results, interpersonal behavior, previous test results, parental reports, teacher observations, medical evaluations, and school grades?
3. What recommendations are feasible?
4. What community or school resources are available to carry out the recommendations?
5. Are follow-up evaluations necessary?

Avoiding Common Pitfalls in Report Writing

This section presents general and specific suggestions to aid in the art of clear writing. The points in this section may help to eliminate or reduce many of the problems that impede communication. In order to promote clarity, focus on the *presence* of a trait or behavior rather than on its absence. An almost infinite number of things that did not characterize the examinee can be cited. Unless it is expected that the report will contain information about pathological symptoms (e.g., brain damage), citing the absence of an attribute is not illuminating. Describe how the examinee actually performed. However, occasionally there are complaints or reports from parents, schools, physicians, or others that the child has a particular problem. When a thorough examination does not reveal what has been presented originally, comment certainly should be made that a specific attribute or behavior was not apparent or not discernible during the evaluation.

If terms that are obscure or only understood by a limited number of people must be used, be sure to describe them in detail. Thus, for example, do not use abbreviations to stand for special programs or refer to room numbers in buildings without describing the referents in sufficient detail. The reader is likely to become perplexed unless obscure details are either eliminated or clarified.

Some report writers have a tendency to dissect or fragment examinees so that they are presented as if various parts of their intellectual ability or personality are independent of one another. The examinee's abilities are always interrelated, but not necessarily in a well-integrated and well-functioning manner. To illustrate the interplay of abilities, use expressions conveying comparison and contrast, such as "however," "but," "on the one hand," "on the other hand," or "in comparison with" to help build an integrated picture of the examinee's abilities.

When mental health agencies share their reports with schools, a variety of problems can arise. The guidelines offered below will help diminish problems that arise in interagency communication and in other settings as well (Drake & Bardon, 1978, pp. 314–315). (You will see that some of the guidelines overlap with those offered later in the chapter.)

- Hearsay or unverified opinions are best omitted, along with information that has little relevance for the educational well-being of a child or that adds little to the school's understanding of him [or her].
- Before a report is sent to a school, it is important to know the reasons for the request and the decisions that need to be made about the child. Such information will enable the writer to focus the report on specific problems and to avoid including information that is unnecessary.
- In writing the report, behavioral descriptions or supporting information are preferable to generalized statements. For example, it is better to write "Johnny refused to be tested and ran away from the office in tears," rather than "Johnny is a negative child who shows hostility toward those who wish to help him."
- Generalized statements should be backed up by specific information. For example, a statement that Johnny needs supplemental help might be supported as follows: "Johnny's academic achievement scores

place him significantly below national norms, while his performance on mental ability tests suggests that he could achieve at a higher level."

- The source of information should be cited if statements that cannot be directly verified are made. Attributions such as "his mother reported," "according to his classroom teacher," or "according to the report prepared by the school psychologist" lend credence to the information.
- If information that is not verifiable or attributable to other sources seems warranted in the opinion of the report writer, qualifiers such as "it appears," "it seems," or "in my professional judgment" should be used to help separate opinion from conclusions based on verifiable information.
- Information that is potentially harmful or damaging to a child were it to be revealed should be excluded from a report if possible. If it is necessary for the school to have such information, it should be conveyed orally to a school-employed mental health worker on a professional basis, with the firm understanding that the information is provided for school professionals only and is not to become part of the school's written records.

A variety of sentences that fail to meet acceptable standards of communication are now presented. The types of problems they demonstrate are grouped into descriptive categories. Although the sentences have been taken out of context, careful study of the sentences and the comments that follow them should help you to recognize and avoid potential problems. Some of the sample sentences have more than one problem and some of the categories overlap, so that placement in a specific category is somewhat arbitrary. Additional guidelines for report writing are shown in Exhibit 26-1, which is on pp. 492–493.

Abstractness

Sentences containing abstract ideas and terms present problems for the reader. The reader must strain for meaning. Information may be lost because vagueness and ambiguity, often a result of abstract phrases, have replaced the directness and simplicity needed for communication.

Example 1. "It is recommended that he be tested again after a three-year period to ascertain whether or not maturation will result in an improved operational level." This is a highly abstract way of saying "Retesting in three years is recommended in order to evaluate developmental changes."

Example 2. "His seemingly conscious withdrawal from conversation coupled with an outwardly stoic nature yield an impression of social impoverishment." "Conscious withdrawal," "stoic nature," and "social impoverishment" are complex concepts. The examiner must be wary of describing the examinee as having traits that he or she may not possess, and of making statements that go beyond an accurate account of the examinee's behavior. To avoid any misinterpretation brought about by the use of the word "stoic," it would be less ambiguous if the examinee's behavior were accurately described (e.g., not showing much emotion during the test). Reticence and a suggested stoical nature need not indicate social impoverishment. The examinee, boxed in stoicism, wrapped and tied in conscious withdrawal, and labeled as socially impoverished, is defenselessly delivered to the reader. Rephrasing is warranted in order to achieve clarity.

Ambiguity

The ambiguous sentence does not clearly inform the reader what the examiner wishes to convey. Be alert to any sentences that may be misinterpreted or that have implications other than those desired.

Example 1. "It is possible that his performance may reflect the lack of proper emotional orientation that is necessary for meaningful and emotionally relevant action." The concept "meaningful and emotionally relevant action" is ambiguous because it has many possible implications that need to be clarified. Furthermore, concrete illustrations of the examinee's performance are needed to enable the reader to understand the interpretation.

Example 2. "Joe lacks language ability." "Lacks" may mean either "is deficient in" or "shows a complete absence of." Therefore, ambiguity is created when the phrase is used. The examiner, in all probability, does not literally mean that there is a complete absence of language ability; rather, he or she desires to convey that the examinee is "below average" or "inadequate" or "retarded" or "slow" or something similar. Preferably, he or she would use one of these terms to convey as precisely as possible the level at which the examinee is functioning. For example, he or she may note that the examinee is below average in language ability or say that language functioning level is approximately two years below chronological age. A gifted examinee can be described as being superior in his or her language ability, or one may say that language functioning is at a level four years above chronological age. It is, of course, possible that in exceptional cases the examinee does "lack" a particular skill. In these cases, a sentence such as "Joe cannot write, speak, or understand the speech of others" conveys the information.

Apologies

Do not make excuses either for the test or for the examinee's test performance. Report, without apology, the results of the evaluation in as objective a manner as possible.

Example 1. "Jill gave the impression of enjoying herself, and at the same time was willing to try to meet the challenge of the seemingly never-ending questions of the examiner." To whom did the questions seem never-ending? Do not apologize for the examination techniques, since apologetic statements tend to belittle indirectly the examiner's professional status and perhaps to diminish the value of the report as well.

Example 2. "The examiner is sorry that Jim achieved an IQ of only 85." Why include "sorry" and "only"? The examiner appears to be belittling the examinee's performance. If other information indicated that the examinee was expected to perform at a higher level of functioning, then this expectation should be noted and the relevant information included; doubts about the representativeness of the results should be clearly brought out. With the use of the term "only," the reader is left in doubt, because he or she does not know why it was included. Perhaps those examinees falling into ranges below the normal do not feel as helpless or as sorry for themselves as we might think they feel. Our personal values should not be imposed or projected on either the examinees or the readers.

Awkwardness

Awkward sentences contain ambiguous, abstract, vague, or superfluous material. Stylistic problems are therefore evident.

Example 1. "His confidence was congruent with his abilities, and although he realized that he was intelligent, he did not appear to overvalue it or undervalue it, but rather seemed to accept it without evaluating it." The examiner appears to be presenting a picture of a normal examinee, yet the statement is so troubled—poor referents and awkward phraseology—that the message is lost. Better: "He displayed a great deal of confidence in his abilities."

Example 2. "He did not appear to be anxious or concerned but was willing to try to succeed within his normal pattern of effort." The examiner does not usually know what is the examinee's "normal pattern of effort." Better: "His motivation was normal."

Content Unimportant

It is sometimes difficult to determine what material to include in the report. Judgment must be used at all times. "I didn't know what to say" is not sufficient justification for including material that is not important.

Focus on statements that will contribute to an understanding of the examinee's performance.

Example 1. "At one time she wanted to use my pencil and draw a picture, but it was explained to her that she had to wait to draw until we were finished. After the test she drew a quick picture and took it with her." Unless this information is serving to illustrate a particular point, why include it? It might be a useful exercise to imagine oneself as the reader, wondering why the material is included in the report.

Example 2. "John told me that he walks to school and that he likes television." Without other relevant details, the information contained in the sentence is not informative. However, if the child's walking to school reflects a recovery from an illness or reflects a development of independence, then such information is valuable and should appear in the report accompanied by an interpretation.

Generalization Inappropriate

Do not overgeneralize from limited data. All available information should be used in arriving at conclusions. Recommendations and interpretations should be based on reliable and sufficient data.

Example 1. "Nancy was weak in areas requiring numerical reasoning, as evidenced by her missing the item on ingenuity at the Average Adult level." Reference to one item is not sufficient justification for concluding that she was weak in numerical reasoning. It is hazardous to generalize from one failure or from one success. A consistent, clear-cut *pattern* of failures or successes should be present before conclusions of this kind are reached. The levels at which the successes and failures occurred will help in guiding the interpretations.

Example 2. "The examinee is small for his age and may feel a need to achieve." Again, if smallness is the only bit of data available

to the examiner about the examinee's achievement needs, this interpretation should not be made.

Example 3. "On the basis of his Full Scale IQ of 107, it is predicted that Mark will do at least average work in school and that he will excel in athletics." Two inappropriate generalizations are contained in this sentence. First, the 107 IQ indicates that he is *capable* of performing at least at a normal level in school; it does not mean that he *will* perform at that level. Second, the statement about athletics cannot be made on the basis of a child's performance on an intelligence test.

Example 4. "Charles demonstrated good attention span, which indicates that he is free from anxiety." Satisfactory performance on the Digit Span or Sentences subtests, for example, does not indicate that the child is free from anxiety. The best that can be said is that anxiety did not appear to affect the child's performance.

Hedging

Statements about the examinee's performance should be presented in a direct and confident manner when sufficient data are present. Do not hedge when the data are clear. While there are occasions when caution is needed, factual data may be presented simply and precisely.

Example 1. "The Intelligence Quotient of 120 on the Stanford-Binet would seem to indicate a High Average to Superior range of functioning." An IQ of 120 is in the Superior classification according to the Stanford-Binet manual. There is no need to hedge about this fact or about similar facts. Referring to an IQ of 120 as being in the High Average range is also incorrect. Better: "The Intelligence Quotient of 120 is in the Superior classification on the Stanford-Binet, Form L-M."

Example 2. "The IQ obtained by Jim was approximately 86." The IQ obtained on any **one occasion** is an estimate of intelligence and, as stressed in this text, should be accompanied by a statement of precision (standard error). However, the examination does permit the calculation of a score, and this score is a specific, exact number. Therefore, in the sentence above, the word "approximately" should be eliminated, and in its place a precision range should be written (e.g., 86 ± 5).

Incorrect Inferential Statements

Inferential statements that assume definite cause and effect relationships should not be made without supporting data.

Example 1. "Mrs. Jones's rejection of Susan has led to her lying and stealing in school." Supporting information is needed. For example, "According to the examiner's interpretation of the TAT data, Susan's lying and stealing may be related to feelings of maternal rejection" (Drake & Bardon, 1978).

Example 2. "Johnny lacks educational skills." Again supporting information is needed. For example, "Johnny's test scores on the X achievement test are at the 13th percentile on national norms for reading comprehension and at the 16th percentile for arithmetic calculation" (Drake & Bardon, 1978).

Inexactitude

Inexact sentences invite a host of problems, including incorrect interpretations.

Example 1. "Her physical appearance suggested no behavioral problems." Rarely will the examinee's physical appearance denote a behavioral problem. Better: "Her appearance was quite ordinary. She was dressed in a loosely fitting sweater and skirt, and her height and weight are normal for her age."

Example 2. "The examinee achieved an IQ of 112. He has just begun kindergarten and needs to develop listening skills and an approach to solving problems." Since the examinee achieved an IQ of 112, it is diffi-

cult to understand how he achieved this score without having developed *some* listening skills and an adequate pattern of solving problems. The examiner may not have meant to relate the two sentences, but may have seen them as two separate facts and failed to indicate this by lack of a transition. If other information leads you to conclude that the examinee is hyperactive or more impulsive than the average examinee of his age, clearly indicate this in the report. To answer the examination questions successfully, the examinee usually must be able to attend to the test questions, concentrate, and respond to the directions. Always consider what the appropriate normative behavior is for the examinee's developmental stage.

Example 3. "Bill's only weakness was shown by his score on the Arithmetic subtest." This sentence was based on WISC-R scaled scores of 13 or more on all of the subtests, with the exception of a 10 on Arithmetic. The interpretation is incorrect because a scaled score of 10 represents average functioning. This child had no significant weaknesses in relation to the standardization group. His score on the Arithmetic subtest, rather, indicates that he is not as well developed in arithmetical skills as he is in other areas of the test.

Irrelevant Statements

Statements that are irrelevant to the purposes of the report should not be included.

Example 1. "Jeffrey's mother has been seen leaving the house at odd hours."

Example 2. "Beverly was sexually molested when a child." If this or the statement in Example 1 is potentially relevant, cite source, use the qualifier "reportedly," or convey such information verbally to the referral source (Drake & Bardon, 1978).

Limited or Too General

A virtue in report writing is to be as complete as possible, while recognizing that the report should be kept within manageable bounds and should include only significant information. However, when the material is too sparse, ambiguity may result. Clarity can be achieved, on some of these occasions, by presenting the data on which the interpretation was based. Comments that are "too general," on the other hand, should be eliminated, except when they pertain to some specific question posed by the referral source.

Example 1. "The examiner would recommend that additional information be gathered in regard to her background and her achievement." In and of itself, this recommendation is acceptable. However, the statement should be more specific so that the reader knows *what* information is needed and *why* it is needed. What does the examiner hope to learn from the additional information? What purpose will it serve? Does the examiner wish to see the examinee for further evaluation after the additional information is obtained? Thus, recommendations should incorporate, at times, the rationale used in their formulation.

Example 2. "Bobby shows indications of strength in numerical reasoning and in nonverbal reasoning, and on tests dealing with nonmeaningful memory. Other areas of strength include. . . ." These are tantalizing sentences because the reader is not given information concerning the examinee's absolute strength. It would be helpful to know how strong the examinee was in these areas and in what ways the strengths were shown. Referring to a percentile rank (or ranks) would help in describing the child's strengths.

Example 3. "She is unable to concentrate." It would be helpful to use supporting information or behavioral descriptions. For example, "During periods of observation, and according to the teacher's report, she seldom completes assigned work and usually does not attend to a specific task for longer than two minutes" (Drake & Bardon, 1978).

Example 4. "Joan demonstrates no progress beyond the preprimer level in reading." Supporting information or behavioral descriptions would be useful. For example, "Joan's classroom teacher reports that she continues to be unable to identify 60 percent of the words in the primer reading book used by the class" (Drake & Bardon, 1978).

Non Sequiturs

Sentences should blend into one another so that abrupt transitions are minimized. Introduce changes in content by use of transitional phrases. The reader should be prepared for what is to follow, and the lead sentence in a paragraph often provides just such preparation.

Example 1. "Richard is above average on memory items. He failed a memory test at a level below his chronological age." The second sentence should be connected with the first sentence by a phrase such as "even though."

Example 2. "Jay has excellent conceptual thinking. Another average ability is memory." The second sentence does not easily follow from the first. An "excellent" ability is first presented, and then, without any warning, an "average" ability is presented. The word "another" is the major problem in the second sentence. It would be better to use the conjunction "but" after the word "thinking" ("but average memory ability") to indicate that another clause is being introduced.

Technical Terms and Information

Since the psychological report may be read by many nonprofessional people, it is preferable to keep technical matters to a minimum. The goal is to describe and interpret the examinee's performance by minimizing technical details and by maximizing common-sense terms. Always consider whether the reader clearly knows what the technical referents mean.

Eliminating technical terms enhances readability, since such terms are difficult to understand for readers not versed in psychological terminology. Historical and technical information about the particular test, too, should be minimized. It is not necessary to mention, for example, that Terman and Merrill revised the Stanford-Binet in 1937, that Pinneau constructed the revised IQ tables for the Stanford-Binet, or that the standard deviation of the IQs is 16 for the Stanford-Binet or 15 for the WISC-R. Technical details should be referred to only in exceptional cases. For instance, a report on the testing of a foreign-born examinee might note that the Stanford-Binet, WISC-R, and WPPSI were standardized on American children.

Example 1. "His language ability should be strengthened, as indicated by his performance on the Minkus Completion test at year level XII." The examiner, in attempting to illustrate the examinee's below-average language ability, refers to a test that is likely to have little, if any, meaning to the reader. Also, as we have previously noted, it is of limited usefulness to refer to a specific test without illustrating the activities required by the test.

Example 2. "When she reached the ceiling level, she became more restless and serious." The technical term "ceiling level" may not be understood by the reader. It is preferable to replace "ceiling level" with "When the more difficult levels of the test were reached, she. . . ." If "ceiling level" is used, it can be followed with "the level at which all tests were failed" in parentheses.

Example 3. "The child was particularly strong in memory-span tests." Instead of saying "strong in memory-span tests," describe the examinee's abilities as follows: "The child has a good memory span." Discuss the examinee's abilities rather than noting the test names.

Undocumented Statements

Statements that refer to circumstances or behaviors that the examiner has not observed firsthand should give the source of the statement.

Example 1. "Billy has uncontrolled temper tantrums." The source for this statement should be cited. For example, "According to Billy's classroom teacher, he cries and stamps his feet when she denies him a privilege. No methods tried by the teacher to prevent the tantrums in these situations have proved successful" (Drake & Bardon, 1978).

Example 2. "The father is an alcoholic." The source also is needed for this statement. For example, "According to the father he is an alcoholic and a member of AA" (Drake & Bardon, 1978).

Technical Aspects of Report Writing

It is a truism that conventional grammatical rules must be followed in writing psychological reports. However, there are some aspects of report writing, concerned with grammatical, stylistic, and structural points, that need special emphasis and discussion. A few areas that I have found to be particularly difficult for the beginning examiner are presented below. A good reference source for technical writing is the American Psychological Association's (1974) *Publication Manual*. Other reference sources should be consulted as needed.

Abbreviations

Abbreviations generally should not be used in the report. Terms such as "etc." can be misleading and should be used only on rare occasions. However, IQ, MA, and CA may be used, since they pertain to intelligence testing. These three terms are always capitalized and are usually written without periods. Preferably, "examiner" and "examinee" should not be abbreviated because the reader may not understand the meaning of the abbreviations.

Capitalization

Proper names of tests should be capitalized. For example, the "V" in Vocabulary test is capitalized. Other tests that have more than one word in their title present difficulties with respect to capitalization. It is recommended that the first letters of major words of test names be capitalized. For example, the test Obeying Simple Commands is written with the first letter of each word in capitals. The classification in which the examinee's IQ falls should be written with the first letter capitalized to gain attention, as in "Normal classification." General areas of intelligence, such as language skills or visual-motor abilities, are not usually capitalized because they do not refer to specific tests in the examination. "Examiner" and "examinee" should not be written in capital letters.

Hyphens

The rules for hyphenation are very complex. It will be helpful to consult a dictionary or other sources, such as *A Manual of Style* published by the University of Chicago Press (1969) or the *Style Manual* published by the United States Government Printing Office (1967). A term such as "7-year-old" is usually hyphenated, especially if it is employed as a compound adjective.

Identifying Data and Test Results

The heading of the report should contain at least the following identifying data: name and address of agency; examinee's name, date of birth, and chronological age; date of examination; date of report; and examinee's grade. In the body of the report, include the IQ, precision range (standard error of measurement), IQ classification, percentile rank, MA (for the Stanford-Binet), and other test scores. It is also helpful to repeat the child's CA when presenting the test results. Finally, the examiner's name (typewritten and signature) should be placed at the end of the report.

Punctuation

The period and the comma are always placed *before* the closing quotation marks, even when the quotation marks enclose only a single word. For example, "Mark said that he was 'nervous,' and that he is uncomfortable around people." Place colons and semicolons after the quotation mark. Similarly, place a question mark after the quotation mark, unless the question is part of the quoted material.

Spacing

If the report is to be sent to an agency, single spacing is preferred. However, for training purposes, reports should be double spaced to allow for corrections and for the supervisor's comments.

Style

Year levels of the examination may be referred to by Roman numerals or by spelling out the numerals. Use of Roman numerals facilitates differentiating the test proper from other information, such as CA and MA, which use Arabic numerals. Thus, for example, when referring to "year level VIII" write the last term in Roman numerals or use the words "year level eight" or "the eight year level."

Tense

The major difficulty encountered in the use of tense is with reference to past and present tenses. When discussing an examinee's level of intelligence, it is preferable to write: "The examinee is of average intelligence." If the past tense had been used in the above sentence, it would sound as if the examinee were deceased or as if he or she were not average at the time the report was written. In general, more enduring traits such as height, weight, intelligence, and sex should be referred to in the present tense. Thus, "John is a muscular, overweight adolescent who was cooperative on the examination." John's physical characteristics are described as existing at the time the report was written. Test behavior, in contrast, is described in the past tense, because the behavior was displayed on a specific past occasion.

Revising the First Draft

After the first draft has been completed, examine the report for errors and for ways to enhance the clarity of the material. Be sure that all findings, interpretations, and recommendations are clearly presented; revise sections that are vague or ambiguous. Like research papers, the psychological report aims "to make the clearest, most comprehensible presentation in the simplest terms, using the smallest possible number of words, dealing only with relevant issues and avoiding undue generalization and speculation. The aim is to clarify and not to make obscure" (Thorne, 1960, p. 343). Some questions to consider are as follows: Can the report be understood by an intelligent layperson? Are there ambiguities, redundancies, or misleading phrases? After the final typing, it is important to proofread the report. Spelling errors, omitted phrases, and grammatical and typing errors should be corrected. With experience, it is less likely that revisions of the report will be needed, but careful proofreading will always be necessary.

Comment on Report Writing

We have seen that psychological reports (a) provide a record of the child's performance, (b) communicate findings, (c) help in providing remediation and treatment suggestions, and (d) facilitate placement decisions. The writer should try to evoke in the reader an active sense of participation and opportunities for involvement, reflective interchange, and mastery of new information (Bachrach, 1974). The following set of guiding principles for report writing summarizes much of the material that has been presented in the chapter (Emerick & Hatten, 1974):

1. Make your presentation straightforward and objective.
2. Edit the report carefully to make certain that spelling, grammar, and punctuation are accurate.
3. Watch your semantics—avoid overused or nebulous words, pet expressions, and stereotyped phrases.
4. Avoid writing a report that is so bland that it would represent anyone. Instead, try to describe a unique, specific child.
5. Make the report "tight."
6. Avoid using the report as a place to display your learning or to parade a large vocabulary.
7. Stay close to the data until you wish to draw your observations together to make some interpretations.

Unfortunately, psychological reports have received their share of criticism.[1] Many of the difficulties that we have just read about have been found in reports written by psychologists in clinics and hospitals. Problems included (a) lack of supporting data or behavioral referents, (b) poor expression (e.g., use of clichés and jargon, loose use of terms, and vagueness), (c) poor organization, (d) inconsistencies, (e) incorrect use of theory, (f) poor differentiation of test data from other data, (g) failure to answer the referral problem, and (h) excessive length and irrelevance. Many surveys, too, have found that psychologists, teachers, and psychiatrists do not always agree on the interpretation of psychological terminology.[2] Thus, every attempt must be made to use precise and well-defined terms in the report.

In a study in which elementary school teachers rated reports written by school psychologists (Rucker, 1967b), *negatively* rated reports were described as "too brief," "lacked form and organization," "results either absent or not explained," "recommendations vague, short, or not answering referral questions," or "unrealistic suggestions made for classroom procedure." In contrast, the *positively* rated reports were described as "understandable," "enjoyable to read," "motivated to follow suggestions," "excellent interpretation of test results," "explained so that the results are understandable even if reader is not familiar with the test," "showed how problem came about," "answered specific referral questions," "recommendations could be implemented in classroom without singling out child," or "conveyed that teacher had asked relevant questions that deserved careful answers."

The best reports incorporated helpful suggestions, clear answers to the referral questions, specific and meaningful interpretations, and awareness of classroom procedures. The poorest reports were overly brief, poorly organized, and inadequate in their presentation of results and recommendations. Overall, the most important factor in evaluating the utility of the report was the quality of the recommendations. The recommendations should aim to increase the teacher's understanding of the child's prob-

EXHIBIT 24-2. Exercises for General Test Interpretation and Report Writing

1. "John had severe perceptual and verbal expression problems." This sentence was then followed by a discussion of arithmetic skills.
2. "His sometimes wandering attention may have contributed to his scatter of subtest scores."
3. "Items that reflect John's ability to learn were not high."
4. "Lower scores were found on items that probably reflect natural endowment as opposed to early educational environment."
5. "Her IQ of 134 predicts excellent success in school."
6. "He does not demonstrate good pencil control at the automatic level yet."
7. "John's visual memory is stronger than his auditory memory. This is usually the case for elementary school children."
8. "If it can be assumed that the WISC-R is an accurate indicator of intellectual functioning, then Jim's IQ of 101 on the test rules out intellectual retardation as the cause of Jim's difficulties."
9. "The Bender-Gestalt has been used as a maturational test of visual-motor functions, a test to explore organic brain damage, and a test of personality."
10. "She scored an IQ score of 111."
11. "Her IQ is indicated to be 80."
12. "This subject is a small girl with a pleasant disposition and rapport."
13. "Ann has shown scores of average intelligence with a lack of intellectual maturity."
14. "All of the errors Tom made on the Bender-Gestalt are significant indicators of brain disorder."
15. "The Bender-Gestalt determines whether or not the person is suffering from distortion in the visual-motor process."
16. "His ability to differentiate essential details contained many inexactitudes and superficial descriptions."
17. "His word fluency tended to be at a simple level, in that he frequently repeated the vocabulary word item within his definition of that item."
18. "In comparison, his interpretation of social situations was below average."
19. "Bill is considered a troublemaker and this may be due to good social judgment and grasp of social conventionality."
20. "Initially it was very difficult to identify the disparate characteristics of her abilities which distinguished her strengths from her weaknesses on all of the subtests comprising the five McCarthy subscale indices." ■

lems and to make, where possible, suggestions for curriculum changes. Any information about the child's style of problem solving and situational conditions that affect the child's learning and performance should be noted. Generally speaking, one of the most important contributions of the psychological report is to help the teacher and parent approach the child in a new way.

Thus, we have seen that report writing is a process of refining ideas, establishing clarity of expression, and using expertise in decision making. The ability to write a clear and meaningful report is highly valued. The psychologist, through the psychological report, contributes to the educational and treatment process, a process which he or she shares with other professionals who are also working toward the goal of enhancing and developing the child's potentialities.

Test Your Skills

The final series of exercises, designed to test your report writing and interpretation skills, is presented in Exhibit 24-2. Read each excerpt shown. In each case there is some inadequacy of description or interpretation. Find the mistake in the sentences. After finishing your evaluations, check them with those in the Answers to Test Your Skills Exercises on p. 544.

Summary

1. The psychological report usually serves as the primary vehicle through which the findings of the evaluation are conveyed. Skill is required to write a report that adequately brings together findings, interpretations, and recommendations. The report

should be written within a few hours or days after the evaluation has been completed.

2. Examiners, in the writing of the report, may play a number of different roles. Which one (or ones) they play will be dependent in part on the nature of the situation. A contextual approach to report writing, as an alternative to a psychodynamic one, stresses the social and descriptive elements of the assessment situation.

3. The psychological evaluation usually includes the following five areas: (1) reason for referral, (2) general observations, (3) test results, (4) recommendations, and (5) summary. When an intelligence test is administered in the battery, it is desirable to report a precision range associated with the IQ. Diagnostic formulations and recommendations should be based on a synthesis of all available information. While specificity is important in making recommendations, long-range predictions are especially hazardous and should be recognized as such in the report.

4. Test-oriented reports and subject-oriented reports are rather arbitrary designations; all reports should include both test-related material and subject-related material.

5. The formulation of a report involves a number of principles. First, consider the kinds of material necessary to include in the report. Guideposts will include the preferences of the referral source and material that emphasizes the examinee's individuality. Second, an attempt should be made to synthesize the test findings with behavioral observations. Variability in performance should be noted and an explanation attempted. The interaction between the examiner and examinee constitutes an important part of the testing situation. Third, carefully selected examples of the examinee's performance can enrich the report. Fourth, the certainty of the statements made in the report should be based in part on the type of data being referred to. Fifth, when the goal of the evaluation is to estimate the child's intelligence, the anchor of the report should be the IQ.

6. Specific examples presented in the chapter illustrate sentences that, for a variety of reasons, fail to communicate adequately. The following kinds of difficulties were enumerated: abstractness, ambiguity, apologies, awkwardness, unimportant content, inappropriate generalization, hedging, incorrect inferential statements, inexactitude, irrelevant statements, limited or too general comments, non sequiturs, technical terms, and undocumented statements. Finally, technical aspects of report writing were discussed.

7. After the first draft is completed, it may be necessary to revise it. Careful proofreading is always needed.

8. Surveys have found that psychological reports in a variety of settings sometimes fail to communicate clearly. Problems center on organization, terminology, content, style, and recommendations. In schools, an important contribution of the report is to help the teacher approach the child in a new way.

9. The psychological report can make a definitive contribution to the assessment process.

CHAPTER 25

Consultation

In my opinion, interdisciplinary work does not mean the meeting of specialists in different disciplines, but rather the meeting of different disciplines in the same individual—an adventure that our system discourages, when it does not absolutely forbid it.

LUCIEN ISRAEL
Conquering Cancer (1978)

EXHIBIT 25-1. Suggestions for Working with Teachers

1. The psychologist should relieve the teacher's uneasy feelings by sympathetically reviewing the problem with him or her.
2. The psychologist and teacher should both help to define the various aspects of the problem or problems.
3. The steps to be taken should be planned together, be they observation, interviewing, testing, etc.
4. The information available should be pooled; the total amount of information will thus be increased, and additional insights may be gained.
5. The psychologist should prepare a specific plan for the teacher, taking into account his or her capabilities as well as his or her limitations.
6. The psychologist might well supplement the written report to the teacher with an oral report. This would help to ensure that the teacher does not place exaggerated value on the written psychological report. To do so might result in the teacher's shunning his or her responsibility, thus placing the entire matter into what he or she feels are the omnipotent hands of the psychologist. She or he may feel that the problem will now be magically solved; this attitude will lead only to frustration and disappointment on the part of the teacher.
7. The psychologist should explore with the teacher the ways in which the personnel and the resources of the school and community may be advantageously used.
8. The teacher should be relieved of the responsibility for behavior of the child over which she or he has no control. She or he might be reminded that the home should share such responsibility.
9. It is the responsibility of the psychologist to make certain that the teacher does not expect immediate results. Such unrealistic expectations would only prove frustrating and disheartening for the teacher.
10. The teacher should be encouraged to adopt a variety of methods in dealing with her or his students; flexible procedures should be stressed.
11. It is the psychologist's responsibility to remain available for help in future consultations, when they are requested. ■

Source: Handler, Gerston, & Handler, 1965, pp. 80–81, with a change in notation.

The psychologist's role does not end with the testing of the child and the writing of a report. Psychologists may be called upon to present their findings at a case conference, to confer with individual teachers and other school personnel regarding the findings, to meet with parents, or to consult with other professionals. In these ways the findings of the psychological evaluation become "alive" and enable psychologists to contribute to the decision-making process. The report, too, represents an important part of the consultant role; it speaks for the psychologist. As a result of the information provided in the report, actions will be taken.

To be effective, psychologists, as consultants, should know as intimately as possible the situations in which change is to take place. If the school is the setting in which consultation occurs, it is necessary to have a harmonious working relationship with the school personnel, knowledge of the child's classroom behavior, and continuous interactions and feedback (Sarason, Levine, Goldenberg, Cherlin, & Bennett, 1966). In working in the larger community, the psychologist should have information about the available agencies, centers, workshops, and inpatient facilities. Ideally, it would be helpful to know what treatments are offered at the various facilities and how effective they are in helping children.

Ethical Standards of Psychologists

The Ethical Standards of Psychologists of the American Psychological Association (1979) serve as a guidepost for psychologists in their professional work. A careful study of the standards (see Appendix E) will enable psychologists (and students-in-training) to understand some of the responsibilities associated with their professional role.

Some of the highlights of the standards, with respect to assessment, are as follows:

1. Psychologists must recognize that their recommendations may alter the lives of others and be aware of their social responsibility.

2. Psychologists must recognize their own competencies and the limitations of their techniques.
3. Public statements made about diagnostic services must be portrayed accurately and objectively.
4. Psychologists must protect the confidentiality of the information obtained in the course of the evaluation. The only exceptions are (a) when consent is given by the client (or guardian) to release the information, (b) when one is working with other professionals within an agency, or (c) when failure to release information would violate the law.
5. Clients must clearly understand the financial costs connected with the assessment.
6. Clients have a right to their test results and should be provided with the basis for the conclusions and recommendations.
7. Security of tests and test results must be maintained.
8. Doubts concerning the reliability or validity of the test results should be clearly stated in the report.
9. Research on assessment must consider the dignity and welfare of the subjects participating in the research project.

Consultation in the Schools

Consultation in schools involves working with the child, the teacher, and the parents. While the psychologist may spend much time with the child and the teacher, the parents are a crucial part of the equation. Their support (or lack thereof) will greatly influence the success or failure of any remediation efforts. Psychologists must be able to reach the parents, as well as the teacher and the child.

While the focus of this and other parts of the chapter is on teachers and parents of handicapped children, psychologists also consult with teachers and parents of normal and gifted children. Many of the principles of consultation and interviewing discussed in this chapter are applicable to these situations as well. Psychologists also make an impact on planning programs for normal and gifted children.

The psychologist in the school should be a *school* psychologist, emphasizing the learning process, particularly as it relates to formal education. This role contrasts with that of (a) the psychometrician, who focuses on test results, and (b) the clinical psychologist, who focuses on psychopathology. The school psychologist must take a broader view than merely focusing on tests or on the child. The school environment, the teacher, and the educational program all are important elements of the learning matrix, as are the child's individual dynamics and the home environment. The thrust of the profession of school psychology may be said to involve three interrelated areas:

1. to facilitate learning by children in the school setting;
2. to apply psychological theory to the solution of school-related problems; and
3. to assist teachers, parents, administrators, and other school personnel to facilitate learning.

The professional functions of school psychologists include assessment, intervention, consultation, research and evaluation, and administration (Cook & Patterson, 1977).

Assessment includes administering, scoring, and interpreting psychological tests, observing the child's behavior, and diagnostic interviewing.

Intervention includes participating in counseling activities, developing educational plans, and designing behavior modification programs. Intervention activities reflect problem-solving approaches developed from the case study.

Consultation refers to work with teachers, principals, other professionals, and nonprofessionals.

Research and evaluation refers to any activity associated with psychoeducational functions, including evaluation of the adequacy of psychological services, fol-low-up of interventions, and follow-up of assessments.

Administration includes the writing of psychological reports, correspondence, preparation time, and attendance at meetings.

School psychologists are called upon to assist not only in their traditional roles as diagnosticians, but also as learning specialists, capable of determining the most appropriate learning environment and types of procedures to facilitate the child's learning process. In order to function successfully in a school setting or as a consultant to schools, one must know about the structure, function, and effectiveness of special education classes, resource rooms, and regular classes for handicapped, exceptional, and normal children. For some children, it may be necessary to consider a trial period in a special education program or a regular day class in order to ascertain the most beneficial type of learning environment. Children also may receive combinations of regular and special class programs, including services of resource specialists (e.g., reading specialists, speech specialists, and counselors), special tutors, and peer counselors.

The psychological evaluation, which plays an important part in consultation, serves various functions (Bardon & Bennett, 1974). The major ones include (a) assessment for classification, (b) description of learning style, (c) class placement, (d) remediation, (e) management, and (f) development of teaching strategies. In order to accomplish these objectives, psychologists need:

1. knowledge of psychological and psychoeducational assessment instruments,
2. knowledge of child psychopathology and exceptionality,
3. knowledge of behavioral and educational intervention,
4. knowledge of Public Law 94-142 and other pertinent laws, and
5. knowledge of the special needs of transitional pupils who are being transferred from special education to regular education.

In working with teachers, the psychologist, as a consultant, (a) assists teachers in clarifying the nature of the problem, (b) determines interventions that have been tried (both successful and unsuccessful ones), and (c) discusses with teachers possible additional alternatives (Lambert, 1976). The primary goal is to help teachers find solutions to pupil problems. The emphasis is on translating the results of the assessment directly into programming activities.

In the consultant role, the psychologist strives to seek the placement that will best facilitate the child's education; assessment should not simply involve arriving at a diagnostic label. Psychological reports and follow-up consultations should aim to (a) help modify teachers' behaviors and help teachers deal more effectively with the child and parents and even with other teachers and school personnel; (b) challenge teachers to be more exhaustive in their thinking and to consider different approaches to problems of individual children; and (c) help provide teachers with a framework to view changes in children over time (Lambert, Yandell, & Sandoval, 1975). Ongoing consultation is required in order to determine whether recommendations must be modified as the child responds, or fails to respond, to recommendations.

Illustrations of some of the recommendations made by school psychologists are as follows:

- placement of the child in special programs or special classes, or with special teachers;
- remedial techniques that could facilitate the child's learning;
- changes in curriculum, subject matter presentation, or learning atmosphere;
- behavior management programs that teachers could implement;
- behavior management programs that parents could implement;
- counseling or therapy by a school counselor or at an outside agency;
- assistance with academic activities at home;
- assistance with interpersonal relations;
- methods for helping parents or teachers make changes in the child's self-concept or attitude.

There is some evidence that teachers are not likely to follow recommendations that require great effort (Frankel & Kassinove, 1974). On the other hand, the effectiveness of school psychological services is likely to be increased when there are follow-up contacts with teachers (White & Fine, 1976). Follow-up contacts lead to greater implementation of recommendations, to greater perceived pupil behavior improvement, and to a greater sense of cooperative planning. Recommendations must consider the assets and limitations of the classroom and what resources are available in the school, home, and community.

Teachers desire that school psychologists be concerned not only with diagnosis but with intervention activities as well (Gilmore & Chandy, 1973). To do this, psychologists will need to identify sources of interference in the educational process, understand their dynamics, and recommend appropriate intervention or remediation strategies.

In consulting, the psychologist should try to create an atmosphere in which parents and teacher feel comfortable and at ease, and able to express their needs and desires. The psychologist must convey a feeling of respect and understanding of the parents' and teacher's problems, and recognize that it will be the teacher and parents who will have to continue to work with the child after the evaluation is completed. The psychologist must obtain the teacher's support for the prescriptive teaching program; if not, diagnostic testing becomes a meaningless procedure that little benefits the child, teacher, or school. Psychologists should try to reduce any feelings of threat generated in parents and teachers, and try to help them become more sensitive to themselves and to their relationship with the child. This can be done, in part, by helping translate the teacher's strengths into potential actions, and by designing the necessary interventions in such a way that they are congruent with the teacher's conception of his or her own role. Useful guidelines for working with teachers are shown in Exhibit 25-1, which began this chapter.

Teachers are in a key position to help in the identification of handicapped children. Teachers, as observers of children's performance in the classroom, are also in an excellent position to develop remediation strategies which, in part, may entail modification in the kind and sequence of instructional objectives, teaching procedures, materials, rate and style of instruction, and reinforcement procedures. In many cases, teachers may not need to refer the child to a psychologist because they have sufficient information to develop appropriate educational programs.

Problems in the consultation process in schools can arise from numerous sources, one of which is the referral process itself. The management and structuring of the referral process is extremely important, not only in schools but in other organizational settings as well. Lauro (1975) proposed that in order to alleviate problems associated with the referral process in schools, a guiding philosophy is needed. He suggested that referrals in school settings be initiated by the classroom teacher and channeled through the principal. The teacher should describe the problem in as much detail as possible. The psychologist should then work with the teacher to develop a systematic study of the child's behavior and academic difficulties. The mutual involvement of psychologist and teacher establishes that both parties can contribute to the diagnostic and remediation process.

Lauro also believes that it is the principal's responsibility to determine whether or not a referral to the psychologist is appropriate and, if so, what priority it should take within the psychologist's scheduled time for that school. The principal, in conference with the teacher, should initially determine what resources are available. Referral problems can be diminished if, at the beginning of the school year, psychologists schedule meetings with teachers, during which time the referral process and techniques for behavioral observation are discussed.

Psychologists should help teachers and other educational specialists recognize when referrals are needed and when they are not. Children should be referred for individual assessment when teachers find that they are unable to help children learn. If the guidelines in this section are followed, it is likely that some of the confusion and frustration surrounding the role of the school psychologist can be reduced. Difficulties arise, in part, because teachers as well as psychologists are not completely sure of the psychologist's role, and because interdisciplinary communication involving psychologists, teachers, physicians, social workers, and principals is often less than satisfactory.

Public Law 94-142

Public Law 94-142, the Education for All Handicapped Children Act of 1975, has important implications for the assessment process and for the practice of psychology in the schools. The law was designed to ensure the right to education for all persons, including handicapped children. Educational programming for the handicapped is a key provision of the law. The law establishes safeguards for the evaluation and placement of children; makes its provisions applicable to private as well as public schools; requires the seeking out of children presently unserved; requires elimination of architectural barriers; requires the education of handicapped children to be in the least restrictive environment, that is, within a regular class as much as possible; calls for the development of individual educational plans; gives parents the right to have access to records and to participate in the development of educational objectives; requires nondiscriminatory assessment procedures; and requires confidentiality of information.

Let us examine in somewhat more detail some of the features of PL 94-142 as they pertain to assessment practices.

1. *Testing and evaluation procedures.* The following procedures must be developed.

State and local educational agencies shall insure, at a minimum, that:

(a) Tests and other evaluation materials:

    (1) Are provided and administered in the child's native language or other mode of communication, unless it is clearly not feasible to do so;

    (2) Have been validated for the specific purpose for which they are used;

    (3) Are administered by trained personnel in conformance with the instructions provided by their producer;

(b) Tests and other evaluation materials include those tailored to assess specific areas of educational need and not merely those which are designed to provide a single general intelligence quotient;

(c) Tests are selected and administered so as best to ensure that when a test is administered to a child with impaired sensory, manual or speaking skills, the test results accurately reflect the child's aptitude or achievement level or whatever other factors the test purports to measure, rather than reflecting the child's impaired sensory, manual, or speaking skills (except where those skills are the factors which the test purports to measure);

(d) No single procedure is used as the sole criterion for determining an appropriate educational program for a child; and

(e) The evaluation is made by a multidisciplinary team or group of persons, including at least one teacher or other specialist with knowledge in the area of suspected disability.

(f) The child is assessed in all areas related to the suspected disability, including, where appropriate, health, vision, hearing, social and emotional status, general intelligence, academic performance, communicative status, and motor abilities. [*Federal Register,* August 23, 1977, Vol. 42, No. 163, pp. 42496–42497, 121a.532]

In addition, "testing and evaluation materials and procedures used for the purposes of evaluation and placement of handicapped children must be selected and administered so as not to be racially or culturally discriminatory" (*Federal Register,* August 23, 1977, Vol. 42, No. 163, p. 42496, 121a.530).

2. *Development of an individualized educational program (IEP).* The individualized educational program (IEP) is a plan designed to help handicapped children achieve particular educational goals. It is a team effort, bringing together the skills and resources of the educational staff. Each word in the term "individualized educational program" has a particular meaning: *individualized* means that the program is directed toward the unique needs of a specific child; *educational* means that the program is directed to learning activities; and *program* refers to specific and clearly formulated goals.

The IEP is a statement of what kind of expectations the educational staff has for the handicapped child. The basic components of an IEP are as follows:

a. A description of the child's present level of educational performance.

b. Annual instructional objectives (or long-range goals) that describe the educational performance to be achieved by the end of the school year. These are concrete statements of what the student will be able to perform. They should be realistic for the student to accomplish in a nine-month period. Examples of some long-term goals are (1) to increase reading level from the first grade to second grade, (2) to improve spelling, (3) to improve practical and applied arithmetical skills, and (4) to improve social interactions with peers.

In arriving at instructional objectives, various factors are considered, including content, conditions in which the learning takes place, and the proposed level of performance. It is important to consider the child's learning style, rate of learning, amount of structure needed, and favored sense modalities. Written goals and objectives serve a number of purposes: they provide for accountability; they can motivate students; they facilitate teacher-parent communication; and they help focus on learning activities.

c. Short-term instructional objectives are similar to long-term instructional objectives, but they focus on specific goals that can be achieved in a short time, such as buttoning and unbuttoning a coat, identifying vowel sounds, walking ten feet, using complete sentences, and making appropriate social responses to peers. These goals are usually in manageable units of instruction.

d. Specific educational services needed by the child, including a description of the following: (a) the special education and related services needed to meet the unique needs of the child, including the type of physical education program in which the child will participate, and (b) all special instructional media and materials that are needed.

e. The date when those services will begin and the anticipated length of time that services will be given.

f. The extent to which the child will participate in regular education programs. Every attempt is made to place the handicapped child in the least restrictive educational alternative.

"Oscar, I do not consider 'beating some sense into their stubborn little heads' an acceptable behavioral objective."

Courtesy of *Phi Delta Kappan* and the artist, Bardulf Ueland.

g. A justification for the type of educational placement which the child will have.

h. A list of the individuals who are responsible for implementation of the IEP.

i. The objective criteria, evaluation procedures, and schedules for determining, on at least an annual basis, whether the instructional objectives are being achieved. At least once a year, according to PL 94-142, the IEP needs to be reviewed and revised if necessary. At the review meeting, parents, teacher, and an administrator should be present. This review usually takes place at the end of the school year, but can also occur when a student transfers to another school district or when there is a change in placement or on the anniversary of the child's original placement.

The annual review serves a number of functions: (1) plans, procedures, and outcomes are reviewed and evaluated; (2) difficulties with the plan are identified; (3) reasons for the difficulties are sought; (4) new goals and procedures are formulated; and (5) feedback is provided to those responsible for the plan and for its implementation.

When an individual assessment is planned, the parents should receive written communication of their child's referral in ordinary wording and in the primary language used in the home. If the procedures described below are followed, the parents' "informed consent" will be ensured. The parents should be invited to attend a meeting with staff personnel. If the parents are unable to appear, the following items should be presented in writing or through documented telephone calls or, possibly, a home visit: (1) description of the problem; (2) assessment needs and procedures, including any anticipated referral of records and to whom; (3) identification and explanation of all tests, records, and information-gathering procedures to be used; (4) possible uses of information gathered; (5) complete information concerning due process, procedural safeguards, confidentiality, and parent access to records. The following items should be sought from parents at the meeting, or in some other manner if no meeting is held: (1) written consent before the assessment starts; (2) written consent for obtaining and sharing information; and (3) parental perception of the child's problem.

The development of IEPs is by no means an easy task. The statements contained in the IEP represent "plans"; they are not foolproof prescriptions. While they represent the best thinking of the educational staff—developed on the basis of assessment information, available resources, and staff compromise—they must be monitored continuously. They should be viewed as guideposts, not as fixed and unchangeable strategies and goals.

3. *Parents' right to an independent educational evaluation.* This provision states that parents have a right to obtain an independent evaluation of the child if they disagree with the evaluation performed at the local educational agency. However, the evaluation is paid for by the school district only upon the recommendation of a hearing officer. If the parents initiate the evaluation, the results must be considered by the state and local educational agency.

4. *Periodic evaluations.* Re-evaluation of the child should be done at least every three years, or more frequently if conditions warrant it.

5. *Parents' right to examine records.* Parents have the right to inspect and review any information in their child's file.

The development of procedural safeguards is an attempt to promote fair classification. It is a recognition that school placement decisions are consequential to the student and family and are not to be undertaken lightly or arbitrarily. Schools are accountable for the accuracy of their classification and the appropriateness of the recommended program. School personnel are obliged to specify the basis up-

on which they classify children and must demonstrate that the programs are likely to benefit the child. Before an assignment to a special program becomes fact, the school should inform the parents and child, explain the proposed action, and indicate what alternatives are available. It is imperative that the parents and child not be coerced or intimidated into accepting the school's decision. Some parents do not understand placement procedures and special education programs. It will require care on the part of psychologists to express decisions about eligibility, placement, program goals, and the review process in clear, jargon-free language using concepts understandable to parents.

6. *Least restrictive environment.* The least restrictive environment provision of PL 94-142 is often referred to as "mainstreaming," that is, the placement of handicapped children in regular classes. While mainstreaming has been of major concern to educators for decades, it has recently received special attention with the advent of PL 94-142. Psychologists, as members of the educational team, aid in arriving at an appropriate placement decision. A key factor to consider is the child's ability to learn in a regular classroom setting—the child's learning handicaps must not be so severe as to preclude their effective remediation in a regular classroom.

Figure 25-1 shows seven different levels of special education services. At the top of the hierarchy is the regular classroom, while the last level depicted shows services that are provided only in an institutional setting. The tapered design depicts the fact that fewer children usually are involved in specialized programs. The most specialized facilities are usually needed by the fewest children.

Advocates of mainstreaming believe that it will remove stigmas; enhance the social status of exceptional children; facilitate modeling of appropriate behavior by handicapped children; provide a more stimulating and competitive environment; offer more

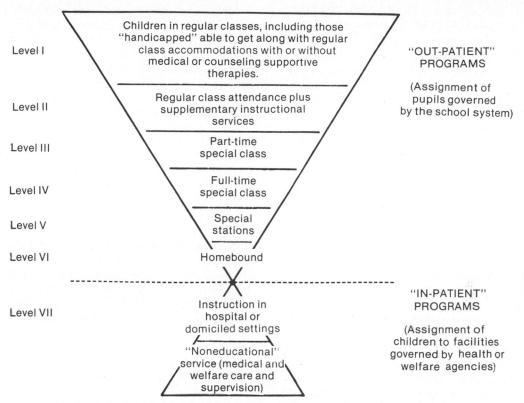

FIGURE 25-1.   The Cascade System of Special Education Service. The tapered design indicates the considerable difference in the numbers involved at the different levels and calls attention to the fact that the system serves as a diagnostic filter. The most specialized facilities are likely to be needed by the fewest children on a long term basis. This organizational model can be applied to development of special education services for all types of disability. Reprinted with permission of the publisher and author from E. Deno, "Special Education as Developmental Capital," *Exceptional Children, 37,* p. 235. Copyright 1970, Council for Exceptional Children.

flexible cost effective service; and be more acceptable to the public and, in particular, to minority groups (Weatherley & Lipsky, 1977). The pressures toward mainstreaming, which have been fermenting during the 1960s and 1970s, stem from a number of sources, including the following:

- *Special education services can now provide specialized programs to handicapped children.* Remediation programs can provide services to children for a few hours each day in resource rooms. Thus increased flexibility in offering services allows for more integration of handi-

capped children with regular class children.

- *Special classes for the mentally retarded supposedly have a debilitating effect on the children's social-personal adjustment and self-image.* The mainstreaming movement is supported in part by the belief that placement of educable mentally retarded children in regular classes would reduce the stigma that accompanied their segregated placement in special classes, and increase their social acceptability to other children. It is not true, however, that children in special education classes always have negative attitudes toward their special class placements. Studies, too, have shown that placement in regular classes does not improve the social status of educable mentally retarded children.[1] Thus, integrated class placements may *not* be accompanied by greater social acceptance of retarded children. The low social status of retarded children is related to teachers' and peers' perceptions of their misbehavior and academic difficulties. Attitudes of teachers toward retarded children may influence peers' acceptance of retarded children who are placed in regular classes (Corman & Gottlieb, 1978).

- *Civil rights actions against school districts have focused on the apparent disproportion of ethnic minorities in special education classes.* Dunn (1968), for example, contended that self-contained special education classes for educable mentally retarded children are "depositories" for ethnic minority and economically deprived children. This allegation, however, has not been clearly supported by research.
- *Special classes are supposedly ineffective in raising the academic capabilities of mentally retarded children.* Research suggests that special classes and regular classes produce similar levels of academic achievement; thus special classes do not handicap children academically (Kolstoe, 1972). Even more importantly, special classes have been found to be superior to regular classes in fostering employment opportunities.

Research findings related to mainstreaming suggest the following trends (Corman & Gottlieb, 1978):

1. Instructional techniques are more important to improved academic achievement than the setting in which children learn.
2. No uniform trends have been reported about the effects of mainstreaming on the academic achievement of mentally retarded children.
3. Attitudes of professional school personnel toward mainstreaming have been both positive and negative.

Mainstreaming is a more complex procedure than simply placing handicapped children in a regular classroom. Consideration must be given to the specialized educational needs of these children, and how the standard curriculum can be modified to accommodate their learning styles. Regular class teachers need special assistance in developing such programs. Further, the social needs of these children must be considered. Integrating the needs of handicapped children with those of regular class children will require special effort.

The success with which handicapped children are placed in regular classrooms will, in the final analysis, depend on the acceptance and consideration of teachers, administrators, parents, and children. A crucial factor is the attitude of the people involved. In determining appropriate placements, the child's educational needs, and not the type of handicap, should be of primary concern. *We must not forget that the slow learner placed either in a regular class or in a special education class still has a learning problem that must be remediated.*

Comment on PL 94-142. While PL 94-142 provides many useful guidelines for providing services for handicapped children, the ultimate test of the usefulness of the law is in the education received by each handicapped child. The American Psychological Association has been concerned about the possibility that some provisions of the law may be implemented inadequately, particularly with regard to the development of IEPs. Their statement of concern and recommendations to promote better implementation of the law are shown in Exhibit 25-2.

Perhaps the weakest aspect of PL 94-142 is its failure to define clearly what is meant by racially or culturally nondiscriminatory procedures. The law fails to specify any acceptable procedures, and yet uses such concepts as "significantly subaverage general intellectual functioning" in its definition of mental retardation. This and other statements suggest that PL 94-142 recognizes the importance of standardized tests

EXHIBIT 25-2. American Psychological Association's Statement on Education for All Handicapped Children Act of 1975 (P.L. 94-142)

The American Psychological Association heartily supports the educational purposes of Public Law 94-142 (Education for All Handicapped Children Act of 1975). Therefore, the APA is concerned that in some cases implementation of P.L. 94-142 may not be proceeding in a manner commensurate with the goal of providing quality education for all handicapped children. The primary problem consists of the possibility of a pro forma procedure which superficially follows the implementation of the law in the development of Individualized Educational Programs (IEPs). The concerns of the APA are expressed in the following statement of principles and recommendations.

1. *Commitment to principle.* The right to the most appropriate education in the least restrictive manner possible is a fundamental right of all children. Full implementation of the rights and procedures of the law should not be contingent in any way on the extent of federal funding made available to assist the states in their current obligations.
2. *Commitment to quality education.* Economic and bureaucratic factors are currently perverting the original goals of the legislation. For example, children are being placed in regular classes without provision of adequate auxiliary services or teacher preparation and training. The APA opposes any such inadequate programming. It is necessary that high-quality education be given to all children and that the needs of the total child be recognized and addressed in school settings.
3. *Commitment to professional functioning.* One major responsibility to the child is to assure that valid assessment procedures are performed by appropriately trained professionals. It is the obligation of psychologists to see that their professional functioning is in the best interest of the child. Such an obligation is reinforced by the ethical code of psychologists which mandates that psychologists must not knowingly permit the misuse of psychological services by others.
4. *Commitment to the development of appropriate IEPs.* Adequate educational strategies must be developed for each individual child. Where appropriate, psychologists should be involved in individualized educational plans, in both the assessment and implementation phases. It is necessary that psychologists and teachers have extensive information about a child's individual competencies and learning style so that appropriate teaching strategies can be written into the IEP.
5. *Commitment to total effective work.* All mandated services and goals must be communicated to parents and teachers in readily understandable terms. This procedure should be used to obtain fully informed parental consent. All material should be transmitted in detailed terms that are educationally relevant. Parent participation should be an integral part of the IEP and not a pro forma ritualistic procedure.
6. *Commitment and use of psychologists and their data in the best interest of the child.* It is the psychologist's responsibility to insure that all assessment procedures are appropriate to investigate all possible strengths and deficits of the handicapped child through criterion referenced and norm referenced tests. These strengths and deficits must be integrated into a program that can be implemented for each child, taking account of the cultural and social milieu of the child and family.
7. *Commitment to continuing generation of knowledge.* The effectiveness of individualized programs should be continually monitored. Constant evaluation and reevaluation should generate information that would improve individualized programs, increase their quality, and aid the individual child. Therefore, teachers should be provided with adequate follow-up consultation and evaluation services.
8. *Commitment to supportive services.* It is necessary that a total network of supportive services be available to assist the child, teacher, and family. ■

Source: Reprinted from *American Psychological Association School Psychology Newsletter,* 1979, *33*(5), p. 8.

in the assessment process. Another serious shortcoming in PL 94-142 is the lack of guidance concerning how to determine the child's *native language*. Ethnic minority children, as we have seen, are often bidialectical, making it extremely difficult to determine whether or not they have a "native language." Overall, PL 94-142 represents an attempt by the federal government to ensure that handicapped children receive a meaningful education.

The Family Educational Rights and Privacy Act of 1974

In an effort to eliminate some of the abuses associated with data gathering and personal files, the Family Educational Rights and Privacy Act of 1974, commonly known as the "Buckley Amendment," was passed by the U.S. Congress. Some of the highlights of the act are as follows (Drake & Bardon, 1978):

1. Parents have access to official educational records of their children.
2. Parental consent must be obtained for release of records to other agencies.
3. Rights transfer to public school pupils at the age of 18 years and to other students, regardless of age, attending post-secondary educational institutions.
4. Schools must provide a hearing, when requested by parents or students, in which records may be challenged.
5. Schools have the responsibility to inform parents of their right of access to the records.
6. Failure to follow these guidelines may result in removal of federal funding for the school.

A survey in New Jersey (Zampardi, 1978) reported that as a result of this Act school psychologists have changed their reports in the following ways: (a) shortened the length of the reports, (b) reduced the technicality of the reports, (c) increased the use of private files or memory aids, (d) ceased to record highly personal or legally sensitive information regarding parent or student, (e) increased verbal communication with other professionals, and (f) changed methods of reporting IQ. The frequency of use of conventional tests has remained generally unchanged. The above changes were reported by over two-thirds of the psychologists surveyed. Thus, unintended consequences have arisen from the Buckley Amendment.

The consequences of the Buckley Amendment have been in some cases positive, and in others negative. On the positive side, the open records policy has led (a) to closer relationships with parents, (b) to a reduction of conjectural and speculative statements in psychological reports, (c) to a reduction of labeling, and (d) to greater attention to the writing of psychological reports. On the negative side, the policy has led (a) to increased paper work, (b) to constricted and watered down reports, (c) to concern about lawsuits, and (d) to concern about the ability of parents to understand the report.

Assessment Procedures and Special Education on Trial

In the late 1960s and throughout the 1970s the procedures used by schools to place children in special education programs have been evaluated by the courts of our nation. Two principal issues surfaced during various trials. (See Table 25-1 for a summary of the outcomes of various suits.) One issue dealt with the overrepresentation of ethnic minority children in classes for the educable mentally retarded. Associated with this issue were related matters concerning (a) the assessment techniques used to certify placement in special education programs and (b) the value and role of special education. A second issue concerned the rights of children, regardless of the degree of handicap, to receive a free and appropriate education. Regarding the last issue, the courts have clearly ruled that handicapped children are entitled to such rights.

Ethnic minorities have argued (a) that they have been overrepresented in classes for the educable mentally retarded, (b) that special education represents a dead end and provides substandard educational programs, (c) that intelligence tests are biased, (d) that pupils with limited facility in English have been administered tests requiring extensive facility in English, and (e) that a full range of assessment techniques has not been used in arriving at placement decisions. Implied in these arguments is that the children were denied equal protection under the Fourteenth Amendment of the Constitution. In most of the cases that have come before the judiciary, both parties have signed consent agreements, which have attempted to rectify any procedures that were unfair to ethnic minorities. In addition, the provisions of PL 94-142 have sought to protect the rights of ethnic minority children. However, in the *Larry P. v. Riles* case, a federal court ordered the State of California to cease to use intelligence tests for the assessment of black children for placement in educable mentally retarded classes. The court did not interpret the provisions of PL 94-142 to mean that intelligence tests must be used in conjunction with other measures to arrive at the diagnosis of mental retardation. In contrast, a federal court in Illinois ruled in the *Parents in Action on Special Education v. Joseph P. Hannon* case that intelligence tests are not culturally biased against black children. Further, this court stipulated that when used with other criteria in the assessment process, intelligence tests comply with

TABLE 25-1.   Representative Court Cases Involving Assessment and Placement of Ethnic Minority Children and Handicapped Children in Special Education Classes

Case	Decision
Hobson v. Hansen—269 F. Supp. 401 (D.D.C. 1967)	A U.S. district court invalidated the District of Columbia school system's educational tracking practices. Special classes, however, were permissible as long as testing procedures were rigorous and retesting was frequent.
Diana v. State Board of Education—C-70 37 RFT (N.D. Cal. 1970)	A U.S. federal court in California invalidated testing procedures that were used to evaluate Mexican-American children for placement in special education classes. The school system agreed that linguistically different children would be tested both in their primary language and in English, that primarily nonverbal tests would be used for the assessment of these children's cognitive skills, and that an interpreter would be used when a bilingual examiner is not available.
Pennsylvania Association for Retarded Children v. Commonwealth of Pennsylvania—343 F. Supp. 279 (E.D. PA 1972)	A U.S. federal court in Pennsylvania ratified a consent agreement assuring that retarded children have the right to publicly supported schooling appropriate to their needs. Extensive remedial education programs were then instituted for those retarded children previously denied an education.
Wyatt v. Stickney—344 F. Supp. 387 (M.D. Ala. 1972)	An Alabama federal court ruled that children in a state institution for the mentally retarded have a constitutional right to treatment.
Guadalupe v. Tempe Elementary School District—Stipulation and Order (January 24, 1972)	A U.S. district court in Arizona agreed to a stipulated agreement that children could not be placed in educable mentally retarded classes unless they scored lower than two standard deviations below the population mean on an approved IQ test administered in the child's own language. It was also stipulated that other assessment procedures must be used in addition to intelligence tests and that parental permission must be obtained for such placements.

(cont.)

TABLE 25-1 (cont.)

Case	Decision
Mattie T. v. Holladay—No. DC-75-31-S (1979)	A U.S. district court in Mississippi approved a consent decree stipulating (a) that classification and placement procedures for special education must be evaluated by outside experts, (b) that a remedy must be devised to solve the problem of large numbers of black children in classes for the mentally retarded, and (c) that all misclassified children are to be identified and given compensatory education through tutoring or vocational training, even beyond the age of 21.
Larry P. v. Riles—No. C-71-2270 RFP (1979)	A U.S. federal district court in California ruled that standardized intelligence tests are culturally biased and cannot be used in the assessment of black children for possible placement in educable mentally retarded classes. The court further stipulated that the number of black children in classes for the educable mentally retarded must closely match their proportion in the population. The case is under appeal as of January 1981.
Parents in Action on Special Education v. Joseph P. Hannon—No. 74 C 3586 (N.D. Ill. 1980)	A U.S. federal district court in Illinois ruled that the WISC, WISC-R, and Stanford-Binet are not racially or culturally biased. Furthermore, when these tests are used in conjunction with other procedures, they do not discriminate against black children in the Chicago public schools. The court believed that the school system was complying with federally mandated criteria for determining an appropriate educational program for a child. The court, which heard from some of the same witnesses who testified for the plaintiffs in the *Larry P.* case, noted that in the *Larry P.* case the judge failed to undertake a detailed examination of the items on the intelligence tests. Without such an examination, the court believed, the issue of cultural bias cannot be properly evaluated.

federal guidelines concerning the use of nondiscriminatory procedures. The issues raised by minorities, as we have seen, are complex, and simple and clear-cut answers are not always available (see Chapter 19).

Consultation with Parents

Parents, on learning that they have a handicapped child, may experience a variety of reactions, including anxiety and emotional distress, grief, disbelief, shock, ambivalence, anger, and disappointment. Parents may feel cheated because they did not produce a "perfect being" (Kaplan, 1971). The clinician may receive some pent-up hostility that has developed from prior encounters with the medical and mental health professions. Feelings of inadequacy may arise from the parents' inability to work with their child, and from their becoming impatient and irritable with their child. These reactions may produce a loss of self-esteem. Finally, guilt may emerge as a result of the parents' anger toward the child and their feelings of inadequacy.

The clinician needs to recognize that by the time a school-aged child is referred for evaluation, the parents may have already experienced much frustration and anguish.

They may have seen other professionals, but are still seeking a "magic solution." They may know that their child has a problem, but they are tired of feeling that they are to blame. In their contacts with the clinician, negative feelings that they have about themselves may interfere with the communication process; such feelings, then, may have to be dealt with during the interview. It may be helpful for the clinician to tell parents that he or she is aware of their possible discomfort at having to come and talk to a virtual stranger. It is also useful to ask the parents how they learned of their child's problem, and what diagnostic information has been made available to them.

The following outline provides valuable additional guidelines for conducting interviews with parents of mentally retarded children and handicapped children and, for the most part, with parents of normal children as well. The goals of the interview, according to Sarason (1959), include (1) a thorough presentation of the child's condition (etiology, severity, and prognosis); (2) planning of a specific program geared to the child's needs and capabilities; (3) recognizing and dealing with the personal problems of the parents as they affect the child or as they are exacerbated by the child's condition; and (4) planning for periodic discussion. The interview can be conceptualized as covering the following four phases.

I. INITIAL PHASE OF THE INTERVIEW

1. Every effort should be made to have both parents present at the interview. This will facilitate obtaining a more objective picture of the facts and will help in enabling the parents to share the responsibilities of caring for the child.
2. Recognize the frustration and hardships that may have been faced by the parents. Help them feel comfortable during the interview and encourage them to talk and to ask questions freely. Convey to them that they have something important to contribute to the discussion.
3. The parents' attitudes about the etiology of their child's condition should be obtained, as well as information about how they have handled the problems that the child has presented and what goals they have set for the child.

II. COMMUNICATING THE DIAGNOSTIC FINDINGS

4. In this phase, inform the parents that you approve of their participation, prepare them for conflict-arousing information, where indicated, and then help them to express any feelings of anxiety, hostility, disappointment, or despair. The diagnostic findings are used, in part, to help the parents give up erroneous ideas, if present, and to adopt a more realistic approach to their child's problems.

III. DISCUSSION OF A SPECIFIC PROGRAM

5. Offer to discuss with the parents a specific program for their child.

IV. TERMINATING THE INTERVIEW

6. Inform the parents that you are available for another session or sessions, especially if all of the goals have not been achieved or if the parents seem to desire further discussion.
7. In cases in which the parents are unable to accept the results of the evaluation, convey to them your understanding of their difficulty in accepting and in adjusting to the material that has been discussed. Make available to them names of other agencies or professionals should they desire another evaluation.

The particular way in which the four phases of the interview unfold will depend on the needs of the parents and your orientation. It is important that you show warmth, understanding, and respect. The crucial test of the effectiveness of the interview, as Sarason pointed out, is whether or not the parents can act on the basis of what they have learned. Erroneous beliefs present before the interview, which have been serving to defend the parents from unpleasant consequences, will probably not be given up after one interview. Consequently, several interviews may be needed, and even a visit to the home may facilitate therapeutic progress.

The clinician, even during the initial interview, must be sensitive to the parents' feelings of self-depreciation, guilt, and anxiety, and should give them an opportunity to talk about these feelings. The clinician needs to help parents feel that together they are engaged in a joint effort to understand the child and to better the child's behavior and functioning. Guilt feelings are best handled by presenting parents with accurate information about the child's handicapping condition and the causes of it. Parents should be helped to understand that handicapped children have the same needs as all children, as well as some that are uniquely their own. The clinician should stress the child's strengths and his or her potential, keeping in mind, of course, the nature of the handicap and the limitations associated with it.

Parents desire that (a) professionals use understandable terminology, (b) they both be present at the conference, (c) reading materials be recommended, (d) copies of reports be given to them, and (e) interdisciplinary communication and information about their child's social behavior and academic performance be presented (Dembinski & Mauser, 1977). Valuable guidelines for working with parents of handicapped children (and with parents of normal children as well), which elaborate on some of these points, appear in Exhibit 25-3.

Discussing the results of the psychological evaluation with parents of the mentally retarded requires tact and skill. The psychologist's role is to help the parents recognize the problem, formulate a plan, and place the plan into action (Milligan, 1971). It is a traumatic experience for most parents to learn that their child is mentally retarded. The sequence of incorporating this knowledge into the family structure may be one of shock, disbelief, fear and frustration, and then intelligent inquiry (Koegler, 1963); or emotional disorganization, reintegration, and mature adaptation (American Medical Association, 1965). The parents should be informed of the limitations of the findings, and should be encouraged to make tentative plans for the child's future. Factual informa-

tion regarding community resources, referral agencies and institutions, and recommended sources for learning about mental retardation (books and pamphlets) will help parents in planning for their child. In order to be successful, the interview should resemble any other therapeutic interview in which the gaining of insight is the objective.

In cases in which the child is diagnosed as having a serious handicap, such as mental retardation or psychosis, the desire of parents to seek a second opinion seems to be a realistic course of action because of the tremendous emotional impact of the diagnosis. However, some parents of handicapped children may "shop around," that is, they may visit a number of different professionals or clinics in order to obtain an acceptable diagnosis. Once the acceptable diagnosis is obtained, they may look endlessly for new treatments or educational programs. "The shopping behavior is maladaptive in that it frequently is costly in time, parental energy, and money; it is disruptive of family life, sometimes involving a family's making long trips or changing its place of residence; it takes the parents' focus off constructive efforts to work with their child" (Anderson, 1971, p. 3). One method of preventing (or alleviating) such behavior is to help parents work through their initial feelings of heartbreak on learning about the child's handicap. Clinicians must be sure that their own reactions to handicapping conditions do not interfere with their ability to help parents learn to accept the child's handicap. Clinicians should recognize that the presence of a handicapped child (or learning that the child has a disability) will be perceived differently by different parents, and that these perceptions need to be discussed during the initial interview or in subsequent interviews.

In school settings, parents are more likely to contact a recommended agency under the following conditions (Conti, 1975):

- the psychologist has expressed confidence in the ability of the recommended service to meet the needs of the child or family;
- a specific agency is named in the referral;

EXHIBIT 25-3. Suggestions for Working with Parents of Handicapped Children

Let the parents be involved every step of the way. The dialogue established may be the most important thing you accomplish. If the parents' presence is an obstacle to testing because the child will not "cooperate" in their presence, the setup should include a complete review of the testing procedure with the parents. (Remote video viewing or one-way windows are great if you are richly endowed.)

Make a realistic management plan part of the assessment outcome. Give the parents suggestions for how to live with the problem on a day to day basis, considering the needs of the child, the capacities of the family, and the resources of the community. Let the parents know that you will suggest modifications if any aspect of the management plan does not work.

Inform yourself about community resources. Give the parents advice on how to go about getting what they need. Steer them to the local parent organization. Wherever possible, make the parents team members in the actual diagnostic, treatment, or educational procedures. It will give you a chance to observe how the parents and child interact.

Write your reports in clear and understandable language. Professional terminology is a useful shortcut for your own notes, and you can always use it to communicate with others of your discipline. But in situations involving the parents, it becomes an obstacle to understanding. Keep in mind that it is the parents who must live with the child, help him or her along, shop for services to meet his or her needs, support his or her ego, and give him or her guidance. You cannot be there to do it for him or her, so the parents *must* be as well informed as you can make them. Information that they do not understand is not useful to them. The goal is parents who understand their child well enough to help him or her handle his or her problems.

Give copies of the reports to parents. They will need them to digest and understand the information in them, to share the information with other people close to the child, and to avoid the weeks or months of record gathering which every application to a new program in the future will otherwise entail.

Be sure the parents understand that there is no such thing as a one shot, final, and unchanging diagnosis. Make sure they understand that whatever label you give the child (if a label must be given) is merely a device for communicating and one which may have all kinds of repercussions, many of them undesirable. Make sure they understand that it says very little about the child at present and even less about the child of the future. Caution them about using that label to "explain" their child's conditions to other people.

Help the parents to think of life with their child in the same terms as life with their other children. It is an ongoing, problem solving process. Assure them that they are capable of that problem solving and that you will be there to help them with it.

Be sure that the parents understand their child's abilities and assets as well as his or her disabilities and deficiencies. What the child *can* do is far more important than what he or she cannot do, and the parents' goal thereafter is to look for, anticipate, expect, and welcome new abilities with joy when they appear. Urge them to be honest with their child. Tell them that the most important job they have is to respect their child, as well as love him or her, and to help him or her "feel good about himself or herself." Tell them that blame, either self blame or blame on the part of the child, must be avoided.

Warn the parents about service insufficiencies. Equip them with advice on how to make their way through the system of "helping" services. Warn them that they are not always helpful. Tell them that their child has a *right* to services. Tell them to insist on being a part of all decisions about their child.

Explain to them that some people with whom they talk (teachers, doctors, professionals of any kind, or other parents) may emphasize the negative. Help train the parents not only to think positively but to teach the other people important in their child's life to do so. ■

Source: "A Lost Generation of Parents" by K. A. Gorham, *Exceptional Children, 41,* 1975, pp. 523–524, with changes in notation. Copyright 1975 by the Council of Exceptional Children. Reprinted with permission.

- families were not previously referred;
- two or three school personnel have made the decision for referral;
- the family appeared highly motivated during the referral conference(s);
- the family has high socioeconomic status;
- there were two or more referral conferences with both parents.

The variables that were not associated significantly with whether or not the family contacted an agency included the age, sex, and grade of the child; the educational level of the parents; the length of the waiting list; the ability of the family to provide transportation and meet service costs; and the number of years the school psychologist had served in the district. No clear explanation was available to account for the pattern of findings. We need to learn more about the factors that are related to parents' follow-up of recommendations made by psychologists.

In cases of divorce, the custodial parent should be consulted before the information is given to the other parent. In those cases in which the custodial parent does not give permission to share the assessment findings with the other parent, the school psychologist, in conjunction with the school administrators, should arrive at a decision.

Another potentially troubling issue concerns the extent to which the student has a say in determining what information the parents receive. While there are still no clear-cut guidelines, as the courts and legislatures are continuing to define the rights of children vis-à-vis their parents, the psychologist should consider that the parents are legally and morally responsible for their child. On the other hand, there is an increasing tendency toward protecting the right of children to make their own decisions. The child's ability to make competent decisions, too, must be considered.

In exploring the possibility of institutionalization with parents, consider differences in the types of available institutions, the degree and type of retardation, and the family situation (Ellis, 1975). Each child must be treated individually, by carefully considering all of the variables involved. Some in-

stitutions have excellent training programs, focusing on self-help habit training, motor skills development, and language acquisition programs. While the residential institution for mentally retarded persons has recently come under attack, institutions still serve an important role, particularly for the profoundly retarded person.

Ethnic minority children who are institutionalized need special consideration (Norris & Overbeck, 1974). The major problems center on (a) how to diminish the deculturating tendencies of the typical institutional milieu and (b) how to consider the cultural mores and roles of the child so as to provide the best rehabilitation service. Every attempt must be made to provide opportunities in the institution for the children to participate in activities that are relevant to their culture. Institutions should make a special effort to employ staff members or consultants who are familiar with the ethnic background and language of the children.

Those engaged in communicating the results of psychological evaluations to parents will find their work rewarding, challenging, and, at times, frustrating and heartbreaking. Especially important in working with mentally retarded children (and with other handicapped children) and their parents is an understanding by examiners of themselves and of their attitude toward handicaps and the handicapped (Thurston, 1963).

The interview represents an important part of the assessment procedure. It can be particularly rewarding, for it allows the psychologist to implement in a purposeful way the results of the evaluation. Following the guidelines presented in this chapter will help to alleviate some of the anxieties associated with the communication of test results to parents of mentally retarded children, to parents of other handicapped children, and to parents of normal children as well.

Consultation in Courts and in Correctional Settings

The forensic application of psychological tests—the use of tests in the legal system or court setting—is one of the most challenging areas of consultation. In such settings, psychological testing may be involved in pretrial competency hearings, court trials, court sentence hearings, criminal investigations, civil court procedures, court-martial proceedings, and Social Security Administration hearings (Weitz, 1976). Psychological testing is important and valuable in forensic matters. It provides information about how the individual functions in the here and now, and reveals information that is not readily available in the interview. Case 25-1 illustrates the use of testing in a pretrial competency hearing.

Psychologists who work in courts or in correctional settings are faced with a number of important and unique issues, which bring into focus situational demands and moral and ethical concerns involved in psychological assessment procedures. These issues are also relevant to the work of psychologists employed in other agencies or in private practice. The following analysis is based on Riscalla's (1971) work.

The duties of the court psychologist include (a) making determinations of an individual's competency to stand trial, (b) deciding whether a juvenile should remain with his or her family, and (c) recommending whether an offender should be incarcerated or receive probation. Psychologists must decide to what extent concern with the offender's rights may conflict with the rights of the community and with the psychologists' employment by the court. Their duties place them in a captive, adversary role, because they may be called upon to support a particular position which is held either by the court or by the offender. They should recognize their own feelings about their role as well as their attitudes toward certain offenses, and should consider how their moral standards will affect their relationship with the offender as well as with the court.

Court psychologists may perceive their role in a number of ways. One is that of the anti-establishment psychologist who takes sides with the offender by rationalizing the offense on the basis of personality dynamics or adverse environmental conditions. A second is that of the punitive, self-righteous

---

CASE 25-1. Pretrial Competency Hearing

[A] criminal matter in which psychological testing proved to be highly significant involved a 17-year-old male, who was accused of murdering a 42-year-old prostitute, when he allegedly fought with her about her fee for services rendered. Following his arrest, the young man signed a confession. I [Weitz] was brought into this case by his defense counsel and subsequently examined the defendant while he was detained at the County Jail. The testing revealed an intelligence classification of "mental defective" on the basis of the Wechsler Scale. The projective techniques confirmed the low level mental acuity. The Gray Standardized Oral Reading Paragraphs indicated that he was a nonreader. In my pretrial testimony, wherein I presented my report, I referred to some of the questions and answers in the confession which the defendant signed:

Question: "Is this a true and voluntary statement made of your own free will?"
Answer: "Yes."
Question: "Can you read and write?"
Answer: "Yes."
Question: "After given an opportunity to read this statement, will you sign it?"
Answer: "Yes."

It quickly became obvious to the court that the defendant could not have read nor was he able to understand the contents of the confession which he signed. The presiding judge declared the confession to be null and void and set the defendant free. During the course of my study, the defendant admitted to me that he was forced to sign the confession out of fear after having been beaten severely with a rubber hose. Ironically, within a few weeks after he was released, the police apprehended two men who proved to be the murderers. ■

Source: Weitz, 1976, pp. 6–7.

---

psychologist who aims to protect the rights of society, and words reports so that the court may take punitive action against the offender. A third role is that of the uninvolved psychologist who is afraid of authority and who preserves his or her neutrality at any price. The fourth and proper role, according to Riscalla, is that of the psychologist who recognizes his or her captive, adversary role and yet tries to limit it, insofar as that is possible, by illuminating issues and pointing out constructive alternatives which might lead to solutions.

Psychologists must recognize that as representatives of the court they may be viewed with suspicion and hostility. Sharing the results of the evaluation with the offender before the report is written is one method that may reduce suspiciousness and facilitate a more harmonious relationship with the client. As by-products of such a procedure, the accuracy of the assessment may be improved, the recommendations may be more realistic, and the clients may gain insight into their behavior. Clients who do not desire to participate in the evaluation should have their wishes respected.

Riscalla also suggested that clients, their representative, or other interested authorized individuals be permitted to discuss the report with the psychologist and to examine it, if necessary, prior to its submission to legal authorities. This and the other procedures discussed above may help psychologists serve their clients better, write more understandable reports, and make the assessment procedure more relevant and meaningful.

Comment on Consultation

This text has been dedicated to the principle that tests of intelligence and special abilities provide a cornerstone for the consultation process. Data gained from interviews, observations, and past records form additional cornerstones. These cornerstones are linked with our knowledge of child development and child psychopathology to form the foundation upon which assessment decisions are based. Ideally, the assessment task should be one that provides a learning opportunity for both the psychologist and the child. A knowledgeable and responsible use of intelligence and special ability tests can be of value to the child, to those responsible for his or her care and education, and, ultimately, to society as a whole.

Summary

1. The consultant role requires a knowledge of the situations in which change is to take place.

2. Psychologists must know the ethical standards of their profession. With respect to assessment, the standards indicate (a) that test limitations must be recognized, (b) that confidentiality must be protected, (c) that clients have a right to know their test results, and (d) that any doubts about the reliability or validity of results must be stated in the report.

3. Psychologists who work in schools (a) help children learn, (b) solve school-related problems, and (c) assist school personnel to facilitate children's learning. Their functions include assessment, intervention, consultation, research and evaluation, and administration.

4. The objectives of the psychological evaluation in schools include (a) classification, (b) description of learning style, (c) class placement, (d) remediation, (e) management, and (f) development of teaching strategies. The aim is to help teachers find solutions to pupil problems.

5. Teachers are more likely to follow recommendations when great effort is not required, when the psychologist has follow-ups with teachers, and when the recommendations are designed in ways that are congruent with the teacher's conception of his or her role.

6. It is important that members of the school staff understand how referrals are initiated, have priorities established for assessments, and know when referrals are needed.

7. Public Law 94-142 has many implications for the assessment of children, particularly within the school setting, but in the community as well. The law is designed to protect the rights of children and parents and to ensure education for all handicapped children. It incorporates many of the ethical principles of the American Psychological Association. It mandates, for example, (a) that consideration be given to the child's native language, (b) that only valid tests be used for the assessment, (c) that more than one assessment technique be used, (d) that

the child's physical handicaps be considered, (e) that all relevant factors be considered in the evaluation, (f) that a team approach be used, (g) that the assessment procedures not be racially or culturally discriminatory, (h) that an individualized educational program be designed, (i) that parents have the right to an independent evaluation, (j) that re-evaluations be performed at least every three years, (k) that parents have the right to examine their child's records, and (l) that the child be placed in the least restrictive educational environment. Two serious shortcomings of PL 94-142 are its failure to specify clearly (a) what is meant by "racially and culturally nondiscriminatory procedures" and (b) how "native language" can be determined.

8. The Family Educational Rights and Privacy Act of 1974 established that parents must have access to their children's records and that parents must be consulted before these records are released to other agencies. It has been found that because of this act, psychologists have modified their reports.

9. Ethnic minorities have gone to the courts to challenge the assessment procedures that apparently have resulted in an overrepresentation of ethnic minorities in educable mentally retarded classes. Most cases have been settled by consent agreements. However, in the case of *Larry P. v. Riles* a federal judge banned the use of intelligence tests in the assessment of black children for placement in educable mentally retarded classes, whereas, in the *Parents in Action on Special Education v. Hannon* case, another federal judge ruled that intelligence tests are not culturally biased. The courts also have ruled that handicapped children have a right to a free and appropriate education.

10. Consultation with parents is a demanding, yet rewarding, activity. The results of the psychological evaluation take on a different color when they must be orally communicated to parents. The interaction should be in the nature of a dialogue in which both participants (the examiner and parents) have the opportunity to clarify the results of the evaluation. Working with parents of mentally retarded children requires considerable skill. Sarason's excellent presentation of the issues involved in consulting with parents of the mentally retarded serves as a model of clarity and insight. He emphasized that the psychologist should help the parents to recognize and adjust to the realities of their child's condition.

11. An important area of assessment involves the forensic application of psychological tests. Psychologists working in courts should recognize their captive adversary role, and yet try to limit it, insofar as possible, by developing constructive alternatives.

12. The proper use and application of intelligence and special ability tests can be of benefit to society as a whole.

Notes

Chapter 3

1. Further details concerning the intelligence testing movement may be found in Boring (1950); Linden and Linden (1968); Peterson (1925); and Tuddenham (1962).
2. Cattell (1963); Horn (1967, 1968, 1972, 1978a, 1978b); Horn and Cattell (1967).
3. Das (1972, 1973a); Das, Kirby, and Jarman (1975); Das and Molloy (1975); Jarman and Das (1977).
4. Bat-Haee, Mehyrar, and Sabharwal (1972); Dodwell (1961); Dudek, Lester, Goldberg, and Dyer (1969); Elkind (1961); Goldschmid (1967); Gottfried and Brody (1975); Humphreys and Parsons (1979); Kaufman (1972b); Keasey and Charles (1967); Keating (1975); Lester, Muir, and Dudek (1970); Orpet, Yoshida, and Meyers (1976); Rogers (1977); Wasik and Wasik (1976).

Chapter 4

1. Birch (1972); Kaplan (1972); Lester (1976); Lloyd-Still (1976); Loehlin, Lindzey, and Spuhler (1975).
2. Bayley (1949); Bayley and Schaefer (1964); Honzik, Macfarlane, and Allen (1948).
3. Jones, Conrad, and Blanchard (1932); Lehmann (1959); McNemar (1942).
4. Broman and Nichols (1975); Fishler, Graliker, and Koch (1965); Fishman and Palkes (1974); Illingworth and Birch (1959); Keogh and Kopp (1978); Knobloch and Pasamanick (1960); VanderVeer and Schweid (1974); Werner, Honzik, and Smith (1968).
5. Butler and Engel (1969); Davis (1971); Engel and Fay (1972); Engel and Henderson (1973); Griesel and Bartel (1976); Hendersen and Engel (1974); Jensen and Engel (1971); Perry, McCoy, Cunningham, Falgout, and Street (1976); Rhodes, Dustman, and Beck (1969).

Chapter 5

1. Exner (1966); Feldman and Sullivan (1971); Hata, Tsudzuki, Kuze, and Emi (1958); Keller (1957); Kinnie (1970); Lantz (1945); Marine (1929); Sacks (1952); Silverstein, Mohan, Franken, and Rhone (1964); Solkoff (1964); Solkoff and Chrisien (1963); Solkoff, Todd, and Screven (1964); Tsudzuki, Hata, and Kuze (1956); Tyson (1968).
2. Berko (1953); Mecham, Berko, and Berko (1960); Mecham, Berko, Berko, and Palmer (1966).
3. Allen (1959); Sievers (1950); Strother (1945).
4. Bice and Cruickshank (1966); Garrett (1952); Lord (1937).
5. Allen (1959); Maurer (1940); Michal-Smith (1955).
6. Mecham et al. (1960); Russ and Soboloff (1958); Sievers (1950).
7. Crowell and Crowell (1954); Klapper and Birch (1966); Kogan (1957); Portenier (1942); Taylor (1961).
8. Auffrey and Robertson (1972); Babad, Mann, and Mar-Hayim (1975); Donahue and Sattler (1971); Egeland (1969); Fiscus (1975); Grossman (1978); Sattler, Hillix, and Neher (1970); Sattler and Winget (1970); Simon (1969).

9. Hersh (1971); Larrabee and Kleinsasser (1967); Schroeder and Kleinsasser (1972).
10. Dangel (1972); Ekren (1962); Gillingham (1970); Saunders and Vitro (1971); Sneed (1976).
11. Busch and Osborne (1976); Clingman and Fowler (1975); Cohen (1970); Cook (1973); Galdieri, Barcikowski, and Witmer (1972); Goh and Lund (1977); Graham (1971); Lyle and Johnson (1973); Miller (1974); Quay (1971); Sweet and Ringness (1971); Tiber and Kennedy (1964); Tufano (1976).
12. Bergan, McManis, and Melchert (1971); Breuning and Zella (1978); Klugman (1944); Saigh and Payne (1976); Sweet and Ringness (1971).
13. Ali and Costello (1971); Edlund (1972); Piersel, Brody, and Kratochwill (1977); Terrell, Taylor, and Terrell (1978).
14. Brannigan, Calnen, Loprete, and Rosenberg (1976); Brannigan, Rosenberg, Loprete, and Calnen (1977); Curr and Gourlay (1956); Davis, Peacock, Fitzpatrick, and Mulhern (1969); Jordan (1932); Kaspar, Throne, and Schulman (1968); La Crosse (1964); Mahan (1963); Masling (1959); Massey (1964); Miller and Chansky (1972); Miller, Chansky, and Gredler (1970); Plumb and Charles (1955); Sattler, Andres, Squire, Wisely, and Maloy (1978); Sattler and Ryan (1973a); Sattler and Squire (1982); Sattler, Winget, and Roth (1969); Schwartz (1966); Scottish Council for Research in Education (1967); Smith, May, and Lebovitz (1966); Walker, Hunt, and Schwartz (1965); Wrightstone (1941).
15. Curr and Gourlay (1956); Davis et al. (1969); Jordan (1932); Kaspar et al. (1968); LaCrosse (1964); Masling (1959); Plumb and Charles (1955); Sattler and Ryan (1973a); Schwartz (1966); Smith, May, and Lebovitz (1966).
16. Bennett (1970); Cattell (1937); Cieutat (1965); Cieutat and Flick (1967); Cohen (1950, 1965); Curr and Gourlay (1956); Davis et al. (1969); Di Lorenzo and Nagler (1968); Green (1960–62); Kaspar et al. (1968); Krebs (1969); Nichols (1959); Oakland, Lee, and Axelrad (1975); Rothman (1974); Sattler (1966b, 1969); Sattler and Theye (1967); Schachter and Apgar (1958); Schwartz and Flanigan (1971); Smith and May (1967); Thomas, Hertzig, Dryman, and Fernandez (1971).
17. Back and Dana (1977); Bradbury, Wright, Walker, and Ross (1975); Cieutat and Flick (1967); Pedersen, Shinedling, and Johnson (1968); Quereshi (1968); Smith et al. (1966).
18. Egeland (1967); Sattler (1973b); Sattler and Martin (1971).

Chapter 6

1. Bachelder and Denny (1977a, 1977b); Estes (1974).
2. Peterson (1925); Pintner (1931); Woodrow (1919).
3. For information concerning the scale in other countries, consult Peterson (1925).
4. Dean (1950); Hofstaetter (1954); Jones (1949, 1954); Stott and Ball (1965).
5. Burt (1939); Goodenough (1942); Krugman (1939); McCandless (1953); Vernon (1937).
6. British Psychological Society (1958); Cattell (1937); Harriman (1939); Kent (1937); Krugman (1939); McCandless (1953); Mitchell (1941).

Chapter 7

1. See, for example, Allen and Jefferson (1962); Sattler and Tozier (1970); Taylor (1961).
2. Two types of modifications also have been proposed that simply involve changing the order of administering the tests. One method, termed the "adaptive method," involves altering the order of administering hard and easy tests. When the adaptive method was tried with poorly adjusted and well-adjusted elementary school children, the poorly adjusted group obtained higher scores with the adaptive method than with the standard method, while the well-adjusted group obtained similar scores under both types of administration (Hutt, 1947). A second method, termed "serial administration," involves grouping tests of the same content together. Children have been found to obtain the same scores under serial and conventional methods of administration (Frandsen, McCullough, & Stone, 1950; Spache, 1942). These two types of modifications, while interesting, do not hold much promise because they are not geared to handicapped children. The research findings, however, do indicate that a modified order of administering the tests may alter some children's performance.
3. Studies using abbreviated tests for the 1960 form have involved mentally retarded children (Forehand & Gordon, 1971; Silverstein, 1963, 1966; Silverstein & Fisher, 1961), black children (Kennedy et al., 1963), children attending a child guidance clinic (Gayton, 1971), developmentally disabled children (Bloom et al., 1977), and normal children (Gordon & Forehand, 1972). Studies reporting on the efficacy of the abbreviated scale for the 1937 forms uniformly showed high correlations (.89 or higher) between the abbreviated and full scales (e.g., Birch, 1955; Brown, 1942; Kvaraceus, 1940; Shotwell & McCulloch, 1944; Spache, 1942; Spaulding, 1945; Wright, 1942). However, the range of difference in IQ points between the abbreviated and full scales was often considerable. For example, Wright reported a range of −17 to +13 points. Kvaraceus found 2 children with more than a 10-point difference, 25 children with a difference between 6 and 10 points, and 187 children with a difference between 0 and 5 points.
4. Birch (1955); Gayton (1971); Silverstein (1963, 1966); Silverstein and Fisher (1961); Wright (1942).

Chapter 8

1. Brown (1941) presents extensive case material that describes how children differ in their reactions to the examination. Since only a small portion of his work is described here, it is recommended that his material be read in full.
2. Garner (1966); Gittleman and Birch (1967); Harris and Shakow (1937); Hendriks (1954); Hunt and

Cofer (1944); Lorr and Meister (1941); McNemar (1942); Schneider and Smillie (1959); Wallin (1917); Wells (1927).

The technical criticisms of the use of scatter on the Stanford-Binet are numerous. Scatter may result from a number of factors inherent in the construction of the test, including lack of perfect correlation among tests, test unreliability, lack of discriminatory power of certain tests, an increase in variability with an increase in absolute mean test performance, and systematic errors in testing due to language handicaps, sensory defects, special training, lack of cooperation, and ambiguous scoring instructions. Scatter can occur even in the absence of any clinically significant variability in the examinee's responses (Garner, 1966). McNemar (1942) concluded it is difficult to see how any clinical meaning can be attached to the concept of scatter. Lorr and Meister (1941) were opposed to the use of scatter as even a crude estimate of the measurement of error of the test for an individual examinee. However, in spite of all the negative criticism, Anderson (1951) was of the opinion that the interpretation of scatter still has clinical usefulness.

3. Berko (1955); Riggs and Burchard (1952); Satter (1955); Schafer and Leitch (1948); Vane, Weitzman, and Applebaum (1966).

4. Brengelmann and Kenny (1961); Cochran and Pedrini (1969); Fisher (1962); Fisher, Kilman, and Shotwell (1961); Giannell and Freeburne (1963); Kangas and Bradway (1971); Kroske, Fretwell, and Cupp (1965); McKerracher and Scott (1966); Wechsler (1955).

Chapter 9

1. **Table. Studies Comparing the WISC-R with Other Ability Tests and Measures of Achievement**

Appelbaum and Tuma (1977)[i]; Bloom, Raskin, and Reese (1976)[o]; Brooks (1977)[o]; Covin (1976a, 1976b)[g]; Covin (1976b)[i]; Covin (1976b)[j]; Covin (1977d, 1977e)[i]; Covin (1977b, 1977e)[n]; Covin and Lubimiv (1976)[s]; Craft and Kronenberger (1979)[q]; Davis and Walker (1977)[e]; DeHorn and Klinge (1978)[i]; Goh and Youngquist (1979)[e]; Hale (1978)[s]; Hartlage and Boone (1977)[a,s]; Hartlage and Steele (1977)[m,s]; Hirshoren, Hurley, and Hunt (1977)[c]; Karnes and Brown (1979)[n]; Kaufman and Van Hagen (1977)[o]; Kendall and Little (1977)[i,k,l]; Lowe and Karnes (1976)[d]; Lowrance and Anderson (1979)[n]; Martin and Kidwell (1977)[n]; Mize, Smith, and Callaway (1979)[i,n]; Nagle and Lazarus (1979)[q]; Naglieri (1980)[e]; Naglieri and Harrison (1979)[e]; Nicholson (1977)[k]; Rasbury, Falgout, and Perry (1978)[f,k]; Rasbury, McCoy, and Perry (1977)[r]; Raskin, Bloom, Klee, and Reese (1978)[o,s]; Reschly and Reschly (1979)[f,p]; Reynolds and Gutkin (1980a)[s]; Richmond and Long (1977)[i]; Sapp, Horton, McElroy, and Ray (1979)[a]; Sattler, Bohanan, and Moore (1980)[i]; Schwarting and Schwarting (1977)[s]; Sewell and Manni (1977)[o]; Smith, Hays, and Solway (1977)[b]; Stedman, Lawlis, Cortner, and Achterberg (1978)[s]; Stokes, Blair, Jones, and Marrero (1979)[f,g,m]; Tebeleff and Oakland (1977)[a]; Vance, Lewis, and DeBell (1979)[i,n]; Vance, Prichard, and Wallbrown (1978)[j]; Wechsler (1974)[o,q,r]; Wikoff (1978)[h].

[a]California Achievement Test; [b]Culture Fair Intelligence Test; [c]Hiskey-Nebraska Test of Learning Aptitude; [d]Lorge-Thorndike Intelligence Test; [e]McCarthy Scales of Children's Abilities; [f]Metropolitan Achievement Tests; [g]Otis-Lennon Mental Ability Test; [h]Peabody Individual Achievement Test; [i]Peabody Picture Vocabulary Test; [j]Pintner-Cunningham; [k]Quick Test; [l]Revised Beta Examination; [m]School grades; [n]Slosson Intelligence Test; [o]Stanford-Binet Intelligence Test; [p]Teacher predictions; [q]Wechsler Adult Intelligence Scale; [r]Wechsler Preschool and Primary Scale of Intelligence; [s]Wide Range Achievement Test.

2. Berry and Sherrets (1975); Brooks (1977); Catron and Catron (1977); Covin (1976c, 1977a, 1977c); Gironda (1977); Hamm, Wheeler, McCallum, Herrin, Hunter, and Catoe (1976); Hartlage and Boone (1977); Hartlage and Steele (1977); Jenson, Hanson, and Young (1976); Klinge, Rodziewicz, and Schwartz (1976); Larrabee and Holroyd (1976); Munford, Meyerowitz, and Munford (1980); Paal, Hesterly, and Wepfer (1979); Pristo (1978); Reschly and Davis (1977); Rowe (1976, 1977); Schwarting (1976); Solly (1977); Stokes, Brent, Marrero, Huddleston, and Rozier (1978); Swerdlick (1978); Tuma, Appelbaum, and Bee (1978); Watkins and McKinney (1978); Weiner and Kaufman (1979); Wheaton and Vandergriff (1978).

3. Kaufman's findings were arrived at by the principal factor analysis method (squared multiple correlations in diagonals as the final estimates of communalities), which was followed by a varimax rotation for the eleven age groups ($6\frac{1}{2}$ to $16\frac{1}{2}$ years) that comprised the total WISC-R standardization sample reported in the WISC-R manual. In this section, the general findings of his analyses are described.

4. The emergence of a large unrotated general factor at each level and the high intercorrelations among the factors (when oblique factor analytic procedures were used) also provided empirical support for the Full Scale IQ concept (Kaufman, 1975a).

5. The procedure used by Kaufman (1975a) was an analysis of the unrotated first principal factor.

6. DeHorn and Klinge (1978); Reynolds and Gutkin (1980b); Schooler, Beebe, and Koepke (1978); Shiek and Miller (1978); Swerdlik and Schweitzer (1978); Vance and Wallbrown (1977); Wallbrown, Blaha, Wallbrown, and Engin (1975).

7. Kaufman recommends that specific interpretations be given to all subtests, with the exception of (a) Similarities for children above $8\frac{1}{2}$ years and (b) Object Assembly for all children; patterns involving these latter two subtests probably are due to measurement error.

8. The Information subtest is not included in the Freedom from Distractibility factor score because

it did not load substantially when other factor analytic procedures were used (Kaufman, 1975a).

9. Exner (1966); Morris, Martin, Johnson, Birch, and Thompson (1978); Sattler (1969).

10. Herrell and Golland (1969); Post (1970); Schwebel and Bernstein (1970).

11. Brannigan, Calnen, Loprete, and Rosenberg (1976); Brannigan, Rosenberg, Loprete, and Calnen (1977); Sattler, Andres, Squire, Wisely, and Maloy (1978).

12. Reid, Moore, and Alexander (1968); Yudin (1966).

13. Dean (1977f); Erikson (1967); Finch, Kendall, Spirito, Entin, Montgomery, and Schwartz (1979); Gayton, Wilson, and Bernstein (1970); Goh (1978); Rasbury, Falgout, and Perry (1978); Satz, Van de Riet, and Mogel (1967); Tellegen and Briggs (1967).

Chapter 11

1. This suggestion was obtained from A. B. Silverstein.

2. Personal communication, A. B. Silverstein, 1980.

3. Johnson and Lyle (1972a, 1972b, 1973); Lyle and Johnson (1973, 1974).

Chapter 12

1. Anthony (1973); Austin and Carpenter (1970); Bach (1968); Barclay and Yater (1969); Crockett, Rardin, and Pasework (1975); Dokecki, Frede, and Gautney (1969); Fagan, Broughton, Allen, Clark, and Emerson (1969); Kaufman (1973b); Oakland, King, White, and Eckman (1971); Pasework, Rardin, and Grice (1971); Plant (1967); Prosser and Crawford (1971); Rellas (1969); Richards (1968); Ruschival and Way (1971); Sewell (1977); Zimmerman and Woo-Sam (1970).

2. Austin and Carpenter (1970); Crockett et al. (1975); Oakland et al. (1971); Wasik and Wasik (1972); Yater, Boyd, and Barclay (1975).

3. Austin and Carpenter (1970); Bach (1968); Dokecki et al. (1969); Krebs (1969); McNamara, Porterfield, and Miller (1969); Plant (1967); Plant and Southern (1968); Yater, Barclay, and Leskosky (1971); Yule, Berger, Butler, Newham, and Tizard (1969).

4. Eichorn (1972); Fagan et al. (1969); Oldridge and Allison (1968).

5. Corey (1970); Fagan et al. (1969); Yule et al. (1969).

Chapter 13

1. The Psychological Corporation, A. S. Kaufman, personal communication, August 1971, has indicated that these are acceptable answers for questions 4 and 9 on the Information subtest.

2. The suggestion courtesy of Professor Joy Rogers.

3. Personal communication, A. B. Silverstein, 1980.

Chapter 14

1. Davis (1975); Davis and Rowland (1974); Davis and Walker (1977); Gerken, Hancock, and Wade (1978); Goh and Youngquist (1979); Harrison and Wiebe (1977); Levenson and Zino (1979); McCarthy (1972); Naglieri (1980).

2. DeForest (1941); Driscoll (1933); Ebert and Simmons (1943); Kawin (1934); Stutsman (1934); Wellman (1938).

3. Allen and Young (1943); DeForest (1941); Driscoll (1933); Gordon (1933); Stutsman (1931); Wellman (1938).

4. Hammill, Crandell, and Colarusso (1970); Rotatori and Epstein (1978); Slosson (1963).

5. Armstrong and Mooney (1971); Armstrong, Mooney, and Jensen (1971); Carlisle, Shinedling, and Weaver (1970); DeLapa (1968); Johnson and Johnson (1971); Jongeward (1969); Lamp and Traxler (1973); Ritter, Duffey, and Fischman (1973); Rotatori, Sedlak, and Freagon (1979); Stark (1975); Stewart and Myers (1974); Stewart, Wood, and Gallman (1971).

6. Baum and Kelley (1979); Jerrolds, Callaway, and Gwaltney (1972); Karnes and Brown (1979); Lamp and Traxler (1973); Lowrance and Anderson (1979); Machen (1973); Maxwell (1971); Pikulski (1973); Stewart and Myers (1974); Stewart, Wood, and Gallman (1971); Vance, Lewis, and DeBell (1979).

7. Carlisle, Shinedling, and Weaver (1970); Hale, Douglas, Cummins, Rittgarn, Breed, and Dabbert (1978); Hammill (1969); Hammill, Crandell, and Colarusso (1970); Houston and Otto (1968); Hutton (1972); Johnson and Johnson (1971); Lamp and Traxler (1973); Lamp, Traxler, and Gustafson (1973); Lessler and Galinsky (1971); Maxwell (1971); Miller (1973); Shepherd (1969); Stewart, Wood, and Gallman (1971); Swanson and Jacobson (1970).

8. Raven (1938, 1960, 1965).

9. Barratt (1956); Burke (1958); Estes, Curtin, DeBurger, and Denny (1961); Fitz-Gibbon (1974); Harris (1959); Jensen (1974c); Johnson (1952); Knief and Stroud (1959); Levine and Iscoe (1955); Malpass, Brown, and Hake (1960); Martin and Wiechers (1954); Moran (1972); Raven (1948); Stacey and Carleton (1955); Wiltshire and Gray (1969).

10. Burke (1958); Corman and Budoff (1974); Keir (1949); MacArthur (1960); MacArthur and Elley (1963); Rimoldi (1948); Wiedl and Carlson (1976).

11. Burns and Velicer (1977); Croake, Keller, and Catlin (1973); Dunn (1967a); Evans, Ferguson, Davies, and Williams (1975); Harris (1963); McGilligan, Yater, and Huesing (1971); Strumpfer and Mienie (1968).

12. Datta (1967); Dunn (1967b); Gayton (1970); Gayton, Wilson, and Evans (1971); Goldstein and Peck (1971); Levine and Gross (1968); Levinson and Block (1977); Pihl and Nimrod (1976); Pikulski (1972); Schaefer and Sternfield (1971); Strümpfer and Mienie (1968); Yater, Barclay, and McGilligan (1969).

13. Ables (1971); Byrd and Springfield (1969); Datta (1967); Dunn (1967b,c); Fine and Tracy (1968); Gayton, Bassett, and Bishop (1970); Gayton, Tavormina, Evans, and Schuh (1974); Gayton, Wilson, and Evans (1971); Lehman and Levy (1971); Pihl and Nimrod (1976); Pikulski (1972); Reisman and Yamokoski (1973); Schaefer and Sternfield (1971).

14. Carlson (1970); Croake, Keller, and Catlin (1973); Johnson and Johnson (1971); Vane (1967).
15. Byrd and Springfield (1969); Dunn (1967b); Gayton et al. (1974); Hartman (1972); Pikulski (1972).
16. Armentrout (1971); Auricchio (1966); Duffey, Ritter, and Fedner (1976); Hartman (1972); Roche (1970).
17. Datta (1967); Dunn (1967c); Pihl and Nimrod (1976); Strümpfer and Mienie (1968).
18. Black (1973); Sharp (1958); Spellacy and Black (1972).
19. Alper (1958); Arnold (1951); Bensberg and Sloan (1951); Bessent (1950); Beverly and Bensberg (1952); Bonham (1974); Gallagher, Benoit, and Boyd (1956); Ollendick, Finch, and Ginn (1974); Ritter (1976); Sharp (1957); Tate (1952).
20. Elliot (1969); French (1964); Pasewark, Sawyer, Smith, Wasserberger, Dell, Brito, and Lee (1967).

Chapter 15

1. Baum (1975); Bossard and Galusha (1979); Cochran and Pedrini (1969); DeBell and Vance (1977); Fortenberry and Broome (1963); Gretzler (1974); Hale, Douglas, Cummins, Rittgarn, Breed, and Dabbert (1978); Harris (1973); Hartlage and Lucas (1976); Hopkins, Dobson, and Oldridge (1962); Jastak and Jastak (1978); Kelly and Amble (1970); Lawson and Avila (1962); McAreavey (1976); Ryan (1973); Sanner and McManis (1978); Scherer (1961); Schwarting and Schwarting (1977); Smith (1961); Smith and McManis (1977); Washington and Teska (1970).
2. Dean (1977c); Lamanna and Ysseldyke (1973); Wilson and Spangler (1974).
3. Baum (1975); Bray and Estes (1975); Burns, Peterson, and Bauer (1974); Davenport (1976); Ollendick, Murphy, and Ollendick (1975); Sitlington (1970); Soethe (1972); Wetter and French (1973); Wilson and Spangler (1974).
4. Herman, Huesing, Levett, and Boehm (1973); Hutcherson (1978); Steinbauer and Heller (1978).
5. Huizinga (1973); Kirk and Kirk (1978); Taddonio (1973).
6. Belford and Blumberg (1975); Burns and Watson (1973); Meyers (1969); Ramanaiah, O'Donnell, and Adams (1978); Sedlak and Weener (1973); Wisland and Many (1969).
7. Burns (1976, 1977); Carroll (1972); Lumsden (1978); Waugh (1978); Wiederholt (1978).
8. These results are based on studies reported in the PPVT-R manual.
9. Ibid.
10. Ibid.
11. Ammons and Ammons (1962); Otto and McMenemy (1965); Sawyer and Whitten (1972); Strandberg, Griffith, and Miner (1969).
12. Hoffman, Preiser, and David (1975); Joesting and Joesting (1971a, 1971b); Lamp and Barclay (1967); Otto and McMenemy (1965); Pless, Snider, Eaton, and Kearsley (1965); Sawyer and Whitten (1972).
13. Ammons and Ammons (1962); Maloney, Ward, Schenck, and Braucht (1971); Staffieri (1971); Strandberg, Griffith, and Miner (1969); Vance and Singer (1979a).

Chapter 16

1. Halpern (1951); Koppitz (1964, 1975); Stellern, Halpern, Vasa, and Little (1976).
2. Frostig, Maslow, Lefever, and Whittlesey (1964); Hammill, Goodman, and Wiederholt (1971); Sabatino, Abbott, and Becker (1974).
3. Allen (1968); Boyd and Randle (1970); Chissom and Thomas (1971); Fretz (1970); Hammill, Colarusso, and Wiederholt (1970); Ohnmacht and Olson (1968); Olson (1968); Olson and Johnson (1970); Silverstein (1965); Silverstein, Ulfeldt, and Price (1970); Smith and Marx (1972).
4. Becker and Sabatino (1973); Corah and Powell (1963); Hueftle (1967); McKinney (1971); Sabatino, Abbott, and Becker (1974); Thomas and Chissom (1973); Ward (1970).
5. Corah and Powell (1963); Mann (1972); Smith and Marx (1972).
6. Black (1974); DuBois and Brown (1973); Frostig et al. (1964); Leibert and Sherk (1970); Ohnmacht and Olson (1968); Olson (1966a, 1966b, 1968); Olson and Johnson (1970); Sabatino et al. (1974); Smith and Marx (1972). These studies have employed such measures as the Gates-MacGinitie Reading Survey, the Gates Reading Readiness Test, the Olson Reading Readiness Test, the Metropolitan Readiness Test, the Wide Range Achievement Test, the Stanford Achievement Test, and letter and word discrimination tasks.
7. Becker and Sabatino (1973); Culbertson and Gunn (1966); DuBois and Brown (1973); Hammill, Goodman, and Wiederholt (1971).
8. Bieger (1974); Frostig et al. (1964); Rosen (1966); Talkington (1968); Walsh and D'Angelo (1971); Wiederholt and Hammill (1971).

Chapter 17

1. Fromme (1974); Gambaro (1944); Patterson (1943); Watson (1951).
2. Collard (1972); Ernhart (1974); Hunt (1974).
3. Abikoff, Gittelman-Klein, and Klein (1977); Glennon and Weisz (1978); Haynes and Kerns (1979); Werry and Quay (1969).

Chapter 18

1. I am grateful to Terry B. Gutkin for this suggestion.
2. Brophy and Good (1970); Dusek and O'Connell (1973); Good and Brophy (1972); Yoshida and Meyers (1975).
3. Budoff, Gimon, and Corman (1974); Budoff and Hamilton (1976); Budoff, Meskin, and Harrison (1971).
4. Arnold (1962); Haworth (1966); Murstein (1963).

Chapter 19

1. Anastasi (1967); Berdie (1965); Bernal (1972); Clark (1967); Eells, Davis, Havighurst, Herrick, and Tyler (1951); Halpern (1971); Johnson and Medinnus (1965); Kagan (1968, 1971); Leland (1971); Levine (1966); Masland, Sarason, and Gladwin (1958); Mundy and Maxwell (1958); Padilla and Ruiz (1973); Palmer (1970); Riessman (1962);

Sarason and Doris (1969); Schmideberg (1970); Schubert (1967); Williams (1970a, 1970b, 1970c, 1971); Zigler and Butterfield (1968).

2. Bossard, Reynolds, and Gutkin (1980); Hall, Huppertz, and Levi (1977); Reschly and Sabers (1979); Reynolds and Hartlage (1979).

3. Bossard, Reynolds, and Gutkin (1980); Hurley, Hirshoren, Hunt, and Kavale (1979); Oakland and Feigenbaum (1979); Oakland and Marrs (1977); Oakland, Tombari, and Parker (1978); Reschly and Reschly (1979).

4. Jensen (1974c); Meyer and Goldstein (1971); Miele (1979); Nichols (1971); Olivier and Barclay (1967); Sandoval (1979).

5. Gutkin and Reynolds (1981); Guy (1977); Kaufman and DiCuio (1975); Kaufman and Hollenbeck (1974); Miele (1979); Reschly (1978); Semler and Iscoe (1966); Silverstein (1973); Vance, Huelsman, and Wherry (1976); Vance and Wallbrown (1978).

6. Anastasi (1958); Farnham-Diggory (1970); Guthrie (1976); Harrison (1977); Haywood (1974); Jordan (1976); Jorgensen (1974); Kagan (1971); Samuda (1975); Tobias (1974); Wrightsman (1972).

7. Abramson (1969); Barnebey (1973); Bucky and Banta (1972); Caldwell and Knight (1970); Canady (1936); Costello (1970); Crown (1971); Dill (1972); Forrester and Klaus (1964); France (1973); Hall, Reder, and Cole (1975); Hanley and Barclay (1979); Jensen (1974b); Jensen and Figueroa (1975); Lipsitz (1969); Marwit and Neumann (1974); Miller and Phillips (1966); Moore and Retish (1974); Pelosi (1968); Ratusnik and Koenigsknecht (1977); Samuel, Grayson, Sherman, Soto, and Winstead (1976); Samuel, Soto, Parks, Ngissah, and Jones (1976); Sattler (1966a); Savage and Bowers (1972); Scott, Hartson, and Cunningham (1976); Smith and May (1967); Solkoff (1972, 1974); Wellborn, Reid, and Reichard (1973); Yando, Zigler, and Gates (1971).

8. Genshaft and Hirt (1974); Hall, Turner, and Russell (1973); Harver, (1977); Levy and Cook (1973).

9. Anttonen and Fleming (1976); Claiborn, (1969); Dusek and O'Connell (1973); Fielder, Cohen, and Feeney (1971); Fleming and Anttonen (1971); Ginsburg, (1970); Gozali and Meyen (1970).

10. Beberfall (1958); Chavez (1956); Perales (1965).

11. Bernal (1972); DeAvila (1976); DeAvila and Havassy (1974a); Padilla and Ruiz (1973).

12. Chandler and Plakos (1969); Eklund and Scott (1965); Galvan (1967); Holland (1960); Keston and Jimenez (1954); Levandowski (1975); Myers and Goldstein (1979); Palmer and Gaffney (1972); Sattler, Avila, Houston, and Toney (1980); Swanson and DeBlassie (1971); Thomas (1977).

13. Dean (1977a, 1979b); Reynolds and Gutkin (1980a).

14. Dean (1979a); Gerken (1978); Milne (1975); Reynolds and Gutkin (1980a); Swanson and DeBlassie (1971).

15. Cundick (1970); Havighurst and Hilkevitch (1944); McAreavey (1976); Peck (1973); Peters (1963); Sachs (1974); St. John, Krichev, and Bauman (1976); Thurber (1976); Turner and Penfold (1952).

16. Cundick (1970); Thurber (1976); Turner and Penfold (1952).

17. Knobloch and Pasamanick (1962); Naylor and Myrianthopoulos (1967); Pasamanick and Knobloch (1958, 1966); Wiener and Milton (1970).

18. Denniston (1975); Eysenck (1971); Herrnstein (1973); Nichols (1974).

19. Anastasi (1961); Barnes (1973); Bereiter (1972); Bridgeman and Buttram (1975); Clarizio (1979b); Cleary, Humphreys, Kendrick, and Wesman (1975); Cole and Bruner (1971); Davis (1971); Flaugher (1974); Goldman (1972); Green (1978); Holtzman (1971); Jensen (1970a); Kagan and Klein (1973); Mercer (1971); Nava (1970); Newland (1970); Ramirez, Taylor, and Petersen (1971); Tucker (1976); Wikoff (1974); E. B. Williams (1971); Williams (1970a).

Chapter 20

1. Klasen (1972); Mattis, French, and Rapin (1975); Satz and Sparrow (1970); Stanley and Hall (1973); Torgesen (1977); Vande Voort, Senf, and Benton (1972).

2. Satz and Friel (1973); Satz, Friel, and Rudegeair (1974a, 1974b); Satz and Sparrow (1970).

3. Bruner (1968); Hunt (1961); Piaget (1926).

4. Barnwell and Denison (1975); Bloom and Raskin (1980); Bloom, Wagner, and Bergman (1980); Sattler (1980); Tabachnick (1979); VanVactor (1975).

5. Altus (1956); Belluomini (1962); Belmont and Birch (1966); Burks and Bruce (1955); Corwin (1967); Dockrell (1960); Ekwall (1966); Goldman and Barclay (1974); Graham (1952); Griffiths (1970); Hunter and Johnson (1971); Kallos, Grabow, and Guarino (1961); Klasen (1972); Lyle and Goyen (1969); McLean (1963); McLeod (1965); Muir (1962); Muzyczka and Erickson (1976); Neville (1961); Paterra (1963); Reid and Schoer (1966); Richardson and Surko (1956); Robeck (1962); Rogge (1959); Rourke, Orr, and Ridgley (1974); Sheldon and Garton (1959); Silberberg and Feldt (1968); Smith, Coleman, Dokecki, and Davis (1977a); Thompson (1963); Vance, Gaynor, and Coleman (1976).

6. Gutkin (1979a); Smith, Coleman, Dokecki, and Davis (1977b); Vance and Singer (1979b).

7. Conners (1970); Nelson and Warrington (1974); Rie and Rie (1979); Rourke and Finlayson (1975); Rourke and Telegdy (1971); Rourke, Young, and Flewelling (1971); Wells (1970).

8. Freeman (1967); Satterfield (1973); Satterfield, Cantwell, Saul, and Yusin (1974).

9. Dean (1977d); Tigay and Kempler (1971); Turner, Mathews, and Rachman (1967).

10. Hamm and Evans (1978); Maxwell (1960); McHugh (1963); Morris, Evans, and Pearson (1978); Petrie (1962); Schoonover and Hertel (1970); Woody (1967).

11. Andrew (1974); Camp (1966); Corotto (1961); Harris (1957); Hays, Solway, and Schreiner (1978); Henning and Levy (1967); Kaiser (1964); Reisman (1973); Richardson and Surko (1956); Saccuzzo and Lewandowski (1976); Shinagawa (1963); Smith (1969); Solway, Hays, Roberts, and Cody (1975); Wiens, Matarazzo, and Gaver (1959).

12. Gilbert and Rubin (1965); Hopkins and McGuire (1966); Tillman (1967a); Tillman and Bashaw (1968); Tillman and Osborne (1969).

13. Brill (1962); Evans (1966); Hirshoren, Kavale, Hurley, and Hunt (1977); Larr and Cain (1959); Lavos (1962); Pickles (1966).

Chapter 21

1. Charles (1953, 1957); Muench (1944).

2. Alper and Horne (1959); Earhart and Warren (1964); Poull (1921); Rushton and Stockwin (1963); Walker and Gross (1970); Walton and Begg (1957).

3. Curtis (1918); Doll (1917); Elwood (1934); Hinckley (1915); Johnson and Blake (1960); Jones (1919); Kennedy-Fraser (1945); Laycock and Clark (1942); Louden (1933); Magaret and Thompson (1950); Martinson and Strauss (1941); McFadden (1931); Perkins (1932); Pressey and Cole (1918); Thompson and Magaret (1947); Townsend (1928); Wallin (1929).

4. Berko (1955); Cassel and Danenhower (1949); Gallagher (1957); Hoakley and Frazeur (1945); Rohrs and Haworth (1962).

5. Vance and Wallbrown (1977); Vance, Wallbrown, and Fremont (1978); Van Hagen and Kaufman (1975).

6. This order is based on studies of the WISC and WISC-R by Kaufman and Van Hagen (1977); Silverstein (1968c); and Vance, Hankins, Wallbrown, Engin, and McGee (1978).

Chapter 22

1. Gardiner and Walter (1977); Glanville, Best, and Levenson (1977); Tomlinson-Keasey, Kelly, and Burton (1978); Wada and Davis (1977).

2. Bryden (1973); Bryden and Allard (1978); Satz, Bakker, Teunissen, Goebel, and Van der Vlugt (1975).

3. Annett (1973); Boll (1973); Dikmen, Matthews, and Harley (1975); Fitzhugh and Fitzhugh (1965); Horn (1970); Hutt (1976).

4. Golden (1979); Reitan and Davison (1974); Selz (1981).

5. Bortner and Birch (1969); Caputo, Edmonston, L'Abate, and Rondberg (1963); Clawson (1962a); Pennington, Galliani, and Voegele (1965); Reed and Fitzhugh (1966); Reed and Reed (1967); Reed and Reitan (1963, 1969); Reed, Reitan, and Kløve (1965); Rowley (1961); Schwartz and Dennerll

(1970). These studies are based on the WISC. However, the findings in all likelihood apply to the WISC-R.

6. Annett, Lee, and Ounsted (1961); Braun and Brane (1971); Hartlage and Green (1972); Pihl (1968). These studies are based on the WISC. However, the findings in all likelihood apply to the WISC-R.

Chapter 23

1. Hingtgen and Bryson (1972); Wing, Yeates, Brierley, and Gould (1976).

2. DeMyer (1976); DeMyer, Barton, and Norton (1972); Hingtgen and Bryson (1972); Rutter (1974, 1978); Rutter and Bartak (1971).

3. DeMyer, Barton, Alpern, Kimberlin, Allen, Yang, and Steele (1974); Lotter (1967); Rutter and Lockyer (1967).

4. Bartak and Rutter (1971, 1973); DeMyer et al. (1974); Gittelman and Birch (1967); Lockyer and Rutter (1969); Rutter and Bartak (1973).

5. DeMyer, Barton, DeMyer, Norton, Allen, and Steele (1973); Lotter (1974, 1978); Rutter (1970, 1974).

6. Bender (1970); Goldfarb, Goldfarb, and Pollack (1969); Kolvin, Humphrey, and McNay (1971); Pollack (1960); Rutter, Greenfeld, and Lockyer (1967); Rutter and Lockyer (1967).

7. Rutter (1977, 1978); Rutter, Shaffer, and Shepherd (1975).

8. Churchill (1972); Cohen, Caparulo, and Shaywitz (1976); Ornitz and Ritvo (1976); Rutter (1965); Rutter and Bartak (1971); Wing and Wing (1971).

Chapter 24

1. Affleck and Strider (1971); Garfield, Heine, and Leventhal (1954); Hartlage and Merck (1971); Lacey and Ross (1964); Moore, Boblitt, and Wildman (1968); Olive (1972); Smyth and Reznikoff (1971); Tallent (1963); Tallent and Reiss (1959a, 1959b, 1959c).

2. Cuadra and Albaugh (1956); Grayson and Tolman (1950); Rucker (1967a); Shively and Smith (1969).

Chapter 25

1. Goodman, Gottlieb, and Harrison (1972); Gottlieb and Budoff (1973); Gottlieb, Semmel, and Veldman (1978); Guskin and Chaires (1966); Iano, Ayers, Heller, McGettigan, and Walker (1974).

Answers to Test Your Skills Exercises

Chapter 8: Exercises for the Stanford-Binet

1. This statement conveys little, if any, meaning to the reader. It and similar statements should be deleted from the report.
2. This is a technical description of the test procedures. It adds little to the report. I recommend that this and similar procedural material be excluded from the report.
3. This is an odd statement. If we interpret it literally we might wonder if Bill went berserk. Maybe he did, but I doubt it. Perhaps the writer meant to say that Bill began to fail more items. The writer must ask himself or herself why this material is being included in the report. What purpose does it serve? What point is being illustrated by including it?
4. A child's level of performance is determined not by the range of successes and failures, but by the actual number of tests passed or failed. The IQ (or MA) should be the focus for making statements about the child's ability level, not the range.
5. This is a vague statement because it does not interpret the meaning or implications of scatter. I recommend that the implications of scatter be evaluated in the report. Further, it is better to discuss scatter as variability of performance because "scatter" is a more technical concept.
6. In most cases there is not a one-to-one relationship between level of test performance and classroom achievement. It is misleading to give such an impression in the report. MA does not indicate level of academic achievement. Academic achievement is measured by appropriate achievement tests.
7. This is an awkward sentence although the writer's intention to connect classroom behavioral observations and test performance is a good one. Better ways of expressing this relationship are as follows: "Her performance in areas measuring judgment and reasoning was below average, and observation of her classroom performance confirmed her below-average functioning in these

541

areas'' or ''Judgment and reasoning skills are at a below-average level, not only on intellectual tasks but also in behaviors displayed in the classroom.''

8. Immaturity is a global description of behavior. While responses to test questions may provide some information about the child's temperament, we need a much more extensive sampling of behavior before we can label a child as ''immature.'' It is better to label certain responses or behaviors as immature, especially those that are typical of a much younger child.

9. This type of meticulous description of the test procedure has little, if any, value in the report. It adds ''empty calories.'' It should be deleted.

10. The reader is interested in learning about the child's abilities. Therefore, reporting about what the test did not reliably measure usually is of little interest. I recommend that this type of statement be deleted. If additional testing is needed for special areas, simply recommend such testing.

11. The child's CA and MA must be taken into account in evaluating the pattern of strengths and weaknesses. The description fails to recognize that tests failed at year level VIII do not indicate weaknesses, for the failures occurred at a level that was one standard deviation above the child's CA.

12. This statement is not very informative or meaningful. Telling the reader that no credits were received, without interpretation, has little value. The numbers in parenthesis are likely to cause confusion.

13. This is a poorly written sentence, and it needs to be rewritten. From the description, there is no way of knowing whether visual-motor development was below average, average, or above average.

14. Confusion reigns! Help! This sentence needs an overhauling. I believe that the writer wants to say that the child has good verbal fluency and general comprehension; however, the communication is poor.

15. A child who obtains an IQ of 97 has functioned on the test in the average range. There is no need to hedge by using a term such as ''probably falls.'' The concept of ''potential'' is a thorny one in psychological assessment. A judgment of potential should be based on all available factors, not only on the IQ.

16. A raw score in a report is usually meaningless to the reader. Why not translate it into an age level (or to a standard score or percentile, if these are available), if you believe that it is necessary to report a score? Usually, it is not necessary to report a score for one test on the Stanford-Binet.

17. This sentence suffers because it does not tell the reader why the scores were significant (e.g., significant relative to what and in which direction).

Chapter 11: Exercises for the WISC-R

1. *Intelligence test scores in and of themselves should never be used as a basis for establishing a learning disability designation.* Many factors, especially a discrepancy between estimates of intelligence and achievement, must be taken into account in arriving at a classification of learning disability. One could write, ''The 15-point discrepancy between Mary's Verbal and Performance Scale IQs indicates that her verbal abilities are better developed than her nonverbal abilities.''

2. The explanation offered for the child's Verbal-Performance discrepancy is interesting but probably incorrect. The items on the WISC-R Performance Scale call for cognitive skills primarily. Visual-motor skills, while necessary for some items, are not the major component for success on the Performance items. Indeed, if the writer's reasoning were correct, there would be no way for children who are maturationally normal to obtain superior nonverbal scores.

3. There is no one-to-one correlation between verbal knowledge, as revealed by

high Verbal subtest scores, and expressive skills. There are many bright individuals who have expressive difficulties (e.g., in writing or in speech). This statement should be supported by behavioral observations and, when available, by reports of others.

4. A reader is likely to be confused by this information. It is better to refer to IQs, percentiles, or even age equivalents than to raw scores or standard scores. Readers desire that the clinician interpret the child's performance, rather than provide numbers that may have limited, if any, meaning to them.

5. The IQ achieved by a child is a specific number. It is not appropriate to say "approximately 98." The notion of "approximately" is handled by the confidence interval or precision range.

6. This sentence mixes up scaled scores and IQs. It is better to report IQs for all three of the scales. For example, "Bill achieved a Verbal Scale IQ of 118, a Performance Scale IQ of 114, and a Full Scale IQ of 118."

7. Including this type of information in a report serves no useful purpose. The clinician's job is to impart meaning, to interpret performance, to assess ability, and to make recommendations.

8. This statement, while technically correct, has little, if any, meaning to the average reader. Providing percentile equivalents of scaled scores is a preferred way of reporting this information.

9. The report should not give a blow-by-blow description of the child's entire performance. This statement conveys little useful information and should not appear in the report.

10. This is an example of providing information about the structural components of the test ("optional subtest") and test procedures ("not used in computing the IQ") that is not needed in the report. I suggest that it be deleted.

11. This is an incorrect interpretation because Digit Span is not *significantly* below the mean of the Verbal Scale subtests.

12. Many children are persistent, yet they also fail items. There is much more involved in success on the Object Assembly items than mere persistence. Persistence may help a child in solving various tasks, but unless it is coupled with cognitive ability, it is likely to account for only a small part of successful performance.

13. This is an awkward sentence. Better: "On the WISC-R she achieved a Verbal IQ of 66."

14. The WISC-R does not use mental ages. Test-age equivalents are available for the various subtests, but these should be used cautiously. The WISC-R and WPPSI (and WAIS-R) are point scales, not age scales, while the Stanford-Binet is an age scale.

15. "Freedom from Distractibility" is a technical term that may not be understood by most readers of the report. Better: "Frank had difficulties with attention and concentration."

16. Scaled scores of 9 or higher on any of the Wechsler subtests do not indicate "poor" ability. A scaled score of 9 is only one-third of a standard deviation below the mean scaled score of 10; it is within the average range.

17. "Lack of" is a very strong statement. If this term is used, it should be in a context as close to literal usage as possible. A scaled score of 8, while slightly below average, reflects a level of ability that still enables a child to function in many situations. It is incorrect to interpret a scaled score of 8 as indicating a "lack of social judgment."

18. The score itself is not retarded. The score reflects a weakness or poor skills. It is preferable to say that "her spatial visualization skills are not well developed, as estimated by her performance on one subtest."

19. What is the basis for writing that the paired words on the Similarities subtest are seemingly opposite? The words are "different," but they are not opposite and indeed are subtly related in an abstract conceptual way.

20. There are many possible reasons why changes may occur in the test scores; therefore, it is potentially misleading to offer only two of those reasons. Differences in test scores may be associated, for example, with maturational changes, growth spurts, changes in item content, motivation, situational variables, or environmental changes. Unless the examiner knows which reasons are most probable, it is better not to offer any. What is most important is to try to determine which IQ (and test performance) is the most reliable and valid and to try to account for the changed performance.

21. This is not a clear description of the task. Coding requires the child to use a key or to learn a key. The symbols may be meaningful to some children. The statement, as written, makes it sound as if the child is required to do something actively—attach a symbol to a number. This is misleading because the symbol-number association (or combination) is given in the subtest. A preferred way for Coding A: "The Coding task is a psychomotor task that requires the child to copy rapidly simple figures associated with different shapes." For Coding B, a preferred way: "The Coding task is a psychomotor task that requires the child to copy rapidly symbols associated with numbers."

22. This is not the proper way to interpret subtest scores. Reading proficiency should be evaluated by reading tests, not by the WISC-R or Stanford-Binet. Reading involves many different components, and only a valid and reliable reading test should be used to evaluate reading proficiency. Intelligence tests can assist in evaluating some cognitive skills of children; however, any one test cannot be used to evaluate every conceivable type of cognitive and perceptual-motor skill.

23. It is interesting to attempt to use patterns of intelligence test scores for developing hypotheses about personality style. However, Verbal-Performance discrepancies in and of themselves should not be used to substantiate such hypotheses. Such discrepancy scores need to be incorporated with other behaviors and test scores when developing hypotheses. Furthermore, a 10-point discrepancy is within the realm of chance on the WISC-R and, as such, is not a significant difference that requires highlighting.

24. I know of no research that supports this interpretation of the Coding subtest. Remember, you have only a sample of the child's performance in a limited, controlled, and organized encounter. It is difficult to know if the level of energy displayed in the test situation can be sustained outside of the test situation.

25. This is an interesting hypothesis, but needs to be supported by much more information before it is offered in the report. A low Information score may be due to a variety of factors, such as limited schooling, few interests, and inadequate stimulation.

26. It is not necessary to report the total scaled score. It is preferable to cite the IQs obtained on the Verbal, Performance, and Full Scales.

27. "She scored 12" is not likely to be understood by most readers. It is not clear whether this is a raw score or a scaled score. It is better to use descriptive terms (e.g., "above average") or percentiles ("at the 84th percentile").

28. This statement is not accurate because it focuses on some of the subtests, rather than the Full Scale, to characterize the child's overall level of ability. Furthermore, "standard deviations" is a technical concept and has little, if any, place in a psychological report.

29. It is not necessary to report the mean score.

Chapter 24: Exercises for General Test Interpretation and Report Writing

1. This description is incomplete because it fails to indicate (a) the type of perceptual problem (e.g., visual or auditory or both), (b) the type of verbal expression

problem (e.g., written word or spoken word or both), and (c) how the problems were manifested in the test situation.

2. "Scatter" is a technical concept and may be misunderstood by lay readers. It is better to use the term "variability" (e.g., "contributed to the marked variability of his subtest scores") in place of scatter. Most protocols have some variability.

3. All items on intelligence tests in some sense reflect the child's ability to learn. Therefore, it is misleading to say that only specific items reflect learning ability. Items differ in the extent to which they tap old or new learning (or content vs. process or crystallized vs. fluid abilities), but all items measure some degree of learning ability.

4. There is no way of separating (or partialing out) items that reflect natural endowment from those that reflect educational or experiential opportunities. Therefore, it is misleading to write that some items reflect natural endowment, because *all* items require some degree of exposure to the environment and some natural endowment.

5. This is an interesting statement. The examiner goes out on the limb, and on the basis of the IQ alone makes a statement about future performance. The IQ should be used primarily to evaluate current level of performance, not to predict future performance. There are many factors (e.g., motivation and study habits) that affect school performance, and the IQ is only one of them. Her IQ of 134 does indicate, however, that she has the ability to excel in school.

6. This is a confusing statement because it is not clear what automatic level refers to. A possible restatement: "John's fine motor control is poorly developed, as can be seen by his inability to write legibly."

7. All such statements should be based on research findings or normative data. It is doubtful that the writer in this case has any such body of information at his or her command. There may not be a one-to-one correspondence between breadth of memory for visual material and breadth of memory for auditory material for any population of children.

8. The reader expects that only valid tests will be used in the examination. If the tests are only to be used for research purposes or if they are experimental editions or if they are only screening devices, then such information should be clearly conveyed. I do not believe that the reader should be asked to decide on the validity of a test instrument. This decision should be made by the psychologist.

9. The function of a report is to describe and evaluate the child's performance. It is not to recount the instrument's uses, unless this information is relevant to the case.

10. This is an awkward sentence. Referring to "IQ" as a score is redundant. A better way to express this finding: "She obtained an IQ of 111," followed by a confidence interval and other descriptive information.

11. This, too, is an awkward sentence. Better: "Her IQ is 80," followed by a confidence interval and other descriptive information.

12. This is also an awkward sentence. Better: "The child is a small girl who has a pleasant disposition. Rapport was easily established."

13. This is a confusing sentence because it does not attempt to account for the reason why the girl lacks intellectual maturity. It also was not followed by any explanation. Further, the concept of "intellectual maturity" is vague. The writer should attempt to define what is meant by intellectual maturity. The two ideas in this sentence also appear to be in conflict with each other.

14. This is a potentially misleading statement. Errors on the Bender-Gestalt may have no relationship to brain damage. They simply may be indicators of maturational difficulties, developmental delays, perceptual difficulties, integration difficulties, and so forth. Referring

to brain disorder in the report on the basis of only Bender-Gestalt errors is misleading. If there are no other supporting signs of brain damage, the examiner is on very shaky grounds when he or she uses such statements in the report.

15. This is an awkward way of describing the abilities required by the Bender-Gestalt. It is better to say simply that the Bender-Gestalt is a measure of visual-motor ability.

16. This is an awkward sentence. Better: "He had difficulty differentiating essential from nonessential details."

17. This may be an incorrect interpretation. Repeating the word in a definition may not indicate a "simple level." Better: "His definitions were at a functional or descriptive level."

18. This sentence is not clear because we do not know what comparison the writer has in mind.

19. "Troublemakers" come from all backgrounds. Why should good social judgment cause one to be a troublemaker?

20. This is a difficult sentence to follow. The writer may be trying to convey that the child's abilities were approximately at the same level, but fails to do so clearly.

APPENDIX A

Publishers of Tests Reviewed

American Association on Mental Deficiency, 5201 Connecticut Ave., N.W., Washington, D.C. 20015.

American Guidance Service, Inc., Publishers' Building, Circle Pines, Minnesota 55014.

American Orthopsychiatric Association, Inc., 1790 Broadway, New York, New York 10019.

Bobbs-Merrill Co., Inc., 4300 West 62nd Street, Indianapolis, Indiana 46268.

William C. Brown Co., Publisher, 2460 Keeper Boulevard, Dubuque, Iowa 52001.

Consulting Psychologists Press, Inc., 577 College Avenue, Palo Alto, California 94306.

The Devereux Foundation Press, 19 South Waterloo Road, Devon, Pennsylvania 19333.

Economy Company, Box 25308, 1901 North Walnut, Oklahoma City, Oklahoma 73125.

Follett Publishing Co., 1010 W. Washington Boulevard, Chicago, Illinois 60607.

Grune and Stratton, Inc., 111 Fifth Avenue, New York, New York 10003.

Guidance Associates of Delaware, Inc., 1526 Gilpin Avenue, Wilmington, Delaware 19806.

Ladoca Project and Publishing Foundation, Inc., East 51st Avenue and Lincoln Street, Denver, Colorado 80216.

Language Research Associates, Inc., 175 East Delaware Place, Chicago, Illinois 60611.

Linguametrics Group, P.O. Box 454, Corta Madera, California 94925.

Charles E. Merrill Publishing Co., 1300 Alum Creek Drive, Columbus, Ohio 43216.

The Psychological Corporation, 757 Third Avenue, New York, New York 10017.

Psychological Test Specialists, Box 1441, Missoula, Montana 59801.

The Riverside Publishing Co., 3 O'Hare Towers, 8420 Bryn Mawr Ave., Chicago, Illinois 60631.

Science Research Associates, 155 North Wacker Drive, Chicago, Illinois 60606.

Slosson Educational Publications, Inc., 140 Pine Street, East Aurora, New York 14052.

Stoelting Company, 1350 South Kostner Avenue, Chicago, Illinois 60623.

Teaching Resources Corporation, 50 Pond Park Road, Hingham, Massachusetts 02043.

University of Illinois Press, Urbana, Illinois 61801.

Western Psychological Services, 12031 Wilshire Boulevard, Los Angeles, California 90025.

Modified Instructions for Administering the WISC-R Performance Scale Subtests to Deaf Children

Pantomime Instructions

Picture Completion

Show child Card 2 from Wechsler Intelligence Scale for Children (WISC) (Wechsler, 1949). This item depicts a table with three legs. Count legs by pointing to each with index finger. Hold up three fingers, then point to missing leg by tracing its designated outline with index finger. Hold up four fingers. Summarize directions by counting each leg with index finger, holding up three fingers, pointing to missing area, and holding up four fingers.

Present age-appropriate initial item from WISC-R Picture Completion booklet. Point to child, point to picture (not to missing part), and point to child again.

Follow instructions in WISC-R manual regarding failure and discontinuation procedures. If child fails to indicate missing part on Cards 1 and 2 within twenty seconds, point to missing part.

Picture Arrangement

Place sample item (SCALE) in front of child in numerical order indicated in WISC-R manual. Point to pictures in general. Arrange pictures in correct order. Point to Picture A and hold up one finger, point to Picture B and hold up two fingers, and point to Picture C and hold up three fingers, thereby designating first, second, and third. Rearrange pictures in original administration order. Point to series in general sweeping motion, and then point to child.

Present age-appropriate initial item from WISC-R Picture Arrangement subtest. Point to series in general sweeping motion, and then point to child. If child does not respond or does not arrange the cards in the correct order for Item 1 (FIGHT) and/or Item 2 (PICNIC), arrange the cards in the correct sequence. Then point to each card, designating first, second, and third. Allow child to look at correct sequence for about ten seconds, and then put the cards in their original numerical order. Point to series in general sweeping motion, and then point to child. If child fails to arrange Item 3 (FIRE) and/or Item 4 (PLANK) in the correct sequence, put the cards in their original numerical order. Take Card "F" or "W" from the array and place it below the other three cards. Point to it and hold up one fin-

---

Reprinted, with change in notation, with permission of the author, P. M. Sullivan, *A Comparison of Administration Modifications on the WISC-R Performance Scale with Different Categories of Deaf Children.* Unpublished doctoral dissertation, University of Iowa, 1978.

ger. Then point to remaining cards in general sweeping motion, and point to child.

In Items 5 to 12, arrange cards in numerical sequence, point to cards in general sweeping motion, and point to child.

Follow instructions in WISC-R manual regarding timing and discontinuation procedures.

Block Design

Design 1. Place four blocks in front of child and turn each block to show the different sides. Point to each different side of each block during this demonstration. Arrange the four blocks into Design 1. Give child four other blocks. Point to child, point to child's blocks, and point to model. If child fails, assemble child's blocks to match modeled design. Point to child's blocks and point to model. Scramble child's blocks. Point to child, point to child's blocks, and point to model.

Design 2. Assemble Design 2 behind a screen. Present model to child in completed form. Point to child, point to child's blocks, and point to model. If child fails on first trial, follow procedure given for Design 1.

Design 3. Display card depicting Design 3. Assemble blocks into Design 3 in full view of child. Point to card and point to blocks. Scramble the blocks. Point to child, point to child's blocks, and point to card. If child fails on first trial, repeat above administration procedure. If child is 8 or older, and subtest begins with this item, follow procedure for designating color patterns and similarities of blocks given at the beginning of section on Design 1.

Designs 4 to 11. Display card showing each respective design. Point to child, point to blocks, and point to card.

Follow instructions in WISC-R manual regarding timing and discontinuation procedures.

Object Assembly

Arrange the pieces of sample item (APPLE) behind shield. Expose array and assemble pieces together. Rearrange pieces in original presentation sequence. Point to child and point to array. If child does not respond, repeat above procedure. Correct any errors.

Items 1 to 4. Arrange pieces behind shield. Expose array, point to child, and point to pieces. Correct errors on Item 1 only.

Follow instructions in WISC-R manual for timing and scoring.

Coding

Coding A. Point to star, circle, triangle, cross, and box in general sweeping motion. Point to

each mark in each geometric form individually. Point to blank sample items and fill in the first circle. Give child pencil, point to child, and point to remaining sample items. Child is stopped after completion of last sample item. Point to subtest items in general sweeping motions for each row. Point to child and point to first item. If child discontinues work after completing first row, point to next row. Follow timing instructions in the WISC-R manual.

Coding B. Point to numbered boxes in general sweeping motion. Then point to each number and its respective symbol individually in the entire array. Point to blank sample items and fill in the first one. Give child pencil, point to child, and point to remaining sample items. Stop child after completion of last sample item. Point to subtest items in general sweeping motion for each row. Point to child and point to first item. If child discontinues work after completing first row, point to next row. Follow timing instructions in the WISC-R manual.

Mazes

Give child booklet. Point to sample item. Point to figure in center of maze and to opening that leads to exit. Demonstrate sample item. On reaching opening to outside of center, pause and, without lifting the pencil, point to blind alley. Then point to correct route and finish the tracing.

Items 1 to 9. Point to center of maze, to exit opening, and to child. Follow discontinuation procedure in WISC-R manual. If child does not begin work in center of maze, stop work, place pencil in center of maze, and point for child to continue.

Follow timing and scoring instructions in the WISC-R manual.

Murphy-Neuhaus-Reed Instructions

Picture Completion

This modification is based on Neuhaus (1967).

Materials. Three pictures are drawn on 3½" × 3½" white cardboard squares. Each item shows a picture with a missing detail on one side accompanied by the same picture with the missing detail filled in on the other side. The three constructed sample items include a picture of an arrow with the tip missing on one side and drawn in on the other, a picture of an elephant with the trunk missing on one side and drawn in on the other, and a picture of a doll with an arm missing on one side and drawn in on the other side.

Procedure. Present Sample Item 1 (ARROW). Show side with missing detail first, turn picture over and show side with completed detail. Point to completed detail. Repeat procedure above. Present Sample Item 2 (ELEPHANT) and Sample Item 3 (DOLL) in the same manner given above.

Present age-appropriate initial item from WISC-R Picture Completion booklet. Follow instructions in WISC-R manual regarding failure and discontinuance procedures. If child fails to indicate missing part on Cards 1 and 2 within twenty seconds, point to missing detail.

Picture Arrangement

This modification is based on Reed (1970).

Materials. One set of three 3½″ × 3½″ white cardboard square cards with the numeral 1 printed on one card, the numeral 2 on one card, and the numeral 3 on one card.

One set of three 3½″ × 3½″ white cardboard square cards with the letter A printed on one card, the letter B on one card, and the letter C on one card. Use the sample item (SCALE) from the WISC-R Picture Arrangement subtest.

Procedure. Present Sample Item 1 (NUMBERS) in order 2, 3, 1 from child's left to right. Arrange cards in correct numerical sequence. Allow child to view for ten seconds. Rearrange cards in original administration order. Motion child to arrange cards by pointing to them in general sweeping motion. If child does not respond or arranges cards incorrectly, arrange cards in their correct sequence. Then rearrange cards in original administration order and motion child to arrange cards. Follow same procedure for Sample Item 2 (LETTERS) and sample item (SCALE) from WISC-R Picture Arrangement subtest.

Present age-appropriate initial item from WISC-R Picture Arrangement subtest. If child does not respond or does not arrange cards in the correct order for Item 1 (FIGHT) and/or Item 2 (PICNIC), arrange the cards in the correct sequence. Allow child to look at correct sequence for about ten seconds and rearrange cards in their original numerical order. Motion to child to rearrange cards. If child fails to arrange Item 3 (FIRE) and/or Item 4 (PLANK) in correct sequence, put the cards in their original numerical order. Take Card "F" or "W" from the array and place it below the other three cards. Motion for child to complete arrangement by pointing to remaining cards in general sweeping motion.

Items 5 to 12. Arrange cards in numerical sequence and motion for child to complete arrangement by pointing to sequence in general sweeping motion.

Follow instructions in WISC-R manual regarding discontinuance and timing procedures.

Block Design

This modification is based on Murphy (1957).

Materials. One white strip of cardboard 4″ × 1″ on which the instructions "Make one like this" are printed.

Procedure. Design 1. Set out four blocks in single line with red color on top. Point to each block in sequence. Repeat this procedure with white and red/white sides aligned in top position of sequence. Arrange the four blocks into Design 1, taking care to use both hands in the process. Give child four other blocks. Give child written instructions. Motion for child to make pattern by pointing to model and to child's blocks. If child fails, assemble child's blocks to match modeled design. Scramble child's blocks and point to instructions, model, and to child's blocks.

Design 2. Assemble Design 2 behind a screen. Present model to child in completed form. Give child written instructions. Motion for child to complete pattern by pointing to model and to child's blocks. If child fails on Design 2, follow procedure given for Design 1.

Design 3. Display card depicting Design 3 in full view of child, taking care to use both hands in the process. Scramble the blocks. Give child written instructions. Motion for child to construct pattern by pointing to card and to child's blocks. If child fails on first trial, repeat above administration procedure. If child is 8 or older, and subtest begins with this item, follow procedure for designating color patterns and similarities of blocks given at the beginning of section on Design 1.

Designs 4 to 11. Display card showing each respective design. Point to written instructions. Motion for child to construct pattern by pointing to card and to child's blocks.

Follow timing, scoring, and discontinuance instructions in WISC-R manual.

Object Assembly

This modification is based on Neuhaus (1967).

Materials. Three pictures drawn on 3½″ × 3½″ white cardboard squares. These pictures consist of an apple, a girl, and a horse.

Procedure. Arrange the pieces of sample item (APPLE) behind shield. Expose array and place Picture 1 (APPLE) beside it. Point to picture. Assemble pieces together.

Items 1 and 2. Arrange pieces behind shield. Expose array and place picture of GIRL or HORSE beside it. Point to picture. Motion child to assemble pieces together by pointing to pieces in general sweeping motion. Correct errors on *Item 1 only*. Time and score as in WISC-R manual.

Items 3 and 4. Arrange pieces behind shield. Expose array. Motion child to assemble pieces together by pointing to pieces in general sweeping motion. Time and score as shown in WISC-R manual.

Coding

This modification is based on Murphy (1957).

Materials. Coding protocol from Wechsler Intelligence Scale for Children (WISC) (Wechsler, 1949). One white strip of cardboard 4″ × 1″ on which the instructions "Do this quickly" are printed.

Procedure. The same procedure will be followed for Coding A and B. Sit next to child and fill out sample items on WISC Coding protocol. Point to each geometric form or number and its respective symbol with pencil before filling in the first three sample items. Work quickly on remaining four sample items and do not point to components of code. Give child WISC-R Coding protocol and point to each geometric form or number and its respective symbol with pencil. Give child pencil and point to sample items. When child has completed sample items, point to subtest items with pencil in general sweeping motions for each row. Place written instructions beside protocol and point to them. If child ceases work after completion of Row 1, redirect attention to Row 2 by pointing to first item in row. Time and score as in WISC-R manual.

Mazes

Materials. Mazes protocol from Wechsler Intelligence Scale for Children (WISC) (Wechsler, 1949). One white strip of cardboard 4″ × 1″ on which the instructions "Start in the middle. Find your way out." are written.

Procedure. Sit next to child and point to sample maze on WISC protocol. Place written directions beside protocol and point to them. Demonstrate sample item. Give child Mazes protocol from WISC-R. Place written directions beside protocol and point to them. Give child pencil and point to center of sample maze.

Items 1 to 9. Point to written directions and to center of each maze. Follow discontinuance procedure in WISC-R manual. If child does not begin work in center of maze, stop work, place pencil in center, and motion for child to continue.

Follow timing and scoring instructions in WISC-R manual.

APPENDIX C

Miscellaneous Tables

TABLE C-1.   Confidence Intervals for Stanford-Binet IQs

IQ	Age Level														
	2-0-0 through 5-8-29					5-9-0 through 13-5-29					13-6-0 through 18-0-0				
	Confidence Level					Confidence Level					Confidence Level				
	68%	85%	90%	95%	99%	68%	85%	90%	95%	99%	68%	85%	90%	95%	99%
140–149	±7	±10	±11	±13	±18	±5	±7	±8	±10	±13	±4	±5	±6	±7	±10
130–139	±6	±9	±11	±13	±17	±5	±8	±9	±10	±14	±4	±6	±7	±8	±11
120–129	±6	±8	±10	±12	±15	±5	±8	±9	±10	±14	±4	±6	±7	±9	±11
110–119	±6	±8	±9	±11	±14	±5	±7	±8	±9	±12	±4	±6	±7	±9	±11
100–109	±5	±8	±9	±10	±14	±4	±6	±7	±9	±12	±4	±6	±7	±9	±12
90–99	±5	±7	±8	±10	±13	±4	±6	±7	±9	±12	±4	±6	±6	±8	±11
80–89	±5	±7	±8	±10	±13	±4	±6	±7	±8	±11	±3	±5	±6	±8	±10
70–79	±5	±7	±8	±9	±12	±3	±5	±6	±7	±10	±3	±4	±5	±7	±9
60–69	±5	±7	±8	±10	±13	±3	±4	±5	±5	±7	±2	±3	±4	±5	±6

Note. Confidence intervals rounded off, with .5 dropped for even numbers.

The formula for computing the confidence intervals, is as follows:

$\sigma_{meas.} = \sigma_1 \sqrt{1 - r_{11}}$, which is used in computing the confidence intervals ($\sigma_{meas.}$), which is used in computing the confidence intervals, is as follows: σ_1 is the standard deviation of the test scores and r_{11} is the reliability coefficient. In order to find the confidence interval which represents the 68% ($\pm 1\ \sigma$) confidence level on the Stanford-Binet for a 3-year-old child with an IQ of 140, the following procedure is used: $16\sqrt{1 - .834}$. The standard deviation of the Stanford-Binet is 16, obtained from the manual, while the reliability coefficient for the child's age and IQ is .834, obtained from McNemar (1942). The confidence interval for the 68% confidence level is also equal to the standard error of measurement. The standard error of measurement is multiplied by the respective z values in order to obtain the confidence intervals for other confidence levels. For example, the confidence interval for the 99% level of confidence (3σ) is $7 \times 2.58 = 18$. The first term is the standard error of measurement, and the second term is the z value for the 99% level of confidence.

TABLE C-2. Stanford-Binet Year Levels Corresponding to Normal Variability for Either a CA or MA Reference Point

Chronological Age (CA)	Normal Variability		Mental Age (MA)
—	II	to II-6	2-00–2-02
2-00–2-02	II	to III	2-03–2-05
2-03	II-6	to III	2-06–2-07
2-04–2-07	II-6	to III-6	2-08–3-00
2-08	III	to III-6	3-01
2-09–3-00	III	to IV	3-02–3-06
3-01	III	to IV-6	3-07
3-02–3-05	III-6	to IV-6	3-08–3-11
3-06–3-08	III-6	to V	4-00–4-02
3-09–3-10	IV	to V	4-03–4-04
3-11–4-03	IV	to VI	4-05–4-09
4-04–4-10	IV-6	to VI	4-10–5-04
4-11–5-06	V	to VII	5-05–5-10
5-07–5-09	VI	to VII	5-11–6-01
5-10–6-08	VI	to VIII	6-02–7-00
6-09	VI	to IX	7-01
6-10–7-05	VII	to IX	7-02–7-09
7-06–7-11	VII	to X	7-10–8-04
8-00–8-03	VIII	to X	8-05–8-08
8-04–9-00	VIII	to XI	8-09–9-05
9-01–9-02	VIII	to XII	9-06–9-07
9-03–9-09	IX	to XII	9-08–10-02
9-10–10-05	IX	to XIII	10-03–10-11
10-06–10-07	X	to XIII	11-00–11-01
10-08–11-05	X	to XIV	11-02–11-11
11-06–11-08	X	to AA	12-00–12-02
11-09–12-06	XI	to AA	12-03–13-00
12-07–12-10	XI	to SAI	13-01–13-04
12-11–14-04	XII	to SAI	13-05–14-07
14-05–14-06	XIII	to SAI	14-08–14-09
14-07–15-07	XIII	to SAII	14-10–15-09
15-08–17-10	XIV	to SAII	15-10–16-08
17-11–18-00	AA	to SAII	16-09–17-01
—	AA	to SAIII	17-02–18-00
—	SAI	to SAIII	18-01–22-10

Note. The child's CA is obtained to the nearest year and month by rounding off the days. For example, 9 years, 11 months, and 16 days is recorded as 10-0, while 9 years, 11 months, and 15 days would be 9-11.

Table C-2 represents a refinement of the one originally published by Kaufman and Waterstreet (1978). Reprinted by permission of the publisher and authors from C. H. Chase and J. M. Sattler, "Determining Areas of Strengths and Weakness on the Stanford-Binet," *School Psychology Review, 9,* p. 176. Copyright 1980, National Association of School Psychologists.

TABLE C-3. **A Conversion of the Stanford-Binet** *Published* **Mental Age Scores into** *Corrected* **Mental Age Scores for 1972 Standardization Sample**

Year	Month											
	0	*1*	*2*	*3*	*4*	*5*	*6*	*7*	*8*	*9*	*10*	*11*
2	—	—	—	2-00	2-01	2-02	2-03	2-03	2-04	2-05	2-06	2-06
3	2-07	2-08	2-09	2-10	2-10	2-11	3-00	3-01	3-02	3-03	3-04	3-05
4	3-06	3-07	3-08	3-09	3-10	3-11	4-00	4-01	4-02	4-03	4-04	4-05
5	4-06	4-07	4-08	4-09	4-10	4-11	5-00	5-02	5-03	5-04	5-05	5-06
6	5-07	5-08	5-09	5-10	5-11	6-01	6-02	6-03	6-04	6-05	6-06	6-07
7	6-08	6-09	6-10	6-11	7-00	7-01	7-02	7-03	7-04	7-05	7-06	7-07
8	7-07	7-08	7-09	7-10	7-11	8-00	8-01	8-02	8-03	8-04	8-05	8-06
9	8-07	8-08	8-09	8-10	8-11	9-00	9-01	9-02	9-03	9-04	9-05	9-06
10	9-07	9-08	9-09	9-09	9-10	9-11	10-00	10-01	10-02	10-03	10-04	10-05
11	10-06	10-07	10-08	10-09	10-10	10-11	11-00	11-00	11-02	11-03	11-04	11-05
12	11-05	11-06	11-07	11-08	11-09	11-10	11-11	12-00	12-01	12-02	12-03	12-04
13	12-05	12-06	12-07	12-08	12-10	12-11	13-00	13-01	13-02	13-03	13-04	13-06
14	13-07	13-08	13-10	13-11	14-00	14-02	14-03	14-04	14-06	14-07	14-08	14-09
15	14-11	15-00	15-01	15-01	15-02	15-03	15-04	15-05	15-06	15-07	15-08	15-09
16	15-09	15-10	15-11	—	—	—	—	—	—	—	—	—

Note. The years and months of the *published* MA scores appear in the first column and row respectively. To find the *corrected* MA of an individual enter the table at the appropriate *published* MA. For example, an individual obtaining a *published* MA of 12 years, 7 months would receive a *corrected* MA of 12 years, 0 months.

From D. N. Shorr, S. E. McClelland, and H. B. Robinson, "Corrected Mental Age Scores for the Stanford-Binet Intelligence Scale," *Measurement and Evaluation in Guidance, 10,* p. 146. Copyright 1977, American Personnel and Guidance Association. Reprinted by permission.

TABLE C-4. Analysis of Functions of Stanford-Binet Tests (Form L-M)

Test (and level)	Functions and Processes	Meeker Structure of Intellect Designation
II		
II, 1. Three-Hole Form Board	Visual-motor ability Recognition and manipulation of forms	NFR
II, 2. Delayed Response	Reasoning Attention Directing ideas in combination with memory span	MFS
II, 3. Identifying Parts of the Body	Language Comprehension of simple speech	CMC
II, 4. Block Building	Visual-motor ability Comprehension of material Spatial relations Ability or desire to imitate and experiment	CFS, EFS, NFR
II, 5. Picture Vocabulary	Language Recall and verbal identification by recognition of familiar objects May reveal child's perceptions and associations, experiences, ability to remember, and special modes of expressing himself or herself	CMU, NMU
II, 6. Word Combinations	Language Meaningful use of two words but not necessarily in a structurally correct manner	NMR
II, A. Identifying Objects by Name	Language Use of verbal symbols in identifying common objects by name	CFU
II-6		
II-6, 1. Identifying Objects by Use	Language Ability to attach definitions to concrete objects	NMR
II-6, 2. Identifying Parts of the Body	See II, 3	CMC
II-6, 3. Naming Objects	Language Comprehension of simple speech—focus is on specific objects	CFU, NMU
II-6, 4. Picture Vocabulary	See II, 5	CMU, NMU

TABLE C-4   (cont.)

Test (and level)	Functions and Processes	Meeker Structure of Intellect Designation
II-6, 5. Repeating 2 Digits	Memory Passive registration of stimuli Auditory recall Attention Ability to follow directions	MSS, MSU
II-6, 6. Obeying Simple Commands	Social Intelligence Purposeful response to verbal directions	CMS, MMR
II-6, A. Three-Hole Form Board: Rotated	Similar to II, 1, but requires reorientation	NFR, CFT
III		
III, 1. Stringing Beads	Visual-motor ability Comprehension Direction of attention	CFS, NFU
III, 2. Picture Vocabulary	See II, 5	CMU, NMU
III, 3. Block Building: Bridge	See II, 4	CFS, NFS, NFU
III, 4. Picture Memories	Memory Comprehension Attention	EFU, MFU
III, 5. Copying a Circle	Visual-motor ability Hand-eye coordination	NFU
III, 6. Drawing a Vertical Line	Visual-motor ability Hand-eye coordination Execution by demonstration	NFU
III, A. Repeating 3 Digits	See II-6, 5	MSU
III-6		
III-6, 1. Comparison of Balls	Reasoning Conceptualization of physical form Identifying relative size	CFR, EFR
III-6, 2. Patience: Pictures	Reasoning Ability to establish part-whole relationships	CFT, CFU, NMT
III-6, 3. Discrimination of Animal Pictures	Reasoning Visual discrimination and perceptual ability	CFC, EFU
III-6, 4. Response to Pictures	Social intelligence Ability to enumerate objects Vocabulary Fluency of speech Sentence combinations Perceptions: Ability to interpret single elements of a whole Comprehension of situations	CMC, EMR

TABLE C-4   (cont.)

Test (and level)	Functions and Processes	Meeker Structure of Intellect Designation
III-6, 5. Sorting Buttons	Reasoning Motor manipulation according to verbal direction	NFC
III-6, 6. Comprehension I	Social intelligence Ability to reasonably evaluate a situation and give a pertinent response	CMI, EMT
III-6, A. Comparison of Sticks	Reasoning Visual-perceptual discrimination	EFR
IV		
IV, 1. Picture Vocabulary	See II, 5	CMU, NMU
IV, 2. Naming Objects from Memory	Memory	MFU
IV, 3. Opposite Analogies I	Conceptual thinking Associative ability	CMR, NMR, DMS
IV, 4. Pictorial Identification	Language Ability to isolate and eliminate items	CMI, NMR, MFU
IV, 5. Discrimination of Forms	Reasoning Ability to compare and contrast visual form perceptions and to apply critical discriminations	CFC, EFU
IV, 6. Comprehension II	See III-6, 6	CMI, EMR
IV, A. Memory for Sentences I	Memory (immediate auditory recall)	MMS
IV-6		
IV-6, 1. Aesthetic Comparison	Social intelligence Comparison and practical judgment involving discriminative ability for aesthetic values	EMR, EFS
IV-6, 2. Opposite Analogies I	Conceptual thinking Association ability	CMR, NMR, DMS
IV-6, 3. Pictorial Similarities and Differences I	Reasoning Ability to discriminate differences by use of visual perception	CFC, CMC, EFU
IV-6, 4. Materials	Social intelligence General information Language comprehension	CMI, CMT
IV-6, 5. Three Commissions	Memory Ability to retain and accomplish verbal directions in sequence	MMS

TABLE C-4   (cont.)

Test (and level)	Functions and Processes	Meeker Structure of Intellect Designation
IV-6, 6. Comprehension III	See III-6, 6	CMI, CMS
IV-6, A. Pictorial Identification	See IV, 4	CMI, NMR, MFU
V		
V, 1. Picture Completion: Man	Visual-motor ability Visual discrimination and perception	CFU, NFI
V, 2. Paper Folding: Triangle	Visual-motor ability Visual-memory and motor coordination	CFT, NFR
V, 3. Definitions	Language Ability to associate verbal symbols with objects General vocabulary	CMU
V, 4. Copying a Square	Visual-motor ability Hand-eye coordination Appreciation of spatial relationships	EFS, NFU
V, 5. Pictorial Similarities and Differences II	See IV-6, 3	CFC, EFU
V, 6. Patience: Rectangles	Reasoning Manipulation of materials involving spatial relationships and perception	CFS, CFT
V, A. Knot	Visual-motor ability Ability to manipulate and imitate	NFR, CFT
VI		
VI, 1. Vocabulary	Language Reasoning Expression of ideas Manner of speech Working habits Personality traits	CMU
VI, 2. Differences	Conceptual thinking Ability to discriminate on an abstract or ideational level	CMT, DMI, CFI, NMC
VI, 3. Mutilated Pictures	Reasoning Perception and part-whole relationships	CFU, MSI
VI, 4. Number Concepts	Numerical reasoning Rote counting ability	MSI, NMR
VI, 5. Opposite Analogies II	See IV-6, 2	CMR, EMR
VI, 6. Maze Tracing	Visual-motor ability Perception General comprehension in making choices	CFI

TABLE C-4   (cont.)

Test (and level)	Functions and Processes	Meeker Structure of Intellect Designation
VI, A. Response to Pictures	See III-6, 4	EMR, CMC
VII		
VII, 1. Picture Absurdities I	Social intelligence Ability to isolate incongruities and absurdities of visual material	EMS
VII, 2. Similarities: Two Things	Conceptual thinking	CMT, CSC
VII, 3. Copying a Diamond	Visual-motor ability	EFS, NFU
VII, 4. Comprehension IV	See III-6, 6	EMT, DMI, NMI
VII, 5. Opposite Analogies III	See IV-6, 2	CMR, NMR
VII, 6. Repeating 5 Digits	See II-6, 5	MSU
VII, A. Repeating 3 Digits Reversed	Memory Remanipulation Reorganization	MSU, MSS
VIII		
VIII, 1. Vocabulary	See VI, 1	CMU
VIII, 2. Memory for Stories: The Wet Fall	Memory Verbal comprehension	MMR, MMU
VIII, 3. Verbal Absurdities I	Reasoning Ability to identify incongruous elements of situations Vocabulary	EMS
VIII, 4. Similarities and Differences	Conceptual thinking Flexibility Comprehension of reversibility Ability to view facts from various angles at the same time and coordinate the multiple relationships involved	CMI, CMT, NMI
VIII, 5. Comprehension IV	See III-6, 6	EMT, NMI, DMI
VIII, 6. Naming the Days of the Week	Social intelligence General information Long-term recall	MMR, MMS
VIII, A. Problem Situations I	Social intelligence Ability to identify practical elements of a situation	EMR, NMI
IX		
IX, 1. Paper Cutting	Visual-motor ability Manipulation in response to verbal directions	CFT, ESR

TABLE C-4 (cont.)

Test (and level)	Functions and Processes	Meeker Structure of Intellect Designation
IX, 2. Verbal Absurdities II	See VIII, 3	EMS
IX, 3. Memory for Designs I	Memory Visuo-memory ability and perception Attention and visual clues combine with recall and motor reproduction	MFU
IX, 4. Rhymes: New Form	Language Controlled association by specific stimulus	DMR
IX, 5. Making Change	Numerical reasoning	NSS, MSI
IX, 6. Repeating 4 Digits Reversed	See VII, A	MFU, MSS
IX, A. Rhymes: Old Form X	See IX, 4	DMR
X, 1. Vocabulary	See VI, 1	CMU
X, 2. Block Counting	Numerical reasoning Perception	CFI, NFI, DFC
X, 3. Abstract Words I	Language Ability to select general characteristics by disregarding irrelevant details	CMU
X, 4. Finding Reasons I	Social intelligence Ability to see the relationship between cause and effect in situations with which the child is familiar	MMR, CMI, EMR, DMI, DMU, NMR
X, 5. Word Naming	Language Verbal expression Linguistic facility Free association	DSU
X, 6. Repeating 6 Digits	See II-6, 5	MSU
X, A. Verbal Absurdities III XI	See VIII, 3	EMS, EMR
XI, 1. Memory for Designs I	See IX, 3	MFU
XI, 2. Verbal Absurdities IV	See IX, 2	EMS, EMR
XI, 3. Abstract Words II	See X, 3	CMU
XI, 4. Memory for Sentences II	Memory Immediate recall of verbal stimuli Familiarity with words Enunciation Auditory accuity Ability to pay attention, to concentrate on a short sequence of stimuli, and to respond to the stimuli	MMS

TABLE C-4 (cont.)

Test (and level)	Functions and Processes	Meeker Structure of Intellect Designation
XI, 5. Problem Situation II	Social intelligence Ability to analyze elements of a situation and to establish relationships	CMI
XI, 6. Similarities: Three Things	Conceptual thinking Ability to test and discard various hypothetical situations Flexibility and factual knowledge	CMT, NMC
XI, A. Finding Reasons II	See X, 4	CMI, MMR, EMR, DMI
XII		
XII, 1. Vocabulary	See VI, 1	CMU
XII, 2. Verbal Absurdities II	See VIII, 3	EMR, EMS
XII, 3. Picture Absurdities II: The Shadow	See VII, 1	EFI, EMS
XII, 4. Repeating 5 Digits Reversed	See VII, A	MSS, MSU
XII, 5. Abstract Words I	See X, 3	CMU
XII, 6. Minkus Completion I	Language Ability to use abstract words for language completion	CMR, EMR, NMI
XII, A. Memory for Designs II	See IX, 3	MFU
XIII		
XIII, 1. Plan of Search	Reasoning Ability to analyze the logical requirements of a problem	CFI
XIII, 2. Abstract Words II	See X, 3	CMU
XIII, 3. Memory for Sentences III	See XI, 4	MMS
XIII, 4. Problems of Fact	Reasoning	CMI, EMR
XIII, 5. Dissected Sentences	Language Ability to place the component parts of a sentence in order	NMS, NMR
XIII, 6. Copying a Bead Chain from Memory	Memory Form perception and discrimination Spatial relations	MFS, NFS
XIII, A. Paper Cutting	See IX, 1	CFT
XIV		
XIV, 1. Vocabulary	See VI, 1	CMU
XIV, 2. Induction	Numerical reasoning Ability to follow a series of events and make a generalization stating the governing principle involved Abstracting a rule from particular instances	CSS, NSR

TABLE C-4   (cont.)

Test (and level)	Functions and Processes	Meeker Structure of Intellect Designation
XIV, 3. Reasoning I	Reasoning	MSS, NMI
XIV, 4. Ingenuity I	Numerical reasoning	CSC, DMT, NSI, DST
	Application of arithmetic to a realistic, properly visualized situation	
	Manipulation of visual imagery	
XIV, 5. Orientation: Direction I	Reasoning	MFS, NFR, CFS
XIV, 6. Reconciliation of Opposites	Conceptual thinking	NMT
XIV, A. Ingenuity II	See XIV, 4	CSC, DMT, NSI, DST
AA		
AA, 1. Vocabulary	See VI, 1	CMU
AA, 2. Ingenuity I	See XIV, 4	CSC, DMT, NSI, DST
AA, 3. Differences Between Abstract Words	Language	CMU, EMU, CMR
	Ability to point out the essential distinction between pairs of stimulus words	
AA, 4. Arithmetical Reasoning	Numerical reasoning	CMS, MSI, NSS
AA, 5. Proverbs I	Conceptual thinking	CMI, NMT, DMS
	Ability to analyze, abstract, and apply result to life situations	
	Rational process of inference	
AA, 6. Orientation: Direction II	See XIV, 5	MFS, NFR, CFS
AA, 7. Essential Differences	Conceptual thinking	CMU, EMR, CMT
AA, 8. Abstract Words III	See X, 3	CMU
AA, A. Binet Paper Cutting	Visual-motor ability	CFT
SA 1		
SA I, 1. Vocabulary	See VI, 1	CMU
SA I, 2. Enclosed Box Problem	Numerical reasoning	MSS, MSI, MFT
SA I, 3. Minkus Completion II	See XII, 6	CMR, EMR, NMI
SA I, 4. Repeating 6 Digits Reversed	See VII, A	MSS, MSU
SA I, 5. Sentence Building	Language	CMU, DMR
SA I, 6. Essential Similarities	Conceptual thinking	CMT, NMT
SA I, A. Reconciliation of Opposites	See XIV, 6	NMT

TABLE C-4   (cont.)

Test (and level)	Functions and Processes	Meeker Structure of Intellect Designation
SA II		
SA II, 1. Vocabulary	See VI, 1	CMU
SA II, 2. Finding Reasons III	See X, 4	MMR, CMI, EMR, DMI, DMU, NMR
SA II, 3. Proverbs II	See AA, 5	CMI, NMT, DMS
SA II, 4. Ingenuity I	See XIV, 4	CSC, DMT, NSI, DST
SA II, 5. Essential Differences	See AA, 7	CMU, EMR, CMT
SA II, 6. Repeating Thought of Passage I: Value of Life	Memory	MMR, CMS, NMU
SA II, A. Codes	Reasoning	CSR, CMR, NSR
SA III		
SA III, 1. Vocabulary	See VI, 1	CMU
SA III, 2. Proverbs III	See AA, 5	CMI, NMT, DMS
SA III, 3. Opposite Analogies IV	See IV-6, 2	CMR, CMU, NMR, DMU
SA III, 4. Orientation: Direction III	See XIV, 5	MFS, NFR, CFS
SA III, 5. Reasoning II	See XIV, 3	NSS, MSI, ESR
SA III, 6. Repeating Thought of Passage II: Tests	See SA II, 6	MMR, CMS, NMU
SA III, A. Opposite Analogies V	See IV-6, 2	CMR, CMU, NMU, DMU

Note. See Appendix C-36 for description of Structure of Intellect designations.

Functions and processes adapted from Contrucci, Korn, Martinson, and Mathias (1962), Sattler (1965), Taylor (1961), and Terman and Merrill (1960). Structure of Intellect designations obtained from Meeker (1969). Templates and SOI profile forms as well as five workbooks to accompany prescriptions based on SOI templates are available from the SOI Institute, 343 Richmond, El Segundo, Ca. 90245.

Meeker informed the writer that validation studies from 1962 to 1974 of the Binet and Wechsler factors indicated a need for a factor pure test. The SOI–Learning Abilities Test is composed of 26 factors which, according to Meeker, carry the heaviest factorial prediction of success in school. The test may be administered individually (to deaf, mentally retarded, or preschool children) or to groups.

TABLE C-5. Confidence Intervals for WISC-R Scales

	Age Level									
	6½ (6-0-0 through 6-11-30)					7½ (7-0-0 through 7-11-30)				
	Confidence Level					Confidence Level				
Scale	68%	85%	90%	95%	99%	68%	85%	90%	95%	99%
Verbal Scale IQ	±4	±6	±7	±8	±11	±4	±6	±7	±8	±10
Performance Scale IQ	±5	±7	±8	±9	±12	±5	±7	±8	±9	±12
Full Scale IQ	±3	±5	±6	±7	± 9	±3	±5	±6	±7	± 9
	Age Level									
	8½ (8-0-0 through 8-11-30)					9½ (9-0-0 through 9-11-30)				
	Confidence Level					Confidence Level				
Scale	68%	85%	90%	95%	99%	68%	85%	90%	95%	99%
Verbal Scale IQ	±4	±6	±6	±8	±10	±4	±5	±6	±7	±10
Performance Scale IQ	±4	±6	±7	±9	±12	±4	±6	±7	±9	±12
Full Scale IQ	±3	±5	±5	±6	± 8	±3	±5	±5	±6	± 8
	Age Level									
	10½ (10-0-0 through 10-11-30)					11½ (11-0-0 through 11-11-30)				
	Confidence Level					Confidence Level				
Scale	68%	85%	90%	95%	99%	68%	85%	90%	95%	99%
Verbal Scale IQ	±4	±5	±6	±7	± 9	±3	±5	±6	±7	± 9
Performance Scale IQ	±5	±7	±8	±9	±12	±4	±6	±7	±9	±11
Full Scale IQ	±3	±5	±5	±6	± 8	±3	±4	±5	±6	± 8

TABLE C-5 (cont.)

	Age Level									
	12½ (12-0-0 through 12-11-30)					13½ (13-0-0 through 13-11-30)				
	Confidence Level					Confidence Level				
Scale	68%	85%	90%	95%	99%	68%	85%	90%	95%	99%
Verbal Scale IQ	±3	±5	±5	±6	± 8	±3	±5	±6	± 7	± 9
Performance Scale IQ	±5	±7	±8	±9	±12	±5	±7	±8	±10	±13
Full Scale IQ	±3	±4	±5	±6	± 8	±3	±5	±5	± 6	± 8

	Age Level									
	14½ (14-0-0 through 14-11-30)					15½ (15-0-0 through 15-11-30)				
	Confidence Level					Confidence Level				
Scale	68%	85%	90%	95%	99%	68%	85%	90%	95%	99%
Verbal Scale IQ	±3	±5	±6	±7	± 9	±3	±5	±6	±7	± 9
Performance Scale IQ	±5	±7	±8	±9	±12	±5	±7	±8	±9	±12
Full Scale IQ	±3	±5	±5	±6	± 8	±3	±5	±5	±6	± 8

	Age Level									
	16½ (16-0-0 through 16-11-30)					Average (Average of 11 Age Groups)				
	Confidence Level					Confidence Level				
Scale	68%	85%	90%	95%	99%	68%	85%	90%	95%	99%
Verbal Scale IQ	±4	±5	±6	±7	± 9	±4	±5	±6	±7	± 9
Performance Scale IQ	±5	±7	±8	±9	±12	±5	±7	±8	±9	±12
Full Scale IQ	±3	±5	±5	±6	± 8	±3	±5	±5	±6	± 8

Note. See Table C-1 for an explanation of method used to arrive at confidence intervals.

TABLE C-6.   Significant Differences Between WISC-R Scaled Scores, IQs, and Factor Scores (.05/.01 significance levels)

	I	S	A	V	C	DS	PC	PA	BD	OA	CO
S	4/5										
A	4/5	4/5									
V	3/4	3/5	4/5								
C	4/5	4/5	4/5	4/5							
DS	4/5	4/5	4/5	4/5	4/5						
PC	4/5	4/5	4/5	4/5	4/5	4/5					
PA	4/5	4/5	4/5	4/5	4/5	4/5	4/6				
BD	3/4	3/5	4/5	3/4	4/5	4/5	4/5	4/5			
OA	4/5	4/6	4/6	4/5	4/6	4/6	4/6	5/6	4/5		
CO	4/5	4/5	4/6	4/5	4/6	4/6	4/6	4/6	4/5	5/6	
M	4/5	4/6	4/6	4/5	4/6	4/6	4/6	5/6	4/5	5/6	5/6

	VSIQ
PSIQ	12/15

	VCIQ	POIQ
POIQ	12/16	
FDIQ	13/18	14/19

Note. Abbreviations: I = Information; S = Similarities; A = Arithmetic; V = Vocabulary; C = Comprehension; DS = Digit Span; PC = Picture Completion; PA = Picture Arrangement; BD = Block Design; OA = Object Assembly; CO = Coding; M = Mazes; VSIQ = Verbal Scale IQ; PSIQ = Performance Scale IQ; VCIQ = Verbal Comprehension IQ; POIQ = Perceptual Organization IQ; FDIQ = Freedom from Distractibility IQ.

Sample reading: A difference of 4 points between scaled scores on the Information and Similarities subtests is significant at the 5 percent level, while a difference of 5 points is significant at the 1 percent level. In like manner, from the first small box, a 12-point difference between the Verbal Scale IQ and Performance Scale IQ is needed for the 5 percent level, and a 15-point difference is needed for the 1 percent level.

The values in this table for the subtest comparisons are overly liberal when more than one comparison is made for a subtest. However, they are more accurate when a priori planned comparisons are made, such as Information vs. Comprehension or Digit Span vs. Arithmetic. The values in this table are based on the average of the eleven age groups.

See Chapter 11, Exhibit 11-2 for an explanation of the method used to arrive at magnitude of differences.

See Table C-8 in the Appendix for the procedure used to obtain the Deviation IQs for the Verbal Comprehension, Perceptual Organization, and Freedom from Distractibility Deviation IQs.

Standard errors of measurement for WISC-R factor Deviation IQs obtained from Gutkin (1979b).

TABLE C-7.   Differences Required for Significance When Each WISC-R Subtest Scaled Score Is Compared to the Mean Scaled Score for Any Individual Child

Subtest	5 Verbal Scale Subtests[a] .05	.01	6 Verbal Scale Subtests .05	.01	5 Performance Scale Subtests[b] .05	.01	6 Performance Scale Subtests .05	.01
Information	2.81	3.37	2.94	3.50	—	—	—	—
Similarities	3.07	3.68	3.22	3.84	—	—	—	—
Arithmetic	3.14	3.76	3.30	3.93	—	—	—	—
Vocabulary	2.74	3.29	2.86	3.41	—	—	—	—
Comprehension	3.15	3.78	3.32	3.95	—	—	—	—
Digit Span	—	—	3.42	4.07	—	—	—	—
Picture Completion	—	—	—	—	3.38	4.06	3.55	4.22
Picture Arrangement	—	—	—	—	3.59	4.31	3.78	4.50
Block Design	—	—	—	—	2.92	3.50	3.03	3.61
Object Assembly	—	—	—	—	3.82	4.58	4.03	4.80
Coding	—	—	—	—	3.70	4.43	3.89	4.64
Mazes	—	—	—	—	—	—	4.03	4.80

Subtest	10 Subtests[c] .05	.01	11 Subtests[a] .05	.01	11 Subtests[b] .05	.01	12 Subtests .05	.01
Information	3.25	3.80	3.29	3.85	3.30	3.86	3.34	3.89
Similarities	3.60	4.21	3.65	4.27	3.66	4.28	3.71	4.32
Arithmetic	3.69	4.32	3.75	4.38	3.76	4.39	3.81	4.44
Vocabulary	3.15	3.69	3.19	3.73	3.20	3.74	3.24	3.78
Comprehension	3.71	4.35	3.77	4.41	3.78	4.42	3.83	4.47
Digit Span	—	—	3.89	4.55	—	—	3.96	4.61
Picture Completion	3.86	4.52	3.92	4.58	3.93	4.59	3.98	4.64
Picture Arrangement	4.14	4.85	4.21	4.92	4.22	4.93	4.28	4.99
Block Design	3.20	3.75	3.24	3.79	3.25	3.80	3.29	3.83
Object Assembly	4.45	5.22	4.53	5.30	4.54	5.31	4.61	5.37
Coding	4.29	5.02	4.36	5.10	4.37	5.10	4.43	5.17
Mazes	—	—	—	—	4.54	5.31	4.61	5.37

Note. Table C-7 shows the minimum deviations from an individual's average subtest scaled score that are significant at the .05 and .01 levels.

The following formula, obtained from Davis (1959), was used to compute the deviations from average that are significant at the desired significance levels: $D = CR \times S_{m((T/m) - Z_1)}$, where D is the deviation from average, CR is the critical ratio desired, and $S_{m((T/m) - Z_1)}$ is the standard error of measurement of the difference between an average subtest scaled score and any one of the subtest scaled scores that entered into the average. The standard error of measurement can be obtained by the following formula:

$$S_{m((T/m) - Z_1)} = \sqrt{\frac{S_{mT}^2}{m^2} + \left(\frac{m - 2}{m}\right) S_{mZ_1}^2}$$

where S_{mT}^2 is the sum of the squared standard errors of measurement of the m subtests, m is the number of subtests included in the average, T/m is the average of the subtest scaled scores, and $S_{mZ_1}^2$ is the squared standard error of measurement of any one of the subtest scaled scores. The critical ratio for the 5 percent level ranges from 2.58 to 2.87, and that for the 1 percent level from 3.09 to 3.34, depending on the number of subtests. These critical ratios were obtained by use of the Bonferroni inequality, which controls the familywise error rate at .05 (or .01) by setting the error rate per comparison at .05/m (or .01/m).

The following example illustrates the procedure. We will determine the minimum deviation of a child's score on the WISC-R Information subtest required to be significantly different from his or her average score on the five standard Verbal Scale subtests (Information, Similarities, Arithmetic, Vocabulary, and Comprehension) needed at the 95 percent level of confidence. We calculate S^2_{mT} by first squaring and then summing the appropriate average standard errors of measurement for each of the five subtests. These standard errors of measurement appear in Table 10 of the WISC-R manual:

$$S^2_{mT} = (1.19)^2 + (1.34)^2 + (1.38)^2 + (1.15)^2 + (1.39)^2 = 8.37.$$

We determine $S^2_{mZ_1}$ by squaring the average standard error of measurement of the subtest of interest, the Information subtest:

$$S^2_{mZ_1} = (1.19)^2 = 1.4161.$$

The number of subtests, m, equals 5.
Substituting these values into the formula yields the following:

$$S_{m((T/m) - Z_1)} = \sqrt{\frac{8.37}{(5)^2} + \left(\frac{5-2}{5}\right)1.4161} = 1.087.$$

The value, 1.087, is then multiplied by the appropriate z value for the 95 percent confidence level to obtain the minimum significant deviation (D). The z value is 2.58 using the Bonferroni correction ($.05/5 = .01$).

$$D = 2.58 \times 1.087 = 2.81.$$

[a]Digit Span excluded.
[b]Mazes excluded.
[c]Digit Span and Mazes excluded.
The figures in the table courtesy of A. B. Silverstein.

TABLE C-8.   Estimated WISC-R Deviation IQs for Verbal Comprehension, Perceptual Organization, and Freedom from Distractibility Factors

Sum	Estimated Deviation IQ			Sum	Estimated Deviation IQ		
	Verbal Comprehension[a]	Perceptual Organization[b]	Freedom from Distractibility[c]		Verbal Comprehension[a]	Perceptual Organization[b]	Freedom from Distractibility[c]
3	—	—	41	40	100	100	122
4	47	42	43	41	101	102	124
5	49	44	45	42	103	103	126
6	50	46	47	43	104	105	129
7	51	47	49	44	106	106	131
8	53	49	52	45	107	108	133
9	54	50	54	46	109	110	135
10	56	52	56	47	110	111	137
11	57	54	58	48	112	113	140
12	59	55	60	49	113	114	142
13	60	57	63	50	115	116	144
14	62	58	65	51	116	118	146
15	63	60	67	52	118	119	148
16	65	62	69	53	119	121	151
17	66	63	71	54	121	122	153
18	68	65	74	55	122	124	155
19	69	66	76	56	124	126	157
20	71	68	78	57	125	127	159
21	72	70	80	58	126	129	—
22	74	71	82	59	128	130	—
23	75	73	85	60	129	132	—
24	76	74	87	61	131	134	—
25	78	76	89	62	132	135	—
26	79	78	91	63	134	137	—
27	81	79	93	64	135	138	—
28	82	81	96	65	137	140	—
29	84	82	98	66	138	142	—
30	85	84	100	67	140	143	—
31	87	86	102	68	141	145	—
32	88	87	104	69	143	146	—
33	90	88	107	70	144	148	—
34	91	90	109	71	146	150	—
35	93	92	111	72	147	151	—
36	94	94	113	73	149	153	—
37	96	95	115	74	150	154	—
38	97	97	118	75	151	156	—
39	99	98	120	76	153	158	—

Note. The formulas used to compute the Deviation Quotients, using subtest scaled scores, are as follows:

Verbal Comprehension Deviation Quotient = 1.47 (Information + Similarities + Vocabulary + Comprehension) + 41.2.
Perceptual Organization Deviation Quotient = 1.60 (Picture Completion + Picture Arrangement + Block Design + Object Assembly) + 36.0.
Freedom from Distractibility Deviation Quotient = 2.2 (Arithmetic + Digit Span + Coding) + 34.
[a]Verbal Comprehension subtests are Information, Similarities, Vocabulary, and Comprehension.
[b]Perceptual Organization subtests are Picture Completion, Picture Arrangement, Block Design, and Object Assembly.
[c]Freedom from Distractibility subtests are Arithmetic, Digit Span, and Coding.
First two columns adapted from Gutkin (1978).

TABLE C-9.   Extrapolated IQ Equivalents of Sums of Scaled Scores for WISC-R

Verbal		Performance		Full Scale[a]	
Sum of Scaled Scores	IQ	Sum of Scaled Scores	IQ	Sum of Scaled Scores	IQ
5	44	5	39	10	36
.	.	6	41	11	37
.	.	7	42	12	38
.	.	8	44	13	39
94	155	.	.	14	39
95	157	.	.	.	.
		.	.	.	.
		91	156	.	.
		92	158	185	161
		93	159	186	162
		94	160	187	163
		95	162	188	163
				189	164
				190	165

Note. WISC-R regression equations:

Verbal IQ = 37.3513 + 1.2552 (scaled score)
Performance IQ = 32.6814 + 1.3580 (scaled score)
Full Scale IQ = 29.3456 + .7124 (scaled score)

[a]Wechsler recommends that a Full Scale IQ should not be calculated unless raw scores greater than 0 are obtained on at least *three* Verbal and *three* Performance Scale subtests.

TABLE C-10. Probability of Obtaining Designated Differences Between Individual WISC-R Verbal and Performance IQs

Probability of Obtaining Given or Greater Discrepancy by Chance	Age Level											
	6½	7½	8½	9½	10½	11½	12½	13½	14½	15½	16½	Av.[a]
.50	4.32	4.32	4.08	3.99	4.08	3.81	3.83	4.16	4.02	4.09	4.02	4.06
.25	7.20	7.20	6.80	6.66	6.80	6.34	6.38	6.93	6.71	6.82	6.70	6.77
.20	8.01	8.01	7.57	7.41	7.57	7.06	7.10	7.71	7.47	7.59	7.45	7.54
.10	10.33	10.33	9.76	9.55	9.75	9.10	9.15	9.94	9.62	9.78	9.61	9.72
.05	12.27	12.27	11.59	11.35	11.59	10.81	10.87	11.81	11.43	11.62	11.41	11.54
.02	14.59	14.59	13.78	13.49	13.77	12.85	12.93	14.04	13.59	13.81	13.57	13.72
.01	16.16	16.15	15.26	14.93	15.25	14.23	14.31	15.54	15.05	15.29	15.02	15.19
.001	20.66	20.66	19.51	19.10	19.51	18.20	18.31	19.88	19.25	19.56	19.22	19.43

Note. Table C-10 is entered in the column appropriate to the examinee's age. The discrepancy that is just less than the discrepancy obtained by the examinee is located. The entry in the same row, first column, gives the probability of obtaining a given or greater discrepancy by chance. For example, the hypothesis that a 6½-year-old examinee obtained a Verbal-Performance discrepancy of 17 by chance can be rejected at the .01 level of significance. Table C-10 is two-tailed. See Chapter 11, Exhibit 11-2 for an explanation of method used to arrive at magnitude of differences.
[a]Av. = Average of eleven age groups.

TABLE C-11. Percentage of Population Obtaining Discrepancies Between WISC-R Verbal and Performance IQs

% in Population Obtaining Given or Greater Discrepancy	Age Level											
	6½	7½	8½	9½	10½	11½	12½	13½	14½	15½	16½	Av.[a]
50	8.66	8.53	8.78	7.74	8.41	8.02	7.61	8.78	8.28	9.26	8.41	8.41
25	14.43	14.22	14.64	12.91	14.01	13.36	12.68	14.64	13.80	15.43	14.01	14.01
20	16.06	15.83	16.29	14.37	15.60	14.87	14.11	16.29	15.36	17.17	15.60	15.60
10	20.71	20.41	21.00	18.52	20.11	19.17	18.19	21.00	19.80	22.13	20.11	20.11
5	24.60	24.24	24.95	22.00	23.88	22.77	21.00	24.95	23.52	26.30	23.88	23.88
2	29.24	28.82	29.66	26.15	28.39	27.07	25.68	29.66	27.96	31.26	28.39	28.39
1	32.38	31.91	32.84	28.96	31.44	29.97	28.44	32.84	30.96	34.61	31.44	31.44
.1	41.41	40.82	42.00	37.04	40.21	38.34	36.37	42.00	39.60	44.27	40.21	40.21

Note. Table C-11 is entered in the column appropriate to the examinee's age. The discrepancy that is just less than the discrepancy obtained by the examinee is located. The entry in the same row, first column, gives the percentage of the standardization population obtaining discrepancies as large as or larger than the located discrepancy. For example, a 6½-year-old examinee with a Verbal-Performance discrepancy of 14 on the WISC-R will be found in between 25 and 50% of the standardization population.

The method used to compute the discrepancy between the Verbal and Performance Scale IQs which reflects the percentage of the population obtaining the discrepancy is as follows: Discrepancy $= \sigma_1 z \sqrt{2 - 2r_{xy}}$. The first term is the standard deviation of the test, the second is the selected z value, and the last is the correlation between the two scales. For example, for a 6½-year-old child the discrepancy between the WISC-R Verbal and Performance Scale IQs which represents 5% of the population is $15(1.96)\sqrt{2 - 2(.65)} = 24.60$.
[a]Av. = Average of eleven age groups.

TABLE C-12.   Validity Coefficients of Proposed WISC-R Short Forms

Dyad		Triad		Tetrad		Pentad	
Short Form	r	Short Form	r	Short Form	r	Short Form	r
V BD	.906	S V BD	.931	I V C BD	.947	S A V PA OA	.963
I BD	.888	I V BD	.929	S V PA BD	.947	S A V PA BD	.962
S BD	.885	I C BD	.928	I C PC BD	.945	S A V BD OA	.960
C BD	.878	I S BD	.925	S A V OA	.944	I C PC BD CO	.960
V OA	.878	V C BD	.924	I V PA BD	.944	I V PC BD CO	.960
V PC	.868	S C BD	.921	I S C BD	.944	S A C PA OA	.960
S V	.864	S V OA	.919	I C PA BD	.944	I S C PA BD	.960
I S	.860	V PA BD	.919	I S PA BD	.943	I V C PC BD	.959
I PC	.858	A V OA	.919	S V PC BD	.943	A V C BD OA	.959
I V	.857	V PC BD	.919	S V BD OA	.943	A V C PA BD	.958

Note. Abbreviations: I = Information; S = Similarities; A = Arithmetic; V = Vocabulary; C = Comprehension; PC = Picture Completion; PA = Picture Arrangement; BD = Block Design; OA = Object Assembly; CO = Coding.
The following formula, obtained from Q. McNemar (*Journal of Clinical and Consulting Psychology*, 1974, *42*, 145–146), was used to compute the part-whole correlations:

$$r = \frac{k + \Sigma\Sigma r_{hj}}{\sqrt{n + 2\Sigma r_{ij}} \sqrt{k + 2\Sigma r_{gh}}}$$

where $\Sigma\Sigma r_{hj}$ is the sum of the correlations between each of the k subtests and all the other subtests, n is the total number of subtests, Σr_{ij} is the sum of the correlations between each of the n subtests, and Σr_{gh} is the sum of the intercorrelations of the k subtests. The term $\sqrt{n + 2\Sigma r_{ij}}$ becomes a constant for all computations. The formula was applied to the average subtest intercorrelations for the eleven age groups that composed the standardization sample ($N = 2200$) to determine the correlations with the Full Scale of all possible short forms of two, three, four, and five subtests. The average subtest intercorrelations are based on the ten standard subtests (Digit Span and Mazes are omitted). The standard errors of estimate for the best dyad, triad, tetrad, and pentad are 6.34, 5.48, 4.82, and 4.04 IQ points, respectively.

TABLE C-13.   Yudin's Abbreviated Procedure for the WISC-R as Modified by Silverstein

Subtest	Items Administered	Multiply Score by
Information	Every 3rd	3
Similarities	Odd only	2
Arithmetic	Odd only	2
Vocabulary	Every 3rd	3
Comprehension	Odd only	2
Picture Completion	Every 3rd	3
Picture Arrangement	Odd only	2
Block Design	Odd only	2
Object Assembly	Odd only	2
Coding	All items	1

Adapted from Silverstein (1968a).

TABLE C-14. WISC-R Structure of Intellect Classifications

INFORMATION

Items 1 to 3	MMU	Memory for Semantic Units	the ability to remember isolated ideas or word meanings
Items 4, 5	MMR	Memory for Semantic Relations	the ability to remember meaningful connections between items of verbal information
Items 6, 11, 25, 28	CMU	Cognition of Semantic Units	the ability to comprehend the meaning of words or ideas
Items 7, 8, 10	MMS	Memory for Semantic Systems	the ability to remember meaningfully ordered verbal information
Item 9	EMR	Evaluation of Semantic Relations	the ability to make choices among semantic relationships based on the similarity and consistency of the meanings
	MMR	Memory for Semantic Relations	the ability to remember meaningful connections between items of verbal information
Items 12, 13, 17	MMR	Memory for Semantic Relations	the ability to remember meaningful connections between items of verbal information
	NMR	Convergent Production of Semantic Relations	the ability to produce a word or idea that conforms to specific relationship requirements
Items 14, 18	MMR	Memory for Semantic Relations	the ability to remember meaningful connections between items of verbal information
Item 15	CMU	Cognition of Semantic Units	the ability to comprehend the meaning of words or ideas
	MMS	Memory for Semantic Systems	the ability to remember meaningfully ordered verbal information
Items 16, 22	MMI	Memory for Semantic Implications	the ability to remember arbitrary connections between pairs of meaningful elements of information
Item 17	MMR	Memory for Semantic Relations	the ability to remember meaningful connections between items of verbal information
	NMR	Convergent Production of Semantic Relations	the ability to produce a word or idea that conforms to specific relationship requirements
Item 19	MFS	Memory for Figural Systems	the ability to remember spatial order or placement of given visual information or to remember auditory complexes of rhythm or melody
Item 20	MSS	Memory for Symbolic Systems	the ability to remember the order of symbolic information
	CMU	Cognition of Semantic Units	the ability to comprehend the meaning of words or ideas
Items 21, 23, 29	NMU	Convergent Production of Semantic Units	the ability to converge on the appropriate name, or summarizing word, for any given information
Item 24	EMR	Evaluation of Semantic Relations	the ability to make choices among semantic relationships based on the similarity and consistency of the meanings

TABLE C-14   (cont.)

INFORMATION (cont.)

Item 26	MMR	Memory for Semantic Relations	the ability to remember meaningful connections between items of verbal information
	NMI	Convergent Production of Semantic Implications	the ability to deduce meaningful information implicit in the given information
Item 27	MMU	Memory for Semantic Units	the ability to remember isolated ideas or word meanings
	NMU	Convergent Production of Semantic Units	the ability to converge on the appropriate name, or summarizing word, for any given information
Item 30	CMU	Cognition of Semantic Units	the ability to comprehend the meaning of words or ideas
	MMR	Memory for Semantic Relations	the ability to remember meaningful connections between items of verbal information

SIMILARITIES

Items 1 to 15	CMR	Cognition of Semantic Relations	the ability to see relations between ideas or meanings of words
	CMT	Cognition of Semantic Transformations	the ability to see potential changes of interpretations of objects and situations
Item 16	CSR	Cognition of Symbolic Relations	the ability to see relations between items of symbolic information
Item 17	CMR	Cognition of Semantic Relations	the ability to see relations between ideas or meanings of words
	CMT	Cognition of Semantic Transformations	the ability to see potential changes of interpretations of objects and situations

ARITHMETIC

Every item	MSI	Memory for Symbolic Implications	the ability to remember arbitrary connections between symbols
	CMS	Cognition of Semantic Systems	the ability to comprehend relatively complex ideas

VOCABULARY

Every item	CMU	Cognition of Semantic Units	the ability to comprehend the meanings of words or ideas

COMPREHENSION

Every item	EMI	Evaluation of Semantic Implications	the ability to judge the adequacy of a meaningful deduction

DIGIT SPAN

Every item	MSS	Memory for Symbolic Systems	the ability to remember the order of symbolic information

PICTURE COMPLETION

Every item	CFU	Cognition of Figural Units	the ability to perceive or recognize figural entities

TABLE C-14 (cont.)

PICTURE COMPLETION (cont.)

	EFS	Evaluation of Figural Systems	the ability to evaluate a system of figural units that have been grouped in some manner
Item 14 (also)	MSS	Memory for Symbolic Systems	the ability to remember the order of symbolic information

PICTURE ARRANGEMENT

Every item	EMR	Evaluation of Semantic Relations	the ability to make choices among semantic relationships based on the similarity and consistency of the meanings
	NMS	Convergent Production of Semantic Systems	the ability to order information into a verbally meaningful sequence

BLOCK DESIGN

Every item	CFR	Cognition of Figural Relations	the ability to recognize figural relations between forms
	EFR	Evaluation of Figural Relations	the ability to choose a form based on the evaluation of what the relations are between the figures or forms in the sequence

OBJECT ASSEMBLY

Every item	CFS	Cognition of Figural Systems	the ability to comprehend arrangements and positions of visual objects in space
	CFT	Cognition of Figural Transformations	the ability to visualize how a given figure or object will appear after given changes, such as unfolding or rotation
	EFR	Evaluation of Figural Relations	the ability to choose a form based on the evaluation of what the relations are between the figures or forms in the sequence

CODING A

Entire subtest	NFU	Convergent Production of Figural Units	the ability to reproduce correctly a form
	EFU	Evaluation of Figural Units	the ability to judge units of figural information as being similar or different

CODING B

Entire subtest	NSU	Convergent Production of Symbolic Units	factorial meaning has not been described
	ESU	Evaluation of Symbolic Units	the ability to make rapid decisions regarding the identification of letter or number sets

MAZES

Every item	CFI	Cognition of Figural Implications	the ability to foresee the consequences involved in figural problems

Note. WISC-R SOI designations obtained from M. Meeker at the SOI Institute. Templates and SOI profile forms as well as five workbooks to accompany prescriptions based on SOI templates are available from the SOI Institute, 343 Richmond, El Segundo, CA 90245

TABLE C-15. Interpretative Rationales, Implications of High and Low Scores, and Instructional Implications for WISC-R Subtests

Ability[a]	Background Factors	Possible Implications of High Scores	Possible Implications of Low Scores	Instructional Implications
		INFORMATION		
Verbal comprehension Range of knowledge Long-range memory	Natural endowment Richness of early environment Extent of schooling Cultural predilections Interests	Good range of information Possession of knowledge associated with the cultural and educational environment Good memory Enriched background Alertness and interest in the environment Intellectual ambitiousness Intellectual curiosity Urge to collect knowledge	Poor range of information Poor memory Hostility to a school-type task Tendency to give up easily Foreign background Low achievement orientation	Stress factual material by having child read newspaper articles, discuss current events, and do memory exercises Use other enrichment activities, including calendar activities, science and social studies information, and projects involving animals and their function in society
		SIMILARITIES		
Verbal comprehension Verbal concept formation Abstract and concrete reasoning abilities Capacity for associative thinking Ability to separate essential from nonessential details Memory	A minimum of cultural opportunities Interests and reading patterns	Good conceptual thinking Ability to see relationships Ability to use logical and abstract thinking Ability to discriminate fundamental from superficial relationships Ability to select and verbalize appropriate relationships between two objects or concepts Flexibility of thought processes	Poor conceptual thinking Difficulty in seeing relationships Difficulty in selecting and verbalizing appropriate relationships between two objects or concepts Overly concrete mode of thinking Rigidity of thought processes Negativism	Focus on recognition of differences and likenesses in shapes, textures, and daily surroundings Stress language development, synonyms and antonyms, and exercises involving abstract words, classifications, and generalizations

TABLE C-15 (cont.)

Ability[a]	Background Factors	Possible Implications of High Scores	Possible Implications of Low Scores	Instructional Implications
ARITHMETIC				
Freedom from distractibility and verbal comprehension Numerical reasoning ability Mental computation Application of basic arithmetical processes Concentration Attention Memory	Opportunity to acquire fundamental arithmetic processes	Facility in mental arithmetic Ability to apply reasoning skills in the solution of mathematical problems Ability to apply arithmetical skills in personal and social problem-solving situations Good concentration Ability to focus attention Ability to engage in complex thought patterns (for upper-level items, particularly) Teacher-oriented student	Inadequate ability in mental arithmetic Poor concentration Distractibility Anxiety over a school-like task Blocking toward mathematical tasks Poor school achievement (perhaps associated with rebellion against authority or with cultural background) Anxiety (e.g., worry over personal problems)	Develop arithmetical skills Develop concentration skills Use concrete objects to introduce concepts Drill in basic skills Develop interesting and "real" problems to solve
VOCABULARY				
Verbal comprehension Language development Learning ability Fund of information Richness of ideas Memory Concept formation	Education Cultural opportunities	Good verbal comprehension Good verbal skills and language development Good family or cultural background Good schooling Ability to conceptualize Intellectual striving	Poor verbal comprehension Poor verbal skills and language development Limited educational or family background Difficulty in verbalization Foreign language background Verbalization not encouraged in culture	Develop a working vocabulary Encourage child to discuss experiences, ask questions, and make a dictionary Use other verbal enrichment exercises, including Scrabble, analogy, and other word games

TABLE C-15 (cont.)

Ability[a]	Background Factors	Possible Implications of High Scores	Possible Implications of Low Scores	Instructional Implications
COMPREHENSION				
Verbal comprehension Social judgment Common sense Use of practical knowledge and judgment in social situations Knowledge of conventional standards of behavior Ability to evaluate past experience Moral and ethical judgment	Extensiveness of cultural opportunities Ability to evaluate and use past experience Development of conscience or moral sense	Good social judgment and common sense Recognizes social demands when practical judgment and common sense are necessary Knowledge of rules of conventional behavior Ability to organize knowledge Social maturity Ability to verbalize well Wide experience	Poor social judgment Failure to take personal responsibility (e.g., overdependency, immaturity, limited involvement with others) Overly concrete thinking Difficulty in expressing ideas verbally Creative individual looking for unusual solutions	Help child understand social mores, customs, and societal activities, such as how other children react to things, how the government works, and how banks operate Discuss the actions of others to help children develop awareness of social relationships and what is expected of them in terms of the behavior of others Role-play situations, such as reporting fires, calling police, and obtaining help for plumbing problems
DIGIT SPAN				
Freedom from distractibility Short-term memory Rote memory Immediate auditory memory Attention Concentration Auditory sequencing	Ability to passively receive stimuli	Good rote memory Good immediate recall ability Ability to attend well in a testing situation Ability to attend to auditory stimuli	Anxiety Inattention Distractibility A possible learning deficit Difficulty in auditory sequencing	Emphasize listening skills by using sequencing activities, reading a short story and asking child to recall details, and seeing if child can follow directions Use short and simple directions and repeat when necessary Use other memory exercises and memory games

TABLE C-15 (cont.)

Ability[a]	Background Factors	Possible Implications of High Scores	Possible Implications of Low Scores	Instructional Implications
PICTURE COMPLETION				
Perceptual organization Ability to differentiate essential from nonessential details Identification of familiar objects (visual recognition) Concentration on visually perceived material Reasoning Visual organization Visual perception (closure) Visual memory	Experiences Alertness to environment	Good perception and concentration Good alertness to details Ability to establish a learning set quickly Ability to differentiate between essential and nonessential details	Anxiety affecting concentration and attention Preoccupation with irrelevant details Negativism ("nothing is missing")	Focus on visual learning techniques stressing individual parts that make up the whole Use perceptual activities that focus on recognizing objects, describing objects, and attention to details (e.g., maps and art work) Improve scanning techniques aimed at identifying missing elements in pictures
PICTURE ARRANGEMENT				
Perceptual organization Planning ability Interpretation of social situations Nonverbal reasoning ability Attention to details Alertness Visual sequencing Common sense	A minimum of cultural opportunities	Planning ability Ability to anticipate in a meaningful way what results might be expected from various acts of behavior Alertness to detail Forethought Sequential thought processes Ability to synthesize parts into intelligible wholes	Difficulty with visual organization (sequencing) Difficulty in anticipating events and their consequences Inattentiveness Anxiety Failure to use cues	Focus on cause and effect relationships, logical sequential presentations, and part-whole relationships Use story completion exercises Discuss alternative behaviors and endings in stories and events

TABLE C-15 (cont.)

Ability[a]	Background Factors	Possible Implications of High Scores	Possible Implications of Low Scores	Instructional Implications
BLOCK DESIGN				
Perceptual organization Visual-motor coordination Spatial visualization Abstract conceptualizing ability Analysis and synthesis	Rate of motor activity Color vision	Good visual-motor-spatial integration Good conceptualizing ability Good spatial orientation in conjunction with speed, accuracy, and persistence Analyzing and synthesizing ability Speed and accuracy in sizing up a problem Good hand-eye coordination Good nonverbal reasoning ability Good trial-and-error methods	Poor visual-motor-spatial integration Visual-perceptual problems Poor spatial orientation	Use puzzles, blocks, spatial-visual tasks, perceptual tasks involving breaking down an object and building it up again, and art work with geometric forms and flannel board Focus on part-to-whole relationships and working with a model or key
OBJECT ASSEMBLY				
Perceptual organization Visual-motor coordination Ability to synthesize concrete parts into meaningful wholes Spatial relations	Rate of motor activity Familiarity with figures Capacity to persist at a task Experience with part-whole relationships Working for an unknown goal	Good visual-motor coordination Ability to visualize a whole from its parts Ability to perceive a whole, with critical understanding of the relationships of the individual parts Successful trial and error Experience in assembling puzzles Persistence	Visual-motor difficulties Visual-perceptual problems Poor planning ability Difficulty in perceiving a whole Minimal experience with construction tasks Limited interest in assembly tasks Limited persistence	Develop perceptual and psychomotor skills through guided practice in assembling parts into familiar configurations Encourage trial-and-error activities Reinforce persistence Work with puzzles and activities centering on recognition of missing body parts Employ construction, cutting, and pasting activities Focus on interpretation of wholes from minimal cues

TABLE C-15 (cont.)

Ability[a]	Background Factors	Possible Implications of High Scores	Possible Implications of Low Scores	Instructional Implications
		CODING		
Freedom from distractibility Visual-motor coordination or dexterity Speed of mental operation Psychomotor speed Short-term memory Visual recall Attentional skills Symbol-associative skills	Rate of motor activity	Visual-motor dexterity Good concentration Sustained energy or persistence Ability to learn new material associatively and reproduce it with speed and accuracy Good motivation or desire for achievement	Visual-motor coordination difficulties Distractibility Visual defects Poor pencil control Disinterest in a school-like task Excessive concern for detail in reproducing symbols exactly Lethargy	Use visual-motor learning exercises, such as having child develop a code for matching geometric figures and numbers, learn Morse Code, and work on tracing activities
		MAZES		
Perceptual organization Planning ability Foresight Visual-motor control Eye-hand coordination Attention and concentration	Visual-motor organization	Good perceptual organization Planning efficiency Speed and accuracy Ability to follow instructions	Poor visual-motor organization Poor planning efficiency Difficulty in delaying action	Focus on planning skills, directionality, visual discrimination, and other paper-and-pencil activities emphasizing planning and anticipation Help child evaluate responses prior to emitting the responses

Note. For each individual examinee, select the appropriate implication (or implications) listed in the columns only after careful consideration of the entire test protocol and background information.

[a]The first entry under "Ability" is based on factor analytic findings. The other entries are derived from clinical and educational interpretations of the subtest functions.

Adapted, in part, from Blatt and Allison (1968), Freeman (1962), Glasser and Zimmerman (1967), Kaufman (1975a), Rapaport, Gill, and Schafer (1968), and Searls (1975).

TABLE C-16. Confidence Intervals for WPPSI Scales

	Age Level									
	4 (3-10-16 through 4-2-29)					4½ (4-3-0 through 4-8-29)				
	Confidence Level					Confidence Level				
Scale	68%	85%	90%	95%	99%	68%	85%	90%	95%	99%
Verbal Scale IQ	±4	±5	±6	±7	± 9	±4	±5	±6	±7	± 9
Performance Scale IQ	±4	±6	±7	±9	±11	±4	±6	±7	±8	±10
Full Scale IQ	±3	±4	±5	±6	± 8	±3	±4	±5	±6	± 8

	Age Level									
	5 (4-9-0 through 5-2-29)					5½ (5-3-0 through 5-8-29)				
	Confidence Level					Confidence Level				
Scale	68%	85%	90%	95%	99%	68%	85%	90%	95%	99%
Verbal Scale IQ	±4	±5	±6	±7	± 9	±3	±5	±6	±7	±9
Performance Scale IQ	±4	±5	±6	±7	±10	±3	±5	±6	±7	±9
Full Scale IQ	±3	±4	±5	±6	± 7	±3	±4	±4	±5	±7

	Age Level									
	6 (5-9-0 through 6-2-29)					6½ (6-3-0 through 6-7-15)				
	Confidence Level					Confidence Level				
Scale	68%	85%	90%	95%	99%	68%	85%	90%	95%	99%
Verbal Scale IQ	±3	±5	±6	±7	±9	±4	±5	±6	±7	±10
Performance Scale IQ	±3	±5	±6	±7	±9	±4	±6	±7	±8	±10
Full Scale IQ	±3	±4	±4	±5	±7	±3	±4	±5	±6	± 8

Note. See Table C-1 for an explanation of method used to obtain confidence intervals.

TABLE C-17.   Significant Differences Between WPPSI Scaled Scores and Between IQs (.05/.01 significance levels)

	I	V	A	S	C	Se	AH	PC	M	GD
V	3/5									
A	4/5	3/5								
S	4/5	3/4	3/5							
C	4/5	3/5	4/5	4/5						
Se	3/5	3/4	3/4	3/4	3/5					
AH	4/5	4/5	4/5	4/5	4/5	4/5				
PC	4/5	3/4	3/5	3/5	4/5	3/4	4/5			
M	3/4	3/4	3/4	3/4	3/4	3/4	4/5	3/4		
GD	4/5	3/5	4/5	3/5	4/5	3/4	4/5	3/5	3/4	
BD	4/5	3/5	4/5	3/5	4/5	3/4	4/5	3/5	3/4	4/5

Box: PSIQ | VSIQ 11/14

Note. Abbreviations: I = Information; V = Vocabulary; A = Arithmetic; S = Similarities; C = Comprehension; Se = Sentences; AH = Animal House; PC = Picture Completion; M = Mazes; GD = Geometric Design; BD = Block Design; VSIQ = Verbal Scale IQ; PSIQ = Performance Scale IQ.

Sample reading: A difference of 3 points between scaled scores on the Information and Vocabulary subtests is significant at the 5 percent level, while a difference of 5 points is significant at the 1 percent level. In like manner, from the small box, an 11-point difference between the Verbal Scale IQ and Performance Scale IQ is needed for the 5 percent level, and a 14-point difference is needed for the 1 percent level. The Sentences subtest was not included in computation of significant differences for the Verbal Scale.

The values in this table for the subtest comparisons are overly liberal when more than one comparison is made. However, they are more accurate when a priori planned comparisons are made, such as Information vs. Vocabulary or Similarities vs. Comprehension. The values in this table are based on the average of the six age groups.

See Chapter 11, Exhibit 11-2 for an explanation of the method used to obtain magnitude of differences.

TABLE C-18.   Differences Required for Significance When Each WPPSI Subtest Scaled Score Is Compared to the Mean Scaled Score for Any Individual Child

Subtest	5 Verbal Scale Subtests[a] .05	.01	6 Verbal Scale Subtests .05	.01	5 Performance Scale Subtests .05	.01	10 Subtests[a] .05	.01	11 Subtests .05	.01
Information	3.05	3.66	3.19	3.80	—	—	3.55	4.16	3.61	4.22
Vocabulary	2.83	3.39	2.94	3.50	—	—	3.25	3.80	3.29	3.85
Arithmetic	2.86	3.43	2.98	3.55	—	—	3.29	3.86	3.34	3.91
Similarities	2.90	3.48	3.02	3.60	—	—	3.34	3.91	3.39	3.96
Comprehension	3.02	3.62	3.15	3.76	—	—	3.51	4.11	3.56	4.16
Sentences	—	—	2.89	3.44	—	—	—	—	3.22	3.76
Animal House	—	—	—	—	3.26	3.91	3.84	4.50	3.90	4.56
Picture Completion	—	—	—	—	2.81	3.37	3.22	3.78	3.27	3.82
Mazes	—	—	—	—	2.61	3.13	2.94	3.45	2.98	3.48
Geometric Design	—	—	—	—	2.96	3.55	3.43	4.02	3.49	4.08
Block Design	—	—	—	—	2.91	3.49	3.36	3.94	3.41	3.99

Note. Table C-18 shows the minimum deviations from an individual's average subtest scaled score that are significant at the .05 and .01 levels. See Note in Table C-7 for an explanation of how the deviations were obtained.
[a] Sentences subtest excluded.
The figures in the table courtesy of A. B. Silverstein.

TABLE C-19. Extrapolated IQ Equivalents of Scaled Scores for WPPSI

Verbal		Performance		Full Scale[a]			
Sum of Scaled Scores	IQ	Sum of Scaled Scores	IQ	Sum of Scaled Scores	IQ	Sum of Scaled Scores	IQ
5	45	5	39	10	35	·	·
·	·	6	40	11	36	178	156
·	·	7	41	12	37	179	157
·	·	8	43	13	38	180	157
95	156	·	·	14	38	181	158
		·	·	15	39	182	159
		·	·	16	40	183	160
		92	157	17	40	184	160
		93	158	18	41	185	161
		94	160	19	42	186	162
		95	161	20	43	187	162
				21	43	188	163
				22	44	189	164
				·	·	190	165
				·	·		

Note. WPPSI regression equations:

$$\text{Verbal IQ} = 38.3946 + 1.2366 \text{ (scaled score)}$$
$$\text{Performance IQ} = 31.7940 + 1.3624 \text{ (scaled score)}$$
$$\text{Full Scale IQ} = 28.17 + .72 \text{ (scaled score)}$$

[a]This column reprinted by permission of the publishers and author from:
A. B. Silverstein, "WISC and WPPSI IQs for the Gifted," *Psychological Reports,* 1968, *22,* 1168. Copyright 1968 Psychological Reports. "WPPSI IQs for the Mentally Retarded," *American Journal of Mental Deficiency, 73,* p. 446. Copyright 1968, American Association on Mental Deficiency.

TABLE C-20.   Probability of Obtaining Designated Differences Between Individual WPPSI Verbal and Performance IQs

Probability of Obtaining Given or Greater Discrepancy by Chance	Age Level					
	4	4½	5	5½	6	6½
.50	3.8	3.7	3.5	3.3	3.3	3.7
.25	6.6	6.2	6.0	5.6	5.6	6.2
.20	7.3	6.9	6.7	6.2	6.2	7.0
.10	9.4	8.9	8.6	8.0	8.0	8.9
.05	11.2	10.6	10.3	9.5	9.5	10.7
.02	13.3	12.6	12.2	11.3	11.3	12.6
.01	14.7	13.9	13.5	12.5	12.5	14.0
.001	18.8	17.9	17.3	16.1	16.0	17.9

Note. Table C-20 is entered in the column appropriate to the examinee's age. The discrepancy that is just less than the discrepancy obtained by the examinee is located. The entry in the same row, first column, gives the probability of obtaining a given or greater discrepancy by chance. For example, the hypothesis that a 4-year-old examinee obtained a Verbal-Performance discrepancy of 17 by chance can be rejected at the .01 level of significance. Table C-20 is two-tailed. See Chapter 11, Exhibit 11-2 for an explanation of the method used to arrive at magnitude of differences.

TABLE C-21.   Percentage of Population Obtaining Discrepancies Between WPPSI Verbal and Performance IQs

% in Population Obtaining Given or Greater Discrepancy	Age Level					
	4	4½	5	5½	6	6½
50	8.1	8.6	8.7	8.2	7.7	8.8
25	13.8	14.7	14.8	14.0	13.1	15.0
20	15.4	16.3	16.5	15.6	14.7	16.8
10	19.7	21.0	21.2	20.0	18.8	21.5
5	23.5	25.0	25.3	23.9	22.4	25.6
2	27.9	29.6	30.0	28.3	26.6	30.4
1	30.9	32.8	33.2	31.4	29.4	33.7
.1	39.6	42.0	42.6	40.2	37.7	43.2

Note. Table C-21 is entered in the column appropriate to the examinee's age. The discrepancy that is just less than the one obtained by the examinee is located. The entry in the same row, first column, gives the percentage of the standardization population obtaining discrepancies as large or larger than the located discrepancy. For example, a 4-year-old examinee with a Verbal-Performance discrepancy of 15 will be found in between 20 and 25% of the standardization population. See Table C-11 for an explanation of the method used to arrive at magnitude of differences.

TABLE C-22.   Validity Coefficients of Proposed WPPSI Short Forms

Dyad		Triad		Tetrad		Pentad	
Short Form	r	Short Form	r	Short Form	r	Short Form	r
I BD	.835	I A PC	.878	I V GD BD	.906	V A S PC GD	.923
I GD	.833	I A MA	.878	I C MA BD	.904	I A C PC MA	.923
I A	.830	A C PC	.877	V A PC GD	.904	V A C PC GD	.923
V A	.828	I V GD	.877	A C PC GD	.904	I V A PC GD	.922
I MA	.828	V A PC	.876	I C GD BD	.904	I A C PC GD	.922
A PC	.828	V A GD	.876	I A PC GD	.904	I A S PC GD	.922
I PC	.823	V A MA	.875	I V A MA	.903	I V A MA BD	.921
A C	.822	A C MA	.875	I A C MA	.903	I V A MA GD	.921
V BD	.822	I V BD	.875	A C PC MA	.903	V A C PC MA	.921
V GD	.820	I C GD	.875	I V MA BD	.903	V A C MA BD	.921

Note. Abbreviations: I = Information; V = Vocabulary; A = Arithmetic; S = Similarities; C = Comprehension; AH = Animal House; PC = Picture Completion; MA = Mazes; GD = Geometric Design; BD = Block Design.

Reprinted by permission of the publisher and author from A. B. Silverstein, "Reappraisal of the Validity of WAIS, WISC, and WPPSI Short Forms," *Journal of Consulting and Clinical Psychology, 34,* p. 13. Copyright 1970, American Psychological Association.

TABLE C-23.   Yudin's Abbreviated Procedure for the WPPSI as Modified by Silverstein

Subtest	Item Used	Multiply Score by
Information	Every 3rd	3
Vocabulary	Every 3rd	3
Arithmetic	Odd only	2
Similarities	Odd only	2
Comprehension	Odd only	2
Animal House	Unchanged	1
Picture Completion	Every 3rd	3
Mazes	Odd only	2
Geometric Design	Odd only	2
Block Design	Odd only	2

Adapted from Silverstein (1968a).

TABLE C-24.   WPPSI Structure of Intellect Classifications

INFORMATION

Items 1, 2, 3, 6	MMU	Memory for Semantic Units	the ability to remember isolated ideas or word meanings
Items 4, 5, 8, 14	MMR	Memory for Semantic Relations	the ability to remember meaningful connections between items of verbal information
	EMR	Evaluation of Semantic Relations	the ability to make choices among semantic relationships based on the similarity and consistency of the meanings
Items 7, 12, 20, 21	CMU	Cognition of Semantic Units	the ability to comprehend the meanings of words or ideas
Item 9	MMR	Memory for Semantic Relations	the ability to remember meaningful connections between items of verbal information
	CMU	Cognition of Semantic Units	the ability to comprehend the meanings of words or ideas
Item 10	MFU	Memory for Figural Units	the ability to remember given figural objects
	CFS	Cognition of Figural Systems	the ability to comprehend arrangements and positions of visual objects in space
Item 11	EFU	Evaluation of Figural Units	the ability to judge units of figural information as being similar or different
Item 13	CFR	Cognition of Figural Relations	the ability to recognize figural relations between forms
	MMU	Memory for Semantic Units	the ability to remember isolated ideas or word meanings
Items 15, 17, 19	EMR	Evaluation of Semantic Relations	the ability to make choices among semantic relationships based on the similarity and consistency of the meanings
Items 16, 18, 22	MSS	Memory for Symbolic Systems	the ability to remember the order of symbolic information
Item 23	MMR	Memory for Semantic Relations	the ability to remember meaningful connections between items of verbal information

VOCABULARY

Every item	CMU	Cognition of Semantic Units	the ability to comprehend the meaning of words or ideas

ARITHMETIC

Items 1 to 4	EFR	Evaluation of Figural Relations	the ability to choose a form based on the evaluation of what the relations are between the figures or forms in the sequence

TABLE C-24   (cont.)

ARITHMETIC (cont.)

Items 5 to 8	MSU	Memory for Symbolic Units	the ability to remember isolated items of symbolic information, such as syllables and words
Items 9 to 20	MSI	Memory for Symbolic Implications	the ability to remember arbitrary connections between symbols
	CMS	Cognition of Semantic Systems	the ability to comprehend relatively complex ideas

SIMILARITIES

Items 1 to 5	EMR	Evaluation of Semantic Relations	the ability to make choices among semantic relationships based on the similarity and consistency of the meanings
	NMS	Convergent Production of Semantic Systems	the ability to order information into a verbally meaningful sequence
Items 6, 8, 10	EMR	Evaluation of Semantic Relations	the ability to make choices among semantic relationships based on the similarity and consistency of the meanings
	CMT	Cognition of Semantic Transformation	the ability to see potential changes of interpretations of objects and situations
Items 7, 9	NMS	Convergent Production of Semantic Systems	the ability to order information into a verbally meaningful sequence
	EMR	Evaluation of Semantic Relations	the ability to make choices among semantic relationships based on the similarity and consistency of the meanings
Items 11 to 16	CMT	Cognition of Semantic Transformation	the ability to see potential changes of interpretations of objects and situations

COMPREHENSION

Every item	EMI	Evaluation of Semantic Implications	the ability to judge the adequacy of a meaningful deduction

SENTENCES

Every item	MMS	Memory for Semantic Systems	the ability to remember ordered verbal information

ANIMAL HOUSE

Every item	NFU	Convergent Production of Figural Units	the ability to reproduce correctly a form
	EFU	Evaluation of Figural Units	the ability to judge units of figural information as being similar or different

TABLE C-24   (cont.)

PICTURE COMPLETION

| Every item | CFU | Cognition of Figural Units | the ability to perceive or recognize figural entities |
| | EFS | Evaluation of Figural Systems | the ability to evaluate a system of figural units which have been grouped in some manner |

MAZES

| Every item | CFI | Cognition of Figural Implications | the ability to foresee the consequences involved in figural problems |

GEOMETRIC DESIGN

| Every item | NFU | Convergent Production of Figural Units | the ability to reproduce correctly a form |

BLOCK DESIGN

Every item	CFR	Cognition of Figural Relations	the ability to recognize figural relations between forms
	EFR	Evaluation of Figural Relations	the ability to choose a form based on the evaluation of what the relations are between the figures or forms in the sequence
	NFR	Convergent Production of Figural Relations	the ability to reproduce correct relationships between forms

Note. WPPSI SOI designations obtained from M. Meeker at the SOI Institute. Templates and SOI profile forms as well as five workbooks and modules for training with accompanying prescriptions based on SOI templates are available from the SOI Institute, 343 Richmond, El Segundo, CA 90245.

TABLE C-25. Interpretative Rationales and Implications of High and Low Scores for WPPSI Subtests

Ability[a]	Background Factors	Possible Implications of High Scores	Possible Implications of Low Scores
INFORMATION			
Verbal comprehension	Natural endowment	Good range of information	Poor range of information
Range of knowledge	Richness of early environment	Good memory	Poor memory
Long range memory	Extent of pre-schooling	Enriched background	Tendency to give up easily
	Cultural predilections	Alertness and interest in the environment	Foreign background
	Interests	Intellectual ambitiousness	Low achievement orientation
		Intellectual curiosity	
		Urge to collect knowledge	
VOCABULARY			
Verbal comprehension	Education	Good verbal comprehension	Poor verbal comprehension
Language development	Cultural opportunities	Good family or cultural background	Limited educational or family background
Learning ability		Good pre-schooling	Difficulty in verbalization
Fund of information		Ability to conceptualize	Foreign language background
Richness of ideas		Intellectual striving	Verbalization not encouraged in culture
Memory			
Concept formation			
Expressive ability			
Verbal fluency			
Word knowledge			
ARITHMETIC			
Verbal comprehension	Opportunity to acquire fundamental arithmetic processes	Facility in mental arithmetic	Inadequate ability in mental arithmetic
Numerical reasoning ability		Good concentration	Poor concentration
Mental computation		Ability to focus attention	Distractibility
Application of basic arithmetical processes			Blocking toward mathematical tasks
Concentration			
Attention			
Memory			
Nonverbal reasoning ability			
Quantitative concepts			

TABLE C-25 (cont.)

Ability[a]	Background Factors	Possible Implications of High Scores	Possible Implications of Low Scores
SIMILARITIES			
Verbal comprehension	A minimum of cultural oppor-	Good conceptual thinking (e.g.,	Poor conceptual thinking (e.g.,
Logical thinking (items 1–10)	tunities	ability to select and verbalize	difficulty in selecting and
Verbal concept formation	Interests	appropriate relationships	verbalizing appropriate rela-
(items 11–16)		between two objects or con-	tionships between two objects
Abstract and concrete reason-		cepts)	or concepts)
ing abilities		Flexibility of thought processes	Overly concrete mode of think-
Capacity for associative think-			ing
ing (items 11–16)			Rigidity of thought processes
Ability to separate essential			Negativism
from nonessential details			
Memory			
Reasoning by analogy			
COMPREHENSION			
Verbal comprehension	Extensiveness of cultural	Good social judgment	Poor social judgment
Social judgment	opportunities	Knowledge of rules of conven-	Failure to take personal respon-
Linguistic skill	Ability to evaluate and use	tional behavior	sibility (e.g., overdependency,
Logical reasoning	past experience	Ability to organize knowledge	immaturity, limited involve-
Common sense	Development of conscience	Social maturity	ment with others)
Use of practical knowledge	or moral sense	Ability to verbalize well	Overly concrete thinking
and judgment in social		Wide experience	Difficulty in expressing ideas
situations			verbally
Knowledge of conventional			
standards of behavior			
Ability to evaluate past			
experience			
Moral and ethical judgment			

TABLE C-25 (cont.)

Ability[a]	Background Factors	Possible Implications of High Scores	Possible Implications of Low Scores
		SENTENCES	
Verbal comprehension Short-term memory Rote memory Immediate auditory memory Attention Concentration Auditory sequencing Verbal facility	Ability to passively receive stimuli	Good rote memory Good immediate recall ability Ability to attend well in a testing situation	Anxiety Inattention Distractibility Difficulty in auditory sequencing
		ANIMAL HOUSE	
Perceptual organization Attention Goal awareness Concentration Finger and manual dexterity Learning ability	Rate of motor activity	Visual-motor dexterity Good concentration Sustained energy or persistence Ability to learn new material associatively and reproduce it with speed and accuracy Good motivation or desire for achievement	Visual-motor coordination difficulties Distractibility Visual defects Lethargy
		PICTURE COMPLETION	
Perceptual organization Ability to differentiate essential from nonessential details Identification of familiar objects (visual recognition) Concentration on visually perceived material Alertness to detail Reasoning Visual organization Visual perception (closure) Visual memory	Experiences Alertness to environment	Good perception and concentration Good alertness to details Ability to establish a learning set quickly	Anxiety affecting concentration and attention Preoccupation with irrelevant details Negativism ("nothing is missing")

TABLE C-25 (cont.)

Ability[a]	Background Factors	Possible Implications of High Scores	Possible Implications of Low Scores
MAZES			
Perceptual organization Planning ability Foresight Visual-motor control	Visual-motor organization	Good perceptual organization Planning efficiency Speed and accuracy Ability to follow instructions	Poor visual-motor organization Poor planning efficiency Difficulty in delaying action
BLOCK DESIGN			
Perceptual organization Visual-motor coordination Spatial visualization Abstract conceptualizing ability Analysis and synthesis	Rate of motor activity Color vision	Good visual-motor-spatial integration Good conceptualizing ability Analyzing and synthesizing ability Speed and accuracy in sizing up a problem Good hand-eye coordination Good nonverbal reasoning ability Good trial-and-error methods	Poor visual-motor-spatial integration Visual-perceptual problems
GEOMETRIC DESIGN			
Perceptual organization Perceptual-motor ability Visual-motor organization	Motor ability	Good perceptual-motor ability Good eye-hand coordination	Poor perceptual-motor ability Poor eye-hand coordination Developmental immaturity

Note. For an individual examinee, select the appropriate implication (or implications) listed in the columns only after careful consideration of the entire test protocol and background information.

[a]The first entry under "Ability" is based on factor analytic findings. The other entries in this column are derived from clinical and educational interpretations of the subtest functions.

Adapted, in part, from Blatt and Allison (1968), Freeman (1962), Glasser and Zimmerman (1967), Herman (1968), Kaufman (1975a), Rapaport, Gill, and Schafer (1968), Searls (1975), and Wechsler (1967).

TABLE C-26.   Constants for Converting Wechsler Composite Scores into Deviation Quotients

2 Subtests			3 Subtests			4 Subtests			5 Subtests		
Σr_{jk}	a	b	Σr_{jk}	a	b	Σr_{jk}	a	b	Σr_{jk}	a	b
.78–.92	2.6	48	2.16–2.58	1.8	46	3.95–4.85	1.4	44	6.96–8.83	1.1	45
.66–.77	2.7	46	1.79–2.15	1.9	43	3.21–3.94	1.5	40	5.50–6.95	1.2	40
.54–.65	2.8	44	1.48–1.78	2.0	40	2.60–3.20	1.6	36	4.36–5.49	1.3	35
.44–.53	2.9	42	1.21–1.47	2.1	37	2.09–2.59	1.7	32	3.45–4.35	1.4	30
.35–.43	3.0	40	.97–1.20	2.2	34	1.66–2.08	1.8	28	2.71–3.44	1.5	25
.26–.34	3.1	38	.77– .96	2.3	31	1.29–1.65	1.9	24	2.10–2.70	1.6	20
.19–.25	3.2	36	.59– .76	2.4	28	.98–1.28	2.0	20	1.59–2.09	1.7	15

Reprinted by permission of the publisher and authors from A. Tellegen and P. F. Briggs, "Old Wine in New Skins: Grouping Wechsler Subtests into New Scales," *Journal of Consulting Psychology, 31,* p. 504. Copyright 1967, American Psychological Association.

TABLE C-27.   Estimated WISC-R and WPPSI Full Scale Deviation IQs for Vocabulary plus Block Design Scaled Scores

Vocabulary plus Block Design Scaled Score	Estimated WISC-R Full Scale IQ	Estimated WPPSI Full Scale IQ	Vocabulary plus Block Design Scaled Score	Estimated WISC-R Full Scale IQ	Estimated WPPSI Full Scale IQ
1	45	43	21	103	103
2	48	46	22	106	106
3	51	49	23	109	109
4	54	52	24	112	112
5	56	55	25	115	115
6	59	58	26	117	118
7	62	61	27	120	121
8	65	64	28	123	123
9	68	67	29	126	126
10	71	70	30	129	129
11	74	73	31	132	132
12	77	76	32	135	135
13	80	79	33	138	138
14	83	82	34	141	141
15	85	85	35	144	143
16	88	88	36	146	147
17	91	91	37	149	150
18	94	94	38	152	153
19	97	97	39	155	156
20	100	100	40	158	159

Note. The estimated Deviation IQs were obtained by the procedure recommended by Tellegen and Briggs (1967).

TABLE C-28.   Percentile Ranks and Suggested Qualitative Descriptions for Scaled Scores on WISC-R, WPPSI, and WAIS-R

Scaled Score	Percentile Rank		Qualitative Descriptions	Educational Descriptions
19	99			
18	99		Very superior	Superior
17	99			
16	98	Strengths		
15	95		Superior	
14	91			
13	84		High average	Bright average
12	75			
11	63		Average or Normal	Average
10	50			
9	37			
8	25		Low average	Low average
7	16			
6	9	Weaknesses	Borderline	Slow learner
5	5			
4	2			Educable mentally retarded
3	1		Mentally retarded	
2	1			Trainable mentally retarded
1	1			

TABLE C-29.   Interpretative Rationales, Implications of High and Low Scores, and Instructional Implications for Wechsler Scales and Factor Scores

Ability[a]	Background Factors	Possible Implications of High Scores	Possible Implications of Low Scores	Instructional Implications
		FULL SCALE		
General intelligence Scholastic aptitude Academic aptitude Readiness to master a school curriculum	Natural endowment Richness of early environment Extent of schooling Cultural opportunities Interests Rate of motor activity Persistence Visual-motor organization Alertness	Good general intelligence Good scholastic aptitude Readiness to master a school curriculum	Poor general intelligence Poor scholastic aptitude Not ready to master school curriculum	Focus on language development activities Focus on visual learning activities Develop concept formation skills Reinforce persistence
		VERBAL SCALE		
Verbal comprehension Application of verbal skills and information to the solution of new problems Verbal ability Ability to process verbal information Ability to think with words	Natural endowment Richness of early environment Extent of schooling Cultural opportunities Interests	Good verbal comprehension Good scholastic aptitude Possession of knowledge of the cultural milieu Good concept formation Readiness to master school curriculum Achievement orientation	Poor verbal comprehension Poor scholastic aptitude Inadequate understanding of the cultural milieu Poor concept formation Bilingual background Foreign background Not ready to master school curriculum Poor achievement orientation	Stress language development activities Use verbal enrichment exercises Focus on current events Use exercises involving concept formation

TABLE C-29   (cont.)

Ability[a]	Background Factors	Possible Implications of High Scores	Possible Implications of Low Scores	Instructional Implications
		PERFORMANCE SCALE		
Perceptual organization Ability to think in terms of visual images and manipulate them with fluency, flexibility, and relative speed Ability to interpret or organize visually perceived material against a time limit Nonverbal ability Ability to form relatively abstract concepts and relationships without the use of words	Natural endowment Rate of motor activity Persistence Visual-motor organization Alertness	Good perceptual organization Good alertness to detail Good nonverbal reasoning ability Good persistence Good ability to work quickly and efficiently Good spatial ability	Poor perceptual organization Poor alertness to detail Poor nonverbal reasoning ability Limited persistence Poor ability to work quickly and efficiently Poor spatial ability	Focus on visual learning activities Focus on part-whole relationships Use spatial-visual tasks Encourage trial-and-error activities Reinforce persistence Focus on visual planning activities Improve scanning techniques
		FREEDOM FROM DISTRACTIBILITY		
Ability to attend and concentrate Ability to screen out extraneous influences and sustain attention on relevant aspects of an academic task	Natural endowment Ability to passively receive stimuli	Good attention Good concentration Good ability to screen out extraneous influences	Poor attention Poor concentration Poor ability to screen out extraneous influences	Develop attention skills Develop concentration skills Focus on small, meaningful units of instruction

[a]This column adapted, in part, from Cohen (1959) and Wallbrown (1979).

TABLE C-30.   Suggested Remediation Activities for Combinations of Wechsler Subtests

Subtests	Ability	Activities
Information, Vocabulary, and Comprehension	General knowledge and verbal fluency	(1) Review basic concepts, such as days of the week, months, time, distances, and directions; (2) have children report major current events by referring to pictures and articles from magazines and newspapers; (3) teach similarities and differences of designs, topography, transportation, etc.; (4) have children make a scrapbook of pictures of animals, buildings, etc.; (5) introduce words, dictionary work, abstract words; (6) have children repeat simple stories; (7) have children explain how story characters are feeling and thinking.
Similarities and Vocabulary	Verbal conceptual	(1) Use show and tell games; (2) have children make a scrapbook of classifications, such as of animals, vehicles, and utensils; (3) have children match abstract concepts; (4) have children find commonality in dissimilar objects; (5) review basic concepts such as days of the week, months, time, directions, and distances.
Digit Span, Arithmetic, Picture Completion, and Picture Arrangement	Attention and concentration	(1) Have children arrange cards in a meaningful sequence; (2) have children learn telephone number, address, etc.; (3) use spelling word games; (4) use memory games; (5) have children learn days of week, months of year; (6) use mathematical word problems; (7) use dot-to-dot exercises; (8) have children describe details in pictures; (9) use tracing activities; (10) use tinker toys.
Block Design and Object Assembly	Spatial-visual	(1) Have children identify common objects and discuss details; (2) use guessing games involving description of a person, place, or thing; (3) have children match letters, shapes, numbers, etc.; (4) use jigsaw puzzles; (5) use block building activities.
Coding, Block Design, Object Assembly, Animal House, and Mazes	Visual-motor	(1) Use paper folding activities; (2) use finger painting activities; (3) use dot-to-dot exercises; (4) use scissor cutting exercises; (5) use sky-writing exercises; (6) have children string beads in patterns; (7) use peg board designs; (8) use puzzles (large jigsaw pieces); (9) have children solve a maze; (10) have children follow a moving object with coordinated eye movements; (11) use tracing exercises (e.g., trace hand, geometric forms, and letters); (12) have children make large circles and lines on chalkboard; (13) have children copy from patterns; (14) have children draw from memory.

TABLE C-31. Confidence Intervals for the McCarthy Scales

	Age Level									
	2½ (2-4-16 through 2-8-29)					3 (2-9-0 through 3-2-29)				
	Confidence Level					Confidence Level				
Scale	68%	85%	90%	95%	99%	68%	85%	90%	95%	99%
Verbal	±3	±5	±7	± 6	± 8	±3	±5	±5	± 6	± 8
Perceptual-Performance	±5	±7	±8	± 9	±12	±4	±5	±6	± 7	± 9
Quantitative	±5	±7	±8	±10	±13	±4	±6	±7	± 8	±11
General Cognitive	±4	±6	±7	± 8	±11	±4	±5	±6	± 7	±10
Memory	±5	±7	±8	± 9	±12	±5	±7	±8	±10	±13
Motor	±4	±6	±7	± 8	±10	±4	±6	±7	± 8	±11

	Age Level									
	3½ (3-3-0 through 3-8-29)					4 (3-9-0 through 4-2-29)				
	Confidence Level					Confidence Level				
Scale	68%	85%	90%	95%	99%	68%	85%	90%	95%	99%
Verbal	±3	±4	±5	±5	± 7	±3	±5	±5	± 6	± 8
Perceptual-Performance	±3	±5	±5	±6	± 8	±4	±5	±6	± 7	± 9
Quantitative	±4	±6	±7	±8	±11	±5	±8	±9	±10	±14
General Cognitive	±3	±5	±6	±7	± 9	±5	±7	±8	± 9	±12
Memory	±4	±6	±7	±8	±11	±4	±6	±7	± 8	±10
Motor	±4	±6	±7	±8	±11	±5	±7	±8	± 9	±12

	Age Level									
	4½ (4-3-0 through 4-8-29)					5 (4-9-0 through 5-2-29)				
	Confidence Level					Confidence Level				
Scale	68%	85%	90%	95%	99%	68%	85%	90%	95%	99%
Verbal	±4	±5	±6	± 7	± 9	±4	±5	±6	± 7	± 9
Perceptual-Performance	±3	±5	±5	± 6	± 9	±4	±5	±6	± 7	±10
Quantitative	±5	±7	±8	± 9	±12	±4	±5	±6	± 7	±10
General Cognitive	±4	±5	±6	± 7	±10	±4	±6	±7	± 8	±10
Memory	±5	±7	±8	±10	±13	±5	±7	±8	±10	±13
Motor	±4	±6	±7	± 8	±11	±4	±6	±7	± 8	±11

TABLE C-31   (cont.)

	Age Level									
	5½ (5-3-0 through 5-11-29)					6½ (6-0-0 through 6-11-29)				
	Confidence Level					Confidence Level				
Scale	68%	85%	90%	95%	99%	68%	85%	90%	95%	99%
Verbal	±4	±5	±6	±7	±9	±4	±6	±6	±8	±10
Perceptual-Performance	±4	±6	±6	±8	±10	±5	±7	±8	±9	±12
Quantitative	±4	±5	±6	±7	±10	±4	±6	±7	±8	±11
General Cognitive	±4	±6	±7	±8	±11	±5	±7	±8	±10	±13
Memory	±5	±8	±9	±10	±14	±4	±6	±7	±8	±10
Motor	±4	±6	±7	±9	±12	±6	±8	±9	±11	±14

	Age Level									
	7½ (7-0-0 through 7-11-29)					8½ (8-0-0 through 8-11-29)				
	Confidence Level					Confidence Level				
Scale	68%	85%	90%	95%	99%	68%	85%	90%	95%	99%
Verbal	±3	±5	±5	±6	±9	±4	±5	±6	±7	±10
Perceptual-Performance	±4	±6	±7	±8	±11	±5	±7	±8	±10	±13
Quantitative	±4	±6	±7	±8	±11	±4	±6	±7	±8	±11
General Cognitive	±4	±6	±6	±8	±10	±4	±6	±7	±9	±12
Memory	±4	±6	±7	±8	±10	±4	±6	±7	±8	±11
Motor	±5	±7	±8	±10	±13	±6	±9	±10	±12	±16

	Age Level				
	Average (Average of 10 age groups)				
	Confidence Level				
Scale	68%	85%	90%	95%	99%
Verbal	±3	±5	±6	±7	±9
Perceptual-Performance	±4	±6	±7	±8	±10
Quantitative	±4	±6	±7	±8	±11
General Cognitive	±4	±6	±7	±8	±11
Memory	±4	±6	±7	±9	±12
Motor	±5	±7	±8	±9	±12

Note. See Table C-1 for an explanation of the method used to arrive at confidence intervals.

TABLE C-32.   Differences Required for Significance When Each McCarthy Scale Index Is Compared to the Mean Scale Index for Any Individual Child

Index	.05	.01
Verbal	8.36	9.97
Perceptual Performance	9.34	11.16
Quantitative	9.87	11.78
Memory	10.22	12.20
Motor	10.57	12.62

Note. See Note in Table C-7 for an explanation of how the deviations were obtained.

TABLE C-33.   Differences Required for Significance When Each Peabody Individual Achievement Test (PIAT) Subtest Is Compared to the Mean Score for Any Individual Child

Subtest	.05	.01
Mathematics	17.68	21.22
Reading Recognition	13.57	16.29
Reading Comprehension	19.02	22.82
Spelling	19.92	23.91
General Information	16.55	19.86

Note. See Note in Table C-7 for an explanation of how the deviations were obtained.
The figures in the table courtesy of A. B. Silverstein.

TABLE C-34. Landmarks of Normal Behavior Development

Age	Motor Behavior	Adaptive Behavior	Language	Personal and Social Behavior
Under 4 weeks	Makes alternating crawling movements Moves head laterally when placed in prone position	Responds to sound of rattle and bell Regards moving objects momentarily	Small, throaty, undifferentiated noises	Quiets when picked up Impassive face
4 weeks	Tonic neck reflex positions predominate Hands fisted Head sags but can hold head erect for a few seconds	Follows moving objects to the midline Shows no interest and drops objects immediately	Beginning vocalization, such as cooing, gurgling, and grunting	Regards face and diminishes activity Responds to speech
16 weeks	Symmetrical postures predominate Holds head balanced Head lifted 90 degrees when prone on forearm	Follows a slowly moving object well Arms activate on sight of dangling object	Laughs aloud Sustained cooing and gurgling	Spontaneous social smile Aware of strange situations
28 weeks	Sits steadily, leaning forward on hands Bounces actively when placed in standing position	One-hand approach and grasp of toy Bangs and shakes rattle Transfers toys	Vocalizes "m-m-m" when crying Makes vowel sounds, such as "ah, ah"	Takes feet to mouth Pats mirror image
40 weeks	Sits alone with good coordination Creeps Pulls self to standing position	Matches two objects at midline Attempts to imitate scribble	Says "da-da" or equivalent Responds to name or nickname	Responds to social play, such as "pat-a-cake" and "peek-a-boo" Feeds self cracker and holds own bottle
52 weeks	Walks with one hand held. Stands alone briefly	Releases cube in cup Tries tower of 2 cubes	Uses expressive jargon Gives a toy on request	Cooperates in dressing "Plays" ball
15 months	Toddles Creeps upstairs	—	Says 3 to 5 words meaningfully Pats pictures in books Shows shoes on request	Points or vocalizes wants Throws objects in play or refusal

TABLE C-34 (cont.)

Age	Motor Behavior	Adaptive Behavior	Language	Personal and Social Behavior
18 months	Walks, seldom falls Hurls ball Walks upstairs with one hand held	Builds a tower of 3 or 4 cubes Scribbles spontaneously and imitates a writing stroke	Says 10 words, including name Identifies one common object on picture card Names ball and carries out two directions, for example "put on table" and "give to mother"	Feeds self in part, spills Pulls toy on string Carries or hugs a special toy, such as a doll
2 years	Runs well, no falling Kicks large ball Goes upstairs and downstairs alone	Builds a tower of 6 or 7 cubes Aligns cubes, imitating train Imitates vertical and circular strokes	Uses 3-word sentences Carries out four simple directions	Pulls on simple garment Domestic mimicry Refers to self by name
3 years	Rides tricycle Jumps from bottom steps Alternates feet going upstairs	Builds tower of 9 or 10 cubes Imitates a 3-cube bridge Copies a circle	Gives sex and full name Uses plurals Describes what is happening in a picture book	Puts on shoes Unbuttons buttons Feeds self well Understands taking turns
4 years	Walks downstairs one step per tread Stands on one foot for 4 to 8 seconds	Copies a cross Repeats 4 digits Counts 3 objects with correct pointing	Names colors, at least one correctly Understands five prepositional directives—"on," "under," "in," "in back of," or "in front of," and "beside"	Washes and dries own face Brushes teeth Plays cooperatively with other children
5 years	Skips, using feet alternatively Usually has complete sphincter control	Copies a square Draws a recognizable man with a head, body, limbs Counts 10 objects accurately	Names the primary colors Names coins: pennies, nickels, dimes Asks meanings of words	Dresses and undresses self Prints a few letters Plays competitive exercise games

Reprinted, with a change in notation, with permission of the publisher and author from S. Chess, "Health Responses, Developmental Disturbances, and Stress or Reactive Disorders: I: Infancy and Childhood." In A. M. Freedman and H. I. Kaplan (Eds.), *Comprehensive Textbook of Psychiatry*, p. 1362, Copyright 1967, Williams & Wilkins, 1967.

TABLE C-35. Standard Scores for the Koppitz Developmental Scoring System

	Chronological age												
Errors	5-0 to 5-5	5-6 to 5-11	6-0 to 6-5	6-6 to 6-11	7-0 to 7-5	7-6 to 7-11	8-0 to 8-5	8-6 to 8-11	9-0 to 9-5	9-6 to 9-11	10-0 to 10-5	10-6 to 10-11	11-0 to 11-11
1	155	138	135	127	122	119	119	112	112	109	107	107	104
2	150	134	130	122	117	114	113	106	105	102	99	98	94
3	146	130	125	118	113	109	107	100	99	95	91	90	83
4	141	125	121	114	108	103	101	94	92	88	83	82	72
5	137	121	116	109	104	98	95	88	85	81	76	73	61
6	132	116	112	105	99	92	89	82	78	74	68	65	51
7	128	112	107	101	95	87	83	76	71	66	60	57	40
8	123	108	103	97	90	82	77	70	65	59	52	48	29
9	119	103	98	92	85	76	71	64	58	52	44	40	19
10	114	99	94	88	81	71	65	58	51	45	36	32	8
11	110	94	89	84	76	66	59	52	44	38	28	23	
12	105	90	85	79	72	60	53	46	37	31	20	15	
13	100	85	80	75	67	55	47	40	30	24	12	7	
14	96	81	75	71	63	50	41	34	24	16	4		
15	91	77	71	67	58	44	35	28	17	9			
16	87	72	66	62	54	39	29	22	10	2			
17	82	68	62	58	49	34	23	16	3				
18	78	63	57	54	45	28	17	10					
19	73	59	53	49	40	23	11	4					
20	69	55	48	45	35	18	5						
21	64	50	44	41	31	12							
22	60	46	39	37	26	7							
23	55	41	35	32	22	1							

Note. These standard scores ($M = 100$, $SD = 15$) are based on a linear transformation of the data obtained from Koppitz's (1975) 1974 normative sample.

Standard scores are useful primarily from 5 to 8 years of age. After the age of 8 years, the low ceiling and the skewed distribution of developmental scores make standard scores not too meaningful.

TABLE C-36.   Definitions of Categories in the Structure of Intellect

OPERATIONS

Major kinds of intellectual activities or processes; things that the organism does with the raw materials of information, information being defined as "that which the organism discriminates."

C   *Cognition.* Immediate discovery, awareness, rediscovery, or recognition of information in various forms; comprehension or understanding.

M   *Memory.* Retention or storage, with some degree of availability, of information in the same form it was committed to storage and in response to the same cues in connection with which it was learned.

D   *Divergent Production.* Generation of information from given information, where the emphasis is on variety and quantity of output from the same source. Likely to involve what has been called *transfer.* This operation is most clearly involved in aptitudes of creative potential.

N   *coNvergent Production.* Generation of information from given information, where the emphasis is on achieving unique or conventionally accepted best outcomes. It is likely that the given (cue) information fully determines the response.

E   *Evaluation.* Reaching decisions or making judgments concerning criterion satisfaction (correctness, suitability, adequacy, desirability, etc.) of information.

CONTENTS

Broad classes or types of information discriminable by the organism.

F   *Figural.* Information in concrete form, as perceived or as recalled, possibly in the form of images. The term "figural" minimally implies figure-ground perceptual organization. Visual spatial information is figural. Different sense modalities may be involved; e.g., visual kinesthetic.

S   *Symbolic.* Information in the form of denotative signs, having no significance in and of themselves, such as letters, numbers, musical notations, codes, and words, when meanings and form are not considered.

M   *seMantic.* Information in the form of meanings to which words commonly become attached, hence most notable in verbal communication but not identical with words. Meaningful pictures also often convey semantic information.

B   *Behavioral.* Information, essentially non-verbal, involved in human interactions where the attitudes, needs, desires, moods, intentions, perceptions, thoughts, etc., of other people and of ourselves are involved.

PRODUCTS

The organization that information takes in the organism's processing of it.

U   *Units.* Relatively segregated or circumscribed items of information having "thing" character. May be close to Gestalt psychology's "figure on a ground."

C   *Classes.* Conceptions underlying sets of items of information grouped by virtue of their common properties.

R   *Relations.* Connections between items of information based on variables or points of contact that apply to them. Relational connections are more meaningful and definable than implications.

S   *Systems.* Organized or structured aggregates of items of information; complexes of interrelated or interacting parts.

T   *Transformations.* Changes of various kinds (redefinition, shifts, or modification) of existing information or in its function.

I   *Implications.* Extrapolations of information, in the form of expectancies, predictions, known or suspected antecedents, concomitants, or consequences. The connection between the given information and that extrapolated is more general and less definable than a relational connection.

TABLE C-37.   Classification Ratings for IQs on Stanford-Binet, Wechsler Scales, and McCarthy Scales

Stanford-Binet		WISC-R, WPPSI, WAIS-R		McCarthy Scales of Children's Abilities	
IQ	Classification	IQ	Classification	GCI	Classification
140–169	Very Superior	130 and above	Very Superior	130 and above	Very Superior
120–139	Superior	120–129	Superior	120–129	Superior
110–119	High Average	110–119	High Average	110–119	Bright Normal
90–109	Normal or Average	90–109	Average	90–109	Average
80–89	Low Average	80–89	Low Average	89–89	Dull Normal
70–79	Borderline Defective	70–79	Borderline	70–79	Borderline
30–69	Mentally Defective	69 and below	Mentally Deficient or Mentally Retarded[a]	69 and below	Mentally Retarded

[a]WISC-R and WPPSI use a classification of Mentally Deficient, whereas WAIS-R uses a classification of Mentally Retarded.
Adapted from Terman and Merrill (1960), Wechsler (1967, 1974, 1981), and McCarthy (1972).

APPENDIX

Highlights of Assessment Measures

Title, Author, and Publisher	Description	Norms/ Reliability/ Validity	Comment
AAMD Adaptive Behavior Scale (ABS) (Nihira, Foster, Shellhaas, & Leland, 1974) American Association on Mental Deficiency	Behavior rating scale for use with institutionalized mentally retarded, emotionally maladjusted, and developmentally disabled individuals. Assesses basic survival skills and maladaptive behaviors. Percentiles are provided. For ages 3-0 to adult. Takes approximately 30 minutes to administer.	Norms are based on institutionalized mentally retarded and are adequate for this population. Interrater reliability satisfactory for survival skill domains but not for maladaptive behavior domains. More information is needed about its validity.	Useful scale for evaluating competencies of institutionalized mentally retarded individuals and other institutionalized individuals. Respondent is attendant, parent, or teacher.
AAMD Adaptive Behavior Scale—Public School Version (ABS-PSV) (Lambert, Windmiller, Cole, & Figueroa, 1975) American Association on Mental Deficiency	Behavior rating scale for use with elementary school children. Similar to ABS, except that some domains eliminated. Percentiles provided. For ages 7 to 13 years. Takes approximately 15 to 30 minutes to administer.	Norm group is limited. Reliability is satisfactory. More information is needed about its validity.	Useful scale for evaluating the competencies of mentally retarded elementary school children. Respondent is teacher or parent.
Abbreviated Symptom Questionnaire (Conners, 1973a)[a]	Ten-item behavior checklist that was developed from the Parent Symptom Questionnaire. Raw scores. For school-aged children. Takes approximately 2 minutes to administer.	No information reported about norm group, reliability, or validity.	Useful quick screening scale for assessing behavior problems of children. Respondent is parent or teacher.
Adaptive Behavior Inventory for Children (ABIC) (Mercer & Lewis, 1978) Psychological Corporation	Behavior rating scale that measures six areas of adaptive behavior: family, peers, community, school, earner/consumer, and self-maintenance. Scaled scores provided for each area and a total score ($M = 50$, $SD = 15$). For ages 5-0 to 11-11 years. Takes approximately 30 minutes to administer.	Norm group is limited. Reliability is satisfactory. More information is needed about its validity.	Useful instrument for evaluating competencies of mentally retarded elementary school children. Respondent is parent.
AML Behavior Rating Scale (Cowen, Trost, Lorion, Dorr, Izzo, Isaacson, 1975)[a]	Eleven-item behavior checklist that is brief and rapid. Contains three measures: acting-out, shyness-timidity-withdrawal, and learning disability. Raw scores. For primary grade children. Takes approximately 2 minutes to administer.	Norm group limited. More information is needed about the scale's reliability and validity.	Useful screening scale for evaluating behavior problems of elementary school children. Respondent is teacher.

Title, Author, and Publisher	Description	Norms/ Reliability/ Validity	Comment
Auditory Discrimination Test (ADT) (Wepman, 1973) Language Research Associates, Inc.	Contains forty word pairs matched for familiarity, length, and phonetic category. Scored on a 5-point scale. For ages 5-0 to 8-0 years. Takes approximately 5 to 10 minutes to administer.	Norm group is limited. Reliability satisfactory. Validity is questionable.	Serves as a rough screening device in assessing discrimination ability.
Balthazar Scales of Adaptive Behavior (Balthazar, 1976) Consulting Psychologists Press, Inc.	Behavior rating scale for use with severely and profoundly mentally retarded individuals. Assesses functional independence and social adaptations. Scores are in percentiles. For ages 5 years to adult. Total time is approximately 90 minutes to administer.	Norms are limited. More information is needed about the scales' reliability and validity.	Useful instrument for measuring competencies of institutionalized mentally retarded individuals. Respondent is attendant.
Bayley Scales of Infant Development (Bayley, 1969) Psychological Corporation	Provides a Mental Developmental Index and a Psychomotor Developmental Index. Both Indexes are standard scores ($M = 100$, $SD = 16$). For ages 2 months to 2-6 years. Takes 45 to 75 minutes to administer.	Norms are excellent. Reliability and validity are satisfactory.	The best measure of infant development available.
Behavior Problem Checklist (Quay & Peterson, 1979)[b]	Behavior checklist with fifty-five items and four subscales: Conduct Problem, Personality Problem, Inadequacy-Immaturity, and Socialized Delinquency. Raw scores. For kindergarten through 6th grade. Takes approximately 5 minutes to administer.	Norm group is limited. Reliability is variable and not satisfactory for one or more of the subscales. Validity is satisfactory.	Useful scale for evaluating behavior problems of children. It is based on a theoretical model of deviancy. Respondent is teacher or parent.
Bender Visual Motor Gestalt Test (Bender, 1938) American Orthopsychiatric Association, Inc.	Consists of nine cards with geometric designs that child copies. Developmental Bender Scoring System provides percentile norms and standard scores ($M = 100$, $SD = 15$). Ages 5-0 through 11-11 on Developmental Bender Scoring System. Takes approximately 5 minutes to administer.	Norm group is limited for Developmental Bender Scoring System. Reliability is minimally satisfactory. Validity is satisfactory when used as a measure of perceptual-motor development.	Useful in evaluating visual-motor abilities.

Title, Author, and Publisher	Description	Norms/ Reliability/ Validity	Comment
Bilingual Syntax Measure and Bilingual Syntax Measure II (Burt, Dulay, & Hernandez, 1976, 1978) Psychological Corporation	Children asked questions about pictures designed to elicit syntactic structures (e.g., plurals, reflexives, and subjunctives) in Spanish and in English. Level of proficiency assigned on a 5-point (or 6-point) scale. For kindergarten through 2nd grade and 3rd through 6th grade. Takes 25 to 30 minutes to administer each form.	No norms. Reliability and validity limited.	Measures limited aspect of language proficiency. Serves as a rough screening measure.
Boehm Test of Basic Concepts (Boehm, 1971) Psychological Corporation	A pictorial multiple-choice test that measures various concepts (direction, amount, and time) considered to be necessary for school achievement. Percentiles available. For kindergarten through 2nd grade. Takes approximately 30 minutes to administer.	Norms are reasonably representative of school systems. Reliability is minimally satisfactory. Validity is satisfactory.	Useful supplementary measure of basic concepts.
Bruininks-Oseretsky Test of Motor Proficiency (Bruininks, 1978) American Guidance Service	Measures gross and fine motor skills with eight subtests. Each subtest provides standard scores ($M = 15$, $SD = 5$). Three composite scores are obtained ($M = 50$, $SD = 10$). For ages 4-6 to 14-6 years. Takes 45 to 60 minutes to administer.	Norm group is excellent. Reliability is satisfactory for Battery Composite score, less satisfactory for Fine and Gross Composites, and unsatisfactory for individual subtests. More information is needed about its validity.	Useful in the assessment of gross and fine motor skills.
Child Behavior Checklist (Achenbach, 1966, 1978; Achenbach & Edelbrock, 1979)[c]	Behavior checklist with 138 items that provides a profile of behavioral deviancy (eight or nine scales) and social competence (three scales). It provides standard scores on each scale ($M = 50$, $SD = 10$). For ages 4-0 to 16-0 years. Takes 30 to 40 minutes to administer.	Norms are limited. Reliability and validity are satisfactory.	Excellent for evaluating behavior problems of children. Based on factor analytic findings. Respondent is parent.
Child Behavior Scale (Lahey, Stempniak, Robinson, & Tyroler, 1978)[d]	Behavior checklist with 110 items and four scales: Conduct Problems, Learning Disabilities, Anxiety-Withdrawal, and Hyperactivity. Raw scores. For grades 4th through 8th. Takes approximately 20 minutes to administer.	Norm group limited. No information about reliability. Validity adequate.	Useful screening instrument to evaluate behavior problems of elementary school children. Respondent is teacher.

Title, Author, and Publisher	Description	Norms/ Reliability/ Validity	Comment
Classroom Adjustment Ratings Scale (CARS) (Lorion, Cowen, & Caldwell, 1975)[e]	Behavior checklist with forty-one items and three scales: Learning Problems, Acting-Out, and Shy-Anxious. Raw scores. For grades 1st through 3rd. Takes 5 to 10 minutes to administer.	Norms limited. No reliability information. Validity adequate.	Useful screening instrument to evaluate behavior problems of young elementary school children. Respondent is teacher.
Classroom Reading Inventory (Silvaroli, 1976) William C. Brown Co.	Measures word reading, paragraph reading, and spelling. Error scores converted to reading levels. For 2nd through 10th grade. Takes 25 to 30 minutes to administer.	No information reported about norm group, reliability, or validity.	Useful screening instrument. Provides information about reading levels, word recognition, and reading comprehension.
Columbia Mental Maturity Scale (CMMS) (Burgemeister, Blum, & Lorge, 1972) Psychological Corporation	Child selects one drawing that is different from the others. Contains ninety-two cards. Measures general reasoning ability. Deviation scores are provided ($M = 100$, $SD = 16$). For ages 3-6 to 9-11 years. Takes 15 to 20 minutes to administer.	Norms are excellent. Reliability and validity are satisfactory.	Serves as a supplementary nonverbal measure of intelligence. May be less culturally loaded than other intelligence tests.
Denver Developmental Screening Test (DDST) (Frankenburg, Dodds, Fradal, Kazuk, & Cohrs, 1975) Ladoca Project and Publishing Foundation, Inc.	Provides information about personal-social, fine motor, language, and gross-motor areas. Scores are pass or delay. For birth to 6 years. Takes approximately 20 minutes to administer.	Norm group limited. More information is needed about its reliability and validity.	A screening instrument with marginal psychometric properties. Caution is needed in using it as a screening instrument.
Detroit Tests of Learning Aptitude (Baker & Leland, 1967) Bobbs-Merrill Co., Inc.	Contains nineteen tests that measure various cognitive, auditory, visual, and motor abilities. Mental ages are provided for each subtest. An IQ can be calculated by ratio method. For ages 3-0 through adult. Takes 60 to 90 minutes to administer.	Inadequate and outdated norms. Reliabilities not reported for subtests. More information is needed about its validity.	Out-of-date test. It should not be used as a primary assessment instrument. Some subtests are helpful as supplementary diagnostic tools.
Developmental Test of Visual Motor Integration (VMI) (Beery, 1967) Follett Publishing Co.	Consists of twenty-four geometric designs that child copies. Age scores are provided. For ages 2-0 through 15 years. Takes approximately 10 minutes to administer.	Norm group is limited. Reliability and validity are satisfactory.	A useful test in evaluating children's visual-motor abilities.

Title, Author, and Publisher	Description	Norms/ Reliability/ Validity	Comment
Developmental Test of Visual Perception (DTVP) (Frostig, Maslow, Lefever, & Whittlesey, 1964) Consulting Psychologists Press, Inc.	Contains five subtests: Eye-Hand Coordination, Figure-Ground Perception, Form Constancy, Position in Space, and Perception of Spatial Relations. A Perceptual Quotient is provided ($Mdn = 100$, $SD = 16$) and perceptual age equivalents. For ages 3-0 to 9-0 years. Takes approximately 40 minutes to administer.	Norm group is not satisfactory. Reliability of Perceptual Quotient is low. Reliabilities of subtests are unsatisfactory. Validity is minimally adequate for Perceptual Quotient.	Serves as a screening instrument to evaluate visual perception, but should not be used as a measure of reading readiness or to predict reading skill.
Devereux Adolescent Behavior Rating Scale (Spivack, Haimes, & Spotts, 1967) The Devereux Foundation	Behavior checklist with eighty-four items that provides a profile of behavior problem areas (twelve behavior factors and three clusters). Standard scores are provided for each scale ($M = 0$, $SD = 1$). For ages 13-0 to 18-0. Takes 10 to 15 minutes to administer.	Norms are limited. Reliability is poor. Validity is satisfactory.	Useful scale for evaluating behavior problems of adolescents. Respondent is attendant or teacher.
Devereux Child Behavior Rating Scale (Spivack & Spotts, 1966) The Devereux Foundation	Behavior checklist with ninety-seven items that provides a profile of behavior competencies (ten scales) and behavior control (seven factors). Standard scores are provided for each scale ($M = 0$, $SD = 1$). For ages 8-0 to 12-0 years. Takes 15 to 20 minutes to administer.	Norms are limited. Reliability and validity are satisfactory.	Useful scale for evaluating behavior problems of elementary school children. Respondent is attendant or parent.
Devereux Elementary School Behavior Rating Scale (Spivack & Swift, 1967) The Devereux Foundation	Behavior checklist with forty-seven items that provides a profile of behavior problem areas (ten behavior competence factors and seven behavior control factors). Standard scores are provided ($M = 0$, $SD = 1$). For kindergarten through 6th grade. Takes 5 to 10 minutes to administer.	Norms are limited. Reliability and validity are satisfactory.	Useful scale for evaluating behavior problems of elementary school children. Respondent is teacher.
Extended Merrill-Palmer Scale (Ball, Merrifield, & Stott, 1978) Stoelting Co.	Sixteen verbal and nonverbal tests grouped into four dimensions: Semantic Production, Figural Production, Semantic Evaluation, and Figural Evaluation. Provides percentile bands. For ages 3-0 to 5-11 years. Takes approximately 1 hour to administer.	Norms not representative of the country. Reliability and validity data are inadequate.	Test has a unique way of organizing abilities. However, it does not provide an overall score or a precise way of evaluating a child's performance. Further research is needed to evaluate its usefulness.

Title, Author, and Publisher	Description	Norms/Reliability/Validity	Comment
Goldman-Fristoe-Woodcock Test of Auditory Discrimination (Goldman, Fristoe, & Woodcock, 1970) American Guidance Service	Measures auditory discrimination under quiet and noisy conditions. Error scores are converted to standard scores ($M = 50$, $SD = 10$). For ages 4 years through adult. Takes 10 to 15 minutes to administer.	Norm group is limited. Reliability is poor. More information is needed about its validity.	A crude measure of auditory discrimination. Its psychometric properties are poor.
Goodenough-Harris Drawing Test (Draw-A-Man) (Harris, 1963) Psychological Corporation	Child is asked to draw a man, woman, and self. Provides a Deviation IQ ($M = 100$, $SD = 15$). For ages 3-0 to 15-11 years. Takes approximately 5 to 15 minutes to administer.	Norms are excellent. Reliability somewhat poor, but validity is satisfactory.	A useful supplementary instrument for measuring cognitive ability. Can be used as a screening instrument. May be less culturally loaded than other intelligence tests.
Halstead Neuropsychological Test Battery (Battery is referred to in Reitan & Davison, 1974) Not available from a commercial publisher.	A battery of cognitive and perceptual-motor tests. Used primarily as a clinical procedure. For ages 9 to 14 years. Takes approximately 4 to 6 hours to administer.	Norms are limited. Little is known about the reliability and validity of the battery.	Useful for the assessment of brain damage.
Health Resources Inventory (Gesten, 1976)[f]	Behavior checklist with fifty-four items and five areas of competence: Good Student, Gutsy, Peer Sociability, Rules, and Frustration Tolerance. Scored on a 5-point scale. For 1st through 6th grades. Takes 5 to 10 minutes to administer.	Norm group limited. Reliability and validity satisfactory.	Useful screening scale for evaluating behavior competencies of elementary school children. More work is needed to evaluate its effectiveness. Respondent is teacher.
Hyperkinesis Rating Scale (Davids, 1971)[g]	Behavior checklist with six items for rating hyperkinesis. Has 6-point rating scale. For school children. Takes 1 to 2 minutes to administer.	No information available about norm group, reliability, or validity.	Useful screening instrument for rating hyperactive behavior, but more work is needed to evaluate its reliability and validity. Respondent is parent or teacher.

Title, Author, and Publisher	Description	Norms/ Reliability/ Validity	Comment
Illinois Test of Psycholinguistic Abilities, Revised Edition (ITPA) (Kirk, McCarthy, & Kirk, 1968) University of Illinois Press	Contains twelve subtests that measure various facets of language ability. Scaled scores are available for each subtest ($M = 35$, $SD = 6$). Ratio method used to compute a psycholinguistic age. For ages 2-4 to 10-3 years. Takes approximately 1 hour to administer.	Norm group is limited. Reliability and validity are satisfactory.	Many subtests are similar to those that appear on intelligence tests. It has limited usefulness in the assessment battery.
Infant Psychological Developmental Scale (Uzgiris & Hunt, 1975) All information needed to administer test contained in text by Uzgiris and Hunt.	Contains eight subscales based on Piagetian theory. Score is the highest number on each scale. For ages 2 weeks to 2 years. Takes approximately 40 to 60 minutes to administer.	Norm group limited. Reliability is satisfactory. More information needed about validity.	A useful addition to the area of infant assessment.
KeyMath Diagnostic Test (Connolly, Natchman, & Pritchett, 1971) American Guidance Service, Inc.	Contains fourteen subtests that measure three areas of arithmetic ability: content, function, and applications. Grade equivalents available. For 1st through 6th grades. Takes approximately 30 minutes to administer.	Excellent norm group. Reliability and validity are satisfactory.	Very useful for the assessment of arithmetic ability of elementary school children.
Kohn Problem Checklist (Kohn, Parnes, & Rosman, 1976)[h]	Behavior checklist with forty-nine items and two dimensions: Apathy-Withdrawal and Anger-Defiance. Standard scores ($M = 0$, $SD = 100$) available. For ages 3-0 to 6-0 years. Takes 10 to 15 minutes to administer.	Norms are limited. Reliability poor. Validity is satisfactory.	Useful screening scale for evaluating behavior problems of preschool children. Respondent is teacher.
Kohn Social Competence Scales (Kohn, Parnes, & Rosman, 1976)[h]	Behavior checklist with sixty-four or seventy-three items and two dimensions: Interest-Participation vs. Apathy-Withdrawal and Cooperation-Compliance vs. Anger-Defiance. Standard scores ($M = 0$, $SD = 100$) are available. For ages 3-0 to 6-0 years. Takes 10 to 15 minutes to administer.	Norms are limited. Reliability is poor. Validity is satisfactory.	Useful screening scale for evaluating the social competence of preschool children. Respondent is teacher.

Title, Author, and Publisher	Description	Norms/ Reliability/ Validity	Comment
Language Assessment Battery (New York City Board of Education) Riverside Publishing Co.	Designed to assess reading, writing, listening comprehension, or speaking in English and Spanish for children in kindergarten through 12th grade. Contains three levels. Percentiles and stanines available by grade level. Time varies by level, from 5 or 10 minutes to approximately 40 minutes.	Norms not representative of the country. Reliability satisfactory. No validity information available.	Measures limited aspects of language proficiency. Serves as a rough screening measure.
Language Assessment Scales (DeAvila & Duncan, 1977) Linguametrics Group	Measures four areas of language in English and in Spanish: phonemic, referential, syntactical, and pragmatic. One form for kindergarten through grade 5; other form for grade 6 and up. No standard scores available. Takes approximately 30 minutes to administer.	Norms are poorly described and extremely limited. Reliability limited for some measures. Validity limited. Scores show no appreciable change as a function of age.	Measures limited aspects of language proficiency. Serves as a rough screening measure.
Leiter International Performance Scale (LIPS) (Leiter, 1948) Stoelting Co.	Age-scale format. Measures intelligence by means of nonverbal items. Ratio method used to compute IQs. For ages 2 years to adult. Takes approximately 30 to 45 minutes to administer.	Norm group poorly described. Reliability and validity satisfactory.	Norms are outdated and standardization is inadequate. It serves as a supplementary measure of intelligence. May be less culturally loaded than other intelligence tests.
Lindamood Auditory Conceptualization Test (LACT) (Lindamood & Lindamood, 1971) Teaching Resources Corporation	One part requires discrimination of individual sounds and the other requires discrimination of longer sound patterns. Raw scores are converted to percentiles for children in kindergarten through 6th grade only. Test reaches a ceiling after 6th grade. For kindergarten through grade 12. Takes 20 to 30 minutes to administer.	Norm group is limited. More information is needed to evaluate its reliability and validity.	Serves as a screening device for the assessment of auditory ability.
McCarthy Scales of Children's Abilities (McCarthy, 1972) Psychological Corporation	Eighteen tests grouped into six scales: Verbal, Perceptual-Performance, Quantitative, Memory, Motor, and General Cognitive. Provides a General Cognitive Index (GCI) ($M = 100$, $SD = 16$). For ages 2-6 to 8-6 years. Takes about 1 hour to administer.	Excellent norms, reliability, and validity.	A useful test. Profile of abilities is an advantage. GCIs may not be interchangeable with Stanford-Binet or WISC-R IQs.

Title, Author, and Publisher	Description	Norms/ Reliability/ Validity	Comment
Merrill-Palmer Scale of Mental Tests (Stutsman, 1931) Stoelting Co.	Thirty-eight verbal and nonverbal tests in 6-month intervals. Ratio method used to compute IQs. For ages 1-6 to 5-11 years. Takes approximately 30 to 40 minutes to administer.	Norms are seriously outdated. Reliability is poor, but validity is satisfactory.	Test provides some information about the cognitive ability of preschool children.
Parent Symptom Questionnaire (Conners, 1973a)[a]	Behavior checklist with ninety-three items that provides eight factor scores covering various areas of behavior problems. Raw scores. For school-aged children. Takes approximately 20 minutes to administer.	Norm group limited. No information about reliability. Validity adequate.	Useful screening scale for evaluating behavior problems of children. Respondent is parent.
Peabody Individual Achievement Test (PIAT) (Dunn & Markwandt, 1970) American Guidance Service	Contains Mathematics, Reading Recognition, Reading Comprehension, Spelling, and General Information subtests. Standard scores are provided ($M = 100$, $SD = 15$). For kindergarten through high school. Takes 30 to 40 minutes to administer.	Norm group is excellent. Reliability and validity are excellent for total score, but less satisfactory for subtests.	A brief, limited screening measure of academic skills. Multiple-choice format for some subtests makes test useful for handicapped children.
Peabody Picture Vocabulary Test—Revised (PPVT-R) (Dunn & Dunn, 1981) American Guidance Service	A nonverbal, multiple-choice test that measures receptive vocabulary. Standard scores ($M = 100$, $SD = 15$) are available. For ages 2-6 through adult. Takes 10 to 15 minutes to administer.	Norm group is excellent. Reliability is marginally satisfactory. Validity is likely to be satisfactory, based on prior edition.	This is a vocabulary test, and should not be used to measure intelligence. Useful as a screening device for measuring extensiveness of vocabulary, particularly for children with expressive difficulties.
Pictorial Test of Intelligence (PTI) (French, 1964) Riverside Press	Contains six subtests: Picture Vocabulary, Form Discrimination, Information and Comprehension, Similarities, Size and Number, and Immediate Recall. Deviation IQs are available ($M = 100$, $SD = 16$). For ages 3-0 to 8-0 years. Takes approximately 45 minutes to administer.	Norms are excellent. Reliability and validity are satisfactory.	Serves as a supplementary nonverbal measure of learning aptitude for young children with motor and speech handicaps.
Preschool Attainment Record (Doll, 1966) American Guidance Service	Behavior rating scale that measures physical, social, and intellectual competencies. Ratio method used to obtain an Attainment Quotient. For ages birth to 7-6 years. Takes 10 to 20 minutes to administer.	Norm group is not described. Reliability and validity satisfactory for total score.	An experimental scale for evaluating the adaptive behavior of young children. It fails to meet acceptable psychometric standards. Respondent is parent.

Title, Author, and Publisher	Description	Norms/ Reliability/ Validity	Comment
Preschool Behavior Questionnaire (Behar & Stringfield, 1974)[j]	Behavior checklist with thirty items and three scales: Hostile-Aggressive, Anxious, and Hyperactive-Distractible. Percentiles available for the three scales and for total score. For preschool children. Takes 5 to 10 minutes to administer.	Norms are limited. Reliability is satisfactory. More information is needed about its validity.	Useful screening device for evaluating behavior problems of preschool children. Respondent is teacher or parent.
Progressive Matrices (Raven, 1938, 1947a, 1947b) Psychological Corporation	Three different forms measuring nonverbal reasoning ability. Task is to discover the missing symbol from matrices that are arranged in increasing order of difficulty. Percentiles are available. For ages 6 years to adult. Takes 15 to 30 minutes to administer.	No norms for U.S. children. Reliability and validity are satisfactory.	Main limitation is that it measures cognitive ability through one process—figural reasoning. Norms are needed for U.S. children (and adults). A useful supplementary measure of nonverbal reasoning ability. It may be less culturally loaded than other intelligence tests.
Purdue Pegboard (Tiffin, 1948) Science Research Associates	A manual dexterity task that measures fine motor coordination. Percentile norms are available (see Gardner, 1979). For ages 5 years through adult. Takes 2 minutes to administer.	Norms are limited. No information about reliability and validity.	Useful measure of fine motor coordination and laterality.
Purdue Perceptual-Motor Survey (Roach & Kephart, 1966) Charles E. Merrill Publishing Co.	Consists of twenty-two items divided into areas of laterality, perceptual-motor matching, and directionality. Scores are assigned on the basis of qualitative judgments (primarily an ordinal scale). For 2nd through 4th grades. Takes 10 to 15 minutes to administer.	Norm group is poor. More information is needed about its reliability and validity.	A supplementary method for evaluating perceptual and motor behavior.
Quick Test (Ammons & Ammons, 1962) Psychological Test Specialists	A nonverbal multiple-choice test that measures receptive vocabulary. Provides mental-age scores. Ratio method used to compute IQs. For ages 2-0 years to adult. Takes 3 to 10 minutes to administer.	Norm group is limited. Reliability and validity are satisfactory.	This is a vocabulary test, and should not be used to measure intelligence. Useful as a screening device for measuring extensiveness of vocabulary, particularly for children with expressive difficulties.

Title, Author, and Publisher	Description	Norms/ Reliability/ Validity	Comment
Reitan-Indiana Neuro-psychological Test Battery for Children (Battery is referred to in Reitan & Davison, 1974) Not available from a commercial publisher.	A battery of cognitive and perceptual-motor tests. Used primarily as a clinical procedure. For ages 5 to 8 years. Takes approximately 4 to 6 hours to administer.	Norms are limited. Little is known about the reliability and validity of the battery.	Useful for the assessment of brain damage.
Revised Visual Retention Test (Benton, 1963) Psychological Corporation	Consists of three forms, with ten geometric designs on each form, that child copies directly and draws from memory. Standard scores available ($M = 100$, $SD = 15$) for ages 5 through 11 (see Rice, 1972). Takes 10 to 15 minutes to administer.	Norms are limited. More information is needed about its reliability and validity.	Useful in evaluating visual-motor ability and visual memory.
San Diego Quick Assessment (LaPray & Ross, 1969)[a]	Consists of graded word lists. Error scores. For preprimer through 11th grade. Takes approximately 5 minutes to administer.	No information reported about norm group, reliability, or validity.	A screening measure of reading skill.
Slosson Intelligence Test (SIT) (Slosson, 1963) Slosson Educational Publications, Inc.	Age-scale format. Items are similar to those on the Gessell and Stanford-Binet. Ratio method used to compute IQs. For ages .5 months to 27 years. Takes 10 to 30 minutes to administer.	No norms are described. Reliability and validity are satisfactory.	Test is poorly standardized and does not use a satisfactory method of computing IQs. It may serve as a screening device.
Southern California Sensory Integration Tests (Ayres, 1972) Western Psychological Services	Contains seventeen tests that measure four areas of perceptual and perceptual-motor functioning: form and space perception, postural and bilateral integration, tactile perception, and motor skills. Raw scores are converted to standard scores ($M = 0$, $SD = 1$). For ages 4 through 8 years. Takes 75 to 90 minutes to administer.	Norm group is limited. Reliabilities are poor. No validity data reported in manual.	For those knowledgeable about perceptual and perceptual-motor areas, the battery may serve as a rough screening guide. Its psychometric properties are poor.
Stanford-Binet Intelligence Scale (SB) (Terman & Merrill, 1960) Riverside Publishing Co.	Primarily a global measure of intelligence. Provides a mental age and a Deviation IQ ($M = 100$, $SD = 16$). For ages 2 years through adult. Takes approximately 1 hour to administer.	Excellent norms, reliability, and validity.	One of the best intelligence tests available.

Title, Author, and Publisher	Description	Norms/ Reliability/ Validity	Comment
Sucher-Allred Reading Placement Inventory (Sucher & Allred, 1973) Economy Company	Contains a Word-Recognition Test and an Oral Reading Test. Identifies three levels of reading proficiency. Error scores converted to reading levels. For primer through 9th grades. Takes approximately 20 minutes to administer.	No information reported about norm group, reliability, or validity.	A screening measure of reading skill.
System of Multicultural Pluralistic Assessment (SOMPA) (Mercer & Lewis, 1978) Psychological Corporation	Incorporates medical, social, and pluralistic information in the assessment of cognitive, perceptual-motor, and adaptive behavior. Standard scores ($M = 50$, $SD = 15$) are provided for the Bender-Gestalt. An estimated learning potential (ELP) score is obtained from the WISC-R based on sociocultural variables. For ages 5-0 to 11-11 years. Takes approximately 5 hours to administer.	Norm group is limited. Reliability is generally satisfactory. Validity has not been established for use of the ELP.	There is no evidence that SOMPA provides nonbiased assessment measures. The use of ELP in any decision-making situation is not justified, unless there is research to support its use.
Teacher Behavioral Description Form (Seidman, Linney, Rappaport, Herzberger, Kramer, & Alden, 1979)[i]	Behavior checklist with twenty-three items and three scales: Anxiety-Withdrawal, Attention Getting—Aggressive, and "Ideal" Student Behavior. Has 3-point rating scale. For 1st and 2nd grades. Takes approximately 5 to 10 minutes to administer.	Norm group limited. Reliability poor. Validity satisfactory.	Useful screening instrument to evaluate behavior problems of young elementary school children. Respondent is teacher.
Teacher Questionnaire (Conners, 1973a)[a]	Behavior checklist with thirty-nine items and four scales: Conduct Problem, Inattentive Passive, Tension-Anxiety, and Hyperactivity. Raw scores. For school children. Takes approximately 10 to 15 minutes to administer.	Norm group limited. No information available about reliability. Validity adequate.	Useful screening instrument to evaluate behavior problems of children. Respondent is teacher.
T.M.R. School Competency Scales (Levine, Elzey, Thormahlen, & Cain, 1976) Consulting Psychologists Press	Behavior rating scale for use with trainable mentally retarded in a school setting. Measures perceptual-motor, initiative-responsibility, cognition, personal-social, and language areas. Percentiles are provided for each scale and total score. For ages 5 years and over. Takes 20 to 30 minutes to administer.	Norm group limited. Reliability is satisfactory. No information given about its validity.	Usefulness is limited because manual fails to provide any validity data. Respondent is teacher.

Title, Author, and Publisher	Description	Norms/ Reliability/ Validity	Comment
Token Test for Children (DiSimoni, 1978) Teaching Resources Corporation	Test employs auditory commands that require child to manipulate tokens varying along three dimensions—color, shape, and size. Standard scores are available ($M = 500$, $SD = 5$). For ages 3-0 to 12-5 years. Takes 10 to 15 minutes to administer.	Norms are limited. More information is needed about its reliability and validity.	Useful as a screening measure to assess auditory comprehension, especially in identifying mild receptive disturbances in aphasic individuals.
Vineland Social Maturity Scale (Doll, 1953) American Guidance Service	Behavior rating scale that measures various competencies, including self-help, self-direction, occupation, communication, and locomotion. Ratio method used to obtain a Social Quotient. For ages birth to 25 years. Takes 20 to 30 minutes to administer.	Norm group is limited and out of date. Reliability and validity appear to be satisfactory, but more information is needed about these factors.	Useful scale for measuring competencies of children and adults. It has inadequate psychometric properties. Respondent usually is parent.
Visual Aural Digit Span Test (VADS) (Koppitz, 1977) Grune and Stratton, Inc.	Contains four subtests that measure short-term memory: Aural-Oral, Visual-Oral, Aural-Written, and Visual-Written. Percentile scores are provided. For ages 5-6 to 12-11 years. Takes approximately 10 minutes to administer.	Norm group is satisfactory. More research is needed about its reliability and validity.	The range of scores is extremely limited, making the test scores difficult to interpret. Its place in the assessment battery is questionable.
Wechsler Intelligence Scale for Children—Revised (WISC-R) (Wechsler, 1974) Psychological Corporation	Twelve subtests grouped into a Verbal Scale and a Performance Scale. Provides subtest standard scores ($M = 10$, $SD = 3$) and Deviation IQs ($M = 100$, $SD = 15$). For ages 6-0 through 16-11 years. Takes approximately 1 hour to administer.	Excellent norms, reliability, and validity.	One of the best intelligence tests available.
Wechsler Preschool and Primary Scale of Intelligence (WPPSI) (Wechsler, 1967) Psychological Corporation	Eleven subtests grouped into a Verbal Scale and a Performance Scale. Provides subtest standard scores ($M = 10$, $SD = 3$) and Deviation IQs ($M = 100$, $SD = 15$). For ages 4-0 to 6-6 years. Takes approximately 1 hour to administer.	Excellent norms, reliability, and validity.	One of the best intelligence tests available.
Wide Range Achievement Test (WRAT) (Jastak & Jastak, 1978) Guidance Associates of Delaware, Inc.	Contains Reading, Spelling, and Arithmetic subtests. Standard scores are available ($M = 100$, $SD = 15$). For ages 5-0 to 64-11 years. Takes 20 to 30 minutes to administer.	Norm group is not representative of the population. Reliability and validity are satisfactory.	A brief, limited screening instrument of academic skills.

Title, Author, and Publisher	Description	Norms/ Reliability/ Validity	Comment
Woodcock-Johnson Psycho-Educational Battery (Woodcock, 1977) Teaching Resources Corporation	Contains twenty-seven tests that cover assessment of cognitive ability, achievement, and interest. Not all areas are tested at every age. Standard scores can be obtained ($M = 100$, $SD = 15$). For ages 3 years through adult. Takes approximately 2 hours to administer.	Norm group is excellent. Reliability and validity are satisfactory.	Manual fails to present standard errors of measurement for each subtest and scale, which impedes profile analysis. Cognitive ability scores may not be interchangeable with WISC-R IQs for learning-disabled children.
Woodcock Reading Mastery Tests (Woodcock, 1973) American Guidance Service	Contains five reading tests: Letter Identification, Word Identification, Word Attack, Word Comprehension, and Passage Comprehension. Raw scores converted to grade scores, age scores, percentile ranks, and standard scores ($M = 50$, $SD = 10$). For kindergarten through grade 12. Takes 20 to 30 minutes to administer.	Excellent norm group. Reliability is satisfactory for most subtests. More information is needed about validity.	Useful in evaluating reading skills.

Note. Appendix A lists addresses of the test publishers.

[a] Scale is reproduced in journal publication.

[b] Behavior Problem Checklist can be obtained from Donald R. Peterson, 39 North Fifth Avenue, Highland Park, New Jersey 08904.

[c] Child Behavior Checklist can be obtained from Thomas M. Achenbach, Department of Child Psychiatry, University of Vermont, Burlington, Vermont 05405.

[d] Child Behavior Scale can be obtained from Benjamin B. Lahey, Department of Psychology, University of Georgia, Athens, Georgia 30601.

[e] Checklist is reproduced in Chapter 17 (Table 17-4). Norm tables available from Emory L. Cowen, Department of Psychology, University of Rochester, Rochester, New York 14627.

[f] Checklist is reproduced in Chapter 17 (Table 17-6).

[g] Checklist is reproduced in Chapter 17 (Table 17-7).

[h] The Kohn Problem Checklist and the Kohn Social Competence Scale may be obtained by contacting Martin Kohn, The William Alanson White Institute, 20 West 74th Street, New York, New York 10023.

[i] Checklist is reproduced in Chapter 17 (Table 17-5).

[j] Teacher Behavioral Description Form can be obtained from Edward Seidman, Department of Psychology, University of Illinois, Champaign, Illinois 61820.

APPENDIX E

Ethical Principles of Psychologists

Psychologists respect the dignity and worth of the individual and honor the preservation and protection of fundamental human rights. They are committed to increasing knowledge of human behavior and of people's understanding of themselves and others and to the utilization of such knowledge for the promotion of human welfare. While pursuing these endeavors, they make every effort to protect the welfare of those who seek their services or of any human being or animal that may be the object of study. They use their skills only for purposes consistent with these values and do not knowingly permit their misuse by others. While demanding for themselves freedom of inquiry and communication, psychologists accept the responsibility this freedom requires: competence, objectivity in the application of skills and concern for the best interests of clients, colleagues, and society in general. In the pursuit of these ideals, psychologists subscribe to principles in the following areas: 1) Responsibility; 2) Competence; 3) Moral and Legal Standards; 4) Public Statements; 5) Confidentiality; 6) Welfare of the Consumer; 7) Professional Relationships; 8) Assessment Techniques; and 9) Research Activities.

Principle 1: Responsibility

In their commitment to the understanding of human behavior, psychologists value objectivity and integrity, and in providing services they maintain the highest standards of their profession. They accept responsibility for the consequences of their work and make every effort to insure that their services are used appropriately.

a. As scientists, psychologists accept the ultimate responsibility for selecting appropriate areas and methods most relevant to these areas. They plan their research in ways to minimize the possibility that their findings will be misleading. They provide thorough discussion of the limitations of their data and alternative hypotheses, especially where their work touches on social policy or might be construed to be detrimental to persons in specific age, sex, ethnic, socioeconomic or other social

---

Reprinted by permission of the publisher. Copyrighted by the American Psychological Association, Inc., 1977. These principles incorporate the proposed amendments that appeared in the *APA Monitor*, 1979, *10*(11), 15–18.

These ethical principles apply to psychologists, to students of psychology, and to others who do work of a psychological nature under the supervision of a psychologist.

623

groups. In publishing reports of their work, they never suppress disconfirming data. Psychologists take credit only for the work they have actually done.

Psychologists clarify in advance with all appropriate persons or agencies the expectations for sharing and utilizing research data. They avoid dual relationships which may limit objectivity, whether political or monetary, so that interference with data, human participants, and milieu is kept to a minimum.

b. As employees of an institution or agency, psychologists have the responsibility of remaining alert to and attempting to moderate institutional pressures that may distort reports of psychological findings or impede their proper use.

c. As members of governmental or other organizational bodies, psychologists remain accountable as individuals to the highest standards of their profession. When the demands of an employer require activities which are in conflict with these ethical principles, psychologists inform their employer of the ethical principles involved and attempt to effect changes within their organization by constructive action while declining to violate these ethical principles.

d. As teachers, psychologists recognize their primary obligation to help others acquire knowledge and skill. They maintain high standards of scholarship and objectivity by presenting psychological information fully and accurately.

e. As practitioners, psychologists know that they bear a heavy social responsibility because their recommendations and professional actions may alter the lives of others. They are alert to personal, social, organizational, financial, or political situations or pressures that might lead to misuse of their influence.

Principle 2: Competence

The maintenance of high standards of professional competence is a responsibility shared by all psychologists in the interest of the public and the profession as a whole. Psychologists recognize the boundaries of their competence and the limitations of their techniques and only provide services, and use techniques that meet recognized standards for which they are qualified by training and experience. In those areas in which recognized standards do not yet exist, psychologists take whatever precautions are necessary to protect the welfare of their clients. Psychologists

maintain knowledge of current scientific and professional information related to the services they render.

a. Psychologists accurately represent their competence, education, training and experience. Psychologists claim as evidence of professional qualifications only those degrees obtained from institutions acceptable under the Bylaws and Rules of Council of the American Psychological Association.

b. As teachers, psychologists perform their duties on the basis of careful preparation so that their instruction is accurate, current and scholarly.

c. Psychologists recognize the need for continuing education and are open to new procedures and changes in expectations and values over time. They recognize differences among people, such as those that may be associated with age, sex, socioeconomic, and ethnic backgrounds. Where relevant, they obtain training, experience, or counsel to assure competent service or research relating to such persons.

d. Psychologists with the responsibility for decisions involving individuals or policies based on test results have an understanding of psychological or educational measurement, validation problems and other test research.

e. Psychologists recognize that personal problems and conflicts may interfere with professional effectiveness. Accordingly, they refrain from undertaking activities in which a personal problem may lead to inadequate professional services or harm to a client. If psychologists become aware of such a personal problem, they seek competent professional assistance to determine whether they should suspend, terminate or limit the scope of their professional and/or scientific activities.

Principle 3: Moral and Legal Standards

Psychologists' moral, ethical and legal standards of behavior are a personal matter to the same degree as they are for any other citizen, except as these may compromise the fulfillment of their professional responsibilities, or reduce the trust in psychology or psychologists held by the general public. Regarding their own behavior, psychologists are sensitive to the prevailing community standards and of the possible impact upon the quality of professional services provided by their conformity to or deviation from these standards. Psychologists are also aware of the possible impact of their public behavior upon the ability of colleagues to perform their professional duties.

a. As teachers, psychologists are aware of the diverse backgrounds of students and, when dealing with topics that may give offense, treat the material objectively and present it in a manner that respects the attitudes and experiences of all students.

b. As employees, psychologists refuse to participate in practices inconsistent with legal, moral and ethical principles regarding the treatment of employees, clients or the general public. Psychologists do not condone practices that are inhumane or that result in illegal or otherwise unjustifiable discrimination on the basis of race, age, sex, religion or national origin in hiring, promotion, or training.

c. In their professional roles, psychologists avoid any action that will violate or diminish the legal and civil rights of clients or of others who may be affected by their actions.

d. As practitioners, psychologists remain abreast of relevant federal, state, local, and agency regulations and Association standards of practice. Psychologists who offer or render direct ameliorative services are either licensed/certified to render said services or render them under the direct supervision of a person so licensed/certified. They are concerned with the development of such legal regulations and policies as best serve the public interest and in changing such existing regulations as are not beneficial to the interests of the public and the profession.

e. As researchers, psychologists remain abreast of relevant federal, state and institutional regulations concerning the conduct of research with human participants or animals.

Principle 4: Public Statements

Public statements, announcements of services, advertising and promotional activities of psychologists serve the purpose of providing sufficient information to aid the consumer public in making informed judgments and choices. Psychologists represent accurately and objectively their professional qualifications, affiliations, and functions, as well as those of the institutions or organizations with which they or the statements may be associated. In public statements providing psychological information or professional opinions or providing information about the availability of psychological products, publica-

tions and services, psychologists base their statements on scientifically acceptable psychological findings and techniques with full recognition of their limits and uncertainties.

a. When announcing or advertising professional services, psychologists may list the following information as a description of provider and services provided: name, highest relevant academic degree earned from a regionally accredited institution, date, type and level of certification or licensure, diplomate status, APA membership status, address, telephone number, office hours, a brief listing of the type of psychological services offered, an appropriate presentation of fee information, foreign languages spoken, and policy with regard to third party payments. Additional relevant or important consumer information may be included if not prohibited by other sections of the *Ethical Principles*.

b. In announcing or advertising the availability of psychological products, publications or services, psychologists do not display any affiliations with an organization in a manner that falsely implies the sponsorship or certification of that organization. In particular and for example, psychologists do not offer APA membership or fellowship in a way that implies specialized professional competence or qualifications. Public statements, defined herein to include, but not be limited to, communications by means of newspaper, book, list, directory, television, radio or motion picture shall not contain: a false, fraudulent, misleading, deceptive, or unfair statement; a misinterpretation of fact; a statement likely to mislead or deceive because in context it makes only a partial disclosure of relevant facts; a testimonial regarding the quality of a psychologist's direct ameliorative services or products; a statement intended or likely to create false or unjustified expectations of favorable results; a statement implying unusual, unique, or one of a kind abilities; a statement intended or likely to appeal to a client's fears, anxieties, or emotions concerning the possible results of the consumer's failure to obtain the offered services; a statement concerning the comparative desirability of offered service; a statement of direct solicitation of individual clients.

c. A psychologist shall not compensate or give anything of value to a representative of the press, radio, television or other communication medium in anticipation of or in return for professional publicity in a news item. A paid advertisement must be identified as such unless it is apparent from the context that it is a paid advertisement. If the paid advertisement is communicated to the public by use of radio or television, it shall be pre-recorded, approved for broadcast by the psychologist and a recording of the actual transmission shall be retained by the psychologist.

d. Psychologists associated with the development or promotion of psychological devices, books, or other products offered for commercial sale make reasonable efforts to insure that announcements and advertisements are presented in a professional, scientifically acceptable and factually informative manner.

e. Psychologists do not participate for personal gain in commercial announcements or advertisements recommending to the general public the purchase or use of any proprietary or single-source product or service.

f. Psychologists present the science of psychology and offer their services, products and publications fairly and accurately, avoiding misrepresentation through sensationalism, exaggeration or superficiality. Psychologists are guided by the primary obligation to aid the public in forming their own informed judgments, opinions and choices.

g. As teachers, psychologists insure that statements in catalogues and course outlines are accurate and not misleading, particularly in terms of subject matter to be covered, bases for evaluating progress and nature of course experiences. Announcements, brochures, or advertisements describing workshops, seminars, or other educational programs accurately represent intended audience and eligibility requirements, educational objectives, and nature of the material to be covered, as well as the education, training and experience of the psychologists presenting the programs, and any fees involved. Public announcements or advertisements soliciting subjects for research, and in which clinical services or other professional services are offered as an inducement, make clear the nature of the services as well as the costs and other obligations to be accepted by the human participants of the research.

h. Psychologists accept the obligation to correct others who may represent the psychologist's professional qualifications or associations with products or services in a manner incompatible with these guidelines.

i. Psychological services and products for the purpose of diagnosing, treating or giving personal advice to particular individuals are provided only in the context of a professional relationship, and are not given by means of public lectures or demonstrations, newspaper or magazine articles, radio or television programs, mail, or similar media unless it has been demonstrated by acceptable standards that self-administered applications of such advice are beneficial and without harmful effects.

Principle 5: Confidentiality

Psychologists have a primary obligation to respect the confidentiality of information obtained from a person in the course of teaching, practice and research. They reveal such information to others only with the consent of the person or the person's legal representative, except in those unusual circumstances in which not to do so would violate the law or would result in clear and imminent danger to the person or to others. Psychologists inform their clients of the limits of confidentiality.

a. Information obtained in clinical or consulting relationships, or evaluative data concerning children, students, employees, and others are discussed only for professional purposes and only with persons clearly concerned with the case. Written and oral reports present only data germane to the purposes of the evaluation and every effort is made to avoid undue invasion of privacy.

b. Psychologists who present information obtained during the course of professional work in lectures, writings or other public forums either obtain adequate prior consent to do so or adequately disguise all identifying information.

c. Psychologists make provisions for maintaining confidentiality in the storage and disposal of records.

d. When working with minors or other persons who are unable to give voluntary, informed consent, psychologists take special care to protect the minors' best interests.

Principle 6: Welfare of the Consumer

Psychologists respect the integrity and protect the welfare of the people and groups with whom they work. When there is a conflict of interest between the client and the psychologist's employing institution, psychologists clarify the nature and direction of their loyalties and responsibilities and keep all parties informed of their commitments. Psychologists fully inform consumers as to the purpose and nature of an evaluative treatment, educational or training procedure, and they freely acknowledge that clients, students, or participants in research have freedom of choice with regard to participation.

a. Psychologists are continually cognizant of their own needs and of their inherently powerful position vis a vis clients, in order to avoid exploiting their trust and dependency. Psychologists make every effort to avoid dual relationships with clients and/or relationships which might impair their professional judgment or increase the risk of client exploitation. Examples of such dual relationships include treating employees, students, supervisees, close friends or relatives. Sexual intimacies with clients are unethical.

b. When a psychologist provides services to a client at the request of a third party, the psychologist assumes the responsibility of clarifying the nature of the relationships to all parties concerned.

c. Where demands of an organization on psychologists go beyond reasonable conditions of employment, psychologists recognize possible conflicts of interest that may arise. When such conflicts occur, psychologists clarify the nature of the conflict and inform all parties of the nature and direction of the loyalties and responsibilities involved.

d. Psychologists make advance financial arrangements that safeguard the best interests of and are clearly understood by their clients. They neither give nor receive any remuneration for referring clients for professional services. They contribute a portion of their services to work for which they receive little or no financial return.

e. The psychologist attempts to terminate a clinical or consulting relationship when it is reasonably clear that the consumer is not benefiting from it.

Principle 7: Professional Relationship

Psychologists act with due regard for the needs, special competencies and obligations of their colleagues in psychology and other professions. Psychologists respect the prerogatives and obligations of the institutions or organizations with which they are are associated.

a. Psychologists understand the areas of competence of related professions, and make full use of all the professional, technical, and administrative resources that best serve the interests of consumers. The absence of formal relationships with other professional workers does not relieve psychologists from the responsibility of securing for their clients the best possible professional service nor does it relieve them from the exercise of foresight, diligence, and tact in obtaining the complementary or alternative assistance needed by clients.

b. If a psychologist is consulted by a consumer who is already receiving similar services from another professional, the psychologist discusses this issue with the consumer so as to minimize the risk of confusion and conflict for the consumer.

c. Psychologists who employ or supervise other professionals or professionals in training accept the obligation to facilitate their further professional development by providing suitable working conditions, consultation, adequate and timely evaluation, and experience opportunities. They accord informed choice, confidentiality, due process and protection from physical and mental harm to their subordinates in such relationships.

d. In conducting research in institutions or organizations, psychologists obtain the same informed consent that they would from individual research participants. They are aware of their obligation to future research workers and insure that host institutions are given adequate information about the research and proper acknowledgment of their contributions.

e. Publication credit is assigned to all those who have contributed to a publication in proportion to their contribution. Major contributions of a professional character made by several persons to a common project are recognized by joint authorship, with the experimenter or author who made the principal contribution identified and listed first. Minor contributions of a professional character, extensive clerical or similar nonprofessional assistance, and other minor contributions are acknowledged in footnotes or in an introductory statement. Acknowledgment through specific citations is made for unpublished as well as published material that has directly influenced the research or writing. A psychologist who compiles and edits material of others for publication publishes the material in the name of the originating group, if any, and with his/her own name appearing as chairperson or editor. All contributors are to be acknowledged and named.

f. When psychologists know of an ethical violation by another psychologist, they attempt, where it is appropriate, to correct the problem by bringing the unethical behavior to the attention of the psychologist. When the violation is more serious or not amenable to such an informal solution, they bring it to the attention of the appropriate local, state, and/or national committee on professional ethics and conduct.

g. Members of the Association cooperate with duly constituted committees of the Association, in particular and for example, the Committee on Scientific and Professional Ethics and Conduct, and the Committee on Professional Standards Review, by responding to inquiries promptly and completely. Members also respond promptly and completely to inquiries from duly constituted state association ethics committees and professional standards review committees.

Principle 8: Assessment Techniques

In the development, publication, and utilization of psychological assessment techniques, psychologists make every effort to promote the welfare and best interests of the client. They guard against the misuse of their test results. They respect the client's right to know the results, the interpretations made and the bases for their conclusions and recommendations. Psychologists make every effort to maintain the security of their tests and assure their appropriate use by others.

a. In using psychological tests, psychologists respect the right of clients to have a full explanation of the nature and purpose of the tests in language that the client can understand, unless an explicit exception to this right has been agreed upon in advance. When the explanations are to be provided by others, the psychologist establishes procedures for providing adequate explanations.

b. Psychologists responsible for the development and standardization of psychological tests utilize established scientific procedures and observe the relevant APA standards.

c. In reporting test results, psychologists indicate any reservations regarding validity or reliability resulting from testing circumstances or inappropriateness of the test norms for the person tested. Psychologists strive to insure that the test results and their interpretations are not misused by others.

d. Psychologists offering test scoring and interpretation services are able to demonstrate that the validity of the programs and procedures used in arriving at interpretations are based on appropriate evidence. The public offering of an automated test interpretation service is considered as a professional-to-professional consultation. The psychologist makes every effort to avoid misuse of test reports.

Principle 9: Research Activities

The decision to undertake research should rest upon a considered judgment by the individual psychologist about how best to contribute to psychological science and to human welfare. Psychologists carry out their investigations with respect for the people who participate and with concern for their dignity and welfare.

a. In planning a study the investigator has the responsibility to make a careful evaluation of its ethical acceptability. To the extent that this weighing of scientific and human values suggests a compromise of any principle, the investigator incurs an increasingly serious obligation to seek ethical advice and to observe stringent safeguards to protect the rights of the human research participants.

b. Responsibility for acceptable ethical practice in research always remains with the individual investigator. The investigator is also responsible for the ethical treatment of research participants by collaborators, assistants, students, and employees.

c. The investigator informs the participant of all aspects of the research that might reasonably be expected to influence willingness to participate, and explains all other aspects of the research about which the participant inquires. Failure to make full disclosure imposes additional force to the investigator's abiding responsibility to protect the welfare and dignity of the research participant.

d. When the methodological requirements of a study necessitate concealment or deception, the investigator promptly provides the participant with a sufficient explanation of this action.

e. Ethical practice requires the investigator to respect the individual's freedom to decline to participate in or withdraw from research. The obligation to protect this freedom requires special vigilance when the investigator is in a position of power over the participant, as, for example, when the participant is a student, client, employee, or otherwise is in a dual relationship with the investigator.

f. Prior to conducting research, the investigator establishes a clear and fair agreement with the research participant that clarifies the responsibilities of each. The investigator has the obligation to honor all promises and commitments included in that agreement.

g. The investigator protects participants from physical and mental discomfort, harm, and danger. If a risk of such consequences exists, the investigator informs the participant of that fact, secures consent before proceeding, and takes all possible measures to minimize distress. Research procedures likely to cause serious or lasting harm to a participant are not used.

h. After the data are collected, the investigator provides the participant with information about the nature of the study and removes any misconceptions that may have arisen. Where scientific or human values justify delaying or withholding information, the in-

vestigator acquires a special responsibility to assure that there are no damaging consequences for the participant.

i. When research procedures may result in undesirable consequences for the individual participant, the investigator has the responsibility to detect and remove or correct these consequences, including, where relevant, long-term after effects.

j. Information obtained about the individual research participants during the course of an investigation is confidential unless otherwise agreed in advance. When the possibility exists that others may obtain access to such information, this possibility, together with the plans for protecting confidentiality, is explained to the participants as part of the procedure for obtaining informed consent.

k. Investigations of human participants using drugs are conducted only in such settings as clinics, hospitals, or research facilities maintaining appropriate safeguards for the participant.

Glossary

AAMD. American Association on Mental Deficiency.

Aberration. An unexpected or severe departure from the normal.

Ability grouping. An organizational strategy in which pupils are grouped for instruction on the basis of specific levels of academic ability in reading, math, and other areas.

Ability test. A test that measures the extent to which a person is capable of performing a certain task.

Abstract ability. The ability to comprehend abstract ideas and relationships.

Acalculia. Inability to manipulate arithmetic symbols or to do simple mathematical calculations.

Accommodation. Focusing of the eye's lens.

Accommodation (Piaget). Restructuring of mental organizations so that new information may be processed.

Achievement test. A test designed for the specific purpose of assessing prior learning.

Acuity. The extent to which a given sensory modality is able to make accurate discriminations between similar stimuli.

Adaptive behavior. Ability of an individual to interact appropriately and effectively with his/her environment.

Affect. Emotion, feeling, or mood.

Age norm. The average score on an aptitude or achievement test made by children of a given chronological age.

Age scale. A scale on which the scores are expressed in age units. For each age, norms (expressed in units of years or months) are available for evaluating the individual's performance.

Agnosia. Impairment or loss of the ability to recognize or comprehend the meaning of stimuli, including familiar objects and symbols.

Agrammatism. Loss of ability to speak coherently. May be due to brain injury or severe mental disturbance, especially schizophrenia.

Agraphia. The inability to write; caused by brain damage.

Alexia. A disturbance of the ability to read or interpret written symbols.

Alternate form reliability. Reliability determined by correlating scores on two forms of a test.

Amblyopia. A refractive defect resulting in dim vision and sometimes associated with cerebral palsy; sometimes called "lazy eye."

Amnesia. The partial or total loss of memory for past experiences due to any cause.

Amnestic aphasia. A disturbance in ability to retrieve words needed for the spoken form of language.

Amniocentesis. A diagnostic procedure used for genetic assessment in which embryonic cells from the amniotic fluid are withdrawn to permit a chromosomal analysis.

Amphetamines. Drugs, such as cocaine, benzedrine, dexedrine, and methedrine, which serve as central nervous system stimulants by increasing activity and suppressing appetite; may cause feeling of well-being. Used in the treatment of hyperactivity.

Amusia. Loss of the ability to produce or to comprehend musical sounds.

Anaclitic depression. Profound sadness of an infant when separated from his or her mother for a prolonged period.

Analytic cognitive style. A style in which the individual uses a stimulus centered, parts-specific approach to thinking; information is extracted from its embedding context.

Anarthria. Loss of the ability to form words accurately due to brain lesion or damage to peripheral nerves that carry impulses to the articulatory muscles.

Angiogram (cerebral). Procedure that allows the study of blood distribution in the brain by the injection of a radiopaque dye into blood vessels in or near the brain.

Anhedonia. Diminished intensity of experienced pain and pleasure and the decreased responsiveness to negative and positive reinforcement.

Animism. Tendency to attribute life to inanimate objects; most prevalent in children between the ages of 2 and 7 years.

Anomia. An inability to name objects or recall and recognize names.

Anoxia. Deficiency or lack of oxygen. It may occur in the newborn during the transition from maternal supply of oxygenated cord blood to independent breathing. Brain cells are particularly vulnerable to continued anoxia.

Antisocial. Exhibiting attitudes and overt behavior contrary to accepted customs, standards, and moral principles of a society.

Apgar (rating). A score derived from assessment of the neonate's heart rate, respiratory effort, muscle tone, cry, and color. Each area is scored 0 to 2. Normal infants score between 7 and 10.

Aphasia. A language disorder, due to brain injury, characterized by a loss of ability to comprehend, manipulate, or express words in speech, writing, or gesture.

Aphonia. Loss or impairment of voice resulting from laryngeal defects or emotional disorders.

Apraxia. Loss of the ability to perform purposeful movements in the absence of paralysis or sensory disturbance; caused by lesions in the cerebral cortex.

Aptitude test. A standardized measure of a person's ability to profit from further training or experience in an occupation or skill.

Arithmetic mean. A measure of the average or central tendency of a group of scores, computed by dividing the sum of the scores by the number of scores.

Articulation. The production of speech sounds.

Assimilation. Perceiving and interpreting new information in terms of existing knowledge and understanding.

Assimilation (Piaget). Perceiving and interpreting new information in terms of currently existing mental organizations.

Astereognosis. A form of agnosia in which there is an inability to recognize objects or geometric forms by touch; thought to be caused by lesions in the central parietal lobe.

Asymbolia. Loss of the ability to use or understand symbols, such as those used in mathematics, language, chemistry, and music.

Ataxia. Impairment of coordination of muscular activity.

Athetosis. Uncontrolled muscular movement in cerebral palsy marked by slow, recurring, weaving, or worm-like movements of arms and legs.

Atonia. Deficient muscular tone.

Atrophy. Degeneration of tissues, as may occur in paralyzed muscles.

Attenuation. A decrease in the magnitude of the correlation between two measures, such as a test and a criterion, caused by unreliability in the measures.

Audiometry. The measurement of sound, especially that in the human speech ranges.

Auditory agnosia. Impaired ability to recognize familiar sounds.

Auditory aphasia. Inability to comprehend spoken words; also known as word deafness or receptive aphasia.

Auditory association. Relating concepts presented orally.

Auditory closure. Recognizing the whole after the presentation of a partial auditory stimulus.

Auditory discrimination. Distinguishing between slight differences in sounds.

Auditory memory. Recalling words, digits, etc., in a meaningful manner; includes memory of meaning.

Auditory perception. Hearing sounds accurately and understanding what they mean.

Auditory sequential memory. Reproducing a sequence of auditory stimuli.

Autism. Thinking governed by personal needs; perceiving the world in terms of wishes as opposed to reality; extreme preoccupation with one's own thoughts and fantasies.

Autonomic nervous system. System that deals with automatic regulation of smooth muscles and glands.

Autosome. Any chromosome other than sex chromosome (not X or Y chromosome).

Autotopagnosia. Disturbance in recognition of body parts.

Average. A general term applied to the various measures of central tendency. The three most widely used averages are the arithmetic mean, the median, and the mode. When the term "average" is used without designation as to type, the most likely assumption is that it is the arithmetic mean.

Aversive conditioning. A form of learning that is brought about through the use of punishment (negative consequences) or by removal of positive reinforcers.

Babbling. Inappropriate vocal play; random articulation; unintelligible jabber, nonsense. Also normal stage in the infant's development.

Babinski reflex. Involuntary response involving upward movement of the big toe and fanning of the other toes when the sole of the foot is stimulated. Usually absent by 12 to 24 months of age unless there is specific neurological dysfunction.

Barbiturate. A class of drugs that act as central nervous system depressants, inducing sleep and muscular relaxation (e.g., Nembutal, Seconal, and pheno-barbital).

Basal age. The highest age level at which all items are passed on tests standardized in mental-age units.

Base line. A characteristic level of performance which can be used to assess changes in behavior resulting from experimental conditions.

Base rate. The proportion of people in a population who possess a characteristic of interest. The base rate must be taken into account when determining the effectiveness of a test in identifying people having the characteristic.

Behavior modification. Use of learning theory principles to bring about changes in specified target behaviors.

Behavioral analysis. A generic term used to classify a variety of approaches that focus on specific observable behaviors and on the observable environmental events, objects, and conditions that affect those specific behaviors.

Behavioral objectives. The specific objectives, expressed in terms of behavioral outcomes, to be achieved by an educational unit or course of study.

Benign. Mild. A nonmalignant disorder, the prognosis for which is favorable.

Bias. Any one of a number of factors that cause test scores to be consistently higher or lower than they would be if measurement were more accurate.

Biased sample. A sample that gives a distorted picture of a group.

Bilateral. Both sides; especially related to hemispheric functioning and the two sides of the body.

Bilingualism. Ability to use two languages.

Biopsy. The excision of a piece of tissue from a living organism for diagnostic purposes.

Biserial correlation coefficient. A measure of the correlation between two variables, such as the relationship between scores on a single test item (1 or 0) and scores on the test as a whole, in which one variable is dichotomized (i.e., has only two possible scores). It is assumed that scores on the dichotomized variable would be normally distributed if the variable were measured more precisely.

Body image. Awareness of one's own body and its orientation, position, and movement in space and time.

Brain damage. Any anatomical or physiological change of a pathological nature in the nerve tissue of the brain.

Brain disorder (syndrome). An organic disorder characterized by impairment of orientation, memory, intellective function, or emotional stability.

Brain lesion. Localized damage to the brain; destruction of brain tissue.

Brain waves. The rhythmic, spontaneous electrical discharges of the living brain, principally the cortex.

Broca's speech area. A portion of the left cerebral hemisphere said to control motor speech.

Catastrophic reaction. A sudden outbreak of inappropriate behavior as a result of stress or frustration.

Ceiling. The upper limit of an ability that can be assessed by a test; the maximum score obtainable on a test.

Central nervous system (CNS). Brain and spinal cord.

Cerebellum. A portion of the brain consisting of two hemispheres located behind and above the medulla. It coordinates motor activities and maintains bodily equilibrium.

Cerebral contusion. A bruising of brain tissue resulting in loss of consciousness; usually associated with fracture of the skull.

Cerebral cortex. The convoluted outer layer of gray matter of the cerebral hemispheres which, together with the corpus callosum, comprises the cerebrum.

Cerebral dominance. Assumption that one cerebral hemisphere of the brain generally leads the other in governing an individual's functions.

Cerebral hemisphere. Either of the two halves that make up the cerebrum.

Cerebral hemorrhage. Bleeding onto brain tissue from a ruptured blood vessel.

Cerebral palsy. Impairment of motor functioning associated with brain lesion; usually a congenital defect in children.

Cerebral trauma. Brain injury as a result of some type of physical force, e.g., a concussion.

Cerebral vascular disease. A condition whereby the blood vessels of the brain attain a pathological state.

Cerebrospinal fluid. A fluid secreted chiefly by the choroid plexuses of the lateral ventricles of the brain, filling the ventricles and the subarachnoid cavities of the brain and the central canal of the spinal cord.

Cerebrum. The main portion of the brain, occupying the upper part of the cranium and consisting of the two cerebral hemispheres. It is united by the corpus callosum and forms the largest part of the central nervous system.

Character disorder. A general term that refers to personality disorders, including disorders of conduct (e.g., stealing, embezzling).

Childhood psychosis. A childhood disorder characterized by disturbed social relationships, impairment of speech, bizarre motor behavior, daydreaming, and irritability.

Childhood schizophrenia. A childhood disorder which manifests itself, after a period of normal development, when the child begins to show severe disturbances in social adjustment and in reality contact.

Chlorpromazine. Generic term for one of the most widely used major tranquilizers, sold under the name Thorazine.

Chorea. A neurological disorder of muscle control characterized by dramatic and rapid, jerky movements, primarily of the arms and legs.

Choreiform movements. Spasmodic or jerky movements that occur quite irregularly and arhythmically in different muscles.

Chronic brain disorder. A relatively permanent and usually irreversible condition resulting from diffuse impairment of brain tissue.

Chronological age (CA). Refers to the number of years and months a person has lived.

Circumstantiality. Indirect conversation, with many tedious, irrelevant details and additions.

Clang association. A stringing together of words similar in sound, with no attention paid to their meaning. For example, "How are you Don, pawn, gone?"

Clonic. Relating to the rapid alternation between muscular rigidity and relaxation that characterizes epileptic contractions.

Closure. The process of achieving completion in a visual, behavioral, or mental act.

CNS. See Central nervous system.

Coefficient of equivalence. The type of reliability coefficient obtained when parallel forms of the same test are administered to the same individuals.

Coefficient of internal consistency. An index of the extent to which various parts of a test measure the same function.

Coefficient of stability. The type of reliability coefficient obtained when the same test is administered twice to the same individuals (test-retest reliability).

Cognition. A general concept for any process whereby an individual becomes aware of or obtains knowledge of an object.

Cognitive processes. Modes of thought, knowing, and symbolic representation, including comprehension, judgment, memory, imagining, and reasoning.

Cognitive style. An individual's characteristic approach to problem solving and cognitive tasks.

Common variance. Refers to that variation which is shared between any two or more tests.

Communality (h²). Proportion of test variability accounted for by common-factor variance; communality equals reliability minus specificity.

Concrete mode. One of the styles of cognitive functioning that describes the child's approach to problem solving at a simple, elementary level. Also, the use of tangible objects in instruction, as opposed to purely verbal instruction.

Concrete operations stage (Piaget). The third period of Piaget's theory of cognitive development, occurring between the ages of 7 and 11 years and marked by logical reasoning in new situations.

Concurrent validity. The extent to which a measurement correlates with a criterion when both are obtained at approximately the same time.

Condensation. Combining fragments of two or more ideas and expressing them in the pattern of a single phrase; telescoping of thoughts.

Conduct disorder/disturbance. An adjustment reaction of childhood, manifested primarily as disturbances in social conduct or behavior.

Confabulation. A type of thinking characterized by the filling of memory gaps with false and irrelevant information and details.

Confidence level. A statistical "degree of certainty" (e.g., 68, 95, or 99 percent) indicating the probability that an obtained value represents the population (or true) value.

Congenital. Present at birth. Congenital does not carry the connotation of a hereditary origin.

Congenital anomalies. Abnormalities that are present at birth. Congenital anomalies are not necessarily inherited.

Conservation (Piaget). A child's ability to realize that an object retains certain essential properties no matter how its form may change.

Construct validity. A type of validity that establishes the degree to which a particular test measures a specified psychological construct.

Content analysis. A method of studying and analyzing communications in a systematic, objective, and quantitative manner to measure the frequency with which certain terms, ideas, or emotions are expressed.

Content (Guilford). Refers to the type of information or material that the intellect operates on.

Content validity. A type of validation that, through a logical analysis of the test content, establishes whether the test measures what it is supposed to measure.

Control group. A group of subjects carefully selected so that it is comparable in every possible respect to the experimental group, except that the treatment variable is not applied to it.

Convergence. The ocular pointing mechanism by which the eyes are "aimed" at a target. It enables one to see a single object at varying distances.

Convergent thinking. The generation of ideas and facts from known information where the emphasis is on finding a single, logical solution to a problem.

Convulsion. Violent, extensive, involuntary, and pathological muscle contractions.

Convulsive disorder. A clinical syndrome, the central feature of which is recurrent muscular seizures; recurrent disturbances of consciousness, with or without muscular components and accompanied by changes in the electrical potentials of the brain.

Corpus callosum. A large band of white fiber connecting the two cerebral hemispheres.

Correlation. A statistical procedure for determining the degree of relationship between two variables.

Correlation coefficient (r). An index of the degree of relationship between two variables. The index varies from +1.00 (perfect positive relationship) through .00 (absence of a relationship) to −1.00 (perfect negative relationship).

Cortical evoked potential. The electrical activity in response to a stimulus, as recorded from the cerebral cortex.

Cretinism. An abnormal condition resulting from thyroid insufficiency in childhood; characterized by severe mental retardation, stunting, patchy hair, protruding abdomen, and a severely underdeveloped personality.

Criterion. A standard against which a test may be validated.

Criterion-referenced measurement. Tests designed to measure to what degree the learner has mastered a specified skill.

Criterion validity. The extent to which a test measures what it is alleged to measure, as indicated by the correlation of test scores with some standard or reference measure.

Cross-dominance. Sensorimotor functioning characterized by right-handed and left-eyed, or left-handed and right-eyed, performance; occasionally refers to dominance of ear or foot as well.

Cross-modal. Involving more than one sensory modality.

Cross-modality perception. The process by which a certain stimulus acquired meaning through the use of more than one sensory modality.

Cross-sectional study. A method of investigating developmental trends based on a comparison of children at different ages during the time of the study.

Cross-validation. The act or process of verifying results obtained with one group by replication with a different, but similar, group.

Crystallized intelligence. Type of intelligence that results from interaction with the culture.

Cultural bias. Refers to test items that may be unfair to a particular group because of undue emphasis on a specific set of learned behaviors and customs.

Cultural deprivation. A relative concept which recognizes that one's past learning and life experiences may retard one's adaptive and intellectual functioning when another cultural orientation is encountered.

Cultural-familial retardation. Refers to individuals diagnosed as mentally retarded in the absence of indications of cerebral pathology, but where there is a history of familial intellectual subnormality.

Culture-fair test. A test designed to minimize biases associated with different sociocultural experiences of the examinees.

Culture-free test. See Culture-fair test.

Cumulative deficit. An increasingly greater deficit in academic skills as the child goes through school.

Cutaneous. Pertaining to the skin or sense organs in skin.

Cyanosis. Blueness of the skin, due to insufficient oxygen in the blood, as a result of poor circulation or, especially in the newborn, delayed or insufficient breathing.

Cystic fibrosis. A chronic and fatal inherited disease that damages the mucus-producing glands, resulting in severe damage to the lungs and the digestive tract.

Decibel (db). A unit of measure for the intensity or loudness of sound.

Decile. A score in a frequency distribution below which either 10% (1st decile), 20% (2nd decile), . . . 90% (9th decile), or 100% (10th decile) of the total number of scores fall.

Decoding. The process by which a receiver translates signals into messages, as in reading.

Deduction. The process in logical thinking whereby one derives specific conclusions from general principles, premises, or propositions.

Degenerative brain disease. A disease or condition that results in progressive deterioration of the brain.

Delusion. A false but persistent belief.

Demographic variable. A quantity or factor that is a function of, for example, age, sex, education, socioeconomic status, or ethnicity.

Demyelinating disease. Any of the diseases of the central nervous system that result in progressive deterioration of the myelin sheath that surrounds and insulates nerve fibers.

Dependent variable. In a psychological experiment, the measure of the behavior that the experimenter observes, but does not manipulate or control.

Developmental disabilities. Disabilities primarily attributable to mental retardation, cerebral palsy, epilepsy, or autism, resulting in the child's failing to develop normally.

Deviation IQ. Intelligence quotient (IQ) obtained by converting raw scores on an intelligence test to a score distribution having a mean of 100 and a standard deviation, such as 16 for the Stanford-Binet or 15 for the Wechsler tests.

Dexedrine. A stimulant drug (dextroamphetamine) used to control hyperactive behavior in children.

Dextral. Consistently right-sided in lateral preference.

Diabetes mellitus. A metabolic disorder caused by insufficient production of insulin from the pancreas, which leads to excessive amounts of unmetabolized sugar in the blood.

Diadochokinesia. Ability to perform alternating movements, such as flexion and extension of a limb.

Diagnostic test. An achievement test composed of items in a number of subareas, with the purpose of diagnosing an individual's relative strengths and weaknesses in the subareas.

Dialect. A regional variation of a language.

Difficulty index. The proportion (percentage) of individuals passing a given test item; the larger the index, the easier the item.

Dilantin (phenytoin). Anticonvulsant drug used for epilepsy.

Diplegia. Paralysis affecting like parts on both sides of the body.

Directional confusion. Tendency to make reversals and substitutions because of a left-right or laterality orientation disorder.

Directionality. Ability to distinguish right from left, forward from backward, and up from down.

Discrimination. Process of detecting differences in stimuli.

Discrimination, auditory. Ability to identify differences between sounds.

Discrimination, visual. Ability to recognize differences between similar but slightly different forms or shapes, such as alphabetic letters.

Discrimination index. An index that indicates how well an item discriminates between the low and high scores on some criterion.

Disinhibition. Lack of ability to restrain oneself from responding to distracting stimuli.

Disinhibition, motor. An unplanned or meaningless motor response in which a child may respond to a given stimulus with inappropriate or excessive motor activity.

Dispersion. The extent to which scores vary or deviate from one another or the average score.

Distortion of ideas. Hyperbole, exaggerations; incorrect details; misrepresentation of fact.

Distractibility. Difficulty in maintaining focused attention due to the influence of extraneous stimuli.

Distribution. A tabulation of scores to show the frequency of each score.

Divergent thinking. Ability to generate a number of possible alternative solutions to a problem presented; thought processes required to produce a novel response.

Dizygotic twins. Twins originating from two fertilized ova and thus having different genetic makeups; fraternal twins.

Dorsi-flexion. The lifting of the foot up toward the body.

Double-blind. Refers to a study of drugs in which neither the subject nor the experimenter knows whether the subject is receiving the drug in question or a placebo.

Down's syndrome (Trisomy 21; Mongolism). A congenital chromosomal anomaly (extra chromosome on 21st) characterized by a flat skull, thickened skin of eyelids, stubby fingers, and a short, stocky body; associated with moderate to severe mental retardation.

DSM-III. Diagnostic and Statistical Manual of Mental Disorder representing the diagnostic classification system officially adopted by the American Psychiatric Association.

Dynamometer. A device for measuring the strength of a muscular response.

Dysarthria. An impairment of speech articulation caused by disease in the central nervous system.

Dyscalculia. Partial inability to calculate, to manipulate number symbols, or to do simple arithmetic.

Dysdiadochokinesis. Inability to perform rapid alternating movements.

Dysgenesis. Failure to mature, e.g., cerebral dysgenesis is failure of parts of the brain to mature as expected.

Dysgraphethesia. Inability to recognize figures or numbers traced on the skin.

Dysgraphia. Partial inability to express ideas by means of writing or written symbols, usually associated with brain dysfunction.

Dyskinesia. Impairment of voluntary movement, resulting in poor coordination.

Dyslalia. Impaired speech ability caused by functional or unknown factors.

Dyslexia. Impaired ability to read or to understand what one reads either silently or aloud.

Dysnomia. Impaired ability to recall names of objects or words.

Dysphagia. Difficulty in swallowing; often found in cerebral palsied children.

Dysphasia. Impairment of speech, consisting of difficulty in arranging words in their proper sequence; results from central nervous system damage.

Dysphemia. Defective articulation of speech, due to functional causes.

Dysphonia. Impairment of voice quality.

Dysphoria. Generalized feeling of anxiety, restlessness, and depression.

Dyspraxia. A partial loss of ability to perform coordinated movements.

Dysrhythmia. Abnormal speech fluency, characterized by defective stress, breath control, and intonation; also a disruption of rhythm, as in abnormal EEG wave patterns.

Dystonia. Impairment of muscle tone.

Dystrophy. Organ atrophy and muscular weakness resulting from faulty nutrition.

Early infantile autism. See Infantile autism.

Echolalia. Inappropriate repetition of speech previously uttered by another speaker.

Echopraxia. Tendency toward automatic imitation of the movements and gestures of others.

Educable mentally retarded (EMR). Mentally retarded children capable of some degree of school achievement; IQs in the 50 to 70 range.

Educational retardation. The difference between a child's intellectual capacity and his or her level of achievement in academic areas.

Ego. In psychoanalytic theory, the predominantly conscious part of the personality, responsible for decision making and for dealing with reality.

Elaboration. Embellishment by the addition of associated ideas, movements, or drawings.

Electroencephalogram (EEG). A recording of the electrical discharges from the brain.

Electroencephalograph (EEG). A device that permits recording of brain waves by placing electrodes on the scalp.

Emotional lability. See Lability.

EMR. See Educable mentally retarded.

Encephalitis (encephalopathy). Acute inflammation of the brain or its meninges resulting from any of a wide variety of infections and toxins.

Encoding. Translating information into a communicable form, as in the process of expressing knowledge or intention through written, oral, or body language.

Endogenous. Arising from causes within the individual; attributable to internal causes associated with hereditary factors.

Epicanthus. The prolonged fold of skin of the upper eyelid over the inner angle or both angles of the eye.

Epilepsy. An organic disorder characterized by irregularly occurring transitory disturbances in consciousness, often accompanied by seizures or convulsions.

Equivalent form. Any of two or more forms of a test that are closely parallel with respect to the nature of the content, number, and difficulty of the items included, and that will yield very similar average scores and measures of variability for a given group. (Also referred to as *alternate, comparable,* or *parallel* form.)

Equivalent forms reliability. A type of reliability in which two forms of a test, designed to meet the same item specifications, are shown to have similar means and variances and to be highly correlated.

Error score. The score that is associated with the unreliability of the test.

Error variance. Residual variance not accounted for by the common and specific variance, due to uncontrolled factors such as test unreliability and sampling errors.

Etiology. Causes of a disease or disorder.

Eugenics. An application of genetics whereby an attempt is made to improve the inborn qualities of a race or breed, with attention to both positive (promote propagation of specially fit) and negative (discourage propagation of "unfit") aspects.

Evoked potential. See Cortical evoked potential.

Exceptional child. Child who deviates significantly from the norm; may be exceptional by virtue of, for example, unusually high or low intelligence, physical disability, or emotional difficulties.

Exogenous. Attributable to external causes.

Expectancy effect. Effects of a person's expectations on another person's behavior.

Experimental design. A plan for collecting and treating the data of an experiment.

Expressive aphasia. Inability to remember the pattern of movement required to speak, write, or use signs, even though one knows what one wants to say; due to brain damage.

Expressive language skills. Skills required to communicate ideas through language, such as writing, gesturing, and speaking.

Extrapolation. The process of extending norms to scores not actually obtained in the standardization program.

Extrinsic tumor. A tumor having its origin outside the limb or organ in which it is found.

Eye-hand coordination. Coordination of eyes and hands in performing motor tasks.

Face validity. The extent to which test items appear to measure what the test is supposed to measure.

Factor. A dimension, trait, or characteristic of intellect or personality discovered by factor analysis. Also, any one of several conditions that together cause an event.

Factor analysis. A statistical technique used to isolate underlying relationships between sets of variables.

Fairness. The extent to which the items on a test are a representative sample of what the examinees have been exposed to.

False negatives. Examinees whose test scores indicate that they will not succeed on the criterion, but who actually do succeed.

False positives. Examinees whose test scores indicate that they will succeed on the criterion, but who actually do not succeed.

Familial retardation. Individuals with mild mental retardation with no known cause.

Field dependence. The organization of the field as a whole dominates perception of its parts; an item within a field is experienced as fused within the organized ground.

Field independence. The ability to perceive items as discrete from the organized field.

Figure-ground disturbance. The inability to differentiate the central stimulus or figure from its background.

Figure-ground perception. The ability to attend to one aspect (figure) of a sensory field while perceiving it in relation to the rest of the field (ground).

Fine motor coordination. Fine muscle control required to do precise movements, as in writing and drawing.

Fine motor skills. Small muscle–dependent skills, such as reaching, grasping, and eye-hand movement.

Finger agnosia. Inability to recognize the names of or identify the individual fingers of one's own hand or of the hands of others.

Five percent level. A statistical level indicating that the obtained results would be expected to occur 5% or less of the time by chance alone.

Flaccid paralysis. Paralysis in which the muscles become weak, soft, or atrophied.

Flexion. Bending of any part of the body, especially joints.

Fluid intelligence. Type of intelligence that is independent of education and experience; it is the basic capacity for learning and problem solving.

Focal lesion. A lesion of a small definite area.

Formal operations stage (Piaget). The final stage of Piaget's theory of cognitive development, occurring between the approximate ages of 11 and 15 years, characterized by systematic reasoning abilities and successful integration of all past intellectual operations.

Fraternal twins. See Dizygotic twins.

Frequency. The number of times a particular score is obtained.

Frequency distribution. A tabulation of scores from high to low (or low to high) showing the number of persons who obtain each score or group of scores.

Frontal lobe. One of the four lobes making up the cerebral cortex; responsible for planning, performance, and execution of all voluntary behavior.

g. A term referring to general intellectual ability.

Gait. The manner or style of walking or running.

Galactosemia. A metabolic disorder caused by a recessive gene; renders the individual unable to metabolize various forms of sugar. Symptoms include cataracts, mental retardation, jaundice, and poor weight gain.

Gaussian distribution. See Normal distribution.

General factor. See g.

Generalization. The process of forming an idea or judgment that is applicable to an entire class of objects, people, or events.

Generic. Relating to or descriptive of an entire group or class; general. Also, commonly available; not protected by trademark; nonproprietary (as in reference to drugs).

Genes. The fundamental transmitters of hereditary characteristics, located on chromosomes.

Genetics. The study of the nature and mechanisms of heredity and variation in biological systems.

Genotype. The genetic makeup of an individual; the qualities or traits shared by members of a biologically defined group.

Gerstmann syndrome. A group of symptoms (agraphia, acalculia, right-left disorientation, and finger agnosia) indicating a disturbance of laterality and of body image.

Gestalt. A term used to express any unified whole whose properties cannot be derived just by adding the parts and their relationships; more than the sum of its parts.

Gifted. Usually those with IQs above 130; talented.

Global. Perceived as a whole without attempt to distinguish separate parts or functions.

Global aphasia. Aphasia that involves all of the functions which make up speech or communication.

Global cognitive style. See Relational cognitive style.

Grade norm. A standard of performance that represents the average performance of a group of pupils in a given grade.

Grand mal seizure. The most common and most dramatic of the epilepsies, involving widespread and abnormal electrical activity in the brain, violent convulsions and loss of consciousness.

Graphesthesia. Sense by which outlines, numbers, words, or symbols traced or written on the skin are recognized.

Gross motor skills. Large muscle–dependent skills such as walking, running, and throwing.

Group factor. In factor analysis, a factor present in more than one test in a set of tests but not present in all.

Group test. A test that may be administered to a number of individuals at the same time.

Hallucination. Perception of a sensory stimulus when there is no real external stimulation.

Halo effect. The tendency in rating to let one of an individual's traits influence ratings on other traits.

Handedness. Hand preference of an individual.

Haptic. Pertaining to the sense of touch.

Hard neurological signs. Physical symptoms of brain injury that can be identified medically.

Hemiopia. The condition where one has only one half of the field of vision in one or both eyes.

Hemiparesis. Weakness or incomplete paralysis of one side of the body.

Hemiplegia. Paralysis of one side of the body.

Hemispheres. The two symmetrical halves of the brain, left and right.

Hemispherical dominance. Refers to the fact that one cerebral hemisphere of the brain generally leads the other in control of body movement, resulting in the preferred use of left or right (laterality).

Heterogeneous. Composed of parts that display marked dissimilarity.

Heterogeneous grouping. The placing of children without regard to achieving homogeneity.

Homogeneity. Similarity or likeness among members of any group, data, or variables. Also, the degree to which a test measures a single variable.

Homogeneous grouping. Placing children with the same characteristics together. Also, arranging a set of variables into like categories.

Homolateral. See Ipsilateral.

Hydrocephalus. Presence of too much cerebrospinal fluid in the ventricles of the brain. Obstruction of normal circulation of cerebrospinal fluid may be due to abnormal brain development, brain infection (such as meningitis), brain hemorrhage, or presence of a lump or cyst.

Hyperactivity. Exceedingly active behavior not typical of most children, and characterized by overactivity, restlessness, distractibility, and limited attention span.

Hyperkinesis. See Hyperactivity.

Hyperthyroidism. Reversible condition caused by oversecretion of the thyroid hormone thyroxin. Characterized by anxiety, irritability, and restlessness. May be accompanied by states of excitement with delusions and hallucinations.

Hypertonia. Excessive muscle tone.

Hypoactivity. Exceedingly inactive behavior not typical of most children, and characterized by lethargy, frequent sleepiness, and little movement.

Hypokinesis. See Hypoactivity.

Hypothyroidism. See Cretinism; Myxedema.

Hypotonia. Decrease in muscle tone.

Iconic memory. Relating to a very short-term, image-like memory; visual-spatial imagery characteristic of the child's second stage of linguistic development.

Ideational agnosia. Inability to visualize or recall construction of words.

Ideational fluency. The flow and number of ideas that an individual can generate.

Idiopathic. Self-originated; of unknown origin.

Impulsive. The tendency to act quickly without thinking.

Inborn error of metabolism. An innate disorder in which the usual coterie of the baby's chemical reactions is disrupted, usually by an enzymatic defect.

Independent variable. Any variable (stimulus) that is assumed to produce an effect on, or be related to, a behavior of interest; a variable manipulated by the experimenter.

Individual test. A test that can be administered only to one individual at a time.

Individualized educational program (IEP). A written program of educational services required by PL 94-142.

Infantile autism. A psychosis of early childhood characterized by early onset, extreme aloneness, mutism or echolalic speech, and intolerance of change in routine.

Innate intelligence. Genetically determined intelligence.

Intelligence. Definitions of intelligence usually include three concepts: (a) the ability to deal with abstractions, (b) the ability to learn, and (c) the ability to cope with new or novel situations.

Intelligence quotient (IQ). An index of rate of development in certain aspects of intelligence during childhood, originally found by obtaining the ratio between mental age (MA) and chronological age (CA); IQ = MA/CA × 100. Preferred current practice is to compute a Deviation IQ (*see* Deviation IQ).

Intelligence test. A psychological test designed to measure cognitive functions, such as reasoning, comprehension, and judgment.

Interindividual. A comparison of one person with another or of one person with a group of individuals.

Internal consistency reliability. The extent to which the items on a test correlate among themselves.

Interpolation. The act of estimating a value between two given values or points.

Intersensory integration. Combining information from more than one sensory modality to form a perception about a certain object.

Interval scale. A measurement scale that does not have an absolute zero point, but whose intervals are equal.

Intervention strategy. The rationale, methods, and materials upon which instruction, treatment, or rehabilitation are based.

Intonation. Pattern of pitch, stress, and juncture in language.

Intracranial neoplasm. New or abnormal growth, such as a tumor, located within the cranium.

Intraindividual. Comparing different characteristics within an individual.

Intrauterine insult. A foreign agent introduced into the uterus during the gestation period (particularly during the first trimester) that interferes with proper fetal development.

Intrinsic tumor. A tumor located entirely within the limb or organ of origin.

Intuitive thought (Piaget). The third stage of Piaget's cognitive development theory, occurring between the approximate ages of 4 and 7. The child's thought patterns are bound by immediate perceptions and experiences rather than by flexible mental functions.

In utero. Pertaining to the time that the human is developing within the womb or uterus—from the time of conception to the time of birth.

Ipsative score. A scoring scheme in which subtest performance is contrasted with the individual's average subtest performance rather than with the average of a reference group, as in normative scoring.

Ipsilateral. Homolateral; occurring on the same side.

IQ. See Intelligence quotient.

Irrelevancies. Words or ideas out of context with the issues being considered.

Item analysis. A general term for procedures designed to assess the usefulness of a test item. (*See also* Difficulty index; Discrimination index.)

Jacksonian epilepsy. A form of epilepsy in which muscle spasms are limited to a particular part of the body, usually without loss of consciousness; caused by irritation of the cerebral cortex.

Kinesthesia. The sensation of bodily position, presence, or movement resulting chiefly from stimulation of sensory nerve endings in muscles, tendons, and joints.

Kinesthetic. See Kinesthesia.

Kinesthetic method. Method of treating reading disability through the systematic incorporation of muscle movement (such as tracing the outline of words) to supplement visual and auditory stimuli.

Kinetic reversal. Transposing letters within words, or numerals within number groups (*aet* for *ate;* 749 for 794).

Kuder-Richardson formula 20 (KR-20). A formula for estimating the internal consistency reliability of a test based on only a single administration of the test.

Kwashiorkor. A nutritional deficiency in young children resulting from severe protein deprivation and characterized by edema, dermatitis, growth failure, and liver damage.

Labeling. Describing exceptional children using terms based on categories of exceptionality, such as mentally retarded, learning disabled, and emotionally disturbed.

Lability. Flexible, free in expression, easily changed; especially pertains to emotions.

Lag. See Maturational lag.

Language test. A test composed of verbal or numerical items, i.e., items involving the use of language.

Lateral confusion. Tendency to perform some acts with a right side preference and others with a left side preference or to shift from right to left for one type of activity.

Laterality. Preference for use of left or right side of body; determined by hemispherical dominance.

Law of effect. The learning principle postulated by Edward Thorndike which states that responses leading to satisfying results will have a tendency to be repeated, while responses leading to annoying states will not.

Learning. A relatively permanent change in behavior occurring as the result of practice.

Learning disability. A disorder in which there is an educationally significant discrepancy between estimated intellectual potential and actual level of performance.

Left-to-right progression. Recognizing letter or word sequences correctly; can be disturbed if laterality has not been established.

Lesion. An injury to tissue from wound, disease, or surgical procedures.

Lobes of the brain. See Frontal lobe; Temporal lobe; Parietal lobe; Occipital lobe.

Local norms. Norms based on a local school or school system and used in place of or in addition to national norms.

Locomotion. Movement from one location to another, such as walking, crawling, and rolling.

Longitudinal study. A study in which data on the same group of individuals are collected repeatedly over a period of time.

Long-term memory. A storage system that enables individuals to retain information for relatively long periods of time.

Loose association. In schizophrenia, an aspect of thought disorder wherein the patient has difficulty sticking to one topic and drifts off on a train of associations evoked by an idea.

Low birth weight. The weight of any newborn child who, regardless of length of gestation, weighs less than 5½ pounds.

Low ceiling. Term applied to a test that is too easy for some examinees.

Machismo. A life pattern in which masculine behaviors are emphasized.

Mainstreaming. The administrative practice of placing handicapped children in regular classroom settings; generally involves the provision of supportive special education services, such as a resource room.

Malapropism. Misapplication of a word; confusion of a word sounding somewhat like the one intended but ludicrously wrong in the context.

Mastery test. A test given with a single objective in mind—that of determining to what extent individuals have learned or mastered a given piece of material or lesson.

Maturation. The attainment of complete psychobiological development, or the process whereby this state is reached.

Maturational lag. Delay in physiological, mental, or neurological development without apparent structural defect.

MBD. See Minimal brain dysfunction.

Mean. The arithmetical average attained by adding up scores and dividing their total by the number of scores.

Measures of central tendency. Those values which closely approximate the middle as opposed to the extremes of a distribution of scores (e.g., mean, median, and mode).

Median (Md). The middle of a distribution or set of ranked scores; the point (score) that divides the group into two equal parts; the 50th percentile.

Medical model. The conceptualization of abnormal behaviors as diseases, analogous to organic diseases; also termed the disease model.

Memory span. Number of items that can be recalled immediately after presentation.

Meningitis. A brain infection involving an acute inflammation of the membranes that cover the brain and spinal cord; characterized by drowsiness, confusion, irritability, and sensory impairments.

Meningocele. A protusion of the membranes of the brain or spinal cord through a defect in the skull or the spinal column.

Meningomyelocele. A protrusion of the membranes and the cord through a defect in the vertebral column.

Mental ability. Term used synonymously with intelligence or cognitive ability.

Mental age (MA). Degree of general mental ability possessed by the average child of a chronological age corresponding to that expressed by the MA score. Also a score on a test.

Mental deficiency. *See* Mental retardation.

Mental retardation. Refers to significantly subaverage general intellectual functioning existing concurrently with deficits in adaptive behavior, and manifested during the developmental period.

Mental retardation, mild. Range of IQs between 52 and 67 (Stanford-Binet) or 55 to 69 (Wechsler).

Mental retardation, moderate. Range of IQs between 36 and 51 (Stanford-Binet) or 40 to 54 (Wechsler).

Mental retardation, profound. Range of IQs 19 and below (Stanford-Binet) or 24 and below (Wechsler, extrapolated).

Mental retardation, severe. Range of IQs between 20 and 35 (Stanford-Binet) or 25 and 39 (Wechsler, extrapolated).

Metabolic dysfunction. Dysfunction in the chemical processes of the body.

Methylphenidate. Generic term for Ritalin; prescribed for children with hyperactivity.

Microcephaly. A condition characterized by smallness of the head, with associated subnormal mental development; produced by incomplete brain development due to a premature closing of the skull.

Midbrain. Smallest of the three principal divisions of the vertebrate brain; concerned mainly with eye movement and reflexes, as well as relay of auditory impulses to the auditory cortex of the temporal lobes.

Mild learning disabilities. Mild perceptual-conceptual deviations that impair the ability of children to process information effectively, thereby serving as barriers to appropriate academic adaptation.

Minimal brain dysfunction (MBD). A relatively mild impairment of brain functioning that is characterized by impulsive behavior and short attention span.

Mixed dominance theory. Theory that language disorders may be due wholly or partly to the fact that one cerebral hemisphere does not consistently lead the other in the control of sensorimotor, perception, or body movements, i.e., hemispherical dominance is not adequately established.

Mixed laterality. Tendency to perform some acts with a right side preference and others with a left, or the shifting from the right to left for certain activities.

Mnemonics. Pertaining to memory or the improvement of memory with the aid of artificial systems.

Modality. The sensory pathways through which an individual receives information and thereby learns.

Mode. The most frequently occurring score in a group of scores (in statistics).

Moderator variables. Variables such as sex, age, race, social class, and personality characteristics that affect the relationship (correlation) between two other variables.

Mongolism. *See* Down's syndrome.

Monoplegia. Paralysis of one limb.

Monozygotic twins. Twins originating from a single fertilized ovum and having identical genetic makeup; identical twins.

Motor area. Portion of the frontal lobe that controls voluntary movement.

Multiple correlation coefficient (R). A measure of the overall degree of relationship, varying between −1.00 and +1.00, of several predictor variables with a single criterion variable.

Multisensory. Making use of more than one sensory modality to bring stimuli to the brain for interpretation.

Multisensory approaches. Educational techniques that require the use of several sensory modalities employed simultaneously or successively to facilitate learning.

Muscular dystrophy. Progressive atrophy of the muscles resulting in neuromuscular impairment and weakness.

Mutism. A refusal or inability to talk due to severe emotional conflicts. Also, the lack of speech, resulting from congenital deafness or lack of proper development of the speech organs.

Myxedema. An acute condition caused by deficiency in thyroid hormone secretion and characterized by poor emotional control, easy fatigability, frequent skin disorders, and hair loss in adults. (*See also* Cretinism.)

N. Symbol used to represent the number of cases in any specified group.

National norms. Norms based on a national sample. (*See also* Norms.)

Naturalistic observation. The examination of behavior under normal or unstructured conditions.

Negative transfer. The interference of a previously learned task with the learning of a new task.

Neologisms. Invention; coinage of new words of the individual's own making.

Neonatal period. The first ten days following birth.

Neonate. The newborn infant.

Neoplasm. Tumor or abnormal new growth.

Nephritis. Inflammation of the kidneys.

Neurological. Pertaining to the nervous system. Neurological problems are those arising from disease, damage, or dysfunction of the nervous system.

Neurological examination. Examination of sensory and motor responses, especially the reflexes, to determine impairments of the nervous system.

Neurological handicap. Impairment of the central nervous system.

Neurological insult. Damage to the brain or spinal cord caused by prenatal, perinatal, or postnatal factors.

Neurological lag. Neurological or nervous system development that is slower than other physical development.

Neurology. Discipline that studies the structure and function of the nervous system.

Neuromuscular. Pertaining to any process that is a joint function of the muscles and nerves.

Neuron. An individual nerve cell; the basic unit of the nervous system.

Neuropsychology. Branch of psychology that deals with the nervous system's impact on behavior (or brain-behavior relationships).

Nominal aphasia. See Anomia.

Nominal scale. A measurement scale that classifies its elements into categories to indicate that the elements are different, but does not classify them according to order or magnitude.

Nonlanguage test. See Nonverbal test.

Nonverbal test. A test consisting of nonverbal and nonlanguage materials for which spoken or written language is not required.

Normal curve. A theoretical frequency distribution for a set of data, represented by a bell-shaped curve symmetrical about the mean.

Normal distribution. See Normal curve.

Normalization. Providing services and opportunities for the handicapped that are as close as possible to those for the nonhandicapped.

Normalized scores. Scores obtained by transforming raw scores in such a way that the transformed scores are normally distributed and have a mean of 0 and a standard deviation of 1 (or some linear function of these numbers).

Norm-referenced measures. Measures that are used to identify an individual's performance in relation to the performance of others on the same measure.

Norms. A list of scores and the corresponding percentile ranks, standard scores, or other transformed scores of a group of examinees on whom a test was standardized.

Nystagmus. Rapid jerky involuntary movement of the eyes, followed by a slower return.

Object permanence (Piaget). A scheme acquired during the sensorimotor stage of development in which children know that an object continues to exist even when it is removed from the visual field.

Objective test. A test scored by comparing the examinee's responses to a list of correct answers determined beforehand.

Objectives. The goals (information, values, and other behavioral changes) or aims of instruction.

Oblique rotation. In a factor analysis, a rotation in which the factor axes are allowed to form acute or obtuse angles. The factors are correlated and a second or third order factor can then be extracted.

Obtained score. See Raw score.

Occipital lobe. One of the four lobes making up the cerebral cortex; responsible for processing information from the visual system.

Ocular. Pertaining to the eye.

Ocular pursuit. Visually following a moving target by successive fixations of the eye.

Oculomotor. Pertaining to eye movements.

Odd-even reliability. The correlation between the scores on the odd-numbered items and even-numbered items on a test, corrected by the Spearman-Brown reliability formula. (See also Spearman-Brown formula.)

Olfactory. Pertaining to the sense of smell.

Omnibus test. A test consisting of a variety of items designed to measure different aspects of mental functioning.

One percent level. A statistical level indicating that the obtained results would be expected to occur 1% or less of the time by chance alone.

Ontogeny. The developmental history of an organism.

Operation (Piaget). A mental process that is integral to an overall system, such as adding, subtracting, dividing, multiplying, or classifying.

Operational definition. A definition that is expressed in terms of the procedures (operations) used to measure a trait or object or process.

Operations (Guilford). Cognitive processes or intellectual actions.

Optic atrophy. Progressive deterioration of the optic nerve.

Optic nerve. Nerve fibers beginning at the back of the retina that converge and connect the retina with the brain's visual centers.

Oral method. Method of teaching communication to deaf or hard-of-hearing persons by speech and lip reading.

Ordinal scale. A non-equal interval measurement scale that does not start from an absolute zero point and assigns values according to ordinal numbers: first, second, etc.

Organic. Pertaining to the biological as opposed to the functional aspects of an organism.

Organic brain damage (OBD). See Brain damage.

Organicity. Refers to impairment of the central nervous system.

Orthogonal rotation. In a factor analysis, a rotation that maintains the independence of factors; that is, the axes are at right angles and therefore uncorrelated.

Paper-and-pencil test. A test that requires written answers; most group tests are paper-and-pencil tests.

Parallel-form reliability. See Equivalent forms reliability.

Parallel forms (equivalent forms). Two tests are equivalent in that they contain the same kinds of items of equal difficulty and are highly correlated.

Paraphasia. The habitual introduction of incorrect and inappropriate words into speech.

Paraplegia. A paralysis of one half of the body—usually the lower half—due to injuries of the spinal cord.

Paresis. Slight or partial paralysis. Also used alone to designate general paresis (dementia associated with syphilitic infection of the brain).

Parietal lobe. One of the four lobes making up the cerebral cortex; responsible for processing somatosensory and visuospatial input from the body.

Partially hearing. Hard of hearing; individuals on the mild to moderate end of the continuum of degree of auditory impairment who can usually understand conversational speech, though some require the benefits of a hearing aid.

Partially sighted. Individuals with visual acuity of 20/70 or less in the better eye with correcting glasses, but still with some functional sight; those with seriously defective vision.

Pathognomic. Characteristic of a disease; a sign or symptom from which a diagnosis can be made.

Percentile band. A range of percentile ranks within which there is a certain probability that an examinee's true score on a test will fall.

Percentile norms. A norm given in terms of the percentile standings of individuals on the test or measure in question.

Percentile rank. A point (score) in a distribution at or below which fall the percent of cases indicated by the percentile. Thus a score coinciding with the 84th percentile is regarded as equaling or surpassing that of 84 percent of the persons in the group, and such that 16 percent of the performances exceed this score.

Perception. The process whereby sensory stimuli are organized, interpreted, and imbued with meaning; dependent on the past experiences of the organism.

Perceptual disorder. A disturbance in the ability to accurately interpret sensory stimulation.

Perceptual handicap. Inadequate ability to attend, recognize, discriminate, and integrate information seen, heard, and touched, resulting in conceptual (cognitive) deviations.

Perceptual-motor. A term describing the interaction of the various channels of perception with motor activity.

Perceptual-motor match. Process of comparing the input data received through the motor system and the input data received through perception.

Performance test. Test composed of items that do not involve the use of language, either oral or visual, except for the interpretation and following of directions. Even directions may be given without words if necessary.

Perinatal. Connected with or occurring during the birth process.

Peripheral vision. Side vision; the ability to see objects, movement, or light on the left and right or at the periphery while looking straight ahead.

Perseveration. Persistence of a previous response in spite of its lack of relation to the present situation.

Petit mal seizures. Epileptic episodes that are marked by brief, frequent attacks of impaired consciousness, staring, disinterest, loss of attention, blinking of the eyes, or loss of normal posture.

Phenotype. The individual's observable traits.

Phenylketonuria (PKU). A hereditary form of mental retardation caused by lack of a necessary enzyme (phenylalanine hydroxylase) in amino acid metabolism.

Phi coefficient. A coefficient of correlation, frequently used in item analysis, that indicates the degree of relationship between two dichotomized variables.

Phobia. A persistent and abnormal fear.

Phoneme. The smallest unit of sound in spoken language, such as |b| in "boy."

Physiognomy. Facial features, especially when regarded as revealing character.

Piagetian stages. See Sensorimotor stage; Preoperational stage; Concrete operations stage; Formal operations stage.

Pica. A strong craving to eat nonnutritive objects, e.g., paint, gravel, or hair.

PKU. See Phenylketonuria.

PL 94-142. The Education for All Handicapped Children Act of 1975.

Placebo. An inert (harmless) substance used in drug experiments as a control.

Placement. The administrative assignment of children to one or more specific instructional settings for which they are believed to be best suited.

Plantar reflex. The flexion of the toes when the sole of the foot is lightly stroked.

Plasticity of development. The quality of an organism to be flexible and adaptive to conditions encountered during its development.

Pneumoencephalogram. A procedure that permits the outlining of the cerebral ventricular system and subarachnoid system.

Point-biserial coefficient. A coefficient of correlation between a dichotomous variable and a continuous variable.

Point scale. A type of test in which each item is assigned a point value and the individual's performance is rated according to the total number of points earned.

Polygenic. The interaction of many genes, each of which adds a little to the development of a trait.

Postnatal. The period immediately following birth.

Power test. A test with ample time limits so that all examinees have time to try all items.

Predictive validity. The extent to which scores on a test are predictive of performance on some criterion measure assessed at a later time; usually expressed as a correlation between the test (predictor) and the criterion.

Prematurity. Infant born after the 27th week and before full term; arbitrarily defined as weighing between 2.2 and 5.5 pounds.

Prenatal. Prior to birth.

Preoperational stage (Piaget). The second major stage of cognitive development, covering approximately the age period between 2 and 7 years.

Preschool intervention. Programs designed to improve or remediate basic academic and personal-social skills in preschool children, usually those between the ages of 4 and 6 years.

Prevalence. The number of cases of a condition or disease identified in a population at a given point in time.

Probability. The degree to which it is likely that an event will occur in a certain way as opposed to other possible ways.

Product-moment correlation coefficient. An index of the relationship between two variables. (*See also* Correlation coefficient.)

Products (Guilford). The forms that result from intellectual operations on different content.

Profile. A graphic representation of the results on several tests (or subtests) when the results have been expressed in some uniform or comparable terms (e.g., standard scores, percentile ranks, or grade equivalents).

Prognosis. Pertaining to the prediction of the duration, course, and outcome of a certain condition.

Prognostic test. A test used to predict success in a specific subject or field.

Projective technique. A method of personality study in which ambiguous stimulus materials are used to elicit subjective responses of an associative or fantasy nature.

Pronoun reversal. A symptom of autistic children in which pronouns are reversed, e.g., child refers to himself or herself as "you" and to other people as "I."

Proprioceptive stimulation activities. Activities providing stimuli to receptors in joints, tendons, or muscles.

Psychoeducational approach. Application of psychological and educational approaches in the school.

Psychoeducational diagnostician. A specialist who diagnoses and evaluates a child who is having difficulty in learning.

Psychogenic. Pertaining to conditions that have no clear-cut organic foundations.

Psycholinguistics. The study of the language and communication processes from the shared viewpoint of the disciplines of psychology and linguistics.

Psychometrics. The measurement of psychological variables, such as intelligence, aptitude, and emotional disturbance. Also, the mathematical, especially statistical, design of psychological tests and measures.

Psychometrist. A person who administers psychological tests. Also, a specialist in the statistical analysis of psychological data.

Psychomotor. Pertaining to the motor effects of psychological processes. Psychomotor tests are tests of motor skill that depend upon sensory or perceptual-motor coordination.

Psychomotor seizure. Epileptic seizure associated with disease of the temporal lobe and characterized by variable degrees of impairment of consciousness. The patient performs a series of coordinated acts which are out of place, bizarre, and serve no useful purpose and for which he/she is amnesic.

Psychosis. A severe mental disorder characterized by disturbance in cognitive, perceptual, and emotional processes.

Psychotropic drugs. Drugs that affect mental activity.

Quadriplegia. Paralysis of all four limbs.

Quartile. A score in a frequency distribution below which either 25% (1st quartile), 50% (2nd quartile), 75% (3rd quartile), or 100% (4th quartile) of the total number of scores fall.

Questionnaire. A list of questions concerning a particular topic, administered to a group of individuals in order to obtain information about their preferences, beliefs, interests, and behavior.

r. A symbol for the coefficient of correlation (Pearson r). (*See also* Correlation coefficient.)

Random sample. A sample obtained by assigning subjects to groups in such a manner that each subject has an equal chance of being in each group.

Range. A rough measure of the spread or variability of a group of scores, computed by subtracting the lowest score from the highest score. The range is unduly influenced by extreme values.

Rank-order correlation (rho). Method of obtaining a correlation coefficient by assigning ranks to each score and determining the relationship between the sets of ranks.

Rapport. Relationship, especially one of mutual trust or emotional affinity.

Rating scale. A scale used by a rater to estimate magnitude of the trait or quality rated.

Ratio IQ. An intelligence quotient obtained by dividing the mental age obtained on an intelligence test by the examinee's chronological age and multiplying by 100.

Ratio scale. A scale of measurement having a true zero and on which equal numerical ratios imply equal ratios of the attribute being measured.

Raw score. An examinee's unconverted score on a test (e.g., the number of correct answers or the number of correct answers minus a certain portion of incorrect answers).

Readiness test. A test that measures the extent to which an individual posesses the skills and knowledge necessary for learning some complex subject such as reading or writing.

Reading age. Score that indicates a child's reading ability in terms of age.

Reading disability. Reading level significantly below measured intellectual capacity or estimated reading level.

Reading readiness. General stage of developmental maturity at which the child can learn to read easily and efficiently.

Reauditorization. Ability to recall the name or sound of visual symbols (letters).

Recall item. An item that requires recall of some information.

Receptive language. Language that is spoken or written by others and received by the individual; includes listening, reading, and understanding sign language.

Recessive gene. A gene that requires another gene like itself in order for the trait to be manifest.

Recognition item. An item that requires recognition of the correct answer in a list of possible answers.

Redundancy (remedial teaching). The art of presenting the same information to as many of the senses as simultaneously as possible in a given task.

Reflex. The automatic elicitation of a specific response without involving higher brain functions.

Regression effect. Tendency for a retest score to be closer to the mean than the initial test score.

Regression equation. An equation for predicting a score on a criterion variable from the scores on one or more predictor variables.

Relational cognitive style. A style in which the individual uses a global, self-centered descriptive method of abstraction; parts have no meaning in themselves; information is embedded in the field.

Reliability. The degree to which a test is consistent in its measurements. (*See also* Equivalent forms reliability; Internal consistency reliability; Split-half reliability.)

Reliability coefficient. An index that varies from .00 to 1.00 and indicates the reliability of a test. (*See also* Reliability.)

Remediation. Procedures used to increase a child's competence in various skills.

Representative sample. A sample that matches the population of which it is a sample with respect to characteristics important for the purposes under investigation.

Resource room. Any room in the school other than the regular classroom in which special education instruction is offered.

Resource teacher. A specialist who works with children with learning disabilities and acts as a consultant to other teachers, providing materials and methods to help children who are having difficulty within the regular classroom.

Response set. Tendency for examinees to respond in relatively fixed or stereotyped ways, such as the tendency to guess, to answer "true," or to give socially desirable answers.

Response style. See Response set.

Retrolental fibroplasia (RLF). Destruction of the retina due to excessive exposure to pure oxygen.

Reversal. A transposition of letters.

Reversibility. The ability to move backward in a sequence of thoughts or previous actions.

Revisualization. Ability to retrieve a visual image of a stimulus (e.g., letter or word or object) that was seen before.

Rh incompatibility. This occurs when the mother has Rh negative blood and the fetus has Rh positive blood. When blood from the fetus mixes in the placenta with the mother's blood, antibodies are produced that destroy the red blood cells of the fetus. This can cause such pathologies as abortions, stillbirth, jaundice, or mental retardation.

Right-left disorientation. Inability to distinguish right from left; confused directionality.

Rigidity. Maintaining an attitude or behavioral set when such a set is no longer appropriate.

Ritalin. A drug used to control hyperactivity.

Rotation. Changing the orientation of a design or letter.

Rubella (German measles). An infectious disease which, if contracted by the mother during the first three months of pregnancy, has a high risk of causing a variety of congenital anomalies, including deafness, cataract, cardiac malformation, and mental retardation.

Saccadic movements. The jerky movements of the eyes from one fixation point to another, as while reading.

Sample. A group drawn from a population which is considered to be representative of that population so that statistical conclusions based on the sample will also be valid for that population.

Schema (Piaget). Term used to describe an individual's action and its underlying mental structure (e.g., grasping schema, sucking schema).

Schizophrenogenic. Causing or contributing to the development of schizophrenia; often applied to the cold, conflict-inducing mother who is alleged to make her children schizophrenic.

Scholastic aptitude. The ability of a person to learn the kinds of skills taught in school.

Scholastic aptitude test. Any test that predicts the ability of a person to learn the kinds of skills taught in school.

School phobia. An acute, irrational dread of attending school, usually accompanied by somatic complaints; the most common phobia of childhood.

Screening. A general term for any rapid selection process, usually not very precise, to select applicants.

Seizures. Convulsions of varying degrees of severity caused by abnormal electrochemical discharges in the brain.

Selection. The use of tests and other devices to choose applicants for a program.

Selection ratio. The percentage of applicants who are chosen for a particular position.

Selective attention. The capacity to choose from an array of competing stimuli those that are relevant to the task or purpose at hand.

Self-concept. The person's sense of his or her own identity, worth, or capabilities.

Self-fulfilling prophecy. An attitude held by one person (believer) about another person that may determine how the believer interacts with the other person; the attitude eventually may lead the other person to change behavior so as to reflect the believer's attitude. Also can apply to an attitude of a person about himself or herself.

Self-report inventory. A personality or interest inventory consisting of a series of items that the examinee rates as being characteristic (true) or not characteristic (not true) of himself or herself.

Semantic aphasia. Inability to understand the meaning of words or phrases.

Semi-interquartile range (Q). Half the distance between the first and third quartiles in a frequency distribution. A measure of variability, the semi-interquartile range is computed as $Q = (Q_3 - Q_1)/2$, where Q_3 is the 75th percentile and Q_1 the 25th percentile.

Sensorimotor. Combination of the input of sense organs and the output of motor activity.

Sensorimotor stage (Piaget). The first stage of cognitive development (0–2 years), in which learning activities are directed toward the coordination of simple sensorimotor skills.

Sensorineural hearing loss. Impaired ability to hear resulting from damage or dysfunction of the inner ear and its associated sensory cells and nerve pathways.

Separation anxiety. A fear experienced when a person is separated from someone on whom he or she is very dependent.

Sequential development. A step-by-step plan of development wherein competency at any given stage implies having achieved competency in all earlier stages.

Sex-linked characteristics. Those inherited characteristics carried by the genes of the X and Y chromosomes.

Shaping. Form of operant conditioning that begins by reinforcing all responses similar to the desired one, then reinforcing only successively closer approximations until the desired response is attained.

Sheltered workshop. A facility that provides occupational training or protective employment for handicapped, retarded, or disturbed individuals.

Short-term memory. The temporary retention of information (usually 30–60 seconds).

Sickle cell anemia. A hereditary disorder, governed by a recessive gene, that results in red blood cells assuming a sickle shape, with resultant obstruction of capillaries.

Significant difference. A discrepancy between two statistics, computed from separate samples, which is of such a magnitude that the probability that the samples were drawn from different populations is greater than some previously set limit.

Skewness. The degree of asymmetry of a frequency distribution.

Slow learner. Usually refers to a child who is performing below grade level.

Social quotient (SQ). An index of a person's ability to look after his or her own needs and to take responsibility for himself or herself.

Socioeconomic status. An individual's position in a given society as determined by wealth, occupation, and social class.

Sociogram. A diagram depicting preferred or actual interactions between members of a given group.

Sociometric. Pertaining to a technique for assessing the degree to which an individual is liked or respected by his or her peers.

Sociometry. A quantitative method for determining and describing the pattern of acceptances and rejections in a group of people.

Soft neurological signs. Signs associated with deficiencies in complex behaviors that are considered uncertain indicators of brain damage.

Somatosensory. Pertains to the ability of the body to recognize various sensory functions, such as recognizing shapes with hands while blindfolded.

Sound blending. The ability to integrate separate word sounds into a meaningful whole.

Space perception. Awareness of the spatial properties of an object, including position, direction, size, form, and distance.

Spastic. Characterized by sudden, violent involuntary contraction of a muscle or a group of muscles, attended by pain and interference with function and producing involuntary movement and distortion.

Spasticity. The state of increase of tension in a muscle; heightened resistance to the extension or flexion of a joint.

Spearman-Brown formula. A formula giving the relationship between the reliability of a test and its length.

Special ability tasks. Tasks that measure special abilities, such as mechanical, clerical, musical, and artistic.

Special class approach. An intervention alternative for exceptional children that involves the placement of children with similar instructional needs in a special class.

Specific language disability. A term usually applied to children with adequate intelligence who have difficulty in learning to read, write, spell, or communicate.

Specific variance. Refers to variance associated with a specific test in contrast to the variance the test has in common with other tests.

Speed test. A test in which individual differences depend entirely on speed of performance.

Spina bifida. A developmental anomaly characterized by defective closure of the bony encasement of the spinal cord through which the cord and meninges may or may not protrude; often associated with lower body paralysis.

Splinter skills. Islands of competence, such as rote repetition of long word lists or early recognition of the printed word, in autistic children. These are highly specific skills that have a limited relationship to other skills.

Split-half reliability. Estimating the reliability of a test by splitting it into comparable halves, correlating the scores from the halves, and adjusting for length using the Spearman-Brown formula.

SQ. See Social quotient.

Standard deviation (SD). A measure of the variability or dispersion of a distribution of scores. Computation of the *SD* is based on the square of the deviation of each score from the mean. The *SD* is sometimes called "sigma" and represented by the symbol σ.

Standard error of estimate. An estimate of the margin of error in an individual's predicted criterion score due to imperfect validity of the test.

Standard error of measurement. An estimate of the margin of error in an individual's score due to the imperfect reliability of an instrument.

Standard scores. Scores that express an individual's distance from the mean in terms of the standard deviation of the distribution. Examples are *T* scores, Deviation IQs, *z* scores, stanines, and sten scores.

Standardization. Administering of a carefully constructed test to a large, representative sample of people under standard conditions for the purpose of determining norms.

Standardized test. A test of empirically selected items which has unambiguous directions for use, adequately determined norms, and reliability and validity data.

Stanine. A standard score scale consisting of the scores 1 through 9 and having a mean of 5 and a standard deviation of 2. Each stanine (except 1 and 9) is one-half *SD* in width, with the middle stanine of 5 extending from one-fourth *SD* below to one-fourth *SD* above the mean.

Statistic. Any value that expresses the end result of statistical manipulation of other values.

Sten score. A linearly transformed standard score yielding 10 single-digit scores with a mean of 5.5 and a standard deviation of 2.

Stereognosis. The ability to perceive and understand objects or forms by touch.

Strabismus. Failure of the eyes to focus properly on the same points, leading to a squint, cross-eye, or wall-eye.

Stratified sample. A sample in which cases are selected so that they closely match the demographic characteristics of the geographical region, community size, and grade (e.g., age, sex, or ethnicity) of the population.

Strauss syndrome. The cluster of symptoms characterizing a type of brain-injured child; includes hyperactivity, distractibility, and impulsivity.

Strephosymbolia. A reading difficulty referring to reversal in perception of left-right order, especially in letter or word order; sometimes called "twisted symbols" (e.g., *was* for *saw*).

Stuttering. Speech impediment characterized by hesitations, rapid repetition of elements, and breathing or vocal muscle spasm.

Subtest. A division of a test designed to measure a particular aspect of that which the test as a whole measures.

Syllabication. A word-attack skill consisting of breaking a word down into its appropriate syllables.

Symbiotic infantile psychosis. Childhood psychosis that appears at the time of a threat of separation from the mother.

Syndrome. A constellation of symptoms and signs that, when occurring together, characterize a particular disorder or disease.

Synkinesia. Involuntary and useless movements accompanying a voluntary movement.

Syntactic. Pertaining to grammar and the rules governing sentence structure and sequence.

Syntax. The way in which words are put together to form phrases and sentences.

T score. A standard score having a mean of 50 and a standard deviation of 10. (*See also* Standard scores.)

Tactile. Pertaining to the sense of touch.

Tactile agnosia. Impaired ability to recognize familiar objects by touch.

Tactile-kinesthetic. Combining sensory impressions of touch and muscle movement.

Tactile perception. Ability to interpret and give meaning to sensory stimuli that are experienced through the sense of touch.

Target behavior. From the behavioral view, refers to the specific and explicitly described observable behavior to be changed.

Task analysis. The examination and description of an instructional task in order to determine its component parts or steps.

Tay-Sachs disease (amaurotic familial idiocy). A disorder of lipoid metabolism caused by a recessive gene that results in a progressive degenerative disease characterized by severe mental retardation, seizures, paralysis, and death.

Temporal. Pertaining to time or time relationships. Also, pertaining to or near the temples of the skull.

Temporal lobe. One of the four lobes making up the cerebral cortex; responsible for processing information from the auditory system. It is closely associated with the limbic system, which has a variety of functions, including regulation of hormones and memory.

Test. An objective and standardized procedure for measuring a behavior sample.

Test anxiety. A feeling of fear or great concern in an individual that he or she will not do well on a test.

Test of significance. A statistical procedure that determines whether the observed variations under various treatment conditions are due to the changes in conditions or to chance fluctuations.

Test-retest reliability. A method of assessing the reliability of a test by administering it to the same group of examinees on two different occasions and computing the correlation between their scores.

Tetrachoric correlation. The correlation between two dichotomized measures. Computation is based on the assumption that the underlying variables are continuous and normally distributed.

Thorazine (chlorpromazine). A major tranquilizer often used in the treatment of schizophrenia; decreases autonomic and motor activity, attention span, and anxiety.

Thought disorder. Impaired thinking in psychotic individuals.

TMR. See Trainable mentally retarded.

Token economy. A behavior modification procedure, based on operant conditioning principles, in which individuals are given artificial rewards for socially desirable behavior; the rewards or tokens can then be exchanged for desired objects and activities.

Token reinforcement. Involves the use of an object or event, such as poker chips, stars, or check marks, to reinforce target behaviors such as completion of assigned work, use of manners, and proper grooming.

Tonic (physiology). Pertaining to a continuing slight stretching usually present in muscles when not in active movement.

Tonic phase (in epilepsy). Unremitting muscular contraction.

Toxemia. Any condition of blood poisoning, especially that caused by bacterial toxins transported through the blood stream from a focus of infection.

Toxicity. The quality of being poisonous.

Tracking. Placing pupils into ability levels or tracks for the purpose of instruction.

Trainable mentally retarded. Mentally retarded children capable of learning few academic skills; IQs in the 30 to 50 range.

Trait. A physical, mental, or behavioral characteristic that distinguishes one person from another.

Transduce. Ability to convey information from one sensory modality to another.

Transfer. The ability to shift information, skills, or strategies learned in one situation to a new situation.

Trauma. Wound or injury, either mental or physical, that inflicts serious damage on the individual.

Tremor. Continual, uncontrollable, involuntary rhythmic muscular motion.

Triplegia. Paralysis of three extremities, most often both legs and one arm.

True score. The hypothetical score that is a measure of the examinee's true knowledge of the test material. In test theory, an examinee's true score on a test is the mean of the distribution of scores that would result if the examinee took the test an infinite number of times.

True variance. Differences in test scores that are due to true differences in the characteristics under consideration.

Tumor (neoplasm). A new growth of tissue in which cell multiplication is uncontrolled and progressive.

Underachievement. Performance poorer than predicted from an aptitude measurement.

Unilateral. One-sided; children who are unilateral use predominantly one side of their body.

Unresponsive. Absence of or inadequate or delayed reaction in the presence of stimuli that usually elicit a reaction.

Validity. The extent to which a test actually measures what it purports to measure. (*See also* Concurrent validity; Construct validity; Content validity; Criterion validity.)

Variability. The spread or dispersion of test scores around their average value, best indicated by their standard deviation.

Variance. A measure of variability of test scores, computed as the mean of the squares of the deviations of raw scores from their arithmetic mean; the square of the standard deviation.

Verbal test. A test in which ability to understand and use words plays a crucial role in determining performance.

Vision screening. A sampling of visual skills for the purpose of assessing visual problems.

Visual acuity. Clarity or sharpness of vision.

Visual agnosia. Impaired ability to recognize familiar objects by sight.

Visual closure. Ability to identify a visual stimulus from an incomplete visual presentation.

Visual evoked potential. Brain waves generated by nerve impulses to the cortex in response to visual stimuli.

Visual field. All of the objects visible to the unmoving eye of a particular observer at a given moment.

Visual-motor coordination. Skills normally performed through visual perception and an integrated motor response; often involves spatial relations and tactile perception.

Visual-motor memory. Ability to reproduce by drawing previously seen objects or designs.

Visual perception. The identification, organization, and interpretation of visual stimuli.

Visual sequential memory. Ability to reproduce sequences of visual items from memory.

Word-attack skills. Ability to analyze unfamiliar words by syllables and phonic elements and to arrive at their pronunciation.

Word blindness. See Alexia.

Word salad. Speech pattern in which words and phrases are combined in a disorganized fashion, seemingly devoid of logic and meaning.

z score. A linearly derived standard score with a mean of zero and a standard deviation of 1. (*See also* Standard scores.)

Thirty-eight terms in this glossary were reprinted by permission of the publisher from *Exceptional Children: A Developmental View,* by M. D. Wyne and P. D. O'Connor (Lexington, Mass.: D. C. Heath and Company, 1979).

References

Abikoff, H., Gittelman-Klein, R., & Klein, D. F. Validation of a classroom observation code for hyperactive children. *Journal of Consulting and Clinical Psychology*, 1977, *45*, 772–783.

Ables, B. S. The use of the Draw-a-Man Test with borderline retarded children without pronounced pathology. *Journal of Clinical Psychology*, 1971, *27*, 262–263.

Abramson, T. The influence of examiner race on first-grade and kindergarten subjects' Peabody Picture Vocabulary Test scores. *Journal of Educational Measurement*, 1969, *6*, 241–246.

Achenbach, T. M. The classification of children's psychiatric symptoms: A factor analytic study. *Psychological Monographs*, 1966, *80*(7, Whole No. 615).

Achenbach, T. M. Comparison of Stanford-Binet performance of nonretarded and retarded persons matched for MA and sex. *American Journal of Mental Deficiency*, 1970, *74*, 488–494.

Achenbach, T. M. The Child Behavior Profile: I. Boys aged 6–11. *Journal of Consulting and Clinical Psychology*, 1978, *46*, 478–488.

Achenbach, T. M., & Edelbrock, C. S. The Child Behavior Profile: II. Boys aged 12–16 and girls 6–11 and 12–16. *Journal of Consulting and Clinical Psychology*, 1979, *47*, 223–233.

Adelson, E., & Fraiberg, S. Gross motor development in infants blind from birth. *Child Development*, 1974, *45*, 114–126.

Adkins, P. G., & Young, R. G. Cultural perceptions in the treatment of handicapped school children of Mexican-American parentage. *Journal of Research and Development in Education*, 1976, *9*, 83–90.

Affleck, D. C., & Strider, F. D. Contribution of psychological reports to patient management. *Journal of Consulting and Clinical Psychology*, 1971, *37*, 177–179.

Akhurst, B. A. *Assessing intellectual ability*. New York: Barnes & Noble, 1970.

Ali, F., & Costello, J. Modification of the Peabody Picture Vocabulary Test. *Developmental Psychology*, 1971, *5*, 86–91.

Allen, M. E., & Young, F. M. The constancy of the intelligence quotient as indicated by retests of 130 children. *Journal of Applied Psychology*, 1943, *27*, 41–60.

Allen, R. M. Psychological assessment procedures for the cerebral palsied. In *Proceedings of the postdoctoral workshop in psychological services for the cerebral palsied*. Coral Gables, Fla.: University of Miami Press, 1959. Pp. 21–24.

Allen, R. M. Factor analysis of the Developmental Test of Visual Perception performance of educable mental retardates. *Perceptual and Motor Skills*, 1968, *26*, 257–258.

Allen, R. M., Haupt, T. D., & Jones, R. W. Visual perceptual abilities and intelligence in mental retardates. *Journal of Clinical Psychology*, 1965, *21*, 299–300.

Allen, R. M., & Jefferson, T. W. *Psychological evaluation of the cerebral palsied person*. Springfield, Ill.: Charles C Thomas, 1962.

Alper, A. E. A comparison of the Wechsler Intelligence Scale for Children and the Arthur adaptation of the Leiter International Performance Scale with mental defectives. *American Journal of Mental Deficiency*, 1958, *63*, 312–316.

Alper, A. E., & Horne, B. M. Changes in IQ of a group of institutionalized mental defectives over a period of two decades. *American Journal of Mental Deficiency,* 1959, *64,* 472–475.

Alpern, G. D., & Kimberlin, C. C. Short intelligence test ranging from infancy levels through childhood levels for use with the retarded. *American Journal of Mental Deficiency,* 1970, *75,* 65–71.

Altus, G. T. A WISC profile for retarded readers. *Journal of Consulting Psychology,* 1956, *20,* 155–156.

American Medical Association. Conference report on mental retardation: A handbook for the primary physician. *Journal of the American Medical Association,* 1965, *191*(3), 117–166.

American Psychiatric Association. *Diagnostic and statistical manual of mental disorders* (3rd ed.). Washington, D.C.: APA, 1980.

American Psychological Association. *Publication manual* (2nd ed.). Washington, D.C.: APA, 1974.

American Psychological Association. American Psychological Association's statement on Education for All Handicapped Children Act of 1975 (P.L. 94-142). *American Psychological Association School Psychology Newsletter,* 1979, *33*(5), 8.

American Psychological Association. Ethical principles of psychologists. *APA Monitor,* 1979, *10*(11), 15–18.

Ammons, R. B., & Ammons, C. H. The Quick Test (QT): Provisional manual. *Psychological Reports,* 1962, *11,* 111–161.

Ammons, R. B., & Ammons, H. S. *The Full-Range Picture Vocabulary Test.* New Orleans: R. B. Ammons, 1948.

Anastasi, A. The concept of validity in the interpretation of test scores. *Educational and Psychological Measurement,* 1950, *10,* 67–78.

Anastasi, A. *Differential psychology* (3rd ed.). New York: Macmillan, 1958.

Anastasi, A. Psychological tests: Uses and abuses. *Teachers College Record,* 1961, *62,* 389–393.

Anastasi, A. Psychology, psychologists, and psychological testing. *American Psychologist,* 1967, *22,* 297–306.

Anastasi, A. More on heritability: Addendum to the Hebb and Jensen interchange. *American Psychologist,* 1971, *26,* 1036–1037.

Anastasi, A. *Psychological testing* (4th ed.). New York: Macmillan, 1976.

Anastasi, A., & Cordova, F. A. Some effects of bilingualism upon the intelligence test performance of Puerto Rican children in New York City. *Journal of Educational Psychology,* 1953, *44,* 1–19.

Anastasi, A., & Schaefer, C. E. Note on the concepts of creativity and intelligence. *Journal of Creative Behavior,* 1971, *5,* 113–116.

Anderson, K. A. The "shopping" behavior of parents of mentally retarded children: The professional person's role. *Mental Retardation,* 1971, *9*(4), 3–5.

Anderson, S., & Messick, S. Social competency in young children. *Developmental Psychology,* 1974, *10,* 282–293.

Anderson, W. F., & Stern, D. The relative effects of the Frostig program, corrective reading instruction, and attention upon the reading skills of corrective readers with visual perceptual deficiencies. *Journal of School Psychology,* 1972, *10,* 387–395.

Andre, J. Bicultural socialization and the measurement of intelligence (Doctoral dissertation, Georgia State University, 1975). *Dissertation Abstracts International,* 1976, *36,* 3675B–3676B. (University Microfilms No. 75-29,904)

Andrew, J. M. Delinquency, the Wechsler P > V Sign, and the I-Level System. *Journal of Clinical Psychology,* 1974, *30,* 331–335.

Annett, M. Laterality of childhood hemiplegia and the growth of speech and intelligence. *Cortex,* 1973, *9,* 4–33.

Annett, M., Lee, D., & Ounsted, C. Intellectual disabilities in relation to lateralized features in the E.E.G. In *Proceedings in the Second National Spastics Society Study Group.* London: Heinemann, 1961. Pp. 86–112.

Anthony, J. J. A comparison of Wechsler Preschool and Primary Scale of Intelligence and Stanford-Binet Intelligence Scale scores for disadvantaged preschool children. *Psychology in the Schools,* 1973, *10,* 297–299.

Anttonen, R. G., & Fleming, E. S. Standardized test information: Does it make a difference in black student performance. *Journal of Educational Research,* 1976, *70,* 26–31.

Appelbaum, A. S., & Tuma, J. M. Social class and test performance: Comparative validity of the Peabody with the WISC and WISC-R for two socioeconomic groups. *Psychological Reports,* 1977, *40,* 139–145.

Appelbaum, S. A. Science and persuasion in the psychological test report. *Journal of Consulting and Clinical Psychology,* 1970, *35,* 349–355.

Appelbaum, S. A. Objections to diagnosis and diagnostic psychological testing diagnosed. In L. W. Field (Chair), *Consultant's dilemma: Decreasing emphasis on training in diagnostic testing.* Symposium presented at the meeting of the American Psychological Association, Chicago, September 1975.

Armentrout, J. A. Effects of perceptual training on children's human figure drawings. *Journal of Genetic Psychology,* 1971, *119,* 281–287.

Armstrong, R. J., & Mooney, R. F. The Slosson Intelligence Test: Implications for reading specialists. *Reading Teacher,* 1971, *24,* 336–340.

Armstrong, R. J., Mooney, R. F., & Jensen, J. A. A short, reliable, easy to administer individual intelligence test for special class placement. *Child Study Journal,* 1971, *1,* 156–163.

Arnold, G. F. A technique for measuring the mental ability of the cerebral palsied. *Psychological Service Center Journal,* 1951, *3,* 171–178.

Arnold, M. B. *Story sequence analysis.* New York: Columbia University Press, 1962.

Arthur, G. The Arthur adaptation of the Leiter International Performance Scale. *Journal of Clinical Psychology,* 1949, *5,* 345–349.

Arvey, R. D. Some comments on culture fair tests. *Personnel Psychology,* 1972, *25,* 433–448.

Ashurst, D. I., & Meyers, C. E. Social system and clinical model in school identification of the educable retarded. In R. K. Eyman, C. E. Meyers, & G. Tarjan (Eds.), *Sociobehavioral studies in mental retardation.*

Monographs of the American Association on Mental Deficiency, 1973, *1,* 150–163.

Auffrey, J., & Robertson, M. Case history information and examiner experience as determinants of scoring validity on Wechsler intelligence tests. *Proceedings of the 80th Annual Convention of the American Psychological Association,* 1972, *7,* 553–554.

Ault, R. L. *Children's cognitive development: Piaget's theory and the process approach.* New York: Oxford University Press, 1977.

Auricchio, E. W. Comparison of several methods of scoring Draw-a-Person tests. *Perceptual and Motor Skills,* 1966, *23,* 1124.

Austin, J. J., & Carpenter, P. The use of the WPPSI in early identification of mental retardation and preschool special education. In R. S. Morrow (Chair), *Diagnostic and educational application of the Wechsler Preschool and Primary Scale of Intelligence (WPPSI).* Symposium presented at the meeting of the American Psychological Association, Miami, September 1970.

Ausubel, D. P., Novak, J. D., & Hanesian, H. *Educational psychology: A cognitive view* (2nd ed.). New York: Holt, Rinehart and Winston, 1978.

Ausubel, D. P., & Sullivan, E. V. *Theory and problems of child development* (2nd. ed.). New York: Grune & Stratton, 1970.

Ayres, A. J. *Sensory integration and learning disorders.* Los Angeles: Western Psychological Services, 1972.

Babad, E. Y., Mann, M., & Mar-Hayim, M. Bias in scoring the WISC subtests. *Journal of Consulting and Clinical Psychology,* 1975, *43,* 268.

Bach, L. C. *A comparison of selected psychological tests used with trainable mentally retarded children* (Doctoral dissertation, University of South Dakota). Ann Arbor, Mich.: University Microfilms, 1968. No. 69-3111.

Bachelder, B. L., & Denny, M. R. A theory of intelligence: I. Span and the complexity of stimulus control. *Intelligence,* 1977, *1,* 127–150. (a)

Bachelder, B. L., & Denny, M. R. A theory of intelligence: II. The role of span in a variety of intellectual tasks. *Intelligence,* 1977, *1,* 237–256. (b)

Bachrach, H. Writing with one's audience in mind: Some thoughts about the reporting of psychological test findings. *Clinical Psychologist,* 1974, *27,* 17–19.

Back, R., & Dana, R. H. Examiner sex bias and Wechsler Intelligence Scale for Children scores. *Journal of Consulting and Clinical Psychology,* 1977, *45,* 500.

Bailey, B. S., & Richmond, B. O. Adaptive behavior of retarded, slow learner, and average intelligence children. *Journal of School Psychology,* 1979, *17,* 260–263.

Baker, H., & Leland, B. *Detroit Tests of Learning Aptitude, revised edition.* Indianapolis: Bobbs-Merrill, 1967.

Baldwin, V. *The relationship of Visual Aural Digit Span and Visual Aural Letter Span (VALS) to reading and spelling achievement of 20 second-grade average and 20 second-grade children with learning problems.* Unpublished masters thesis, University of New Mexico, 1976.

Balinsky, B. Review of L. M. Terman & M. A. Merrill, *Stanford-Binet Intelligence Scale, manual for the third revision, Form L-M. Personnel and Guidance Journal,* 1960, *39,* 155–156.

Ball, R. S., Merrifield, P., & Stott, L. H. *Extended Merrill-Palmer Scale.* Chicago: Stoelting, 1978.

Balthazar, E. E. *Balthazar Scales of Adaptive Behavior.* Palo Alto, Ca.: Consulting Psychologists Press, 1976.

Bannatyne, A. Diagnosis: A note on recategorization of the WISC scaled scores. *Journal of Learning Disabilities,* 1974, *7,* 272–273.

Bannatyne, A. Review of the Goldman-Fristoe-Woodcock Test of Auditory Discrimination. *Journal of Learning Disabilities,* 1975, *8,* 130–132.

Baratz, S. S., & Baratz, J. C. Early childhood intervention: The social science base of institutional racism. *Harvard Educational Review,* 1970, *40,* 29–50.

Barclay, A., & Yater, A. C. Comparative study of the Wechsler Preschool and Primary Scale of Intelligence and the Stanford-Binet Intelligence Scale, Form L-M, among culturally deprived children. *Journal of Consulting and Clinical Psychology,* 1969, *33,* 257.

Bardon, J. I., & Bennett, V. C. *School psychology.* Englewood Cliffs, N.J.: Prentice-Hall, 1974.

Bardon, J. I., Bennett, V. C., Bruchez, P. K., & Sanderson, R. A. Psychosituational classroom intervention: Rationale and description. *Journal of School Psychology,* 1976, *14,* 97–104.

Barkley, R. A., & Cunningham, C. E. The effects of methylphenidate on the mother-child interactions of hyperactive children. *Archives of General Psychiatry,* 1979, *36,* 201–208.

Barnebey, N. S. The effect of race of examiner on test performance of Negro and white children. *Proceedings of the 81st Annual Convention of the American Psychological Association,* 1973, *8,* 647–648.

Barnes, E. J. The utilization of behavioral and social sciences in minority group education: Some critical implications. In W. R. Rhine (Chair), *Ethnic minority issues on the utilization of behavioral and social science in a pluralistic society.* Symposium presented at the meeting of the American Psychological Association, Washington, D.C., September 1971.

Barnes, E. J. IQ testing and minority school children: Imperatives for change. *Journal of Non-White Concerns in Personnel and Guidance,* 1973, *2,* 4–20.

Barnwell, A., & Denison, H. WISC scale discrepancies: Are they diagnostically significant for learning disabilities? *Journal of Pediatric Psychology,* 1975, *3,* 9–11.

Barratt, E. S. The relationship of the Progressive Matrices (1938) and the Columbia Mental Maturity Scale to the WISC. *Journal of Consulting Psychology,* 1956, *20,* 294–296.

Barron, R. C. A comparison of patterns of intellectual and psycho-linguistic abilities among first graders with average and very low reading ability (Doctoral dissertation, University of Minnesota, 1971). *Dissertation Abstracts International,* 1971, *32,* 1817B. (University Microfilms No. 71-22,182)

Bartak, L., & Rutter, M. Educational treatment of autistic children. In M. Rutter (Ed.), *Infantile autism: Concepts, characteristics and treatment.* London: Churchill Livingstone, 1971.

Bartak, L., & Rutter, M. Special educational treatment of autistic children: A comparative study—I: Design of study and characteristics of units. *Journal of Childhood Psychology and Psychiatry and Allied Disciplines,* 1973, *14,* 161–179.

Bartak, L., & Rutter, M. Differences between mentally retarded and normally intelligent autistic children. *Journal of Autism and Childhood Schizophrenia,* 1976, *6,* 109–120.

Bat-Haee, M. A., Mehyrar, A. H., & Sabharwal, V. The correlation between Piaget's conservation of quantity tasks and three measures of intelligence in a select group of children in Iran. *Journal of Psychology,* 1972, *80,* 197–201.

Baum, D. D. A comparison of the WRAT and the PIAT with learning disability children. *Educational and Psychological Measurement,* 1975, *35,* 487–493.

Baum, D. D., & Kelly, T. J. The validity of the Slosson Intelligence Test with learning disabled kindergartners. *Journal of Learning Disabilities,* 1979, *12,* 268–270.

Bauman, M. K. Blind and partially sighted. In M. V. Wisland (Ed.), *Psychoeducational diagnosis of exceptional children.* Springfield, Ill.: Charles C Thomas, 1974.

Baumeister, A. A. Use of the WISC with mental retardates: A review. *American Journal of Mental Deficiency,* 1964, *69,* 183–194.

Baumeister, A. A., & Muma, J. R. On defining mental retardation. *Journal of Special Education,* 1975, *9,* 293–306.

Baxley, G. B., & LeBlanc, J. M. The hyperactive child: Characteristics, treatment, and evaluation of research design. In H. W. Reese (Ed.), *Advances in child development and behavior* (Vol. 11). New York: Academic Press, 1976.

Bayley, N. Consistency and variability in the growth of intelligence from birth to eighteen years. *Journal of Genetic Psychology,* 1949, *75,* 165–196.

Bayley, N. *Bayley Scales of Infant Development: Birth to two years.* New York: Psychological Corporation, 1969.

Bayley, N., & Schaefer, E. S. Correlations of maternal and child behaviors with the development of mental abilities: Data from the Berkeley growth study. *Monographs of the Society for Research in Child Development,* 1964, *29*(6, Serial No. 97), 1–80.

Beberfall, L. Some linguistic problems of the Spanish-speaking people of Texas. *Modern Language Journal,* 1958, *42,* 87–90.

Beck, R., & Talkington, L. W. Frostig training with Headstart children. *Perceptual and Motor Skills,* 1970, *30,* 521–522.

Becker, J. T., & Sabatino, D. A. Frostig revisited. *Journal of Learning Disabilities,* 1973, *6,* 180–184.

Beery, K. E. *Developmental Test of Visual-motor Integration.* Chicago: Follett Educational Corporation, 1967.

Behar, L., & Stringfield, S. A behavior rating scale for the preschool child. *Developmental Psychology,* 1974, *10,* 601–610.

Belford, B., & Blumberg, H. M. Factor analytic study of the Revised Illinois Test of Psycholinguistic Abilities (ITPA). *Perceptual and Motor Skills,* 1975, *40,* 153–154.

Belluomini, H. M. *Wechsler Intelligence Scale for Children: Predicting success in corrective reading.* Unpublished masters thesis, Sacramento State College, 1962.

Belmont, L., & Birch, H. G. Lateral dominance, lateral awareness, and reading disability. *Child Development,* 1965, *36,* 57–71.

Belmont, L., & Birch, H. G. The intellectual profile of retarded readers. *Perceptual and Motor Skills,* 1966, *22,* 787–816.

Bender, L. A Visual Motor Gestalt Test and its clinical use. *American Orthopsychiatric Association Research Monograph,* 1938, No. 3.

Bender, L. *Manual for instruction and test cards for Visual Motor Gestalt Test.* New York: American Orthopsychiatric Association, 1946.

Bender, L. The life course of schizophrenic children. *Biological Psychiatry,* 1970, *2,* 165–172.

Bennett, D. K. *The tester and intelligence testing: An examination of protocol interpretation* (Doctoral dissertation, Harvard University). Ann Arbor, Mich.: University Microfilms, 1970. No. 70–20,142.

Bensberg, G. J., Jr., & Sloan, W. Performance of brain-injured defectives on the Arthur adaptation of the Leiter. *Psychological Service Center Journal,* 1951, *3,* 181–184.

Benton, A. L. Cerebral disease in a child. In A. Burton & R. E. Harris (Eds.), *Clinical studies of personality.* New York: Harper, 1955.

Benton, A. L. *Right-left discrimination and finger localization.* New York: Hoeber-Harper, 1959.

Benton, A. L. *Benton Visual Retention Test* (Rev. ed.). New York: Psychological Corporation, 1963.

Benton, A. L. Clinical neuropsychology of childhood: An overview. In R. M. Reitan & L. A. Davison (Eds.), *Clinical neuropsychology: Current status and applications.* Washington, D.C.: V. H. Winston & Sons, 1974.

Benton, A. L. Developmental dyslexia: Neurological aspects. In W. J. Friedlander (Ed.), *Advances in neurology* (Vol. 7). *Current reviews of higher nervous system dysfunction.* New York: Raven Press, 1975.

Berdie, R. F. The Ad Hoc Committee on Social Impact of Psychological Assessment. *American Psychologist,* 1965, *20,* 143–146.

Bereiter, C. The relation of social class and educational aptitude. *Canadian Psychologist,* 1972, *13,* 329–340.

Bergan, A., McManis, D. L., & Melchert, P. A. Effects of social and token reinforcement on WISC Block Design performance. *Perceptual and Motor Skills,* 1971, *32,* 871–880.

Bergan, J. R. *Behavioral consultation.* Columbus, Ohio: Charles E. Merrill, 1977.

Berger, M. The third revision of the Stanford-Binet (Form L-M): Some methodological limitations and their practical implications. *Bulletin of the British Psychological Society,* 1970, *23,* 17–26.

Berger, M., & Yule, W. Cognitive assessment in young children with language delay. In M. Rutter & J. A. M. Martin (Eds.), *The child with delayed speech.* London: Wm. Heinemann/S.I.M.P., 1972 (Clinics in Developmental Medicine No. 43).

Berko, M. J. Some factors in the mental evaluation of cerebral palsied children. *Cerebral Palsy Review,* 1953, *14*(5–6), 6, 11, 15.

Berko, M. J. A note on "psychometric scatter" as a factor in the differentiation of exogenous and endogenous mental deficiency. *Cerebral Palsy Review,* 1955, *16*(1), 20.

Berman, A., & Siegal, A. A neuropsychological approach to the etiology, prevention, and treatment of juvenile delinquency. In A. Davids (Ed.), *Child personality and psychopathology: Current topics* (Vol. 3). New York: Wiley, 1976.

Bernal, E. M., Jr. *Assessing assessment instruments: A Chicano perspective.* Paper prepared for the Regional Training Program to Serve the Bilingual/Bicultural Exceptional Child, Montal Educational Associates, Sacramento, California, February 1972.

Berry, K. K., & Sherrets, S. A comparison of the WISC and WISC-R scores of special education students. *Journal of Pediatric Psychology,* 1975, *3*, 14.

Bersoff, D. N. School psychology as "institutional psychiatry." *Professional Psychology,* 1971, *2*, 266–270.

Bersoff, D. N. Silk purses into sow's ears: The decline of psychological testing and a suggestion for its redemption. *American Psychologist,* 1973, *28*, 892–899.

Bessent, T. E. A note on the validity of the Leiter International Performance Scale. *Journal of Consulting Psychology,* 1950, *14*, 234.

Best, B., & Roberts, G. Early cognitive development in hearing impaired children. *American Annals of the Deaf,* 1976, *121*, 560–564.

Beverly, L., & Bensberg, G. J. A comparison of the Leiter, the Cornell-Coxe and Stanford-Binet with mental defectives. *American Journal of Mental Deficiency,* 1952, *57*, 89–91.

Bice, H. V., & Cruickshank, W. M. The evaluation of intelligence. In W. M. Cruickshank (Ed.), *Cerebral palsy: Its individual and community problems* (2nd ed.). Syracuse, N.Y.: Syracuse University Press, 1966. Pp. 101–134.

Bieger, E. Effectiveness of visual perceptual training on reading skills of nonreaders: An experimental study. *Perceptual and Motor Skills,* 1974, *38*, 1147–1153.

Binet, A. Recherches sur les mouvements de quelques jeunes enfants. *La Revue Philosophique,* 1890, *29*, 297–309. (a)

Binet, A. Perceptions d'enfants. *La Revue Philosophique,* 1890, *30*, 582–611. (b)

Binet, A. *Introduction à la psychologie expérimentale.* Paris: Alcan, 1894.

Binet, A. *L'étude expérimentale de l'intelligence.* Paris: Schleicher, 1903.

Binet, A. Nouvelles recherches sur la mésure du niveau intéllectuel chez les enfants d'école. *L'Année Psychologique,* 1911, *17*, 145–210.

Binet, A., & Henri, V. La mémoire des mots. *L'Année Psychologique,* 1895, *1*, 1–23. (a)

Binet, A., & Henri, V. La mémoire des phrases. *L'Année Psychologique,* 1895, *1*, 24–59. (b)

Binet, A., & Henri, V. La psychologie individuelle. *L'Année Psychologique,* 1895, *2*, 411–465. (c)

Binet, A., & Simon, T. Méthodes nouvelles pour le diagnostic du niveau intéllectuel des anormaux. *L'Année Psychologique,* 1905, *11*, 191–244.

Binet, A., & Simon, T. Le développement de l'intelligence chez les enfants. *L'Année Psychologique,* 1908, *14*, 1–94.

Binet, A., & Simon, T. The development of intelligence in children. (E. S. Kit, trans.) Baltimore, Md.: Williams & Wilkins, 1916.

Binet, A., & Simon, T. L'intelligence des imbéciles. *L'Année Psychologique,* 1909, *15*, 1–147.

Birch, H. G. Malnutrition, learning, and intelligence. *American Journal of Public Health,* 1972, *62*, 773–784.

Birch, H. G., & Gussow, J. D. *Disadvantaged children: Health, nutrition and school failure.* New York: Grune & Stratton, 1970.

Birch, J. W. The utility of short forms of the Stanford-Binet tests of intelligence with mentally retarded children. *American Journal of Mental Deficiency,* 1955, *59*, 462–484.

Black, F. W. Neurological dysfunction and reading disorders. *Journal of Learning Disabilities,* 1973, *6*, 313–316.

Black, F. W. Achievement test performance of high and low perceiving learning disabled children. *Journal of Learning Disabilities,* 1974, *7*, 178–182.

Blackstock, E. G. Cerebral asymmetry and the development of early infantile autism. *Journal of Autism and Childhood Schizophrenia,* 1978, *8*, 339–353.

Blatt, S. J. The validity of projective techniques and their research and clinical contribution. *Journal of Personality Assessment,* 1975, *39*, 327–343.

Blatt, S. J., & Allison, J. The intelligence test in personality assessment. In A. I. Rabin (Ed.), *Projective techniques in personality assessment.* New York: Springer, 1968. Pp. 421–460.

Bloom, A. S., Klee, S. H., & Raskin, L. M. A comparison of the Stanford-Binet abbreviated and complete forms for developmentally disabled children. *Journal of Clinical Psychology,* 1977, *33*, 477–480.

Bloom, A. S., & Raskin, L. M. WISC-R Verbal-Performance IQ discrepancies: A comparison of learning disabled children to the normative sample. *Journal of Clinical Psychology,* 1980, *36*, 322–323.

Bloom, A. S., Raskin, L. M., & Reese, A. H. A comparison of WISC-R and Stanford-Binet Intelligence Scale classifications of developmentally disabled children. *Psychology in the Schools,* 1976, *13*, 288–290.

Bloom, A. S., Wagner, M., & Bergman, A. A comparison of intellectually delayed and primary reading disabled children on measures of intelligence and achievement. *Journal of Clinical Psychology,* 1980, *36*, 788–790.

Bloom, B. S. *Stability and change in human characteristics.* New York: Wiley, 1964.

Bloom, G. E., & Jones, A. W. Bases of classification of reading disorders. *Journal of Learning Disabilities,* 1970, *3*, 606–617.

Boder, E. Developmental dyslexia: A diagnostic approach based on three atypical reading-spelling patterns. *Developmental Medicine and Child Neurology*, 1973, *15*, 663–687.

Boehm, A. E. *Boehm Test of Basic Concepts*. New York: Psychological Corporation, 1971.

Boll, T. J. Effect of age at onset of brain damage on adaptive abilities in children. *Proceedings of the 81st Annual Convention of the American Psychological Association*, 1973, *8*, 509–510.

Boll, T. J., & Reitan, R. M. Comparative ability interrelationships in normal and brain-damaged children. *Journal of Clinical Psychology*, 1972, *28*, 152–156.

Bonham, S. J., Jr. Predicting achievement for deaf children. *Psychological Service Center Journal*, 1974, *14*, 35–44.

Boring, E. G. *A history of experimental psychology* (2nd ed.). New York: Appleton-Century-Crofts, 1950.

Bornstein, H. L., Hamilton, K., Saulnier, K., & Roy, H. (Eds.). *The signed English dictionary for preschool and elementary levels*. Washington, D.C.: Gallaudet College, 1975.

Bortner, M., & Birch, H. G. Perceptual and perceptual-motor dissociation in cerebral palsied children. *Journal of Nervous and Mental Disease*, 1962, *134*, 103–108.

Bortner, M., & Birch, H. G. Patterns of intellectual ability in emotionally disturbed and brain-damaged children. *Journal of Special Education*, 1969, *3*, 351–369.

Bossard, M. D., & Galusha, R. The utility of the Stanford-Binet in predicting WRAT performance. *Psychology in the Schools*, 1979, *16*, 488–490.

Bossard, M. D., Reynolds, C. R., & Gutkin, T. B. A regression analysis of test bias on the Stanford-Binet Intelligence Scale. *Journal of Clinical Child Psychology*, 1980, *9*, 52–54.

Bouchard, T. J., Jr. Current conceptions of intelligence and their implications for assessment. In P. McReynolds (Ed.), *Advances in psychological assessment* (Vol. 1). Palo Alto, Ca.: Science & Behavior Books, 1968.

Bowd, A. D. Some determinants of school achievement in several Indian groups. *Alberta Journal of Educational Research*, 1972, *18*, 69–76.

Boyd, L., & Randle, K. Factor analysis of the Frostig Developmental Test of Visual Perception. *Journal of Learning Disabilities*, 1970, *3*, 253–255.

Bradbury, P. J., Wright, S. D., Walker, C. E., & Ross, J. M. Performance on the WISC as a function of sex of *E*, sex of *S*, and age of *S*. *Journal of Psychology*, 1975, *90*, 51–55.

Bradway, K. P., & Thompson, C. W. Intelligence at adulthood: A twenty-five year follow-up. *Journal of Educational Psychology*, 1962, *53*, 1–14.

Braen, B. B., & Masling, J. M. Intelligence tests used with special groups of children. *Journal of Exceptional Children*, 1959, *26*, 42–45.

Braginsky, D. D., & Braginsky, B. M. *Hansels and Gretels; studies of children in institutions for the mentally retarded*. New York: Holt, Rinehart and Winston, 1971.

Brannigan, G. G. Wechsler Picture Arrangement and Comprehension scores as measures of social maturity. *Journal of Psychology*, 1975, *89*, 133–135.

Brannigan, G. G. Children's social desirability response tendencies and Wechsler Comprehension and Picture Arrangement performance. *Psychological Reports*, 1976, *38*, 1194.

Brannigan, G. G., & Ash, T. Cognitive tempo and WISC-R performance. *Journal of Clinical Psychology*, 1977, *33*, 212.

Brannigan, G. G., Calnen, T., Loprete, L. J., & Rosenberg, L. A. A comparison of WISC and WISC-R scoring criteria for Comprehension, Similarities, and Vocabulary responses. *Journal of Clinical Psychology*, 1976, *32*, 94.

Brannigan, G. G., Rosenberg, L. A., Loprete, L. J., & Calnen, T. Scoring of WISC-R Comprehension, Similarities, and Vocabulary responses by experienced and inexperienced judges. *Psychology in the Schools*, 1977, *14*, 430.

Braun, J. S., & Brane, M. Comparison of the performance of children with dysrhythmia grade 1 and normal EEG on psychological tests. *Proceedings of the 79th Annual Convention of the American Psychological Association*, 1971, *6*, 457–458.

Bray, N. M., & Estes, R. E. A comparison of the PIAT, CAT, and WRAT scores and teacher ratings with learning disabled children. *Journal of Learning Disabilities*, 1975, *8*, 519–523.

Brazelton, T. B. *Neonatal Behavioral Assessment Scale*. Philadelphia: J. B. Lippincott, 1973.

Brengelmann, J. C., & Kenny, J. T. Comparison of Leiter, WAIS and Stanford-Binet IQ's in retardates. *Journal of Clinical Psychology*, 1961, *17*, 235–238.

Bretzing, B. H. *IQ and achievement tests: Is there a difference?* Paper presented at the meeting of the American Psychological Association, San Francisco, September 1977.

Breuning, S. E., & Zella, W. F. Effects of individualized incentives on norm-referenced IQ test performance of high school students in special education classes. *Journal of School Psychology*, 1978, *16*, 220–226.

Bridgeman, B., & Buttram, J. Race differences on nonverbal analogy test performance as a function of verbal strategy training. *Journal of Educational Psychology*, 1975, *67*, 586–590.

Brill, R. G. The relationship of Wechsler IQ's to academic achievement among deaf students. *Exceptional Children*, 1962, *28*, 315–321.

Brim, O. G., Jr. American attitudes toward intelligence tests. *American Psychologist*, 1965, *20*, 125–130.

British Psychological Society. Appendix I—the 1937 version of the Stanford-Binet Scale—a critical appraisal. *Bulletin of the British Psychological Society*, 1958, *35*, 13–15.

Brittain, M. The WPPSI: A Midlands study. *British Journal of Educational Psychology*, 1969, *39*, 14–17.

Brody, E. B., & Brody, N. *Intelligence: Nature, determinants, and consequences*. New York: Academic Press, 1976.

Broman, S. H., & Nichols, P. L. *Early mental development, social class, and school-age IQ*. Paper presented at the meeting of the American Psychological Association, Chicago, September 1975.

Brooks, C. R. WISC, WISC-R, S-B, L & M, WRAT: Relationships and trends among children ages six to ten referred for psychological evaluation. *Psychology in the Schools*, 1977, *14*, 30–33.

Brooks, P. H., & Baumeister, A. A. A plea for consideration of ecological validity in the experimental psychology of mental retardation: A guest editorial. *American Journal of Mental Deficiency,* 1977, *81,* 407–416.

Brooks, R. Psychoeducational assessment: A broader perspective. *Professional Psychology,* 1979, *10,* 708–722.

Brophy, J. E., & Good, T. L. Teachers' communication of differential expectations for children's classroom performance: Some behavioral data. *Journal of Educational Psychology,* 1970, *61,* 365–374.

Brown, A. L., & French, L. A. The zone of potential development: Implications for intelligence testing in the year 2000. *Intelligence,* 1979, *3,* 255–273.

Brown, A. M., Matheny, A. P., Jr., & Wilson, R. S. Baldwins' kindness concept measure as related to children's cognition and temperament: A twin study. *Child Development,* 1973, *44,* 193–195.

Brown, E. W. Observing behavior during the intelligence test. In E. Lerner & L. B. Murphy (Eds.). Methods for psychology study of personality in young children. *Monographs of the Society for Research in Child Development,* 1941, *6*(Whole No. 4), 268–283.

Brown, F. A comparison of the abbreviated and the complete Stanford-Binet Scales. *Journal of Consulting Psychology,* 1942, *6,* 240–242.

Brown, F. The SOMPA: A system of measuring potential abilities? *School Psychology Digest,* 1979, *8,* 37–46.

Bruininks, R. H. *Bruininks-Oseretsky Test of Motor Proficiency.* Circle Pines, Minn.: American Guidance Service, 1978.

Bruner, F. G., Barnes, E., & Dearborn, W. F. Report of committee on books and tests pertaining to the study of exceptional and mentally deficient children. *Proceedings of the National Education Association,* 1909, *47,* 901–914.

Bruner, J. S. The course of cognitive growth. In N. S. Endler, L. R. Boulter, & H. Osser (Eds.), *Contemporary issues in developmental psychology.* New York: Holt, Rinehart and Winston, 1968.

Bruner, J. S. Poverty and childhood. *Oxford Review of Education,* 1975, *1,* 31–50.

Bryden, M. P. Perceptual asymmetry in vision: Relation to handedness, eyedness, and speech lateralization. *Cortex,* 1973, *9,* 418–432.

Bryden, M. P., & Allard, F. Dichotic listening and the development of linguistic processes. In M. Kinsbourne (Ed.), *Assymetrical function of the brain.* London: Cambridge University Press, 1978.

Buckley, K. J., & Oakland, T. D. *Contrasting localized norms for Mexican-American children on the ABIC.* Paper presented at the meeting of the American Psychological Association, San Francisco, August 1977.

Bucky, S. F., & Banta, T. J. Racial factors in test performance. *Developmental Psychology,* 1972, *6,* 7–13.

Budoff, M., Gimon, A., & Corman, L. Learning potential measurement with Spanish-speaking youth as an alternative to IQ tests: A first report. *Revista Interamericana de Psicologia,* 1974, *8,* 233–246.

Budoff, M., & Hamilton, J. L. Optimizing test performance of moderately and severely mentally retarded adolescents and adults. *American Journal of Mental Deficiency,* 1976, *81,* 49–57.

Budoff, M., Meskin, J., & Harrison, R. H. Educational test of the learning-potential hypothesis. *American Journal of Mental Deficiency,* 1971, *76,* 159–169.

Bühler, C. The Ball and Field test as a help in the diagnosis of emotional difficulties. *Character and Personality,* 1938, *6,* 257–273.

Burgemeister, B. B. *Psychological techniques in neurological diagnosis.* New York: Harper & Row, 1962.

Burgemeister, B. B., Blum, L. H., & Lorge, I. *Columbia Mental Maturity Scale* (3rd ed.). New York: Harcourt Brace Jovanovich, 1972.

Buriel, R. Relationship of three field-dependence measures to the reading and math achievement of Anglo American and Mexican American children. *Journal of Educational Psychology,* 1978, *70,* 167–174.

Burke, H. R. Raven's Progressive Matrices: A review and critical evaluation. *Journal of Genetic Psychology,* 1958, *93,* 199–228.

Burks, H. F., & Bruce, P. The characteristics of poor and good readers as disclosed by the Wechsler Intelligence Scale for Children. *Journal of Educational Psychology,* 1955, *46,* 488–493.

Burma, J. H. *Spanish-speaking groups in the United States.* Durham, N.C.: Duke University Press, 1954.

Burns, C. J., & Velicer, W. F. Art instruction and the Goodenough-Harris Drawing Test in fifth-graders. *Psychology in the Schools,* 1977, *14,* 109–112.

Burns, E. Effects of restricted sampling on ITPA scaled scores. *American Journal of Mental Deficiency,* 1976, *80,* 394–400.

Burns, E. The effects of skewness on the interpretation of ITPA scaled scores. *Journal of School Psychology,* 1977, *15,* 219–224.

Burns, E., Peterson, D., & Bauer, L. The concurrent validity of the Peabody Individual Achievement Test. *Training School Bulletin,* 1974, *70,* 221–223.

Burns, G. W., & Watson, B. L. Factor analysis of the revised ITPA with underachieving children. *Journal of Learning Disabilities,* 1973, *6,* 371–376.

Burstein, A. G. Review of the Wechsler Intelligence Scale for Children. In O. K. Buros (Ed.), *The sixth mental measurements yearbook.* Highland Park, N.J.: Gryphon Press, 1965. Pp. 843–845.

Burt, C. The measurement of intelligence by the Binet tests. *Eugenics Review,* 1914, *6,* 36–50, 140–152.

Burt, C. The latest revision of the Binet intelligence tests. *Eugenics Review,* 1939, *30,* 255–260.

Burt, M. K., Dulay, H. C., & Hernandez, C. E. *Bilingual Syntax Measure technical handbook.* New York: Harcourt Brace Jovanovich, 1976.

Burt, M. K., Dulay, H. C., & Hernandez, C. E. *Bilingual Syntax Measure II manual: English edition.* New York: Harcourt Brace Jovanovich, 1978.

Busch, J. C., & Osborne, W. L. Significant vs meaningful differences in the effects of tangible reinforcement on intelligence test achievement and reliability of TMR subjects. *Psychology in the Schools,* 1976, *13,* 219–225.

Butcher, H. J. *Human intelligence: Its nature and assessment.* London: Methuen, 1968.

Butler, B. V., & Engel, R. Mental and motor scores at eight months in relation to neonatal photic responses. *Developmental Medicine and Child Neurology,* 1969, *11,* 77–82.

Butler, K. G. Review of the Lindamood Auditory Conceptualization Test. In O.K. Buros (Ed.), *The eighth mental measurements yearbook.* Highland Park, N.J.: Gryphon Press, 1978. Pp. 1464–1465.

Byrd, C., & Springfield, L. A note on the Draw-a-Person Test with adolescent retardates. *American Journal of Mental Deficiency*, 1969, *73*, 578–579.

Cain, L. F., Levine, S., & Elzey, F. F. *Cain-Levine Social Competency Scale.* Palo Alto, Ca.: Consulting Psychologists Press, 1963.

Caldwell, M. B., & Knight, D. The effect of Negro and white examiners on Negro intelligence test performance. *Journal of Negro Education*, 1970, *39*, 177–179.

Camp, B. W. WISC performance in acting-out and delinquent children with and without EEG abnormality. *Journal of Consulting Psychology*, 1966, *30*, 350–353.

Campbell, S. B. Hyperactivity: Course and treatment. In A. Davids (Ed.), *Child personality and psychopathology: Current topics* (Vol. 3). New York: Wiley, 1976.

Canady, H. G. The effect of "rapport" on the I.Q.: A new approach to the problem of racial psychology. *Journal of Negro Education*, 1936, *5*, 209–219.

Cantwell, D. P. (Ed.). *The hyperactive child: Diagnosis, management, current research.* New York: Spectrum, 1975.

Caparulo, B. K., & Cohen, D. J. Cognitive structures, language, and emerging social competence in autistic and aphasic children. *Journal of the American Academy of Child Psychiatry*, 1977, *16*, 620–645.

Caputo, D. V., Edmonston, W. E., Jr., L'Abate, L., & Rondberg, S. R. Type of brain damage and intellectual functioning in children. *Journal of Consulting Psychology*, 1963, *27*, 184.

Caputo, D. V., & Mandell, W. Consequences of low birth weight. *Developmental Psychology*, 1970, *3*, 363–383.

Carlisle, A. L., Shinedling, M. M., & Weaver, R. Note on the use of the Slosson Intelligence Test with mentally retarded residents. *Psychological Reports*, 1970, *26*, 865–866.

Carlson, J. S. A note on the relationships between the Draw-a-Man Test, the Progressive Matrices test, and conservation. *Journal of Psychology*, 1970, *74*, 231–235.

Carlson, J. S., & Wiedl, K. H. Toward a differential testing approach: Testing-the-limits employing the Raven Matrices. *Intelligence*, 1979, *3*, 323–344.

Carlson, L. C., & Reynolds, C. R. *Specific variance of the WPPSI subtests at six age levels.* Paper presented at the meeting of the American Psychological Association, Montreal, Canada, September 1980.

Carroll, J. B. Review of Illinois Test of Psycholinguistic Abilities. In O. K. Buros (Ed.), *The seventh mental measurements yearbook.* Highland Park, N.J.: Gryphon Press, 1972. Pp. 819–823.

Carrow, E. Comprehension of English and Spanish by preschool Mexican-American children. *Modern Language Journal*, 1971, *55*, 299–306.

Carter, D., & Clark, L. MA intellectual assessment by operant conditioning of Down's syndrome children. *Mental Retardation*, 1973, *11*(3), 39–41.

Carter, G. L., & Kinsbourne, M. The ontogeny of right cerebral lateralization of spatial mental set. *Developmental Psychology*, 1979, *15*, 241–245.

Carter, R. B. A study of attitudes: Mexican American and Anglo American elementary teachers' judgments of Mexican American bilingual children's speech (Doctoral dissertation, University of Houston, 1977). *Dissertation Abstracts International*, 1977, *37*, 4941A– 4942A.

Carver, R. P. Reading tests in 1970 versus 1980: Psychometric versus edumetric. *Reading Teacher*, 1972, *26*, 299–302.

Cassel, R.H., & Danenhower, H. S. Mental subnormality developmentally arrested: The Primary Mental Abilities Test. *Training School Bulletin*, 1949, *46*, 94–104.

Catron, D. W., & Catron, S. S. WISC-R vs. WISC: A comparison with educable mentally retarded children. *Journal of School Psychology*, 1977, *15*, 264–266.

Cattell, P. Stanford-Binet IQ variations. *School and Society*, 1937, *45*, 615–618.

Cattell, P. *Cattell Infant Intelligence Scale.* New York: Psychological Corporation, 1940.

Cattell, P. *The measurement of intelligence of infants and young children.* New York: Psychological Corporation, 1950.

Cattell, R. B. Measurement versus intuition in applied psychology. *Character and Personality*, 1937, *6*, 114–131.

Cattell, R. B. Theory of fluid and crystalized intelligence: A critical experiment. *Journal of Educational Psychology*, 1963, *54*, 1–22.

Cattell, R. B., & Drevdahl, J. E. A comparison of the personality profile (16 P.F.) of eminent researchers with that of eminent teachers and administrators, and of the general population. *British Journal of Psychology*, 1955, *46*, 248–261.

Chandler, C. R. Value orientations among Mexican Americans in a southwestern city. *Sociology and Social Research*, 1974, *58*, 262–271.

Chandler, J. T., & Plakos, J. Spanish-speaking pupils classified as educable mentally retarded. *Integrated Education*, 1969, *7*(6), 28–33.

Charles, D. C. Ability and accomplishment of persons earlier judged mentally deficient. *Genetic Psychology Monographs*, 1953, *47*, 3–71.

Charles, D. C. Adult adjustment of some deficient American children—II. *American Journal of Mental Deficiency*, 1957, *62*, 300–304.

Chase, C. H., & Sattler, J. M. Determining areas of strengths and weaknesses on the Stanford-Binet. *School Psychology Review*, 1980, *9*, 174–177.

Chavez, S. J. Preserve their language heritage. *Childhood Education*, 1956, *33*, 165, 185.

Chess, S. Healthy responses, developmental disturbances, and stress or reactive disorders: I: Infancy and childhood. In A. M. Freedman & H. I. Kaplan (Eds.), *Comprehensive textbook of psychiatry.* Baltimore: Williams & Wilkins, 1967.

Chiappone, A. D. Use of the Detroit Tests of Learning Aptitude with EMR. *Exceptional Children*, 1968, *35*, 240–241.

Chinn, P. C., Drew, C. J., & Logan, D. R. *Mental retardation: A life cycle approach.* St. Louis: Mosby, 1975.

Chissom, B. S., & Thomas, J. R. Comparison of factor structures for the Frostig Developmental Test of Visual Perception. *Perceptual and Motor Skills,* 1971, *33,* 1015–1019.

Christensen, E. W. Counseling Puerto Ricans: Some cultural considerations. *Personnel and Guidance Journal,* 1975, *53,* 349–356.

Christian, W. P., Jr., & Malone, D. R. Relationships among three measures used in screening mentally retarded for placement in special education. *Psychological Reports,* 1973, *33,* 415–418.

Churchill, D. W. The relation of infantile autism and early childhood schizophrenia to developmental language disorders of childhood. *Journal of Autism and Childhood Schizophrenia,* 1972, *2,* 182–197.

Cieutat, V. J. Examiner differences with the Stanford-Binet IQ. *Perceptual and Motor Skills,* 1965, *20,* 317–318.

Cieutat, V. J., & Flick, G. L. Examiner differences among Stanford-Binet items. *Psychological Reports,* 1967, *21,* 613–622.

Ciminero, A. R., & Drabman, R. S. Current developments in behavioral assessment of children. In B. B. Lahey & A. E. Kazdin (Eds.), *Advances in clinical child psychology* (Vol. 1). New York: Plenum, 1977.

Claiborn, W. L. Expectancy effects in the classroom: A failure to replicate. *Journal of Educational Psychology,* 1969, *60,* 377–383.

Clarizio, H. F. Commentary on Mercer's rejoinder to Clarizio. *School Psychology Digest,* 1979, *8,* 207–209. (a)

Clarizio, H. F. In defense of the IQ test. *School Psychology Digest,* 1979, *8,* 79–88. (b)

Clark, K. B. *Dark ghetto.* New York: Harper & Row, 1967.

Clark, L. D. Multiple schedule discrimination in autistic children. Unpublished data, University of Utah, 1971.

Clark, M. *Health in the Mexican-American culture.* Berkeley: University of California Press, 1959.

Clarke, A. D. B., & Clarke, A. M. Mental retardation and behavioural change. *British Medical Bulletin,* 1974, *30,* 179–185.

Clawson, A. Relationship of psychological tests to cerebral disorders in children: A pilot study. *Psychological Reports,* 1962, *10,* 187–190. (a)

Clawson, A. *The Bender Visual Motor Gestalt Test for Children: A manual.* Beverly Hills: Western Psychological Services, 1962. (b)

Cleary, T. A., Humphreys, L. G., Kendrick, S. A., & Wesman, A. Educational uses of tests with disadvantaged students. *American Psychologist,* 1975, *30,* 15–41.

Clingman, J., & Fowler, R. L. The effects of contingent and noncontingent rewards on the I.Q. scores of children of above-average intelligence. *Journal of Applied Behavior Analysis,* 1975, *8,* 90.

Coates, S. Field independence and intellectual functioning in preschool children. *Perceptual and Motor Skills,* 1975, *41,* 251–254.

Cochran, M. L., & Pedrini, D. T. The concurrent validity of the 1965 WRAT with adult retardates. *American Journal of Mental Deficiency,* 1969, *73,* 654–656.

Cohen, D. J., Caparulo, B., & Shaywitz, B. Primary childhood aphasia and childhood autism: Clinical, bio-logical and conceptual observations. *Journal of the American Academy of Child Psychiatry,* 1976, *15,* 604–645.

Cohen, E. Is there examiner bias on the Wechsler-Bellevue? *Proceedings of Oklahoma Academy of Science,* 1950, *31,* 150–153.

Cohen, E. Examiner differences with individual intelligence tests. *Perceptual and Motor Skills,* 1965, *20,* 1324.

Cohen, J. The factorial structure of the WISC at ages 7-6, 10-6, and 13-6. *Journal of Consulting Psychology,* 1959, *23,* 285–299.

Cohen, L. The effects of material and non-material reinforcement upon performance of the WISC Block Design subtest by children of different social classes: A follow-up study. *Psychology,* 1970, *7*(4), 41–47.

Cohen, R. L., & Netley, C. Cognitive deficits, learning disabilities, and WISC Verbal-Performance consistency. *Developmental Psychology,* 1978, *14,* 624–634.

Cole, D. Communication and rapport in clinical testing. *Journal of Consulting Psychology,* 1953, *17,* 132–134.

Cole, M., & Bruner, J. S. Cultural differences and inferences about psychological processes. *American Psychologist,* 1971, *26,* 867–876.

Coleman, H. M., & Dawson, S. T. Educational evaluation and visual-perceptual-motor dysfunction. *Journal of Learning Disabilities,* 1969, *2,* 242–251.

Collard, R. R. Review of the Preschool Attainment Record, research edition. In O. K. Buros (Ed.), *The seventh mental measurements yearbook.* Highland Park, N.J.: Gryphon Press, 1972. Pp. 759–760.

Conners, C. K. Cortical visual evoked response in children with learning disorders. *Psychophysiology,* 1970, *7,* 418–428.

Conners, C. K. Rating scales for use in drug studies with children. *Psychopharmacology Bulletin: Pharmacotherapy with Children* (DHEW, Health Services and Mental Health Administration Publication No. 73-9002). Washington, D.C.: U.S. Government Printing Office, 1973. (a)

Conners, C. K. What parents need to know about stimulant drugs and special education. *Journal of Learning Disabilities,* 1973, *6,* 349–351. (b)

Connolly, A. J., Nachtman, W., & Pritchett, E. M. *The KeyMath Diagnostic Arithmetic Test.* Circle Pines, Minn.: American Guidance Service, 1971.

Conti, A. P. Variables related to contacting/not contacting counseling services recommended by school psychologists. *Journal of School Psychology,* 1975, *13,* 41–50.

Contrucci, V. J., Korn, E. F., Martinson, M. C., & Mathias, D. C. *Individual test interpretation for teachers of the mentally retarded.* Bulletin No. 18. Madison, Wis.: Wisconsin State Department of Public Instructions, 1962. (ERIC Document Reproduction Service No. ED 011 712)

Cook, L. C. The effects of verbal and monetary feedback on the WISC scores of lower-SES Spanish American and lower- and middle-SES Anglo students (Doctoral dissertation, New Mexico State University, 1973). *Dissertation Abstracts International,* 1973, *34,* 1693A-1694A. (University Microfilms No. 73-23,317)

Cook, V. J., & Patterson, J. G. Psychologists in the schools of Nebraska: Professional functions. *Psychology in the Schools*, 1977, *14*, 371–376.

Corah, N. L., & Powell, B. J. A factor analytic study of the Frostig Developmental Test of Visual Perception. *Perceptual and Motor Skills*, 1963, *16*, 59–63.

Corey, M. T. The WPPSI as a school admissions tool for young children. In R. S. Morrow (Chair), *Diagnostic and educational application of the Wechsler Preschool and Primary Scale of Intelligence* (WPPSI). Symposium presented at the American Psychological Association, Miami, September 1970.

Corman, L., & Budoff, M. Factor structures of Spanish-speaking and non-Spanish-speaking children on Raven's Progressive Matrices. *Educational and Psychological Measurement*, 1974, *34*, 977–981.

Corman, L., & Gottlieb, J. Mainstreaming mentally retarded children: A review of research. In N. R. Ellis (Ed.), *International review of research in mental retardation* (Vol. 9). New York: Academic Press, 1978.

Corotto, L. V. The relation of Performance to Verbal IQ in acting out juveniles. *Journal of Psychological Studies*, 1961, *12*, 162–166.

Corwin, B. J. The relationship between reading achievement and performance on individual ability tests. *Journal of School Psychology*, 1967, *5*, 156–157.

Costello, J. Effects of pretesting and examiner characteristics on test performance of young disadvantaged children. *Proceedings of the 78th Annual Convention of the American Psychological Association*, 1970, *5*, 309–310.

Covin, T. M. Comparison of Otis-Lennon Mental Ability Test, Elementary I Level and WISC-R IQs among suspected mental retardates. *Psychological Reports*, 1976, *38*, 403–406. (a)

Covin, T. M. Correlations between the Pintner, Otis-Lennon, Peabody, and Wechsler Intelligence Scale for Children–Revised. *Psychological Reports*, 1976, *39*, 1058. (b)

Covin, T. M. Comparability of WISC and WISC-R Full Scale IQs for elementary school children with learning difficulties. *Psychological Reports*, 1976, *39*, 280. (c)

Covin, T. M. Comparability of WISC and WISC-R scores for 30 8- and 9-year-old institutionalized Caucasian children. *Psychological Reports*, 1977, *40*, 382. (a)

Covin, T. M. Comparison of SIT and WISC-R IQs among special education candidates. *Psychology in the Schools*, 1977, *14*, 19–23. (b)

Covin, T. M. Comparisons of WISC and WISC-R Full Scale IQs for a sample of children in special education. *Psychological Reports*, 1977, *41*, 237–238. (c)

Covin, T. M. Relationship of Peabody and WISC-R IQs of candidates for special education. *Psychological Reports*, 1977, *40*, 189–190. (d)

Covin, T. M. Relationship of the SIT and PPVT to the WISC-R. *Journal of School Psychology*, 1977, *15*, 259–260. (e)

Covin, T. M., & Lubimiv, A. J. Concurrent validity of the WRAT. *Perceptual and Motor Skills*, 1976, *43*, 573–574.

Cowen, E. L., Trost, M. A., Lorion, R. P., Dorr, D., Izzo, L. D., & Isaacson, R. V. *New ways in school mental health: Early detection and prevention of school maladaptation.* New York: Human Sciences Press, 1975.

Craft, N. P., & Kronenberger, E. J. Comparability of WISC-R and WAIS IQ scores in educable mentally handicapped adolescents. *Psychology in the Schools*, 1979, *16*, 502–504.

Craig, R. J. An illustration of the Wechsler Picture Arrangement subtest as a thematic technique. *Journal of Projective Techniques and Personality Assessment*, 1969, *33*, 286–289.

Croake, J. W., Keller, J. F., & Catlin, N. WPPSI, Rutgers, Goodenough, Goodenough-Harris I.Q.'s for lower socioeconomic, black, preschool children. *Psychology*, 1973, *10*(2), 58–65.

Crockett, B. K., Rardin, M. W., & Pasewark, R. A. Relationship between WPPSI and Stanford-Binet IQs and subsequent WISC IQs in Headstart children. *Journal of Consulting and Clinical Psychology*, 1975, *43*, 922.

Crockett, B. K., Rardin, M. W., & Pasewark, R. A. Relationship of WPPSI and subsequent Metropolitan Achievement Test scores in Head-Start children. *Psychology in the Schools*, 1976, *13*, 19–20.

Cronbach, L. J. *Essentials of psychological testing.* New York: Harper, 1949.

Cronbach, L. J. *Essentials of psychological testing* (2nd ed.). New York: Harper, 1960.

Cronbach, L. J. *Essentials of psychological testing* (3rd ed.). New York: Harper & Row, 1970.

Cronbach, L. J. Five decades of public controversy over mental testing. *American Psychologist*, 1975, *30*, 1–14.

Crowell, D. H. Sensory defects. In C. M. Louttit (Ed.), *Clinical psychology of exceptional children* (3rd ed.). New York: Harper, 1957. Pp. 425–491.

Crowell, D. H., & Crowell, D. C. Intelligence test reliability for cerebral palsied children. *Journal of Consulting Psychology*, 1954, *18*, 276.

Crown, P. J. The effects of race of examiner and standard vs. dialect administration of the Wechsler Preschool and Primary Scale of Intelligence on the performance of Negro and white children (Doctoral dissertation, Florida State University). *Dissertation Abstracts International*, 1971, *32*, 232A–233A. (University Microfilms No. 71-18,356)

Croxen, M. E., & Lytton, H. Reading disability and difficulties in finger localization and right-left discrimination. *Developmental Psychology*, 1971, *5*, 256–262.

Cruickshank, W. M. Myths and realities in learning disabilities. *Journal of Learning Disabilities*, 1977, *10*, 51–58.

Cuadra, C. A., & Albaugh, W. P. Sources of ambiguity in psychological reports. *Journal of Clinical Psychology*, 1956, *12*, 109–115.

Culbertson, F. M., & Gunn, R. C. Comparison of the Bender-Gestalt Test and Frostig Test in several clinical groups of children. *Journal of Clinical Psychology*, 1966, *22*, 439.

Cundick, B. P. Measures of intelligence on Southwest Indian students. *Journal of Social Psychology*, 1970, *81*, 151–156.

Curr, W., & Gourlay, N. Differences between testers in Terman-Merrill testing. *British Journal of Statistical Psychology*, 1956, *9*, 75–81.

Curtis, J. N. Point Scale examinations on the high-grade feeble-minded and the insane. *Journal of Abnormal Psychology,* 1918, *13*, 77–118.

Curtis, W. S., & Donlon, E. T. Severe multisensory disorders and learning disabilities. In M. R. Burkowsky (Ed.), *Orientation to language and learning disorders.* St. Louis, Mo.: Warren H. Green, 1973.

Cutler, C. M., Hirshoren, A., & Cicirelli, V. G. Comparison of discrimination and reproduction tests of children's perception. *Perceptual and Motor Skills,* 1973, *37*, 163–166.

Damasio, A. R., & Maurer, R. G. A neurological model of childhood autism. *Archives of Neurology,* 1978, *35*, 777–786.

Dangel, H. L. Biasing effect of pretest referral information on WISC scores of mentally retarded children. *American Journal of Mental Deficiency,* 1972, *77*, 354–359.

Das, J. P. Patterns of cognitive ability in nonretarded and retarded children. *American Journal of Mental Deficiency,* 1972, *77*, 6–12.

Das, J. P. Cultural deprivation and cognitive competence. In N. R. Ellis (Ed.), *International review of research in mental retardation* (Vol. 6). New York: Academic Press, 1973. (a)

Das, J. P. Reply of an eclectic to a developmentalist. *American Journal of Mental Deficiency,* 1973, *77*, 749–750. (b)

Das, J. P., Kirby, J., & Jarman, R. F. Simultaneous and successive syntheses: An alternative model for cognitive abilities. *Psychological Bulletin,* 1975, *82*, 87–103.

Das, J. P.; & Molloy, G. N. Varieties of simultaneous and successive processing in children. *Journal of Educational Psychology,* 1975, *67*, 213–220.

Datta, L. E. Draw-a-Person Test as a measure of intelligence in preschool children from very low income families. *Journal of Consulting Psychology,* 1967, *31*, 626–630.

Davenport, B. M. A comparison of the Peabody Individual Achievement Test, the Metropolitan Achievement Test, and the Otis-Lennon Mental Ability Test. *Psychology in the Schools,* 1976, *13*, 291–297.

Davids, A. An objective instrument for assessing hyperkinesis in children. *Journal of Learning Disabilities,* 1971, *4*, 499–501.

Davis, E. E. Concurrent validity of the McCarthy Scales of Children's Abilities. *Measurement and Evaluation in Guidance,* 1975, *8*, 101–104.

Davis, E. E., & Rowland, T. A replacement for the venerable Stanford-Binet? *Journal of Clinical Psychology,* 1974, *30*, 517–521.

Davis, E. E., & Slettedahl, R. W. Stability of the McCarthy Scales over a 1-year period. *Journal of Clinical Psychology,* 1976, *32*, 798–800.

Davis, E. E., & Walker, C. McCarthy Scales and WISC-R. *Perceptual and Motor Skills,* 1977, *44*, 966.

Davis, F. B. Interpretation of differences among averages and individual test scores. *Journal of Educational Psychology,* 1959, *50*, 162–170.

Davis, F. B. The measurement of mental capability through evoked potential recording. *Educational Records and Research Bulletin,* 1971, *1*, 1–171.

Davis, F. B. Psychometric research on comprehension in reading. *Reading Research Quarterly,* 1972, *7*, 628–678.

Davis, W. E., Peacock, W., Fitzpatrick, P., & Mulhern, M. Examiner differences, prior failure, and subjects' WAIS Arithmetic scores. *Journal of Clinical Psychology,* 1969, *25*, 178–180.

Davis, W. M., Jr. Are there solutions to the problems of testing black Americans? In M. M. Meier (Chair), *Some answers to ethnic concerns about psychological testing in the schools.* Symposium presented at the meeting of the American Psychological Association, Washington, D.C., September 1971.

Davison, L. A. Introduction. In R. M. Reitan & L. A. Davison (Eds.), *Clinical neuropsychology: Current status and applications.* Washington, D.C.: V. H. Winston & Sons, 1974.

Dean, D. A. A factor analysis of the Stanford-Binet and SRA Primary Mental Abilities Battery at the first grade level. In *Pennsylvania State College Abstracts of Doctoral Dissertations, 1950* (State College, Pa.), 1950, *14*, 394–397.

Dean, R. S. Analysis of the PIAT with Anglo and Mexican-American children. *Journal of School Psychology,* 1977, *15*, 329–333. (a)

Dean, R. S. Canonical analysis of a jangle fallacy. *Multivariate Experimental Clinical Research,* 1977, *3*, 17–20. (b)

Dean, R. S. Internal consistency of the PIAT with Mexican-American children. *Psychology in the Schools,* 1977, *14*, 167–168. (c)

Dean, R. S. Patterns of emotional disturbance on the WISC-R. *Journal of Clinical Psychology,* 1977, *33*, 486–490. (d)

Dean, R. S. Reliability of the WISC-R with Mexican-American children. *Journal of School Psychology,* 1977, *15*, 267–268. (e)

Dean, R. S. The validity and reliability of abbreviated versions of the WISC-R. *Educational and Psychological Measurement,* 1977, *37*, 1111–1116. (f)

Dean, R. S. Distinguishing patterns for Mexican-American children on the WISC-R. *Journal of Clinical Psychology,* 1979, *35*, 790–794. (a)

Dean, R. S. Predictive validity of the WISC-R with Mexican-American children. *Journal of School Psychology,* 1979, *17*, 55–58. (b)

Dearborn, G. The determination of intellectual regression and progression. *American Journal of Psychiatry,* 1926, *83*, 725–741.

DeAvila, E. A. Mainstreaming ethnically and linguistically different children: An exercise in paradox or a new approach? In R. L. Jones (Ed.), *Mainstreaming and the minority child.* Reston, Va.: Council for Exceptional Children, 1976.

DeAvila, E. A., & Duncan, S. E. A few thoughts about language assessment: The Lau Decision reconsidered. *Proceedings of the National Conference on Research and Policy Implications, Lau Task Force Report.* Austin, Tex.: Southwest Educational Development Laboratory, 1976.

DeAvila, E. A., & Duncan, S. E. *Language Assessment Scales* (2nd ed.). Corte Madera, Ca.: Linguametrics Group, 1977.

DeAvila, E. A., & Havassy, B. *IQ tests and minority children.* Austin, Tex.: Dissemination Center for Bilingual Bicultural Education, 1974. (a)

DeAvila, E. A., & Havassy, B. The testing of minority children: A neo-Piagetian approach. *Today's Education,* 1974, *63*(4), 72–75. (b)

De Bell, S. M., & Vance, H. B. Concurrent validity of three measures of arithmetic achievement. *Perceptual and Motor Skills,* 1977, *45,* 848.

De Forest, R. A study of the prognostic value of the Merrill-Palmer Scale of Mental Tests and the Minnesota Preschool Scale. *Journal of Genetic Psychology,* 1941, *59,* 219–223.

DeHorn, A., & Klinge, V. Correlations and factor analysis of the WISC-R and the Peabody Picture Vocabulary Test for an adolescent psychiatric sample. *Journal of Consulting and Clinical Psychology,* 1978, *46,* 1160–1161.

DeLapa, G. The Slosson Intelligence Test: A screening and retesting technique for slow learners. *Journal of School Psychology,* 1968, *6,* 224–225.

Dembinski, R. J., & Mauser, A. J. What parents of the learning disabled really want from professionals. *Journal of Learning Disabilities,* 1977, *10,* 578–584.

DeMyer, M. K. The nature of the neuropsychological disability in autistic children. In E. Schopler & R. J. Reichler (Eds.), *Psychopathology and child development: Research and treatment.* New York: Plenum, 1976.

DeMyer, M. K., Barton, S., Alpern, G. D., Kimberlin, C., Allen, J., Yang, E., & Steele, R. The measured intelligence of autistic children. *Journal of Autism and Childhood Schizophrenia,* 1974, *4,* 42–60.

DeMyer, M. K., Barton, S., DeMyer, W. E., Norton, J. A., Allen, J., & Steele, R. Prognosis in autism: A follow-up study. *Journal of Autism and Childhood Schizophrenia,* 1973, *3,* 199–246.

DeMyer, M. K., Barton, S., & Norton, J. A. A comparison of adaptive, verbal, and motor profiles of psychotic and non-psychotic subnormal children. *Journal of Autism and Childhood Schizophrenia,* 1972, *2,* 359–377.

Denniston, C. Accounting for differences in mean IQ (Review of *Educability and group differences* by A. R. Jensen). *Science,* 1975, *187,* 161–162.

Deno, E. Special education as developmental capital. *Exceptional Children,* 1970, *37,* 229–237.

Denton, L. R. Intelligence test performance and personality differences in a group of visually handicapped children. *Bulletin of the Maritime Psychological Association,* Dec., 1954, 47–50.

Des Lauriers, A., & Halpern, F. C. Psychological tests in childhood schizophrenia. *American Journal of Orthopsychiatry,* 1947, *17,* 57–67.

Deutsch, M., Fishman, J. A., Kogan, L., North, R., & Whiteman, M. Guidelines for testing minority group children. *Journal of Social Issues,* 1964, *20*(2), 129–145.

Dikmen, S., Matthews, C. G., & Harley, J. P. The effect of early versus late onset of major motor epilepsy upon cognitive-intellectual performance. *Epilepsia,* 1975, *16,* 73–81.

Dill, J. R. A study of the influence of race of the experimenter and verbal reinforcement on creativity test performance of lower socioeconomic status black children (Doctoral dissertation, New York University, 1971). *Dissertation Abstracts International,* 1972, *32,* 6071B. (University Microfilms No. 72-11,449)

Di Lorenzo, L. T., & Nagler, E. Examiner differences on the Stanford-Binet. *Psychological Reports,* 1968, *22,* 443–447.

Dingman, H. F., & Meyers, C. E. The structure of intellect in the mental retardate. In N. R. Ellis (Ed.), *International review of research in mental retardation* (Vol. 1). New York: Academic Press, 1966. Pp. 55–76.

DiSimoni, F. G. *Token Test for Children.* Boston: Teaching Resources, 1978.

Dlugokinski, E., Weiss, S., & Johnston, S. Preschoolers at risk: Social, emotional and cognitive considerations. *Psychology in the Schools,* 1976, *13,* 134–139.

Dockrell, W. B. The use of Wechsler Intelligence Scale for Children in the diagnosis of retarded readers. *Alberta Journal of Educational Research,* 1960, *6,* 86–91.

Dodwell, P. C. Children's understanding of number concepts: Characteristics of an individual and of a group test. *Canadian Journal of Psychology,* 1961, *15,* 29–36.

Dohrenwend, B. P., & Chin-Shong, E. Social status and attitudes toward psychological disorder: The problem of tolerance of deviance. *American Sociological Review,* 1967, *32,* 417–433.

Dokecki, P. R., Frede, M. C., & Gautney, D. B. Criterion, construct, and predictive validities of the Wechsler Preschool and Primary Scale of Intelligence. *Proceedings of the 77th Annual Convention of the American Psychological Association,* 1969, *4,* 505–506.

Doll, E. A. A brief Binet-Simon Scale. *Psychological Clinic,* 1917, *11,* 197–211, 254–261.

Doll, E. A. *The Oseretsky Tests of Motor Proficiency: A translation from the Portuguese adaption.* Minneapolis: Educational Test Bureau, 1946.

Doll, E. A. Vineland Social Maturity Scale. In A. Weider (Ed.), *Contributions toward medical psychology: Theory and psychodiagnostic methods* (Vol. 2). New York: Ronald Press, 1953.

Doll, E. A. *PAR, Preschool Attainment Record, research edition manual.* Circle Pines, Minn.: American Guidance Service, 1966.

Donahue, D., & Sattler, J. M. Personality variables affecting WAIS scores. *Journal of Consulting and Clinical Psychology,* 1971, *36,* 441.

Doppelt, J. E., & Kaufman, A. S. Estimation of the differences between WISC-R and WISC IQs. *Educational and Psychological Measurement,* 1977, *37,* 417–424.

Douglas, V. I. Differences between normal and hyperkinetic children. In C. K. Conners (Ed.), *Clinical use of stimulant drugs in children.* Amsterdam, The Netherlands: Excerpta Medica, 1974.

Down, J. L. *On some of the mental affections of childhood and youth.* London: J. & A. Churchill, 1887.

Drake, E. A., & Bardon, J. I. Confidentiality and interagency communication: Effect of the Buckley Amendment. *Hospital and Community Psychiatry,* 1978, *29,* 312–315.

Driscoll, G. P. The developmental status of the preschool child as a prognosis of future development. *Child Development Monographs.* New York: Teachers College, Columbia University, 1933, No. 13.

Dubey, D. R. Organic factors in hyperkinesis: A critical evaluation. *American Journal of Orthopsychiatry,* 1976, *46*, 353–366.

Du Bois, N. F., & Brown, F. L. Selected relationships between Frostig scores and reading achievement in a first grade population. *Perceptual and Motor Skills,* 1973, *37*, 515–519.

Du Bois, P. H. *A history of psychological testing.* Boston: Allyn and Bacon, 1970.

Du Bois, P. H. Increase in educational opportunity through measurement. *Proceedings of the 1971 Invitational Conference on Testing Problems.* Princeton, N.J.: Educational Testing Service, 1972.

Dudek, S. Z., Lester, E. P., Goldberg, J. S., & Dyer, G. B. Relationship of Piaget measures to standard intelligence and motor scales. *Perceptual and Motor Skills,* 1969, *28*, 351–362.

Duffey, J. B., Ritter, D. R., & Fedner, M. Developmental Test of Visual-Motor Integration and the Goodenough Draw-a-Man Test as predictors of academic success. *Perceptual and Motor Skills,* 1976, *43*, 543–546.

Duncan, O. D. Ability and achievement. *Eugenics Quarterly,* 1968, *15*, 1–11.

Duncan, P. M., & Millard, W. *A manual for the classification, training, and education of the feeble-minded, imbecile, & idiotic.* London: Longmans, Green & Co., 1866.

Dunn, J. A. Inter- and intra-rater reliability of the new Harris-Goodenough Draw-a-Man Test. *Perceptual and Motor Skills,* 1967, *24*, 269–270. (a)

Dunn, J. A. Note on the relation of Harris' Draw-a-Woman to WISC IQs. *Perceptual and Motor Skills,* 1967, *24*, 316. (b)

Dunn, J. A. Validity coefficients for the new Harris-Goodenough Draw-a-Man Test. *Perceptual and Motor Skills,* 1967, *24*, 299–301. (c)

Dunn, L. M. Special education for the mildly retarded—Is much of it justifiable? *Exceptional Children,* 1968, *35*, 5–22.

Dunn, L. M., & Dunn, L. M. *Peabody Picture Vocabulary Test-Revised.* Circle Pines, Minn.: American Guidance Service, 1981.

Dunn, L. M., & Markwardt, F. C., Jr. *Peabody Individual Achievement Test.* Circle Pines, Minn.: American Guidance Service, 1970.

Dunsdon. M. I. *The educability of cerebral palsied children.* London: Newnes Educational Company, 1952.

Dunsing, J. D. Perceptual-motor factors in the development of school readiness: An analysis of the Purdue Perceptual-Motor Survey. *American Journal of Optometry,* 1969, *46*, 760–765.

Dusek, J. B., & O'Connell, E. J. Teacher expectancy effects on the achievement test performance of elementary school children. *Journal of Educational Psychology,* 1973, *65*, 371–377.

Dyer, C. O., Neigler, C., & Milholland, J. E. Rater agreements in assigning Stanford-Binet items to Guilford's Structure of Intellect operations categories. *Journal of School Psychology,* 1975, *13*, 114–118.

Earhart, R. H., & Warren, S. A. Long term constancy of Binet IQ in retardation. *Training School Bulletin,* 1964, *61*, 109–115.

Earl, C. J. C. *Subnormal personalities.* London: Baillière, Tindall and Cox, 1961.

Eaton, L., & Menolascino, F. J. Comprehensive treatment for the child with cerebral dysfunction. *Pediatrics Digest,* 1970, *12*, 19–27.

Ebbinghaus, H. Über eine neue Methode zur Prüfung geistiger Fähigkeiten und ihre Anwendung bei Schulkindern. *Zeitschrift für Angewandte Psychologie,* 1897, *13*, 401–459.

Ebel, R. L. The social consequences of educational testing. *School and Society,* 1964, *92*, 331–334.

Ebel, R. L. Criterion-referenced measurements: Limitations. *School Review,* 1971, *79*, 282–288.

Ebel, R. L. Educational tests: Valid? Biased? Useful? *Phi Delta Kappan,* 1975, *57*, 83–89.

Ebert, E., & Simmons, K. The Brush Foundation study of child growth and development: I, psychometric tests. *Monographs of the Society for Research in Child Development,* 1943, *8*(2, Serial No. 35).

Edgerton, R. B., & Karno, M. Mexican-American bilingualism and the perception of mental illness. *Archives of General Psychiatry,* 1971, *24*, 286–290.

Edlund, C. V. The effect on the behavior of children, as reflected in the IQ scores, when reinforced after each correct response. *Journal of Applied Behavior Analysis,* 1972, *5*, 317–319.

Eells, K., Davis, A., Havighurst, R. J., Herrick, V. E., & Tyler, R. W. *Intelligence and cultural differences.* Chicago: University of Chicago Press, 1951.

Egeland, B. Influence of examiner and examinee anxiety on WISC performance. *Psychological Reports,* 1967, *21*, 409–414.

Egeland, B. Examiner expectancy: Effects on the scoring of the WISC. *Psychology in the Schools,* 1969, *6*, 313–315.

Eggers, C. Course and prognosis of childhood schizophrenia. *Journal of Autism and Childhood Schizophrenia,* 1978, *8*, 21–36.

Eichorn, D. H. Review of the Wechsler Preschool and Primary Scale of Intelligence. In O. K. Buros (Ed.), *The seventh mental measurements yearbook.* Highland Park, N.J.: Gryphon Press, 1972. Pp. 806–807.

Eisenson, J. *Examining for aphasia.* New York: Psychological Corporation, 1954.

Eisenson, J. *Aphasia in children.* New York: Harper & Row, 1972.

Eklund, S., & Scott, M. Effects of bilingual instructions on test responses of Latin American children. *Psychology in the Schools,* 1965, *2*, 280–282.

Ekren, U. W. *The effect of experimenter knowledge of a subject's scholastic standing on the performance of a reasoning task.* Unpublished masters thesis, Marquette University, 1962.

Ekwall, E. E. *The use of WISC subtest profiles in the diagnosis of reading difficulties* (Doctoral dissertation, University of Arizona). Ann Arbor, Mich.: University Microfilms, 1966. No. 66-10,207.

Elkind, D. Children's discovery of the conservation of mass, weight, and volume: Piaget replication study II. *Journal of Genetic Psychology,* 1961, *98*, 219–227.

Elkind, D. Border-line retardation in low and middle income adolescents. In R. M. Allen, A. D. Cortazzo, & R. P. Toister (Eds.), *Theories of cognitive development: Implications for the mentally retarded.* Coral Gables, Fla.: University of Miami Press, 1973. (a)

Elkind, D. Infant intelligence. *American Journal of Diseases of Children,* 1973, *126,* 143–144. (b)

Elkind, D. *Children and adolescents: Interpretive essays on Jean Piaget* (2nd ed.). New York: Oxford University Press, 1974.

Ellenberger, H. F. *The discovery of the unconscious.* New York: Basic Books, 1970.

Ellett, C. D., & Bersoff, D. N. An integrated approach to the psychosituational assessment of behavior. *Professional Psychology,* 1976, *7,* 485–494.

Elliott, R. N., Jr. Comparative study of the Pictorial Test of Intelligence and the Peabody Picture Vocabulary Test. *Psychological Reports,* 1969, *25,* 528–530.

Ellis, N. R. Issues in mental retardation. *Law and Psychology Review,* 1975, *1,* 9–16.

Ellis, N. R., Barnett, C. D., & Pryer, M. W. Operant behavior in mental defectives: Exploratory studies. *Journal of Experimental Analysis of Behavior,* 1960, *3,* 63–69.

Elwood, M. I. *A statistical study of results of the Stanford Revision of the Binet-Simon scale with a selected group of Pittsburgh school children.* Unpublished doctoral dissertation, University of Pittsburgh, 1934.

Eme, R. F. Sex differences in childhood psychopathology: A review. *Psychological Bulletin,* 1979, *86,* 574–595.

Emerick, L. L., & Hatten, J. T. *Diagnosis and evaluation in speech pathology.* Englewood Cliffs, N.J.: Prentice-Hall, 1974.

Engel, M. Some parameters of the psychological evaluation of children. *Archives of General Psychiatry,* 1960, *2,* 593–605.

Engel, R., & Fay, W. Visual evoked responses at birth, verbal scores at three years, and IQ at four years. *Developmental Medicine and Child Neurology,* 1972, *14,* 283–289.

Engel, R., & Henderson, N. B. Visual evoked responses and IQ scores at school age. *Developmental Medicine and Child Neurology,* 1973, *15,* 136–145.

Engin, A. W., & Wallbrown, F. H. The stability of four kinds of perceptual errors on the Bender-Gestalt. *Journal of Psychology,* 1976, *94,* 123–126.

Erikson, R. V. Abbreviated form of the WISC: A reevaluation. *Journal of Consulting Psychology,* 1967, *31,* 641.

Ernhart, C. B., Reviews of the Preschool Attainment Record, the Preschool Inventory and the Quick Test. In W. K. Frankenburg & B. W. Camp (Eds.), *Pediatric screening tests.* Springfield, Ill.: Charles C Thomas, 1974.

Escalona, S. K. The use of a battery of psychological tests for diagnosis of maladjustment in young children—a case report. *Transactions of the Kansas Academy of Science,* 1945, *48,* 218–223.

Esquirol, J. E. D. *Des maladies mentales considérées sous les rapports médical, hygiénique et médicolegal.* 2 vols. Paris: Baillière, 1838.

Estes, B. W., Curtin, M. E., DeBurger, R. A., & Denny, C. Relationships between 1960 Stanford-Binet, 1937 Stanford-Binet, WISC, Raven, and Draw-A-Man. *Journal of Consulting Psychology,* 1961, *25,* 388–391.

Estes, W. K. Learning theory and intelligence. *American Psychologist,* 1974, *29,* 740–749.

Evans, L. A comparative study of the Wechsler Intelligence Scale for Children (Performance) and Raven's Progressive Matrices with deaf children. *Teacher of the Deaf,* 1966, *64,* 76–82.

Evans, R., Ferguson, N., Davies, P., & Williams, P. Reliability of the Draw-a-Man Test. *Educational Research,* 1975, *18,* 32–36.

Exner, J. E., Jr. Variations in WISC performances as influenced by differences in pretest rapport. *Journal of General Psychology,* 1966, *74,* 299–306.

Eyman, R. K., Boroskin, A., & Hostetter, S. Use of alternative living plans for developmentally disabled children by minority parents. *Mental Retardation,* 1977, *15*(1), 21–23.

Eysenck, H. J. Intelligence assessment: A theoretical and experimental approach. *British Journal of Educational Psychology,* 1967, *37,* 81–98.

Eysenck, H. J. *The IQ argument: Race, intelligence and education.* New York: Library Press, 1971.

Eysenck, H. J. *The measurement of intelligence.* Baltimore, Md.: Williams & Wilkins, 1973.

Fagan, J., Broughton, E., Allen, M., Clark, B., & Emerson, P. Comparison of the Binet and WPPSI with lower-class five-year-olds. *Journal of Consulting and Clinical Psychology,* 1969, *33,* 607–609.

Falberg, R. M. The psychological evaluation of prelingually deaf adults. *Journal of Rehabilitation of the Deaf,* 1967, *1*(2), 31–46.

Farnham-Diggory, S. Cognitive synthesis in Negro and white children. *Monographs of the Society for Research in Child Development,* 1970, *35*(2, Serial No. 135).

Farris, C. E., & Farris, L. S. Indian children: The struggle for survival. *Social Work,* 1976, *21,* 386–389.

Fedio, P., & Mirsky, A. F. Selective intellectual deficits in children with temporal lobe or centrencephalic epilepsy. *Neuropsychologia,* 1969, *7,* 287–300.

Feldman, S. E., & Sullivan, D. S. Factors mediating the effects of enhanced rapport on children's performance. *Journal of Consulting and Clinical Psychology,* 1971, *36,* 302.

Felner, R. D., Stolberg, A., & Cowen, E. L. Crisis events and school mental health referral patterns of young children. *Journal of Consulting and Clinical Psychology,* 1975, *43,* 305–310.

Feuerstein, R. *The dynamic assessment of retarded performers: The learning potential assessment device, theory, instruments, and techniques.* Baltimore: University Park Press, 1979.

Fielder, W. R., Cohen, R. D., & Feeney, S. An attempt to replicate the teacher expectancy effect. *Psychological Reports,* 1971, *29,* 1223–1228.

Finch, A. J., Jr., Kendall, P. C., Spirito, A., Entin, A., Montgomery, L. E., & Schwartz, D. J. Short form and factor analytic studies of the WISC-R with behavior problem children. *Journal of Abnormal Child Psychology,* 1979, *7,* 337–344.

Fine, M. J., & Tracy, D. B. Performance of normal and EMR boys on the FRPV and GHDT. *American Journal of Mental Deficiency,* 1968, *72,* 648–652.

Fischer, C. T. Contextual approach to assessment. *Community Mental Health Journal,* 1973, *9,* 38–45.

Fischer, C. T. Undercutting the scientist-professional dichotomy: The reflective psychologist. *Clinical Psychologist,* 1976, *29,* 5–7.

Fischer, C. T. Individualized assessment and phenomenological psychology. *Journal of Personality Assessment,* 1979, *43,* 115–122.

Fiscus, E. D. The effects of pre-test information on school psychologists' scoring of the Wechsler Intelligence Scale for Children. *Dissertation Abstracts International,* 1975, *36,* 1387A.

Fisher, G. M. A note on the validity of the Wechsler Adult Intelligence Scale for mental retardates. *Journal of Consulting Psychology,* 1962, *26,* 391.

Fisher, G. M., Kilman, B. A., & Shotwell, A. M. Comparability of intelligence quotients of mental defectives on the Wechsler Adult Intelligence Scale and the 1960 revision of the Stanford-Binet. *Journal of Consulting Psychology,* 1961, *25,* 192–195.

Fishler, K., Graliker, B. V., & Koch, R. The predictability of intelligence with Gesell Developmental Scales in mentally retarded infants and young children. *American Journal of Mental Deficiency,* 1965, *69,* 515–525.

Fishman, M. A., & Palkes, H. S. The validity of psychometric testing in children with congenital malformations of the central nervous system. *Developmental Medicine and Child Neurology,* 1974, *16,* 180–185.

Fiske, D. W. The subject reacts to tests. *American Psychologist,* 1967, *22,* 287–296.

Fitz-Gibbon, C. T. The identification of mentally gifted "disadvantaged" students at the eighth grade level. *Journal of Negro Education,* 1974, *43,* 53–66.

Fitzhugh, K. B., & Fitzhugh, L. C. Effects of early and later onset of cerebral dysfunction upon psychological test performance. *Perceptual and Motor Skills,* 1965, *20,* 1099–1100.

Flanagan, J. C. Review of *Measuring Intelligence* by Terman and Merrill. *Harvard Educational Review,* 1938, *8,* 130–133.

Flaugher, R. L. Some points of confusion in discussing the testing of black students. In L. P. Miller (Ed.), *The testing of black students: A symposium.* Englewood Cliffs, N.J.: Prentice-Hall, 1974.

Flaugher, R. L. The many definitions of test bias. *American Psychologist,* 1978, *33,* 671–679.

Flaugher, R. L., & Rock, D. A. Patterns of ability factors among four ethnic groups. *Proceedings of the 80th Annual Convention of the American Psychological Association,* 1972, *7,* 27–28.

Flavell, J. H. *Cognitive development.* Englewood Cliffs, N.J.: Prentice-Hall, 1977.

Fleming, E. S., & Anttonen, R. G. Teacher expectancy or My Fair Lady. *American Educational Research Journal,* 1971, *8,* 241–252.

Fogelman, C. J. (Ed.) *AAMD Adaptive Behavior Scale Manual, 1974 Revision.* Washington, D.C.: American Association on Mental Deficiency, 1974.

Forehand, R., & Gordon, D. A. Application of two short forms of the Stanford-Binet with retardates. *American Journal of Mental Deficiency,* 1971, *75,* 763–764.

Forrest, D. W. *Francis Galton: The life and work of a Victorian genius.* New York: Taplinger, 1974.

Forrester, B. J., & Klaus, R. A. The effect of race of the examiner on intelligence test scores of Negro kindergarten children. *Peabody Papers in Human Development* (George Peabody College for Teachers, Nashville, Tenn.) 1964, *2*(7), 1–7.

Fortenberry, W. D., & Broome, B. J. Comparison of the Gates Reading Survey and the reading section of the Wide Range Achievement Test. *Journal of Developmental Reading,* 1963, *7,* 66–68.

Foster, A. Writing psychological reports. *Journal of Clinical Psychology,* 1951, *7,* 195.

France, K. Effects of "white" and of "black" examiner voices on IQ scores of children. *Developmental Psychology,* 1973, *8,* 144.

Francis-Williams, J., & Davies, P. A. Very low birthweight and later intelligence. *Developmental Medicine and Child Neurology,* 1974, *16,* 709–728.

Frandsen, A. N., McCullough, B. R., & Stone, D. R. Serial versus consecutive order administration of the Stanford-Binet Intelligence Scales. *Journal of Consulting Psychology,* 1950, *14,* 316–320.

Frank, G. Measures of intelligence and conceptual thinking. In I. B. Weiner (Ed.), *Clinical methods in psychology.* New York: Wiley, 1976.

Frankel, E., & Kassinove, H. Effects of required effort, perceived expertise, and sex on teacher compliance. *Journal of Social Psychology,* 1974, *93,* 187–192.

Frankenburg, W. K., Camp, B. W., & Van Natta, P. A. Validity of the Denver Developmental Screening Test. *Child Development,* 1971, *42,* 475–485.

Frankenburg, W. K., Camp, B. W., Van Natta, P. A., Demersseman, J. A., & Voorhees, S. F. Reliability and stability of the Denver Developmental Screening Test. *Child Development,* 1971, *42,* 1315–1325.

Frankenburg, W. K., & Dodds, J. B. The Denver Developmental Screening Test. *Journal of Pediatrics,* 1967, *71,* 181–191.

Frankenburg, W. K., Dodds, J. B., Fandal, A. W., Kazuk, E., & Cohrs, M. *Denver Developmental Screening Test* (Rev. ed.) Denver: Ladoca Project and Publishing Foundation, 1975.

Freeman, F. S. *Theory and practice of psychological testing.* New York: Holt, 1955.

Freeman, F. S. *Theory and practice of psychological testing* (3rd ed.). New York: Holt, Rinehart and Winston, 1962.

Freeman, R. D. Special education and the electroencephalogram: Marriage of convenience. *Journal of Special Education,* 1967, *2,* 61–73.

French, J. L. *Manual: Pictorial Test of Intelligence.* Boston: Houghton Mifflin, 1964.

French, J. L. Review of the Peabody Individual Achievement Test. In O. K. Buros (Ed.), *The seventh mental measurements yearbook.* Highland Park, N.J.: Gryphon Press, 1972. P. 34.

French, J. L. The gifted. In M. V. Wisland (Ed.), *Psychoeducational diagnosis of exceptional children.* Springfield, Ill.: Charles C Thomas, 1974.

Fretz, B. R. Factor structure of intellectual, visual perception, and visuomotor performance of poorly coordinated boys. *Journal of Motor Behaviors,* 1970, *2,* 69–78.

Fromm, E. Projective aspects of intelligence testing. In A. I. Rabin & M. R. Haworth (Eds.), *Projective techniques with children.* New York: Grune & Stratton, 1960. Pp. 225–236.

Fromm, E., Hartman, L. D., & Marschak, M. Children's intelligence tests as a measure of dynamic personality functioning. *American Journal of Orthopsychiatry,* 1957, *27,* 134–144.

Fromme, D. K. On the use of the Vineland Social Maturity Scale as an estimate of intellectual functioning. *Journal of Clinical Psychology,* 1974, *30,* 67–68.

Frostig, M., & Horne, D. *The Frostig program for the development of visual perception.* Chicago: Follett, 1964.

Frostig, M., Maslow, P., Lefever, D. W., & Whittlesey, J. R. B. The Marianne Frostig Developmental Test of Visual Perception, 1963 standardization. *Perceptual and Motor Skills,* 1964, *19,* 463–499.

Galdieri, A. A., Barcikowski, R. S., & Witmer, J. M. The effect of verbal approval upon the performance of middle- and lower-class third-grade children on the WISC. *Psychology in the Schools.* 1972, *9,* 404–408.

Gallagher, J. J. A comparison of brain-injured and non-brain-injured mentally retarded children on several psychological variables. *Monographs of the Society for Research in Child Development,* 1957, *22*(2, Whole No. 65).

Gallagher, J. J., Benoit, E. P., & Boyd, H. F. Measures of intelligence in brain damaged children. *Journal of Clinical Psychology,* 1956, *12,* 69–72.

Gallagher, J. J., & Moss, J. W. New concepts of intelligence and their effect on exceptional children. *Exceptional Children,* 1963, *30,* 1–5.

Gallagher, J. J., & Wiegerink, R. Educational strategies for the autistic child. In E. Schopler & R. J. Reichler (Eds.), *Psychopathology and child development: Research and treatment.* New York: Plenum, 1976.

Gallo, P. S., Jr., & Dorfman, D. D. Racial differences in intelligence: Comment on Tulkin. *Representative Research in Social Psychology,* 1970, *1,* 24–28.

Galvan, R. R. *Bilingualism as it relates to intelligence test scores and school achievement among culturally deprived Spanish-American children* (Doctoral dissertation, East Texas State University). Ann Arbor, Mich.: University Microfilms, 1967. No. 68-1131.

Gambaro, P. K. Analysis of Vineland Social Maturity Scale. *American Journal of Mental Deficiency,* 1944, *48,* 359–363.

Gardiner, M. F., & Walter, P. O. Evidence of hemispheric specification from infant EEG's. In S. Harnad, R. W. Doty, L. Goldstein, J. Jaynes, & G. Krauthamer (Eds.), *Lateralization in the nervous system.* New York: Academic Press, 1977.

Gardner, R. A. *The objective diagnosis of minimal brain dysfunction.* Cresskill, N.J.: Creative Therapeutics, 1979.

Gardner, W. I. *Children with learning and behavior problems: A behavior management approach.* Boston: Allyn and Bacon, 1974.

Garfield. S. L. Abnormal behavior and mental deficiency. In N. R. Ellis (Ed.), *Handbook of mental deficiency.* New York: McGraw-Hill, 1963. Pp. 574–601.

Garfield, S. L., & Affleck, D. C. A study of individuals commited to a state home for the retarded who were later released as not mentally defective. *American Journal of Mental Deficiency,* 1960, *64,* 907–915.

Garfield, S. L., Heine, R. W., & Leventhal, M. An evaluation of psychological reports in a clinical setting. *Journal of Consulting Psychology,* 1954, *18,* 281–286.

Garfinkel, R., & Thorndike, R. L. Binet item difficulty then and now. *Child Development,* 1976, *47,* 959–965.

Garner, A. M. Intelligence testing and clinical practice. In I. A. Berg & L. A. Pennington (Eds.), *An introduction to clinical psychology* (3rd ed.). New York: Ronald Press, 1966. Pp. 67–105.

Garrett, J. F. Cerebral palsy. In J. F. Garrett (Ed.), *Psychological aspects of physical disability.* Washington, D.C.: U.S. Government Printing Office, 1952. Pp. 60–67.

Garrison, M., Jr., & Hammill, D. D. Who are the retarded? *Exceptional Children,* 1971, *38,* 13–20.

Garza, E. T., & Lipton, J. P. Culture, personality, and reactions to praise and criticism. *Journal of Personality,* 1978, *46,* 743–761.

Gath, D., & Tennent, G. High intelligence and delinquency: A review. *British Journal of Criminology,* 1972, *12,* 174–181.

Gayton, W. F. Validity of the Harris Quality Scale with a child guidance population. *Perceptual and Motor Skills,* 1970, *31,* 17–18.

Gayton, W. F. An evaluation of two short forms of the Stanford-Binet, Form L-M, for use with a child guidance population. *Psychological Reports,* 1971, *28,* 355–357.

Gayton, W. F., Bassett, J. E., & Bishop, J. S. The Harris revision of the Goodenough Draw-a-Man Test: Suitability for a retarded population. *Journal of Clinical Psychology,* 1970, *26,* 522–523.

Gayton, W. F., Tavormina, J., Evans, H. E., & Schuh, J. Comparative validity of Harris' and Koppitz' scoring systems for human-figure drawings. *Perceptual and Motor Skills,* 1974, *39,* 369–370.

Gayton, W. F., Wilson, W. T., & Bernstein, S. An evaluation of an abbreviated form of the WISC. *Journal of Clinical Psychology,* 1970, *26,* 466–468.

Gayton, W. F., Wilson, W. T., & Evans, H. E. Comparative validity of Harris Point and Quality Scales. *Perceptual and Motor Skills,* 1971, *33,* 1111–1113.

Gear, G. H. Accuracy of teacher judgment in identifying intellectually gifted children: A review of the literature. *Gifted Child Quarterly,* 1976, *20,* 478–490.

Genshaft, J. L., & Hirt, M. Language differences between black children and white children. *Developmental Psychology,* 1974, *10,* 451–456.

Gerken, K. C. Performance of Mexican American children on intelligence tests. *Exceptional Children,* 1978,

44, 438–443.

Gerken, K. C. Assessment of high risk preschoolers and children and adolescents with low incident handicapping conditions. In D. J. Reschly & G. D. Phye (Eds.), *School psychology: Perspectives and issues.* New York: Academic Press, 1979.

Gerken, K. C., Hancock, K. A., & Wade, T. H. A comparison of the Stanford-Binet Intelligence Scale and the McCarthy Scales of Children's Abilities with preschool children. *Psychology in the Schools,* 1978, *15,* 468–472.

Gesten, E. L. A health resources inventory: The development of a measure of the personal and social competence of primary-grade children. *Journal of Consulting and Clinical Psychology,* 1976, *44,* 775–786.

Getman, G. N., Kane, E. R., Halgren, M. R., & McKee, G. W. *Developing learning readiness.* St. Louis: Webster Division, McGraw-Hill, 1968.

Giannell, A. S., & Freeburne, C. M. The comparative validity of the WAIS and the Stanford-Binet with college freshmen. *Educational and Psychological Measurement,* 1963, *23,* 557–567.

Gibbs, N. Some learning difficulties of cerebral palsied children. *Spastics Quarterly,* 1959, *8,* 21–23.

Gibson, E. J. Learning to read. In N. S. Endler, L. R. Boulter, & H. Osser (Eds.), *Contemporary issues in developmental psychology.* New York: Holt, Rinehart and Winston, 1968.

Gilbert, J. G., & Levee, R. F. Performances of deaf and normally-hearing children on the Bender-Gestalt and the Archimedes Spiral Tests. *Perceptual and Motor Skills,* 1967, *24,* 1059–1066.

Gilbert, J. G., & Rubin, E. J. Evaluating the intellect of blind children. *New Outlook for the Blind,* 1965, *59,* 238–240.

Gillingham, W. H. *An investigation of examiner influence on Wechsler Intelligence Scale for Children scores* (Doctoral dissertation, Michigan State University). Ann Arbor, Mich.: University Microfilms, 1970. No. 70-20,458.

Gilmore, G. E., & Chandy, J. M. Educators describe the school psychologist. *Psychology in the Schools,* 1973, *10,* 397–403.

Ginsburg, R. E. *An examination of the relationship between teacher expectancies and students' performance on a test of intellectual functioning* (Doctoral dissertation, University of Utah). Ann Arbor, Mich.: University Microfilms, 1970. No. 71-922.

Gironda, R. J. A comparison of WISC and WISC-R results of urban educable mentally retarded students. *Psychology in the Schools,* 1977, *14,* 271–275.

Gittleman, M., & Birch, H. G. Childhood schizophrenia: Intellect, neurologic status, perinatal risk, prognosis, and family pathology. *Archives of General Psychiatry,* 1967, *17,* 16–25.

Glanville, B. B., Best, C. T., & Levenson, R. A cardiac measure of cerebral asymmetries in infant auditory perception. *Developmental Psychology,* 1977, *13,* 54–59.

Glasser, A. J., & Zimmerman, I. L. *Clinical interpretations of the Wechsler Intelligence Scale for Children.* New York: Grune & Stratton, 1967.

Glennon, B., & Weisz, J. R. An observational approach to the assessment of anxiety in young children. *Journal of Consulting and Clinical Psychology,* 1978, *46,* 1246–1257.

Goddard, H. H. The Binet and Simon tests of intellectual capacity. *Training School,* 1908, *5,* 3–9.

Goddard, H. H. A measuring scale of intelligence. *Training School,* 1910, *6,* 146–155.

Goh, D. S. *New method in the design of intelligence test short forms—the WISC-R example.* Paper presented at the meeting of the American Psychological Association, Toronto, Canada, 1978.

Goh, D. S., & Lund, J. M. Verbal reinforcement, socioeconomic status, and intelligence test performance of preschool children. *Perceptual and Motor Skills,* 1977, *44,* 1011–1014.

Goh, D. S., & Youngquist, J. A comparison of the McCarthy Scales of Children's Abilities and the WISC-R. *Journal of Learning Disabilities,* 1979, *12,* 344–348.

Golden, C. J. *Clinical interpretation of objective psychological tests.* New York: Grune & Stratton, 1979.

Goldfarb, W. *Childhood schizophrenia.* Cambridge, Mass.: Harvard University Press, 1961.

Goldfarb, W. Childhood psychosis. In P. H. Mussen (Ed.), *Carmichael's manual of child psychology* (3rd ed.). New York: Wiley, 1970. Pp. 765–830.

Goldfarb, W., Goldfarb, N., & Pollack, R. C. Changes in IQ of schizophrenic children during residential treatment. *Archives of General Psychiatry,* 1969, *21,* 673–690.

Goldman, H. Psychological testing of blind children. *American Foundation for the Blind, Research Bulletin,* 1970, No. 21, 77–90.

Goldman, L. *Using tests in counseling.* New York: Appelton-Century-Crofts, 1961.

Goldman, L. Tests and counseling: The marriage that failed. *Measurement and Evaluation in Guidance,* 1972, *4,* 213–220.

Goldman, M., & Barclay, A. Influence of maternal attitudes on children with reading disabilities. *Perceptual and Motor Skills,* 1974, *38,* 303–307.

Goldman, R., Fristoe, M., & Woodcock, R. W. *Goldman-Fristoe-Woodcock Test of Auditory Discrimination.* Circle Pines, Minn.: American Guidance Service, 1970.

Goldschmid, M. L. Different types of conservation and nonconservation and their relation to age, sex, I.Q., M.A., and vocabulary. *Child Development,* 1967, *38,* 1229–1246.

Goldstein, H. S., & Peck, R. Cognitive functions in Negro and white children in a child guidance clinic. *Psychological Reports,* 1971, *28,* 379–384.

Good, T. L., & Brophy, J. E. Behavioral expression of teacher attitudes. *Journal of Educational Psychology,* 1972, *63,* 617–624.

Goodenough, D. R., & Karp, S. A. Field dependence and intellectual functioning. *Journal of Abnormal and Social Psychology,* 1961, *63,* 241–246.

Goodenough, F. L. *Measurement of intelligence by drawings.* New York: World Book, 1926.

Goodenough, F. L. Review of the Merrill-Palmer Scale of Mental Tests. In O. K. Buros (Ed.), *The 1940 mental measurements yearbook.* Highland Park, N.J.: Gryphon Press, 1940. Pp. 229–230.

Goodenough, F. L. Studies of the 1937 revision of the Stanford-Binet Scale. I. Variability of the IQ at successive age-levels. *Journal of Educational Psychology,* 1942, *33,* 241–251.

Goodenough, F. L. *Mental testing.* New York: Rinehart and Company, 1949.

Goodman, H., Gottlieb, J., & Harrison, R. H. Social acceptance of EMRs integrated into a nongraded elementary school. *American Journal of Mental Deficiency,* 1972, *76,* 412–417.

Goodman, J. F. Wanted: Restoration of the mental age in the 1972 revised Stanford-Binet. *Journal of Special Education,* 1978, *12,* 45–49.

Goodman, J. F. "Ignorance" versus "stupidity"—the basic disagreement. *School Psychology Digest,* 1979, *8,* 218–223. (a)

Goodman, J. F. Is tissue the issue? A critique of SOMPA's models and tests. *School Psychology Digest,* 1979, *8,* 47–62. (b)

Goodstein, H. A., Kahn, H., & Cawley, J. F. The achievement of educable mentally retarded children on the KeyMath Diagnostic Arithmetic Test. *Journal of Special Education,* 1976, *10,* 61–70.

Gordon, D. A., & Forehand, R. The relative efficiency of abbreviated forms of the Stanford-Binet. *Journal of Clinical Psychology,* 1972, *28,* 86–87.

Gordon, R. G. The Merrill-Palmer Scale of Intelligence Tests for pre-school children applied to low-grade mental defectives. *British Journal of Psychology,* 1933, *24,* 178–186.

Gorham, K. A. A lost generation of parents. *Exceptional Children,* 1975, *41,* 521–525.

Goslin, D. A. *The search for ability: Standardized testing in social perspective.* New York: Russell Sage Foundation, 1963.

Gottfried, A. W. Intellectual consequences of perinatal anoxia. *Psychological Bulletin,* 1973, *80,* 231–242.

Gottfried, A. W., & Brody, N. Interrelationships between and correlates of psychometric and Piagetian scales of sensorimotor intelligence. *Developmental Psychology,* 1975, *11,* 379–387.

Gottlieb, J., & Budoff, M. Social acceptability of retarded children in nongraded schools differing in architecture. *American Journal of Mental Deficiency,* 1973, *78,* 15–19.

Gottlieb, J., Semmel, M. I., & Veldman, D. J. Correlates of social status among mainstreamed mentally retarded children. *Journal of Educational Psychology,* 1978, *70,* 396–405.

Gozali, J., & Meyen, E. L. The influence of the teacher expectancy phenomenon on the academic performances of educable mentally retarded pupils in special classes. *Journal of Special Education,* 1970, *4,* 417–424.

Graham, E. E. Wechsler-Bellevue and WISC scattergrams of unsuccessful readers. *Journal of Consulting Psychology,* 1952, *16,* 268–271.

Graham, G. A. The effects of material and social incentives on the performance on intelligence test tasks by lower class and middle class Negro preschool children. *Dissertation Abstracts International,* 1971, *31*(7-B), 4311.

Grayson, H. M., & Tolman, R. S. A semantic study of concepts of clinical psychologists and psychiatrists. *Journal of Abnormal and Social Psychology,* 1950, *45,* 216–231.

Grebler, L., Moore, J. W., & Guzman, R. C. *The Mexican-American people: The nation's second largest minority.* New York: Free Press, 1970.

Green, B. F., Jr. In defense of measurement. *American Psychologist,* 1978, *33,* 664–670.

Green, F. The examiner as a possible source of constant error in intelligence testing. In R. L. Cromwell (Ed.), *Abstracts of Peabody studies in mental retardation* (Vol. 2). Nashville: George Peabody College for Teachers, 1960–1962, Abstract No. 36.

Greenberg, J. W., & Alshan, L. M. Perceptual-motor functioning and school achievement in lower-class black children. *Perceptual and Motor Skills,* 1974, *38,* 60–62.

Greene, E. B. *Measurements of human behavior.* New York: Odyssey Press, 1941.

Greenstein, J., & Strain, P. S. The utility of the Key-Math Diagnostic Arithmetic Test for adolescent learning disabled students. *Psychology in the Schools,* 1977, *14,* 275–282.

Gretzler, A. F. The use of the Arthur Adaptation of the Leiter International Performance Scale in comparison with the Stanford-Binet Form L-M in diagnosing children with central nervous system dysfunctioning. *Dissertation Abstracts International,* 1974, *35*(1-A), 257–258.

Gridley, G., & Mastenbrook, J. ABIC, sociocultural, IQ, and achievement. In M. Kaplan (Chair), *Research on Mercer and Lewis' Adaptive Behavior Inventory for Children (ABIC).* Symposium presented at the meeting of the American Psychological Association, San Francisco, September 1977.

Griesel, R. D., & Bartel, P. R. The visual evoked response in relation to measures of intelligence and development in a group of four-year-old children. *South African Journal of Psychology,* 1976, *6,* 33–42.

Griffiths, A. N. Dyslexia: Symptoms and remediation results. *Quarterly Journal of the Florida Academy of Sciences,* 1970, *33,* 1–16.

Grossman, F. D. The effect of an examinee's reported academic achievement and/or physical condition on examiners' scoring of the WISC-R Verbal IQ. *Dissertation Abstracts International,* 1978, *38,* 4091A.

Grossman, H. J. *Manual on terminology and classification in mental retardation.* 1973 Revision. American Association on Mental Deficiency. Baltimore: Garamond /Pridemark Press, 1973.

Guilford, J. P. The structure of intellect. *Psychological Bulletin,* 1956, *53,* 267–293.

Guilford, J. P. *The nature of human intelligence.* New York: McGraw-Hill, 1967.

Gunzburg, H. C. Subnormal adults. In P. Mittler (Ed.), *The psychological assessment of mental and physical handicaps.* London: Methuen, 1970. Pp. 289–317.

Guskin, S. L., & Chaires, M. C. Research implications: Implications of research on peer acceptance. *Education and Training of the Mentally Retarded,* 1966, *1,* 185–189.

Guthrie, R. V. *Even the rat was white.* New York: Harper & Row, 1976.

Gutkin, T. B. Some useful statistics for the interpretation of the WISC-R. *Journal of Consulting and Clinical Psychology,* 1978, *46,* 1561–1563.

Gutkin, T. B. Bannatyne patterns of Caucasian and Mexican-American learning disabled children. *Psychology in the Schools,* 1979, *16,* 178–183. (a)

Gutkin, T. B. The WISC-R Verbal Comprehension, Perceptual Organization, and Freedom from Distractability Deviation Quotients: Data for practitioners. *Psychology in the Schools,* 1979, *16,* 359–360. (b)

Gutkin, T. B., & Reynolds, C. R. Factorial similarity of the WISC-R for Anglos and Chicanos referred for psychological services. *Journal of School Psychology,* 1980, *18,* 34–39.

Gutkin, T. B., & Reynolds, C. R. Factorial similarity of the WISC-R for White and Black children from the standardization sample. *Journal of Educational Psychology,* 1981, *73,* 227–231.

Guy, D. P. Issues in the unbiased assessment of intelligence. *School Psychology Digest,* 1977, *6*(3), 14–23.

Haeussermann, E. *Developmental potential of preschool children.* New York: Grune & Stratton, 1958.

Hagin, R. A., Silver, A. A., & Corwin, C. G. Clinical-diagnostic use of the WPPSI in predicting learning disabilities in grade 1. *Journal of Special Education,* 1971, *5,* 221–232.

Hale, R. L. The WISC-R as a predictor of WRAT performance. *Psychology in the Schools,* 1978, *15,* 172–175.

Hale, R. L., Douglas, B., Cummins, A., Rittgarn, G., Breed, B., & Dabbert, D. The Slosson as a predictor of Wide Range Achievement Test performance. *Psychology in the Schools,* 1978, *15,* 507–509.

Hall, B. F. The trial of William Freeman. *American Journal of Insanity,* 1848, *5*(2), 34–60.

Hall, V. C., Huppertz, J. W., & Levi, A. Attention and achievement exhibited by middle- and lower-class black and white elementary school boys. *Journal of Educational Psychology,* 1977, *69,* 115–120.

Hall, V. C., Turner, R. R., & Russell, W. Ability of children from four subcultures and two grade levels to imitate and comprehend crucial aspects of standard English: A test of the different language explanation. *Journal of Educational Psychology,* 1973, *64,* 147–158.

Hall, W. S., Reder, S., & Cole, M. Story recall in young black and white children: Effects of racial group membership, race of experimenter, and dialect. *Developmental Psychology,* 1975, *11,* 628–634.

Hallahan, D. P., Ball, D. W., & Payne, J. S. Factorial composition of the short form of the Stanford-Binet with culturally disadvantaged Head Start children. *Psychological Reports,* 1973, *32,* 1048–1050.

Halpern, F. The Bender Visual Motor Gestalt Test. In H. H. Anderson & G. L. Anderson (Eds.), *An introduction to projective techniques.* New York: Prentice Hall, 1951.

Halpern, F. C. Clinicians must listen! *School Psychologist Newsletter,* 1971, *25*(2), 15–17.

Halpin, G., Halpin, G., & Tillman, M. H. Relationships between creative thinking, intelligence, and teacher-rated characteristics of blind children. *Education of the Visually Handicapped,* 1973, *5,* 33–38.

Hamm, H. A., & Evans, J. G. WISC-R subtest patterns of severely emotionally disturbed students. *Psychology in the Schools,* 1978, *15,* 188–190.

Hamm, H. A., Wheeler, J., McCallum, S., Herrin, M., Hunter, D., & Catoe, C. A comparison between the WISC and WISC-R among educable mentally retarded students. *Psychology in the Schools,* 1976, *13,* 4–8.

Hammill, D. D. The Slosson Intelligence Test as a quick estimate of mental ability. *Journal of School Psychology,* 1969, *7*(4), 33–37.

Hammill, D. D., Colarusso, R. P., & Wiederholt, J. L. Diagnostic value of the Frostig Test: A factor analytic approach. *Journal of Special Education,* 1970, *4,* 279–282.

Hammill, D. D., Crandell, J. M., Jr., & Colarusso, R. The Slosson Intelligence Test adapted for visually limited children. *Exceptional Children,* 1970, *36,* 535–536.

Hammill, D. D., Goodman, L., & Wiederholt, J. L. Use of the Frostig DTVP with economically disadvantaged children. *Journal of School Psychology,* 1971, *9,* 430–435.

Hammill, D. D., Goodman, L., & Wiederholt, J. L. Visual-motor processes: Can we train them? *Reading Teacher,* 1974, *27,* 469–478.

Hammill, D. D., & Larsen, S. C. The effectiveness of psycholinguistic training. *Exceptional Children,* 1974, *41,* 5–14.

Handler, L., Gerston, A., & Handler, B. Suggestions for improved psychologist-teacher communication. *Psychology in the Schools,* 1965, *2,* 77–81.

Hanley, J. H., & Barclay, A. G. Sensitivity of the WISC and WISC-R to subject and examiner variables. *Journal of Black Psychology,* 1979, *5,* 79–84.

Hanson, R. A. Consistency and stability of home environmental measures related to IQ. *Child Development,* 1975, *46,* 470–480.

Harari, C., & Shwast, J. Class bias in psychodiagnosis of delinquents. *Crime and Delinquency,* 1964, *10,* 145–151.

Hardy, J. B. Birth weight and subsequent physical and intellectual development. *New England Journal of Medicine,* 1973, *289,* 973–974.

Hardy, J. B., Welcher, D. W., Mellits, E. D., & Kagan, J. Pitfalls in the measurement of intelligence: Are standard intelligence tests valid instruments for measuring the intellectual potential of urban children? *Journal of Psychology,* 1976, *94,* 43–51.

Harriman, P. L. Irregularity of successes on the 1937 Stanford Revision. *Journal of Consulting Psychology,* 1939, *3,* 83–85.

Harris, A. J., & Shakow, D. The clinical significance of numerical measures of scatter on the Stanford-Binet. *Psychological Bulletin,* 1937, *34,* 134–150.

Harris, D. B. A note on some ability correlates of the Raven Progressive Matrices (1947) in the kindergarten. *Journal of Educational Psychology,* 1959, *50,*

228-229.

Harris, D. B. *Children's drawings as measures of intellectual maturity: A revision and extension of the Goodenough Draw-a-Man Test.* New York: Harcourt, Brace & World, 1963.

Harris, M. L. *A comparison of the Wechsler Intelligence Scale for Children with the Wide Range Achievement Test when used with educable mentally retarded children.* Unpublished master's thesis, Mississippi State University, 1973.

Harris, R. A comparative study of two groups of boys, delinquent and non-delinquent, on the basis of their Wechsler and Rorschach test performances. *Bulletin of the Maritime Psychological Association,* 1957, *6,* 21-28.

Harrison, D. K. The attitudes of Black counselees toward White counselors. *Journal of Non-White Concerns in Personnel and Guidance,* 1977, *5,* 52-59.

Harrison, K. A., & Wiebe, M. J. Correlational study of McCarthy, WISC, and Stanford-Binet scales. *Perceptual and Motor Skills,* 1977, *44,* 63-68.

Harrison, P. L., & Naglieri, J. A. Extrapolated general cognitive indexes on the McCarthy Scales for gifted and mentally retarded children. *Psychological Reports,* 1978, *43,* 1291-1296.

Hartlage, L. C., & Boone, K. E. Achievement test correlates of Wechsler Intelligence Scale for Children and Wechsler Intelligence Scale for Children-Revised. *Perceptual and Motor Skills,* 1977, *45,* 1283-1286.

Hartlage, L. C., & Green, J. B. EEG abnormalities and WISC subtest differences. *Journal of Clinical Psychology,* 1972, *28,* 170-171.

Hartlage, L. C., & Lucas, T. L. Differential correlates of Bender-Gestalt and Beery Visual Motor Integration Test for black and for white children. *Perceptual and Motor Skills,* 1976, *43,* 1039-1042.

Hartlage, L. C., & Merck, K. H. Increasing the relevance of psychological reports. *Journal of Clinical Psychology,* 1971, *27,* 459-460.

Hartlage, L. C., & Steele, C. T. WISC and WISC-R correlates of academic achievement. *Psychology in the Schools,* 1977, *14,* 15-18.

Hartman, R. K. An investigation of the incremental validity of human figure drawings in the diagnosis of learning disabilities. *Journal of School Psychology,* 1972, *10,* 9-16.

Harver, J. R. Influence of presentation dialect and orthographic form on reading performance of Black, inner-city children. *Educational Research Quarterly,* 1977, *2,* 9-16.

Haskell, S. H., Barrett, E. K., & Taylor, H. *The education of motor and neurologically handicapped children.* London: Croom Helm, 1977.

Hata, Y., Tsudzuki, A., Kuze, T., & Emi, Y. Relationships between the tester and the subject as a factor influencing on the intelligence test score: I. *Japanese Journal of Psychology,* 1958, *29,* 99-104.

Havighurst, R. J., & Hilkevitch, R. R. The intelligence of Indian children as measured by a performance scale. *Journal of Abnormal and Social Psychology,* 1944, *39,* 419-433.

Havighurst, R. J., & Janke, L. L. Relations between ability and social status in a midwestern community.

I. Ten-year-old children. *Journal of Educational Psychology,* 1944, *35,* 357-368.

Hawkes, G. R., & Taylor, M. Power structure in Mexican and Mexican-American farm labor families. *Journal of Marriage and the Family,* 1975, *37,* 807-811.

Haworth, M. R. *The CAT: Facts about fantasy.* New York: Grune & Stratton, 1966.

Haynes, S. N., & Kerns, R. D. Validation of a behavioral observation system. *Journal of Consulting and Clinical Psychology,* 1979, *47,* 397-400.

Hays, J. R., Solway, K. S., & Schreiner, D. Intellectual characteristics of juvenile murderers versus status offenders. *Psychological Reports,* 1978, *43,* 80-82.

Haywood, H. C. Introduction to clinical neuropsychology. In H. C. Haywood (Ed.), *Brain damage in school age children.* Washington, D.C.: National Education Association, Council for Exceptional Children, 1968.

Haywood, H. C. Intelligence, distribution of. *Encyclopaedia Britannica* (15th ed.), 1974, *9,* 672-677.

Hebb, D. O. *A textbook of psychology* (2nd ed.). Philadelphia: Saunders, 1966.

Hebb, D. O. Whose confusion? *American Psychologist,* 1971, *26,* 736.

Heidbreder, E. *Seven psychologies.* New York: Century, 1933.

Heil, J., Barclay, A., & Endres, J. M. B. A factor analytic study of WPPSI scores of educationally deprived and normal children. *Psychological Reports,* 1978, *42,* 727-730.

Heiskanen, O., & Kaste, M. Late prognosis of severe brain injury in children. *Developmental Medicine and Child Neurology,* 1974, *16,* 11-14.

Henderson, N. B., & Engel, R. Neonatal visual evoked potentials as predictors of psychoeducational tests at age seven. *Developmental Psychology,* 1974, *10,* 269-276.

Henderson, R. W., & Rankin, R. J. WPPSI reliability and predictive validity with disadvantaged Mexican-American children. *Journal of School Psychology,* 1973, *11,* 16-20.

Hendriks, J. *De kwalitatieve analyse van de intelligentie-test van Terman en Merrill.* (The qualitative analysis of the intelligence test of Terman and Merrill.) Amsterdam, The Netherlands: N. V. Standaardboek-handel, 1954.

Hennessy, J. J., & Merrifield, P. R. A comparison of the factor structures of mental abilities in four ethnic groups. *Journal of Educational Psychology,* 1976, *68,* 754-759.

Henning, J. J., & Levy, R. H. Verbal-Performance IQ differences of white and Negro delinquents on the WISC and WAIS. *Journal of Clinical Psychology,* 1967, *23,* 164-168.

Herman, D. O. A study of sex differences on the Wechsler Preschool and Primary Scale of Intelligence. *Proceedings of the 76th Annual Convention of the American Psychological Association,* 1968, *3,* 455-456.

Herman, D. O., Huesing, P. D., Levett, C. A., & Boehm, A. E. *A follow-up study of the BTBC standardization sample: Correlation with later measures of achievement.* Unpublished paper, Psychological Corp., 1973.

Hermelin, B., & Frith, U. Psychological studies of childhood autism: Can autistic children make sense of what they see and hear? *Journal of Special Education,* 1971, *5,* 107–117.

Herrell, J. M., & Golland, J. H. Should WISC subjects explain Picture Arrangement stories? *Journal of Consulting and Clinical Psychology,* 1969, *33,* 761–762.

Herrnstein, R. J. *I.Q. in the meritocracy.* Boston: Little, Brown, 1973.

Hersh, J. B. Effects of referral information on testers. *Journal of Consulting and Clinical Psychology,* 1971, *37,* 116–122.

Hill, K. T. Anxiety in the evaluative context. In W. W. Hartup (Ed.), *Young child* (Vol. 2). Washington, D.C.: National Association of the Education of Young Children, 1972.

Hill, K. T., & Eaton, W. O. The interaction of test anxiety and success-failure experiences in determining children's arithmetic performance. *Developmental Psychology,* 1977, *13,* 205–211.

Hill, K. T., & Sarason, S. B. The relation of test anxiety and defensiveness to test and school performance over the elementary-school years: A further longitudinal study. *Monographs of the Society for Research in Child Development,* 1966, *31*(2, Whole No. 104).

Himelstein, P. Research with the Stanford-Binet, Form L-M: The first five years. *Psychological Bulletin,* 1966, *65,* 156–164.

Himelstein, P. Use of the Stanford-Binet, Form L-M, with retardates: A review of recent research. *American Journal of Mental Deficiency,* 1968, *72,* 691–699.

Himelstein, P. Review of the Pictorial Test of Intelligence. In O. K. Buros (Ed.), *The seventh mental measurements yearbook.* Highland Park, N.J.: Gryphon Press, 1972. Pp. 748–749.

Hinckley, A. C. The Binet tests applied to individuals over twelve years of age. *Journal of Educational Psychology,* 1915, *6,* 43–58.

Hingtgen, J. N., & Bryson, C. Q. Recent developments in the study of early childhood psychoses: Infantile autism, childhood schizophrenia, and related disorders. *Schizophrenia Bulletin,* 1972, No. 5, 8–54.

Hinshelwood, J. *Congenital word-blindness.* London: H. K. Lewis, 1917.

Hirsch, E. A. The adaptive significance of commonly described behavior of the mentally retarded. *American Journal of Mental Deficiency,* 1959, *63,* 639–646.

Hirshoren, A., Hurley, O. L., & Hunt, J. T. The WISC-R and the Hiskey-Nebraska Test with deaf children. *American Annals of the Deaf,* 1977, *122,* 392–394.

Hirshoren, A., Kavale, K., Hurley, O. L., & Hunt, J. T. The reliability of the WISC-R Performance Scale with deaf children. *Psychology in the Schools,* 1977, *14,* 412–415.

Hiscock, M., & Kinsbourne, M. Ontogeny of cerebral dominance: Evidence from time-sharing asymmetry in children. *Developmental Psychology,* 1978, *14,* 321–329.

Hoakley, Z. P., & Frazeur, H. A. Significance of psychological test results of exogenous and endogenous children. *American Journal of Mental Deficiency,* 1945, *50,* 263–271.

Hobbs, N. *The futures of children.* San Francisco: Jossey-Bass, 1975.

Hoffman, S., Preiser, M., & David, G. Preschool intellectual assessment with the Ammons Quick Test. *Psychology in the Schools,* 1975, *12,* 430–431.

Hofstaetter, P. R. The changing composition of "intelligence": A study in T-technique. *Journal of Genetic Psychology,* 1954, *85,* 159–164.

Holden, R. H. Review of the Bayley Scales of Infant Development. In O. K. Buros (Ed.), *The seventh mental measurements yearbook.* Highland Park, N.J.: Gryphon Press, 1972. P. 729.

Holland, W. R. Language barrier as an educational problem of Spanish-speaking children. *Exceptional Children,* 1960, *27,* 42–50.

Holmen, M. G., & Docter, R. F. *Educational and psychological testing: A study of the industry and its practices.* New York: Russell Sage Foundation, 1972.

Holroyd, J., & Wright, F. Neurological implications of WISC Verbal-Performance discrepancies in a psychiatric setting. *Journal of Consulting Psychology,* 1965, *29,* 206–212.

Holtzman, W. H. The changing world of mental measurement and its social significance. *American Psychologist,* 1971, *26,* 546–553.

Honzik, M. P. Environmental correlates of mental growth: Prediction from the family setting at 21 months. *Child Development,* 1967, *38,* 337–364.

Honzik, M. P., Macfarlane, J. W., & Allen, L. The stability of mental test performance between two and eighteen years. *Journal of Experimental Education,* 1948, *17,* 309–324.

Hopkins, K. D., Dobson, J. C., & Oldridge, O. A. The concurrent and congruent validities of the Wide Range Achievement Test. *Educational and Psychological Measurement,* 1962, *22,* 791–793.

Hopkins, K. D., & McGuire, L. Mental measurement of the blind: The validity of the Wechsler Intelligence Scale for Children. *International Journal for the Education of the Blind,* 1966, *15,* 65–73.

Hopkins, K. D., & McGuire, L. IQ constancy and the blind child. *International Journal for the Education of the Blind,* 1967, *16,* 113–114.

Horn, J. L. Intelligence—why it grows, why it declines. *Trans-action,* 1967, *5,* 23–31.

Horn, J. L. Organization of abilities and the development of intelligence. *Psychological Review,* 1968, *75,* 242–259.

Horn, J. L. Organization of data on life-span development of human abilities. In L. R. Goulet & P. B. Baltes (Eds.), *Life-span developmental psychology.* New York: Academic Press, 1970.

Horn, J. L. Intelligence: Why it grows, why it declines. In J. M. Hunt (Ed.), *Human intelligence.* New Brunswick, N. J.: Transaction Books, 1972.

Horn, J. L. Human ability systems. In P.B. Baltes (Ed.), *Life-span development and behavior* (Vol. 1). New York: Academic Press, 1978. (a)

Horn, J. L. The nature and development of intellectual abilities. In R. T. Osborne, C. E. Noble, & N. Weyl (Eds.), *Human variation: The biopsychology of age, race, and sex.* New York: Academic Press, 1978. (b)

Horn, J. L. Trends in the measurement of intelligence. *Intelligence,* 1979, *3,* 229–239.

Horn, J. L., & Cattell, R. B. Age differences in fluid and crystallized intelligence. *Acta Psychologica*, 1967, *26*, 107–129.

Houston, C., & Otto, W. Poor readers' functioning on the WISC, Slosson Intelligence Test and Quick Test. *Journal of Educational Research*, 1968, *62*, 157–159.

Howard, J. L., & Plant, W. T. Psychometric evaluation of an Operation Headstart program. *Journal of Genetic Psychology*, 1967, *111*, 281–288.

Hubschman, E., Polizzotto, E. A., & Kaliski, M. S. Performance of institutionalized retardates on the PPVT and two editions of the ITPA. *American Journal of Mental Deficiency*, 1970, *74*, 579–580.

Hudson, L. Intelligence, race, and the selection of data. *Race*, 1971, *12*, 283–292.

Hudson, L. The context of the debate. In K. Richardson, D. Spears, & M. Richards (Eds.), *Race and intelligence: The fallacies behind the race-IQ controversy*. Baltimore, Md.: Penguin Books, 1972.

Hueftle, M. K. A factor analytic study of the Frostig Developmental Test of Visual Perception, the Illinois Test of Psycholinguistic Abilities, and the Wechsler Intelligence Scale for Children. *Dissertation Abstracts*, 1967, *28*, 2139B–2140B.

Hug, N., Barclay, A., Collins, H., & Lamp, R. Validity and factor structure of the Preschool Attainment Record in Head Start children. *Journal of Psychology*, 1978, *99*, 71–74.

Huizinga, R. J. The relationship of the ITPA to the Stanford-Binet Form L-M and the WISC. *Journal of Learning Disabilities*, 1973, *6*, 451–456.

Humphreys, L. G. Theory of intelligence. In R. Cancro (Ed.), *Intelligence: Genetic and environmental influences*. New York: Grune & Stratton, 1971.

Humphreys, L. G. Statistical definitions of test validity for minority groups. *Journal of Applied Psychology*, 1973, *58*, 1–4.

Humphreys, L. G. Race and sex differences and their implications for educational and occupational equality. In M. L. Maehr & W. M. Stallings (Eds.), *Culture, child and school*. Belmont, Ca.: Brooks/Cole, 1975.

Humphreys, L. G., & Parsons, C. K. Piagetian tasks measure intelligence and intelligence tests assess cognitive development: A reanalysis. *Intelligence*, 1979, *3*, 369–382.

Hunt, E. Quote the Raven? Nevermore! In L. W. Gregg (Ed.), *Knowledge and cognition*. Potomac, Md.: Erlbaum, 1974.

Hunt, E., Frost, N., & Lunneborg, C. Individual differences in cognition: A new approach to intelligence. In G. H. Bower (Ed.), *The psychology of learning and motivation: Advances in research and theory: VII*. New York: Academic Press, 1973.

Hunt, J. McV. *Intelligence and experience*. New York: Ronald Press, 1961.

Hunt, J. McV. *Utility of ordinal scales derived from Piaget's observations*. Paper presented at the meeting of the American Psychological Association, Montreal, August 1973.

Hunt, J. McV., & Cofer, C. N. Psychological deficit. In J. McV. Hunt (Ed.), *Personality and the behavior disorders*. (Vol. II). New York: Ronald Press, 1944. Pp. 971–1032.

Hunt, J. McV. Review of the Preschool Attainment Record. In W. K. Frankenburg & B. W. Camp (Eds.), *Pediatric screening tests*. Springfield, Ill.: Charles C Thomas, 1974.

Hunter, E. J., & Johnson, L. C. Developmental and psychological differences between readers and nonreaders. *Journal of Learning Disabilities*, 1971, *4*, 572–577.

Hurley, O. L., Hirshoren, A., Hunt, J. T., & Kavale, K. Predictive validity of two mental ability tests with black deaf children. *Journal of Negro Education*, 1979, *48*, 14–19.

Hurst, J. G. A factor analysis of the Merrill-Palmer with reference to theory and test construction. *Educational and Psychological Measurement*, 1960, *20*, 519–532.

Hutcherson, R. Correlating the Boehm and PPVT. *Academic Therapy*, 1978, *13*, 285–288.

Hutt, M. L. A clinical study of "consecutive" and "adaptive" testing with the Revised Stanford-Binet. *Journal of Consulting Psychology*, 1947, *11*, 93–103.

Hutt, S. J. Cognitive development and cerebral dysfunction. In V. Hamilton & M. D. Vernon (Eds.), *The development of cognitive processes*. New York: Academic Press, 1976.

Hutton, J. B. Relationships between teacher judgment, screening test data and academic performance for disadvantaged children. *Training School Bulletin*, 1972, *68*, 197–201.

Iano, R. P., Ayers, D., Heller, H. B., McGettigan, J. F., & Walker, V. S. Sociometric status of retarded children in an integrative program. *Exceptional Children*, 1974, *40*, 267–271.

Ilg, F. L., & Ames, L. B. *School readiness: Behavior tests used at the Gesell Institute*. New York: Harper & Row, 1965.

Illingworth, R. S., & Birch, L. B. The diagnosis of mental retardation in infancy. A follow-up study. *Archives of Disease in Childhood*, 1959, *34*, 269–273.

Ingalls, R. P. *Mental retardation: The changing outlook*. New York: Wiley, 1978.

Ingram, T. T. S. The development of higher nervous activity in childhood and its disorders: General introduction. In P. J. Vinken & G. W. Bruyn (Eds.), *Handbook of clinical neurology* (Vol. 4). Amsterdam, The Netherlands: North-Holland, 1969.

Ingram, T. T. S., Mason, A. W., & Blackburn, I. A retrospective study of 82 children with reading disability. *Developmental Medicine and Child Neurology*, 1970, *12*, 271–281.

Jacobson, L. I., Bernal, G., & Lopez, G. N. Case histories and shorter communications. *Behavior Research & Therapy*, 1973, *11*, 143–145.

Jamison, C. B. Review of the Purdue Perceptual-Motor Survey. In O. K. Buros (Ed.), *The seventh mental measurements yearbook*. Highland Park, N. J.: Gryphon Press, 1972. Pp. 1283–1284.

Janke, L. L., & Havighurst, R. J. Relations between ability and social status in a midwestern community. II. Sixteen-year-old boys and girls. *Journal of Educational Psychology*, 1945, *36*, 499–509.

Jarman, R. F., & Das, J. P. Simultaneous and successive syntheses and intelligence. *Intelligence*, 1977, *1*, 151–169.

Jastak, J. F., & Jastak, S. *The Wide Range Achievement Test* (rev. ed.). Wilmington, Del.: Jastak Associates, 1978.

Jenkins, J. J., & Paterson, D. G. (Eds.) *Studies in individual differences*. New York: Appleton-Century-Crofts, 1961.

Jensen, A. R. How much can we boost IQ and scholastic achievement? *Harvard Educational Review*, 1969, *39*, 1–123.

Jensen, A. R. A theory of primary and secondary familial mental retardation. In N. R. Ellis (Ed.), *International review of research in mental retardation* (Vol. 4). New York: Academic Press, 1970. Pp. 33–105. (a)

Jensen, A. R. Another look at culture-fair testing. In J. Hellmuth (Ed.), *Disadvantaged child* (Vol. 3). New York: Brunner/Mazel, 1970. Pp. 53–101. (b)

Jensen, A. R. Can we and should we study race differences? In C. L. Brace, G. R. Gamble, & J. T. Bond (Eds.), *Race and intelligence*. Washington, D.C.: American Anthropological Association, 1971.

Jensen, A. R. Cumulative deficit: A testable hypothesis? *Developmental Psychology*, 1974, *10*, 996–1019. (a)

Jensen, A. R. The effect of race of examiner on the mental test scores of white and black pupils. *Journal of Educational Measurement*, 1974, *11*, 1–14. (b)

Jensen, A. R. How biased are culture-loaded tests? *Genetic Psychology Monographs*, 1974, *90*, 185–244. (c)

Jensen, A. R. Review of T. Dobzhansky, *Genetic diversity and human equality*. *Perspectives in Biology and Medicine*, 1974, *17*, 430–434. (d)

Jensen, A. R. The price of inequality. *Oxford Review of Education*, 1975, *1*, 59–71.

Jensen, A. R. Cumulative deficit in IQ of Blacks in the rural South. *Developmental Psychology*, 1977, *13*, 184–191.

Jensen, A. R. The nature of intelligence and its relation to learning. *Journal of Research and Development in Education*, 1979, *12*(2), 79–95. (a)

Jensen, A. R. g: Outmoded theory or unconquered frontier? *Creative Science and Technology*, 1979, *11*, 16–29. (b)

Jensen, A. R. *Bias in mental testing*. New York: The Free Press, 1980.

Jensen, A. R., & Figueroa, R. A. Forward and backward digit span interaction with race and IQ: Predictions from Jensen's theory. *Journal of Educational Psychology*, 1975, *67*, 882–893.

Jensen, A. R., & Osborne, R. T. *Forward and backward digit span interaction with race and IQ: A longitudinal developmental comparison*. Berkeley: University of California, 1979. (ERIC Document Reproduction Service No. ED 173 384)

Jensen, D. R., & Engel, R. Statistical procedures for relating dichotomous responses to maturation and EEG measurements. *Electroencephalography and Clinical Neurophysiology*, 1971, *30*, 437–443.

Jenson, G., Hanson, J., & Young, M. A study of the comparability of WISC and WISC-R intelligence quotients. *Guidelines for Pupil Services*, 1976–77, *15*(1), 27–30.

Jerrolds, B. W., Callaway, B., & Gwaltney, W. K. Comparison of the Slosson Intelligence Test and WISC scores of subjects referred to a reading clinic. *Psychology in the Schools*, 1972, *9*, 409–410.

Jinks, J. L., & Fulker, D. W. Comparison of the biometrical genetical, MAVA, and classical approaches to the analysis of human behavior. *Psychological Bulletin*, 1970, *73*, 311–349.

Joesting, J., & Joesting, R. Comparison of scores on Quick Test and Stanford-Binet, Form L-M. *Psychological Reports*, 1971, *29*, 1178. (a)

Joesting, J., & Joesting, R. The Quick Test as a screening device in a welfare setting. *Psychological Reports*, 1971, *29*, 1289. (b)

Johns, J. Review of the Sucher-Allred Reading Placement Inventory. In O. K. Buros (Ed.), *The eighth mental measurements yearbook*. Highland Park, N.J.: Gryphon Press, 1978. P. 1227.

Johns, J. L. Can teachers use standardized reading tests to determine students' instructional levels? *Illinois School Research*, 1975, *11*(3), 29–35.

Johnson, D. L. The influences of social class and race on language test performance and spontaneous speech of preschool children. *Child Development*, 1974, *45*, 517–521.

Johnson, D. L., & Johnson, C. A. Comparison of four intelligence tests used with culturally disadvantaged children. *Psychological Reports*, 1971, *28*, 209–210.

Johnson, E. G., & Lyle, J. G. Analysis of WISC Coding: 1. Figural reversibility. *Perceptual and Motor Skills*, 1972, *34*, 195–198. (a)

Johnson, E. G., & Lyle, J. G. Analysis of WISC Coding: 2. Memory and verbal mediation. *Perceptual and Motor Skills*, 1972, *34*, 659–662. (b)

Johnson, E. G., & Lyle, J. G. Analysis of WISC Coding: 4. Paired-associate learning and performance strategies. *Perceptual and Motor Skills*, 1973, *37*, 695–698.

Johnson, E. Z. Sex differences and variability in the performance of retarded children on Raven, Binet and Arthur tests. *Journal of Clinical Psychology*, 1952, *8*, 298–301.

Johnson, G. O., & Blake, K. A. Learning and performance of retarded and normal children. Syracuse University special. *Educational Rehabilitation Monographs*, 1960, No. 5.

Johnson, M. S. Review of the Sucher-Allred Reading Placement Inventory. In O. K. Buros (Ed.), *The eighth mental measurements yearbook*. Highland Park, N.J.: Gryphon Press, 1978. Pp. 1225–1226.

Johnson, R. C., & Medinnus, G. R. *Child psychology: Behavior and development*. New York: Wiley, 1965.

Jones, C. T. Very bright and feeble-minded children: The study of qualitative differences. *Training School Bulletin*, 1919, *16*, 137–141, 155–164, 169–180.

Jones, H. E., Conrad, H. S., & Blanchard, M. B. Environmental handicap in mental test performance. *University of California Publication in Psychology*, 1932, *5*, 63–99.

Jones, L. V. A factor analysis of the Stanford-Binet at four age levels. *Psychometrika*, 1949, *14*, 299–331.

Jones, L. V. Primary abilities in the Stanford-Binet, age 13. *Journal of Genetic Psychology*, 1954, *84*, 125–147.

Jongeward, P. A. A validity study of the Slosson Intelligence Test for use with educable mentally retarded students. *Journal of School Psychology*, 1969, *7*(4), 59–63.

Jordan, J. S. Reliability of Stanford-Binet intelligence quotients derived by student examiners. *Journal of Educational Research*, 1932, *26*, 295–301.

Jordan, T. E. *The mentally retarded* (4th ed.). Columbus, Ohio: C. E. Merrill, 1976.

Jorgensen, C. C. Racism in mental testing: The use of IQ tests to mislabel black children. In A. A. Harrison (Ed.), *Explorations in psychology*. Monterey, Ca.: Brooks/Cole, 1974.

Kagan, J. On cultural deprivation. In D. C. Glass (Ed.), *Environmental influences*. New York: Rockefeller University Press, 1968. Pp. 211–250.

Kagan, J. *Understanding children*. New York: Harcourt Brace Jovanovich, 1971.

Kagan, J., & Klein, R. E. Cross-cultural perspectives on early development. *American Psychologist*, 1973, *28*, 947–961.

Kagan, J., Rosman, B. L., Day, D., Albert, J., & Phillips, W. Information processing in the child: Significance of analytic and reflective attitudes. *Psychological Monographs*, 1964, *78*(1, Whole No. 578).

Kagan, J., Sontag, L. W., Baker, C. T., & Nelson, V. L. Personality and IQ change. *Journal of Abnormal and Social Psychology*, 1958, *56*, 261–266.

Kagan, S. Preferred levels of achievement and aspiration in rural Mexican and urban Anglo American children. *Journal of Comparative Cultures*, 1975, *2*, 113–126.

Kagan, S. Social motives and behaviors of Mexican-American and Anglo-American children. In J. L. Martinez, Jr. (Ed.), *Chicano psychology*. New York: Academic Press, 1977.

Kagan, S., & Zahn, G. L. Field dependence and the school achievement gap between Anglo-American and Mexican-American children. *Journal of Educational Psychology*, 1975, *67*, 643–650.

Kaiser, M. D. *The Wechsler Intelligence Scale for Children as an instrument for diagnosing sociopathy* (Doctoral dissertation, Florida State University). Ann Arbor, Mich.: University Microfilms, 1964. No. 64-10,571.

Kallos, G. L., Grabow, J. M., & Guarino, E. A. The WISC profile of disabled readers. *Personnel and Guidance Journal*, 1961, *39*, 476–478.

Kamin, L. J. A positive interpretation of apparent "cumulative deficit." *Developmental Psychology*, 1978, *14*, 195–196.

Kangas, J., & Bradway, K. P. Intelligence at middle age: A thirty-eight-year follow-up. *Developmental Psychology*, 1971, *5*, 333–337.

Kaplan, B. J. Malnutrition and mental deficiency. *Psychological Bulletin*, 1972, *78*, 321–334.

Kaplan, B. L. Counseling with mothers of exceptional children. *Elementary School Guidance and Counseling*, 1971, *6*, 32–36.

Kaplan, H. E., & Alatishe, M. Comparison of ratings by mothers and teachers on preschool children using the Vineland Social Maturity Scale. *Psychology in the Schools*, 1976, *13*, 27–28.

Karnes, F. A., & Brown, K. E. Comparison of the SIT with the WISC-R for gifted students. *Psychology in the Schools*, 1979, *16*, 478–482.

Kaspar, J. C., Throne, F. M., & Schulman, J. L. A study of the inter-judge reliability in scoring the responses of a group of mentally retarded boys to three WISC subscales. *Educational and Psychological Measurement*, 1968, *28*, 469–477.

Katz, E. A "Survey of Degree of Physical Handicap." *Cerebral Palsy Review*, 1954, *15*(11), 10–11.

Katz, E. Success on Stanford-Binet Intelligence Scale test items of children with cerebral palsy as compared with non-handicapped children. *Cerebral Palsy Review*, 1955, *16*(1), 18–19.

Katz, E. The pointing scale method: A modification of the Stanford-Binet procedure for use with cerebral palsied children. *American Journal of Mental Deficiency*, 1956, *60*, 838–842.

Kaufman, A. S. A short form of the Wechsler Preschool and Primary Scale of Intelligence. *Journal of Consulting and Clinical Psychology*, 1972, *39*, 361–369. (a)

Kaufman, A. S. Piaget and Gesell: A psychometric analysis of tests built from their tasks. *Child Development*, 1972, *42*, 1341–1360. (b)

Kaufman, A. S. Comparison of the performance of matched groups of Black children and White children on the Wechsler Preschool and Primary Scale of Intelligence. *Journal of Consulting and Clinical Psychology*, 1973, *41*, 186–191. (a)

Kaufman, A. S. Comparison of the WPPSI, Stanford-Binet, and McCarthy Scales as predictors of first-grade achievement. *Perceptual and Motor Skills*, 1973, *36*, 67–73. (b)

Kaufman, A. S. The relationship of WPPSI IQs to SES and other background variables. *Journal of Clinical Psychology*, 1973, *29*, 354–357. (c)

Kaufman, A. S. Factor analysis of the WISC-R at 11 age levels between 6½ and 16½ years. *Journal of Consulting and Clinical Psychology*, 1975, *43*, 135–147. (a)

Kaufman, A. S. Factor structure of the McCarthy Scales at five age levels between 2½ and 8½. *Educational and Psychological Measurement*, 1975, *35*, 641–656. (b)

Kaufman, A. S. Do normal children have "flat" ability profiles? *Psychology in the Schools*, 1976, *13*, 284–285. (a)

Kaufman, A. S. A four-test short form of the WISC-R. *Contemporary Educational Psychology*, 1976, *1*, 180–196. (b)

Kaufman, A. S. A new approach to the interpretation of test scatter on the WISC-R. *Journal of Learning Disabilities*, 1976, *9*, 160–168. (c)

Kaufman, A. S. Verbal-performance IQ discrepancies on the WISC-R. *Journal of Consulting and Clinical Psychology*, 1976, *44*, 739–744. (d)

Kaufman, A. S. A McCarthy short form for rapid screening of preschool, kindergarten, and first-grade children. *Contemporary Educational Psychology*, 1977, *2*, 149–157.

Kaufman, A. S. *Intelligent testing with the WISC-R.* New York: Wiley-Interscience, 1979. (a)

Kaufman, A. S. The role of speed on WISC-R performance across the age range. *Journal of Consulting and Clinical Psychology,* 1979, *47,* 595–597. (b)

Kaufman, A. S. WISC-R research: Implications for interpretation. *School Psychology Digest,* 1979, *8,* 5–27. (c)

Kaufman, A. S., & DiCuio, R. F. Separate factor analyses of the McCarthy Scales for groups of black and white children. *Journal of School Psychology,* 1975, *13,* 10–18.

Kaufman, A. S., & Doppelt, J. E. Analysis of WISC-R standardization data in terms of the stratification variables. *Child Development,* 1976, *47,* 165–171.

Kaufman, A. S., & Hollenbeck, G. P. Comparative structure of the WPPSI for blacks and whites. *Journal of Clinical Psychology,* 1974, *30,* 316–319.

Kaufman, A. S., & Kaufman, N. L. Sex differences on the McCarthy Scales of Children's Abilities. *Journal of Clinical Psychology,* 1973, *29,* 362–365.

Kaufman, A. S., & Kaufman, N. L. *Clinical evaluation of young children with the McCarthy Scales.* New York: Grune & Stratton, 1977.

Kaufman, A. S., & Van Hagen, J. Investigation of the WISC-R for use with retarded children: Correlation with the 1972 Stanford-Binet and comparison of WISC and WISC-R profiles. *Psychology in the Schools,* 1977, *14,* 10–14.

Kaufman, A. S., & Waterstreet, M. A. Determining a child's strong and weak areas of functioning on the Stanford-Binet: A simplification of Sattler's SD method. *Journal of School Psychology,* 1978, *16,* 72–78.

Kavajecz, L. G. *A study of results on the Wechsler Preschool and Primary Scale of Intelligence of inadequate readers.* (Doctoral dissertation, Colorado State College) Ann Arbor, Mich.: University Microfilms, 1969. No. 70-7135.

Kawin, E. *Children of pre-school age.* Chicago: University of Chicago Press, 1934.

Keasey, C. T., & Charles, D. C. Conservation of substance in normal and mentally retarded children. *Journal of Genetic Psychology,* 1967, *111,* 271–279.

Keating, D. P. Precocious cognitive development at the level of formal operations. *Child Development,* 1975, *46,* 276–280.

Keir, G. The Progressive Matrices as applied to school children. *British Journal of Psychology, Statistical Section,* 1949, *2,* 140–150.

Keller, J. E. The relationship of auditory memory span to learning ability in high grade mentally retarded boys. *American Journal of Mental Deficiency,* 1957, *61,* 574–580.

Kelly, R. R. Hemispheric specialization of deaf children: Are there any implications for instruction? *American Annals of the Deaf,* 1978, *123,* 637–645.

Kelly, R. R., & Tomlinson-Keasey, C. Information processing of visually presented picture and word stimuli by young hearing-impaired and normal-hearing children. *Journal of Speech and Hearing Research,* 1976, *19,* 628–638.

Kelly, R. R., & Tomlinson-Keasey, C. Hemispheric laterality of deaf children for processing words and pictures visually presented to the hemifields. *American Annals of the Deaf,* 1977, *122,* 525–533.

Kelly, T. J., Sr., & Amble, B. R. IQ and perceptual motor scores as predictors of achievement among retarded children. *Journal of School Psychology,* 1970, *8,* 99–102.

Kendall, P. C., & Little, V. L. Correspondence of brief intelligence measures to the Wechsler Scales with delinquents. *Journal of Consulting and Clinical Psychology,* 1977, *45,* 660–666.

Kennedy, W. A., Moon, H., Nelson, W., Lindner, R., & Turner, J. The ceiling of the new Stanford-Binet. *Journal of Clinical Psychology,* 1961, *17,* 284–286.

Kennedy, W. A., Van de Riet, V., & White, J. C., Jr. Use of the Terman-Merrill abbreviated scale on the 1960 Stanford-Binet Form L-M on Negro elementary school children of the Southeastern United States. *Journal of Consulting Psychology,* 1963, *27,* 456–457.

Kennedy-Fraser, D. *The Terman-Merrill Intelligence Scale in Scotland.* Malham House, Bickely Kent: University of London Press, 1945.

Kent, G. H. Suggestions for the next revision of the Binet-Simon scale. *Psychological Record,* 1937, *1,* 409–433.

Keogh, B. K. A compensatory model for psychoeducational evaluation of children with learning disorders. *Journal of Learning Disabilities,* 1971, *4,* 544–548.

Keogh, B. K., & Kopp, C. B. From assessment to intervention: An elusive bridge. In F. D. Minifie & L. L. Lloyd (Eds.), *Communicative and cognitive abilities—early behavioral assessment.* Baltimore, Md.: University Park Press, 1978.

Keogh, B. K., Vernon, M., & Smith, C. E. Deafness and visuo-motor function. *Journal of Special Education,* 1970, *4,* 41–47.

Kephart, N. C. *The slow learner in the classroom* (2nd ed.). Columbus, Ohio: C. E. Merrill, 1971.

Kernberg, P. F. The problem of organicity in the child: Notes on some diagnostic techniques in the evaluation of children. *Journal of the American Academy of Child Psychiatry,* 1969, *8,* 517–541.

Kessler, J. W. *Psychopathology of childhood.* Englewood Cliffs, N.J.: Prentice-Hall, 1966.

Keston, M. J., & Jimenez, C. A study of the performance on English and Spanish editions of the Stanford-Binet Intelligence Test by Spanish American children. *Journal of Genetic Psychology,* 1954, *85,* 263–269.

Kiernan, C., & Jones, M. *Behaviour assessment battery.* Atlantic Highlands, N.J.: Humanities, 1977.

Kilian, J. B., & Hughes, L. C. A comparison of short forms of the Wechsler Intelligence Scale for Children-Revised in the screening of gifted referrals. *Gifted Child Quarterly,* 1978, *22,* 111–115.

King, J. D., & Smith, R. A. Abbreviated forms of the Wechsler Preschool and Primary Scale of Intelligence for a kindergarten population. *Psychological Reports,* 1972, *30,* 539–542.

King, W. L., & Seegmiller, B. Performance of 14- to 22-month-old black, firstborn male infants on two tests of cognitive development: The Bayley Scales and the Infant Psychological Development Scale. *Developmental Psychology,* 1973, *8,* 317–326.

Kinnie, E. J. *The influence of nonintellective factors on the IQ scores of middle- and lower-class children* (Doctoral dissertation, Purdue University). Ann Arbor, Mich.: University Microfilms, 1970. No. 71-9414.

Kinsbourne, M., & Caplan, P. J. *Children's learning and attention problems.* Boston: Little, Brown, 1979.

Kinsbourne, M., & Warrington, E. K. Developmental factors in reading and writing backwardness. *British Journal of Psychology,* 1963, *54,* 145–156.

Kirk, S. A., & Kirk, W. D. Uses and abuses of the ITPA. *Journal of Speech and Hearing Disorders,* 1978, *43,* 58–75.

Kirk, S. A., McCarthy, J. J., & Kirk, W. D. *The Illinois Test of Psycholinguistic Abilities.* Urbana: University of Illinois Press, 1968.

Kirk, W. D. *Aids and precautions in administering the Illinois Test of Psycholinguistic Abilities.* Urbana: University of Illinois Press, 1974.

Kirkland, M. C. The effects of tests on students and schools. *Review of Educational Research,* 1971, *41,* 303–350.

Kissel, S. Schizophrenic patterns on the WISC: A missing control. *Journal of Clinical Psychology,* 1966, *22,* 201.

Klapper, Z. S., & Birch, H. G. The relation of childhood characteristics to outcome in young adults with cerebral palsy. *Developmental Medicine and Child Neurology,* 1966, *8,* 645–656.

Klasen, E. *The syndrome of specific dyslexia.* Baltimore: University Park Press, 1972.

Kleinpeter, U. Social integration after brain trauma during childhood. *Acta Paedopsychiatrica,* 1976, *42,* 68–75.

Klinge, V., Rodziewicz, T., & Schwartz, L. Comparison of the WISC and WISC-R on a psychiatric adolescent inpatient sample. *Journal of Abnormal Child Psychology,* 1976, *4,* 73–81.

Klugman, S. F. The effect of money incentive versus praise upon the reliability and obtained scores of the Revised Stanford-Binet test. *Journal of General Psychology,* 1944, *30,* 255–269.

Knief, L. M., & Stroud, J. B. Intercorrelations among various intelligence, achievement, and social class scores. *Journal of Educational Psychology,* 1959, *50,* 117–120.

Knight, G. P., & Kagan, S. Development of prosocial and competitive behaviors in Anglo-American and Mexican-American children. *Child Development,* 1977, *48,* 1385–1394.

Knobloch, H., & Pasamanick, B. Environmental factors affecting human development before and after birth. *Pediatrics,* 1960, *26,* 210–218.

Knobloch, H., & Pasamanick, B. Mental subnormality. *New England Journal of Medicine,* 1962, *266,* 1045–1051.

Koegler, S. J. The management of the retarded child in practice. *Canadian Medical Association Journal,* 1963, *89,* 1009–1014.

Koenke, K. A comparison of three auditory discrimina-

tion-perception tests. *Academic Therapy,* 1978, *13,* 463–468.

Kogan, K. L. Repeated psychometric evaluations of preschool children with cerebral palsy. *Pediatrics,* 1957, *19,* 619–621.

Kohlberg, L., & Zigler, E. The impact of cognitive maturity on the development of sex-role attitudes in the years 4 to 8. *Genetic Psychology Monographs,* 1967, *75,* 89–165.

Kohn, M. *Social competence, symptoms, and underachievement in childhood: A longitudinal perspective.* Washington, D.C.: V. H. Winston, 1977.

Kohn, M., Parnes, B., & Rosman, B. L. *A rating & scoring manual for the Kohn Problem Checklist & Kohn Social Competence Scale* (Rev. ed.). Unpublished manuscript, The William Alanson White Institute of Psychiatry, Psychoanalysis & Psychology, 1976.

Kohn, M., & Rosman, B. L. Relationship of preschool social-emotional functioning to later intellectual achievement. *Developmental Psychology,* 1972, *6,* 445–452.

Kohn, M., & Rosman, B. L. Social-emotional, cognitive, and demographic determinants of poor school achievement: Implications for a strategy of intervention. *Journal of Educational Psychology,* 1974, *66,* 267–276.

Kolstoe, O. P. Programs for the mildly retarded: A reply to the critics. *Exceptional Children,* 1972, *39,* 51–56.

Kolvin, I. Infantile autism or infantile psychoses; late onset psychosis. *British Medical Journal,* 1972, *3,* 753–755, 816–817.

Kolvin, I., Humphrey, M., & McNay, A. VI. Cognitive factors in childhood psychosis. *British Journal of Psychiatry,* 1971, *118,* 415–419.

Koppitz, E. M. *The Bender Gestalt Test for young children.* New York: Grune & Stratton, 1964.

Koppitz, E. M. *The Bender Gestalt Test for young children* (Vol. 2): *Research and application, 1963–1973.* New York: Grune & Stratton, 1975.

Koppitz, E. M. *The Visual Aural Digit Span Test.* New York: Grune & Stratton, 1977.

Krager, J. M., & Safer, D. J. Type and prevalence of medication used in the treatment of hyperactive children. *New England Journal of Medicine,* 1974, *291,* 1118–1120.

Krashen, S. D. Lateralization, language learning, and the critical period: Some new evidence. *Language Learning,* 1973, *23,* 63–74.

Krasner, B. R., & Silverstein, L. The Preschool Attainment Record: A concurrent validity study with cerebral palsied children. *Educational and Psychological Measurement,* 1976, *36,* 1049–1054.

Kratochwill, T. R. The movement of psychological extras into ability assessment. *Journal of Special Education,* 1977, *11,* 299–311.

Kratochwill, T. R., & Demuth, D. M. An examination of the predictive validity of the KeyMath Diagnostic Arithmetic Test and the Wide Range Achievement Test in exceptional children. *Psychology in the Schools,* 1976, *13,* 404–406.

Krebs, E. G. *The Wechsler Preschool and Primary Scale of Intelligence and prediction of reading achievement in first grade* (Doctoral dissertation, Rutgers State University). Ann Arbor, Mich.: University Microfilms, 1969. No. 70-3361.

Krippner, S. WISC Comprehension and Picture Arrangement subtests as measures of social competence. *Journal of Clinical Psychology*, 1964, *20*, 366-367.

Kroske, W. H., Fretwell, L. N., & Cupp, M. E. Comparison of the Kahn Intelligence Tests: Experimental form, the Stanford-Binet, and the WAIS for familial retardates. *Perceptual and Motor Skills*, 1965, *21*, 428.

Krugman, M. Some impressions of the Revised Stanford-Binet Scale. *Journal of Educational Psychology*, 1939, *30*, 594-603.

Krywaniuk, L. W., & Das, J. P. Cognitive strategies in native children: Analysis and intervention. *Alberta Journal of Educational Research*, 1976, *22*, 271-280.

Kubany, E. S., & Sloggett, B. B. The role of motivation in test performance and remediation. *Journal of Learning Disabilities*, 1971, *4*, 426-429.

Kubota, M. Memory span and intelligence. *Japanese Journal of Psychology*, 1965, *36*(2), 47-55.

Kvaraceus, W. C. Pupil performances on the abbreviated and complete new Stanford-Binet Scales, Form L. *Journal of Educational Psychology*, 1940, *31*, 627-630.

Lacey, H. M., & Ross, A. O. Multidisciplinary views on psychological reports in child guidance clinics. *Journal of Clinical Psychology*, 1964, *20*, 522-526.

LaCrosse, J. E. *Examiner reliability on the Stanford-Binet Intelligence Scale (Form L-M) in a design employing white and Negro examiners and subjects.* Unpublished master's thesis, University of North Carolina, 1964.

Lahey, B. B., Stempniak, M., Robinson, E. J., & Tyroler, M. J. Hyperactivity and learning disabilities as independent dimensions of child behavior problems. *Journal of Abnormal Psychology*, 1978, *87*, 333-340.

Lamanna, J. A., & Ysseldyke, J. E. Reliability of the Peabody Individual Achievement Test with first-grade children. *Psychology in the Schools*, 1973, *10*, 437-439.

Lambert, N. M. Children's problems and classroom interventions from the perspective of classroom teachers. *Professional Psychology*, 1976, *7*, 507-517.

Lambert, N. M. The Adaptive Behavior Scale—Public School Version: An overview. In W. A. Coulter & H. W. Morrow (Eds.), *Adaptive behavior: Concepts and measurements.* New York: Grune & Stratton, 1978. (a)

Lambert, N. M. Application of adaptive behavior measurement in the public school setting. In W. A. Coulter (Chair), *What's new with adaptive behavior: Current/future status in assessment.* Symposium presented at the meeting of the American Psychological Association, Toronto, Canada, 1978. (b)

Lambert, N. M., & Nicoll, R. C. Dimensions of adaptive behavior of retarded and nonretarded public-school children. *American Journal of Mental Deficiency,* 1976, *81*, 135-146.

Lambert, N. M., Windmiller, M., Cole, L., & Figueroa, R. A. Standardization of a public school version of the AAMD Adaptive Behavior Scale. *Mental Retardation*, 1975, *13*(2), 3-7.

Lambert, N. M., Yandell, W., & Sandoval, J. H. Preparation of school psychologists for school-based consultation: A training activity and a service to community schools. *Journal of School Psychology*, 1975, *13*, 68-75.

Lamp, R. E., & Barclay, A. The Quick Test as a screening device for intellectually subnormal children. *Psychological Reports*, 1967, *20*, 763-766.

Lamp, R. E., & Traxler, A. J. The validity of the Slosson Intelligence Test for use with disadvantaged Head Start and first grade school children. *Journal of Community Psychology*, 1973, *1*, 27-30.

Lamp, R. E., Traxler, A. J., & Gustafson, P. P. Predicting academic achievement of disadvantaged fourth grade children using the Slosson Intelligence Test. *Journal of Community Psychology*, 1973, *1*, 339-341.

Landis, D. Review of the Purdue Perceptual-Motor Survey. In O. K. Buros (Ed.), *The seventh mental measurements yearbook.* Highland Park, N.J.: Gryphon Press, 1972. Pp. 1284-1285.

Lantz, B. Some dynamic aspects of success and failure. *Psychological Monographs*, 1945, *59*(1, Whole No. 271).

LaPray, M., & Ross, R. The graded word list: Quick gauge of reading ability. *Journal of Reading*, 1969, *12*, 305-307.

Larr, A. L., & Cain, E. R. Measurement of native learning abilities of deaf children. *Volta Review*, 1959, *61*, 160-162.

Larrabee, G. J., & Holroyd, R. G. Comparison of WISC and WISC-R using a sample of highly intelligent children. *Psychological Reports*, 1976, *38*, 1071-1074.

Larrabee, L. L., & Kleinsasser, L. D. The effect of experimenter bias on WISC performance. Unpublished manuscript, Psychological Associates, St. Louis, 1967.

Larsen, J. J., Tillman, C. E., Ross, J. J., Satz, P., Cassin, B., & Wolking, W. D. Factors in reading achievement: An interdisciplinary approach. *Journal of Learning Disabilities*, 1973, *6*, 636-644.

Lauro, L. *Managing the referral process: Key to effective school psychology practice.* Paper presented at the meeting of the American Psychological Association, Chicago, September 1975.

Lavos, G. W.I.S.C. psychometric patterns among deaf children. *Volta Review*, 1962, *64*, 547-552.

Lawson, J. R., & Avila, D. Comparison of Wide Range Achievement Test and Gray Oral Reading Paragraphs reading scores of mentally retarded adults. *Perceptual and Motor Skills*, 1962, *14*, 474.

Laycock, S. R., & Clark, S. The comparative performance of a group of old-dull and young-bright children on some items of the Revised Stanford-Binet Scale of Intelligence, Form L. *Journal of Educational Psychology*, 1942, *33*, 1-12.

Layzer, D. Science or superstition? (A physical scientist looks at the IQ controversy.) *Cognition,* 1972, *1,* 265–299.

Layzer, D. Heritability analyses of IQ scores: Science or numerology? *Science,* 1974, *183,* 1259–1266.

Lehman, E. B., & Levy, B. I. Discrepancies in estimates of children's intelligence: WISC and human figure drawings. *Journal of Clinical Psychology,* 1971, *27,* 74–76.

Lehmann, I. J. Rural-urban differences in intelligence. *Journal of Educational Research,* 1959, *53,* 62–68.

Leibert, R. E., & Sherk, J. K. Three Frostig visual perception sub-tests and specific reading tasks for kindergarten, first, and second grade children. *Reading Teacher,* 1970, *24,* 130–137.

Leiter, R. G. *Leiter International Performance Scale.* Chicago: Stoelting Co., 1948.

Leiter, R. G. Part I of the manual for the 1948 Revision of the Leiter International Performance Scale: Evidence of the reliability and validity of the Leiter tests. *Psychological Service Center Journal,* 1959, *11,* 1–72.

Lejeune, Y. A. Projective interpretation of intelligence tests. *Journal of South African Logopedic Society,* 1955, *3,* 9–12.

Leland, H. Testing the disadvantaged. In W. C. Rhodes (Chair), *Use and misuse of standardized intelligence tests in psychological and educational research and practice.* Symposium presented at the American Psychological Association, Washington, D.C., September 1971.

Leland, H. Theory into practice: From concept to measurement of adaptive behavior. In W. A. Coulter (Chair), *What's new with adaptive behavior: Current/future status in assessment.* Symposium presented at the meeting of the American Psychological Association, Toronto, Canada, 1978.

Lerner, I. M. *Heredity, evolution and society.* San Francisco: W. H. Freeman, 1968.

Lesser, G. S., Fifer, G., & Clark, D. H. Mental abilities of children from different social-class and cultural groups. *Monographs of the Society for Research in Child Development,* 1965, *30*(4, Whole No. 102).

Lessler, K., & Galinsky, M. D. Relationship between Slosson Intelligence Test and WISC scores in special education candidates. *Psychology in the Schools,* 1971, *8,* 341–344.

Lester, B. M. Psychological and central nervous system consequences of protein-calorie malnutrition: A review of research findings and some implications. *Revista Interamericana de Psicologia,* 1976, *10,* 17–31.

Lester, E. P., Muir, R., & Dudek, S. Z. Cognitive structure and achievement in the young child. *Canadian Psychiatric Association Journal,* 1970, *15,* 279–287.

Leva, R. A. Relationship among the self-direction, responsibility, and socialization domains of the Adaptive Behavior Scale. *American Journal of Mental Deficiency,* 1976, *81,* 297–298.

Levandowski, B. The difference in intelligence test scores of bilingual students on an English version of the intelligence test as compared to a Spanish version of the test. *Illinois School Research,* 1975, *11*(3),

47–51.

Levenson, R. L., Jr., & Zino, T. C., II. Assessment of cognitive deficiency with the McCarthy Scales and Stanford-Binet: A correlational analysis. *Perceptual and Motor Skills,* 1979, *48,* 291–295.

Levine, B., & Iscoe, I. The Progressive Matrices (1938), the Chicago Non-Verbal, and the Wechsler-Bellevue on an adolescent deaf population. *Journal of Clinical Psychology,* 1955, *11,* 307–308.

Levine, E. S. *The psychology of deafness.* New York: Columbia University Press, 1960.

Levine, H. A., & Gross, M. Suitability of the Harris revision of the Goodenough Draw-a-Man Test for a psychiatric population. *Journal of Clinical Psychology,* 1968, *24,* 350–351.

Levine, M. Psychological testing of children. In M. L. Hoffman & L. W. Hoffman (Eds.), *Review of child development research* (Vol. 2). New York: Russell Sage Foundation, 1966. Pp. 257–310.

Levine, M. N., Allen, R. M., Alker, L. N., & Fitzgibbons, W. *Clinical profile form for the Leiter International Performance Scale.* Chicago: Stoelting, 1974.

Levine, S., Elzey, F. F., Thormahlen, P., & Cain, L. F. *Manual for the T.M.R. School Competency Scales.* Palo Alto, Ca.: Consulting Psychologists Press, 1976.

Levinson, B. M., & Block, Z. Goodenough-Harris drawings of Jewish children of orthodox background. *Psychological Reports,* 1977, *41,* 155–158.

Levy, B. B., & Cook, H. Dialect proficiency and auditory comprehension in standard and black nonstandard English. *Journal of Speech and Hearing Research,* 1973, *16,* 642–649.

Levy, P. Short-form tests: A methodological review. *Psychological Bulletin,* 1968, *69,* 410–416.

Lewis, L. L. The relation of measured mental ability to school marks and academic survival in the Texas School for the Blind. *International Journal for the Education of the Blind,* 1957, *6,* 56–60.

Lewis, M. Infant intelligence tests: Their use and misuse. *Human Development,* 1973, *16,* 108–118.

Lezak, M. D. *Neuropsychological assessment.* New York: Oxford University Press, 1976.

Lichtman, M. V. *Intelligence, creativity, and language: An examination of the interrelationships of three variables among preschool, disadvantaged Negro children* (Doctoral dissertation, George Washington University). Ann Arbor, Mich.: University Microfilms, 1969. No. 70-13,956.

Lietz, E. S. Perceptual-motor abilities of disadvantaged and advantaged kindergarten children. *Perceptual and Motor Skills,* 1972, *35,* 887–890.

Lillywhite, H. Doctor's manual of speech disorders. *JAMA: Journal of the American Medical Association,* 1958, *167* (Part 2), 850–858.

Lindamood, C., & Lindamood, P. *Lindamood Auditory Test of Conceptualization.* Boston: Teaching Resources, 1971.

Linden, K. W., & Linden, J. D. *Modern mental measurement: A historical perspective.* Boston: Houghton Mifflin, 1968.

Lipsitz, S. *Effect of the race of the examiner on results of intelligence test performance of Negro and white children*. Unpublished master's thesis, Long Island University, 1969.

Livingston, J. S. *An evaluation of a photographically enlarged form of the Revised Stanford-Binet Intelligence Scale for use with the partially seeing child* (Doctoral dissertation, New York University). Ann Arbor, Mich.: University Microfilms, 1957. No. 21,712.

Lloyd-Still, J. D. *Malnutrition and intellectual development*. Littleton, Mass.: Publishing Sciences Group, 1976.

Locke, J. L. Review of the Auditory Discrimination Test. In F. L. Darley (Ed.), *Evaluation of appraisal techniques in speech and language pathology*. Reading, Mass.: Addison-Wesley, 1979.

Lockyer, L., & Rutter, M. A five- to fifteen-year follow-up study of infantile psychosis. III: Psychological aspects. *British Journal of Psychiatry*, 1969, *115*, 865–882.

Lodge, G. T. How to write a psychological report. *Journal of Clinical Psychology*, 1953, *9*, 400–402.

Loehlin, J. C., Lindzey, G., & Spuhler, J. N. *Race differences in intelligence*. San Francisco: W. H. Freeman, 1975.

Lombard, T. J., & Riedel, R. G. An analysis of the factor structure of the WISC-R and the effect of color on the Coding subtest. *Psychology in the Schools*, 1978, *15*, 176–179.

Long, P. A., & Anthony, J. J. The measurement of mental retardation by a culture-specific test. *Psychology in the Schools*, 1974, *11*, 310–312.

López, M., & Young, R. K. The linguistic interdependence of bilinguals. *Journal of Experimental Psychology*, 1974, *102*, 981–983.

Lord, E. E. *Children handicapped by cerebral palsy*. New York: Commonwealth Fund, 1937.

Lorion, R. P., Cowen, E. L., & Caldwell, R. A. Normative and parametric analyses of school maladjustment. *American Journal of Community Psychology*, 1975, *3*, 291–301.

Lorr, M., & Meister, R. K. The concept scatter in the light of mental test theory. *Educational and Psychological Measurement*, 1941, *1*, 303–310.

Lotter, V. Epidemiology of autistic conditions in young children. II. Some characteristics of the parents and children. *Social Psychiatry*, 1967, *1*, 163–173.

Lotter, V. Factors related to outcome in autistic children. *Journal of Autism and Childhood Schizophrenia*, 1974, *4*, 263–277.

Lotter, V. Follow-up studies. In M. Rutter & E. Schopler (Eds.), *Autism: A reappraisal of concepts and treatment*. New York: Plenum, 1978.

Louden, M. V. Relative difficulty of Stanford-Binet vocabulary for bright and dull subjects of the same mental level. *Journal of Educational Research*, 1933, *27*, 179–186.

Louttit, C. M. *Clinical psychology of exceptional children* (3rd ed.). New York: Harper, 1957.

Lovell, K., & Shields, J. B. Some aspects of a study of the gifted child. *British Journal of Educational Psychology*, 1967, *37*, 201–208.

Lowe, J. D., & Karnes, F. A. A comparison of scores on the WISC-R and Lorge-Thorndike Intelligence Test for disadvantaged black elementary school children. *Southern Journal of Educational Research*, 1976, *10*, 152–154.

Lowrance, D. S. Psycho-educational assessment of the learning disabled child. *Dissertation Abstracts International*, 1977, *38*, 2667A–2668A.

Lowrance, D., & Anderson, H. N. A comparison of the Slosson Intelligence Test and the WISC-R with elementary school children. *Psychology in the Schools*, 1979, *16*, 361–364.

Lubin, B., Wallis, R. R., & Paine, C. Patterns of psychological test usage in the United States: 1935–1969. *Professional Psychology*, 1971, *2*, 70–74.

Lumsden, J. Review of the Illinois Test of Psycholinguistic Abilities, revised edition. In O. K. Buros (Ed.), *The eighth mental measurements yearbook*. Highland Park, N.J.: Gryphon Press, 1978. Pp. 578–580.

Luria, A. R. *Higher cortical functions in man*. New York: Basic Books, 1966. (a)

Luria, A. R. Human brain and psychological processes. New York: Harper & Row, 1966. (b)

Lutey, C. L. *Individual intelligence testing: A manual*. Greeley, Colo.: Author, 1967.

Lyle, J. G., & Goyen, J. Performance of retarded readers on the WISC and educational tests. *Journal of Abnormal Psychology*, 1969, *74*, 105–112.

Lyle, J. G., & Johnson, E. G. Analysis of WISC Coding: 3. Writing and copying speed, and motivation. *Perceptual and Motor Skills*, 1973, *36*, 211–214.

Lyle, J. G., & Johnson, E. G. Analysis of WISC Coding: 5. Prediction of Coding performance. *Perceptual and Motor Skills*, 1974, *39*, 111–114.

Lyman, H. B. Review of the Peabody Individual Achievement Test. *Journal of Educational Measurement*, 1971, *8*, 137–138.

Lynn, R. The intelligence of the Japanese. *Bulletin of the British Psychological Society*, 1977, *30*, 69–72.

MacArthur, R. S. The Coloured Progressive Matrices as a measure of general intellectual ability for Edmonton grade III boys. *Alberta Journal of Educational Research*, 1960, *6*, 67–75.

MacArthur, R. S., & Elley, W. B. The reduction of socioeconomic bias in intelligence testing. *British Journal of Educational Psychology*, 1963, *33*, 107–119.

Maccoby, E. E., & Jacklin, C. N. *The psychology of sex differences*. Stanford, Ca.: Stanford Univ. Press, 1974.

Machen, L. H. A validity and reliability study of the Slosson Intelligence Test (SIT) with an atypical population: Gifted children. *Dissertation Abstracts International*, 1973, *33* (7-A), 3296.

Machover, K. A. *Personality projection in the drawing of the human figure*. Springfield, Ill.: Charles C Thomas, 1949.

Madaus, G. F. Divergent thinking and intelligence: Another look at a controversial question. *Journal of Educational Measurement*, 1967, *4*, 227–235.

Madden, T. M. A note on the administration and scoring of the WISC Mazes subtest. *Psychology in the Schools*, 1974, *11*, 143–146.

Madsen, W. *Mexican-Americans of South Texas*. New York: Holt, Rinehart and Winston, 1964.

Magaret, G. A., & Thompson, C. W. Differential test responses of normal, superior and mentally defective subjects. *Journal of Abnormal and Social Psychology*, 1950, *45*, 163–167.

Mahan, T. W., Jr. Diagnostic consistency and prediction: A note on graduate student skills. *Personnel and Guidance Journal*, 1963, *42*, 364–367.

Maloney, M. P., Ward, M. P., Schenck, H. U., & Braucht, G. N. Re-evaluation of the use of the Quick Test with a sample of institutionalized mentally retarded subjects. *Psychological Reports*, 1971, *29*, 1155–1159.

Malpass, L. F., Brown, R., & Hake, D. The utility of the Progressive Matrices (1956 Edition) with normal and retarded children. *Journal of Clinical Psychology*, 1960, *16*, 350.

Malter, R. F. *Conceptualization processes and memory: Implications for the diagnosis and remediation of learning disabilities*. Paper presented at the meeting of the American Psychological Association, San Francisco, August 1977.

Mann, L. Review of the Marianne Frostig Developmental Test of Visual Perception. In O. K. Buros (Ed.), *The seventh mental measurements yearbook*. Highland Park, N.J.: Gryphon Press, 1972. Pp. 1274–1276.

Manuel, H. T. *Spanish-speaking children of the Southwest: Their education and the public welfare*. Austin: University of Texas Press, 1965.

Marine, E. L. The effect of familiarity with the examiner upon Stanford-Binet test performance. *Teachers College Contributions to Education*, 1929, No. 381.

Marjoribanks, K. Environment, social class, and mental abilities. *Journal of Educational Psychology*, 1972, *63*, 103–109.

Marland, S. P., Jr. *Education of the gifted and talented: Report to the Congress of the United States by the Commissioner of Education*. Washington, D.C.: U.S. Government Printing Office, 1972.

Marsden, G., & Kalter, N. Bodily concerns and the WISC Object Assembly subtest. *Journal of Consulting and Clinical Psychology*, 1969, *33*, 391–395.

Martin, A. W., & Wiechers, J. E. Raven's Colored Progressive Matrices and the Wechsler Intelligence Scale for Children. *Journal of Consulting Psychology*, 1954, *18*, 143–144.

Martin, J. D., & Kidwell, J. C. Intercorrelations of the Wechsler Intelligence Scale for Children–Revised, the Slosson Intelligence Test, and the National Educational Developmental Test. *Educational and Psychological Measurement*, 1977, *37*, 1117–1120.

Martinson, B., & Strauss, A. A. A method of clinical evaluation of the responses to the Stanford-Binet Intelligence Test. *American Journal of Mental Deficiency*, 1941, *46*, 48–59.

Martinson, R. A. Children with superior cognitive abilities. In L. M. Dunn (Ed.), *Exceptional children in the schools: Special education in transition*. New York: Holt, Rinehart and Winston, 1973.

Marwit, S. J., & Neumann, G. Black and white children's comprehension of standard and nonstandard English passages. *Journal of Educational Psychology*, 1974, *66*, 329–332.

Masland, R. L., Sarason, S. B., & Gladwin, T. *Mental subnormality*. New York: Basic Books, 1958.

Masling, J. M. The effects of warm and cold interaction on the administration and scoring of an intelligence test. *Journal of Consulting Psychology*, 1959, *23*, 336–341.

Massey, J. O. *WISC scoring criteria*. Palo Alto, Ca.: Consulting Psychologists Press, 1964.

Massey, J. O., Sattler, J. M., & Andres, J. R. *WISC-R scoring criteria*. Palo Alto, Ca.: Consulting Psychologists Press, 1978.

Mastenbrook, J. *Analysis of the content of Adaptive Behavior and two instruments*. Paper presented at the meeting of the American Psychological Association, San Francisco, September 1977.

Mastenbrook, J. Future directions in adaptive behavior assessment: Environmental adaptation measure. In A. T. Fisher (Chair), *Impact of adaptive behavior: ABIC and the environmental adaptation measure*. Symposium presented at the meeting of the American Psychological Association, Toronto, Canada, 1978.

Mastenbrook, J., Scott, L., & Marriott, S. *Use of the ABIC in special education: Problems and solutions*. Paper presented at the meeting of the American Psychological Association, Toronto, Canada, September 1978.

Matarazzo, J. D. *Wechsler's measurement and appraisal of adult intelligence* (5th ed.). Baltimore, Md.: Williams & Wilkins, 1972.

Mateer, F. *The unstable child*. New York: D. Appleton & Co., 1924.

Matějček, Z. Specific learning disabilities. *Bulletin of the Orton Society*, 1977, *27*, 7–25.

Matheny, A. P., Jr., Dolan, A. B., & Wilson, R. S. Bayley's Infant Behavior Record: Relations between behaviors and mental test scores. *Developmental Psychology*, 1974, *10*, 696–702.

Mattis, S., French, J. H., & Rapin, I. Dyslexia in children and young adults: Three independent neuropsychological syndromes. *Developmental Medicine and Child Neurology*, 1975, *17*, 150–163.

Maurer, K. M. Mental measurement of children handicapped by cerebral palsy. *Physiotherapy Review*, 1940, *20*, 271–273.

Maxwell, A. E. Discrepancies in the variances of test results for normal and neurotic children. *British Journal of Statistical Psychology*, 1960, *13*, 165–172.

Maxwell, M. T. The relationship between the Wechsler Intelligence Scale for Children and the Slosson Intelligence Test. *Child Study Journal*, 1971, *1*, 164–171.

McAreavey, J. P. An analysis of selected educationally handicapped South Dakota Sioux Indian children's responses to the Wechsler Intelligence Scale for Children and Wide Range Achievement Test of Reading. *Dissertation Abstracts International*, 1976, *36*, 5154A–5155A.

McCall, R. B. Childhood IQ's as predictors of adult educational and occupational status. *Science*, 1977, *197*, 482–483.

McCall, R. B. The development of intellectual functioning in infancy and the prediction of later I.Q. In J. D.

Osofsky (Ed.), *Handbook of infant development.* New York: Wiley, 1979.

McCall, R. B., Appelbaum, M. I., & Hogarty, P. S. Developmental changes in mental performance. *Monographs of the Society for Research in Child Development,* 1973, *38*(3) (Serial No. 150), 1–83.

McCall, R. B., Hogarty, P. S., & Hurlburt, N. Transitions in infant sensorimotor development and the prediction of childhood IQ. *American Psychologist,* 1972, *27,* 728–748.

McCandless, B. R. Review of the Revised Stanford-Binet Scale. In O. K. Buros (Ed.), *The fourth mental measurements yearbook.* Highland Park, N.J.: Gryphon Press, 1953. Pp. 464–465.

McCandless, B. R. Review of the Boehm Test of Basic Concepts. In O. K. Buros (Ed.), *The seventh mental measurements yearbook.* Highland Park, N.J.: Gryphon Press, 1972. P. 626.

McCarthy, D. Administration of Digit Symbol and Coding subtests of the WAIS and WISC to left-handed subjects. *Psychological Reports,* 1961, *8,* 407–408.

McCarthy, D. A. *Manual for the McCarthy Scales of Children's Abilities.* New York: Psychological Corporation, 1972.

McClintock, C. G. Development of social motives in Anglo-American and Mexican-American children. *Journal of Personality & Social Psychology,* 1974, *29,* 348–354.

McConnell, R. E. The origin of mental tests. *Education,* 1930, *50,* 464–473.

McFadden, J. H. Differential responses of normal and feebleminded subjects of equal mental age on the Kent-Rosanoff Free Association Test and the Stanford Revision of the Binet-Simon Intelligence Test. *Mental Measurements Monographs,* 1931, No. 7.

McFie, J. Intellectual impairment in children with localized post-infantile cerebral lesions. *Journal of Neurology, Neurosurgery, and Psychiatry,* 1961, *24,* 361–365.

McFie, J. The diagnostic significance of disorders of higher nervous activity: Syndromes related to frontal, temporal, parietal and occipital lesions. In P. J. Vinken & G. W. Bruyn (Eds.), *Handbook of Clinical Neurology* (Vol. 4). Amsterdam, The Netherlands: North-Holland, 1969.

McFie, J. *Assessment of organic intellectual impairment.* New York: Academic Press, 1975.

McGilligan, R. P., Yater, A. C., & Huesing, R. Goodenough-Harris Drawing Test reliabilities. *Psychology in the Schools,* 1971, *8,* 359–362.

McGinnis, M. A. *Aphasic children.* Washington, D.C.: Alexander Graham Bell Association for the Deaf, 1963.

McGuire, T. R., & Hirsch, J. General intelligence (*g*) and heritability (*H²*, *h²*). In I. C. Uzgiris & F. Weizmann (Eds.), *The structuring of experience.* New York: Plenum Press, 1977.

McHugh, A. F. WISC performance in neurotic and conduct disturbances. *Journal of Clinical Psychology,* 1963, *19,* 423–424.

McIntire, J. T. The incidence of feeble-mindedness in the cerebral palsied. *American Association on Mental Deficiency Proceedings,* 1938, *43*(2), 44–50.

McKerracher, D. W., & Scott, J. I.Q. scores and the problem of classification. *British Journal of Psychiatry,* 1966, *112,* 537–541.

McKinney, J. D. Factor analytic study of the Developmental Test of Visual Perception and the Metropolitan Readiness Test. *Perceptual and Motor Skills,* 1971, *33,* 1331–1334.

McLaughlin, B. Second-language learning in children. *Psychological Bulletin,* 1977, *84,* 438–459.

McLean, T. K. *A comparison of the subtest performance of two groups of retarded readers with like groups of non-retarded readers on the Wechsler Intelligence Scale for Children* (Doctoral dissertation, University of Oregon). Ann Arbor, Mich.: University Microfilms, 1963. No. 64-5402.

McLeod, J. A comparison of WISC sub-test scores of pre-adolescent successful and unsuccessful readers. *Australian Journal of Psychology,* 1965, *17,* 220–228.

McNamara, J. R., Porterfield, C. L., & Miller, L. E. The relationship of the Wechsler Preschool and Primary Scale of Intelligence with the Coloured Progressive Matrices (1956) and the Bender Gestalt Test. *Journal of Clinical Psychology,* 1969, *25,* 65–68.

McNemar, Q. *The revision of the Stanford-Binet Scale.* Boston: Houghton Mifflin, 1942.

McNemar, Q. Lost: Our intelligence? Why? *American Psychologist,* 1964, *19,* 871–882.

McNemar, Q. Correction to a correction. *Journal of Consulting and Clinical Psychology,* 1974, *42,* 145–146.

McWilliams, B. J. Clinical use of the Peabody Picture Vocabulary Test with cleft palate pre-schoolers. *Cleft Palate Journal,* 1974, *11,* 439–442.

Meadow, K. P. Early manual communication in relation to the deaf child's intellectual, social, and communicative functioning. *American Annals of the Deaf,* 1968, *113,* 29–41.

Meadow, K. P. The development of deaf children. In E. M. Hetherington (Ed.), *Review of child development research* (Vol. 5). Chicago: University of Chicago Press, 1975.

Mecham, M. J., Berko, M. J., & Berko, F. G. *Speech therapy in cerebral palsy.* Springfield, Ill.: Charles C Thomas, 1960.

Mecham, M. J., Berko, M. J., Berko, F. G., & Palmer, M. F. *Communication training in childhood brain damage.* Springfield, Ill.: Charles C Thomas, 1966.

Meeker, M. N. *The structure of intellect.* Columbus, Ohio: Charles E. Merrill, 1969.

Mehr, H. M. The application of psychological tests and methods to schizophrenia in children. *The Nervous Child,* 1952, *10,* 63–93.

Meichenbaum, D. H., & Goodman, J. Training impulsive children to talk to themselves: A means of developing self-control. *Journal of Abnormal Psychology,* 1971, *77,* 115–126.

Melear, J., & Boyle, J. The relationship of the Columbia Mental Maturity Scale to the WISC with reference to low achieving Anglo and Spanish bilingual children. *Colorado Journal of Educational Research,* 1974, *14,* 8–10.

Mercer, J. R. Sociocultural factors in labeling mental retardates. *Peabody Journal of Education*, 1971, *48*, 188–203.

Mercer, J. R. Pluralistic diagnosis in the evaluation of Black and Chicano children: A procedure for taking sociocultural variables into account in clinical assessment. In C. A. Hernandez, M. J. Haug, & N. N. Wagner (Eds.), *Chicanos: Social and psychological perspectives* (2nd ed.). St. Louis: C. V. Mosby, 1976.

Mercer, J. R. *System of Multicultural Pluralistic Assessment technical manual.* New York: Psychological Corporation, 1979.

Mercer, J. R., & Lewis, J. F. *System of Multicultural Pluralistic Assessment.* New York: Psychological Corporation, 1978.

Messick, S., & Anderson, S. Educational testing, individual development, and social responsibility. *Counseling Psychologist*, 1970, *2*(2), 80–88.

Meyer, W. J., & Goldstein, D. Performance characteristics of middle-class and lower-class preschool children on the Stanford-Binet, 1960 Revision. ERIC: ED 044 429, 1971.

Meyers, C. E. What the ITPA measures: A synthesis of factor studies of the 1961 edition. *Educational and Psychological Measurement*, 1969, *29*, 867–876.

Meyers, C. E. Review of the Balthazar Scales of Adaptive Behavior. In O. K. Buros (Ed.), *The eighth mental measurements yearbook.* Highland Park, N.J.: Gryphon Press, 1978. Pp. 696–698.

Michal-Smith, H. Problems encountered in the psychometric examination of the child with cerebral palsy. *Cerebral Palsy Review*, 1955, *16*(3), 15–16, 20.

Mickelson, N. I., & Galloway, C. G. Verbal concepts of Indian and non-Indian school beginners. *Journal of Educational Research*, 1973, *67*, 55–56.

Miele, F. Cultural bias in the WISC. *Intelligence*, 1979, *3*, 149–164.

Milgram, N. A. Danger: Chauvinism, scapegoatism, and euphemism. In G. J. Williams & S. Gordon (Eds.), *Clinical child psychology: Current practices and future perspectives.* New York: Behavioral Publications, 1974.

Miller, C. K., & Chansky, N. M. Psychologists' scoring of WISC protocols. *Psychology in the Schools*, 1972, *9*, 144–152.

Miller, C. K., Chansky, N. M., & Gredler, G. R. Rater agreement on WISC protocols. *Psychology in the Schools*, 1970, *7*, 190–193.

Miller, H. R. WISC performance under incentive conditions: Case report. *Psychological Reports*, 1969, *24*, 835–838.

Miller, J. O., & Phillips, J. A preliminary evaluation of the Head Start and other metropolitan Nashville kindergartens. Unpublished manuscript, George Peabody College for Teachers, 1966.

Miller, M. D. Discrimination between two types of learning disabilities by Wechsler Intelligence Scale for Children subtest patterns (Doctoral dissertation, Southern Illinois University, 1976). *Dissertation Abstracts International*, 1977, *37*, 5747A.

Miller, R. A. Social milieu and the effects of reinforcement on I.Q. tests. *Dissertation Abstracts International*, 1974, *35* (1-B), 517–518.

Miller, W. D. Classroom usefulness of intelligence tests in estimating reading potential. *Yearbook of the National Reading Conference*, 1973, *22*, 162–168.

Millham, J., Chilcutt, J., & Atkinson, B. Criterion validity of the AAMD Adaptive Behavior Scales. In J. Millham (Chair), *Reliability and validity of the Adaptive Behavior Scales.* Symposium presented at the meeting of the American Psychological Association, Washington, D.C., September 1976.

Milligan, G. E. Counseling parents of the mentally retarded. In J. H. Rothstein (Ed.), *Mental retardation* (2nd ed.). New York: Holt, Rinehart and Winston, 1971. Pp. 492–502.

Milne, N. D. M. Relationships among scores obtained on the Wechsler Intelligence Scale for Children, Columbia Mental Maturity Scale and Leiter International Performance Scale by Mexican-American children. *Dissertation Abstracts International*, 1975, *35*(10-A), 6516.

Milofsky, C. D. Why special education isn't special. *Harvard Educational Review*, 1974, *44*(4), 437–458.

Minde, K., Weiss, G., & Mendelson, N. A 5-year follow-up study of 91 hyperactive school children. *Journal of the American Academy of Child Psychiatry*, 1972, *11*, 595–610.

Mitchell, M. B. Irregularities of university students on the Revised Stanford-Binet. *Journal of Educational Psychology*, 1941, *32*, 513–522.

Mittler, P. The psychological assessment of autistic children. In J. K. Wing (Ed.), *Early childhood autism: Clinical, educational and social aspects.* London: Pergamon Press, 1966.

Mittler, P., & Ward, J. The use of the Illinois Test of Psycholinguistic Abilities on British 4-year-old children: A normative and factorial study. *British Journal of Educational Psychology*, 1970, *40*, 43–54.

Mize, J. M., Smith, J. W., & Callaway, B. Comparison of reading disabled children's scores on the WISC-R, Peabody Picture Vocabulary Test, and Slosson Intelligence Test. *Psychology in the Schools*, 1979, *16*, 356–358.

Montagu, A. Sociogenic brain damage. *American Anthropologist*, 1972, *74*, 1045–1061.

Moore, C. H., Boblitt, W. E., & Wildman, R. W. Psychiatric impressions of psychological reports. *Journal of Clinical Psychology*, 1968, *24*, 373–376.

Moore, C. L., & Retish, P. M. Effect of the examiner's race on black children's Wechsler Preschool and Primary Scale of Intelligence IQ. *Developmental Psychology*, 1974, *10*, 672–676.

Moore, M. V. Pathological writing. *Asha*, 1969, *11*, 535–538.

Morales, E. S., & George, C. *Examiner effects in the testing of Mexican-American children.* Paper presented at the meeting of the American Psychological Association, Washington, D.C., September 1976.

Moran, R. E. Progressive matrices and the educationally disadvantaged. *Mental Retardation*, 1972, *10*(3), 9.

Moriarty, A. E. Coping patterns of preschool children in response to intelligence test demands. *Genetic Psychology Monographs*, 1961, *64*, 3–127.

Moriarty, A. E. Review of the Denver Developmental Screening Test. In O. K. Buros (Ed.), *The seventh mental measurements yearbook.* Highland Park, N.J.: Gryphon Press, 1972. Pp. 733–734.

Morris, J. D., Evans, J. G., & Pearson, D. R. The WISC-R subtest profile of a sample of severely emotionally disturbed children. *Psychological Reports,* 1978, *42,* 319–325.

Morris, J. D., Martin, R. A., Johnson, E., Birch, M. C., & Thompson, D. Subtest order and WISC-R scores of a sample of educable mentally retarded subjects. *Psychological Reports,* 1978, *43,* 383–386.

Muench, G. A. A followup of mental defectives after eighteen years. *Journal of Abnormal and Social Psychology,* 1944, *39,* 407–418.

Muir, M. The WISC test pattern of children with severe reading disabilities. *Reading Horizons,* 1962, *2*(Winter), 67–73.

Mulcahy, R. F. Autism: Beautiful children. *Mental Retardation Bulletin,* 1972-3, *1,* 73–77.

Mundy, L., & Maxwell, A. E. Assessment of the feebleminded. *British Journal of Medical Psychology,* 1958, *31,* 201–210.

Munford, P. R., Meyerowitz, B. E., & Munford, A. M. A comparison of Black and White children's WISC/WISC-R differences. *Journal of Clinical Psychology,* 1980, *36,* 471–475.

Münsterberg, H. Zur Individualpsychologie. *Centralblatt fur Nervenheilkunde und Psychiatrie,* 1891, *14,* 196–198.

Murdoch, K. Rate of improvement of the feeble-minded as shown by standardized educational tests. *Journal of Applied Psychology,* 1918, *2,* 243–249.

Murphy, G. Psychological views of personality and contributions to its study. In E. Norbeck, D. Price-Williams, & W. M. McCord (Eds.), *The study of personality.* New York: Holt, Rinehart and Winston, 1968. Pp. 15–40.

Murphy, K. P. Tests of abilities and attainments. In A. W. G. Ewing (Ed.), *Educational guidance and the deaf child.* Manchester: Manchester University Press, 1957. Pp. 213–251.

Murphy, L. B. The appraisal of child personality. *Journal of Consulting Psychology,* 1948, *12,* 16–19.

Murphy, L. B. The stranglehold of norms on the individual child. In M. D. Cohen (Ed.), *Testing and evaluation: New views.* Washington, D.C.: Association for Childhood Education International, 1975. (ERIC Document Reproduction Service No. ED 109 143)

Murstein, B. I. *Theory and research in projective techniques.* New York: Wiley, 1963.

Muzyczka, M. J., & Erickson, M. T. WISC characteristics of reading disabled children identified by three objective methods. *Perceptual and Motor Skills,* 1976, *43,* 595–602.

Myers, B., & Goldstein, D. Cognitive development in bilingual and monolingual lower-class children. *Psychology in the Schools,* 1979, *16,* 137–142.

Myers, E. T. *A survey of sight-saving classes in the public schools of the United States.* New York: The National Society for the Prevention of Blindness, 1930.

Nagle, R. J., & Lazarus, S. C. The comparability of the WISC-R and WAIS among 16-year-old EMR children. *Journal of School Psychology,* 1979, *17,* 362–367.

Naglieri, J. A. Comparison of McCarthy General Cognitive Index and WISC-R IQ for educable mentally retarded, learning disabled, and normal children. *Psychological Reports,* 1980, *47,* 591–596.

Naglieri, J. A., & Harrison, P. L. Comparison of McCarthy GCI's and WISC-R/Binet IQ's for EMR children. In *Proceedings of the National Association of School Psychologists/California Association of School Psychologists and Psychometrists.* San Diego, Ca., 1979.

Nalven, F. B. Classroom-administered Digit Span and distractibility ratings for elementary school pupils. *Psychological Reports,* 1969, *24,* 734.

Nalven, F. B., & Puleo, V. T. Relationship between digit span and classroom distractibility in elementary school children. *Journal of Clinical Psychology,* 1968, *24,* 85–87.

Nava, J. Cultural backgrounds and barriers that affect learning by Spanish-speaking children. In J. H. Burma (Ed.), *Mexican-Americans in the United States: A reader.* Cambridge, Mass.: Schenkman Publishing Co., 1970. Pp. 125–133.

Naylor, A. F., & Myrianthopoulos, N. C. The relation of ethnic and selected socio-economic factors to human birth-weight. *Annals of Human Genetics,* 1967, *31,* 71–83.

Needleman, H. L. Lead poisoning in children: Neurologic implications of widespread subclinical intoxication. In S. Walzer & P. H. Wolff (Eds.), *Minimal cerebral dysfunction in children.* New York: Grune & Stratton, 1973.

Neeman, R. L. Perceptual-motor attributes of normal school children: A factor analytic study. *Perceptual and Motor Skills,* 1972, *34,* 471–474.

Nelson, H. E., & Warrington, E. K. Developmental spelling retardation and its relation to other cognitive abilities. *British Journal of Psychology,* 1974, *65,* 265–274.

Nelson, R. O. An expanded scope for behavior modification in school settings. *Journal of School Psychology,* 1974, *12,* 276–287.

Nelson, R. O. The use of intelligence tests within behavioral assessment. In R. P. Hawkins (Chair), *Theoretical and methodological issues in behavioral assessment.* Symposium presented at the meeting of the American Psychological Association, Chicago, September 1975.

Neuhaus, M. Modifications in the administration of the WISC Performance subtests for children with profound hearing losses. *Exceptional Children,* 1967, *33,* 573–574.

Neville, D. A comparison of the WISC patterns of male retarded and non-retarded readers. *Journal of Educational Research,* 1961, *54,* 195–197.

Newcomer, P. L., & Hammill, D. D. ITPA and academic achievement: A survey. *Reading Teacher,* 1975, *28,* 731–741.

Newland, T. E. Psychological assessment of exceptional children and youth. In W. M. Cruickshank (Ed.), *Psychology of exceptional children and youth*

(2nd ed.). Englewood Cliffs, N.J.: Prentice-Hall, 1963. Pp. 53–117.

Newland, T. E. Testing minority group children. *Clinical Child Psychology Newsletter,* 1970, *9*(3), 5.

Newland, T. E. Review of the Pictorial Test of Intelligence. In O. K. Buros (Ed.), *The seventh mental measurements yearbook.* Highland Park, N.J.: Gryphon Press, 1972. Pp. 749–750.

Nichols, P. L. The effects of heredity and environment on intelligence test performance in 4 and 7 year white and Negro sibling pairs (Doctoral dissertation, University of Minnesota, 1970). *Dissertation Abstracts International,* 1971, *32,* 101B–102B. (University Microfilms No. 71-18, 874)

Nichols, P. L., & Anderson, V. E. Intellectual performance, race, and socioeconomic status. *Social Biology,* 1973 *20,* 367–374.

Nichols, R. C. The effect of ego involvement and success experience on intelligence test results. *Journal of Consulting Psychology,* 1959, *23,* 92.

Nichols, R. C. Review of *Genetics and education* by A. R. Jensen. *Educational Studies,* 1974, *5,* 35–38.

Nicholson, C. L. Correlations between the Quick Test and the Wechsler Intelligence Scale for Children–Revised. *Psychological Reports,* 1977, *40,* 523–526.

Nicolosi, L., & Kresheck, J. D. Variability in test scores between Form A and Form B on the Peabody Picture Vocabulary Test. *Language, Speech, and Hearing Services in Schools,* 1972, *3*(2), 44–47.

Nihira, K. Factorial dimensions of adaptive behavior in adult retardates. *American Journal of Mental Deficiency,* 1969, *73,* 868–878. (a)

Nihira, K. Factorial dimensions of adaptive behavior in mentally retarded children and adolescents. *American Journal of Mental Deficiency,* 1969, *74,* 130–141. (b)

Nihira, K., Foster, R., Shellhaas, M., & Leland, H. *AAMD Adaptive Behavior Scale* (Rev. ed.). Washington, D.C.: American Association on Mental Deficiency, 1974.

Noll, V. H. Review of the Boehm Test of Basic Concepts. *Journal of Educational Measurement,* 1970, *7,* 139–140.

Norris, P., & Overbeck, D. B. The institutionalized mentally retarded Navajo: A service program. *Mental Retardation,* 1974, *12*(3), 18–20.

Nunnally, J. C., Jr. *Psychometric theory.* New York: McGraw-Hill, 1967.

Oakland, J. A. WISC Coding as a measure of motivation. *Journal of Clinical Psychology,* 1969, *25,* 411–412.

Oakland, T. Research on the ABIC and ELP: A revisit to an old topic. *School Psychology Digest,* 1979, *8,* 209–213. (a)

Oakland, T. Research on the Adaptive Behavior Inventory for Children and the Estimated Learning Potential. *School Psychology Digest,* 1979, *8,* 63–70. (b)

Oakland, T., & Feigenbaum, D. Multiple sources of test bias on the WISC-R and Bender-Gestalt Test. *Journal of Consulting and Clinical Psychology,* 1979, *47,* 968–974.

Oakland, T. D., King, J. D., White, L. A., & Eckman, R. A comparison of performance on the WPPSI, WISC, and SB with preschool children: Companion studies. *Journal of School Psychology,* 1971, *9,* 144–149.

Oakland, T., Lee, S. W., & Axelrad, K. M. Examiner differences on actual WISC protocols. *Journal of School Psychology,* 1975, *13,* 227–233.

Oakland, T., & Marrs, S. *Predictive validity of readiness measures for middle and lower class black, Mexican-American, and Anglo children.* Paper presented at the meeting of the American Psychological Association, San Francisco, August 1977.

Oakland, T., Tombari, M., & Parker, E. *Factors influencing reading and math achievement: An examination of social class and racial-ethnic differences.* Paper presented at the meeting of the American Psychological Association, Toronto, Canada, 1978.

Offord, D. R., & Cross, L. A. Adult schizophrenia with scholastic failure or low IQ in childhood: A preliminary report. *Archives of General Psychiatry,* 1971, *24,* 431–436.

Ogdon, D. P. *Psychodiagnostics and personality assessment: A handbook.* Los Angeles: Western Psychological Services, 1967.

Ohnmacht, F. W., & Olson, A. V. Canonical analysis of reading readiness measures and the Frostig DTVP. *Educational and Psychological Measurement,* 1968, *28,* 479–484.

Oldridge, O. A., & Allison, E. E. Review of the Wechsler Preschool and Primary Scale of Intelligence (WPPSI). *Journal of Educational Measurement,* 1968, *5,* 347–348.

Olive, H. Psychoanalysts' opinions of psychologists' reports: 1952 and 1970. *Journal of Clinical Psychology,* 1972, *28,* 50–54.

Olivier, K., & Barclay, A. Stanford-Binet and Goodenough-Harris Test performances of Head Start children. *Psychological Reports,* 1967, *20,* 1175–1179.

Ollendick, D. G., Murphy, M. J., & Ollendick, T. H. Peabody Individual Achievement Test: Concurrent validity with juvenile delinquents. *Psychological Reports,* 1975, *37,* 935–938.

Ollendick, T. H., Finch, A. J., Jr., & Ginn, F. W. Comparison of Peabody, Leiter, WISC, and academic achievement scores among emotionally disturbed children. *Journal of Abnormal Child Psychology,* 1974, *2,* 47–51.

Olson, A. V. The Frostig Developmental Test of Visual Perception as a predictor of specific reading abilities with second-grade children. *Elementary English,* 1966, *43,* 869–872. (a)

Olson, A. V. Relation of achievement test scores and specific reading abilities to the Frostig Developmental Test of Visual Perception. *Perceptual and Motor Skills,* 1966, *22,* 179–184. (b)

Olson, A. V. Factor analytic studies of the Frostig Developmental Test of Visual Perception. *Journal of Special Education,* 1968, *2,* 429–433.

Olson, A. V., & Johnson, C. I. Structure and predictive validity of the Frostig Developmental Test of Visual Perception in grades one and three. *Journal of Special Education,* 1970, *4,* 49–52.

Ornitz, E. M. The modulation of sensory input and motor output in autistic children. In E. Schopler & R. J. Reichler (Eds.), *Psychopathology and child development: Research and treatment.* New York: Plenum, 1976.

Ornitz, E. M., & Ritvo, E. R. The syndrome of autism: A critical review. *American Journal of Psychiatry,* 1976, *133,* 609–621.

Orpet, R. E., Yoshida, R. K., & Meyers, C. E. The psychometric nature of Piaget's conservation of liquid for ages six and seven. *Journal of Genetic Psychology,* 1976, *129,* 151–160.

Ortego, P. D. The education of Mexican Americans. In E. Ludwig & J. Santibañez (Eds.), *The Chicanos, Mexican American voices.* Baltimore: Penguin Books, 1971.

Osgood, C. E. Motivational dynamics of language behavior. In *Nebraska symposium on motivation.* Lincoln: University of Nebraska Press, 1957.

Otto, W., & McMenemy, R. A. An appraisal of the Ammons Quick Test in a remedial reading program. *Journal of Educational Measurement,* 1965, *2,* 193–198.

Owens, E. P., & Bowling, D. H. Internal consistency and factor structure of the Preschool Attainment Record. *American Journal of Mental Deficiency,* 1970, *75,* 170–171.

Paal, N., Hesterly, S. O., & Wepfer, J. W. Comparability of the WISC and the WISC-R. *Journal of Learning Disabilities,* 1979, *12,* 348–351.

Padilla, A. M. Child bilingualism: Insights to issues. In J. L. Martinez, Jr. (Ed.), *Chicano psychology.* New York: Academic Press, 1977.

Padilla, A. M., & Ruiz, R. A. *Latino mental health: A review of literature.* Rockville, Md.: National Institute of Mental Health, DHEW Pub. no. (ADM) 74-113, 1973.

Palmer, F. H. Socioeconomic status and intellective performance among Negro preschool boys. *Developmental Psychology,* 1970, *3,* 1–9.

Palmer, J. O. *The psychological assessment of children.* New York: Wiley, 1970.

Palmer, M., & Gaffney, P. D. Effects of administration of the WISC in Spanish and English and relationship of social class to performance. *Psychology in the Schools,* 1972, *9,* 61–64.

Paraskevopoulos, J., & Kirk, S. A. *The development and psychometric characteristics of the revised Illinois Test of Psycholinguistic Abilities.* Urbana: University of Illinois Press, 1969.

Pasamanick, B., & Knobloch, H. The contribution of some organic factors to school retardation in Negro children. *Journal of Negro Education,* 1958, *27,* 4–9.

Pasamanick, B., & Knobloch, H. Retrospective studies on the epidemiology of reproductive casualty: Old and new. *Merrill-Palmer Quarterly,* 1966, *12,* 7–26.

Pasewark, R. A., Rardin, M. W., & Grice, J. E., Jr. Relationship of the Wechsler Pre-School and Primary Scale of Intelligence and the Stanford-Binet (L-M) in lower class children. *Journal of School Psychology,* 1971, *9,* 43–50.

Pasewark, R. A., Sawyer, R. N., Smith, E. A., Wasserberger, M., Dell, D., Brito, H., & Lee, R. Concurrent validity of the French Pictorial Test of Intelligence. *Journal of Educational Research,* 1967, *61,* 179–183.

Pasewark, R. A., Scherr, S. S., & Sawyer, R. N. Correlations of scores on the Vane Kindergarten, Wechsler Preschool and Primary Scale of Intelligence and Metropolitan Reading Readiness Tests. *Perceptual and Motor Skills,* 1974, *38,* 518.

Paterra, M. E. A study of thirty-three WISC scattergrams of retarded readers. *Elementary English,* 1963, *40,* 394–405.

Patterson, C. H. The Vineland Social Maturity Scale and some of its correlates. *Journal of Genetic Psychology,* 1943, *62,* 275–287.

Payne, R. The psychotic subnormal. *Journal of Mental Subnormality,* 1968, *14,* 25–34.

Peck, R. L. A comparative analysis of the performance of Indian and white children from north central Montana on the Wechsler Intelligence Scale for Children (Doctoral dissertation, Montana State University, 1972). *Dissertation Abstracts International,* 1973, *33,* 4097A (University Microfilms No. 73-2647).

Pedersen, D. M., Shinedling, M. M., & Johnson, D. L. Effects of sex of examiner and subject on children's quantitative test performance. *Journal of Personality and Social Psychology,* 1968, *10,* 251–254.

Pelosi, J. W. *A study of the effects of examiner race, sex, and style on test responses of Negro examinees* (Doctoral dissertation, Syracuse University). Ann Arbor, Mich.: University Microfilms, 1968. No. 69-8642.

Pennington, H., Galliani, C. A., & Voegele, G. E. Unilateral electroencephalographic dysrhythmia and children's intelligence. *Child Development,* 1965, *36,* 539–546.

Perales, A. M. The audio-lingual approach and the Spanish-speaking student. *Hispania,* 1965, *48,* 99–102.

Perkins, R. E. A study of the relation of brightness to Stanford-Binet test performance. *Journal of Applied Psychology,* 1932, *16,* 205–216.

Perry, N. W., Jr., McCoy, J. G., Cunningham, W. R., Falgout, J. C., & Street, W. J. Multivariate visual evoked response correlates of intelligence. *Psychophysiology,* 1976, *13,* 323–329.

Peters, H. Performance of Hopi children on four intelligence tests. *Journal of American Indian Education,* 1963, *2,* 27–31.

Petersen, C. R., & Hart, D. H. Factor structure of the WISC-R for a clinic-referred population and specific subgroups. *Journal of Consulting and Clinical Psychology,* 1979, *47,* 643–645.

Petersen, N. S., & Novick, M. R. An evaluation of some models of culture-fair selection. *Journal of Educational Measurement,* 1976, *13,* 3–29.

Peterson, J. *Early conceptions and tests of intelligence.* Yonkers-on-Hudson, N.Y.: World Book, 1925.

Petrie, I. R. J. Residential treatment of maladjusted children: A study of some factors related to progress in adjustment. *British Journal of Educational Psychology*, 1962, *32*, 29–37.

Philips, I. Psychopathology and mental retardation. *American Journal of Psychiatry*, 1967, *124*, 29–35.

Piaget, J. *The language and thought of the child.* London: Routledge and Kegan Paul, 1926.

Pickles, D. G. The Wechsler Performance Scale and its relationship to speech and educational response in deaf slow-learning children. *Teacher of the Deaf*, 1966, *64*, 382–392.

Pierce, C. M. Problems of the Negro adolescent in the next decade. In E. B. Brody (Ed.), *Minority group adolescents in the United States.* Baltimore, Md.: Williams & Wilkins, 1968.

Pierce, C. M. Psychiatric problems of the black minority. In G. Caplan (Ed.), *American handbook of psychiatry* (Vol. 2). *Child and adolescent psychiatry, sociocultural and community psychiatry* (2nd ed.). New York: Basic Books, 1974.

Pierce, H. O. Errors which can and should be avoided in scoring the Stanford-Binet Scale. *Journal of Genetic Psychology*, 1948, *72*, 303–305.

Piersel, W. C., Brody, G., & Kratochwill, T. R. A further examination of motivational influences on disadvantaged minority group children's intelligence test performance. *Child Development*, 1977, *48*, 1142–1145.

Pihl, R. O. The degree of the Verbal-Performance discrepancy on the WISC and the WAIS and severity of EEG abnormality in epileptics. *Journal of Clinical Psychology*, 1968, *24*, 418–420.

Pihl, R. O., & Nimrod, G. The reliability and validity of the Draw-a-Person Test in IQ and personality assessment. *Journal of Clinical Psychology*, 1976, *32*, 470–472.

Pikulski, J. J. A comparison of figure drawings and WISC IQ's among disabled readers. *Journal of Learning Disabilities*, 1972, *5*, 156–159.

Pikulski, J. J. Predicting sixth grade achievement by first grade scores. *Reading Teacher*, 1973, *27*, 284–287.

Pinderhughes, C. A. Understanding Black Power: Processes and proposals. *American Journal of Psychiatry*, 1969, *125*, 1552–1557.

Pintner, R. *Intelligence testing* (2nd ed.). New York: Henry Holt, 1931.

Pintner, R. Intelligence testing of partially-sighted children. *Journal of Educational Psychology*, 1942, *33*, 265–272.

Pintner, R., Dragositz, A., & Kushner, R. Supplementary guide for the Revised Stanford-Binet Scale (Form L). *Applied Psychology Monographs*, 1944, No. 3.

Piotrowski, R. J. The effect of omitting a limited number of subtests on the Full Scale reliability of the WISC-R. *Psychology in the Schools*, 1976, *13*, 298–301.

Plant, W. T. Cited by D. Wechsler, *Manual for the Wechsler Preschool and Primary Scale of Intelligence.* New York: Psychological Corporation, 1967. P. 34.

Plant, W. T., & Southern, M. L. First grade reading achievement predicted from WPPSI and other scores obtained 18 months earlier. *Proceedings of the 76th Annual Convention of the American Psychological Association*, 1968, *3*, 593–594.

Pless, I. B., Snider, M., Eaton, A. E., & Kearsley, R. B. A rapid screening test for intelligence in children: A preliminary report. *American Journal of Diseases of Children*, 1965, *109*, 533–537.

Plumb, G. R., & Charles, D. C. Scoring difficulty of Wechsler Comprehension responses. *Journal of Educational Psychology*, 1955, *46*, 179–183.

Pollack, M. Comparison of childhood, adolescent, and adult schizophrenias. Etiologic significance of intellectual functioning. *Archives of General Psychiatry*, 1960, *2*, 652–660.

Pollack, M. Mental subnormality and childhood schizophrenia. In J. Zubin & G. A. Jervis (Eds.), *Psychopathology in mental development.* New York: Grune & Stratton, 1967. Pp. 460–494.

Popovich, D. A. *Prescriptive behavioral checklist for the severely and profoundly retarded.* Baltimore, Md.: University Park Press, 1977.

Portenier, L. G. Psychological factors in testing and training the cerebral palsied. *Physiotherapy Review*, 1942, *22*, 301–303.

Post, J. M. *The effects of vocalization on the ability of third grade students to complete selected performance subtests from the Wechsler Intelligence Scale for Children* (Doctoral dissertation, University of South Carolina). Ann Arbor, Mich.: University Microfilms, 1970. No. 70-19,602.

Poull, L. E. Constancy of I.Q. in mental defectives, according to the Stanford-Revision of Binet tests. *Journal of Educational Psychology*, 1921, *12*, 323–324.

Pressey, S. L., & Cole, L. W. Irregularity in a psychological examination as a measure of mental deterioration. *Journal of Abnormal Psychology*, 1918, *13*, 285–294.

Price, T. L. Sioux children's Koppitz scores on the Bender-Gestalt given by white or native American examiners. *Perceptual and Motor Skills*, 1976, *43*, 1223–1226.

Price-Williams, D. R., & Ramirez, M., III. Divergent thinking, cultural differences, and bilingualism. *Journal of Social Psychology*, 1977, *103*, 3–11.

Pristo, L. J. Comparing WISC and WISC-R scores. *Psychological Reports*, 1978, *42*, 515–518.

Proger, B. B. Review of Boehm Test of Basic Concepts. *Journal of Special Education*, 1970, *4*, 249–252.

Proger, B. B. Review of the Balthazar Scales of Adaptive Behavior. *Journal of Special Education*, 1973, *7*, 95–101.

Prosser, N. S., & Crawford, V. B. Relationship of scores on the Wechsler Preschool and Primary Scale of Intelligence and the Stanford-Binet Intelligence Scale Form LM. *Journal of School Psychology*, 1971, *9*, 278–283.

Quay, H. C. Dimensions of problem behavior and educational programming. In P. S. Graubard (Ed.), *Children against schools.* Chicago: Follett Educational Corporation, 1969. Pp. 203–215.

Quay, H. C. Patterns of aggression, withdrawal, and immaturity. In H. C. Quay & J. S. Werry (Eds.), *Psychopathological disorders of childhood.* New York: Wiley, 1972. Pp. 1–29.

Quay, H. C. Classification. In H. C. Quay & J. S. Werry (Eds.), *Psychopathological disorders of childhood* (2nd ed.). New York: Wiley, 1979.

Quay, H. C., & Peterson, D. R. *Behavior Problem Checklist.* Miami, Fl.: Authors, 1979.

Quay, L. C. Language dialect, reinforcement, and the intelligence-test performance of Negro children. *Child Development,* 1971, *42,* 5–15.

Quay, L. C. Negro dialect and Binet performance in severely disadvantaged black four-year-olds. *Child Development,* 1972, *43,* 245–250.

Quay, L. C. Language dialect, age, and intelligence-test performance in disadvantaged black children. *Child Development,* 1974, *45,* 463–468.

Quay, L. C., & Weld, G. L. Visual and auditory selective attention and reflection-impulsivity in normal and learning disabled boys at two age levels. *Journal of Abnormal Child Psychology,* 1980, *8,* 117–125.

Quereshi, M. Y. Intelligence test scores as a function of sex of experimenter and sex of subject. *Journal of Psychology,* 1968, *69,* 277–284.

Rabin, A. I., & McKinney, J. P. Intelligence tests and childhood psychopathology. In B. B. Wolman (Ed.), *Manual of child psychopathology.* New York: McGraw-Hill, 1972.

Radin, N. Maternal warmth, achievement motivation, and cognitive functioning in lower-class preschool children. *Child Development,* 1971, *42,* 1560–1565.

Radin, N. Three degrees of maternal involvement in a preschool program: Impact on mothers and children. *Child Development,* 1972, *43,* 1355–1364.

Radin, N. Observed paternal behaviors as antecedents of intellectual functioning in young boys. *Developmental Psychology,* 1973, *8,* 369–376.

Ramanaiah, N. V., O'Donnell, J. P., & Adams, M. A test of the theoretical model of the revised Illinois Test of Psycholinguistic Abilities. *Applied Psychological Measurement,* 1978, *2,* 519–525.

Ramirez, M., III. Identification with Mexican family values and authoritarianism in Mexican-Americans. *Journal of Social Psychology,* 1967, *73,* 3–11.

Ramirez, M., III. Identification with Mexican-American values and psychological adjustment in Mexican-American adolescents. *International Journal of Social Psychiatry,* 1969, *15,* 151–156.

Ramirez, M., III, & Castañeda, A. *Cultural democracy, bicognitive development, and education.* New York: Academic Press, 1974.

Ramirez, M., III, Taylor, C., Jr., & Petersen, B. Mexican-American cultural membership and adjustment to school. *Developmental Psychology,* 1971, *4,* 141–148.

Ramsey, P. H., & Vane, J. R. A factor analytic study of the Stanford-Binet with young children. *Journal of School Psychology,* 1970, *8,* 278–284.

Rapaport, D., Gill, M. M., & Schafer, R. *Diagnostic psychological testing* (Rev. ed.). New York: International Universities Press, 1968.

Rasbury, W. C., Falgout, J. C., & Perry, N. W., Jr. A Yudin-type short form of the WISC-R: Two aspects of validation. *Journal of Clinical Psychology,* 1978, *34,* 120–126.

Rasbury, W. C., McCoy, J. G., & Perry, N. W., Jr. Relations of scores on WPPSI and WISC-R at a one-year interval. *Perceptual and Motor Skills,* 1977, *44,* 695–698.

Raskin, L. M., Bloom, A. S., Klee, S. H., & Reese, A. The assessment of developmentally disabled children with the WISC-R, Binet and other tests. *Journal of Clinical Psychology,* 1978, *34,* 111–114.

Ratusnik, D. L., & Koenigsknecht, R. A. Cross-cultural item analysis of the Columbia Mental Maturity Scale: Potential application by the language clinician. *Language, Speech, and Hearing Services in Schools,* 1976, *7,* 186–190.

Ratusnik, D. L., & Koenigsknecht, R. A. Biracial testing: The question of clinicians' influence on children's test performance. *Language, Speech, and Hearing Services in Schools,* 1977, *8,* 5–14.

Raven, J. C. *Progressive Matrices.* London: Lewis, 1938.

Raven, J. C. *Advanced Progressive Matrices.* London: Lewis, 1947. (a)

Raven, J. C. *Coloured Progressive Matrices.* London: Lewis, 1947. (b)

Raven, J. C. The comparative assessment of intellectual ability. *British Journal of Psychology,* 1948, *39,* 12–19.

Raven, J. C. *Guide to using the Standard Progressive Matrices.* London: Lewis, 1960.

Raven, J. C. *The Coloured Progressive Matrices Test.* London: Lewis, 1965.

Read, K. H. *The nursery school* (6th ed.). Philadelphia: Saunders, 1976.

Reed, H. B. C., Jr., & Fitzhugh, K. B. Patterns of deficits in relation to severity of cerebral dysfunction in children and adults. *Journal of Consulting Psychology,* 1966, *30,* 98–102.

Reed, H. B. C., Jr., & Reitan, R. M. Intelligence test performances of brain damaged subjects with lateralized motor deficits. *Journal of Consulting Psychology,* 1963, *27,* 102–106.

Reed, H. B. C., Jr., Reitan, R. M., & Kløve, H. Influence of cerebral lesions on psychological test performances of older children. *Journal of Consulting Psychology,* 1965, *29,* 247–251.

Reed, J. C., & Reed, H. B. C., Jr. Concept formation ability and non-verbal abstract thinking among older children with chronic cerebral dysfunction. *Journal of Special Education,* 1967, *1,* 157–161.

Reed, J. C., & Reitan, R. M. Verbal and Performance differences among brain-injured children with lateralized motor deficits. *Perceptual and Motor Skills,* 1969, *29,* 747–752.

Reed, M. Deaf and partially hearing children. In P. Mittler (Ed.), *The psychological assessment of mental and physical handicaps.* London: Methuen, 1970. Pp. 403–441.

Reese, H. W., & Lipsitt, L. P. *Experimental child psychology.* New York: Academic Press, 1970.

Reeve, R. E., Hall, R. J., & Zakreski, R. S. The Wood-cock-Johnson Tests of Cognitive Ability: Concurrent validity with the WISC-R. *Learning Disability Quarterly*, 1979, *2* (2), 63–69.

Reeves, J. W. *Thinking about thinking*. London: Secker and Warburg, 1965.

Reichler, R., & Schopler, E. Observations on the nature of human relatedness. *Journal of Autism and Childhood Schizophrenia*, 1971, *1*, 283–296.

Reid, W. B., Moore, D., & Alexander, D. Abbreviated form of the WISC for use with brain-damaged and mentally retarded children. *Journal of Consulting and Clinical Psychology*, 1968, *32*, 236.

Reid, W. R., & Schoer, L. A. Reading achievement, social-class and subtest pattern on the WISC. *Journal of Educational Research*, 1966, *59*, 469–472.

Reisman, J. M., & Yamokoski, T. Can intelligence be estimated from drawings of a man? *Journal of School Psychology*, 1973, *11*, 239–244.

Reisman, M. N. WISC Verbal and Performance IQ differences in delinquents. *Journal of Community Psychology*, 1973, *1*, 200.

Reitan, R. M. Methodological problems in clinical neuropsychology. In R. M. Reitan & L. A. Davison (Eds.), *Clinical neuropsychology: Current status and applications*. Washington, D.C.: V. H. Winston & Sons, 1974.

Reitan, R. M., & Davison, L. A. (Eds.). *Clinical neuropsychology: Current status and applications*. Washington, D.C.: V. H. Winston & Sons, 1974.

Rellas, A. J. The use of the Wechsler Preschool and Primary Scale (WPPSI) in the early identification of gifted students. *California Journal of Educational Research*, 1969, *20*, 117–119.

Reschly, D. J. WISC-R factor structures among Anglos, Blacks, Chicanos, and Native-American Papagos. *Journal of Consulting and Clinical Psychology*, 1978, *46*, 417–422.

Reschly, D. J., & Davis, R. A. Comparability of WISC and WISC-R scores among borderline and mildly retarded children. *Journal of Clinical Psychology*, 1977, *33*, 1045–1048.

Reschly, D. J., & Reschly, J. E. Validity of WISC-R factor scores in predicting achievement and attention for four sociocultural groups. *Journal of School Psychology*, 1979, *17*, 355–361.

Reschly, D. J., & Sabers, D. L. Analysis of test bias in four groups with the regression definition. *Journal of Educational Measurement*, 1979, *16*, 1–9.

Resnick, L. B. Social and scientific conceptions of intelligence. *International Review of Applied Psychology*, 1975, *24*, 131–138.

Resnick, L. B. The future of IQ testing in education. *Intelligence*, 1979, *3*, 241–253.

Reuter, J., & Mintz, J. Columbia Mental Maturity Scale as a test of concept formation. *Journal of Consulting and Clinical Psychology*, 1970, *34*, 387–393.

Reynell, J. Children with physical handicaps. In P. Mittler (Ed.), *The psychological assessment of mental and physical handicaps*. London: Methuen, 1970. Pp. 443–469.

Reynolds, C. R. Factor structure of the Peabody Individual Achievement Test at five grade levels between grades one and 12. *Journal of School Psychology*, 1979, *17*, 270–274.

Reynolds, C. R. The fallacy of "two-years below grade level for age" as a diagnostic criterion for dyslexia. *Journal of School Psychology*, 1981, *19* (4), in press.

Reynolds, C. R., & Gutkin, T. B. A regression analysis of test bias on the WISC-R for Anglos and Chicanos referred for psychological services. *Journal of Abnormal Child Psychology*, 1980, *8*, 237–243. (a)

Reynolds, C. R., & Gutkin, T. B. Stability of the WISC-R factor structure across sex at two age levels. *Journal of Clinical Psychology*, 1980, *36*, 775–777. (b)

Reynolds, C. R., & Hartlage, L. Comparison of WISC and WISC-R regression lines for academic prediction with Black and with White referred children. *Journal of Consulting and Clinical Psychology*, 1979, *47*, 589–591.

Rhodes, L. E., Dustman, R. E., & Beck, E. C. The visual evoked response: A comparison of bright and dull children. *Electroencephalography and Clinical Neurophysiology*, 1969, *27*, 364–372.

Rice, J. A. *Benton's Visual Retention Test: New age, scale scores, and percentile norms for children*. Paper presented at the meeting of the American Psychological Association, Honolulu, September 1972.

Richards, J. T. *The effectiveness of the Wechsler Preschool and Primary Scale of Intelligence in the identification of mentally retarded children* (Doctoral dissertation, University of Virginia). Ann Arbor, Mich.: University Microfilms, 1968. No. 60–4019.

Richards, J. T. Internal consistency of the WPPSI with the mentally retarded. *American Journal of Mental Deficiency*, 1970, *74*, 581–582.

Richardson, H. M., & Surko, E. F. WISC scores and status in reading and arithmetic of delinquent children. *Journal of Genetic Psychology*, 1956, *89*, 251–262.

Richmond, B. O., & Long, M. WISC-R and PPVT scores for black and white mentally retarded children. *Journal of School Psychology*, 1977, *15*, 261–263.

Rie, E. D., & Rie, H. E. Reading deficits and intellectual patterns among children with neurocognitive dysfunctions. *Intelligence*, 1979, *3*, 383–390.

Rie, H. E., Rie, E. D., Stewart, S., & Ambuel, J. P. Effects of methylphenidate on underachieving children. *Journal of Consulting and Clinical Psychology*, 1976, *44*, 250–260.

Riessman, F. *The culturally deprived child*. New York: Harper, 1962.

Riessman, F. *The inner-city child*. New York: Harper & Row, 1976.

Riggs, M. M., & Burchard, K. A. Intra-scale scatter for two kinds of mentally defective children. *Training School Bulletin*, 1952, *49*, 36–44.

Rimoldi, H. J. A. A note on Raven's Progressive Matrices Test. *Educational and Psychological Measurement*, 1948, *8*, 347–352.

Riscalla, L. M. The captive psychologist and the captive patient: The dilemma and alternatives. In S. L. Brodsky (Chair), *Shared results and open files with the client: Professional irresponsibility or effective involvement?* Symposium presented at the American

Psychological Association, Washington, D.C., September 1971.

Ritter, D. R. Intellectual estimates of hearing-impaired children: A comparison of three measures. *Psychology in the Schools*, 1976, *13*, 397–399.

Ritter, D. R. Preschool attainment record as a measure of developmental skills. *Journal of Consulting and Clinical Psychology*, 1977, *45*, 1184.

Ritter, D., Duffey, J., & Fischman, R. Comparability of Slosson and S-B estimates of intelligence. *Journal of School Psychology*, 1973, *11*, 224–227.

Ritter, D., Duffey, J., & Fischman, R. Comparability of Columbia Mental Maturity Scale and Stanford-Binet, Form L-M, estimates of intelligence. *Psychological Reports*, 1974, *34*, 174.

Roach, E. G., & Kephart, N. C. *The Purdue Perceptual-Motor Survey*. Columbus, Ohio: Charles E. Merrill, 1966.

Robb, G. P., Bernardoni, L. C., & Johnson, R. W. *Assessment of individual mental ability*. Scranton, Pa.: Intext Educational, 1972.

Robeck, M. C. Children who show undue tension when reading: A group diagnosis. *International Reading Association Conference Proceedings*, 1962, *7*, 133–138.

Robinson, N. M., & Robinson, H. B. *The mentally retarded child: A psychological approach* (2nd ed.). New York: McGraw-Hill, 1976.

Roche, D. On the concurrent validity of the Goodenough-Harris Draw-a-Person Test. *Papers in Psychology*, 1970, *4*, 5–7.

Rockwell, G. J., Jr. WISC Object Assembly and bodily concern. *Journal of Consulting Psychology*, 1967, *31*, 221.

Rodman, H. Family and social pathology in the ghetto. *Science*, 1968, *161*, 756–762.

Roe, A. *The making of a scientist*. New York: Dodd, Mead, 1953.

Roe, A., & Shakow, D. Intelligence in mental disorder. *Annals of the New York Academy of Sciences*, 1942, *42*, 361–490.

Rogers, S. J. Characteristics of the cognitive development of profoundly retarded children. *Child Development*, 1977, *48*, 837–843.

Rogge, H. J. *A study of the relationships of reading achievement to certain other factors in a population of delinquent boys* (Doctoral dissertation, University of Minnesota). Ann Arbor, Mich.: University Microfilms, 1959. No. 60-944.

Rohrs, F. W., & Haworth, M. R. The 1960 Stanford-Binet, WISC, and Goodenough Tests with mentally retarded children. *American Journal of Mental Deficiency*, 1962, *66*, 853–859.

Rosen, C. L. An experimental study of visual perceptual training and reading achievement in first grade. *Perceptual and Motor Skills*, 1966, *22*, 979–986.

Rosenthal, R. *Experimenter effects in behavioral research*. New York: Appleton-Century-Crofts, 1966.

Rosenthal, R., & Jacobson, L. *Pygmalion in the classroom*. New York: Holt, Rinehart and Winston, 1968.

Rosenthal, W. S. Review of the Visual Aural Digit Span Test. In F. L. Darley (Ed.), *Evaluation of appraisal techniques in speech and language pathology*. Reading, Mass.: Addison-Wesley, 1979.

Rosner, J. Language arts and arithmetic achievement and specifically related perceptual skills. *American Educational Research Journal*, 1973, *10*, 59–68.

Ross, A. O. *The practice of clinical child psychology*. New York: Grune & Stratton, 1959.

Ross, A. O. A clinical child psychologist "examines" retarded children. In G. J. Williams & S. Gordon (Eds.), *Clinical child psychology: Current practices and future perspectives*. New York: Behavioral Publications, 1974.

Ross, R. T. Behavioral correlates of levels of intelligence. *American Journal of Mental Deficiency*, 1972, *76*, 545–549.

Rossman, B. B., & Horn, J. L. Cognitive, motivational and temperamental indicants of creativity and intelligence. *Journal of Educational Measurement*, 1972, *9*, 265–286.

Rotatori, A. F., & Epstein, M. The Slosson Intelligence Test as a quick screening test of mental ability with profoundly and severely retarded children. *Psychological Reports*, 1978, *42*, 1117–1118.

Rotatori, A. F., Sedlak, B., & Freagon, S. Usefulness of the Slosson Intelligence Test with severely and profoundly retarded children. *Perceptual and Motor Skills*, 1979, *48*, 334.

Rothman, C. Differential vulnerability of WISC subtests to tester effects. *Psychology in the Schools*, 1974, *11*, 300–302.

Rourke, B. P., & Finlayson, M. A. J. Neuropsychological significance of variations in patterns of performance on the Trial Making Test for older children with learning disabilities. *Journal of Abnormal Psychology*, 1975, *84*, 412–421.

Rourke, B. P., Orr, R. R., & Ridgley, B. A. *The neuropsychological abilities of normal and retarded readers: A three-year follow-up*. Paper presented at the meeting of the Canadian Psychological Association, Windsor, Canada, June 1974.

Rourke, B. P. & Telegdy, G. A. Lateralizing significance of WISC Verbal-Performance discrepancies for older children with learning disabilities. *Perceptual and Motor Skills*, 1971, *33*, 875–883.

Rourke, B. P., Young, G. C., & Flewelling, R. W. The relationships between WISC Verbal-Performance discrepancies and selected verbal, auditory-perceptual, visual-perceptual, and problem-solving abilities in children with learning disabilities. *Journal of Clinical Psychology*, 1971, *27*, 475–479.

Rowe, H. A. H. *The comparability of WISC and WISC-R*. Hawthorn, Victoria, Australia: Australian Council for Educational Research, 1976 (Occasional Paper No. 10).

Rowe, H. A. H. "Borderline" versus "mentally deficient." *Australian Journal of Mental Retardation*, 1977, *4*, 11–14.

Rowley, V. N. Analysis of the WISC performance of brain damaged and emotionally disturbed children. *Journal of Consulting Psychology*, 1961, *25*, 553.

Royer, F. L. Information processing in the block design task. *Intelligence*, 1977, *1*, 32–50.

Rubin, R. A., & Balow, B. Perinatal influences on the behavior and learning problems of children. In B. B. Lahey & A. E. Kazdin (Eds.), *Advances in clinical child psychology* (Vol. 1). New York: Plenum, 1977.

Rucker, C. N. Technical language in the school psychologist's report. *Psychology in the Schools,* 1967, *4,* 146–150. (a)

Rucker, C. N. Report writing in school psychology: A critical investigation. *Journal of School Psychology,* 1967, *5,* 101–108. (b)

Rudel, R. G., Teuber, H. L., & Twitchell, T. E. Levels of impairment of sensori-motor functions in children with early brain damage. (Swed) *Neuropsychologia,* 1974, *12,* 95–108.

Rugel, R. P. WISC subtest scores of disabled readers: A review with respect to Bannatyne's recategorization. *Journal of Learning Disabilities,* 1974, *7,* 48–55.

Ruschival, M. L., & Way, J. G. The WPPSI and the Stanford-Binet: A validity and reliability study using gifted preschool children. *Journal of Consulting and Clinical Psychology,* 1971, *37,* 163.

Rushton, C. S., & Stockwin, A. E. Changes in Terman-Merrill I.Q.s of educationally sub-normal boys. *British Journal of Educational Psychology,* 1963, *33,* 132–142.

Russ, J. D., & Soboloff, H. R. *A primer of cerebral palsy.* Springfield, Ill.: Charles C Thomas, 1958.

Rutter, M. The influence of organic and emotional factors on the origins, nature and outcome of childhood psychosis. *Developmental Medicine and Child Neurology,* 1965, *7,* 518–528.

Rutter, M. Prognosis: Psychotic children in adolescence and early adult life. In J. K. Wing (Ed.), *Early childhood autism: Clinical, educational and social aspects.* London: Pergamon Press, 1966.

Rutter, M. Autistic children: Infancy to adulthood. *Seminars in Psychiatry,* 1970, *2,* 435–450.

Rutter, M. Childhood schizophrenia reconsidered. *Journal of Autism and Childhood Schizophrenia,* 1972, *2,* 315–337.

Rutter, M. The development of infantile autism. *Psychological Medicine,* 1974, *4,* 147–163.

Rutter, M. Research report: Institute of Psychiatry, Department of Child and Adolescent Psychiatry. *Psychological Medicine,* 1976, *6,* 505–516.

Rutter, M. Infantile autism and other child psychoses. In M. Rutter & L. Hersov (Eds.), *Child psychiatry: Modern approaches.* Oxford: Blackwell Scientific, 1977.

Rutter, M. Diagnosis and definition. In M. Rutter & E. Schopler (Eds.), *Autism: A reappraisal of concepts and treatment.* New York: Plenum, 1978.

Rutter, M., & Bartak, L. Causes of infantile autism: Some considerations from recent research. *Journal of Autism and Childhood Schizophrenia,* 1971, *1,* 20–32.

Rutter, M., & Bartak, L. Special educational treatment of autistic children: A comparative study: II. Follow-up findings and implications for services. *Journal of Child Psychology and Psychiatry and Allied Disciplines,* 1973, *14,* 241–270.

Rutter, M., Greenfeld, D., & Lockyer, L. A five to fifteen year follow-up study of infantile psychosis: II. Social and behavioural outcome. *British Journal of Psychiatry,* 1967, *113,* 1183–1199.

Rutter, M., & Lockyer, L. A five to fifteen year follow-up study of infantile psychosis: I. Description of sample. *British Journal of Psychiatry,* 1967, *113,* 1169–1182.

Rutter, M., Shaffer, D., & Shepherd, M. *A multi-axial classification of child psychiatric disorders: An evaluation of a proposal.* Geneva, Switzerland: World Health Organization, 1975.

Ryan, L. E. An investigation of the relationship between the scores earned by selected Negro and White children on the Wechsler Intelligence Scale for Children and the Wide Range Achievement Test (Doctoral dissertation, Mississippi State University, 1973). *Dissertation Abstracts International,* 1973, *34,* 2398A–2399A. (University Microfilms No. 73-25,711)

Sabatino, D. A., Abbott, J. C., & Becker, J. T. What does the Frostig DTVP measure? *Exceptional Children,* 1974, *40,* 453–454.

Saccuzzo, D. P., & Lewandowski, D. G. The WISC as a diagnostic tool. *Journal of Clinical Psychology,* 1976, *32,* 115–124.

Sachs, D. A. The WISC and the Mescalero Apache. *Journal of Social Psychology,* 1974, *92,* 303–304.

Sacks, E. L. Intelligence scores as a function of experimentally established social relationships between child and examiner. *Journal of Abnormal and Social Psychology,* 1952, *47,* 354–358.

Safer, D. J., & Allen, R. P. Factors associated with improvement in severe reading disability. *Psychology in the Schools,* 1973, *10,* 110–118.

Saigh, P. A., & Payne, D. A. The influence of examiner verbal comments on WISC performances of EMR students. *Journal of School Psychology,* 1976, *14,* 342–345.

Salvia, J., & Ysseldyke, J. E. *Assessment in special and remedial education.* Boston: Houghton Mifflin, 1978.

Sameroff, A. J. (Ed.). Organization and stability of newborn behavior: A commentary on the Brazelton Neonatal Behavior Assessment Scale. *Monographs of the Society for Research in Child Development,* 1978, *43* (5–6, Serial No. 177).

Sameroff, A. J. The etiology of cognitive competence: A systems perspective. In R. B. Kearsley & I. E. Sigel (Eds.), *Infants at risk: Assessment of cognitive functioning.* Hillsdale, N.J.: Lawrence Erlbaum, 1979.

Samuda, R. J. *Psychological testing of American minorities: Issues and consequences.* New York: Dodd, Mead, 1975.

Samuel, W., Grayson, S., Sherman, B., Soto, D., & Winstead, K. *Motivation, race, social class, and IQ: A follow-up study.* Paper presented at the meeting of the American Psychological Association, Washington, D.C., September 1976.

Samuel, W., Soto, D., Parks, M., Ngissah, P., & Jones, B. Motivation, race, social class, and IQ. *Journal of Educational Psychology,* 1976, *68,* 273–285.

Sandoval, J. The WISC-R and internal evidence of test bias with minority groups. *Journal of Consulting and Clinical Psychology,* 1979, *47,* 919–927.

Sandoval, J., & Miille, M. P. W. Accuracy of judgments of WISC-R item difficulty for minority groups. *Journal of Consulting and Clinical Psychology*, 1980, *48*, 249–253.

Sanner, R., & McManis, D. L. Concurrent validity of the Peabody Individual Achievement Test and the Wide Range Achievement Test for middle-class elementary school children. *Psychological Reports*, 1978, *42*, 19–24.

Sapp, G. L., Horton, W., McElroy, K., & Ray, P. An analysis of ABIC score patterns of selected Alabama school children. In *Proceedings of the National Association of School Psychologists/California Association of School Psychologists and Psychometrists*. San Diego, April 1979.

Sarason, S. B. *Psychological problems in mental deficiency* (2nd ed.). New York: Harper, 1953.

Sarason, S. B. *Psychological problems in mental deficiency* (3rd ed.). New York: Harper, 1959.

Sarason, S. B., & Doris, J. *Psychological problems in mental deficiency* (4th ed.). New York: Harper & Row, 1969.

Sarason, S. B., Levine, M., Goldenberg, I. I., Cherlin, D. L., & Bennett, E. M. *Psychology in community settings: Clinical, educational, vocational, social aspects*. New York: Wiley, 1966.

Sargent, H. D. Psychological test reporting: An experiment in communication. *Bulletin of the Menninger Clinic*, 1951, *15*, 175–186.

Sartain, H. W. Instruction of disabled learners: A reading perspective. *Journal of Learning Disabilities*, 1976, *9*, 489–497.

Satter, G. Psychometric scatter among mentally retarded and normal children. *Training School Bulletin*, 1955, *52*, 63–68.

Satterfield, J. H. EEG issues in children with minimal brain dysfunction. *Seminars in Psychiatry*, 1973, *5*, 35–46.

Satterfield, J. H., Cantwell, D. P., & Satterfield, B. T. Pathophysiology of the hyperactive child syndrome. *Archives of General Psychiatry*, 1974, *31*, 839–844.

Satterfield, J. H., Cantwell, D. P., Saul, R. E., & Yusin, A. Intelligence, academic achievement, and EEG abnormalities in hyperactive children. *American Journal of Psychiatry*, 1974, *131*, 391–395.

Sattler, J. M. Analysis of functions of the 1960 Stanford-Binet Intelligence Scale, Form L-M. *Journal of Clinical Psychology*, 1965, *21*, 173–179.

Sattler, J. M. Statistical reanalysis of Canady's "The effect of 'rapport' on the I.Q.: A new approach to the problem of racial psychology." *Psychological Reports*, 1966, *19*, 1203–1206. (a)

Sattler, J. M. Comments on Cieutat's "Examiner differences with the Stanford-Binet IQ." *Perceptual and Motor Skills*, 1966, *22*, 612–614. (b)

Sattler, J. M. Effects of cues and examiner influence on two Wechsler subtests. *Journal of Consulting and Clinical Psychology*, 1969, *33*, 716–721.

Sattler, J. M. Racial "experimenter effects" in experimentation, testing, interviewing, and psychotherapy. *Psychological Bulletin*, 1970, *73*, 137–160.

Sattler, J. M. Intelligence testing of ethnic minority group and culturally disadvantaged children. In L. Mann and D. Sabatino (Eds.), *The first review of special education* (Vol. 2). Philadelphia: The JSE Press, 1973. Pp. 161–201. (a)

Sattler, J. M. Examiners' scoring style, accuracy, ability, and personality scores. *Journal of Clinical Psychology*, 1973, *29*, 38–39. (b)

Sattler, J. M. Racial experimenter effects. In K. S. Miller & R. M. Dreger (Eds.), *Comparative studies of blacks and whites in the United States*. New York: Seminar Press, 1973. Pp. 8–32. (c)

Sattler, J. M. Scoring difficulty of the WPPSI Geometric Design subtest. *Journal of School Psychology*, 1976, *14*, 230–234.

Sattler, J. M. The effects of therapist-client racial similarity. In A. S. Gurman & A. M. Razin (Eds.), *Effective psychotherapy: A handbook of research*. Elmsford, N.Y.: Pergamon Press, 1977. Pp. 252–290.

Sattler, J. M. Review of McCarthy Scales of Children's Abilities. In O. K. Buros (Ed.), *The eighth mental measurements yearbook*. Highland Park, N.J.: Gryphon Press, 1978. Pp. 311–313.

Sattler, J. M. Standard intelligence tests are valid instruments for measuring the intellectual potential of urban children: Comments on pitfalls in the measurement of intelligence. *Journal of Psychology*, 1979, *102*, 107–112.

Sattler, J. M. Learning-disabled children do not have a perceptual organization deficit: Comments on Dean's WISC-R analysis. *Journal of Consulting and Clinical Psychology*, 1980, *48*, 254–255.

Sattler, J. M., & Anderson, N. E. Peabody Picture Vocabulary Test, Stanford-Binet, and Stanford-Binet Modified with normal and cerebral palsied preschool children. *Journal of Special Education*, 1973, *7*, 119–123.

Sattler, J. M., Andres, J. R., Squire, L. S., Wisely, R., & Maloy, C. F. Examiner scoring of ambiguous WISC-R responses. *Psychology in the Schools*, 1978, *15*, 486–489.

Sattler, J. M., Avila, V., Houston, W. B., & Toney, D. H. Performance of bilingual Mexican American children on Spanish and English versions of the Peabody Picture Vocabulary Test. *Journal of Consulting and Clinical Psychology*, 1980, *46*, 782–784.

Sattler, J. M., Bohanan, A. L., & Moore, M. K. Relationship between PPVT and WISC-R in children with reading disabilities. *Psychology in the Schools*, 1980, *17*, 331–334.

Sattler, J. M., & Bowman, G. E. A Comparison between the Koppitz and SOMPA norms for the Koppitz Developmental Bender-Gestalt Scoring System. *School Psychology Review*, 1981, *10*, 396–397.

Sattler, J. M., & Feldman, G. I. Comparison of 1965, 1976, and 1978 Wide Range Achievement Test norms. *Psychological Reports*, 1981, *49*, 115–118.

Sattler, J. M., & Gwynne, J. Ethnicity and Bender Visual Motor Gestalt Test performance. *Journal of School Psychology*, 1982, *20*(1), in press.

Sattler, J. M., Hillix, W. A., & Neher, L. A. Halo effect in examiner scoring of intelligence test responses.

Journal of Consulting and Clinical Psychology, 1970, *34*, 172–176.

Sattler, J. M., & Kuncik, T. M. Ethnicity, socioeconomic status, and pattern of WISC scores as variables that affect psychologists' estimates of "effective intelligence." *Journal of Clinical Psychology*, 1976, *32*, 362–366.

Sattler, J. M., & Martin, S. Anxious and nonanxious examiner roles on two WISC subtests. *Psychology in the Schools*, 1971, *8*, 347–349.

Sattler, J. M., & Ryan, J. J. Scoring agreement on the Stanford-Binet. *Journal of Clinical Psychology*, 1973, *29*, 35–38. (a)

Sattler, J. M., & Ryan, J. J. Who should determine the scoring of WISC Vocabulary responses? *Journal of Clinical Psychology*, 1973, *29*, 50–54. (b)

Sattler, J. M., & Squire, L. Scoring difficulty of the McCarthy Scales of Children's Abilities. *School Psychology Review*, 1982, *11*, 83–88.

Sattler, J. M., Squire, L., & Andres, J. Scoring discrepancies between the WISC-R Manual and two scoring guides. *Journal of Clinical Psychology*, 1977, *33*, 1058–1059.

Sattler, J. M., & Theye, F. Procedural, situational, and interpersonal variables in individual intelligence testing. *Psychological Bulletin*, 1967, *68*, 347–360.

Sattler, J. M., & Tozier, L. L. A review of intelligence test modifications used with cerebral palsied and other handicapped groups. *Journal of Special Education*, 1970, *4*, 391–398.

Sattler, J. M., & Winget, B. M. Intelligence testing procedures as affected by expectancy and IQ. *Journal of Clinical Psychology*, 1970, *26*, 446–448.

Sattler, J. M., Winget, B. M., & Roth, R. J. Scoring difficulty of WAIS and WISC Comprehension, Similarities, and Vocabulary responses. *Journal of Clinical Psychology*, 1969, *25*, 175–177.

Satz, P., Bakker, D. J., Teunissen, J., Goebel, R., & Van der Vlugt, H. Developmental parameters of the ear asymmetry: A multivariate approach. *Brain and Language*, 1975, *2*, 171–185.

Satz, P., & Friel, J. Some predictive antecedents of specific learning disability: A preliminary one year follow-up. In P. Satz & J. J. Ross (Eds.), *The disabled learner: Early detection and intervention.* Rotterdam, The Netherlands: Rotterdam University Press, 1973.

Satz, P., Friel, J., & Rudegeair, F. Differential changes in the acquisition of developmental skills in children who later become dyslexic: A three year follow-up. In D. G. Stein, J. J. Rosen, & N. Butters (Eds.), *Plasticity and recovery of function in the central nervous system.* New York: Academic Press, 1974. (a)

Satz, P., Friel, J., & Rudegeair, F. Some predictive antecedents of specific reading disability: A two-, three-, and four-year follow-up. In *The Hyman Blumberg Symposium on Research in Early Childhood Education.* Baltimore, Md.: Johns Hopkins University, 1974. (b)

Satz, P., & Sparrow, S. S. Specific developmental dyslexia: A theoretical formulation. In D. J. Bakker & P. Satz (Eds.), *Specific reading disability: Advances in theory and method.* Rotterdam, The Netherlands: Rotterdam University Press, 1970.

Satz, P., Van de Riet, H., & Mogel, S. An abbreviation of the WISC for clinical use. *Journal of Consulting Psychology*, 1967, *31*, 108.

Saunders, B. T., & Vitro, F. T. Examiner expectancy and bias as a function of the referral process in cognitive assessment. *Psychology in the Schools*, 1971, *8*, 168–171.

Savage, J. E., Jr., & Bowers, N. D. *Testers' influence on children's intellectual performance.* Washington, D.C.: U.S. Office of Education, 1972. (ERIC microfiche No. 064 329)

Sawyer, R. N. An investigation of the reliability of the French Pictorial Test of Intelligence. *Journal of Educational Research*, 1968, *61*, 211–214.

Sawyer, R. N., & Whitten, J. R. Concurrent validity of the Quick Test. *Psychological Reports*, 1972, *30*, 64–66.

Scarr, S. From evolution to Larry P., or what shall we do about IQ tests? *Intelligence*, 1978, *2*, 325–342.

Schachter, F. F., & Apgar, V. Comparison of preschool Stanford-Binet and school-age WISC IQs. *Journal of Educational Psychology*, 1958, *49*, 320–323.

Schaefer, C. E., & Sternfield, M. Comparative validity of the Harris Quality and Point Scales. *Perceptual and Motor Skills*, 1971, *33*, 997–998.

Schafer, S., & Leitch, M. An exploratory study of the usefulness of a battery of psychological tests with nursery school children. *American Journal of Psychiatry*, 1948, *104*, 647–652.

Scherer, I. W. The prediction of academic achievement in brain injured children. *Exceptional Children*, 1961, *28*, 103–106.

Schmideberg, M. The socio-psychological impact of IQ tests. *International Journal of Offender Therapy*, 1970, *14*, 91–97.

Schneider, J., & Smillie, D. The use of scatter on the Stanford-Binet. *Psychological Service Center Journal*, 1959, *11*, 73–75.

Schooler, D. L., Beebe, M. C., & Koepke, T. Factor analysis of WISC-R scores for children identified as learning disabled, educable mentally impaired, and emotionally impaired. *Psychology in the Schools*, 1978, *15*, 478–485.

Schoonover, S. M., & Hertel, R. K. Diagnostic implications of WISC scores. *Psychological Reports*, 1970, *26*, 967–973.

Schroeder, H. E., & Kleinsasser, L. D. Examiner bias: A determinant of children's verbal behavior on the WISC. *Journal of Consulting and Clinical Psychology*, 1972, *39*, 451–454.

Schubert, J. Effect of training on the performance of the W.I.S.C. 'Block Design' subtest. *British Journal of Social and Clinical Psychology*, 1967, *6*, 144–149.

Schubert, J., & Cropley, A. J. Verbal regulation of behavior and IQ in Canadian Indian and white children. *Developmental Psychology*, 1972, *7*, 295–301.

Schwarting, F. G. A comparison of the WISC and WISC-R. *Psychology in the Schools*, 1976, *13*, 139–141.

Schwarting, F. G., & Schwarting, K. R. The relationship of the WISC-R and WRAT: A study based upon a selected population. *Psychology in the Schools*, 1977, *14*, 431–433.

Schwartz, M. L. The scoring of WAIS Comprehension responses by experienced and inexperienced judges. *Journal of Clinical Psychology,* 1966, *22,* 425–427.

Schwartz, M. L., & Dennerll, R. D. Neuropsychological assessment of children with, without, and with questionable epileptogenic dysfunction. *Perceptual and Motor Skills,* 1970, *30,* 111–121.

Schwartz, R. H., & Flanigan, P. J. Evaluation of examiner bias in intelligence testing. *American Journal of Mental Deficiency,* 1971, *76,* 262–265.

Schwebel, A. I., & Bernstein, A. J. The effects of impulsivity on the performance of lower-class children on four WISC subtests. *American Journal of Orthopsychiatry,* 1970, *40,* 629–636.

Scott, L. S. *Texas Environmental Adaptation Measure: Its use in classification and planning.* Paper presented at the meeting of the National Association of School Psychologists, San Diego, March 1979.

Scott, R., Hartson, J., & Cunningham, M. Race of examiner as a variable in test attainments of preschool children. *Perceptual and Motor Skills,* 1976, *42,* 1167–1173.

Scottish Council for Research in Education. *The Scottish standardisation of the Wechsler Intelligence Scale for Children.* London: University of London Press, 1967.

Searls, E. F. *How to use WISC scores in reading diagnosis.* Newark, Del.: International Reading Association, 1975.

Sears, R. R. Obituary: Maud Merrill James (1888–1978). *American Psychologist,* 1979, *34,* 176.

Seashore, H. G., Wesman, A. G., & Doppelt, J. E. The standardization of the Wechsler Intelligence Scale for Children. *Journal of Consulting Psychology,* 1950, *14,* 99–110.

Sechrest, L., Fay, T. L., & Zaidi, S. M. H. Problems of translation in cross-cultural research. *Journal of Cross-cultural Psychology,* 1972, *3,* 41–56.

Sedlak, R. A., & Weener, P. Review of research on the Illinois Test of Psycholinguistic Abilities. In L. Mann & D. A. Sabatino (Eds.), *The first review of special education.* Philadelphia: JSE Press, 1973.

Seidman, E., Linney, J. A., Rappaport, J., Herzberger, S., Kramer, J., & Alden, L. Assessment of classroom behavior: A multiattribute, multisource approach to instrument development and validation. *Journal of Educational Psychology,* 1979, *71,* 451–464.

Selz, M. Halstead-Reitan Neuropsychological Test Battery for children. In G. W. Hynd & J. E. Obrzut (Eds.), *Neuropsychological assessment and the school-age child: Issues and procedures.* New York: Grune & Stratton, 1981.

Selz, M., & Reitan, R. M. Rules for neuropsychological diagnosis: Classification of brain function in older children. *Journal of Consulting and Clinical Psychology,* 1979, *47,* 258–264.

Semler, I. J., & Iscoe, I. Structure of intelligence in Negro and white children. *Journal of Educational Psychology,* 1966, *57,* 326–336.

Sewell, T. E. A comparison of the WPPSI and Stanford-Binet Intelligence Scale (1972) among lower SES black children. *Psychology in the Schools,* 1977, *14,* 158–161.

Sewell, T. E., & Manni, J. Comparison of scores of normal children on the WISC-R and Stanford-Binet, Form LM, 1972. *Perceptual and Motor Skills,* 1977, *45,* 1057–1058.

Shankweiler, D. P. A study of developmental dyslexia. *Neuropsychologia,* 1964, *1,* 267–286.

Shapiro, M. B. An experimental approach to diagnostic psychological testing. *Journal of Mental Science,* 1951, *97,* 748–764.

Sharp, H. C. A comparison of slow learner's scores on three individual intelligence scales. *Journal of Clinical Psychology,* 1957, *13,* 372–374.

Sharp, H. C. A note on the reliability of the Leiter International Performance Scale 1948 Revision. *Journal of Consulting Psychology,* 1958, *22,* 320.

Sharp, S. E. Individual psychology: A study in psychological method. *American Journal of Psychology,* 1898, *10,* 329–391.

Sheldon, M. S., & Garton, J. A note on "A WISC profile for retarded readers." *Alberta Journal of Educational Research,* 1959, *5,* 264–267.

Shepherd, C. W., Jr. Childhood chronic illness and visual motor perceptual development. *Exceptional Children,* 1969, *36,* 39–42.

Sherman, M., Chinsky, J. M., & Maffeo, P. Wechsler Preschool and Primary Scale of Intelligence Animal House as a measure of learning and motor abilities. *Journal of Consulting and Clinical Psychology,* 1974, *42,* 470.

Shiek, D. A., & Miller, J. E. Validity generalization of the WISC-R factor structure with 10½-year-old children. *Journal of Consulting and Clinical Psychology,* 1978, *46,* 583.

Shinagawa, F. Studies on the relationship between intelligence structure and personality traits: An analysis of WISC discrepancy. *Japanese Psychological Research,* 1963, *5,* 55–62.

Shinn, M. Father absence and children's cognitive development. *Psychological Bulletin,* 1978, *85,* 295–324.

Shipe, D., Vandenberg, S., & Williams, R. D. B. Neonatal Apgar ratings as related to intelligence and behavior in preschool children. *Child Development,* 1968, *39,* 861–866.

Shively, J. J., & Smith, A. E. Understanding the psychological report. *Psychology in the Schools,* 1969, *6,* 272–273.

Shorr, D. N., McClelland, S. E., & Robinson, H. B. Corrected mental age scores for the Stanford-Binet Intelligence Scale. *Measurement and Evaluation in Guidance,* 1977, *10,* 144–147.

Shotwell, A. M., & McCulloch, T. L. Accuracy of abbreviated forms of the Revised Stanford-Binet Scale with institutionalized epileptics. *American Journal of Mental Deficiency,* 1944, *49,* 162–164.

Shouksmith, G. *Intelligence, creativity and cognitive style.* New York: Wiley, 1970.

Sievers, D. J. *Psychometric problems related to cerebral palsy.* Unpublished master's thesis, University of New Mexico, 1950.

Sigel, I. E. How intelligence tests limit understanding of intelligence. *Merrill-Palmer Quarterly,* 1963, *9,*

39–56.

Silberberg, N. E., & Feldt, L. S. Intellectual and perceptual correlates of reading disabilities. *Journal of School Psychology,* 1968, *6,* 237–245.

Silvaroli, N. J. *Classroom Reading Inventory* (3rd ed.). Dubuque, Iowa: William C. Brown, 1976.

Silverman, H. L. Factors in emotional disturbance in children: The role of the clinician, therapist, and teacher. *International Journal of Experimental Research in Education,* 1970, *7,* 79–92.

Silverstein, A. B. An evaluation of two short forms of the Stanford-Binet, Form L-M, for use with mentally retarded children. *American Journal of Mental Deficiency,* 1963, *67,* 922–923.

Silverstein, A. B. Comparison of two item-classification schemes for the Stanford-Binet. *Psychological Reports,* 1965, *17,* 964.

Silverstein, A. B. A further evaluation of two short forms of the Stanford-Binet. *American Journal of Mental Deficiency,* 1966, *70,* 928–929.

Silverstein, A. B. Validity of a new approach to the design of WAIS, WISC, and WPPSI short forms. *Journal of Consulting and Clinical Psychology,* 1968, *32,* 478–479. (a)

Silverstein, A. B. WISC and WPPSI IQs for the gifted. *Psychological Reports,* 1968, *22,* 1168. (b)

Silverstein, A. B. WISC subtest patterns of retardates. *Psychological Reports,* 1968, *23,* 1061–1062. (c)

Silverstein, A. B. WPPSI IQs for the mentally retarded. *American Journal of Mental Deficiency,* 1968, *73,* 446. (d)

Silverstein, A. B. The internal consistency of the Stanford-Binet. *American Journal of Mental Deficiency,* 1969, *73,* 753–754.

Silverstein, A. B. Reappraisal of the validity of the WAIS, WISC, and WPPSI short forms. *Journal of Consulting and Clinical Psychology,* 1970, *34,* 12–14. (a)

Silverstein, A. B. Reappraisal of the validity of a short short form of Wechsler's Scales. *Psychological Reports,* 1970, *26,* 559–561. (b)

Silverstein, A. B. Deviation social quotients for the Vineland Social Maturity Scale. *American Journal of Mental Deficiency,* 1971, *76,* 348–351.

Silverstein, A. B. Another look at sources of variance in the Developmental Test of Visual Perception. *Psychological Reports,* 1972, *31,* 557–558. (a)

Silverstein, A. B. Review of the Balthazar Scales of Adaptive Behavior. *American Journal of Mental Deficiency,* 1972, *77,* 361. (b)

Silverstein, A. B. Note on prevalence. *American Journal of Mental Deficiency,* 1973, *77,* 380–382.

Silverstein, A. B. Note on the construct validity of the ITPA. *Psychology in the Schools,* 1978, *15,* 371–372. (a)

Silverstein, A. B. Note on the norms for the WRAT. *Psychology in the Schools,* 1978, *15,* 152–153. (b)

Silverstein, A. B., & Fisher, G. M. An evaluation of two short forms of the Stanford-Binet, Form L-M, for use with mentally retarded adults. *American Journal of Mental Deficiency,* 1961, *65,* 486–488.

Silverstein, A. B., Mohan, P. J., Franken, R. E., & Rhone, D. E. Test anxiety and intellectual performance in mentally retarded school children. *Child Development,* 1964, *35,* 1137–1146.

Silverstein, A. B., Ulfeldt, V., & Price, E. Clinical assessment of visual perceptual abilities in the mentally retarded. *American Journal of Mental Deficiency,* 1970, *74,* 524–526.

Simon, W. E. Expectancy effects in the scoring of vocabulary items: A study of scorer bias. *Journal of Educational Measurement,* 1969, *6,* 159–164.

Sisco, F. H., & Anderson, R. J. Current findings regarding the performance of deaf children on the WISC-R. *American Annals of the Deaf,* 1978, *123,* 115–121.

Sitkei, E. G., & Meyers, C. E. Comparative structure of intellect in middle- and lower-class four-year-olds of two ethnic groups. *Developmental Psychology,* 1969, *1,* 592–604.

Sitlington, P. L. *Validity of the Peabody Individual Achievement Test with educable mentally retarded adolescents.* Unpublished master's thesis, University of Hawaii, 1970.

Sloan, W., & Birch, J. W. A rationale for degrees of retardation. *American Journal of Mental Deficiency,* 1955, *60,* 258–264.

Slosson, R. L. *Slosson Intelligence Test (SIT) for children and adults.* New York: Slosson Educational Publications, 1963.

Small, L. *Neuropsychodiagnosis in psychotherapy.* New York: Brunner/Mazel, 1973.

Smith, A. Neuropsychological testing in neurological disorders. In W. J. Friedlander (Ed.), *Advances in neurology* (Vol. 7). *Current reviews of higher nervous system dysfunction.* New York: Raven Press, 1975.

Smith, A. L., Hays, J. R., & Solway, K. S. Comparison of the WISC-R and Culture Fair Intelligence Test in a juvenile delinquent population. *Journal of Psychology,* 1977, *97,* 179–182.

Smith, B. S. The relative merits of certain verbal and non-verbal tests at the second-grade level. *Journal of Clinical Psychology,* 1961, *17,* 53–54.

Smith, H. W., & May, W. T. Individual differences among inexperienced psychological examiners. *Psychological Reports,* 1967, *20,* 759–762.

Smith, H. W., May, W. T., & Lebovitz, L. Testing experience and Stanford-Binet scores. *Journal of Educational Measurement,* 1966, *3,* 229–233.

Smith, M. D., Coleman, J. M., Dokecki, P. R., & Davis, E. E. Intellectual characteristics of school labeled learning disabled children. *Exceptional Children,* 1977, *43,* 352–357. (a)

Smith, M. D., Coleman, J. M., Dokecki, P. R., & Davis, E. E. Recategorized WISC-R scores of learning disabled children. *Journal of Learning Disabilities,* 1977, *10,* 437–443. (b)

Smith, M. K., & McManis, D. L. Concurrent validity of the Peabody Individual Achievement Test and the Wide Range Achievement Test. *Psychological Reports,* 1977, *41,* 1279–1284.

Smith, N. C., Jr. Factors underlying WISC performance in juvenile public offenders (Doctoral dissertation, Ohio State University, 1969). *Dissertation Abstracts International,* 1969, *30,* 1888B–1889B. (University Microfilms No. 69-15,966)

Smith, P. A., & Marx, R. W. Some cautions on the use of the Frostig Test: A factor analytic study. *Journal of Learning Disabilities*, 1972, *5*, 357–362.

Smyth, R., & Reznikoff, M. Attitudes of psychiatrists toward the usefulness of psychodiagnostic reports. *Professional Psychology*, 1971, *2*, 283–288.

Sneed, G. A. An investigation of examiner bias, teacher referral reports, and socioeconomic status with the WISC-R. *Dissertation Abstracts International*, 1976, *36*, 4367A.

Snow, R. E. Review of R. Rosenthal and L. Jacobson, *Pygmalion in the classroom*. *Contemporary Psychology*, 1969, *14*, 197–199.

Snow, R. E. Theory and method for research on aptitude processes. *Intelligence*, 1978, *2*, 225–278.

Soethe, J. W. Concurrent validity of the Peabody Individual Achievement Test. *Journal of Learning Disabilities*, 1972, *5*, 560–562.

Solkoff, N. Frustration and WISC Coding performance among brain-injured children. *Perceptual and Motor Skills*, 1964, *18*, 54.

Solkoff, N. Race of experimenter as a variable in research with children. *Developmental Psychology*, 1972, *7*, 70–75.

Solkoff, N. Race of examiner and performance on the Wechsler Intelligence Scale for Children: A replication. *Perceptual and Motor Skills*, 1974, *39*, 1063–1066.

Solkoff, N., & Chrisien, G. Frustration and perceptual-motor performance. *Perceptual and Motor Skills*, 1963, *17*, 282.

Solkoff, N., Todd, G. A., & Screven, C. G. Effects of frustration on perceptual-motor performance. *Child Development*, 1964, *35*, 569–575.

Solly, D. C. Comparison of WISC and WISC-R scores of mentally retarded and gifted children. *Journal of School Psychology*, 1977, *15*, 255–258.

Solway, K. S., Hays, J. R., Roberts, T. K., & Cody, J. A. Comparison of WISC profiles of alleged juvenile delinquents living at home versus those incarcerated. *Psychological Reports*, 1975, *37*, 403–407.

Sontag, L. W., Baker, C. T., & Nelson, V. L. Mental growth and personality development: A longitudinal study. *Monographs of the Society for Research in Child Development*, 1958, *23*(2, Whole No. 68).

Spache, G. Serial testing with the Revised Stanford-Binet Scale, Form L, in the test range II-XIV. *American Journal of Orthopsychiatry*, 1942, *12*, 81–86.

Spaulding, P. J. Comparison of 500 complete and abbreviated Revised Stanford Scales administered to mental defectives. *American Journal of Mental Deficiency*, 1945, *50*, 81–88.

Spearman, C. *The nature of intelligence and the principles of cognition*. London: Macmillan, 1923.

Spearman, C. E. *The abilities of man*. New York: Macmillan, 1927.

Spellacy, F., & Black, F. W. Intelligence assessment of language-impaired children by means of two nonverbal tests. *Journal of Clinical Psychology*, 1972, *28*, 357–358.

Spence, A. G., Mishra, S. P., & Ghozeil, S. Home language and performance on standardized tests. *Elementary School Journal*, 1971, *71*, 309–313.

Spivack, G., Haimes, P. E., & Spotts, J. *Devereux Adolescent Behavior Rating Scale Manual*. Devon, Pa: Devereux Foundation, 1967.

Spivack, G., & Spotts, J. *Devereux Child Behavior Rating Scale Manual*. Devon, Pa.: Devereux Foundation, 1966.

Spivack, G., & Swift, M. *Devereux Elementary School Behavior Rating Scale Manual*. Devon, Pa.: Devereux Foundation, 1967.

Spivack, G., & Swift, M. The classroom behavior of children: A critical review of teacher-administered rating scales. *Journal of Special Education*, 1973, *7*, 55–89.

Sprague, R. *Learning difficulties of first grade children diagnosed by the Frostig Visual Perceptual Tests: A factor analytic study*. Unpublished doctoral dissertation, Wayne State University, 1963.

St. John, J., Krichev, A., & Bauman, E. Northwestern Ontario Indian children and the WISC. *Psychology in the Schools*, 1976, *13*, 407–411.

Staats, A. W. *Social behaviorism*. Homewood, Ill.: Dorsey Press, 1975.

Stacey, C. L., & Carleton, F. O. The relationship between Raven's Coloured Progressive Matrices and two tests of general intelligence. *Journal of Clinical Psychology*, 1955, *11*, 84–85.

Staffieri, J. R. Performance of preschool children on the Quick Test (QT). *Psychological Reports*, 1971, *29*, 472.

Stafford, J. Review of the Sucher-Allred Reading Placement Inventory. In O. K. Buros (Ed.), *The eighth mental measurements yearbook*. Highland Park, N.J.: Gryphon Press, 1978. Pp. 1227–1228.

Stanley, G., & Hall, R. A comparison of dyslexics and normals in recalling letter arrays after brief presentation. *British Journal of Educational Psychology*, 1973, *43*, 301–304.

Stanley, J. C. The study and facilitation of talent for mathematics. In National Society for the Study of Education (Ed.), *The gifted and the talented: Their education and development. Seventy-eighth yearbook of the National Society for the Study of Education*. Chicago: University of Chicago Press, 1979.

Stark, F. R. An analysis of the effectiveness of the Slosson Intelligence Test for the identification of mentally retarded preschool children, using the Stanford-Binet as the base test (Doctoral dissertation, American University, 1975). *Dissertation Abstracts International*, 1975, *36*, 1440A.

Stedman, J. M., Lawlis, G. F., Cortner, R. H., & Achterberg, G. Relationships between WISC-R factors, Wide Range Achievement Test scores, and visual-motor maturation in children referred for psychological evaluation. *Journal of Consulting and Clinical Psychology*, 1978, *46*, 869–872.

Steinbauer, E., & Heller, M. S. The Boehm Test of Basic Concepts as a predictor of academic achievement in grades 2 and 3. *Psychology in the Schools*, 1978, *15*, 357–360.

Stellern, J., Vasa, S. F., & Little, J. *Introduction to diagnostic-prescriptive teaching & programming*. Glen Ridge, N.J.: Exceptional Press, 1976.

Sterling, H. M., & Sterling, P. J. Experiences with the QNST. *Academic Therapy*, 1977, *12*, 339–342.

Stern, W. *The psychological methods of testing intelligence*. Baltimore, Md.: Warwick & York, 1914.

Sternlicht, M. A downward application of the 1960 Revised Stanford-Binet with retardates. *Journal of Clinical Psychology*, 1965, *21*, 79.

Stewart, K. D., & Myers, D. G. Long-term validity of the Slosson Intelligence Test. *Journal of Clinical Psychology*, 1974, *30*, 180–181.

Stewart, K. D., Wood, D. Z., & Gallman, W. A. Concurrent validity of the Slosson Intelligence Test. *Journal of Clinical Psychology*, 1971, *27*, 218–220.

Stoddard, G. D. *The meaning of intelligence*. New York: Macmillan, 1943.

Stokes, E. H., Blair, G., Jones, A. M., & Marrero, B. Comparison of intellectual ability and school achievement. In *Proceedings of the National Association of School Psychologists/California Association of School Psychologists and Psychometrists*. San Diego, Ca., 1979.

Stokes, E. H., Brent, D., Marrero, B., Huddleston, N. J., & Rozier, J. S. A comparison of WISC and WISC-R scores of sixth-grade students: Implications for validity. *Educational and Psychological Measurement*, 1978, *38*, 469–473.

Stormer, G. E. *Dimensions of the intellect unmeasured by the Stanford-Binet* (Doctoral dissertation, University of Illinois). Ann Arbor, Mich.: University Microfilms, 1966. No. 66-12,432.

Stott, L. H., & Ball, R. S. Infant and preschool mental tests: Review and evaluation. *Monographs of the Society for Research in Child Development*, 1965, *30*(3, Whole No. 101).

Strandberg, T. E., Griffith, J., & Miner, L. Child language and screening intelligence. *Journal of Communication Disorders*, 1969, *2*, 268–272.

Strother, C. R. Evaluating intelligence of children handicapped by cerebral palsy. *Crippled Child*, 1945, *23*, 82–83.

Strümpfer, D. J. W., & Mienie, C. J. P. A validation of the Harris-Goodenough Test. *British Journal of Educational Psychology*, 1968, *38*, 96–100.

Strunk, W., Jr., & White, E. B. *The elements of style*. New York: Macmillan, 1959.

Student, M., & Sohmer, H. Evidence from auditory nerve and brainstem evoked responses for an organic brain lesion in children with autistic traits. *Journal of Autism and Childhood Schizophrenia*, 1978, *8*, 13–20.

Stutsman, R. *Mental measurement of preschool children*. Yonkers-on-Hudson, N.Y.: World Book, 1931.

Stutsman, R. Factors to be considered in measuring the reliability of a mental test, with special reference to the Merrill-Palmer Scale. *Journal of Educational Psychology*, 1934, *25*, 630–633.

Sucher, F., & Allred, R. A. *Sucher-Allred Reading Placement Inventory*. Oklahoma City: Economy Company, 1973.

Sullivan, A. M., & Skanes, G. R. Differential transfer of training in bright and dull subjects of the same mental age. *British Journal of Educational Psychology*, 1971, *41*, 287–293.

Sullivan, P. M. *A comparison of administration modifications on the WISC-R Performance Scale with different categories of deaf children*. Unpublished doctoral dissertation, University of Iowa, 1978.

Sullivan, P. M., & Vernon, M. Psychological assessment of hearing impaired children. *School Psychology Digest*, 1979, *8*, 271–290.

Sundberg, N. D., Snowden, L. R., & Reynolds, W. M. Toward assessment of personal competence and incompetence in life situations. In M. R. Rosenzweig & L. W. Porter (Eds.), *Annual review of psychology*, 1978, *29*, 179–221.

Suppes, P. A survey of cognition in handicapped children. *Review of Educational Research*, 1974, *44*, 145–176.

Swanson, E. N., & DeBlassie, R. Interpreter effects on the WISC performance of first grade Mexican-American children. *Measurement and Evaluation in Guidance*, 1971, *4*, 172–175.

Swanson, M. S., & Jacobson, A. Evaluation of the S.I.T. for screening children with learning disabilities. *Journal of Learning Disabilities*, 1970, *3*, 318–320.

Sweet, R. C., & Ringness, T. A. Variations in the intelligence test performance of referred boys of differing racial and socioeconomic backgrounds as a function of feedback or monetary reinforcement. *Journal of School Psychology*, 1971, *9*, 399–409.

Swerdlik, M. E. Comparison of WISC and WISC-R scores of referred Black, White and Latino children. *Journal of School Psychology*, 1978, *16*, 110–125.

Swerdlik, M. E., & Schweitzer, J. A comparison of factor structures of the WISC and WISC-R. *Psychology in the Schools*, 1978, *15*, 166–172.

Tabachnick, B. G. *WISC-R scatter in learning disabled children*. Paper presented at the annual meeting of the Western Psychological Association, San Diego, April 1979.

Taddonio, R. O. Correlation of Leiter and the visual subtests of the Illinois Test of Psycholinguistic Abilities with deaf elementary school children. *Journal of School Psychology*, 1973, *11*, 30–35.

Talkington, L. W. Frostig visual perceptual training with low-ability-level retarded. *Perceptual and Motor Skills*, 1968, *27*, 505–506.

Tallal, P., & Piercy, M. Developmental aphasia: Impaired rate of non-verbal processing as a function of sensory modality. *Neuropsychologia*, 1973, *11*, 389–398.

Tallent, N. *Clinical psychological consultation*. Englewood Cliffs, N.J.: Prentice-Hall, 1963.

Tallent, N., & Reiss, W. J. Multidisciplinary views on the preparation of written clinical psychological reports: I. Spontaneous suggestions for content. *Journal of Clinical Psychology*, 1959, *15*, 218–221. (a)

Tallent, N., & Reiss, W. J. II. Acceptability of certain common content variables and styles of expression. *Journal of Clinical Psychology*, 1959, *15*, 273–274. (b)

Tallent, N., & Reiss, W. J. III. The trouble with psychological reports. *Journal of Clinical Psychology*, 1959, *15*, 444–446. (c)

Tansley, A. E., & Gulliford, R. *The education of slow learning children* (2nd ed.). London: Routledge & Kegan Paul, 1960.

Tate, M. E. The influence of cultural factors on the

Leiter International Performance Scale. *Journal of Abnormal and Social Psychology,* 1952, *47,* 497–501.

Taylor, E. M. *Psychological appraisal of children with cerebral defects.* Cambridge, Mass.: Harvard University Press, 1961.

Taylor, H. D., & Thweatt, R. C. Cross-cultural developmental performance of Navajo children on the Bender-Gestalt Test. *Perceptual and Motor Skills,* 1972, *35,* 307–309.

Taylor, R. L., Slocumb, P. R., & O'Neill, J. A short form of the McCarthy Scales of Children's Abilities: Methodological and clinical applications. *Psychology in the Schools,* 1979, *16,* 347–350.

Teagarden, F. M. Review of the Vineland Social Maturity Scale. In O. K. Buros (Ed.), *The fourth mental measurements yearbook.* Highland Park, N.J.: Gryphon Press, 1953. Pp. 162–163.

Tebeleff, M., & Oakland, T. *Relationships between the ABIC, WISC-R and achievement.* Paper presented at the annual meeting of the American Psychological Association, San Francisco, August 1977.

Tellegen, A., & Briggs, P. F. Old wine in new skins: Grouping Wechsler subtests into new scales. *Journal of Consulting Psychology,* 1967, *31,* 499–506.

Tennent, G., & Gath, D. Bright delinquents: A three-year follow-up study. *British Journal of Criminology,* 1975, *15,* 386–390.

Terman, L. M. The Binet-Simon scale for measuring intelligence: Impressions gained by its application. *Psychological Clinic,* 1911, *5,* 199–206.

Terman, L. M. *The measurement of intelligence.* Boston: Houghton Mifflin, 1916.

Terman, L. M. A symposium. Intelligence and its measurement. *Journal of Educational Psychology,* 1921, *12,* 127–133.

Terman, L. M. *Genetic studies of genius* (Vol. 1). Stanford, Ca.: Stanford University Press, 1925.

Terman, L. M., & Childs, H. G. A tentative revision and extension of the Binet-Simon Measuring Scale of Intelligence. *Journal of Educational Psychology,* 1912, *3,* 61–74, 133–143, 198–208, 277–289.

Terman, L. M., & Merrill, M. A. *Measuring intelligence.* Boston: Houghton Mifflin, 1937.

Terman, L. M., & Merrill, M. A. Tests of intelligence. B. 1937 Stanford-Binet Scales. In A. Weider (Ed.), *Contributions toward medical psychology* (Vol. 2). New York: Ronald Press, 1953. Pp. 510–521.

Terman, L. M., & Merrill, M. A. *Stanford-Binet Intelligence Scale.* Boston: Houghton Mifflin, 1960.

Terman, L. M., & Oden, M. H. *The gifted group at midlife.* Stanford, Ca.: Stanford University Press, 1959.

Terrell, F., Taylor, J., & Terrell, S. L. Effects of type of social reinforcement on the intelligence test performance of lower-class Black children. *Journal of Consulting and Clinical Psychology,* 1978, *46,* 1538–1539.

Thomas, A., Hertzig, M. E., Dryman, I., & Fernandez, P. Examiner effect in IQ testing of Puerto Rican working-class children. *American Journal of Orthopsychiatry,* 1971, *41,* 809–821.

Thomas, J. R., & Chissom, B. S. Note on factor structure of the Frostig Developmental Test of Visual Perception. *Perceptual and Motor Skills,* 1973, *36,* 510.

Thomas, P. J. Administration of a dialectical Spanish version and standard English version of the Peabody Picture Vocabulary Test. *Psychological Reports,* 1977, *40,* 747–750.

Thompson, B. B. A longitudinal study of auditory discrimination. *Journal of Educational Research,* 1963, *56,* 376–378.

Thompson, C. W., & Magaret, G. A. Differential test responses of normals and mental defectives. *Journal of Abnormal and Social Psychology,* 1947, *42,* 285–293.

Thorndike, E. L. *The measurement of intelligence.* New York: Bureau of Publications, Teachers College, Columbia University, 1927.

Thorndike, R. L. The measurement of creativity. *Teachers College Record,* 1963, *64,* 422–424.

Thorndike, R. L. Review of R. Rosenthal and L. Jacobson, *Pygmalion in the classroom. American Educational Research Journal,* 1968, *5,* 708–711.

Thorndike, R. L. *Stanford-Binet Intelligence Scale, Form L-M, 1972 norms tables.* Boston: Houghton Mifflin, 1973.

Thorndike, R. L., & Hagen, E. P. *Measurement and evaluation in psychology and education* (4th ed.). New York: Wiley, 1977.

Thorne, F. C. Operational psychological report writing. *Journal of Clinical Psychology,* 1960, *16,* 343–349.

Thurber, S. Changes in Navajo responses to the Draw-a-Man Test. *Journal of Social Psychology,* 1976, *99,* 139–140.

Thurston, J. R. Counseling the parents of mentally retarded children. *Training School Bulletin,* 1963, *60,* 113–117.

Thurstone, L. L. Primary mental abilities. *Psychometric Monographs,* 1938, No. 1.

Tiber, N., & Kennedy, W. A. The effects of incentives on the intelligence test performance of different social groups. *Journal of Consulting Psychology,* 1964, *28,* 187.

Tiffin, J. *Manual for the Purdue Pegboard.* Chicago: Science Research Associates, 1948.

Tigay, B., & Kempler, H. L. Stability of WISC scores of children hospitalized for emotional disturbance. *Perceptual and Motor Skills,* 1971, *32,* 487–490.

Tillman, M. H. The performance of blind and sighted children on the Wechsler Intelligence Scale for Children: Study I. *International Journal for the Education of the Blind,* 1967, *16,* 65–74. (a)

Tillman, M. H. The performances of blind and sighted children on the Wechsler Intelligence Scale for Children: Study II. *International Journal for the Education of the Blind,* 1967, *16,* 106–112. (b)

Tillman, M. H. Intelligence scales for the blind: A review with implications for research. *Journal of School Psychology,* 1973, *11,* 80–87.

Tillman, M. H., & Bashaw, W. L. Multivariate analysis of the WISC scales for blind and sighted children. *Psychological Reports,* 1968, *23,* 523–526.

Tillman, M. H., & Osborne, R. T. The performance of blind and sighted children on the Wechsler Intelligence Scale for Children: Interaction effects. *Education of the Visually Handicapped,* 1969, *1,* 1–4.

Tobias, P. V. IQ and the nature-nurture controversy. *Journal of Behavioural Science,* 1974, *2,* 1–24.

Tolor, A. Assessment myths and current fads: A rejoinder to a position paper on nonbiased assessment. *Psychology in the Schools,* 1978, *15,* 205–209.

Tomlinson-Keasey, C., Kelly, R. R., & Burton, J. K. Hemispheric changes in information processing during development. *Developmental Psychology,* 1978, *14,* 214–223.

Torgesen, J. K. The role of nonspecific factors in the task performance of learning disabled children: A theoretical assessment. *Journal of Learning Disabilities,* 1977, *10,* 27–34.

Torgesen, J. K. Factors related to poor performance on memory tasks in reading disabled children. *Learning Disability Quarterly,* 1979, *2*(3), 17–23.

Townsend, R. R. Tests of the Stanford Revision of the Binet-Simon scale most frequently failed by children in orthogenic backward classes. *Psychological Clinic,* 1928, *17,* 200–203.

Tsudzuki, A., Hata, Y., & Kuze, T. A study of rapport between examiner and subject. *Japanese Journal of Psychology,* 1956, *27,* 22–28.

Tucker, J. A. Operationalizing the diagnostic-intervention process. In T. Oakland (Ed.), *Non-biased assessment of minority group children with bias toward none.* Lexington, Ky.: Coordinating Office for Regional Resource Centers, University of Kentucky, 1976.

Tuddenham, R. D. The nature and measurement of intelligence. In L. J. Postman (Ed.), *Psychology in the making.* New York: Knopf, 1962. Pp. 469–525.

Tufano, L. G. The effect of effort and performance reinforcement on WISC-R IQ scores of black and white EMR boys. *Dissertation Abstracts International,* 1976, *36,* 5961A.

Tuma, J. M., Appelbaum, A. S., & Bee, D. E. Comparability of the WISC and the WISC-R in normal children of divergent socioeconomic backgrounds. *Psychology in the Schools,* 1978, *15,* 339–346.

Turnbull, W. W. Intelligence testing in the year 2000. *Intelligence,* 1979, *3,* 275–282.

Turner, G. H., & Penfold, D. J. The scholastic aptitude of the Indian children of the Caradoc Reserve. *Canadian Journal of Psychology,* 1952, *6,* 31–44.

Turner, R. K., Mathews, A., & Rachman, S. The stability of the WISC in a psychiatric group. *British Journal of Educational Psychology,* 1967, *37,* 194–200.

Tyler, L. E. *The psychology of human differences* (3rd ed.). New York: Appleton-Century-Crofts, 1965.

Tyler, L. E. *Individuality: Human possibilities and personal choice in the psychological development of men and women.* San Francisco: Jossey-Bass, 1978.

Tyson, M. H. *The effect of prior contact with the examiner on the Wechsler Intelligence Scale for Children scores of third-grade children* (Doctoral dissertation, University of Houston). Ann Arbor, Mich.: University Microfilms, 1968. No. 69-784.

United States Government Printing Office. *Style manual* (Rev. ed.). Washington, D.C.: USGPO, 1967.

University of Chicago Press. *A manual of style* (12th ed.). Chicago: University of Chicago Press, 1969.

Urbach, P. Progress and degeneration in the "IQ debate." *British Journal of the Philosophy of Science,* 1974, *25,* 99–135, 235–259.

Uzgiris, I. C., & Hunt, J. McV. *Assessment in infancy: Ordinal scales of psychological development.* Urbana: University of Illinois Press, 1975.

Valencia-Weber, G. Training American Indians in psychology. In K. D. Sandvold (Chair), *Psychology graduate training for minority bicultural students.* Symposium presented at the meeting of the American Psychological Association, San Francisco, September 1977.

Valentine, C. A. Deficit, difference, and bicultural models of Afro-American behavior. *Harvard Educational Review,* 1971, *41,* 137–157.

Valett, R. E. A clinical profile for the Stanford-Binet. *Journal of School Psychology,* 1964, *2,* 49–54.

Vance, H. B., Gaynor, P., & Coleman, M. Analysis of cognitive abilities for learning disabled children. *Psychology in the Schools,* 1976, *13,* 477–483.

Vance, H. B., Hankins, N., Wallbrown, F., Engin, A., & McGee, H. Analysis of cognitive abilities for mentally retarded children on the WISC-R. *Psychological Record,* 1978, *28,* 391–397.

Vance, H. B., Huelsman, C. B., Jr., & Wherry, R. J. The hierarchical factor structure of the Wechsler Intelligence Scale for Children as it relates to disadvantaged white and black children. *Journal of General Psychology,* 1976, *95,* 287–293.

Vance, H. B., Lewis, R., & DeBell, S. Correlations of the Wechsler Intelligence Scale for Children–Revised, Peabody Picture Vocabulary Test, and Slosson Intelligence Test for a group of learning disabled students. *Psychological Reports,* 1979, *44,* 735–738.

Vance, H. B., Prichard, K. K., & Wallbrown, F. H. Comparison of the WISC-R and PPVT for a group of mentally retarded students. *Psychology in the Schools,* 1978, *15,* 349–351.

Vance, H. B., & Singer, M. G. Correlations between the Quick Test Forms 1 and 3 and Peabody Picture Vocabulary Test for children and youth with learning problems. *Psychological Reports,* 1979, *44,* 315–318. (a)

Vance, H. B., & Singer, M. G. Recategorization of the WISC-R subtest scaled scores for learning disabled children. *Journal of Learning Disabilities,* 1979, *12,* 487–491. (b)

Vance, H. B., & Wallbrown, F. H. Hierarchical factor structure of the WISC-R for referred children and adolescents. *Psychological Reports,* 1977, *41,* 699–702.

Vance, H. B., & Wallbrown, F. H. The structure of intelligence for black children: A hierarchical approach. *Psychological Record,* 1978, *28,* 31–39.

Vance, H. B., Wallbrown, F. H., & Fremont, T. S. The abilities of retarded students: Further evidence concerning the stimulus trace factor. *Journal of Psychology,* 1978, *100,* 77–82.

Van der Keilen, M. Some effects of a special Indian culture oriented program on attitudes of white and Indian elementary school pupils. *Canadian Journal of Behavioural Science,* 1977, *9,* 161–168.

VanderVeer, B., & Schweid, E. Infant assessment: Stability of mental functioning in young retarded children. *American Journal of Mental Deficiency*, 1974. *79*, 1-4.

Vande Voort, L., Senf, G. M., & Benton, A. L. Development of audiovisual integration in normal and retarded readers. *Child Development*, 1972, *43*, 1260-1272.

Van Duyne, H. J. Age and intelligence factors as predictors of the development of verbal control of nonverbal behavior. *Journal of Genetic Psychology*, 1974, *124*, 321-331.

Vane, J. R. An evaluation of the Harris revision of the Goodenough Draw-a-Man Test. *Journal of Clinical Psychology*, 1967, *23*, 375-377.

Vane, J. R., Weitzman, J., & Applebaum, A. P. Performance of Negro and white children and problem and nonproblem children on the Stanford Binet Scale. *Journal of Clinical Psychology*, 1966, *22*, 431-435.

Van Hagen, J., & Kaufman, A. S. Factor analysis of the WISC-R for a group of mentally retarded children and adolescents. *Journal of Consulting and Clinical Psychology*, 1975, *43*, 661-667.

VanVactor, J. C. A field study of the use of the WISC to differentiate children with learning disabilities from emotionally disturbed and clinically normal. *Dissertation Abstracts International*, 1975, *35*(11-A), 7161-7162.

Varon, E. J. Development of Alfred Binet's psychology. *Psychological Monographs*, 1935, *46*(3, Whole No. 207).

Vega, M., & Powell, A. The effects of practice on Bender Gestalt performance of culturally disadvantaged children. *Florida Journal of Educational Research*, 1970, *12*, 45-49.

Vellutino, F. R. Toward an understanding of dyslexia: Psychological factors in specific reading disability. In A. L. Benton & D. Pearl (Eds.), *Dyslexia: An appraisal of current knowledge*. New York: Oxford University Press, 1978.

Vellutino, F. R., Steger, B. M., Moyer, S. C., Harding, C. I., & Niles, J. A. Has the perceptual deficit hypothesis led us astray? *Journal of Learning Disabilities*, 1977, *10*, 375-385.

Vernon, M. C. Fifty years of research on the intelligence of the deaf and hard-of-hearing children: A review of literature and discussion of implications. *Journal of Rehabilitation of the Deaf*, 1968, *1*(4), 1-12.

Vernon, M. C. Deaf and hard of hearing. In M. V. Wisland (Ed.), *Psychoeducational diagnosis of exceptional children*. Springfield, Ill.: Charles C Thomas, 1974.

Vernon, M. C., & Brown, D. W. A guide to psychological tests and testing procedures in the evaluation of deaf and hard-of-hearing children. *Journal of Speech and Hearing Disorders*, 1964, *29*, 414-423.

Vernon, P. E. The Stanford-Binet Test as a psychometric method. *Character and Personality*, 1937, *6*, 99-113.

Vernon, P. E. *The structure of human abilities*. New York: Wiley, 1950.

Vernon, P. E. Ability factors and environmental influences. *American Psychologist*, 1965, *20*, 723 -733.

Vernon, P. E. *Intelligence and cultural environment*. London: Methuen, 1969.

Vernon, P. E. *Intelligence: Heredity and environment*. San Francisco: W. H. Freeman, 1979.

Vincent, J. P., Williams, B. J., & Elrod, J. T. Ratings and observations of hyperactivity: Multitrait-multimethod analyses. In M. Kessler (Chair), *Hyperactive child: Fact, fiction, and fantasy*. Symposium presented at the meeting of the American Psychological Association, San Franciso, September 1977.

Wachs, T. D. Relation of infants' performance on Piaget scales between twelve and twenty-four months and their Stanford-Binet performance at thirty-one months. *Child Development*, 1975, *46*, 929-935.

Wada, J. A., & Davis, A. E. Fundamental nature of human infant's brain asymmetry. *Le Journal Canadien des Sciences Neurologiques*, 1977, *4*, 203-207.

Walker, K. P., & Gross, F. L. I.Q. stability among educable mentally retarded children. *Training School Bulletin*, 1970, *66*, 181-187.

Walker, R. E., Hunt, W. A., & Schwartz, M. L. The difficulty of WAIS Comprehension scoring. *Journal of Clinical Psychology*, 1965, *21*, 427-429.

Wallbrown, F. H. *A factor analytic framework for the clinical interpretation of the WISC-R*. Paper presented at the meeting of the National Association of School Psychologists/California Association of School Psychologists/Psychometrists, San Diego, March 1979.

Wallbrown, F. H., Blaha, J., Counts, D. H., & Wallbrown, J. D. The hierarchial factor structure of the WISC and revised ITPA for reading disabled children. *Journal of Psychology*, 1974, *88*, 65-76.

Wallbrown, F. H., Blaha, J., Wallbrown, J. D., & Engin, A. W. The hierarchical factor structure of the Wechsler Intelligence Scale for Children-Revised. *Journal of Psychology*, 1975, *89*, 223-235.

Wallbrown, F. H., Blaha, J., & Wherry, R. J. The hierarchical factor structure of the Wechsler Preschool and Primary Scale of Intelligence. *Journal of Consulting and Clinical Psychology*, 1973, *41*, 356-362.

Wallbrown, F. H., Wallbrown, J. D., & Engin, A. W. Test-retest reliability of the Bender-Gestalt for firstgrade children. *Perceptual and Motor Skills*, 1976, *42*, 743-746.

Wallin, J. E. W. The phenomenon of scattering in the Binet-Simon scale. *Psychological Clinic*, 1917, *11*, 179-195.

Wallin, J. E. W. A statistical study of the individual tests in ages VIII and IX in the Stanford-Binet Scale. *Mental Measurements Monographs*, 1929, No. 6.

Wallin, J. E. W. The results of multiple Binet re-testing of the same subjects. *Journal of Exceptional Children*, 1940, *6*, 211-222.

Walsh, J. F., & D'Angelo, R. Effectiveness of the Frostig program for visual perceptual training with Head Start children. *Perceptual and Motor Skills*, 1971, *32*, 944-946.

Walton, D., & Begg, T. L. Cognitive changes in lowgrade defectives. *American Journal of Mental Deficiency*, 1957, *62*, 96-102.

Ward, J. The factor structure of the Frostig Developmental Test of Visual Perception. *British Journal of Educational Psychology,* 1970, *40,* 65–67.

Wardrop, J. L. Review of the Sucher-Allred Reading Placement Inventory. In O. K. Buros (Ed.), *The eighth mental measurements yearbook.* Highland Park, N.J.: Gryphon Press, 1978. Pp. 1226–1227.

Washington, E. D., & Teska, J. A. Correlations between the Wide Range Achievement Test, the California Achievement Tests, the Stanford-Binet, and the Illinois Test of Psycholinguistic Abilities. *Psychological Reports,* 1970, *26,* 291–294.

Wasik, B. H., & Wasik, J. L. Patterns of conservation acquisition and the relationship of conservation to intelligence for children of low income. *Perceptual and Motor Skills,* 1976, *43,* 1147–1154.

Wasik, J. L., & Wasik, B. H. A note on use of the WPPSI in evaluating intervention programs. *Measurement and Evaluation in Guidance,* 1970, *3,* 54–56.

Wasik, J. L., & Wasik, B. H. Use of the WPPSI and the WISC with culturally deprived children. *Measurement and Evaluation in Guidance,* 1972, *5,* 280–285.

Watkins, D. B., & McKinney, D. *WISC and WISC-R comparisons among learning disabled children.* Unpublished manuscript, 1978. Greensboro Public Schools, Greensboro, NC 27402.

Watson, R. I. *The clinical method in psychology.* New York: Harper, 1951.

Waugh, R. P. Review of the Illinois Test of Psycholinguistic Abilities, revised edition. In O. K. Buros (Ed.), *The eighth mental measurements yearbook.* Highland Park, N.J.: Gryphon Press, 1978. P. 583.

Weatherley, R., & Lipsky, M. Street-level bureaucrats and institutional innovation: Implementing special-education reform. *Harvard Educational Review,* 1977, *47,* 171–197.

Wechsler, D. *Manual for the Wechsler Intelligence Scale for Children.* New York: Psychological Corporation, 1949.

Wechsler, D. *Manual for the Wechsler Adult Intelligence Scale.* New York: Psychological Corporation, 1955.

Wechsler, D. *The measurement and appraisal of adult intelligence* (4th ed.). Baltimore: Williams & Wilkins, 1958.

Wechsler, D. *Manual for the Wechsler Preschool and Primary Scale of Intelligence.* New York: Psychological Corporation, 1967.

Wechsler, D. *Manual for the Wechsler Intelligence Scale for Children-Revised.* New York: Psychological Corporation, 1974.

Wechsler, D. *Manual for the Wechsler Adult Intelligence Scale-Revised.* New York: Psychological Corporation, 1981.

Wechsler, D., & Weider, A. Tests of intelligence. C. Wechsler Intelligence Scale for Children. In A. Weider (Ed.), *Contributions toward medical psychology* (Vol. II). New York: Ronald Press, 1953. Pp. 522–529.

Weiner, S. G., & Kaufman, A. S. WISC-R vs. WISC for black children suspected of learning or behavioral disorders. *Journal of Learning Disabilities,* 1979, *12,* 100–105.

Weithorn, C. J. Hyperactivity and the CNS: An etio-logical and diagnostic dilemma. *Journal of Learning Disabilities,* 1973, *6,* 41–45.

Weitz, R. Forensic applications of psychological testing. In L. W. Field (Chair), *Contribution of psychological testing to clinical practice.* Symposium presented at the meeting of the American Psychological Association, Washington, D.C., September 1976.

Wellborn, E. S., Reid, W. R., & Reichard, C. L. Effect of examiner race on test scores of black and white children. *Education and Training of the Mentally Retarded,* 1973, *8,* 194–196.

Wellman, B. L. *The intelligence of preschool children as measured by the Merrill-Palmer Scale of Performance Tests.* University of Iowa Studies, New Series No. 361; Studies in Child Welfare, Vol. 15, No. 3. Iowa City: University of Iowa, October 1938.

Wells, C. G. *A comparative study of children grouped by three basic score patterns on the Wechsler Intelligence Scale for Children* (Doctoral dissertation, University of Northern Colorado). Ann Arbor, Mich.: University Microfilms, 1970. No. 71-14,543.

Wells, F. L. *Mental tests in clinical practice.* Yonkers-on-Hudson, N.Y.: World Book, 1927.

Wells, F. L., & Kelley, C. M. Intelligence and psychosis. *American Journal of Insanity,* 1920, *77,* 17–45.

Wener, B. D., & Templer, D. I. Relationship between WISC Verbal-Performance discrepancies and motor and psychomotor abilities of children with learning disabilities. *Perceptual and Motor Skills,* 1976, *42,* 125–126.

Wepman, J. M. *The Auditory Discrimination Test.* Chicago: Language Research, 1973.

Werner, E. E. Review of the Denver Developmental Screening Test. In O. K. Buros (Ed.), *The seventh mental measurements yearbook.* Highland Park, N.J.: Gryphon Press, 1972. Pp. 734–736.

Werner, E. E., Honzik, M. P., & Smith, R. S. Prediction of intelligence and achievement at ten years from twenty months pediatric and psychologic examinations. *Child Development,* 1968, *39,* 1063–1075.

Werry, J. S. The childhood psychoses. In H. C. Quay & J. S. Werry (Eds.), *Psychopathological disorders of childhood* (2nd ed.). New York: Wiley, 1979.

Werry, J. S., & Quay, H. C. Observing the classroom behavior of elementary school children. *Exceptional Children,* 1969, *35,* 461–467.

Wesman, A. G. Intelligent testing. *American Psychologist,* 1968, *23,* 267–274.

Wesman, A. G. Symposium: Tests and counseling: I. Testing and counseling: Fact and fancy. *Measurement and Evaluation in Guidance,* 1972, *5,* 397–402.

Westman, A. S. Review of Southern California Sensory Integration Tests. In O. K. Buros (Ed.), *The eighth mental measurements yearbook.* Highland Park, N.J.: Gryphon Press, 1978. Pp. 1408–1409.

Wetter, J., & French, R. W. Comparison of the Peabody Individual Achievement Test and the Wide Range Achievement Test in a learning disability clinic. *Psychology in the Schools,* 1973, *10,* 285–286.

Whalen, C. K., & Henker, B. Psychostimulants and children: A review and analysis. *Psychological Bulletin,* 1976, *83,* 1113–1130.

Wheaton, P. J., & Vandergriff, A. F. Comparison of

WISC and WISC-R scores of highly gifted students in public school. *Psychological Reports*, 1978, *43*, 627-630.

Wheldall, K., & Jeffree, D. Criticisms regarding the use of the E.P.V.T. in subnormality research. *British Journal of Disorders of Communication*, 1974, *9*, 140-143.

White, D. R., & Jacobs, E. The prediction of first-grade reading achievement from WPPSI scores of preschool children. *Psychology in the Schools*, 1979, *16*, 189-192.

White, J. L. Guidelines for black psychologists. *Black Scholar*, 1970, *1*, 52-57.

White, L. Organic factors and psychophysiology in childhood schizophrenia. *Psychological Bulletin*, 1974, *81*, 238-255.

White, P. L., & Fine, M. J. The effects of three school psychological consultation modes on selected teacher and pupil outcomes. *Psychology in the Schools*, 1976, *13*, 414-420.

Wiebe, M. J., & Harrison, K. A. *Relationships of psychological processes in the McCarthy Scales, Stanford-Binet, and Detroit Tests*. Unpublished manuscript, Texas Women's University, Department of Special Education, 1977.

Wiederholt, J. L. Review of the Illinois Test of Psycholinguistic Abilities, revised edition. In O. K. Buros (Ed.), *The eighth mental measurements yearbook*. Highland Park, N.J.: Gryphon Press, 1978. Pp. 580-583.

Wiederholt, J. L., & Hammill, D. D. Use of the Frostig-Horne Visual Perception Program in the urban school. *Psychology in the Schools*, 1971, *8*, 268-274.

Wiedl, K. H., & Carlson, J. S. The factorial structure of the Raven Coloured Progressive Matrices Test. *Educational and Psychological Measurement*, 1976, *36*, 409-413.

Wiener, G., & Milton, T. Demographic correlates of low birth weight. *American Journal of Epidemiology*, 1970, *91*, 260-272.

Wiens, A. N., Matarazzo, J. D., & Gaver, K. D. Performance and Verbal IQ in a group of sociopaths. *Journal of Clinical Psychology*, 1959, *15*, 191-193.

Wikoff, R. L. Subscale classification schemata for the Stanford-Binet, Form L-M. *Journal of School Psychology*, 1971, *9*, 329-337.

Wikoff, R. L. Danger: Attacks on testing unfair. In G. J. Williams & S. Gordon (Eds.), *Clinical child psychology: Current practices and future perspectives*. New York: Behavioral Publications, 1974.

Wikoff, R. L. Correlational and factor analysis of the Peabody Individual Achievement Test and the WISC-R. *Journal of Consulting and Clinical Psychology*, 1978, *46*, 322-325.

Willerman, L., Broman, S. H., & Fiedler, M. F. Infant development, preschool IQ, and social class. *Child Development*, 1970, *41*, 69-77.

Willerman, L., & Fiedler, M. F. Intellectually precocious preschool children: Early development and later intellectual accomplishments. *Journal of Genetic Psychology*, 1977, *131*, 13-20.

Williams, A. M., Marks, C. J., & Bailer, I. Validity of the Peabody Picture Vocabulary Test as a measure of hearing vocabulary in mentally retarded and normal children. *Journal of Speech and Hearing Research*, 1977, *20*, 205-211.

Williams, E. B. Testing of the disadvantaged: New opportunities. In F. H. Wright (Chair), *Uses and abuses of psychology: A program for constructive action*. Symposium presented at the American Psychological Association, Washington, D.C., September 1971.

Williams, R. L. Danger: Testing and dehumanizing black children. *Clinical Child Psychology Newsletter*, 1970, *9*(1), 5-6. (a)

Williams, R. L. From dehumanization to black intellectual genocide: A rejoinder. *Clinical Child Psychology Newsletter*, 1970, *9*(3), 6-7. (b)

Williams, R. L. Black pride, academic relevance and individual achievement. *Counseling Psychologist*, 1970, *2*(1), 18-22. (c)

Williams, R. L. Abuses and misuses in testing black children. *Counseling Psychologist*, 1971, *2*(3), 62-73.

Williams, R. L. *The BITCH-100: A culture-specific test*. Paper presented at the meeting of the American Psychological Association, Honolulu, Hawaii, September 1972.

Williams, R. L., & Mitchell, H. What happened to ABPsi's moratorium on testing: A 1968 to 1977 reminder. *Journal of Black Psychology*, 1977, *4*(1,2), 25-42.

Wilson, J. D., & Spangler, P. F. The Peabody Individual Achievement Test as a clinical tool. *Journal of Learning Disabilities*, 1974, *7*, 384-387.

Wilson, J. J., Rapin, I., Wilson, B. C., & Van Denburg, F. V. Neuropsychologic function of children with severe hearing impairment. *Journal of Speech and Hearing Research*, 1975, *18*, 634-652.

Wilson, R. S. Twins: Patterns of cognitive development as measured on the Wechsler Preschool and Primary Scale of Intelligence. *Developmental Psychology*, 1975, *11*, 126-134.

Wilson, R. S. Sensorimotor and cognitive development. In F. D. Minifie & L. L. Lloyd (Eds.), *Communicative and cognitive abilities—early behavioral assessment*. Baltimore, Md.: University Park Press, 1978.

Wilson, R. S., & Harpring, E. B. Mental and motor development in infant twins. *Developmental Psychology*, 1972, *7*, 277-287.

Wiltshire, E. B., & Gray, J. E. Draw-a-Man and Raven's Progressive Matrices (1938) intelligence test performance of reserve Indian children. *Canadian Journal of Behavioural Science*, 1969, *1*, 119-122.

Wing, L., & Wing, J. K. Multiple impairments in early childhood autism. *Journal of Autism and Childhood Schizophrenia*, 1971, *1*, 256-266.

Wing, L., Yeates, S. R., Brierley, L. M., & Gould, J. The prevalence of early childhood autism: Comparison of administrative and epidemiological studies. *Psychological Medicine*, 1976, *6*, 89-100.

Wisland, M. V., & Many, W. A. A study of the stability of the Illinois Test of Psycholinguistic Abilities. *Educational and Psychological Measurement*, 1967, *27*, 367-370.

Wisland, M. V., & Many, W. A. A factorial study of the Illinois Test of Psycholinguistic Abilities with children having above average intelligence. *Educational and Psychological Measurement*, 1969, *29*, 367–376.

Wissink, J. F., Kass, C. E., & Ferrell, W. R. A Bayesian approach to the identification of children with learning disabilities. *Journal of Learning Disabilities*, 1975, *8*, 158–166.

Wissler, C. The correlation of mental and physical tests. *Psychological Review*, 1901, *3*(Monogr. Suppl. 16).

Witkin, H. A., Faterson, H. F., Goodenough, D. R., & Birnbaum, J. Cognitive patterning in mildly retarded boys. *Child Development*, 1966, *37*, 301–316.

Witkin, H. A., Price-Williams, D., Bertini, M., Bjorn, C., Oltman, P. K., Ramirez, M., & Van Meel, J. *Social conformity and psychological differentiation.* Princeton, N.J.: Educational Testing Service, 1973.

Wolf, R. The measurement of environments. In A. Anastasi (Ed.), *Testing problems in perspective.* Washington, D.C.: American Council on Education, 1966.

Wolf, T. H. Alfred Binet: A time of crisis. *American Psychologist*, 1964, *19*, 762–771.

Wolf, T. H. The emergence of Binet's conception and measurement of intelligence: A case history of the creative process. *Journal of the History of the Behavioral Sciences*, 1969, *5*, 113–134. (a)

Wolf, T. H. The emergence of Binet's conceptions and measurement of intelligence: A case history of the creative process. Part II. *Journal of the History of the Behavioral Sciences*, 1969, *5*, 207–237. (b)

Woodcock, R. W. *Woodcock Reading Mastery Tests.* Circle Pines, Minn.: American Guidance Service, 1973.

Woodcock, R. W. *Woodcock-Johnson Psycho-Educational Battery: Technical report.* Boston: Teaching Resources, 1977.

Woodrow, H. H. *Brightness and dullness in children.* Philadelphia: J. B. Lippincott, 1919.

Woodward, C. A., Santa-Barbara, J., & Roberts, R. Test-retest reliability of the Wide Range Achievement Test. *Journal of Clinical Psychology*, 1975, *31*, 81–84.

Woody, R. H. Diagnosis of behavioral problem children: Electroencephalography and mental abilities. *Journal of School Psychology*, 1967, *5*, 116–121.

Wright, B. A. An analysis of attitudes: Dynamics and effects. *New Outlook for the Blind*, 1974, *68*, 108–118.

Wright, C. A modified procedure for the abbreviated Revised Stanford-Binet Scale in determining the intelligence of mental defectives. *American Journal of Mental Deficiency*, 1942, *47*, 178–184.

Wrightsman, L. S. *Social psychology in the seventies.* Monterey, Ca.: Brooks/Cole, 1972.

Wrightstone, J. W. *A supplementary guide for scoring the Revised Stanford-Binet Intelligence Scale, Form L.* New York: Board of Education, 1941.

Yacorzynski, G. K., & Tucker, B. E. What price intelligence? *American Psychologist*, 1960, *15*, 201–203.

Yando, R., Zigler, E., & Gates, M. The influence of Negro and white teachers rated as effective or non-effective on the performance of Negro and white lower-class children. *Developmental Psychology*, 1971, *5*, 290–299.

Yater, A. C., Barclay, A. G., & Leskosky, R. Goodenough-Harris Drawing Test and WPPSI performance of disadvantaged preschool children. *Perceptual and Motor Skills*, 1971, *33*, 967–970.

Yater, A. C., Barclay, A. G., & McGilligan, R. Interrater reliability of scoring Goodenough-Harris drawings by disadvantaged preschool children. *Perceptual and Motor Skills*, 1969, *28*, 281–282.

Yater, A. C., Boyd, M., & Barclay, A. G. A comparative study of WPPSI and WISC performances of disadvantaged children. *Journal of Clinical Psychology*, 1975, *31*, 78–80.

Yerkes, R. M. The Binet versus the point scale method of measuring intelligence. *Journal of Applied Psychology*, 1917, *1*, 111–122.

Yerkes, R. M., Bridges, J. W., & Hardwick, R. S. *A Point Scale for measuring mental ability.* Baltimore: Warwick & York, 1915.

Yoshida, R. K., & Meyers, C. E. Effects of labeling as educable mentally retarded on teachers' expectancies for change in a student's performance. *Journal of Educational Psychology*, 1975, *67*, 521–527.

Ysseldyke, J. E., & Sabatino, D. A. Identification of statistically significant differences between scaled scores and psycholinguistic ages on the ITPA. *Psychology in the Schools*, 1972, *9*, 309–313.

Ysseldyke, J. E., & Samuel, S. Identification of diagnostic strengths and weaknesses on the McCarthy Scales of Children's Abilities. *Psychology in the Schools*, 1973, *10*, 304–315.

Yudin, L. W. An abbreviated form of the WISC for use with emotionally disturbed children. *Journal of Consulting Psychology*, 1966, *30*, 272–275.

Yule, W., Berger, M., Butler, S., Newham, V., & Tizard, J. The WPPSI: An empirical evaluation with a British sample. *British Journal of Educational Psychology*, 1969, *39*, 1–13.

Yule, W., Rutter, M., Berger, M., & Thompson, J. Over- and under-achievement in reading: Distribution in the general population. *British Journal of Educational Psychology*, 1974, *44*, 1–12.

Zajonc, R. B. Family configuration and intelligence. *Science*, 1976, *192*, 227–236.

Zampardi, M. G. *School psychologists' opinions and practices regarding the Buckley amendment.* Paper presented at the meeting of the American Psychological Association, Toronto, Canada, 1978.

Zigler, E., Abelson, W. D., & Seitz, V. Motivational factors in the performance of economically disadvantaged children on the Peabody Picture Vocabulary Test. *Child Development*, 1973, *44*, 294–303.

Zigler, E., & Butterfield, E. C. Motivational aspects of changes in IQ test performance of culturally deprived nursery school children. *Child Development*, 1968, *39*, 1–14.

Zimmerman, I. L., Steiner, V. G., & Pond, R. L. Language status of preschool Mexican-American children: Is there a case against early bilingual education? *Perceptual and Motor Skills,* 1974, *38,* 227–230.

Zimmerman, I. L., & Woo-Sam, J. The utility of the Wechsler Preschool and Primary Scale of Intelligence in the public school. *Journal of Clinical Psychology,* 1970, *26,* 472.

Zintz, M. V. Problems of classroom adjustment of In-

dian children in public elementary schools in the Southwest. *Science Education,* 1962, *46,* 261–269.

Zuelzer, M. B., Stedman, J. M., & Adams, R. Koppitz Bender Gestalt scores in first-grade children as related to ethnocultural background, socioeconomic class, and sex factors. *Journal of Consulting and Clinical Psychology,* 1976, *44,* 875.

Name Index

Subject Index